£4 —

The Younger Pitt

THE
YOUNGER PITT

THE YEARS OF ACCLAIM

JOHN EHRMAN

CONSTABLE LONDON

First published in Great Britain 1969
by Constable and Company Limited
10 Orange Street London WC2H 7EG
Copyright © 1969 by John Ehrman
This paperback edition first published 1984
ISBN 0 09 465990 7

Set in Monotype Baskerville 11pt by
The Anchor Press, Tiptree, Essex
Printed in Great Britain by
St Edmundsbury Press
Bury St Edmunds, Suffolk

To Susan

Contents

Contents

PART FIVE

Illustrations

Introduction

About ten years after the younger Pitt died in January 1806, some of his friends and associates began to discuss the possibility of a Life based on his papers. Several authors were mentioned, but none of them was chosen, for one of Pitt's executors was Bishop Pretyman Tomline, his old Cambridge tutor and sometime secretary, and the Bishop was determined to write the book himself. The prospect filled the rest of the group with gloom, for Tomline's only claim was his long though much interrupted friendship with his patron. But there was nothing to be done, the work went ahead, and the first instalment appeared in 1821, carrying the story to the opening of the wars with France in 1793. It was as inadequate as had been feared, although the volumes sold well enough; as Lord Rosebery, a later biographer, observed, 'there is no greater proof of Mr Pitt's hold on the interest and affection of his countrymen than the fact that they absorbed four editions of his "Life" by Tomline'. But the reviews were such that the Bishop decided not to publish the rest of the work, and after this unpromising start nothing more appeared for forty years. When it did so, however, the result was very different, for the author was peculiarly well fitted to the task. The fifth Earl Stanhope, historian, man of affairs, and the grandson of Pitt's early friend and brother-in-law, possessed a cultivated mind, an easy style, and an inherited love and knowledge of his subject. His four-volume Life in 1861–2 ranks among the best of Victorian political biographies, and it held the field for fifty years. It was supplemented, and in some respects replaced, in 1911, when John Holland Rose, later to be the first Professor of Naval and Imperial History at Cambridge, published his biography in two successive volumes. These have been the three occasions on which a full scale Life has been undertaken from original material, and all other studies since the 1820s, including Rosebery's brilliant sketch, have been very largely indebted to one or more of these works.

Another half century has now passed, and there is perhaps room – however daunting the task – for another attempt to erect 'a moment's memory to that laurelled head'. It would be strange if no developments had taken place in historians' knowledge and views in the interval, and in fact there have been several of considerable importance. The Namier revolution, or restoration, has occurred in the field of political history, and however its significance is appraised no one can now assume that Pitt began his career within the structure of a definite two party system. Other work has been under way on the study of late eighteenth-century government, particularly, in recent years, on finance and imperial affairs. As a result we can look again at Pitt's Parliamentary setting, at the ways in which he met the conditions and turned them to advantage. We may also hope to see rather more clearly some of the conditions and problems of government – the setting for his daily work, the detail of which tended earlier to be neglected in comparison with his Parliamentary efforts. We can in fact try to strike the balance afresh and to explain Pitt's life once more, against these various developments in our knowledge of his times.

All historical figures of course need their degree of explanation in such terms. But it is particularly important in the case of Pitt, who of all the great British Prime Ministers lived most exclusively for public affairs. It is not only that his policies and actions must be seen in the conditions of his day, so far as we can reconstruct them; it is also that his mind and personality emerge most clearly from his public acts. His interest was so much concentrated on politics and government, his private life was so restricted and simple, that he is revealed most convincingly and fully in his work. His handling of his problems greatly affected the course of the events to which it responded; it is also the mosaic in which a pattern of behaviour may be traced. If a close attention to his circumstances, therefore, is needed in order to help explain him, it is equally desirable in order not to explain him away.

This has been a lengthy study, and I have been very fortunate in the help I have received. Papers have been made freely available – on a few occasions in microfilm or photostat – and I must record my obligations to their owners and custodians for allowing me to read and cite them. Her Majesty The Queen gave me gracious permission to consult the Royal Archives at Windsor. I am very grateful also to the Marquess of Abergavenny, the Marquess Camden, the Marquess of Lansdowne, the late Earl Stanhope (and Miss O. N. Shotter), Lord Bolton, Lord Kenyon, Lord Northbrook (and Major T. L. Ingram), Sir Edward Hoare Bart, Mr H. M. Adams, the late Mr George Fortescue, Mr W. S. Lewis, Mr Hector Monro (and the Manuscript Department of Edinburgh University Library), Captain G. M. T. Pretyman (and Mr D. Charman of the Ipswich and East Suffolk Record Office), Messrs Berry Brothers and Rudd (particularly Mr Anthony Berry), Messrs Coutts and Company (particularly Mr Seymour Egerton and Miss Veronica Stokes), and the Master and Fellows of Pembroke College, Cambridge. I wish to thank the authorities of the Bodleian Library, the British Museum, the Cambridge University Library, the

History of Parliament Trust, the India Office Library, the John Rylands Library, Manchester, the Kent County Record Office, the National Library of Scotland (particularly Dr William Beattie and Mr J. S. Ritchie), the Public Record Office (particularly Mr Kenneth Timings), the Scottish Record Office, the Brotherton Collection in the University of Leeds, Duke University, North Carolina, the Huntington Library and Art Gallery, California (particularly Miss Jean Preston), and the William L. Clements Library in the University of Michigan.

I am greatly indebted to those who have answered my questions, read parts of the book, or eased my path in other ways: to Dr M. S. Anderson, Dr Daniel A. Baugh, Mr Mark Bence-Jones, Dr J. E. D. Binney, Professor G. C. Bolton, the Hon. Robert Boscawen, Mr John Brooke, Mr Cecil Clarabut, the Financial Agent to the Earl of Derby, Commander Douglas Doble, Mr Francis Egerton, Mr Roger Ellis, Professor Holden Furber, Professor Gerald Graham, Professor R. W. Greaves, Professor W. B. Hamilton, Mr Guy Hartcup, Professor D. B. Horn, Dr Edward B. Jones, Dr G. S. R. Kitson Clark, Dr M. J. Mannheim, Dr P. J. Marshall, Mrs Murdoch Mitchison, the late Sir Lewis Namier, Mr Philip Robinson, the Hon. John St Aubyn, Dr R. C. Smail, Sir Wilfrid Sheldon, Mr E. Anthony Smith, Dame Lucy Sutherland, Dr Franklin B. Wickwire, the late Dr O. C. Williams; to Dr P. L. Hull of the Cornwall County Record Office, Mr P. T. Best of Messrs Farrer and Company, Mr David Leggatt of the Greenwich Public Libraries, George Harding's Bookshop, the Clerk of the Worshipful Company of Merchant Taylors, Miss W. D. Coates and Lieutenant Colonel White while they were at the National Register of Archives, the Librarian of the Sheffield City Libraries, the authorities of Harvard University Library (including the Kress and Houghton Libraries), and those of Yale University Library (including the Osborn Collection). I am equally grateful to the City and Borough Corporations of Birmingham, Leeds, Leicester, Liverpool, Manchester, Newcastle upon Tyne, Nottingham, Plymouth, Sheffield, Wolverhampton, and York. And I must further record my thanks for permission to read unpublished theses or papers by Miss P. K. Crimmin, Dr Murray S. Downs, and Miss E. J. Southall, and to include material from my book *The British Government and Commercial Negotiations with Europe 1783–1793*, of which the copyright is held by the Syndics of the Cambridge University Press.

Illustrations have been reproduced by kind permission of Mr and Mrs Paul Mellon (frontispiece), the Trustees of the National Portrait Gallery (figs. 1, 5, 6, 12, 14, 16), the Administrative Trustees of the Chevening Estate (fig. 2), the Trustees of the British Museum (figs. 7, 10, 18, 19, 21), the Marquess of Bute (fig. 8: photo, Scottish National Portrait Gallery), Miss V. M. E. Dundas of Arniston and the Trustees of the Arniston Estates (fig. 9: photo, Scottish National Portrait Gallery), the Controller of H.M. Stationery Office (fig. 11, from a

Crown copyright document in the Public Record Office), the Master and Fellows of University College, Oxford (fig. 13), the Courtauld Institute of Art (photo, fig. 15), the Governing Body of Christ Church, Oxford (fig. 17: photo, Royal Academy of Arts), the Marquess of Bath (fig. 20: photo, Courtauld Institute of Art). Miss Angela Lewi of the National Portrait Gallery gave me welcome aid in my inquiries.

Three of my friends have been associated with the book throughout. Miss Jean Dawson undertook some of the early research, and later, in her spare time, the laborious task of typing my manuscript. I am very grateful indeed for her skilled and unremitting help. Mr Ralph Arnold and Professor I. R. Christie have done me the great and prolonged service of reading the drafts of every chapter as these appeared. They have corrected the faults as far as is possible, and suggested improvements; but neither they nor any of those I have already mentioned can be held responsible for the remaining defects. And finally I cannot end without an affectionate tribute to the memory of G. M. Trevelyan, with whom I discussed the prospect of this biography, who lived to comment on the opening chapters of this first volume, and who once remarked – I thought perhaps more readily than he might have done as a younger man – that, all in all, he looked on the younger Pitt as the greatest of British Prime Ministers. Such general comparisons of course are sadly out of date. Nevertheless, this work is really an attempt to examine the material on which a judgment of that kind can be based.

December 1968   J. E.

A number of factual errors and misprints have been corrected for this paperback edition.

September 1984   J.E.

Abbreviations

A.C.	*The Journal and Correspondence of William, Lord Auckland,* ed. The Bishop of Bath and Wells (4 vols, 1861–2).
Ashbourne	The Right Hon. Edward Gibson, Lord Ashbourne, *Pitt: Some Chapters of his Life and Times* (1898).
B.M.	British Museum.
Buckingham	The Duke of Buckingham and Chandos, *Memoirs of the Courts and Cabinets of George the Third* (2 vols, 1853).
Ec. H.R.	*The Economic History Review.*
E.H.R.	*The English Historical Review.*
H.C.J.	*Journals of the House of Commons.*
H.M.C.	Publications of the Historical Manuscripts Commission.
H. of P.	Sir Lewis Namier and John Brooke, *The History of Parliament: The House of Commons 1754–1790* (3 vols, 1964).
Holland Rose	J. Holland Rose, *William Pitt and National Revival* (1911).
L.C.G.III	*The Later Correspondence of George III,* ed. A. Aspinall (5 vols, 1962–).
P.H.	*Cobbett's Parliamentary History of England . . . 1066 to 1803,* ed. William Cobbett (36 vols, 1806–20).
P.R.	*The Parliamentary Register: or, History of the Proceedings and Debates of the House of Commons [House of Lords],* John Debrett (45 vols, 1780–96).
P.R.O.	Public Record Office.
Stanhope	Earl Stanhope, *Life of the Right Honourable William Pitt* (4 vols, 1861–2).
Tomline	George Tomline, *Memoirs of the Life of the Right Honorable William Pitt* (2nd edn., 3 vols, 1821).
Trans.R.H.S.	*Transactions of the Royal Historical Society.*

Part One

CHAPTER I

Early Years

I

When you motor from central London to Sevenoaks, perhaps the least irksome route runs by Clapham Common and the edge of Croydon over Hayes Common to Farnborough. As it crosses Hayes Common, you are in the middle of what was, within living memory, still celebrated as Pitt country. To the south of the road, by Keston, once stood old Holwood House, the younger Pitt's country villa during almost the whole of his first long Ministry; and two miles away to the north lies Hayes itself, where Chatham for many years had his favourite retreat, and where his second son was born.

Hayes today is a typical outer suburb of London. Not a trace remains among its neat streets and gardens of Chatham's Hayes Place – 'dear Hayes', where if anywhere his restless spirit was at ease – except in the names of Chatham and Pittsmead Avenues, in a small piece of ornamental water amid the civic amenities of the Husseywell Recreation Grounds, and perhaps in a cottage near the corner of what was once the village street. There is nothing now except the old maps to guide one to the site of the only house in England where a future Prime Minister was born in the course of his father's Administration.

That event took place on 28 May 1759. It was an auspicious moment. 'Annus mirabilis', the year when 'our bells are worn threadbare with ringing for victories',[1] was above all Pitt's triumph. As news of the successes rolled in – of Goree and Guadeloupe, Minden, Lagos, Quiberon Bay, Quebec – his prestige and popularity soared to a peak unequalled until our own day; and the new son was baptised with a name of incomparable lustre. Nothing thereafter could alter that fact. The younger Pitt was always conscious that his father held a unique place in the history of the times and the affections of the country.

The triumph was a chapter in family as well as national history. It is notoriously dangerous to try to explain personality too closely in hereditary terms; but the younger Pitt was descended on both sides from notable families, each marked by strong and widely held features. There was indeed an unusually high concentration of vivid and sometimes curious character in one branch of the Pitts over some five

1. Horace Walpole to George Montagu, 21 October 1759 (*The Letters of Horace Walpole. . .*, ed. Mrs Paget Toynbee, IV (1903), 314).

generations. From the time of Governor Pitt of Madras in Queen Anne's reign to that of the second Lord Camelford and (allowing for the Stanhope contribution) Lady Hester Stanhope, they were a distinctive lot. The old Governor himself, the founder of their short-lived fortunes, was a formidable, masterful man, and his qualities descended in good measure through what he called his 'cockatrice brood'. Over the next hundred years, the same dominant traits tended to reappear – an imperious and often quarrelsome temper, extravagant behaviour and emotion, a marked inability to understand other people, and a fundamental simplicity which sometimes gave its possessors a surprisingly sweet and winning charm. This strongly transmitted nature was dangerously unstable, most noticeably (perhaps from the addition through their mother of some Villiers blood) in the case of the Governor's grandchildren. Chatham himself was, in our terms, a manic depressive. His favourite sister Ann died in Dr Duffell's home for the mentally disturbed. Another sister, Elizabeth, was clearly affected in the same way.[1] The strain, which left the next generation by comparison unscathed, reappeared more obviously in the younger Pitt's nephew Camelford and in Hester Stanhope. Thereafter it seems to have burnt out, after one of those still inexplicable eruptions that sometimes occur in the history of an otherwise unexciting line.

Chatham's genius dominated his children's early years. The impression on William was particularly strong. But it fell on a nature very different in many ways from that of Chatham himself. For the younger Pitt was not only a Pitt; he was also a Grenville, and his mother's family possessed a character as firmly marked, though not so dramatic, as that of his father's. Hester Grenville herself was a noble woman. Married to the elder William Pitt when she was thirty-three and he forty-six, she devoted herself until he died entirely to his interests. Passionately aware of his greatness, and deeply in love, she shared his periods of elation, comforted as best she could those of black despair, shielded him when necessary from the outside world, supported without illusions all his extravagances, and dealt as far as possible with the resulting tangle of his affairs. Her resolution and staying power were typical of her family at its best. For the Grenvilles, whether individually attractive or not – and in this they varied greatly – came of capable and pertinacious stock. In many ways, they formed a contrast to the Pitts. Where the Pitts' energies were fitful and unpredictable, theirs were stubborn. The Pitts were inclined to violence and brilliance: the Grenvilles were methodical, uncreative, and cultivated. The Pitts dissipated their strength as a family: the Grenvilles concentrated theirs. The Pitts were often unworldly in their expectations and demands: the Grenvilles dealt in conventional coin. Such qualities as the two families shared were moreover held in such different ways that the similarities

1. And of the other four brothers and sisters, certainly one – Thomas – and possibly another – Mary – shared, to a lesser degree, the prevailing instability.

seem more verbal than real. Both were immensely proud. But where the Pitts were moved by a fierce sense of individuality, the Grenville pride was a collective affair, cold and dense and withdrawn. Both were to be counted, the Grenvilles particularly, as political families. But while Chatham, from mid-career, ostentatiously courted independence of both King and party, the Grenvilles were content, in theory as in practice, to abide by the accepted rules. Nor were their tastes the same. Chatham was absorbed by foreign affairs, empire and war: the two Grenville Prime Ministers, George and William Wyndham, inclined more naturally to finance and administration. In two respects, however, these very different families were perhaps alike. The members of both were fearless, and, though socially active, often at a loss when dealing with their fellow men.

The younger Pitt's kinship with the Grenvilles has been generally remarked. One has only to compare his portraits with his mother's to see the physical likeness; and in character and interests, too, he owed much, though by no means all, to them. But it was inevitably as Chatham's son that he thought of himself. The experience must indeed have been exciting for an impressionable boy. The young Pitts were soon given to understand, in true eighteenth-century style, that they were objects of attention. When William, aged seven, was sent with his brothers and sisters for a spell of sea air at Weymouth, the party was greeted by the bells in Yeovil as they passed, and a deputation of Mohican chiefs, on passage to London with a petition for the King, waited upon the children of the great Pitt as soon as they arrived. The next summer, the bells were rung and flowers strewn as they went to Brighton; and again, a few years later, when they set off on holiday to Lyme Regis. Such occasions were rare, for the children as a family did not go much abroad. But their lives, though quiet and regular, always had as background the affairs of the great world. Newspapers were eagerly scanned; important visitors came and went when Chatham was at Hayes; and well or ill, retired or active, no one could fail to be aware that he remained a centre of interest.

The effect on William was profound and lasting. He seems very soon to have become his father's favourite. Chatham and his wife were devoted parents, and the family – Hester, born in 1755, John in 1756, Harriot in 1758, William the next year, and James Charles in 1761 – grew up happily in an atmosphere of affection. But there is a special note in the parents' references to their second son. While Hester and Harriot were lively and intelligent girls, attention of course fastened on the boys; and he was so obviously the star. The early epithets, 'Sweet William', 'Stout William', 'William the Great', turn in a few years to 'Eager Mr William', 'the Young Senator', 'the Orator', 'the Philosopher'. 'Of William', reported Lady Chatham when he was seven, 'I said nothing, but that was because he cannot be *extraordinary* for *him*'. 'William (our Constant Theme)', wrote Chatham a few years later,

'. . . was ever such a Pen my dear Life, under such Command, as this sweet Boy's?' 'How can I employ my reviving Pen so well', runs a rather pathetic letter from him towards the end, in 1777, 'as by addressing a few lines to the *Hope* and *Comfort* of my Life, my Dear William?'[1]

The youthful pen which Chatham admired runs oddly to our ears.

> I flatter myself [wrote William to his father at the age of eleven] that the Sun shone on your expedition, & that the views were enough enliven'd thereby to prevent the drowsy Morpheus from taking the opportunity of the heat to diffuse his poppies upon the eyes of any of the travellers.[2]

But Chatham demanded a certain type of eloquence; and when it was not required, the descriptive powers he sought found more direct expression.

> A neat House, a sweet Garden, and a summer-House divine: A King's Lieutenant has just passed under the Window, and a King's Cutter lies here: Players are just arrived in Town.[3]

The letters to his mother and his brothers and sisters are lively and unaffected. The finer efforts were reserved for his father and elder relations.

Whenever time or the state of his mind allowed, Chatham bent his formidable powers of education upon the precocious boy. They were directed to one end. William received a good grounding in the classics, English history and literature, and mathematics, for all of which he appears to have shown equal aptitude. From 1765, the family had as tutor the Reverend Edward Wilson, a graduate of Pembroke Hall, Cambridge, and an acute and intelligent man. But the general education was given a particular flavour by Chatham himself. As a child, the younger Pitt was absorbed by his father's political career. At the age of seven, he told Wilson that ' "he was glad he was not the eldest son, but that he could serve his country in the House of Commons, like his papa" '.[4] Six years later, he took a leading hand in writing a play, 'Laurentius, King of Clarinium', for family theatricals: the plot is

1. Lady Chatham to Chatham, 5 May 1766 (P.R.O. 30/8/9); Chatham to Lady Chatham n.d. but possibly 1773 (P.R.O. 30/8/5); William Stanhope Taylor & John Henry Pringle, *Correspondence of William Pitt, Earl of Chatham*, IV (1840), 440 (and see facsimile, op. cit., facing p. 1).

2. 31 July 1770 (J. Holland Rose, *Pitt and Napoleon* (1912), 95).

3. Pitt to Lady Chatham, Lyme Regis, 7 June 1773 (P.R.O. 30/8/11).

4. Wilson to Lady Chatham, 2 July 1766, reporting a conversation of 'three months ago' (*Chatham Correspondence*, III (1839), 27). The wording is often misquoted. The little boy must have been thinking of the peerage granted to his mother a few years before, for Chatham would not then have taken his own peerage.

political, and turns on a contest provoked by a Regency.[1] Chatham naturally seized on such a disposition. No budding politician can ever have received such a training in debate. The boy was exhorted to found his style on Barrow's Sermons, Thucydides, Polybius – and 'Junius'. His elocution was formed by reading aloud from Shakespeare and from Milton. He was enjoined to train himself in the ready choice of speech by translating passages from the classical authors as he read, pausing at any point until he had found the right word. Above all he was set, in Chatham's presence, to address a Parliamentary audience. The results were to be seen when he was in his teens. Macaulay has handed down the tradition of how, while still up at Cambridge, the young Pitt listened to a debate in the House of Lords in company with Fox, who was already a leading Parliamentary orator. As it proceeded, 'Pitt repeatedly turned to him, and said, "But surely, Mr. Fox, that might be answered thus"; or "Yes; but he lays himself open to this retort" '.[2] In later life, his critics twitted him with having been 'taught by his dad on a stool'.[3]

The precept was not confined to education. 'If I should smoke', Chatham once observed, 'William would instantly call for a pipe'.[4] Pitt's habits in maturity suggest the force of this remark. His pleasures remained largely those of his father: he rode, he farmed when time allowed, above all he followed Chatham's favourite pastime of land-scape gardening. The similarity was equally marked in his attitude to his personal affairs. Chatham loved magnificence and drama: he was attended on his journeys by postillions in blue and silver livery, he turned inns upside down, he swathed himself in bandages and all the paraphernalia of the invalid. His son, by comparison, lived unostenta-tiously. But both were sublimely indifferent to the cost. Pitt was brought up against the background of his father's extravagance. Chatham was apt to refer to Hayes as if it had been a cottage. It was in fact a good deal more than that. On purchasing the property, he immediately pulled down the old house and built himself one in the modern taste. As described in the sale catalogue a decade after his death, it was an 'Elegant Spacious Villa', with twenty-four bedrooms, brewhouse, laundry, and dairy, stabling for sixteen horses, and standing for four carriages. There were kitchen gardens of over two acres, a

1. Macaulay could not resist the comment that the result read like the work of a Pittite poetaster at the end of the Regency crisis in 1789 (*The Miscellaneous Writings of Lord Macaulay*, II (1860), 306).

2. Op. cit., 311.

3. Perhaps he really was. According to a local tradition at Hayes, Chatham used to put him on a mounting block in the garden, tell him to imagine that the trees in the park were members of the House of Commons, and set a subject for address. The block itself, preserved by successive owners of Hayes Place, was cut up for firewood by a coachman towards the end of the last century. (Canon [H. P.] Thompson, *A History of Hayes in the County of Kent* (1935), 45).

4. *Chatham Correspondence*, IV, 207 n1.

pinery and a peachery, a fenced park of some sixty acres, and about 110 acres of pasture beyond. '*The Pleasure Ground*', continues the description, 'is disposed with Taste, fringed with Rich Plantations maturely grown, and the Timber scattered with Pleasing Negligence. *The Paddock* refreshed with a Sheet of Water, and the Grounds adorned with Seats, Alcoves, &c'.[1] Chatham's hand may be recognised in this. But he was not content with the property as it stood. He began at once to buy or rent adjoining fields and buildings, and over the years acquired most of the land surrounding the village. An estate map, compiled in the middle sixties and thereafter kept up to date, shows a scattered property of several hundred acres. The sale catalogue of 1789, when most of the leaseholds had gone, speaks of two farms, pasture and woods of some ninety acres, two freehold messuages 'with large gardens', and the Manor of Farnborough with the manorial rights. An undated assessment of the estate for the poor rates, during Chatham's lifetime, puts it at £300 a year.

These activities, though not on a great scale, were not negligible. It was at his other property, Burton Pynsent in Somerset, that Chatham really let himself go. Here indeed he had plenty of scope. The house was large, the situation, above Sedgemoor, commanding, the property extensive and worth between £3,000 and £4,000 a year. It came to him unexpectedly in 1765, as a bequest from the eccentric Sir William Pynsent, whom he appears never to have seen; and he took possession forthwith, despite legal attempts to dispute the will. Burton Pynsent, indeed, represented to Chatham much that he desired and felt himself entitled to claim. It provided the kind of base that counted in the country, the landed position which sustained a political family; and it had fallen to him in a manner peculiarly appropriate to his conception of his career. It was perhaps no coincidence that he claimed a peerage at the first opportunity, as Earl of Chatham and Viscount Burton Pynsent.

Building and landscaping began at once. A new wing – all that now remains of the house – was added for a library and a 'bird room' for Lady Chatham. A column, 140 feet high, was raised to the memory of Sir William Pynsent. Roads were made through the estate to join the highways to Taunton and Langport. Woods were felled and planted, farmyard buildings erected on 'Tuscan pillars', and farming experiments conducted on a princely scale. Reynolds was later set to paint a series of portraits for the ballroom of Chatham's old associates in politics and war. At first, Hayes was sold; but in little more than a year it was bought back at a higher price, when Chatham found he could not do without it. Meanwhile he retained until 1770 his house in the Circus at Bath. The results soon followed. With an income which has been reckoned at £7,000 a year at least, he found himself in the 1770s heavily in debt.

1. Christie's Sale Catalogue for 7 May 1789, copy in Till Mss, U.468, Q.5/5 (Kent County Archives, Maidstone).

The retrenchments were carried out by his wife. Chatham's contribution was to accept substantial loans from his friends as if they were his due. He was in fact entirely unaffected by the state of his finances, and life, if embarrassed and somewhat reduced, continued amply enough. It was scarcely surprising if the younger Pitt inherited, along with the family improvidence, the conviction that this was how a great man lived.

This background and education were uninterrupted by absence at school. Chatham had been at Eton, and the rigours of life as an Oppidan had made a deep impression. 'He scarcely observed a boy who was not cowed for life' by the experience; and his sons were accordingly educated at home. In William's case the decision may have been supported by the state of his health. From the age of about six until he was fourteen, he was delicate and often ill. Indeed, from the frequent references to his illness in the family correspondence, from his lack of robustness, and from his exhaustion and death at the age of forty-six, the impression gained ground at the time, and has been widely accepted since, that the childhood weakness persisted throughout life. This does not in fact appear to have been so. According to those closest to Pitt – his tutor at Cambridge, and his family – he was entirely free of it after the age of fourteen; the symptoms of later years were by no means the same; and the life he led in the interval could scarcely have been pursued by anyone with an excessively weak constitution. It seems likely, indeed, from such evidence as can be produced, that the trouble sprang from recurring infection of the nose and throat, and at times the sinuses. If it could have been diagnosed, and his tonsils and adenoids removed, perhaps the boy would have been able to lead a healthier life.[1]

As it was, he endured the attentions of the age. Chatham suffered from diffused gout. His son was presumed to have inherited it, and was treated accordingly. Soot bark and blisters, with a 'cordial confection', formed the staple of his cure, prescribed by the doctor at Hayes and approved by Chatham's physician, Dr Addington. It says something for Pitt's constitution that the 'Effort of Nature', in Addington's words, 'to root out . . . something morbid that had long lurk'd in it',[2] should have proved finally successful.

By the time that Pitt was fourteen, Chatham had decided to send him to the University. The eldest brother was destined for the army, the youngest for the navy: William was in theory reserved for the Bar. The choice may seem surprising, for Chatham loathed lawyers. But it is

1. I am indebted to Sir Wilfrid Sheldon for this diagnosis. He points to the typical symptoms recorded at different times – rigors followed by a crisis, swollen glands in the neck, regular colds in the spring producing debility, loss of weight, and occasional difficulty in concentration; culminating, in the last attack at the age of fourteen, in prolonged lassitude and fever, with loss of appetite and a bad cough. It would also be typical to shake clear of the infection at the age of puberty. But it must be stressed that the evidence is sketchy.
2. To Lady Chatham, 30 October 1773 (P.R.O. 30/8/15).

doubtful if either he or his son looked on the profession as more than a stopgap, and something to fall back on if politics should fail. In April 1773, Pitt was accordingly placed on the books of Pembroke Hall, Cambridge. Chatham himself was an Oxford man; but he was content to follow Wilson's advice, and send his son to the tutor's College. By the standards of the day, fourteen was young. The age of entrance had been rising since earlier in the century, and it was now more usual to go up at seventeen, though fifteen or sixteen was still not uncommon. But Wilson and Chatham were satisfied that this was an exceptional case.

> I could not have acted with more prudence than I have done [wrote Wilson to his wife in December 1772] in the affaire of Pembroke Hall. Mr. Pitt is not the child his years bespeak him to be. He has now all the understanding of a man, and is, and will be, my steady friend thro' life. He has sound principles, a grateful and liberal heart, and *talents unequal'd*. He will go to Pembroke, not a weak boy to be made a property of, but to be admir'd as a prodigy; not to hear lectures, but to spread light. His parts are most astonishing and universal. He will be fully qualified for a wrangler *before he goes*, and be an accomplish'd classick, mathematician, historian, and poet. This is no exaggeration, believe me, but as it will one day shew itself fully.[1]

Chatham himself was prepared to believe that 'too young for the irregularities of a man, . . . he will not, on the other hand, prove troublesome by the Puerile sallies of a Boy'.[2] Nor was the judgment mistaken, for Pitt impressed others at this time. The poet Hayley, meeting him that summer, pronounced him 'the wonderful youth';[3] and the effect on the Fellows of Pembroke was much as those at home had forecast. He had indeed the stamp of true precocity, which Wilson hit in the telling phrase that Pitt 'seemed never to learn but merely to recollect'.[4]

When he went to the University, the lines of Pitt's talents and character had in fact been laid. His nature, at once impressionable and distinctive, had already taken a mature and lasting cast. The compound of exceptional precocity, an affectionately dominating father, a close and spirited family circle, and an intensive, cloistered education set

1. Ashbourne, 7–8. The mathematical qualifications need not be overestimated. According to his tutor at Cambridge, Pitt had read 'the first six books of Euclid's Elements, Plane Trigonometry, the elementary parts of Algebra and . . . Rutherforth's Natural Philosophy' (Tomline, 1, 4). This was indeed ample for the purpose. Although mathematics was becoming the favourite subject at the University, the standard of examination was still very low by that of the following century (see D. A. Winstanley, *Unreformed Cambridge* (1935), 53–5).
2. To Joseph Turner [Fellow of Pembroke], 3 October 1773 (Lord Rosebery, *Pitt* (1891), 8).
3. *Memoirs of William Hayley, written by Himself*, I (1823), 127.
4. Quoted by Tomline, I, 3–4.

against the background of an exciting and illusorily familiar world – a world seen from Chatham's unusual point of vision – had made its enduring mark. Brilliant, idealistically ambitious, concentrated, and supremely confident, he faced his introduction to a larger scene.

II

Cambridge in the 1770s was much, though not quite, the same place that it had been for the best part of the century. The stagnant calm of the Augustan University was still barely disturbed by the catspaws of domestic reform. Noblemen (so defined as to include baronets and the sons of peers) were distinguished by their privileges and, if they wished, their clothes; few of the dons were notably industrious except in University politics, and not a few were odd; and the isolation of the Eastern counties preserved, as in a vacuum, the lineaments of a conservative and idiosyncratic society. It was the Cambridge of Gunning. But it was also the Cambridge of John Jebb, the academic reformer whose proposal that noblemen and fellow-commoners should be examined like other undergraduates was defeated by one vote in Pitt's second year.[1] The failure ensured that a nobleman was not required to show any qualification for a degree for another half century. But the voting indicated that there were doubts abroad, and if the University was moribund it contained some seeds of renewal. In comparison with Oxford, it had indeed a certain reputation for diligence; even noblemen and fellow-commoners sometimes did more than was asked of them; and in the better Colleges at least, a man could be soundly taught along the orthodox lines. Pembroke was such a College in the second half of the century: Pitt himself described its reputation as 'sober' and 'staid', with 'nothing but solid study there',[2] and both his tutors in succession were conscientious men. In the event, the reading of his Cambridge years sufficed, with little addition, as a basis for the rest of his life.

Academic conservatism, moreover, as so often, did not necessarily conflict with a more liberal view of other issues. The survival of the whig tradition in England as anything more than a political convenience depended largely on the dissenting chapels and academies, and a section of the established clergy. The latter owed a good deal to the Cambridge spirit. In the 1770s, some few resident Fellows of Colleges were directly involved in the movements for liturgical, ecclesiastical, and Parliamentary reform. But perhaps the more significant contribution of such men was to transmit to wider circles, often no doubt formally and with little of its earlier vigour, the main stream of Lockeian

1. And the defeat was in the Non-Regent House, the stronghold of the senior Masters of Arts. It was believed that, had the Grace passed, the Regent House would have approved it by eleven votes (Winstanley, op. cit., 327).
2. To Chatham, 8 October 1773 (*Chatham Correspondence*, IV, 289).

political philosophy and latitudinarian churchmanship which remained associated with the University's name. Whether or not Chatham was influenced by such considerations in sending his son to Cambridge, the atmosphere was rather more propitious than it was at Oxford to the dissemination of 'true whig' ideas.

In his first year, however, Pitt was hardly there. Accompanied by Wilson, he arrived at Pembroke on 8 October 1773, and was given the fine rooms over the gate once occupied by the poet Gray. On the 21st he had the worst attack yet of his old illness. Wilson acted promptly. Dr Glynn, a leading medical man in the University, was summoned from the convenient proximity of King's; Dr Addington, informed the next morning, came up a few days later from London; and Lady Chatham dispatched the children's nurse, Mrs Sparry. The crisis soon passed; but it left the boy very weak and listless, and it was the beginning of December before he was pronounced fit to go home. By then he seemed to be regaining his strength; but the doctors were still disturbed. Glynn, who considered the recovery unnaturally slow, even had doubts of 'his Patient's living to Manhood';[1] and while Addington was more sanguine, he was also more convinced than ever that the boy had inherited his father's gout, and it was probably from this time that he prescribed the drinking of a bottle of port a day.[2]

In the event the attack proved to be the crisis, and Pitt was not troubled by the complaint again. But it had naturally alarmed his parents, and fear of its recurrence governed his life for the next two years. It was the summer of 1774 before he returned to Cambridge, accompanied once more by Wilson; but he left for Hayes when the new term began in October, and spent the winter with his family. He went back to Cambridge in May 1775, and remained there until September: the following winter was again passed at home. Not until the summer term of 1776 was he able to enter on a normal University year.

Pitt was thus at Cambridge only intermittently from 1773 to 1776, and then as much in the vacation as in the term. This had two results. It did nothing to distract him from a studious life; and it brought him in those years more into the society of the dons than of the

1. Wilson to Lady Chatham, 15 December 1773 (P.R.O. 30/8/67).

2. It is difficult to be sure exactly when the Doctor gave his celebrated piece of advice. That it was his seems certain. Mrs Pretyman Tomline, the wife of Pitt's Cambridge tutor and lifelong friend, later ascribed it definitely to this occasion (notes of October and November 1801 on Pitt, in Stanhope Mss, Chevening, 'Mr Pitt II'). As Pretyman's wife, and a close friend of Pitt's favourite sister Harriot, she was in a good position to know; and her statement receives some support from Addington's correspondence with Lady Chatham (P.R.O. 30/8/15). There is no reference there at any time during his early years to Pitt's drinking port. But Addington, though Chatham's doctor, acted only as a consultant for the children, and it looks as if he had no direct experience of these attacks before 1773, when he discussed the symptoms in some detail.

undergraduates. Cambridge in the summer months was then indeed

> A habitation sober and demure
> For ruminating creatures,[1]

and Pitt spent them reading, walking and riding, with an occasional expedition to the sights of Wimpole or Houghton. His most regular companions were Dr Glynn, a noted conversationalist as well as a doctor, the friend of Mason and Gray and a well-known Cambridge figure; and, towards the end of the period particularly, his tutor, Dr Pretyman.

In 1773, Pitt had been put under the supervision of the two principal College lecturers, Joseph Turner and George Pretyman, and there had of course been Wilson as well. But in 1775 Wilson left the family to take up his duties as rector of Binfield in Berkshire, and thereafter Pretyman was placed in sole charge. He continued so until Pitt went down from Cambridge. The somewhat unusual circumstances caused him to see an unusual amount of his pupil. The difference in age was small (Pretyman was eight years older than Pitt), and there were few undergraduates in the College of enough social standing to claim comparable attention.[2] The association proved important, for Pretyman (or Tomline as he was later known, after inheriting property) remained intermittently close to Pitt until the latter's death. He acted as an unpaid private secretary to the Prime Minister, living with him in Downing Street, until created by his former pupil Bishop of Lincoln and Dean of St Paul's, was with him on his deathbed, and as literary executor wrote the official biography. His descendant still possesses the remains of Pitt's library, and an important, though diminished, collection of his papers.

Pretyman has not fared well at the hands of those concerned with Pitt. Nor is this surprising. As literary executor he has been widely suspected of destroying some of the papers; and as a biographer he was nothing short of disastrous. When the first instalment of his work appeared, *The Edinburgh Review* (admittedly a politically hostile organ) remarked that it seemed to have been composed 'not by means of his Lordship's memory, but of his scissars';[3] and indeed, apart from a few early reminiscences, it might have been written by a complete stranger, relying for his information on the pages of *The Parliamentary History* and *The Annual Register*. 'The worst biographical work of its

1. Wordsworth, *The Prelude*, Book Third, 'Residence at Cambridge'.
2. Of the fifty-five men admitted to Pembroke from 1773 to 1779 inclusive, none was entered as a nobleman and eight were fellow-commoners (Pembroke College Mss, Cambridge, Admission Book, 1616–1797).

It was now more usual than not for a peer's son, unless himself bearing a courtesy title, to be entered as a fellow-commoner. The fees were lower, and the privileges not greatly different.
3. *The Edinburgh Review*, XXXV, no. LXX (July 1821), 450–1.

size in the world', Macaulay called it.[1] It was perhaps as well that the second part did not see the light of day.

It is not unfair to judge Pretyman by his book. Dull writers, of course, are very often far from being dull men – Fox himself wrote a remarkably lifeless fragment of a history of James II. But the Bishop's book is inept as well as dull. It was not stimulating to construct a biography largely on reports of the Parliamentary debates. But to do so when the author knew (as he was reminded by some of those who read his draft) that many of them were based on versions put out in newspapers hostile to Pitt argues a political innocence amounting to stupidity. Pretyman was in fact an upright, businesslike cleric – a reasonable scholar, a capable mathematician, but not generally distinguished in manner or mind – who served Pitt well as a faithful friend. He had no pretensions to influence: his merits were his competence, his devotion, and the comfort of a familiar face. It is not particularly surprising that a young politician, thrust quickly into a position of power, should have been glad of such services; or that he should later have rewarded them, and perhaps suited himself, by making his friend a Bishop. But, anxious though he was at the time to show that he commanded the necessary royal support, Pitt should hardly have pressed Tomline's claims in 1805 for the vacant Archbishopric of Canterbury.

Under his tutor's supervision, Pitt read steadily and hard. It seems likely, indeed, that he did not later enlarge significantly on the education he then acquired. At the end of his life, his library divided into two parts. One contained a large collection of the classics, and lesser collections of English literature, history, law and philosophy, French history and literature, mathematics and science. Some of the volumes were bought later, particularly the French. But most of the authors are those of whom we hear at Cambridge – the favourite classics, Thucydides, Polybius, Plutarch, Quintilian, Pliny, Cicero, Sallust; Shakespeare and Milton, Johnson's *Lives of the English Poets*; Blackstone and Bacon, Bolingbroke and Locke; the histories of Clarendon, Burnet, Rapin, Coxe, Robertson, and Hume; Newton's *Principia*, and works on mathematics and chemistry. The other part consisted of books and pamphlets bearing – as one might expect – on contemporary affairs, on landscape gardening and farming, and in later years on war.[2]

1. *Miscellaneous Writings*, II, 308.
2. 'Catalogue of the Library at Walmer Castle late belonging to the Right Honble. Wm. Pitt, taken 12 Feby, 1806' (Pretyman Ms 562:21). There were stated to be 1,095 volumes, 47 pamphlets, and seven maps. From lists of Pitt's effects at Downing Street at about the same time, he seems to have kept few of his books there then.

Some seven hundred volumes from this library, mostly falling in the first category, are in the possession of Captain G. M. T. Pretyman at Orwell Park House in Suffolk. They show that in many cases, particularly with his classics, Pitt later bought new or collected editions of authors already represented. Although the earlier acquisitions cannot be dated directly, they are often clearly distinguished from the later by their appearance, as well as sometimes by the dates of the editions.

The two portions are distinct. When Pitt, as was long his custom if not otherwise engaged, set aside a part of the late afternoon or early evening for a book, it was usually to return to an old favourite or to study something relating to public affairs.

In his attitude to contemporary letters, Pitt was indeed a philistine. He wrote some verse as a child, and at Cambridge he is said to have had 'an elegant taste for the beauties of the English poets'.[1] But it seems to have been mainly for the poets of the past, and while his memory would not allow him to forget what he had read, the interest was not maintained.[2] He showed little feeling later for emergent talent, whether in verse or prose; but equally he held a low opinion of Johnson's style and a lower one of Gibbon's, and apart from the political economists few of his significant contemporaries found room on his shelves. His official lack of patronage of literature aroused some comment at the time, and has been rightly reprobated since. His interests lay in other directions. But in those the effect of his Cambridge reading endured. For Pitt's powers of digestion were by then phenomenal, and an equally remarkable memory ensured that the results were not lost. At breakfast one day over twenty years later, he astonished a knowledgeable company by discussing nice points of classical etymology and quoting 'from *Memory* in a manner that seemed, as they said, "as if he had been doing nothing at all in his life but studying Greek and Latin".' Towards the end of his life, he was still able to settle a difficult passage from Thucydides at sight.[3] His appetite for the classics at Cambridge was indeed omnivorous: Pretyman was obliged to study with him even 'the obscure and in general uninteresting work of Lycophron'.[4] His powers of translation, thanks to his early training, were exceptional – at the age of fourteen he 'could read 400 pages of

1. Tomline, I, 13. There are four sets of verses, dating from 1771 and thereabouts, in Sir Timothy Hoare's Mss, K.35/8.

2. Pitt's memory was as comprehensive in this as in every other respect. It was perhaps not surprising that he could quote at will from his favourite Milton. It was more so that he could declaim extempore an appropriate passage from Waller's 'The Queen', when seeking on one occasion to rouse Addington's ambition (The Hon. George Pellew, *The Life and Correspondence of the Right Honble. Henry Addington, First Viscount Sidmouth,* I (1847), 38).

But the only specimen of contemporary poetry in his library, other than those contained in Robert Anderson's twelve-volume *Works of the British Poets* of 1795, was 'Grove Hill, a descriptive Poem' – an unremarkable piece of versification by Thomas Maurice of the British Museum which appeared in 1797, and was acquired (if it was not presented) presumably because the subject related to a feature of the countryside near Hayes, and the author was a fervent Pittite.

3. Mrs Pretyman Tomline to Tomline, 22 December 1801 (Stanhope Mss, 'Mr. Pitt II'); *Memorials and Correspondence of Charles James Fox,* ed. Lord John Russell, II (1853), 3.

4. Tomline, I, 10. Fox also tackled Lycophron, in his case during his retirement in the late 1790s. (*Correspondence of the late Gilbert Wakefield, B.A. with the late Right Honourable Charles James Fox . . .* (1813), 110, 128).

Thucydides off at once with as much ease as he could read English'[1] – and as always he was absorbed by methods of presentation and style. A morning would be spent in dissecting the structure of a few pages of narrative, or comparing the arguments of opponents in a debate. He showed an equal interest in mathematics and 'natural philosophy', to an extent indeed that seems to have somewhat alarmed his tutor. Newton's *Principia* fascinated him, and he used later to say that such studies had been particularly useful, not only on account of their intrinsic importance but also for 'the habit of close attention and patient investigation' they required.[2] His other favourite reading lay in English history and political philosophy. His knowledge of French literature was adequate. He enjoyed, but was not addicted to, philosophy. Not even Pretyman could claim that his interest in theology was marked.

Pitt's reading owed little directly to the University's demands. Noblemen and fellow-commoners were not required to do much in practice in the way of attending lectures, and he appears to have confined himself at different times over a period of six years to a course on Quintilian, another on 'experimental philosophy' (almost certainly by George Atwood), Dr Hallifax's lectures on civil law, and some by John Hey, Fellow of Sidney Sussex, on 'Morality'. Nor did he sit for his degree by examination. He had in fact intended to do so; but when the time came in 1776 he had not kept enough terms, and so took his M.A., as he was entitled, without further ado.[3] Nevertheless, the *genius loci* had its effect. For Pitt's attainments were, and remained, preeminently those of a Cambridge education. They reflected its limits, and almost epitomised its strengths. His whole cast of mind might be called, without caricature, that of a Cambridge rather than an Oxford man. The prominence accorded to mathematics; the subordination of Platonic and Aristotelian moral philosophy (still regnant in Oxford) to modes of thought deriving from Newton and Locke; the practical emphasis, in the classical education itself, on composition and translation; the strength of whig interpretations in the teaching of theology, philosophy, and history: all suited his tastes and talents and did something to develop them. Circumstance and his own interests left the early foundations largely undisturbed. No great new intellectual influence was added later to those of his youth. Pitt never enjoyed contemporary letters, in the manner of Shelburne or Fox. He could not read extensively in European languages, as did North. In particular, the great stream of French rationalism virtually passed him by. His general knowledge and cultivation were essentially those of the Cambridge

1. Mrs Pretyman Tomline's 'Common Place Book', record of conversation with Bishop Tomline, November 1802. (Pembroke College Mss, 29, I, 35:3).
2. Tomline, I, 12.
3. Noblemen entered as fellow-commoners did not thereby forfeit their right to proceed to a degree without examination.

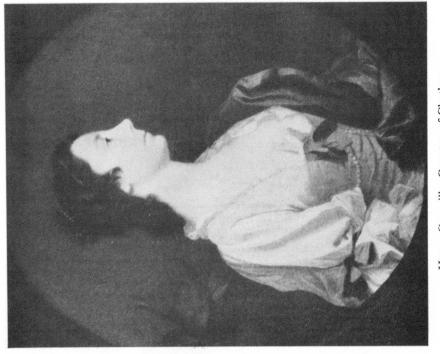

Hester Grenville, Countess of Chatham
by Hudson

William Pitt, Earl of Chatham
Studio of W. Hoare

Burton Pynsent, Somerset. *Engraved by T. Bonnor*

tripos, brought to a very high point, and extended and given form by his feeling for politics. Within that structure – and it was capacious – he moved with masterful ease. He was not much concerned with what might lie beyond.

When he began to keep regular terms, from 1776, Pitt had his first real opportunity to make his friends. Among the closest were Edward James Eliot, Henry Bankes, John Pratt, Lord Euston, St Andrew St John, J. C. Villiers, Lord Westmorland, William Lowther, and towards the end Charles Long. Others included Lord Granby (who went down in 1774, but lived nearby at Cheveley), Lord Althorp, and Westmorland's friend William Meeke. Some of them became his colleagues, and almost all were associated with different aspects of his career. Granby, as Duke of Rutland, was Lord Lieutenant of Ireland in his first Administration; Westmorland later became Joint Postmaster General, Lord Lieutenant of Ireland, and Lord Privy Seal; Pratt (Lord Camden), a member of the Admiralty and Treasury Boards, Lord Lieutenant of Ireland, Secretary of State for War and the Colonies, and Lord President of the Council; Eliot and Long, members of the Treasury Board, Long having been Joint Secretary to the Treasury; Villiers, a member of the Board of Trade. The rest were also associated, by birth or inclination, in differing degrees with politics. Bankes sat in the Commons for most of his life. Meeke went with Westmorland to Ireland, became Clerk of the Parliament in Dublin until the Union, and then for a time a Member at Westminster. Euston was Pitt's Parliamentary colleague for Cambridge University. Lowther sat for a succession of northern seats. And St John, who alone ceased to be a friend of Pitt's after leaving Cambridge, was a faithful follower and at one time an Under-Secretary of Fox.

Such a group reflects an element long constant in University life. Its members were all, like Pitt himself, fellow-commoners or noblemen – 'young men', as Pretyman called them, 'of his own age and station in life'[1] – linked by family or school acquaintance and a taste, usually inherited, for public affairs. It was not an exceptionally close or brilliant set – in neither respect can it compare with Fox's circle at Oxford a decade before. It was not a dissolute set – which was why Wilberforce, soon to become one of Pitt's closest friends, saw little of it. In so far as it was a set, its interests were steadier and its amusements milder, and a certain seriousness lay behind the natural acceptance of the life of a governing class. Pitt was a leading member from 1776. 'In society', Wilberforce later observed, he was always 'remarkably cheerful and

---

1. Tomline, I, 7. They were emphatically not a College group. Only Eliot and Pitt came from Pembroke. Pratt, Euston, Lowther and Althorp (and Granby) were Trinity men; St John and Villiers were at St John's; Westmorland, Meeke and Long at Emmanuel. Bankes was at Trinity Hall.

Pitt's closest friends in the College itself, other than Eliot, were probably John Hamilton, afterwards Earl of Abercorn, and Robert Wharton.

pleasant, full of wit and playfulness.'[1] At Cambridge, no pressures had yet arisen to hide these qualities from all but a very few. 'His society', according to Pretyman, 'was universally sought, and from the age of seventeen or eighteen he constantly passed his evenings in company.'[2] In such surroundings he was lively and gay, 'abounding in playful wit and quick repartee'.[3] Otherwise his life continued much as before – reading in his room, discussion with Pretyman, the attendance at Chapel, the regular ride.

Pitt was in residence at Cambridge until the end of 1779: a total, on and off, of over six years. Towards the end, as at the start, he was away a good deal, but until the winter of 1779 not long enough to fail to keep a term. His prolonged stay arose mainly from the wish to make up for his earlier absence. He relished 'the sober Hours and Studies of College', particularly after a spell elsewhere,[4] and as late as June 1779 remained anxious to enjoy them while he could. 'This place', he wrote to his mother, 'has so many Advantages for Study, and I have unavoidably lost so much Time lately, and can spare so little for the Future, that I cannot help wishing to continue here a considerable Part of the Summer'[5]. But he may also have been influenced shortly afterwards by the prospect of an exciting opportunity. In May 1779 the old Duke of Rutland died, and Pitt's friend Granby succeeded. The occasion threw the University into a state of excitement, for Granby had been one of its Burgesses in Parliament since he went down in 1774, and a successor must be found. He himself had been an opponent of Government; but in the ensuing by-election, in June, the seat went to James Mansfield, a supporter of Government and soon to be one of its law officers. The new Member's tenure, however, appeared somewhat insecure. The political scene was dark, the Ministry was harassed, and it seemed possible, though it would be unusual, that Parliament would soon be dissolved well in advance of the statutory limit. The various Opposition interests in the University were therefore on the alert, and at the beginning of July Pitt received an offer of support if he was prepared to stand at a general election. It is not clear who was responsible for the invitation: possibly Granby exerted himself on his friend's behalf. Nor was Pitt by any means the only candidate in view. But at least a chance had come his way, and precisely of the kind he would have wished. In such circumstances, as he informed his mother, 'the Scenes of Cambridge are become doubly interesting to me'.[6] Political prospects now

1. 'Sketch of Mr. Pitt' (*Private Papers of William Wilberforce*, ed. A. M. Wilberforce (1897), 68).
2. Tomline, I, 8.
3. Op. cit., 7.
4. Pitt to Lady Chatham, 4 November 1777 (P.R.O. 30/8/11). And see also his letter to her of 19 April 1779 (P.R.O. 30/8/12).
5. Same to same, 28 June 1779 (loc. cit.).
6. Same to same, 3 July 1779 (loc. cit.).

combined with his own inclination to keep him there for at least a few more months.

III

When Pitt was not at Cambridge, he was now often in London. There were several reasons for his visits. In May 1778 Chatham died, and since the eldest son John was with his regiment at Gibraltar it fell to William to help settle his father's affairs. Chatham left an embarrassed estate. By selling stock and raising mortgages on Burton Pynsent and Hayes, he – or his wife – had managed to pay back his friends' largest loans. Parliament now met the outstanding debts to the tune of £20,000, and voted an annuity of £4,000 in perpetuity to the Earldom of Chatham. Lady Chatham herself became the recipient of an annuity of £3,000, granted to her husband by the King in 1761 for the period of three lives. These measures enabled her to continue living at Burton Pynsent; but they could do little more than remove the immediate threat of debt. The annuity of £3,000 (in effect £2,000 when fees and taxes had been met) was in arrears when Chatham died, and Pitt was soon engaged in protracted efforts to get the payments brought up to date and secured regularly for the future. All the family had meanwhile to wait, in varying degrees, for the money due to them from the mortgaged property. It was not in fact possible for the executors to produce a comprehensive statement until 1785, when Hayes was sold. Pitt's own fortunes at that date may be summarised here, for he had been living in the interval on his expectations from them.

Chatham had raised a mortgage of £13,175 on Burton Pynsent in 1774, and one of £10,000 on Hayes in 1778. Pitt was assigned £1,500 on the former at the time, and £8,500 on the latter by his mother in February 1782. He was assigned a further £244–2–8 on the earlier mortgage in November 1780, when his younger brother, James Charles, died suddenly and his share was distributed between the rest of the family. In theory therefore Pitt's capital was £1,500 on coming of age in May 1780, £1,774–2–8 in 1781, and £10,244–2–8 from February 1782.[1] Of this total, he appears to have received nothing until Hayes was sold in May 1785 for £8,540. He was then paid a sum of £4,396–8–4.[2] Meanwhile, his income amounted to £600 a year,

1. Chatham also left Pitt a legacy of £3,500. But this could not of course be paid, and while it figures in Pitt's own financial transactions it was not included in the trustees' statements covering the distribution of the estate.

2. Two accounts, one undated but clearly drawn up as a result of the sale of Hayes (in P.R.O. 30/8/10), the other dated 1785 (in Pretyman Ms 435/14), agree that Pitt's 'fortune' was £10,244-2-8, and that he had received (and according to the first account, from the sale of Hayes itself) £4,396-8-4 of it. The second account has in addition a heading 'By Cash pd. him [Pitt] on further Accot.'. But this was left blank at the time, and although there is a pencilled entry against it of £1,643-11-8, this would seem, from Pitt's subsequent financial transactions, to have been a much later insertion.

being a grant from his elder brother of which half was in fact a payment from the same source to his mother, made over by her to him. It was on this basis that he lived on coming down from Cambridge, and raised money as he found necessary or convenient.

It was not long before the latter process began. Thus in August 1780, wishing to ease his mother's current difficulties and to repay sums advanced before he was of age, Pitt borrowed £1,000 at five per cent from Thomas Coutts, the family's banker – a proven friend, and a seasoned investor in young men of note or promise – in return for assigning to him Chatham's unpaid (and unpayable) legacy of £3,500.[1] And a few months later, he was granted an annuity of £300 by Rutland for a capital payment (how made is uncertain) of £3,500. The situation was reflected in the steps he took when the time came to house himself in London. In January 1777 he had been admitted to Lincoln's Inn, and towards the end of the following year it looked as if some rooms might become available. But the occupant wished to sell the lease rather than to let; and the price was £1,100. This, Pitt thought, sounded 'a frightful sum'.[2] But there was no other likely set in view, and it seemed not much more expensive to buy the lease outright than to rent similar rooms later. Lady Chatham approved. But she could not find the money, and her brother, Lord Temple, therefore agreed to advance £1,000 against Pitt's expectations. The lease was accordingly bought, and the first instalment paid. Fortunately the rest was not required for some time, for Temple died in September 1779 without redeeming his promise, and in the autumn Pitt was anxiously preparing to borrow elsewhere (and in fact did borrow the outstanding £100 from Coutts) on the security of his uncle's obligation. In the event, he was able to take possession in December. But a year later he and his elder brother mortgaged the lease, together with that of another set of rooms in Lincoln's Inn, to a certain Solomon Henry for a loan of £1,500 at five per cent. Pitt thereby raised some ready money on the basis of a property itself bought, so far as his share was concerned, with loans secured on future expectations. He had begun to spin the web in which he was to be entangled for the rest of his life.

Pitt went to live in Lincoln's Inn, in the rooms 'on the north side of the attic of staircase number 4 of Stone Buildings',[3] early in 1780. But the business of eating dinners in preparation for the Bar had taken him there from time to time over the previous two years. Family duties, too, had continued to demand his presence in London. Chatham's affairs kept him in town at intervals from the early summer of 1778, and in the following spring and summer he had also to deal with an awkward problem affecting his younger brother James Charles, who as a young officer in the fleet at Portsmouth had become involved in the disputes

1. See p. 19, n.1 above.
2. Pitt to Hester Countess of Chatham, 30 November 1778 (Stannope, I, 25).
3. Holland Rose, 67.

arising from the famous Keppel court-martial, to an extent that made it desirable for him to be moved (as eventually he was) to another appointment. These various commitments had one great merit in Pitt's eyes. They gave him the opportunity, when Parliament was sitting, to listen to the debates. He had already done so a few times – certainly in January 1775, and again in May and September 1777 – when Chatham was delivering his philippics on America; and he was in the House of Lords on the great occasion of his father's dying speech in April 1778 – the consummation of the heroic legend in which he had been brought up. He now took full advantage of his time in London to attend whenever possible. His letters, at first from Nerot's hotel in King Street, St James's, later from Lincoln's Inn, are full of the doings at Westminster. He was present at some of the most stirring events in the last phase of that most stirring of Parliamentary sessions – when the Commons delivered an address of thanks to Keppel, while the London mob crowded to the door of the Chamber; when Burke introduced his Plan for Economical Reform, and the Government was defeated ('a scene which I never saw before')[1] on his motion to abolish the Board of Trade; when Shelburne spoke in the Lords on the Spanish Manifesto and the Armed Neutrality; and Tommy Townshend, Dunning, Burke and Fox assailed Lord North's motion, so full of consequences for Pitt's own later measures, to set up Parliamentary Commissioners to examine the public accounts. Watching the speakers from the gallery of the Commons, 'perfectly unobserv'd',[2] Pitt became particularly interested in Burke. He noted the mixture of 'real beauties and ridiculous affectations'.[3] But he could not withhold his admiration in the debates on Economical Reform. 'I must have the Malice to remind you', he wrote to Eliot at Cambridge, 'that you have lost the two most interesting Debates this Century. Burke's Extempores have both Times exceeded his corrected Publication, which (entre nous) is in my Opinion much the worse for revision. I had no Idea till now of his Excellence'.[4]

Such scenes absorbed most of Pitt's attention. He spared some time for the 'incidental Engagements that are unavoidable in a London life'.[5] 'I am just come', runs one letter when the season was in full swing, 'from behind the Throne in the House of Lords, and preparing to take my Station in Fop Alley'.[6] The big receptions, at the Duchess of Bolton's or Northumberland House; the opera (he had been fond of music at Cambridge, and later subscribed to the Treasury Box);[7] the

1. Pitt to Hester Countess of Chatham, 14 March [1780] (Stanhope, I, 38).
2. Same to same, n.d. but 13 or 14 April 1778 (P.R.O. 30/8/11).
3. Same to same, 14 March [1780] (Stanhope, I, 38).
4. 14 March [1780] (Pretyman Ms 435/39).
5. Pitt to Hester Countess of Chatham, 2 March [1780] (P.R.O. 30/8/12).
6. Pitt to Eliot, 15 February [1779] (Pretyman Ms 435/39).
7. Though, according to Pretyman – and later Windham – 'he had no ear' (The Earl of Rosebery, *Bishop Tomline's Estimate of Pitt, Together with Chapter XXVII of the Unpublished Fourth Volume of the Life* (1903), 34 & n.2).

occasional visit to the Pantheon, are recorded without much comment. Some of them at least were clearly a duty. It is scarcely surprising to learn that Pitt avoided dances when he could; and when he went to the masquerade, at the Pantheon in Oxford Street, 'as I had hardly the pleasure of plaguing or being plagued by any body, I was heartily tired of my domino before it was over'.[1] He was happier when summoned to dine with one of his father's friends, where there would be leading men among the guests and the talk turned on public affairs.

To this normal life of the town was added, in June 1780, the dramatic experience of the Gordon riots – the worst case of mob violence in the capital in a century of spasmodic violence, and one which those who saw it were not quick to forget. Pitt had already glimpsed the London crowd in action, at the time of Keppel's acquittal sixteen months before. The disturbances now were on a different scale. Lincoln's Inn, surrounded for a spell by 'flames on all sides',[2] was put into a state of defence, with eight hundred men of the Northumberland Militia and a volunteer corps of 'very respectable lawyers . . . with muskets on their shoulders, to the no small diversion of all spectators'.[3] It was during this episode that the celebrated encounter took place between Pitt and Gibbon, when the latter came as a guest to one of the dinners given by members of the Inn to the officers of the militia. Pitt was not a great admirer of the historian, whose politics he disliked as much as his style. 'I wish', he had written to Eliot only three months before, when the Board of Trade, of which Gibbon was a member, was under attack, 'you had heard Fox on the subject of your Friend Gibbon, who came in his helpless State last Night, on the hazard of his life for the sake of his Place; a strange Principle of self-Preservation'.[4] The occasion itself was described by Gibbon's host, the young lawyer James Bland Burges.[5]

1. Pitt to Hester Countess of Chatham, 4 April [1780] (Stanhope, I, 39).
2. Same to same, 8 June (op. cit., 41).
3. Same to same, Thursday (ibid).
4. 14 March [1780] (Pretyman Ms 435/39).
5. *Selections from the Letters and Correspondence of Sir James Bland Burges, Bart. . . .*, ed. James Hutton (1885), 60-1.

Two biographers of Gibbon, J. M. Robertson and Mr D. M. Low, have challenged the truth of this anecdote. They do so on two grounds: the improbability of Gibbon's behaviour, and the later statement of Lord Sheffield (Holroyd) that when Gibbon met Pitt at a dinner party in 1793 'he was not acquainted' with him.

Sheffield published his statement in 1796: Burges wrote his reminiscences towards the end of a life that ended in 1824. It is therefore fair to say that memory may have played more tricks with Burges than with Sheffield. At the same time, the two arguments do not seem to me conclusive. We cannot now properly judge the improbability of Gibbon's behaviour: Burges's account is uncomfortably explicit, and if we must allow for the great historian's well-known politeness we must also allow for his well-known vanity. As to Sheffield's statement, I cannot see that it really amounts to much. A single conversation, thirteen years before, with an unknown young man in a large company, scarcely constitutes acquaintance. And if it is thought to do so, Sheffield may have overlooked the occasion, or preferred to ignore it. Mr Low asks how this last could have happened, when there would have been witnesses to remind

22

Mr. Gibbon, nothing loath, took the conversation into his own hands, and very brilliant and pleasant he was during the dinner and for some time afterwards. He had just concluded, however, one of his best foreign anecdotes, in which he had introduced some of the fashionable levities of political doctrine then prevalent, and, with his customary tap on the lid of his snuff-box, was looking round to receive our tribute of applause, when a deep-toned but clear voice was heard from the bottom of the table, very calmly and civilly impugning the correctness of the narrative, and the propriety of the doctrine of which it had been made the vehicle. The historian, turning a disdainful glance towards the quarter whence the voice proceeded, saw, for the first time, a tall, thin, and rather ungainly-looking young man, who now sat quietly and silently eating some fruit. There was nothing very prepossessing or very formidable in his exterior, but, as the few words he had uttered appeared to have made a considerable impression on the company, Mr. Gibbon, I suppose, thought himself bound to maintain his honour by suppressing such an attempt to dispute his supremacy. He accordingly undertook the defence of the propositions in question, and a very animated debate took place between him and his youthful antagonist, Mr. Pitt, and for some time was conducted with great talent and brilliancy on both sides. At length the genius of the young man prevailed over that of his senior, who, finding himself driven into a corner from which there was no escape, made some excuse for rising from the table and walked out of the room. I followed him and, finding that he was looking for his hat, I tried to persuade him to return to his seat. 'By no means', said he. 'That young gentleman is, I have no doubt, extremely ingenious and agreeable, but I must acknowledge that his style of conversation is not exactly what I am accustomed to, so you must positively excuse me.' And away he went in high dudgeon, notwithstanding that his friend [Holroyd, serving as an officer in the militia] had come to my assistance. When we returned to the dining room we found Mr. Pitt proceeding very tranquilly with the illustration of the subject from which his opponent had fled, and which he discussed with such ability, strength of argument, and eloquence, that his hearers were filled with profound admiration.

The riots ended a few days before Pitt was called to the Bar. Since February 1780 he had been 'attending' in Westminster Hall, and at the end of July he joined the Western Circuit, 'sitting', he wrote from Winchester, 'in Expectation of Attorneys'.[1] Some seem to have called,

Sheffield of the conversation. But the same consideration applies equally, if not more strongly, to Burges's detailed account, which surely stood a strong risk of being challenged if it was materially false.

1. To Hester Countess of Chatham, 25 July [endorsed by Pretyman 1780, though there is a later attribution by Stanhope of 1781] (P.R.O. 30/8/12).

23

in the two summers he was present. He picked up a number of retainers in cases of *crim.con.* – criminal conversation, the predecessor of the modern action for divorce – and gained some modest distinction at Exeter assizes. How far he ever became interested in the law it is hard to say: 'Certainly', according to one who knew him quite well then and later, 'he always relished the Society of Lawyers'.[1] He was a popular member of the Mess – 'among lively Men of nearly his own time of Life . . . almost the most lively'[2] – joined a Western Circuit Club in London, and for several years held an annual dinner at Richmond with some of his erstwhile fellow Counsel. No doubt, had things gone differently, he would have entered politics in the course of a successful career at the Bar.

As it was, the business of the Circuit came to take second place. Throughout the first half of 1780, Pitt's interest had remained centred on the prospects of an election. On at least two occasions he had been given a half promise of a seat in Parliament: by one cousin, Thomas Pitt, for Old Sarum – the family borough for which his father had sat at the start of his career – and by another, the new Lord Temple, for Buckingham. But either would depend, to an unknown extent, on the intentions of the sitting Members; and moreover Pitt remained anxious to try his fortunes at Cambridge, for a University seat – 'of all others most desirable, as being free from expense, perfectly independent, and I think in every respect extremely honourable'[3] – carried a distinction denied to the representation of a proprietary borough. He had kept up his canvass, at the College feasts in the winter and again in the summer before going on Circuit; and in the middle of the Circuit itself the long-awaited moment arrived. On 1 September 1780, Parliament was suddenly dissolved, to reassemble at the end of October. As soon as he heard the news, Pitt left Exeter for Cambridge.

The circumstances for Opposition were not as propitious as had earlier been hoped. North's Government had weathered the storm of the previous winter and spring, and indeed had regained some ground at the end of the session in May and June. The forces of change and reform seemed to have been momentarily checked, a process which was underlined by the reaction to the Gordon riots. Having survived the threat of a dissolution under pressure, the Minister and the King were now able to consider one in conditions more to their liking. In July, after making the not unusual offer of a coalition to some of their opponents, they examined the prospects of an election afresh; they thought themselves ready towards the end of August; and at the end of that month they moved.

1. Amendments to his Reminiscences by J. Jekyll, 6 May 1820 (Pretyman Ms 562:1820).
2. Reminiscences of J. Jekyll, 4 May 1820 (loc.cit). The wording of the ms differs somewhat from that printed by Tomline, to whom the paper was addressed, in I, 42n.
3. Stanhope, I, 31.

Government had kept its counsel well. The Opposition groups were taken by surprise, and few if any had prepared in detail for an election precisely at that time. Pitt's chances at Cambridge in any case were not high. There were four other candidates for the two available seats, and all, unlike himself, had canvassed the University before. James Mansfield, a sitting Member and the newly appointed Solicitor General, again represented the Government interest. John Townshend, who had recently come second to him in the contest for Granby's vacant seat, was a follower of Lord Rockingham and thus assured of the support of the principal Opposition party. Lord Hyde in turn had run Townshend close in the election of 1779. And Richard Croftes, though inactive, had occupied the other seat for the University for the past nine years. Not all of these candidates had earlier been definitely in the field. But Pitt's own prospects had always been doubtful, as indeed both Temple and Rockingham had made clear at the start, in 1779; and they had not improved since, though inexperience and a native optimism sometimes persuaded him that they had.[1] When the result was announced he was at the bottom of the poll, with Mansfield and Townshend in the first two places.[2]

In November, Pitt was therefore back at work in Westminster Hall. But he had not long to wait for another opportunity of a seat, and this time without any uncertainty. Among the friends who were anxious to see him in Parliament was the new Duke of Rutland, with whom Pitt went to stay on the morrow of his defeat, and whose political connexions included Sir James Lowther, the great boroughmonger of the north. In the autumn, Lowther was making his final arrangements to meet the anomalies produced, as usual after a general election, by having put in some of his candidates for more than one seat. It was therefore a good season for Rutland's approach; and since Sir James was prepared to oblige the Duke, Pitt was offered a vacancy, with all expenses paid, at his borough of Appleby. Under such conditions there was no question of failure: the candidate did not have to visit his constituents. The only doubt in Pitt's mind – and still more in his mother's – was whether or not to accept a seat of this sort. He had earlier been disinclined to take up Temple's vague offer of Buckingham, in case it could not 'be done

1. In the early part of 1780, Pretyman warned Pitt that he could expect very little support, and even urged him not 'to persevere in standing' should Parliament be dissolved before he came of age. (Undated letter in Pretyman Ms 435/45. I ascribe it to the early part of 1780 because it bears an endorsement of that year, and because Pitt's twenty-first birthday fell in May.)

For Pitt's renewed optimism as late as June and July, after earlier doubts, see his letters to Lady Chatham of 21 June and 7 July [1780] in P.R.O. 30/8/12. (Both may be dated 1780 from their references to the forthcoming Circuit.) And see also *H.M.C., Tenth Report, Appendix, Pt. IV*, 25.

2. The figures, on 16 September, were Mansfield 277, Townshend 247, Hyde 206, Croftes 150, Pitt 142 (Charles Henry Cooper, *Annals of Cambridge*, IV (1852), 399).

on a *liberal, Independent* Footing'.[1] Temple was at least a cousin, brought up in much the same political tradition as himself. Lowther was neither. He had, it was true, supported Opposition, and at times Chatham himself. But his objects were essentially those of an independent interest; he kept a notoriously strict hold on his Members; and his reputation as a borough manager was unsavoury by the standards of the age. At first sight, it was not an ideal banner under which to enlist. But to give him credit, Lowther in this instance (as in one other, that of the former Speaker's son) waived his usual demands. The formal offer at the end of November was made, Pitt reported, 'in the handsomest Manner. Judging from my Father's Principles He concludes that mine would be agreeable to his own, and on that Ground, to me of all others the most agreeable, desires to bring me in. No Kind of Condition was mentioned, but that if ever Our Lines of Conduct should become opposite, I should give Him an Opportunity of chusing another Person. On such Liberal Terms', Pitt continued firmly, 'I could certainly not hesitate to accept the Proposal, than which Nothing could be in any respect more agreeable'.[2] It was indeed a fortunate one. A seat at Cambridge was no longer in sight, candidature for an open borough (assuming a vacancy had been in prospect) was out of the question if only on the ground of expense, and here was an immediate haven to be gained without any outlay, in which he was assured of safety and a very reasonable freedom of movement. The election duly took place in December, allowing Pitt to enter the House when it reassembled in January 1781 after the Christmas recess. 'I shall be in Time', he had written to his mother on accepting Lowther's offer, 'to be Spectator and Auditor *at least*, of the Important Scene after the Holidays'.[3] Twenty months later, he was Chancellor of the Exchequer.

1. Pitt to Hester Countess of Chatham, 27 March 1780 (P.R.O. 30/8/12).
2. Same to same, 'Thursday Night' [endorsed November 1780] (loc. cit.).
3. Ibid.

CHAPTER II

The World of Westminster

I

The visitor to Parliament in the last quarter of the eighteenth century would normally approach by way of Parliament Street or King Street, the two thoroughfares into which Whitehall divided at the southern end, and round the houses flanking the entry to Westminster Bridge. As he emerged into New Palace Yard, he saw before him a range of variegated buildings clustered round the historic centre of Westminster Hall. The Palace of Westminster, in which the Lords had sat since at least the fourteenth and the Commons since the mid-sixteenth century, was still the medieval palace, under constant alteration and slightly enlarged, but retaining many of the features of an abandoned royal court – the tradesmen and coffee-houses in the purlieus, the houses, gardens and stables of sinecure officials, as well as the concentration of legal, Parliamentary and (now marginal) administrative business that had once marked the principal residence of the King. In its precincts, covering almost exactly the area that Barry's Houses of Parliament occupy today, ancient and modern structures, for the most part overcrowded, insanitary and damp, spread and huddled together, the haphazard accretions of a long and vigorous history in which the vestigial remains of the distant past appeared, like petrified trunks, as features in the landscape of more recent times. The cloister of St Stephen's Chapel was to be seen in the passages of the Auditor of the Exchequer. Alice's coffee-house and Bellamy's kitchen clung like barnacles to the Court of Requests, itself the old Little Hall of the Norman court, where in 1782 Fox and Burke were watched as they paced up and down discussing whether to break with Shelburne and resign from the Government. Westminster Hall was partly filled by the Law Courts, crammed also into buildings on its western side. The gabled houses of the Exchequer, and the gardens of its officers, bordered the river. The outer part of the Tudor Court of Wards, a few yards from the Commons' lobbies, which some decades before harboured a coffee-house and an auction room, had recently been thrown into new Parliamentary accommodation stretching into a building with façades based on designs by Kent. The topography of the old palace was something of a microcosm of constitutional development, and Pitt and his contemporaries moved in a setting, strange to us, that embodied much of the inheritance of their age. It was perhaps not unfitting that the venerable rabbit-warren should have been largely destroyed in the 1830s, the decade which in so many ways saw the emergence of a new political world.

The House of Commons itself was approached from one of two directions: through Westminster Hall, as Members and officials of the House come today, passing by the Courts of Chancery and King's Bench which occupied its southern end, up the steps, and into the outer lobby of the Chamber; or from Old Palace Yard opposite the Abbey, through a passage by a coffee-house, up a staircase to the level of the Court of Requests, and out into a 'new and commodious passage', completed by the 1770s, which ran along the southern side of Westminster Hall to the lobbies. This new passage building was a sign of the times. Until the latter half of the century, the Commons were restricted to much the same space as that which they had been given over two hundred years before – the Chamber and inner lobby in St Stephen's Chapel, a small outer lobby, and the Speaker's Chamber. In the later seventeenth century, a little elbow room was gained from adjoining areas; but in general matters remained much as they had been. No officer of the House – not the Speaker himself till 1794 – lived in the Palace until well into the eighteenth century; committees were generally restricted to the use of the Speaker's Chamber and two small rooms above the lobbies; and papers seem to have been kept in such spaces as could be prised out of other hands. By the 1760s and '70s the situation was becoming impossible. Accommodation that had long been inadequate was fast growing more so as the business of the House increased, a process aggravated when Grenville's Act of 1770 swelled the number of committees on election petitions. The clerical organisation was becoming rather more elaborate and informed by something of a new spirit, stimulated no doubt by the appointment of John Hatsell as Clerk in 1768. More ample facilities could scarely be postponed further. A real effort was made at last to provide them. New offices and committee rooms for the Commons were put in hand in an open space to the south of St Stephen's Chapel. Others were carved out of the old Court of Wards. Above all, a handsome building, known as the Stone Building in St Margaret's Lane, was erected by stages on the western side of the Palace between the Law Courts and Old Palace Yard, the southern extremity forming a new approach to the House and most of the accommodation being appropriated to its purposes. The year 1780, when most of these changes had taken place, 'marked', it has been said, 'an epoch in the topography of the House of Commons'.[1] Cramped as its amenities remained compared with those of a later generation, it had nevertheless almost doubled the extent of its premises in two decades,

1. Orlo Cyprian Williams, 'The Topography of the Old House of Commons' (unpublished monograph, 1953), 18.

had acquired a new and more dignified approach, and begun that process of expansion which over the next fifty years was to bring under its control half the area of the Palace. It was not inappropriate that Burke's Plan for the Economical Reform of the Civil and Other Establishments should have been put forward at the very time when the Commons were most rapidly enlarging their own facilities.

The Chamber of the House remained fundamentally what it had been since it was first occupied by the Commons. When St Stephen's Chapel was turned over to their use, under Edward VI, the internal arrangements seem to have been disturbed as little as possible. The Speaker's chair was put upon the altar steps, the table for the recording clerks replaced the lectern in the middle of the choir, and the collegiate stalls (for St Stephen's had been a collegiate foundation), ranged in tiers along the walls as they are in many college and school chapels today, were made into benches for the Members. The screen also was left, turning the ante-chapel into a lobby, while its 'return stalls' provided 'cross-benches' facing the Table and the Speaker's Chair. The only substantial alterations were that the ceiling was lowered and some windows were changed. The Commons thus had to make the best, as in principle they still do, of the arrangements of a college chapel, suffering the resulting inconveniences and adjusting their proceedings to the physical facts. More alterations, some superficially considerable, took place over the next century and a half. The length of the benches was extended to the level of the Speaker's Chair. A door was cut in the end wall behind it, which came to be known as Solomon's Porch – where Pitt, one winter's night early in 1783, 'was obliged to retire from the House . . . by a violent sickness' during a speech by Fox.[1] Under Wren's supervision, the ceiling was lowered farther, the eastern windows were altered, galleries were built on three sides (primarily for Members, later used by Strangers as well), new furniture and lights were introduced, and the whole was panelled. It was in this redecorated Chamber that the eighteenth-century Commons met. The lofty medieval chapel had become an intimate, panelled room, not much, if at all, bigger than a large reception room in a great country house.[2] It remained, curiously enough, not unlike a chapel – but of the Reformed variety rather than the Gothic splendour that St Stephen's had been.[3] An idea of its size may be gained from the present St Stephen's Hall, the passage of approach to the modern House of Commons. Lord Mansfield's statue marks the level of the screen, and less than the length of a cricket pitch away the exit door to the Central Hall stands on the site of the end wall

1. *Private Papers of William Wilberforce*, 53.
2. The dimensions were: length 57'6", breadth 32'10", height 30'. The narrow galleries projected some 15' above floor level.
3. The resemblance was noted by the Lutheran Pastor Moritz from Berlin (*Travels through Various Parts of England in 1782*, in *The British Tourist* . . . [ed.] William Mavor, IV (1798), 26).

of the Chamber. 'Crammed', as Cobbett put it later, into their 'little hole' in its medieval shell, and pushing out piecemeal into the territory of a royal palace, the Commons might indeed be taken as an epitome of the political world itself: a world whose realities were often clothed in older forms, moulded at every turn by historical detail, inseparable from the antique organism which thereby pulsed tenaciously with life.

II

The simple *ad hoc* arrangements of the sixteenth century left their mark on the nature, as well as the appearance and procedure, of the House. Two features may be noticed in particular. The Chamber was, as (now designedly) it still is, too small to seat all the Members at the same time. And they faced each other in two main groups across a dividing floor. These physical characteristics, the result of chance, gave a certain flavour to developments themselves determined broadly on other grounds. The first – the small size of the Chamber – meant that debate, and indeed life in general in the House, was a very intimate affair. Whether the oratory was spacious or conversational, according to the fashion of the time, the speaker could not escape an audience that sat all around him – or melted away. Nor could he disregard its atmosphere, easy and casual for the most part, sometimes crowded and tense, but always informal and critical, disconcertingly responsive to a favourite and impatient of a bore. Such a setting favoured the arts of argument *ad hominem*, which were demanded in any case by the composition and balance of the House. For perhaps the strongest strain in the character of that complex assembly was its belief in its independence. All the pressures and inducements at the disposal of the party managers did not disguise the fact that the Commons were liable to have a will of their own. Indeed, they paid tribute to it, in the sense that hypocrisy, in Johnson's definition, is the tribute that vice pays to virtue. The independence of the individual Member was a cardinal article of faith, often treated of course as articles of faith are apt to be. Whatever the current practice, all subscribed to the ideal. This independence was not to be construed as irresponsibility: on the contrary, it was regarded as the reverse of faction, which involved opposition for opposition's sake. Nor was it confined, though it was often directed, to the promotion of local issues. Its purpose and justification were rather to provide a body of free and representative judgment, unbeholden to patronage of any kind, which could act as a guide, and thus a check, to the King's Government on its Parliamentary occasions. Unity, not division, was the end, though division had often to be the means. The watchword of the independent Member, it has been well said, was 'attachment to the Crown but no obligation to Ministers'.[1] Two quotations from members of the Pitt family illustrate the attitude.

> If you are in Parliament [wrote Governor Pitt to his son in 1705] show yourself on all occasions a good Englishman, and a faithful servant to your country. . . . Avoid faction, and never enter the House pre-possessed; but attend diligently to the debate, and vote according to your conscience and not for any sinister end whatever. I had rather see any child of mine want than have him get his bread by voting in the House of Commons.[2]

Three-quarters of a century later, the same note was struck more diffidently.

> We are now both in Parliament [wrote William Morton Pitt, the younger Pitt's distant cousin, to his friend Lord Herbert after the election of 1780.] . . . I believe we shall agree that it is better as well as more prudent not to appear to come with a predetermined intention of siding uniformly with one set or another. Surely it is possible to act an upright, independent and respectable part in Parliament: yet I am told not. I hope you feel yourself bold enough to try it: be assured of one thing that if a number, and even a very small number fall into that channel they must acquire consideration, and collect a greater force daily.[3]

Such a hope pointed the difficulties, as well as the tenacity, of the point of view. For the end to which it pointed was of course impossible. The independent Member by definition was attached to no formed group; and if he and his fellows were to combine, they could not do so for long without some continuing bond of opinion or interest, and something, too, of an organisation to support their collective voice. They would in fact become, in however loose a sense, a Parliamentary party – the very thing they conceived it their duty to avoid. Such rare attempts as some of them made to act as a body were therefore unsuccessful; when they moved predominantly in one direction, it was in association with other elements in the House. The independents were in fact essentially unattached, amateur politicians, who gloried in the role: the representatives of their 'countries' at Westminster, whose roots and allegiances were embedded in local soil. It was often difficult, if not impossible, to get them to attend, when local business, or race meetings (where it was discussed), or hunting held prior claim. It was often equally difficult to tell how they would vote when they were present, or if they would vote at all. These habits, perhaps a legacy

1. Sir Lewis Namier, 'Monarchy and the Party System', in *Personalities and Powers* (1955), 25.
2. Quoted op. cit., 26.
3. Quoted in Ian R. Christie, *The End of North's Ministry 1780–1782* (1958), 192–3.

from generations when Parliaments were infrequent, persisted through-out others in which the business of central government remained small. For, as Disraeli observed in due course, 'there was not much business then'. Government brought few public bills by later standards, not many of those were the subject of party strife, and the course of a Parliamentary session varied little from year to year. The more exciting debates were sandwiched between Christmas and Easter; otherwise the average back-bencher was not unduly troubled, and between the great set-pieces the House became 'a mere club'.[1] Much of the energy of the party leaders and managers, like the back-benchers', was therefore devoted to local affairs – the enclosure bills and election petitions, the measures for turnpikes or canals or Corporations, which figure so largely in the Parliamentary Journals. Wider issues were rare by comparison, particularly in the middle reaches of the century, and persuasion then could take various forms – an appeal to family or local connexion already tested from day to day, an equally familiar hospitality and entertainment, and, not least, the force of argument in debate. It was for this last reason that the Parliamentary orator was so important to his associates. On him fell the task of convincing a notoriously difficult audience of the justice of his cause. It was indeed no coincidence, though it might appear a paradox, that the classical age of Parliamentary eloquence should have come to fruition in the long heyday of Sir Francis Headpiece and Squire Bluster.[2]

The importance of the independent Member was both numerical and symbolic; and it is not easy, perhaps not necessary, to distinguish too sharply between the two. Estimates of numbers fluctuate, according to the character of the times and the issue, and the point from which the individual independent is assessed. He was not by nature an easy creature to define. It was often the custom to equate him with the County Members, and it was indeed largely on an addition to their numbers that the Parliamentary reformers of the 1770s and '80s,

1. *Endymion*, ch. LXXVI.
2. Whose family from the time of Elizabeth had 'frequently represented the shire in parliament, being chosen to present addresses, and given laws at hunting matches and races' (Johnson, in *The Rambler*, no. 142).

The audience, nevertheless, may have had its restrictive effect on the eloquence. The extent of classical quotation in the late eighteenth-century Parliaments is a favourite tradition. But there were limits. According to Sir Nathaniel Wraxall – an unreliable witness, but one who is better for custom and atmosphere than for specific events – Pitt, 'who well knew how large a part of his audience, especially among the country gentlemen, were little conversant in the writings of the Augustan Age, or familiar with Horace, always displayed great caution in borrowing from these classic sources'; Fox and Sheridan, too, 'though not equally severe in that respect, yet never abused or injudiciously expended the stores of antient literature that they possessed'; and while Burke was 'more frequently carried . . . away into the times of Virgil and Cicero', Barré 'usually condescended, whenever he quoted Latin, to translate for the benefit of the county members' (*The Historical and the Posthumous Memoirs of Sir Nathaniel William Wraxall 1772–1784*, ed. Henry B. Wheatley (1884), III, 12).

including Pitt himself, pinned their hopes of a return to the ancient 'purity' of the House. The counties, it is true, were in general less subject than other constituencies to 'influence', private or govern- mental: their contests, when local rivalries were fierce, were apt to be too expensive for the more professional politicians to wish to engage. But the independents were not really confined so closely to one type of seat. The country gentlemen who, more justifiably, were taken as the epitome of the type, sat for the boroughs as well as for the counties; and the Drakes of Amersham, the Whitmores of Bridgnorth, the Grosvenors of Chester could be every bit as independent as any knights of the shire. There were also Members of the same disposition outside or temporarily parted from the landed interest, principally merchants sitting for close boroughs or for the open boroughs of the sizeable towns. On the other hand, many men of independent origin were not content to act as such. An ambitious Member would take service in the ranks of Government or a private group: there was no other way in which he could hope to exercise his talents; and others, less concerned with the national business, the party game or personal advancement, were still prepared to support, however casually, a connexion which to them was primarily of local or family interest. The borderlines were often difficult to trace. Independence, in fact, was a matter of degree. It was the product not so much of a certain type of seat as of two qualities to which the seat was at best a likely guide. The first was property – most commonly landed property, and then often the inheritance of an eldest son, but property of any valid kind, the wealth of the merchant or even a decent inde- pendent competence, which would preserve its holder from all tempta- tions but those of ambition. And the second qualification was this lack of ambition outside its natural home, a distaste for the active political life of London which would combine with the possession of property to save the independent from the perils of a place.

Such men could not be classified by the party managers without reference to the occasion. The issue might be such that some of them could safely be counted as supporters of Government or its opponents. Alternatively, they might be in the ranks – not necessarily confined to themselves – of the 'Uncertains'. In the House of Commons elected in 1780, it has been reckoned that some 200 Members could be classed as independent. Of these, the Secretary of the Treasury estimated early in 1781 that about 130 were entirely unconnected with any party at the time. A similar list at the end of 1783 produced 104; another in 1788, 108. These last figures accounted, on specific occasions, for slightly less than a fifth of the House.

Depending on the circumstances, the independent Members might therefore tip the balance of a division. Towards the end of the century, their direct effect was perhaps on the decline; but the last two years of North's Administration showed that it could still be potent, for it was his abandonment by the country gentlemen that led to his fall. But numbers were not the sole test of the independent's significance. His weight was felt beyond the immediate effect of his vote. The uncommitted Members were something more than the sum of what was left when all the Members who could be labelled had been counted. The very fact that they are so difficult to classify exactly points their pervasive influence. For whatever else divided the various Parliamentary groups, it was not social background; and the values of the assembly were those of the country gentleman himself. The increase in his fortunes over the century, the growing variety within his class, only underlined its identity and strength. Its highest political expression remained the House of Commons, and the ethos of the House was very largely its own. The gentlemen of England were assembled in St Stephen's; and the very symbol of the gentry was the independent Member.

To more active politicians, he was often thoroughly annoying. But his attitudes could not be disregarded, if only because they penetrated those of the active politicians themselves. The country gentleman might talk of Whigs and Tories. But with the virtual disappearance from national politics[1] of the main issues over which they had fought – above all the definition of the nature of the monarchy, and the nature of the settlement between Church and Dissent – he had reverted in practice to simpler conceptions. His poles of reference at Westminster were now indeed more like the ancient cries of 'Court' and 'Country' than anything else. The pressures which he feared – and in this he was typical of the political class as a whole – were above all still those of the Crown. 'Distrust of the Executive', Sir Thomas Hanmer had observed early in the century, 'is the principle on which the whole of our Constitution is based':[2] the attitude had not altered in the interval, and the executive remained the King's. It was to repel such encroachments that the Commons had built their historic defences – the rules of procedure, the limitations on placemen, the scrutiny of finance – and in the heat of the American War the old cries, seldom entirely dormant, were actively revived. Taken to its extremes, this was 'Country' policy. But country gentlemen under the Hanoverians were seldom inclined to extremes. In a world of small, shifting parties their desire for unity was not dimmed. Distrust of faction remained the counterpoise to distrust of the executive; if it was necessary to defend the independence of the House against pressure by the Crown, it was equally necessary to avoid the dangers of 'a formed opposition'. The strength of this sentiment was proved by the career of Fox, whose persistent attacks on the royal prerogative ended by shocking a mass of the country gentlemen as well as George III. But Fox, devoted as he became to the idea of party, was in many ways not a typical party leader. Very few were prepared to risk the double loss

1. Though not always from local politics. Or perhaps it would be truer to say that the terms were retained more often in local politics to cover local purposes.
2. Quoted in Betty Kemp, *King and Commons 1660–1832* (1957), 4–5.

of the King's confidence and that of the uncommitted Members of Parliament. The cries of the average party politician were the realities of the independent. They were also, in a sense, the realities of the party politicians themselves.

The defence of party therefore turned on the claim that is was something other than faction. The argument achieved classic form in Burke's *Thoughts on the Cause of the Present Discontents*. In many ways, this said nothing new. It was true that the idea of party had long received little theoretical support, and indeed for some time had been explicitly out of favour. But the legacy of an earlier, formative age could not be finally dismissed. Eighteenth-century politicians often explained their actions in terms of late seventeenth-century conflicts, and the tradition of party as an embodiment of political principle remained potent if ill-defined. 'The fashionable levities of political doctrine'[1] overlay deeper currents, easily forced to the surface when the times seemed propitious. The period of the American Revolution was such a time. Issues were again brought to the fore, real political alternatives posed, in a way that had not been known since the early part of the century; and how could such a situation be met better than by 'a body of men united, upon some particular principle in which they are all agreed'?[2] When principles were in question, parties alone could represent them; they had a right, if the principles meant anything, to try to carry them through; and in so doing, to make a claim on the conscience of the individual Member.[3] True parties, indeed, were not only morally superior to factions; they should also be more effective, for the purpose in hand.[4] It was a powerful appeal, which has echoed ever since. We must be the more careful to recognise to whom, and in what circumstances, it was made.

As so often with pamphlets produced in the heat of political warfare, it is not always easy to tell when Burke was voicing a hope and when he was claiming to describe the facts. His luxuriant imagination did not always distinguish clearly between the two. But in either case he was using the idiom of his day. The party of which he spoke was very far from that familiar to a later age, alike in its inner pressures and its external conditions. It was not distinguished or bound by broad political programmes. It could not hold office on its own terms. It did not command a unified organisation in any way binding on all its members. It existed, indeed, in a very different sort of world: one in which the Crown retained powerful prerogatives even if its Parliamentary patro-

1. See p. 23 above.
2. Edmund Burke, *Thoughts on the Cause of the Present Discontents* (1770), in *The Works of the Right Honourable Edmund Burke* (1826), II, 335.
3. Op. cit., 330–1.
4. See the whole concluding passage of the pamphlet for Burke's insistence on the need for effectiveness – which in Parliamentary terms implied stability and size.

nage should be reduced, in which many Members of Parliament would respond to the appeal of party only on their own terms, and good party men themselves owed their strongest allegiance to their leader, rather than to the association with which he might be connected at the time.

Such conditions determined what a party could hope to achieve. They also suggested some of the obstacles to success. Thus leading politicians might assure the House, as almost all did, that they did not mean to pursue a preconceived party line. But if their followings were not to be looked on simply as opportunist cliques, a good deal of effort had to be devoted to justifying the past; and such exercises did not appeal to those for whom 'a patriotic line of conduct' was far from synonymous with a rigid, or forced, consistency. On the other hand, when a party compromised with its past, and moved as a unit to fresh positions, it could be accused of faction, 'the mean and interested struggle for place and emolument'.[1] While an alternative conception of political duty prevailed, and the parties themselves were variously imbued with it, party remained an ambiguous term.

For it was not only that many Members were unwilling to pay that kind of allegiance. Parties themselves were not so constituted as to make good Burke's hope, or claim. 'Bodies of men', he called them, 'bound together by common opinions, common affections, and common interests'.[2] Such a description applied more to a small group, or to the nucleus of a larger party, than to a party of any size as it appeared in the managers' lists. Throughout the eighteenth century, men were accustomed to seek political leadership in one of three sources – in the King, in a family or individual disposing of Parliamentary influence, or occasionally in an outstanding personality. These were the poles of political attraction, around which connexions formed; and all were subject to constant variations in strength. One of the most valuable possessions of the propertied class, confirmed and strengthened in its struggles against the Crown, was political property. Over a third of the Members of the Commons in the second half of the century represented directly private patrons. At the same time, no patron controlled in this way more than eight or nine seats, very few could lay claim to more than half that number, and control itself was often far from complete. The property held so tenaciously was in fact widely diffused. No one magnate or group of magnates was ultimately in a position to browbeat or ignore the rest; nor were the King himself or any of the leading Parliamentary men of talent. The political map was a patchwork, and power was achieved by coalition – often of interests within a group, always between groups themselves. An effective party, in these circumstances, was likely to comprise various elements, and the more effective it was the more varied they were likely to be. Some of the strongest links that held them were not strictly political at all. Family or local con-

1. Op. cit., 336.
2. Op. cit., 335.

nexions, ties of personal friendship or dependence, were primary loyalties which it would take a good deal to upset, and from which the average leader, in the long years of stagnation, had come to look for his normal means of support. The fluctuations of groups in quiet times were not necessarily governed by, though they were usually referred to, issues of national policy; and when such issues arose, the familiar landmarks did not disappear. Other elements then came to the fore. Ideas would be canvassed, often in the partly irrelevant terms of earlier battles; new, more exciting political figures might be thrown up, possibly to attract their own rather different kinds of following; independents would rally in some degree to one side or another. The parties would tend to coalesce, for the purpose in hand, into two large opposing groups. But if the picture thus appeared simpler, it was not necessarily so. Loyalties still centred on the smaller unit, 'the subdivision', 'the little platoon',[1] and the connecting links were weaker than the units themselves. Both the periods in which party stability appeared most marked in the first half-century of George III's reign – the years of the American Revolution, and those of the long ascendancy of the younger Pitt – ended abruptly in a confused manœuvring of groups, reminiscent of the state of affairs before they began.

Such considerations apply most strongly to the parties of the private interests. Judged by the acid test of the division lists, the most stable following in the Commons was generally the so-called party of the Crown – the group of agents and supporters of the King's Government, whose hard core voted for whatever Ministers he might favour at the time. But in some ways this was hardly a party at all: its character was affected by administrative as well as political needs, and it lacked the political leadership from which Cabinets were formed. In so far as this was to be found in the Commons, it had to come from the private interests, so that some kind of working partnership was necessary. The House of Commons which Pitt joined in 1780 may serve as an illustration, the better perhaps because on the surface the party picture then appeared exceptionally simple and clear. The followers of Government at that time could be divided into four main parties – that of the Crown itself, and those of Lord North, Lord Sandwich, and Lord Gower – allied with a number of small independent or semi-independent connexions, and supported, decreasingly, by some of the uncommitted Members. Opposition comprised one large party, Lord Rockingham's, in alliance with two smaller ones, Lord Shelburne's and Sir James Lowther's, and supported by a growing number of independents. But Rockingham's party was itself formed from a number of smaller groups, brought into a closer alliance by the exceptional nature of the times. The Cavendish and Bentinck connexions, centred on the Duke of Portland, and the circle of Charles James Fox were powerful and steady auxiliaries: other followings, such as those of the Dukes of Bolton

---

1. Burke, *Reflections on the Revolution in France* (1790), in *Works*, V, 100.

and Rutland, Lords Abingdon, Bristol and Derby, and Edward Eliot, brought lighter and in some cases less reliable support. The various groups had their distinctive flavours. Some of the smaller ones were based exclusively on family connexion; others, like Lowther's for instance, on a blend of family connexion and territorial interest. Some included prominent 'men of business' – the active politicians and lawyers who took service under a private patron when they did not do so under the Crown; some, particularly the followings of Sandwich and North after their long years in power, were swelled by their leaders' professional or commercial connexions – by men whom hope of favours to come or gratitude for favours received attached to a political chieftain rather than to Government itself. Some again counted men who followed their leaders – North and Shelburne were examples, and Fox was the archetype – out of personal friendship or political sympathy, as well as, or in spite of, family tradition or material interest.

These diversities reflected the leaders' personalities and aims, as well as, in most cases, the sources of their electoral power. Thus Abingdon's temperament combined with the nature of his influence to produce a somewhat unmanageable and ineffectual group; Lowther's, to produce a not much larger but notably united following, which could always make itself felt when he wished. On the other hand, Lowther's approach to politics was essentially that of an independent northern chieftain, and his party was formed and generally employed on that basis: North, by contrast, managed to turn a looser and less powerful connexion into the nucleus of a much wider following, as the result of an active political career. The great magnates themselves were not handed success on a plate. Rockingham and Portland would not have been powerful politicians if they had not been the Marquess of Rockingham and the Duke of Portland, born to electoral influence and great estates. But others inherited the same kind of fortune, and their own prominence at Westminster rested on a combination of persistent field work in the provinces and a disposition for national politics sufficiently marked to attract and hold the necessary men of talent. No political leader could in fact count on more than a very small proprietorial following. The rest – if he wanted more – depended on his success with other proprietors and interests, and the figure he or his associates cut in the House of Commons. He could not control outright more than the core of his party, and even that was not always easy to define. Local factions might shift or dissolve, families or friends might quarrel, ambitious or needy men transfer allegiance, powerful interests be captured by a hostile clique. And in all the more successful parties at least – for it was a mark of their success – there were those who did not really look on themselves as bound to party at all: men like Robert Gregory, the faithful follower of Fox, who 'though strongly attached to [him] and to the party acting with him . . . disdained to be considered as a devoted partisan', and who, riled on one occasion to find his support taken for granted, was

said to have told the House that he was 'connected with no set of men
... being as independent in my seat and in my principles as any individual within these walls'.[1] Many who figured regularly in the party
lists did so on some such understanding, and no connexion seeking
power could disregard their effect.

The benches on either side of the House were not therefore occupied by
two clearly distinguished groups, recognisable as such under two different party names. One can only talk in those decades of Government
and Opposition,[2] bearing in mind that their ranks were liable to frequent change. When it came to a division, Members present had to
vote 'aye' or 'no'. But divisions were not the only means of taking the
sense of the House: they were not a necessary consequence of debate,
and they were often sparsely attended. Nor do Members seem to have
ranged themselves on either side of the Chamber on anything approaching strict party lines. The evidence is inconclusive; but while the leaders
of Government and Opposition, accompanied by their firm supporters,
now normally sat on opposite sides of the House, and while the choice
of seats by prominent figures out of office had become significant,
custom does not appear to have hardened. It was even possible for an
office-holder to sit facing his colleagues – Rigby did so as Paymaster
General in the seventies and early eighties, though the fact that it was
remarked suggests that the practice was exceptional – and many Members seem to have settled much as they pleased or as they could. There
can have been little of the invidious prominence attached to 'crossing
the floor' which later politicians are supposed to have felt.[3]

Such arrangements were probably more fluid for back-benchers than
for the leaders, and they could not bind the leaders of Opposition as
they bound those of the Government. There were indeed visible differences between them. The occupants of the Treasury Bench, as it had
come to be called, formed a distinctive group as they had done at least
since Tudor times. Contrary to the general rule, they filled their seats

1. Wraxall, *Historical Memoirs*, II, 108.

2. An example of the term Opposition, in the sense of 'a sort of public body',
occurs (on p. 174) in a pamphlet of 1791 or 1792 – *A Review of the Principal Proceedings
of the Parliament of 1784* – which was quoted in approval by George Rose, Pitt's
joint Secretary of the Treasury, and is said to have been passed by Pitt himself.

3. There is, however, an example of the term being used in a political sense in 1788.
It would also be interesting to know when the term 'honourable friend' became the
regular way of referring to a member of the same party. It had certainly not done
so yet, though the term was sometimes used in the '70s and '80s, even by an independent like Sir George Savile; and see North's expressions in December 1783, in
P.R., XII (1784), 478. But expressions of affinity seem to have been the exception
rather than the rule; and, when they were used, were sometimes linked with the
seating arrangements – 'the hon. gentlemen who sit before me', 'hon. gentlemen on
this side' – which perhaps suggests a less permanent form of alliance.

as of right;[1] and, unlike their fellow Members, they and some of their supporters always appeared in full dress – on North's fall in 1782, the force of the change struck the House when familiar figures were seen in unfamiliar clothes as well as on unfamiliar benches, and Fox's choice of dress was always apt to reflect the state of his political fortunes and ideas. Ministers in fact appeared as the Ministers of the Crown, present, as chosen Privy Councillors had always been present, to announce the King's measures and obtain the necessary support. Through all the great changes that had occurred in their relations with the rest of the House, there was this visible reminder that they owed an allegiance beyond its walls.

The nature and extent of that allegiance was the great continuing political question of the century. In the later years of the American War, it often took the form of an attack upon the nature of the King's following in the House itself. Ministers drew their support in the Commons from two main sources – their own followers, and the King's Friends or the adherents of Government and the Court. It was not always easy, of course, to distinguish exactly between the two while an Administration lasted; but there was an essential distinction neverthe-less. The first were attached, for whatever reason and in whatever degree, to a political leader who might or might not be in office: the second to the sovereign as the Head of Government, and to Ministers as long as they enjoyed his confidence. This last phalanx, as opponents were apt to call it, contained various types: 'efficient' Government officials, serving officers, courtiers, holders of sinecures who did not fall into any of those classes, merchants holding Government contracts, aspirants to favour, and some, shading into the independents, whose loyalties were quite simply fixed on the Crown. Such a body of men, centred on the one permanent source of official favour, might be expected to behave more predictably than the supporters of a private interest; and so, to judge by the division lists, they did. Throughout the second half of the century, the followers of the Crown formed the largest and most stable voting element in the House.

At one time it had looked as if this would not be so. In the late seventeenth and early eighteenth centuries, Place Bills had been intro-duced on several occasions to exclude from the Commons all persons holding offices of profit under the Crown. But they were thrown out in one House or the other, and the measures which passed referred to certain office-holders only. By 1742, the date of the last important Place Act of the century, the list included the Commissioners of Customs and

1. Having, probably in the course of the century, ejected prominent Privy Coun-cillors who were not, or no longer, of their number. The Members for London and York also had a customary right to their own seats in the Chamber; so did Members who had received the thanks of the House when in their place; and the practice had grown up in recent years of allowing a few prominent Members (Chatham was one) always to occupy the same seats when they were present.

of Excise and the officers engaged in the management of the other revenue duties, various colonial and naval officials and some in the Irish revenue departments, certain pensioners of the Crown 'at pleasure', and, broadly speaking, the lesser officials in the Treasury, the Exchequer, the Admiralty, the offices of the Treasurer of the Navy and the Paymaster General, and those of the Secretaries of State. But it did not include the senior office-holders in the more important departments, several of whom indeed were excepted by name – and who, thanks to a liberal interpretation of the term 'new office', were joined in the course of the century by holders of new 'effective' posts. There was thus a body of important officials and what we would call junior Ministers who were in their own persons politicians and administrators both. The emphasis varied, partly according to function, perhaps more according to personality. There were usually a few men – Philip Stephens of the Admiralty and Sir Charles Frederick of the Ordnance spring to mind at this time – who were by nature administrators pure and simple, and who sat in the House by virtue of their posts and scarcely engaged in politics at all. There were others, like Charles Jenkinson, who suffered a political career largely for the sake of its administrative opportunities; others again, like William Eden, who used their administrative talents in the service of an active political career. There was a whole spectrum of degree, and no certain rule by which to judge what sort of man would hold what office. Parliamentary seats depended on vacancies, so that a useful political administrator might be temporarily out of the House: on the other hand, a post which had apparently become non-political might suddenly be filled by a politician. These ambiguities, and the varied nature of Parliamentary placemen as a whole, emphasised the links between the administrative and political worlds. There was no figure more typical of the times than the patronage Secretary of the Treasury, calculating the Parliamentary odds from his office off Whitehall.

But while this group of 'efficient' office-holders, taken by and large, provided the brains and stiffening of the party, it was not numerically strong. In 1780 it consisted of between thirty and forty Members, and another 28, it has been reckoned, then held places at Court. But the total number of placemen – that is to say, holders of some office under the Crown – was then in the region of 165;[1] and many of them were much less firmly attached to Government or the King. Over forty held sinecures, in many cases granted for life, and another forty-odd were serving officers who held no other place, and who, in the closing years of the American War, were not all supporters of North. The placemen's behaviour could not in fact be taken entirely for granted – perhaps it would be truer to say, it could be taken for granted only after much hard work. A great deal of management was required, by the King himself, by some of his Ministers, and by the patronage Secretary of the Trea-

1. Some of course holding more than one office.

sury, to keep so large a following sweet. The King's Friends, indeed, were not entirely an exception to the general rule. Their strength was the result not so much of the monolithic power of the King, as of the success with which he could combine his powers with others.

This was the more so because places were filled by various means. For the Crown itself disposed of only a limited number of Parliamentary seats, and was thus obliged to bargain its extensive official patronage against electoral favours from the private patrons who could supply the balance. In the election of 1780, it has been reckoned that Government returned twenty-four Members to Parliament, and that another 221 seats lay more or less at the disposal of 119 private persons. If the Crown was to be certain of providing the basis of a Government party in the Commons, it could therefore do so only in co-operation with other interests.

It was indeed a measure of its strength that Members so elected should normally have proved as reliable as they did. Election itself, though needing careful preparation, was not the greatest worry. The patronage of the Crown, energetically managed, was ramifying enough to secure the necessary return from private patrons; and in fact no Government lost a general election in the course of the century. It was more difficult to secure firm allegiance throughout a session, although the Crown held a naturally strong hand in treating with its placemen and friends. Even so, not all its cards were good. Thus, places were granted for services rendered rather than for services to come. Only a few could be filled afresh each session, so that while many placemen had come to owe loyalty to the King rather than to a given set of Ministers, some who were out of sympathy with the Government of the day could not be replaced. And there was always the possiblity, as the case of North showed, that a King's Friend would transfer allegiance from the King to a Minister who might then leave office. But in general conditions favoured the Crown. Most placemen would remain loyal, out of inclination as well as interest; and if some drifted away from the King, others, elected to support Government at the instance of a private patron, would continue to do so even if the patron himself later withdrew. It was indeed this weighting of the scales in what seemed a dangerously unfair manner that may have accounted for the feeling behind the cries, widespread at this time, of corruption on the part of the Crown. In themselves, these were often cynical or wild. Some of the attacks were allowed to lapse when their authors came into office. The number of Government boroughs was not disproportionately high compared with the number of those at the disposal of the greater private patrons, nor was it on the increase, as sometimes alleged, but if anything on the decline. Crown boroughs were not exceptionally venal, and the Crown did not spend exceptionally large sums of money on elections: its influence, particularly with its allied patrons, was of a different kind. But it may have been precisely that which caused so much unease

– the fear that the Crown, inherently strong, had unduly strengthened its ties with other sources of power, and was encroaching too far on other people's property. No responsible politician was prepared to deny that the King's Government should be justly represented in the House. But there was a traditional feeling – exploited perhaps, but not manufactured, by interested parties – that in politics, as still to some extent in finance, 'the King should live of his own'.

III

Such fears were expressed the more strongly in the Commons because the Crown's electoral allies were well represented in the Lords. Of the 221 seats which in 1780 were controlled by 119 private patrons, 113 lay at the disposal of 52 peers. The House of Lords at the time consisted of 232 members, of whom 26 were bishops and three were royal dukes. A quarter of the temporal peers of Parliament were therefore in a position to exercise direct control over a fifth of the members of the House of Commons. But their influence did not necessarily stop there. The provision of the Place Act of 1707, whereby a Member of Parliament had to seek re-election whenever he took one of a large number of offices under the Crown, helped to maintain if not increase the number of Ministers found from the Lords, with a corresponding increase in the official patronage of the upper House. And there were less formal ties. In the winter of 1780, 67 legitimate sons of British peers sat in the lower House;[1] and other seats were occupied by near relations of peers of Parliament. Not all of them, of course, followed their noble kinsmen's politics even if they did not represent their boroughs. But many did, and when Chatham called the House of Commons 'a parcel of younger brothers' he was drawing attention to a political as well as a genealogical fact. Even prominent politicians in the Commons – the Grenvilles are a notable example – were apt, like Chinese mandarins, to consult the head of the family before they made a move. Politically conscious peers, as long as their rent-rolls were in good order, were *ipso facto* in a position of great strength.

The Commons as a body accepted and resented this state of affairs. On the one hand, there appeared to be a natural allegiance between the Houses viewed as the counter-balance to the Crown. Together, as Blackstone put it, they 'checked, and kept within due bounds' the executive power;[2] and the Revolution Settlement of 1689, the constitutional charter of the eighteenth century, was the undisputed memorial to their success. The cohesion of the governing class turned this constitutional alliance into something like a family compact – with all

1. That is to say, men born sons of peers – the fathers were not all living at that date.
2. William Blackstone, *Commentaries on the Laws of England*, I (1765), 150.

the strains and divisions to which families are prone. While the nobility and gentry were always conscious of the former's 'decent, regulated pre-eminence',[1] they did not lead separate lives away from Westminster; and, particularly as general elections came to be more widely spaced, the peerage balanced the increasing power of the Commons by increasingly exploiting the social relations between them. At the same time, the Commons were acutely conscious of this increase in their power, and sensitive to anything that appeared to threaten it. Their constitutional position was now, fairly obviously, much stronger than that of the Lords, and they were not inclined to let the fact be overlooked. Irrespective of party alignments, there was thus a certain jealousy between the two bodies, shown in a number of ways. It was noticeable, for instance, that those First Lords of the Treasury who appealed most to the country gentlemen – Walpole, Pelham, North, and the younger Pitt – were themselves in the lower House. They were all in fact good House of Commons men, a matter which had its implications for the Lords as well as for the Crown.

Tension between the Houses was of course always liable to rise with the political temperature. In the 1770s, when 'corruption' was a prominent issue, the Commons' suspicions were aggravated by the Crown's inherent advantages in the Lords. It normally controlled the election of the representative Scottish peers. It had its placemen, as in the lower House. It appointed and promoted the bishops. Above all, it held the vital key to social eminence in an aristocratic age, the creation and advancement of the temporal peers themselves. If the King was an active and skilful politician, these powers of the Crown could be deployed to support his personal interest: the cries of the great Whig lords and their parties in the Commons, the more general uneasiness in that House, were stimulated by the fact that George III was using his advantages to the full. In doing so, neither he nor the average peer considered himself to be departing from his natural role. For the ethos of the upper House was quite different from that of the lower. The peerage, as a body, looked on itself as the natural support of the Crown, the ancient source of counsel and still the most splendid Estate of the Realm. Its members, unlike the Commons, did not originally have to be summoned to give advice on special occasions, but enjoyed a permanent right of access to their sovereign – a right which indeed they could still invoke. 'Except on very particular occasions indeed', Lord Hillsborough told the restive Lord Carmarthen in 1781, 'the nobility should always co-operate with the Crown, from whom alone they derived their consequence'.[2] The peers filled the great Household Offices, the surviving Great Offices of State, the *ex officio* seats on the Privy Council. Their personal links with the monarch were venerable and strong, and

1. Burke, *Reflections on the Revolution in France*, in *Works*, V, 109.
2. *The Political Memoranda of Francis Fifth Duke of Leeds . . .*, ed. Oscar Browning (1884,) 45.

if the Whig grandees sniffed at the Hanoverian Succession, they still combined with their brethren to fill the places around the throne, and to emphasise, by one means or another, the rights of their order against the third Estate.

This mixture of tension and alliance between the Houses, and between each of them and the Crown, was regarded by the constitutional theorists as the secret of the constitution itself, that mysterious entity which excited so much reverence at home and – though perhaps now decreasingly – so much interest abroad. Few Englishmen doubted that it was a wonderful achievement: George III himself voiced the general opinion when he called it 'the most beautiful Combination that ever was framed'.[1] It was more difficult to say exactly what the combination was, and how it worked. In an age dominated by legal thought, the favourite approach was the lawyer's. The French *parlementaire* Montesquieu, the Swiss jurist De Lolme, and Mr Justice Blackstone provided the classic interpretations of an historically complex theme. Taking as their starting point the liberty of the individual, they stressed the limits within which authority must lie; and since authority, as Blackstone saw, was in the last resort the expression of the King in Parliament,[2] it was upon the mutual checks of King, Lords and Commons that attention chiefly fastened. The beauty of the result lay in the exquisite way in which their respective natures and powers were separated and combined.[3]

And herein indeed [wrote Blackstone in a famous passage] consists the true excellence of the English government, that all the parts of it form a mutual check upon each other. In the legislature, the people are a check upon the nobility and the nobility a check upon the people; by the mutual privilege of rejecting what the other has resolved: while the King is a check upon both, which preserves the executive power from encroachments. And this very executive power is again checked, and kept within due bounds by the two houses, through the privilege they have of enquiring into, impeaching, and punishing the conduct (not indeed of the King, which would destroy his constitutional independence; but, which is more beneficial to the

1. *The Correspondence of King George III from 1760 to 1783,* ed. the Hon. Sir John Fortescue, V (1928), no. 2991.

2. The ancient tradition of natural law as an overriding moral restraint on the positive law of Parliament could still be invoked, but now with little effect.

3. Even Montesquieu, who placed his emphasis on the separation of powers, did not deny that they must also be combined in some respects. He observed that 'the executive power . . . ought to have a share in the legislature', and that, since the relations between King, Lords and Commons could not be so balanced in practice as to be entirely static, 'the three powers' ought 'to move in concert' (*The Spirit of Laws,* transl. Mr [Thomas] Nugent (2nd edn., 1752), 227, 228).

public) of his evil and pernicious counsellors. Thus every branch of our civil policy supports and is supported, regulates and is regulated, by the rest; for the two houses naturally drawing in two directions of opposite interest, and the prerogative in another still different from them both, they mutually keep each other from exceeding their proper limits; while the whole is prevented from separation, and artificially connected together by the mixed nature of the crown, which is a part of the legislative, and the sole executive magistrate.[1]

This was the theory, and it had its effect. With whatever short-comings and excesses, King, Lords and Commons all thought of them-selves as standing for something unique and essential to the constitution, and were genuinely disturbed when they suspected that their proper functions were being weakened or confused. Exactly how those func-tions were to be interpreted was liable to be a matter of dispute, in a setting accepted for most of the century as fixed and secure. It was not less so in a period when the setting was beginning to change, while most of the old assumptions still held good. The precise relations bet-ween the King and his Ministers, between Ministers themselves, between them and their followers, and in a lesser degree between the two Houses, were the very stuff of Pitt's political life. But it was always accepted that there were proper connexions, which should be as har-monious as possible. Both Houses of Parliament responded to the need for co-operation with the executive as well as for independence from it; both contained elements standing generally more for the one than for the other; but no element denied that co-operation was its end. It was indeed one of the difficulties of party leaders in opposition that they had to disclaim, as a sign of faction, the role of opposition for opposition's sake. Fox voiced the argument well on one of the occasions when he was hopeful of office. 'You think', he wrote to Rockingham at the beginning of 1779, 'you can best serve the country by continuing in a fruitless opposition; I think it impossible to serve it at all but by coming into power, and go even so far as to think it irreconcilable with the duty of a public man to refuse it, if offered to him in a manner consistent with his private honour, and so as to enable him to form fair hopes of doing essential service'.[2] These were traditional sentiments, which were naturally held more strongly in more old-fashioned quarters. 'To be sure', the Duke of Marlborough observed to his Member William Eden, in the early days of Pitt's Administration in 1784, 'the more the late Members of Opposition keep together, the more the present Govern-ment will be embarrassed – But that does not seem to me to be a good reason for keeping together. I should hope that they would not keep together, but that some of the late Opposition who are Men of Business,

1. *Commentaries on the Laws of England*, I, 150–1.
2. *Memorials and Correspondence of Charles James Fox*, I, 207.

would think it for the good of the Country to offer their assistance and come over, or be Rats, if you please'.[1] There were different loyalties; but loyalty to the Crown was deep-rooted, perhaps for many men the most deep-rooted of all. It was the duty of Government to govern; it was the first though not necessarily the ultimate duty of well disposed men to lend support; and if they had to oppose there were limits beyond which they should not go. To many, indeed, the royal influence in Parliament was a necessary corollary of the argument, one of the legitimate buttresses of the King's prerogative which enabled him to avoid falling 'into the leading-strings of party'.[2] But whatever the restrictions placed upon this point of view, there was a widespread instinctive feeling that opposition should be the exception rather than the rule, and that a limited monarchy, because of its very limits, should receive a proper measure of support.

The House of Commons was now indisputably the focus of the political scene, and it was there that such sentiments were most effectively displayed. For Parliamentary government in the lower House could in fact be sustained only on a basis of co-operation. The King allied himself with private patrons to produce a following for the Crown; that following was allied with private interests to produce a Government; and no combination of the two could afford in the end to neglect the uncommitted Members. No element in the House, indeed, could safely be disregarded for long. The very fluctuations of the movements, the kaleidoscopic pattern of the House itself, pointed the existence of factors making for unity. The House of Commons was not the Polish Diet. If its structure was complex, it was immensely strong; and its character was not the less firmly marked for its diversity. The diffusion of propertied rights produced a network of separate interests, which the unity of the propertied class bound in a network of connexions. The Commons prided themselves on resisting the power of the Crown: they were thereby led to share with it increasingly in the work of government. Independence of the executive, and the need to support it, were two sides of the same coin. Foreign rulers and observers in official positions often looked on the House as the home of misrule. Its own members were imbued with the sense of its dignity and strength.

Eighteenth-century politics, in fact, like any others, had their own moral tone. If the constitution was delicately balanced, it was a matter of personal responsibility – of personal honour – to see that it was not grossly abused. It was this which made convention and precedent so important, and endowed the often squalid contests over conduct and place with a genuine feeling. 'Our Constitution is so happily tempered',

1. B.M. Add. Ms 34419, f. 385. When Eden did rat, at the end of the following year, he excused himself to his late associates on much the same grounds.
2. J. Douglas, *Seasonable Hints from an Honest Man* (1761), quoted in S. Neville Williams, *The Eighteenth-Century Constitution 1688–1815* . . . (1960), 76.

ran one panegyric in 1789, 'and its machinery so well constructed, that it requires less *skill* than it does *good intentions*, to keep it in order'.[1] Such a sentiment would strike a responsive chord in most eighteenth-century men of affairs; and it was one that was kept constantly vibrating from the very fact that conventions are liable to be interpreted in different ways. It echoes in the fervour, allowing for his temperament, of George III's disgust with some of the claims of the politicians, and in the real indignation with which they sometimes attacked the influence of the Crown. It lies behind much of the political language, the frequent protestations of 'manliness' and honour. It heightens the interest felt in private character as a guide to public conduct. It is something that cannot be ignored in assessing the careers of Fox and Pitt.

1. *Considerations on the Present State of the Nation . . . By a Late Under-Secretary of State* [William Knox] (1789), 20.

The Old House of Commons, from the River Gardens
Etched by J. T. Smith after Thomas Sandby

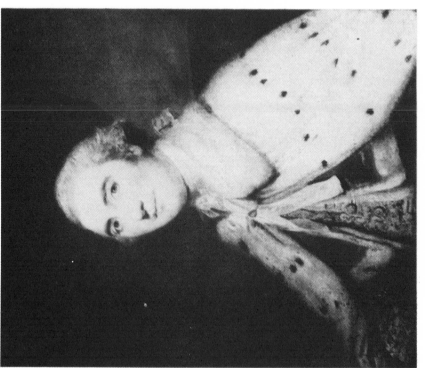

Lord Mahon. *Engraved after J. Sayers*

The Earl of Shelburne. *After Reynolds*

CHAPTER III

The Young Member and the Movements for Reform

I

When Pitt entered Parliament at the beginning of 1781, the outlook for the country was clouded, but Government's prospects seemed quite good. The whole position hinged, as it had done for the past five years, on the course of operations in the American colonies. In 1780 these had at last taken a turn for the better. There was no longer any real hope of crushing the Americans as a result of a comprehensive strategic plan. But the policy of limited expeditions and sporadic attacks, co-ordinated where possible with loyalist risings, to which the British command had been reduced over the past two years, was for the first time proving quite successful. The main effort was concentrated in the south. By the middle of 1780 Cornwallis had cleared South Carolina of organised opposition, and in August he gained a victory at Camden in North Carolina. Rodney's ships held a temporary advantage in the Caribbean and up the coast. And growing reports of low American morale were dramatically underlined by Benedict Arnold's desertion in November. Operations farther north were indecisive, and the loyalists everywhere, on whom much depended, were in fact weaker than was believed. But the immediate situation seemed not unpromising; it was even possible to argue that the Americans might still be worn down; and there was certainly no particular reason, from the state of the campaign itself, to expect a decisive reverse within a year.

The improvement in America enabled Ministers to discount the news from Europe and the East. Since the spring of 1778 Britain had been at war with France, and since June 1779 with Spain. Operations against the colonies had thus become part of a major war, with all that this meant to a maritime power. The implications were the more serious because for once we were isolated in Europe, without an ally or even the comfort of a benevolent neutral. The reconciliation of France and Austria after the Seven Years' War had produced an unfamiliar and unfavourable situation: old enemies remained hostile, old friends were now at best indifferent. The position grew worse in the course of 1780. Russia, which had soon found cause to quarrel with our interpretation

49

of neutral rights at sea, formed a League of Armed Neutrality with the other Baltic powers in March; and in November, when the Dutch seemed likely to join this defensive confederacy and to recognise the United States of America, we declared war on Holland to forestall both moves.

At the beginning of the new year the naval strength was therefore badly stretched. The humiliation of 1779, when the combined French and Spanish fleets had cruised undisturbed in the Channel for almost two months, was not repeated in 1780. But we remained dangerously weak at home and in the Mediterranean, where Gibraltar was under siege, and there was now the further embarrassment in Europe and the East of having to watch the Dutch. Meanwhile, in India itself the Mahratta war continued, and Hyder Ali was ranging the Carnatic and threatening Madras. In such circumstances it would have been a very bold stroke to reinforce the squadrons in American waters. At the same time, the position was not entirely black. It was known from intercepted letters that the French were unhappy about the cost of the war, and that their relations with the Americans were strained. Warren Hastings was organising energetically in India. And if British possessions overseas were threatened, those of the allied powers were likewise not immune from attack: at the turn of the year, an expedition sailed for the Dutch-held Cape of Good Hope. The war was not going well. There were no victories to celebrate except the limited successes in the Carolinas. But a resolute Government might still hope and plan for better things.

The closest danger of all had moreover been temporarily checked. One of the darkest features of a dark scene in 1779 had been the threat of violence in Ireland. Her trade was hard hit by the war, the example of the American colonies had been taken to heart, and the familiar means of control from London, through the Lord Lieutenant in Dublin, wholly failed to meet the growing clamour of the Parliamentary class. The Volunteer Movement, in which mercantile and political grievances were fused, gave warning of a challenge by the Anglo-Irish Ascendancy itself – a settlers' revolt in nationalist form. Paralysed by indecision, the Cabinet shut its eyes and fumbled. In the autumn of 1779 the situation accordingly came to the boil. The merchants and gentry were arming, the Irish Parliament threatened the supplies, the mob growled and rioted in the Dublin streets. At the beginning of November, one percipient observer forecast that 'a very few weeks, if not days, will produce events which will disunite the interests of Great Britain and Ireland'.[1] But, apparently at the last minute, the British Government moved. In December North introduced a programme of commercial concessions; and when these had passed into law in January 1780 they were found to have a sudden, indeed a surprising, effect. The measures met the most pressing economic grievances. They might be taken as a promise of

1. John Beresford to John Robinson, 5 November 1779 (*The Correspondence of the Right Hon. John Beresford* . . . ed. by the Right Hon. William Beresford, I (1854), 73).

better things. And while they could not be expected to cure a deep-rooted disease in themselves, they proved enough to bring the Irish Parliament uneasily to heel, and to remove the immediate danger of insurrection.

In the second half of 1780, Government in fact enjoyed something of a breathing space. Indeed, they could once more claim something like public support. The war was not unpopular as long as it was not too openly mishandled, and if 1780 was not an inspiring year it was a great deal better than 1779. The Gordon riots in June, moreover, swung opinion sharply in favour of the authorities. The average man was badly frightened; the supporters of reform paused; and the great weight of moderate opinion, in Parliament and beyond, rallied to the forces of order embodied in the Ministers of the Crown. With the advantage of hindsight, we can see that this was only a lull. North and his colleagues had been too deeply shaken by their earlier buffetings to do more now than carry on in the absence of bad news. Only a few months before, North himself had been suffering from something like a nervous break-down, his Cabinet was depressed and divided, and the machinery of government was failing to engage. An Administration which so recently had been in such a state could not be transformed simply by a run of better luck, or even by the mistakes of its opponents. Its members remained at the mercy of events, and if there was another defeat, especially in America, both their appeal and their resolution were open to doubt. Meanwhile the pressures had eased, North had apparently regained much of his poise, and Ministers could again look with some confidence to those weighty forces which were normally ranged behind the Government of the day.

In this lowered temperature, Opposition found it difficult to maintain its earlier impetus. Parliament assembled in November, after the general election. In the short period before Christmas, North held his own. In the more testing weeks between Christmas and Easter he regained much of his old control. At the end of January 1781, Government weathered an attack on the subject of the war with Holland. On 26 February, after some anxious moments, they defeated a motion to reintroduce Burke's bill for Economical Reform – the great stalking-horse of Opposition in the previous spring. By the end of March, they had comfortably survived a series of debates on North's handling of the latest Government loan, and Opposition seemed to one of his colleagues to be 'if not dead at least asleep'.[1] In May the Minister was able to move to the attack, and to carry without great difficulty some measures for India and finance.

It was in these somewhat dispiriting circumstances that Pitt appeared on the scene, at the end of January 1781. His speeches over the next

1. Earl of Hillsborough to William Eden, 21 March 1781; quoted in Christie, *The End of North's Ministry*, 256–7.

five months, few in number though they were, formed one of the brightest features of an uninspiring session for his associates. The new recruit was accepted at once as a major figure. Within eighteen months of taking his seat he was in the Cabinet, and four months earlier he had felt able to reject junior office in advance. He was then twenty-two, and had been on his feet a dozen times.[1] As a Parliamentary performance, its success was immediate and complete.

Pitt made his maiden speech on 26 February 1781, in the course of the second reading of Burke's motion to reintroduce his bill for Economical Reform. He had apparently not intended to take part; but the House was anxious to hear Chatham's reputedly brilliant son, and quite early in the proceedings a group of Opposition Members called on him by name. Taken somewhat by surprise, he rose and spoke 'directly in answer to matter that had fallen out in the course of the debate'.[2] This in itself was a remarkable thing to have done. A maiden speaker has traditionally never been asked to do more than try his powers in a set speech, not particularly related to what has gone before. It was altogether exceptional on such an occasion to make a debating reply, and Pitt's confidence in doing so astonished the House. So did the speech itself, and the manner of its delivery. 'His voice', *The Parliamentary Register* recorded, 'is rich and striking, full of melody and force; his manner easy and elegant; his language beautiful and luxuriant. He gave in this first essay, a specimen of eloquence, not unworthy the son of his immortal parent'.[3] When he sat down, Fox hurried up to congratulate him. North declared it the best first speech he had ever heard. Burke is said to have remarked, 'He is not a chip of the old block: he is the old block itself!' For the next fifty years and more, the speech remained a standard by which budding orators were judged.

Pitt spoke only twice more in the course of the session – on 31 May, in a debate on North's Commissioners of the Public Accounts, and on 12 June, to defend his father's views on the American War. On both occasions he confirmed the impression he had already made. By the summer recess he was accepted not only as a leading debater, but as someone from whom 'his fellow-subjects . . . were destined, on some future day, to derive the most important services'.[4]

1. It was in his thirteenth recorded speech, on 8 March 1782, that Pitt announced himself uninterested in 'a subordinate situation' (see pp. 79-80 below). Not every speech by Members was necessarily recorded – one occasion in 1782, for instance, was described as 'a most tedious and desultory debate, in which near half the members present took part' (*P.R.*, VII (1782), 223). But in view of the marked attention which that same authority, and the Opposition newspapers on whose original material it was partly based, paid throughout these months to Pitt's recorded contributions, it seems unlikely that anything more than a mere interjection on his part was allowed to pass unnoticed.
2. *P.R.*, II (1781), 17.
3. Ibid.
4. Henry Dundas's words, on 12 June 1781 (op. cit., III (1781), 571).

How exactly had he done it? What were the qualities which, then and always, so impressed the House? Few things are more dead than old speeches, particularly Parliamentary speeches. The sense of occasion, the speaker's arts, almost always escape the published report, and in this case the style of oratory itself has changed beyond recall. It is difficult enough to recapture the flavour of a speech by Pitt or Fox, let alone their different kinds of flavour, when we have something like a proper text. The difficulties are not lessened by the knowledge that with Pitt this is seldom the case. Parliamentary reporting in the late eighteenth century, though improving, was still suspect and therefore unreliable, and even when Members supplied their own versions they were not always exact.[1] In any case Pitt hardly ever did so, and we have therefore normally to rely for his words on the accounts of other Members, and the memories – perhaps from the middle eighties supplemented by long-hand notes – of a few 'newswriters' squashed into the jostling back bench of the gallery, half hidden from the nearer end of the Chamber, and working, again at least until the middle eighties, without reliefs. 'Memory' Woodfall himself could not hope in such circumstances to provide much more than a lifelike impression. Sometimes he could not identify the speaker, or properly catch what was said, from his inconvenient perch. Sometimes he was tired, particularly when an important debate had obliged him to attend early in order to secure a place, and had kept him there for perhaps ten or thirteen hours. Sometimes he could not be present at all, when there was an interesting debate to be reported in the Lords, or the gallery of the Commons was cleared, or the crowd at the door prevented him from getting in.[2] And when these obstacles had been overcome, and the weary reporter was free to turn his memories or notes into a collected account, the result was normally subject to the discipline or caprice of a newspaper. Woodfall himself, as a reporter, had higher standards than his rivals in the early eighties, and did his best with the meagre space available. But as an editor he was not noticeably less partisan, and was usually careful

1. E.g. p. 21 above.

2. Thus he was in the House of Lords on 27 February 1782, when Pitt made a speech on the American War 'which was allowed on all hands to be the best and most forcible in point of argument, and the most brilliant, splendid, and powerful in point of eloquence, of any he had before delivered in parliament' (*The Morning Chronicle, & London Advertiser*, 28 February); and he, with most of the reporters, failed to force his way into the gallery on 7 May 1782, to hear Pitt introduce his motion on Parliamentary reform, and was thus 'unable to give any account of the Debate from himself' (loc. cit., 8 May; and see p. 70 below). Reporters do not seem to have been given any reliable priority in securing seats until after the end of the Napoleonic Wars.

The gallery could (as it still can) be cleared whenever a Member on the floor of the House chose to 'spy Strangers'; and in the later 1770s this had happened a good deal. More often, however, – and this was the case down to the 1850s – it was cleared automatically when a division was taken and was then not reopened, so that the proceedings thereafter could be reported only by Members themselves.

to see that the Tory dogs did not have the best of it. Pitt was in fact reported more fully in these early sessions than he was later on, when his break with Fox lost him the advantage of the old Rockingham party's journalistic contacts. But while we need not therefore be too nice about accepting the record of the Opposition press as an honest attempt, we cannot expect from it more than a few hints of the effect he produced.

It is clear, of course, that the House was amazed at the very start by Pitt's assurance in handling so finished a style. The sentences were rounded; the proportions were observed; the flashes of brilliance were seldom forced; there were light and shade in the measured tones. Here was a matured debater of great skill and range. This, however, takes us only some of the way. Pitt, after all, was not the only orator whose initial brilliance was allowed. Sheridan was fast developing talents thought, at least by some, to be equal to his; and even the young Lord Maitland, who spoke for the first time on the same day as Pitt, was bracketed with him in some quarters as 'highly distinguished by . . . ability and eloquence'.[1] Yet there is no question as to their comparative success. What was it, behind the easy manner and the beautiful language, that so attracted this particular audience?

One incident may suggest one of the reasons. In his first speech, Pitt destroyed the argument of his immediate predecessor, Lord Nugent, by showing that it was based on a misreading of a clause in the bill under debate. He did so with ease and effect. The matter was introduced quite naturally, at an appropriate moment in the speech. It did not disturb the flow. It was simply an unanswerable fact, which removed much of the point of Lord Nugent's contribution. This was always to be a great feature of Pitt's style. Like all good debaters, he excelled at picking on an opponent's weakness, particularly a factual omission or mistake, as part of the development of his own case. 'After a variety of particular arguments, all strongly applicable to what Lord North had suggested, Mr. Pitt resumed his general argument'.[2] This excerpt from the report of his second speech is typical of a method which has always appealed to the House of Commons.

It was incorporated in a style that was both closely reasoned and comprehensive. Pitt liked to move along well-ordered lines, his argument gathering a logical momentum. One must remember, of course, that these early speeches were some of the very few that he ever made in Opposition, and they reflect a freedom he was soon to lose. Moreover, despite his virtuosity he was still a young man, apt to strike an attitude and discover a principle. But one of the things that impressed the House about this particular young man was that he spoke like a Minister from the Opposition benches; and his inexperience in debate

1. *The Annual Register . . . for the Year 1781* (3rd edn., 1800), 183. And cf. Wraxall, op. cit., II, 78.
2. *P.R.,* III, 471.

was never very marked. Pitt's style of argument was already in fact what it remained throughout his life – logical, balanced, absolutely controlled. And in this, as in so many ways, he was the antithesis of Fox, whose strength lay in what one contemporary called his 'lightning' style[1] – a battery of arguments, poured out with extraordinary force, spilling over one another in a dazzling sequence. Pitt himself was no impressionist. He built on classical lines, and, like a great classical architect, gained his originality from the assurance with which he stamped his impress on a common form. When you listened to a great speech by Fox, you were conscious of hearing something unique: 'la baguette du Magicien', as Pitt is said once to have called it,[2] could belong to no one else. A great speech by Pitt was of a different order. You were not swept along with the orator in his headlong triumphant course, confronted by a succession of sudden brilliant views. You did not share his own sense of adventure, were not involved in his emotions. Rather, you followed a supremely convincing exposition: the arguments unrolled, the objections were crushed, the case built up towards its appointed triumphant end. You were not breathlessly watching a tight-rope walker who you knew would not fall. You were being steered through a difficult channel to a sure harbour by a pilot who was not going to run aground. Both men had that quality of the born orator, that they spoke in a speaker's, not a writer's, style; both knew, none better, how to speak to the House of Commons. Unlike Burke, for instance, who came late to the game from a suspect background, they had the feeling of the place in their bones, respected its prejudices and echoed its tone. They never committed the sin of trying the House beyond its strength; on the contrary, they did supremely well what the average Member would like to have done himself. 'An orator', reflected Hazlitt of the Parliamentary champions of his youth, 'can hardly get beyond *commonplaces*'.[3] But the commonplaces were transformed in the case of Fox by a flashing intelligence and intuition, and in that of Pitt by a mind of distinction and a character of weight.

For it was Pitt's character, allied to his gifts, that seems to have struck the House most forcibly from the start. Many years later, Wraxall singled out 'the judgment, the diction, and the solemnity' as the outstanding features of his maiden speech;[4] and the recollection is unlikely to have been the result of hindsight alone. Towards the end of the summer session in 1781, Henry Dundas, who knew a good prospect when he saw one, referred to 'the happy union of . . . first-rate abilities, high integrity, a bold and honest independency of conduct, and the most persuasive eloquence';[5] and if the compliment implied in the third

1. *The Morning Post*, 15 September 1806.
2. Robert Isaac Wilberforce and Samuel Wilberforce, *The Life of William Wilberforce*, I (1838) 38.
3. *On the Difference between Writing and Speaking.*
4. *Historical Memoirs*, II, 77.
5. *P.R.*, III, 571.

of these qualities was common political form, it was the combination of the rest which made men talk of Pitt, after only a few months, as a born Minister as well as a born debater. The judgment seemed as mature as the argument and the style. The House had expected to hear a clever young man. It was surprised to find 'the statesman, not the student, or the advocate, or the candidate for popular applause'.[1]

The meeting of Pitt and his audience was indeed something of a marriage of true minds. He entered Parliament fully armed, a born House of Commons man. The ease with which he made this clear owed a very great deal to his birth and to the nature of the assembly itself. When he rose to make his second speech, 'the House received him with all that silent attention which his former display of abilities, and the recollection of his illustrious descent, could not fail to command'.[2] As Chatham's son, he was the only new Member who could count on such general interest and goodwill; and if comparisons might be drawn later, all that mattered for the moment was the great chance of a favourable hearing. As Sheridan could tell the fortunate young man, there was everything to be said for being born with a Parliamentary golden spoon. And for someone who could profit by the fact, the conditions can seldom have been more propitious. The mixture of eligibility and talent was exactly to the taste of the old House of Commons; and its ear for debating ability was at its keenest in those decades. Oratory was becoming more and more a feature of debate: it was precisely at this time that speeches were growing longer, and that the recognised performer was allowed increasingly to set the pace. The great age of the Parliamentary gladiator had recently dawned, and Pitt had been trained for such a role by a master hand. His remarkable combination of qualities was exactly suited to the situation. There is something inevitable about his early success.

From the time that he entered the House, in January 1781, until he was given office at the beginning of July 1782, Pitt spoke, as far as can be ascertained, on twenty occasions.[3] About half of these were of no great importance. The more substantial speeches were devoted to three main subjects – the conduct and objects of the war; the relations between Parliament and the Crown; and the reform of Parliament itself. The first was of course the burning topic of the day, particularly after the disaster at Yorktown again plunged Government into difficulties in the

1. Wraxall, II, 77.

2. *P.R.*, III, 464.

3. This does not include his separate remarks on the three occasions on which he spoke twice in a day's debate; but it does include the few times he rose briefly to make a point, the one occasion on which he gave notice of his intention to introduce a motion, and another on which the speaker is named simply 'Mr. Pitt', so that it might have been his cousin Thomas or his more distant relation William Morton Pitt.

winter of 1781–2. It was almost obligatory for a rising politician to express his views; Pitt had a heriditary interest in doing so; and his remarks, though effectively expressed, were not particularly original. But, like his more important contributions on Economical and Parliamentary Reform, they show the stock of ideas, largely inherited, with which he began his political life, and which determined his first party affinities.

Pitt's views on America were in fact his father's. Opposition on this great question had always been divided into two camps. The main corps, led by Rockingham, applauded the colonists' struggle for independence. They drank their toasts to Washington, their young men wore the buff and blue. Chatham and his followers, on the other hand, condemned Government's measures with equal fervour as likely to sever the connexion of the colonies with the Crown. Both parties joined in attacking the policy that had led to war, and the war itself. But one did so in the hope, the other in the fear, that the result would be the emergence of a new State. Chatham's dying speech had been made in protest at the Rockinghams' views. It was not surprising that Pitt should have echoed his arguments.

Chatham's mantle had been inherited by a small party. He himself – it had been his pride – had never built up a large connexion, and his later vagaries and absences had pared what there was to the bone. Its leader was now Lord Shelburne, the associate of his later age; and a very curious and interesting leader he was. His effect on Pitt will be considered later, when the two men sat together in Cabinet. At this early stage he bulked large in the young man's life. When Temple and Rockingham had declined to help Pitt in the Cambridge by-election,[1] Shelburne and Rutland busied themselves on his behalf. When Pitt came to London, it was Shelburne and Camden, his father's old Chancellor, of whom he saw most among the older generation. In the awkward incident of his brother's imbroglio at Portsmouth,[2] it was to Shelburne that he turned principally for advice. Although strictly speaking he was Lowther's Member, and owed strong obligations to Rutland,[3] his natural ties lay with Shelburne among the Parliamentary leaders, and in so far as he looked to anyone for support it was to him.

The ties were not so strong that Pitt could be counted as one of Shelburne's followers. It was not in his nature to play second fiddle, he was a figure in his own right from the first, and he very soon staked out a distinctive position. But he stood a great deal closer to Shelburne's

1. See p. 25 above.
2. Pp. 20–1 above.
3. 'Let me . . . hope that I shall have the satisfaction of fighting under your banner in the cause to which we are both attached, and of proving to the world how much I know the value and feel the honour of such a connexion' (Pitt to Rutland, 9 March 1781; *H.M.C., Fourteenth Report, Appendix, Pt. I,* 40). Rutland was himself a protégé of Shelburne's.

group than he did to the more imposing party of Rockingham, Portland and Fox, in whose hands the main fortunes of Opposition lay. His relations with the latter were cordial enough. The Rockinghams were the leaders in a campaign which he had followed with rapt attention from his Cambridge days. He admired their orators, his immediate sympathies were theirs, like them he rejoiced in the name of Whig at a time of common effort. 'I do not wish . . .', he had declared when soliciting support in his first by-election, 'to call myself any Thing but an *Independent Whig*';[1] and the Rockinghams were carrying the burden of the struggle against the Court. When Fox was involved in a duel in the winter of 1779, 'I am very glad', Pitt wrote to his mother, 'that [the] Wound is so slight, as, just at present, His Life may I think be considered as precious'.[2] And Fox for his part gladly hailed the new star. His compliments were generous, he was ready to welcome such a recruit to his circle, and within a month of Pitt taking his seat Fox put him up for Brooks's.[3] Here indeed was a potentially valuable acquisition to a party priding itself on talent, not least because it would be at the expense of Shelburne. In varying degrees of amity, the groups and personalities coalesced. But the alliance was coloured by their distinct and sometimes divergent traditions. America was a bone of contention as well as a bond. But another division – one indeed central to whig thought itself – was suggested by the attitude of the Rockinghams on the one hand, and of Shelburne and Pitt on the other, to the great questions of Economical and Parliamentary Reform.

II

Reform lay very close to Pitt's heart at the outset. His maiden speech was made, though inadvertently, on the subject of Economical Reform. His first motion, the only one he sponsored before he became a Minister, was for an inquiry into the possibility of a measure of Parliamentary reform. And apart from the obvious subject of the American War, all his speeches of any substance as a private Member in 1781–2 were concerned with some aspect of reform, or with the relations between Parliament and the executive on which such questions impinged. It is

1. Pitt to Westmorland, 26 July 1779 (Ms at Duke University, North Carolina). 'Which', he added, 'in words is hardly a distinction, as every one alike pretends to it'.
2. 3 December 1779 (P.R.O. 30/8/12). Fox further recommended himself to the family a few weeks later by attacking, in a Parliamentary debate, the way in which the payments on the Chatham pension had been allowed to fall into arrears (Pitt to Hester Countess of Chatham, 26 February 1780; loc. cit.).
3. It is usually stated that this occurred immediately after Pitt had made his maiden speech on 26 February. He was in fact elected on the 28th. But according to the inscription on his portrait at Brooks's, Fox had put him up on the 20th. (See *Memorials of Brooks's from the Foundation of the Club 1764 to the Close of the Nineteenth Century* . . . (1907), 27.)

therefore fair to say that reform was the subject which chiefly excited Pitt's interest at this time.

This was perhaps scarcely surprising. Reform was becoming a prominent issue when Pitt began to follow politics, and the movement reached a climax just as he entered the House. It was indeed a European phenomenon, in an age when Enlightened rulers were gingerly applying the idioms of the *philosophes* to the complex structures of their inherited institutions. Their efforts were normally directed to administrative ends. In England, the great strength of Parliamentary institutions was shown by the fact that the issues were political, and centred on Parliament itself. The mystique of the constitution, indeed, governed reformers and their opponents alike. The Glorious Revolution, it was generally agreed, had set the scene for an ideal balance between Crown, aristocracy and people, guaranteeing the proper rights and liberties of each. In the growing disturbances of the sixties and seventies, culminating in an unsuccessful war, the question was whether the balance had not been upset – by the Crown at the expense of aristocracy and people, or perhaps by Crown and aristocracy acting in uneasy collusion. If this was so, the remedy must lie within the institution in which all three interests met, and reform must be concentrated on the House of Commons. Such an aim was essentially conservative: to restore something thought to have been lost. There was no question, to the bulk of the reformers, of radically altering the system itself – of dissociating the executive from the Crown, or extending the franchise very far. The political nation remained to most of them essentially what it had been, with a modest shift of emphasis in favour of 'the middling sort'. If the symptoms of reform were sometimes disturbing, its objects were less so. While there were radicals who drew on other, more extreme traditions – which indeed gave the cause much of its lasting theoretical strength –, its immediate success depended on its appeal to the enlightened self-interest of a stable but troubled governing class.

The early stirrings in the sixties had produced a wide range of plans. But common to them all were two cries which were to endure: one for shorter Parliaments – whether annual or triennial – instead of the more recent rule of seven years, and one for a transfer of seats from the decayed boroughs to the counties and some of the larger towns. Such demands drew their life from the 'Wilkes and Liberty' campaign, that remarkable and genuinely popular metropolitan movement; and when it declined they survived as the programme of a small if vociferous minority. But the expense and deadlock of the American War enlarged the area of discontent, and as trade began to suffer and taxation to rise, dismay turned to anger among merchants and gentry alike. By 1780, economic and 'collateral difficulties . . . [had] put the people out of temper little by little, and at last provoked them to "turn their eyes inward upon themselves".'[1] Something like a Country movement, in the

1. Pitt's description, looking back in 1783 (*P.R.*, IX (1783), 690).

old seventeenth-century style, seemed to be emerging. The agitation for reform became at once more formidable and more confused.

The pattern developed largely between 1779 and 1781. When Pitt entered Parliament, therefore, the position had changed a great deal from that of Chatham's later years, let alone from the time when he had been actively interested in reform. For Pitt's concern was not aroused by the general picture alone; his approach was shaped, once more, by hereditary interest. Chatham had been one of the first, and far the greatest, of the leading politicians to associate himself with the reformers. Indeed, the origins of the movement may not unreasonably be traced to the events following his resignation in 1761. It was Chatham's name which Wilkes invoked at the start of his explosive career, and if their later relations were frequently stormy Chatham was the only great Parliamentarian who remained consistently, if often disapprovingly, in touch with the metropolitan groups. He was something of an admirer of the republican Thomas Hollis, and a friend of John Sawbridge, the father of the demands for shorter Parliaments in the House itself. Their attitudes and aspirations appealed to his radical streak. More than any other leading political figure of his time except his brother-in-law Temple, he expressed himself in favour of a measure of constitutional change.

When it came to the point, however, the measure was not very large; and if the more thoroughgoing reformers could sometimes shelter beneath the great man's name, they came to be chary of his activities and ideas. Their dealings with him, indeed, reflected the awkwardness inherent in the relations between a prominent Member of Parliament and the forces of discontent outside. Chatham's patronage in the event proved cautious and vacillating. By the early seventies he was willing to accept triennial Parliaments in principle; but only in principle, and the opposition of 'families of all descriptions' soon convinced him that immediate action was 'totally inadvisable'.[1] As for a reform of the House of Commons itself, his remedy was an increase in the number of County Members, 'who', he was reported as saying in his most explicit statement on the subject, 'approach nearest to the constitutional representation of the country, because they represent the soil'.[2] Rotten boroughs were by and large undesirable, and sometimes a disgrace. The influence of corruption which they often enshrined should certainly be checked. But this could be done more judiciously by strengthening the purer part of the House than by tampering with the defective element itself. 'The limb is mortified, but the amputation might be death'.[3] These sentiments were scarcely calculated to satisfy the theorists, or those urban forces on which Chatham still liked to call.

Such arguments concerned the reform of Parliament itself. But as the

1. To Shelburne, 22 April 1771 (*Chatham Correspondence*, IV, 157).
2. *P.H.* (1813), XVI, 754.
3. Ibid.

political climate changed in the course of the later seventies, they became entangled with the demands of the associated but distinct movement for Economical Reform. The connexion between the two causes was clear in the circumstances of the time. The targets of Economical Reform were the expense of government, swollen by the war, and the political influence of the Crown which it fostered, and which was held to be the source of inefficiency and corruption. The evils of the times, so the argument ran, lay in a set of incompetent Ministers, fettered to the King and enabled to flout public opinion by the passive allegiance of the bought cohorts of the Crown. The object must therefore be to narrow the field of Crown activity, by abolishing or reducing some of its offices, disfranchising some of its officials, and disqualifying some of its placemen and contractors from the right of election to the House of Commons. These aims, in the restricted version in which they were presented to Parliament, became the distinguishing mark, if not the property, of the Rockingham party. But they were equally acceptable to the various groups of Parliamentary reformers, themselves concerned to scotch the old bogy of an over-powerful executive. As early as 1770, indeed, the metropolitan radicals had gone farther in this direction than the Rockinghams themselves; and ten years later, when reform had been taken up more widely in the provinces, the Yorkshire Association called for similar measures without reference to the Parliamentary party.

Nevertheless, the different groups approached the issue in different ways. To the Economical Reformers, the programme they advocated was an end in itself. When the Crown had been duly curbed, all would be well. To the Parliamentary reformers, of whatever brand, such a programme was a necessary preliminary to the wider panacea of a reform of the House of Commons. The immediate connexion, indeed, barely disguised the contradictions between the leaders of the various movements. Where the Economical Reformers sought their ideal balance within the House as it stood, the Parliamentary reformers looked to some change in the representation. Parliamentary reformers were concerned with a redistribution or an alteration in the balance of seats: Economical Reformers with the nature of the Members who held what already existed. The roots of the movements for Parliamentary reform lay outside Parliament, and their leaders sought the politicians' support as far as possible on their own terms. Economical Reform, as it came to fruition, was the product of a Parliamentary party, whose leaders sought a useful measure of public support. Parliamentary reform was directed perhaps as much against the politicians as against the Crown. Economical Reform came to be directed by politicians against the Crown.

This last was indeed the great distinguishing feature of the Rockinghams' programme. All politicians in opposition in the later eighteenth century were of course apt to cry corruption and attack the influence of the Crown. All the same, there was a certain difference between the Rockinghams and the rest. They went farther than anyone else in proclaiming as theory what most politicians would happily have wrung from the King in practice; and whatever their reservations in practice, they went farther than anyone else in applying the theory as a condition of office. Economical Reform to them was, quite openly, the latest weapon of the great Whig families in their traditional defence of freedom against the Crown; and the belief became, in adverse circumstances, something of an obsession. The attitude governed the programme of reform itself. It would probably be unfair to say that Burke's scheme, and the associated measures, were concerned only with the political value of retrenchment, and not with retrenchment for its own sake. The issues were generally recognised to be serious – some Members believed that Burke introduced his bill with North's connivance – and in its original form at least his plan comprised a quite comprehensive group of reforms, which with proper drafting would have had real merits.[1] It might be more true to say that the administrative and political objects were held to be inseparable, and that the former came increasingly to be conditioned by the latter. It was common ground to all parties – to Shelburne's as well as to Rockingham's – that the primary object of the Parliamentary campaign was to reduce the political influence of the Crown.[2] But the Rockinghams ended by restricting their proposals to that object, and often fighting those that did not bear directly on it. Thus they opposed the reduction of places held for life as distinct from those held 'on pleasure', on the argument that the holders were financially independent of the Crown. And they refused to investigate the salaries paid in 'efficient' departments, or even to pry into the size of individual pensions. Such measures, after all, affected patronage as a whole, not merely the patronage at the direct disposal of the King. They embarrassed the reformers as well as the Crown. They might weaken the influence of the defenders of freedom themselves.

The same attitude governed the Rockinghams' views on Parliamentary reform. Their position here was in essence perfectly simple. They looked with dismay on any serious attempt to alter the relations between Parliament and the public. The whole object of their efforts, in fact, in so far as they were not merely a bid for power, was so to restore the balance between Parliament and the Crown that the complementary question need not be aired. Such concessions as the party made to the Parliamentary reformers were therefore tactical, designed to win

1. This is a debatable point among historians. For the discussion, see the Note on Sources for ch. IV below.

2. E.g. Dunning's remark in the House of Commons in February 1780: 'the saving of money, is but a secondary object. The reduction of the influence of the crown, is the first.' (*The Parliamentary Register . . .*, ed. John Almon, XVII (1780), 133). Dunning was one of Shelburne's principal lieutenants.

support for its own campaign; and where it could not hope to manage, it opposed a movement whose aims it disliked and whose implications it feared. The Rockinghams were prepared to reduce the duration of Parliaments from the conventional seven to three years – 'the term . . . fixed at the Revolution' of 1688.[1] But this was only in answer to pressure from outside; and the complementary programme to amend the representation struck them as dangerous in the extreme. So did the appearance of associations outside Parliament which they did not direct themselves. Both the proposals and the methods, the ends and the means, threatened the foundations of all they held dear. The constitution was strong, but it was delicately poised. Tamper with the framework – abolish rotten boroughs, increase the number of County Members, interfere with the conduct of elections, allow the initiative to shift beyond Parliament's control – and the beneficent balance might easily be destroyed.[2] Liberty was the product of a regulated property: lay your hands on property, and liberty would suffer. The great Whig lords were not entirely selfish, they could point to a venerable party tradition in support of their views, and a century of stability had seemed to endorse this conservative strain. The Rockinghams genuinely believed that they were the guardians of a system which was the envy of the world. The problem, as they saw it, was to restore that system to health without it being damaged in the process by ignorant well-wishers.

The Rockinghams' marriage with the Parliamentary reformers was thus at best one of convenience, and was always liable to end in divorce. It was the more surprising at first sight that their closest contacts in 1780–2 should have lain with the extreme metropolitan wing. Relations between the two groups had long been uneasy, and Rockingham himself was the most powerful of Yorkshire politicians at a time when that county was challenging the capital for leadership of the movement. The Londoners' views, indeed, were not at all to the Rockinghams' taste. They were far too sweeping on Economical Reform itself; and a programme which called for annual Parliaments, the abolition of rotten boroughs, and even a radical extension of the franchise, held no appeal for the 'snug chaste corps'[3] led by a Wentworth, a Cavendish and a

1. George Thomas, Earl of Albemarle, *Memoirs of the Marquis of Rockingham and his Contemporaries*, II (1852), 404.
2. The argument could be ingeniously applied. Thus Portland opposed an addition to the number of County Members – generally considered to be the guardians of independence against the aristocracy and the Crown – on the ground that it would *increase* unduly the weight of the aristocracy, by encouraging 'the most opulent families' at the expense of 'the middling gentlemen', thus weakening the representatives' regard for the freeholders' opinion and proving 'prejudicial to the democratical part of the Constitution' (loc. cit., 412–13). This was indeed an argument which Pitt had later to meet (see p. 74, n. 2 below).
3. The description is William Burke's, Edmund's somewhat disreputable relation (quoted in N. C. Phillips, 'Edmund Burke and the County Movement, 1779–1780', *E.H.R.*, LXXVI, no. 299, 261).

Bentinck. The alliance between these dissimilar partners, fluctuating and partial as it was, owed its existence in fact chiefly to the adventurous activities of Charles Fox, whose sudden success as a candidate for the City of Westminster gave him and his associates a better chance of controlling a popular movement than was offered by the more staid and independent Yorkshire Association.

For the Foxites were in a somewhat different, and much more interesting position. They supported wholeheartedly the campaign for Economical Reform. They subscribed in general to the Rockinghams' views. But they were also implicated, to an extent that disturbed some of their colleagues, in the most radical of the movements for Parliamentary reform. Fox's hunger for office, unappeased since he had quarrelled with North in 1774, and aggravated by more recent hopes and disappointments, was now indeed leading him along some strange paths. At the end of 1779 he turned to popular politics, with the violent facility which marked everything he did. Adopted early in the new year as prospective candidate for Westminster, he was soon the idol of the most famous of open constituencies. 'Charles James Cub Esq?', the target of the Wilkite prints of the early seventies, had become the Man of the People, 'bowing and sweltering' in Westminster Hall with Wilkes on his right hand and the radical John Jebb on his left. His dazzling talents, at this moment of high excitement, drew his two unlikely sets of associates together. By restoring to the London movement the support of a leading Parliamentary figure, and with a far greater intimacy than Chatham had ever allowed, he temporarily bridged the gap between Wentworth Woodhouse and the butchers of Covent Garden.

It was perhaps not entirely a matter of opportunism; or if it was, the occasion was blessed. Fox himself did not conceal his impatience for office, and the ruinous state of his finances combined with his sense of unused powers to force him along a characteristically reckless course. The gambler of Brooks's was raising the stakes, and the result was an old story, which sober men did not much like.

> *Achitophel*, grown weary to possess
> A lawful Fame, and lazie Happiness,
> Disdained the Golden Fruit to gather free
> And lent the Croud his Arm to shake the Tree.[1]

George III voiced a common opinion when he remarked at this time that Fox had never had any principles at all.

1. Dryden, *Absolom and Achitophel* (1681), lines 200–4. There is an instructive similarity between some of the fears aroused in 1680 by 'Achitophel' Shaftesbury – that gifted, ambitious man who, if anyone, could surely share with the devil the title of first Whig – and those aroused by Fox a century later.

The case, however, was not as simple as that. If Fox lacked scruples he also lacked guile, and when he said that, despite appearances, he believed in what he was doing, we may be sure that he believed what he said. He was exceptionally prone to self-deception; but when the issue was a great one he was not cynical about the cause. He was a selfish, dangerous gambler; but he was also a great deal more than that. His profound, unselfconscious egoism made him soar as well as fall. The campaign into which he had plunged was moreover not unsuited to his tastes. Aristocratic radicalism is a familiar story. There may have been something in Fox's heredity which, in the right conditions, favoured such a bent.[1] And if his fortunes were not to be linked with an aristocracy in possession, this was a not untypical example of aristocracy in revolt. The Rockinghams were uneasily prepared to allow demands which they feared from a movement which they hoped to control. Fox himself revelled in the excitement, absorbed by every aspect of a cause he had made his own.

The positions of Shelburne and of Pitt – for there were shades of emphasis between them – bore only a limited resemblance to those of either the Rockinghams or Fox. Both men approved the objects of Economical Reform; but against a rather different background from the Rockinghams', and with rather different interests from theirs. Pitt, particularly at the start, went with them for much of the way. Neither his mother's nor his father's family stood close to the Court. George III disliked Grenvilles, whatever their politics; old Temple had returned the feeling with interest; and Chatham himself had been feared and finally hated at St James's, his funeral boycotted[2] and the payments on his pension allowed to fall into arrears. His son entered public life with a healthy suspicion of the King – a suspicion which he was never to lose. At the same time, he was no mere aristocratic cadet. Neither the Grenvilles nor the Pitts belonged to the clan of great Revolution families, and if Chatham had spent much of his life in fighting the Court, he had made it very clear that it was not out of love or respect for them. Pitt inherited this feeling of contempt – a feeling which again he was never to lose. His instinctive dislike of the great magnates was as marked as his suspicion of George III, and if it was necessary to restrain the royal influence it was not in order to elevate that of the territorial peers. Such sentiments prevented him from following the Rockinghams in their more extreme denunciations of the powers of the Crown, or in the claims they made for themselves. Like Shelburne, he was heir to a

1. Certainly two of the most radical politicians in the early eighties were Fox and his uncle the Duke of Richmond – both descendants of Charles II.
2. 'The Court did not honour us with their countenance, nor did they suffer the procession to be as magnificent as it ought' (Pitt to Hester Countess of Chatham, 9 June 1778; Stanhope, I, 22).

tradition in which party, in Burke's sense, had theoretically no place. His few early constitutional maxims are thoroughly innocuous. 'It neither became them [the Commons] to settle the men that were to come in, nor to adjust or investigate the measures they were to pursue. The Crown had the undoubted right to appoint its own Ministers; it was the province of that House to watch and examine the conduct of Ministers'.[1] 'A patriot King, presiding over a united people'.[2] These were traditional commonplaces, with no hint of the Rockinghams' more debatable views. Pitt, like Shelburne, subscribed to the respectable whig doctrine of the growing influence of the Crown. Like Shelburne, he is not on record as attacking the royal prerogative.[3]

At the same time, both Shelburne and Pitt proved more radical than the Rockinghams on the substance of Economical Reform. Shelburne indeed openly criticised the limits to the party's programme. His action reflected not only his political position, but also his conception of what reform itself involved. Like Chatham, he did not attack the influence of the Crown in order to increase that of the Revolution families. Like Chatham's son, he was genuinely concerned in administration for its own sake.

For this was perhaps the greatest difference between the Rockinghams on the one hand and Shelburne and Pitt on the other. Unlike Fox, to a far greater extent than Burke, in quite another sense indeed from most leading politicians, they were interested in the processes of government as such. The consequences perhaps should not be drawn too sharply: the Rockinghams and their successors did not entirely lose sight of domestic reform once their original measures had passed, while neither Shelburne nor Pitt could hope always to honour his professions. It was rather that there was a change in the climate of thought. Where the Rockinghams saw administrative problems largely in political terms, Shelburne and Pitt were prepared to tackle them in their own right. The Rockinghams inhabited, even while they helped transform, a familiar, restricted political world. Shelburne and Pitt, in their temperamentally different ways, looked out on a wider scene, in which Adam Smith had come to maturity and Bentham was growing up.

Something of the same spirit informed their attitude to Parliamentary reform. Both men could claim, by apprenticeship or birth, an affinity with the cause. Both were conscious of their links with the one Parliamentary leader of recent times who had appealed to the people at large.

---

1. Speech of 15 March 1782, on Sir John Rous's motion for withdrawing the confidence of Parliament from His Majesty's Ministers. (*P.R.*, VI (1782), 474).

2. The same occasion (*P.H.*, XXII (1814), 1190).

3. Cf. Shelburne's observation in the House of Lords of 14 April 1780: 'in distinction of the influence from the prerogative of the crown, . . . he approved and respected the latter to the full as much as he disliked and dreaded the former' (*The Parliamentary Register* . . . ed. Almon, XV (1780), 232).

Both were abreast of the latest currents in political thought. Their vision of politics was wider than the Rockinghams'. It was also steadier at this point than Fox's fitful gleams.

Given their background, one might perhaps have expected Shelburne and Pitt to work in some degree with the London reformers and their allies. Chatham's example, Shelburne's own early experience, might have made this seem a natural course. In fact, however, nothing of the kind happened. Throughout the critical years 1780 to 1783, neither man sat or was represented on the committee of the Westminster Association. They never worked closely with Fox. And as the Parliamentary reformers differed increasingly among themselves, both sided with the opponents of the London radicals. As time went by, indeed, their sympathies came to lie increasingly with a quite different organisation, and one of which the Rockinghams had been chary from the start. Shelburne from 1780, Pitt from 1783, broadly supported the aims of the Yorkshire movement.

It was not surprising that Rockingham should have felt uneasy about his fellow Yorkshiremen. Guided by a firm and disinterested leadership, they were a good deal more formidable than the Londoners. From the time that they first came together, in 1779, they were determined to rely as little as possible on any political party; and they made this uncomfortably clear from the start. Such an aim was of course common to all reformers. But the character of the northern movement gave it a particular point. For the Yorkshire Association was genuinely representative of that most powerful political force, the gentlemen and freeholders of a great county; and its very respectability and weight posed a more serious challenge than the familiar clamour of the metropolitan groups. Nor were its demands much more congenial to the Rockinghams than its methods. The Yorkshiremen went as far as the Londoners on Economical Reform; and while they rejected the more extreme proposals for an extension of the franchise, and became increasingly inclined to postpone the issue of shorter Parliaments, this last concession was made in order to favour the chances of amending the representation, most notably by an increase in the number of County Members. The Rockinghams preferred more radical demands, standing little chance of acceptance, coming from a movement which they might hope to control, to a moderate programme, on lines which they still disliked, coming from a substantial and less malleable source.

Shelburne and Pitt, on the other hand, were not circumscribed in this way. They welcomed reform, and the Yorkshire programme in particular held much to appeal to them. For, allowing for the march of events, the Yorkshiremen's approach was not unlike that of Chatham, and as the reformers' dissensions grew the fact became increasingly clear. Like Chatham, the Yorkshiremen came to oppose extreme ideas. Like him, they were prepared to compromise on shorter Parliaments. Like him, they placed their faith in the County Members. The position, of course, had altered a good deal since his day. Fresh issues had emerged, Parliamentary forces were shifting, ideas themselves had been more widely discussed. No programme in the early eighties could have been the same as one of ten years before. But attitudes were more stable than arguments, and as the Yorkshiremen's limits and priorities hardened, Chatham could have recognised a spirit akin to his own.

This in itself might not account for the way in which Pitt came to work in the end so closely with the northern movement. Parliamentary developments also played their part. When Shelburne first supported the Yorkshiremen's aims, in the spring and summer of 1780, it was not to the exclusion of other groups, but because he hoped a national movement would thereby emerge. Nor was Pitt himself at first committed to one set of reformers at the expense of another. But Shelburne's action led to a quarrel with the Rockinghams and his temporary withdrawal from politics; the Foxites meanwhile strengthened their hold on the Westminster Association; and the subsequent manœuvres and discords in the Parliamentary Opposition could not but affect those among the reformers themselves. The London movement inevitably was involved in Fox's fortunes, and as they became increasingly ambiguous its own could not escape. Meanwhile its disagreements with the Yorkshiremen became pronounced. Pitt had not long been active in the cause when the lines were finally drawn. His alliance with the Yorkshire Association was strengthened by the course of party politics, as party politics were moulded by the attitudes which the issues of reform brought to light.

III

Despite the similarity of their views on Parliamentary reform, Pitt was not brought into the movement by Shelburne. He owed his introduction to Charles, Lord Mahon, the husband of his eldest sister Hester, and the grandson of the first Earl Stanhope and Chatham's aunt Lucy Pitt. These marriages bound the two families closely together, the more so because both were attended by the same sad fate. Both Lucy and Hester died as the result of childbirth, the one leaving orphaned twins and the other three small girls. Mahon's father and aunt had accordingly been brought up in the charge of old Governor Pitt, and they remained on good terms with their cousin Chatham when they grew older. Chevening and Hayes were only eight miles apart; Mahon's mother and Lady Chatham corresponded almost weekly when the Stanhopes went abroad for some years; Mahon's own marriage to Hester Pitt took place as soon as they returned; and her children in due course were to come under Pitt's protection, as they rebelled against Mahon's rule. The connexion has left its mark on more recent times. Mahon's grandson, the fifth Earl Stanhope, is Pitt's best biographer, and built up his own collection of the statesman's papers.[1]

Mahon and Pitt had thus known each other for some years when Pitt first came to London, and at that time they knew each other well. Together they supported Chatham on his final appearance in the House of Lords, and two months later they were the principal mourners at his funeral. Pitt was in and out of the Mahons' house in Harley Street on his visits from Cambridge, and when he came down at the beginning of 1780 Hester's illness and death threw the brothers-in-law much together. They had, in any case, a good deal in common. Mahon, like many Englishmen over the past two centuries, had been educated almost entirely in Geneva, to which his parents removed when he was ten years old, and unlike many of them his tastes and accomplishments bore witness to the fact. An inherited talent for mathematics had been encouraged, systematic readings in law and political philosophy had taken effect, and the young man returned to England frugal, serious and zealous, a competent scientist and filled with a lively sense of public duty. Such interests and qualities naturally appealed to Pitt, and indeed the two men were, even physically, in some ways not unlike. Both were thin and rather awkward – Mahon once knocked Pitt on the head with one of his see-saw gestures when speaking in a debate from behind the Treasury bench – both had a natural simplicity and a naturally strong reserve, both were incorruptible and obstinate and nursed their independence. Both were excited by the reform movement as it spread to the counties at the end of 1779.[2] In January 1780 Mahon became chairman of the newly formed Kent committee, and in October Pitt was elected to it.

In the course of 1780 and 1781, delegates from the counties attended a series of meetings in London, designed to hammer out a national organisation and a national plan. Mahon was one of the Kentish representatives; and he soon struck up a working partnership with the leader of the Yorkshire Association, the Reverend Christopher Wyvill, who was then fast taking the lead of the movement as a whole. They shared much the same aims and objects, they liked and respected each other, and they were soon closely allied in their efforts to get the Yorkshire Association's priorities accepted as the programme of a united organisation. Wyvill, chary of undue Parliamentary interference but anxious for the necessary Parliamentary support, found Mahon's activities increasingly useful as his differences with the Rockinghams grew. Mahon, for his part, was glad to act as Wyvill's principal contact with other reformers and with the House of Commons itself.[3] Pitt was

1. See Note on Pitt's Papers below.
2. For Pitt's sentiments, see Ghita Stanhope and G. P. Gooch, *The Life of Charles Third Earl Stanhope* (1914), 37–8.
3. To which he was returned in October 1780 as a Member for Shelburne's borough of Chipping Wycombe.

not directly involved in any of this. He met Wyvill once, at Mahon's house in the spring of 1780; but he did not do so again for over two years, he did not attend the meetings of the combined reformers in London, and as far as can be seen did not correspond with their leaders outside Parliament during that time.[1] He kept in touch with events rather through the politicians themselves: through Mahon, and possibly through the Duke of Richmond, a former adherent of Chatham's who was now the main link between the Rockinghams and Shelburne, and was flirting uncertainly with the more extreme ideas of reform. The divisions had not finally hardened, though they could not be ignored. Pitt's first active contribution was indeed to reflect the fact.

At the end of March 1782, North's Government fell, and Rockingham and Shelburne came into office. The reformers' hopes revived, and at the end of April a meeting was held at Richmond's house which Wyvill and Pitt attended, to concert a plan for Parliamentary action. It was agreed that Pitt – now a figure of interest to the House and the public, and bringing a fresh and uncommitted voice – should sound the ground. On 1 May he accordingly gave notice that 'on Tuesday next . . . he intended to move for a Select Committee to take into consideration the present state of the representation of the Commons of England'.[2]

On the morning of Tuesday 7 May 'the avenues' to the House 'were crowded; but few were fortunate enough to get admission to the gallery', which had to be closed an hour after it was unlocked.[3] Pitt rose in the late afternoon, 'and was upon his legs for an hour and a half'.[4] The occasion is of interest not only as marking his début as a Parliamentary reformer, but also for the unusual degree of unity it evoked among the reformers themselves. This of course was greatly helped by the fact that Pitt made no detailed proposals: he was there to rally support and sympathy, and test the feeling of the House. The speech accordingly had something for everyone. It attacked the influence of the Crown with a vigour which pleased the Economical Reformers. It connected Parliamentary with Economical Reform by an argument – 'the people were loud for a *more equal representation,* as one of the most likely means to protect their country from danger, and themselves from oppressive taxes' – which had earlier been that of the Yorkshire Asso-

1. It is sometimes stated that Pitt was a member of the Society for Promoting Constitutional Information, founded by the veteran reformer Major Cartwright in April 1780. This does not seem to have been so. His name has come to be included probably because he attended the meeting of reformers at the Thatched House Tavern in May 1782 (see p. 71 below), which was held under the Society's auspices. In point of fact, the Society very soon proved a thorn in his flesh, as it was in Wyvill's.

2. *P.R.,* VII (1782), 105. This is not mentioned in *P.H.,* XXII.

3. *The Morning Herald & Daily Advertiser,* 8 May 1782; *The Morning Chronicle,* 8 May 1782.

4. *Morning Chronicle,* from Members' reports.

ciation.[1] And it defined the nature of representation itself – 'equal, easy, practicable, and complete'[2] – in terms acceptable to the theorists and the London radicals. At the same time Pitt did his best not to frighten the House.[3] His motion, he stressed, was one of inquiry only; and if he mentioned schemes for shorter Parliaments, and for transferring seats from some of the close boroughs, it was as well known possibilities in a situation which would have to be explored as a whole. His attack on the rotten boroughs themselves was indeed markedly cautious, stressing the obvious targets of the newly rich patron such as (shades of Governor Pitt) the Indian nabob. The object was general – to seek the best means of removing defects from 'a beautiful frame of government'; 'and it would not be innovation . . ., but recovery of constitution, to remove them'. Pitt looked therefore to 'a moderate and substantial reform', and he appealed to Chatham's example against accusations of raising 'vague and chimerical speculations, inconsistent with practice and expediency'. If he had made himself responsible for a motion which his father had never brought, it was because the times now made it more necessary, and more likely to succeed.[4]

The motion was lost by 161 votes to 141. Even allowing for absenteeism among North's disorganised followers and the embarrassed corps of King's Friends, the defeat was respectable and the size of the minority encouraging. Pitt indeed, with his usual optimism, had even looked to success, though he admitted that only 'a very small Party' was 'heartily' for the motion.[5] Had the reformers but known it, they were not in fact to do so well for another forty-eight years. Fired by a new sense of hope and purpose, they prepared to organise a wave of petitions to Parliament, as they had done two years before; and at an enthusiastic meeting on 18 May, at the Thatched House Tavern in St James's, Pitt wrote the minutes carrying Wyvill's resolutions to that effect.[6] From this moment the two men began to draw closer together, and at an interview in June Wyvill was also assured of Shelburne's goodwill. For the first time it

1. This passage comes from Pitt's winding-up, not his opening speech (*The London Chronicle*, 7–9 May, which alone attempts a verbatim report of his final reply). But it is perhaps the clearest expression of an argument which the main speech also contained. For the parallel with the Yorkshire Association's approach, see Wyvill's *Political Papers . . . chiefly respecting a Reformation of the Parliament of Great Britain . . .* I (1794).

2. *P.R.*, VII, 12.

3. He did not entirely succeed. His cousin Thomas Pitt, for instance, was alarmed that the motion seemed to lead to 'a principle of equal representation' – a remark at which Pitt himself apparently shook his head (*P.H.*, XXII, 1423).

4. This last remark comes from his speech in reply at the end of the debate (*London Chronicle*, 7–9 May); the rest from the opening speech (*P.R.*, VII, 120–6).

5. To Hester Countess of Chatham, n.d. but clearly May 1782. 'The failure of My Motion was rather unexpected, and might perhaps have been prevented if so strong an Opposition had been foreseen' (P.R.O. 30/8/12).

6. The fact was brought up against him twelve years later, when war broke out, by the defendants on trial under his Act of Traitorous Correspondence with the Enemy.

looked as if the forces centred on the Yorkshire Association might be brought into a working alliance with front-rank politicians.

But even while this was happening, there were less hopeful signs. Wyvill approached Rockingham in June 1782, as well as Shelburne; but in this case without much success. The new First Lord of the Treasury was prepared, at Richmond's request, to countenance a further Parliamentary discussion of reform. But he showed no sign of being willing to support measures of reform themselves, and before the month was out there was disquieting evidence of the party's views. In May, Mahon had introduced a bill to amend the conduct of elections, particularly by taking effective steps to suppress bribery and by holding a poll at different places successively within a constituency instead of at one centre on one occasion. This latter clause was attacked by Fox in committee, and on 21 June it was thrown out in the House, Pitt in Mahon's words, speaking for it 'like an angel', while Fox opposed it 'with the greatest asperity'.[1] The crippled bill was accordingly withdrawn, and the reformers' hopes of unity suffered something of a blow.

Worse was soon to follow. The Rockingham and Shelburne parties had never been on easy terms. On 1 July Rockingham died, and with him went the last real hopes of a united Ministry. Fox, with the Cavendishes and Burke, resigned a few days later, and Shelburne was left to form a Government on his own. The Parliamentary disputes had their effect on the cause of reform, itself suffering again from the reformers' conflicting views. On 18 July, the London radicals pressed for a petition to Parliament in the most general terms, which would cover, as they acknowledged, a 'diversity of sentiment'.[2] Wyvill could scarcely oppose this. But the implication of wider, unspecified reforms was precisely what he feared, and as the summer went by he wondered increasingly how best to circumvent it. On the one hand he was determined, as always, not to become involved in the party game: not to forfeit Fox's goodwill by adopting courses congenial only to Mahon and Pitt. On the other, he undoubtedly agreed with Mahon that the 'friends to reform, are divided; and the seceding part violent to a degree'.[3] In the course of the autumn he therefore evolved a modified programme, designed to meet a delicate situation without losing sight of his principal aims. The first priority, as always, was an increase in the number of County Members, to which Wyvill was now prepared to add a demand for more

1. To Wyvill, 22 June 1782 (quoted in Ian R. Christie, *Wilkes, Wyvill and Reform* (1962), 149).

2. Quoted op. cit., 155.

3. On 17 July, Fox had attacked Shelburne violently before the Westminster Association, for not being a true friend to a radical Parliamentary reform (Wyvill, *Political Papers*, II (1794), 164–70).

Members from the metropolis. At the same time, fifty of the most 'obnoxious' boroughs should be abolished, the electors receiving financial compensation and the grant of the county franchise. The Septennial Act should be repealed. The conduct of Scottish elections should be reformed, and the number of Scottish Members increased. And – a new idea for Yorkshire – the English county franchise should be extended to the more substantial, forty shilling copyholders, thus adding to the weight of the lesser freeholders as a counterpoise to that of the greater landed men.

These proposals were passed by the Yorkshire Association at the beginning of November 1782, and the rest of the movement was urged to petition Parliament when it reassembled in the new year. Wyvill himself was prepared if necessary to forgo the abolition of the fifty boroughs, which he recognised must be a controversial demand. But in the event his programme ran into more general trouble. For the London reformers, reluctant in any case to follow Yorkshire's lead, opposed its ideas as being too specific; and this fresh dissension, combined with the extremists' propaganda, discouraged reforming Associations elsewhere. Although Wyvill had his way, the results were not what he had hoped. Outside Yorkshire itself, the new campaign attracted a markedly varying amount of support. In the counties there was undoubtedly less interest than there had been two years before: twelve petitions were now sent in, compared with 26 in 1780, and while some had more signatures than their predecessors, most had less. The appeal did better in the boroughs – 23 petitions reached Parliament, compared with 12 in 1780. But few of the larger towns were enthusiastic apart from London and its neighbours, and some were very conspicuous by their absence. Scotland and Wales hardly responded, the former much to Wyvill's disappointment. The great wave of pressure for a fresh Parliamentary effort had failed to gather way; and by the time that the effort itself could be mounted, the Parliamentary scene had taken a further turn for the worse.

The reformers had apparently assumed that Pitt would bring a new motion for reform, based on the Yorkshire programme, early in 1783. But the comparative failure of the petitions gave him pause and influenced his plans. At the beginning of the year, he 'found himself not yet enabled, by any sufficient declaration of the people, to attempt the abolition of fifty boroughs'.[1] He was in any case involved during these months in the preoccupations and struggles of the Shelburne Ministry. And when he finally decided to present a motion, he felt free to follow his own ideas. Even so, these were a great deal closer to Wyvill's programme than to anything else. Pitt had indeed now rejected outright the radicals' more extreme views – 'the speculative principles of some, that

1. Op. cit., IV, 260 n.

had given alarm'[1] – and was in correspondingly bad odour with the Society for Promoting Constitutional Information. He was prepared to ask for an extra hundred County Members (a figure beyond Wyvill's expectation, and one indeed on which the Yorkshire leader had been prepared at one time to hedge) to be found in proportion to the size of the counties.[2] He accepted Wyvill's argument that Scotland should be subjected to some electoral reform. He would not commit himself, though he looked favourably, on the possibility of more Members for the metropolis. He would not move for the repeal of the Septennial Act. And while he could not agree to the outright abolition of fifty 'obnoxious' boroughs – an idea which he was sure stood no chance of success – he proposed that they should be gradually abolished as opportunities arose to disfranchise them for bribery.

Wyvill, not surprisingly, was heartened by these plans. Pitt had come down firmly against the extremists, he was at one with the Yorkshiremen on the vital question of the County Members, and while he had rejected parts of their programme he had gone as far as could reasonably be expected of any Parliamentarian at the time. Whatever the omissions, Wyvill was therefore prepared to bless the surviving proposals as being 'nearly coincident' with his own.[3]

Pitt discussed his intentions with the Yorkshire leader at a private meeting on 5 May 1783. On the 7th – the anniversary of his first speech on the subject – he introduced his motion for a measure of Parliamentary reform. Once again 'an immense concourse of people assembled early in the lobby and avenues leading to the House', and on this occasion the gallery was filled by noon.[4] The House itself was unusually crowded – the division figures show 447 Members present, and according to one account there were another 50 or so in the Chamber who had paired[5] – and the debate lasted from shortly after four in the afternoon until about half-past two the next morning. The interest, clearly,

1. Quoted, or perhaps paraphrased, from his letter to the committee of the Suffolk Association, probably early in April 1783 (*The Life and Correspondence of Major Cartwright*, ed. by . . . F. D. Cartwright, I (1826), 155).

2. This was designed to meet the objection that more Members for the smaller counties would merely play into the hands of a few great interests – which were not so dominant in the larger counties.

Professor Christie has pointed out (*Wilkes, Wyvill and Reform*, 177) that Shelburne, while First Lord of the Treasury, believed he had gained a promise from George III to support an increase in the county representation. Any such undertaking, of course, was no longer valid by the time that Pitt brought his motion, for the Shelburne Ministry was then no more (see p. 77 below). But it is highly doubtful in any case if it affected Pitt one way or the other: it was not out of hope of support from the King's Friends that he made this proposal.

3. Wyvill, op. cit., IV, 59. And see also loc. cit., 5–7.

4. *Morning Herald*, 8 May 1783.

5. *Parker's General Advertiser: and Morning Intelligencer*, 8 May 1783. The 447 include the four Tellers and the Speaker. Cf. *P.H.* XXIII (1814), 826, 'there was an uncommonly numerous attendance, nearly 500 members being present'.

was as great as before. But the chances of a respectable failure were much less, and victory was inconceivable. Detailed proposals for legislation were a different matter from a demand for an inquiry; and in the interval the political temperature had changed once more. In May 1782 Rockingham, Fox and Shelburne had been, in whatever sense, colleagues in office: in May 1783 Rockingham was dead, and Shelburne, his successor, had recently been driven from office by Fox. This moreover had been achieved by Fox's notorious coalition with North, and while the Foxite party was still pledged to reform its allies outside Parliament were pardonably confused, and North himself was adamant that all proposals of reform must be rejected. The bulk of the old Rockingham party thus had every excuse for abstaining; the Foxites were in a thoroughly ambiguous position; and Shelburne and his colleagues could no longer hope to influence the mass of Ministerial votes. Pitt was therefore under no illusion, as he rose to open the debate, about 'the arduous and very difficult task he had ventured to undertake'.[1]

Pitt's proposals followed the lines – though not exactly – that he had outlined to Wyvill, set in a context designed to reassure the House. As on the previous occasion, he stressed the moderate nature of his demands. Indeed, he emphasised the degree to which he had since departed from the more radical of his earlier expressions. 'His object at present was not to innovate, but rather to renew and invigorate the spirit of the constitution, without deviating materially from its present form'. He rejected the 'spirit of speculation' and the 'variety of schemes, founded in visionary and impracticable ideas', which had been thrown up in the intense excitement three years before.[2] A radical extension of the franchise was impractical, and indeed 'subversive of liberty'. Rotten boroughs were 'deformities, which in some degree disfigured the fabric of the constitution, but which he feared could not be removed without endangering the whole pile'.[3] The object must be rather 'to defeat the effect of undue influence in them', which would be achieved by disfranchising those found guilty on any occasion of electoral malpractices, and above all by introducing the 'counter-balance' of more Members for the counties and the metropolis. He therefore moved that effectual measures should be taken to prevent bribery at elections; that boroughs convicted of corruption by a select committee of the House should be disfranchised, and the innocent voters transferred to the county roll; and that 'an addition' – with no number specified – should

1. *P.R.*, IX, 689. All quotations in the next paragraph are taken from this source.
2. So *P.R.* and (almost identically) *P.H.*, XXIII, 829, both of which appear to follow the *Morning Herald*'s account. The *Morning Chronicle* put it more strongly: 'Let not the House suppose that he meant with the mad zeal of modern visionaries and speculative reformers, rashly and sacrilegiously to attempt an innovation'.
3. Cf. Chatham's remark on p. 60 above.

be made to the number of knights of the shire, and (in this instance bettering his statement to Wyvill)[1] to the number of Members for the metropolitan boroughs.

The motion was defeated handsomely, by 293 to 149. Fox did his duty by speaking for it, and his lieutenants did the same. But some of the Rockinghams abstained, and the parties of North and the Court, backed by a large cross-section of the House, voted decisively against it. The size of the majority showed that Members had still to be convinced of the need for any reform – a scarcely surprising result in view of the comparative failure of the petitions. Nevertheless, there were some consoling features for Wyvill and Pitt. The minority included nearly half the County Members, and a significant proportion of the newer Members, returned in or since 1780. Tributes had been paid from several quarters to Pitt's own moderation and good sense, and a few Members had acknowledged in debate that this would influence their votes.[2] And decisive though its verdict was, the House of Commons had shown itself ahead of feeling in the country, in which scarcely ten per cent of the electorate had recently been persuaded to petition for reform. Wyvill was therefore not disposed to lose heart, or to doubt that *'a moderate but efficacious plan'* would in the end 'turn the scales completely to the side of Reformation'.[3] And Pitt himself looked forward to a time when public opinion or his own fortunes should encourage him to try again.

1. See p. 74 above.
2. Including the astute Henry Dundas (*P.R.*, IX, 726).
3. *The York Chronicle*, 30 May 1783 (quoted in Christie, op. cit., 187).

CHAPTER IV

Office under Shelburne

I

B y the time that he made his second speech on Parliamentary reform, Pitt had been in and out of office. On 13 July 1782 he became Chancellor of the Exchequer, and on 31 March 1783 he resigned.

This brief spell marked one of the turns of fortune in the confused period between North's long reign and that of Pitt himself. The years 1782–4 are indeed something of a political nightmare: they certainly appear so to us, and they seem to have been viewed as such even at the time. The end of a long Ministry was of course always a signal for intensive manœuvres. The completeness of North's fall, in the last stages of an unsuccessful war, left a vacuum which both encouraged them and revealed their inadequacy. For the familiar conflicts of the Parliamentary groups were now imposed on a really disturbed situation, which their heightened vigour only made worse. By the time that Pitt came into office again, it was no exaggeration to talk of 'the present distracted state of public affairs'.[1] It was scarcely surprising that European rulers and their Ministers in the eighties should have been 'taught', as one British envoy put it, 'to look upon a ministerial revolution' in England 'as the natural and infallible consequence of a war'.[2]

North's position had deteriorated fast in the winter of 1781–2. A week or two before Parliament was due to meet on 27 November, he and his opponents alike looked forward, with differing sentiments, to a quiet session. But on the 25th the news reached London that Cornwallis had surrendered to the Americans at Yorktown, and Government was saddled with the one kind of reverse it could scarcely hope to bear. Even then Opposition did not reap the benefit at once. The Ministry weathered the immediate attacks, and its majorities at the end of December were not much smaller than at the start. But, faced by such a blow, Ministers were again losing their nerve, and when this became apparent the rot soon spread. At the end of January 1782, North capi-

1. As the freeholders of Yorkshire did in a Loyal Address to George III in March 1784 (*Life of Wilberforce*, I, 388).

2. Robert Liston [Minister in Madrid] to the Marquess of Carmarthen [Foreign Secretary] 23 October 1787 (P.R.O., F.O.72/11). He was not the only British envoy to make the point.

tulated to a demand from some of his followers, led by the shrewd and forceful Henry Dundas, to drop the unpopular Secretary for the American Colonies, Lord George Germain. In the course of February the Parliamentary attack mounted, and on the 27th Government suffered its first defeat of the session. On 8 and 15 March, it survived two motions of no confidence with derisory majorities; and when a group of country gentlemen gave notice a few days later of another motion to the same effect, North at last persuaded the King to let him go. On the 20th, amid scenes of uproar, he forestalled the debate by announcing his resignation to the House.

In the last few weeks of North's Administration, George III had made reluctant attempts to find a basis for a new Government. They ranged over all the most obvious material. The King tried North's former colleagues, who had left him at various times – Gower and Weymouth, who had resigned in 1779, and Grafton, who had gone in 1775. He tried Shelburne: he tried Rockingham; but in every case without success. For, anxious if possible to retain North himself, and at least the support of his followers, George III was manœuvring on the familiar lines, to bring dissident forces of sufficient strength into some form of coalition; and this time, in these strange circumstances, the normal solution did not work. No other group, it transpired, was prepared to bolster North in office. But none was prepared to replace him on the King's terms.

It was the moment for which the Rockinghams had waited, the opportunity which at last seemed attuned to their ideas. George III had tried, as he acknowledged, 'every description of men', and found them 'equally unwilling to stand forth'.[1] Rockingham held the key, and it really looked as if he might dictate conditions, more openly than any candidate for office – including himself – had been able to do since the early part of the reign. Even in less promising circumstances, when North had offered a coalition in the summer of 1780,[2] he had laid down specific terms for policy and place. Now it seemed likely that they would be accepted, and that the King must agree in advance to men and measures he disliked. Of course Rockingham, even so, could go only so far. Even in his awkward situation George III held some good cards. He managed to avoid a direct negotiation – which he seems always to have thought a sign of weakness – and to conduct the talks through the Lord Chancellor and, at the end, through Shelburne. And he had the qualified satisfaction of seeing Shelburne himself in the Cabinet, a fact which was to prove crucial to the Rockinghams' fate. All the same, the King was obliged to bow to a set of demands, formally presented, which were more extensive than those he had refused two years before: the end of the war in America; 'no Veto' on that policy from the throne; 'peace in general if possible'; 'economy in every branch', and certain

1. To Lord Thurlow, 10 March 1782 (quoted in Christie, *The End of North's Ministry*, 350).
2. See p. 24 above.

measures of Economical Reform in particular; and permission to Rockingham to form a Government which would exclude *'obnoxious Ministers'* and others held to be creatures of the King himself.[1] These were notable concessions, and they were extracted in an unusually specific way. Whig historians have not been wrong in claiming that the occasion was something exceptional, though they need not have added the gloss that the exceptional was constitutionally correct. At the end of March 1782, Burke was not alone in thinking that the new Ministry might be an earnest of 'a new system'.[2]

It lasted three months, and the reverberations of the failure echoed for years. 'Unless they change their ideas of government, and personal behaviour to the King', Henry Dundas observed at the outset, 'I do not believe they will remain three months';[3] and his reasoning, at least in part, was as acute as his estimate of time. The new Administration was not united from the start, and the most powerful element never earned – it never had the chance of earning – the trust of George III. For while Rockingham was able to rule out any serious coalition with his late opponents, he could not avoid the continued partnership of his most prominent allies. 'You can stand without me', Shelburne had told him on the eve of North's collapse, 'but I could not without you'.[4] But the Shelburnites' debating talents, and the King's own wishes, were strong enough for the party to gain a substantial share of the spoils. Rockingham became First Lord of the Treasury, and nominated the holders of five of the other ten Cabinet posts. But Shelburne became Secretary of State for the Home Department, and managed to secure another three Cabinet offices for his friends. Outside the Cabinet, the balance was much the same. Portland was Lord Lieutenant of Ireland, and Burke, Sheridan and Fitzpatrick figured in the list of Rockinghamite appointments. But Shelburnites, headed by Barré and Orde, also filled subordinate places, and even the influence of North's old Chancellor Thurlow and his Lord Advocate Dundas, who survived the change, did not entirely disappear. Nor were the Rockinghams sole beneficiaries of the major reshuffle in the Court itself. They had won a famous victory, but they had not 'stormed the closet', and they looked on Shelburne with the more impatience because their pretensions had stood so high.

There was one notable omission from the list of offices. Pitt was not given a place. Perhaps it was not surprising. Only a fortnight before the

1. *Memoirs of the Marquis of Rockingham*, II, 452–3, corrected by Christie, *The End of North's Ministry*, 350–1. For the demands of 1780, see the same author's 'The Marquis of Rockingham and Lord North's Offer of a Coalition, June–July 1780' (*E.H.R.*, LXIX, no. 272, 388–407).
2. *The Correspondence of Edmund Burke*, ed. John A. Woods, IV (1963), 422.
3. Henry to Robert Dundas, 25 March 1782; quoted in Cyril Matheson, *The Life of Henry Dundas, First Viscount Melville* (1933), 79.
4. Lord Edmond Fitzmaurice, *Life of William, Earl of Shelburne ...*, III (1876), 131.

new Ministry was formed, the young man had announced in the Commons that 'he never would accept of a subordinate situation'.[1] There is a story that Pitt had misgivings about his words as soon as he sat down;[2] but in fact they fairly represented his attitude. He was determined to reserve, and to show that he reserved, his freedom of choice; and it was a tribute to his success in the past year that the House accepted the claim. Although the uncompromising statement may have caused some surprise, and have seemed rather rash to Pitt himself, it evoked no hostile reaction and was apparently not regarded as absurd. At the same time, it would not necessarily meet with a response, and Pitt may have suspected, as he sat down, that he had committed himself to a waiting game. For if his claim was not presumptuous, it was not exceptionally strong. He was not – as he stressed – one of Shelburne's followers. But, as events were very soon to make clear, he fell within Shelburne's orbit, and Shelburne's own freedom of manœuvre was fairly strictly circumscribed. Anxious as he undoubtedly was to see Pitt in the Cabinet, he had a prior duty to his own party, and he also needed the co-operation of some experienced figures of weight. It was therefore rather doubtful if a Cabinet place would be left when these prior demands had been met.

The answer turned on Rockingham; and the Rockinghams felt no pressing obligation. Their relations with Pitt were quite cordial, but they were scarcely more than that. The young man had his own friends and his own club, which despite Fox's opening was not Brooks's; and, apart possibly from Keppel, he does not seem to have seen much of the leaders of the party.[3] Nor was he attached to them by more than general ties of Opposition.[4] His claims to high office were therefore only those of

1. On 8 March 1782 (*P.R.,* VI, 412). Newspaper reports give the same words.

2. There are two sources for this: Horace Walpole, in his *Last Journals* (II, 46), and a story told to Rockingham's biographer Lord Albemarle, many years after the event, by the old Foxite Robert Adair, who claimed to have had it from his uncle, Admiral Keppel, to whom Pitt confided his doubts. Adair is not a reliable witness, and his memory may or may not have been correct. Nor is Horace Walpole a particularly good guide in his old age. By contrast, Tomline (I, 66) states that Pitt 'had indeed determined, as he soon afterwards declared publicly, never to accept any subordinate office' – which sounds as if the remark in the House had been thought out. But of course he may well have repented of making it, even though he meant it.

3. Apart from sitting next to Keppel in the debate of 8 March 1782 – which did not necessarily mean much – he dined with him 'and a few of the diligent People who are in Town' on at least one occasion towards the end of January (Pitt to Hester Countess of Chatham, n.d. but certainly of that month, P.R.O. 30/8/12). This, however, seems to have been at the instance of Tommy Townshend, who was friendly with both wings of Opposition, rather than of Keppel himself.

For Pitt's club activities, see pp. 106–7 below.

4. The whole weight of evidence points to this; and Pretyman later went so far as to say that Pitt at this time had 'very little acquaintance with Lord Rockingham or any of his party' (Tomline, I, 66 n.). There is a statement by Robinson, then Secretary of the Treasury, in a letter of 25 March 1782, that at a meeting of some sixty Opposition Members 'Mr. Wm. Pitt has declared full Attachment to the

talent; and in the circumstances – the Rockinghams in a strong Parliamentary position, and so many more intimate obligations to be met after the locust years – these were not enough. Offers were made, through Shelburne, of various junior places, the most serious apparently being that of one of the two Vice-Treasurers of Ireland – worth about £5,000 a year, and the first office which Chatham had held. But Pitt had rejected such approaches in advance, and although it seemed at one moment that Shelburne's efforts might prove successful,[1] the Rockinghams in the event were not prepared to surrender another Cabinet post. Pitt therefore was not in the Government, and, as he professed to his Cambridge friend William Meeke, then contemplating the Bar, seemed 'at least as likely to continue a lawyer as you are to commence one'.[2]

He did not continue so for long. The Rockingham Ministry was known to be divided at the start, and in its few months of office the divisions did not heal. They were caused by differences alike of personality and of principle. It was unfortunate – soon fatal – that Shelburne was not the man to overcome Fox's initial distrust; and their enmity focused the disagreements within a Cabinet all too easily at odds. Even the policies on which the two wings were generally agreed gave rise to difficult and disagreeable debate. Thus, while both were committed to legislation on Economical Reform, Shelburne joined with Thurlow in opposing some of the Rockinghams' proposals, and the Rockinghams attacked some of Shelburne's more far-reaching ideas. And while Ministers were at one in seeking to meet fresh trouble in Ireland by granting greater independence, Shelburne's handling of the issue was criticised by Fox. These disputes were significant rather than important. They did not prevent four measures of Economical Reform from reaching the statute book, or an immediate policy for Ireland being agreed and carried through. Nor was Parliamentary reform, for all its implications, regarded as a subject of Ministerial confidence. But if the visible

Rockinghams, who think themselves strong enough to beat all parties joined together and seek occasion to quarrell with Ld Shelburne' (to Charles Jenkinson; B.M.Add. Ms 38218, f.50). Robinson of course was not there, and he was grasping at straws. It seems possible, from the rest of his letter, that Pitt's remarks in fact referred to the immediate tactics to be pursued against a tottering Government; and if they had a more general application, it seems likely that it was to stress his comparative independence of Shelburne's party rather than to claim membership of Rockingham's. Two months later, Shelburne himself stated that Pitt was 'certainly hostile' to the Rockinghams (*Correspondence of King George III*, VI, no. 3765).

1. On 28 March, Lady Chatham wrote to him of 'the high honour done her son William, which increases that enjoyed by her on the propitious change that has taken place' (Fitzmaurice, *Life of Shelburne*, III, 136). This sounds as if something agreeable to Pitt had been on the cards at one point, and through Shelburne's prompting. And see John Norris, *Shelburne and Reform* (1963), 150.

2. Endorsed June 1782 (Stanhope Mss, 'Pitt Papers, Part i').

damage was slight, the symptoms were serious. The differences of opinion were less disturbing than the suspicions and divergences they revealed.

The great question facing the Ministry, however, was that of making peace – a problem, thorny enough in itself, which in these conditions was explosive. With the best will in the world, the Rockinghams and Shelburne would have found it hard to reconcile their views on America.[1] As it was, there was very little good will to spare. It was the more unfortunate that the negotiations should have fallen to Shelburne and Fox and, following a recent administrative reform, equally between them. For at the end of March 1782 the old Secretaries of State's office was replaced by a new Home Office and Foreign Office, the first of which took charge of American and colonial affairs. Shelburne, as Home Secretary, was thus responsible for the talks with America, Fox as Foreign Secretary for those with France, Holland and Spain. Their policies, as might have been expected, were diametrically opposed. Fox welcomed American independence, and based his tactics on the fact. He hoped to see a quick peace secured with the former colonies by an immediate recognition of the United States, armed with which he could bring France more easily to terms. He would then bargain with the European Governments for a general return to the position before the war, while his colleague bargained with the Americans on the details of boundaries and trade. Shelburne's tactics and objects were entirely different. He was prepared to concede more than Fox to the Americans over boundaries and trade, but not to accept a total separation of the two countries. His alternative was not unlike that in prospect for Ireland – freedom in domestic affairs, but some continued connexion, by mutual consent, in foreign policy and commerce. Such terms, moreover – and this proved the crux – should be negotiated as a whole, and no treaty with America should be signed in advance. These differences of policy, as so often, were brought to the point by a personal quarrel. For the talks with both America and France were to be carried on in Paris, and the two Secretaries accordingly sent their representatives there. It was not long before Fox was accusing Shelburne's agent of undermining the work of his own, and asking the Cabinet to have him sent home. And when, at the end of June, he failed to get his way, it seemed possible that Fox himself would resign.

Such was the background to the drama which was about to break, and which over the next eighteen months settled the fates of Fox and Shelburne and of Pitt himself. The underlying animosities within the Government had now been harnessed to an issue on which action could be taken and old scores perhaps be paid. It is difficult to say what would have happened if Fox had resigned from a Ministry of which Rockingham was the head. It was fairly clear that Fox himself could not become First Lord of the Treasury: neither the King nor the Whig magnates

1. See p. 57 above.

were likely to approve. But he was determined that Shelburne should not fill the place, and he accordingly proposed Rockingham's old ally, the Duke of Portland. It was an unexceptionable choice, if George III agreed. But the King saw his chance, and was quick to grasp it. On 2 July Shelburne was offered Rockingham's place. Over the next two days he took soundings, while Fox and his friends debated what do to. By the 5th both men had made up their minds. Fox went to Court that day with his Seals in a bag, and on hearing that Shelburne meant to accept the Treasury handed them to the King.

When the dust died down, Shelburne had three Cabinet posts to fill. His own promotion left the Home Office vacant, Fox had left the Foreign Office, and Lord John Cavendish resigned as Chancellor of the Exchequer. The other Ministers stayed, Rockinghams included, convinced that Fox had shown bad judgment in the cause on which he chose to leave. There was therefore room for Pitt, and Shelburne was anxious to have him. He had two possibilities in mind, the Home Office and the Exchequer, and the King himself seems to have preferred the first.[1] But it proved difficult to find the right man to fill the Exchequer, and in the event Pitt became Chancellor. He was not, as he might have been, a Secretary of State. But he was a member of the Cabinet at the age of twenty-three.

I I

When Pitt answered the letters of congratulation, he referred to his appointment as 'unexpected'. Certainly there was no particular reason to suppose that it would come when and as it did. Rockingham had not been well for some time, but he had not been expected to die until almost the end, and when he did so no one could tell exactly what would happen. Pitt had undoubtedly been sounded in advance – 'I believe', he wrote to his mother on 2 July, 'the Arrangement may be of a Sort in which I *may*, and probably *ought* to take a Part . . . I only know what were the strong Wishes of *Some* who foresaw the Event' – but a week

---

1. On 1 July, the day that Rockingham died, George III mentioned the possibility of Shelburne being 'succeeded by Mr. Pitt as Secretary for the Home Department and British Settlements' (*Correspondence of King George III*, VI, no. 3825). And on the 4th he wrote, 'I tried to get Mr. Townshend to come to the Treasury [as Chancellor of the Exchequer] but that will not do . . . He does not wish to be in any situation but Secretary at War, a hint that His Wife may hereafter have a Peerage might perhaps satisfy him and place Mr. Pitt at once in the home Department, His abilities would make that the most creditable nomination' (to Shelburne; Lansdowne Mss, Bowood). The next day, Pitt himself was under the impression that 'My Lot will be either at the Treasury as Chancellor of the Exchequer, or in the Home Department as Secretary of State' (to Hester Countess of Chatham; Stanhope, I, 83); and the latter rumour seems to have been widespread. 'W. Pitt, Secretary of State!', wrote the horrified Mornington – later one of Pitt's most reliable lieutenants – from Ireland on 12 July (*H.M.C., Dropmore*, I, 162).

before he had been making his arrangements for the Circuit and the weeks of leisure beyond.[1] Now he had to cancel them, and to take advantage of the Parliamentary recess to learn something of the ways of office and move into his new house.

In the first half of 1782, Pitt was still living in his rooms at Lincoln's Inn, although in the summer months he stayed with his brother in Grafton Street. Number 10 Downing Street was still in occupation by North, for neither Rockingham, as First Lord of the Treasury, nor Lord John Cavendish, as Chancellor of the Exchequer, had wanted it. Shelburne likewise was adequately housed, in his palace of Shelburne House in Berkeley Square. The reversion fell therefore to Pitt, and in the course of July he prepared to move into 'the best Summer Town House possible'.[2] The preparations indeed were on quite a handsome scale, to judge by the bill of over £700.[3] But by mid-August the new incumbent was settled, 'as far as a Bachelor can be', in a part of his 'vast awkward House'.[4]

Meanwhile he was entering on his official duties. The summer recess was not an active time at the Treasury, which was just as well for a Chancellor who had never held office before. The Board met every other day on an average throughout the second half of July and the whole of August, but the business was almost entirely routine and Pitt had time in which to look around and discover something of the ways of Whitehall. He had indeed plenty to learn. Applicants for places cannot have been encouraged to hear that the new Minister did not know what lay within his gift; and his ignorance was matched by his lack of concern, even when the appointment concerned himself.

> My secretary, whom you wish to know, [he wrote to the experienced and anxious Lady Chatham] is a person, whose Name you may probably never have heard, a Mr. Bellingham, an Army friend of my Brother – You will wonder at a Secretary from the *Army*; but as the office is a perfect Sinecure, and has no Duty but that of receiving about four Hundred a yr., No Profession is unfit for it. I have not yet any private Secretary, nor do I perceive, at least as Yet, any Occasion for It.[5]

He was indeed probably occupied at the start more by Cabinet than by Treasury business, for the progress of the peace negotiations, and Shelb-

1. Stanhope, I, 81–2.
2. To Hester Countess of Chatham, 16 July (P.R.O. 30/8/12).
3. Household accounts, 1780–2 ('Mr Pitt II', Stanhope Mss). Pitt employed the firm of Graham and Lichfield.
4. Pitt to Hester Countess of Chatham, 10 August, 30 July (P.R.O. 30/8/12).
5. Same to same, 10 August (loc.cit.; see Stanhope, I, 85). But it should be noted that North had not immediately appointed a secretary as Chancellor of the Exchequer, and George III did not employ a private secretary until 1805.

urne's activity, kept Ministers in London a good deal during those months.

The Ministry itself was on an uncertain footing. It was difficult to tell how the Parliamentary forces would settle down in advance of the event – as Jack Robinson, late of the Treasury, observed in August, 'in a state so rent as this has lately been . . . it is the hardest task that can be to class them'.[1] But one estimate two months later – it was relayed by Gibbon – put Shelburne's followers and the King's Friends at 140, Fox's followers at 90, and North's at 120. The rest were independent or very loosely attached. One obvious possibility for Shelburne was therefore to follow the well tried path of seeking some form of coalition with either of the other organised parties.

But this would have been to ignore several important factors, not least the temperament of Shelburne himself. In the first place, a resolute Government could always hope to better its position given a modicum of competence and of the King's goodwill. Such a combination would normally earn the independents' support or acquiescence, which in turn would affect the professionals' calculations. A good showing in the new session should therefore help the Ministry's chances, and Dundas might be followed by others from the ranks of Fox or North. North himself moreover was still quiescent, and seemed more likely to go on acting within the traditional limits of Opposition than to plunge into the sort of extreme campaign he had himself endured. The most immediate danger came from Fox; and Fox was hamstrung in the short run unless he combined with North – which seemed highly unlikely in the summer and autumn of 1782. Shelburne could therefore reasonably hope to strengthen his forces in the coming months by a judicious accession of individual 'rats'.

This was in any case the sort of line he favoured. For Shelburne's political ideas were those which Chatham had professed. More important, they were held from much the same point of view. It was common enough to decry the idea of party as a threat to individual independence and the legitimate powers of the Crown. But Chatham and Shelburne were equally concerned with the effect on government: it was the 'lounging opinions'[2] of the average party notable that filled them particularly with alarm. Their idea of a Ministry was an assembly of talents, and in its absence they were apt to go their own ways. Both men in fact often felt stifled by the air of the lobbies; both were conscious of gifts which needed room to expand. The decisive difference between them was that Chatham was enough of a politician in his earlier days to temper his demands, and in his prime was a compulsive

1. *Parliamentary Papers of John Robinson 1774–1784*, ed. W. T. Laprade (1922), 42. This is the Jack Robinson of Sheridan's famous phrase, when he was called on in debate to name the man whom he had accused of seducing members of Opposition into the ranks of Government, 'Yes, I could name him as soon as I could say Jack Robinson'.

2. A phrase attributed to Shelburne (*Memorials and Correspondence of Charles James Fox*, I, 454).

force. Shelburne, by contrast, had no personal magnetism, and was constitutionally unfitted to relate theory to practice[1].

It was perhaps because of this that he so puzzled his contemporaries, and has remained a puzzle ever since. Certainly the inconsistencies are baffling and real. Shelburne was a subtle and imaginative statesman, one of the most impressive of British Prime Ministers in his intellectual range: the patron of Bentham and Dumont, of Priestly and Price, the systematic correspondent of Mirabeau and Franklin and Romilly and Adam Smith, a man of imperial vision, a good European, the champion of economic liberalism and administrative reform. He was also one of the most distrusted politicians of his day, 'Malagrida', 'the Jesuit of Berkeley Square', disliked by his colleagues and unpopular in his department. Nor was it a simple case of intellect versus character. As a negotiator, Shelburne could be patient, reasonable and firm. He gained the confidence of many with whom he dealt, in Ireland, America and France. As a patron he was generous and understanding; in the right setting he did not lack charm. But he never could gain the trust, or even the respect, of the English political world.

It is difficult now to see exactly why this should have been so. 'Do you know', runs a well known story of Goldsmith trying to pay a compliment, 'that I never could conceive why they call you Malagrida, for Malagrida was a very good sort of man?'[2] Many have felt inclined to echo this Irish remark. No doubt the impression of duplicity was assiduously fed by Shelburne's opponents, in the bitter disputes of 1782–3. But it was already widespread, and there is little point in trying to gainsay so decisive a verdict. Perhaps it was partly that Shelburne had a European rather than an English mind. His passion for ideas, his modes of thought, were distinctly continental: he might have made a great Minister of an enlightened despot, a Pombal, a Turgot, a Floridablanca. Nor does his personality seem to have been such as to offset this disadvantage. Shelburne was not a clubable man; but neither was he the sort of unclubable man that clubable men will accept. He was a patron, not a leader; and the same obliqueness of sympathy often attracted him to his formal opponents rather than to those who were supposed to be his friends. He never seems to have been at ease with his fellow men, or able to get alongside them except under cover of a predetermined relationship – patron to dependant, Secretary of State to foreign representative. This native uncertainty was evident in his manner, by turns reserved and effusive, autocratic and ingratiating, not the sort of thing his peers much liked. Something doubtless was

1. He himself wrote at the end of his life of 'the imposture of Mr. Pitt's [Chatham's] character' (Fitzmaurice, *Life of Shelburne*, I, 84). Of course Shelburne was not alone in this opinion; but it is significant that he never was close to, and in fact rather disliked, the man whose political mantle he inherited.

2. Francis Hardy, *Memoirs of the Political and Private Life of James Caulfield, Earl of Charlemont* (1810), 177. Malagrida was a Jesuit, notorious for his alleged duplicity in recent Portuguese politics.

attributable to a most unhappy childhood, alternately bullied and neglected in the deep Irish south. But the sense of loneliness was inborn, and a lifetime of politics underlined the fact. For the trouble was that Shelburne was not really a politician at all: with all his imaginative sympathy, and despite a great air of knowingness, he never could see why men acted as they did. The result was an ingrained suspicion of his world, which his world returned with interest, and to which his reasoning powers gave the more intense effect. It was typical of Shelburne that he should have sat down to analyse his duties as a landowner; it was equally typical that he should have found the 'natural enemies' of a landlord's benevolence to be his agent, his tenants, his lawyer and his neighbours.[1] Sagacious and blinkered, strong-willed and unsure, gifted and flawed, he is impressive and pathetic. In very many ways he reminds one of Lord Curzon.

Not the least baffling aspect of Shelburne is the extent of his influence on Pitt. At first sight it might seem substantial. 'To understand Mr. Pitt', Disraeli announced, 'one must understand one of the suppressed characters of English history, and that is Lord Shelburne';[2] and much can be said to lend colour to that view. Pitt had seen a good deal of Shelburne on entering the great world; he had received counsel and support, and now received office at his hands. Shelburne himself moreover was at the height of his powers, in his middle forties, brimming with ideas and eager to carry them out. He was in an inherently strong position to influence the younger man; and if parallels are drawn some remarkable similarities can be cited. Shelburne supported the Yorkshire brand of Parliamentary reform: Pitt worked increasingly closely with Wyvill. Shelburne took over the reform of government where the Rockinghams left off: Pitt pursued it, at his own pace, throughout his career. Shelburne and his friend Richard Price held strong views on the management of a sinking fund to help redeem the National Debt: Pitt reformed the same fund for the same purpose. Shelburne envisaged a comprehensive commercial settlement with Ireland: Pitt suffered one of his greatest early defeats in that cause. Shelburne opposed the tradition of inveterate hostility to France, and strove for a peace treaty which would include a greater measure of free trade: Pitt concluded an Anglo-French commercial treaty, the most notable monument of commercial liberalism between the American and French Revolutionary Wars. Other parallels may be suggested from the methods of the two men. Pitt, like Shelburne, could be cavalier in Cabinet, and worked very closely with a chosen circle, not all necessarily Cabinet colleagues. Like Shelburne, he was thoroughly professional in his approach, insisting on the facts and ranging widely to get them. His outlook on government, his sense of priorities, resembled those of the older man. How far was he Shelburne's brilliant disciple?

1. For his paper, see Fitzmaurice, op. cit., II, 329–61.
2. *Sybil*, ch. III.

There is no direct evidence. Little correspondence survives, and neither man ever made claims in respect of the other. Shelburne was later icily neutral, and finally hostile, towards Pitt; Pitt rid himself of all connexion with Shelburne. That of course means nothing in itself. Debts are not always acknowledged by the debtor, or pressed by the creditor. The similarities, however, need to be looked at more closely before we can hazard a guess how much they really yield. Thus Shelburne was not solely responsible for the development of Pitt's ideas on Parliamentary reform; there were varied influences at work, several of which would seem to have been more immediate than his.[1] Pitt's financial and administrative reforms, too, though broadly akin to Shelburne's plans, were moulded in detail – and detail in such matters is all-important – by the reports of various Parliamentary commissions and committees, particularly those of the Commissioners for Examining the Public Accounts set up and encouraged by Lord North, and by discussion with advisers who owed little or nothing to Shelburne. Again, the Anglo-French commercial treaty was not in some respects what Shelburne would have liked; more important, Pitt's conduct of the negotiations, and of a number of parallel negotiations with other European powers, differed markedly in feeling and often in object from Shelburne's handling of the peace treaties. Such examples suggest a significant difference of temperament, which was equally reflected in the two men's methods of work. It was typical of Shelburne that he liked to rely largely on non-official sources, to conduct his own bureau of information and take private advice. Seeking to force officials and politicians into line with enlightened theory, he tended to impose his own fully detailed schemes. Pitt proceeded in quite a different way, making full use of official advice and, increasingly, taking objections into account. His strength indeed lay in the extent to which he helped enlarge Government's capacity: his weakness, in the limits he accepted to his stimulating powers. For in matters of policy, as distinct from personal conduct, Pitt always showed a ready respect for the odds, and a few reverses early on made him disinclined to force the pace. 'Patience', he is said to have replied towards the end of his life, when asked the most necessary quality of a Minister;[2] and patience and persistence are not always the same. In Shelburne's case they were. His patience – for he could be patient – was precisely the persistence which will not let a project rest. He was remarkably active and pertinacious; too much so for prolonged success. Pitt achieved, and would always achieve, far more. He did so while being far more easily discouraged.

1. See pp. 68, 70 above.

2. This well known remark rests on the evidence of Lord Brougham's *Historical Sketches of Statesmen who Flourished in the Time of George III*, I (1839), 278. He does not reveal his source, and when questioned in 1861 could not recall it. But he thought it might have been Wilberforce or Canning, and was satisfied that the story came from good authority. ('Lord Stanhope's Notes and Correspondence on his *Life of Pitt*,' Stanhope Mss).

Intellectual affinities were therefore balanced by differences of temperament. The question of influence must be judged in the light of that fact. It took a little time – though not very long – for the temperamental contrast to emerge, and Pitt's debt to Shelburne is clearest in his early measures. Even so there were significant changes of method and detail from the start, as there later remained broadly similar intentions. But if the older man's influence can be exaggerated in specific issues, there can be little doubt that Pitt learned a good deal by example. His brief apprenticeship had allowed him to watch innovation in action, and to observe Shelburne's virtues and his equally strongly marked mistakes. His first experience of office was under the man whose views on government most resembled his own; and the fact that he was difficult and fallible doubtless also had its effect. Pitt was never anxious again to be associated with Shelburne. But in the longer perspective the association endures.

III

To a biographer of Pitt, the relations between the two men furnish the chief interest of their brief spell together; for nine months in office, dominated by the need to make a peace, scarcely allowed an effective pattern of policy to emerge. Not that a pattern was lacking. Shelburne was determined from the start to bring about 'a general and grand reform',[1] and some at least of his thoughts were disclosed when Parliament reassembled in December. The King's Speech then indeed amounted to something suspiciously like a programme – certainly a notice of intention a great deal more detailed than King's Speeches were used to contain. After dealing with the overriding question of making peace, Shelburne turned to some favourite themes. The National Debt, much swollen by the war, should be subject to a stricter scheme of redemption, and the terms of the navy, victualling and ordnance bills, all carrying large discounts, should in particular be closely reviewed. Office establishments and payments were being inspected with a view to making certain regulations in common. The Indian territories required 'some fundamental laws, which may make their connection with Great Britain a blessing'; and the liberal principles already applied to commerce with Ireland[2] should be extended to 'a revision of our whole trading system'.[3] Much of this programme, of course, was centred on the Treasury – though effective action might often prove to be beyond its powers. Pitt was therefore placed in direct contact with Shelburne's reforming schemes, more directly perhaps than if he had been a Secretary of State.

1. His first speech in the House of Lords as First Lord of the Treasury, 3 July 1782 (*P.R.,* VIII (1783), 350).
2. See p. 50 above.
3. *P.R.,* XI (1784), 7.

The schemes started, for better or worse, where the Rockinghams left off. In its three months in power, the party had carried its chief measures of Economical Reform. On 19 June, Crewe's Act came into force, disfranchising the revenue officers of the Crown. On the same day Clerke's Act disqualified holders of Government contracts from sitting in the Commons. And on 11 July, Burke's Civil List Act at last triumphantly received the royal assent.[1] The achievement was not as complete as its authors would have wished. While Clerke's bill was strengthened in its passage through committee, Burke's was weakened in the final version, and two minor bills connected with it had to be dropped. Nor did the combined measures fully meet their objects. The Civil List Act in particular suffered from major defects, the result of its author's preconceptions and inexperience of office. Departments, including the Board of Trade, were suppressed whose loss was found to be inconvenient, the discharge of the Crown's debt was assigned to funds which could not be redeemed, future economies were upset by ignorant drafting. Nor were the results satisfactory when tested by the great touchstone of political influence. The Act curtailed payments for the Home Secret Service, because those were thought to feed the royal patronage; but in fact the bulk of such expense was not borne on that fund. It abolished forty-seven places under the Crown tenable with a seat in the Commons; but nine months later the experts reckoned that the number then affected was in practice twenty-two, the rest being held by peers or men out of Parliament. Crewe's and Clerke's Acts, likewise, though effective as far as they went, had lesser consequences than had been expected; and while the combined measures may have somewhat increased the difficulties of Parliamentary management, they cannot be said to have affected it very deeply. The fact was that the Rockinghams had misjudged the nature of much of the Crown's influence: it was both more pervasive and less decisive than they thought. They had made their great direct assault, and the defences were dented slightly here and there. But the shift in power which they envisaged remained to be achieved gradually by other means, and then it was with rather different results.

Shelburne had earlier criticised the Rockinghams' proposals. He now had to deal with their consequences, while pursuing his own plans. A good deal of his time was spent in settling the extensive subject of the Civil List on its revised basis; and before he left office, Pitt too had become well acquainted with a measure which in due course he would have to amend. Meanwhile the first stage of the 'general and grand reform' was being put in hand. In one instance, indeed, it was carried into effect. At the end of 1782 the business of the Treasury office was

1. Burke also carried an Act to transfer the Paymaster General's accounts to the custody of the Bank of England – a measure designed to end the notorious inconvenience and peculation hitherto attaching to them. But this stood somewhat apart from the other measures.

remodelled and all fees were abolished by funding, increased salaries being paid out of the fund. Other Government offices were required to make reports, or be investigated: the revenue and spending departments to submit details of fees and in some cases of their handling of public money, the Excise to report on the laws affecting smuggling and the possible consolidation of its duties, the Customs on the abolition of patent places, the Comptroller of Army Accounts on the methods of his office; the Mint, and the management of the Crown Lands, to open their records to inquiry. As a result, several measures were put in train in the winter: for a comprehensive regulation of fees, for a reform of the Customs, for the supply of stationery, and for the post.

Shelburne was therefore quite justified in claiming later that a 'considerable beginning' had been made to this part of his general plan.[1] Other claims, and suppositions, were less well founded. The recalcitrant powers of Government departments are notoriously well developed, and Shelburne was predictably exasperated by them. But it was inaccurate and ungenerous to say that apart from Richmond at the Ordnance, 'no one man in Administration or Opposition was in earnest in the support of any reform'.[2] Movements of this sort arise very seldom from the impulse of a single man, and if Shelburne was exceptional in the way in which he viewed reform as a subject, he was far from being the only person in public service to be roused by the need for specific reforms. There was concern and sometimes action in varied, and surprising, quarters; and indeed, when one comes to look into the origins of some of Pitt's subsequent measures, the difficulty is often to allocate proper credit between the proposals already to hand. The Rockinghams no doubt had proved rather ineffectual, though not entirely from lack of will. But North's years in office had yielded some real if unspectacular gains – Shelburne's own regulations at the Treasury, for instance, were explicitly based on those of 1776[3] – and it was equally disingenuous to ignore the recent reports of the Parliamentary Commissioners for Examining the Public Accounts, who had made several recommendations akin to Shelburne's, and given them the publicity which he rightly thought essential to success. It was still further unwise to contrast his own efforts with 'the little which has been done in that line since'.[4] Shelburne himself could scarcely have been expected to do more, in the months available, than achieve some reforms within his own department. But he might have admitted, had he not been so angry by the time he wrote, that the North–Fox Coalition soon afterwards did for the Exchequer – and more effectively –

1. In an undated, unfinished memorandum, quoted Fitzmaurice, III, 328–37.
2. Loc. cit., 328–9.
3. See the wording of the Treasury Board minute of 30 November 1782 (P.R.O., T.29/52, f. 517). And see p. 62 above for one view of North's attitude to the Civil List bill itself.
4. Fitzmaurice, III, 330.

what he had done for the Treasury, that Pitt in his turn embarked on reform, and that indeed two of his own most important projects were brought before the Commons soon after his fall by his late Chancellor of the Exchequer, acting in the second case as a private Member.

The contents of these bills, indeed, throw some light on Shelburne's approach, as well as on his claim to be the only genuine reformer at the time. For Pitt followed faithfully the plans already drawn up, and his proposals fairly reflect his former master's intentions. The first bill, introduced four days after Shelburne resigned, was concerned with the Customs. Based on a scheme devised and perhaps initiated by the 'very active' Commissioner Sir William Musgrave,[1] it was a sweeping measure. All patents for life were to be abolished, patents 'at pleasure' (which could be superseded) alone being retained and granted in future, and certain other 'useless' places were also to go. All fees on business done, other than some allowed specifically by earlier Acts, were to be discontinued. The duties of all surviving offices were to be vested in the deputies who exercised them in practice. And patent and fee holders affected by the Act were to receive compensation. These proposals met with an instructive response. Three main objections were successfully raised. The merchants, it was claimed, did not want so many fees abolished, a step which they feared might only lead to a raising of duties in compensation. Patents at pleasure instead of for life tended to increase the influence of the Crown.[2] And – a reflection of the same argument – it was dangerous to abolish by statute places granted for life by patent (as had indeed been done in a few instances in Burke's Civil List Act), thus invoking the law against the law and indulging in something like what we should call retroactive legislation. The bill was accordingly defeated in the Commons. Its reception and fate left their mark on Pitt's later line of approach.

The second measure, generally known as the Public Offices Regulation Bill, though also unsuccessful, fared better in the Commons. Introduced at the beginning of June 1783, it brought together the results of several of Shelburne's inquiries. The sale of places was to be checked, fees and perquisites were to be regulated in five large departments, and incidental expenses were to be reduced, particularly in the supply of Government stationery – one of the ripest of Georgian abuses, on which Pitt thought it possible to save £40,000 a year. The detail of the plan sprang from the Treasury in Shelburne's day; but the whole had been vetted, and evidence was to be taken, by the Parliamentary Commissioners for Examining the Public Accounts, a body now

1. 'Proceedings respecting Customs fees since the Introduction of the Bill in 1783' (P.R.O. 30/8/285). P.R.O., T.29/53, f. 107 also suggests that Musgrave was responsible for introducing the plan.

2. Ibid. Musgrave himself, indeed, had stated that 'very few' sinecures in the Customs had 'been given to any Persons for their Support of Government', but that places usually went to private nominees—often children—of 'the Ministers for the Time being' (to Shelburne, 10 December 1782; copy in P.R.O. 30/8/285).

acknowledged to be 'favourites with the public',[1] or in other words with the independent Members. This wise provision may have helped the measure to pass the House of Commons. But despite some cogent advocacy it failed in the Lords. The new Ministry, notably unenthusiastic in the lower House, rallied its forces. Much was heard of the drawbacks of involving Parliamentary Commissioners in Treasury business; and the increase in the powers of the Treasury itself, which the scheme necessarily entailed, was said – and probably with justice – to excite some alarm. So ended Pitt's attempt to bring into force the administrative plans of Shelburne's Treasury Board.

These matters are of some importance to an understanding of Pitt's development. They were of less interest to a public concerned with the political drama arising from the outcome of the negotiations for peace. Begun by Rockingham's Ministry in April 1782, these took a distinctive shape when Shelburne came to power in July. For the treaties which he prepared and others carried were, even in their final incomplete form, Shelburne's most original achievement. His systematic vision, here set free to range a world-wide scene, was clear and comprehensive and remarkably far-reaching, his handling of the problems incisive and judicious. If his grasp of domestic issues was less sure than he thought, he rose to real heights on the international stage.

Shelburne's design for the peace was a connected whole – and not only because the signing of a treaty with America was made dependent on the signing of the treaty under negotiation with France.[2] The United States, whose complete independence he had at last been brought to swallow, were to be granted very great concessions. Their claims to marginal territory – in the south towards the Mississippi, in the northwest towards the Great Lakes – were freely met, in the latter instance at Canada's expense. They were thereby handed a valuable part of the fur trade, and a no less valuable chain of fortified posts. They were admitted to the fisheries off the Newfoundland coast. Provided that they honoured past debts and compensated the loyalists for their losses, they were in fact given the chance to build a viable, expanding State.

Such terms cut much of the ground from under the French, and indeed allowed Shelburne more and more to play on their misgivings. For France looked to a sphere of influence in the New World as the reward for her intervention, and was correspondingly disenchanted with the Americans' demands. On the other hand, she could scarcely risk another year's campaign in a fading cause. If English resources were strained, so were hers, and the last months of war did not bring the European allies much success. Rodney in the Caribbean, Hastings and Eyre Coote in India, Eliott at Gibraltar, saved England from a

1. Portland's phrase when discussing the bill (*P.R.*, XI, 263).
2. See p. 82 above.

shameful peace. The French had to rest content with Tobago and the captured island of St Lucia in the West Indies, all the other conquests there being handed back. They were granted fishing rights in the west of Newfoundland and along the Labrador coast, and undisputed possession of the off-lying islands of St Pierre and Miquelon. They regained a base for their gum trade on the Senegal river in West Africa, the English holding theirs on the Gambia. And they were given an *enclave* round Pondicherry and Karikal in Madras – a meagre return for years of effort and expense.

French anxieties, in turn, were used to restrain the Spaniards' claims. We gave up our pretensions to Minorca and surrendered the Floridas – an acquisition which, however, was later to cause trouble for Spain with the United States. But we regained the islands in the Bahamas which had been lost during the war, we established, though imprecisely, our rights to continue felling timber in Honduras – a practice which had led to British settlement along the coast – and we kept Gibraltar, though both Shelburne and George III would gladly have bargained the Rock for some Spanish territory across the Atlantic. Meanwhile France was mediating with Holland. As a result, the Dutch were obliged to drop the discussion of neutral rights – the question which above all had occasioned war – and to allow free navigation by British shipping in the spice-laden Eastern Seas. On the other hand they were able to secure the restoration of Trincomalee, 'the key to the Indian Ocean', in return for ceding the inconsiderable Indian port of Negapatam.

Shelburne could thus point to some real tactical successes, at a time when his country needed all the tactical finesse he could command. But his conception of the peace went deeper than that. When he pursued the familiar swopping of territory, his moves were related where possible to a clearly held, ambitious plan.

It was a plan for trade, an attempt to use the peace as a forcing-house for 'a revision of our whole trading system'.[1] 'You will already have recognized in the treaties . . .', Shelburne wrote to the Abbé Morellet, 'the great principle of free trade, which inspires them from beginning to end. I have no hesitation in saying that in my opinion, a peace is good in the exact proportion that it recognizes that principle'.[2] His actions suggest that he meant what he said, and strove to make good his purpose wherever he could.[3] Opportunity to trade was the foundation of the treaty with the United States. Nor was this surprising, for the 'continental colonies', as they were officially called, formed one of the

1. p. 89 above.
2. Fitzmaurice, III, 323.
*3. It has been held that 'this argument that liberalism made the treaty can be carried too far' (Norris, *Shelburne and Reform*, 262). Probably it can; the design was not always applicable, and events were sometimes too strong. But I think that Shelburne undoubtedly set great store by his ideal, and related it to his actions in a way that no other politician would have done.

most valuable elements of British commerce. The growing population and wealth of an unindustrialised community made them an ideal market for British manufactures; the rising level of incomes in England led to a greater demand for the new materials of the southern colonies and the West Indies; the Americans extracted a favourable balance of payments from the West Indian islands by the sale of timber and fish; and there was thus a booming triangular trade, involving a substantial amount of British shipping and little movement of bullion such as was required in the trade with the Far East. By the early 1770s, when the serious troubles began, the future United States were the largest importers after Europe of British goods and re-exports – larger than Ireland, larger than the rest of America, the West Indies and Asia combined –, and the transatlantic traffic accounted for about half the total tonnage of British shipping. How then was this state of affairs, already damaged by the war, to be restored and safeguarded now that the colonies had broken away?

To Shelburne, the disciple of Dean Tucker and Adam Smith, the answer was obvious. The Americans must be given every inducement to buy British by way of a freer trade. On the one hand, their territorial ambitions must be satisfied at once. Indeed, the wider their boundaries inland the greater the market for British goods. Let the Americans incur the responsibility and expense of developing the Mississippi valley and the north-west. We would supply the growing community with the necessary manufactures. But on the other hand they must be able to pay, and given incentives to maintain their sales to us. Shelburne there-fore looked to a commercial treaty following the treaty of peace, where-by the United States would enjoy equal advantages with us in their trade with our possessions, and the continuation of their former rights in trading with ourselves. The fewer restrictions the better. Reciprocity was the aim. This was the principle, reconciliatory, progressive, which had guided our recent concessions to Ireland. 'Why should we not reach it out also to America?'[1]

A freer trade was also desirable in Europe, and Shelburne accepted an undertaking in the peace treaties to open commercial talks with France, Spain and Holland – a demand made by them in the hope of exploiting a favourable situation, but welcomed by him, given time, in the firm belief that an easement of restrictions would benefit us. In the Eastern hemisphere his aims were more traditional: not so much the revision of a trading system (though future discussion of the Indian market was accepted) as the protection of opportunity to trade. The effort to retain Trincomalee, the anxieties about French designs on the Cape of Good Hope, the insistence on rights of navigation among the Dutch East Indian islands: all reflected, in more primitive conditions and more familiar ways, the same pursuit of strength by trade that underlay the plans for reciprocity elsewhere.

1. Shelburne in the House of Lords, 17 February 1783 (*P.R.*, XI, 68).

95

This was an imaginative, subtle and audacious design. It was, for those very reasons, a difficult one to carry out. Shelburne needed all the cards he could play in an intricate game. But the belated victories which strengthened his hand abroad weakened him at home. The war had never been unpopular in itself: it was mismanagement and misfortune that had brought it into disrepute. Now that things seemed to be going better the old feelings revived, and most of those who accepted the need for peace were not disposed to yield too much. Such feelings entered the Cabinet itself. Richmond and Keppel disliked the large concessions to the United States, and bitterly opposed Shelburne's wish to barter Gibraltar; and they could sometimes call on other, rather wavering support. Doubts on policy were moreover heightened by Shelburne's personality and methods of work. He was always strongly inclined to go his own way. Now he was convinced, and probably rightly, that the negotiations must be kept strictly within his grasp, and – also probably rightly – that an assorted group of colleagues would not approve or indeed understand his intentions as a whole. The result was that he became increasingly secretive and dictatorial. The Cabinet, which seems to have met fairly regularly in the summer and early autumn, was summoned in the winter only when absolutely necessary, and the atmosphere was correspondingly strained. Richmond remained personally friendly; but Grafton resigned in protest against the First Lord of the Treasury 'becoming *Prime* Minister', as distinct from 'holding the principle office in the Cabinet', and Camden was forced to acknowledge in the end that his old associate could no longer hope to survive the 'personal dislike'.[1]

Shelburne managed to conclude the preliminary treaties of peace before he fell; and they were ratified in due course by those who brought him down. But even if he had remained in office it seems unlikely that he could have carried his complementary plans for a revision of trade. Here indeed the opposition was bound to be more intense, for changes hinted at in the territorial were made explicit in the commercial settlements. The Commons might perhaps be expected to pass the undertakings for commercial talks with the European powers, for the discussions were required to be completed only by the end of 1785. They were much less likely to approve a treaty of trade with the United States which ran counter to the whole pattern of the mercantile system and the tradition of mercantile thought. The bill admittedly was brought forward at a particularly unfortunate moment, at the beginning of March 1783. Shelburne had just resigned, the Ministry was in fragments, and Pitt introduced the measure as spokesman for a caretaker

1. *Autobiography and Political Correspondence of John Henry Third Duke of Grafton K.G.,* ed. Sir William R. Anson (1898), 361, 364. The 'dislike' did not arise entirely from Shelburne's handling of the peace negotiations: Grafton, for instance, resigned because he had not been consulted about Cabinet appointments. But the ground had been prepared by the experience of recent months.

Government. But the chances of success were slim at best. It was asking a great deal of the House to admit the Americans to our West Indian trade, on terms which might well be against the interests of our remaining loyal colonists; to encourage a growing shipping industry, once a source of strength but now become a rival in the vital carrying trade; and to complicate our future dealings with other foreign powers by granting the citizens of the new United States the commercial privileges of British subjects. The strength of such objections was indeed to be seen over ten years later, when Pitt cautiously revived the idea of a treaty on which Shelburne and later Fox had been defeated. His concessions then were strictly limited; as a result they were refused in the United States; and although a settlement was reached it bore little resemblance to the earlier liberal plan. The seeds of the war of 1812 were sown in the failure of 1783 and the inadequate success of 1794.

It is possible, however, that Pitt had doubts about Shelburne's measure at the time. He spoke of it in studiously non-committal terms: it was, so the report ran, 'an experiment hazarded in a great measure upon conjecture'.[1] This of course may have been largely because the Government was on the defensive. It may also have been because Pitt had not been actively involved in the drafting of the bill. That had been entrusted by Shelburne to a certain John Pownall, recently one of the Commissioners of Trade, and the result followed his reports, prepared at speed at the end of January. It was never a good time for Ministers to give much thought to commercial questions – officials complained throughout the decade of the way in which the Parliamentary session caused such matters to be put aside – and on this occasion Pitt was largely preoccupied with a growing political storm. He saw Pownall's final report, of course,[2] and was not prepared to disapprove. But when he was quoted as saying that he had considered the subject 'as well as the small portion of his leisure would allow',[3] he could no doubt support his reservations by an appeal to the facts.

Pitt indeed seems to have acted here, as he did in some other cases, the part of a dutiful lieutenant and legatee.[4] The same applies to his role in the peace talks themselves. He took his full share of Cabinet responsibility, attending all the meetings of which record exists. He was one of Shelburne's principal supporters in the sometimes acrimonious proceedings. He was a bulwark of the Ministry in the House of Commons. But there is no evidence to suggest that he was admitted at all fully into Shelburne's thoughts, or knew much more than most of his colleagues about the progress of the negotiations. The Prime Minister held his cards very close to his chest. Even Grantham, the Foreign Secretary, was sometimes not consulted. Pitt did his duty by his chief,

1. *P.R.,* IX, 440.
2. Dated 2 February. It is among Pitt's papers (P.R.O. 30/8/343).
3. *P.R.,* IX, 440.
4. E.g. pp. 91–3 above.

and clearly approved his intentions. But his grasp of detail could be faulted – he earned George III's rebuke for telling the House that peace with America was irrevocable whenever peace with France should be signed, even if the current negotiation failed[1] – and it seems likely that his heart was more in the programme of reform than in foreign affairs. At the Treasury he stood fairly close to Shelburne, personally and officially. In the conduct of the peace, he seems to have proved no exception to the rule that the Prime Minister 'neglected his Cabinet colleagues, leaving them as far as possible in the dark'.[2]

IV

The preliminary treaties with the United States, France and Spain were presented to Parliament on 27 January 1783, and a debate had already been arranged for 17 February. The moment for battle had come, and the Ministry was in a poor state to fight.

Shelburne had based his hopes on attracting recruits from the ranks of North and Fox, and a growing sympathy from among the independents. But for this he needed a show of strength which the Cabinet altercations undermined, and in its absence he gave no hint of concessions. Inept politician that he was, he did not realise until too late that his power was slipping away. His confidence, though excessive, was not absurd at the start of the Parliamentary session, when Members' reactions had still to be tested. But as the dissensions in Cabinet grew over the turn of the year, and his opponents began to show greater interest in a working partnership with one another, he still could not bring himself to any real accommodation.

The reason lay partly in Shelburne's faith in the power of the Crown. When he told the sceptical William Grenville in mid-December that there was 'a moral certainty' of a sure foundation for Government – and one that a wise man would not expect him to explain[3] – it was this potent fact, as he saw it, to which he referred. Certainly the Crown had so far done what it could. The King had pressed North to persuade the country gentlemen not to embarrass the Ministry – an appeal which met with a qualified response. He had sanctioned – possibly arranged – the appearance of a trusted 'man of business', Charles Jenkinson, as an intermediary between North and the Government. He backed the Minister consistently, if not always enthusiastically, in his troubles with his colleagues. Shelburne was right in thinking that he had George III's

1. See p. 93 above.
2. Vincent T. Harlow, *The Founding of the Second British Empire 1763–1793*, I (1952), 336. This work gives the fullest account of the peace negotiations.
3. W. W. Grenville to Lord Temple, 15 December 1782 (Buckingham, I, 89). See also p. 74, n2. above for Shelburne's expectations from the Crown in the matter of Parliamentary reform.

support. It is a measure of his over-confidence in the result that he later blamed his fall on George's III treachery.

The miscalculation was typical. The Crown's powers were certainly not to be underrated. It had electoral strength, a large influence in appointments, the steadiest of Parliamentary parties. But it could not be expected, particularly in a lively session, to produce confidence in a Ministry which was narrowly based and known to be at odds. Nor were Shelburne's policies such as to enlarge the base. A programme of thoroughgoing reform was hazardous in itself. It was not rendered more generally acceptable by hints about the role of the Crown. For the trouble was that Shelburne was prepared to act strictly by Chathamite ideas – an exercise which had driven Chatham himself into retirement. 'The Constitution of Great Britain', he told an American, 'is sufficient to pervade the whole world';[1] and in that exalted conception the royal prerogative had its accepted place. Freed from its recent association with reaction and defeat, it was now to be restored to its legitimate share in a balanced system. Served by a reformed administration, strong in a reformed finance, the patriot King would rule in harmony with the general sense of a reformed Parliament; for 'this country ought not to be governed by any party or faction'.[2] This was all very well. Much of the sentiment was familiar. But Shelburne was not Chatham in his prime, and the prospect of continuous innovation was no more to the politicians' taste – or indeed always to that of the King himself[3] – for being linked with a defence of the royal functions. His programme might gain some support from the uncommitted Members; but he had chosen, even there, a highly debatable form of appeal.

Meanwhile North and Fox and their followers watched. North held the key to an open situation. If he decided broadly to support the peace, or at least not actively to oppose, the Government would almost certainly survive. If he threw his weight against it, he was likely – though not certain, for his party held a large variegated fringe – to bring down the Government. Since November there had been soundings to discover how he felt, and Jenkinson at times was hopeful of the result. But if North was to hold his hand, his followers would expect a return. He himself would like to see Shelburne's reforms curtailed; some of them looked in addition to a share of office.

As Shelburne was brought to recognise his danger, he considered this second prospect. At times he seemed not averse to what he thought might be involved. But what he thought was not in line with the facts. The groups which looked to North might be a varied federation, but

1. Henry Laurens to James Bourdieu, 10 August 1782 (quoted Harlow, op. cit., 267).
2. Speech of 10 July 1782 (*P.R.*, VIII, 365).
3. Shelburne's statement that '*the Court* was averse' to his reforms (Fitzmaurice, III, 328) was made from the bitterness of his retirement. But it is a sad commentary on a policy for which he relied on the Crown's support.

they were held together largely out of regard for their leader, and Shelburne did nothing to conciliate that sentiment. There was never any real question of his abandoning his policy. He was also not prepared to face the possibility of a coalition on anything like equal terms, or indeed to offer any office, at least immediately, to North himself.

This last disqualification put paid to an arrangement, even though in fact North was not anxious for a post. His followers could scarcely be expected to bolster up a shaky Ministry when their leader had been thus proscribed. But Shelburne was neither anxious nor free to act otherwise. He had no wish to add North to his councils; and he knew in any case that such a move would rouse intense opposition from a quarter he could not ignore. For the most uncompromising disapproval of an alliance with North came from Pitt, and in the Cabinet as it stood Pitt's support was indispensable. To the young man, indeed, North was something of a bogy: the villain of his youth, the target of his father's attacks and those others which he had followed so intently from Cambridge, the inept and discredited Minister of an unjust war, a leader of resistance to Parliamentary reform. He was not particularly enthusiastic about North's followers – almost a year later Dundas was not sure that 'some of those prejudices do not continue to operate in his mind'.[1] He was quite resolved to have nothing to do with North in person. His determination clinched the doubts which other Chathamites felt. When Dundas was allowed at the last minute to make a limited overture to North's party, it came too late even to be considered.

The alternative, then, was to seek some form of alliance with Fox. In some ways this was more to the Chathamites' taste. True, Fox had broken up the Whig Cabinet, and indulged in constant recrimination since. But some of the former differences of opinion with the Rockinghams had disappeared with Shelburne's recognition of the United States, and several of his colleagues would be glad to think, however optimistically, of 'the Whigs once more united'.[2] Shelburne himself was pardonably unenthusiastic. But he allowed himself to be persuaded into Pitt's making an approach, and the King with equal reluctance agreed. On 10 or 11 February Pitt and Fox met on their own. The result was fateful. By the best account, Pitt 'asked one question, viz., whether there were any terms on which he [Fox] would come in. The answer was, None, while Lord Shelburne remained; and so it ended'.[3] According to tradition, the two men never met alone in private again.

1. Quoted in *L.C.G. III*, I, xxix.
2. *Autobiography of Grafton*, 355.
3. This account is by W. W. Grenville, who had the story from Pitt on 11 February, the day on which, according to Grenville, the meeting took place (Buckingham, I, 148). But as George III's reply to Shelburne's letter giving the news is dated 9.20 a.m. on the 11th, it seems more likely that the meeting was held on the 10th. There are two other accounts of this famous interview which merit attention. William Adam, one of North's lieutenants, heard something of it from Dundas, and recorded (later?) that 'Pitt drew himself up' on hearing Fox's answer (*Correspondence*

Shelburne's calculations until almost the end had been based on the assumption that Fox and North would not join forces.[1] The whole history of the past few years, the unusual bitterness of Fox's attacks, the real discrepancies between their positions, seemed to endorse such a belief. But in fact tentative discussions had been going on for some weeks between members of either party. The principals themselves had their misgivings. North swung unhappily between conflicting advisers; and Fox too was torn – 'he felt the greatest objections . . . and yet perhaps it was best, though he agreed it could not be lasting'.[2] But there were men in either camp to urge them on: to play on Fox's resentment of Shelburne, and his deep belief – fast becoming an obsession – that the Ministry had betrayed the cause to the Crown; to persuade North that he held a key which would grow rusty with disuse, and that if he did not soon declare himself against a Minister who refused him office his followers would begin to desert and his influence for good government fade away. Time was now drawing very short. The debate on the peace was due to start within a week of the day on which Pitt saw Fox. The intermediaries worked hard. On the 14th Fox met North and 'the infamous coalition' was arranged. On the 17th, Government was defeated in the Commons by 224 to 208 – a better showing on its part than might have been expected. Four days later, on a second test, it was beaten by 207 to 190. On 24 February, Shelburne resigned.

It is arguable that he should not have done so: that he should have tried to fight it out with the King's support, and made continued efforts, in the excitement aroused by the Coalition, to detach some of its more doubtful adherents. But Shelburne was in fact already half inclined to go. He was beginning to lose his bearings in a struggle he despised, his

---

of Charles James Fox, II, 33). Tomline's version is more dramatic. When Fox had made his reply, 'Mr. Pitt observed, that if that was his determination, it would be useless for him to enter into any farther discussion, "as he did not come to betray Lord Shelburne" ' (I, 89). Tomline's account of the whole affair is not entirely satisfactory – he dates it to a period 'before the meeting of Parliament' (I, 88) –, his is the only evidence for these words, and what his source was I do not know. But Adam's story, if relayed correctly, suggests that Pitt responded with spirit.

1. Adam stated that on 12 February 'Dundas told him, that some time ago Ministers had thought the best thing that could happen to them would be a junction of Mr. Fox with Lord North; that Mr. Pitt had wished for it, thinking the Ministry would thereby gain supporters from both' (*Correspondence of Fox*, II, 32–3). It is fairly clear, from all the evidence, that Ministers towards the end did not know where they stood, and this thought, if held, would seem to have been one of many. In so far, moreover, as they took the possibility into account, they did not expect it to come about so soon – and with the imminent prospect of the debates on the peace, timing was all-important. On 18 February, Pitt wrote that the Government's defeat came 'rather sooner than I imagined, though certainly not quite unexpected' (Stanhope, I, 98).

2. *Autobiography of Grafton*, 355, reporting a conversation in February.

excessive optimism now gave way to a sudden suspicion of the Court, and he thought that with his disappearance some at least of his policies might prevail. His retirement was followed by five weeks of utter confusion.

For George III did not intend to submit. He had lost his Minister, but he held the power of appointment, and he was horrified at the prospect of admitting North and Fox. He had fought obstinately, and with some success, against submission to the Rockinghams. This 'unnatural and factious coalition'[1] was a great deal worse. Nor was the King convinced that such a fate was necessary. The division figures showed that the new allies were not mustering their full voting strength, and he judged that a growing bewilderment and resentment would operate in his favour. His first thought, therefore, was to defy the threat with the aid of a Minister from Shelburne's Cabinet.

Shelburne's own preference was for Pitt. He had said as much to Dundas over a week before he resigned, and he repeated the suggestion on the very eve. That hardy politician was caught by the idea. He paid tribute to the young man's 'great and splendid' qualities. But it was his youth which, added to them, held particular appeal.

> There is scarcely any other Political Character of consideration in the Country to whom many people from Habits, from Connections, from former Professions, from Rivalships and from Antipathies will not have objections. But he is perfectly new ground . . .

Dundas was therefore 'completely satisfied . . . that, young as He is, the appointment of Him to the Government of the Country is the only step that can be taken in the present moment attended with the most distant chance'.[2] He urged the outgoing Minister to press the suggestion on the King.

The King needed little pressing, particularly as the Lord Chancellor gave him similar advice. He sent for Pitt the same afternoon. The first impression was promising. Both George III and Dundas thought that Pitt would accept, and both remained optimistic for the next two days. Dundas exerted himself with his former colleagues in North's party to give the new arrangement a chance, and by the 27th all seemed set fair. At eleven o'clock that morning he left Pitt, as he thought, 'perfectly resolved to accept First Lord of the Treasury'.[3] Three hours later all was over.

1. To Shelburne, 22 February 1783 (*Correspondence of King George III*, VI, no. 4131).
2. 'Melville Papers, unbound'; William L. Clements Library, University of Michigan. This copy of the letter is undated and unsigned. From the description and abbreviated quotation of another copy in Holland Rose, 125, it was dated 24 February, a.m.
3. Henry Dundas to his brother, Lord Arniston, 27 February 1783, 5 p.m. (Stanhope, I, 108).

I have just been at your house, [Pitt wrote to Dundas at two o'clock in the afternoon] to tell you, which I must do with great pain, what has passed in my mind since I last saw you . . . What you stated to me this morning seemed to remove all doubt of my finding a majority in Parliament, and on the first view of it, joined to my sincere desire not to decline the call of my friends, removed at the same time my objections to accepting the Treasury. I have since most deliberately reconsidered the ground, and, after weighing it as fully as is possible for me to do, my final decision is directly contrary to the impression then made on me. I see that the main and almost only ground of reliance would be this, – that Lord North and his friends would not continue in a combination to oppose. In point of prudence, after all that has passed, and considering all that is to come, such a reliance is too precarious to act on. But above all, in point of honour to my own feelings, I cannot form an administration trusting to the hope that it will be supported, or even will not be opposed, by Lord North, whatever the influence may be that determines his conduct. The first moment I saw the subject in this point of view, from which I am sure I cannot vary, *unalterably* determined me to decline . . .[1]

'Nothing', the King wrote that evening, 'could get him to depart from the ground he took'.[2]

This was a remarkable, and impressive, decision. On the face of it, Pitt had almost every inducement to accept. The King was perforce behind him. Shelburne had wished him well, and so did the rest of the Cabinet. His accession, he was told, would restore North's neutrality, an event which must severely strain the coalition with Fox at the moment of its birth. And on that basis he could count on much general goodwill. Nor was he disinclined to take the prize. 'I am not less ambitious to be great and powerful', he had declared only a week before, 'than it is natural for a young man with such brilliant examples before him, to be'.[3] It was a combination of arguments which almost led him to accept. That he ended by refusing is a tribute to his sense of prudence and of purpose. The decision, while it shocked those who had counted on him, placed him in an unassailable position. He had earned the right, by an irrefutable test, to attack the Coalition, and beyond that had served notice that he would not come to power on others' terms. When he proclaimed that 'he could not coalesce with those whose principles he knew to be diametrically opposed to his own',[4] his words must now carry a conviction which such sentiments seldom earned. He had kept clear of party at a moment when the party game was reaching a dangerous climax, without delivering himself to the King. He had

1. Loc. cit., 107.
2. To Shelburne (Holland Rose, 126).
3. In the debate of 21 February (*P.R.*, IX, 349).
4. Ibid.

immensely strengthened the impression that he stood on 'perfectly new ground'.[1] And he had done so on a realistic, shrewd assessment of the odds. It was a strikingly precocious example of his political good sense.

The King had therefore to look elsewhere. Over the next four weeks he ranged the political world. He even considered Thomas Pitt, Pitt's first cousin, a respected member of the Gower group but scarcely Ministerial timber – 'Mr. Thomas Pitt or Mr. Thomas anybody'.[2] Above all he tried to get North to come in on some acceptable basis. But despite some differences with his new allies, North refused to act alone, and the Coalition's terms were even worse than George III had feared. The Lord Chancellor (normally the King's personal representative in the Cabinet) was to go, and the Duke of Portland, whom North and Fox proposed for First Lord of the Treasury, was to be granted an audience at which he would require approval for his list of Ministerial appointments. This was invading the prerogative with a vengeance. In growing desperation, the King turned again to Pitt. On 20 March he asked him once more to form a Government, and over the next four days Pitt re-examined the odds. Once more Dundas had hopes; but the answer was the same. The King was now in the deepest distress. He thought of appealing to Parliament as a body. He drafted a message of abdication. But at the end of the month, his hand forced by 'the total stagnation of Public Business',[3] he submitted to 'the most daring and unprincipled faction that the annals of this Kingdom ever produced'.[4] On 31 March Pitt announced his resignation as Chancellor of the Exchequer. On 1 April the Duke of Portland became First Lord of the Treasury, and North and Fox took the Seals as Secretaries of State.

1. P. 102 above.
2. Dunning [Lord Ashburton]'s account of an interview with the King on 9 March (Fitzmaurice, III, 375). Thomas Pitt's name was considered again near the end of the month.
3. Memorandum by the King, n.d. but early April 1783 (*Correspondence of King George III*, VI, no. 4271).
4. To Pitt, 25 March (Stanhope, I, Appendix iii).

CHAPTER V

Brief Leisure

I

Pitt was now, as he had falsely anticipated a few weeks earlier, 'a
Free Man'.[1] But the Parliamentary session was likely to last for
about another three months, and until it ended he was held in or
near London. He moved quickly out of Downing Street, perhaps with
the less regret because the house had been undergoing large repairs and
alterations. The chambers in Lincoln's Inn were in process of being
sold; but there was always a bed to be had at his brother's, and for much
of the spring and early summer, an unusually fine one that year, he
based himself on Wilberforce's villa at Wimbledon.

In the days when London ended to the west of Hyde Park, when the
villages of Brompton and Fulham lay among quiet lanes and market
gardens, and the Old Berkeley hounds hunted up to Kensington Palace,
the farther bank of the Thames seemed remote from the town. 'From
my retirement at Wimbledon', Wilberforce quoted Milton in praise of
' "each rural sight, each rural sound" '.[2] The practice had been
growing for some time of politicians and men of affairs keeping an
establishment which could be reached within the half day from London.
In Pitt's first Administration Dundas and Grenville had houses by
Wimbledon Heath, the Foreign Secretary, Carmarthen, one at North
Mimms, the Home Secretary, Sydney, lived at Chislehurst, Jenkinson
at Addiscombe, Eden when in England at Beckenham, and Pitt himself
rented a villa near Putney and then bought Holwood House near
Hayes. There was much coming and going, as business allowed; and
Pitt, who liked riding and had been advised at Cambridge to pursue it
for his health, spent a good deal of time in the saddle between Westminster and the nearby countryside.

His health, if not outstanding, now seemed normal. The delicate boy
who at fourteen had weighed just over six stone had grown into a thin,
angular but not ill built young man. He had a full but longish face, a
questing nose, and fine auburn hair – he kept the colour to his death;[3]
stood about six foot tall, and in March 1783 weighed 11 stone $11\frac{1}{2}$

1. To Hester Countess of Chatham, 2 March (P.R.O. 30/8/12. See Stanhope, I,
109).
2. To his sister, 5 June 1783 (*Life of Wilberforce*, I, 29–30).
3. There is a lock of it at Chevening; and the colour is suggested in a sketch,
preserved at Pembroke, said to have been done of Pitt while he was at the College.

pounds in 'shoes and frock' dress on Berry's (then Clarke's) scales in St James's Street. His stomach was never strong, and it was at this time that he is pictured 'actually holding Solomon's porch door open with one hand' during a debate, 'while vomiting during Fox's speech to whom he was to reply'.[1] It did not prevent him from speaking for two and three-quarter hours, 'most capitally'.[2] Work and drink had not yet taken their toll, and such indispositions as are recorded did not much affect his daily life. His constitution was not robust, but he was resilient and energetic, and his fortitude and good spirits carried him along. Throughout these years, Pretyman later remarked, 'he was usually considered . . . as a healthy man'.[3]

He was also considered a highly sociable one by his friends – an opinion certainly not shared by the political world at large. For the complete contrast between Pitt's public and private personalities was already marked. 'I know', wrote Shelburne to Barré, who was going to see the Minister in 1784, 'the coldness of the climate you go into, and that it requires all your animation to produce a momentary thaw'.[4] Shelburne was a bitter witness. But he wrote as though he was referring to an accepted fact, and others had found that Pitt could keep his distance. Fox himself had failed to charm the young man into Brooks's: he was not 'dazzled or won', and 'held back'.[5] Yet he was often – for a time continually – in the clubs he favoured. Those who knew him at White's, which he joined in 1783, recalled his 'uncommon vivacity'.[6] But it was in 'the small society' of Goostree's[7] that he was most at home.

The history of Goostree's is typical of the founding period of the subscription club. In 1773, James Goostree graduated from a coffee-house in St James's Street to a house in Pall Mall – on part of the site now occupied by the British Legion's offices – where, in the manner of Almack, Brooks and Boodle, he opened a club bearing his name. It was indeed neighbour to Brooks's and Boodle's over the next few years, and its briefer career showed many of the features of their early life. Like Boodle's, like Brooks's later, it was controlled at first by a committee of 'managers'; like them, it was liable to sudden revolutions in member-

1. *Life of Wilberforce*, I, 26. This was not the occasion mentioned by Wilberforce on p. 29 above, when Pitt had to retire into Solomon's porch. That had occured four nights before.

2. Ibid.

3. Tomline, Box 29, i, 35.2, undated (Pembroke College, Cambridge, Mss).

4. Fitzmaurice, III, 422.

5. Wraxall, op. cit., II, 79. And of course he 'rarely, if ever' went there (ibid) after he broke with Fox. Brougham (*Historical Sketches of Statesmen who Flourished in the Time of George III*, I, 201 n) relates that, passing the club one night in 1803, Pitt told his companion Charles Long that he had not been in 'since the Coalition of [*sic*] 1784'.

6. Mrs Pretyman Tomline's notes, October and November 1806, quoting Edward Eliot as 'one of my authorities' ('Mr Pitt II', Stanhope Mss).

7. The phrase is James Hare's, Fox's friend, in December 1781 (*H.M.C., Carlisle*, 555).

ship and character under cover of the same name. In the middle seventies Goostree's was a purely social affair, enjoying a rich and fashionable membership and a reputation for staging lavish fêtes and routs. But this did not last long, probably because the members left *en bloc* to join the Savoir Vivre at its elegant new quarters round the corner; and when the club was revived it was on a different footing. In the later months of 1780 it was taken over by a group of politically minded young men, many of them friends from Cambridge and all in Opposition. Pitt, fresh to London, was a leading spirit. Edward Eliot, Bankes, Pratt, St John, Euston, Althorp had been in his circle at the University. There were his brother Chatham and his cousin William Grenville. And among others who now began to figure in his life were Wilberforce, Thomas Steele, Robert Smith, and the lawyer Pepper Arden, who had rooms on Pitt's staircase in Lincoln's Inn and became Solicitor General under Shelburne. There were some twenty-five in all, 'very nice in their admissions',[1] who constituted the club until its demise in about 1787.

Here Pitt felt free to let himself go, in the way that always charmed his friends and surprised those who met him for the first time off the public stage. We have a few glimpses of him elsewhere: in a room off the House of Commons, with Wilberforce, Euston and others, 'singing and laughing *à gorge déployée*' so that old George Selwyn, who saw them, could 'wish for one night to be twenty';[2] at a party at the Boar's Head in Eastcheap, 'in high spirits, quoting and alluding to Shakespeare';[3] talking to Wyvill about his reform bill while Mahon and Wilberforce, left upstairs, were 'making such a noise . . . and laughing so heartily' that Harriot Pitt next door could hardly go on with her letter.[4] But Goostree's was the focus of his social life. He supped there, Wilberforce tells us, every night during the winter of 1780–1, and he continued to frequent it over at least the next two years. At first there was a good deal of gambling. But Pitt, who felt its 'increasing fascination',[5] soon decided that he must stop, and perhaps as a result play was discouraged. James Hare, of Brooks's, may have been right in forecasting that this would shorten the club's life. It is more likely that the intimacy of a small society suffered as members grew busier or were scattered, and as Pitt himself was immersed in office. Meanwhile he entered happily into all that was going on. Looking back on this time, Wilberforce reflected 'He was the wittiest man I ever knew'.[6]

Life passed pleasantly at Goostree's and Wimbledon. 'Eliot, Arden, and I', runs a note to Wilberforce, 'will be with you before curfew, and

1. Ibid.
2. *George A. Selwyn, His Letters and His Life,* ed. E. S. Roscoe & Helen Clergue (1899), 217.
3. Jekyll's reminiscences, in Tomline, I, 43n.
4. *The Letters of Lady Harriot Eliot 1766–1786,* ed. Cuthbert Headlam (1914), 76.
5. *Life of Wilberforce,* I, 18.
6. Ibid.

expect an early meal of peas and strawberries'. 'To Wimbledon', noted Wilberforce in his diary, 'with Pitt and Eliot at their persuasion'. 'Fine hot day, went on water with Pitt and Eliot fishing'. 'Delicious day, – lounged morning at Wimbledon with friends, *foining* at night, and run about the garden for an hour or two'.[1] Pitt had the taste for horseplay of his class and age. Dudley Ryder's dress hat was found strewn about the flower beds one morning, and Shelburne, seeking political news from Bowood after the Government's resignation, had to be satisfied with a lighter tale.

> I have had no opportunity of particular conversation with Mr. P. [wrote one of his lieutenants] since yr. Ldship left London . . . He passes, as usual, most of his time with his young Friends in a Society sometimes very lively – Some little excess happen'd lately at Wimbledon . . . In the Evening some of the Neighbours were alarmed with noises at their doors, but Nobody, I believe, has made any ill natured reflection upon a mere frolic – It has only been pleasantly remarked, that the Rioters were headed by Master P. – late Chancellor of the Ex-, and Master Arden, late Sollicitor Genl.-[2]

There is no mention of women in all this. Pitt's reputed indifference on the subject was, as one might expect, a public joke at the time.

> 'Tis true, indeed, we oft abuse him
>   Because he bends to no man;
> But Slander's self dares not accuse him
>   Of stiffness to a woman.[3]

The gossips were probably right. Pitt was not a misogynist. As a young man he went through the motions of attending the usual entertainments – partly, one may suspect, because his sister Harriot kept him up to the mark. Hester Stanhope always maintained that he had a keen eye for a pretty woman and a pretty dress. He was an easy and agreeable guest, as well as obviously a catch of whom a hostess could feel proud. He enjoyed being taken up by the lively Duchess of Gordon for some years, after Harriot died. He liked women's company when it came his way. But that of course does not mean that he was ever attracted to a woman, there is no real sign that he was, and his one serious effort, in his later thirties, ended in embarrassed escape. This, again, was probably not because he was strongly attracted sexually to men, though

---

1. Loc.cit., 25, 28–9. 'Foining' is thrusting or fencing.

2. Thomas Orde to Shelburne, 17 July 1783 (Lansdowne Mss, Bowood).

3. *Political Miscellanies*, in *The Rolliad, in Two Parts; . . . Probationary Odes for the Laureateship; and Political Miscellanies* (1795), 21. There are ten more epigrams of the same sort in this publication; and the point is repeated and suggested to exhaustion in caricatures and newspapers over the years.

the inference was sometimes obliquely drawn.[1] If he had any homo-sexual 'potential' if would seem to have been very mild, and it is much more likely that he had no strong sexual inclinations at all. The qualities, in his friendships and his life, most often stressed by those who knew him, were cheerfulness, simplicity, candour, purity, disinterested-ness. The attributes are revealing. 'His heart was formed for the sensibilities of friendship'[2] rather than for the splendours and miseries of possessive love.

In this respect, Pitt's character and his conduct were of a piece. Some of the difficulties which sometimes arise in interpreting his reaction to events may be caused by his very lack of complication and involvement, and the consequent sense of uncertainty when the un-expected occurred. His simple, boyish optimism was often disap-pointed and as often survived; but at the necessary cost sometimes of tactical surrender. That the cost met the need, that the surrenders left no lasting wound, suggests the extent to which Pitt's temperament affected his inherited disposition. Chatham too had been baffled by the outside world; but in his case with a very different result. He had transmitted his vision to his favourite son. He bequeathed something of his family's temperament. But the tragic quality of his nature was mercifully diminished, by an infusion of Grenville staying power and an inherent lack of passion.

These contrasts produced their own blend. It underlay, for instance, the discrepancy between Pitt's public and his private manner. For this was no gradual development, brought on by experience of the world. On the contrary, one might say that it sprang from a lasting inexpe-rience: certainly it existed undisguised from near the start. The chilly tone in public was of course deliberate, designed to serve Pitt's concep-tion and defence of his role. It was not only that he was a very young man among experienced politicians. He was also a penniless younger son, seeking and holding a position which the great magnates liked to

1. It is difficult for instance, to see what else is meant by the following paragraph in *The Rolliad*. Such stuff of course means very little in itself. But it is perhaps fair to quote the most suggestive passage of the kind I have found. The stanza which it follows alludes to Pitt's stay at Brighton in the summer of 1784, when his chief pleasure was alleged to have lain in discussing affairs of state with his cronies.
'. . . Where beauteous Brighton overlooks the sea,
These be his joys; and Steele shall make the Tea.
How neat! how delicate! and how unexpected the allusion in the last couplet! These two lines alone include the substance of whole columns, with which the ministerial papers entertained the public last summer, on the *sober*, the *chaste*, the *virtuous*, the *edifying* manner in which the immaculate young man passed the recess from public business: not in riot and debauchery, not in gaming, not in attendance on ladies, modest or immodest, but in drinking Tea with Mr. *Steele*, at the *Castle* in *Brighthelm-stone*. Let future ages read and admire.' (*Criticisms on the Rolliad, Part the First : Corrected and Enlarged* (1785), 77). A somewhat similar passage occurs in the *Political Eclogues* included in the later editions, which is quoted in part by Holland Rose, 285-6.
2. Tomline, Box 29, i, 35.3, undated notes (Pembroke College, Cambridge, Mss).

claim if possible as their own. But if the adoption of the image was deliberate, that does not mean it was not involuntary. This was Pitt's natural reaction to the circumstances of his choice. It stemmed very largely from Chatham's example, and the legacy of Pitt and Grenville pride: William Wyndham Grenville, for instance, behaved in something of the same way. It preserved the Pitts' overbearing, uneven self-confidence in the Grenvilles' freezing chill. It was also, by way of contrast, a shy man's defence,[1] and shielded a nature which made the mildest of personal demands while identifying itself with an exacting public ideal.

The character that emerged, and set, very early was strong on its own terms. Pitt's temperament softened the aggressiveness that distinguished his father's family, and the acquisitive touchiness that sometimes marked his mother's. It gave stability, and its own consistency, to a curious inheritance. But the inheritance was there, to define the achievement. There were large areas of human interest which Pitt was simply not equipped to understand. Nor was the stability itself achieved without tension. Pitt's steadiness and cheerfulness were the wonder of his friends. They were particularly so to those who, like Dundas, saw that he had another side to his nature, and that he could easily be 'either in a garrett or a cellar'.[2] 'I take it', wrote James Harris, the ambassador, '. . . that there enters a good deal of marble into his composition'.[3] The remark was just, and the marble was of fine quality. But the quarry from which it came held its share of fractured pieces.

The Parliamentary recess began on 16 July. Six days before, after a characteristically lethargic courtship, Pitt's elder brother Chatham had married Mary Townshend, the daughter of Tommy Townshend, recently made Lord Sydney. Pitt began his holiday by calling in on them at Hayes on his way to his cousin Temple at Stowe, a house which he had not visited before. Early in August he went down to Brighton, where he was seen by Rutland's tame Member, Daniel Pulteney, showing 'the *monstrari digito* whenever he appears abroad'.[4] Then, after returning briefly to London, he paid a visit to his mother at Burton Pynsent, and thence to Bankes in Dorset, where he joined Eliot and Wilberforce for a little shooting.[5] Another short spell in and near Lon-

---

1. 'For he was one of the shyest men I ever knew' (*Private Papers of Wilberforce*, 65, n1).

2. To Lord Spencer, 17 November 1801; quoted in Keith Grahame Feiling, *The Second Tory Party 1714–1832* (1938), 166.

3. *Diaries and Correspondence of James Harris, First Earl of Malmesbury*, ed. by his Grandson, II (1844), 257.

4. *H.M.C., Fourteenth Report, Appendix, Pt. I*, 70. The letter may be dated 10 August, rather than 3rd or 10th as given there.

5. Pitt enjoyed shooting, and it may be noted, in view of the rarity of pheasants at the time, that he sometimes mentions them as well as the more usual partridges.

don, and on 11 September the three friends met in Kent, and the next day sailed from Dover for France.

Pitt had thought of going abroad in the previous two summers; but the Western Circuit had intervened in 1781, and his sudden appointment to office in 1782. He now revived the plan, proposing to spend a few weeks at a provincial town in France to improve his grasp of the language, before paying a brief visit to Paris and Versailles. With Eliot and Wilberforce, he accordingly made his way to Rheims. Their arrival was not particularly auspicious. Pitt never paid any attention to his private affairs, and neither he nor his companions had bothered to equip themselves with that essential item of eighteenth-century travel, the letter of introduction. A last-minute demand on Robert Smith produced from his friend Thellusson the banker the name of a business correspondent in the town. But he turned out to be 'a very little grocer', quite unable to prove an *entrée* into local society. For some days, therefore, the three Englishmen studied their grammar together, 'not having a single French acquaintance'.[1] At length the lieutenant of police came to their rescue, and told the Archbishop and others of their existence. Thereafter their stay was quite agreeable. According to one account, the Archbishop had a nephew living with him, the young Talleyrand-Périgord; but if this was so, we know nothing of his conversations with Pitt. Wilberforce noted a few other scraps of information. It was at this time that Pitt paid his tribute to Fox's 'magician's wand',[2] and once, after listening to an account of French institutions, he remarked that there was no political liberty, but more civil liberty than was generally supposed.

At the end of the first week in October the party moved on to Paris, where they spent a few days in seeing the sights. But the Court was at Fontainebleau, with everyone of interest, and they accordingly rounded off their stay by going to view 'all the magnificence of France'.[3] They were presented to the King – 'clumsy, strange figure' – and to the Queen, who had heard of their visit to the grocer. They met the Ministers Vergennes and de Castries, Madame de Polignac and Madame de Lamballe, Lafayette and Benjamin Franklin, Marmontel and Noailles. They supped and dined, attended the opera, played 'cards, trictrac, and backgammon'.[4] Pitt went stag hunting one day. He found himself an object of general curiosity. 'They all, men and women, crowded round [him] in shoals; and he behaved with great spirit, though he was sometimes a little bored when they talked to him about the parliamentary reform'.[5]

To one ambitious mother, he was something more. Madame Necker –

1. *Private Papers of Wilberforce*, 55.
2. See p. 55 above.
3. Pitt to Hester Countess of Chatham, 15 October (Stanhope, I, 132).
4. *Life of Wilberforce*, I, 40.
5. Wilberforce to Bankes, 28 October 1783 (loc. cit., 44).

the Suzanne Curchod who had once refused Gibbon, and was now the wife of the fallen Director General of the Finances – decided that Pitt would make a desirable husband for her daughter. Horace Walpole, a close friend, is said to have been asked to convey the news, which he did by way of John Pratt. Nothing more was heard of it. Mademoiselle Necker herself disliked the idea, and it is not even certain if she and Pitt ever met. One can only speculate on what might have happened if he had married the girl who became Madame de Staël.

As it was, he left France unscathed. The Parliamentary session was liable to begin soon, and a special messenger suddenly summoned him home. The three friends left Paris at once, and on the night of 22 October Pitt was back in London.[1] He never crossed the Channel again.

II

There is no indication who sent the special messenger. But Pitt had not neglected to keep in touch during the recess. He took care to attend the King's levee when in London,[2] and the date of his arrival in Paris was timed so as to catch George Rose, a former Secretary of the Treasury under Shelburne, travelling home from a visit with Lord Thurlow to Spa. He was indeed, as he well knew, in an interesting, perhaps potentially a key position.

This was common knowledge. The politicians' gossip, wrote Daniel Pulteney in August, was that 'Pitt may be Prime Minister as soon as he will', and it seemed that he had 'the real confidence of every man of every description'.[3] The forecast was wide of the mark, for George III was in no position to act as he might wish, and Pulteney knew moreover that his patron Rutland would like such a report. But it was true that Pitt's reputation stood generally high, and that the King still had an eye on him. He had emerged well from his brief period in office, and best of all from the manner of his going. Shelburne could perhaps reflect, with some sense of grievance, that if his young lieutenant had not insisted on regarding North as untouchable it might have eased his own belated attempt at manœuvre. But whatever his feelings he could have no serious quarrel, and Pitt's resolute defence of the Ministry's policies, followed by his refusal to form a Government, impressed the average politician and the inner ring alike. 'Mr. Pitt', wrote Sir Charlton Leighton, an independent Member, at the time of Shelburne's fall, 'retires with a character for ability that is only equalled by that for

1. Wilberforce states that *he* returned to England on the 24th (loc. cit., 42). Perhaps Pitt went on ahead. At any rate he was reported by several newspapers, some of them appearing on the 24th and 25th, as having reached London on the night of Wednesday 22nd. (See the relevant files in B. M. Burney Collection 739b.)

2. On 8 August (*Morning Herald* and *Morning Chronicle*, 9 August 1783) and 10 September (Stanhope, I, 129). And see also Stanhope, I, 128.

3. *H.M.C., Fourteenth Report, Appendix, Pt. I*, 70.

integrity'.[1] 'The good judgment of so young a man', Grafton commented, 'who not void of ambition, on this trying occasion, could refuse this splendid offer, adds much to the lustre of the character he had acquired'.[2]

This enviable reputation lasted to the end of the session. Pitt of course was not uniformly successful in debate, and once he had distinctly the worst of it, at Sheridan's hands. The two men indeed were antipathetic by nature,[3] and Sheridan was one of the very few speakers of whom Pitt learned to be careful. On this occasion (it was towards the end of the first, long debate on the peace, on 17 February) he had advised Sheridan to reserve his amusing phrases for the stage – an ill-natured remark, made perhaps the more readily because Pitt was feeling ill,[4] for of course the theatre, like Sheridan himself, was socially suspect. But the sarcasm laid him open to 'the severest retort that he ever in his life received'.[5] For Sheridan at once replied that if he engaged in such activities again he would be tempted to try to improve on one of Ben Jonson's best creations – the character, in *The Alchymist*, of the Angry Boy.

But in general Pitt maintained his reputation in the House, and some of his speeches, particularly at the start, were morally damaging to the Coalition. His famous exclamation at the outset – 'If . . . this ill-omened marriage is not already solemnised, I know a just and lawful impediment, and in the name of the public safety I here forbid the Banns' – has achieved a lasting fame.[6] He was enormously helped in his attacks by his own undamaged rectitude, which shone if anything the more brightly when the new Ministry became involved in the mismanaged Powell and Bembridge affair.[7] Men did not shrink in the eighteenth

1. To the Marquess of Carmarthen, 24 February (B.M. Add. Ms 28060, f.23v).

2. *Autobiography of Grafton*, 369.

3. Sheridan, too, seems to have been obstructive in the matter of the Chatham pension soon afterwards, when he was a Secretary of the Treasury under the Coalition. (Pitt to Hester Countess of Chatham, 11 November 1783 (P.R.O. 30/8/12).)

4. See pp. 29 n1, 106 n1 above.

5. Stanhope's phrase (I, 97).

6. *P.H.*, XXIII, 552. There is some mystery about this remark. It first appears in W. S. Hathaway's edition of *The Speeches of William Pitt* in 1806; and it is repeated by Tomline (I, 124). But the paragraph in which it is contained is not given in *P.R.*, IX (349), or in the identical report of Pitt's speech in *The Gentleman's Magazine* (June 1783). But the *Morning Post* of 22 February, *Parker's General Advertiser* of the same date, and the *Whitehall Evening Post* of 25–27 February include the phrase about forbidding the banns, though the wording of the passage differs in one case.

There is a further ground for accepting such evidence. Like other celebrated remarks this may have been inspired by an earlier occasion, and indeed have gained point from it. In December 1782, when Shelburne was the centre of speculation, 'David Hartley had a conceit . . . to get up [in the Commons] & proclaim the banns of Matrimony between the Lord North & the Earl of Shelburne & If any person knows any cause why these two persons should not be joined let him declare it' (Sir Grey Cooper to Charles Jenkinson, 20 December 1782; B.M. Add. Ms 38218, f.149).

7. For a succinct account of this episode, which was highly damaging to the Foxites, see Steven Watson, *The Reign of George III 1760–1815* (1960), 260 n1.

century from protesting their virtues. It was common form, and the audience was left to assess the claim. Pitt made his share of declarations, which did not fail of their effect, and perhaps the best known example of all, when the moral was pointed by omission, must be read in the knowledge that it convinced and thrilled the House.

'Laudo manentem', he quoted, referring to his resignation, 'Si celeres quatit
Pennas, resigno quae dedit
. . . probamque
Pauperiem sine dote quaero'.[1]

He had paused at the word 'dedit', passing over the phrase 'et mea Virtute me involvo'. The quotation deeply impressed his audience, and none more than the minority which really knew its Horace.[2]

Pitt therefore remained in a strong position if the King should feel free to change his Government. Towards the end of the session Ministers feared that this might be so, when they suddenly found themselves committed to the first of a weary series of applications for the financial relief of the Prince of Wales. Emerging with a bound from the last restraints of his minority, the heir to the throne was already well in debt, and he now greeted the approach of his twenty-first birthday with a request for an annual establishment which his father rightly found excessive. The affair was conducted with the acrimony common to the Hanoverians' dealings with their heirs, not lessened in this case by the fact that the heir was the boon companion of Fox. For a moment it really looked as if George III might try to rid himself of 'my son's Ministry'. But the matter was settled, the session ended, and Ministers could look forward to surviving the recess.

Fox appears to have suspected Pitt of working with George III on this occasion. In fact he had not, but after it was over he received a tentative, indirect approach. It seems likely that, stirred by the fracas, the King was casting round generally, for the names of Gower and Weymouth were mentioned, and Temple, recently recalled from Ireland where he had been Shelburne's Lord Lieutenant, was also

1. 'I praise her [Fortune] while she abides. If she flutter her swift wings for flight, I renounce her gifts . . . and woo honest dowerless, poverty' (Horace, *Odes*, Bk.III, 29). The occasion was the debate of 21 February.
2. As so often with a famous Parliamentary story, there is again some confusion of evidence. Wraxall, who is not reliable, states that Pitt paused deliberately, drew his handkerchief across his lips once or twice while the House watched intently, and then, striking his hand on the Table, added the last lines (*Memoirs*, III, 11–12). Wilberforce (*Private Papers*, 53) states that he had 'no recollection whatever' of this byplay, though he would never forget the impression produced by the quotation itself. Pretyman, in one of the rare personal reminiscences which he thought worthy of the dignity of history, records the immediate effect of the omission on his neighbour in the gallery (Tomline, I, 129 n.)

consulted. It is indeed from Pitt's letters to Temple that we know of the incident, for the two were now in close communication. Their attitude emerges clearly from the correspondence.

The approach was made in July by Thurlow, now also in the wilderness but personally close to the King.[1] It was guarded, but the intention was clearly to see if Pitt and his friends were prepared to make a bid for power, supposing they could count on the Crown's support. In that event, if they succeeded, how far was Pitt still committed to Parliamentary reform? The answer was unequivocal.

> I stated in general, that if the King's feelings did not point strongly to a change, it was not what we sought; but that if they did, and we could form a permanent system, consistent with our principles, and on public grounds, we should not decline it. I reminded him how much I was personally pledged to Parliamentary Reform on the principles I had publicly explained, which I should support on every seasonable occasion. I treated as out of the question any idea of measures being taken to extend influence, though such means as are fairly in the hands of Ministers would undoubtedly be to be exerted; and I said that I wished those with whom I might act, and the King (if he called upon me), to be fully apprized of the grounds on which I should necessarily proceed.

'My opinion at present', Pitt added, 'is, that though he [Thurlow] was sounding to see whether something might not be formed more on the foundation of the old politics of the Court, he will see that that is out of the question; but that such a Government may, nevertheless, be formed as will be justly much more acceptable to the King than the present. I think, therefore, what has passed will not tend to delay our having the offer whenever things are ripe for it'.[2] Temple cordially agreed, and when Pitt dined with Thurlow a few days later nothing more was heard. But it would have been surprising if he had acted otherwise at this point. It was obviously far wiser to bide his time, to keep his freedom of manœuvre, and let it be known that if he came in it would not be solely on the King's terms.

For the time was not ripe. There was no particular temptation for anyone in opposition to try to form a Government that summer. Much has been said, and was said at the time, of the iniquities of the Coalition, and certainly its appearance startled the political world. The fact that

1. On the 19th. Pitt's letter to Thurlow is almost certainly wrongly dated the 22nd from the copy published in *H.M.C., Dropmore*, I, 215–16. The copy at Chevening, which is published in Earl Stanhope, *Miscellanies, Second Series* (1872), 23–6, is dated the 20th.
2. Stanhope, *Miscellanies, Second Series*, 25–6.

it was known at once as 'the Coalition' in an age of coalitions shows that it was looked on as something extraordinary.[1] Normally, there was nothing unusual in an alliance being made by men who had recently been abusing each other. In the party system as it stood, much of the value of an effective assault lay in its use as a bargaining counter with the assaulted party. But the past few years had seen a more fundamental struggle, in which the Rockinghams, and Fox with them, had proclaimed their role to be of a different kind.[2] It was not only that the party warfare had been exceptionally violent, and Fox's language such as to make it seem really unlikely that he could combine with North. The two men had become identified, rightly or wrongly, with wholly different policies and wholly different attitudes to the throne. Their junction was bound to shock many of Fox's supporters, in and out of Parliament. It was equally bewildering to many of North's, and to many of the sympathetic independents.

All this is true, and easy to see, especially in retrospect. No one has been harder on Fox in this affair than some of the nineteenth-century liberals, to whom it was an aberration in a line of development that had still to be drawn. But the effect was not so clear-cut at the time. Indeed, when the first suprise died down the Coalition looked to be doing quite well. Politicians, like most people, soon adapt themselves to a change, and the resources available to a Government, even with a reluctant captive King, remained large as long as the leaders did not lose heart. Both North and Fox, moreover, could make a case for what they had done. North could claim to be acting not only against Shelburne's innovations, but equally as a damper on Fox; as 'the moderating party' who, by combining his superior numbers with the former Rockinghams, could best form 'a stable Government' and above all set proper limits to reform.[3] That this indeed was an interpretation which many could accept is shown by the fact that Bute, George III's faithful if obtuse 'dear friend', advised his son to vote for the Coalition under the impression that the King approved.[4] At the same time, North had his own reservations about the role of the Crown. If he had seemed to be its creature in the later stages of the American war, this was by no means to his taste. He looked on himself, and with cause, as above all a House of Commons man, he regretted his lack of control in Cabinet from which the King had appeared to benefit, and while he was personally

1. The phrase occurs in letters and newspapers in the spring and summer, before the later dramatic turn of events.

2. Fox had never gone all the way with the pure Rockingham doctrine of opposition, or at least with what Rockingham was saying in 1779 (see p. 46 above). But he was bracketed firmly with the party in the public mind. Much turned, of course, on the definition of 'private honour' in a given case (loc. cit.).

3. The quotations come from the correspondence in the previous summer of Eden and Loughborough, two of the most persuasive of North's followers in favour of such a step (*A.C.*, I. 9–10; B.M. Add. Ms 34419, ff. 92–3).

4. See *L.C.G. III*, I, no. 749. I owe this reference to Professor Christie.

reluctant to play a part again, and must have felt uneasy about the extreme conditions imposed on the King, he could not entirely object to an arrangement which depended on his mediation.[1] Fox for his part presented, and saw, the issue in simple terms. His quarrel with North had been over the war, and the war was at an end. The great object now was to get rid of Shelburne, and curb the King's swollen power as the Rockinghams had tried and failed to do. There was no other issue comparable with this. It was not betraying but crowning the struggle to secure a potent ally.

Each party could thus find grounds on which to justify its action, though some of the most substantial were scarcely complimentary to the other. Whether for such reasons or simply out of loyalty or prudence, most of the rank and file were content to follow their leaders. At the very outset there was some falling away,[2] largely from shock and confusion, perhaps also because Shelburne's Government had not yet actually gone. But the Coalition was not in serious trouble once it came in. Some influential supporters and independents were lost. Some of the attacks, Pitt's in particular, did a certain amount of damage. But when it was clear that the King was not going to risk an immediate challenge, members of the Government were confident enough. In July, Fox thought that the Coalition was gaining strength and credit, and that its only source of weakness lay in George III's dislike. In September, North's lieutenant William Adam reported that it seemed generally not unpopular, and that in Scotland it was steadily making ground. Early in November, Portland reckoned that Opposition was likely to be in a poor way. Pitt himself would go no farther in September than to say that 'the field is open'. He drew comfort from the King's refusal so far to create Government peers; but he recognised that the Ministry was not likely to be dismissed without 'some ostensible ground of complaint'.[3] None then existed. Pitt could point only to the possibility of attacks on incompetence or corruption. But in fact the requirement was about to be met. A week after Parliament reassembled Fox introduced his East India bill.

1. The less so, perhaps, since George III, hitherto so generous, was behaving unreasonably and embarrassingly over the debt for election expenses in 1780 which North had incurred on his behalf.
2. See p. 102 above.
3. To Temple, 10 September 1783 (Stanhope, *Miscellanies, Second Series,* 35).

CHAPTER VI

The Struggle for Power

I

India was a major factor in English – and Scottish – politics in the last thirty years of the eighteenth century. It raised in a unique combination some of the most important problems of the age – the nature of British power in an Eastern setting, how far mercantile, how far territorial; the character of Englishmen's dealings with native powers and native populations; the effectiveness of control by a Chartered Company founded in very different circumstances and linked uneasily to Government; the relations between Ministers and interests which they had always to handle with kid gloves. For the peculiar prominence of Indian affairs was caused by the extent to which they penetrated the fabric of English life. The Company's resources, though often mismanaged, were not only very large; they were also widely deployed, and the fortunes of its members and servants, from the nabobs and the ships' captains to the soldiers and the clerks in Bengal and Madras, affected a spreading network of families, which looked to East India House as others looked to the Treasury or the Court. The great trading companies had long stood in a special relation to Government. John Company was unique, in the range of its patronage and the semi-Governmental nature of its concerns.

These concerns were now undermining its stability. While the Company had been limited to trade and the protection of the necessary bases the system of management had worked well enough. But its increasing involvement in politics and war proved an excessive strain. By the early 1770s it was in a parlous state, virtually bankrupt, a hive of faction at home and of quarrels and corruption abroad. Only the Government, it seemed, could provide financial help; but that meant that it must be drawn, reluctantly, into reform, and over the next ten years it sought alternately to tackle and evade the issue. The scene was set by North's Regulating Act of 1773, a product of the earlier and more forceful period of his Ministry. This turned the Governor of Bengal into a Governor-General, with a Council and superintending powers over Bengal and Madras; set up a Supreme Court, appointed by the Crown over the judicial system of Bengal; gave selected Ministers the right to see political and military despatches from India; and made various regulations for the conduct of the Company's business and its servants' behaviour. It was an honest attempt, as far as it went. But in a complex situation it did not go far enough, and after a few more years of scandal – furious quarrels in Madras, Warren Hastings at odds with his Council in Bengal, their supporters manipulating the embattled interests at home – Ministers were obliged to consider fresh legislation. In 1778, a scheme of quite radical reform was drawn up by John Robinson, a leading Indian expert as well as North's patronage secretary. But the Ministry was now in no shape to face the inevitable row, North evaded the issue over the next two years, and in the summer of 1781, in the temporary lull,[1] he was content to renew the Company's Charter for ten years in return for a few modest alterations.

But affairs in India did not oblige the Ministry by standing still. While the new Act was being prepared the quarrels in Bengal were reaching a climax, Hyder Ali swept through the Carnatic, and a French fleet arrived in the East. This combination of events produced a Parliamentary explosion. In the first half of 1781 two committees came into being: the famous Select Committee of the Commons, soon to be dominated by Burke, set up to investigate the judicial system of Bengal, and the Secret Committee, of which the leading members were Charles Jenkinson and Dundas, appointed to examine the causes of the Carnatic War. Neither body confined itself to its terms of reference. Both soon strayed into the wider fields of administrative and financial reform. And between them, thanks largely to Burke's inspiration, they thrust Indian affairs inescapably to the fore, and virtually monopolised discussion of a problem which Government itself was in no position to face.

For, in the confusion following North's fall, neither Rockingham nor Shelburne had time to deal with India. The former could only grant the Company some more temporary financial help, the latter resigned before he could introduce his contemplated 'fundamental laws'.[2] But by then the means lay to hand for a comprehensive settlement, if a Ministry could be found prepared to see it through. Burke was marshalling his ideas against the background of the Select Committee, and Dundas had gone so far as to prepare a bill from his experience on the Secret Committee which, though unsuccessful, later became the model for Pitt's India Act.

By the summer of 1783 there was thus a widespread public interest, an important group of second-rank politicians with expert knowledge and strong views, and a situation which could scarcely allow of much more delay. It was in these circumstances that Fox decided, with natural apprehension, that 'the first business' of the winter session must be 'of a very delicate nature, I mean the East India business'.[3]

1. See p. 51 above.
2. See p. 89 above.
3. To the Earl of Northington, 17 July 1783 (*Memorials and Correspondence of Fox,* II, 119).

Fox had given notice of his intention before the House rose in July, and his scheme was under draft in the recess, the guiding hand being probably Burke's. Action was foreshadowed in the King's speech on 11 November, and exactly a week later the first bill was introduced. Any serious legislation on such a subject was of course bound to be controversial. The nature of Fox's settlement made it full of risk.

For, as Fox himself remarked, his main bill was 'vigorous and hazardous'.[1] It was concerned with the structure of the Company, leaving a second measure (introduced on the 26th) to deal with the structure of government in India itself. The central feature was the provision of a Board of seven Commissioners, to be nominated by Parliament and hold office for at least four years, 'who should be invested with full power to appoint and displace officers in India, and under whose control the whole government of that country should be placed'.[2] Under them would be nine[3] Assistant Commissioners, in charge of the Company's trade, who would also be nominated at first by Parliament, though subsequently by a vote of the Court of Proprietors at East India House. By this scheme, Fox was doing three things. He was removing all political and military control from the Company, reducing it to its original role of a purely commercial body. He was transferring that control not to the Crown but to a board nominated by Parliament. And he was proposing to bring the Governor-General and his Council, on whom the day-to-day rule of the Indian territories rested, more firmly under the supervision of the Commissioners at home.

The plan was not a good one, and there is little doubt that it would have worked less satisfactorily than the scheme later carried by Pitt.[4] It held no solution to the great problems of government in India itself, which could not be overcome by restricting the Governor-General's authority. It placed overriding powers in the hands of a board chosen by the Ministers of the day, but liable to survive them and come into conflict with their successors. It divided matters of government from matters of trade with a sharpness that was probably impractical. It left untouched the important question of the Crown's rights over the Indian territories. But these were not the grounds on which the main bill was most bitterly attacked, and the attack itself almost certainly did Fox an injustice. Indeed, one may well feel some sympathy with him at this crisis in his fortunes. He could have proposed a less controversial measure without immediate discredit, and avoided the worst risk of

1. Loc. cit., 171.
2. *P.R.*, XII, 42.
3. At first eight.
4. Cf. Bentham's verdict in 1790, quoted in Mary P. Mack, *Jeremy Bentham, an Odyssey of Ideas, 1748–1792* (1963), 396–7.

upsetting a Ministry which might otherwise easily have survived. He knew, and did not much relish, the dangers; and some at least of his difficulties may have arisen from an attempt to apply to a complex case the arguments of his party over the past few years. For the Rockinghams had consistently declared – and it was in accord with all their professions – that the patronage of the Company should not simply be transferred to the Crown, or its servants in India given greater powers with which to tyrannise and corrupt. The new bill was an attempt to translate these principles into practice, and if it was fallible it was not necessarily insincere. Fox can be convicted often enough of misjudgment and misconduct. His judgment was bad here: Burke could be a dangerous guide. But he was almost certainly not governed, though he was doubtless affected, by the motives of which he was to be so widely accused.

For the bill opened up an obvious and highly damaging line of attack. It placed the Company's patronage in one fell swoop in the Commissioners' hands, and so, it could be held, in those of the Administration which appointed them. Never, it could be said, had Ministers raided other people's property with such profit; never had they tried to seize such a mass of influence, under the plea that it could not be allowed to fall to the Crown. Burke and his fellows had been crying out for years about the dangers of the Indian patronage. Now they planned to take it over, by way of their nominees. Fox's defence, that his scheme on the contrary was the only way to keep such powers out of Ministers' hands, cut little ice in view of his well known attitude to the Crown; and indeed he would not have been Fox if he had not perceived the party advantage and accepted the hazard involved. One need only envisage his reaction to such a move by another party. 'If Lord North had proposed this bill', one observer rightly remarked, 'Fox would have called a meeting of his constituents and mounted the rostrum in Westminster Hall the next day'.[1]

The attack was strengthened by the secrecy in which the measure had been shrouded. For, well aware of the risks, Fox moved at first with circumspection. There were five distinct, though related, factors of which he had to take account: his allies in the Coalition, the East India Company, the House of Commons, the House of Lords, and the King. Their interaction over the next few weeks tested and threw light on the workings of the balanced constitution.

Fox's early moves went well. Rumours of his, or Burke's, intentions were abroad in the autumn, and he must have known that North and his associates felt grave doubts about what they heard. While they were informed of the principles, they were accordingly given little advance notice of the detail of the bill – as late as 15 November their friends in the Company were still trying to find out – and North himself seems at

---

1. Philip Yorke to the Earl of Hardwicke, 21 November 1783 (B.M. Add. Ms 35381, ff. 161–4). He was referring of course to North in his earlier form of existence.

this stage to have held conspicuously aloof. He did not attend the usual meeting of Government supporters on the eve of session, and he was remarkable for his absence from the House throughout the next fortnight. But when it came to the point he dared not risk a split – a sad commentary on the claims his party had earlier been making[1] – and his son seconded the first reading of the bill on the 18th. With party unity thus adequately if reluctantly secured, Fox could count on success in the Commons, particularly as he was acting at the start of the session, before many of the independent country gentlemen would be in town.[2] His reasoning was correct. Despite the hasty efforts of Opposition to whip up support, the bill passed easily through its various stages. The Coalition's majorities never fell below a hundred,[3] and on 9 December the measure was ready to go to the Lords.

Meanwhile, of course, the Company was in a ferment. All its varied, centrifugal interests were outraged in various ways. The secrecy and speed with which Fox moved prevented these feelings at first from being reflected in the Commons: of the 58 Members who may be said to have been connected with Indian and Company interests, it has been reckoned that 41 were prepared to support Government at the outset, and that only some twelve changed sides in the course of November.[4] But the manœuvre, doubtless necessary, recoiled upon its author. Fox's unprepared allies in the Company could not hope to calm the burst of fury at East India House; the Chairman of the Directors, who was among them, was forced to resign; and on 21 November a General Court set up a committee of defence.

The most notable members of the committee of nine were Governor Johnstone, the veteran Laurence Sulivan, and, most actively, Richard Atkinson: all prominent in the connexion which supported Warren Hastings and had long opposed the Rockingham Whigs. The Company's defence in fact was now firmly in the hands of what was known as the 'Old Party', which had hitherto owed Parliamentary allegiance to North and had been carefully built up for him by Robinson, Jenkinson and Dundas. The ramifications in Leadenhall Street, the names of the politicians, are generally less well known than their counterparts at Westminster. But their influence on national politics was not negligible, and at this critical moment it had one important result. For it brought to a point Robinson's growing dissatisfaction with North, and Robinson was to be a key figure over the next few weeks. His experience of Company politics was matched by his experience of Parliament: as patronage Secretary of the Treasury for twelve years, his detailed 'States' had supplied the raw material on which Ministers could act. Hitherto he had managed, with increasing misgivings, to combine his

1. P. 116 above
2. See pp. 31–2 above.
3. It was 109 on the vital second reading, and either 106 or 107 on the third.
4. C. H. Philips, *The East India Company 1784-1834* (1940), 24.

two familiar loyalties, to the King and to his leader. But when the two finally clashed, and North seemed to be jeopardising his role in Parliament and the Company, Robinson took with him to Opposition a unique fund of knowledge and expertise.

There was scarcely time to do anything about the bill in the Commons. It passed its second reading on 27 November, which was probably just about the date on which Robinson joined Jenkinson and Dundas in talks with the committee of nine. The object must therefore be to prepare the ground as fast as possible so as to influence and profit from the likely obstruction in the Lords.

For the Lords were a source of some worry to the Coalition. In numbers and debating power it was rather weak in the upper House. Opposition peers had shown something of their potential in June, when Temple and Thurlow had rallied support for Pitt's Public Offices bill.[1] They might well be more formidable now, particularly as Fox's cause lay mainly in the hands of two spokesmen, Stormont and Loughborough, who were of North's party and known to be lukewarm to the measure.[2] Above all there was the King, whose attitude was still unknown, but who, given the chance and inclination, could bring great pressure to bear on the peers. It was presumably for these reasons that Fox had earlier thought of approaching Thurlow, the former Lord Chancellor whose removal had been one of the Coalition's triumphs a few months before. But the idea could not be seriously entertained: Thurlow was too much the King's man; and all things considered Ministers were prepared to hope for the best. They expected a clear majority after their demonstration of strength in the Commons. And if they could keep up the pace, so as to deny the King any real chance of mobilising against them, they would soon be safe and in good order to face the rest of the session.

For the King had still to show his hand. So far he had said nothing, and some of the Coalition leaders later claimed that his silence had misled them. This may have been a genuine impression; or they may have been disingenuous. It was of course true that no measure of this kind could be brought before Parliament without the King's approval, and he had not objected to the mention of an East India bill in the Speech from the Throne. But given the state of his relations with his Ministers, it seems unlikely that he knew more than an outline of the plan; and he may well have been content to let it go at that. If this was so, his subsequent quiescence could not necessarily be taken for consent. In all the circumstances, it might as easily be a preparation for battle.[3]

1. Pp. 92–3 above.
2. Stormont in fact finally voted against the bill.
3. *The Annual Register* for 1784 later declared (69–70) that the Ministry could scarcely have adopted such a measure in ignorance or defiance of the King's views.

In point of fact, George III had not yet made up his mind. He was waiting attentively to see what would happen. He was certainly anxious to try to break the Government if he thought he stood a chance. But, as in the summer, he preferred the initiative to come from elsewhere,[1] and when Temple and Thurlow suggested, on 1 December, that he should acquaint the Lords with his disapproval of the bill, he showed no immediate sign of accepting their advice.[2] He needed an estimate of the Parliamentary forces before he decided to act, and a Minister in the Commons who would be prepared to see the business through.

The estimates were under way in the first days of December. While the committee of nine mobilised its forces at East India House, the small expert group of politicians began to take the Parliamentary pulse. As early as the 3rd, Atkinson thought that 'everything stands prepared for the blow if a certain person has the courage to strike it'.[3] The results were drawn up in great secrecy over the next few days. Robinson's first draft 'State' of the Commons was ready on the 6th. The canvass of the Lords seems to have been complete by the 8th. By the 9th, he was ready to present a report. In the Lords there were said to be 79 'hopeful', 66 'con', 26 'doubtful', and 42 'absent'.[4] The position in the Commons was thought to be as follows.[5]

	Pro	Hopeful	Doubtful	Contra
In the present Parliament	149	104	74	231
After an election	253	116	66	123

These papers were studied at once by Dundas, Thurlow and Pitt. They agreed as a result that there was now 'no *manly* ground of apprehension'.[6] It would be interesting to know if they had anything else to guide them to this important decision; for a forecast of the state of affairs *after* an election would seem to have been scarcely enough in

This was presumably written either by or with the approval of Burke. There were also rumours at the time that George III had favoured the bill in advance. But it seems to me highly unlikely that Fox would not have pressed the matter much farther if he could have produced any evidence, or that independent Members would not then have continued to give him stronger support throughout the ensuing crisis.

1. Cf. Pitt's view in July, p. 115 above.

2. The dated memorandum is in Buckingham, I, 288–9. Thurlow's part in it is described in Stanhope, I, 147. For peers' rights of access and advice to the sovereign see p. 44 above.

3. *H.M.C., Tenth Report, Appendix, Pt. VI*, 61. The person was presumably the King.

4. B. M. Facs. 340 (2), ff. 290–2. The document is undated. For its probable dating see *H.M.C., Tenth Report, Appendix, Pt. VI*, 61–2.

5. *Parliamentary Papers of John Robinson 1774–1784*, ed. William Thomas Laprade (1922), 55–105. For the dating, see Robinson to Jenkinson, 7 & 9 December 1783 (B.M. Add. Ms 38567, ff. 167–8, 169–70).

6. Atkinson to Robinson, 8 December (B.M. Facs. 340 (2), f. 293).

itself. It was in fact highly doubtful if an election could be held for some time. 'When gentlemen talk of a dissolution', wrote William Eden a month later, 'they are not aware of its difficulties, which at all times are great upon any Government, but which would be found quite insuperable in the present circumstances and period of the Session'.[1] It was not only that an election took some little time to prepare, particularly if it was to be held (as this was) far in advance of the conventional seven year span; nor that such a step was bound to be unpopular because of the disturbance and expense. There was also essential Parliamentary business to be completed soon. The Land Tax, and an Act to make good the financial deficiencies of the previous year, had to be passed by 5 January, and the various annual supplies and the Mutiny Act by 25 March. There was therefore no time to stage an election at once; and not much time to do so, and to take the Mutiny bill through its stages, in the interval between 5 January and 25 March, if an election had to be fitted in then. Pitt and his allies had thus to consider the likely trend of opinion in the House of Commons as it stood; and one would expect them to have called for the necessary calculation.

It should perhaps be noted at this point that there is one, not immediately contemporary, source which challenges this reconstruction of events. Many years later, William Wyndham Grenville sat down to write his memoirs. As Pitt's cousin, Temple's brother, and the close associate of both, his evidence is clearly important; and he claimed that on the eve of taking office they all believed that Parliament could be dissolved at once, and an election held. They did so, according to Grenville, because George Rose of the Treasury (Thurlow's friend)[2] had told them that there was enough money in the Exchequer for a Government to dispense with the need for immediate supplies. Indeed, this was the great difference between the spring and the winter of 1783, giving the King in the latter instance the free hand which he had earlier been denied. But 'it was the misfortune of the new Ministers', when they came in, 'to find . . . they had been deceived as to the state of the Public Treasury. It now appeared that three months must necessarily elapse, before the Parliament could be dissolved, and in that interval the annual supplies must be obtained from a House of Commons devoted to their Adversaries'.[3] This explanation, however, raises serious doubts. No one employed it until Grenville himself did so, many years later. Pitt, arguing soon afterwards against the King's wish for a dissolution, referred to the uncertainty and unpopularity of an immediate election, and said nothing to suggest that he had hoped it would

1. Quoted in *L.C.G. III*, I, xxxiii.
2. See p. 112 above.
3. 'Commentaries of my own Political Life and of Public Transactions connected with it', ch. 2; n.d., Fortescue Mss, Boconnoc, Cornwall. I am much indebted to Professor W. B. Hamilton for lending me his microfilm of this long document, which in his view was written after 1813.

take place; George III gave no sign that he had counted on the financial calculation; and no one ever seems to have pointed an angry finger at Rose. The universal and protracted silence is curious, though not inexplicable, considering how widely the crisis was discussed. But in any case Rose was not at the Treasury at the relevant time: he had left in April, after Shelburne's resignation, and he did not return until 27 December, when he was reappointed joint Secretary by Pitt. Any information that he gave was therefore unofficial. Perhaps he had told Ministers in the spring, when he had been at the Treasury, that a dissolution was impossible for financial reasons; and perhaps he gave advice in the opposite sense, from his private station, in early or mid-December. But one would have hardly thought that this last could be decisive. It was very shaky ground on which to take such a hazardous step.

There is another piece of evidence, moreover, which has to be considered. At some point in these fateful days, an estimate *was* prepared of possible trends in the existing Parliament; and it gave those who had called for it the desired result. 'If all Persons set heartily to exert themselves', there could be a working majority in the existing House of between 23 and 43 in due course. This favourable report cannot, alas, be dated exactly. It was almost certainly composed by 22 or 23 December, probably by the 17th or 18th, and perhaps by the 9th.[1] One cannot be more precise; but it is at least possible that the figures were known before Pitt took office, whether or not they affected the result.

For Pitt, of course, was the potential Minister. He had not, as it happened, shone as brightly as usual in the recent debates, or taken a line entirely helpful to the King. The other Opposition leaders appreciated at once that the obvious issue was that of patronage. But he appeared equally concerned with the purely financial aspects of the case; his attack in general seemed somewhat weak;[2] and his remarks on patronage itself were not unambiguous. There was, he observed as late as 1 December, 'a paradox' in Fox's plan: it diminished the influence of the Crown immediately in favour of Ministers, but in the end served to increase it. As one newspaper commented, this was an argument

---

1. A copy of the document (Dundas's) is in the Melville papers, in the National Library of Scotland, Ms 63B. It is given in part in Laprade, op. cit., 51–3. The fact that this paper, alone of the estimates still extant, contains a 'Recapitulation', which Robinson mentions on 9 December (see p. 124, n5 above), may suggest the earlier date. On the other hand, it gives three seats as 'vacant' which were not vacant until later in the month, though the prospect may (in two cases probably) have been known to Robinson beforehand: in one, however, (West Looe) it was possibly determined only by the death of the sitting Member on the 16th. The terminal date would seem to be set by the death, on the 21st, of the Member for St Albans, whose name is included in the list.

2. Notes, clearly for his speech on the second reading, are in P.R.O. 30/8/197. For a comment on Pitt's part in the debates, see B.M. Add. Ms 35381, ff. 180–1.

more congenial to country gentlemen than to the Court.[1] But it made no difference to Pitt's prospects: whatever doubts George III may have felt after the experience of March, there was no comparable figure in the Commons to whom he could turn. And Pitt for his part felt no hesitation about accepting, after he had been persuaded that he did not face a hopeless task. His earlier refusal had sprung from a rooted objection to placing himself in pawn to North. He had no objection to coming into office over the body of the Coalition, as long as he did not have to give pledges of his future conduct to the King. His views in fact were those he had expressed in July,[2] and there was no suggestion now of royal conditions in advance. Pitt therefore committed himself freely once he had decided to risk the odds. With his consent, the way was clear for the King to act.

Events now moved fast. On 10 December George III was informed that 'certain persons' were ready 'to receive the burthen, to which a reply was made full of assurances that he would go every length they desired him'.[3] The next day Temple had an audience, and carried away with him on a card the precious statement, which he had earlier failed to gain,[4] to the effect that 'His Majesty allowed Earl Temple to say, that whoever voted for the India Bill was not only not his friend, but would be considered by him as an enemy; and if these words were not strong enough, Earl Temple might use whatever words he might deem stronger and more to the purpose'.[5] The intention was apparently to wait a few more days, so that the secret preparations might have their fullest impact. But rumours soon spread, the King himself was talking, and on the 15th the Opposition peers carried by eight votes a motion to adjourn the debate on the bill. Two days later, they threw out the measure by a majority of nineteen. On the night of the 18th, when North and Fox showed no sign of resigning, the King sent for their Seals. The next morning Pitt kissed hands as First Lord of the Treasury and Chancellor of the Exchequer.

II

On the afternoon of 19 December, Pepper Arden – not an impressive figure at the best of times – entered the House of Commons to move a new writ for the borough of Appleby, 'in the room of the right honour-

1. *P.R.*, XII, 285; *Morning Chronicle*, 2 December.

2. See p. 115 above.

3. Atkinson to Robinson, 12 December 1783 (*H.M.C., Tenth Report, Appendix, Pt. VI*, 62).

4. See p. 124 above.

5. This is the version normally given. It comes from Buckingham, I, 285. Dr Murray S. Downs, in an unpublished paper 'The British Constitution in 1783: George III Dismisses the Coalition', quotes in full an interesting variant from B.M. Add. Ms 38716, f. 142, given, on quite good authority, at third hand.

able William Pitt, who, since his election, had accepted the places of First Commissioner of his Majesty's Board of Treasury, and Chancellor and Under Treasurer of his Majesty's Exchequer'.[1] The announcement was greeted with a shout of laughter. Such was the first reaction to the news, and to the quality of the herald.

> A sight to make surrounding nations stare;
> A Kingdom trusted to a school-boy's care.[2]

The great struggle between Pitt and Fox in the winter of 1783–4 is one of the most famous stories in English political history, and it has been told again and again. Throughout the nineteenth century the emphasis was on Pitt's astonishing courage in defying the Coalition, and his skill in destroying its majorities over the next three months. Since Robinson's papers began to be studied, some fifty years ago, the achievement has seemed less miraculous, and it has sometimes been held that the new Minister had only to stay put in order to reap the assured reward. This last verdict may be accepted, if the implications of staying put are grasped. Pitt could scarcely have taken the plunge without the comfort of Robinson's advice. But it was still a plunge. The expected result would be gained only if 'all Persons set heartily to exert themselves';[3] and the first and most demanding exertions fell on Pitt himself.

For if Governments could count on winning their elections it was because they had prepared the ground, and things could easily go wrong on this occasion if the new Ministry proved incapable. The Crown's need to work in alliance with a host of private interests made it necessary to consider their opinions as an election approached; the reluctance to displace a sitting Member, which was strong throughout the century, made it necessary to find that opinion largely in the pre-election Parliament.[4] If the Coalition managed to hold its recent majorities in the Commons – let alone if it decided as a result to bring Government business to a halt – the Crown could not easily risk the dissolution which alone could bring hope of success. Of course it had very powerful resources of place and favour on which to draw. But they were not all-embracing, they could be sensibly weakened if Ministers seemed unlikely to hold their own, and in this extraordinary state of

1. *P.R.*, XII, 450. Until 1919 a Member of Parliament had always, and until 1926 almost always, to seek re-election on accepting a permissible office of profit from the Crown.

2. *Criticisms on The Rolliad*, 21.

3. P. 126 above.

4. Robinson's detailed State in Laprade, op. cit., 66–105, shows the extent to which he relied on a change of sides by the *sitting* Members, as well as on the introduction of fresh support at the election itself. There were 163 new Members in the event, out of a House of 558. In the elections of 1774 and 1780 there were 166. Many of them were of course nominated by boroughmongers (peers and MPs) whose allegiances had to be sought in the earlier Parliament.

affairs, when the King and his late, powerful Government were openly at war, such a possibility was by no means out of the question. The two factors reacted on each other. The Crown counted on private allies to assure it electoral success. The private allies co-operated with the Crown on the assumption that it held the rewards. This was the basis, traditional, proven, on which Robinson's figures were largely built. But with the King on the defensive, and opinion so wildly disturbed, the proof this time rested heavily on the immediate course of events.

Persuasion moreover could not be confined to what Robinson called '*civility and attention*'. He had also to reckon with the less manageable sort of independent. 'Sir Edward Astley will often [be] *for* and perhaps sometimes against.' 'Sir William Middleton does not attend much, but his part is more doubtful.' 'Lord Fife . . . varies and is uncertain without explanation.'[1] Many of these men had still to appear on the scene, and their minds would be made up largely by the Ministry's bearing and presentation. Governments were generally sensitive to the current of feeling among the uncommitted Members, as much for the moral as for the immediate numerical effect. It was the more important now that the King was out to gain a clear-cut result. For George III saw the contest as personal, the third and decisive round of the battle he had been fighting for almost two years. He dreaded a situation in which, even if the Coalition could not win, Fox might yet be able to force himself into partnership with Pitt, and so bring once more into office his detestable views on the role of the Crown.[2] The King badly needed a Minister who could outface and beat the foe. The need was equally pressing for Pitt, once he was fully committed to the struggle, if he was not to depend too much on the King.

Pitt therefore took office in the knowledge that he could hope to beat the Coalition, provided he showed himself determined and capable enough to reassure the weighty forces which would then support the Crown. He had to rally a varied mass of calculation and opinion that was waiting to be convinced. His initial difficulties were clearly shown when he set about forming his Government. Temple was available; so

1. *Parliamentary Papers of John Robinson*, 69, 99. Lord Fife held an Irish peerage. These (and other) forecasts proved accurate. In the lists of supporters of Pitt and Fox, and absentees from the debates, on the back of successive editions of Dean Tucker's *The Beauties and Deformities of Fox, North, and Burke* . . . in the first quarter of 1784, Astley appears as a supporter of Pitt, Middleton and Fife as absentees.

2. George III did in fact allow Pitt to discuss the possibility of 'an accommodation' with the Coalition on 21 December, as the result of a rumour – so he was told – that Fox might not be averse (*L.C.G. III*, I, no. 3). But he was satisfied in his own mind that nothing would come of it, and indeed that the rumour was not serious.

In point of fact, the first move in this abortive business came from Pitt himself. But as he insisted that North must not be in the Cabinet, and that Fox's India bill could not be accepted as it stood, the offer might seem to have been as much an attempt to turn away the wrath of Fox's anticipated attack as a serious move for an immediate alliance, which Pitt must have guessed stood little chance (see Feiling, *The Second Tory Party*, Appendix I; and *L.C.G. III*, I, 4, n9).

was Thurlow; and the veteran Lord Gower, the leader of the former Bedford connexion, gallantly volunteered. But other men of weight were not anxious to take leading Cabinet posts. Grafton, Camden, Cornwallis, Grantham refused. Richmond would take the Ordnance, as long as he was not in the Cabinet. Pitt had even to approach and be refused by Lord Sackville, formerly the controversial Lord George German – a particularly galling introduction to the demands of office. Sydney, at first considered too weak, had to be made Home Secretary against his wish; the untried Carmarthen had to be made Foreign Secretary. At Court, the Lord Chamberlain, the Earl of Hertford, thought it prudent to decline a dukedom.

All this was bad enough. But in the midst of his efforts Pitt suffered what at the moment seemed a far worse blow. On 22 December, Temple resigned. The reason has remained obscure to this day. It was not, as used to be thought, that the King had refused him a dukedom for his services as Lord Lieutenant of Ireland; nor, almost certainly, that he wanted an immediate election which Pitt was not prepared to recommend; nor yet that he preferred to face as a private person the accusations which had been made between 15 and 18 December against his conduct in taking the King's message of the 11th.[1] If this last had been so, he would scarcely have accepted office on the 19th, unless indeed, as his brother later stated, he believed that Parliament would be dissolved at once.[2] If he really thought this was going to happen, he might have panicked when it did not. But it seems more likely that he had simply not appreciated the potential violence of the objections, and now made haste to disclaim the possible offence, and also disembarrass the new Ministry, by vacating a post so dangerously exposed.[3] The immediate effect was severe. Temple had been in the forefront of the battle. He had been entrusted with the Seals returned by North and Fox. He was the Ministry's destined Leader in the House of Lords. Small wonder that the forthright Dundas was furious – 'damned dolterheaded coward', 'uncharged blunderbuss' – or that the King never forgave this latest example of Grenville behaviour.[4] Pitt showed less distress. He sent Temple two friendly notes the next day, he continued to consult him about appointments, and his brother Chatham believed that the two men 'acted cordially together to the last'.[5] Perhaps he

1. P. 127 above.
2. P. 125 above.
3. The evidence is complicated. The two most recent surveys, which reach rather different conclusions, are by Professor Aspinall in *L.C.G. III*, I, xxvii–xxviii and 6, n2, and by Mr E. Anthony Smith in *The Historical Journal*, 6, no. 1, 91–7. Whether or not Temple was moved chiefly by a desire to help Pitt, that motive did not contradict any personal apprehension he may have felt; and it could reasonably be represented, to himself as well as to others, as the cause of his action.
4. *L.C.G. III*, I, xxvii–xxviii for Dundas; loc. cit., no. 502 for the King's unabated resentment in April 1789.
5. To Hester Countess of Chatham, 2[3] December (P.R.O. 30/8/13).

foresaw or accepted the explanation of a blessing in disguise: if there had been an unconstitutional flavour about the defeat of the India bill, Temple could be said to have purged the sin. Perhaps he was simply reluctant to quarrel with a powerful cousin who had lately been a close ally. But if Pitt did not show resentment he was nonetheless shaken. He told Pretyman that the news had kept him awake all night – 'the only event, of a public nature, which I ever knew disturb Mr. Pitt's rest, while he continued in good health' – , and though Wilberforce the next morning thought him 'nobly firm', he was in fact far from confident how the day would end.[1]

By the evening of the 23rd, however, a Cabinet had been formed. Thurlow was Lord Chancellor, Gower Lord President of the Council, the Duke of Rutland Lord Privy Seal, Lord Howe First Lord of the Admiralty, and Sydney and Carmarthen were the two Secretaries of State. It was not an impressive list. Thurlow, while far from easy as a colleague, was a formidable figure in the upper House. Gower brought experience, connexions, and some welcome prestige – Dundas indeed thought that he might well have been made First Lord of the Treasury, as Portland had been in the Coalition. But the rest were lightweights in debate and, except perhaps for Rutland, in influence, poor substitutes for the more familiar notables who had already declined. Nor was it an encouraging sign that all, except for Pitt himself, were in the Lords;[2] for while it may reasonably be calculated that no 'efficient' Cabinet of the reign had contained more than three members of the House of Commons, and although George Grenville and North had each been in Pitt's position for a time, he could have done with some show of support from Cabinet colleagues in so serious a crisis. Such strength, indeed, as Pitt could muster at first in the lower House lay in a few able or knowledgeable figures of the second rank – good men of business in management or debate, but not, at least as yet, to be admitted into Cabinet with the peers. Nor were there many of these. Pepper Arden was an undistinguished, Thurlow's protégé Lloyd Kenyon a reluctant, Law Officer. The respectable Sir George Yonge was no great help as Secretary at War. George Rose had had a brief experience under Shelburne as joint Secretary of the Treasury, but his colleague, Pitt's young friend Steele, was appointed because the Shelburnite Thomas Orde refused the post. Of the minor figures, some were by nature civil servants, and the rest – the junior lords at the Treasury and the Admiralty, where hopeful young men were apt to start – showed no particular promise. Pitt could count on only two really useful lieutenants: Dundas, now Treasurer of the Navy, and William Grenville, Paymaster of the Forces.

1. Tomline, I, 233; *Life of Wilberforce*, I, 48; Pitt to George III, 23 December 1783 (*L.C.G. III*, I, no. 4).
2. Carmarthen's was a courtesy title, as heir to the Duke of Leeds. But he sat in the Lords as Baron Osborne of Kniveton, in which title he had been called up in 1776.

Both indeed were already, as they increasingly became, something more. Henry Dundas had worked closely with Pitt over the past ten months, and had recently been the most active fartherer of his interests. Ambitious, decisive, a keen judge of form, he had soon become convinced that his future lay with the young man, and the disappointments of the spring had not led him to hedge his bet. He brought substantial political assets – respectable debating ability, an expert knowledge of Indian affairs, above all a growing Scottish interest, cultivated over a decade. But his personal qualities were perhaps more important in the long run. For Dundas had many of the attributes that Pitt needed in a second-in-command: a firm temper and ready address, robust humanity, a capacity for hard work, administrative skill. It was the habit of Pitt's early friends – notably Pretyman and Wilberforce – to deplore his influence; but this may not in fact have been as harmful as they thought. Dundas looked at things with a wordly eye: he played by the rules of a corrupt age. But he exercised his patronage carefully and sympathetically, he was not devoid of principles – he had started life with whiggish sentiments, and he had a very real appreciation of his leader's mind – and, as the experience of the war later proved, he was far from being insensitive. 'He was made', it has been well said, 'on a large manly scale',[1] and he rose to the opportunities he created for himself. His tastes were coarse by the rising evangelical standards. But they were not vicious, Pitt in any case was not ethereal, and the sessions of horseplay and drinking, the effects of which began to be noticed in the middle nineties, may well have been a necessary outlet for the younger man in a life of increasing loneliness and strain. Dundas was, as he said himself, 'a cement of political strength';[2] he was also a good and by no means an unperceptive friend. Real as his influence on Pitt became, there was never any question of their relative stations. Pitt addressed Dundas as 'dear Dundas', until he made him a peer. Dundas to the end addressed Pitt as 'my dear Sir'.

Grenville was another matter. As one of a prominent political clan he started on a higher rung of the ladder than Dundas, and potentially he had a considerable standing of his own. His talents, his very appearance, were in many ways like Pitt's. Grenville had the family aptitude for administration and finance. He had a good mind, a strong character, and his share of the family pride. He was indeed something of a caricature of his cousin – he really was as steady, as unbending, as industrious as the Prime Minister seemed to the world. Lacking any of Pitt's mercurial brilliance, his influence was perhaps the stronger. Such a character, placed in close contact with a more impressionable nature, was bound to have an effect; and so it did through a succession of posts, ending with that of Foreign Secretary. The influence was liberal in peacetime – the cousins studied Adam Smith together as young men –,

1. Feiling, *The Second Tory Party*, 169.
2. Quoted loc. cit., 170.

unyielding in war. Grenville was one of the most reliable agents of administrative and financial reform, and the strongest opponent of any idea of reconciliation with a republican France. Less sympathetic than Dundas, his effect was perhaps more telling. His was the least fissile character in the inner circle, and the fact became more obvious with time.

Three omissions from the Government are worthy of note. Robinson, Jenkinson and Shelburne did not take office. Robinson may have preferred, or agreed, to stay a private Member in his awkward situation; but neither of the other two was offered a post. Jenkinson, as a prominent King's man, might have been thought in the circumstances to be a natural candidate. But it was precisely because of the circumstances that Pitt passed him by. While the accusations of backstairs influence which had long been brought against him were generally false, he bore a reputation which at this moment would do the young reformer no good, and his appointment would strengthen an element in the Ministry which Pitt was very anxious to restrain. Thurlow was indispensable, and had to be accepted; Jenkinson was merely given assurances of 'attention' and 'regard'. Shelburne of course was quite another matter. His abilities were splendid, and Pitt owed him a great debt. But the debt had been at least partly paid over the past twelve months, and the prospective liabilities could be said to outweigh the assets. Shelburne was unpopular, he had not endeared himself recently by refusing to attend Parliament,[1] and, perhaps above all, he had proved difficult to work with. Many years later Pitt remarked that any crimes he had committed as a Minister had been paid for by his experience in Shelburne's Ministry. He was not prepared now to saddle himself with so distrusted and awkward a colleague; nor, we may guess, did he welcome the idea of a former chief in his Cabinet. 'This young man', Dundas wryly observed, 'does not choose to suffer it to be doubtfull who is the effectual Minister'.[2] The exclusion of Jenkinson and Shelburne, at their different levels, underlines Pitt's determination to show that he believed in himself.

The House, which had risen over Christmas, reassembled on 12 January. The general opinion was that Pitt could not last long. 'Depend upon it', said the Whig hostess Mrs Crewe a few days before the Christmas recess, 'it will be a mincepie administration'. 'Billy's painted galley', observed Gibbon, 'will soon sink under Charles's black collier'. 'The present Ministry not having the prospect of a long continuance', wrote the independent Benjamin Keene on 11 January, 'can hardly

1. Cf. pp. 101–2 above.
2. Quoted by Orde in a letter to Shelburne, 18 December 1783 (Lansdowne Mss, Bowood).

expect the support of persons unconnected as I am'.[1] If Robinson was satisfied that his estimates were sound, most politicians still saw a very different picture.

Fox moved confidently, almost gaily, to the attack; the more so as he had extracted from Dundas and Bankes before the recess (Pitt being temporarily excluded from the House while the new writ for Appleby was passing) assurances that the Minister did not mean to ask for an immediate dissolution. He rested his case on what one can only call the supremacy of the House of Commons. A bill, carried by a large majority of the House, had been thrown out at the King's instigation by the Lords. The King had then dismissed his Ministers, and called in others who did not enjoy the confidence of the House. Not enjoying that confidence, they were in a morally untenable position. Pitt must resign, in favour of a Government which could once more command a majority on recognisably vital issues, and even if he were to be included in a fresh arrangement, it could be only after he had thus acknowledged 'having come into office upon unconstitutional grounds, and upon such principles as were disgraceful to himself.'[2]

Fox's digust with Pitt was no pretence. It sprang from the hopes and suspicions of the past eighteenth months. From the start he had tried to win the young man to his side, and he did not abandon the prospect until the last minute. 'If Mr. Pitt could be persuaded (but I despair of it)', he wrote in September 1783, 'I am convinced if he could, he would do more real service to the country than any man ever did';[3] and when Parliament met in November, and North's support of the India bill still seemed to be in doubt, he hastened to make an offer of alliance.[4] The refusal confirmed his suspicions. Pitt's ambition matched his talents, and for all his fine talk he would not scruple to gratify it as he could. 'Scruples' to Fox by now referred always to relations with the King, and since the summer of 1782 he had suspected the young man of faint-heartedness or worse. 'They look to *you*', he had told Pitt at the time of Rockingham's death; '*without you* they cannot succeed; *with you* I know not whether they will or no'. Pitt had answered that 'they' might find themselves mistaken. But Fox was not so sure. 'I believe', he told his friends, 'they will *not* be mistaken'.[5] Events since then had gone

1. *Life of Wilberforce*, I, 48; *Reminiscences of Charles Butler Esq. of Lincolns Inn* (1822), I, 161; *L.C.G. III*, I, xxxii. Keene was not very secure in his seat for the borough of Cambridge.

2. *P.R.*, XII, 536. As far as one can tell from the reports, the case was not presented fully in these terms at the very outset. Fox then concentrated on the related issue of the right of dissolution. But I think this is a fair summary of its development by the end of January.

3. To Lord Ossory, 9 September 1783 (*Memorials and Correspondence of Fox*, II, 208).

4. This offer is quoted by Downs, loc. cit., from a letter of Temple's to Lady Temple on 15 November. It appears also in *Correspondence of King George III*, VI, no. 4520.

5. *Memorials and Correspondence of Fox*, I, 446–7. And for earlier, less pronounced, misgivings, see loc. cit., 325.

far to convince him that the same might happen again, and now he saw no further need to doubt it.

Fox was always liable to be captivated by his impressions. But there is no need to discount the fact of Pitt's ambition. Of course he was ambitious. The times were out of joint, there was much that he wanted to do, he had enormous self-confidence, he was longing to come in. Nor must one overlook the history of the past nine months. This was the fourth time he had been sounded, and the third time he had received a direct invitation. 'Three times is a lot'. He could not stay indefinitely in his tent, waiting for the field to be arranged to his liking. It was pointless to accept if there was no chance of success, on the terms he chose. But to refuse again, when there was a chance, might mean forfeiting much of the prestige and some of the best allies he had gained.

Nor were the terms now unacceptable. Pitt's Ministry at the start certainly did not enjoy the sort of backing he would have chosen. Too much perhaps has been made of the fact that it included some of North's old associates – though it is true that Pitt had seemed prepared to swallow even Germain. Gower, one of the two men most concerned, had left North's Government three years before it fell, and although Dundas had remained in office, he became increasingly critical and had thrown in his lot with Pitt since the spring of 1782. More to the point was the fact that Pitt owed a great deal to the Court. He could obviously be accused of having sold himself to the King.

> Oft may the Statesman, in St. Stephen's brave,
> Sink in St. James's to an abject slave;[1]

And it was a charge which would be pressed home if he failed to gain a much wider support. His immediate defence was that he had not acted unconstitutionally. His justification lies in the fact that he did not intend to let the forecast come true, and that he had judged the odds pretty well.

The rights and wrongs of the King's action were highly debatable: in a constitution governed by conventions this was bound to be so. But Fox undoubtedly went too far along the line he followed. The open use of pressure on the Lords was extraordinary. It stretched the prerogative to the limit. But it could be held to have been justified in the circumstances of the case. Unless the argument was to be accepted that the King had no reserved powers at all, Fox's own doctrine of a responsible Ministry surely implied that it was the responsibility of Ministers to tell the King in proper detail what their legislation contained. If, as seems likely, they failed to do so here, it is difficult to see what else George III could have done about a measure he opposed, unless he was to apply the royal veto after the bill had passed both Houses – a step which

1. *Criticisms on The Rolliad*, 23.

might have been considered more objectionable than the one he took. It could not be denied that he was free to listen to advice from outside his Ministry, although such behaviour might now be held to be exceptional. Nor could his right to dismiss and appoint his Ministers be gainsaid, except on Fox's very shaky doctrine of the rights of the House of Commons. As the veteran reformer Sir William Dolben observed, the contention that 'the Ministers must be chosen by that House and the people . . . contradicted every idea he had read of or met with relative to the British constitution'.[1] The King's action had been high-handed and unusual, to be defended on the ground that he had himself been misused. There were many, including some who opposed the East India bill, who were unhappy about it and held aloof from the new Government. But that was a different matter from accepting all the implications of Fox's version of the case.

Pitt had little difficulty in claiming to be consistent. He had always remained within the Chathamite tradition: his views on the prerogative were orthodox.[2] If he had joined the Rockingham Whigs in attacking the undue influence of the Crown, he shared Shelburne's attitude to its legitimate powers, and had denounced the extreme terms on which the Coalition demanded office. The proof of this pudding was in the eating. Seventeen years later, Pitt resigned without demur on realising that he had committed himself to a policy – Catholic emancipation – which the King refused to support.

We must not mistake Pitt's attitude. He did not leap into the lists as a champion of the Crown. His first reaction to the India bill scarcely suggests that he was immediately impressed by the constitutional dangers, and while he took the prerogative as he found it he was no fervid protector of George III. His chief concern on forming a Government was in fact to preserve his independence; and he was satisfied, from the King's need and his own self-confidence, that this could be achieved. Nor was he under an illusion as to the probable trend: on the contrary, his vision was remarkably clear. When he was asked, on his visit to France, what part of the British constitution might be expected to decay first, he answered 'the prerogative of the King, and the authority of the House of Peers'.[3] His emphasis in this respect differed from Shelburne's – indeed Shelburne and Fox, with contrasting objects, shared much the same view of the Crown's potential. Both rated it very high, and gave it a prominent place in their policies: Fox as something to be curbed, Shelburne as something to be reformed and incorporated in his general plan. Such an estimate of course was partly a product of the times. As the passions and confusion of the early eighties died down, the issue no longer seemed so acute. But Pitt in any case seems to have been less impressed; perhaps, as has been argued, he was

1. In the debate on 16 January 1784 (*P.R.*, XII, 588).
2. See p. 66 above.
3. *Life of Wilberforce*, I, 38.

less interested.[1] He advocated his reforms, when it came to the point, without particular reference to the Crown, or to any doctrine other than those of economy and efficiency. And he trusted to himself from the start to avoid compromising his position, within his conception of what that involved. He accepted the King's invitation because he wanted to come in, and because he saw no reason in principle why he should not.

The events of the next three months set the political stage for the next few years – one may almost say for the rest of the decade. Pitt and Fox are among the great opposites of our history; and to contemporaries as to posterity, their rivalry came to seem almost pre-ordained. But in point of fact their perpetual opposition was not inevitable, and more than once it seemed possible that they might be allies. Sharp and increasingly deep as their political differences were, they were no sharper and, for a long time, no deeper than those of earlier opponents who had coalesced for a while, or than those of Fox himself and North before their ill-fated junction. The result of the election of 1784 ruled out such a possibility for a time, and the great divide which preceded it had its roots in the events of the past two years. But there were moments in those years when the two men seemed to be drawing together. Fox, as we have seen, had not entirely despaired of Pitt; and Pitt was not averse to working with Fox if he could.[2] The final split was caused not so much by their mutual opposition as by the fact that each had an enemy with whom the other became allied. It was Fox's hostility to George III and Pitt's hostility to North that, with Shelburne acting as catalyst, ranged Pitt and Fox against each other.

But, this being so, the personal gulf was never bridged. For if the impression of inevitable rivalry was due partly to chance, it was also the product, as with Gladstone and Disraeli, of strongly contrasting personalities. Something no doubt may be allowed for the growth of legend. Pitt and Fox were heirs to their fathers' conflicts, and their own lifelong opposition satisfied a gladiatorial sense already aroused. The picture was heightened by the extraordinary difference in their fortunes. The fact that from 1784 Pitt was almost always in, and Fox always out of office underlined, in a sense created, their contrasting roles; and the contrast grew harsher with the growing rigour of the times. By the middle nineties, 'I believe', wrote the Duke of Leeds, Pitt's former Foreign Secretary, 'it would be very difficult to find any one quarter of the Kingdom where one or other was not by the Majority considered as nearly approaching to Perfection, and the other looked upon as entirely composed of mischievous and unconstitutional ingredients'.[3]

1. See Richard Pares, 'The Younger Pitt', in *The Historian's Business and Other Essays* (1961), 127.
2. Pp. 129 n2, 134 above.
3. B.M. Add. Ms 27916, f. 62. The paper is unsigned and undated; but it is in Leeds's hand, and may be ascribed from internal evidence to the years 1792–5.

The contrast may have been crudely drawn, but it was real enough. Pitt and Fox were in truth, as they appeared, different in kind, and the implications could be glimpsed even at this early stage. 'Two Young men', Jenkinson called them, '. . . both of great parts & great Ambition, & from their different Tempers & Characters I am afraid, irreconcilable'.[1] Fox was gregarious, easy, delightful, the darling of a wide circle. Pitt presented a chilling front to the world. Fox fascinated women. Pitt did not. Fox lived life to the full in a corrupt and glittering society. Pitt had simpler tastes and a less voracious appetite. Fox was emotional and impulsive. Pitt kept his mild emotions and his impulsive streak largely in check. Fox exploited, and fell victim to, an overpowering charm. Pitt could never have relied on such a weapon. Fox was an egoist through and through: his causes were always splendid, his failures never his fault. Pitt's lofty self-confidence could be splintered, and he was intellectually honest. Fox indulged his nature, in whatever sphere he moved. Pitt placed a greater strain on himself, serving an ideal of public conduct. Both liked gambling; but Pitt did not gamble. Both were improvident; but Pitt despised a public 'job'. Fox could dazzle men, but his political judgment was bad. Pitt was often disconcerted by men, but he grew politically circumspect. Fox was an assiduous and for long a successful party leader. Pitt was openly uninterested in his followers. The one compelled affection, the other compelled respect. Fox's was a private character, projected onto a public stage. Pitt's was essentially a public character, geared to public ends. Fox could shine, as indeed he did, in a variety of situations. Pitt was fitted peculiarly for one life and one situation, and they were those which he followed and held.

When Parliament reassembled on 12 January after the Christmas recess, Pitt's first concern was simply to hang on: to rebut the charges of unconstitutional action – somewhat easier now that Temple had gone – and to put up enough of a show to discourage Opposition from interfering with the supplies. This was his greatest anxiety, in his weak position. But in fact, as Mahon had told him, it was 'the very thing which they will not venture to do'.[2] To hamper the government of the country, by withholding the necessary financial grants, would have discredited the late Ministers in and out of doors. There were limits to opposition. This would be an unprecedented step. And in the event Fox did not take it.[3]

He did just about everything else at the start. On the first day, in a House filled to bursting and with a gallery 'holding as many persons as ever were wedged together',[4] he set out to show his strength. He inflicted

1. To Mrs Johnson, February 1784 (B.M. Add. Ms 38309, f. 88).
2. *Life of Wilberforce*, I, 49.
3. See p. 47 above.
4. *Morning Chronicle*, 13 January 1784.

two defeats on the Government in the lobbies, by majorities of 39 and 54 – the second on a motion that the King's name had been used unconstitutionally – and carried five other motions without a division. He attacked Pitt ferociously, and, more woundingly, with contempt. He stopped him from reading a royal message – normally communicated at once – until every one of Opposition's motions had been carried. And according to a later tale, he appeared on the Opposition benches in full dress, to signify that, though dismissed by the King, he was still the Minister of the House's choice.[1] Pitt appears to have been momentarily shaken by this display.[2] But his colleagues rallied round, Richmond indeed offered to join the Cabinet as a gage of support[3] – a gesture that was gladly accepted –, Pitt himself refused to seek a way out, however conveniently, by dissolution; and the fight went on. The next fortnight remained exciting, but things were never again as black as on the 12th. On the 16th Fox carried a motion that the Ministry was unconstitutional, but by the reduced majority of 21; and a week later he stopped Pitt's attempt to pass an India bill by the small majority of eight – an interesting example of the way in which Members voted according to what they thought to be the merits of the case – and gained leave, without a vote, to introduce his own measure. When the House adjourned for a few days on the 26th, Ministers were still fully conscious of the dangers, but they could reflect that at least they had survived so far.

The slightly better atmosphere was probably due to two developments. The Government had not been idle, and addresses were beginning to come in from friendly Corporations, favourable to the King and Pitt. Nor could all, perhaps even most, of them be dismissed as the result purely of manipulation: some at least reflected a genuine wave of sentiment.[4] At the same time, the independents were stirring in the House itself. Suggestions had already been made that this dangerous quarrel should be composed, and a new Ministry formed which could include the leaders of both parties. On 26 January, some 53 Members met at the St Alban's Tavern and passed a resolution to that effect; and on 2 February their chairman, Robert Grosvenor, carried a motion unanimously in the Commons that 'a firm, efficient, extended, united Administration' was to be desired.[5]

This last development was not at all to the King's liking. He wanted a victory which would keep out Fox. Pitt was not, and could not afford to be, so cavalier. He had already shown himself prepared to discuss an

1. See p. 40 above. The story is told by Sir George Cornewall Lewis in *Essays on the Administrations of Great Britain from 1783 to 1830* (1864), 70, n2. He does not give his authority.
2. Most of his biographers have denied this. But the statement by Carmarthen in *The Political Memoranda of Francis Fifth Duke of Leeds*, 94, seems to me convincing.
3. See p. 130 above.
4. E.g. the dowager Lady Spencer's remarks, quoted in *L.C.G. III*, I, xxxi–xxxii.
5. *P.R.*, XIII (1784), 27.

arrangement, on his own terms, with Fox; and he would have been ill advised to refuse to do so now. He had always sought the independents' favour; he needed it badly at this point; and when the issue was squarely presented he agreed to consider it. In any case he may have guessed what Opposition's reaction would be. For Fox, bent on victory, was still in no mood to compromise. He insisted at once that Pitt must resign, or at least step down, before a fresh arrangement could be reached; and this Pitt naturally enough refused to do. By the middle of February the talks seemed therefore to have failed. But the independents still felt strongly, and, as so often, their attitude could not be disregarded. On the 16th and 18th Fox carried two more motions, by 29 and 12, the second to postpone consideration of the supplies for the Ordnance. But he could no longer ignore the pressure for a settlement, and he now set himself to extract from it what advantage he could. While he continued to carry damaging motions against Pitt, his language was noticeably softer in debate. He offered behind the scenes to amend his India bill so as to remove some of the more objectionable features. And when Pitt amplified his position by stating, once again, that he would not serve with North, North at once announced that he would withdraw. The climate of opinion was affected by these moves. But in fact a solution was most unlikely, for neither Fox nor Pitt was prepared by now to go very far. Both were angling for the favour of the uncommitted Members rather than seeking a settlement; and it was easy enough to find insuperable objections. Fox still insisted that Pitt must first resign; and the King, now driven reluctantly to take a hand, laid down, with Pitt's agreement, that a new Ministry should be on 'a fair and equal footing'.[1] In view of the Coalition's past demands this was unlikely to be accepted; and so it proved. Although not everyone was convinced, by 1 March the negotiation had failed. Fox then carried another motion which included a demand for Pitt's dismissal, a sign that the fight was to continue as before. The episode had shown the independents' influence, and the limits to their effectiveness when trying to take the initiative themselves.[2]

The last stage of the battle was ushered in dramatically. On the evening of 28 February Pitt went down to the City to receive its Freedom, voted by an excited Common Council earlier in the month. His return was adventurous.

He was attended [wrote his brother Chatham, who was with him and Mahon in the carriage, many years later] by a great concourse of people, many of the better sort, all the way down the Strand, as well

1. Stanhope, I, Appendix, vii–viii; *L.C.G. III*, I, no. 37. Cf. this attitude with Pitt's conditions on 21 December (p. 129, n2 above).
2. See p. 31 above.

as by a considerable Mob – the Populace insisted on taking off the Horses and drawing the Coach – A Mob is never very discreet, and unfortunately they stopped outside Carlton House and began hissing, and it was with some difficulty we forced them to go on. As we proceeded up St. James's Street, there was a great Cry, and an attempt made to turn the Carriage up St. James Place to Mr. Fox's house (he then lived at Ld Northingtons) in order to break his windows and force him to light [them], but which we at last succeeded in preventing their doing. I have often thought this was a trap laid for us, for had we got up, there, into a Cul de Sac, Mr. Pitt's situation, would have been critical indeed. – This attempt brought us rather nearer in contact with Brooks, and the moment we got opposite . . . a sudden and desparate attack was made upon the Carriage . . . by a body of Chairmen armed with bludgeons, broken Chair Poles – (many of the waiters, and several of the Gentlemen among them) – They succeeded in making their way to the Carriage, and forced open the door. Several desperate blows were aimed at Mr. Pitt, and I recollect endeavouring to cover him, as well as I cou'd, in his getting out of the Carriage. Fortunately however, by the exertions of those who remained with us, and by ye timely assistance of a Party of Chairmen, and many Gentlemen from Whites, who saw his danger, we were extricated from a most unpleasant situation, and with considerable difficulty, got into some adjacent houses, . . . and from thence to White's. The Coachmen, and the Servants were much bruised, and the Carriage nearly demolished. I do not recollect having particularly seen Genl. Fitzpatrick [a crony of Fox], but I distinguished Mr. Hare, and the present Lord Crewe extremely active . . . I never went to Brooks any more, and I was never able to ascertain further what passed or what first led to the Outrage that night. . . .[1]

Fox himself could show, so the story goes, that he had not been actively involved. When he was questioned about his part, he replied that he had been in bed with his mistress Mrs Armistead, 'who was ready to prove it on oath'.[2]

Such was the atmosphere in which battle was resumed. Another three and a half weeks were to pass before Parliament was dissolved; but in point of fact Pitt had already won. With the failure of the negotiation Members had finally to choose, and the tide was now flowing against Fox. Pitt's earlier refusal to ask for a dissolution – difficult though not impossible as such an arrangement would have been – was reaping its reward. He had not, it was true, carried all the independents with him:

1. To Tomline, enclosure to letter of 4 February 1821 (Pretyman Ms 562:1821).
2. The first account I have found of this tale is in *The Olio: A Collection of . . . Anecdotes . . . by the late Francis Grose* (2nd edn. 1796) 190. It was therefore published, under the name of a celebrated antiquary, while Fox and Mrs Armistead were alive.

some, and some of the most important, ended the negotiation in sympathy with Fox. Many Members, too, were unhappy about the way in which he had defied a succession of adverse votes on major issues; a course which Pitt himself defended only because a majority in one House was straining the accepted usage of the constitution. But the whole varied weight of that usage was now making itself felt. Pitt's sticking power allowed the blend of management and opinion to come into play. The fact that the King's Minister was still there, assured of the King's support, was the indispensable condition for the Treasury's activities; and a new dimension had been added by Pitt's own performance. Starting from a posture of great weakness in a series of gruelling debates, he had held his own, virtually singlehanded, against a formidable array, and had slowly forced Fox himself, at the height of his vigour, to recognise an ultimately hopeless position. A new Parliamentary leader had clearly emerged. The political situation, as always, quickly adjusted itself to the fact.

Fox's bolt was shot at the end of the first week in March. On the 5th he carried a motion, by a majority of nine, to postpone discussion of the Mutiny bill. But as he had announced a fortnight before that he would not stop the supplies, this was merely a delaying action. His motion of the 1st[1] had been carried by only twelve votes. When he moved a similar resolution on the 8th it was carried by one. This was effectively the end. By the 16th Pitt thought 'our present situation a triumph, at least compared with what it was', and on the 19th the Cabinet held a 'very merry' dinner at the Duchess of Rutland's.[2] The supplies were now passing without any great fuss, and as soon as they were secured Pitt asked for a dissolution. The King came down to the House of Lords on the 24th, and the next day Parliament was formally dissolved.

III

Everything about this struggle seemed fated to be dramatic. Early on the morning of 24 March, a few hours before the King was due to dissolve Parliament, the Great Seal of England was stolen from the Lord Chancellor's house. The apparently opportune theft made no difference in the event. A Council was hurriedly held, the craftsmen worked through the twenty-four hours, and a temporary Seal was ready on the 25th. The affair remains a mystery; no one was brought to book. It naturally provided a further nine days' wonder – 'the sole topic of conversation among all ranks of people'[3] – and brought fresh grist to the cartoonists' mill.

For the cartoons were flying, faster perhaps than ever before or since.

1. P. 140 above.
2. Stanhope, I, 199; *H.M.C., Fourteenth Report, Appendix, Pt. I*, 81.
3. *Morning Chronicle*, 26 March 1784.

'L'Angleterre', ran a later French verdict,[1] 'est une monarchie composée, mitigée par des caricatures'; and the *genre* was already accepted by the 1780s as characteristically English, though in fact the flavouring element of personal satire had been imported quite recently from Italy, probably as a result of the Grand Tour. It reached new heights with the Coalition and the ensuing struggle. Fox said himself that Gillray's print of 'Carlo Khan' riding the Indian elephant did more harm than did anything else, and in the prodigious flow of those months a whole gallery of the new professional school – Sayers, Collings, Rowlandson, Isaac Cruikshank, William Dent – was represented and partly introduced. Their products attracted the greater attention from the spread of the printshop in the West End: the Humphreys had been there for the last few years, and Fores and Holland had just set up shop. The intense excitement of the winter gave a notable fillip to a vogue that was fast becoming a recognisable trade.

The political caricaturists drew their matter chiefly from the newspapers. Sheridan attacked Dundas on one occasion for a speech which 'might fairly be deemed hints for paragraphs and sketches for prints'.[2] The old weekly or bi- or tri-weekly news-sheet, in which domestic and foreign intelligence was sparsely scattered among the advertisements and shipping news, was being transformed by the Parliamentary reports and comments into the daily paper with a distinctive political sense. The process was still in its infancy: at the end of 1783 there were only nine daily newspapers in Great Britain,[3] all published in London, of which five were still advertising journals, and the circulation of journals of every kind, metropolitan and provincial, was in the aggregate something like one to every three hundred persons. But it was advanced enough for foreigners to note the avidity with which the debates were discussed, and for politicians to feel the effects – as Pitt's correspondence bears witness – in the stream of unsolicited advice from coffee-house readers. The newspaper and the caricature had now to be added to the pamphlet – still, to a greater extent than the others, the work of the amateur or the politician himself – as weapons in the shaping of public opinion.

As such, of course, they were ripe for influence or control. Since the invention of printing, the publicist was as familiar a figure as the politician he served, and he had his place on the Bishops' bench and in the clubs as well as in Grub Street. Every Government had its literary placemen and pensioners, some of them actively employed, and allocated a quota of Secret Service money to literary ends. Shelburne's

1. It was Charles Nodier's; quoted in M. Dorothy George, *English Political Caricature to 1792* (1959), 2, n2.
2. 12 January 1784 (*P.R.*, XII, 518).
3. And possibly one Sunday newspaper – which by an Act of Charles II was illegal. I am not sure if *The British Gazette and Sunday Monitor*, started in about 1780, was still extant.

short-lived Ministry spent some £1,800 on pamphleteers and editors, and in 1784 some £229 was paid to the well known printer Stockdale 'for various pamphlets and publications', another £200 to unnamed persons 'for the writing in the newspapers', and a further £1,000 at least seems to have gone in subsidies to the press.[1] The new Ministry may well have counted, too, on some of the caricaturists, though the great Gillray himself was not yet committed. But it was some time before Pitt was able to rival the contacts with the London daily press, in the vital matter of Parliamentary reports, which the Rockinghams bequeathed to the Foxites, and the fact worried his colleagues during the early years. 'I perfectly recollect', wrote Grenville on this topic, 'how long and how much it was the subject of complaint amongst us, that while the greatest diligence and labour was employed to give weight to all that was urged against him, justice was rarely, if ever, done to him or his cause'.[2] A reading of the newspapers that survive lends some colour to the claim.

The use of such weapons formed one aspect of the politicians' treatment of the public. In a senatorial age, public opinion had a place and a meaning which it needs a conscious effort for us to understand. The shift of interest over the centuries as the issues changed, away from the Just Prince and the Sovereign People to the Balanced Constitution, had removed the role of the final authority rather to the edge of the stage. No one now was much concerned with the people as such, except in relation to the Parliamentary equipoise, and when Parliamentarians had to consider the problem they were uncertain what to say. There was a general feeling that the public will was not to be resisted in the last resort. But there was an equally strong, almost a mystical, feeling that this will was most truly expressed by Parliament, where the popular interest was best interpreted by its natural leaders and balanced in conjunction with those of the aristocracy and the Crown. North and Burke, while still opposed to each other, were at one in deploring formal pressures from the constituencies, except where those were fostered by the Parliamentary forces themselves; and one of Fox's greatest difficulties in 1784 was to reconcile his earlier championship of the people, in the popular assemblies at Westminster Hall, with his more recent defence of the Commons as the sole palladium of their liberties.

The validity of such doctrine depended on how the political public was defined. Most public men would have agreed with a use of the adjective going back to the sixteenth century: something to be 'enjoyed, shared, or competed for, by all persons legally or properly qualified'.[3] The qualifications were those of religion and property; and if there was a growing dispute about their limits, and a movement to extend them,

1. A. Aspinall, *Politics and the Press c.1780–1850* (1949), 67, 68, 153, 163.
2. To Tomline, 26 March 1818 ('Pitt Papers: Autograph Letters from Colleagues &c, II'; Stanhope Mss).
3. So *O.E.D.*, giving examples 'as in . . . *public worship, public school*'.

'Master Billy's Return from Grocer Hall'. *March 1784*

King George III *by Allan Ramsay*

this was because it was argued that the newcomers would conform to existing standards, not generally because it was thought that the standards should be changed. The public in fact was the political nation, 'the well-informed and weighty parts of the community', whose numbers Burke in the nineties put at 400,000 – something under five per cent of the probable population of England, Scotland and Wales.[1] It was entirely distinct from, indeed to be contrasted with, the crowd. 'John Bull in a crowd', said 'Memory' Woodfall, 'is always John Bull in a mob';[2] and the mob had no right to a place in the framing of opinion.

But if this was the public which the politicians would have liked, and were normally content to address, it was not exactly what they got at elections. The anomalies and distortions of an ancient franchise produced an electorate in which the antiquarian could rejoice, but which in its haphazard diversity – forty-shilling freeholders in the counties, 'pot-wallopers', 'scot and lot' men, holders of burgage tenures, freemen of Corporations in the boroughs – yielded to no coherent explanation. The 'vulgar' were often let in, the 'well-informed and weighty' kept out. The result seemed to many to have a certain craggy charm; it was a feature of old England that should not be disturbed. It was also said to play a valuable part in the general scheme: 'time was its parent, silence was its nurse',[3] there was much unconscious wisdom stored in their keeping, a reasonable system must take account of its irrational elements. 'Dead forms were made to serve live forces'.[4] The process obliged the political class to use all the weapons at its command – outright possession or an agreed division of the votes where possible; propaganda, threats, bribes, the bread and circuses of the elections where not. It also encouraged an unreformed assembly, already concerned more with a balance of interests than a counting of heads, to defend itself on the ground of 'virtual' or 'indirect' representation.

In an age when sectional interests were strong and national issues fairly rare, it was at least true that the pressures on Parliament were themselves usually indirect. Opinion was brought to bear far more often through the normal contacts of a peer or a Member with his neighbours or associates than by the occasional petition or election. In

1. The quotation is from Lord Brougham (Arthur Aspinall, *Lord Brougham and the Whig Party* (1939), 82); Burke's estimate (which included Scotland) occurs in his *First Letter on a Regicide Peace* (1796), in *Works*, VIII, 140. 'This', he asserted, 'is the British publick' (loc. cit., 141). The same figure, as Professor Christie reminds me, had been given over twenty years earlier by James Burgh in his *Political Disquisitions*, I (1774), 36–8.

2. Quoted Aspinall, *Politics and the Press*, 37. He was in fact referring to his colleagues, the Parliamentary reporters.

3. Gladstone's tribtue to the unreformed system, in *Gleanings of Past Years*, I (1887), 134.

4. Sir Lewis Namier, *The Structure of Politics at the Accession of George III* (2nd edn. 1957), 63.

that sense, the Parliamentarians really did pay heed to the interests they reflected or served; it was indeed a defence of the rotten borough down to the time of Gladstone that it furnished the surest means of leavening the mass with unrepresentative men of ability or promise. But, by the same token, Members did not like to think of themselves merely as delegates. 'They were not sent there', said North in 1784, '. . . to represent a particular province or district' – or, he might have added, trade; '. . . they were sent there as trustees, to act for the benefit and advantage of the whole Kingdom'.[1] The old medieval conception of the Commons as a meeting of the shires and boroughs still held good; but when Members met, they formed the *'deliberative assembly* of *one* nation'.[2]

Changes of sentiment or allegiance were therefore normally signalled in the course of a session, rather than on the infrequent occasions when a Parliament came to an end. The general election of 1784 has often been regarded as exceptional, even epoch-making, because for once it enshrined a genuine statement of the public will. Certainly the nature of the Government's success at the polls had not been foreseen. The King's Ministers, of course, were as always bound to get a working majority; otherwise an election would not have been held so far in advance of the statutory date. But the quality of the victory came as a shock. So did its size, to the Opposition leaders. At the end of March, Portland was talking of a party of about 200 in the new House of Commons facing some 250 Ministerial supporters; and Eden thought that the first figure was on the low side. Such a forecast, counting steady friends only, might perhaps have been accepted two months before, though Robinson would have disagreed. By now it was definitely out of date. Even so, everyone was surprised when the results came in. 'So complete a rout', remarked *The Annual Register*, a publication still connected with Burke, '. . . . is scarcely to be credited'. 'The Election', noted Carmarthen,[3] 'went far more favourably to Government than its most sanguine friends could have imagined'. 'We are more successful everywhere, with only a very few exceptions', wrote Pitt, 'than can be imagined'. 'It exceeds all expectation', cried Robinson himself.[4]

Some of these reactions need some explaining, for the incoming Ministers had been led at the start to expect an even bigger victory than that which they gained. In December 1783, Robinson had forecast a majority of 180 after an election, taking the sum of 'pros' and 'hopefuls'

1. 16 June, 1784 (*P.R.*, XV (1784), 195).
2. Burke's *Speech to the Electors of Bristol* (1774), in *Works*, III, 20.
3. See p. 131 above.
4. The quotation from Pitt may be found in *Private Papers of Wilberforce*, 6–8; the others in Mrs Eric George, 'Fox's Martyrs; The General Election of 1784' (*Trans. R.H.S.*, 4th Series, XXI, 166–7).

against that of 'doubtfuls' and 'cons'.[1] In the event, Government could count on a normal majority of about 120 in a full House.[2] Why then did Robinson and those he served greet the results so enthusiastically?

Because of the ways in which they were achieved. Closely knit societies are always sensitive to the differences within their ranks; the more solidly confident the establishment, the subtler and stronger its distinctions become. Just as there was a vast difference between an English duke and the 'shabbier' sort of Irish peer,[3] or between a landed country gentleman and the shadier sort of dependent Member, so there was a hierarchy of constituencies, generally accepted and broadly marked. Governments could do a great deal to manipulate majorities; but moral success turned on the response or the fortunes of men who mattered, either on their own account or because of the nature of their seats. It was the unexpected defeat of some of the most prominent and respectable Foxites, and the marked swing of opinion among the more respectable and significant constituencies, that were responsible for Ministers' delight.

For while Robinson's overall forecast was proved optimistic, a more important failure was the extent to which his proportions and his details were wrong. He expected too much of the English close boroughs, Scotland and Wales – the constituencies where Government influence could most obviously be brought to bear. He had not expected enough of the counties and some of the open boroughs, where Government influence was traditionally more uncertain. The most unexpected success, indeed, came from the counties, where the figures were 48 for Government, 29 against, and 3 doubtful, compared with Robinson's estimate (taking 'pros' and 'hopefuls' against 'doubtfuls' and 'cons') of 40 versus 40. In the open boroughs (as defined by him) Government did much as he had forecast in the aggregate – 125 against 96, with 11 doubtful, compared with an estimate of 138 versus 94 – but sometimes better than expected in the most significant constituencies, those of the London area and the larger provincial boroughs. In the close boroughs (on the same definition) he proved far too optimistic: the result was 109 to 61, with 7 doubtful, compared with an estimate of 131 to 46. Wales was worse – 9 to 12, with 3 doubtful, compared with an estimate of 18 to 6; and Scotland, too, was very disappointing – 24 to 15, with 6 doubtful, against an estimate of 42 to 3. The forecast in short – and it was made by the best informed expert of the day – had two great shortcomings. It underrated the consistency of party feeling, as expressed in the close constituencies under the control of Coalition men who failed to turn; and it took no account of the strength of opinion in the more open constituencies, where the swing to Government was,

1. P. 124 above. And he had remarked then that his figures were conservative.
2. This figure, taken from *H. of P.*, I, 89, is perhaps conservative.
3. 'Ld Strangford is a very poor and a very *shabby* Peer' (Duke of Portland to Fox, 28 April 1782; B.M. Add. Ms 47561).

irregularly, marked. Perhaps the most significant figures of all were those for the most respectable plus the largest constituencies – the English counties, and the boroughs with over a thousand voters apiece. Government ended with 90 such seats against 53, and 3 doubtful. At the election of 1780, North's Ministry ended with 35 against 111.[1]

The general picture, moreover, was heightened by a number of dramatic gains. 'Fox's Martyrs'[2] included a number of well known figures, some of them defeated surprisingly and unambiguously. Lord John Cavendish, Coke of Norfolk, Lord Sheffield, 'Poodle' Byng, Sir Thomas Bunbury, Sir Robert Clayton – these were among the victims, and the fact was sometimes scarcely credible. Coke in Norfolk, Bunbury in Suffolk, had attained a local command which only a quite exceptional upheaval would overturn. Others were ejected from seats enjoying a special prestige. 'Yorkshire and Middlesex', Fox used to say, 'between them make all England';[3] and here was Byng out of Middlesex and Lord John Cavendish out of York. Nor were they solitary cases: both these regions, so largely hostile to Government four years before, were now ranged almost solidly behind it. Wilberforce's success for the county in Yorkshire was an equally telling blow, and Fox's famous triumph at Westminster was in fact one of the Coalition's only two victories in the London area. Results of this sort were of course not typical of the whole; the bulk of Fox's Martyrs might better be described as martyrs for North, for they were removed largely from boroughs in which the Treasury had placed them at earlier elections. But typical or not, they underlined a trend which could be observed elsewhere, and in a highly personal system of politics they were important in their own right.

All these signs meant a great deal to men at the time. They must not be taken out of their context by us. The occasion may have been exceptional, but an exception implies a rule, and the election of 1784 had all the ingredients of the ordinary pre-Reform election. If we acknowledge a distinction between 'open' and 'close' seats, we must not press it too far. It was a matter of degree, and at neither end of the scale did opinion necessarily have free play. The openness of an open constituency consisted in an opportunity for manœuvre by major interests, formed along the usual lines and wielding the usual pressures and inducements. Nor were there enough open constituencies, in any case, to decide the result on their own. There was all the usual management, which as always was the basis of success; despite all the exceptions, Members were chosen very largely for reasons that had nothing to do

1. All these figures are taken from *H. of P.*, I, 91–3. Variants may be found elsewhere, but the emphasis is clear. 'Support' and 'opposition' are of course general terms, denoting the normal, not necessarily the invariable, attitudes of Members.

2. The name, taken from Foxe's 'Book of Martyrs', given to the Coalition men who did not reappear in the next Parliament.

3. *Life of Wilberforce*, II, 133.

with national politics; a national issue, as always, was refracted through personal and local interests. Only a series of regional and special studies would show us the true variety and proportions of this blend, and only one such study has yet been made in depth.[1] But we know enough to see all the familiar processes at work, and to realise that when the politicians assessed the results they did so on a situation unlike our own. Opinion could be expressed only in certain cases, and then often in ways that seem to us indirect. The election itself, indeed, might not always be the decisive feature. There were no more contested polls, broadly speaking, than usual – only 83 out of a possible 314. But opinion had in fact often been earlier brought to bear, when a candidate withdrew, or even did not stand, for lack of support. On this occasion, too, the issue might have been fought out over the question of the constituency's loyal address, a feature of the struggle since mid-January which was exceptional in scale.[2] By the end of March, more than two hundred addresses had been sent in to the King, all but a handful hostile to the Coalition, and the election sometimes merely confirmed the result of this earlier test of strength. In other cases, attention might fasten on the degree to which politics could invade, without upsetting, normal non-political practices: on the way, for instance, in which they might affect the choice from a list of potential candidates drawn up on local and personal grounds. Or it might be a question of inducing electors to spare one vote for politics in a constituency returning two Members. The assessment of opinion depended as always on the sum of hundreds of special cases, which this time seemed to add up to an unusual result. Historians must necessarily point the similarities between this and other elections of the age: contemporaries were impressed by the marginal but cumulatively decisive differences. The ordinary processes were responding, in their own way, to an extraordinary occasion. 'Within the limits of the system, a mandate could scarcely have been more emphatic'.[3]

The blend of personal and political pressures was shown in Pitt's own election, as a Burgess for Cambridge University. As was not uncommon, particularly for prominent politicians, he was put up for other seats as well: for the City of London, which he declined, and for Bath, where he allowed his name to go forward, presumably as a hedge, but which he did not visit and where in the event he came third and last on the poll of 58 votes. But the University was his goal. It had been the earliest object of his ambition,[4] and now more than ever it was the sort of seat he thought suitable for himself. He set out for Cambridge on 25 March for a quick canvass.

1. N. C. Phillips, *Yorkshire & English National Politics 1783–1784* (1961).
2. See p. 139 above.
3. Mrs Eric George, loc. cit., 167.
4. See p. 24 above.

The prospects at first seemed uncertain. 'There will be a notable Bustle in the Varsity', wrote Lord Hardwicke, who knew of what he spoke,[1] and the University politicians had in fact been at work for some weeks. By the time Pitt arrived, many engagements had been entered into. The sitting Members, the Foxites James Mansfield and John Townshend, were standing again and of course were well known, and Pitt's friend Euston could count on much support from his own large college of Trinity, as well as some from the fact that he was heir to the Chancellor of the University. But the presence of the Minister himself, though brief, soon had its effect. His own college of Pembroke was a solid base – he collected a vote from every resident and all but three of its non-resident graduates – and his calls on dons elsewhere were naturally in the main well received. 'His appearance', wrote the senior tutor at Pembroke, '. . . did immense service',[2] and within a few days his managers were reaping the rewards. Even by the 28th Pretyman thought that he might conceivably head the poll, and while opinion generally was that 'it will be a very near struggle', it was clear that Pitt was 'gaining ground daily'.[3] Sentiment divided to some extent by colleges: Pembroke, Clare, Corpus Christi, Caius, Trinity, Trinity Hall, Magdalene, Emmanuel were strongly for Pitt and Euston, King's and St John's more for Mansfield and Townshend. But other colleges followed no marked line, and many electors opted for a combination of political opponents. Thus the Provost of King's chose Mansfield and Pitt, over twenty of the voters from Trinity chose Euston and Townshend, Dr Glynn, who had looked after Pitt in his illness at Pembroke, coupled his name with Mansfield's. One graduate, already engaged to Mansfield and Townshend, promised to support whomever Pitt advised in the county.[4] There was a fairly typical cross-section of individual and party interest, affected of course by the fact that the Minister personally had intervened. When the poll was held on 3 April Pitt was at its head with 359 votes, Euston followed with 309, and the two former Members joined Fox's Martyrs, Townshend with 281 votes, Mansfield with 185. It was a triumph for Pitt, after his failure three and a half years before. He remained a Member for the University for the rest of his life.

'The influence of the Crown', the historian William Belsham stated in the 1790s, 'being now combined with the inclination and independent interest of the country, at the general election' of 1784 'the effect

1. To Charles Philip Yorke, 30 March 1784 (B.M. Add. Ms 35382, f. 44v).
2. J. T[urner] to Pretyman, [27 March 1784] (P.R.O. 30/8/315).
3. Yorke to Lord Hardwicke, 29 March 1784 (B.M. Add. Ms 35382, f. 43).
4. John Beverley, M.A., *The Poll for the Election . . . for the University of Cambridge, on Saturday, 3d April, 1784* (?1784); C. Garrick to Pitt, 29 March 1784 (P.R.O. 30/8/315).

produced was prodigious'.[1] If this verdict was correct – and I think
most authorities today would judge that it was – there is perhaps little
point in trying to assess the relative importance of the different contributions. Their effect rose precisely from their combination. Various
explanations were given at the time to help account for Government's
success, most – though not quite all – doubtless correct as far as they
went. Treasury money of course was spent, as well as money raised
from well affected individuals. But the amount seems to have been less
than North's Ministry, for instance, had spent on the election of 1780 –
and as usual a good deal was laid out in vain.[2] The Crown also drew
as usual on its patronage and favour: two of the four peers created at
Pitt's request in January 1784 were borough owners, as were four of the
ten created or promoted after the election, in May 1784. But again
these numbers were not out of the way. While Pitt made ample use of
'such means as are fairly in the hands of Ministers',[3] he did no more than
was customary, and in some respects perhaps a little less.

This, however, it might be argued, was because the Treasury could
count on a powerful financial ally. The gold of the East India Company
was said to have been spent freely in a cause so vital to its fortunes. In
fact, the amounts seem not to have been exceptional, and much of the
effect was gained more by skill than by wealth. The Company's most
telling contribution to the campaign was its use of the press, an art in
which Warren Hastings's defenders had been adept for some years; and
while of course subsidies were provided, much of the most effective
writing was done without pay by the Governor-General's friends. The
Company also published a pamphlet in its defence, it circularised other
Corporations – 'Our Charter is at stake: Look to Your Own' –, and as
usual there were sympathetic nabobs standing for Parliamentary seats.
All these activities were normal, and certainly played their part. But
they were not such as to account in themselves for the nature of the
result.[4]

It is in fact very difficult in this case to distinguish exactly between
subsidised and voluntary expressions of opinion. The struggle arising
from the East India Bill was 'one of that kind which holds no middle
place in the political system',[5] and attitudes were genuinely held as well
as skilfully exploited. Both the King and Pitt were borne along on a wave
of public approval, and each in his own way could feel strengthened
thereby. The King could claim, in a very personal sense, to have been
vindicated in his actions, and to have proved the moral and material

1. *Memoirs of the Reign of George III* . . ., III (1795), 357.
2. Some £9,200, for instance, to keep Fox out of Westminster, and £2,000 to keep
Sawbridge out of London. For details here and in the rest of this paragraph, see
H. of P., I, 95, which modifies the impression conveyed by *L.C.G. III*, I, xxxv.
3. P. 115 above.
4. See Lucy S. Sutherland, *The East India Company in Eighteenth-Century Politics*
(1952), 411–13.
5. *A Review of the Principal Proceedings of the Parliament of 1784*, 1.

strength of the Crown. Without its steady support, its active influence, Pitt could not have survived and won. His Parliamentary success had been gained in defence of the royal prerogative, his electoral triumph could not have been achieved except in alliance with the throne. But if the King was necessary to the Minister, the Minister was valuable to the King. It was no accident that the turning point in George III's fortunes came with his choice of Pitt; and it was a choice which Pitt's own talents and standing had virtually dictated. After many misadventures, the Crown was associated with a Minister in whom the public placed high hopes; with the 'perfectly new ground' which Dundas had been seeking, with the promise of reforming efficiency which Shelburne had less happily held out. Pitt brought a fresh face, a breath of fresh air, to a stale and heated scene. He was acceptable alike to many of those who looked for a programme of reform, and to those who thought that the attacks on the Crown had gone too far. He came at the right moment, and struck just the right note.

One of his greatest assets, in that acceptance world, was his disdain of a 'job'. He had given a widely quoted example in the past few months. A sinecure post, the Clerkship of the Pells, had become vacant in January. It was worth £3,000 a year, and it fell within Pitt's gift. There was no reason, by all the precedents, why he should not take it for himself, and in view of his poverty his friends urged him to do so. Instead he gave it to the veteran Shelburnite Barré, in place of a comparable pension bestowed on that Member by the Economical Reformer Rockingham. The action was unexpected, effective, and unforced. The country was saved a pension, the Rockinghamites' – the Foxites' – professions were dealt a further shrewd blow, a man with a small private income for once refused to profit from public funds. The Coalition were naturally infuriated by what they saw as a morally extravagant gesture; and of course it was meant to be exactly that. Pitt knew the value of what he was doing. But he need not have done it, very few would have blamed him if he had not, and this was a striking way of showing that he stood to lose by what he professed. The sacrifice may not perhaps have been as great as it seemed to others, for Pitt did not care about money, and he may even have been relieved to act as he wished in a matter affecting no one but himself. But it was a sacrifice which was not to be dismissed, and it came as a welcome change. 'Sir', said Barré himself to Pretyman, 'it is the act of a man, who feels that he stands upon a high eminence, in the eyes of that country, which he is destined to govern'.[1] There was something in Pitt that made the gesture carry conviction and weight.

The election confirmed his belief that he had the country behind him; that he did not owe his position solely to the King. He was disposed to feel that in any case – it was in his nature – and the feeling could not always be translated into practical terms in the daily work of

1. Tomline, I, 254.

government and handling the House. But it was something which counted in Pitt's approach to that work, and to George III. Many years later, when he was out of office and there was a question of his return, he announced that he would wait for public opinion to declare itself. The objection was raised that it could not do so, 'quite alone and unaided'. ' "Yes", said he, "often in a way not only unknown, but in a manner as if it had no concerted beginning" '.[1] He was drawing by then on a long experience, but perhaps most vividly on that of 1784, when the election crowned the struggle which opened a Ministry of seventeen years.

1. *Diaries and Correspondence of Malmesbury*, IV, 112–13.

Part Two

CHAPTER VII

Ends and Means

I

Minister taking office at the end of 1783 was faced, almost wherever he looked, with the consequences of the American War. Thanks to Shelburne's skilled negotiation aided by some belated military and naval success, the terms of peace were not as severe as might have been expected. We surrendered Trincomalee and our claims to Minorca, both strategically important places. Otherwise the territorial loss was not pronounced outside the American colonies themselves.[1] The armed forces were at a low ebb, and the country had suffered a shock after the glories of the Seven Years' War. Our finances were disordered, we were diplomatically weak, and it would take some skill and a little time to regain our influence in Europe. But the balance had been tilted before without lasting effect, as we now had cause to know. France, Spain and Holland had suffered a strain equal to our own. Given normal conditions, the wound might not have gone very deep.

But were the conditions normal? Men at the time were not sure. In the first place, they were badly frightened by the unprecedented growth of the National Debt. At the start of the Seven Years' War this had been under £75 million: at the end it had almost doubled, to over £134 million in 1764. But after ten years of peace there had been a slight reduction, to under £128 million in 1774. Now, ten years later again, the figure stood at just under £243 million. It was mortifying to reflect this this enormous rise had been caused by an unsuccessful war. It was terrifying, for a generation which believed that a national debt of such size should be paid off, to think that the sum had been more than trebled in under thirty years. The voices which had earlier been raised to defend a permanent deficit, as 'one great branch of solid property'[2] which public investment could safely support, were now stifled by its headlong growth, and the no less alarming growth of the annual charge. It was one thing to accept a debt costing some £2 million a year out of an income of some £7 million, or later some £4 million out of an income of £10 or £11 million; quite another to be faced by an

1. Pp. 93–4 above. The definitive treaties with the United States, France and Spain were signed in September 1783; that with Holland only in May 1784. But the terms followed those of the preliminaries negotiated by Shelburne.
2. Sir James Steuart, *An Inquiry into the Principles of Political Oeconomy* (1767), II, 447.

annual charge of over £8 million out of an income which had risen only to between £12 and £13 million.[1] There was a very real fear of national bankruptcy by the end of the war, and the rising school of liberal economists took it perhaps more seriously than anyone else. Looking back on that time from the vantage of some forty years, William Grenville remarked that 'the nation gave way . . . to an almost universal panic on this subject'.[2]

The general fear was matched by a general agreement on the form of a remedy. The answer, if there was one, must lie in a sinking fund, from which the deficit could gradually be redeemed. Such a fund had indeed existed ever since Walpole's day; but it had had a chequered history, and would have to be placed on a new footing. Various schemes were advanced, naturally differing from each other. But all rested on the same postulates and raised the same implications. A sinking fund required an annual surplus from revenue. A surplus required economy in government and, still more, a higher yield from taxes. Effective taxes required a healthy economy. A healthy economy, for Britain, rested largely on overseas trade.[3]

But how should Britain adjust its trade to the fact of the American revolution? Commerce had fared badly in the course of the war. The country remained adequately stocked in most respects, though the volume and pattern of imports were disturbed; but sales abroad were harder hit. During the Seven Years' War, the official total value of British exports and re-exports had risen in the best years by a quarter above the immediate pre-war figure, and never dropped below it. Between 1775 and 1782 their value dropped in the worst years by a third below the immediate pre-war figure, and never rose above it.[4] This last movement, moreover, contained a far more serious decline in some of the most important markets in the western Atlantic. Throughout the century this area had been steadily taking a higher proportion of British exports, while continuing to provide a preferential source of supply. Europe's share had been falling, the western colonies' rising, in the commercial graph. The Colonial System was embracing an increasingly large amount of British trade. And now the loss of the American colonies 'had split the single cloth from which the old colonial policy had been made'.[5]

1. B. R. Mitchell & Phyllis Deane, *Abstract of British Historical Statistics* (1962), ch. XIV, tables 1, 2, 5; J. E. D. Binney, *British Public Finance and Administration 1774–1792* (1958), Appendices I, II.

2. Lord Grenville, *Essay on the Supposed Advantages of a Sinking Fund* (1821), 19.

3. How largely is disputable. Perhaps a third to a fifth of Britain's manufactures now left the country. But this of course was only part of the story. The repercussions of overseas trade were widespread, and the economy was attuned to them.

4. Phyllis Deane & W. A. Cole, *British Economic Growth 1688–1959: Trends and Structure* (1962), table 85. Chapter II and Appendix I of this work discuss the figures' serious limitations. See also Mitchell & Deane, op. cit., ch. XI, table 10.

5. W. R. Brock, *The Effect of the Loss of the American Colonies upon British Policy* (Historical Association, 1957), 4.

A major upset of this sort was bound to provoke a major debate. Opinion was sharply divided. For a decade and more, there had been rising doubts about the value of the Colonial System as it stood, and particularly about its application to the American territories. Josiah Tucker, Richard Price, James Anderson – the Aberdonian economist to whom Pitt later entrusted a survey of the British fisheries –, Adam Smith himself, voiced the growing impatience with the burdens of protection, and the growing confidence in British manufactures to find their own best outlets. Why export our reserves of labour, and foster their semi-independent growth? Why restrict and distort our vast trading potential in an outmoded cause? Overseas possessions were expensive, and their communities would respond to their own needs. Let the economic laws, wherever possible, respect the free play of our economic strength. When Adam Smith wrote at the end of the war that he felt 'little anxiety about what becomes of the American commerce',[1] he was basing his confidence on the prospect of better markets elsewhere.

Such views were not unrepresentative. But the combination was new, and unproved. The average Member of Parliament had some grounds for shrinking from a radical change of system, even when the issue was restricted to the commercial argument alone. Adam Smith hoped that, under a freer trade, we would gain more in Europe than we lost in America. But how could we be sure on the eve of fresh talks with France and Spain, when they (and possibly others) would try to strike a fresh – and perhaps illiberal – bargain?[2] European industry was in competition to our own; and the virgin markets of Africa and, more particularly, the East, undoubtedly hopeful though they were, could not be counted on immediately to redress a balance that might be badly upset. Nor could an exchange of goods with the former colonies be considered on its own. The United States might perhaps prove good customers under a freer system; but would they agree to such a system unless the freedom was extended to the carrying trade, to 'navigation'? This raised problems which were thought to strike at the heart of British wealth and power. What would happen, in the first place, to our protected access to the West Indian trade, one of the pillars of Atlantic prosperity? What would happen, beyond that, to the whole structure of British shipping, which had always been taken as the basis of a profitable exchange of goods? It was only recently that the economists had begun to lay greater stress on the value of freight as an item in the ledger. But the economic merits of protection were debatable here as elsewhere, and they were not the most important point. The crux of the matter lay in the need to protect the supply of the ships themselves, and the men.

For the greatest threat raised by the loss of the American colonies was the threat to our maritime strength. Our shield was the navy, and the

1. To William Eden, 15 December 1783 (*A.C.*, I, 65).
2. See pp. 95, 96 above.

navy needed a thriving marine. Private ships were valuable for wartime privateering – as Paul Jones had recently shown; a large pool of skilled seamen was vital to an enlarged wartime fleet. The British Atlantic community had formed a single unit. The products of Portsmouth, New Hampshire, and Plymouth, Massachusetts, were as fine as those of the Channel ports; the fisheries of Newfoundland and the Banks were – or were thought to be – the nurseries of blue-water men. The former colonies were now not only our rivals in the carrying trade: their loss had robbed our naval power of one element of its strength. It was more necessary than ever to safeguard what remained. To abandon the system of protection might conceivably give us 'a country of opulent merchants for a time'. But 'we should find ourselves, like the Dutch, rich perhaps, as individuals, but weak, as a State'.[1]

This was the point of intersection between the demands of power and those of wealth. It lay at the centre of the politicians' and pamphleteers' debate. It was a focus for a wider feeling of unease. For 'the great business of America'[2] covered a large field. How would the successful revolt affect the rest of the Old Empire? How would change in the Empire affect England herself? George III had warned that if the American colonies were lost the West Indies and Ireland would follow; and the last part of his prophecy had seemed all too likely for a time. As it was, the commercial system had had to be altered; the spectre of independence had been raised; the Irish question had been thrust inescapably to the fore. Its violent persistence was mercifully hidden in the future. But the pressure was immediate, and the shadow had been cast. 'The Constitution of Great Britain is sufficient to pervade the whole world'.[3] Now that the panacea had been challenged by so many of the recipients, it could not but be questioned, if only for reassurance, at home. The colonial upheaval forced men to take sides, 'to turn their eyes inwards',[4] as no purely foreign war was likely to do. It jolted the national pride, and the national system. It underlined and revealed defects in administration. It pointed the weakness of Government finance, and the uncertain assumptions for trade. It saw the biggest political fight since the days of Queen Anne. It stirred a normally somnolent public to unusual reflections and demands. Not all the problems, of course, were brought into being by the war; many of them existed already, or were latent, and would doubtless have grown in other ways, at a different pace. But the experience was a stimulant where it was not a cause. It sharpened the self-consciousness of a

1. John Lord Sheffield, *Observations on the Commerce of the American States* (edn of Feb. 1784), 238. This powerful pamphlet went through six editions between the spring of 1783 and the summer of 1784; the earlier editions do not contain this passage.

2. Edward Gibbon to Dorothea Gibbon, 31 January 1775 (*The Letters of Edward Gibbon*, ed. J. E. Norton, II (1956), no. 290).

3. P. 99 above.

4. See p. 59 above.

complacent age. It gave its own flavour to ideas and reactions that were common to much of Europe. It was the first great political experience of Pitt's generation. It bequeathed the situation with which he had now to deal.

II

The prospect looked serious, even critical. It proved to be nothing of the kind. In the early 1780s England was weakened abroad and shaken at home. Within a few years she was settled and prosperous, and had regained her normal place in Europe; a generation later she was the greatest power in the world. At the time, the American War appeared ominous in the extreme. We can see that it came on the eve of the most rapid expansion in English history.

The undeniable reverse was shrugged off with undeniable ease. This may have been aided – it was certainly accompanied – by a marked lack of sentiment. The loss of America roused real fears; but they were fears for the home country rather than for an imperial idea. It was indeed the Americans themselves, and their agents here, who had once talked most of the bonds of Empire, and speculated most on their limits and their meaning. In England, overseas possessions were valued primarily as possessions; for what they could contribute to British strength and wealth. Their place in a larger system, their indigenous development, had seldom been a subject of much interest or thought. There was little feeling in London for Empire as such, other than as a weight in the balance of power; its responsibilities, where recognised, were viewed often with reluctance, and the designs of Chatham and Shelburne were more significant for the future than at the time. The American revolution certainly influenced imperial thought. It helped mould the treatment of Canada, for instance, which Pitt and Grenville introduced, and which became one of the models in the control of a new Empire. But that Empire emerged very largely on the lines of an earlier pattern, which the failure in America seemed to justify and confirm. Overseas possessions were necessary, to nourish overseas trade; but they should involve as few commitments for government as possible. The revolution forced Ministers to think out some of the implications afresh. It was a formative experience, with ramifying effects. But the disturbance was safely absorbed, confidence was soon regained, and the secession was not allowed to overturn a system of trade which shortly revived, not least with the Americans themselves.

The liberal political economists were in fact proved right, though not entirely in the ways they had imagined. The loss was not vital, as many had feared. It did not undermine the basis of national strength. There was indeed little room for sentiment in an age of expansion and technological change. In the first place imperial interests were very widely spread, in a pattern developed, largely unconsciously, over the past two or three decades. The North Atlantic complex itself proved adjustable to the shock, mainly because the problems of the remaining colonies were not new. Political difficulties in Canada, economic difficulties in the West Indies, may have been thrown into relief, but they were not created, by the war. Nor, in either area, was the British response fundamentally changed. The West Indies remained a major factor in the system of power and wealth, expansion in and around the Caribbean an element in policy. The role of Canada was strengthened by the needs and measures suggested by the débâcle. Close ties could be maintained, the volume of Atlantic traffic increased. There were in fact strong seeds of recovery in the West itself. But of course the war was followed by a period of doubt and some conscious reaction, which helped to fix attention on the welcome possibilities in the East. These indeed had been recognised as considerable for some time: even before the war, there were those who contrasted them with the problems of the Atlantic. The wealth of India had long been exciting; but other openings lay farther afield, affecting the role of the sub-continent itself. From Suez to Manila, and northward to Canton, new opportunities beckoned, which the British seemed well placed to exploit. Not all were viewed with equal favour in London: Warren Hastings's interest in Egypt, and again in Bhutan, were firmly restrained. But the coasts of China and Malaya invited fresh ventures based on Calcutta and Madras; and the Pacific Ocean itself was not to be ignored. The farthest explorations had caught the imagination of the times – 'the latest Discoveries', it was claimed in the eighties, 'appear to engross conversation'[1] – and this enlightened interest aided, and sometimes covered, a search for trade and bases which had been steadily growing as European rivalries stimulated the chase. Much of the search was officially inspired. If Dalrymple and Chapman made their voyages for the East India Company, Anson and Byron, Wallis and Cook had sailed under the white ensign, with secret instructions. The Borneo Enterprise, the search for *Terra Australis*, marked an interest in the East which the ensuing defeat in the West helped further to underline. The new pattern, moreover, met the immediate mood, suggesting as it did a maritime expansion free of large colonial commitments. The strategic implications could be accepted – perhaps because they could not all yet be foreseen. The Falkland Islands had attracted attention in the sixties; now there was some interest in the Cape of Good Hope, and a good deal more in Ceylon. One cannot say that there was a departure of policy, that a new Empire was being deliberately sought in place of the old. On the contrary, the British position was strong because no such choice had to be made, nor was there any clear sign that Ministers' minds worked in this way. The Atlantic trade remained far more important

1. Quoted in E. A. Benians, ch. I, *The Cambridge History of the British Empire*, II (1940), 3.

to Britain than that of Asia, existing ties were not to be loosened, one made the best of all one had. But it was not surprising that the prospects in the East should have been welcomed at such a time, and fresh energies applied with growing effect.

The efforts, moreover, could be defended with greater force than before. For the Eastern trade, with all the wealth it raised, had never yielded a profit on the national ledgers. It supplied some valuable raw materials, and tea and cheap cottons for resale; but the balance was adverse for Britain, and the loss of bullion had long been criticised. Now, however, the outlook seemed much more promising. Bullionist doctrines carried less weight, fresh markets were opening up, above all these might be of the kind which the cheaper British goods could fill. At first, hopes had been roused by the great unknown.

> The American colonies are generally supposed to contain two million people . . . The number of inhabitants in the Southern Continent is probably more than 50 millions . . . the scraps from this table would be sufficient to maintain the power, dominion and sovereignty of Britain by employing all its manufactures and ships.[1]

This was a prophecy of the later sixties, which Captain Cook was soon to disprove. But substitute China, Malaya and the East Indies, and adjust the rules of trade to suit, and the argument was increasingly attractive as Manchester and the Midlands got into their stride. For the interest in the East reflected not only a partial revulsion from the West; it was also an expression of confidence in the progress of industry at home.

Nor of course was this misplaced, though the balance, as measured hitherto, was not so soon to be redressed in the East itself. The world-wide results, in the eighties alone, surpassed all calculations. 'The vast increase of the Trade of this Country since the termination of the last War', wrote the Inspector-General of Imports and Exports to Pitt in 1790, 'must be a matter of astonishment even to those who are the best acquainted with the flourishing State of our Manufactures and our internal industry'.[2] The eventual dimensions of the process could not possibly be foreseen.

For the country was in fact embarked on the greatest change it had ever known. Gibbon divided facts into three classes: those that prove nothing beyond themselves; those than can be used to establish a partial conclusion, to determine a motive or illustrate a character; and those that dominate the general system, and move its springs. The Industrial

1. The quotation, in Harlow, *The Founding of the Second British Empire*, I, 38, is from Alexander Dalrymple's *An Historical Collection of the several Voyages and Discoveries in the South Pacific Ocean* (2 vols., 1770–1).
2. P.R.O. Customs 17/12.

Revolution was emphatically one of the last. It made Britain the world's greatest workshop, and sustained her fortunes for a hundred years. It settled the shape of life as we know it in the modern world. It raised entirely new problems for society, and gave a new dimension to human experience. By any standard, this was one of the turning points for mankind. And the impetus is first recognisable in England, in the reign of George III. It gives that period in these islands a vital importance: the results of the victory over France, the emergence of the democratic idea itself, gain much of their significance from the fact of industrialisation. The 1780s saw a spurt in the process that had long been under way. Earlier advances were yielding results and stimulating successors,[1] the scale of business was growing, the factors that made the revolution were being combined with increasing effect. The results began to stimulate exports even as the war drew to a close. 'The commerce of England', observed a prescient observer in 1782, '. . . may be aptly compared to a spring of mighty power, which always exerts its force in proportion to the weight of its compression'.[2]

The causes of the take-off, as economists call it, are still under debate. But if their proportions are hard to determine, the ingredients themselves are fairly clear. A striking growth in population – perhaps over 25 per cent between the 1750s and the 1790s – supplied the necessary labour force. The prolonged if uneven agricultural revolution, increasing its pace as the century progressed, not only helped sustain this growth but also gave the landowning interest, controlling what was still the largest industry in the country, the means for more flexible investment, a greater purchase of manufactured goods, and the maintenance of prices at a rewarding level. Trade did much the same, if again unevenly, for the merchant interests, allowing them to invest more amply in land, as they had always done, in industry and Government stock. Money was mostly cheap, facilities for credit were growing, and the pressures of strong government in the past, and of private enterprise now, combined to set an atmosphere favourable to expansion. There were few legal and comparatively few corporative restrictions, a fund of mercantile experience buttressed large-scale organisation, there was no lasting conflict of interest between agriculture and trade. The governing class was well disposed, the social and economic climate propitious.

Governments were the beneficiaries rather than the initiators of the results. But in one field at least their policies may have had a direct effect. For the ease with which money is made available depends largely on the rates of interest, and in settling those rates Government had its part to play. The yield on gilt-edged stocks may be said to have set the

1. In the 1750s, 92 patents were taken out; in the 1760s, 195; in the '70s, 294; in the '80s, 517 (Mitchell & Deane, op. cit., ch. X, table 13).

2. George Chalmers, *An Estimate of the Comparative Strength of Great Britain during the Present and Four Preceding Reigns* . . . (1782), 5–6.

pattern for other long-term yields, and thus to have affected the whole structure of legal rates; and from the fifties to the nineties, the Treasury usually (though not always – Pitt himself was a partial exception) borrowed at between 3 and 4 per cent. Such a level, whatever its minor variations, was conducive to improvement and risk. Of course there were plenty of exceptions and failures in a still rudimentary system, and perhaps the provision of credit was not as important at the start as it later became. Much improvement was financed directly from savings and profits; much borrowing was done at local, customary rates, not all of which responded to more general or even regional movements; and it is difficult to be precise about those movements themselves, or their effects. Certainly credit could be easily shaken. Bad harvests, the chances of war, over-confidence could have swift results. But amid all the dangers and setbacks the incentive remained. The industrial revolution was financed increasingly by cheap capital, itself underwritten by the public's readiness to invest in Government loans.[1]

The facilities for a take-off were thus quite highly developed. But still they cannot account for the take-off itself. Two further, direct propellants were required for that event: an adequate supply of power, and the scientific knowledge to exploit it. Both were now present, the former in the shape of water and coal, the latter in an astonishing, sustained burst of technological invention. Such a series of discoveries was naturally unexpected. Even so, it can scarcely be held to have been just the result of chance. The spirit of course bloweth where it listeth, and genius knows no rules; but simple, unskilled communities cannot advance on such a front at such a rate. The Industrial Revolution was made possible by the earlier scientific revolution, by the achievements of such giants as Newton and Leibnitz and Descartes and Boyle. It was nurtured very largely by a particular educational system: by the Scottish universities and schools and the English dissenting academies, and, springing often from that background, the societies and institutions for discussion and improvement which were so characteristic of the time. This harnessing of talent in an inventive people had a snowball effect. Discoveries reacted on one another as the process gathered pace, and the process itself reacted on the conditions in which it had been conceived. The social and political implications were barely visible on the horizon; meanwhile the achievements themselves could be welcomed as a fresh addition to Britain's strength, a fresh tribute to her vigour and the wisdom of her ways. The new manufactures in their early stages seemed a reassurance rather than a menace to the society which in due course they were to undermine.

For if the old order was about to face a convulsion, the fact was not

1. For some of the discussion of this subject, which is controversial, see the Notes on Sources to this chapter.

apparent. This was still a confident age; there was no real chill in the air. So much that we call typically eighteenth century can be ascribed to the later seventeenth century. But from the further growth of prosperity sprang much that cannot. A hundred years before, Englishmen had been well pleased with themselves; but they could scarcely have claimed to set the pace in any material sense for Europe. Now they had largely – and for much the same reasons – assumed the educative role of the Dutch: their institutions, their social habits, were consciously mature, and the results enriched the comity of the civilised world. In France itself, the great arbiter, Anglomania was rife. The Englishman's comfort, in house and inn, the Englishman's coaches and horses and dogs, the yield of his crops, his landscapes and gardens, his pastimes and tastes, were accepted abroad. Much of the interest aroused by his legal and political arrangements was due to the fact that they flourished in so enviable a State.

> Thy Seasons moderate as thy Laws appear,
> Thy Constitution wholesome as the Year:
> Well pois'd, and pregnant in thy annual Round
> With Wisdom, where no fierce Extreme is found . . .
> Where Strength and Freedom in their Prime prevail,
> And Wealth comes wafted on each freighted Gale.[1]

This was the spirit in which men of that time faced conditions they felt they could understand.

The strength of the spirit indeed was shown when the conditions were tested. The bitterness of the struggle with a revolutionary France, many of the ugly things done at home, were born of the propertied classes' feeling for the values they knew, and their fear – the more unreasoning from their respect for reason – of the forces, always lurking, which now threatened to break the mould. Thoughtful men were convinced that they had achieved a rational order, in which improvement, carefully weighed, could be safely absorbed. These were the assumptions of pre-revolutionary liberal thought, applied as naturally to manufacture as to everything else. They were held almost universally, whatever the consequences drawn: intelligent men, of whatever profession, looked at the world from much the same point of view. There was a unity of culture; no great division between feeling and thought, or between thought and the approach to affairs. The lines and the limits of Pitt's comprehension were the more strongly marked because in so many ways he was intellectually up to date.

Pitt was indeed as well equipped for his tasks as a politician could reasonably hope to be. That of course is not to say that he would always recognise their implications. The events that seem important at the time

1. *The Isle of Wight, A Poem in Three Cantos* (1782); quoted by Asa Briggs, *The Age of Improvement* (1959), 8.

are often, as we know, not those of underlying importance. But statesmen can hardly be expected always to divine the latter – historians find it difficult enough – nor is it always necessary that they should. They work with what they have, they try to control what others can see, and when their own vision is too distant so usually are the results. In this case, moreover, it was really impossible to guess what lay ahead. How could anyone foretell the unprecedented movement from a static to a dynamic world? Under industrialisation the nature of society is transformed. 'Growth becomes its normal condition. Compound interest becomes built, as it were, into its habits and institutional structure'.[1] Of course the transformation was not sudden, or complete at any given time. Early, even mid-Victorian society in some respects was not unlike that of half a century before. But its basis was very different, and the structure itself was not the same. When Pitt came to office, England still lay on the far side of the watershed; the pace of life and of policy was still that of the sailing ship and the horse. Statesmen pursued their art on traditional lines, their problems were familiar and seemed manageable, their responses could be viewed and discussed as a whole. The significance of Pitt's peacetime career is largely that it lay in the foothills of change. One need not demand that his generation should have known of the mountains beyond.[2]

It would be a mistake to think of Pitt simply as a disciple of the liberal political philosophers. In many ways he certainly was, and his debt was marked and is well known; but he had other strands in his make-up, and his reactions can be surprising if one assumes that they will necessarily conform to the doctrine according to Adam Smith. He had a strong independent intelligence, and a sometimes disconcerting openness of mind. Some at least of his decisions, I think, are to be so explained, rather than by the simple assumption that he must have surrendered to pressure. But of course Pitt was constantly under pressure, to which he had often to yield. Like any politician, he had to live by political and administrative facts; like most politicians, he could take for fact what might itself have yielded to pressure. He had his share of defeats, and he tended increasingly to avoid them. He also moved as he did on occasions because he was not thinking on the lines one might expect.

Governing his approach to many of the issues were two general considerations. Far more than most leading politicians, Pitt was interested in administration. He wished to improve its pattern, and he was prepared to move in his own ways for change. But this was not always easy within a political framework which he and his contemporaries were glad to accept. The fact was that a theory of politics which was relevant to the feelings and needs of the time decreed a place for administration which was becoming less so. The American War had

1. W. W. Rostow, *The Stages of Economic Growth* . . . (1960), 7.
2. Bentham himself did not fully develop the social philosophy which bears his name until the early years of the nineteenth century.

just shown that the structure of government was clumsy and the result disproportionately expensive. But any reform meant tampering with political institutions which many held to be sacrosanct, and which the young Minister himself did not wish to undermine. It was not that the importance of government was dismissed – one has only to read the eighteenth-century historians to see its prominent role. It was rather that Governments, at least in England, were assumed to have produced a reasonable society, which could now get along pretty well on its own. As a result, 'the characteristic instrument of social purpose was not the individual, or the State, but the club',[1] from the Jockey Club and the Dilettanti to the Freemasons and Lloyds, from the Society for the Reformation of Manners and the Chamber of Manufacturers to the literary and dining clubs in the taverns. This zest for voluntary association swelled the demands for official retrenchment. But even to retrench, and to aid the play of natural voluntary forces, meant some legislative and administrative change. 'Laissez-faire' itself involved some Governmental action, which would immediately be suspect for its political effects. This was Pitt's dilemma; a dilemma of his age. Before we can judge of his response, we must therefore try – and it is not altogether easy – to trace the pattern and spirit of government itself.

III

The course and temper of a Parliamentary session throw some light on the way in which government was viewed. For the freedom of the individual Member, the nature and limits of party principles themselves, were influenced by the scale of administration as well as by the structure of politics. 'The Government existed, in those days, not in order to legislate but in order to govern: to maintain order, to wage war, and, above all, to conduct foreign affairs';[2] and on all these matters, affecting the peace and strength of the realm, there was a presumption that the average Member would support the Crown. Only if the maintenance of order touched a traditionally sensitive Parliamentary chord, if a war seemed to be going badly, or a major development in foreign relations was in question, were Ministers likely to find themselves embarrassed. It was a reflection of this fact, as also no doubt of Members' indifference to figures, that the peacetime financial demands, seldom varying much, now seldom provoked much debate, the Estimates were seldom challenged in detail, and as long as taxes remained steady the Government was normally left to spend its money as it liked. It was perhaps a further reflection that when public bills were proposed, preparatory resolutions were often debated in the House sitting as a Committee, where the rules of debate were wider, the attitude was more

1. T. S. Ashton, *The Industrial Revolution 1760–1830* (repr. 1957), 127.
2. Richard Pares, *King George III and the Politicians* (1953), 4.

that of a jury, and the sense of the assembly could be taken so as to improve the prospects of the bill passing without a division, thus satisfying the ideal that on legislation the vote should be unanimous. 'Distrust of the Executive'[1] did not normally mean distrust of policy, except where that was thought to affect the relations between Ministers and Parliament.

The pace and rhythm of business, over half a century of domestic peace and maritime war, had defined the flavour of the administrative system. In an age when the number of places under the Crown was a subject of political attention, the number of 'efficient offices', as they were often called – the posts whose occupants did the work in London – was small. The system of central government was indeed, in a literal sense, archaic; a rambling historic structure, whose medieval and early Tudor character was only partly disguised by late Stuart additions, and much of whose outworks had not been tinkered with at all. Public opinion for most of the century had been happy to let the building alone, and to confine repairs to damage by storm. The inconveniences were noted, but the architecture was generally admired. Men indeed looked on an institution then as we now tend to look on an ancient building itself. It was a distinctive, irreplaceable feature of the English scene, which should not be altered unless absolutely necessary, and then as inconspicuously as possible.

The pattern of central administration reflected such an attitude. In 1784, *The Royal Kalendar* – a *Whitaker* of the day – arranged under various headings the hitherto undifferentiated list of offices and departments of the Crown. Many of the results would have seemed more curious sixty or seventy years later than they would have done two hundred years before. Thus, some of the senior Ministers and their departments – those of the Lord Privy Seal and the Secretaries of State – and what later became the diplomatic service, were listed with the Court and the royal households. The army and navy were administered not simply by the War Office and the Admiralty, but by a whole string of authorities – thirteen in the case of the navy – enjoying varying and often substantial degrees of independence. The departments of the law included not only what we should recognise as law courts and legal offices, but the most venerable financial department, the Court of Exchequer. The whole formal structure of government was closer to the system under Henry VIII or Edward VI – in many important respects, under Henry VI and Edward IV – than what which emerged in the earlier part of Queen Victoria's reign.

It is not merely for convenience that one thus may refer to the reigns of monarchs. In the late eighteenth century, the government of the kingdom was still very much the King's affair. The offices of the Lord Privy Seal and the Secretaries of State were grouped with the Court and the royal households because those Ministers had derived their powers

1. See p. 34 above.

directly from the throne. The Privy Seal and the Signet had been the two main instruments of royal administration since the fifteenth century; their custodians, the Lord Privy Seal and the King's Secretary, were correspondingly close to the royal person; and as business grew, first under the Privy Council and then under emergent departments, so did the need for a strong link with the sovereign himself. The Secretaries of State in particular had been well placed to provide it. They owed their importance to the fact. And in a century in which change was gradual and seldom explicit, the familiar connexion had not disappeared. In the 1770s and '80s, it was still not anomalous to associate two of the most important Ministers and their staffs with the personal officers and servants of the Crown. The same applied, in the context, to His Majesty's Ministers abroad. They were in a very real sense His Majesty's Ministers, as much, it could be claimed, as his Ministers at home. 'If any good is ever done', wrote the British envoy at The Hague, in typical ambassadorial exasperation, to a junior colleague at Berlin in 1785, 'it must be effected through the King's Ministers abroad and not by those about his person';[1] and the phraseology was not entirely absurd when British envoys received their salaries from the King's civil list, bore his personal credentials to foreign Courts in an age when Courts were centres of power, and took instructions from a Secretary who had normally submitted them first to the royal eye. Although the Foreign Office started its life in 1782, as one of the offices of the Secretaries of State, it was almost another twenty years before Ambassadors and Ministers abroad were removed, in the year books, from the pages of the Court.

The King's connexion with his armed forces was also close and in some ways direct. He knew many of the officers, kept a close eye on their appointments, and claimed their personal loyalties. The royal authority remained a major factor in a situation shaped also by Parliament's financial concern and the administrative conditions set by the armed services themselves. The effect was to be seen particularly in the case of the army, of which the sovereign was traditionally the active head and which lay particularly close to the hearts of the Hanoverian Kings. The War Office was the office of the Secretary at War, a minor Ministerial figure, not of Cabinet rank, who shared with greater authorities the management of military affairs. While he had come to answer for the army on administrative questions in the House of Commons, he had only an indirect or subordinate interest in much that went on. Thus patronage and policy remained the business of the sovereign, the Secretaries of State, and the Commander-in-Chief when he existed; boards of General Officers were appointed to advise on questions of general interest; and if the War Office prepared the estimates, the Paymaster General drew the money and distributed it to the forces.

1. Sir James Harris to William Ewart, 15 March 1785 (*Diaries and Correspondence of Malmesbury*, II, 112–13).

The conditions of service, moreover, enabled the regiments to retain many of the functions later associated with Whitehall. Colonels were still very much in charge of all that concerned their men, and in peacetime at least they and their agents made their own arrangements. Nor did the War Office control, in these limited ways, more than the regular cavalry and infantry. The 'unembodied' militia and volunteers were the responsibility of a Secretary of State, the troops in India largely of John Company, the artillery and engineers, with all ordnance supplies, of the Ordnance Board under its Master General. Small wonder that under this system 'a British army . . . had no more uniformity of movements, of discipline, and appearance . . . than one composed of the troops of different sovereign states'.[1]

The position of the navy was rather different. The Admiralty had inherited the precedence and powers of the Lord High Admiral, and these were reinforced by the conditions of naval life, which demanded a high degree of co-ordination. The direction and maintenance of the fleet was the most complex single business in the country; it could not be left entirely to amateurs and chance. The Board of Admiralty was a powerful and not unprofessional body. But it was by no means the sole occupant, or the master, of its house. Subordinate boards, particularly the Navy Board, claimed their separate origins, enjoyed their own patronage in differing degrees, and often followed semi-independent lines. And while the Admiralty supervised the life of the fleet more closely than any of the military departments supervised the troops, it again was not responsible for the ordnance supplies, which were provided by the Ordnance, or necessarily for strategic dispositions, although the First Lord could seldom be ignored. Practice varied with personalities; but the Secretaries of State were very powerful, and the Board on occasion could be kept at least partly in the dark. The distribution of naval business, indeed, illustrated by its very need for compactness the constitutional conditions. The management of the most intricate and vital of administrative services reflected the haphazard development of the system of control.

The armed forces were far the greatest of the charges on Government. In a normal peacetime year they absorbed about three-quarters of its current expenditure,[2] and their wartime needs, more than anything else, developed the system of financial control. It was war, and the rise of the National Debt, that were responsible for the growth of the financial and revenue departments. The historical background again accounted for the ways in which that development took place.

For another impression conveyed by the lists of offices is of the archaic complexity of the financial organisation. The Exchequer itself formed part of a medieval court of law, and its establishments and

1. Castlereagh's words, referring to this time (C. M. Clode, *The Military Forces of the Crown* . . ., II (1896), 359).
2. I.e., its expenditure other than provision for past debt.

procedures were the result of Tudor experiments within what remained a Plantagenet institution. The whole system still rested on its original basis, the personal obligation of a feudal inferior to guard his lord's money against fraud and misappropriation; and its 'old and obstinate' processes, as North once called them,[1] were designed entirely with that end in view. This hoary relic was imbedded in a system of estimate and supply which had reached its highest point of development in the wars of the later Stuarts. Faced with a rapidly rising debt, and the complementary growth of Parliament's concern, the machinery of taxation and appropriation had then evolved new forms. The Treasury, placed in commission for much of the period, found itself supervising a more elaborate system of revenue collection. Six new boards came into existence in the last forty years of the seventeenth century, and the older boards of Customs and of Excise then began their uninterrupted lives. Their relations with their superior varied over the following decades; but while some were left more free than others to manage their appointments and affairs, the degree of supervision fluctuated from case to case and time to time. Treasury control of expenditure, however, was always less complete. The department, of course, was responsible for allocating payments from the various funds to the various services, and its power grew when the funds were short or the debts became too pressing. But without such incentives – and they were often lacking – it scarcely pretended to control the 'several great offices of the State' which were normally acknowledged to be 'distinct and independent'.[2] Neither the naval nor the military authorities, the great spenders of government money, submitted annual estimates to the Treasury for amendment as a matter of course;[3] and as long as the Treasurer of the Navy and the Paymaster General of the Forces could prove that their demands fell within the scope of the Parliamentary grants, they normally received what they asked from the Exchequer without much ado. The Treasury in fact was still far from being undisputed master of the whole financial field, or, as a result, the co-ordinating department of government. It was of course a very powerful department, as the Lord High Treasurer had been a very powerful Great Officer of State. Its sources of patronage, through the Exchequer and the revenue boards, were unrivalled. But it had not yet confirmed its primacy over its colleagues, and the First Lord was not yet departmentally a Prime Minister.

The financial system, indeed, showed perhaps most clearly the strengths and the weaknesses of the executive system as a whole. On the one hand there was the tradition of strong government, centred on

1. Quoted in Binney, *British Public Finance and Administration 1774–92*, 237.
2. Lord Stormont, opposing Pitt's Public Offices Regulation Bill of 1783, which he said would give the Treasury 'a painful pre-eminence over all of them' (*P.R.*, XI, 266).
3. Nor for that matter did the Parliamentary committee which estimated the needs of the 'unembodied' militia. The Ordnance Board, however, did in some respects.

the Crown, which the Norman and Angevin kings had bequeathed and the Tudors renewed. On the other there was the counterpoise, equally rooted in medieval thought, which sought to reconcile the claims of the monarch with the liberties of the Estates. The ancient partnership persisted through all the conflicts of the partners, its proportions varying with their fortunes and the nature of the times. The struggles of the seventeenth century, culminating in the Glorious Revolution, settled its form for a quieter age. The last extension of the central power, in the wars of the later Stuarts, had benefited the Parliamentary class at least as much as the Crown; and in the perennial balance between efficiency and liberty, considered as extremes, the scales were now weighted decidedly in favour of liberty. The attitude penetrated government itself. Departments valued their independence as well as individuals; and the large collection of administrative resources, built up over some six hundred years, proved only partly relevant to the tasks which were now allowed to be carried out. The natural results soon followed. The pattern of administration became at once rigid and diffuse, and in an age when political interest ran as high as ever, but great political issues were rarely in dispute, attention was focused on office almost entirely as a personal perquisite or political prize. The means of strong government remained, and they remained in much the same hands. But government itself was at something of a discount, and its weapons were retained more often for their value than for their use.

The physical whereabouts of the Government reflected this legacy of the past. As the Court had moved over the centuries, from Westminster to Whitehall and from Whitehall to St James's, it left behind a mixed assembly of functions grouped originally round the Crown. The last remove having been from Whitehall, most of the important departments were now in or off that street, sharing with lodgings and private houses – some a good deal larger than the offices – the site of the palace burned down in 1698. But there were still outcrops elsewhere. A few offices, including the Secretary of State's office which in 1782 became the Foreign Office, remained with the King, in or near St James's. Others were still to be found in and around the Palace of Westminster. And there was a large collection of mostly subordinate boards and departments scattered about the town – in the nooks and crannies of the Inns of Court, off the Strand and in the City, as far as Tower Hill and the Tower itself. The geographical distribution of business was not untypical of the pattern of government; and it was a sign of the times when the Foreign Office, as a result once more of fire, moved to Whitehall in the later eighties, and some of the naval and financial departments were concentrated in the same decade in the new government building of Somerset House.

The comparative size of the different central staffs told a similar tale.

173

The higher the department, of course, the smaller it was apt to be. The Admiralty, by its nature, was not as large as the Navy Office, the Treasury as the Exchequer or the offices of some of the revenue boards. That was normal enough, when business was subdivided; though even so, such staffs – the Admiralty with one of 29, the Treasury one of 30, the Secretaries of State between them (after the American department had gone) with one of 38[1] – were small by any standard, including that of comparison with similar offices in the greater western European states. It was more typical of the age that the different establishments, when compared, bore little relation to their functions. Thus the office of the Lord Privy Seal and the Signet Office, whose duties were largely formal, had a staff of eight each, while the Secretaries of State had only thirteen and fifteen subordinates respectively, including their office servants, and shared another ten for common purposes. The Tax Office, responsible for the collection of a gross revenue of some £2½ million in 1780, had an establishment of nineteen, including two office servants and excluding the commissioners themselves: four other smaller boards, handling a gross revenue of under £1¼ million, were allowed between them over two hundred staff. Yet other financial departments had larger establishments: the Excise Office one of over 250, while the Customs Office and the Exchequer boasted over 300 each.

It was significant that these last two departments, the largest of all, should both have been of medieval origin. Both in fact were able to draw on organisations that had survived the decline of the original procedures to provide a mass of places which could now be used for other ends. The Customs was particularly well adapted to this purpose, thanks to its widespread system of collection. In 1784, there were 103 'ports and creeks' at which dues could be levied, and since the duties of the medieval officials had been superseded while their posts remained, there were two largely separate lists of appointments to be filled. It was therefore perhaps not surprising that about a third of the revenue officials in the country should have been borne on the Customs' books. The department, in fact, was a haven for patronage, designed, it sometimes seemed, 'less for the collection of revenue than for the collection of favours'.[2] The central office yielded a rich crop of sinecure posts; but it was in the outports that the greater political possibilities lay. Customs' men, whether working officials or absentees, could be a notorious means of influence in the coastal boroughs, as could naval officials in the dockyard towns and excisemen inland. The revenue officers in general, comprising as they did perhaps six or seven per cent

1. The Admiralty staff including ten office servants, and excluding the Marine Department and the Court of Admiralty; the Treasury and the Secretaries of State's office including ten office servants each.

2. Elizabeth E. Hoon, *The Organization of the English Customs System 1696–1786* (1938), 202.

of the electorate, were indeed an obvious instrument of electoral power until their disfranchisement in 1782. The Exchequer did not offer the same kind of opportunities. Its main establishment was confined to London, and its attraction lay purely in its sinecure posts. But these were peculiarly inviting. The combination of an elaborate hierarchy and a largely archaic routine was a heaven-sent answer to the sinecurist's prayer. With only five exceptions on the administrative side, every senior officer of the department performed his arcane rites by deputy; and many of the deputies were themselves sinecurists on a smaller scale.

No other Government department could rival the Customs and the Exchequer in the profusion of such posts. But few did not carry their share in what was the historian of one office has called 'the age of deputies'.[1] It was difficult to tell why some posts became sinecures and others did not. Why, for instance, should the Collectors Inwards and Outwards of the Customs be the Dukes of Newcastle and Marlborough, and the Inspector-General of Import Duties a working official? Why should the Surveyorship of the Meltings and the Clerkship of the Irons at the Mint have provided an income for George Selwyn, while the Assay-Master remained an effective member of the staff? It was not only redundant offices that were treated in this way, but on the other hand some lucrative posts escaped. The workings of the system defied precise analysis: there were always some conventions to be found in the making, while others were the outcome of 'usage . . ., uninterrupted usage, from a very early period'.[2]

Sinecures were not confined to sinecurists pure and simple. The holders of 'effective offices' often received such a reward. One of the most eminent of all, the First Lord of the Treasury, was often Lord Warden of the Cinque Ports when a vacancy occurred, and prominent 'men of business' and even faithful officials naturally looked to such means of support. There was also some pluralism among the working posts themselves, many officials holding more than one 'effective' appointment in the same department. The practice, indeed, was sometimes not unreasonable. Salaries varied a good deal in comparable instances; but some at least were low, and in the case of others which were not office-holders might be required to pay a substantial security in advance. Government servants without other means or employment were therefore often justifiably glad of the extra income. It was the more acceptable if the salary itself accounted for only a part. Many posts still commanded more in the way of fees, and indeed the fee system was one of the most obvious attractions of service under the Crown. The Exchequer sinecurists did best, as might have been expected – when their fees and gratuities (and indeed their places) were discontinued in 1785, the Auditors of the Imprests, who had been salaried at the princely rate of £66-13-4, received in compensation

1. Sir John Craig, *The Mint* (1953), heading to ch. XIII.
2. Sir James Graham on the powers of the Admiralty (*H.C. 438* (1861), 653-4).

£7,000 a year.[1] But such an example was exceptional only in degree; and while working officials on the whole were perhaps apt to do less well, some could count on large amounts over and above their official income. The Chief Clerk at the Navy Office, whose salary was some £250 a year, took at least another £2,500 in gifts; the perquisites of some Customs officials, according to Adam Smith, were worth more than double or treble their salaries; and on one occasion when a Chief Clerk at the Foreign Office was promoted to Under-Secretary, he complained that the loss of his fees and 'private Agencies' made the appointment financially not worth while.[2]

The fee and incident system was obviously a cause of abuse. Although there was a clear distinction in theory between what was allowed and what was not, there was an insensible drift throughout the century from the latter to the former, and in practice in any case the line was indistinct. The authorised fees themselves occasioned much inconvenience and worse. Officials, retired in all but name, would cling to office for their sake; they discouraged and raised the cost of much government business; and they were one of the props of the sinecure system, which thereby fell less heavily as a charge on the Crown. But they were unlikely to disappear until the attitude to government changed. As long as the King was left to run the civil and foreign services, and to do so on the fixed income of the civil list, no very radical amendment was liable to take place. On the whole, moreover, fees were preferred to salaries by the office-holders themselves. It was considered rather degrading to take the King's money: it affected a man's standing; the less he had to rely on payment by the Crown the better he was pleased. If you charged the public its fees, you were being properly paid for your services. If you drew nothing but a salary you were nothing but a dependant, with no pretensions to a position of your own. For this attitude to fees disclosed a certain attitude to office itself – and one not without advantages in the conditions of the day. Its most explicit form was the claim to a freehold place.

The idea of freehold had long lain at the very centre of English public life. It was 'a privilege held by grant or prescription, by which men enjoy some benefit beyond the ordinary subject'.[3] The possession of freehold property gave a man a vote, and allowed him to represent his

1. This was not a direct calculation of the difference between their former salaried and non-salaried incomes. It was the value set on the loss of their freehold place (see below). But that of course itself depended on the size of the annual income, far the greatest part of which came from fees and gratuities.

2. *P.R.*, X (1783), 179; *An Inquiry into the Nature and Causes of the Wealth of Nations*, ed. Edwin Cannan (1904), II, 380; 'The Case of Mr Aust delivered to Lord Grenville'. 27 March 1795 (B. M. Egerton Ms 3505).

3. Definition in G. Jacob's *Law Dictionary* of 1729, quoted in David Ogg, *England in the Reigns of James II and William III* (1953), 54.

Henry Dundas *by Reynolds*

'Cicero in Catilinam': Pitt and Fox in the House of Commons
Engraved after Sayers, March 1785

fellows in Parliament and hold certain offices in the state. Conversely, it was a medieval tradition, defended victoriously in more recent times – as the Fellows of Magdalen had taught James II – that certain offices, granted for life, were the property of their occupants. 'These places', Burke remarked of some sinecures in 1780, 'and others of the same kind have been considered as property. They have been given as provision for children; they have been the subject of family settlements; they have been the security of creditors'. 'What the law respects', he went on significantly, 'shall be sacred to me'. 'I have considered the office which I hold', wrote Chatham's friend Camden of one of the Teller-ships of the Exchequer, 'as a freehold which I have inherited'. 'Property', observed the younger Pitt's cousin Buckingham of the same office, 'which is as much mine as the Crown is the King's'.[1] Possessions of this kind were perhaps not quite of the same order as land or mercantile or industrial wealth: they were held for life and granted by patent, so that, in however slight a degree, they involved dependence on someone else. But their inalienable rights were never challenged in the courts; and when Pitt put in hand his administrative reforms, he thought it necessary to compensate the holders of some freehold offices which he wished to abolish, and to wait for others to die before their places were allowed to lapse.

The freehold principle, indeed, was widely regarded as a bulwark of liberty, a shelter from undue dependence on Ministers or the King.[2] Old Horace Walpole, for instance, indulged his criticisms of George III from the Crown appointments of Usher to the Exchequer, Clerk of the Estreats, and Comptroller of the Pipe. Strictly speaking, the principle applied only to certain places held for life; but in practice it was not confined to them. Many office-holders 'at pleasure' were virtually life tenants, and some could hope, though less confidently, to secure a reversion for a nominee. It was this combination of patronage and independence which gave the eighteenth-century system its peculiar flavour. Nor can the two be distinguished too precisely, for independence was often fostered by the ways in which patronage worked. In the first place, the patrons were many and varied. The King himself was only *primus inter pares*; Ministers of course held wide powers of appointment; they in turn had to pay attention to the wishes of their colleagues and supporters; and throughout the country there was a web of conventional rights and interests, closely watched and often passionately preserved. Territorial peers and prominent gentlemen, private Members of Parliament whatever their political colour, mayors and councillors and aldermen, directors of Chartered Companies, were among the

---

1. All quoted in S. E. Finer, 'Patronage and the Public Service' (*Public Administration*, XXX, 356). It was significant that a movement under the later Stuarts to replace life patents and reversions in the Exchequer by offices granted 'at pleasure' should have been decisively reversed in the period of the early Hanoverians.

2. E.g., pp 62, 92 above

more obvious powers outside Crown service with claims, often contested among themselves, to influence particular Crown appointments. And the same conventions and disputes operated within the ranks of Government, defining the relations between senior and junior boards, between departments and their semi-independent servants (Admirals and Governors, Colonels of regiments, Collectors and Receivers), between the claimants to patronage in every branch and at every level of official life. The Treasury Commissioners could not consistently ignore the wishes of the subordinate commissioners of revenue; the Admiralty had always to reckon with the Navy Board, the Navy Board with the dockyard commissioners. The administrative map, like the political, was a patchwork of interests. If the influence of the Crown, seen from Parliament, appeared politically formidable, the influence of the whole political world permeated the services of the Crown.

Patronage came into play whenever there was a place to be filled. The game had its rules, constantly altering but widely understood. Some posts were accepted as falling, more or less unchallenged, within a particular gift: others were the subject of contests between recognised patrons. These might include the working office-holders themselves. Certain places were apt to be reserved within a department for promotion by seniority, or, less predictably, for promotion from one department to another. Such appointments naturally attracted vested interests of their own. Some of the senior officials had their means of influence, and the same names might appear in the same kind of posts over more than one generation. Something of an official clan had indeed grown up – had probably long existed – within the miscellaneous body of political nominees. We need to know a good deal more in order to generalise – despite recent research into some offices, Whitehall in the later eighteenth century still awaits its Namier, and indeed remains largely an unknown world. But clearly Government service at the working levels had a certain cohesion, and was something of a family affair. The departments were not only filled to some extent from the same family connexions, or the same districts, or even the same schools;[1] they had their own traditions and atmospheres, some almost their own ways of life. At the Post Office, many of the staff lived on the spot 'in collegiate surroundings', and small boys could be brought up to receive what a later Parliamentary Report called 'a good Post Office education'.[2]

This, however, was one feature of a highly varied scene. Promotion and appointments, even among the working posts, were in the last resort unpredictable. The political nation looked after its own, and the outcome of its internecine contests could never be taken for granted. Men

1. 'I look upon it', wrote one Under-Secretary of State to another in 1753, when a third was under pressure, 'as a general attack upon Westminster and Christchurch' (quoted by W. R. Ward in 'Some Eighteenth-Century Civil Servants: the English Revenue Commissioners, 1754–98'; *E.H.R.*, LXIX, no. 274, 44 n2).

2. Kenneth Ellis. *The Post Office in the Eighteenth Century* (1958), 20–1.

could not be sure how far they would rise by application or seniority. They could only count, with very rare exceptions, on not being removed from what they held.

For if the chances of appointment and promotion were uncertain, the chances of dismissal were remote. Patronage indeed could scarcely be effective in the long run if places were not reasonably secure. From the great sinecurists to the junior clerks, officials on the establishment now usually held their appointments undisturbed. It was possible in theory for an office-holder to be ejected for political reasons, and there were some posts from which he might be expected to resign with his official patron. But in practice a Minister would wait for a vacancy to introduce a nominee,[1] and the conventions attaching to resignation were vague. As long as a man was content to stay put, he had little to fear: once he had secured his appointment, he could usually go his ways undisturbed if he wished. Placemen were not always amenable after they had been placed. It was not unknown for revenue officers to vote contrary to their patrons' wishes, for departmental officials to act as laws unto themselves, for sinecurists to hold their posts while denouncing the Government of the day. It was the ambitious man, or one in need of money, who was apt to lose his freedom of manœuvre – though he too, if he was capable, had his cards to play. Patronage was decisive when there was a place to be filled, but it remained important to the successful candidate only if he then wanted something else.

This comparative independence had diverse results. On the one hand, it cumbered the departments with a mass of useless lumber, both in the sinecurist and the working posts. On the other, it enabled the small body of hard-working officials to maintain and in places develop a not ineffective system of business. British power in the eighteenth century could scarcely have grown otherwise, even in an age of 'laissez-faire' – and 'laissez-faire' was by no means universal. Much of the improvement doubtless fell towards the end of the century; but the men responsible for it were themselves products of the system, and if Pitt was able to make good use of such officials as William Fawkener and William Fraser, Richard Frewin and Thomas Irving, Evan Nepean and William Stiles, the departments in which they learned their jobs cannot be entirely condemned. Again we do not know enough to be categorical; but as the administration of the armed forces and the revenue is examined more closely, the less easy it is to dismiss it always with contempt. Amid all the abuses and complacency, there were conscientious and imaginative men at work. A patronage system, indeed, need not be altogether a spoils system. Compared with their counterparts in some of the leading continental states, English officials under the old order were by no means to be despised.

But of course it was the old order, and if the system survived the

1. There was a widespread dismissal of officials for political reasons in 1763. But it was regarded as extraordinary at the time, and was not repeated.

century it was because the conditions were never quite bad enough to destroy it, or to force Ministers and officials to do more than just enough – often with the help of dormant powers or traditions – to meet the pressures of a period of strain. The small scale of business enabled the political and social demands to be met. For to most men a place remained above all a source of income and a barometer of the patron's importance; and administration could be no more self-sufficient than the administrators themselves.

Government, in fact, shared the values of politics. Such a connexion was vital to the eighteenth-century balance. For in an age of largely autonomous institutions, the ancient partnership of Crown and Estates depended on the extent to which each could informally influence and penetrate the others' domain. Patronage provided the answer – a patronage which held the political nation in the service of the Crown, and turned service under the Crown into a political asset. Both politics and administration suffered from the results. But, in all their jobbery and incoherence, these reflected and preserved the unifying forces of the state.

IV

It was therefore around the system of influence that the constitutional conventions revolved. In the course of the next century an alternative emerged. By the time that Bagehot replaced Blackstone as the oracle of the constitution, the Cabinet had become 'a *hyphen* which joins, a *buckle* which fastens the legislative part of the state to the executive part of the state'.[1] But in the later eighteenth century this was far from being the case. Cabinet government has flourished in what we may call its classic form when Cabinet Ministers are drawn from the party holding a majority in the House of Commons, recognise the leader of that party as Prime Minister, owe a collective responsibility for their actions to Parliament, and hold office as the political heads of departments staffed on a common basis by non-political civil servants, and acting on policies endorsed by the Cabinet itself. The Hanoverian system was entirely different. The King was the head of the executive; departments were run on largely independent lines, and were jealous of the fact; not all matters of interest to Ministers were treated in Parliament as matters of confidence in Government; and political majorities were obtained not from coherent parties but from the limited alliances of fluctuating groups, supported for the purpose in hand by unattached individuals. Ministers therefore had no real basis on which to build an assured collective power. They were not firmly bound together by either political or administrative ties, and while there might be effective Cabinets there could scarcely be an effective Cabinet system. One

1. Walter Bagehot, *The English Constitution* (1867), 15.

Ministry might speak with a single voice: the members of the next might have little more in common than that they were all peers or Members of Parliament and all servants of the King.

This is not to say that Cabinets did not recognise themselves as such, or that something of a regular procedure had not developed. The history of any policy-making committee is likely to be elusive if not obscure, and that of the successive offshoots of the Privy Council from the later seventeenth century – Lords Justices, Cabinet Council, *conciliabilium*, 'Inner' and 'Outer' Cabinets – is no exception. The principle of the process is not hard to understand. The King's advisory council becomes too unwieldy for the confidential and efficient handling of business. A few of the important members accordingly meet more or less regularly among themselves, sometimes in the King's presence, more often in the course of the eighteenth century without him. The meetings (perhaps running parallel while the King remains a possible attendant) tend to become formalised, particularly in war when decisions have constantly to be taken by the same men working together. The attendants acquire a distinct identity, and the fact begins to attract notice. Other members of the larger, formal council try to gain admission, and some succeed. An inner group begins once more to withdraw. Some such process is typical of government by council or committee at any time. The difficulties in the eighteenth century are to gauge the degree of formal continuity between one body and the next, and to tell how far Ministers were independent of their royal master at any stage and how far they were dependent on one another.

Given the political and administrative situation, it would be surprising to find that they were anything like self-contained in either respect. No set of Ministers could function except by reference to the King. He usually interviewed them individually in his closet, and exchanged individual advice; he could insist on any member of the Privy Council attending a meeting of the Cabinet; he was not bound to ask the advice of his Cabinet on any given issue, and could indeed, in all constitutional propriety, seek advice elsewhere; and at the beginning of the 1780s, the initiation of Cabinet business was recognised as subject to his control. Such facts suggest the authority of one who was still a considerable patron on his own account, and occupied a strategic position in the appointment and dismissal of Ministers themselves.

Yet the fact that the King could so affect Cabinet business implies that there was a Cabinet which operated in this way. If he saw Ministers individually in the closet, he scarcely ever attended their collective discussions, and in any case they could often decide informally what to say before they were called.[1] Cabinet membership and its privileges

1. The King sometimes still sat in the 'Grand' or 'Honorary' Cabinet, at which the King's Speech was read before the opening of a Parliamentary session, and in the so-called 'Hanging' Cabinets which were summoned from time to time to receive the reports of the Recorder of London. But these were purely vestigial remains of

were, as to some extent they always are, fluid and arbitrary; but certain Ministers now had something of a claim to be included, and if the duties and rights of the company were ambiguous they were formal enough to cause dispute. The Cabinet could perhaps not claim the right to discuss any given question, and when it did so individual members sometimes recorded their dissent; but if collective advice was tendered, it was doubtful how far the King could finally disregard it. Ministers owed individual responsibility to the King and to Parliament sitting as a court of law rather than as a political assembly:[1] they did not always resign if they were overruled in Cabinet on a matter important to them, or seek its approval for their Parliamentary measures; and the Cabinet itself was not clearly bound by a joint responsibility. But both King and Ministers knew that the latter's strength lay in their collective opinions, even if collective pressures did not necessarily follow. The control of a department lay with the King, the Minister concerned, and to some extent a First Minister if he was effective; but when co-ordination between departments was required constantly over a period – as in war – there was a tendency for decisions to be formally recorded in the main Ministerial committee. Cabinet minutes may not have been regularly taken, or considered binding in the last resort; but when there was a minute it was not to be ignored.

There was now in fact no serious alternative to the Cabinet as the effective Ministerial body, if a given set of Ministers could be said to be effective at a given time. The tradition was impressive enough for a strong Minister or Ministry to invoke it. The two did not necessarily go together. A Minister might win concessions from the Crown without thereby strengthening his ties with his colleagues – neither the elder nor the younger Pitt was a particularly good Cabinet man, though both could be said to have advanced the powers of Ministers in one way or another at the King's expense. But all advantages gained by a Minister benefited Ministers as a class, and thus in the long run the development of a Cabinet system. This indeed is obvious when one considers the emergence of the First or Prime Minister himself, from his shadowy existence in the eighteenth century to his Victorian glory. Exactly how far any Minister can be said to have filled such an office under the Georges is a matter of debate: the only golden rule is that there was no golden rule. No one Minister stood, on a firm constitutional basis, in quite the same relation to his colleagues or to the King as his successor: no one Ministerial office was occupied automatically by the leader of a

the old Cabinet Council, long become large and formal, of an earlier day.

Richard Pares has pointed out how Ministerial consultation outside the closet was facilitated by the procedure of the Court and the geography of the palace, enabling those with the *entrée* to the closet to assemble in the ante-room (*King George III and the Politicians*, 148–9). For the evolution of the arrangements at St James's, see Hugh Murray Baillie, 'Etiquette and the Planning of the State Apartments in Baroque Palaces', *Archaeologia*, CI (1967).

1. Impeachment was a legal process.

Ministry. The First Lord of the Treasury was usually recognised as *primus inter pares*. But he was not necessarily so: one or other of his colleagues – particularly if he was a Secretary of State – might be at least as strong as himself, as the elder Pitt was with Newcastle, and Fox and Shelburne were with Rockingham; and even when he had no obvious rival, his powers might not be exercised to match his position. In the closing years of the American War, the person who denied most warmly that North was First Minister was North himself; and he was not altogether wrong, as his colleagues and George III agreed. It was far from easy to tell where authority lay within a Ministry, or how far it was independent of the King. When Robert Beatson first published his *Political Index* in 1786, he put in a single list the 'Prime Ministers and Favourites from the Accession of Henry VIII to the present Time'.[1] Having thus, in traditional style, linked the favoured Minister with the throne, he was unable to name anyone except Walpole as sole Prime Minister after 1714. In every other instance two, three, four or even more names are grouped together, and for the years 1770 to 1782 the list takes refuge in the collective vagueness of 'Lord North etc.'. The position was not in fact usually as obscure as that. More often than not there was a First Minister, however uncertain his status, to voice pretensions to the main say in Ministerial appointments or even over much of the royal patronage, and to assemble collective opinions with which to confront the King. Such claims accumulated as useful precedents to be exploited as occasion arose. But it remained difficult to predict when that might be, while power was shared by a politically active monarch and a set of Ministers with no reliable institutional authority behind them.

It was scarcely to be expected that Pitt, young and inexperienced as he was, would have formed close relations with his Cabinet at the start. Nor did he do so for a long time. The Cabinet itself lacked any real cohesion, after the upheavals of the past two years. The mantle of Chatham, that coat of many colours, might be said to have covered a part. Sydney and Richmond[2] had been his followers, and more recently colleagues of Shelburne – Richmond after disagreeing with his nephew Fox –, Rutland was of the same persuasion, and when he went to Ireland as Lord Lieutenant in February 1784 his successor Camden, Chatham's Chancellor, strengthened the flavour. Of the four other members, three had been belated opponents of the American War. Gower, a leader in his own right, had led his connexion along various paths; in support of Chatham, and then of North, but finally in an opposition which did not involve him closely with the Rockinghams. Howe had likewise joined North's opponents in the later seventies, and

1. *A Political Index to the Histories of Great Britain and Ireland* . . . (1786), I, 7.
2. See p. 139 above.

then opposed the Coalition in 1783. Carmarthen broke with North in 1780, was connected loosely with Rockingham, and accepted the Versailles Embassy from Shelburne shortly before the Minister fell. Thurlow, by contrast, had stayed with North to the end, continued with Rockingham and with Shelburne, and owed his loyalty simply to the King.

There was thus no recognisable party in the Cabinet similar to the Rockinghams. But neither was there any recognisable connexion. No set of Ministers was linked by firm ties of family or area; there was no territorial group like Rockingham's, no Grenville or Cavendish 'cave'. No Minister indeed disposed of a solid influence: even Gower, who had the most, could not thereby claim Pitt's ear. Without such natural foci, the Cabinet's character must turn largely on its treatment by Pitt himself; and Pitt, by his youth and temperament, was ill fitted to respond. He was, and remained, a lonely figure from the start. Rutland, an early friend and patron, went to Ireland almost at once, and his departure left a personal gap which the others could not fill. Sydney was an acquaintance, and now the young Chatham's father-in-law; Richmond had been a colleague under Shelburne, and a fellow worker for Parliamentary reform; Camden, as his father's friend, had seen something of Pitt when he first came to town. But they were all older men, and none was in Pitt's circle – the young man, indeed, was a contemporary of Camden's son. Howe was a distinguished Admiral, Gower a veteran statesman, both more than thirty years older than himself. He had never been close to Carmarthen, who was nearer his age.

Given Pitt's shyness and reserve, none of this was very hopeful. Nor were the characters and attainments of his colleagues, with one partial exception, such as to break the ice. Howe, taciturn and grave, confined himself to sea affairs. The affable grandee Gower lent his prestige rather than his efforts. Camden, who had refused office at first, was experienced and shrewd, but indecisive and rather tired. These were all occupants of 'dignified' or specialised posts. More to the point was the mediocrity of the two Secretaries of State, normally the linchpins of an Administration. Sydney is remembered, if at all, for his mention in Goldsmith's verse on Burke --

> Though fraught with all learning, yet straining his throat
> To persuade Tommy Townshend to lend him a vote –

and for the fact that he gave his title, while Home Secretary, to the capital of New South Wales. He was, in effect, an average politician of the second rank – assiduous, a fair debater, but noted less for his ability than for his interest and connexions – whose qualities were not such as greatly to excite Pitt. Although he had been Home Secretary before, under Shelburne, he did not in fact really aspire to high office. He would have been content on that occasion with the Secretaryship at

War,[1] and he was not at all anxious to enter the Cabinet now. His colleague Carmarthen was simply the heir to the Duke of Leeds. An amiable, idle, impulsive young man, fond of theatricals and light verse, he was more celebrated in the early eighties for a memorable scandal – he had divorced his wife for eloping with John Byron, the father of the poet – than for his political achievements and gifts. Not that he took himself lightly. He had plunged into Opposition towards the end of the American War, losing indeed a Lord Lieutenancy and a post at Court for his pains; and while he now accepted the Foreign Office rather reluctantly – his heart was still in the frustrated Embassy at Versailles – he did his duty as best he could, prided himself on his ideas, and resigned in the end because his advice was ignored. His contribution to foreign policy, over a period which embraced three major crises, was thrown into sharp relief by the fact that his successor was William Grenville.

These then, for one reason or other, were not the men to work closely with Pitt. Nor again were the two most interesting of his colleagues. Thurlow was in the Cabinet because he could not be kept out; because he represented the King, and his gifts were needed in the Lords. But, able as he was, he had long proved a mixed blessing, rude, suspicious, and for all his thunder disinclined to take a risk. Physically impressive – 'no man', Fox was supposed to have said, 'could *be* so wise as Thurlow *looked*'[2] – he used his presence to the full. Nor indeed was it entirely misleading. Thurlow had risen by a quick mind and a bold spirit which were not easily put down, and he now thoroughly enjoyed his formidable reputation.

> The rugged *Thurlow*, who with sullen scowl,
> In surly mood, at friend and foe will growl,[3]

exacted a lively respect from Society, and from his fellow peers. In council he was less impressive, for he could never take his eyes off the main chance. Admirable as he was in many ways – he hid unexpected kindnesses, he was something of a scholar, he had a real reverence for the law and used his patronage well – there was something cankered in his disposition; in the way he flaunted his coarsenesses, and lay low or blustered where he could not command. Pitt thoroughly disliked him, and he thoroughly disliked Pitt. Political necessity held them together for more than eight years.

Richmond, 'the Radical Duke', was another matter. Intellectually, he was more attractive than any of his colleagues. As Shelburne conceded, he had a lively interest in reform, and was really concerned to do something about it. He was an active Master General of the Ord-

1. P. 83, n1 above.
2. John Lord Campbell, *The Lives of the Lord Chancellors* . . ., V (1846), 661.
3. *Criticisms on The Rolliad, Part the Second* (1785), 49.

nance, a keen Parliamentary reformer, an energetic Minister while his sympathy was engaged. All this drew Pitt towards him, and for a time Richmond could count on a ready hearing. He was a regular attendant in Cabinet – more regular than Gower or Thurlow –, he had definite ideas – more definite than Camden, Sydney or Carmarthen –, he saw a certain amount of the Prime Minister outside office hours. Steele,[1] now admitted to Pitt's circle, had come from under his wing. But his temperament was awkward, and he was always prone to extremes. 'I pass in the world', he acknowledged himself, 'for very obstinate, wrong-headed, and tenacious of my opinions';[2] and he was at odds with almost all his family, and sooner or later with whomever he worked. Tactless, irritable, unsociable, he became a burden and something of a bore: his gifts, which were real, were not exercised best in council. He had not been and he never became an intimate of Pitt's, and after the first few years he went his own way.

The Cabinet, therefore, was not an effective body. It had been scraped together at a bad moment, and it lacked the cohesion which Pitt alone could give. For the first five years, the Prime Minister worked more closely with other men – with a variety of politicians whose abilities he came to respect, with favoured officials, above all with Grenville and Dundas. He bore his isolation lightly in his several capacities: in the conduct of business, in the House of Commons, and not least in his relations with the King.

For the King was a more considerable figure than any member of this Cabinet. Always a force to be reckoned with, recent events had spotlighted his role. The Crown was the centre of controversy, George III himself a leading politician. No one could have guessed, when Pitt came to office, that the late upheaval had in fact marked a climax in this respect.

At the end of 1783, George III was forty-five years old, and he had been twenty-three years on the throne. Corpulent, voluble, energetic, sharing many of the leading tastes of the time – a scientific farmer, a keen collector, a devotee of music – he was a model, in a dissolute age, of simple domestic virtue. His Court was remarkably free of scandal, he was faithful to his Queen, he had just had his fifteenth child, he preferred a modest life at Kew or Buckingham House to the splendours of a palace. The fashionable world found him rather ridiculous, and inexpressibly dull: *his* careful habits preserved a sanctum from the world to which duty called. For duty was the keynote of George III's existence; it sustained his every effort, it was the rock on which he built. As a boy he had been backward, idle, and ill at ease; the unwilling object of political ambitions, guarded by a censorious mother, made very conscious of his faults and determined to do better. Brought early to the throne, he faced the future with diffidence, distaste and resolu-

1. See p. 131 above
2. Quoted in Alison Gilbert Olson, *The Radical Duke* (1961), 12.

tion; and as his immature hopes faded, and his troubles increased, he clung the more to a faith in his conduct which was always naturally strong. He had his full share of sexual passion, which he could have indulged of course where he wished: he continued to live an exemplary domestic life. He found his subjects ungrateful, his Ministers factious: he went steadily on, by the letter of the law. This single-minded devotion made him a formidable figure, largely against his will. For George III did not set out or normally wish to be aggressive. He was determined to do his duty as King; and he knew that, in England, Kings must respect the constitution. Indeed he did so with all his heart: he saw himself as its champion. The trouble was that he did not feel easy in a system based on conventions. 'He . . . will seldom do wrong', it had been noted in his youth, 'except when he mistakes wrong for right'.[1] Stubbornly and resentfully he plunged through the shifting sands, and his struggles, as he claimed defensive, seemed menacing to others. He has been compared to a bull;[2] but sometimes he appeared, as indeed he was described at the outset of the Coalition, more like a startled and recalcitrant horse. At the time of his triumph over Fox he was a tired and excited man, and it is not altogether surprising that he was glad, so far as duty allowed, to retire in the years that followed towards the wings of the stage.

But he remained a force. After twenty-three years on the throne he had learned a lot. He had conquered his laziness, he was now meticulous and indefatigable, he could not be faulted on his rights. He had a royal memory, he knew the detail of business better than most of his Ministers, and his comments, seldom imaginative, were very often to the point. He could be dangerous when threatened. His equipment had greatly improved. But his nature remained the same, passionate, prejudiced, well-meaning, literal, obstinate, and lonely. Near its centre there lay, as there had always done, the desire for someone in whom to confide. But Pitt was not the man to take that place, and he did not intend to try. Each looked warily on the other, from the vantage of his position. Each respected the other's role, and gave credit where credit was due. But Pitt never went out of his way to conciliate the King, and the King never warmed to the Minister with whom he had to work for almost twenty years.

1. James Earl Waldegrave, *Memoirs* (1821), 8–9.
2. See Pares, *King George III and the Politicians*, 67.

CHAPTER VIII

The First Two Years:
India and Ireland

I

'No one who had not been an eye-witness', wrote Wilberforce, many years later, of the morrow of the election of 1784, 'could conceive the ascendancy which Mr. Pitt then possessed over the House of Commons'. 'If', he went on, 'he had then generously adopted the resolution to govern his country by *principle* rather than by *influence*, it was a resolution which he could then have carried into success.'[1] This counsel of perfection can be tested by Pitt's experiences over the next two years.

The first, unavoidable task to be faced was India, the cause of the recent crisis. It was no more agreeable than before. '*That*', remarked the Clerk of the Commons, John Hatsell, 'will be the Rock Mr. Pitt will split upon, as his Predecessors did; for he is so circumstanc'd, that he cannot avoid attempting to do something, & will be able to do nothing'.[2] The rock was really the East India Company, to whose support Pitt was obviously indebted, and which was so difficult to please. Hatsell was in fact proved wrong. Pitt did succeed in doing something, which lasted in its essentials for over seventy years. But the ways in which he did so, and many of his subsequent difficulties, reveal the strength of the pressures to which he was subject, even in the flush of success.

For when the immediate danger was past the old Company factions revived. While the general election was under way in April, other elections were being held in the great building in Leadenhall Street; to the Court of Directors, followed by those to the several 'Chairs'. The most important of the latter was the chairmanship of the Directors, and Pitt was urged by Richard Atkinson, his chief link with the Company,[3] to take advantage of his new found strength to turn this into a Government nomination. But perhaps wisely on the long term, the Minister refused to intervene, and Atkinson was accordingly thrown back on the familiar system of alliances. The results raised plenty of trouble for the immediate future. The most obvious candidate for the Chair was

1. *Private Papers of Wilberforce*, 72–3.
2. To John Ley, 25 April [1784] (Ley Mss).
3. See pp. 122–7 above.

Laurence Sulivan, a power in the Company since the days of his opposition to Clive, and the leader of the largest party, the 'Indian interest', which had recently thrown its weight behind Pitt. But he was also Warren Hastings's most prominent ally, and while Pitt and Dundas were by no means committed against the great proconsul, they were far from happy about him and obviously not prepared to jeopardise their freedom of manœuvre. Nothing therefore was said officially; but unofficially an 'absolute negative' to Sulivan was conveyed.[1] Meanwhile his supporters had been elected to three of the six vacancies – all lost by Foxites – on the Court of Directors, where they were already strong. In this awkward situation Atkinson was forced to pull out every stop to achieve the old champion's defeat. He succeeded, by one vote; but the Ministry had split its recent supporters, and the promise of stability had been temporarily lost. The disappointed Sulivan was in command of a a majority of the Directors, 'and in whatever way a compromise of power is made with him, he will keep it no longer than Kings keep Treaties'.[2]

It was against this rather unpromising background that Pitt introduced his India bill early in July 1784. It was firmly based on Dundas's abortive measure of the year before, itself very largely the product of his work with Robinson and Jenkinson on the Commons' Secret Committee. This earlier measure had had four main objects: to strengthen the Governor-General of Bengal in his relations with his Council, and his powers and those of the Council in day to day administration; to strengthen the Governors of the Presidencies in India in their relations with their Councils; to strengthen the Directors of the Company at home in their relations with the General Court, while increasing the powers of Government in relation to the Company (Dundas himself was flirting with the idea of a third Secretaryship of State for Indian affairs); and lastly – this no doubt in view of the proceedings of Burke and the Select Committee – to investigate and settle the affairs of the native rulers of Tanjore and Arcot, in which Hastings and the Government of Madras had been controversially concerned.[3]

The terms of Dundas's plan had been sensible and shrewd. They drew on the experience of earlier attempts and the mass of information from the Parliamentary committees. But they called for some adjustment when Pitt came to consider them, in the light of other Parliamentary comments and his own needs. With Dundas at his elbow, he soon dropped most of the increased powers for the Governor-General, he strengthened the measures against abuses by the Company's servants in India, and in answer to Atkinson's objections he abandoned

1. Atkinson to Dundas, n.d. but possibly June 1784 (P.R.O. 30/8/355).
2. Same to same, 22 July 1784; quoted in Holden Furber, 'Henry Dundas and the East India Directors in 1784' (*Journal of Modern History*, V, no. 4, 483).
3. See pp. 119–20, 122 above.

the tentative idea of a new Secretary of State. His provisions and his tactics were indeed very warily framed, reflecting the care with which he felt obliged to act.

In its final form, Pitt's bill set up a Board of Commissioners (soon to be known as the Board of Control) to be appointed by the King and to consist of one of the existing Secretaries of State, the Chancellor of the Exchequer, and four other Privy Councillors, one of the first two Ministers normally being President. This Board would have 'the superintendence and control over all the British territorial possessions in the East Indies and over the affairs of the Company'. It would 'superintend, direct and control' all matters relating to civil or military government and the revenues. Its members would have access to all the Company's papers, and were to be shown the Directors' correspondence with India except in cases of urgency, signifying the Board's decision within fourteen days – though the Directors could appeal to the King in Council. Acting through a secret committee of not more than three of the Company's Directors, it could send secret orders, and instructions for negotiations with Indian princes, to India. But it could not appoint or nominate any of the Company's servants, from the Governor-General down.

In India, the Councils of the Presidencies were to be limited to three members other than the Governor, of whom one must be the settlement's (or if present the Company's) Commander-in-Chief. The Governor, and the Governor-General on his Council, should have a casting vote. Either the Crown or the Directors could recall the Governor-General, or any of the Company's servants. No authority in India could make a treaty likely to lead to war, or embark on hostilities: if they entered into a treaty, or found themselves at war, they must report to the Directors of the Company at once. Justice in India was to be answerable when required to the British courts, and the Company's corrupt or disobedient servants would be liable to trial by a commission of peers and Members of Parliament.

In London, the Court of Proprietors was deprived of its power to veto a decision of the Directors if approved by the Board.

The measure also provided for inquiries into the Arcot debts and the system of land tenure in India, and for various reforms in the government of the British territories. It was to come into force at home on receiving the royal assent, and in India on 1 January 1785.[1]

Opinion has differed widely on the merits of the bill. It has sometimes been held to have followed Fox's so closely, except in the matter of patronage, that it was really very largely a cheat. This was not Fox's opinion. He condemned the measure not only for the nature and allegiance of the Board of Control – a Ministerial not an independent body, responsible to the Crown not to Parliament – but also for the fact that the authorities in India were left largely undisturbed. 'If the Bill

1. See the Act, 24 Geo. III, c. 25.

had been framed by the delinquents themselves, it could not . . . have been more directly and clearly calculated to perpetuate the abuses'.[1] Allowing for the rigours of debate, his indignation was probably genuine. In so far as the two bills agreed, it was in bringing the Company's activities more directly under Government's control; but this was an object common to all Parliamentary experts since 1781, and in his provisions for a common purpose Pitt followed the ideas of Dundas, and through him Robinson and Jenkinson, rather than – often in contrast to – those of Fox and Burke. One could in fact argue that the bill was weak in not following its model more closely. The Company had certainly extracted some real concessions. It suffered fresh restraints; but the Directors' authority remained substantial – a good deal more so in some respects than had seemed likely at the start. It was not surprising that the Governor-General's powers should have been less than those which Dundas at first proposed – his own misgivings about Hastings would account for that – nor that those of the Directors should have been raised against the Company's General Court, for the latter was less easily amenable to Ministerial pressure. But the right of appeal to the King in Council (nugatory though this turned out to be), the firm retention of all patronage, the involvement of the Directors in secret correspondence – these points were extracted by Company spokesmen, either in January when Pitt first drew up a bill,[2] or in June when he was drafting the final measure. Some of his difficulties, of course, were caused by the turn of Parliamentary events: after Fox's effort, he could scarcely do much about patronage himself. More arose from the need to conciliate sections of the Company, in return for their support of the bill as a whole.

Some of the concessions, therefore, were important, and they drew comment at the time. But Pitt and Dundas were thereby able to achieve a good deal. They laid a foundation on which, however imperfect, it was possible to build for the future – at home, by steady if at first anxious pressure from a Ministerial Board on the Company's Directors; in India, by a gradual enlargement to the powers of authorities brought slowly under Government's control. 'The unending criss-cross of relationships between Calcutta and Westminster, Leadenhall Street and Downing Street, the Directors and the Whips . . . that also is part of the lost landscape';[3] and that landscape was planted, unevenly but continuously, in the decades that followed Pitt's India Act. The key was there, which Fox's more drastic scheme did not provide; and if the lock yielded slowly, that perhaps was better than trying to break down the door. The Company remained a great nuisance to Ministers. But at least its co-operation had been enlisted, and its servants' responsibilities were sustained. The terms of the alliance

1. *P.R.*, XVI (1784), 77–8.
2. P. 139 above.
3. G. M. Young, 'Burke', in *Today and Yesterday* (1948), 98.

were imprecise in detail – so much so that the result has been called a 'clever, dishonest bill'.[1] But if Pitt might perhaps have been bolder, it must be remembered that he first drafted his measure in January at a time of considerable risk, and he could scarcely alter it greatly within a few months, even if (which was very doubtful) the situation allowed. And after Burke's devastatingly obvious plan it was perhaps only politic to be vague, and to refrain from underlining the Ministry's hopes of gradually having its way.

The bill passed through Parliament with conspicuous ease. This was due to two facts. First, if Pitt had had to be cautious in January, so had the Company: much of its bargaining was done at a time when it was shaken and ready to help. Even then it was not unduly enthusiastic, and there were some anxious debates in Leadenhall Street. But in the end all the major interests felt it safest to consent, so that they could scarcely back out in the summer when the subject was raised again. Even Sulivan, whatever his reservations, was broadly committed to the measure, and Pitt could count in the last resort on his uneasy allies. And secondly, Parliament itself was temporarily tired of India; the recent upheaval had momentarily exhausted the emotions of the past few years. Members in any case were apt to be restive in the later part of the session; particularly so that year, perhaps, because July was very hot. Fox himself acknowledged 'the disinclination . . . to hear more debate than was absolutely necessary',[2] and Pitt contrived in this lassitude to keep the political temperature low. He had kept Dundas out of sight as much as possible – he and he alone interviewed the Company's representatives in January –, he went out of his way to claim the Company's agreement and stress the Company's rights, and if the bill itself was not 'clever and dishonest' it was carefully and cleverly presented. Perhaps the Directors themselves did not appreciate the extent to which the compromise might be weighted against them. Certainly they could not voice their fears too openly at the time. The measure passed with some amendments, and on 13 August it became law.

The new arrangement was put in hand at once. The Board of Control consisted of Sydney, Pitt, Dundas, William Grenville, Lord Mulgrave and Lord Walsingham. Dundas soon took charge. Over the next four years he presided at almost two out of every three meetings, his views on policy always commanded respect, and he was given virtual *carte blanche* in the vital matter of the Ministry's efforts to influence appointments. It was not long before he was recognised as the Government's Indian expert, to whom Pitt was happy in the next few years to leave the bulk of an ungrateful task.

1. Philips, *The East India Company 1784–1834*, 34. The phrase seems to me somewhat to overestimate Pitt's initiative and control of the situation.
2. *P.R.,* XVI, 14.

For Pitt had a healthy respect for the Company's nuisance value. Even when it was quiet he wondered what was going on. 'I have heard nothing of our friends the Directors', he wrote to Sydney later in 1784, 'I hope they will give us no fresh trouble';[1] and by that time rumours of a schism were already rife. Part of the trouble lay, as so often, in the question of appointments, always a symbol of underlying divisions and a crucial test of power and prestige. The Directors – supported, it was rumoured, by the King – had chosen a new Commander-in-Chief of whom Government disapproved. It was the first of several such clashes, most of them bitter and prolonged. 'The Court of Directors', exclaimed Pitt on one occasion, 'deserve to be hanged'.[2]

But Ministers were soon involved in a more important quarrel. One of the most virulent controversies of the past few years had been over the question of the Arcot debts, owed by the Nawab to Company servants (or extracted by them from him) and involving an intricate network of British agents and officials. It had greatly interested Burke, an investigation had been promised by Fox, and Pitt had been obliged in his own bill to provide for an inquiry.[3] But he cannot have done so with much pleasure, for Richard Atkinson, his closest supporter, was intimately concerned, as the London agent for the largest of the creditors. It was indeed this clause in Fox's bill which, as much as anything else, had decided Atkinson to throw in his lot with Pitt, and in the summer of 1784 the 'Arcot interest' asked for the payment of the debts in full without an investigation. Sulivan and the 'Indian interest' strenuously opposed the claim, and succeeded in defeating it in the Court of Directors. But in October the Board of Control ordered a full settlement. The clause in the Act was thus ignored, the decision seemed arbitary and suspect, it gave the pamphleteers a new bone to worry – 'that pure, holy, and glorious triumvirate, composed of Mr. Pitt, Mr. Dundas, and Mr. Atkinson'[4] –, and it thrust Sulivan finally into opposition.

The Ministry was thus in bad odour with a majority of the Directors, at a time when their relations particularly needed to be good. For, inescapably and urgently, the great question of Hastings was coming to a head; and while the recent arguments had nothing directly to do with this issue, they antagonised the Indian interest at a very awkward point. The decision in favour of the Arcot interest, coming on top of Sulivan's disappointment of his Chair, seemed ominous to Hastings's supporters and to Hastings himself. In point of fact, Pitt was far from having made up his mind. He certainly was not anxious to pronounce against the Governor-General; but he was uneasy, and Dundas's influence inclined

1. 14 October 1784 (Clements Library Mss, University of Michigan).
2. To Dundas, 8 September [1787] (Clements Mss). And see Dundas's reply in P.R.O. 30/8/157.
3. P. 190 above.
4. *A Key to the Parliamentary Debates* . . . (n.d. but probably 1785), 32.

him even more to wait and see. For Dundas had been a party to the report of the Secret Committee of the Commons in 1782, which had led to a vote of censure on some of Hastings's activities; and while he was not prepared to take steps against Hastings in person, he frankly admitted that he would be glad if the Governor-General would retire. When Pitt came in, with the support of a united 'Old Party' including Sulivan, it seemed possible that the tide might be reversed. But Hastings himself was not unduly hopeful, he became progressively less so, and at the beginning of 1785 he made up his mind. The failure of Pitt's Act to extend the Governor-General's powers seemed to him decisive.[1] He submitted his resignation in January, and a few months later sailed for home.

His decision at once gave fresh life to his opponents, and the Ministry had to face the possibility of renewed debate. It had also to consider, with the Company, whom to appoint in Hastings's stead. No more awkward choice could be imagined in an explosive atmosphere; and it was embarrassed almost at once by a fresh complication. One possible candidate for the post was the Governor of Madras, the energetic and peremptory George Macartney, who had been sent out a few years before to clean up the province, and had succeeded to some extent. His efforts had gained him the Government's admiration. But they included a wartime decision to put a temporary stop to the vexed affair of the Arcot debts by vesting the revenues on which payment depended in the Government of Madras; and when Macartney wished to perpetuate this arrangement, he was overruled by Hastings. The final settlement in London enraged Hastings's supporters; but it also enraged Macartney by recognising the debtors' case. Never a patient man, he decided to resign. Meanwhile Dundas, all unaware, had resolved to press for him as Hastings's successor, and he engaged Pitt's rather lukewarm support.[2] Macartney was appointed in February 1785, by a single vote. But on learning the news a few months later he promptly refused the post, and in turn sailed for England to see what was going on. By the autumn of 1785, when a Parliamentary attack on Hastings was stirring, relations between the Government and the Company were therefore unhappy, the Governor-Generalship was in a vacuum, and Ministers were striving uneasily to enforce the authority of the Board of Control without being drawn into declaring their attitude to Hastings himself.

II

It is not easy to decide exactly what Pitt thought about Indian affairs in these early years. One may suspect that he was not prepared to

1. For his last effort to influence the new Government, see his letter to Pitt of 11 December 1784, in C. C. Davies, 'Warren Hastings and the Younger Pitt'; *E.H.R.*, LXX, no. 277, 609–22.

2. Pitt certainly had not thought of Macartney seriously a few months before: see his letter to Sydney of 14 October 1784, in Clements Mss.

probe them more deeply than he had to. He seems rather to have hoped to settle immediate issues with as little fuss as possible; and in this his hands of course were largely tied by the fact that he had risen by Fox's fall. But he does not give the impression of having been deeply shocked by Fox's bill.[1] His own was framed, on the basis of Dundas's, to impose as much Governmental control as was compatible with keeping sectional interests quiet. He was prepared to pay the price, or so it seemed to many, by allowing the settlement of the Arcot debts. And he left Company and Indian business as far as could to Dundas.[2] India was an explosive and intricate subject, in which he had not been closely involved; and he looked on the Company itself and its parties with a bored distaste. His reactions to its affairs in 1784 and 1785 are typical of his behaviour when he was embarrassed and his attention was not really engaged.

For this was a side of Pitt's character which was to be shown in other fields over the years. He could be quite inactive or indecisive when his concern was not aroused, or had dropped. In this instance, where action could not be avoided and a plan lay to hand, he was content to be tactically adroit. He behaved in a very different way over the other great contemporary problem, that of a commercial settlement with Ireland.

Walter Bagehot maintained, in his review of the first two volumes of Stanhope's *Life* of Pitt, that one of the most important things about the young Minister was that 'he came to power with a fresh mind'. 'An old man of the world has no great objects, no telling enthusiasm, no large proposals, no noble reforms' (Bagehot did not live to experience Gladstone in his old age). But Pitt was exempt at the start from this sad decay, and his electoral triumph gave him the power 'to do what he would'.[3] The last part of this judgment needs qualifying: Pitt was far from being free to act always as he wished. And we must recognise the directions and limits of his enthusiasm: there were areas of darkness between the beams of light. But the beams were very strong where they fell, and Bagehot of course was right. Pitt was eager, as a young man should be, for large proposals and noble reforms. Nor did he ever entirely lose his youthful hopes; the confident, enthusiastic strain in his nature was always waiting for the occasion – to an extent indeed that had marked repercussions when the occasion failed. He could always take fire, though it was not always easy to predict the cause. Given the right subject and conditions, he, like Shelburne – like Chatham – loved a comprehensive scheme.

Ireland was such a subject. It lay near the heart of the complex of

1. See p. 126 above.

2. Out of 116 meetings of the Board of Control in the years 1784–6, Pitt attended one (the opening meeting) in 1784, eight in 1785 (all in the last quarter), and eight in 1786 (India Office Library, Board of Control Minutes, vol. 1).

3. 'William Pitt' (1861), in *Biographical Studies*, ed. Richard Holt Hutton (1881), 141–2.

problems bequeathed by the recent war.[1] The whole nature of her connexion with England – commercial, juridical, strategic – had still to be finally settled in the light of the successful American revolt. Much had been done in the past few years; but it had necessarily been done piecemeal, and a stubborn variety of interests had frustrated the hopes of a balanced solution. Irish trade had been partly freed by North's Acts of 1780[2] – British colonial markets were now open on the terms available to British manufacturers, woollens and glass could be exported, access to the Levant was allowed, gold and silver coin could be accepted from whatever quarter. Two years later, under further pressure, a degree of self-government was bestowed. Poyning's Law, and the Act of George I governing relations with Ireland, were repealed; the Irish Parliament became independent, subject only to the veto of the Privy Council; the Irish judicature was freed from the supervision of the British courts. These measures of Rockingham's Government were confirmed by Shelburne's Renunciation Act,[3] after various incidents had thrown doubt on their application. Much therefore had been done, and done by all parties, to meet the claim for 'a distinct kingdom', though one that should be, as the great Irish leader Grattan put it, 'inseparably annexed to the Crown of Great Britain'.[4]

Much; but not enough. For the very degree of independence raised the question of future links. How was the 'distinctness' of Ireland now to be reconciled with her 'inseparable annexation' to the parent Crown? To English Ministers, all convinced that a continuing connexion was indispensable, some formal compact, presumably by treaty, seemed necessary to this end. They said as much to the Irish. But despite professions of goodwill no practical suggestion came from Dublin; rather, as two bad harvests hit the country in 1783 and 1784, there were fresh cries for commercial help. Perhaps not surprisingly, these met with little response from Ministers all of whom had already tried to meet earlier demands. Shelburne became convinced that his Renunciation Act was 'a damned thing', North was flatly opposed to any new concessions, Fox was equally determined that 'the account must be considered as having been closed'.[5] This last reaction, had he read it, would have seemed to George III a suitable judgment on the folly of opening floodgates under pressure.[6]

But while they reacted sharply against the renewed agitation, both Shelburne and Fox had a broad idea of the lines a settlement should

1. See p. 160 above.
2. P. 50 above
3. Passed after his fall, but prepared by him.
4. *Memoirs of the Life and Times of the Rt. Hon. Henry Grattan.* By his son, Henry Grattan, II (1839), 236–8.
5. Shelburne's remark was made to Townshend (Buckingham, I, 113); Fox's in a letter to the Earl of Northington, 1 November 1783 (*Life of Grattan*, III, (1841), 107).
6. See his note to North of 24 July 1783 (*Correspondence of King George III*, VI, no. 4426).

take. Their views are of great interest, not least for the effect on Pitt. Both men freely granted the rights of the Irish Parliament and judicature, and the devolution of domestic authority on the Lord Lieutenant. But in 'external affairs' the Irish must acknowledge 'the superintending Power and Supremacy to be where Nature has placed it', and – a cardinal point for Shelburne – they should pay 'a proportionate contribution . . . for the general protection of the empire' in return for past concessions and the promise of 'an extended commerce'. The issue of sovereignty thus did not arise; on the contrary, the question was how Ireland could again become 'a useful and co-ordinating part of the British Empire'.[1] The means lay chiefly in the support of her industry and the enlargement of her trade. The price – the more necessary now that American resources had been removed – was a guaranteed contribution to imperial defence.

So far Fox and Shelburne shared common ground. Their differences were those of detail and, still more, of tactics,[2] and Shelburne in particular was undecided how to act. 'It is the only subject', he told George III at the start, 'through which I do not see some sort of way';[3] and he remained pessimistic to the end. Indeed he had good cause. Admittedly things improved in Ireland in the later part of 1782; and English Ministers, including Anglo-Irish absentees like Shelburne himself, were always apt to hope that a combination of patronage and firmness would do the trick. But from the Castle in Dublin the prospects looked unsure. Successive Lord Lieutenants felt that they faced an unpredictable future, which might not prove amenable to the familiar inducements and restraints. 'It is no longer the Parliament of Ireland that is to be attended to', lamented Portland, '– It is the whole of this Country';[4] and while he was writing at a bad moment in a situation that could suddenly improve, it had always to be borne in mind that it could as suddenly deteriorate. In 1783, with a bad harvest, the atmosphere worsened once more; but no one in office had the time or the will to regain the initiative. So difficult a task must now await a breathing space in England, and the approach would come more easily from a fresh and uncommitted hand.

Pitt had some acquaintance with the detail of Irish issues when he formed his Government. As Chancellor of the Exchequer he had been marginally concerned with the consequences of revising the Irish trade, and he took his share in Cabinet discussions of the situation as a whole.

1. These quotations are all from Shelburne: to Portland on 18 May and 9 June 1782 (P.R.O., H.O. 100/1, 100/2), and to Grenville in December (Buckingham, I, 86–7).
2. See p. 81 above.
3. Letter of 14 May 1782 (*Correspondence of King George III*, VI, no. 3743).
4. To Shelburne, no. 2, 24 April 1782 (P.R.O., H.O. 100/1).

But his connexion with the Grenvilles, at a time when Temple was Lord Lieutenant and William Grenville was Temple's Secretary, had drawn him closer to the heart of the problem. He did not dissent from Shelburne's policy, and the Grenvilles themselves maintained a certain reserve.[1] But when William Grenville visited London to press for a Renunciation Bill, he involved Pitt in its drafting;[2] and Pitt spoke to the measure in the subsequent debates. His views indeed must have been coloured by his cousins' impressions; for both were seized – perhaps too much – by the urgency of the Irish problem, they were correspondingly dismayed by Shelburne's caution, and the fact that the Coalition in its turn was cautious may have further stimulated Pitt to act.

He was the more ready to do so because the issue centred once more on trade. For the wheel had come full circle since 1780. The national movement had been founded in distress; commercial had been followed by constitutional concessions; and now a constitutional settlement hung on that of commerce. This was precisely the sort of challenge that appealed to Pitt. He was always excited by problems of trade and finance, and here they impinged on others of the same nature with which he would have to deal. It would clearly be helpful to take the Irish questions in conjunction with their counterparts in Britain – examination of the customs duties, and of the Navigation Act – which he had in mind or were already under way; and they could scarcely be divorced from the review of our commercial relations with European powers, which in one case – that of Portugal – had already come up, and to which in others we were committed by the treaties of peace.[3] There were therefore cogent reasons for Pitt to tackle the subject, and they were of the kind to which he would gladly listen.

He could not move at once. The political struggle took all his time until April 1784, and then the India bill and other business claimed priority before the recess. The excitement in England, too, was reflected in Ireland, perhaps the more so because Pitt had no Lord Lieutenant at first. Cornwallis had refused the post, and it was February before Rutland arrived, accompanied in the key appointment of Chief Secretary by the able Shelburnite Thomas Orde.[4] They found it difficult for a time to command a reliable Parliamentary majority, and, as at home, the Government did not settle down until the spring. Meanwhile distress continued and unrest increased. There was fresh rioting in Dublin, merchants and shopkeepers were tarred and feathered, soldiers beaten up. The Irish Parliament was restive, and the Castle soon began to press for something to be done. Pitt seemed sympathetic,[5]

1. William Grenville, when asked by Pitt, refused to move the address on the peace terms in the Commons.
2. See Buckingham, I, 124.
3. P. 95 above.
4. See pp. 130, 183 above.
5. See Mornington's report to Rutland of 31 May 1784 (*H.M.C., Fourteenth Report, Appendix, Pt. I,* 99–100).

and a visit by Orde to London in June and July turned the scale. When he left, it had been arranged that he should return with some colleagues in the autumn, and that meanwhile the Irish Government should draft a preliminary commercial plan. This was produced by early September, the work principally of Orde and John Foster, the Irish Chancellor of the Exchequer; and by the middle of that month the result was in Pitt's hands.

The proposals concentrated on three immediate objects: a revision of the Navigation Act, the regulation of certain duties (including a measure of protection), and the definition of Ireland's position in treaties with foreign states. But it became clear at once that these limited targets would not satisfy Pitt. On 19 September he wrote an important letter to Orde, which reveals at the very start a far more radical, systematic approach.[1]

The points that now present themselves for discussion are not without delicacy and difficulty; but what appears to me more delicate and difficult than the arrangement of any one or all the specific points that can be stated, is to endeavour to establish some fixed principles which may from time to time be applied to new circumstances as they arise in the relative situations of the two countries. It is not enough if we settle what shall be the modification of the Navigation Act, or what shall be the proportion of duties on certain commodities. We must, in order to make a permanent and tranquil system, find some line according to which the Parliaments of the two countries may exercise the rights of legislation, without clashing with each other on the one hand, or, on the other, being encumbered by the necessity of actual and positive concert on every point of common concern.

It is certainly on general principles desirable *(though with some reservations arising from the actual circumstances)* that the system of commerce should be so arranged as to extend the aggregate wealth of Great Britain and Ireland to its utmost limit, without partiality or preference to one part of the Empire or the other. But for this purpose two things seem fundamentally requisite. One, that Ireland, which will thus gain upon England in relative strength and riches, should proportionately relieve her of the burden which she now sustains exclusively. The other, that this increase of strength and riches in Ireland may really prove either a positive addition to that of the Empire at large, or at least a transfer only from one member of it to the other, and may not in the end be *so much taken from ourselves and given* to a separate country. . . .

One distinct object, and indeed the principal one in this view of the matter, is that of naval strength. It is of the utmost importance to have that well considered in any settlement to be made. . . . The operation, indeed, of many of these speculations is remote. It may be

1. Ashbourne, 85–7.

long before the industry and the capital of Ireland are sufficient to bring forward the application of them in practice. But in such a question as this we must look to remote as well as to immediate consequences; and it is always possible that, in so great a change as that made in the situation of Ireland by what has been done, and perhaps may yet remain to be done, that [*sic*] the effects may be more rapid than any calculations can now foresee. . . . After all, the great question remains: *What is it* that in truth will give satisfaction and restore permanent tranquillity to Ireland? Much has been given already, and the effect has been very little in proportion. It will be idle to make concessions without having good ground to think that they will attain their object.

He ended by suggesting the possibility of some Irish Parliamentary reform.

The principles were repeated to Rutland a fortnight later.[1]

I own to you the line to which my mind at present inclines (open to whatever new observations or arguments may be suggested to me) is, *to give Ireland an almost unlimited communication of commercial advantages,* if we can receive in return some security that *her strength and riches will be our benefit, and that she will contribute from time to time in their increasing proportions to the common exigencies of the empire.* And having, by holding out this, removed, I trust, every temptation to Ireland to consider her interest as separate from England, to be ready, while we discountenance *wild and unconstitutional attempts, which strike at the root of all authority,* to give real efficacy and popularity to Government, by acceding (if such a line can be found) to a *prudent and temperate reform of Parliament,* which may guard against or gradually cure *real* defects and mischiefs, may show a sufficient regard to the interests and even prejudices of individuals who are concerned, and may unite the Protestant interest in *excluding the Catholics from any share in the representation* or the government of the country.

He did not depart from this line of argument throughout the coming year.

Pitt's policy was thus very largely that of his predecessors, to be applied more generously, more searchingly, and as an act of grace, and with the distinctive addition of some measure of Parliamentary reform. But there was of course a host of interests through which he would have to weave his way. As he himself conceded, success 'must depend upon the actual temper and disposition of men's minds',[2] and there were very serious obstacles to be overcome. In England, the Cabinet must be

1. *Correspondence between the Right Honble William Pitt and Charles Duke of Rutland . . . 1781–1787* (1890), 43–4.
2. Op. cit., 44.

carried and commercial interests reassured, while the Irish Government, working with this support through its own institutions, must satisfy its merchants and nationalists that the bargain was worth while. All would hang on tactics and timing, in a situation which no one so far had managed properly to control.

Rutland and Orde were optimistic at first. 'I think I can venture to assure you', wrote the latter to Pitt in mid-October, 'that we shall experience little difficulty' over an Irish contribution to naval defence.[1] But this sanguine mood did not last long. At the end of the month the Irish Government's deputation arrived in London,[2] and as the talks progressed a serious difference of view emerged. The emissaries – principally Foster and John Beresford, the influential M.P. and Customs Commissioner who now came increasingly to the fore – could not quarrel with the object of the commercial plan itself. 'I have found both Mr. Pitt and Mr. Dundas very liberal in their ideas', wrote Beresford; and indeed they were prepared in principle to extend 'a system of perfect equality in trade'.[3] But the price to be paid was another matter. The Irish Government saw enormous difficulties in agreeing to a fixed annual contribution to defence. There was bound to be an outcry against a specific immediate payment in return for a more distant and unpredictable gain; and the payment, whatever form it took, must be related to Ireland's own needs, and should not be removed entirely from her own control. It would therefore be much wiser not to impose a sum from outside, but to leave the amount of the contribution to Irish goodwill.

Pitt was not impressed. The Irish problem had seized his imagination. It was 'a subject', he wrote to Orde, 'I have so much at heart'; 'one of the most interesting subjects', he told Rutland, 'that can occupy our attention in the course of our lives'.[4] In such a frame of mind, Rutland's warnings seemed jeremiads, and moreover Pitt was convinced that he had found the key. The principle of a settlement was clear: 'the only one on which the whole plan can be justified, is . . . that for the future the two countries will be to the most essential purposes united';[5] and he was satisfied, from his calculations, that such unity as could be achieved in trade would benefit Ireland as much as Britain. In that case, he was confident that he had an answer to the vexed question of the contribution. We certainly could not rely simply on Irish goodwill; not only because English opinion would demand a guaranteed *quid pro quo*, but

1. 10 October 1784 (copy in Bolton Mss, no. 196, Letter Book I).
2. See p. 199 above. In the event, Orde himself could not come.
3. To Orde, 27 October, 5 November 1784 (Bottom Mss, loc. cit). Dundas, as a good Scot in the great age of Scottish Enlightenment, had indeed agreed with Adam Smith on the subject of Ireland five years before.
4. To Orde, 7 January 1785 (Bolton Mss, no. 193); to Rutland, 6–7 January 1785 (*Correspondence between Pitt and Rutland*, 74).
5. *Correspondence*, 65–6.

also because it was essential to the principle of the scheme that the guarantee should not rest solely with the beneficiaries. But equally it was only fair that the peacetime payment should match the advantage – as the latter rose or fell, so should the former. Pitt believed that he had lighted on the perfect medium for this purpose: the income from a fund known as the Irish hereditary revenue.[1] For since this was made up mainly of the customs and excise duties, it could be taken as an index of national prosperity. Let the contribution, then, be regulated by the fortunes of this fund. Let an aggregate be taken of its yield over the past four or five years, and any annual surplus be paid in future to the common naval defence. If Irish trade suffered in any year under the new commercial arrangements, the Irish contribution would automatically decrease; but if, as Pitt expected, it benefited from them, the size of the contribution would reflect the fact. Such an arrangement was strictly equitable in peace – indeed it might well favour Ireland at first, if the commercial benefits were delayed. In the event of war, Pitt was content to rest on Irish goodwill.

The more Pitt studied the subject, the more he liked his plan; and indeed it offered a hopeful, and one might have thought an honourable, prospect. The 'fixed principle' was established, to which future problems could be referred; it was neatly embodied in existing arrangements, which need not be disturbed; and the result could be logically defended against objections from either side. It should go a long way towards meeting those of the English protectionists, by converting a proportion of the Irish gain under a freer trade into a subscription to naval defence. It should meet the Irish reluctance to granting a fixed specific sum which would be open to attack as conditions changed. 'If the bargain is unfair . . . it is not calculated for the situation of two countries connected as Great Britain and Ireland ought to be. But it is of the essence of such a settlement [as mine] that both the *advantage* and the *obligation* should be reciprocal; one cannot be so without the other',[2] and the proportions would be automatically attuned by a self-regulating financial scale. The whole arrangement was a good example of the way in which Pitt's mind liked to work.[3]

But there was a snag – and one which was underlined by the choice of this particular fund. For the hereditary revenue was devoted, like the Civil List in England, to the normal peacetime expenses of government; and, like the Civil List, it was failing to keep pace. If any increased revenue, therefore, was to be earmarked for predominantly British

1. This comprised revenues vested in the Crown, under Charles II, in exchange for former Crown lands distributed, under the Commonwealth, between the English soldiers settled in Ireland.

2. Pitt to Rutland, 6–7 January 1785 (*Correspondence*, 71–2).

3. It is interesting that Grenville, who claimed later to have disliked the scheme, acknowledged and indeed stressed this fact. The idea, he thought in retrospect, was 'impossible'. But it reflected Pitt's habitual 'fondness in every difficulty for complicated expedients'. ('Commentaries of my own Political Life . . .'; Fortescue Mss).

purposes, the Irish budget would not benefit from the increased trade, and fresh supplies must still be raised. In fact the Irish could claim that the concession was not as great as it appeared: no specifically Irish need was served, the more that was gained the more was handed over, and moreover by an agreement which removed the money from their annual control. Rutland and his advisers therefore continued to protest that they doubted if this form of painless extraction would be gratefully received.

But if it were not; if the Irish Parliament refused the offer, the results might be serious indeed. Pitt soon managed to carry the English Ministers with him, rather to the Irish Government's surprise – 'I sat long enough in your Cabinet', Rutland wrote later, 'to be acquainted with the cavil and pertinacity of some of your colleagues'[1] – and on 5 January 1785 the heads of the proposals were laid before the King. But the next step, it was agreed in London, must be taken in Dublin; the Irish Commons must accept this 'essential part' of the scheme before the British Commons were asked to accept the rest.[2] This argument was reinforced by threatening noises from Opposition, and Ministers accordingly redoubled their pleas and commands to Rutland and Orde. At the same time they were unwilling to modify the scheme itself. The Lord Lieutenant was told that some money might be devoted to the purchase of naval stores in Ireland, or alternatively it might be allocated to the reduction of the British (and thus, by inclusion) the Irish National Debt. But the Admiralty refused – as they always did, and rightly – to reserve special funds for special aspects of defence, and Pitt himself was not prepared to compromise on this. The scheme had therefore to go forward as the British Government wanted. Its reception was much as the Irish Government had feared.

On 7 February, after as much delay as could be decently gained by 'a *lucky* cold',[3] Orde introduced ten resolutions to the Irish Commons. They followed the lines laid down in the conversations in London three months before. There would be freedom of trade between the two countries in their own products, and reciprocity in their duties, including an amendment of excise duties where the total impost would otherwise be unequal. Bounties on exports would be cancelled except for those on corn, meal, malt, flour and biscuit, and bounties on mutual re-exports from the British plantations would be cancelled or equalised. Imports from foreign states would be mutually regulated. And – by article 10 – the future surplus from the revenue of the Irish hereditary fund, above a sum to be decided, would be appropriated 'towards the support of the naval force of the empire'.[4]

1. 14 July 1785 (P.R.O. 30/8/330).
2. See, most explicitly, Sydney to Rutland, 6 January 1785 (P.R.O., H.O. 100/16).
3. Rutland to Pitt, 6 [actually 7] February 1785 (*H.M.C., Fourteenth Report, Appendix, Pt. I*, 175).
4. *The Parliamentary Register: or History . . . of the House of Commons of Ireland*, IV, (1785), 120–5.

The result was catastrophic. There were protests from every quarter against article 10 – from Grattan and from Beresford, from the Law Officers and the Dublin press – and it was soon clear to the Castle that only an amendment would save the day. Working at high speed amid scenes of great excitement, the Irish Government therefore took the plunge, and agreed to withdraw the offending clause. Instead, a new article 10 was introduced, deploring the increase of the Irish National Debt, and resolving that the annual revenue should be made equal to the expenses; and a further article 11 was added, providing that the surplus of the hereditary revenue over and above £656,000 a year should go to the naval defence of the Empire, in peacetime after the Irish budget had been balanced, in wartime regardless of whether it had or not.

The concession did the trick – as well it might. The Irish Commons quietened at once, and the resolutions passed on 11 February.

To the sorely tried Rutland and Orde, this was a happy deliverance. To Ministers in London it seemed a calamitous reverse. The Lord Lieutenant had had no time to consult, and the unexpectedness of the news increased the sense of grievance. Sydney, the Home Secretary, conveyed the Government's displeasure; the King expressed his horror to Pitt; and Pitt himself was so convinced that the English Commons would now reject the scheme that he thought seriously of 'suspending' it until the Irish Government could find a way out.[1]

In the event he went ahead. He was probably right. It would have been awkward not to report the passing of the Irish Resolutions, and the best hope of countering Opposition was to make an early statement of the Government's case. But Pitt could scarcely do more than that, while he tried to unsort the tangle; and on 22 February he opened the debate in that sense. Avoiding excessive detail, he dwelt on the object of his plan, and insisted on the need for a generous approach. But he was equally insistent on the need for a guaranteed Irish annual contribution, and he therefore asked the Commons merely to approve the principle of the Resolutions 'till the Parliament of Ireland should have considered the matter' still under dispute.[2]

Opposition naturally mounted a fierce attack. But the House was content to await events, and to allow a week before resuming the debate. The two Governments meanwhile set to work to bridge the gap.

By the second week of March it looked as if they might succeed.

1. Pitt to the Marquess of Buckingham, 20 February 1785 (Holland Rose, 253).
2. *P.R.*, XVII (1785), 247–60. The tone of his speech, and Orde's subsequent correspondence with George Rose of the Treasury (Bolton Mss, no. 196, Letter Book II), suggest that Lecky was mistaken in supposing that 'the English Government took no step to disavow their representatives in Ireland' (*A History of Ireland in the Eighteenth Century* (1892 edn.), II, 442).

Rutland was sure that the Irish Commons would guarantee a contribution, as long as it was not embodied in the earlier obnoxious form. Some wording must therefore be devised which would separate 'contribution and economy' (i.e. the Irish budget), and recognise the legitimate and equal needs of both. Pitt could not drop the principle of his original article 10. But he was prepared to rephrase it if the Irish would drop their own two articles, and to accompany the rephrased Resolutions, as passed by the British Commons, with an Address acknowledging the need for 'an economical administration' in Ireland which was recognised as being the Irish Parliament's concern. The proviso of a balanced budget would thus be removed, but its principle retained; and further detailed Resolutions (which Pitt drafted) or a bill would then be presented in Dublin, to meet the twin policies as approved at Westminster. The Irish Government was not entirely happy; but it fell into line, and agreed to present an Appropriation Bill which would meet Pitt's demands. On 10 March Orde was sent to London to work out the final terms, and when he left Dublin he thought that agreement might be reached in 'a few hours'.[1]

It is impossible to say if these tactics would have worked. There was always the danger of a procedural snag, and the difference of principle was not entirely removed. But they were never put to the test; for by the time that Orde reached London the picture had changed. The Ministry was in trouble, Pitt himself was despondent, and Orde, who had expected to be back in Ireland within a matter of days, found himself held in England over the next three weeks.

What had gone wrong? Pitt himself had been optimistic only a week before. 'If we succeed now', he had written to Orde – and he made it clear that he thought they would – 'we shall have the satisfaction to reflect, notwithstanding the temporary interruption which has been unavoidable, that this great work has been carried thro' with infinitely less difficulty than any man living cd. some months ago have ventured to hope'.[2] He was convinced that the new proposals would meet the Irish case; and that being so, 'the whole principle is preserved, recognised and approved'.[3]

Such assurance may seem excessive. But Pitt was not relying on his new formula alone. He also believed that he could count on the acquiescence of most of the English manufacturers. At the end of January, the Committee of Trade had been ordered to report on the question of settling reciprocal duties with Ireland, and of continuing the preferences in her favour against imports from foreign states. Evidence

1. To Evan Nepean [an Under-Secretary of State at the Home Office], 10 March 1785 (P.R.O., H.O. 100/16).
2. 3 March 1785 (Bolton Mss, no. 196, Letter Book II). And see his letter of the same date to Rutland, in Ashbourne, 116–18.
3. Edward Cooke [Under-Secretary of State in Dublin] to Rutland, reporting a conversation with Pitt, 3 March 1785 (Bolton Mss, no. 196, Letter Book II).

was taken from the industrialists over the next few weeks, and on the whole with heartening results. Some spokesmen were naturally less well disposed than others – the textile manufacturers were more doubtful than the iron founders and the potters, the silk mercers than the cotton manufacturers, the cotton manufacturers than the wool merchants. All were concerned that competition should be really equal, that English taxes should be reviewed, Irish internal levies curtailed, and Irish bounties on exports reduced. But given such satisfaction, none opposed the principle of reciprocity, for 'undampted, unchecked and untaxed' the British manufacturer 'will be equal, if not superior, to any other manufacturer in the world'.[1] Pitt therefore felt free, from such evidence as well as from his own soundings, to tell the Commons on 22 February that 'the manufacturers . . . had not been alarmed at the prospect'.[2] Ten days later the Government's impression remained the same. 'There seems no reason', Sydney remarked on 3 March, 'to expect delay from Addresses sent from Commercial Towns'.[3]

Yet within a week the commercial towns were mustering their forces, and the addresses were beginning to pour in. What had occasioned such an extraordinary reverse? In the first place, the Committee of Trade's inquiries had not covered the whole field. They were excluded by their terms from reference to the Navigation Act, which left a wide area open to speculation. Nor could the evidence itself be taken as definitive: it was perforce hedged about with provisions, and subject to approval of the detailed terms. Many of those who attended the Committee were aware that they could not speak fully for all their competitors, and it would not be difficult to play on the fears of an adverse turn of events. The ground was less firm, the balance more even, than the answers might suggest. There had already been mutterings when the Irish Government stressed the advantages for Irish trade. Now they suddenly swelled to a chorus as the result of a tactical error by Pitt.

For Pitt was as determined as ever to control, and force, the pace. He was sure that the greatest danger lay in delay – and the course of some of his later commercial negotiations suggests that he was not far wrong. But such a strategy demanded both nerve and finesse, and while Pitt had not lacked confidence his tactics failed at this delicate point. The debate on the Irish Resolutions was resumed on 3 March.[4] The Minister opened it by announcing that he would move their adoption in a week's time, unless fresh evidence or protests had meanwhile been received in due form.[5] This was scarcely in accord with the earlier sense of the House, which had agreed to postpone the debate so as to

1. From the evidence of the Manchester cotton delegation (quoted in Harlow, op. cit., I, 595). And cf. loc. cit., 594, 596.
2. *P.R.*, XVII, 255.
3. To Rutland (quoted Harlow, loc. cit., 585).
4. See p. 204 above.
5. *P.R.*, XVII, 313–14.

allow papers to be properly prepared and considered. Opposition at once grasped the opportunity, and accused Pitt of indecent haste.

The charge undoubtedly had an effect. It worried many of the independents, and it must have been partly responsible for the way in which Government's arguments were largely ignored. Pitt did not in fact neglect to publish a statement of his evidence. Early in March – perhaps at the beginning – he put on sale a shortened version of the advance draft of the Committee of Trade's report, with a selection of the manufacturers' replies.[1] The pamphlet might perhaps have been fuller, and supported with greater publicity. It did not answer, as it might have done, some of the objections that were being raised. But even so it dealt convincingly with much of Opposition's case, and in a calmer atmosphere one might have expected it to be widely noticed.

As it was, the publication seems to have been largely ignored. This, however, was by no means the result entirely of chance. It is possible, though perhaps not probable, that merchants and manufacturers would soon have had second thoughts in any case, and might have combined to express them effectively. It is also possible that they would not have done so at this point without some further stimulus. Certainly the stimulus was there. 'The truth is at this hour & you best know it', wrote William Eden to his associate Lord Sheffield when all was over, 'that if you & I had not work'd up that Irish Business, Ld. North would have slept thro the Session at Bushy & Mr. Fox at St. Anne's Hill'.[2] This was probably claiming too much: both North and Fox were interested in Ireland, they had already scented their chance, and the nature of the session in general was scarcely such as to send them to sleep. But Eden and Sheffield undoubtedly supplied the ammunition and the organising power on which the party's case was fought; and one can hardly imagine that without their efforts it would have taken the course it did.

The two men had 'worked up business' before, most notably in the debates on commercial relations with the United States. They made quite a formidable pair. Sheffield – John Holroyd, Gibbon's friend[3] – was a firm and persuasive exponent of an up-to-date form of protection. An accomplished pamphleteer,[4] he entered the field as soon as the Irish Resolutions passed in Dublin, his genuine convictions reinforced by a personal distrust of Pitt. Eden was a more complex and less attractive character. Able and experienced – he had been a Commissioner of Trade, a Commissioner to America, and later Chief Secretary in

1. Both Stockdale and Almon printed, and sold, the *Report of the Lords of the Committee of Council* . . . (1785) in similar versions, obviously at the Treasury's behest. The report itself, as published, was dated 1 March, and came from the draft of the approved document which was passed by the Privy Council, as Harlow points out (*The Founding of the Second British Empire I*, 598), only on the 16th.

2. 22 October 1785 (B.M. Add. Ms 45728).

3. His host, indeed, on the occasion of the historian's encounter with Pitt (p. 23 above).

4. See p. 160, n1 above.

Ireland under North, and a Vice-Treasurer of Ireland under the Coalition – he was also a highly ambitious politician, with a growing family to support, whose genuine interest in administration was matched by a hunger for personal advancement which recently had forced him into political decline. An active protagonist of the Coalition, he had suffered from its fall, and was now determined to recoup his fortunes without delay. Ireland gave him his chance. If he could triumph in an issue on which he was an acknowledged expert, he would again be 'considered . . . by no means an insignificant Character'.[1] With the nervous intensity which marked all the manœuvres of a long and distinguished career, he applied his powers of debate and intrigue to bringing the Government down.

The effects were soon felt. In February Sheffield published his *Observations on the Manufacture, Trade, and Present State of Ireland,* dwelling mainly (as in his pamphlet on America) on the possible threat to the Navigation Act. This was a damaging line of attack; for the subject had been excluded from the Committee of Trade's review, Sheffield had great influence with the Atlantic merchants, and the powerful West Indian interest, already involved in talks with Government over the islands' trade, were feeling uneasy about the possible repercussions of the Irish scheme. In the last week in February they opened negotiations with Pitt, and when they failed to receive immediate satisfaction a minority broke bounds and launched an attack in the press. Pitt's statement of 3 March brought tempers to the boil. A resolution, on the 9th, to join the manufacturers in a combined opposition was defeated only by the promise that the Minister would be confronted with a detailed questionnaire.

For meanwhile the manufacturers had moved, or been jockeyed, into action. They had indeed taken a momentous step. On 8 March, a representative meeting was called at the London Tavern, resolutions were passed against the Government, and a 'Great [later General] Chamber of the Manufacturers of Great Britain' was set up, to oppose the Irish Resolutions in their current form and to act thereafter as a permanent industrial association. This was a striking development. Extra-Parliamentary associations were always viewed with wary respect until they proved to have shot their bolt, they had caused a lot of trouble in the past few years, and it was something new for manufacturers to combine in this way. Political associations were familiar, on extraordinary occasions. Mercantile committees were acknowledged, and sometimes influential – the West India Planters' and Merchants' Committee was perhaps the most notable example. But this was the first time that industrialists had formally combined – a few years before, they were described by Adam Smith as being 'in a sort of tacit, but constant and uniform combination'[2] – and tried to exert political

1. To Morton Eden, 29 August [1784] (B.M. Add. Ms 34419, f. 405v).
2. *An Inquiry into the Causes of the Wealth of Nations*, ed. Cannan, I, 68.

pressure on a national scale. Such a step seemed scarcely likely to lie within their unaided powers: the activities of Eden and Sheffield, the expert look of the draft rules for the Chamber, suggested an experienced political source.[1] So did the choice of the first chairman of the executive committee. For this was none other than Josiah Wedgwood – Wedgwood of all men, who had recently spoken in favour of a freer trade. But he was a friend of Eden and Sheffield, with whom he was known to have been in close touch; and it was therefore perhaps not surprising, though it was certainly unfortunate, that the first deputation from the new Chamber should have had a frosty reception from Pitt. There was no question, they were informed on 10 March, of the Government's timetable being voluntarily altered. Wedgwood accordingly called a special meeting, and on the 12th published a notice of opposition in the press. When the unsuspecting Orde reached London that day, it was therefore to find Ministers with plenty of trouble on their hands.

This was in fact the turning point. Pitt never fully regained his power of choice. He was not at the end of his resources; he was still determined to find a way. But it was now the way of compromise, and the planned sequence of persuasion was lost.

The tangled story of the next five months seems as wearying and infuriating now as it must have seemed to Pitt at the time; and at least he had the consolation, almost to the end, of momentary hopes of success. The tale need not be told in detail, for it was much what one might expect: an attempted defence of the reciprocal duties by concessions to the supporters of the Navigation Act, and by ever more elaborate safeguards of the Irish contribution to defence; a battered agreement in England which the Irish then refused to accept.

The sudden opposition threw Pitt off balance at first. Orde's letters to Dublin show the Minister contending with a startled and doubtful Cabinet, himself momentarily shaken and depressed. Fresh petitions and evidence were pouring in, the Parliamentary debates had to be postponed, the Opposition press continued the attacks largely un-

1. As indeed did the argument which weighed so heavily with the manufacturers at this point. Under the proposed equalization of duties it was intended that the lower scale, which was Irish, should apply to both countries; and since this was in no instance below 10½ per cent, the British article in the home market would still be protected to that extent. But the industrialists were led to believe, by articles in the Opposition press, that the arrangement involved an imposition of *additional* duties, under which protection in the home market would necessarily suffer. The misrepresentation might have been exposed at the start had the Committee of Trade's findings been published more fully. As it was, I find it hard to disagree with Harlow (*The Founding of the Second British Empire,* I 608) that 'the play of commercial opinion was turned . . . by a trick'.

checked.[1] Pitt thought it necessary to yield ground at once on his weakest flank. The West India merchants were quickly assured that their interests would be protected, and the East India Company soon extracted a similar promise for its Far Eastern trade. These provisions had to be worked into the main scheme, itself under scrutiny in the light of the manufacturers' attacks. The results were to be seen when the debate was resumed in May. The original Resolutions were now transformed into sixteen Propositions; the sanctity of the Navigation Act was confirmed and, by the fourth Proposition, applied to Ireland as it was to Britain; French and Spanish colonial products were not allowed into Britain in Irish ships, imports of rum and other spirits were forbidden by way of Irish ports, some compensating duties were levied on Irish products which might otherwise undercut their British counterparts. The concessions were substantial. But, supported by such palliatives and the Treasury's efforts behind the scenes, Government rallied again and was not unhopeful of success. Pitt himself recovered his poise, his opening speech – earnest, practical, detailed – did something to remove the recent bad impression, and Opposition helped, as the debate went on, by broadening and confusing its case. North and Eden concentrated with effect on the protection of British interests. But Fox and Sheridan, with an eye to Ireland where the issue might finally have to be joined, moved on to attack the fourth Proposition as infringing Irish legislative independence; and while they may have had some success in Dublin, their sudden concern amused and disgusted a large part of their audience at home. Nevertheless, it was an anxious time.

> Do not imagine [wrote Pitt near the start][2] because we have had two triumphant divisions, that we have everything before us. We have an indefatigable enemy, sharpened by disappointment, watching and improving every opportunity. It has required infinite patience, management, and exertion to meet the clamour without doors, and to prevent it infecting our supporters in the house. Our majority, though a large one, is composed of men who think, or at least act, so much for themselves, that we are hardly sure from day to day what

1. Government's counter-attack was indeed curiously muted – a reflection, no doubt, of that weakness with the press which had contributed to the neglect of its publication of the Committee of Trade's draft report. George Rose produced a pamphlet anonymously, *The Proposed System of Trade with Ireland Explained*; and there were others, notably by George Chalmers in England, and Sir Lucius O'Brien and Hervey Redmond Morres in Ireland. But they seem to have had little popular effect. There is a ms. among Pitt's papers, 'The Opposition to the Irish Arrangements Traced' (P.R.O. 30/8/321), which may have been intended for publication.

2. To Rutland, 21 May 1785 (*Correspondence*, 105–6). This, and other letters from Pitt and Rose to Orde in Bolton Mss no. 196, Letter Book I, suggest that Wraxall exaggerated when he stated that Members divided on purely party lines because they despaired of following the detailed case (*Memoirs*, IV (1884), 132–4). The country gentlemen may well have failed to understand all the arguments. But many of them would seem to have judged all the more by the tone of the debate.

impression they may receive. We have worked them up to carry us through this undertaking in its present shape; but we have had awkwardness enough already in many parts of the discussion. The idea of having stirred this question first in Ireland, without taking previously the sense of the Parliament of England; the necessity we have been under to make explanations and amendments (which, though perfectly consistent with the general tenor of the original resolutions, are for this purpose magnified and misrepresented by opposition); the inference attempted to be drawn from hence, that the propositions were not at first properly considered; and the argument drawn for farther delay, from stating the danger which would have followed if they had been passed as we first proposed them; all these topics, enforced and aggravated as you will imagine them, have damped, and, perhaps, in some instances discontented our friends, even in the moment of victory. Any new circumstance of embarrassment might have the effect, sooner than can almost be imagined, of reversing our apparent situation of strength and security.

But in the end, with some further amendments, Government won through. The Propositions, increased to twenty, passed the Commons on the night of 30/31 May; they were manœuvred slowly through the Lords over the next six weeks; and on 25 July the alterations were agreed by both Houses. The last act had now to be played out in Dublin.

There had been frenzied preparations in London for that event. While Pitt fought in the Commons for a greater freedom of trade, he was walking a tightrope with the Irish Government – on the one hand, pressing for more elaborate safeguards to the annual contribution, on the other trying to conciliate the rising anger at his concessions. Pressure was tried first. Orde had managed to avoid committing himself too deeply in March; but in April the Cabinet insisted on detailed provisions for collecting the hereditary revenue, and on fresh exceptions (other than war) to the rule that the appropriated surplus should have regard to the state of the Irish budget. There was much agitated correspondence over the next two months, and by the time that the Propositions passed in London Rutland and Orde were close to despair. The fourth Proposition in particular had roused a fresh storm in Ireland, Grattan was thundering once more, the Parliamentary forces were disordered. In the middle of June, Beresford was sent over to consult on how best to present the revised scheme. His letters over the next five weeks convey an air of mingled excitement and exhaustion.

For Ministers and officials were pretty jaded by this time. It had been a strenuous session, with several hard fought battles other than the Irish business itself. 'For many weeks past', George Rose complained to-wards the end of May, 'I have been obliged to see people from 7 o'clock in the morning, often earlier, till 11. From that time till 3 with Mr. Pitt and at the Treasury & the rem^r. of the day & evening at the House of Commons till midnight – on our great question till 7 or 8 o'clock in the morning'.[1] The Parliamentary pressure was less now; but it left a group of tired men to tackle a set of still intractable problems. How should the necessary bill be put before the Irish Commons – with the Propositions, or without them but with a complementary and conciliatory Address? Should it be presented now, in what was left of the session, or allowed to wait until the winter? Could it be framed so as to maintain the sense of the more objectionable Propositions, without hopelessly offending Irish susceptibilities? Could Grattan be persuaded of the Ministry's goodwill in advance of the draft itself? The atmosphere changed incessantly as the letters went to and fro. 'I never saw men more dejected', Beresford reported at one moment of Pitt, Grenville and Dundas. A few days later, more favourable news 'has raised their spirits enough. There is no occasion to raise them too high, lest a fever might ensue'. Later again, 'P., R. [Rose], G. & D.' were 'unhinged'.[2] The Cabinet were unhappy, Pitt was having trouble with Gower and Camden, and the final preparation of a draft bill was exhausting in the extreme. At the beginning of July, Beresford spent a working week-end with the Minister at Putney. The meetings went on throughout the next week – 'Of the last 28 hours', he wrote on the 5th, 'I have spent 20 in Downing Street, & yet I am now . . . not further advanced than at the beginning'[3] – interspersed by consultations with the Cabinet and Grenville, Rose and Dundas. At last, on the 8th, a draft was sent to Dublin. Ten days later it was returned with alternative proposals. On the 22nd, the Cabinet decided – as it had threatened before against Pitt's advice – not to try to pass, but only to present, a bill in Dublin that summer. 'Good heavens!', exclaimed Orde, 'I am almost distracted'.[4] But the Prime Minister did not relax – for two days, wrote Rose, 'I have lived without sleep and almost without meat'[5] – and by the end of the month he had managed once more to reconcile all parties. A bill was finally drafted which satisfied the Irish Government; the Propositions would not be directly presented after all; a conciliatory Address would be sent, reaffirming Irish legislative independence. The Castle meanwhile was lobbying its supporters, and hopes rose once more. By 6 August Orde was prepared to forecast that 'the bill ought to do well'.[6] Pitt himself, now at Burton Pynsent resting from 'the scene which has lasted so long', could 'hardly see' two days later 'how accident or malice can raise any essential obstacle'.[7]

1. To Orde, 27 May 1785 (Bolton Mss, no. 196, Letter Book I).
2. To Orde, 18 June, 23 June, 1 August 1785 (Bolton Mss, no. 195).
3. To Orde (loc. cit.).
4. To Rose, 28 July (Bolton Mss, no. 196, Letter Book I).
5. To Orde, 31 July (Bolton Mss, no. 196, Letter Book II).
6. To Rose (Bolton Mss, no. 196, Letter Book I).
7. To Rutland, 8 August 1785 (*Correspondence*, 110).

Alas for the hopes. To the framers of the measure, emerging wearily from their maze, the final version obviously bore 'the stamp of fairness & liberality';[1] to Grattan and Flood and the Patriots, it was simply the old Propositions writ large. Rutland and Orde had deceived themselves. The bill did not stand a chance. On 13 August Orde moved for leave to present it to the Irish Commons – a motion that was normally carried with ease. It passed by only 19 votes, after a damaging debate. Over the next forty-eight hours the Castle took hasty soundings, and came to the conclusion that nothing could be done. It dared not risk an outright defeat. On the 15th, Orde accordingly announced that the measure would be dropped. Dublin was illuminated that night, and the crowds thronged the streets.

The defeat of the Irish Propositions marked Pitt's most serious failure in his first two years in office, and he did not suffer another like it for almost six years. It was something of a landmark for him, and he must have reflected on what went wrong – indeed, we can see him starting to do so even before the end of the affair.[2] Historians have reflected since. Some have gone so far as to suggest that the whole effort was misconceived; and certainly it is true that the failure had no immediate adverse result. On the contrary, Ireland became quieter and more prosperous over the next few years, and it is ironic that the attempts to relieve her distress should have reached a climax at a time when her agriculture and trade were in fact on the turn. Much of the credit for this result may be given to Foster's Corn Law of 1784, which soon increased the extent of arable, and encouraged the export of cereals to Britain's fast growing population. A healthy agriculture, as in England, greatly stimulated manufactures, and the process was helped by heavy industrial subsidies and the recent access to British colonial markets. When the Propositions failed, and the system of protection was left intact, Ireland's economy flourished for the best part of a decade.

It is doubtful if Pitt would have been much affected if he could have foreseen this event. He never denied the need for protection in trade with foreign powers when an easing of restrictions seemed of doubtful advantage. But the whole point of his Irish policy was that Ireland was not a foreign power; the fundamental principle, 'the only one on which the whole plan can be justified, is . . . that for the future the two countries must be to the most essential purposes united'.[3] The commercial scheme, in his eyes, was not only hopeful in itself: it was also the key to everything else. It would draw Ireland back into the web of Empire, it would lead to a common policy in foreign trade, it would help define more clearly the relations between the two Parliaments, it might pave

1. Orde to Rose, 6 August 1785 (Bolton Mss, no. 196, Letter Book I).
2. P. 211 above.
3. P. 201 above.

the way for a measure of Irish Parliamentary reform. It would achieve – what we had so dismally failed to achieve with the Americans – a new and more intimate connexion based on a greater mutual respect.

Pitt's policy, therefore, was settled. Could different tactics have brought success? The critical point was clearly at the end of February and early in March, when the fate of the Resolutions in Dublin gave Opposition its chance. Pitt was then thrown irretrievably on the defensive. But the extent to which this was so was determined by the degree of his surprise; he had not been prepared for delay, or for so marked a swing of sentiment. Perhaps it was unwise to have introduced the scheme in Ireland rather than in England. But this last would not have been easy while Irish reactions were still unknown, and if English agreement had been gained Irish agreement would still have had to follow. The real need, in fact, was to be reasonably sure of the Irish Parliament, at whatever stage its consent was required. And this meant either relying on the normal means of persuasion and pressure, or adjusting the British policy to suit.

Part of the charge against Pitt, therefore, is that he misconceived the situation in Dublin. It has been suggested that he might have done better to wait until he had tackled the question of Irish Parliamentary reform, for which indeed there had recently been ample preparation in Ireland itself.[1] But, as one of the most zealous advocates of reform appreciated, the Irish Government would have disapproved,[2] and if Pitt was not to leave the commercial questions in the air he had to tackle the assembly as it stood. It was not one of which he held a high opinion. Like most British Ministers, he could not equate the Irish with the British Commons; like them, he assumed that the Irish could always be brought into line. He did not propose, or wish, to trust to such pressures alone. He did his best to produce a plan which would meet all objections. But on this reasonable basis he expected Rutland and Orde to manage, and their eventual defeat struck him as 'almost incomprehensible'.[3] In the inevitable post-mortem he did not mince his words, or disguise his opinion that some of the deserters should be punished.[4] Reform the Irish Parliament by all means, and as soon as possible; but meanwhile Pitt did not relish seeing the Castle defied by men accustomed to listen to what they were told.

These assumptions about Ireland – which he continued to hold – may have stiffened Pitt's resolve not to yield too much on his plan at the start. But he was not disposed to do so in any case, for he was convinced that the plan was right. He had been at great pains to proportion each side's obligations to its needs, and he appreciated that the result could

1. Holland Rose, 249.
2. Richmond to Pitt, 24 December 1784 (P.R.O. 30/8/330). See also R. B. McDowell, *Irish Public Opinion 1750–1800* (1944), 111–12.
3. To Rutland, 17 August 1785 (*Correspondence*, 118).
4. Pitt to Orde, 23 August, 31 August 1785 (Bolton Mss, no. 193).

be all too easily unbalanced. This was his answer to the objections that he was offending Irish goodwill, and insisting on too definite a bargain – a word he himself disliked. Pitt in fact believed wholeheartedly in his proposals – one might almost say that he was in love with the arithmetical beauty of his design. He was not blind to the possible objections; but he was sure that he had met them in advance. The plan was reasonable precisely in the extent to which it should disarm prejudice; it took the measure, he was convinced, of the 'temper and disposition of men's minds'.[1] He was the more disappointed and disconcerted to find that it did not.

The result indeed was a personal blow. Pitt had a radical intelligence, in the sense that it sought the root of a problem. He very much disliked patching, particularly in a cause that he had at heart. He never changed in this respect, or in his instinctive optimism; he was always strongly inclined to believe he would find a way. But he was less inclined hereafter to believe that he could impose it if the argument seemed good. He had pledged himself to a scheme which was his in a very real sense: it was he who had shaped the initial response from earlier ideas, who risked a comprehensive effort and forced the pace, who lighted on the device of the hereditary revenue fund. His was the guiding hand throughout, he had worked extremely hard, and the failure was the more bitter because he hoped for success to the last.

For Pitt's optimism was perhaps the most striking feature of the whole affair. It could be a source of great strength as the problems grew. 'I am so sensible', wrote Orde, 'of the manly and noble part which Mr. Pitt has acted that I will die by inches in the cause of his support'.[2] Such devotion and skill were the more impressive because Pitt could not really bear to envisage defeat, or even a truncated version of his original scheme. He was not afraid to face the facts, even as they altered; but he was most reluctant to believe that they would alter, until in fact they did. Perhaps his hopes had been too high; they were certainly held with dangerous strength. '*I cannot allow myself to doubt*', he wrote early on of one of his points.[3] He had to discipline himself the harder when things began to go wrong.

The failure left its mark. Pitt's vision of a large-minded settlement had ended in quibblings and distrust. The immediate result, it is true, was by no means as black as he feared. '. . . Let this business of Ireland terminate well', he had written, 'let peace continue for five years, and we shall again look any Power in Europe in the face'.[4] But the disappointment had no obvious effect on Britain's recovery, or on Ireland itself, or even on the standing of his Government. The consequences

1. P. 200 above.
2. To Rose, 16 July 1785 (Ashbourne, 136).
3. To Rutland, 6/7 January 1785 (*Correspondence*, 57).
4. To Rutland, 8 August 1785 (op. cit., 111–12). And see also his remark in the debate of 12 May (*P.R.*, XVIII (1785), 266–7).

were less direct, and of longer term; but they were none the less significant for that. A great chance had been lost to build a framework in which Ireland's deeper troubles might be tackled; and Pitt himself had undergone an experience which he did not wish to repeat.

CHAPTER IX

The First Two Years:
the Westminster Scrutiny and
Parliamentary Reform

I

The Parliamentary struggle over the Irish Propositions came at an unfortunate time; for in the first four months of 1785 Pitt suffered two defeats on other questions, neither of them involving the fate of his Ministry but both of some consequence to himself. That session indeed, embracing a period always liable to be contentious,[1] proved more disappointing than any he had encountered so far, or was to encounter again for some years.

Pitt of course could not hope always to remain unassailed on his personal pedestal. Sooner or later he was bound to do something of which independent opinion disapproved. The occasion came with his handling of the later stage of the Westminster scrutiny, 'this cursed business' as one of his annoyed back-benchers called it.[2]

The Westminster election of 1784 was a famous affair. It had gone on for forty days – 'forty days' poll, forty days' riot, and forty days' confusion'[3] – and at the end Fox had triumphed in a three-cornered contest over one of his Ministerial opponents, Sir Cecil Wray, and come second on the poll to Lord Hood in a constituency returning two Members. But he had not in fact been returned, for when the final count was taken Wray demanded a scrutiny, on the grounds of corruption and false votes, and this the high bailiff granted with suspicious ease. Westminster was therefore unrepresented when the new Parliament met, Fox was present only as Member for the Tain Burghs in the far north – which a Whig patron had hastily taken the precaution of winning for him –, and it seemed not at all unlikely that he would eventually be removed from the popular seat by which he and Government alike set such considerable store.

1. See p. 32 above.
2. Daniel Pulteney to Rutland, 10 February 1785 (*H.M.C., Fourteenth Report, Appendix, Pt. I,* 177).
3. Pitt in the House of Commons, 8 June 1784 (Tomline, I, 549. This is one of the few occasions on which Tomline prints a speech *verbatim* which is only barely reported in *P.R., P.H.,* and Stockdale).

For Westminster had its own atmosphere and prestige. The constituency was numerically the largest in the kingdom, it was the only one in which every male 'inhabitant householder' had the vote, it was the home of Parliament itself and the Court, with Westminster Hall now a popular forum inside the palace precincts. Above all it was Fox's constituency, the scene of his greatest triumphs, an element in his strength which he was determined to hold. As the Coalition's fortunes crashed elsewhere, and the list of Martyrs grew, all eyes turned on his own desperate struggle.

The result has passed into legend. Westminster elections were usually pretty boisterous affairs, and that of 1784 was in fact no rowdier – probably less so – than that of 1774. But the personal drama was so acute, Fox's fate so compelling, the issue so long in doubt, that every move was followed with breathless attention. Both sides flung in all they had. The Ministry spent perhaps a quarter of its total election expenses, the local magnates pulled out every stop, the King had a detachment of the Guards marched to the hustings to vote. Ministerial bullies, dressed as sailors, fought Fox's Irish chairmen up and down the town. The Whigs could not call on the royal troops, or many of the royal tradesmen. But they had the rather doubtful asset of the Prince of Wales, and the very definite asset of a famous circle of beauties – the incomparable Georgiana, Duchess of Devonshire, and 'the other *Women of the People*' as Pitt ungallantly called them[1] (a not unprophetic description, for their spirit was really very much the same as that of the liberal French *aristos* four to five years later). The excitement rose as the battle was prolonged almost a month after the other results came in. At last, in mid-May, Fox got home by 236 votes. His supporters staged an uproarious procession through the streets, and on the day that the King rode down the Mall to open Parliament the Prince of Wales, dressed in the buff and blue, held a garden party for Fox at Carlton House.

When Wray demanded a scrutiny, therefore, and it was granted at once, Opposition were clearly not going to take this lying down. As soon as Parliament met they called for a motion of censure on the high bailiff. Two questions were really involved: 'first, the legality of the scrutiny, under the circumstances of the case; and secondly, its expediency'.[2]

Pitt confided the legal defence to Lloyd Kenyon, the future Lord Chief Justice, who had been made Attorney General five months before and had now just become Master of the Rolls. Kenyon made the best of a weakish case. Opposition's argument rested mainly on an Act of William III, which required a sheriff charged with the duty of returning an election writ to do so on or before the day that Parliament should

1. To Wilberforce, 8 April (Stanhope, I, 209). Lady Salisbury was thrown in unavailingly as a counter-attraction. But who could have rivalled Georgiana canvassing in a crisis for her beloved Charles Fox?
2. *The Annual Register . . . for the Years 1784 and 1785* (2nd edn, 1800), 175.

deliver it to the clerk of the Crown in Chancery. Since the high bailiff was a subordinate officer of the sheriff, he had therefore no power of his own volition to delay the process. The provisions of this statute, moreover, were reinforced by Grenville's Act of 1770 for the regulation of elections and contested returns. But Kenyon managed to throw doubt on the argument by reminding the House that an election writ did not differ in its legal nature from other writs, that writs could be issued by courts other than Chancery, and that if the sheriff gave a sufficient reason to such a court it could permit him to delay his return. The reason in this instance lay in the bailiff's inability to swear that the persons returned had the majority of legal votes. Kenyon, and other Government speakers, therefore declared that the bailiff and his counsel should be examined on the evidence before the House sitting as a court, and that meanwhile no return could justifiably be allowed.

This may, perhaps, have been good law; but it is doubtful how far it applied here, for the sheriffs of Westminster had not in fact sought, or any court directed, a delay in the return of this particular writ. The high bailiff indeed had closed the poll at the time he did precisely in order to meet the statutory date. So good a lawyer as John Scott, the future Lord Eldon, then a young Member, rejected Kenyon's arguments, and Kenyon himself was impressed by some of the objections later raised. But he had put the case with enough skill to achieve its immediate object, and to enable Pitt to repeat it over the next few weeks. Indeed, Pitt went farther. If Kenyon, he maintained, was correct in law, the Commons had no right to censure the high bailiff by ordering him to pass the result of the poll against his will. Opposition had asked why the issue should not go before the select committee of the House which normally dealt with contested returns under Grenville's Act. But then there must be a sitting Member to be confirmed or removed – which was impossible in this instance unless the high bailiff's action was overruled. They were not in fact faced with the normal situation, in which a petition was heard against someone already returned. In this case a returning authority was himself dissatisfied, and it was not within the comeptence of the House to order him to proceed.

This was a very dubious extension of an already dubious case; for the House could certainly censure a returning officer, even without hearing him,[1] or it could, after hearing him, direct a return of the writ – precisely as it did in this case in the end. But Pitt knew the temper of his audience when he argued as he did.[2] He had been more cautious at the start. In fact, while he naturally stood by the high bailiff and supported a scrutiny, he had then been privately prepared to let the case

1. For earlier instances, see John Simeon, *A Treatise on the Law of Elections, in all its Branches* (1789), 140.
2. He seems to have done so most fully on 8 June, though the argument was implicit in his remarks of 25 May. He left the initial statement of the defence, on 24 May, very largely to Kenyon and Mahon.

go to a committee of the House. It was a matter of tactics – 'the choice of the alternative is delicate'. But either could be accepted, though the Ministry had defended the first, for 'in either case I have no doubt of Fox being thrown out'.[1]

For this of course was the point. If Fox could be ejected from Westminster – not from Parliament, as has sometimes been stated, for he would still have sat for his northern seat – it would be a real feather in the Government's cap. The contest had been long and bitter, the constituency suited Fox like a glove, his removal would crown the Ministry's triumph, not least in the London area.[2] His victory had been Opposition's great, almost its only, solace. It would be a rare day's work if the result could be set aside.

Nor at this point were there widespread qualms – there were some – about the prospect. Passions still ran high; no quarter was being given. There had obviously been corruption all round, and it was widely known that if Fox had not beaten Wray on the poll he would have asked for an inquiry (not necessarily a scrutiny) himself. Now that the tables had been turned he could not really complain if he found his opponents in punitive mood. The new House, as it later proved, was not a purely docile assembly: Pitt was not sure of its reaction when the question was first raised.[3] But of course it was weighted against Fox, particularly on an electoral dispute, and as long as legality was not flouted the quality of mercy might well be strained. The gambler had played high and lost; let him abide by the consequences. This was certainly Pitt's own feeling, after the storms of the past few months. He had flung himself into the battle when battle had finally to be joined – *'tear the enemy to pieces'*, he had written to Wilberforce in York.[4] There was no suggestion at the time that he was personally involved in the high bailiff's action, and it seems very unlikely from his attitude at the start of the debates.[5] But since the action had been taken, and Opposition had contested it, he was certainly not going to disavow his supporter and let the matter drop.

In such an atmosphere, Government had its way. Opposition's motions and petitions were consistently defeated, by majorities ranging, on matters of substance, from 78 to 168 in divisions of between 260 and 400. On 8 June, after a final vigorous debate, the high bailiff was ordered to begin the scrutiny 'with all practicable dispatch'.[6]

---

1. To Rutland, 24 May 1784 (*Correspondence*, 15).
2. See p. 148 above.
3. To Rutland, 24 May 1784 (*Correspondence*, 15).
4. 24 March (Stanhope, I, 202).
5. I think his letter of 24 May to Rutland bears this interpretation.
6. *H.C.J.*, XL, 104. The M.P. Francis Baring reported to Shelburne that 419 Members voted in the division on 24 May (25 May 1784; Lansdowne Mss, Bowood). But this is not borne out by the published figures.

No one can have been much surprised when the dispatch was not very marked. The relevant precedents were not encouraging; the last scrutiny at Westminster itself had been abandoned with little to show for it after five months. Pitt had declared that a scrutiny was better, on the ground of convenience, than a petition to the select committee of the House, which could not hope to complete its processes before the end of the year. In the event, the scrutiny lasted beyond that term.

At the beginning of 1785, Opposition therefore raised the matter afresh. Only the lawyers had benefited in the past eight months, and at this rate the proceedings could drag on for another two years. The scrutiny in fact was defeating its object: whether or not it was legal, it was certainly not expedient.

This very soon proved to be the sense of the House. A feeling began to spread that the business should be dropped. Almost a year had now elapsed since the general election; passions no longer ran high, the whole affair was stale. But Pitt would not yield an inch. If the scrutiny had been legal before, it was legal now. Fox himself was largely responsible for the delay, by his obstructive tactics. Government could have no wish to prolong the uncertainty, when its enemy was sitting in the House while its supporters, Hood and Wray, were not. But that should not lead them to abandon a decision of which they had approved, simply because those whom it did not suit were doing their best to frustrate it.

The arguments did not appeal. If it had seemed fair enough for Fox to accept the result of a losing game before, it seemed fair enough for Pitt to accept it now. His legalistic approach, in a matter in which the legality was always suspect, seemed unrealistic and petty, and now vindictive as well. The division figures soon proved the point. The debates began on 1 February. On the 9th, the Ministry had a majority of 39 on a vote of 309; on the 21st, one of nine on a vote of 281;[1] on 3 March they found themselves in a minority of 38 on a vote of 286. Although they defeated a motion on the 9th to expunge the earlier resolution to proceed with the scrutiny from the journals of the House, the original return was accepted, and Hood and Fox took their seats for Westminster.

Why did Pitt act as he did? He laid himself open to the obvious charge – the most damaging he could suffer – of personal revenge, whether he lost or won. Indeed, so obvious was this charge that he must have had some other impulse to carry on, when it might have been more graceful to withdraw. There is no evidence that he was persuaded by the King, as has sometimes been claimed. Pretyman, who after all was close to the

1. On a motion to continue the scrutiny. They had a majority of 58 earlier on the same day, in a division of 348, on a motion that counsel should be heard on the question.

Minister at this time, maintained that he was convinced that Wray had a genuine majority of legal votes, and that the scrutiny itself was a lawful procedure. Holland Rose, rather similarly, has suggested that Pitt was championing the purity of elections, on the eve of a fresh attempt at Parliamentary reform. If so, he may have been influenced by the fact that Wray was himself a well known reformer, whose victory would throw Fox's impurities into greater relief. But if this was really his object it was curiously naive, for no one could pretend that there had not been corruption on both sides, or that the scrutiny would not be subject to the same kinds of pressure. Nor does Pitt's attitude at the start convince one that he was committed to a scrutiny in principle. It seems more likely that he was affected by a feeling more in keeping with the realities of the day. The whole point of the Westminster election was that Fox was the Man of the People, standing for a constituency with the most popular franchise in the land. If he could be proved to have really come bottom of the poll, his pretensions would be most effectively upset. He could hardly claim to speak with the same authority if he had been rejected at Westminster, and was representing the delegates (not even the voters) of Wick and Dornoch and Kirkwall.[1]

With his earlier majorities behind him, Pitt was prepared to force such a result. It came as a shock when the majorities melted, and even his supporters were dismayed.[2] He was in fact badly out of touch; he had been betrayed by his obstinacy; he had not seen – it had not struck him – how his reaction would be received. He was ungenerous because he was unimaginative, and not prepared to appear inconsistent, and satisfied that he could teach Fox a lesson which the House would support. The lesson was his; and it was not lost. Six years later, armed with far more damaging material, Pitt treated his great rival in a very different way.

The defeat came at a bad moment, at a crisis for the Irish scheme.[3] Some people indeed thought that the shock was partly responsible for Pitt's sudden concessions in that affair. This may or may not have been so. Hostile votes on one question did not necessarily apply to another – and even on the scrutiny itself, Wraxall was probably right in pointing to the Ministry's final majority on 9 March as showing that the House wished only to restrain, not overturn, the Government.[4] There were other adequate reasons for Pitt to have yielded ground on the Irish Resolutions. But the sudden loss of sympathy was certainly upsetting, 'amongst the most vexatious and harassing occurrences in the whole

1. The Scottish burghs, except Edinburgh, were unique in having an indirect system of election, by delegates themselves elected by the borough councils.
2. See Pretyman's words in Tomline, II, 26.
3. Pp. 204–9 above.
4. P. 221 above. *Memoirs*, IV, 98. He might also have cited the Government's success, in June, on its bill for regulating the duration of polls and scrutinies in elections, which arose from the Westminster scrutiny and was carried, on a low vote, against Opposition.

course of his administration'.[1] The affair had got quite out of hand, as such personal excitements are apt to do; to the public, it seemed perhaps 'the most prominent feature of the present session';[2] and it reached its peak at a time when the Minister needed all his authority, not only to calm suspicions over Ireland, but also to rally support for the personal effort which he was about to make again for Parliamentary reform.

II

Pitt had in fact been contemplating such an effort at least since December 1784. He had indeed hoped to introduce a reform bill in February 1785, but the long debates on the Westminster scrutiny, the delay in the programme for Ireland, and some unexpected complications in Parliamentary business, combined to postpone the event to the middle of April.

There had scarcely been an opportunity to move before the winter. The defeat of Pitt's last attempt, in May 1783, had been followed by the political crisis at the end of the year, and in the spring and summer of 1784 he had scarcely the time or indeed the wish to raise the subject afresh. He had his India bill and some financial measures to attend to, and a whole list of problems and negotiations to master. Nor was it the moment, so soon after entering office, to try to whip up support for so personal a plan. When the indefatigable Sawbridge moved in June for an instalment of reform, Pitt – unsuccessfully of course, knowing Sawbridge – begged him to postpone the question.

Even five months later there was still no sign that the Minister meant to try again. Wyvill, the Yorkshire leader with whom he had acted before, planned to start an extended tour abroad early in December. But on reaching London *en route* he was summoned to Downing Street, and as a result the journey was called off. For Pitt, it seemed, had now suddenly made up his mind; he would 'put forth his whole power and credit, *as a man* and *as a minister, honestly* and *boldly* to carry a plan of reform'.[3] Abandoning at once the prospective delights of the continent, Wyvill therefore plunged into the familiar business of organising an extra-Parliamentary campaign.

There is no reason to doubt that Pitt was acting from conviction. This was by no means universally believed at the time. It was not only Opposition that questioned his motives; some of his own associates and supporters were in doubt. Of course it was easy to argue that he was being moved by expediency: that he could hardly afford to abandon a

1. Pretyman's expression (Rosebery, *Bishop Tomline's Estimate of Pitt . . .*, 31).
2. *The Annual Register for 1784 and 1785*, 174.
3. Wyvill to James Wilkinson, 9 December 1784 (Wyvill, *Political Papers*, IV, 119).

cause with which he had been so prominently associated, and which moreover had helped to win him some important seats in the election. This impression was strengthened by the strategy he thought it necessary to pursue. For Pitt was very anxious that his effort should be a Ministerial responsibility, that Government itself should be involved more fully than had ever been possible before. Only so, he judged – and rightly – could the necessary votes be rallied, the general lukewarmness met and overcome. The theme runs through his, and his supporters', letters. Success, Rutland was warned, was 'essential to the credit, if not the stability of the present administration'. 'Mr. Pitt's character as well as his Administration is in some danger of being shaken' by failure, urged Camden. The bill, wrote Wyvill, was to be considered 'as the measure of *Government*, or of *the majority of the cabinet*'.[1] Pitt himself was very careful to involve the Home Secretary in the communication of his plans.[2] Above all he was eager, as Shelburne had been, to disarm the Court; he sought the benevolent neutrality, if not the active support, of the King. All this made him wary of too close a connexion with the reforming movements themselves. While he relied on their efforts to produce the necessary wave of petitions, 'I wish', he wrote in January, 'Mr. Wyvill had been a little more sparing of my name'.[3] His very determination to 'put forth his whole power and credit ... *as a minister*' could give rise to suspicions that he was less deeply committed '*as a man*'.

One must also take his temperament into account: the intense reluctance to confide his hopes to more than the congenial few. Thus Daniel Pulteney, who as Rutland's link with London saw a good deal of Pitt at this time, could never decide if he was 'encumbered or enamoured with . . . this Yorkshire reform'; and Sydney, the Home Secretary, professed himself 'persuaded that . . . the necessity of bringing it forward is the only motive of his conduct'.[4] But with those whom Pitt thought more sympathetic he shed his reserve. Camden, Wilberforce, Robert Smith[5] knew that he was in earnest; Rutland in Ireland was kept posted of his hopes; Wyvill himself never doubted,

1. Pitt to Rutland, 12 January 1785 (*Correspondence*, 84); Camden to Grafton, 19 March 1785 (*Autobiography of Grafton*, 398); Wyvill to William Mason, 5 January 1785 (copy in P.R.O. 30/8/192). The same note is struck in Pitt to Gower, 19 March 1785 (P.R.O. 30/29/384).

2. See Pitt to Rutland, 11 January 1785 (*Correspondence*, 76). Sydney was perhaps drawn in at first because Irish reform was also being discussed. But see n4 below for his similar role in the later discussion with George III.

3. To Rutland, 12 January 1785 (*Correspondence*, 84). The King had just made a predictable comment on the combination of his Minister and 'a known demagogue' (to Sydney, 4 January; *L.C.G. III*, I, no. 159).

4. Pulteney to Rutland, 19 April 1785 (*H.M.C., Fourteenth Report, Appendix, Pt. I,* 202); Sydney to George III, 19 March 1785 (*L.C.G. III,* I, no. 183). I do not think that Sydney was being entirely disingenuous in the tactical needs of the moment.

5. See p. 107 above. Smith was a keen Parliamentary reformer, who seconded Sawbridge's motion in June 1784.

amid the later disappointments, that in 1785 the Minister was sincere.[1]

He was also, as so often, very optimistic at the start. 'You will hardly believe me', he wrote to Wilberforce in December 1784, 'if I tell you that I entertain the strongest hope of coming very near, if not absolutely succeeding'. 'I really think', he told Rutland in January, 'that I see more than ever the chance of effecting a safe and temperate plan'.[2] At first, indeed, there seemed to be some ground for his hopes. Yorkshire was still a powerful base, despite the tacit hostility of the old Rockingham interests, and there was some support elsewhere in the north-east, and in Nottinghamshire and Norfolk. But as the weeks went by it was obvious that the rest of the country did not care. The north-west and the midlands, even Birmingham, failed to live up to Wyvill's expectations – perhaps partly because of recent taxes and their fright over Pitt's Irish scheme.[3] No petitions came in from the south, except from Launceston and Lyme Regis. Scotland, on which great hopes had been placed, did not organise in time. In London, conservatives and radicals alike ignored the Yorkshire programme. Once again, as two years before, the campaign largely misfired, and when Pitt introduced his bill he could not point to much public response.

He had also by that time failed to shift the King. If Shelburne had ever been correct in thinking that George III would support a limited reform,[4] the occasion had passed and was not to be repeated. The King disliked any such idea, and made no bones about it. He had shown Pitt what he thought in the summer of 1783;[5] he was unlikely to approve the measure now unless he could be persuaded that it was a matter of Ministerial confidence. But George III was well aware that the Cabinet was largely unenthusiastic on a question that had never been regarded in that light before, and he at once disclaimed any responsibility for the result. Indeed, he turned the tables rather neatly on Pitt. The Minister had hinted at the 'fatal' effect of a defeat caused partly by 'those who are supposed to be connected with government'.[6]

> Mr. Pitt [the King replied] must recollect that though I have ever thought it unfortunate that He had early engaged himself in this measure, yet that I have ever said that as He was clear of the propriety of the measure He ought to lay his thoughts before the House; that out of personal regard to Him I would avoid giving any opinion

1. For Camden, see *Autobiography of Grafton*, 398–9; For Wilberforce and Smith, *Correspondence of Wilberforce*, I, 4, and *Life of Wilberforce*, I, 77–8; for Wyvill, *Political Papers*, IV, 16. Rutland, faced with the cares of office, had in fact grown less enthusiastic: 'knight errantry' was now his description of Pitt's effort.

2. *Private Papers of William Wilberforce*, 10; *Correspondence*, 84.

3. Thus one of the leading Manchester reformers, Thomas Walker, was prominent in the business of the General Chamber of Manufacturers.

4. See p. 74, n2 above.

5. P. 115 above.

6. Pitt to George III, 19 March 1785 (*L.C.G. III*, I, no. 182).

to anyone on the opening of the door to Parliamentary Reform except to Him. . . .[1]

In other words, he would keep silence precisely because Pitt's reform bill was Pitt's own affair. If the King was not going to be openly hostile – and the Minister's friends made the most of the fact – that was not much consolation when his neutrality implied that Government's credit was not at stake.

For in that case the measure did not really stand much chance. Two-thirds at least of the independent Members were thought in January to dislike the prospect, and several members of the Treasury bench were 'very unreserved in their declarations against it'.[2] Nor could Pitt expect much sympathy from the Foxites, after the earlier break within the reform movement[3] and his own recent treatment of Fox. When it came to the point, Fox in fact voted for the bill. But he managed to do so while condemning almost all its main provisions, and over a third of those who did not vote for it, but had done so for its predecessor, were connected with the Foxite party in various ways. The Minister therefore, unsupported by any obvious public pressure, could not count on a firm basis in any quarter of the House.

The contents of the bill reflected this state of affairs. No evidence survives of Pitt's thoughts in December, when Wyvill was so pleased with what he heard; but the scheme in its final version was 'safe and temperate' indeed.[4] It was ready in all its essentials by the third week in March.[5] The central feature was explained succinctly by Camden: 'the general idea of the plan is to purchase out the small boroughs by the consent of the electors, and to add to the present number of the county representatives'.[6] The number of boroughs in contemplation was thirty-

1. George III to Pitt, 20 March 1785 (Donald Grove Barnes, *George III and William Pitt, 1783–1806* (1939), 127). He could not resist adding the comment that the behaviour of some of Pitt's 'most intimate friends' on the Westminster scrutiny showed the limits there could be to the persuasion of 'friendship'.

2. Pulteney to Rutland, 27 January 1785 (*H.M.C., Fourteenth Report, Appendix, Pt. I*, 169).

3. See pp. 72, 76 above

4. See p. 225 above.

5. Holland Rose (200, n1) cites an undated paper from the Pretyman Mss – 'Notes on Reform of Parliament' – which did not contain the proposals for compensation when a constituency was extinguished (see below). Since he assumed that the memorandum was a rough draft of Pitt's speech in moving the measure, he suspected that this important provision was added at the last minute, possibly to conciliate Dundas. But the 'Heads of a Bill' which Pitt sent to the King on 19 March (*L.C.G. III*, I, no. 182) and to Wyvill at about the same time (Wyvill, IV, 103–9), and the explanation which he gave to Philip Yorke (see *L.C.G. III*, I, 141, n2), show that it was in fact contemplated then, so that the undated paper is presumably earlier than Holland Rose thought.

6. To Grafton, 19 March 1785 (*Autobiography of Grafton*, 399).

six, and the electors' consent would be purchased from a special fund starting probably at about £1,000,000. There would be no compulsion, save where a constituency was disfranchised – as it could be already – for corruption; the process would be voluntary, slow, and piecemeal, and its management would be in the hands of a committee of the House. The number of seats affected – a maximum of 72 – would be distributed as they fell between the counties and the metropolis. Meanwhile the electorate would be somewhat enlarged by the inclusion of forty-shilling copyholders and certain leaseholders, and some of Mahon's proposals for the better regulation of elections would be brought into force.[1] The bill in short was framed so as to command the widest possible assent, and to avoid any fears of 'democratic' innovation. It touched neither the size of the House nor the length of the sessions. It offered a modest extension of the franchise, and a more equitable management of the poll. The redistribution of seats, on well canvassed lines, would be effected by voluntary action; no private rights would be overruled – a lesson learned perhaps from Fox's great mistake on India. If Parliamentary reform was to be admitted at all, it could scarcely have been in a more conciliatory shape.

But Parliamentary reform was not going to be admitted. On 18 April, Pitt moved for leave to bring in his bill. Once again the House was full; 450 Members perhaps were present, and 422 voted in the division – more than in any of the debates on the Westminster scrutiny. No doubt this was largely because Pitt himself was involved: the division on Sawbridge's motion in the previous June had numbered almost a hundred less. He did his best moreover to ensure a good attendance by moving the bill on the day before the mid-sessional 'call of the House', which ensured that Members were in town;[2] and the immediate summons was impressively ceremonious.

> At four o'clock, the *Chancellor of the Exchequer*, in order to give greater solemnity to the business he was going to introduce, moved, that the Serjeant at Arms should repair with the mace to the different avenues leading to the House, and summon all the Members he should meet, to attend their duty in their places. The motion was carried . . .[3]

And no doubt the laggards hurried in. In the event, Pitt did better than in 1783. The majority against him was 74, compared with one then of 144. But even so the defeat was disheartening considering that he was now in office, he carried not much more than a third of those present, two members of the Treasury bench – Rose and Grenville – were

---

1. See p. 72 above.
2. He had done the same in February, on the first call, with the Irish Resolutions.
3. *Morning Herald*, 19 April 1785. I have not found this incident reported elsewhere.

against him, and, perhaps most significantly, there was a marked drop in support from the County Members. Given the change in Pitt's position over the past two years, one might indeed say that the Commons were no better disposed to reform than before. According to one observer, the Minister 'was heard indeed, with great attention, but with that sort of civil attention which people give to a person who has a good claim to be heard, but with whom the hearers are determined to disagree'.[1] There were probably contributory reasons for the defeat, particularly among the independents: Pitt had forfeited some sympathy from his recent behaviour over Fox, and his command of the House was uneven at this time. But the main reason lay really in the fact that the issue was no longer a live one; there was not enough public pressure to interest the party notables, and the party scene itself had changed. The Yorkshire movement had been born, the metropolitan movements flourished, in a period of discontent. Now that the American War was over things were settling down. Trade was recovering, confidence returning, a great political crisis was past. Such a process had many aspects; but the results were identified largely with Pitt himself. His failure in this instance owed a good deal to his success elsewhere.

He did not try again. A meeting at the Thatched House Tavern soon afterwards underlined the divisions between the reformers, when a motion by Wyvill in favour of Pitt's plan was defeated by the metropolitan radicals and the Foxites. The Yorkshire movement thereafter died away, the London movements were moribund, and the great subject of Parliamentary reform sank to the status of a toast at the annual dinners of the societies for commemorating the Glorious Revolution. Only in Scotland did it survive, and indeed gather strength; but purely Scottish movements carried little weight farther south. Parliament itself remained apathetic. In May 1786, a further motion of Mahon's (now Lord Stanhope) for regulating the poll, introduced by Wilberforce in the Commons, was defeated in the Lords; and although Stanhope carried a limited plan for the same purpose in 1788, it was repealed a year later, before it came into operation. Meanwhile Sawbridge's annual efforts suffered their usual fate. Pitt spoke for the first of Stanhope's motions;[2] but he did not move for anything more comprehensive, and, as Wyvill admitted, it would have been pointless if he had. He had done more for the cause in recent years than any other leading politician, and he could scarcely be blamed for desisting when there was no chance of success.

III

'The conclusion of our session', wrote Pitt to Rutland, when Parlia-

1. Pulteney to Rutland, 19 April 1785 (*H.M.C., Fourteenth Report, Appendix, Pt. I*, 202).
2. Not, as far as one can tell, for the second; but the records of the debate are sparse.

ment had risen for the summer recess of 1785, 'has been in all respects triumphant. The zeal of our friends seems more confirmed than ever; and everything essential to the strength of our Government as satisfactory as possible'. 'The Ministry', wrote one of his opponents a few weeks later, 'wants Strength & Consistency & effect'.[1] Allowing for the fact that both views were expressed with certain objects in mind – Pitt was trying to encourage Rutland, and Eden by then was looking for a post – where did the truth lie? Pitt had certainly had a trying year. The honeymoon period was over; how did he stand now?

The issues we have been trying to follow were not of course the whole story. There had been other questions, other bills, under debate in these two years. Most of them were financial, and on most – though not all – Pitt's approach was approved: it was indeed because the Minister was 'in the plenitude of power and popularity upon every other question'[2] that his defeat on the Westminster scrutiny came to him as such a shock. The greater part of Government business passed without undue fuss. But this was not in fact of particular moment. The greater part of Government business was always uncontroversial; neither the Government nor the House expected anything else.[3] The significance of these four occasions was not that they covered the whole field of debate, but on the contrary that they were exceptional, and that on three of them – the three on which he held decided personal views – Pitt retreated or lost.

These last three occasions, moreover, followed quickly on one another, in the space of some five months. It was very unusual for a Minister to suffer in this way; particularly, one might have thought, a Minister who had recently enjoyed such success. In the light of Pitt's fortunes in the session of 1785, what had happened to the 'ascendancy' which so impressed Wilberforce in 1784?[4]

The answer might be made that it had never existed, in the form which Wilberforce supposed. He had confined his observation to the Commons, and no Ministry could ignore the Lords. But its application was very doubtful even as it stood. General respect and goodwill after victory were not enough in themselves; a Parliamentary leader needed something more – or less – to bite on. For Pitt to have managed the lower House without the use of 'influence', as Wilberforce thought might have been done, he must have worked from an assured base, and in the end through a moral discipline which Wilberforce himself might not have liked. We have no estimate of the size of Pitt's personal following in the Commons at this time; of 'the Party attached to Mr. Pitt' – to use the words of a slightly later estimate – as distinct from the

1. Pitt to Rutland, 8 August 1785 (*Correspondence*, 111); William Eden to Morton Eden, 8 September (B.M. Add. Ms 34420, f. 106v).
2. Tomline, II, 26.
3. See pp. 168–9 above.
4. P. 188 above.

'Detached Parties' of other colleagues and supporters and the 'Party of the Crown'.[1] But it was certainly not large, and the more reliable inner core probably numbered no more than 20 or 25. For all the size of Government's normal majorities, this was a small party compared with that which Fox could still call his own; nor, by his standards or those of Government, was it particularly reliable. On the question of the Westminster scrutiny, Pitt was hurt at 'finding some of his most respectable friends, both private and political' in opposition or absent; he was hurt again when Henry Bankes spoke against his plan for compensation in the debate on Parliamentary reform; and again when Mahon published an attack the next year on his most cherished financial scheme.[2] The latitude enjoyed by the inner group did not indeed please all its members. Pretyman in particular thought that Bankes and Wilberforce went much too far. When they served on election committees, for instance, 'considering themselves *as private friends of* Mr Pitt, from an *excess* of *Candor, Liberality* and *fear of being biassed* in their judgment [they] seemed absolutely to make a point of deciding *against* friends to the Government in every possible case'. And the worst of it was that 'Mr Pitt encouraged this *absurd refinement*'.[3] Another generation bore witness to the same state of affairs. 'Ask Mr. Bankes', wrote the indignant W. E. Tomline to his Parliamentary patron Lord Falmouth, who had rebuked him for not voting for a measure of which he himself approved, 'how often he both spoke & voted against Mr. Pitt upon most important points & went home to sup with him after the Debate as cordial friends as ever'.[4]

Bankes and Wilberforce, and Mahon, were not of course typical party supporters. Bankes's 'English obstinacy'[5] made him really more of an independent than anything else, and Wilberforce was fast losing interest in the daily stuff of politics. But Pitt's toleration of such behaviour may have had its effect on what was already recognised as an unusually independent House. The differences in tone between successive Parliaments are often curious, and hard to explain; certainly the Parliament of 1784 seems at the outset to have been a rather awkward one to control. The back-bencher Daniel Pulteney called it 'perhaps *too independent*'. 'This of all Parliaments I have known', observed Fox, 'is the most difficult to gain attention from upon points that do not come to a direct question'. Pitt himself drew attention to the independence of his majority. He might at times have echoed his father's remark of thirty

1. See Namier, *Personalities and Powers*, 31–2.
2. Tomline, II, 26; *P.R.,* XVIII, 83. For Mahon's action in 1786, see pp. 267–8 below; he had also voted against the Government's bill of June 1785 following the end of the Westminster scrutiny (see p. 222, n4 above), and refused to take the chair in committee as Pitt wished.
3. Mrs Pretyman Tomline's notes, October–November 1801 (Stanhope Mss, 'Mr Pitt II'). She must have been echoing her husband's opinion.
4. 27 March 1828 (Pretyman Ms 562:1828).
5. *Criticisms on the Rolliad*, 176.

years before – 'they are not disciplined troops, and he must be an able general indeed who can answer for them'.[1]

Pitt himself was still in process of working out his generalship. In many ways he was a very odd leader indeed. Chatham was his model. But it was Chatham in his later rather than his early years. The Great Commoner at the start had in fact been sociable, even delightful: his son from the start emphatically was not. 'Pitt does not make friends', Wilberforce noted sadly in his diary;[2] and while the remark applied to a bad moment, it was generally true. Most of the Cabinet found him uncommunicative – he was particularly difficult to talk to, Thurlow recalled, in these early years – and he did nothing to entertain the political world at large. His one contemplated gesture in that direction, of holding a series of 'assemblies' at Downing Street 'to *take in everybody*',[3] was abandoned when the health of his hostess, his sister Harriot, began to fail. In the House of Commons, he paid no attention to his back-benchers at all.

> From the instant that Pitt entered the doorway . . ., he advanced up the floor with a quick and firm step, his head erect and thrown back, looking neither to the right nor to the left, nor favouring with a nod or a glance any of the individuals seated on either side, among whom many who possessed five thousand pounds a year would have been gratified even by so slight a mark of attention.[4]

'It was not thus', Wraxall added, 'that Lord North or Fox treated Parliament'. '. . . In vain to talk to him', the Speaker complained in the summer of 1783, about helping to restrain the temper of the House;[5] his guidance in such matters was always impersonal and remote. The average Government supporter had to get used to the idea that the Minister was unapproachable, and generally uninterested in his followers' affairs.

Nor was he generally prepared – though there were exceptions – to stretch a point in their favour. A good illustration of his attitude was

1. Pulteney to Rutland, 4 March 1785 (*H.M.C., Fourteenth Report, Appendix, Pt. I*, 186); he also called it 'the present *virtuous* house' (loc. cit., 178). Fox to Eden, n.d. and with later endorsement 'early in 1784', but from internal evidence more probably early 1785 (B.M. Add. Ms 34419, f. 357v). For Pitt, see pp. 210–11 above. Chatham is quoted in *H. of P.*, I, 194.

2. 10 March 1785 (*Life of Wilberforce*, I, 78).

3. *Letters of Lady Harriot Eliot*, 137. She was obliged to admit that a series of balls, which would have been more popular, would not 'at all answer'.

4. Wraxall, *Memoirs*, III, 217.

5. Orde to Shelburne, 17 July 1783 (Lansdowne Mss, Bowood), reporting a conversation between Barré and Speaker Cornwall. Cornwall was a weak man making excuses, and he owed his Speakership to North; Orde was reporting to a disgruntled Shelburne. But the story rings true.

provided at about this time. Since Pitt's last years as an undergraduate, his friend Rutland had been working, from his seat at Cheveley, to break the Yorke family's hold over the representation of the county and borough of Cambridge. By 1780 he had found a possible agent and ally in the young local banker John Mortlock, then busy laying the foundations of the chequered career which was to make him 'the Master of Cambridge' for a quarter of a century. In 1784 Mortlock was elected a Member for the borough with Rutland's approval, a plum, it might seem, ripe for plucking by Pitt. But the plucking had its price. Since 1781 Mortlock had been Receiver-General of the Land Tax for the county, a profitable post under Government which he was required to surrender if returned to Parliament. The necessary transaction occurred at an unfortunate time, for the Commissioners of Taxes – possibly as a political manœuvre – had recently come down on their Receiver for alleged arrears of £50,000, which caused a run on his bank. The worst of the trouble was surmounted, however, and Mortlock was unwilling to lose contact with his Government post. In April 1784 he accordingly asked for it to be given to his business partner, Samuel Francis – a promise probably extracted before he stood for Parliament himself. The appointment was made; but not in the way that Mortlock had hoped. Francis was made Receiver for one year only, and despite Rutland's efforts Pitt refused to reappoint him when the year was up. The result, as the Duke and his henchman Pulteney had foreseen, was that Mortlock was unreliable. He held his hand from the start, while he saw which way the wind would blow. He showed signs of mutiny in the summer of 1784; by November, Pulteney was hinting at the need for a knighthood – an exceptional step; and early in 1785, Mortlock voted against Pitt on the Westminster scrutiny. Even then, as later events suggested, he might have been bought back. But Pitt on the contrary reaffirmed his disapproval. In the spring of 1786 Mortlock was accused of tampering with the list of the Commissioners of the Land Tax for Cambridgeshire, and the matter was brought to the notice of the House. Fox and Sheridan defended him, while Rutland's connexion did their best with Pitt behind the scenes. But the Minister would not listen. The Treasury spokesmen were mobilised against Mortlock, and although they could not carry a motion for an immediate inquiry the matter was adjourned to a later debate. In the meantime, a number of 'Mr. Pitt's general supporters told him they took it ill his taking such a part against an individual'.[1] Probably as a result – shades of the Westminster scrutiny – he agreed to drop the charge, and Mortlock escaped with an apology to the House. But Pitt had made his point. He had shown his severe displeasure at a breach of the law, and his resolve not to support it in a possible adherent. He had certainly lost Mortlock for the immediate future: three months later, Fox and Sheridan were made honorary freemen of the borough of Cambridge.

1. Pulteney to Rutland, 2 June 1786 (*H.M.C., Fourteenth Report, Appendix, Pt. I*, 306).

The episode throws some light on the ways in which Pitt thought, and could afford to act. He did not stop the unsavoury appointment of Francis in the first place, probably because promises had already been extracted from the Yorkes and from Rutland.[1] Instead he limited its duration and refused to renew it. He did nothing to conciliate Mortlock, at a time when Rutland was hoping to secure him. He tried to set up an inquiry into Mortlock's activities, which might have led to censure or even to expulsion from the House. He dropped it in the end, when urged by Rutland's emissaries and some Government supporters, because, according to Pulteney, it might be said to smack of persecution.

All this was done, and was possible, because Mortlock was playing fast and loose with the rules. This was usually the point at which Pitt drew the line. It was not, of course, always an easy point to determine; but a reforming Minister could at least say what lay definitely beyond. Pitt's course seemed clear as regards himself. He set the highest standards for his own conduct; he must be above reproach, he would not tolerate proven irregularities, and if they reached the stage of Parliamentary inquiry he would judge the case as it deserved. Mortlock or Warren Hastings, it was all the same: he was not going to be swayed by personal or party considerations. This indeed was his pride; it may have been his sanctuary. Whatever compromises he accepted in matters in which he was not solely concerned, he would not tarnish his personal code of behaviour. The same standards applied to those who thought like himself. Bankes and Wilberforce, for instance, not in office, should follow their consciences free of pressure, even if the Minister was sometimes annoyed or hurt by the result. But beyond these narrow limits he must rely on the accepted rules, as the best, the only, means of regulating conduct. His control over such matters was far from complete; there were large areas of government where his superintending powers were delicate or vague.[2] But in every area, including his own, there were subtle and valid distinctions between what was acceptable and what was not. Pitt never questioned the propriety, the necessity, of the normal modes of appointment and pressure; they were the normal ways in which business and government must be carried on. 'Such means as are fairly in the hands of Ministers would undoubtedly be to be exerted'.[3] Political virtue consisted in not extending them illegitimately, and in seeing that they were not improperly applied.

A reforming Minister, indeed, was peculiarly subject to the difficulties and dangers of a double standard. One might almost say that they were unavoidable in a case such as Pitt's. Perhaps, too, in his case, they were increased by his temperament; by the short range of his human sympathies, and his intense distaste for the unsympathetic. Patronage and

1. On the evidence for the promise, see Dr R. Plumptre to Lord Hardwicke, 21 July 1782 (B.M. Add. Ms 35629, f. 141).
2. See pp. 176–80 above.
3. P. 115 above.

private business – honours, rewards, the management of private bills –, the stuff of life to a Walpole or a Newcastle, the intimate concern of a North and a Fox, made Pitt merely 'bilious'.[1] He did not much care who wanted what, he was bored or embarrassed by the unavoidable routine. Sometimes, indeed, he managed to avoid it. There were complaints from the start that requests were ignored, and they did not grow less with time; often a decision was left to someone else as long as the proprieties were observed. Normally the Minister did what he had to, provided that the rules were not being broken. But sometimes, when he was roused, his distaste could take a contrary form. The Westminster scrutiny, the aftermath of the defeat of the Irish Propositions, showed a party leader working on the familiar lines with familiar weapons. Pitt in fact was quite content to use the stick, though he disliked offering the carrot. If his blood was up, he had little compunction in seeing that his opponents took the consequences, particularly if he had decided that they were fighting by their own rules. Thus, Fox had brought the Westminster scrutiny on himself; it was said to be legal: let it proceed. Irish M.P.s were thoroughly corrupt: let them be punished in their own coin. The punitive measures were not much affected by personal concern; they were sometimes supported, particularly in his youth, by the feeling with which Pitt took up a cause. The measures in which he was closely interested were generally presented with great care. He mastered the facts, he considered the objections – he was always receptive to reasoned argument –, he made a very real effort to win consent by conviction. If the design was then threatened or ruined by corrupt or factious men, it was not unjust to fight them on their own terms.

Pitt's pecularities as a party notable did not matter much in the end, because of his other qualities. When Wraxall remarked that North and Fox did not treat Parliament thus, he added, 'nor from them would Parliament have so patiently endured it'.[2] There seems to be no golden rule for political effectiveness, and if this kind of leadership was unusual it had its own style, and could be very strong. But it was the kind of leadership that placed a premium on success; the effect grew with time, as Pitt was seen to deliver the goods. It could not be taken for granted so easily in the early days; and Pitt for his part was then still engaged in striking a balance with the House. The setbacks of 1785 played their part in the process. Pitt was very careful in the next few years not to invite such treatment again. He let Parliamentary reform lie; he took care to avoid accusations of personal spite; above all, he was more wary in his handling of controversial issues. He did not surrender the initiative, or alter his ways. He always remained enthusiastic and confident when a policy seemed attractive; no one could ever induce him to bother with his followers' affairs. But his very refusal to do so made it the more necessary to act with care: his judgment of situations, which

1. Quoted in Feiling, *The Second Tory Party*, 165.
2. *Memoirs*, III, 217–18.

could be so acute, must do duty for his ignorance of men. If he was to ensure his ascendancy over the House he must respect its temper, and not try his normal majorities too high.

The more in fact Pitt wanted to do, the more he must rely on his conventional means of support. Like any other Minister, he must appeal to varied elements: to independent opinion, which was indeed his pride, and to the alliances, seldom stable, between private interests and the Crown. The elements were not always distinct, let alone contrasting: independents could influence parties, parties had their contacts with independent men. But no leader could live for long by one element alone. It was absurd, for instance, to suppose with Richard Watson, the egregious Bishop of Llandaff, that one could approve of Pitt's proposing a bill for Parliamentary reform but not of his using Ministerial influence in so pure a cause.[1] Influence did not have to be impure for it to be necessary; nor would its unprincipled use in fact have long sufficed by itself. The behaviour of parties, the cohesion of majorities, did not turn solely on bribes and threats; such things occurred within a wider spectrum. Influence was a mirror of society. It was embedded with natural strength in the very foundations of government, on which a Minister must try to build a structure of his own appropriate design. No Minister of principle could avoid a balance with other men's interests and principles; and if the result could always be questioned – and the more closely in a 'virtuous' career – the task itself lay at the heart of all that he tried to do. To argue that Pitt should have 'adopted the resolution to govern his country by *principle* rather than by *influence*'[2] was to pose an alternative that was largely unreal. One need not always applaud his methods, or agree with his judgment, to see that he must govern by the means which government provided, and seek to mould a situation which he could not bypass or ignore.

It was a situation, moreover, which served him well in many ways. If it forced him to watch his step, it gave him a chance to recover his balance. Ministers might not often be defeated – that was a luxury which firm government could not readily afford; but when they were, they did not necessarily have to resign. Pitt's sudden run of setbacks may have been unusual. It may have had a significant effect on himself. But when all is said and done, it had no effect on the life of his Government: he was right in claiming that 'everything essential' to the Ministry's strength had been preserved.[3] In the first place, Government itself was only once fully involved. Neither the Westminster scrutiny nor, for all Pitt's efforts, the question of Parliamentary reform, was regarded as a matter of confidence; and in the case of Ireland, it must be remembered that defeat did not come from the British House of Commons, but from the Irish, which was not the same. A Government measure had failed,

1. See his letter to Wyvill of 22 December 1784 (Wyvill, *Political Papers,* IV, 421).
2. P. 188 above.
3. P. 229 above.

but the Government's existence was not at stake – as North himself in fact was quick to point out.[1] It was indeed usually very difficult to bring down a Ministry from outside, unless it was already ripening for a fall from within. The built-in advantages of office were very great indeed; the point of weakness normally lay in the shifting relations of the incumbents. And in 1785 Pitt held a strong hand, although the cards were rather different from what Wilberforce supposed. His opponents were out of favour, in the House, the country and the closet, and there was no serious alternative within the Ministry to himself. He enjoyed general goodwill; there was a general desire for political quiet; his conduct of affairs was generally approved. The matter of the scrutiny was regarded as a personal mistake, Parliamentary reform largely as a young man's whim. There was no real question of wishing to bring so hopeful a prospect to an end: the whole situation was very different from that of 1782–4. Pitt's defeats are significant not because they threatened his position, but rather because they suggested how he might buttress its strength.

1. To William Eden, 21 August 1785 (B.M. Add. Ms 34420, f. 80).

Part Three

CHAPTER X

Finance

I

'T hough the pressing business of the day is over', wrote Pitt at the end of the summer session of 1784, 'and the immediate contests of party here leave no longer anything formidable, the real situation of the country, and its permanent concerns, leave enough upon our hands'.[1] Such a distinction could be carried too far; however party may be defined, Parliamentary leaders cannot afford to be too cavalier about party contests. But the statement reflected an attitude with which most Ministers would sympathise at times, and it was true enough. There was a mass of very real problems to be tackled in the aftermath of the war. Ireland was one; but that soon became a party issue. Others did not excite so much Parliamentary concern.

The greatest of these 'permanent' concerns at the outset were finance and trade. Finance offered in many ways the prospect of more immediate results. The position looked thoroughly discouraging. Methods of accounting did not yet allow anything approaching an accurate answer; but clearly the balance for 1783 had once again been highly adverse, and the deficit may in fact have been of the order of £10,833,000 on a net expenditure of £23,510,000.[2] The prospect for 1784 was of course a good deal better, for this would be the first full year of peace, and despite Pitt's intention of spending some money on the fleet, the armed forces were bound to cost very much less than the £13-odd million of the past twelve months. The yield of the taxes, too, might rise as prosperity returned. But even with these advantages – and the extent in each case must be doubtful – there seemed likely to be a deficit once more unless revenues could be raised. Not everyone agreed on its probable size; the ingenious Sir John Sinclair, for instance, who bombarded Pitt with advice, put it at about £1½ million.[3] But early in the year official opinion was inclined to place it at £2 to £2½ million at least. The expenses of civil government were running at just above £1¼ million, and another £9 to £9¼ million was thought to be absorbed

1. To Rutland, 9 August 1784 (*Correspondence*, 35–6).
2. See Mitchell & Deane, *Abstract of British Historical Statistics*, ch. XIV, tables 1, 2. This was a mid-nineteenth century calculation. Figures to the nearest thousand pounds; the year ending 10 October.
3. See his *Hints Addressed to the Public: on the State of Our Finances* (1783), 57–8.

by the charges on debt. To meet this total of some £10½ million, the 'permanent' taxes (i.e., all those other than the land and malt taxes) were thought likely to yield just over £10 million. The armed forces, which could not possibly cost less than the pre-war average of £4 million, must be serviced by the land and malt taxes, producing some £2½ million. There was therefore a prospective deficit on current account of at least £2 million, and in the event Pitt found it necessary to budget for just under £7½ million for the fighting services. These were all running expenses. But there was also the pressing need, as it was seen, to redeem or fund the short-term debt – thought to be some £14 million over and above the National Debt itself – which was floating in navy bills and ordnance debentures issued mostly during the past few years.[1]

All this seemed bad enough. But it was not just a question of filling the gap. The largest single item of peacetime expenditure was the interest on the National Debt, and the size of the debt itself was fast becoming a nightmare.[2] Discounting the fears of national bankruptcy, which were very real, this large annual charge could be lessened only by an annual *surplus* of income, to be placed in a sinking fund for the reduction of the capital of the debt. As things stood, the Government was in a vicious circle. It was having to pay an annual charge which was largely responsible for an annual deficit which in turn was increasing the debt on which an annual charge must be paid. On the figures at his disposal, Pitt had therefore not only to check but to reverse the current process.

There were three ways in which to do so: by curbing expenditure, by raising the yield from existing taxes, and by levying others. All three involved administrative as well as financial action, and the former could not always be quickly applied. New taxes themselves, moreover, were usually reserved for the budget, and again could not all be introduced in one fell stroke. But there was one important set of measures which could be taken quickly on its own. By the summer of 1784, Pitt was able to strike at the smugglers.

Smuggling had long been a major trade; it was now one of the largest in the land. The American War had greatly swollen the scale of opera-

1. The most succinct expression of these official estimates is to be found in the retrospective *A Brief Examination into the Increase of the Revenue, Commerce, and Navigation, of Great Britain, since the Conclusion of the Peace in 1783* (1792), which was by George Rose. Pretyman took it (with some slight mistakes) as the basis for his summary in Tomline II, 483–4. That the figures proved to be somewhat inaccurate is immaterial here. Pitt's final estimate for the armed forces is in *P.R.*, XV, 273; his estimate of the unfunded navy bills and ordnance debentures, loc. cit., 276.

There was of course a spate of other, sometimes very interesting, estimates in the Parliamentary debates and in pamphlets. But these carried no official sanction.

Some lists of the recent yields from taxes, on which Pitt based his calculations, are in P.R.O. 30/8/304.

2. See pp. 157–8 above.

tions which, already substantial, had been more or less stationary for the previous two decades. Figures of course are unknown; but the annual value of illicit imports may well have amounted to some £2 or £3 million, in a period when official imports totalled £12 to £13 million a year at the most.[1] Such statistics were if anything more modest than the impression they conveyed. To the average inhabitant of the coastal counties, the situation must have seemed quite out of hand. The smugglers were taking over, as the revenue service and the home forces were milked for the war. Private bands roamed almost at will. As many as 700 armed men could accompany the convoys inland; as many as 1,000, Pitt was informed, gathered on the beaches to unload; in London itself it was 'no unusual thing to see Gangs of 10, and 15, and 20 Horsemen riding even in the Day time with Impunity'.[2] 'The gentlemen' of course could always count on a good deal of sympathy; Charles Lamb as usual voiced an old feeling when he said that they robbed 'nothing but the revenue'.[3] But at a time when mob rule was something really to be feared, their operations were beginning to alarm respectable men. 'Will Washington take America', asked Lord Pembroke, 'or the Smugglers England first?'[4]

Perhaps the largest, certainly one of the most profitable, of the contraband trades was that in tea, and its fortunes seem to have been something of a yardstick for the rest. The business was perhaps the most highly organised of all and may have covered other activities; bulky goods such as brandy were often shipped with tea as ballast, and the precious leaf was widely believed throughout much of the century to be 'by far the most considerable Commodity that is run'.[5] In the seventies and early eighties, moreover, the 'runs' had a direct political effect, for they were undermining the precarious finances of the East India Company. Again estimates differed: the Company maintained that $7\frac{1}{2}$ million lb of tea was smuggled in each year, the Excise suggested a figure of 7 million lb, some of Pitt's sources put it as low as 3 million lb. But if an average of 4 to 6 million lb is accepted – and there is reasonable evidence for this – the smuggler was accounting for almost, perhaps quite, as much as the Company itself. Given such a drain on the revenue, and the peculiar prominence of the Company's affairs, it is not

1. W. A. Cole, 'Trends in Eighteenth-Century Smuggling' (*Ec.H.R.*, *Second Series*, X, no. 3, 409). Re-exports were thus also affected; but not most exports, for few manufactured British goods paid duty, and smuggling was confined in the main to the owl-men's raw wool.

An undated paper, submitted to Pitt probably in 1782 or 1784, put the total annual value of smuggled goods in the main coastal counties as high as £3,264,000 (P.R.O. 30/8/283).

2. P.R.O. 30/8/283.

3. 'The Old Margate Hoy', in *The Last Essays of Elia*.

4. To Lord Carmarthen, 9 November 1781 (*Pembroke Papers (1780–1794)*, ed. Lord Herbert (1950), 179).

5. See Cole, loc. cit., 407.

surprising that this branch of the trade was attracting attention by the end of the war.

The question indeed was under review when Pitt entered office. Evidence had been assembled, an answer would soon be proposed. There had been preliminary inquiries by Shelburne's Ministry, and the Customs and the Excise had been set to work. A more comprehensive examination was set on foot in the summer of 1783, when the Coalition Government appointed a committee of the Commons to inquire into 'smuggling, and other illicit practices'. Its three reports, of 24 December 1783 and 1 and 23 March 1784, gave Pitt the facts and suggested the lines on which he might act. The committee proposed some improvements to the laws against the smuggling gangs themselves; but it did not expect much from them, and it was convinced that the most effective check on their 'daring practices' would be 'lowering the duties, so as to make the temptation no longer adequate to the risk'.[1] Tea, 'the staple as it were of smuggling', was the article chosen for the experiment, though spirits or tobacco were possible alternatives. This conclusion may have been influenced by a lesson from the past, for a reduction of the tea duties in the 1740s had led to a marked reduction in contraband, which was reversed when the duties began once more to rise piecemeal. But in any case it was an intrinsically hopeful design. As usual, however, there was a price to be paid. For the fall in duties which hurt the smuggler would also hurt the revenue – perhaps by as much, if the fall was pronounced, as $£1\frac{1}{2}$ million or more a year. Whatever the long-term merits of the scheme, such an immediate loss could not be accepted; there must therefore be a compensating increase in taxation elsewhere. It was proposed to meet this need by a graduated rise in the existing window tax, taking the size of houses, measured by their windows, as a guide to the presumed consumption of tea.

The committee had drawn on a wide range of evidence and calculation, much of it necessarily produced by the East India Company itself. As the Company's saviour, Pitt in his turn was given every facility, and he made good use his of allies. He worked very closely with William Richardson, the deputy accountant-general at East India House – who probably knew more of the background than anyone else –, with Atkinson and his friends, above all perhaps with Francis Baring, a director of the Company, a Member of Parliament and one of Shelburne's financial advisers. But Pitt did not confine himself to the Company's advice. He already knew something of the subject from his earlier period at the Exchequer,[2] he consulted other sources,[3] and he

---

1. *Reports from Committees of the House of Commons . . .*, XI (1803), 284.

2. See his papers of that period in P.R.O. 30/8/293, and Richardson's statement in his letter to the East India Company's Committee of Warehouses, March 1786 (P.R.O. 30/8/294). For Richardson's and Atkinson's advice, see also an interesting anonymous letter to Pretyman of 26 June 1821, in Pretyman Ms 562:1821.

3. E.g. his papers on the quantities of smuggled tea in P.R.O. 30/8/283, and his acknowledgement of Mahon's advice (which was not decisive) in *P.R.*, XV, 236.

kept in particularly close touch with the tea merchants through their leader Richard Twining. In carrying his measure into effect, he imposed a firm and detailed guidance – much more obviously successful here than in the purely political field – on those sections of the Company which were necessary to his purpose.

For the measure itself was only the first stage. Pitt introduced his bill in June 1784. It followed broadly the proposals of the Parliamentary committee – themselves not so very different from the tentative plan of Shelburne's day. The duties on tea would be reduced from an average of 119% to between 12½ and 30% of the value per lb; the window tax would be sharply increased on a graduated scale according to number. The immediate gain to the revenue was forecast as nearly £200,000 a year; the gain to the Company would be great, in sales and in shipping. Opposition could scarcely reject a scheme which they had helped to father, and the Commutation Bill, as it came to be called, passed its first reading with little fuss.

Objections indeed were more likely to turn on practical difficulties than on principle. Pitt was well aware of the potential dangers. If the Act was to prove effective, the prices of tea must be regulated and adequate stocks guaranteed. Otherwise there would be confusion and shortage, which would simply play into the smugglers' hands. The complications were soon apparent. The Company objected to the effects on its existing stock, and as a result the rates of duty were altered to a uniform 25% on value, and permissible prices, kinds and quantities of tea for sale were laid down. The revised proposals passed again with little opposition, and on 20 August the bill became law.

The Government had now made itself responsible for the provisions governing the market in tea. Pitt was faced with the task of seeing that its objects were secured. He had to act vigorously from the start, for the smugglers at once transferred their activities from the coasts to the auction room. At the first of the Company's autumn sales, 'a number of persons with silk handkerchiefs around their neck and weatherbeaten countenances'[1] forced up the prices to levels that threatened to wreck the scheme. The Minister went down to Leadenhall Street the next day, and conferred first with Twining and then with the Company. Emergency stocks were mustered, buyers were encouraged to return purchases for re-sale, the Government's support was privately pledged if extra tea had to be bought from Europe. These measures had a temporary effect; but it did not last long. Prices soon rose again, the Opposition press was in full cry, and the dealers themselves and the Company were beginning to quarrel. For the legal stocks of tea were now under pressure, the Company was falling back on inferior leaf, and the buyers were grumbling at the combination of quality and price.

---

1. *Public Advertiser*, 27 September 1784; quoted in Hoh-Cheung & Lorna A. Mui, 'William Pitt and the Enforcement of the Commutation Act, 1784–1788' (*E.H.R.*, LXXVI, no. 300, 453 n2).

Pitt was in an awkward position. He dared not act too openly, so as to antagonise either party; but if nothing was done, the smugglers would win. The crisis came at the turn of the year. At the December sales, the dealers refused to buy any of the offered stock, most of which by now was indeed distinctly poor. Such an impasse must clearly be broken; and broken it was. A silk merchant, Richard Constable, suddenly appeared, and bid for the whole amount at a penny a lb above the reserve. His action had the desired effect. The tea dealers in alarm authorised Twining to compete on their behalf, and the two men soon divided the stock at reasonable prices.

There seems little doubt that Pitt was involved in this move.[1] He was certainly kept posted of all that went on, and he was closely connected with what followed. In the autumn, a group of anonymous gentlemen had advertised proposals to set up a large warehouse for the sale of tea, at prices lower than those at which the dealers were retailing. This group was almost certainly headed by an M.P., Robert Preston, who had made his fortune in the Company's service, was identified with its shipping interest, and was a friend of Richardson.[2] Constable sold his large purchases in December to Preston. The two men, with Richardson's help, bought a warehouse immediately afterwards; and Preston had already waited on Pitt 'to receive . . . instructions' on the rates at which the tea should be sold.[3] Where the capital came from is not known; but Atkinson's and Baring's names were mentioned in the press. All this points strongly to the Minister's knowledge and consent, if not to his prompting. It was the more gratifying that the measures soon did the trick. Both Constable and the regular dealers sold their purchases at lower levels, and prices in general responded early in 1785.

The immediate challenge had thus been met. But the future remained in doubt. If prices were to be held down, the Company must greatly enlarge its stocks, and the necessary supplies from China could scarcely be built up in under two years. Meanwhile, substantial purchases would have to be made in Europe. Once more Pitt was closely concerned. He had already arranged for an advance of £300,000 from the Bank of England, and promised Parliament's support if more was required; his associates were well represented on the purchasing committee which the Company set up; and two of its three active members were Atkinson and Baring. The Minister was thus in touch with the business from its start in the autumn of 1784. From the spring of 1785 he was at its centre.

For the purchases on the continent soon began to alarm the European dealers, and early in the new year a *modus vivendi* was proposed. The suggestion came from the old-established house of Voute in Amsterdam,

---

1. See Mui, loc. cit., 456–7 for a discussion of the evidence.
2. See p. 242 above.
3. Richardson to Pitt, 24 December 1784 (P.R.O. 30/8/293), and in general Mui, loc. cit., 455–8.

acting for a consortium of European merchants. The partners offered to supply all the tea that the Company needed, at prices lower than those on the open market, so long as none was bought elsewhere in Europe and neither the Court of Directors nor the purchasing committee itself was informed of the nature of the arrangement. Baring was entrusted with the details, which he passed on to Pitt, and the two men decided to accept the offer. But clearly the committee might prove awkward, and in the event Pitt was forced to take a hand. He intervened in April and again in November to prevent stocks being bought elsewhere, and when the committee objected in the following January to these constant purchases from a single source, he used the big stick at once.[1] His unexplained pressure was resented, and the committee finally rebelled. In August 1786 it cancelled the latest contract with Voute. But by that time the scheme had largely served its purpose. In 1785 and 1786 the Company bought a total of over 8 million lb of tea from Amsterdam, at prices that ensured the success of the Act. By 1787 the necessary supplies were coming in from China, and a steadily growing legal market could be profitably satisfied. In 1788, more than 13 million lb of tea passed through the Customs, and the East India Directors were talking of re-exporting some to Europe; in 1789, they were looking forward to a near monopoly of the China trade. The Company's revenues and shipping had been fortified, with good effect on the general trade with the East – though there was no sign as yet of a favourable balance. The yield to the Exchequer, from the duty and the window tax, was rather higher than before. The smuggler had been dealt a critical blow in this important traffic. The whole operation had proved a tremendous success. But without some firm and secret handling it might well have failed.

Encouraged by the result, Pitt applied the same medicine elsewhere. In 1785, he slightly lowered the duties on rum and on British spirits. In 1786 and 1787, the duties on French wines and brandies were progressively reduced, and those on other European wines were brought into line in the latter year. Other French goods benefited from the rates settled by treaty in 1786, and in 1787 a general consolidation of customs duties disguised widespread fractional increases by more obvious abolitions and reductions. These measures were not taken solely with an eye to contraband; they were part of a wider process of commercial negotiation and financial reform. But the smuggler remained a prime target, as Pitt made clear in 1787, when at the conclusion of the French treaty he lowered the duty on all brandies by 40 per cent.[2] All this dealt 'the gentlemen' another heavy blow. But Pitt did not rely on lower duties alone to achieve his purpose. He used a variety of weapons to strike at

1. By threatening to open the ports – in other words, to remove all duty.
2. See his remarks as reported in *P.R.*, XXI (1787), 246.

evasion and fraud. The smuggler was not the only threat to the revenue; he had his allies, and his rivals, inland. Wines and spirits and tobacco – the great staples of contraband other than tea – passed through many hands, and some of the spirits were distilled in this country. Their terms of sale could be controlled by the Excise as well as, sometimes better than by, the Customs, and there were good reasons why this should be done. The Excise was the more efficient department, searches could be extended to different stages in the process, the adulteration of quality could be checked more readily. The reduction of the rates on British spirits in 1785 was a prelude to tightening up the laws on quality, and redistributing the duties on all spirits between the two departments. Special regulations were made for Scotland in 1786, 1789 and 1790, and Pitt had earlier brought a long-standing exemption within the jurisdiction of the northern board.[1] In 1786 he transferred the greater part of the duties on wines from the Customs to the Excise, and raised those on the 'sweets' used for adulteration. Three years later he turned to the vexed problem of tobacco – one of the rocks on which Walpole's famous Excise Bill had foundered half a century before. After a spirited but far less serious fight, he carried a similar scheme. Duty in this case was not lowered; but three-fifths of it was transferred to the Excise, and the department was made responsible for inspection and warehousing at the listed ports. All these measures were a pronounced success. The yield on wines rose from £625,000 in 1783 to £804,000 in 1790, that on spirits from £561,000 in 1784 to an average of £915,000 in 1787–90, that on tobacco from an average of £424,000 in 1786–9 to an average of £590,000 in 1789–92.[2]

Pitt thus concentrated on fiscal attack, as the Parliamentary committee had recommended. But he did not ignore its complementary suggestions for strengthening the deterrents.[3] In July 1784, he extended the 'Hovering Act' of 1780 so that vessels might be searched and seized within four (instead of two) leagues from the coast; he made it legal for forfeited vessels to be destroyed if the Customs did not want them, and for the construction of ships building on smuggling lines to be stopped at any stage; he obliged armed vessels to obtain a licence to sail beyond a certain distance from the coasts; increased the penalites for smuggling; and made it a capital felony to shoot at revenue officers and craft. Two years later, the 'Manifest Act' tightened the rules of clearance with the Customs. These statutes were useful additions to the prosecution's

1. That of the great distilleries at Ferrintosh, belonging to Forbes of Culloden, bought out, by an arbitrary process, for over £21,000 in 1784.

> 'Thee, Ferintosh! O sadly lost!
> Scotland lament frae coast to coast!
> . . . For loyal Forbes' charter'd boast
> Is ta'en awa!'

(Burns, 'Scotch Drink', 1785/6. The poet himself had not yet become an exciseman.)

2. *A Brief Examination . . .*, 5, 7, 8.

3. P. 242 above.

armoury in making a legal charge; but they could still do little in themselves to increase the chance of an arrest. Pitt did what he could with the forces he had. One notable coup illustrates his difficulties, and his grasp.[1] In January 1785, a period of winter gales forced the smugglers at Deal to draw their boats high up the beach. As soon as he learned of this, the Minister asked the War Office to send troops to cordon off the area while the vessels were destroyed. The Secretary at War replied that this could not legally be done. But he soon learned his mistake. The First Lord of the Treasury had the right to call on the forces of the Crown to protect the revenue, and Pitt was in no mood to stand for delay. The men were sent, and the operation was a complete success. Such opportunities of course were rare, and the smugglers more often remained immune. Complaints of their activities continued throughout the decade, and one cannot tell at all exactly how much the 'runs' were reduced. The evidence is indirect; but the general impression is clear. The varied measures took a heavy toll, though they could not of course stamp out the traffic. The Parliamentary committee of 1783–4 had estimated that the revenue might benefit by some £2 to 3 million if smuggling could be checked. By Pitt's computation eight years later, about £1 million had been gained directly;[2] and part of the further £2 million of income gained from the general increase in consumption could certainly be attributed to the transfer of illicit into licit trade.[3]

II

To save the revenue from 'frauds' was part of the whole business of increasing the yield from existing taxes. Two other means lay in improving the system of management, and that of the accounts. Both were of the greatest importance, and both were prominent in Pitt's mind. But neither could be tackled comprehensively at once; the former involved the sacred matter of places, which must be approached with care, the latter awaited the detailed answer to the question of redeeming Government debt. Meanwhile the annual deficit had to be met. Given its size, the only possible stopgap was as usual to raise a loan; but this in turn meant raising fresh money to pay the annual charge, which as things stood could be supplied only by fresh taxes. Pitt had estimated his deficit at about £6 million for 1784, and he was anxious to fund £6,600,000 – the most the market would take – of the floating debt.[4] To cover the interest on these operations, and on the rest of the short-term

1. For this incident, see Binney, op. cit., 279. Other examples of Pitt's early efforts may be found in the Treasury Board's Minutes, P.R.O. T. 29/55–56.
2. Speech of 17 February 1792 (*P.H.*, XXIX (1817), 830).
3. For just one instance, the Customs estimated that about £¼ million had been extracted 'chiefly' from the smugglers' profits by the commercial treaty of 1786 with France (Thomas Irving's note of 1788, in B.M. Add. Ms 34427, f. 365v).
4. See pp. 239–40 above.

debt, he reckoned that he would need rather more than £900,000. In his first budget, introduced at the end of June 1784, he therefore proposed extra taxes (other than the increased window tax, already put forward) amounting to that 'enormous', indeed 'unexampled' sum.[1]

Theories of taxation in the middle and later eighteenth century were in something of the same position as theories of politics. Certain strands within a conservative but variegated tradition were emerging with an emphasis more telling for the future than at the time. Like so much else, the pattern had been formed in the middle and later seventeenth century. Two ideas descended from that intellectually active age, to become the assumptions of its less exacting successor. No man, it was argued, should be exempt from liability for tax, in return for the protection afforded by the state; but taxes should fall as lightly as possible on the poor, for the sake of social justice (and indeed of social quiet), and because the cost of labour would otherwise be raised. From these premises, two divergent lines of thought could follow. First, taxes should fall on consumption, and particularly on 'luxuries'. Certain dues were levied on 'necessaries', to which everyone in principle was subject; but conspicuous expenditure was the recognised target, with customs and excise duties, chiefly the former, bearing most of the load. Drink and tobacco, the finer materials, china and plate, fruit and sugar and glass: such 'superfluities' were among the main sources of extra income, as the pressures of trading interests and policy allowed.

Indirect taxation in fact was the staple of revenue in quiet times. But from the wars of William III and Queen Anne to that of the American revolution, Governments found that they needed more than such sources were allowed by public opinion to supply. In times of greater expense direct taxes had also to be levied; and these, once imposed, seldom entirely disappeared. Taxes on property or occupation – the poll tax in its final form, those on carriages and coaches which partly replaced it, on servants, on auctions, on fire insurance, on legal documents and probate, the house tax, the window tax, the land tax – all these direct assessments were the products of war. Their distribution roused heated debate, and some of the proposals were blocked or repealed; but the principle was confirmed as the needs increased. It received a strong theoretical stimulus at the start of the American War. In the year that North began his list of additions to the direct taxes and stamps, Adam Smith published his Inquiry into the Wealth of Nations. With his emphasis on rents and a freer trade, he favoured the ideal of direct taxation. Indirect levies were inescapable, and they had their uses in fiscal policy. But they tended to hamper commerce, and to obscure the true principles of taxation itself. 'The consumprions of the people', he had already stated, 'are not always according to what they possess'; taxes on expenditure thus contained an inherent inequality;

1. *P.R.*, XV, 280. See p. 242 above for the window tax. The highest level of taxation at which North had aimed in the war was £800,000.

and – harking back to the seventeenth century – the revenue should more properly rest on equal contributions, proportioned to the individual's ability to pay.[1] 'Rent, Profits and Wages' should all play their respective parts. Such doctrine held the germ of an income tax. But, in common with earlier theorists whose views led them in the same direction, Adam Smith would not admit so radical an end. The administrative difficulties seemed too great, the privacy of the citizen was too precious; both in practice and in principle, men could not be subject to 'endless vexation'.[2] Taxes should therefore fall as far as possible on certain settled bases and yardsticks of wealth; on certain possessions, on certain earnings, above all on houses and land.

It would be rash to claim too precise an effect for Adam Smith's great work. Its influence was seminal rather than specific. One can seldom be confident that a given act of policy stemmed directly from his advice, any more than such acts in our own time can be laid solely at the door of Maynard Keynes. But his pronouncements on taxation suited Ministers well at the time; they made the added impositions respectable, as North's speeches gratefully suggest.[3] Perhaps they affected the choice between similar possibilities; the house tax of 1778 in particular may well have drawn support, if not inspiration, from Adam Smith. They certainly fostered the widespread acceptance of a group of familiar expedients – just as later they may have helped delay acceptance of an income tax itself.

By the end of the American War, the net of taxation was thus in theory quite widely spread. It was indeed stretching too thinly and unevenly over too much ground. The potential discrepancies of method were covered by necessity. Levies on consumption, assessments on property and certain items of income, were called on indifferently as occasion allowed, and the taxes on 'necessaries' themselves were reluctantly increased from time to time. Compared with the response of the next generation, in the later stages of the French wars, the effort was unheroic in the Gladstonian sense; the heterogeneous collection of imposts did not cut very deep, and higher costs were mostly met by plunging more heavily into debt. Compared with the achievement of the later 1780s, the result was inefficient; the taxes did not bring in the expected amounts. Neither the doctrine nor the system of management was in fact adequate to a long war, particularly one in which trade was so sharply upset. But neither was easily changed in a conservative age,

1. *Lectures on Justice, Police, Revenue, and Arms*, ed. Edwin Cannan (1896), 240; *Wealth of Nations*, II, 310–11. For a discussion of what this last argument implied in the way of 'progressive' taxation, see the two books of that name by E. R. A. Seligman (1908) and F. Shehab (1953). William Kennedy, *English Taxation 1640–1799* . . . (1913), discounts Adam Smith's emphasis on direct taxation, principally because the master disapproved of an income tax itself.

2. This argument was stated most clearly in respect of profits; but it also applied to all forms of property yielding a capitation tax.

3. E.g. in particular his budget speech of 1777 (*P.H.*, XIX (1814), 241–9).

and within their limits the effort seemed very real. 'Where was he to find taxes', asked North, 'to produce 800,000 l?' 'The immense taxes with which [Britain] is loaded', ran a typical pronouncement, 'must alarm every thinking man'.[1] It was the burden of taxation above all else, when the war became unpopular, that swelled the ranks of the Yorkshire movement for Parliamentary reform.

Pitt broadly respected these limits throughout his nine years of peace; nor does he seem to have had any marked preference for a particular class of tax. His first budget has been called 'old-fashioned', his second 'belonged to the old order of things';[2] and the style endured for the rest of the decade. Taking the taxes by themselves, such comment is perfectly true. The budget of 1784 might have been produced by Legge or by Pelham, twenty or even forty years before. Almost all the proposals that passed had already been tried or thought of – taxes on pleasure horses and hackney coaches, on various licences for retail trade in exciseable goods, on sporting (i.e. shooting) certificates, on bricks and tiles, candles, linens and calicoes; supplemented soon afterwards by levies on gold and silver plate, on imported silk and exported lead, by higher rates of postage, by a tightening of the rules for franking letters (not as great as Pitt would have wished, and then very largely evaded), and a further slight extension of the licences for trade. Two innovations – a tax on men's hats, and one on ladies' ribbons (the latter soon cancelled in favour of the duty on silk) – had their nearest equivalents in the sumptuary laws.

The pattern was much the same in 1785, when fresh taxes were still needed to achieve the surplus for reducing debt. In the budget itself, the levy on employers of menservants was increased, that on salt was tidied up, and new taxes were laid on post horses, on gloves, on the employers of female servants, on pawnbrokers' licences, and – most controversially – on retail shops. Later, the shooting licence was extended to cover gundogs and sporting guns, and taxes were imposed on attorneys, on bachelors according to the number of servants they kept (an idea proposed by Fox), on coachmakers' licences and new carriages. In 1786, perfumes and powders (most notably hair powder) were taxed, and the duty on imported gin was raised;[3] in 1789 the rates were increased on pleasure horses, race horses and carriages, and on a number of stamp duties – on newspapers and advertisements, cards and dice, legacies and wills and probate.

1. North to William Knox, January 1782 (*H.M.C., Various Collections*, VI, 274); Francis Dobbs, Esq., *Thoughts on the Present Mode of Taxation in Great Britain* (1784), 1.
2. Holland Rose, 186, 188.
3. A higher rate of duty on some Baltic timber was also proposed, but withdrawn when it seemed likely to have a bad effect on a commercial negotiation then under way with Russia.

This last crop of taxes was designed to compensate for the repeal of the shop tax of 1785, which had been under attack since its introduction. In general, the finances were healthier, and little was needed during those years. But in 1790 there was a threat of war with Spain, for which the preparations cost just over £3 million. Pitt's response was again on strictly traditional lines. Over two-thirds of the expense was met by anticipating revenue with an issue of exchequer bills, and by appropriating some public balances lying in the Bank of England. The rest was to be covered by improving the methods of collecting the receipt tax and the tax on bills of exchange, first brought in by other Ministries seven and eight years before; by raising the taxes on houses, menservants, pleasure horses and carriages, each by 10 per cent; by doubling the tax on gamekeepers, and raising the stamps on licences by a third; and increasing the duties on spirits, rum and brandy, sugar and malt. Two years later, some of these levies were reduced and others abolished; and in the same happy lull, a few of the earlier taxes were eased.

If one takes this list of measures, its nature is clear. The emphasis fell on luxuries, as these had long been defined, and on traditional forms of assessment. When the latter were extended, it was largely in the direction of attorneys and retail trade; but only the shop tax suggested a significant innovation, and significantly enough that was withdrawn. Some necessaries were taxed in the sternest years, 1784 and 1790. But a few of these levies were later reduced, and in general such objects were left alone or the tax was disguised as a trading licence. The whole picture is one of reliance on familiar methods, with no strong preference between them. Expenditure, income and possessions were called on indifferently, as opportunity allowed. None of the taxes approved by Parliament marked a departure of principle; nor, for that matter, did the few that were not approved.

For Pitt was not uniformly successful, and he was sometimes given a hard run. He could count on an exceptionally wide measure of support at the start. 'There appeared a spirit in all ranks of people', George Rose observed later, 'to support any exertion which might afford a chance of extricating the Country from its difficulties'. 'So sensible was he of the necesssity of raising taxes', said Fox in the budget debate of 1784, 'that there were hardly any taxes . . . that he should have thought himself . . . intitled to oppose'.[1] But even so it was not all plain sailing. Taxation was perhaps even more unpopular in the eighteenth century than is normally the case; how could it be otherwise in the great age of the idea of propertied freedom? Nor were the propertied classes alone in resenting such 'oppression'; the 'inferior set of people' – the small farmer, the small shopkeeper, the apprentice, the wage-earner – were

1. *A Brief Examination into the Increase of the Revenue . . .*, 4; *P.R.*, XV, 289–90.

quick to express their feelings, sometimes violently if they could. The whole of society in different ways was keenly on the watch. New taxes were a fruitful source of riot, they always brought the House of Commons to life, they were handled very cautiously by all but the boldest Minister. Pitt was in a strong position. But he did not escape. The caricaturists and the versifiers sprang into action at once. Dent's 'Free-Born Briton or a Perspective of Taxation' was a slightly later classic of the printshops; but the newspapers were already contributing their rhymes.

> On this side and on that, in the air, on the ground,
> By Act upon Act now so firmly we're bound,
> One would think there's not room one new impost to put,
> From the crown of the head to the sole of the foot;
> Like Job, thus John Bull his condition deplores,
> Very patient, indeed, and all covered with sores.[1]

These of course were obvious reactions as the net of taxation spread: they had been voiced more elegantly, for instance, by Burke in the course of the American War. But there were certain imposts which Parliament particularly disliked, whether or not it managed to defeat them. Pitt faced his most determined opposition in 1784 and 1785, and a lesser burst in 1790. In 1784, indeed, he lost two budget proposals – to include hop planters among the traders in exciseable goods subject to licences; and to alter the tax on coals from its long-established form of a levy on cargoes carried by sea to a levy on coal at the pit, which would have been more fair and more comprehensive. He had in fact run up against a combination of sentiment and interest the force of which he would feel again. There was a general reluctance to tax the poor too widely, particularly when other taxes on necessaries were in view; there was also rising pressure from manufacturers, beginning to test their strength, against any imposition likely to raise their prices. The former was a largely unco-ordinated feeling, which might or might not prove effective; when Pitt came down on malt again, in 1790, he succeeded in spite of widespread distaste. The latter could be really formidable, as the story of the Irish Propositions showed; and in 1784 he had not fully gauged its strength. The coal tax gave him little opportunity to do so, for the manufacturers did not need to mount a concerted attack. Pitt 'found men's minds so adverse'[2] that he dropped the proposal in a week. But the occasion was significant for his first encounter with an interest which very soon was to give him much more trouble.

1. Quoted from a verse of 1784 in Stephen Dowell, *A History of Taxation and Taxes in England . . .*, II (2nd edn, 1888), 188. For caricatures, see *Catalogue of Political and Personal Satires . . . in the British Museum*, VI.
2. Statement of 7 July (*P.R.*, XVI, 19). Stockdale (II, 394) states 8 July.

For it was not only the Irish Propositions that suffered in the spring of 1785. The manufacturers then forced the repeal of one of the taxes of the year before. The two questions were indeed connected, and reacted on each other. If the scheme for Ireland was responsible for the formation of the General Chamber,[1] the earlier tax had drawn some of its most prominent members together and supplied one of their most powerful arguments at the start.

The tax on linens and calicoes[2] was hotly resented from the first: not only for the duty itself, but because collection was placed under the Excise. *'Excise'*, most Englishmen still agreed, was 'a hateful tax'.[3] It 'fettered and embarrassed' a man's liberty, and in this case some of the regulations were technically inept. As early as August 1784 the leading manufacturers were collecting subscriptions for a committee of protest; when they were asked to give evidence on the plan for Ireland, their opportunity lay to hand. The representations were ill received, and the manufacturers' tempers rose. They were prepared to accept fair competition, but only if they were 'undampted, unchecked and untaxed'.[4] The cotton men of Manchester and Glasgow were eager for a General Chamber, and their case was supported by the ironfounders of the midlands and west. Shaken by the turn of events, and fighting to salvage his Irish scheme, Pitt gave way in April. He did not admit the arguments, and he suspected that some of them had been 'infused' from outside. But 'the opinions . . . nay, even prejudices and errors' of 'so large . . . and respectable a body of men' were important enough at that moment for him to submit.[5]

The first half of 1785 was an unfortunate time. Scarcely had Pitt repealed this tax when he introduced another that ran into trouble. The tax on female servants caused some fuss, and more amusement – the special debate which it occasioned might almost have been arranged for Members to air their jokes.[6] But the opposition to the shop tax was a much more serious matter. Some of the objections echoed those raised a quarter of a century before, when a similar proposal had been withdrawn, and again when the Coalition's receipt tax had passed in 1783. The levy would fall on a class of persons many of whom were small men, and whose prosperity was essential to the spread of trade. The assessment was also said to be unjust in that it fell on rents, which did not

1. Pp. 205–9 above.
2. P. 250 above.
3. *'Excise*. A hateful tax levied upon commodities . . .'* (Johnson's *Dictionary of the English Language*, 1755).
4. See p. 206 above.
5. Pitt on 20 April 1785 (*P.R.*, XVIII, 95).
6. There were actually two debates under this title, after the budget. But the second was really the occasion for a supplementary budget statement.
The jokes ('perhaps not very diverting, and certainly not very decorous' – Stanhope, I, 255) were of course echoed in prints and papers, where they relied for much of their point on Pitt's attitude to women.

always bear much relation to the size of business in the larger towns.[1] Pitt acknowledged some of the arguments, and made some amendments. But he defended the principle of the tax on the ground that the burden would be passed on in higher prices, so that in the end it was the consumer, not the shopkeeper, who would pay. The levy, he agreed, was 'severe', and 'attended with a more violent and more universal opposition than most others'. But the very 'universality of the opposition' argued 'the universality of the operation', which was justifiable when the country was striving to lighten the burden of debt.[2]

The tax became law. But it was, and remained, highly unpopular. Shopkeepers were not all the respectable men that they have since become. The smaller sort had been active in the Wilkite riots, they attracted their share of prosecutions for sedition in the French wars (in France, they were well represented among the *sansculottes*), Francis Place himself kept his shop at Charing Cross. They were inflammable material, and neither they nor their larger confrères took the Act lying down. There were riots in London in June – Pitt was burned in effigy, John Beresford arrived from Ireland to see Downing Street besieged, and Eden, who was living there, was delighted to find that 'it grows dangerous to live in the Neighbourhood of the popular Minister';[3] and although the violence was short-lived the resentment endured.[4] The shopkeepers of London and Westminster continued to petition, and in 1786 they managed to enlist Fox's support. His motions for repeal were defeated over the next two years; but, as he suspected, time was on his side. The Westminster by-election of 1788 gave the question a new lease of life, and by the time that Fox tried again in 1789, Pitt was ready to withdraw the tax. It would be interesting to know more about the shopkeepers' methods. They produced a signal triumph for a pressure group working through a weakened Opposition at a time when the Minister was at the height of his prestige.

The campaign against the shop tax was exceptional in its persistence. The passions roused so readily were more often quick to die. In September 1785, when memories of the budget and the Irish plan were still fresh, Fox to his surprise was fêted in Manchester; in October, Dundas could report that the northern manufacturers were 'coming very quickly

1. To which, even at the end of the century, Napoleon's nation of shopkeepers was still largely confined. The village shop was only just beginning to replace the travelling packman, as the roads, and so the means of distribution, improved.

2. Stockdale, III, 235. These remarks are not reported in *P.R.*, XVIII.

3. *L.C.G. III*, I, no. 218, n2; Beresford to Orde, 15 June 1785 (Bolton Mss, no. 193); Eden to Sheffield, 'Friday' (B.M. Add. Ms 45728).

4. Thus when Pitt, accompanied by Richmond, went down to a City feast in November, they met with 'some *rough compliments* from ye Mob' and had their carriage windows broken. This was the work, it was said, of apprentices; the City fathers gave them a good welcome (Lady Harriot Eliot to Hester Countess of Chatham, 10 November [1785]; *The Letters of Lady Harriot Eliot*, 116–17).

round'.[1] The General Chamber lost its impetus before a year was out, and Pitt's troubles then receded as the finances improved. He could take comfort in the fact that most of his policies had survived attack. Equally, he now knew the limits he should normally respect. Certainly he remained conservative in his later trials. Even when the French War began, he would not increase the land tax. He reimposed the assessments of 1790, but did not raise their levels until 1796. And when the crisis of the following year forced him into sterner measures, he turned again to traditional methods before he would hazard an income tax. His policies in fact did not vary much from those of his earliest years. Their consistency suggests that he largely shared the reactions he sometimes aroused.

For the pattern is clearly marked, in times of pressure as of ease. Pitt preferred to raise his balance in the budget from a wide variety of sources, rather than by a simpler and more comprehensive attack on the main yardsticks of wealth. Nor did he necessarily reject old-fashioned means in his adherence to such an end. Thus he resorted to an annual lottery, not only as a douceur for loans as North had done, but as a regular item of income when there was no loan in sight.[2] And he even returned in one instance – that of the stamp duty on licences for post horses – to farming a tax to individuals, a practice more readily associated with the Stuart kings than with the name of Pitt.[3] It might well be asked why all this should have been so. Why should Pitt of all men, with his interest in theory and in simplifying the finances, have been content with such a heterogeneous approach? Why should he not at some point, for instance, have increased the house tax to a level that would have rendered some at least of the minor levies redundant?[4] The answer would seem to be that he did not think such a course worth while unless it proved necessary, and that he banked on the fact that this would not be so. 'Clear simple taxes', wrote one of his correspondents, 'have always been avoided on the notion that they wd be too alarming to the Subject';[5] the whole tenor of Pitt's policy suggests that he would have agreed with this as a guide. And while such alarm might have had to be faced if the situation demanded, he never really seems to have believed

1. *Correspondence of Fox*, II, 270–1; Dundas to Pitt, 23 October (P.R.O. 30/58/157).
2. Pitt never shared the growing hostility to lotteries, which arose largely on moral grounds, though there are signs that he regarded them as expedients to meet special expense – he devoted the proceeds very largely to satisfying the claims of the American loyalists from the recent war. He may have been influenced by the fact that the Treasury could use the cash – usually £1½ million at least – free of interest until the prizes were paid. At any rate, he persisted with lotteries throughout the peacetime years, carried a bill for their better management in 1787, and defeated a Parliamentary attempt to stop them in 1792.
3. He did this in 1787, because he was convinced that the abuse in its collection could not be overcome within the department. The farm was quite widespread.
4. For a possible reason at the start, see below; but this scarcely applied at the end of the decade.
5. 'Plan from Mr. [Jonathan] Pitman', 31 December 1783 (P.R.O. 30/8/275).

that it would. He refused to impose a crop of extra taxes to secure a large surplus in 1786, 'on the conviction', as it was reported, 'that he should be able to render the revenue so productive as to make any addition unnecessary'.[1] His tax proposals, in fact, must be placed in a wider context. The increased levies fed the balance after the rest of the revenue had been raised; and essential as it was, that balance was proportionately small. Pitt never had to find more than £1 million by such means, out of an income that rose in peacetime from some £13¼ to some £18½ million; and if that sum seemed formidable, it was also occasional – in all but two of the years the demand was very much less. In the first of those moreover, in 1784, he may well have been deterred from proposing a more comprehensive form of taxation in the budget by the fact that he had already done so in the Commutation Bill.[2] The budgets themselves, in fact, cannot be viewed in isolation; in almost every year, Pitt attended to the revenue as well by other means. And it was chiefly in those means that he sought his answers, which if successful would further reduce his dependence on budgetary support.

For Pitt's main object was to increase the yield from *existing* taxes. It was here that he moved forward, with considerable effect. The Commutation Act, the consolidation of duties, improved methods of assessment and collection – it was in such financial and administrative measures that he placed his hopes and reaped his reward. He could not expect even then to avoid all need for extra taxes; as the experienced Hatsell remarked, 'other funds must [still] be found, or the subsisting taxes must be collected with a degree of rigour and exactness that would give too good a handle for clamour and opposition'.[3] But the need could be further reduced, and in the narrowed margin old means would serve. The best ways to increase income were to provide conditions for increased prosperity, and to improve the system of management and accounts. Theories of taxation demanded review only in the light of the results. Pitt's methods must be seen with this background in mind.

III

All these efforts were devoted to one supreme object: the steady reduction of the public debt. Pitt shared the almost universal fear of the consequences if the situation was allowed to stand. A debt of over £240 million, costing £8 to 9 million a year in charges alone, seemed an insupportable burden. A surplus of revenue was essential to lighten the load.[4]

1. William Morgan, F.R.S., *A Review of Dr. Price's Writings, on the subject of the Finances of this Kingdom* . . . (1792), 51. This was said to have been Pitt's reply to one of the plans which Price submitted for a sinking fund.
2. When he proposed to increase the window tax, to compensate for the expected fall in the revenue from tea (see p. 242 above).
3. To William Eden, 5 November 1785 (*A.C.*, I, 355).
4. See pp. 157–8 above.

But pending that happy event, fresh loans must still be raised. Pitt's first task was to see that the terms were not too expensive. They had swung sharply against Government in the course of the American War. There were three possible ways in theory in which to float a public loan: by open subscription, the Treasury then allotting the amounts between subscribers; by accepting offers made in private on the Treasury's invitation, the terms being subject to bargaining and the allocations again being made by the Treasury; or by a close subscription from a few persons on terms already settled by the Treasury, the subscribers being responsible for announcing the amounts they would provide. The first had seldom been successful, for it depended on too many individuals, and the second had become the accepted method, which North used for most of the war. It had the advantages, when conditions were right, of allowing some room for negotiation, and of saving the Treasury from the accusation of fixing terms that might prove too lenient in the event. But the boot might be on the other foot, as became abundantly clear in the later stages of the war. By the end of the seventies loans were being raised on effectively worse terms, and there was a premium on the scrip itself. This was bad enough; but it had political implications, for since the Treasury made the allocations it could be accused of corruption as well as extravagance. In 1781, the premium on the scrip reached almost 10 per cent, so that 'every 10,000 l allotted to a private friend was precisely the same thing as putting a thousand pounds bank note into his hand'.[1] The handling of the loan swelled the ammunition for the attacks on influence; and political pressures, as so often, succeeded where purely economic pressures had failed.

For the traditional method was not applied in the same form again. Pitt has always been rightly praised for the terms of his first loan. He has also been credited – he was at the time – with having started a new system. But in fact there had been changes over the past two years, and he could profit from the experience of the Coalition and of North himself. In 1782 and 1783, the Treasury managed to place the loan largely – in the first year entirely – with one syndicate which offered to contract for the whole. It also managed unofficially to secure some competition beforehand, and in 1782 North declined to be responsible for any allocations that might be made. These experiments, particularly the first, paved the way for Pitt's improvements. He may also have drawn on an abortive plan worked out with Shelburne for the loan of 1783, the details of which were never disclosed, but which would probably have followed North's revised method in principle.[2] When the time came in 1784, he therefore confirmed the recent trend, and placed the management of the loan on a basis that endured. He encouraged com-

1. The Rt Hon. George Rose, *Observations Respecting the Public Expenditure, and the Influence of the Crown* (1810), 27.
2. See Shelburne's important admission in his speech in the Lords of 5 May 1783 (*P.H.*, XXIII, 812).

petition between two syndicates, insisted that they should accept responsibility for the final allocation, and called for sealed tenders on which a decision would be taken in accordance with terms fixed by the Treasury, also under seal in advance.

This was a bold affirmation of Government's integrity, which the market was now conditioned to accept. It removed suspicions of political pressure, and promised a better financial return. But the promise of course depended on the lenders' co-operation, and this was not complete in 1784. Pitt could still not secure the terms he would have liked; in 1785, when his need was less, he therefore avoided a public loan, and borrowed the £1 million he required direct from the Bank of England.[1] Taxes and short-term bills sufficed thereafter, except in 1789. Probably so as not to increase the amount of long-term redeemable debt, the Minister then resorted to 'the unusual mode of a tontine' – a type of loan that had been tried in England only twice before, in 1693 and 1766, and had proved a fiasco on the second occasion.[2] It failed again now, and the terms were altered next year to his disadvantage. Pitt had shown skill and courage in the way he stated his conditions at the start. His greatest achievement in the matter of loans over the next eight years was that he had scarcely to trouble the market.

The complex structure of the public debt can be described in various ways, according to the purpose. To a Minister in 1784 one immediate fact stood out. The long-term debt was funded – that is to say, each annuity and loan, as it was issued, had been assigned a specific fund of revenue, on which payment of the interest (and sometimes repayment of capital) was a first charge. The sum of these annuities and loans was generally called the National Debt. But there was also a group of unfunded short-term debts, met by issuing navy bills, ordnance debentures and exchequer bills, on which interest was paid from unappropriated revenue without a specific guarantee.[3] At the end of 1783, the navy bills and ordnance debentures were thought to amount to over

1. This had the added advantage that the Bank lent sums out of the £1 million as they were called for, and interest was paid only as they were lent. For the terms in 1784, see J. J. Grellier, *The Terms of All the Loans Which have been Raised for the Public Service during the Last Fifty Years* . . . (1799), 32.

2. *The History of the National Debt, from the Revolution of 1688 to the Beginning of the Year 1800* . . . By the late J. J. Grellier (1810), 353. The tontine was a method of granting life annuities, by which the benefit to survivors increased proportionately as the orignial nominees died off. Pitt may have been attracted to it, despite the earlier failures in England, by the success of an Irish tontine in 1777; there is also a Dutch study of the subject among his papers (P.R.O. 30/8/277).

3. Not all exchequer bills were unfunded. Like the navy bills and ordnance debentures, they were issued by the department in order to anticipate revenue; and since the Exchequer was in a position to anticipate appropriated revenue, some of its bills created funded debt. Others did not. In January 1784, the proportions were roughly equal – £4,489,000 in funded bills, £4,172,000 unfunded.

£14 million, and the former were circulating at a discount of no less than 21 per cent. Such debts had been funded, in less drastic conditions, at the end of the Seven Years' War. It was obviously desirable to repeat the process now.

Funding meant creating stock. Pitt at this time shared the prediliction, common in Shelburne's circle, for as high a rate of interest as possible. '. . . A four per cent. was preferable to a three per cent. and a five per cent. better than a four'.[1] Such a conclusion might seem odd, for higher interest meant a higher annual charge; but the answer lay in the anxiety to reduce the *capital* of the debt. The theory ran thus. Government usually issued low-yielding stock in return for a loan – say, £2 million of 3 per cent stock to meet a loan of £1 million offered at 6 per cent. If a higher-yielding stock had been issued, it would have created less capital debt, though incurring a greater annual charge by way of interest. There was a point at which these two considerations could be balanced, so that a net saving would eventually be gained; for instance, an investor holding £75 of stock yielding 4 per cent would receive the same annual payment as one holding £100 of 3 per cent stock, and there would be 25 per cent less capital to be paid off. This was a favourable case. There would usually be a greater annual cost to Government at the higher rate; but there would still be less stock to be redeemed, and if the terms were worked out properly there would be an advantage in the end. At a time when the weight of indebtedness pressed on men's minds, anything that promised quicker redemption seemed highly important. Nevertheless, of course, lenders might not welcome such a promise, which they feared – contrary to the experience of their successors today – would tend in the interval to depress the price of the stock. North had used to say that 'in order to establish a 5 per cent stock "certain poor ignorant men on the other side of Temple bar must concur" ';[2] and this in fact was what Pitt found when raising his first loan. But he was in a stronger position with the short-term debt, since the wartime navy bills themselves carried 5 per cent. They could probably not all be funded at once, for the market would have been swamped; but it looked as if £6 million of the £14 million might be dealt with in 1784.[3] Pitt's first plan on such lines failed, for he tried to compensate for the discount on the bills by converting them into an equivalent lesser amount of stock – on the ground, it would seem, that they were now largely an object of speculation, bought far more cheaply than they had been by the original assignees. But, however justified his suspicions, such a settlement would have been a breach of

1. Pitt's speech of 30 June 1784 (*P.R.*, XV, 277).
2. Francis Baring's notes to Dr Price on a public loan ('Sir Francis Baring, Bart., M.P., Memoranda, 1782–1790'; transcripts in Northbrook Mss).
3. But Thomas Coutts told Pitt that the whole operation could be undertaken provided the payments were spaced out, and was distinctly upset when his advice was ignored (Ernest Hartley Coleridge, *The Life of Thomas Coutts . . .*, I (1920), 185).

precedent, and indeed of faith in the original terms. It was so represented; the proposal was dropped, and a more equitable conversion arranged. The accepted terms were repeated in 1785, when Pitt funded the rest of the wartime navy bills and ordnance debentures – now found to total a further £10 million – at 5 per cent.[1] In that year, too, he managed to borrow his £1 million from the Bank at the same rate.[2] By 1786, the floating debt consisted only of peacetime navy bills and exchequer bills, which continued to be issued as always to provide immediate support.

By then the way seemed open to tackle the National Debt itself. Pitt had been able to announce an increased revenue in the budget of 1785; he was confident of the future; and he was therefore ready to announce a plan in 1786, even if the surplus did not reach the ideal figure by then.

The plan was for the annual application of a surplus of revenue to the sinking fund. The idea was not new. There had been a sinking fund since 1716, surpluses had been applied to redeeming debt as recently as the early seventies,[3] and while the lean years thereafter made any such process impracticable, the prospect had been revived as soon as the war came to an end. On 4 December 1783, a fortnight before Pitt took office, the Parliamentary Commissioners for Examining the Public Accounts – set up by North almost four years before – produced their Eleventh Report, on the funded debt. It was a powerful document.

> A Plan must be formed for the Reduction of this Debt, and without Delay . . . The Evil does not admit of Procrastination, Palliatives, or Expedients: It presses on, and must be met with force and firmness.

The remedy was obvious: it was

> the Creation of a Fund, to be appropriated, and invariably applied, under proper Direction, in the gradual Diminution of the Debt: This Fund must be the Surplus of the Annual Income, above the Annual Expences of the State, to be obtained and increased by the Extension and Improvement of the Sources of Revenue, and by a frugal Administration of the Produce.[4]

Such a conclusion might have been designed as a blueprint for Pitt's policies over the next nine years.

It certainly gave him invaluable support, for the Commissioners

1. But even here he thought it wise to meet the lenders' fears of an early redemption by stipulating that the new stock would be irredeemable until £25 million of debt in the older stocks at 3 and 4 per cent had been redeemed.
2. See p. 258 above.
3. See p. 157 above.
4. *H.C.J.*, XXXIX, 782.

carried real weight. Above all they had stressed the point which was vital to any new plan, the 'invariable application' of the surplus to its specified purpose. For it was the failure to protect this guarantee which had chiefly hampered past efforts, and brought the idea itself into some disrepute. Ever since Walpole's day, the fund had been raided by Chancellors under pressure. Now that the task to be faced was so much larger than before, the regular allocations must obviously be left intact.

Pitt was the more impressed by this need because, like many others, he attached great importance to the operations of compound interest. The argument was simple; the consequences, once stated, made men blink. If you took a sum, of whatever size, and left it alone to gather interest, you created a larger capital sum each year on which a larger sum in interest would be paid. The rate of increase by this compound process was astonishingly high. The celebrated Dr Price had put it thus, in a famous passage in an influential work:

ONE PENNY, put out at our Saviour's birth to 5 *per cent. compound* interest, would, before this time, have increased to a greater sum, than would be contained in A HUNDRED AND FIFTY MILLIONS OF EARTHS, all solid gold. – But if put out to *simple* interest, it would, in the same time, have amounted to no more than *seven shillings and four pence half-penny*.[1]

Pitt himself calculated that a sum of £1 million, thus 'annually improved', could become £4 million in twenty-eight years.[2]

There is no doubt that Pitt was fascinated by the prospects thus opened up. It is difficult to say how deeply he had thought about the problem of the debt before. Doubtless he had studied some of the proposals lying in the Treasury in Shelburne's day; some at least found their way into his papers.[3] But the time was not ripe to do anything about them, and he seems first to have tackled the subject in detail in 1785. In April, he told the Commons that he hoped the next year to have a surplus of £1 million, which could be applied to a sinking fund: he must have studied Price's work, or perhaps some papers that the Doctor sent him, in the summer recess, for at the end of September he was 'half mad with a project which will give our supplies the effect almost of magic in the reduction of debt'.[4] He was gathering informa-

1. Richard Price, D.D., F.R.S., *An Appeal to the Public, on the Subject of the National Debt* (1772), 19.
2. Speech of 29 March 1786 (*P.R.*, XX (1787), 16).
3. See P.R.O. 30/8/275. Unfortunately there are no endorsements to indicate when they did so.
4. To Wilberforce, 30 September 1785 (*Correspondence of Wilberforce*, I, 9). For the fact that Price sent papers to Pitt in 1785, see Pitt to Price, January 1786 (William Morgan, *A Review of Dr. Price's Writings on the Subject of the Finances of this Kingdom*, 19–20). One may have been a scheme submitted to Shelburne in August 1782, which is in P.R.O. 30/8/275.

tion in the next few months – he made notes of individual charges on the funded debt, and of the capital and annual cost, he received a scheme from Sinclair in October, and another from William Knox, the retired Under-Secretary for America, via Temple probably in the winter[1] – , and by January 1786 he had drafted a provisional plan. It was sent to Price for his comments; in reply, four plans were sent back.[2] They all assumed a surplus of £1 million a year. The first and second proposed schemes for converting some of the existing 3 per cent stocks, which made up most of the debt, into 4 per cent, paying for the stock itself out of the £1 million and for the increased interest out of fresh taxes amounting to £800,000 a year. The fourth, with the same object, proposed the payment of interest out of £1 million, leaving only £200,000 with which to buy up and cancel stock. The third, unlike the others, proposed no plan of conversion, but simply the buying up of stock out of the £1 million, with no fresh taxes.

Price much preferred his schemes of conversion to this third plan; and of those three schemes, he liked the first and second best. He was in fact enamoured of the idea of an upward conversion of stock, which he had pressed from the start and held strongly to the end. The main advantage was that of a high interest when quick redemption was the object: there would be less capital debt to be paid off, in return for a somewhat higher annual charge. But this advantage would be increased if the stock to be converted was standing well below par, for the holder could then be granted a smaller holding of stock at higher interest. Thus, to take a favourable example, £75 in 4 per cents would yield the same as £100 in 3 per cents, and if the 3 per cents were low enough the 4 per cents would seem attractive. Since the 3 per cents were in fact standing at under 60 in the summer of 1785, Price urged the desirability of a large-scale upward conversion at once.

Pitt had been attracted by Price's arguments in the past. Even in January 1786 he seems to have envisaged a conversion from 3 into 5 per cents.[3] But his earlier faith in high interest stocks was becoming more

Price, who was Shelburne's pet economist, had published his views in three pamphlets: *Observations on Reversionary Payments* . . . (1771), *An Appeal to the Public* . . . (1772), and *The State of the Public Debts and Finances* (1783). The first two went quickly into several editions, and the third was reprinted before the end of the year. Pitt had a copy of the first at least (see the list of his books at Downing Street, in Pretyman Ms 562:21).

1. P.R.O. 30/8/275. Other schemes, preserved among Pitt's papers, were doubtless sent in at about this time; but one cannot tell. Temple may have forwarded Knox's plan (which was later printed by its author) during the winter, in response to a letter from Pitt in November discussing the prospect of a sinking fund. Sinclair (see p. 239 above) was a regular correspondent at this period.

2. They are to be found in P.R.O. 30/8/275. The first three, which were sent together, are published in *A Select Collection of Scarce and Valuable Tracts . . . on the National Debt and Sinking Fund* (1857) [ed. J. R. McCulloch, for Lord Overstone].

3. At least according to William Morgan, in his *Review of Dr. Price's Writings*, 20–1. Unfortunately, no copy appears to have survived of Pitt's first, tentative plan.

selective as a result of his experience over the past two years. He was not sure, he said in April 1785, if he would always wish to borrow at 5 per cent; and a few years later he seems to have been returning to 'the sweet simplicity of the three per cents'.[1] The arguments for a lower rate could indeed be used particularly against conversions in the funds. To exchange an amount in low interest stock for a smaller amount at higher interest was a direct invitation to exchange capital for income; and Pitt's doubts were increased by the fact that the 3 per cents were rising in price late in the year. He said as much to Price in January 1786; but the point was ignored in the Doctor's reply. Nor was Pitt happy about the cost of the increased interest. He was not prepared to levy much in the way of fresh taxes for the purpose, just when the revenue was otherwise adequate; nor did he relish the alternative, which would leave him only a fifth of his surplus for the purchase of stock. When the final scheme was produced in March 1786, it therefore did not follow Price's preference, but was a great deal closer to his third, 'weakest' plan.[2]

Exactly how close, and how dependent, became and has remained a matter of dispute. Price himself made no pressing claim: he was not the sort of man to do so, and in any case he was somewhat disappointed with Pitt's final response.[3] But he died in 1791, and his executor, William Morgan, was of a different calibre. On reading the Doctor's papers he leapt to the conclusion that injustice had been done, and the next year, without asking Pitt's permission or checking his facts, he published the Minister's correspondence with Price to prove the point.[4] According to Morgan, Pitt drew his ideas from Price in the first place, was saved by Price from embarking on a defective scheme of his own,

1. For his statement in 1785, see *P.R.*, XVIII, 35. In 1791 he considered, but did not adopt, a plan for converting the 'Bank Long Annuities' into 5 per cent stock. But in 1792, according to Pretyman, he intended to convert 4 per cents into 3½ per cents, and would probably have done so but for the war (Tomline, III, 299). He may by then have been taking into account the effect of Government's rate on the whole structure of interest rates; certainly he recognised the latter's significance in his budget speech of that year (see p. 273 below). But he was probably more concerned with the loan market's reaction.

2. Morgan, op. cit., 40.

3. He did write, in a letter to Stanhope of 15 May 1786, that 'the plan which Mr. Pitt has adopted is that which I have been writing about, and recommending for many years'. (*P.R.*, XX, *House of Lords* (1787), 80). But he then immediately recommended 'an unspeakable improvement of it', and I think it is clear from other evidence, which appears below, that he was referring to the principle of tne plan rather than to its mode of operation, of which he could not disapprove, but which he would not have chosen himself.

4. Pitt had been warned that this would happen (see Richard Bevan to Pitt, 26 March 1791 (P.R.O. 30/8/113)), but seems to have taken no step to get in touch with Morgan.

sought Price's help in return, was afraid to carry out his best suggestion because it would involve fresh taxes, fell back accordingly on his least favourite alternative and further weakened it in the process, and finally never acknowledged any obligation.[1]

How far was all this true? Morgan's pamphlet infuriated some of Pitt's circle. According to Mrs Pretyman Tomline, Pretyman and Eliot 'were more indignant than I ever saw them', and Pitt himself agreed that 'such an accusation *ought not* to pass uncontradicted'. But 'the pressure of public business at that time occasion'd the *intended answer* to be postponed till *contempt* had taken the place of *indignation*, and it was then thought better to let it go unnoticed'.[2] If this was so it was a pity, for Morgan's charges were certainly extravagant, and a reply would have been of service to Pitt and to Price himself.

For Pitt did owe a great deal to Price, in his approach. There were a good many pamphlets on the National Debt in the seventies and early eighties. But it was Price's that caught the imagination, and drove the theories home. Any Minister, no doubt, must have tackled the problem after the war, as the Commissioners for Examining the Public Accounts made clear. Most Ministers, no doubt, would have tried to protect the sinking fund. But Pitt's intellectual stimulus – the project with 'the effect almost of magic' which made him 'half mad'[3] – was sparked off by Price's writings, and took its shape at least in part from them. The Doctor had influenced the Minister already in the matter of high interest rates. He did so again in his exposition of the workings of compound interest, and the consequent overriding need for a strictly inviolable fund. In this sense, Grenville was justified later in calling Price 'the original proposer' and 'real author' of Pitt's efforts.[4] Whatever the differences in the means, he had moulded Pitt's mind in its view of the ends.

It was not therefore surprising that the Minister should have sought Price's advice when the time came. As Mrs Pretyman Tomline herself admitted, 'Mr. Pitt had a high opinion of Dr. Price as a Calculator, [and] from character, and expected to derive much advantage from his plan'.[5] The Doctor commented usefully on the provisional proposals, though not as critically as Morgan implied. But his own alternatives were not as helpful as had been hoped. Pitt's ideas began to harden as he got down to detail, in company with a group of advisers and friends. Pretyman, Grenville and possibly Mahon, Rose, Richard Frewin of the Customs and George Atwood, may have already been at work, on their own calculations and on a number – according to Pretyman 'an almost

1. *A Review of Dr. Price's Writings*, 10–46.
2. Mrs Pretyman Tomline's Common Place Book, 1800 (Pembroke College, Cambridge, Tomline Ms 35:3).
3. P. 261 above.
4. *Essay on the Supposed Advantages of a Sinking Fund*, 59, 63.
5. Pembroke College, Tomline Ms 35:3.

incredible number' – of projects received.[1] Certainly Pretyman and Pitt discussed their objections with Price – unsuccessfully as it turned out.[2] The examination went on, with Pitt himself now very much in charge,[3] and on 29 March he presented his bill to the Commons.

It was based on the expectation of a £1 million surplus of revenue. Pitt's hopes in this respect had been virtually confirmed by a Select Committee of the Commons appointed in March, under Grenville's chairmanship, to examine the anticipated future annual income and expenditure. The estimate was for a surplus of £900,000; Pitt accordingly levied taxes for the year amounting to £100,000.[4] This million pounds would be appropriated, by equal quarterly instalments, to form a sinking fund, which would then be applied entirely to the purchase of Government stocks on which past loans had been raised. Various stipulations were made in order to ensure the object. The Exchequer was required, by Act of Parliament, to give priority to the fund in making its payments – a provision facilitated by the instruction to make quarterly issues. Stock was to be bought on 'every transfer day in the quarter, and in equal sums' each time. And the fund itself was removed from the immediate control of Ministers and of Parliament, and placed under a body of Commissioners for Reducing the National Debt, consisting of the Speaker, the Chancellor of the Exchequer, the Master of the Rolls, the Accountant-General of the Court of Chancery, and the Governor and Deputy Governor of the Bank of England.[5] The choice of stock for purchase was left to them, but they were required as a first priority to buy any standing below par; by a later amendment, they could also buy stocks at par and above, if there was no alternative. The purchased stock, if below par, was not to be cancelled (which might in any case have been a breach of the original contract), but simply transferred to the Commissioners, the interest being credited to their account. Lapsed annuities, likewise, were to be transferred to them. The principle of accumulation would thus be safeguarded and enforced.[6]

1. See loc. cit. for Pretyman, Grenville, Mahon and Atwood; Rose to Pretyman, 7 December 1806 (Pretyman Ms 435/44) for Rose; ? to Pretyman, 26 June 1821 (Pretyman Ms 562:821) for Frewin. The accuracy of this last source may be tested by its verifiable references to other events. Pretyman's phrase is in Tomline, II, 142. For Atwood, see pp. 16 above and 324 below.

2. Pembroke College, Tomline Ms 35:3 for Pretyman; Price to Pitt, 1 and 12 February (P.R.O. 30/8/169), and Morgan, op. cit., 51, for Pitt. Pretyman claimed (in his wife's version) that the objections came first from him, for Pitt at the start still 'seemed to depend . . . much' upon Price's preference, '(he not having *then* examined it)'. (Tomline Ms 35:3).

3. Rose to Pretyman, 7 December 1806 (Pretyman Ms 435/44); Tomline, II, 143. There is a rough draft of the bill in his hand in P.R.O. 30/8/196.

4. See p. 263 above.

5. The list followed that originally envisaged by Pitt, his only doubt being the inclusion of the Master of the Rolls (undated notes in Pitt's hand, P.R.O. 30/8/275).

6. 26 Geo. III, c. 21.

The scheme met the objects of Price's third plan in substance. That this was widely recognised is suggested by the only real amendments proposed. Little direct opposition was encountered in the Commons. But a group of experienced Members – Sir William Pulteney, Sir Adam Fergusson, Sinclair, George Dempster, and Henry Beaufoy – had second thoughts in April, and took steps to get hold of three of the Doctor's four plans. Their comments were not entirely to the point, for, perhaps under Sinclair's influence, they were still enamoured of the idea of conversion; but on this basis they were critical of Price's ideas, preferring others, particularly one by a certain S. Gale (probably Samuel Gale) which they arranged to send to Pitt.[1] In informing him of this, Pulteney referred to 'the 3 plans offered to you by Dr Price the third of which you have adopted'.[2] Similarly, Stanhope in the Lords, proposing a major addition of his own to the Government's bill, quoted Price as stating that Pitt's scheme was 'that which I have been . . . recommending for many years'.[3]

Pitt's advisers would have endorsed this, if at all, with strong reservations. They knew that he had been stimulated by Price, that he was predisposed in his favour at the start, and that some of Price's aims and proposals were satisfied by the bill. But equally they could point to others that were not, and they might well have denied that Price was solely responsible for all that were. Thus, he had recommended the appointment of independent Commissioners. But he was not the first to have had the idea; the French had earlier set up a sinking fund – like the British, to be strictly preserved in all conditions – under independent Directors; and information on their arrangements was available to Pitt.[4] By the time that the Government's bill was ready, many plans had been consulted, many calculations made; and the most recent impression in the Minister's circle was in fact of disagreement with Price. His favourite proposals for the size of the fund, and for extra taxation, had been rejected; so had his pet scheme of an upward conversion of stock. What remained was largely common to many advocates of a sinking fund; the outlines had been endorsed by the Commissioners for Examining the Public Accounts themselves. Pretyman was not being disingenuous when he called it ' "childish to talk of the Plan adopted as *any one person's* plan in particular" ',[5] though he probably went too far in playing down Price's initial role. It is the old problem of assessing different contributions, particularly when Governments invite or are prompted by outside advice. No harm would have been done – rather

1. It is in P.R.O. 30/8/275, and had apparently already appeared as a pamphlet. Sinclair had recently published his own plan for conversion, in his *History of the Public Revenue of the British Empire* (1785).
2. To Pitt, 18 April 1786 (P.R.O. 30/8/169).
3. See p. 263, n3 above.
4. See P.R.O. 30/8/275.
5. Mrs Pretyman Tomline put these words in double quotation marks, as coming from her husband (Tomline Ms 35:3).

the reverse – if Pitt had publicly mentioned the Doctor. But there was no compelling reason why he should, and his words would have had to be carefully phrased. Perhaps he came to regret the omission, or at least the charges it produced. Was it coincidence that he paid his well known tribute to Adam Smith in 1792, the year in which Morgan published – a tribute which in fact has had its own partly misleading effect?[1]

The bill passed with few amendments, in May 1786. No one was prepared to quarrel seriously with an effort which had been urged since the end of the war, and Pitt was widely praised for tackling the problem so energetically. Opposition queried the figures on which he claimed his surplus, as the methods of accounting indeed permitted them to do; but Ministers appeared to have the best of the argument, and Members were overwhelmingly on their side.[2] Two helpful minor amendments were made, by Fox and by Pulteney; there was only one division in the passage of the bill through the lower House.

Only one major attack, indeed, was mounted from any quarter.[3] To Pitt's sorrow and annoyance, it came from Mahon, now Lord Stanhope. Relations between the two men were no longer as close as they had once been. Mahon had not seen eye to eye with Pitt on the shop tax, or in the aftermath of the Westminster scrutiny, and more recently he had been decidedly half-hearted in his support of the Ministry's plan to fortify the dockyards, an issue on which they badly needed every voice.[4] Now, after working on the National Debt, he swung into open opposition. In April he published a critical pamphlet, and in May he spoke in the House of Lords.[5]

Stanhope had two main objections to Pitt's bill. By purchasing stock which stood well below par – and most of it now stood at about 70 – the Commissioners would force up the prices to levels that would defeat them in the end. You might redeem some of the debt on advantageous

1. '. . . An author of our own times now unfortunately no more (I mean the author of a celebrated treatise on the Wealth of Nations), whose extensive knowledge of detail, and depth of philosophical research, will, I believe, furnish the best solution to every question connected with the history of commerce, or with the systems of political economy' (*P.H.*, XXIX, 834. The wording follows Tomline, III, 288, here to be preferred to *P.R.*, XXXI (1792).) Pitt spoke in the Commons on 17 February; Morgan published in April or May. But Pitt had been warned (see p. 263, n. 4 above).

2. See Tomline, II, 161 n. for the atmosphere on the first reading, and the text of the Speaker's address to the King (*H.C.J.*, XLI, 859) for the 'unanimity' on the third.

3. Stormont and Loughborough voiced, but did not press, some doubts in the Lords.

4. For the shop tax, see Charles Earl Stanhope, F.R.S., *Observations on Mr. Pitt's Plan, for the Reduction of the National Debt* (1786), 24; for the aftermath of the scrutiny, p. 230, n. 2 above. The question of the dockyards is discussed in ch. XVII, section I below.

5. *Observations on Mr. Pitt's Plan; P.R.*, XX, *House of Lords*, 72–87. It was his maiden speech there.

terms; but if the rest rose steeply as a result, the aggregate value would not be reduced. The answer, according to Stanhope, lay in an upward conversion, from the 3 per cents which made up most of the stock into a lesser amount of 4 per cents, the holders of the new issue receiving priority on the order of redemption. This arrangement, moreover, would have the virtue of supporting Stanhope's answer to what he saw as the second difficulty. The bill, in his view, did not protect the fund as it was meant to do: there was still nothing to prevent the Commissioners' balance being raided by Parliament in the last resort. But if the state guaranteed the redemption of the 4 per cent stock, the arrangement with the holders would be as sacred as that by which annual interest was paid. The fund would really become inviolable, the operation of compound interest would really be preserved, Pitt's objects would really be achieved, and in the most economical way.

Stanhope's arguments had no immediate effect; no doubt because investors had already shown themselves reluctant to profit from early redemption.[1] The only result – scarcely surprisingly, in view of his uncompromising language – was to widen the gap between the 'honest and independent Citizen' and Pitt.[2] But his theories received some recognition six years later, when further arrangements were made. In 1792, Pitt felt free to add £400,000 to the fund from the revenue[3] – a precedent followed annually by statute for a decade to the tune of £200,000 a year. At the same time, he set a limit to the accumulation of interest and lapsed annuities in the account:[4] when the fund reached £4 million, stock would be cancelled as it was bought up. He also provided for a distinct new fund to redeem new debt, which would be fed at the rate of 1 per cent a year on the nominal capital borrowed, except where there was a stipulation to pay off that capital in a period of 45 years.[5] There were thus alternative means of paying off debt within a given time, so that Stanhope's insistence on guaranteed redemption was tacitly accepted. With these additions and amendments the structure of the fund was complete. It remained unaltered thereafter until its closing years in the 1820s.

The whole idea by then was falling into disrepute. A series of influential pamphlets pointed out the fallacies of the past. There had really been only one, in principle if not in operation;[6] but it was one which effectively vitiated the object. For whatever the merits of the various proposals for redeeming funded debt, they must all rely for success on a surplus of revenue over expenditure. As soon as there was a deficit, the

1. P. 259 above.
2. Stanhope's description of himself (*Observations*, 3).
3. 32 Geo. III, c. 12.
4. See p. 265 above.
5. 32 Geo. III, c. 55.
6. The operation might be said to have been qualified by the fact that there was still no check on the creation of *unfunded* debt. In the event, exchequer bills increased steadily, and navy bills rapidly in the later eighties.

whole system broke down; and by the middle nineties, wartime deficits were the rule. This danger had in fact been mentioned at the start, rather diffidently, by Fox; and the Commons' resolution following the first debate in 1786 had approved the bill in conditions of *surplus*.[1] But the overriding need to protect the fund, where all earlier efforts had failed, placed it in a statutory strait-jacket from which it did not escape. Given a long and expensive war – one of quite unfamiliar expense – and the country's refusal to tax itself beyond a certain point, surpluses were out of the question and debt swiftly piled up. When this began to happen, the fund became a curse; money needed for current expenses had to be sunk in an account devoted to paying off the loans which the increasing expense required. The arrangement might have been designed to make a bad position worse. But still an Act of Parliament was needed to undo an Act, and no one in this case was prepared to take the step. No one in fact was prepared to recognise that the earlier advantage had gone. Without an inviolable fund the payments, and the problem, might simply have lapsed; as it was, men clung grimly to the system, convinced that they were saving their children from doom. The fears of an earlier generation were too deeply graven on their minds; so too was the relief with which it had greeted the prospect of rescue. The Act of 1786 was successful in the right conditions. The Commissioners received just over £8 million in just under seven peacetime years, with which they bought up almost £10¼ million of stock. But this very success was secured by a safeguard which could become a fetter, and men forgot, as they admired its design, that a lock can imprison as well as protect.

IV

No one can hope to borrow money for long from the same lenders without the promise of adequate security. Government borrowing in the eighteenth century was based on appropriations: the produce of specific sources of revenue was assigned to the payment of interest on specific loans. Whatever its drawbacks, this system met its immediate object; from the 1690s to the 1770s British Governments underwrote the cost of war without too steep a rise in current taxation. But it played havoc with the system of national accounts. In 1786 there were eleven loan stocks in existence, fed by 103 accounts each of which had to be kept separate from the rest. So far as can be reckoned, in fact – and their bewildering complexity does not make it easy –, only 21 of the Exchequer's revenue accounts were not devoted to the funding system. Nor was this all. Of the 103 accounts, 14 were used for direct payments to the funds and were themselves fed directly from revenue; 12 more were

1. *H.C.J.*, XLI, 462.

used for direct payments but were themselves fed indirectly from other accounts; and no fewer than 77 were mere conduits for receiving revenue, as it was paid into the Exchequer and then paid out under other heads. As taxes and duties changed, further complications arose; particular appropriations might suffer, to the point at which the funds might be called on to act as security for the deficiencies, and transfers made 'backwards' from themselves to the accounts.[1] The stockholder's security was preserved; but at what a cost! The processes of the Exchequer, already cumbrous, were further bedevilled, and the difficulties of reaching a reckoning immeasurably increased.

But perhaps the most serious effect was that on the great sources of revenue themselves; on the excise and still more on the customs, which together mainly nourished the accounts. The inconvenience and loss had long been notorious. The rigid subdivision of revenue accounts, as allocations were made to the funds, meant that every parcel of dutiable goods must be dealt with separately: on goods subject to customs, thirteen or fourteen distinct duties might have to be paid. Faced with this frightful paperwork, merchants shifted the burden to the Customs officials, feeing them for their services, and the department then set to work on the 68 separate accounts involved. On duties subject to excise, the manufacturers and merchants were obliged themselves to declare the value, before the officials subdivided the produce into the 23 accounts.[2] Such a system – if it deserved the name – was a standing temptation to fraud: Customs men in particular had every inducement to exploit the merchants, by deciding the values and then hastening or delaying the proceedings. It also invited loss to the revenue, as the values were divided into fractions which the departments were liable to reduce to the nearest whole. The result, as Pitt stated, was that trade was 'loaded' with 'clogs and fetters', while the revenue laboured under 'obscurity' where it should be 'clear and distinct'.[3]

So much was universally agreed. The problem had been recognised for some time. There had been talk of consolidating customs duties as early as the middle fifties, and North had examined and set on foot plans for customs, excise and stamps. In 1782, a Select Committee of the Commons, reporting on the cost of the war and the state of the debt, recommended consolidation of the customs dues; and three years later that branch of the revenue was reviewed by the Commissioners for Examining the Public Accounts. They had no hesitation in calling for 'One Head of Duties only, under the Title of "Customs"... the entire Sum

1. *House of Commons, Accounts and Papers, 1890–1, XLVIII*, 4; Binney, op. cit., 106–7. And see Binney, 70–1, for the way in which Pitt's lower duties on tea affected the relevant accounts.

2. The same disadvantages affected the collection of stamp duties; but not to the same extent.

3. Speech of 26 February 1787 (*P.R.,* XXI, 331).

... to be carried, when paid into the Exchequer, to the Sinking Fund'.[1]

Given this background, one might say with Pitt that 'it was more difficult to account for [reform] having been delayed so long, than to prove the propriety of now adopting it'.[2] In point of fact, there had been two reasons for the delay. One was the fear of breaking faith with the lender if the identity of his security was changed – detailed appropriations, after all, had proved the foundation of public confidence. The other was the sheer magnitude of the work involved. 'Who is the bold Man who would undertake it?', the joint Secretary of the Treasury, Sir Grey Cooper, was supposed to have exclaimed under North;[3] and when Pitt moved his bill, he introduced 2,537 separate resolutions. It needed a Minister of real decision and grasp to pilot such a measure, and a combination of circumstances which would facilitate the task. Both were present in 1787. Pitt had the necessary qualities, proved and developed in the past three years; and two very helpful conditions had recently been fulfilled. The sinking fund itself had been reformed – a great incentive to reform the funds that fed it – and the famous commercial treaty with France had just been brought into force. This last achievement was most important for a consolidation of customs duties, for a very desirable adjunct to that effort was a comprehensive settlement of rates. In 1786, commercial talks were under way with four major states – with Portugal, Spain and Russia as well as with France – and a Consolidation Bill must if possible await the outcome in each case.[4] Three of the negotiations hung fire or failed; but that with France succeeded, and its success led to some alterations of duties on goods imported from elsewhere. Given the incentives for a general consolidation, the time was therefore favourable to the task.

The bill indeed soon became linked with the debates on the treaty with France – to an extent which Opposition attacked as misleading and unfair. It was introduced at the end of February 1787, and received the royal assent on 25 April. It was perhaps the most impressive piece of legislation that Pitt ever undertook. Much evidence existed from the inquiries of North's day; more was now collected, from revenue officials and port officers, merchants, stockjobbers and annuitants.[5] The object of the bill was simple: 'that all duties of customs, excise, and certain duties of stamps, do cease and determine, and that other duties be substituted in their stead'.[6] These were fixed, article by article, as a single duty in each case, all fractions being abolished, sometimes by

1. Thirteenth Report, 18 March 1785 (*H.C.J.*, XL, 672). Examples of the appalling complexity of calculating duties may be found in Appendix 66 to the Report (loc. cit., 713–31).

2. *P.R.*, XXI, 328.

3. At least according to Rose's recollection of their meetings (to Tomline, 8 August 1816; Pretyman Ms 562:1816).

4. For this, see ch. XVI below.

5. For some of it, see Pitt's papers in P.R.O. 30/8/305.

6. *P.R.*, XXI, 334. Certain exceptions were specified in the motion.

reduction to the nearest whole but more often by addition. The processes of valuation were simplified, and further regulations against fraud introduced. A schedule was added settling new rates. The produce of the duties, with that of the various taxes and royal hereditary property, was to be carried to eight consolidated accounts, and the total then transferred to one consolidated fund. This would serve all public expenditure (except the cost of funded exchequer bills) so far as that was met by issues from the Exchequer.

Since one fund was now responsible for meeting so many diverse costs, a scheme of priority was needed if stockholders' rights were to be satisfied. The funded debt came first, as the Sinking Fund Act had guaranteed.[1] The earlier loan funds were abolished, and the stockholders' consent was sought by a given date; in future their money would be in one class of holding, on the security of the consolidated fund. The Civil List came next; then the heads of current expenditure for which Parliament had voted the year's supplies. These were the arrangments for the national income and expenses as they stood; but future new taxes would be accounted for separately, the yield being reported to the Commons.[2]

There was little direct opposition; on the contrary, the bill was warmly approved. Fox and Burke vied with each other in its praises; Sheridan was silent; even the wary Grey Cooper 'had not the least objection to the scheme'.[3] It was indeed a good one. Pitt had cut a tangled web, and his system of statutory priorities met the public creditor's needs. Given such safeguards, there was indeed no reason why he should not return very largely to the earlier system whereby the stockholder's security was the general credit of the state. The appropriations in fact had now become something of a farce, as the transfers between accounts grew ever more complicated and the position in each fund more obscure. Under such conditions, it was true to say that 'the annuitants were scarcely aware of their own privilege', and Pitt was right in thinking that the nettle could be grasped. In the event, 'not a single stockholder . . . objected to the plan'.[4]

The effects were soon felt. The Treasury account books were reduced from sixty or seventy folios to about a dozen, the Exchequer's tallies with the Receiver-General of the Customs from 1,700 to some 200 a

1. P. 265 above.
2. 27 Geo. III, c. 13. It should be made clear that this Consolidation Act was not responsible for the creation of Consols. There were already several issues of these on the market, the first dating from 1751, when Pelham consolidated certain 3 per cent annuities into one loan stock.
3. *P.R.*, XXI, 334. These remarks apply to the contents of the bill, not to the complicating issue of the commercial treaty with France, which affected its presentation.
4. Tomline, II, 240, 249.

year. There was a vast and beneficent simplification of the national book-keeping. It was not, as has sometimes been stated, complete. The servicing of funded exchequer bills was not included in the consolidated fund; the Civil List annuities, the land and malt taxes, still required distinct accounting within the consolidated accounts; the dates on which the different accounts were settled, which had never been properly reconciled, remained unreconciled for another sixteen years. Future taxes were not brought within the system, which applied only to the position as it stood at the time. Nor did the arrangement comprehend every item of national revenue and expenditure, for it was limited to the receipts and issues of the Exchequer,[1] and some expenses were met from revenue before the departments' payments to the Exchequer were made. The Commissioners for Examining the Public Accounts had looked forward to the day when the consolidation of duties would lead to 'the Formation of One Fund, into which shall flow every Stream of the Public Revenue, and from which shall issue the Supply for every Public Service'.[2] That day had not dawned yet, and it did not do so until 1857. But Pitt's extensive Act – and it was his in a very real sense – was a milestone. Five years later, he claimed that 'the public accounts ... are at length freed from that obscurity and intricacy in which they were formerly involved, and are rendered so clear and intelligible, that there is no man who may not, with a small degree of attention, become as fully master of the subject, as those whose official duty has led them to make it their peculiar study'.[3] His remarks did not refer to the Consolidation Act alone: there were other, administrative, reforms which affected the Exchequer and the departments.[4] But the reform of the duties and the funds was the greatest of such measures, and it crowned the financial structure designed in the past few years. As long as the limits of the achievement are properly defined, it would be pedantic and ungenerous to quarrel with Pitt's claim.

V

It was made on a great occasion. In his budget speech in February 1792, Pitt reviewed the progress of the economy since the end of the American War. The survey has gained in drama – and dramatic irony – from the fact that it was itself made in the last full year of peace; the unexpected onset of a far greater war was soon to turn a review into a valediction. But it marked a stage in any case, a point at which to pause and look back, for Pitt by then had done what he set out to do at

1. P. 272 above.
2. *H.C.J.*, XL, 673.
3. Speech of 17 February 1792 (*P.H.*, XXIX, 816–17).
4. See ch. XI below.

the start. We are lucky in having for once a proper text of his speech, as well as the extensive notes on which it was based.[1]

It was a tale of success. As Pitt presented the figures, income had risen steadily over the past four years, from £15,565,000 to £16,730,000.[2] Expenditure for the past year was calculated at just over £16 million, and after meeting various outstanding commitments there should be a surplus in April of almost £½ million. This would allow him to allocate an extra £400,000 to the sinking fund in the current year, and the computations of a Select Committee recently set up to estimate future income and expenditure suggested that the surplus would not fall. The Minister could therefore reduce taxation at once by almost £¼ million, and still expect to allocate an extra £200,000 a year to the fund.[3]

This was indeed a happy state of affairs, after the experiences of that generation. 'I expected', wrote the Scottish M.P. George Dempster, who had recently retired from the House, 'to see a prolongation of life by living in the country, but to live to see such a load of taxes repealed never enter'd my brain'.[4] How had the position been reached? Essentially, by an increase in production and trade. Pitt was not much concerned here with its detailed proportions: he was interested chiefly in the phenomenon itself. It was difficult to illustrate from domestic figures, for these were not compiled to suit his purpose; but the Customs' books gave a pointer to the progress of overseas trade. According to them, imports had risen from £9,714,000 in 1782 to £19,130,000 in 1790; exports and re-exports, from £12,239,000 to £20,120,000. On the figures as thus presented, the balance of trade did not appear to have improved. But, in the context, this did not worry Pitt. In the first place, the presentation was known to be incomplete; it was distorted by omissions and the use of obsolete values. Even on gross barter terms, the terms of trade had in fact probably been improving, markedly so over the past two years.[5] Nor was the balance itself regarded in quite the same light as of old; bullionist theories were dying, there was a more flexible approach. But Pitt in any case was less concerned in this instance with the balance than with the *volume* of trade. 'Causes of rapid Encrease since the Peace –', he wrote in his notes, 'Industry aided

---

1. *P.H.*, XXIX, 816–38. This was in fact one of the few Parliamentary speeches which Pitt checked for publication, and Pretyman published the text (see p. 267, n1 above). The notes are in Stanhope Mss, 'Notes by Mr. Pitt re Budget Speech December 1798. etc.'. There is also a full transcript of a memorandum by Pitt on the state of the finances at the start of the year, in Bland Burges Mss, Bodleian Library ('Transcripts of Sir James Burges's Letters and Papers').

2. On the same basis, it had been calculated as some £12,322,000 for 1784–5 (*Reports from Committees*, XI, 41).

3. See pp. 251, 268, above.

4. To Sir Adam Fergusson, 10 March 1792 (*Letters of George Dempster to Sir Adam Fergusson 1756–1813 . . .*, ed. James Fergusson (1934), 211).

5. See Deane & Cole, *British Economic Growth 1688–1955*, 48 and Appendix I.

by Improvements in Skill &c, Facility in Credit (Country Banks), Extension of Markets [he noted specifically the commercial treaty with France], Liberal Commercial Policy . . ., *Nature* of Capital (State of Trade &c. from the Commencement of the Century), Influx of Capital from East Indies'.[1]

'Increase' in fact was the key to the progress of the past decade; that 'increase of commerce and manufactures' which underlay the 'constant accumulation of capital' which in turn would hasten the growth of industry and trade. The nation's appetite was voracious, and the cake was still being baked. Adam Smith had explained the principle; the full results had yet to be seen.

> This accumulation of capital arises from the continual application of a part at least, of the profit obtained each year, to increase the total amount of capital to be employed in a similar manner, and with continued profit in the year following. The great mass of the property of the nation is thus constantly increasing at compound interest; the progress of which, in any considerable period, is what at first view would appear incredible. Great as have been the effects of this cause already, they must be greater in future: for its powers are augmented in proportion as they are exerted. It acts with a velocity continually accelerated, with a force continually increased,
> 'Mobilitate viget, viresque acquirit eundo'.[2]

After the fears of the recent past, this was stirring hearing.

Given such rapid domestic improvement, an overall profit was assured. Merchandise and manufactures would find their own channels: Government's role was that of a benevolent referee. It must protect the nation's advantage in talks with foreign powers, it should place as few restrictions as possible in the way of expansion at home. Pitt could point with pride to what had been done: the load of debt was being lightened, the accounts were simplified, duties were reformed, confidence was restored. The price of Government stocks had risen, taxes were now being reduced. The existing order had proved its power to absorb and encourage new trends.

Pitt's great survey can be shown, by hindsight, to have been fed by inaccurate figures. He knew that the Customs' entries were 'necessarily imperfect'; the calculations of surplus, too, were sometimes incorrect. In 1786, indeed, when he counted on a surplus of almost £1 million, there was probably a final net deficit of about £1,700,000; more

1. Stanhope Mss, 'Notes by Mr. Pitt . . .'. Cf. the central portions of the speech itself.
2. *P.H.*, XXIX, 834.

recently, on the other hand, the results had perhaps been better than he supposed.[1] The accounts in fact, even when improved, could not provide a true answer; nor were the budgets themselves designed to cover the whole financial field. The annual statement dealt with expenditure to be voted for or in the year, with the corresponding taxes and duties, and with the moneys drawn from the sinking or the consolidated fund. It did not have to deal with expenditure already sanctioned specifically or in perpetuity, or therefore with the revenues designed to meet such costs. Since the reign of Queen Anne, 'no complete statement has ever been made up, of the total income and expenditure of the country' – so Sir John Sinclair asserted in 1785, and he was able to repeat his comment in 1804.[2] When the irregularities of the accounts themselves are imposed on such a foundation, it is scarcely surprising that the calculations should often have proved inexact.

Doubts were naturally raised at the time as to some of Pitt's figures. Sheridan in particular made it his business to question the results.[3] The queries were legitimate; but their success was doubtful, while so many ambiguities and complexities remained. It could also be argued that the Minister was being praised for an improvement that would have come about in any case. 'It is provoking', wrote Sheffield as early as 1785, 'that the Publick shd. be so ridiculous as to give credit to the Young Gentleman, because a load of taxes produce largely' from the process of national growth.[4] The point of course was fair enough, and Pitt himself stressed the factors involved. Industrial improvement and a venturesome spirit in seeking gains abroad, aided by easier facilities for private loans and by foreign peace and 'internal tranquillity' – these were 'the peculiar circumstances to which these effects are to be ascribed'.[5] Political shocks had indeed been short-lived, economic shocks were of limited scope. There was only one, relatively mild, recession, in 1787–8, and that was itself brought on by over-confidence and over-expansion

1. Mitchell & Deane, *Abstract of British Historical Statistics*, ch. XIV, tables 1, 2. Other, unpublished, calculations suggest some amendments.

2. *The History of the Public Revenue of the British Empire*, II (3rd edn, 1804), 58. Nor indeed was the annual statement always delivered under the title of budget – in 1792 itself, for instance, it was given in a debate on 'the state of public income and expenditure'.

3. The correspondence of William Eden, while still in opposition, also throws light on such doubts (e.g. letters from Price, 15? June 1785, from Hatsell, 10 October [1785], from Grey Cooper, 5 November 1785; B.M. Add. Ms 34420, ff. 29, 124, 152v, the last two printed in *A.C.*, I, 354, 358–9).

4. 6 November 1785 (B.M. Add. Ms 34420, f. 155). William Morgan, in *A Comparative View of the Public Finances from the beginning to the close of the Late Administration* (1801), 5–6, made the same point, and it was not only opponents who recognised its substance. Just before Pitt presented his budget in 1792, his colleague Camden observed that he had been helped by 'a most unexpected increase of the Revenue' (to Lady Frances Stewart, 5 February 1792; Pratt Mss, Box C3, Kent County Record Office, Maidstone).

5. *P.H.*, XXIX, 833.

in the cotton industry. Given the best part of a decade of widespread and rapid growth, how could the Government's measures fail to profit by the results?

And to what extent could those measures really be ascribed to Pitt? He had carried them into effect; but how far were they properly his? One has often read in the older text-books – the general impression perhaps still exists – that a new reforming era sprang into being after the American War, from the brain of the youthful Minister at one remove from that of Adam Smith. This is to do both Pitt's age and himself an injustice. It obscures what he owed to others, and the real nature of what he achieved. If one examines his policies, one is struck precisely by the way in which he handled his inheritance; and that inheritance was considerable – much was projected, something had been done. Pitt's debt is clearly visible in the content and the area of his financial reforms. He advanced where advance was favoured; he marked time where it was not. He was conservative in taxation – in some ways, perhaps, more conservative than North. He built his method of raising a loan on the foundations of North and, more debatably, the Coalition. His ideas on the rates of interest were at first those of Shelburne's circle. The remodelling of the sinking fund had been widely discussed for some time. North had left a plan, and useful data, for consolidating the duties. The reports of a series of Parliamentary committees, and above all of the Commissioners for Examining the Public Accounts, supplied a wealth of information and advice on which action could be based. To ignore this crowded background is to see Pitt in a false light. His part gains in meaning from the other actors' parts.

It is ironical that his closest precursor in many ways should have been North – the one man of whom he always felt bound to disapprove. Shelburne, it might seem, would have offered more, and in one sense perhaps he did; his belief in the relevance of intellectual standards, his determination to identify Government with the cause of improvement, appealed strongly to Pitt and may have helped colour his style at the start. Some of North's innovations, too, had become standard practice, so that Pitt would not necessarily relate his further developments to that source. Nevertheless, when it came to the point, it was usually North who had been there before him, and formed or adopted conclusions that most nearly resembled his own. For North had in fact been a notably shrewd and capable Chancellor, even in the later stages of a difficult war. He enjoyed his work at the Treasury – the more so perhaps as all else began to fail –, and he combined a formidable experience with a natural financial sense. His grasp of detail was not exceptional, but he made good use of what he was told. His success was acknowledged in the middle seventies, and he never entirely lost his touch. If the war had not submerged him, these achievements might later have received their due; if there had been no war, he would have had others to his credit. He was as much the product of a reforming age as his successors, and where their answers differed his are not lightly to be dismissed. He encouraged inquiry and improvement – he fathered the Commissioners for Examining the Public Accounts. His financial measures were varied and hopeful. His ideas often anticipated Pitt's.

The harvest had thus been largely sown. It had still to be reaped. Much of Pitt's achievement lay in the choices he made from competing plans, and in the skill and determination with which he carried them out. He realised many hopes; he did so by avoiding many pitfalls. He moved steadily forward, and each step paved the way for the next. His sense of priorities was sound, his sense of possibilities acute; he drew on and nursed the widespread goodwill which generally existed in financial matters – taxation excepted – and which was his for the asking at the start. His success indeed stemmed largely from a blend of courage and conciliation which was remarkably well proportioned to the task. For while Chancellors should be firm, they cannot hope for long to dictate. Their calculations may be desiccated, but the customers are warm. In financial matters, of all others, there must be some reconciliation of weighted interests, and within the circle of those he consulted – and beyond which he had scarcely to look – Pitt grew very skilful at gauging reactions and needs. There was the occasional head-on collision, which caused him to withdraw: over the tax on cottons and the shop tax, for instance, when he retreated slowly, over the proposed levies on coals and on hop planters' licences, and the first scheme for funding navy bills, when he gave way at once.[1] But normally he took careful soundings, so that opposition was forestalled or could be overcome. His almost uniform success from 1786 to the early period of the war with France reflected his readiness to listen to objections in advance. Wilberforce tells a story which illustrates the point.

> He had formed a plan of importance (I think in some Revenue matter) on which it was necessary for him to consult with the Attorney-General of the day . . . He was as usual full of his scheme, and detailed it to his professional friend with the warmth and ability natural to him on such occasions . . . But the Attorney-General soon became convinced that there were legal objections . . . which must be decisive . . . These therefore he explained to Mr. Pitt, who immediately gave up his plan with the most unruffled good-humour, without attempting to hang by it, or to devise methods of propping it up . . .[2]

The effect of this quality was enhanced by Pitt's confidence in tackling major issues. For however real the contributions of others, and the support on which he could count, the problems were daunting and the work itself was hard. He soon won general admiration by the spirit

1. See pp. 252–4, 259–60 above.
2. *Private Papers*, 66–7.

in which he tackled the task. 'We must meet our situation fairly', he announced at the outset, 'we must look it in the face';[1] and the note had been struck which marked his whole peacetime career. He set to work at once, and he did not slacken pace for the next five years. By then, he had attacked all the financial questions that seemed outstanding at the end of the war. Nor had he had to surrender on any of the essentials; his concessions had been marginal, his major schemes had won general support. When he repealed the cotton tax, he said that he was glad to meet the manufacturers' wishes 'when the point in question was such as could with any safety be given up'.[2] This was not merely a face-saving remark.

The order of the programme was Pitt's own; so, in the last resort, were the contents of the measures. The knowledge again enhanced the value of his accessibility to ideas. In his treatment of detail he steered a middle course between North, who built on figures which he seldom questioned, and Shelburne's self-confident, opinionated approach. Pitt's understanding of his subject could really be compared with his officials' – an unusual attribute in a leading politician in a consciously amateurish age. The fact was soon noted, by experts and public alike. Baring, who had good opportunity to judge, observed that the young man was 'not only fully informed, but appears equally well to comprehend the whole extent' of the Commutation Bill. '. . . Sensible thinking People are astonished', remarked Lady Gower in 1785. 'So perfect a knowledge of the Commerce, Funds, and Government of the Country that one must imagine, to hear him on these subjects, that he had the experience of fifty years'.[3] This professionalism was crowned by his debating powers. Budget statements had been improving for some time, but these expositions were something new. No one had ever led the country gentlemen so lucidly through the maze; no one had treated the House and the country so candidly, and given them such fare. The speeches remained a model for Peel and for Gladstone himself. The range of statement had indeed been established to which we are still accustomed, with an intellectual distinction to which we are not. The results were formidable and, as Members found, very difficult to challenge. Pitt made his mistakes, and his estimates necessarily had their limitations; but the general conclusions appeared unassailable, and it was dangerous to try to trip him up. The achievements seemed the more impressive to his audience because a grasp of figures was not its strong point. They were the more popular because they fitted the acknowledged needs so exactly; they met widely voiced demands, and

1. Speech of 30 June 1784 (*P.R.*, XV, 272).
2. *P.R.*, XVIII, 95.
3. Baring to Shelburne, 4 August 1784 (Lansdowne Mss, Bowood); Lady Gower to Lord Granville Leveson Gower, 19 [? February, 1785] (*Lord Granville Leveson Gower . . . Private Correspondence, 1781 to 1821*, ed. Castalia Countess Granville, I (1916), 5–6).

they did not venture far beyond.[1] Pitt found plenty on his plate. He cleared it, and then he stopped; for the country did not want more, and neither did he himself. He respected, because he shared, the attitudes of his time; reform was required to re-establish a position, progressively damaged, which was soundly based. New developments must be met, old institutions improved, to justify an order that must now be brought up to date. But its values remained unquestioned, and its prejudices were treated with care. No one tax must be too oppressive, freedom must not be unduly curtailed, there must always be good reason – very good reason – for a change. In the balance struck, in the choices made, Pitt left his mark on the thought he accepted. His Ministerial gifts never showed more clearly than in his handling of finance.

It was perhaps his favourite occupation, the work in which he felt most at home. He knew that most people were bored by the subject, and at least at the beginning he sometimes pretended to agree that it could be 'irksome' or 'fatiguing'.[2] But the pleasure of his Cambridge days survived in 'the habit of . . . patient investigation'.[3] A financial issue could always rouse him, when apparently greater issues might not – it had done so in 1783 in the Indian crisis,[4] it did so again in 1802 when he was refusing to stir against Addington's conduct of foreign affairs. His detailed interest sometimes seemed inappropriate in a statesman, particularly to diplomats and European Courts. 'Now that we have *raised* his attention', wrote the Foreign Secretary in a crisis to the British Minister at The Hague, 'we must . . . not suffer Holland to be sacrificed either to lawn or cambric'; and the Russian Minister in London was once moved to insist that Pitt was more 'qu'un financier impolitique'.[5] Nor were such doubts confined to such circles; Wilberforce for instance believed that his friend suffered from 'the necessity of . . . speaking upon subjects of a low and vulgarising quality, such as the excise on tobacco, wine, &c. &c.'.[6] These impressions could be dangerous, when a clerk-like care for figures was not much admired. But in the right hands, as Pitt well knew, it was a source of the greatest strength. 'The Revenue of the State is the State', wrote Burke.[7] He would certainly have concurred, and he wished that the consequences might be more clearly drawn.

1. Perhaps the transfer of so many duties from Customs to Excise is a partial exception; though here again the ground had been partly cleared (see pp. 291–2 below).

2. E.g. *P.R.*, XV, 272, 287.

3. See p. 16 above.

4. P. 126 above.

5. *Diaries and Correspondence of Malmesbury*, II, 258; Count Simon Vorontsov to Count Michael Vorontsov, 6 June 1786 (*Arkhiv Knyazya Mikhaila Illarionovicha Vorontsova*, ed. P. I. Bartenev, IX (1876), 55). 'Vous voyez donc', Vorontsov concluded after explanations, 'qu'il a été plus politique et homme d'état que simple financier'. He was referring to the case mentioned in p. 250, n3 above.

6. *Private Papers*, 79.

7. *Reflections on the Revolution in France* (*Works*, IV, 358).

... In the conduct of the affairs of this country, [he told Dundas, when the experience of war had reinforced that of peace] there should be an avowed and real minister possessing the chief weight in council and the principal place in the confidence of the King. In that respect there can be no rivality or division of power. That power must rest with the person generally called the First Minister; and that Minister ought ... to be the person at the head of the finances.[1]

The conclusion was not new. North for example had said something of the sort, referring to 'critical times'. But Pitt was talking generally, and his grasp of detail gave the judgment greater point. For as he sifted and examined and decided the multifarious problems of the revenue – the day to day work which persisted through all his other tasks – he was not only laying the foundations for his control of financial policy, but also sharpening the only sure weapons with which he could hope to probe the departments as a whole.

1. Pellew, *Life and Correspondence of Addington,* II, 116; quoting Dundas, who in turn was quoting Pitt.

CHAPTER XI

Administration

I

As First Lord of the Treasury and Chancellor of the Exchequer, Pitt presided directly over the most extensive sector of government. The army and the navy each had more men, and were responsible for more material; but neither was in so central a position or disposed of so many appointments, and control of the army was in any case fragmented. The Treasury and Admiralty Boards stood at the head of the two largest pyramids of administration, and administratively speaking the First Lord of the Treasury was *primus inter pares*, particularly if he combined his office with that of Chancellor of the Exchequer. In one or other capacity, he intervened in the work of other, independent authorities; in that of the Paymaster General of the Forces and the Treasurer of the Navy, of the Ordnance Board and the Court. But his own departments formed an impressive group – the Treasury itself, the Exchequer, and the Treasury's subordinate boards and offices, which in 1784 were the Boards of Customs, Excise, Stamps, Salt, Taxes, Hackney Coach and Chair Licences, Hawkers' and Pedlars' Licences, the two Surveyors General of Crown Lands and of Woods and Forests, the Post Office, and the Mint.

It was in this financial sphere, and above all within his departments, that Pitt could place his greatest hopes of administrative reform. It was in this sphere, too, that he wanted most to achieve it. The tangled state of the finances was his earliest sustained concern, their consolidation and expansion his perennial interest. There is indeed no clear distinction, in this context, between his purely financial and administrative work; the division here has been made largely for convenience. But in the context of administration itself a line can usefully be drawn. Pitt's task was a good deal easier within the area for which he was directly responsible than he could ever expect it to be outside.

Even then it was not easy. Pitt moved with care. Improvements mostly came piecemeal; there was little sudden sweeping change. The results in the tax departments throw some light on his approach. For here, it might seem, was a case for a clear stroke. If the revenue was to be properly tapped, its collection must be improved, and the costs of administration where possible reduced. The group of tax boards, other than Customs and Excise, appeared ill proportioned as it stood. The Board of Taxes itself, responsible for the land tax, the older assessed taxes, and after 1786 for some small items of Crown land revenue, had seven salaried Commissioners in charge of a central staff of under twenty. Four other boards, for salt, stamps and licences, had eighteen Commissioners between them, and central staffs totalling about 200. This seemed clumsy and extravagant, and a remedy had recently been proposed. The Commissioners for Examining the Public Accounts had suggested, in their Second Report in 1781, that these last four boards and their staffs should be combined with the Taxes' Board and Office, and the Treasury itself had agreed. Pitt therefore, like his immediate predecessors, had the incentive to act on such lines if he wished – an incentive which in other cases he was often glad to accept. In this instance, however, he left the separate authorities as they were. Instead, in February 1785 he transferred the collection of some assessed taxes – the scope of which he was enlarging in his first two budgets[1] – from the Stamps and the Excise to the Taxes' Board; and despite a hint that he might abolish the Boards for Hackney Coach Licences and Hawkers' Licences, these and the other bodies survived untouched for many more years.[2]

Pitt thus rejected direct institutional change.[3] He decided to seek his ends within the existing organisation. His hand fell chiefly on the Taxes' Office, which found itself doing more work. He continued the practice which North had begun, of requiring it to help prepare new taxes; and as the fresh assessments were levied, they fell mostly within its charge. There was some recruitment from the Treasury, as places fell due to be filled; but the extra labours were rewarded with little extra help, and no extra reward. The office staff was slightly enlarged, and some cramped accommodation was found for it in Somerset House, where it has remained and expanded ever since. But salaries were not raised, Pitt ignored the complaints, and there was precious little of the sinecure about a post in the Taxes' Office.

Much of the extra work arose from the pressures applied to the local machinery – the final touchstone of effectiveness, on which the shape of central reform must so largely depend. Pitt had to act here in different

1. P. 250 above.
2. Speech of 17 February 1785 (*P.R.*, XVII, 188). The Act was 25 Geo. III, c. 47; the taxes were those on coaches, carriages and wagons, on carriage horses, draught horses and riding horses, and on menservants.
3. He does seem to have thought, in the autumn of 1785, of creating a new 'Superintendent of the collection of the Revenue', to supervise reforms and also to assist the Committee of Trade in matters affecting merchants' and manufacturers' interests. But nothing came of the idea. The Committee of Trade disliked it, and there would have been political difficulties since the post was designed for William Eden, a new and generally unpopular recruit from Opposition. (See P.R.O. 30/8/110, and B.M. Add. Ms 34420, ff. 127–8v).

ways, according to the nature of the material. In the case of the land tax itself, he could not do very much. For the management of that most intimate of imposts had always been confided in the main to the propertied classes themselves – an equivalent, in the field of revenue, to the role of the J.P.s in that of the law. They and their dependants were responsible for assessment and collection, and for transferring the net receipts to the Taxes' Board. No salaries were paid, fees being the sole remuneration, parish officers were appointed by county Commissioners themselves nominated by individual M.P.s, and Treasury appointments were confined to the county Receivers-General who held and paid over the balances.[1] The system and its rewards were thus safely in the hands of the local gentry and professions, and Government, which did not pay the piper, was in no position to call the tune. Pitt's efforts conformed to the fact. They were confined very largely to inspection and exhortation, and Treasury control remained almost entirely indirect. Within his compelling limits, the Minister did what he could. The Treasury badgered the Taxes' Board, the Board badgered the local Commissioners. The Receivers-General were urged to use their influence, to hasten their payments, to reduce the large balances which they often held. Many of the balances were reduced; but the speed of payments and the yields rose only slightly, and in the middle nineties the Board was still confessing that it could do little more. Real as its efforts were, under Pitt's steady pressure, the effect perforce was limited while the old system of appointment and profit endured.

Much more could be achieved in the case of the assessed taxes. For here the assessments were made by salaried local surveyors, appointed by the Treasury, supervised by salaried 'general' surveyors, and checked by salaried inspectors. The Crown therefore had greater powers, Pitt greater freedom to act. The results were soon apparent. In 1785 he began to overhaul the organisation. The class of general surveyor was abolished, its members being retired or allowed to resign, and was replaced by additional inspectors, working from London. Local surveyors were to be vetted before appointment, and trained for three months. Deputies were forbidden, but trainees could act if a surveyor was ill. A system of promotion was established, from surveyor to inspector; powers were given to move officers about the country; the Taxes' Office was given a small examiners' department to supervise the whole. 'Nothing like this set of minutes had been seen before in the history of this branch of the administration'.[2] The short-term effect was a modest decrease in evasion and fraud; the long-term result was later seen in the machinery for the first income tax.

Pitt's methods are instructive. They were governed by two main considerations. In an age when the structures of government and of

1. E.g. p. 232 above.
2. W. R. Ward, 'The Administration of the Window and Assessed Taxes, 1696–1798' (*E.H.R.*, LXVII, no. CCLXV, 539).

politics were cemented by patronage, the forms of administration were political forms as well. Terms of appointment, rights of place, were of critical importance; there could be no effective improvement if this reality was ignored. The recent spate of Economical Reform had not altered the position: in some ways, indeed, it had underlined it. The political nature of the measures had largely dictated the administrative content; the administrative results left their mark on the political approach. No Ministry was anxious, when it came to the point, to reduce its influence further by obvious change. But equally it was less prepared than ever to reduce the countervailing rights of individuals, now enshrined even more strongly as the bulwark of liberty against the Crown. A reformer, because he was a reformer, must tread a winding maze; he could seldom hope to cut down the hedges, as Shelburne and Pitt had already found. Government was a mosaic, and mosaics demand skilled treatment. Greater efficiency depended on the manipulation of other concerns.

The pattern of improvement, in fact, was shaped by the conditions in each case. What applied in one instance did not necessarily apply in another. Thus Pitt could act with the assessed taxes as he could not hope to do with the land tax, because he was dealing with officials who fell more directly under Government's review. Abuses had crept in; but they had not been converted into rights, and the Treasury had corrective powers if it was prepared to act. To attack the machinery of the land tax would have been quite another matter: it would have meant extending Treasury control over a new area, or even creating Government posts at the expense of the influence of individual M.P.s. No Minister was anxious to stir up fresh accusations of increasing the influence of the Crown, least of all if he had been connected in any way with the movement for Economical Reform.

But there was also the question of economy itself. The unsalaried land tax officials certainly had their faults; but they were unsalaried, and the costs of assessment and collection were low. The House of Commons' Select Committee on Finance in 1797 thought that British taxes were the cheapest to administer in Europe. The land and assessed taxes were distinctly cheaper than the rest. The aggregate rate from 1789 to 1792 was some £3.8s per cent of the net produce, compared with £5.5s for the excise, £5.19s for the salt duties, £6.14s for the customs, £8.2s for hackney coach licences, and no less than £48.12.6 for hawkers' licences.[1] It was probably no higher a few years before, and the fact weighed heavily with Pitt. He was keeping costs down to the limit in the rest of the department – the Taxes' Office got little extra, the new inspectors of assessed taxes replaced a vanished class of general surveyors. He would think very hard before raising a charge that was already providentially low.

1. To the nearest shilling in each case. Proportionately, but not relatively, different figures can be produced if the percentage is taken on the gross produce; see the Finance Committee's Fourth Report, in *Reports from Committees*, XII (1803), 54–5.

This approach was repeated elsewhere. It was indeed typical of Pitt. True economy, no doubt, is impossible without efficiency; but the efficiency may involve an immediate expense. What, in such a case, was a Minister to do, particularly one whose prime concern was a surplus in an age of low taxation? Much of Pitt's achievement in the peacetime years lay in the way in which he avoided the choice, within the area of the financial departments. He made very skilled use, by and large, of the tangle he was trying to clear. For if the undergrowth was dense, it could yield a good deal to a patient woodsman, who knew his way about and the kind of weapons he might use. Much could be accomplished by unspectacular, detailed work; by putting fresh life into old forms, by specific individual changes, sometimes by purely financial action which would have administrative effects. The results were not always far-reaching. They generally fell short of the ideal. They might sometimes have been sought more boldly. The task was sometimes shirked. But in the end they were impressive, the more so because the choice itself was clear to Pitt. Economy was the object, and it must be served by greater efficiency. But if improvement involved much expense, the scheme would usually be amended, or turned, or dropped.

These political and financial pressures moulded Pitt's approach. They go far to explain his decision not to amalgamate the tax departments. There may also have been some strictly administrative reasons. It might have been awkward to combine the management of the salt and assessed taxes when the latter was about to be reformed, the Salt Office really fell more easily (as was proved on its eventual abolition in 1798) in the sphere of the Excise than in that of the Taxes' Office, the operations of the Stamp Office must always have remained largely distinct. But even if the main scheme itself was rejected, something might have been done; the two minor licencing boards, for instance, might perhaps have been absorbed. Pitt's alternative owed much more to other considerations. To have combined the local officials effectively would have meant a reduction in staff, which however would presumably have fallen on the unpaid land tax officials; and this would have meant risking a major political fuss, while actually increasing the cost of assessment and collection. The most obvious saving, in fact, might have been in the salaries of the eighteen Commissioners themselves[1] – or in the net reduction after the Taxes' Board had been appropriately enlarged. But revenue commissioners in any form were not easily removed: the places were too useful in a variety of ways. They served as rewards for different services, in the country, in Parliament or at Court. Since they could not be held with a seat in the Commons, they could be used to secure a vacancy – the undesirable Mortlock, for instance, was finally disposed of in this way.[2] They supplemented

1. P. 283 above.
2. See p. 232 above. For the Place Acts, see pp. 40–1 above.

inadequate salaries for 'efficient' officials. They supported indigent gentlemen and retired secretaries, even young lawyers with careers to make. And whatever the motive of the appointment, tenure was regarded as safe. Although the places were not granted for life, 'they have always been understood to be so held, unless in cases of misconduct'.[1] The one wholesale dismissal, in the sixties, had left sharp and unpleasant memories;[2] nor could Ministers generally claim that the places lay solely within their gift. The dividing lines were blurred, but patronage was varied, and the Commissioners' own wishes could not be entirely ignored. Appointments to the taxes' boards throughout the eighties were thus made much as before, on the few occasions on which a vacancy occurred. Shelburne himself gave his secretary a seat on the Hackney Coach Licences' Board, and of Pitt's eight appointments from 1784 to 1792, it has been reckoned that two were of active administrators, two of royal servants, one was to obtain a Parliamentary vacancy, and three were for political or social purposes.[3] The pattern in fact could hardly be changed unless the places themselves were abolished; and this was hardly likely without some compelling extraneous cause. When Pitt hoped, for instance, to do away with the Board of Hawkers' and Pedlars' Licences, it was because he intended to abolish the licences themselves. But the shopkeepers objected, the licences remained, and that being so he was not prepared to raise a fuss. The same applied elsewhere. Larger schemes of amalgamation at the centre might have caused political trouble, which would not have been worth while unless the local officials could be combined. And this in turn would not have been easy – and would certainly have been unpleasant – without a change in the strucure of the taxes themselves. While Pitt remained content with the familiar policy,[4] he had to content himself with minor, if useful, improvements to the old machine. It is significant that the first large remodelling of the taxes' boards and departments began in 1797, when a remodelling of the assessed taxes preceded the introduction of an income tax.

The same pressures, and the same response to change induced by other means, may be seen in the greater departments of the Customs and the Excise. The size of the revenue, the number of men involved, were of course on a larger scale. The two departments between them were responsible for about two-thirds of the national income, for central staffs of almost 600, and for at least two-thirds of the total number of

1. Sixth Report of the Select Committee on Finance, 1797 (*Reports from Committees*, XII, 155).
2. See p. 179, n1 above.
3. W. R. Ward, 'Some Eighteenth Century Civil Servants: The English Revenue Commissioners, 1754–98' (*E.H.R.*, LXX, no. CCLXXIV, 30–43).
4. See pp. 255–6 above.

revenue officials.[1] The scale of their operations, and the tangled state of the Customs, suggested a particularly fruitful field for reform.

A certain amount could be done to strengthen the boards themselves, at least that of the Customs, which stood to benefit most. From 1784 to 1792, Pitt appointed three active administrators to the Customs Commission (one from the Commission for Examining the Public Accounts and two from the department itself), two experienced former officials, and one 'man of business' with roots in Cambridge.[2] This balance was somewhat exceptional. Places on the Excise Board, by contrast, still generally went to nominees with political and social claims – five of the six appointments in this period can be so described, the other going to a royal servant.[3] The categories, of course, should not be distinguished too sharply: one of the politicians at least, Robert Nicholas, became a conscientious Excise Commissioner, while the former Commissioner of Public Accounts left his Customs seat in due course to his son. Appointments with an 'effective' flavour, moreover, might themselves be influenced by jobbery: John Pownall (now a virtually retired official, but still capable of good advice) filled a vacancy on the Customs Board which had been bought from its former occupant by the politician John Luttrell, who then, with Pitt's consent, took Pownall's seat on the Excise Board. This was in fact a distinctly curious business for a 'virtuous' Minister to have approved, for a Commissioner's freedom to dispose of his place had never been complete, and outright sales, never common, were now increasingly frowned upon. Whatever the background, it can hardly qualify as a borderline case; it lay pretty clearly beyond the line which Pitt was normally careful to draw.[4] The transaction stands beside the list of less objectionable appointments, and the two important ones, of Frewin and Stiles to the Customs Board.

For it was in promotions or transfers of this last kind that Pitt really sought his ends. The more blatant political appointments were on the wane, and the political world itself could provide its quota of adminis-

1. Mitchell & Deane, op. cit., ch. XIV, table 1 for net income (estimated gross figures give much the same proportion); p. 174 above for the central staffs, and customs officials; P.R.O., T. 44/10-12 for the excisemen.

2. William Roe, Richard Frewin and William Stiles; Sir Alexander Munro and John Pownall; and Joah Bates, a Fellow of King's and once secretary to Sandwich.

3. John Luttrell (later Luttrell Olmius), Timothy Caswell, John Buller, Robert Nicholas, and Mulgrave's son Augustus Phipps; and Henry Reveley. These appointments to both boards were spread over the period.

4. For this affair, which took place early in 1785, see Ward, loc. cit., 44 n1, 49. Luttrell's letters to Pitt are in P.R.O. 30/8/153, 164. The appointment was allowed to go ahead in return for Luttrell vacating his Parliamentary seat, in which he had supported Fox. Pitt seems to have been influenced by a readiness to help the retiring Commissioner, Thomas Allen (North's former secretary), who was going blind, and to have seized the chance of doing so without Government incurring expense (Luttrell Olmius to Pitt, 2 March 1793; P.R.O., 30/8/164). But the business was irregular, and looks dubious. For Pownall himself, see pp. 97 above and 339–40 below.

tratively minded men. They were spearheaded by a handful of active officials, whose fortunes Pitt encouraged and whom he used to the full. Frewin and Stiles are prime examples. One or other of them, or both, were involved in every major investigation of Customs business between 1782 and 1792. Stiles, then secretary to the Board, had helped prepare Musgrave's report to Shelburne on sinecures and fees;[1] he and Frewin did much of the donkey work on Pitt's Consolidation Act; and they, together with one of the Scottish Customs Commissioners, were charged in 1789 with a fresh investigation of the fee system, and the drafting of what proved to be an abortive bill.

The preparation of this bill, indeed, is of interest. It reveals Pitt's ideas of what might be done, and the obstacles to success. In the spring of 1783 he had tried to carry Shelburne's scheme for abolishing Customs sinecures and fees, and the experience had clearly impressed him. No further legislation on sinecures was proposed over the next eight years; instead, Pitt simply failed to appoint to such places as they fell in. When the Commissioners for Examining the Public Accounts turned to the Customs, in 1785–6, they recommended the abolition of 180 patent and sinecure offices. By the end of 1792, one patent had been revoked. But a further 28 of the places were vacant, two after resignation, and the other 26 as the result of death.[2] There was in fact a quiet and piecemeal suppression of sinecures as opportunity offered. No attempt was made to force the pace, no principle publicly invoked.

The savings were modest – some £8,100 a year, out of the £31,430 recommended by the Commissioners of Public Accounts. How would the picture look if an attack were made on fees? There had been little incentive to launch one following the failure of Shelburne's bill. But the Commissioners of Public Accounts' reports drove the Treasury to re-examine the question. By the spring of 1788 it had taken soundings all round, from the merchants in the outports and from a General Meeting of merchants in London.[3] Contrasting views were expressed: the provincial merchants, as in 1782,[4] wanted fees retained, fearing the increased cost in duties or tax of compensating the officials; the London merchants, on the other hand, looked to a total abolition, pending

1. P. 92 above.

2. Five of the 29 in London, 24 in the outports. One of these last was filled up again, but 'effectively', in 1792. One other sinecure (the only one) was refilled as a sinecure in this period, to honour a promise made by an earlier Ministry.

A further 17 offices were recommended for consolidation, of which 4, all 'fallen in', were treated by the end of 1792.

Details taken, by date, from the lists for 1784–92 in the Fourth Report of the Finance Committee of 1797, Appendices B2, C1, and from the memorandum in Appendix C2 (*Reports from Committees*, XII, 66, 68–9, 74). According to George Rose (*Observations Respecting the Public Expenditure*, 9) Pitt resolved at the end of 1784 to abolish 196 Customs sinecures, worth £42,000 a year, 'as they fell in'.

3. This last seems in fact to have been a semi-permanent body, summoned and interrogated on several occasions from 1786 to 1788.

4. See p. 92 above.

which they would like to see a temporary table of permissible charges. Faced by this division of opinion, and lacking a comprehensive account of all emoluments – allowances, perquisites and gratuities as well as fees and salaries themselves –, the Government set up a fresh inquiry within the Customs Office, from which Frewin's and Stiles's reports emerged in 1790–1.

Their verdict was distinctly cautious. In 1788, fees and the like had accounted for over a third of the Customs officials' emoluments. Of that total, less than a third might be saved on offices earlier recommended for abolition; meanwhile, the immediate cost of dispensing with fees would be over £127,000 a year. Total abolition thus seemed impracticable: it would be far too expensive in increased salaries. Frewin and Stiles recommended instead that the fees on examination of goods and many of the forms required in coastal trade (involving fees) should be abolished, at a cost to the revenue of some £61–66,000 a year, that all other fees should be strictly listed by law, and some more of the sinecures proposed for abolition be statutorily wound up.[1] A bill on these lines was prepared. Pitt thereby consented to renew the attack on sinecures, on a limited scale, by law. But war broke out soon afterwards, he was busy on other matters, and no more was heard for the next four years of such reform by legislation.

Legislation, indeed, was avoided whenever possible. Thus there were certain old statutory rights, of 'prisage' and 'butlerage', granted by the Crown to certain great nobles, and commuted by them into annual payments from the customs dues. But while the Scottish exception to the excise was removed,[2] these deductions were left alone, Pitt presumably being impressed by the dangers of tackling the grantees outright. As with the taxes, in fact, action came in other ways. The Treasury continued to press for greater efficiency in the Customs, as it had been doing for some time. Redundancies were pared away – 104 offices, other than those reviewed by the Commissioners of Public Accounts, were abolished between 1784 and 1797 –, regulations were steadily issued affecting attendance and conduct. Such pressures were not dramatic, nor indeed were they new. They may have made the relatively efficient rather more efficient; they can hardly have touched the 'Country Foxhunters, Bankrupt Merchants' and other lights of society who filled so many of the less arduous posts.[3] The effect, in fact, if cumulatively useful, was irregular and slow. As so often, the greater changes came from another quarter: from acts of financial policy rather than from direct administrative attack. For if the department's structure remained much the same, the nature and scope of its work was revised.

1. Frewin and Stiles, second and third reports, 19 March, 3 May 1791 (*Reports from Committees*, XII, 79–81); 'Notes respecting the Customs bill of 1792', P.R.O. 30/8/285.
    2. See p. 246 above.
    3. Commissioner Musgrave's description in 1782 (see Hoon, *The Organization of the English Customs System*, 205).

The Consolidation Act fundamentally altered the character of the Customs' accounts, with such repercussions that 'the year of its passage . . . may be taken to symbolize the downfall of the old eighteenth-century system'.[1] A simplification of this order was bound to have administrative consequences, however cautiously considered and however long postponed; meanwhile it helped rationalise existing practice, and enabled the existing organisation to cope more effectively with the business brought on by the growing volume of trade. The measure was central to the Customs' operations. They were also aided by Pitt's transfer of duties and inspection to the Excise, where that department was better suited to the task.

For the Excise was a strong candidate for greater responsibilities. It was the favourite of investigating bodies, 'the good boy' of the revenue departments.[2] There was far less wastage and fraud than usual despite the range of the duties, revenue reached the Exchequer quickly, sinecures and fees were unimportant. Little needed to be done, by current standards, in the way of structural reform, though there were some unrealised proposals for reducing staff in order to raise the survivors' salaries.[3] It was much more a question of revising the department's scope. Pitt's moves in this direction were all to the good. Having relieved the Excise of certain taxes which fell more properly to the Taxes' Board, he extended its powers and expertise over a more appropriate field.[4] The new distribution of business soon proved its worth. Aided by simpler accounting, and drawing on its experience, the Excise absorbed the burden which the Customs had found a strain.

But however likely the improvement, the proposals were not without risk; in the light of past history, Pitt indeed could feel pleased with the result. For the Excise was traditionally suspect, and the suspicions still carried weight. Its methods of assessing value, falling squarely on producers and retailers, were resented; its powers of inspection, and the processes of judgment, offended private freedom and the common law. 'The proceedings of the Excise', Blackstone had declared, 'are . . . summary and sudden';[5] and the larger the amount at stake the less real chance there was of redress. For the 'hateful tax' was 'adjudged not by the common judges of property, but wretches hired by those to whom excise is paid'[6] – in other words by J.P.s and the Excise Commissioners themselves –, right of appeal lay to the Court of Exchequer where costs were notoriously high, and the onus of proof, *contra bonum morem*, rested on the appellant. In 1785 there was an effort to redeem this state of affairs by statute; and while the bill failed – it was a private bill introduced by Henry Beaufoy – the Solicitor General agreed that in principle

1. Op. cit., 4.
2. Binney, op. cit., 40.
3. Papers are in P.R.O. 30/8/290.
4. See p. 246 above.
5. *Commentaries on the Laws of England,* I, 308.
6. Johnson's *Dictionary.*

the indictment was correct.[1] Greater powers for the department were therefore still controversial, and Pitt can scarcely have been encouraged by the fate of earlier attempts. Walpole's Excise Bill in the thirties had had to be withdrawn, Dashwood's cider tax in the sixties had led to the downfall of Bute's Ministry. The atmosphere, it was true, had improved since then; proposals for some transfer of duties had been aired more widely, Adam Smith had come out in favour, the department had been commended by the Commissioners of Public Accounts. The aftermath of the Commutation Act had shown that effective warehousing discouraged smuggling, and the Excise was obviously suited to help in this task. Nor, towards the end of the process, was Opposition in good shape, after its battering in the Regency crisis. Pitt therefore had better cause than his predecessors to hope for success. But it could still not be taken for granted; old passions could easily be roused. The comparative ease with which his measures passed, particularly the transfer of tobacco duties, was in part a sign of his growing strength and the growing acquiescence in his judgment.

The improvements, moreover, were effected without expense. The central establishment of the department increased by some 35 per cent between the end of 1783 and the end of 1792, and costs rose by about 11 per cent – a modest increase seeing that so little could be absorbed in fees.[2] But there was a large reduction of local staffs in 1789, which produced a net saving, and since revenue itself rose significantly as the measures took effect, the proportion of management costs over the last four years of peace fell more sharply in the Excise than in any other revenue office.[3] It was something of a triumph for the department, and for Pitt himself. In this instance, the instrument responded pretty well to the demands.

The boards of taxes, licences and duties were the staple of the revenue system. There were two smaller branches of income with which Pitt was concerned. He was again fully responsible for the first, as head of the Treasury; his powers over the second were considerable but not complete.

As every schoolboy knows, when George III came to the throne he surrendered much of the Crown's hereditary revenue, in return for an annual Parliamentary grant on which he ran – or tried to run – the Civil List. The bulk of this revenue derived from the Crown lands, for which two Surveyors General were now responsible to the Treasury. A minor complication was removed in 1786, when Pitt did away with a

---

1. Pitt seems later to have become concerned about the position, judging by the papers he gathered on it (P.R.O. 30/8/290). For Beaufoy, see pp. 266 above and 351–2 below.
2. P.R.O., T. 44/10, 44/12.
3. See *Reports from Committees*, XII, 54–5.

body of trustees formed by Charles II to manage and sell certain Crown rents, and transferred their operations to the Taxes' Board. But the Surveyors General themselves continued, in charge of Crown lands and of Woods and Forests, served by a group of sinecurist Receivers[1] and unsalaried Collectors. As one might perhaps expect, the management was highly incompetent; virtually no income reached the Exchequer, and such as did so was long delayed. Shelburne had begun inquiries; but these lapsed under the Coalition, and in 1786 Pitt revived them on a different basis. A statutory commission was set up, including the formidable Comptroller of the Navy, Sir Charles Middleton (representing the department to which much of the Crown timber was, or should have been, sold), and over the next six years it produced a series of detailed reports. In 1793 it recommended a complete overhaul of the system, and the abolition of the Surveyors General in favour of a new commission for the Crown lands. Some of the proposals were acted on in 1794, but the Board itself had to wait until early in the next century. Its successor survives today, managing a wide range of properties, from Regent's Street and the Nash terraces to most of the foreshore along the coasts.

Even when reformed, the Crown lands yielded only a moderate revenue. The Post Office, potentially at least, was a much more important source. Pitt's efforts to increase its income adorn a tale and point the moral of the shifts to which a reformer might find himself reduced.

It was no coincidence that they resulted from the one sustained frontal attack which Pitt made in the peacetime years on an institution falling within his sphere. Part of the ensuing trouble arose from the fact that his control was not exclusive; other authorities, some well entrenched, were also involved. For the Post Office, serving a number of purposes, served a number of masters, and had developed a distinctive character of its own. As a revenue collector it was subordinate to the Treasury, under which it had been placed by an Act of 1711. But this arrangement was imposed on an organisation which did not thereby wholly disappear. The postal services had long been farmed, like so much else, to individuals, and when the farms were taken away the place of Postmaster General was retained. Throughout most of the eighteenth century it was divided into two, providing minor office for peers who would 'give lustre, vigour and firmness to His Majesty's Government'.[2] The second quality was not conspicuous in the long Augustan noonday, and the practices of earlier ages survived and grew with the volume of work. The Court Post, the London Penny Post, the Bye-Letter Office, all with their origins in private enterprise, remained semi-independent concerns, and in so far as any one authority supervised the whole it was the Secretary, ruling over his officials and paramount on the Board. But the Post Office was not only a revenue office. It was

1. Of whom Fox had earlier been one, until he sold the office to his deputy.
2. Pitt's description (Ellis, *The Post Office in the Eighteenth Century*, 9).

responsible for Government mails, for some Government intelligence and Government propaganda, and it had its links with departments other than the Treasury itself. Its sailing packets brought it into contact with the Foreign Office, the Home Office and the Admiralty – the Admiralty indeed gave some of the packet captains their commissions –, intelligence work was done, under warrant from the First Lord of the Treasury and the Secretaries of State, for themselves and for the King. The scope of operations was wide, their management largely fragmented. But a connecting link was found, in true contemporary style, in overlapping interests. There was a range of conventions affecting patronage and duties, and at the centre sat the Secretary, with a finger in every pie.

If there was to be improvement, therefore, the Secretary should be well disposed. In 1784 he was Anthony Todd, who had held the place with one brief interval since 1768. Unfortunately, Pitt soon found himself up against the redoubtable Todd. It was not altogether surprising, and the fault was not all on one side. Pitt saw a prospect of raising revenue and stimulating efficiency. But it involved him in expedients of which the Office could legitimately disapprove, and the plan centred on a controversial figure who became a focus of competing interests.

The figure was John Palmer, the inventor of the mail coach system. The system itself was the prospect which appealed to Pitt. It was indeed a hopeful one. In the early eighties the posts were notoriously slow and insecure, and net income was failing to rise with the growing volume of traffic. Palmer proposed a revolutionary change, in the shape of fast special coaches, carrying some passengers, in charge of their own armed guards and freed from the need to pay turnpike tolls. In return for such a service, postal rates would be increased, and the privilege of franking (i.e. free postage) drastically reduced. Palmer himself was to be given a senior position in the Post Office with the reversion of the Secretaryship, and his salary was to be supplemented by a poundage of $2\frac{1}{2}$ per cent on the net surplus arising from his scheme.

Pitt was first told of the idea in 1782, when he was Shelburne's Chancellor of the Exchequer. He encouraged Palmer to work on it, as did the Coalition in 1783. By the time that Pitt was back in the Treasury the detail was complete, the Post Office had been informed, and its answer received. Like most innovations, the scheme had its drawbacks, which were pointed out. But the climate of opinion was against the department, and Pitt himself wished to go ahead. He may have been the more disposed to do so because the plan partly followed a precedent he knew – the introduction of the cross-country posts by another outsider, his father's friend Ralph Allen, who had been similarly rewarded by a poundage on the revenue produced. But the moment of decision came unexpectedly, and it would seem without much thought. It was in fact brought on by Pitt's hasty withdrawal of the coal tax in June

1784, and the need, as he saw it, to find an immediate substitute.[1] Higher postal rates seemed one of the answers, and they would be eased by Palmer's scheme. On 21 June Pitt accordingly summoned the postal officials to the Treasury, and announced that the first mail coach would run from Bristol to London on 1 August.

This arbitrary decision was asking for trouble. Palmer was obviously being given extensive powers, but his status and remuneration had not been fixed, and the manner of the announcement gave great offence. The meeting was stormy and confused, and Pitt left it abruptly.[2] Todd and the Office then settled down to wreck Palmer and his scheme.

The fight lasted for some three years. Given ill will, it was easy enough to exploit the likely difficulties, and the Post Office often appeared about to win. But the mail coaches emerged triumphant, to become a famous feature of the English scene. They did so because Pitt ensured that the Treasury stood by Palmer throughout the struggle, and forced Todd and his colleagues in the end to admit defeat. But if the system survived, its author did not. The Secretary could withdraw in good order, make his peace with Palmer, and dig in afresh; but Palmer himself was dogged by troubles which his exposed position – and his temperament – did not equip him to overcome.

The consequences seriously embarrassed Pitt. Palmer's original terms had been accepted verbally, on the Minister's behalf, by Pretyman. But they could not be carried quickly into effect. Pitt had intended to secure Palmer's position by giving him an appointment for life by patent; but the law officers found that this was illegal under the Post Office Act, and the department itself blocked an appointment 'under pleasure'. It also refused to sanction the projector's poundage on the receipts. Meanwhile the unfortunate man had to pay the costs of his scheme himself. His credit soon began to fail, in 1786 he was facing ruin, and his fall would clearly involve that of the mail coach system. The opposition, rather surprisingly, was now headed by one of the Postmasters General – not normally a quarter from which trouble was expected. It came, moreover, from a nominee of Pitt's. In 1784, the joint Postmasters General were Lord Tankerville and Lord Carteret, the latter an appointment of North's which survived under Shelburne and the Coalition, the former an appointment of Shelburne's revoked by the Coalition and now restored. Tankerville seems to have been a well-meaning, self-important, rather ineffectual man, who wished to leave his mark as a reformer; and his zeal led him impartially into conflict with Todd, with Carteret and with Palmer, whose system he attacked and whose terms of payment he

1. Palmer's evidence of his meeting with Pitt, given in 1797 (*Report of the Committee . . . Appointed to consider the Agreement made with Mr Palmer . . .*, 1797, 104). And see p. 252 above.

2. Something of the atmosphere is conveyed in the heading of a document among his papers, in another hand: 'Ideas of what seemed to be concluded at the Treasury June 21, 1784' (P.R.O. 30/8/233).

condemned. The delay caused by Todd enabled him to block the proposed poundage, and his formal opposition, in 1786, came at an unfortunate time. But meanwhile he had become embroiled with Todd and Carteret over the running of the packet boat service – an argument that ended typically with Todd surrendering his private profits in return for a higher salary –, and he now brought matters to a head by reporting Carteret to Pitt for buying personal furniture at the Office's expense. Carteret in turn appealed to the Minister, and Pitt seized his chance. The charge could not be made to stick, Pitt stood by Carteret, and in August 1786 Tankerville was dismissed. With Carteret and Todd now showing signs of coming to terms, the way was clear for Palmer's appointment to an official place, and a verbal promise to settle his debts.

Tankerville was naturally furious. He left vowing vengeance, and within a year the storm began to blow. In May 1787, his kinsman the young Charles Grey – Lord Grey of the Reform Bill – demanded an investigation in the Commons into abuses in the Post Office. The debate grew bitter – Grey challenged Pitt to a duel – and Government was forced to accept an inquiry, which began forthwith. The instrument chosen was the existing Commission for Enquiry into Fees in the Public Offices, set up by Pitt himself a year before with different objects in view. It submitted its conclusions at the end of May 1788. Palmer's system was highly praised, Carteret was cleared – largely by silence – of most of Tankerville's charges, but in general the Office was severely attacked. The Commission deplored the system of fees, enumerated widespread abuses, and declared that the sailing packets were wastefully run. It was one of the strongest reports in a decade of critical reports.

It was not, however, entirely accurate. The names of the Commissioners command respect – of the three, Sir John Dick and William Molleson were the Comptrollers of Army Accounts, and Francis Baring was a shrewd and knowledgeable M.P. – and many of their recommendations later bore fruit. But the postal service was varied and complex, their judgment was sometimes ill informed, and some of their statements proved to be incorrect. It is hard to say how far Pitt grasped these weaknesses at once. They may have contributed to his reaction; so may the fact that the Commission had recently produced a crop of other reports, on the navy, which alo looked like causing trouble. At any rate, hostile and obstinate, he did nothing with the findings, and the Commission was not employed again. Perhaps the Minister counted on reform coming more quietly from the department itself. If so, he was again the victim of his hopes. For a new figure now appeared, to carry the matter to its conclusion; and if he was indeed bent on reform, it was not particularly quiet. When Tankerville was dismissed, Lord Clarendon succeeded him; but Clarendon died almost at once, and in July 1787 Lord Walsingham, who had earlier wanted it, was given the place. Walsingham was a man to be reckoned with – fearless, capable, short in temper but long in determination, the sort of administrator that Tankerville would have liked to be. In different circumstances, Pitt must have applauded his efforts: as it was, he could scarcely object. The new Postmaster started with a grudge, for he was just in time to be adversely involved in the Commission of Enquiry, and he settled down at once to refute the charges and investigate afresh. His examination was thorough and protracted, and it revealed some curious goings-on in Palmer's department, which the Commissioners had overlooked or ignored. Contracts were being given without proper record, staff was recruited and employed irregularly, some of the accounts were confused and incomplete. Palmer was acting arbitrarily, usurping other people's patronage, interfering with their business and possibly mismanaging his own.

All this was due in part to a clash of responsibilities. Pitt had always given Palmer to understand that he had the Treasury's support, and was directly accountable to the Board. It was also due in part to Palmer's own personality: he was not easy to get on with, and his experiences had not helped. He was probably not in fact dishonest; but he employed some doubtful characters, and, soured by frustration, he meant to go his own way. By the turn of the decade he had reached the point of recommending an overhaul of the Office, the subordination or supersession of the Secretary, and freedom of action for himself. Walsingham was not the man to take this sort of thing lying down, and he could count on Todd's skilled if muted support. There were soon some clashes, in which Palmer badly overreached himself. By the summer of 1790 there was something of a crisis, Walsingham sent a report to the Treasury in the autumn, and Pitt, who had so far avoided action, was forced to take a hand. He tried to arrange a compromise; for another year he supported Palmer; but in the spring of 1792 he had finally to decide. In March, the Postmasters General suspended their unruly official, and Walsingham produced proof of his responsibility for some of his department's financial sins. Confronted by these facts, Pitt had no choice. In June the Treasury confirmed Palmer's removal from his appointment, and granted him a pension of £3,000 a year.

There was still a weary epilogue to come, for Palmer challenged his fate. The whole affair was re-examined in 1797 by a special committee of the Commons, and the Post Office itself was again investigated, with the other departments, by the Select Committee on Finance in the same year. It had been a sad and tangled story. But certain conclusions emerge. Pitt saw in Palmer's plans at the start the sort of scheme he always liked: one that would combine the primary object of raising revenue with that of a more efficient service. He made full use, in the ensuing troubles, of the Treasury's powers; without repeated Treasury approval Palmer could not have survived, and Pitt certainly encouraged his man to suppose himself mainly responsible to the senior board. He was not particular about forms of place or remuneration; he was prepared to give Palmer an appointment by life patent, and he allowed him poundage, a mode of payment increasingly frowned on elsewhere. But these expedients, and Pitt's growing embarrassments, sprang directly from his decision to impose an unpopular arrangement on a department which proved more obstinate than he had supposed. Perhaps the quarrel could not have been avoided, and the Post Office in these years was in any case becoming a troubled place. But the chain of events can be traced, link by link, to Pitt's initial action. Neither party won as it hoped. The mail coach system was forced through, and Palmer placed in the department against its will. But he was finally dismissed, Pitt had meanwhile to accept an unwelcome inquiry, and Walsingham vindicated the authority of the Postmaster General. The Treasury's powers were considerable; but the Post Office was sufficiently well entrenched for its own, obstructive, powers to be highly developed. The result no doubt was much affected by chance; given different personalities, there might well have been a different ending. But given the system, the effect of personality was at a premium. Perhaps it was not surprising that the reforming Walsingham should have done down the reforming Palmer. It was also perhaps not surprising that Pitt should have been led into such compromising courses by his most uncompromising intervention in the affairs of a revenue office.

II

At the centre of the financial system stood the Treasury itself and the Exchequer, with the Mint. Little happened at the Mint in these years; the department which had once had Newton for its Deputy Master, and attracted the debate of Lowndes and Locke, was now comatose and stagnant. A little gold was minted for the Bank, silver was not minted at all, copper – and its imitations and tokens – entirely by private hands. There had been a recoinage of gold in the middle seventies, and an inquiry into the office at Shelburne's request in 1782. But the former was of limited importance, and the latter was not followed up. In the background, Charles Jenkinson, the author of the recent recoinage, was pursuing his studies on the currency, which were to bear fruit in the great Committee on Coin in 1798. Meanwhile the country exchanged a bewildering variety of pieces, most of them old, many debased, and many of them counterfeit; and the officials in the Tower slumbered virtually undisturbed.

The Treasury, too, suffered little change; but for different reasons. Most of the abuses which excited attention in the years of Economical Reform had now been tackled, and some removed. North had suggested a way of countering the element of corruption in raising loans; Crewe's Act had disfranchised the revenue officers, many of them directly under

Treasury patronage; Shelburne had pooled the department's fees in a fund for higher salaries.[1] Not all these measures were complete or satisfactory; Pitt had to elaborate on North's experiment for dealing with loans,[2] Shelburne's fee fund did not prove large enough for the purpose. Nor could the reforms themselves revolutionise daily practice. But by and large the Treasury was in reasonable shape by the standards of the day. There was pluralism, of course – George Rose himself, the joint Secretary, was also Master of the Pleas in the Exchequer, and later Clerk of the Parliaments with the new journals' office attached. But it was not always a bad thing that 'effective' officials, possibly underpaid in one capacity, should be able to deploy their expertise in others. Some of the routine was complex, and much of it was slow; but again by contemporary standards it was not mishandled. Pitt's greatest contribution to its improvement was once more the Consolidation Act, which so greatly reduced the elaboration of the accounts. Otherwise he built on his predecessors' foundations, and particularly on those of North and Shelburne, who had steadily tightened up and rearranged the duties. The department's processes and regulations, in fact, were by now adequately settled: it was far more a question of seeing that they were put into effect. Pitt kept a strict eye on the work, by regular attendance at Board meetings, and, always aided by Rose, by his grasp of business and its forms. The establishment itself scarcely altered between 1782 and 1793: as the Commissioners for Enquiring into Fees in the Public Offices acknowledged in 1786, there was little need.[3] And when it was again enlarged, in the early years of the war, the additions met a growing volume of business which had not yet overwhelmed the staff.

'Brain and body, Treasury and Exchequer, were inseparably linked'.[4] The one regulated the finances, the other received them and paid them out. But if the brain was reasonably active, the body was old and clumsy and slow. 'Nobody can understand the full intricacies of Stuart finance or appreciate the niceties of the Hanoverian Treasury and its placemen, without steeping himself in the procedure of the medieval clerks of the exchequer'.[5] The ancient institution, in its ancient home, would indeed still have seemed largely familiar to the later Plantagenets. The Barons still sat in their Court, sheriffs (or their deputies) made their Proffers of Accounts in response to Summons of the Pipe and the Greenwax, and were given their *Quietus* after a recital by officials of the Pipe and the Lord Treasurer's Remembrancer, the clerks of the Audi-

1. See pp. 257, 90–1 above.
2. Pp. 257–8 above.
3. For their highly favourable report, see *House of Commons Accounts and Papers* (1806), VII, particularly 56, 60. One clerk was added in 1787, before further additions were made in and after June 1793 (see Fifteenth Report of the Select Committee on Finance, 1797; *Reports from Committees*, XII, 286–9).
4. Binney, op. cit., 183.
5. Anthony Steel, *The Receipt of the Exchequer 1377–1485* (1954), 369.

tors of the Exchequer engrossed the Declared Accounts in Roman figures, defaulting accountants were liable to the medieval Writs of *Distringas* and *Capias*, Tellers dropped their bills of receipt for the revenues down the pipe to the Tally Court, where the tallies of Pro and Sol were notched and cut, the Clerk of the Pells' office checked the Writs of *Liberate*, the Treasury Orders and Debentures, which mostly awaited his *Recordatur* before the departments could be paid. A few inescapable innovations had been introduced; much of the audit had been improved in the hands of the Auditors of the Imprests, and the Bank of England in practice replaced the Tellers in their handling of issues and receipts. But the antique structure remained, bewilderingly anachronistic, a haven for sinecures, a stumbling block to modern finance. It was not inappropriate that the old Palace of Westminster should have been burned down in the end by Exchequer tallies, and that the most fashionable exponent of the Gothick taste should have held three Exchequer posts.[1]

The administrative drawbacks were obvious. But they were not likely to be removed. Some limited action had been taken in the heat of recent years. In 1783, the Coalition had provided for the disappearance of eight Exchequer places when the holders retired or died, and funded the fees as a contribution to higher salaries. But far-reaching reform was virtually out of the question. The processes of the Exchequer were rooted in law; the department was partly a court, its forms were largely judicial, and in an age devoted to legality there was little prospect of radical change. Law and precedent would have been outraged; so, too, would a host of private interests. For the department was not really a great bulwark of the influence of the Crown; on the contrary, that influence had been earlier defeated, and a multiplicity of patent places sheltered the political world at large. Such defences were strong and varied, and they held out for another half century. The eventual overhaul of the Exchequer barely preceded that of the other courts of law.

Pitt therefore went quietly. But he left some mark on the department. The Consolidation Act reduced the great bulk of the accounts, though it could not affect the forms of their course; and thereby, to a lesser extent, the size of the Exchequer fees. So too, though again slightly, did an Act of the year before, designed to tidy up the regulation of payments under the Civil List Act.[2] The savings were modest: Pitt's own annual fees and gratuities as Chancellor shrank in these years from £53–16–0 to £35–5–0, but only because he lost a New Year's Gift from the Auditors of the Imprests.[3] And this loss was quite unusual, for it resulted

1. See p. 177 above.
2. 26 Geo. III, c. 99. For the reductions in the two years, see the Twenty-Second Report of the Finance Committee of 1797, Appendices D2–12 (*Reports from Committees*, XII, 467–9).
3. Loc. cit., 468.

from the outright abolition of a post; Pitt had dropped his earlier talk, learned from Shelburne, of wholesale suppression,[1] places were simply left to wither on the branch, and very few fell in before the war. His action in this case in fact was a sole, and a notable, exception to the rule. As might be expected, it arose from a special situation. The Auditors of the Imprests were one of the two main audit authorities within the Exchequer,[2] and they were responsible among other things for the armed forces' accounts. But when the Commissioners for Examining the Public Accounts investigated the position in 1783, they found that the navy was really doing the work for itself. Hardly any naval vouchers had been submitted since the reign of Charles II, and the Exchequer's approval was formally given to ledgers passed by the Navy Board. There was thus no proper check on the spending of one of the most expensive of Government departments; of more immediate consequence, there was no check on the accumulation of its arrears. For the Treasurer of the Navy – like the Paymaster General of the Forces until the past few years[3] – still held his balances on private account until his public accounts were declared; and by the time that the ships' books were settled, this might take a decade and more. In July 1780, in fact, the last Treasurer's account to be passed was that of 1758, and the sums outstanding amounted to some £75 million; meanwhile, former officials were free to put the moneys to personal use. However effectively the Auditors of the Imprests may have discharged their other duties, this gap was so large that their operations seemed 'unnecessary', and might perhaps even 'be dispensed with'.[4]

Feeling on the subject of the arrears was strong; strong enough indeed for it to be reflected among the Auditors of the Imprests themselves. Two years after this report was received, they felt obliged to echo its findings, though they naturally dissented from its unwelcome conclusion. In January 1785, Lord Mountstuart wrote to Pitt on behalf of himself and his colleague Lord Sondes.[5] He recommended the appointment of a temporary private commission to help them deal with the Services' accounts, which should consist of the two Comptrollers of Army Accounts, a Treasury clerk, and one other qualified person. Pitt acted at once. He set up a new commission much on these lines, gave it

1. See the report of his remarks on sinecures, in moving his Public Offices Regulation Bill in 1783 (*P.R.*, X, 182).

2. The others being the Auditors of the Land Revenue. But they did not cover the whole field. Sheriffs' and certain court accounts were handled in other ways within the Exchequer, some public issues (e.g. for secret service) were made without audit, and there were auditors outside the Exchequer, of whom the most important was the Auditor of the Excise.

3. See p. 90, n1 above.

4. Eighth Report of the Commissioners for Examining (*H.C.J.*, XXXIX, 55). See also their Third and Sixth Reports, in *H.C.J.*, XXXVIII.

5. P.R.O. 30/8/282. The Commissioners' Eighth Report had in fact been swiftly followed by a Ninth on the Auditors and the army accounts. But this, though critical, was less damaging.

powers to examine public accountants on oath, required it to submit all 'extraordinary' accounts to the Treasury, and placed the appointment of its staff under Treasury control. But instead of the private group of assistants for whom Mountstuart had asked, he created a statutory body, the Commission for Auditing the Public Accounts;[1] and this replaced the Auditors of the Imprests themselves. When the Act passed in July 1785, the unhappy Mountstuart and Sondes found themselves removed from their posts.

The transaction was significant and unusual in several ways. It gave statutory authority for the first time to subsidiary auditors, and extended the Treasury's authority over them. It involved considerable immediate expense, for the Auditors of the Imprests had to be compensated, to the tune of £7,000 a year apiece.[2] Above all, it suppressed life patents by statute – a generally suspect proceeding, as Pitt himself had earlier found.[3] He acted as he did in this instance because he could count on widespread support for a renewed attempt to end a notorious scandal.

It is doubtful how far he hoped to achieve anything more. Certainly, if he did so he was doomed largely to disappointment. The Act of 1785 contained helpful provisions for tackling the immediate task. By 1787, indeed, the Commissioners themselves reckoned that their work was done. 'The system of examining and passing the Public Accounts', in their view, had by then been 'essentially changed and regulated', and they therefore concluded that they might be wound up.[4] This judgment of course was expressed in the light of the Consolidation Act; but in so far as it referred to the Commissioners' own achievements it was decidedly optimistic, and they were not in fact allowed to disappear. Something had certainly been done. The Services' arrears had been investigated, though many were still outstanding, and the Treasurers of the Navy's private balances transferred to the custody of the Bank of England. Some departmental accounts had been simplified, some auditing processes improved.[5] But the sum total of the changes was modest: they referred only to the accounts transferred to the new Commission, which did not include those of the land tax and assessed

1. To be distinguished from the earlier Commissioners for Examining the Public Accounts. The Act was 25 Geo. III, c. 52.

2. See pp. 175–6 above.

3. See p. 92 above.

4. There is a slight mystery about the date of the Commissioners' statement. The copy of the minutes of their meeting in Pitt's papers (P.R.O. 30/8/282) gives it as 15 January 1787; but he endorsed this as having been received on 20 June, and it is possible that the copying clerk misread 'June' for 'Jan'. The meeting itself seems to have been an 'extraordinary' one, for there is no mention in the Commission's own minute book (P.R.O., A.O. 6/3) of these remarks, either on 15 January (when in fact no meeting is recorded) or in the minutes of 15 June.

5. And, in the process, a valuable historical service performed. The Commissioners' reports, which were issued (by J. Lane) in three volumes shortly after they were submitted to Parliament, provide the only public discussion, so far as I know, of the form of the declared accounts.

taxes, or of the excise and some colonial dues; and in the case of the navy itself, *current* accounting went on much as before. The Commission indeed, if potentially useful, really fell between two stools. Pitt refused – and rightly – to follow the proposal of the Commissioners for Examining the Public Accounts that a departmental audit might be hived off to a department. But he did not give his new body the powers required to carry out more than a limited task. Perhaps, it has been suggested, he did not appreciate the need – did not see that current methods of audit could not go far enough.[1] Perhaps; it is hard to say, for Pitt neither endorsed nor rejected the Commissioners' own assessment of their work. Certainly it was 'easier', as the Commissioners for Examining had earlier admitted, 'to see the Defects than to supply the Regulation'.[2] But whether the remedy was not recognised, or was simply not applied, the root cause in either case would seem to have been the same. For the restrictions which Pitt suffered here, consciously or unconsciously, reflected a certain conception or acceptance of the Treasury's possible role. They suggest, in this technical but highly important field, the sort of limits which he saw to his authority in relation to other departments of state, and particularly perhaps to those of the armed forces of the Crown.

III

A few years after Pitt died, one of his young men, himself soon to become Prime Minister, wrote to another who was then holding Rose's old Treasury post. 'Mr. Pitt', he remarked, 'must have felt, and his colleagues must have felt also, that he had such comprehensive talents and powers, that he was himself essentially the Government in all its Departments'. 'Yet even under these circumstances', he added, 'I have understood from you that Mr. Pitt himself could not in all Departments control expenditure as he wished'.[3] The tone of Spencer Perceval's observations was a tribute to Pitt's achievement. They also pointed the nature of the situation through which he had always to work, which yielded so often to his touch and so partially to change.

For control of expenditure was the key to effective administration. It gave the necessary focus to a departmental system which could normally show no other. The desire for a crisper direction, a clearer pattern, had long been voiced intermittently: George II, George III, Lord North, had all on occasions said much the same. But how could this be reconciled with a limitation of powers, the one sure bulwark of freedom and a conception which pervaded the structure of government as it regulated

1. Binney, op. cit., 281.
2. Third Report (*H.C.J.*, XXXVIII, 251).
3. Spencer Perceval to William Huskisson, 21 August 1809 (*English Historical Documents 1783–1832,* ed. A. Aspinall & E. Anthony Smith (1959), 129).

the structure of politics? When the 'several great offices of the State' thought of themselves as so largely 'distinct and independent',[1] it was not easy to alter their relations without seeming to threaten the constitution itself.

No real answer had been found; an answer indeed was seldom sought. The demand was confined mostly to periods of stress in the course of a hard fought war. The one great success of recent times, Chatham's wartime Ministry, was 'for obvious reasons . . . an exception' to the rules.[2] His methods, applied to a short-term need, had been as unusual as the man himself, and he never solved, or really tried to tackle, the problems of peacetime administration. 'A Government of Departments'[3] remained the norm; and one that was very hard to change. Of course Prime Ministers in peacetime are never administrative dictators: their impact on government always rests on political standing and personality. But that does not lessen the importance of the administrative structure in defining how they operate, and what they can and cannot hope to do. Sir Robert Peel, it has often been said, owed his pre-eminence to the fact that he could do the work of every departmental Minister himself. He was also the last Prime Minister to be in that position (and perhaps the only one to exploit it fully), before the scale of business grew beyond any one man's direct control. Pitt inherited less business than Peel; but he also inherited less power, and he had greater resistance to overcome. In an age when efficiency was seldom valued above liberty and economy, the system might yield to a Minister, but it was not shaped to give him strength. The Cabinet was as effective as its leader might make it; its members owed their responsibilities to Parliament and the Crown. With no assured party basis, and no clear administrative control, he must achieve a superiority which owed little to institutional support. Pitt's 'talents and powers' made a growing impression in his Ministry's first decade. They buttressed a growing political strength, from which he shaped the Government more to his liking. His methods seemed largely successful, in the fields he cared for most. But success itself was measured by standards that in many ways were modest, and if Pitt taught the system something, it taught him at least as much.

The Treasury's departmental powers were thus crucial to the authority of its First Lord. They were much clearer in respect of the revenue than they were in respect of expenditure. Pitt advanced most obviously in this latter sphere in his control of the Civil List – the subject on which indeed he had first been heard at the start of his career. His maiden speech, on that theme, had included the significant passage that 'the

1. P. 172 above.
2. Henry Dundas to Pitt, 9 July 1794 (P.R.O. 30/8/157).
3. North's phrase (*Memorials and Correspondence of Fox*, II, 38).

people, who granted that revenue, . . . were justified in resuming a part of it, under the pressing demand of an altered situation'.[1] In the middle eighties, he put this doctrine largely into effect.

The situation by then certainly called for further action. Burke's recent answer was proving inadequate.[2] When George III surrendered the bulk of his hereditary revenues on coming to the throne, he was given an annual grant of £800,000 on which to run the civil government of the country. This was 'a disadvantageous exchange for his Majesty'[3] – more had been needed on average over the past decade – and Parliament had to pay debts amounting to some £1,133,000 over the next seventeen years. Even so, more had still to be met, and the grant was raised to £900,000 in 1777, £50,000 a year being reserved for that purpose. But the remaining £850,000 was still not enough. Another £95,000 of debt had to be paid off in the next eight years, and in 1786 the Commons were faced with a further call for £210,000. The economies of Economical Reform had failed to meet the demands, and these constant *ad hoc* interventions by Parliament were clearly unsatisfactory.

Much of the trouble, as so often, lay in a lack of information. Driven by political pressures, Burke had moved without really knowing the facts. He had no proper estimate of future, or even full statements of current, expenditure; and his allocation of funds to the various charges simply failed to meet the needs. Nor was his plan for paying off the arrears a practical proposition; he hoped to redeem the exchequer bills issued for the purpose out of revenue saved on the places abolished, but the savings proved inadequate and the bills could not be fully met. Ignorance and inexperience vitiated an effort that was in any case beset by problems. For whatever the Act's shortcomings, Burke was caught in one of the great dilemmas of the age. How was he – how was anyone – to reduce administrative costs at a time when administration was slowly expanding? Some fees might be abolished, some places suppressed. But then salaries must be increased, and some departments had quite genuinely to be enlarged. Unless there was to be a fundamental overhaul of offices, which was highly unlikely, the creeping demands of government would more than balance any savings that might be made. Even if some sections of the Civil List could still reasonably be pared, the real need was to regulate the proportions on a knowledgeable basis, and to ensure a better system of estimate and review.

Pitt had already witnessed a major effort to achieve further savings. It was part of his education under Shelburne, and it had had mixed results. The Civil List comprised many heads of expenditure; but it could be divided broadly into three classes, those of the civil Government departments and legal offices, non-departmental payments – pensions and bounties, and home and foreign secret service –, and the

1. *P.R.*, II, 21–2. And see p. 52 above.
2. See p. 90 above.
3. The Rt Hon. George Rose, *Considerations on the Debt of the Civil List* (1802), 31.

royal properties and households. Shelburne had begun inquiries over almost the whole field; but his most immediate plans centred on the Court and the pensions list, on which he proposed to save some £50,000 a year. He soon had a comprehensive scheme, which of course soon ran into trouble, and despite some real successes the immediate savings were not as great as he had hoped. His final estimate of £40,000 a year was decidedly optimistic, and with the advent of the Coalition the pressure soon dropped.[1] Pitt was circumspect in his turn, after the recent agitation. The charges of the privy purse settled broadly on the basis which Shelburne had left, and there was little further alteration in the numbers of the Court. The Royal Family cost the Civil List rather more in the course of the eighties, as the royal children grew up.[2] But as long as earlier items remained more or less steady, and pensions were not allowed to rise, the Minister, while watchful, seems to have been content.

Pitt therefore did not achieve much in the way of savings. But he brought the expenses more directly under Parliamentary control. The opportunity came in 1786–7. At the end of March 1786, George III was forced once more to approach his faithful Commons, who agreed to pay off the outstanding debt, leaving the annual grant free of past encumbrances. Pitt seized the chance to secure the detailed return of classes of payment which Burke – and Shelburne – had lacked; and he set on foot a statutory inquiry into the management of most of the Crown revenues.[3] Armed with these facts and prospects, he moved decisively in the following year. The Consolidation Act included the Civil List in its comprehensive scheme. The expenses were assigned second priority in the order of annual payments; the record of income became a subdivision of the consolidated accounts.[4] Certain items were still reserved for the Crown's private use and management. But Parliament now had the detailed information on which to honour its direct responsibility for meeting the annual costs of the Civil List. No more 'extraordinary' grants were made, and the charges until 1793 settled at an average of rather more than £900,000 a year.[5]

This passage, one might say, was characteristic of Pitt. He did not raise a constitutional issue, as had been done a few years before: the

1. For the figures, see Mitchell & Deane, op. cit., ch. XIV, table 2; for Shelburne's effort, Norris, *Shelburne and Reform*, ch. X, to which George Rose's *Observations Respecting the Public Expenditure, and the Influence of the Crown* is a useful appendix. There is material on the subject in Pitt's papers, P.R.O. 30/8/229.

2. The Prince of Wales's debts were a separate matter.

3. Pp. 292–3 above.

4. See p. 272 above.

5. The exact figure is difficult to determine, for the List was burdened each year with extra sums for miscellaneous services, not all properly attributable to it, which were to be repaid in the following session. The average annual net cost including all such charges, from 1786 to 1792 inclusive, was £1,125,000, the net cost minus the charges £907,000. Rose (*Considerations on the Debt of the Civil List*, 39) reckoned the true average cost for this period at £922,000 a year.

Crown's prerogative and influence were not mentioned, its revenues and payments were not openly attacked. Shelburne's pioneering reorganisation was gently given up. But something was quietly accomplished that had not proved possible before; and almost incidentally, as a by-product of something else. Pitt could not have completed this transfer of responsibility without his predecessors' efforts; he could scarcely have succeeded so easily had the atmosphere not changed. But it was still remarkable that, when he moved, not a dog was heard to bark. There is no reference to the subject in the King's correspondence, there were no cries of joy or protest in Parliament itself. Yet the last great sector of expenditure had been brought within the range of the Commons' detailed control, and the Treasury was extending its authority in a direction which would earlier have roused bitter debate.

'The people, who granted that revenue', had thus 'resumed' it.[1] But the total cost was not reduced. Pitt effected some economies, but he was obliged to spend more elsewhere. He realised one ambition which he had earlier voiced: the supply of Government stationery was centred in a new Stationery Office. Pitt had told the Commons in 1783 that perhaps £40,000 a year was being wasted here, and he already had a plan in his possession, sent through Mahon by a certain Mr Woodmason, for setting up a single department for supervision and supply.[2] In 1786 he felt free to act, and H.M. Stationery Office began its life under the Treasury. The full benefit could not be reaped at once. The new arrangements did not supersede long-term contracts already made – the Home and Foreign Offices, for instance, did not reorganise their demands until the later nineties – and there were perquisites and commissions (such as old Horace Walpole's for stationery to the Exchequer) which did not lapse until the beneficiaries died. But the pressure was gradually felt, the savings steadily took effect, and a whole crop of abuses began to wither away.

In some other directions, Pitt was forced to expand. The Board of Control for India was a fresh responsibility, and other extra charges fell on the Civil List after the cuts of the past few years. Some of the reductions had in fact been ill conceived, and had to be clarified or amended; and one important department, entirely suppressed, had to be brought to life again. The Board of Trade, abolished in 1782, left a gap which was further enlarged by the abolition of the Secretaryship of State for America. The end of the war, the terms of peace themselves, demanded an urgent review of commercial policy; the Home Office, to

1. P. 305 above.
2. See p. 92 above for Pitt's statement. Woodmason's scheme, and Mahon's covering letter stating that it was received on 5 January 1783, are in P.R.O. 30/8/231. Woodmason seems to have been a leading private stationer (*The Gentleman's Magazine*, LII (1782), 151).

which the Board of Trade's staff had been transferred, seemed unlikely to provide the necessary attention; and in March 1784 Pitt established a new Committee of Trade and Plantations, primarily to conduct the inquiries, already under way, into the future of the West Indian and American trade. In order perhaps to avoid Parliamentary debate, and certainly to preserve economy, the new body was formed as a standing Committee of Council and not as a department. Its members could thus be unpaid as such, and the small staff simply transferred from the charge of the Home Office to the Privy Council. But in 1786 it was reconstituted to meet the growing needs of imperial business and commercial negotiations with foreign powers. The membership was changed, a slightly more expensive and larger staff was placed on its books, and the Committee was given more commodious quarters in the Old Treasury Building, which it proceeded at once, very sensibly, to furnish from the firm of Haig and Chippendale.

The officials of the Committee of Trade were recompensed partly by fees, as those of the old Board had been. They thereby cost Government less than they might otherwise have done. But this of course was only part of the picture; fees led to abuses and so to expense, and Pitt remained committed in principle to abolition. In the winter of 1784–5 he revived his attempt to inquire into the system in some of the principal departments. The bill passed both Houses – the Lords this time did not obstruct – and a Commission of Enquiry into Fees in the Public Offices was set up at the end of August 1785.[1] It was also empowered 'to examine into any abuses which may exist'. But its form differed significantly from that proposed earlier. In 1783, Pitt had tried to enlist the aid of the Commissioners for Examining the Public Accounts, a body responsible to the Commons whose reports were published by the House. But the new Commission was established by Order in Council; it was responsible to the King in Council, and its findings were not made known.[2] This change of constitution undoubtedly contributed to the fate of its reports, which had no effect on the civil departments and remained unpublished for some twenty years.[3] The subjects for inquiry outside the armed forces were the Secretaries of State, the Treasury, and the Post Office. The report on the first contained recommendations which were completely ignored, that on the second had nothing to say, and the report on the Post Office saw the end of the Commission.[4] The Secretaries of State in fact did not comment on the findings until 1794, and no action was considered until a Commons' committee investigated

1. The Act was 25 Geo. III, c. 10. See pp. 92–3 above for Pitt's earlier attempt.
2. One of the Commissioners is reported as having told the Commons that the Commission's responsibility lay to the Treasury (Francis Baring, 28 May 1787; *P.R.*, XXII (1787), 407). This was formally incorrect.
3. They eventually appeared in *House of Commons Accounts and Papers* (1806), VII. There was a Parliamentary request for publication in 1793, but without result (*H.C.J.*, 48, 876).
4. For the last two reports, see pp. 299 and 296 above.

again three years later.[1] Such a passive response would have been most unlikely had the reports been laid on the table of the House. Shelburne always said that effective publicity offered the only real hope of reform. The failure of Pitt's method suggests that he was not far wrong.

But was it in fact a failure? How much action did the Minister really want? His choice of means might be held to suggest that he was paying lip-service to an old ideal. It is hard to say. Pitt acted as he did at least partly because the Commissioners for Examining were still engaged on other inquiries,[2] and he may well have preferred a small official expert body to a further, untried Parliamentary commission.[3] But he was well aware that its task might prove difficult: 'success depended undoubtedly upon a willing government'.[4] The result soon showed what could happen when a department was unwilling. For whatever Pitt's feelings towards his inquiry – and one might perhaps give him the benefit of the doubt – or about the contents of the reports themselves, the Secretaries of State's inaction was symptomatic of their constitutional independence. The Home Office and the Foreign Office, indeed, were very much powers in their own right. The eighteenth century had been 'the golden age for the Secretaries of State',[5] and their position was scarcely diminished when their respective duties were more closely defined. North and Fox, as Home and Foreign Secretaries, were the leaders of Portland's Ministry in 1783, and almost twenty years later Addington offered to share power with Pitt as Secretaries of State, a peer being placed at the Treasury. The Secretaries' powers remained far-ranging; they were still the maids of all work for a Government, the main agents and reporters of its policy – Pitt's Foreign Secretaries probably called more Cabinet meetings before the war than any other Minister, including Pitt himself[6] –, and a traditional link with the Crown. The bulk of their correspondence, indeed, was greater with the King than with the Treasury: the Home Office papers in particular, from 1782 to 1793, contain 23 volumes of letters to George III compared with twelve to that department. Most of this material was routine – concerned with appointments and protocol in the first case, with salaries and allowances in the second. But such routine was very important; it was the basis of

1. See the Sixteenth Report of the Finance Committee of 1797 (*Reports from Committees*, XII, particularly 297–8). Baring remarked that the Commissioners themselves 'were never spoken to, or consulted, with regard to their reports, except in the case of Mr. Palmer' ('Sir Francis Baring . . . Memoranda, 1782–1790'; transcripts in Northbrook Mss). He was referring to the period after the reports were completed.

2. See his statement in the Commons on 17 February 1785 (*P.R.*, XVII, 191).

3. I think there is a hint of this in *P.R.*, XXII, 408. For the members, see p. 296 above.

4. Francis Baring to Lansdowne, reporting a conversation with Pitt, 16 April 1785 (Lansdowne Mss, Bowood).

5. Mark A. Thomson, *The Secretaries of State 1681 to 1782* (1932), 162.

6. The word 'probably' is necessary here, for information is scattered and tenuous. But one certainly gains this impression.

other relations, it was defined by past developments, and it affected those that might be evolved. King, Secretaries of State and First Lord of the Treasury were still dancing their old quadrille, and there were many years yet to go before the dance was no longer performed.

The relative importance of these Ministers was in fact a matter of personality and political fortune, shaping rather than being shaped by the system itself. A weak First Lord of the Treasury might depend on the Secretaries, a strong First Lord might control or ignore them, there might be a close or an uneasy combination, whether or not the King intervened. This indeed could be seen by the situation which developed soon after Pitt's death, and in the views which continued to be expressed by his successors. Fox's relations then with Grenville, the chaos of Portland's second Ministry, the comments of Lord Holland on the one hand and Lord Liverpool on the other, suggest a state of affairs not very different from that obtaining before he took office, and showed how personal the successes and failures of a First Minister could be. But Pitt's own experience also reflected the fact. Political chance had provided him with two weak Secretaries at the outset,[1] and he continued with them until the turn of the decade. The results were soon apparent: Pitt directed policy himself, he drafted most of the important despatches, he sometimes took over a question entirely when his interest was roused. His pre-eminence was reflected in the critical matter of their more important appointments, in which the First Lord of the Treasury had long had an undefined influence. Sydney offered to share the Home Secretary's patronage at the start,[2] and Pitt often entered into diplomatic appointments whether or not they were made on political grounds.[3] His wishes might even be observed within the Foreign Office itself – his friend Dudley Ryder went there briefly as an Under-Secretary against Carmarthen's inclination, and Pitt won a battle with Carmarthen on the debatable ground of an appointment in the Secret Office of the Post Office.[4] But this personal activity, because it was personal, could always be reduced or reversed, and when Sydney and Carmarthen disappeared a change could be observed. Their successors, Dundas and Grenville, supplied what Pitt had hitherto lacked – a more efficient conduct of business and a more co-operative service. But their departmental powers were thereby fortified, and Grenville in particular

1. See pp. 184–5 above.

2. Stanhope, I, 228–9.

3. The most notable examples of Pitt's influence here were perhaps in the appointment of Harris to The Hague, of William Eden to Versailles and then Madrid and then The Hague, and of Joseph Ewart to Berlin. Domestic politics entered into the first two cases, but not the third.

4. Which fell officially, in the last resort, within the Treasury's gift. But the Secret Office served the Secretaries of State (see p. 294 above), and the Foreign Secretary in particular was accustomed to have a say in its affairs. For Carmarthen's first reaction to Ryder's appointment, see his letter to Pitt of 27 July 1789, in P.R.O. 30/8/151.

became very much master in his own house. The system worked smoothly on these lines, because Dundas was loyal and Grenville was prepared to co-operate in the stress of war. But it was a highly personal system, and it could easily change again. A First Lord of the Treasury – a First Minister – might dominate or bypass ineffectual colleagues, or he might work closely with efficient men. But he could not rely on his powers as First Lord of the Treasury, or First Minister, to secure the arrangements which he must win for himself.

This applied perhaps above all to any question of reform. Such efforts as were made from the Treasury's corner had no effect before the war. They were not indeed very vigorous; the emphasis fell mainly, as one might expect, on curbing expense. A 'new arrangement' for salaries in the Home Office, discussed in the autumn of 1792, was rejected presumably because of the cost, and Pitt persuaded Dundas and Grenville to take less in the way of fees. Whether the former received anything at once by way of compensation seems doubtful – he acquired a fresh salary in 1793 as President of the Board of Control for India; the latter was given an Auditorship of the Exchequer in lieu.[1] Establishments scarcely grew, the pattern of salaries and fees remained otherwise unchanged. But where purely administrative innovations were suggested they fell on deaf ears. Some improvements took place in the conduct of business; but they came strictly from the departments, and recommendations from the Commission of Enquiry were disregarded until the Home Office was reorganised under pressure of war. Here as elsewhere, indeed, war caused larger changes than had proved possible in a decade of peacetime reform. Meanwhile Pitt worked within a system which might make his office *primus inter pares*, but which placed compelling limits on the administrative results.

The average cost of civil government was just over £1½ million a year from 1784 to 1792. The armed forces in that period never cost less than £4 million a year.[2] The army, the navy and the ordnance together were far the greatest charge on Government. Their departments were also largely immune from central Ministerial control.

This was very noticeable in the sphere of finance itself. We have seen the restricted view which the Commissioners for Auditing the Public Accounts took of their work.[3] There was a similar weakness of super-

1. For the plan for the Home Office, see a paper of 10 September 1792 in P.R.O. 30/8/282; for the voluntary reduction in the Secretaries of State's fees, Sixteenth Report of the Finance Committee of 1797, Appendices E1–3 (*Reports from Committees* XII, 321–22), H.M.C., *Dropmore*, II, 512–13 for Grenville, and Dundas to Pitt (? February 1793) in John Rylands Library, Manchester, English Ms 907 (summarised in J. Holland Rose, *William Pitt and the Great War* (1911), 124–5).

2. Mitchell & Deane, op. cit., ch. XIV, table 2. The lowest figure for the armed forces was £4,178,000, in 1787; the highest for civil government, £1,886,000, in 1791 (both to the nearest thousand pounds).

3. P. 302 above.

vision at an earlier stage. The Service departments apart from the Ordnance (itself only partially affected) presented their annual estimates to Parliament without any check from the Treasury, and the amounts went through virtually unchallenged. Occasionally there was no alteration at all; more often the figures were scaled down in rough and ready fashion to the nearest round figure, as a notional mark of the Commons' authority. Nor, despite a crop of reports from reforming commissions, were the processes of departmental accounting modified by the Treasury in any way. The various authorities retained their old powers, and made their calculations largely on the old lines: the navy, for instance, founded its figures on an estimated cost per man per month which had not changed materially since the days of Cromwell. Pitt's reform of the central accounts gave a much clearer picture of total income and expenditure. It did not affect the bases of calculation by the armed forces themselves.

The only alteration, indeed, came from within a department – perhaps rather surprisingly from the Ordnance Office, long a byword for inefficiency. But the reforming Duke of Richmond had been at work there since the time of Rockingham and Shelburne, when he had settled the establishment and substituted salaries for fees.[1] He had also begun to tighten his control over the estimates, a process he now continued as far as he could. Of course he did not do all he wanted; but there were noticeable results. Departmental debt carried less discount, credit was improved, there was no need for 'extraordinary' grants from 1786 to 1788. This was one facet of an activity which lasted at least until the later eighties, when Richmond was losing heart, and which included improvements in gunpowder and weapons, the founding of a Corps of Royal Artificers (the forerunners of the Royal Engineers), and an inquiry into the security of the dockyards and defence against invasion.[2] But all this activity was inspired entirely from the department itself. Although Pitt and the Government became involved in the plan for fortifying the dockyards, they did so at Richmond's prompting and left the inquiry to him.

Richmond was able to act as he did because his unusual zeal was matched by unusual opportunities. There was an exceptional concentration of powers in the Master General of the Ordnance. Nothing need be said of the army in this period, because it was organised on 'a principle of multiple fission',[3] and there was no unduly energetic Minister or official. The most likely cause of explosion was always when both ingredients were present: when an active reformer was harboured

1. See p. 91 above.

2. And also the encouragement of surveying, though until 1791 Richmond had to act here in association with the King in their private capacities. The Trigonometrical Survey, which became the Ordnance Survey, started life on a shoestring in that year.

3. Richard Glover, *Peninsular Preparation, The Reform of the British Army, 1795–1809* (1963), 15. And see pp. 170–1 above.

in a system in which the responsibilities were dispersed. This was the case in the navy, where by the turn of the decade the consequences had embroiled the whole department and deeply engaged Pitt himself.

The navy of course held a special place in the affections of the propertied classes. As the greatest British soldier of the age later put it, the fleet was 'the characteristic and constitutional force of Britain'.[1] Not only was it the first line of defence, the bulwark of the state; it was also a symbol and guarantee of freedom. The navy stood for everything that a standing army did not. No sailors were quartered on the country, none were readily available to impose the will of the Crown; only the press gang might violate individual liberty. 'Rule Britannia', ran the song, 'Britons never, never, never shall be slaves'; and the sentiment echoed defiance to domestic as well as foreign tyranny. Pitt himself shared the instinctive concern in 'the sea affair'. He had seen something of the fleet in his younger brother's day, his early letters home from London were full of its doings, and when he came to office he did his best to support it. The navy was the greatest exception to his first plans for retrenchment. He naturally looked to a large cut in spending at the end of the war, and much of his effort thereafter was devoted to keeping down the costs. But economy was not designed at the expense of efficiency, and by the normal peacetime standards Pitt did not skimp the fleet. He raised the peacetime establishment in 1784 from 15,000 to 18,000 men, and in the same difficult year earmarked £2,400,000 for shipbuilding; and in 1788, after an abortive attempt to achieve a mutual reduction with the French, he again increased the numbers by a further 2,000 men. Thereafter the navy had to be brought intermittently onto something like a war footing; and when Pitt finally cut expenditure, in the lull of 1792, it was in reaction from a recent exceptional rise in costs.

The results were impressive by the standards of the day. Thirty-three ships of the line were built between 1783 and 1790, and when war threatened in the latter year a force of 93 sail was mobilised. Pitt took a detailed interest in what was going on. 'It was no uncommon thing', recalled an officer who spoke of what he had heard, 'for Mr. Pitt to visit the Navy Office to discuss naval matters with the Comptroller, and to see the returns made from the yards of the progress in building and repairing the ships of the line; he also desired to have a periodical statement from the Comptroller of the state of the fleet, wisely holding that officer responsible personally to him, without any regard to the Board'.[2] Pitt's own papers and correspondence bear out this picture.

1. Sir Arthur Wellesley in a Commons' debate of 3 June 1808 (*Cobbett's Parliamentary Debates* . . ., XI (1808), 814).
2. *Letters and Papers of Admiral of the Fleet Sir Thos. Byam Martin G.C.B.,* ed. Sir Richard Vesey Hamilton, III (1901), 381. Byam Martin's father had been resident Commissioner at Portsmouth from 1780 to 1790, and Comptroller of the Navy from 1790 to 1794.

Such supervision from the leader of a Ministry was very rare in peace.

It was largely aided, perhaps made possible, by a special situation in the Navy Office itself. For the Comptroller in question was Sir Charles Middleton, later Lord Barham, one of the greatest administrators the navy has ever had. He had occupied the post since 1778, and Pitt greatly admired his abilities. As often when a good man was available, the Minister made the most of the fact; as sometimes happened in such cases, he used him to try to short-circuit the department. There is indeed a marked similarity between Pitt's relations with Middleton and his relations with Palmer at the Post Office. There is also some resemblance between the respective results.

For Middleton, like Palmer and with greater weight and knowledge, was fighting for a programme of far-reaching reform. The state of the navy in point of fact can be too easily condemned. The business drew on hard experience, there were often competent men at work, somehow or other they managed to cope with a century of maritime expansion. But their task, inherently difficult, grew more so as its scale increased, and the powers of Government were eroded by the spread of private conventions and rights. Compared with most other departments, the naval authorities were not inefficient: they may well have been generally more efficient than most. But the demands on them were higher, the results of failure more obvious, and their operations were liable to involve far greater expense. The recent war had roused violent criticism, and led to a series of inquiries into an organisation which broadly speaking had changed little since the days of Pepys. The point of departure was financial – 'the Navy being the most popular as well as the most expensive Department is that which requires the greatest Attention'[1] – and the findings were contained largely in financial reports. The Commons' Finance Committees of 1782 and 1786, the Commissioners for Examining the Public Accounts, the Commissioners for Enquiring into Fees in the Public Offices, were all involved in their various ways. Middleton's proposals thus developed against a background of widespread conern, which might seem to have promised an unusually hopeful prospect of success.

But the forces of resistance of course were strong. Authority was diffused, there were well entrenched vested interests, and the navy's very popularity was a two-edged weapon in the amount of attention its affairs aroused. Middleton's greatest difficulty perhaps lay in the degree of support he could expect from his First Lord. For while that potentate's powers might be far from complete within the naval departments in practice, they were theoretically very great, and a determined Comptroller, as chairman of the Navy Board, working with a determined First Lord of the Admiralty would obviously be a highly formi-

1. Lord Mulgrave to Pitt, 'Observations upon the Naval Establishments in Peace', endorsed 1785 (P.R.O. 30/8/250). Mulgrave was joint Paymaster General with Grenville, and had served in the navy for most of his life.

dable combination. The trouble was that two such men, each aware of his rights, were quite as likely to fight each other as to combine; on the other hand, without a strong First Lord a strong Comptroller might not succeed. Middleton, like most reformers, was not easy to get on with: he had irritated Sandwich, he thought little of Keppel, and now he failed to atttact Howe. 'Black Dick' indeed was not the man to unbend to a subordinate, an officer of the Navy Board who held only captain's rank. Their relations were strained from the start, and they later became really bad, when Howe – quite correctly, by the precedents – refused to sanction Middleton's promotion to Rear Admiral while remaining Comptroller.

This contretemps proved important, for it lay at the centre of a dispute which was soon to lead to Howe's disappearance. The event caused few regrets, for the Admiral held aloof from the rest of the Cabinet, he was at odds with Richmond and Dundas, and on distant terms with Pitt himself. There had long been dissatisfaction in the inner circle at the difficulty of 'connecting the department . . . with the rest of the Administration, which has never yet been the case under Pitt's Government, even in the smallest degree'.[1] The Admiralty's screen in Whitehall, which had originally been built to keep out sailors demanding their pay, might rather have seemed to Howe's Ministerial colleagues designed to shelter him from them. But the argument over promotions gave Pitt his chance. Middleton's case was one of a number which roused intense feeling in the fleet – always easy enough, as the quarrels of recent years had shown –, and early in 1788 the affair sparked off a major Parliamentary row. As usual on such occasions, all sorts of interests were involved, and at one point the Ministry, supporting Howe, felt itself endangered. This was not good enough: the First Lord was unpopular in the Commons, Pitt would not be sorry to see him go, and the Minister was moreover very anxious to give Middleton his promotion. Howe resigned in July, and Pitt had already chosen a successor. He 'must be a landsman' – the first since Sandwich – 'as there is no seaman who is altogether fit'.[2] He must also be a landsman who would allow Pitt greater access to the Board. An easy answer lay to hand: the new First Lord was Pitt's brother Chatham. 'To those who know him', wrote Grenville defensively, 'there can be no doubt that his abilities are equal to the undertaking'. But those who did not might be reassured by the fact that he would be given 'Sir Charles Middleton and Hood for assistants'.[3]

1. Grenville to Buckingham, 16 May 1788 (Buckingham, I, 385).
2. Pitt to Wilberforce, 28 June 1788 (*Private Papers of Wilberforce*, 22).
3. Buckingham, I, 385. Middleton continuing (as a Rear Admiral) as Comptroller, Hood joining the Admiralty Board.
Pitt was a little anxious about the appointment, in case it looked 'too much like Monopoly' (to Hester Countess of Chatham, 19 June 1788; Stanhope I, 376). But he wanted someone who would co-operate, and he was not prepared to say that his brother could not do the job. Chatham indeed was no fool: his main drawback proved

The changes came at an important time, for Middleton's reforms had just been presented. They appeared under the aegis – one might say in the guise – of reports from the Commission of Enquiry into Fees. Moving by seniority of departments, the Commissioners turned to the navy in the summer of 1786, after they had tackled the Treasury and the Secretaries of State. Two years and seven reports later their investigation was complete. They had covered the whole field, from the Admiralty to the dockyards and the victualling depots. The recommendations were largely those of Middleton himself. Salaries should replace fees – a return to the days of William III and Anne –, premiums should not be paid on appointments, vacancies should be filled by seniority subject to proper qualifications. The Navy Board should be enlarged, and divided for day to day work into three committees. Dockyard regulations and payments should be tightened up – the abuses were listed in proliferating detail. All establishments and their duties were examined afresh. The reports amounted to a comprehensive overhaul of the civil organisation.

Middleton knew very well that the findings would be unpopular. He counted on Pitt and Chatham to bring about results. He had some grounds for doing so, from the nature of the new appointment and from the Minister's interest, publicly expressed. Had not Pitt told the Commons a year before that no one who knew the Navy Office 'would wish that its examination and reform should be delayed a single hour'?[1] But the hopes were destined to be disappointed. The Commission's reports had to be taken together – a point which Middleton himself was inclined to dispute – and the last appeared on the eve of the summer recess. It was never the best time of year for business, and on this occasion Pitt was preoccupied with foreign affairs. The Comptroller had to wait until the autumn before he could gain a proper hearing; he was then assured – at least he received the impression – that orders would soon be given to carry out the reforms. But this required the prior instructions of the Privy Council, to which the reports were addressed,[2] and when George III fell ill at the end of October the business had to be postponed. In March 1789, when the Regency crisis was over, Middleton returned to the charge. He was told that although the King was much better, he should not be troubled yet with a question on which he 'would probably wish to be fully apprised'. Nor had the Council itself 'in the unsettled state of things' examined the reports, and there would not be much opportunity while Parliament was in session.[3]

to be lethargy. As a young man he was better than Pitt at chess (*The Works of Jeremy Bentham*, ed. John Bowring, X (1843), 105), and according to George III he wrote in a 'clearer and better' style (*The Farington Diary by Joseph Farington R.A.*, ed. James Greig, I (1922), 20).

1. Speech of 28 May 1787 (*P.R.*, XXII, 409).
2. See p. 308 above.
3. Chatham to Middleton, 7 March 1789 (*Letters and Papers of Charles, Lord Barham . . . 1758–1813*, ed. Sir John Knox Laughton, II (1910), 319).

The Comptroller now feared the worst. He contemplated, but did not send, a memorial to the King; he hung on for another year; and in March 1790 he resigned.

The resignation did not lead to a break with Pitt and Chatham. Middleton paid tribute to Pitt's support, and he acted as unofficial naval adviser to the brothers over the next four years. He could not in fact really bear to lose the ear of Ministers, whoever they might be – when Pitt seemed likely to be ousted in the Regency crisis, he flirted with Sandwich. But he recognised that he could no longer expect to bring them up to the scratch. It is not clear exactly why the naval reforms were eventually laid aside – Middleton himself talked of 'causes or motives unaccountable by him'.[1] But the short answer would seem to be that the favourable moment was sacrificed through mischance, and that by the time the political crisis was over Pitt had lost his sense of urgency. The reasons given for delay were perfectly good, as far as they went. Priorities were always all-important when the machinery of government was so easily strained, and the priority of the naval reforms had slipped as the months went by. Pitt was no longer ready, in the press of new affairs, to make an immediate issue of the business. Middleton may have persuaded him once; he could not do so twice. There would certainly have been strong opposition to overcome, within the department and in Parliament, and the Minister can scarcely have wished to risk a revival of the passions displayed in the recent debates – the less so as fresh commitments claimed the Commons' time.[2] If Chatham had thrown his weight behind Middleton – if Chatham had had more weight – Pitt might still perhaps have decided to go ahead. As it was, he contented himself with bringing the Admiralty more closely under his review. The shelving of the naval reforms strengthens the familiar impression that it was generally easier to exploit than to alter a given state of affairs.

IV

This of course is usually the case. It was the case then in an unusual degree. Bearing that in mind, what effects may we say that Pitt had on the structure of peacetime government? Men at the time would have put the question with an emphasis different from our own. What interested them above all else was the effect on the influence of the Crown; how far had a Minister strengthened or weakened the sinews of political power? Few financial or adminsitrative measures could be divorced from this context. '. . . A nation', ran a typical passage on the National Debt, 'is not only heavily burdened, to defray the interest of

1. Loc. cit., 349.
2. It is true that most of the regulations could have been put into effect without consulting Parliament. But the funding or removal of fees for salaries would have meant legislation, and so debate.

its debts, but is also obliged to maintain a number of officers, to collect such branches of the revenue, as are appropriated to that purpose . . . And in a limited monarchy such a circumstance has a tendency to produce, very important alterations in the nature of its Government'.[1] George Rose struck the same note almost a generation later. '. . . *The Influence of the Crown*', he wrote in his pamphlet of that title, summarising Pitt's achievements at the Treasury, 'and the *Public Expenditure;* the last indeed as important with reference to the former, as from its own substantial effects'.[2]

Judged by this contemporary test, Pitt did a great deal in the course of his career, on foundations laid, largely by himself, during the pre-war period. Concise figures are hard to come by for that decade. Pretyman claimed a net reduction of 441 revenue places between December 1783 and February 1793, and he must almost certainly have taken his calculations from Rose, who was an expert guide.[3] But such a saving, though important, was not the whole answer. Rose himself discussed other forms of 'imperceptible influence' – Government contracts, Government loans, leases of Crown lands, home secret service funds, methods of accounting for public money. In most of these cases, the treatment developed during these years. Pitt dealt with Government contracts most conspicuously after the start of the war, and he could do little about the Crown lands in peacetime, for the final report had not yet been received. But he held home secret service issues to the level fixed by Burke's Civil List Act, he dealt a final blow at the means of influence implicit in tendering for loans, and his various measures for the public accounts subjected the accountants to stricter review. Many old loopholes were closed, many old rights withered away, as one conception of the King's service was slowly replaced by another.

The process took a long time, the best part of two generations, from the later stages of the American War to the 1830s and '40s. Pitt's measures and attitude were a very important contribution, and the attitude was perhaps as important as the measures themselves. For Pitt, as has already been suggested, does not seem to have shared in a marked degree the primary concern of so many politicians at the time that he

1. Sir John Sinclair, *History of the Public Revenue of the British Empire,* I, 369. First published in 1785.

2. *Observations Respecting the Public Expenditure and the Influence of the Crown,* 2. Published in 1810.

3. Tomline, III, 538, 527. He stated that the places were 'abolished'. But he must have meant a *net* reduction, for at least 900 offices were suppressed in that time (largely in the Excise, see p. 292 above) as against several hundred newly established by redistribution and expansion of work.

The whole passage follows Rose's treatment in his pamphlet (n2 above), Pretyman submitted the draft of his book to Rose, and there are some calculations in the latter's papers which look as if they might have been made for that purpose (National Library of Scotland Ms 3796, f. 194). But Rose's own published figures, in his pamphlet and elsewhere, are so assembled that this result cannot be extracted from them.

entered politics.[1] He was not moved chiefly by a desire to attack or defend the powers of the Crown as generally understood. Indeed, if he took away with the one hand he gave, to a lesser extent, with the other. Much corruption was suppressed; but the fountain of honour played as freely as usual – the Garter establishment was enlarged in 1786, and new peerages were created on an unprecedented scale.[2] The gentler inducements of social recognition did partial duty for a loss of places and profit, and in all this activity the monarch had his accustomed part to play. Pitt did not challenge the royal prerogative, or the fact that he was the King's Minister. His measures were influenced much more directly by what he took to be the facts of the case, and his methods could vary from case to case with what he took to be the demands. The gradual overhaul of government affected the whole political world, and if the King was the greatest loser other interests lost as well. Pitt pursued his objects, as best he could, without any particular bias: he was trying to depersonalise the workings of the executive within the balanced constitution. But this was a process which was bound in time to affect the balance itself, more fundamentally perhaps than an immediate direct assault.

If he thought it necessary and feasible, Pitt could be high-handed. He was quite prepared to cut across the conventions, and take constitutional points in his stride. The summary withdrawal of their 'charter'd boast' from the owners of the Ferrintosh distilleries, the proposals for Palmer's place and payment in the Post Office, the handling of the purchase of tea from Voutes, the first plan for funding navy bills, the almost casual take-over of the Civil List, are all suggestive examples of this frame of mind. It was, one may say, a pragmatic approach, not unduly shackled as to detail by theory. But the pragmatic quality must be carefully defined. Pitt liked to take a problem on its merits: to study facts and objections, and produce an answer which allowed for them all. But the sort of problem he liked to take was one which allowed of such an answer; his vision was practical, but it was not the less real for that. It rested on detail. But detail satisfied him fully when it served a prepared end, above all a comprehensive plan. Given such an object he might well engage, strongly, enthusiastically, using his grasp of ways and means as ingenuity might suggest. Without such an object, he might be attracted by the detail for its own sake; but he was not inherently interested in patching, and it was difficult to predict how, or if, he would act.

Nor indeed can it always have been easy to predict what the object might be. It was likely to be one in which situations bulked larger than personalities. Pitt had a very shrewd idea of public opinion, so largely

1. See pp. 66, 136–7 above.
2. See ch. XIX below.

reflected in Parliamentary opinion, though of course he made his mistakes like anyone else. This indeed was one of his greatest strengths; he could never have achieved what he did without it. But he was wholly uninterested in personal problems outside his immediate circle, and in many ways unsuited to tackle problems which turned on specific personal concerns. He was very much a child of his time: he grasped its assumptions and reactions. But he was not in the least involved with the mass of men who produced them. His touch could be very sure in matters of policy which demanded an instinct for public attitudes. He was not so well equipped to carry policies which upset individual interests and rights.

Financial reform thus came more easily to him than administrative reform; and much of his administrative reform came in the wake of his financial measures. This is not to say that he failed to carry out a great deal. By the standards of the day – by any reasonable standard – he could claim much success. The whole revenue system, the largest sector of government, looked very different when he had finished with it; and he had laid his clear impress in peacetime on the general direction of affairs. Where he failed it was by the standards of a reforming ideal which suffered from a paucity of resources and often faced serious obstruction. For the difficulties of course were very real; and the hopes themselves must not be exaggerated. Pitt did not expect, and he did not try, to effect sweeping changes in the methods of government; nor was he trying generally to extend its range. It is pointless to look at his early efforts through the eyes of the next generation, or even through those of his own generation in a different setting. In Ireland, for instance, where the demands were greater and other institutions undeveloped, Government was beginning to enlarge its scope in ways still unknown in England itself. But there seemed less need for action here, the climate was hostile to fresh departures and, despite the recent loss of confidence, only intermittently in favour of reform. Nor could Pitt count on highly disciplined support. He might be willing to upset his opponents, but he must not upset the varied mass of his friends. He knew very well – Shelburne's example had taught him – that he could not overload uncommitted opinion with a continuous series of controversial schemes. And in any case he himself was selective in what he wanted to do. He had no intention of overtaxing a cumbrous machinery of government; he would have agreed with the reforming Commissioners for Examining the Public Accounts that 'to disturb, to confound, or to delay' were 'Effects not unfrequent, when Novelty of Form is introduced, and new Principles applied to an old Office'.[1] His object was to *improve*. When he pushed ahead, it was where he thought that a specific push was needed, and where and while he thought it could succeed. He seldom forced the pace; he gained valuable ground as a result. One may question his judgment quite often as to the strength of opposition; but

1. Third Report; *H.C.J.*, 38, 251.

he showed much skill in choosing his targets, and the strategy was sound enough.

One should not therefore enter a verdict without giving Pitt the benefit of reasonable doubt. We must always make due allowance for the forces of resistance, and the inescapable restrictions on his own speed of advance. For it was not only that the system of government was diffuse, and encrusted with vested rights; or that uncommitted opinion had to be taken into account. It was also that a Minister had slender resources, which must be carefully deployed. If one attack was mounted, another was likely to be postponed. Only so much – not very much – could be done at any one time. Effective staffs were very small; there were perhaps some 1100 administrative and clerical places in the central offices in London[1] – roughly the number of equivalent posts in the local government of Wolverhampton in the mid 1960s –, but many of the holders did little or nothing, some were absentees, and there were probably no more than thirty or forty active men in responsible 'efficient' non-Ministerial posts. Information was often hard to gather, habits could not be changed overnight. It was always easier to do business at some times of year than at others, and a minor check could easily lead to major delay. The form of the business itself was important; if it needed Parliamentary attention, it needed Parliamentary time. Too much legislation was never popular: a public bill was quite an event; it usually placed a heavy burden on Ministers and officials. Pitt stepped up the legislative pace beyond the rising level at which he found it. But there were stringent limits. The conduct of affairs became congested while Parliament was sitting, and a contentious or complicated subject might easily be shelved. And when Parliament was not sitting, there were well marked periods of relaxation when Ministers and officials, like the rest of Society, took themselves out of town. The first half of the summer recess in particular was a general holiday, in which routine was lethargically discharged and decisions were hard to obtain. '. . . During the Recess of Parlt.', William Eden once observed sardonically of the Foreign Office, 'a Secretary of State amuses Himself; & . . . during the Session he is occupied by Parlty. Business'.[2] The best time for administrative action was in the autumn and early winter; and even then the pace could be very slow. The British system was not inefficient compared with those elsewhere. But there were many interests to be consulted, and the forces of inertia were strong. The most active men of business led a life of ease by late Victorian standards. When the energetic Middleton could complain of having to work from ten to five each weekday at the height of the American War, and could

1. Meaning places other than those such as warehousemen, landwaiters, tide-waiters, boatmen etc. in the Customs and Excise and naval offices in London; die-casters, engravers etc. in the Stamp Office; office keepers, porters, messengers etc. in all departments; and places of any degree at Court. But this is a round estimate.
2. To Morton Eden, 6 November 1792 (B.M. Add. Ms 34445, ff. 195v–6).

take long week-ends off for a month while Parliament was sitting, how was the average official spending his time? The conduct of business was deliberate in that leisured age, and anything smacking of innovation required particular care. It was not therefore surprising that priorities were all-important. A reforming Minister must be a good butcher; but of measures rather than of men.

These were compelling facts. Pitt's temperament underlined them. He was both hopeful and wary, confident and uncertain. His natural optimism was tremendous – it seemed to many of his friends excessive. It faded only with his strength, and when it broke he died. But it survived for so long – it could survive – only at the cost of many of its objects. Pitt soon learned to face disappointment; but only by turning to something else. He was a born politician, a born Minister, and good Ministers are hopeful men. But they do not devote themselves in the highest office to crusading for a single cause. A Wilberforce, a Romilly, a Shaftesbury may have more specific achievements to his credit; but he does not aim to live in Downing Street, and he would not stay there long. Pitt's very need for hope and action meant that he abandoned many hopes. His very belief in his capacity, his assurance that he could solve a problem, often led to a sharp reaction when he found that he could not. The fact that he saw the force of objections so clearly – his great strength when he formed a policy – might be a source of weakness if the objections were not subdued. He could then become very indecisive, and his interest could easily drop. He was not as self-confident as he seemed in public, when things began to go wrong. The façade remained unbroken; he did not appear to lose his poise. But when his arguments were not accepted he might find it hard to regain his balance. If he was not sure of the answer, he could be easily influenced. If he could not satisfy himself, he was content to satisfy others. Dundas once warned him of 'the yielding nature of your temper where you are anxious upon a subject ' – meaning in the context uncertain –,[1] and one of Pitt's early acquaintances stressed the same point. '. . . His quickness of decision on the first view of a subject – his easiness in being led from it'; so wrote James Bland Burges, in some restrospective notes for a character sketch: 'His suppos'd obstinacy, and real subservience to the plans and views of those inferior to him . . . His want of judgement when to push on or when to relinquish doubtful matters'.[2] This was far from being the whole story, and Burges was not unprejudiced. But he had had some chance to judge, and there is evidence to support his remarks. Pitt could be vigorous and thorough; he could also be volatile or evasive. It depended on the state of his interest, itself very largely at the

1. To Pitt, 13 October 1794 (John Rylands Library, Manchester, English Ms 929).
2. Notes at the end of 'Concise Diary of Events by Sir James Burges, 1752–1806' (Bland Burges Mss, Bodleian Library). They were written possibly quite a long time after the latter date.

mercy of events. Of course he could not attend to everything; it is sometimes amazing that he coped with as much as he did. He had to take matters as they came up, and the more that came up the less the area of choice. But within that area it was hard to tell what the outcome would be, when Pitt was adjusting his strong instinct for perfection to his equally strong instinct for the possible.

This conflict may perhaps be seen particularly clearly in his efforts for administrative reform, which had perforce to be taken piecemeal as and when occasion offered. In finance he could see ahead and hope to proceed step by step; there was a grand design to be realised, and he moved with purpose and skill. It was in many ways far more difficult to see clearly through the maze of government, and the inevitable disappointments blunted Pitt's appetite for the task. He was not trying to achieve the impossible; he was content to work with the grain. But even this was far from easy, and as time went by he rather lost heart. One need not condemn him whenever he failed, or more often refused to act. Some of the refusals, and more occasional failures, may not in any case seem important. But they are not to be glossed over, for Pitt's disposition threw into relief the pressures existing here, and the inducements to submit.

Those who have learned how to work a machine are not always in any case the best men to strive for change. As Pitt grew more skilled in his use of the system, he tended in his difficulties to accept it. The precise nature of this skill may not be immediately apparent. Pitt's habits were by no means those one associates with a good administrator. The extreme disorder of his later years crept on him with time. But he was never methodical: very much the reverse. He stuffed papers away and forgot all about them – there were odd documents of the 1780s still lying about his room in 1806[1] – and he was notoriously bad at answering letters. 'You have had too much of my Correspondence', he wrote to Eliot, 'ever to wonder at its want of Punctuality'; 'Idleness', he admitted to his former tutor, Wilson, 'the old Enemy to our Correspondence'.[2] He never changed, and he remained unmoved by the vociferous complaints. His papers, and those of others, are full of angry and wounded remonstrances, from hopeful projectors of schemes, from grandees requiring honours and titles, from British envoys abroad and supporters at home. Neither the identity of the writer nor sometimes the occasion mattered much. The Duke of Dorset, while Ambassador in France, received no reply for over a year to his requests for a Garter; Lord

1. See the contents of P.R.O. 30/58/1, cleared from Downing Street on his death.
2. Pitt to Eliot, 22 August [1783] (Pretyman Ms 435:39); Pitt to Wilson, 3 September 1777 (Duke University, North Carolina, Mss). Writing to his friend Meeke in the late seventies, while the latter was abroad, he forgot to pay the postage, and the letters were opened by the authorities. (Stanhope Mss, 'Pitt Papers, Part i').

Abergavenny, despite his influence in Sussex, heard nothing at all when he asked for the Order of St Patrick; no answer could be extracted for at least four months – if it ever was – to a letter from the directors of the Dutch East India Company. 'Is it impossible', exclaimed the British Minister at The Hague, 'to move him who *speaks* so well to write one poor line . . .?'[1] Pitt had none of that scrupulous respect for order which was so marked, for instance, in George III.

He was more considerable than that; and his grasp showed in other ways. 'A statesman's most pregnant function lies in the choice and use of instruments'.[2] That judgment was itself made by an instrument – by a civil servant – and the emphasis perhaps reflects the fact. But it must be accounted a part of the truth, and Pitt triumphantly passes the test. He always had an eye for quality, and tried to secure it in the ranks of Government; the more so, no doubt, as the chances of politics gave him so mediocre a Cabinet for so long. He liked to work as far as possible with a few chosen associates and subordinates, with some more or less continuously, with others on a given case. Dundas and Grenville, and less closely Jenkinson at the Committee of Trade, among non-Cabinet Ministers; Nepean and Fraser at the Home Office and the Foreign Office; Orde for a few years in Ireland; Eden – accepted from the ranks of Opposition –, Harris, and (less fortunately) Ewart among the envoys; William Fawkener of the Committee of Trade and the Privy Council, and to a lesser extent George Chalmers; the trio of Frewin, Stiles and Thomas Irving at the Customs;[3] the unfortunate Palmer at the Post Office; Middleton at the Navy Board; Rose and the legal expert William Lowndes at the Treasury – these were among the small group of men, at the various levels, on whom Pitt called regularly or intermittently. He was quick to spot possible talent. He brought George Atwood to London probably because he had heard him lecture at Cambridge, and Bland Burges seems first to have attracted his notice – it was later withdrawn – as the result of a useful procedural suggestion in the course of the India crisis. Of course Pitt could choose or favour his instruments only within fairly narrow bounds; his views were often not decisive, he was sometimes not concerned in senior appointments, and he could not go too far in short-circuiting the established channels. But while he could not always bend the system very greatly to his liking, he grew very skilful at extracting something useful from it. He may have been influenced in his approach by his father's and Shelburne's examples – by their determination to learn the facts and make their wishes felt. But if he was less dynamic than Chatham had been, he was also less disruptive; and he avoided Shelburne's habit of irritating the

---

1. Sir James Harris to Carmarthen, 18 July 1786 (quoted in Alfred Cobban, *Ambassadors and Secret Agents* . . . (1954), 80).

2. Henry Taylor, *The Statesman* (1836), title of ch. III.

3. Curiously enough no outstanding official seems to have emerged at the Excise, that competent department.

departments. He did not try to impose clear-cut solutions formed largely in consultation with outside advisers. Of course, like all Ministers in that formative age of public associations, he had his links with sectional interests, and often sought unofficial opinion. He consulted expert advice when it came his way: the Scottish economist James Anderson, for instance, was asked to report on the northern fisheries, and Adam Smith himself, visiting London in 1787, is said to have been sent official papers for a study of a subject now unknown.[1] But such contacts bore little resemblance to the extensive private information service built up by Shelburne, and if Pitt picked and chose his official sources he did not bypass those that had something to say. In methods as in policy he worked with the grain. His object was to get the most out of the system, not to override it.

He often delved very fully into detail himself. Indeed, this was one of his distinctive strengths. He did not feel diffident about going out to seek the information: he visited the City to consult the tea merchants and the East India Company, he went down to the Navy Office to keep abreast of the shipbuilding programme. When he decided to take a hand he immersed himself in the subject, and those whom he consulted were soon made aware of the fact. One has only to read his correspondence with envoys abroad to see the results and sense the atmosphere. Their tone becomes brisker and more businesslike, interested and confident; they let themselves go, with a knowledge that they will be understood at the other end. And Pitt, for his part, soon becomes master of the material. When he seized on a question, his powers of assimilation were very great. He called for papers, he plunged into the problems, and when he emerged he was formidably well briefed. Nor was the answer likely to be decided by any marked preconceptions: Pitt took the facts and the varying views, and worried them until he had found a solution which very likely had not occurred to him before. The full play of his intellect was brought to bear, at that moment but not sooner, usually very fast and often in a spell of sustained hard work. The way in which he reached a decision about Warren Hastings, and about the nature of the sinking fund, are by no means exceptional examples of this approach.[2] He did not like to make up his mind until he had gone fully into the case; and that process could be exhaustive – he once shut himself up for ten days with Dundas to master the intricacies of the Bengal revenues. It was this rapid and thorough grasp by an unprejudiced intelligence that so deeply impressed his associates in complicated issues. And these major displays were rooted in an apprehension of the system which was not always so readily appreciated or so obviously deployed. Thus Burges catalogued Pitt's failings, as he saw

1. For the episode of Adam Smith, see George Wilson to Jeremy Bentham, 14 July 1787 (*Works of Jeremy Bentham*, X, 173–4). His visit to London and his meetings with Pitt are described in John Rae's *Life of Adam Smith* (1895).
2. See pp. 444–8 below and 261–7 above.

them, during these peacetime years. But he noted in the course of the list, and referring specifically to the same period, that 'His talents, quickness, temper and application well qualified him to have been a Prime Minister in the real sense of the word'.[1]

---

1. Notes in 'Concise Diary of Events' (Burges Mss, Bodleian Library). Another, better disposed though less knowledgeable, official stressed the same combination. 'What I have found remarkably agreeable', wrote John Fordyce, one of the Commissioners for Examining the Crown Lands, 'in any conversation I have had with Mr. Pitt on business is not only the extreme quickness of his apprehension but the undivided and unprejudiced attention which he gives' (to Henry Dundas, 1 September 1789; Rylands Eng. Ms 678). Fordyce himself, admittedly, may not have been entirely unprejudiced. For his earlier career in Scotland, which doubtless made him anxious to please Dundas, see Binney, op. cit., 62–4.

Part Four

CHAPTER XII

Colonies and Trade in the West:
The Role of the Atlantic

I

'Every one must perceive', said Pretyman's son in a posthumous tribute to his father's old friend, 'that the history of Mr. Pitt's administration would necessarily involve not only the history of this Country, but of all Europe, nay, of almost the whole globe, during a period the most eventful in the annals of the world'.[1] This indeed is one of a biographer's difficulties, and it is the more noticeable precisely when we turn to overseas affairs, even before the war. For while Pitt's handling of finance and administration – the latter particularly in its financial aspects – was very much his own, his role in the great complex of questions involving trade, empire and diplomacy was necessarily less personal and less continuously sustained. He was at their centre, and he sometimes took one of them into his own hands. But it is often easier in a sense to see the nature of his influence from other quarters than to trace it by reference specifically to himself.

Those quarters were the Home Office, the Foreign Office, the Board of Control, and the Committee of Trade. The Foreign Office had been in exclusive charge of correspondence with sovereign powers since its foundation in 1782. A year later, when the Secretaryship of the American Department was abolished, the Home Secretary's domestic duties were extended to all British territories other than India. This did not mean that he became solely responsible for correspondence and instructions: other authorities – not only the naval and military and ordnance departments, but also the Treasury, the Customs and the Post Office – likewise acted overseas as they acted at home; and the Privy Council, after the temporary disappearance of the old Board of Trade, retained its own formal but significant jurisdiction. The Home Secretary nevertheless was the leading authority in this sphere – as George III put it, he was the 'Secretary for the Home Department and British Settlements'.[2] In 1784, the Board of Control was charged, nominally

1. William Edward Pretyman Tomline, *A Speech on the Character of the Right Hon. William Pitt, Delivered in Trinity College Chapel, Cambridge, Dec. 17, 1806. Being Commemoration Day* (1806), 1.
2. To Shelburne, 1 July 1782 (*Correspondence of King George III*, VI, no. 3825). He was then discussing the possibility that Pitt would be given the post.

under his part chairmanship, with the direction of policy for India.[1] And in that same year the old Board of Trade and Plantations, abolished in 1782, was refounded as a committee of Council, initially to relieve the Home Office of colonial commercial investigations.

The Board of Control for India was an independent executive body, in no way beholden to the Secretaries of State. The Home Secretary indeed complained at the start that it was invading his patronage.[2] But its working head was not a Cabinet Minister, and neither for several years was the working head of the Committee of Trade. This last body, even after its expansion in 1786,[3] was in fact constitutionally subordinate; it could not negotiate or correspond with foreign powers, it had no executive authority in the colonies or Ireland, it sent no despatches, and its business was seldom submitted directly to the King. In theory, it remained a purely consultative organ. But in practice it soon became much more. A great weight of commercial and imperial policy was falling on the Boards of Control and Trade by the middle eighties, and the latter's views were fast acquiring executive and even legislative force.

There was some administrative precedent for this, for the Board of Trade before 1782 had acquired considerable powers. But the extent to which it now came about was mainly a result of personalities. Given more effective Secretaries of State – particularly a more effective Home Secretary – there might perhaps have been a somewhat different outcome. But Sydney and Carmarthen were unimpressive, Pitt did not rely on them, and neither they nor Camden, the Lord President of the Council to which the Committee was in theory responsible, were attracted in any case by the increasingly complex subject of trade. The Secretaries were very pleased to leave Indian affairs to Dundas – there was no serious attempt in their term of office to poach on his preserves. And Pitt immediately found a strong trio of advisers on commercial policy, in Dundas himself, William Grenville, and the skilled and knowledgeable Jenkinson.

Charles Jenkinson, later Lord Hawkesbury and later still first Earl of Liverpool, had posed something of a conundrum for Pitt at the start. One of the villains of popular mythology in the bitter closing years of the American War, as an allegedly leading backstairs confidant of George III, he had been held at arm's length by the new Ministry and had not immediately been offered a post.[4] Nor was he in fact particularly keen to join. While the accusations against him had been very largely untrue, he looked on himself, like his friend John Robinson, as essentially a King's man, and he retained this attitude to the end. He knew that he was a political liability, and he had his own reservations at first: he was reluctant to ask for places for his friends for almost two

1. P. 190 above.
2. Sydney to Pitt, 24 September 1784 (Stanhope, I, 228–9).
3. See p. 308 above.
4. See p. 133 above.

years. 'I support the present Government', he wrote late in 1784, 'because it is what my Sovereign has chosen, and it Deliver'd Him from the hands of Men he did not like'. 'But', he went on, 'I cannot . . . place implicit Confidence in them till I have seen more of their Behaviour'.[1] As time went by, and he gained more power, that confidence grew. But his steady association with his colleagues, which lasted for so many years, owed more to the fact that they were all the King's Ministers than to any personal attachment.

Jenkinson was not in any case easily inclined to form such links. He certainly never became intimate with Pitt. Of an older generation – he was fifty-seven in 1784 – and coming from a suspect political stable, he conspicuously lacked the personal qualities to overcome such drawbacks. He seems to have been one of those unfortunate men who create a small pool of discomfort round them: not a freezing chill like Pitt when he wished, but a mild persistent sense of unease. His manner, though not unassured, was negative and faintly putting off – at once rather deprecating and, in his later days, rather pompous. He looked at the ground or the ceiling when he spoke, he was ungainly, he moved carefully about a room. He was the dedicated man of business, regular, tenacious, slightly absurd. Descended from a respectable Oxfordshire county family, which had produced the Elizabethan traveller Anthony Jenkinson, he managed to give the disastrous impression that he was rather ill bred. He had none of the easy bonhomie which served Dundas so well. It became something of a habit in Pitt's circle, as his consequence grew, to call him 'the great man'.[2]

But the term was revealing in more than one way. It held a note of wry respect. For if Jenkinson did not wine and dine much with the inner group, he none the less became a force. As has been well said, he was 'the indispensable odd man out',[3] and he was very well aware of his value. He was already a most useful, and he ended as a great, public servant. Starting as Under-Secretary for the North as long ago as 1761, he had been employed continuously in various departments over the next twenty-one years. He had climbed the lower rungs of the ladder, as he claimed, 'by industry, by attention to duty',[4] and in the early eighties his experience was not to be despised. Nor was his ability. Jenkinson was a skilful administrator, with a special interest in trade and international law. He had published a work on neutrality as a

1. To J. Home, 16 November 1784 (B.M. Add. Ms. 38309, f. 98v).
2. Bland Burges to Anne Burges, 13 October 1789 ('Sir J. Burges, Political Transcripts, 1751–90', Box 3; Bodleian Library); Grenville to Buckingham, 4 February 1791 (Buckingham, II, 187). And cf. Pitt himself to Eden 22 June [n.d. but in the 1790s]: 'I am threatened with the honor of a visit from Addiscombe' (where Hawkesbury lived); B.M. Add. Ms 46519, f. 32.
3. Harlow, *The Founding of the Second British Empire*, II (1964), 251.
4. Replying to the sneers of Tommy Townshend (Sydney) at his social background, in a debate in 1770. This was an occasion when he had to remind the House that he came of good family.

young man, and in 1785 he brought out what became a standard collection of treaties. He was an obvious choice, like Dundas and Grenville, for membership of the new Committee of Trade in 1784, and his political reservations did not prevent him from taking a leading part in its affairs. When the Committee was reconstituted in 1786, Pitt decided to put him in charge. Anxious to forestall accusations that the King was behind the appointment, the Minister went out of his way to take the responsibility. He made Jenkinson a peer – a step, he admitted, that 'will sound a little strange at a distance, and with a reference to former ideas; but he has really fairly earned and attained it at my hands'.[1] The influence of the new President of the Committee (or Board) of Trade was thereafter steady and substantial. He was already, as he claimed, 'very much in Mr Pitt's Confidence, & He brings every Question he can to the Committee of Council at which I preside & where I meet the Secretaries of State twice a week sitting under me'.[2] Pitt indeed was always glad to leave an area of business to a reliable man when he found one, and Jenkinson laid an unambiguous stamp on imperial commercial policy. Stern and sometimes thrusting in his choice of means, conservative in aim, he husbanded British resources and nurtured a fresh growth of shipping and trade. Perhaps the most competent administrator in the Government, he was as much an architect of empire as Pitt himself. He was the third but not the least effective member of the triumvirate which worked with the Minister on these matters, at first bypassing the older channels, later – when Dundas and Grenville became the Secretaries of State, and Jenkinson himself one of the Cabinet – more directly through them.

It was fitting that the Committee of Trade should have been re-established to look into the future of the West Indian commerce.[3] For despite some ominous cracks in their old prosperity, and some recent doubts as to their real value, the British West Indies were almost universally regarded as still the most desirable facet of empire, and their attraction derived entirely from their wealth and functions as a source of supply.[4] There was little attempt in London to interfere much with the local government: the 'old representative system' was in full force, and the colonists would have resented closer control. But the pattern of their trade was a different matter, vitally affecting the British system; and it was on the problems of com-

1. To Hester Countess of Chatham, 13 July 1786 (Stanhope, I, 306).
2. To Lord Gower, July 1786 (P.R.O. 30/29/1).
3. P. 308 above.
4. The doubts, expressed by Adam Smith among others, centred on the balance of capital formation in the West Indies and at home, deriving from what was recognised to be an important trade. This was said to favour the West Indies. But the argument was disputed at the time – it remains disputable – , and it did not affect later policy.

merce and shipping that attention chiefly fastened in the peacetime decade.

At the end of 1783 the questions were immediate, and appeared fundamental. The relative importance of the islands' commerce had been barely diminished by recent events. They were now the fifth, instead of the fourth, largest customer of English goods, and in value still easily the largest source of supply.[1] In certain respects indeed they had gained during the war, picking up some of the trade that had earlier gone straight to the mainland colonies. But the new status of those former colonies now threatened their own, for the West Indies' prosperity turned very largely on their role in the general Atlantic traffic, and their prospects were deeply involved in the relations between Britain and the United States. The problems indeed were a focus for those of the whole western Atlantic trade, and the Committee's inquiry embraced the treatment of American shipping and the potential of Canadian supply.

It raised, in acute form, a question of even wider import. Which was to be preferred, the great sugar or the great shipping interest? These two powerful forces – the producer and the carrier – had never come into basic conflict before, and the result was highly significant for the shape of British policy at large. The triangular Atlantic trade had rested in theory on a rough equilibrium of gain and loss between the partners. The mainland colonies, viewed as a whole, had taken more goods from Britain than they supplied; they offset their loss by selling timber and provisions and some African slaves to the British West Indies, and part of their lesser purchases of tropical produce from the islands, on favoured terms, to the home country; and the home country and the islands, in turn, lost on one leg of the triangle to gain on the other. Such a system had two great advantages. Little bullion needed to be moved, in contrast to the trades with other areas; and since the goods had to be carried, by the Navigation Acts, in British or colonial vessels, shipping was encouraged and maritime strength sustained. But now that the United States were a foreign power, what was going to happen? One of the props had been removed: how would the edifice stand? The West Indian planters were in no doubt as to the answer. There must be a free trade between themselves and the mainland, and American shipping must enter their ports on the old terms. Otherwise they would be starved of their supply of timber and provisions, and the economy of the Sugar Islands would be entirely upset.

The planters' case was urgent, for adverse regulations were already in force. Shelburne's bill for a free trade with the United States,

---

1. Elizabeth Boody Schumpeter, *English Overseas Trade Statistics 1697–1808* (1960), tables V, VI. See also table XVII for the continued pre-eminence of sugar as a dutiable product among the principal imports, until it was challenged by tea from the East after 1784. The figures in each case apply to England and Wales only.

presented by Pitt, had been lost in March 1783,[1] and despite the Americans' early hopes, and Fox's efforts, the Coalition proved less sympathetic. Three Orders in Council had been issued between July and December of that year, allowing West Indian inhabitants to trade with the United States in specified commodities, on the old export duties from the islands, but only if the cargoes were carried either way in British ships. United States' vessels were thus excluded from West Indian ports. This system was to stay in force, experimentally, for six months in each case: the afflicted merchants set to work at once to prevent its continuation. They were a powerful, organised lobby, well used to such a task. They bombarded the Coalition Ministers, and when the Coalition fell they bombarded Pitt. Lord Penrhyn, the chairman of their standing committee, 'frequently attended' him and Sydney in January 1784, the Privy Council was petitioned in February, and the Minister set up the inquiry in March.[2]

The result appeared, with exemplary speed and thoroughness, at the end of May. Like the proceedings, which he soon took over, the report bore Jenkinson's mark. It may be described as a victory for the shipping over the sugar interest,[3] and, in terms of Government policy, for tradition over experiment. For the arguments of Sheffield and of Shelburne, canvassed earlier, were fought out over the body of the Caribbean planters.[4] Should the Americans' share of the Atlantic carrying trade, already substantial, be allowed to continue in expectation of the prospects for British manufacturers in the United States? Or did the threat to British shipping, on some of the busiest of deep-sea lanes, outweigh an arguable commercial disadvantage to the home country and the West Indies themselves? The answer turned on the assessment of the Americans' reaction to a stiff policy, and, if it should prove adverse, on the possibilities of supplies for the Caribbean islands from elsewhere. The Orders in Council had already forbidden the West Indians to take American meat and fish, in favour of Ireland and Newfoundland respectively. The Canadians now argued that Canada could provide the other necessaries, hitherto imported from the mainland provinces farther south. The Committee of Trade was not much impressed by this claim. It did not think much of Canada's immediate potential. But nor did it expect the Americans to retaliate fiercely if the recent restrictions were allowed to stand. They still had access to West Indian markets; they would still need British goods; on balance it seemed unlikely that they would cut off their nose to spite their face. And given such an estimate, the response was clear. The West Indies'

1. Pp. 96–7 above.

2. Copies of the committee's representations are among Pitt's papers in P.R.O. 30/8/352.

3. Many of the West Indian merchants, in point of fact, were themselves owners or part owners of ships; but mainly as a facet of their trade in sugar and molasses.

4. See pp. 94–5, 159–60 above.

economy would not be ruined, the American market would not be lost, and continued protection would give a very necessary support to British 'navigation'.[1] For unless the risks were extreme, this was the prime object, particularly since the removal of American tonnage had recently sparked off a boom in domestic shipbuilding. The carrying trade was a nursery for seamen and a bulwark of commerce itself. It must not be jeopardised without the promise of a very favourable return. The Orders in Council were therefore allowed to stand, and reimposed at six-monthly intervals until 1788.

How did Pitt view this decision? He was on record as having presented a bill in the opposite sense, and more recently, out of office, he had called for 'a complete commercial system, suited to the novelty of our situation'.[2] It is doubtful if this new report was the kind of response he had had in mind. But it is also doubtful how far he had really been committed to Shelburne's 'experiment',[3] and he was not now prepared to ignore the evidence he received. There is no sign that he was much concerned in the inquiry itself. He was not a member of the Committee of Trade until over two years later, and while he was shown the findings in advance he does not seem to have kept in close touch with the work.[4] Of course he was busy at the time, with his measures for India and finance. It would of course have been a major task to challenge so powerful a cause, or perhaps to overrule the report of his own committee. But one should not assume too readily that such pressures were the whole answer, and that Pitt simply surrendered a cause which he had at heart. In the first place, he did not admit the evidence uncritically. He examined the report in detail: he queried the prices of freight, the planters' complaints, the prospect for Canadian supplies.[5] As a result, he was content to confirm the recommendations, and to accept that the objects could be met without a major change.

But more important perhaps was the fact that his attitude thereafter remained much the same. For Pitt never sacrificed 'navigation' to the principle of free trade. Where he eased old restrictions he expected both trade and navigation to benefit, or recognised that strict protection was simply not satisfying proven facts. He always wished to be as liberal as possible: he was convinced of the value of a freer exchange. But his

1. This term must be defined, for the relevant usage, which was a good one, has long been obsolete. It covered 'shipping business: trade or intercourse carried on by sea or water' (*O.E.D.*), as in the title of David Macpherson's popular *Annals of Commerce, Manufactures, Fisheries, and Navigation* . . . (1805), or indeed in that of successive Navigation Acts, 'for the encouragement and increasing of shipping and navigation'.

2. Speech of 11 November 1783 (*P.R.*, XII, 10).

3. P. 97 above.

4. Copies of what appear to be parts of the Committee's draft report are in P.R.O. 30/8/351, 352. But there is no hint of Pitt's participation in the earlier processes, among his own papers or Jenkinson's, or those of the Committee.

5. See his undated memorandum, 'Precis – Committee of Trade', in P.R.O. 30/8/195.

conception of the possible was itself fairly strict. Adam Smith himself had argued that 'perfect freedom of trade' could be subject to restrictions, particularly when an industry was necessary to national defence. And since the power of Britain rested so largely on 'its sailors and shipping', 'the act of navigation . . . very properly endeavours to give [them] the monopoly of the trade of their own country'.[1] Pitt certainly acted in that sense throughout the peacetime years. His first great effort for a freer trade, with Ireland, was made precisely in order to fortify the imperial connexion, to complement a thriving navigation, and to sustain naval strength. When a foreign power was involved, these factors were very carefully weighed.

Pitt's plan for Ireland failed; and the failure increased his inclination not to move too fast without very good hopes of success. His cautious streak became more pronounced, and he listened carefully to Jenkinson's advice.[2] He did not always accept it. He sometimes overruled it, or held it in check, particularly when he could count on Grenville's support. Indeed, in 1786 he made Grenville Vice-President of the reconstituted Committee of Trade, with responsibility for its affairs in the Commons, so that he had a balance of weight in his counsels. But the disagreements turned on means rather than on ends, and they referred mostly to problems of European trade. There was little dissent on matters of colonial trade and empire; that was partly why Pitt gave Jenkinson so free a hand in this sphere. He moved as he thought suitable to the occasion; he had no detailed preconceptions; he was willing to foster a change in policy when the balance of advantage seemed clear. But the onus of reasonable proof lay almost always on the prosecution. Only once in these peacetime years did the Minister hazard a really open venture – in 1790–1, when he risked the prospect of a transfer of trade from Russia to Poland. But that was not a purely commercial question: foreign policy was involved; and it was the exception to a general rule. Pitt's assessment of the factors concerned was often more imaginative than Jenkinson's. He was far more flexible and adroit, he was glad to move forward when he could. But he was not prepared to do so unless he thought the issue favourable, and he could fight as hard for an old-fashioned bargain as for a newer look.

His great object, in fact, was to bring his weapons up to date: to gain his ends, where conditions were changing, by newer modes of measure-

1. *Wealth of Nations*, I, 427–9. It is true that Adam Smith wished, at the end of 1783, to make an exception of the West Indies (to William Eden, 15 December 1783; *A.C.*, I, 64–5). But this was because he feared the effect of the British monopoly on the islands' economy, a point on which Pitt felt reassured a few months later, when the Committee of Trade reported.

2. And, it may be, to that of the permanent officials. Certainly Chalmers at the Committee of Trade and Irving at the Customs, to both of whom Pitt was inclined to pay attention, were resolutely in favour of preserving the navigation system – Chalmers used this sometimes disputed phrase – in all its force for the Atlantic (see their papers for Grenville, in the Fortescue Mss at Boconnoc, 'West Indies').

ment and thought. The picture itself as a result might begin to assume a rather different aspect; but the time was still far distant when its proportions would be changed. Pitt subscribed, like some colleagues and officials, to the recent trends in economic thought which revealed the shortcomings of the old bullionist school. The balance of trade should no longer be gauged solely by the movements of gold and silver; the true ingredients were more elaborate, measurements should be redefined. But this did not mean that the idea of a balance itself had disappeared, or that the processes of wealth could be divorced from those of power. There was no ready-made distinction to be observed between liberal and traditional policies: the term liberal itself could mean different things according to the case. The contrast indeed could appear irrelevant in the uneven evolution of an expanding world, and Pitt's 'complete system', if it could be said to exist, was a mongrel by Shelburne's or Sheffield's standards. In the debate between them, he inclined when he could to Shelburne's side. But it was not untypical that in this very first instance he should have adopted Sheffield's policy.

It was equally typical that a few years later he should have supported exceptions to it. For the policy did not stand the test of experience in every respect. It had its own shortcomings, and it needed to be supplemented. British shipping proved unable to meet all the demands of the triangular trade. Ocean-going vessels were not well suited to the shortest leg, between the islands and the mainland; they were uneconomical, and they could not time their passages to make the best of the seasonal markets. Smuggling therefore flourished, and was openly winked at, from the French and Spanish Caribbean and the American coast. When Captain Nelson of the West Indies squadron tried to enforce the law, he had to stay aboard his ship for two months to keep out of harm's way; and by 1786 the Committee of Trade was becoming startled by the scale of the traffic. '... Unless this Vile practice is put an end to, All Your Lordship has done is in Vain': so one of the clerks wrote to Jenkinson,[1] and the Government decided to act. Early in 1787 imports were forbidden from the foreign West Indies except in emergency, the existing Orders in Council were replaced by statute in 1788,[2] and the navy and the local courts were told to deal strictly with offenders. But the remedy only nourished another disease. The West Indian economy had been disturbed since the end of the war: tropical produce was fetching lower prices as trade settled down again, embargoes forced up the cost of imports and sometimes led to shortage, and from 1780 to 1786 there was an unprecedented total of six hurricanes in seven years. The local Assemblies and Governors were already calling for help,

1. Grey Elliott to Lord Hawkesbury, 23 July 1786 (B.M. Add. Ms 38219, f. 28).
2. 27 Geo. III, c. 7; 28 Geo. III, c. 6.

and their cries became more urgent as the new measures began to bite.

One of the colonists' demands, very naturally, was for the enlargement of their only loophole in times of distress, whereby the Governors were empowered to declare an emergency and open their ports to foreign ships. Equally naturally perhaps, these demands did not get very far: the duration of the period was always watched closely in London.[1] Other forms of help were given: grants were made after hurricane damage, the growing plantations of coffee and cotton encouraged. But no breach was allowed for some years in the regulations for trade. This was perhaps partly because, once again, the interested parties were themselves divided. The merchants and shippers were calling for a return to an earlier system of permanent free ports, started successfully in the sixties and ended in practice by the recent war, which, by permitting specified foreign imports in foreign ships to pass duty free through certain harbours, gave a vent to British and local exports in return. The planters agreed, so long as the policy applied to American goods and ships as well; but otherwise they demurred, lest rival produce – above all sugar – should be included in the imports allowed. Faced by this disagreement, Government was the more inclined to do nothing, a course of action in any case congenial at a time when it was trying to repair the bulwarks of navigation. But after a few years it began to think again. The arrangements for the West Indies were not working well; the old free ports had fostered trade; it seemed necessary at least to re-examine the possibilities. The Committee of Trade was set to work on the problem in 1786; a year later, the free ports were resuscitated on a temporary basis and in a limited sense. Listed articles – mostly raw materials, but not imported provisions, sugar or molasses, or exported iron, tobacco or naval stores – could now be carried into specified harbours in four of the British islands by vessels not exceeding seventy tons belonging to the subjects of a European state. The tonnage limit was removed three years later, though the ships had to still be single-deckers; in 1792, the regulations were made permanent, and foreign sugar and coffee were admitted to certain islands; and more ports were added to the list in 1793.[2] Three further Acts in the course of the nineties extended the range and scope of the system, as peacetime restrictions were further eased by the pressures of war.

These moves breached earlier policy – Sheffield himself at first argued against them. But they by no means implied its reversal, or even a radical change. The planters were able to keep out foreign sugar and coffee entirely for a time, and out of the most important plantation islands throughout the peacetime years. More important, the legislation as a whole was fashioned to serve a precisely circumscribed end. For the

1. For an example of the Committee of Trade's reaction to emergencies, carrying Pitt's agreement, see Harlow, op. cit., II, 260–1.
2. 27 Geo. III, c. 27; 30 Geo. III, c. 29; 32 Geo. III, c. 37 and 43; 33 Geo. III, c. 50.

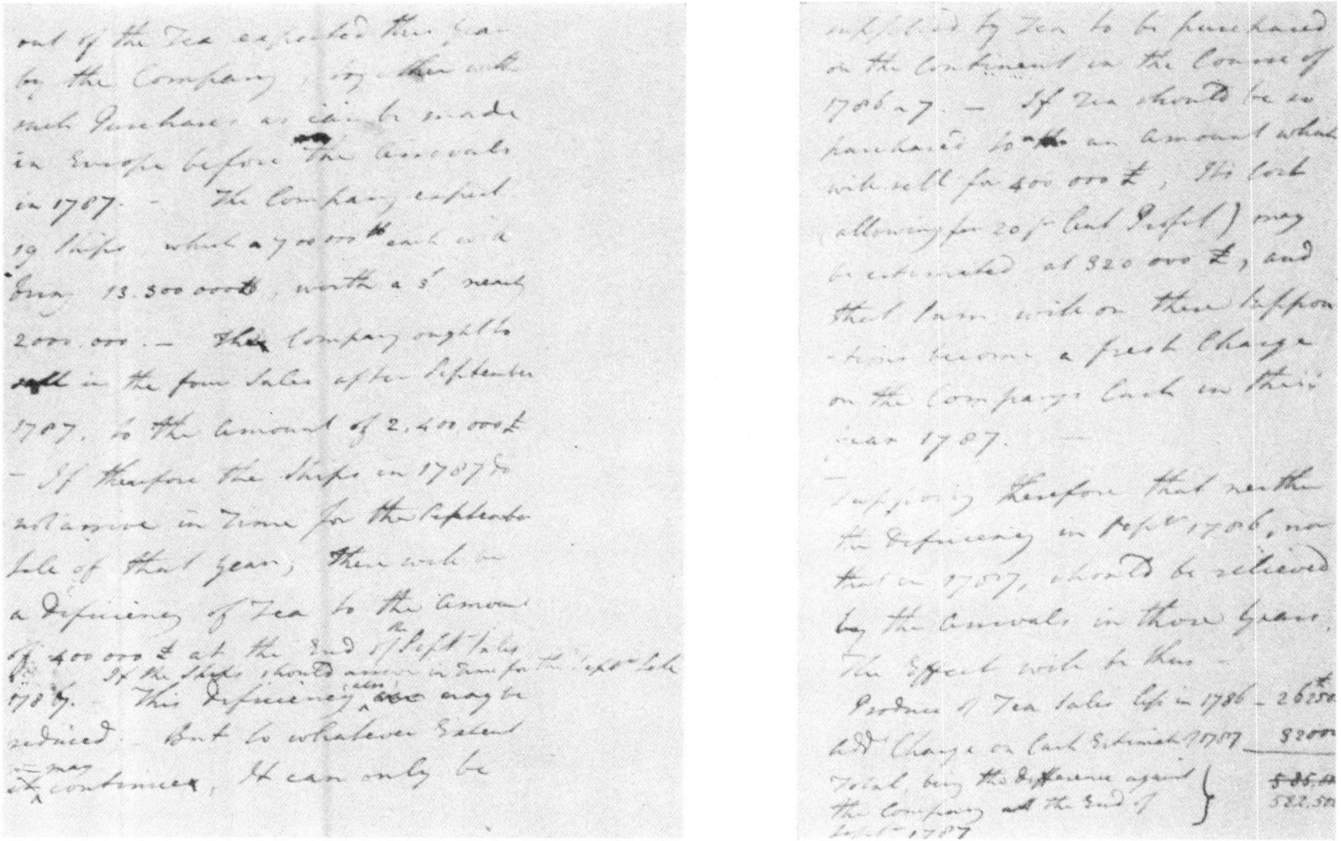

Pitt's Handwriting (P.R.O. 30/8/294)

William Wyndham Grenville *by Hoppner*

free ports were re-established for two reasons, one involuntary, one deliberate; and the balance of emphasis was suggested by the contents of the Acts. The harbours were opened to French and Spanish Caribbean shipping partly because the Government could no longer prevent it. If smuggling and distress were to be countered, something of the sort had to be done. But the concessions were framed so as in turn to support a British initiative, and they did not embrace all the colonists' demands. They were in fact designed very largely, as the shipping and merchant interests had made clear, as part of an attack on foreign markets throughout the New World. This had been the original purpose of the system: it was now revived in a decade in which an earlier favourable balance of trade was being reduced as more foreign-grown cotton had to be bought for the British mills. The regulations were thus a two-edged weapon, aggressive as well as conciliatory, and the result was less a reversal than a restatement of protection. United States' shipping was still excluded; the nature of the islands' trade was well defined; there was no general relaxation of the policy laid down in 1784. Ministers seem to have been united in their approach. It would indeed have been surprising if they had sanctioned a major departure at this point, for the first of the free port bills was presented early in 1787, less than a year after the Government had strengthened that bastion of protection, the Navigation Act.

II

The Navigation Act of 1786 was the central feature of the monument which Jenkinson built to a revived imperial system. The intention was clear, and categorically stated: 'if proper means could be devised to secure the navigation trade to Great Britain, though we had lost a dominion, we might almost be said to have gained an empire'.[1] That empire was, as it has been called, 'fundamentally a ledger-book empire',[2] and the account presented here was cast in conventional form. The result was protection refurbished, old policy reconditioned, a fresh restatement of a long tradition which was soon to face the trial of the Napoleonic Wars.[3]

The bill began to be prepared early in March. It underwent the thorough process which had now become a feature of the Committee of Trade. Evidence was heard; prices and costs were collected for British and foreign ships; the expert John Pownall, who had once helped Shelburne, took charge of a report from the Customs; the Law Officers

1. Jenkinson in the Commons, 11 April 1786 (*P.R.*, XX, 89–90).

2. A. F. McC. Madden, 'The Imperial Machinery of the Younger Pitt', in *Essays in British History Presented to Sir Keith Feiling*, ed. H. R. Trevor-Roper (1964), 189.

3. In short, 'Neo-Mercantilism under Lord Hawkesbury', as the latest account has called it (Harlow, op. cit., II, title of ch. V).

were consulted, and the appropriate Cabinet Ministers informed. Jenkinson's methods of business, as always, command respect. He was ready for Parliament in April – a remarkable feat – and the long measure became law in June. Its object was to reanimate the Navigation Acts by stopping up the loopholes, and thereby foster a large marine which might capture a larger share of an expanding traffic. All other considerations must be subordinate to that end. If a given trade – whether direct between a colony and the home country, or part of the entrepôt trade from a colony to foreign markets through British ports – seemed to be temporarily damaged, that could not be helped. Virtue would bring its reward in due course: the volume would rise, the balance respond; meanwhile the nation's most precious possession, seamen and ships, would be fortified. A thriving marine was the basis of commerce. It was also the basis of wartime strength. For trade was not the sole consideration; there were also the needs of defence, and the bill, as its author proclaimed, was largely 'a Bill for the increase of Naval Power'.[1] The means used were not very subtle. The ends were not always attained. Their pursuit may sometimes have done more harm than good, in the retaliations and troubles it provoked. Some of the successes themselves might perhaps have been gained without that particular policy. But there were certainly successes to record, the case had been clearly put, and when the storms broke in the nineties men on the whole were very glad to have accepted it.

The provisions of the Act were strict.[2] No foreign-built vessel (except those seized and confirmed as lawful prize) would in future qualify for the advantages of British ownership even if owned by a British subject. A British subject resident abroad would not qualify as owner or part-owner of a British vessel, unless he belonged to a British 'factory' in the territory concerned or to a commercial house trading in Great Britain or Ireland. Vessels built in the American colonies, or owned by persons now citizens of the United States, during the period when trade with those colonies was forbidden by British law, were specifically excluded from the advantages of British registration; and such registration must be acquired, on the new terms, by all vessels down to 15 tons trading in the coastal waters of the British Isles or those of British territories. The rest of the Act was devoted to preventing evasion and fraud – an exercise which led to the creation of the first reliable register of British shipping.

This was a logical expression of conservative policy facing changing conditions. It was welcomed by the House of Commons, and by opinion at large. There were complaints, of course: from British merchants and agents abroad, and from shipbuilders intent on restricting potential rivals in Canada. But these were confidently parried, and the bill encountered very little opposition – Jenkinson indeed claimed later that

1. Jenkinson's phrase, quoted loc. cit., 268.
2. 26 Geo. III, c. 60.

it was the only important measure to pass unanimously in the course of fifty years.[1] As far as can be seen, Pitt took little part in the proceedings[2] or the preparations. He was still not a member of the Committee of Trade (he joined the reconstituted board in August), and there is no significant reference to him in this instance among his papers or those of others. He left the business to Jenkinson, and there is no reason to doubt his support. It had been implicit in his decision on the West Indies' trade in 1784, and a year later it was stated clearly, in a way which suggested that Pitt meant what he said. When John Adams, the United States' envoy, paid one of his rare visits to Downing Street – for the only business interview, in fact, that he was ever granted or sought –, he argued the ill effects of continued protection. He was told in reply that the Navigation Act 'would not answer its end, if we should dispense with it towards you'. Americans could not blame Englishmen 'for being attached to their ships and seamen which are so essential to them'. 'Englishmen were much attached to their navigation'.[3]

III

In the same interview Pitt went on to talk, in 'a long, rambling conversation', about the future of the Atlantic fisheries. It was not surprising that he should have done so, for the subject was on his mind at the time, and its treatment was an integral part of the navigation system and a further bone of contention with the United States.

There were two sets of problems to consider, those of Newfoundland and those of the whale fisheries. Both had been placed in a new perspective by the result of the war, though the prospects in either case were of a different kind. The problem of the Newfoundland fisheries was one of preservation under attack. The old enemy, the French, were now admitted by the peace treaty to long contested rights of catch off some of the coasts, and some facilities ashore. The Americans, who shared the Banks, were no longer subject to British statutes, and while excluded from the island itself had gained some rights of access to the

1. It all depends of course on what is meant by 'important'. The ideal, though not the practice, of the House was in fact to show unanimity on important legislation (see pp. 168–9 above); and the records of divisions are far too uncertain for one to check Jenkinson's claim. No doubt he was right.

In the following year, the Irish Parliament completed the arrangements by passing a similar Act.

2. Again it is hard to be sure, for only very brief reports of the debates on the second and third readings have survived in newspapers (there are none in the published collections). His contribution to the first reading was confined to introducing a complementary bill (see p. 246 above) tightening up the regulations for clearing Customs. *The Morning Post* of 17 June 1786 contains a summary of his remarks on the third reading.

3. Adams to Secretary Jay, 25 August 1785 (*The Works of John Adams . . .*, by his Grandson, Charles Francis Adams, VIII (1853), 306).

neighbouring mainland. And the conduct of the fishery was steadily changing, quite apart from these encroachments, and slipping from its former complete dependence on the British Isles. Ever since early attempts at colonisation had failed under the Tudors, Newfoundland had been regarded as 'a great English ship moored near the Banks . . ., for the convenience of the English Fishermen'.[1] The vessels had sailed from England – from Poole and the West Country –, returning at the end of the season before the winter set in. This was still largely the case; but over the past few decades settlements had been growing up in the island. There was now a sizeable resident population, living by the fishery and necessarily importing the bulk of their supplies. They did so in part from the home country, in part from Canada and (much more) New England. But the New England provinces now fell outside the Colonial System. The British Government was therefore faced with the prospect of more intensive foreign competition, and the possibility of a growing colonial settlement – always potentially troublesome – which might come to depend increasingly on the United States.

Such a state of affairs could not be accepted lightly. The Newfoundland fishery was a misty jewel of the British Crown. Dried cod was an article of diet on both sides of the Atlantic, above all in the British West Indies and the Catholic south of Europe. It was a factor in our Caribbean economy and in our trade with Spain and Portugal, and not the least part of its value lay in the ships it filled. The British monopoly of the carrying trade from Newfoundland helped force the return freights to England into British bottoms; it was also a further contribution to the maritime strength which the fisheries in general were supposed to sustain. For the prime object of all British fisheries, as defined by statute, was 'the raising and maintaining a number of seamen for the speedy manning of our fleets in time of danger'; and no better seamen were to be found than in

> 'that hardy crew
> Who on the frozen beach of Newfoundland
> Hang their white fish amid the parching winds'.[2]

It was this fact which had led the Board of Trade in the sixties to declare that Newfoundland was worth more than Louisiana and Canada together. The question now was how far altered conditions would allow old benefits to be held.

The Government acted on much the same lines as it acted over the West Indies. It enforced the spirit of the Navigation Acts as strictly as it thought that circumstances would bear. This did not mean that it

1. William Knox's evidence before a committee of the House of Commons 'on the State of the Trade to Newfoundland', 1793 (*Reports from Committees*, X (1803), 413).
2. John Dyer, *The Fleece* (1757). The governing statute was 10 & 11 Will. III, c. 25.

blinked facts, or responded unreasonably in its own terms: on the contrary, it dealt sternly with sectional interests which proved less liberal than itself. But the object of policy was clear. No needless risks should be taken. Sensible methods must be employed to serve traditional ends.

Ceded rights and foreign rivalry had perforce to be accepted. The great question was how far the Americans should be allowed to supply the population of Newfoundland. For the future of the island and its relations with Britain might turn on the answer. The British shipping and merchant interests were naturally in no doubt. With an urgency almost equal to that of the West India merchants, they sought to extract from Government an exactly contrary response. No imports of any kind should enter the island from the United States: the home country and Canada should have the monopoly of supply. The Committee of Trade began to look into the problem at the end of 1784, and the report – as thorough as ever – was ready early in the following year. It was stern, judicious and unambiguous. The case was dismissed. Jenkinson and his colleagues were satisfied that certain basic provisions would always find their way in from New England, and that an attempted monopoly from Britain and Canada would force up local prices too high. The population might suffer distress; smuggling would certainly increase. American bread, flour and livestock should therefore be admitted, in British-registered ships.

The recommendation was put into effect by statute in March 1785.[1] It was another example of Jenkinson's resolve to contain a vested interest. But it did not point to anything in the nature of a general change. No other American supplies were sanctioned; the produce must still come in British-registered ships; and while the island's population was to be saved from distress, any hint of independence was to be discouraged. These facts were underlined in the following year. The Navigation Act of 1786 tightened up the registration of British shipping, and an Act for the reorganisation of the Newfoundland fishery sought to discourage foreign competition and to protect the home country's interests in the island.[2] Bounties were increased on the cargoes of British-registered ships working the deep-sea grounds – a move in favour of the larger vessels which sailed from the British ports –, and a great effort was made to control the size and nature of the resident population. Ownership of property was strictly regulated; the Governor was given more effective powers; everything possible was done to secure the 'great English ship' to her distant moorings. This vigilance was not relaxed. Two years later, British subjects from Bermuda fishing the Banks were forbidden to land on the island, for 'it would not be

---

1. The Act was 25 Geo. III, c. 1. For the debates on it, see *P.R.*, XVII, 67–79, 144–59, 168–74.
2. 26 Geo. III, c. 26.

advisable to depart from the principle on which the Trade to Newfoundland had hitherto been carried on'.[1]

The attempt to hold the clock steady was a partial success. The volume of shipping from the British Isles to the fishing grounds rose between 1785 and 1792, from its rather depressed level after the end of the American War.[2] But the local tonnage rose more, and in fact the shift of emphasis could not be checked. In Newfoundland as in the British West Indies, old defences would be turned in the end. The danger was recognised;[3] but the defences were mounted, and indeed the fact may have helped delay the process. Meanwhile, as the sales of fish were sustained and the fleet was adequately manned in the peacetime crises, neither Jenkinson nor Pitt felt that their policy was wrong.

Pitt, however, was always happier in attack than defence. He would fight to preserve, and gave little away; he grew wary of failure. But his intellect was essentially constructive, and he responded most readily to the thought of advance. In matters of commerce his theme was expansion, where the prospects, well scrutinised, looked inviting. And the most inviting prospects in the fisheries were those of the growing whaling industry, which stretched from Greenland to the Cape of Good Hope and Cape Horn and beyond.

Whalebone had long been one of the staples of an unindustrialised economy, performing some of the simpler functions of processed metals today. It was still imported in growing quantities in the 1780s. But the real interest in the sperm whale now lay in another direction, in its oil. For whale oil was a valuable substance in the early days of the Industrial Revolution. It lubricated the machines, it lit the lamps in the streets – a not unimportant contribution to manners and safety –, it was an equivalent in many ways of the later shale oil and petroleum fuel. There was an unsatisfied demand, which would support a greatly increased fishing fleet.[4] And the ships that brought the whale 'fins' and oil also catered for another market, that of the skins and oil from the seals which were to be found in the same distant regions. As the voyages of discovery ranged ever farther afield, the commercial possibilities seemed increasingly attractive.

They were the more so at this point because the main pattern of supply had been upset. The whale fisheries were first exploited chiefly by the

1. Minute of the Committee of Trade, 29 January 1789 (quoted Harlow, op. cit., II, 279). The regulation was put into force by 29 Geo. III, c. 53.

2. This was not acknowledged by the British merchants, who continued to bemoan the growing competition. But their figures were chosen as great interests' figures are apt to be.

3. See e.g. Thurlow to Grenville, 21 April 1791, in *H.M.C. Dropmore*, II, 56.

4. Not always immediately apparent; Pitt talked of a 'glut' in 1786 (*P.R.*, XX, 105). But it became clear by the late eighties that there was room for all the oil that could be supplied.

Dutch, the Portuguese, and the North American colonists. But by the 1770s the Americans had captured most of the trade, and a virtual monopoly of the British market. Only some twenty English and Scottish vessels, if that, took part; the rest sailed from the New England ports. This pattern was broken by the war. British whalers were encouraged by bounties, and in 1783 a high duty was placed on American oil. The Government thereafter was not alone in exploring the opportunities: 'all Europe was considering which nation should be so fortunate as to secure, or engross that fishery'.[1] The old Dutch interest was reviving, the French were said to be alert. It would have been surprising in such circumstances if Jenkinson and Pitt had held aloof.

They did nothing of the kind. They thrust strongly forward, to a point which in 1790 brought the country to the verge of war. The ball was set rolling, perhaps not surprisingly, by some groups of dissident Americans. The home of the whaling industry was Nantucket, off the coast of Massachusetts – 'that famous old island . . . the place where the first dead American whale was stranded'.[2] It depended almost entirely on fishing, its people had tried to keep out of the war, and when hostilities opened some of the men came to England, in the service of a few powerful New England whaling merchants who transferred their activities here. It was a significant move, for the merchants in question were engaged in the fishery of the southern Atlantic, which was still fairly new and potentially exciting. The Americans were therefore welcomed, and encouraged by premiums, and by the end of the war they were established as the core of a small but expanding British venture. Early in 1786 they asked for protection in the form of a bounty, and for Government support in extending the area of their operations beyond the Cape of Good Hope.

The Ministry's reply had to be linked with its policy for the northern whale fishery, which it was about to decide at this very time. For the Nantucketers had by now raised other, and more awkward, questions. The first small migration to England was part of a wider movement. In 1785, some families – as distinct from individuals – went to Nova Scotia, and others joined the early settlers here. Both lots intended to live by fishing; but they posed different problems from the earlier group, for while their admission into the British system would bring some obvious advantages, there was also the danger that the larger settlements would not be properly absorbed. The Nantucketers in Nova Scotia would strengthen a colonial, not a domestic trade – a prospect which, as in the case of Newfoundland, was viewed with caution if not alarm –, and both groups were engaged mainly in the Greenland (rather than the southern) fishery, where there was now a quite substantial British

1. Jenkinson in the Commons on 5 May 1786, as reported in *The Morning Post* of the 6th. The debate is included only in summary in *P.R.* and Stockdale, and not at all in *P.H.*
2. *Moby Dick.*

interest which they must not be allowed to rival or exploit. Their reception was correspondingly cool: the entrants into the Maritime Provinces were hedged about with restrictions, and those into England finally rebuffed. Pitt saw the leader of this group, a Mr Roach, in the summer of 1785 – a few weeks before he discussed the fisheries with John Adams. But the subsequent talks with Jenkinson failed. Roach's terms were too high, the Government was suspicious – 'I know New Englanders too well', wrote one official, 'to imagine any proposition of theirs can be without some latent View '[1] –, and the Nantucketers eventually set up shop in France. These developments, and the reactions they aroused, led to an examination of the Greenland Fishery by the Committee of Trade. It began in February 1786, the month in which the Southern Whale Fishery's petition was received, and the report was issued in April.

It was in line with the general tenor of the Ministry's thinking. It related a system of protection to the facts as they appeared. The British partakers of the Greenland Fishery had been given a wartime bounty on their cargoes of 40/– a ton, on which their numbers and operations had thrived. They were now further aided by a high duty on American oil. They argued that this level of protection must be continued if they were to secure a future preponderance of a valuable market. Government, however, was not so sure. The price of oil had risen under this system by almost 15 per cent in the past decade, over £80,000 had been paid in bounties in 1785, and there was not even the excuse that this was done to ensure a pool of seamen for naval use, for only a third of the crews in this case were legally required to be British, and a high proportion of those was exempted from the press. The Customs Commissioners argued that the industry was being featherbedded. Jenkinson agreed, though he still thought that some protection was required. He therefore proposed to lower the bounty to 30/– a ton. Pitt 'very earnestly' supported him, and a bill to that end was passed.[2] Protection was not removed; but it was more closely geared to the economic need, in a case where no immediate naval advantage was involved.

Meanwhile the Ministry was making up its mind about the southern enterprise. It was reluctant to sanction a bounty, which had proved so expensive in the north, and in the end the system of premiums was confirmed and elaborated. But the crux of the matter lay in the admission of the whalers into the waters round the Cape of Good Hope and Cape Horn; for these were reserved by charter to the South Sea and East India Companies, which were not going to welcome an infringement of their rights. Pitt took careful soundings, from the Committee

1. Grey Elliott to ? Jenkinson, 24 January 1786 (P.R.O., B.T. 6/95).
2. The Act was 26 Geo. III, c. 41. For Pitt's speech of 12 April 1786, see *P.R.*, XX, 104–7, and for a derogatory comment Sheffield to Eden, 28 April 1786 (*A.C.*, I, 367). His 'earnestness' was mentioned in *The Morning Post* of the 13th.

of Trade and from Admiral Sir Hugh Palliser, an expert on the fisheries and a former Governor of Newfoundland. As a result, he decided to support the new adventurers, to tackle the Companies, and if necessary amend their charters by law. The South Sea Company was the less formidable of the two. It had long been a mere financial shell, and it was bought off by an agreement that the whalers should purchase licences for each voyage made through its seas. But John Company of course was a much tougher proposition, and in April and May 1786 a battle royal was fought with East India House. Pitt and Dundas presided over a series of meetings between the Company, the Committee of Trade and the southern whalers, the last led by the former Bostonians the Samuel Enderbys, father and son. It ended in a qualified but substantial victory for the whaling interest. Their ships were allowed to fish in the region of the Cape of Good Hope, though not to the east, or in the west farther north than the latitude of 30° south. They were also allowed to fish down to Cape Horn within 500 leagues of the American coast, and to round the Cape and operate in the Pacific south of the equator. These provisions were incorporated in an Act 'for the Encouragement of the Southern Whale Fishery' in June.[1]

The encouragement also took the form of inducements to join. The Americans already engaged were fully recognised by law, and the Act in its first form encouraged more Nantucketers – up to the number of forty ships – to migrate to England with their families. The clause had to be dropped on opposition from the Customs, who were growing alarmed at the prospect of complications and fraud; but it was resuscitated two years later, in a further Act.[2] The offer by then was associated with another scheme, with which the Ministry flirted for some time, to attract a large American fishing colony to the magnificent natural harbour of Milford Haven. This was indeed a stimulating design, and the efforts of Charles Greville, the projector, make an interesting story – his negotiations with Jenkinson and Pitt, his visit to Nantucket, his building of quays and roads and his plans for a town, opposed by the earlier immigrants and the growing British interest of which they were the nucleus, intermittently favoured and neglected by Government, and finally, in 1795, approved too late for the necessary capital to be raised.[3] It is curious that the first project for the great haven, like its most recent successor, should have been based on oil. Its frustration was due in part to the growing success of a native southern fishery from other ports.

For when the first restrictions were removed at the Capes, the whalers

1. 26 Geo. III, c. 50. For the premiums, see also 26 Geo. III, c. 81, art. IV.
2. 28 Geo. III, c. 20.
3. The tale is well told in Harlow, op. cit., II, 307–15. Greville's letters to Pitt are in P.R.O. 30/8/140. He was the nephew of the owner of the property, Sir William Hamilton – to whom he introduced his mistress Emma. He persisted with Milford Haven for some ten years, the efforts reaching a climax in 1792–3.

began to thrust far afield. The East India Company had feared that any concession would prove to be the thin end of the wedge. It was quite right. The battle was renewed within a year. In 1788 the whalers were granted permission to sail the southern Pacific westward as far as the date line, and the Indian Ocean up to the equator and as far east as the waters of Madagascar; they tried, though unsuccessfully, for ampler limits in 1789; and throughout the next decade they steadily eroded the Companies' privilege. But legal attack was only part of the story. The oceans could not be preserved from poaching, or indeed from penetration on other grounds, and the Enderbys' ships, for example, gained an entry into forbidden areas by carrying convicts to Australia and then fishing their way home. 'We intend', wrote the elder Samuel to Pitt of one such voyage, '. . . that [the vessel] shall Circumnavigate the Globe'.[1] The fisheries were coming near to linking Greenland's icy mountains and India's coral strand.

They did so with Ministers' full, if perforce sometimes muted, approval. For the Government was keenly alert to the opportunities opening up. In the middle eighties, its thoughts were directed to snatching an Atlantic trade from the Americans: by the early nineties it was also envisaging a new pattern of commerce in the East, from the Pacific coast of America to the South Sea Islands and Canton. The whalers were among the foremost skirmishers, and Pitt encouraged and supported them. He had taken their part against the older British Companies; he was equally willing to challenge foreign powers.

The first occasion for such an encounter arose in 1789. It was of a familiar kind. English attacks on Spanish claims over trade and territory in the western hemisphere had long been a feature of European life. The Falkland Islands' dispute had almost led to war in the sixties; the American War left an unresolved conflict over settlers' rights in the Gulf of Honduras; our penetration of South and Central American markets was a running sore. The Government kept an eye on Spanish attempts to foster a whaling industry in the middle eighties. Its own success led to a collision at the end of the decade. As the British vessels moved more freely in the eastern Pacific, they became increasingly attracted by the prospects of hunting seals as well as whales. Sealskins and blubber were profitable, the animals were to be found on the rocky American shores, and the crews took to landing in pursuit. The authorities in London gave them leave, as long as they stuck to unoccupied territory: the Spaniards, as always, claimed exclusive jurisdiction over the coasts. In April 1789 they expelled two British whalers from Patagonia, and in the autumn the Government prepared a protest to Madrid.

The complaint was never sent in that form, for it was overtaken by a far more serious quarrel, whose roots stretched back into the previous decade. In 1776 Captain Cook, on his last voyage, had been instructed

1. 25 November 1790 (P.R.O. 30/8/133).

to explore the north-east Pacific, to find a channel which might open the long sought North-West Passage from Hudson's Bay. He failed, in the course of a long and painful search which took him through the Bering Strait. But the expedition had two results. Cook found an accessible base in Nootka Sound, on the western shores of what is now Vancouver Island, where furs and otterskins were to be had – commodities known to be prized in China and Japan. And when the account of the voyage was published, in 1784, it gave a more reliable picture than had yet existed of a long and deeply indented coast, whose detail however remained very largely unknown. The news caused great excitement, and a race was soon under way to exploit the promise of a new trade and the possibility of still discovering the Passage. Russians, Frenchmen, Americans rivalled Englishmen in plans for the chase. A confused situation developed in the later eighties, with English adventurers in the lead, some attached loosely to the East India Company and others in independent groups, while the Admiralty prepared a further expedition in the background. Neither the Company nor the Government, indeed, had made up their minds exactly how to treat the prospect; but two factors remained constant in a disturbed scene. A settlement should be established in territory unoccupied by Europeans; and the resulting trade at Nootka Sound should be triangular – British goods for the local trappers and hunters, furs and otterskins for China and Japan, and whales and seals to complement the Eastern wares and tea which the ships would then bring home.

A settled base was all-important to any such design, and some progress was made towards this end in 1788. But the Spaniards were not disposed to recognise a development which would infringe their historic claims on the Pacific coast. In May 1789 two Spanish warships sailed into Nootka Sound. A series of incidents followed, reaching a climax in June and July. The Spaniards hauled down the British flag, arrested the British traders and their vessels, and formally proclaimed the coast as far north as Alaska to be the possession of the Spanish Crown.

When the news reached London, which it did progressively between the following January and April, there was a violent explosion. The Government demanded redress and withdrawal, and it looked as if there would be another War of Jenkins' Ear. The crisis was acute and persistent until the autumn of 1790.[1] It ended in a British victory: the traders were compensated, and the settlement was confirmed. The foundations of British Columbia had been laid. But the agreement contained a further clause. British subjects would not be 'disturbed or molested' in pursuing the whale fishery 'in the Pacific Ocean, or in the South Seas'.[2]

1. Nootka Sound, a meeting place of East and West, made its mark on many aspects of policy. For its relation to the Eastern trade, see ch. XIV; for its impact on international affairs, chs. XIII and XVII below.
2. See *P.R.*, XXVIII (1791), 37.

The fishery indeed lay near the heart of the whole dispute. The northern trade with Asia could scarcely flourish unless it was combined with whaling and sealing, and the whaling merchants were perhaps best suited to undertake the northern trade. That at least was Government's view. The various early syndicates and individuals were not impressive, the East India Company was uncertain, and the Enderbys and their like, already ranging the Pacific, seemed a more hopeful bet. The two causes were therefore linked – the Southern Whale Fishery, it was remarked at the height of the crisis, was 'perhaps an object of full as much importance in point of national advantage as Nootka Sound itself'[1] –, and when both had been secured the Ministry went ahead. In January 1791, the whaling merchants sought guidance from the Committee of Trade on the implications of the agreement with Spain. They were asked in return – apparently to their surprise – if they would be prepared to start trading in the northern Pacific. On reflection, they agreed to do so. The Government then tackled the East India Company afresh. Pitt, now steeped in the matter, presided over a series of meetings attended by Grenville, Dundas and Hawkesbury, and the Directors' representatives. The Ministers pressed the Company hard, though it put up a strong defence. In the end a bill was prepared, in April, admitting the Southern Whale Fishery and 'the *Trade* at large' to do business freely with Canton. But the measure was never presented. A mission to China based on Indian interests – Macartney's famous mission – was in the air; the Company's charter in any case was soon due for renewal; and when that event occurred, in 1793, the intended freedom of commerce was somewhat curtailed. The Company had to permit outside interests to trade by licence between the coast of north-west America and Japan, Korea and Canton. But it was able to lay down conditions, and no onward passage was allowed. The whalers accordingly turned their attention more strictly to the southern Pacific, in which they consolidated their gains as the years went by. Almost a generation was to pass before they began to visit Japan and northern Asia in any numbers. Meanwhile they acted as the spearhead, albeit a narrow one, of a trade with South America which was later to have momentous results.

Although it did not get all that Ministers wanted, the Southern Whale Fishery was a success. The number of ships working from Britain rose steeply – perhaps fourfold – in the peacetime decade, and the value of the produce from some £14,000 to some £110,000.[2] The Americans' near monopoly was broken, other foreign rivals were contained. But the enterprise was more than a profitable commercial proposition. It was an agent of discovery and empire on acceptable terms. No new colonies were involved, new spheres of influence were opened up, the sinews of

---

1. Duke of Leeds [Carmarthen] to Pitt, 2 June 1790 (P.R.O. 30/8/151).

2. Figures, particularly of ships, are hard to pin down. There are great differences between the various returns in the Committee of Trade's and Pitt's own papers.

power were strengthened without incurring onerous commitments. The whalers seemed an appropriate instrument, more so on the whole than the East India Company. Pitt was firmly on their side, and he played a possibly decisive role. Jenkinson could not have fought the Company on his own, and without a knowledge of the Minister's views Dundas might not have co-operated as much as he did.[1] The Committee of Trade and the Board of Control were united in a case that might well have divided them. Pitt was an active member of both by the late eighties, he kept closely in touch, and the direction of his influence was clear.

The Government did not respond so positively to the demands of the fisheries nearer home. But in the middle eighties it found itself committed to a series of measures which encouraged the industry and rounded off the structure of the maritime system. Paradoxically enough, in view of what followed, the Treasury took the first step. In 1784, Pitt commissioned the economist James Anderson, who had recently published a tract on the Scottish fisheries, to report on the prospects of improving trade and industry in the west. The result was disconcerting,[2] for the inquiry focused the pertinacious efforts of that remarkable group of public-spirited Scotchmen which flourished in the age of the northern Enlightenment. It also attracted the attention of the active independent M.P. Henry Beaufoy, an associate of Shelburne, sympathetic to Pitt, and a frequent speaker on trade and finance,[3] who had some connexions with Scotland and represented the fishing borough of Great Yarmouth. The combination proved powerful. In March 1785, Dundas secured the appointment of a Commons' committee, under Beaufoy, to examine the state of the British fisheries. Its reports appeared over the next four months, and in July Beaufoy introduced 'a chain of motions' based on the findings.[4] He called for a simplification of the salt tax, which as it stood was working against the fishermen in favour of the more highly organised curers, and for the removal of many restrictions on the fishing operations and craft. The industry in fact was 'clogged' with too many 'unreasonable restraints'.[5] It could not flourish until the laws were made simpler and the duties reduced.

1. He acted indeed in this instance more as a scourge than a defender of the Company, committing the Directors, or going beyond their known views, on several occasions in the earlier talks, and later coming down in favour of the whaling merchants against some of the alternative groups (including that of his future son-in-law) which had connexions with East India House. His influence was visible in the limits to the ground recovered by the Company in 1793.

2. And the sequel unhappy. Anderson later accused Pitt of withholding payment for the work.

3. See pp. 266, 292 above and 389 below.

4. *P.R.*, XVIII, 525.

5. First Report from the Committee Appointed to Enquire into the State of the British Fisheries, 11 May 1785 (*Reports from Committees*, X, 13).

Beaufoy went out of his way to state that he was not asking for an immediate revision of the salt tax. But even so the proposals seem to have disconcerted Pitt. Their 'obvious tendency', he remarked, 'was to give up the whole of the revenue arising from the fisheries', and he wanted time to consider the effects.[1] Beaufoy was willing to grant it; but the feeling of the House was against the Minister, and the motions passed. Putting a good face on the decision, Pitt accompanied the Act with one to prevent frauds in the curing of fish and to stop the curers from dealing in salt.[2]

A year later, the indefatigable Beaufoy went farther. He obliged the Government to accept a group of resolutions on the east coast turbot fishery; and as chairman of a second Commons' committee on the state of the British fisheries, he produced the material for a comprehensive Act. As a result, fresh premiums and bounties were settled, and the excise on home consumption was lowered. A further Act in 1787 cleared up some ambiguities, and removed the remaining duties on British-caught fish for home consumption.[3]

So, by a typical mixture of protection and liberalism, the domestic fisheries were encouraged. Despite his early impetus, the process owed little to Pitt except Parliamentary time. To judge by his startled reaction, he had not followed what was going on,[4] and his instinctive answer was that of a Chancellor who had not thought out the case. As Beaufoy rightly hinted, he was acting very differently in other instances – he was lowering duties to aid consumption and simplifying the law.[5] Nor was his initial response consistent with that support of navigation, that 'encouragement of seamen', which was generally his policy. It was indeed the pressure of this popular cause which made him yield so quickly the immediate advantage of a hungry revenue to a wider interest. Jenkinson can scarcely have been displeased, in the midst of his not dissimilar labours. Nor was the navy ungrateful for this contribution to the strength of its reserve. When Admiral Rodney, dining at Carlton House, found herrings on the menu, he told his host that a thriving coastal fishery could add '20,000 hardy seamen' to the fleet.[6] The English fisheries in fact flourished. It was ironical, and sad, that the

1. *P.R.*, XVIII, 534.
2. 25 Geo. III, c. 65; c. 63.
3. 26 Geo. III, c. 81; 27 Geo. III, c. 10. Bounties on pilchards had been raised separately, by 25 Geo. III, c. 58 and 26 Geo. III, c. 45, following reports from a Commons' committee on the state of the pilchard fisheries.
4. Beaufoy's motions in July 1785 were based on the recommendations of his committee's second report, which had appeared in June. And Anderson by then was ready with the results of his inquiry, to much the same effect.
5. It is interesting, indeed, that Pitt seems to have taken no notice of a proposal in 1785 by the younger John Calcraft (the son of Chatham's old follower) to commute the salt tax, only a year after he himself had passed his Commutation Act on tea.
6. *Proceedings of the British Society, at the London Tavern, 1789;* quoted in Gerald S. Graham, *Sea Power and British North America 1783–1820* (1941), 95–6.

Scottish did not. For while the Parliamentary success stimulated the building of lighthouses and the formation of a Fishery Society north of the border, the difficulties in the western Highlands and islands proved too great, as so often since. Land was bought on a joint stock basis, and settlements were started. But within a decade they began to die. The Society's monuments survive in some early houses and ruins at Ullapool and Tobermory. Only the harbour of Pulteneytown at Wick, a later offshoot in a different area, can boast a living connexion with a hopeful scheme.

CHAPTER XIII

Colonies and Trade in the West: The American Continent and Africa

I

In the fashion of his age, Pitt was a great reader of maps. He had voyages and gazeteers and pilots in his library, and his study at Downing Street by the end held four 'sets of maps', three 'fitted to bookcases'.[1] Grenville noted how his eyes would turn to them during the years of war. But a foreign visitor had earlier been intrigued to see a volume lying open on his desk.[2] When he turned to the Atlantic and the Pacific, one familiar fact stood out. Access from the one ocean to the other lay solely in the south. The long search for a North-West Passage was still under way, designed to circumvent the land-mass separating Europe from the fabled East. It was indeed reaching a final climax, as Alexander Mackenzie followed the Arctic rivers and the sailors of many nations probed ever farther up the western coasts. But a new dimension had been added in the process to the British expeditions. When the last sailed under Captain Vancouver in 1791, it was ordered as a first object to explore the north Pacific for a 'water communication' which might 'facilitate an intercourse for the purpose of commerce between the north-west coast and the countries upon the opposite side of the continent . . . inhabited or occupied by His Majesty's subjects'.[3] Canada had entered the reckoning of a world-wide conception of trade. It was a recent entry, and the implications were obscure.

For Canada[4] was not ranked highly after its conquest in the Seven

1. 'An Inventory of the Household Furniture & the Property of the Late Rigt. Honble Willm Pitt taken at his Late House in Downing Street . . . March 3d 1806' (Pretyman Ms 562:22).
2. Michel Ogínski, *Sur La Pologne et les Polonnais, depuis 1788 jusqu'a la fin de 1815*, I (1826), 94. He called on Pitt in the winter of 1790.
3. Grenville to the Lords Commissioners of the Admiralty, 11 February 1791 (Vincent Harlow and Frederick Madden, *British Colonial Developments 1774–1834, Select Documents* (1953), 41).
4. I have used the word Canada throughout this chapter for convenience. The contemporary term was British North America, comprising Quebec Province and the Maritime Provinces on the eastern seaboard.

354

Years' War. The acquisition of Quebec province was received with mixed feelings once the excitement died down, and opinion was slow to change. The Canadian economy rested largely at the start on its links with the West Indies – an exchange of fish and timber and agricultural produce for coffee and sugar, molasses and rum. But the trade remained small – still only a few thousand pounds' worth on the eve of the American War –, and a foreign population, much larger than the main British fringe in the colony of Nova Scotia, was absorbed reluctantly for the sake of guarding New England from the threat of French attack. Some of the strongest early claims in Canada's favour came from the associates and followers of Chatham; but it took another and ironically different struggle to raise the level of general interest. The end of the American, not the Seven Years', War saw the real entry of Canada into British imperial thought. The area changed, strategically and politically, from a defence and partner of the American colonies into a weight and if necessary a barrier against the United States. The balance of its population altered with the advent of large numbers of English-speaking American loyalists. Its potential as a source of naval supply became more important as supply from the Baltic became uncertain. And the pivot of interest moved from an outward-looking seaboard with few natural resources to the prospect of a 'vestibule of trade'[1] for the great hinterland to the south and west.

Such a shift of emphasis raised a host of problems, which Pitt's Ministry had to face over the next decade. What form of government was best suited to the changed population? How far could Canadian developments be fostered without damaging other imperial interests? Could they be strengthened better by conciliation with, or at the expense of, the United States? This last was indeed the central question for the immediate future. Pitt inherited a choice of policies in a confused situation.

The choice was bedevilled by that most obstinate of issues, a frontier problem. Shelburne's border settlement had been the result of tactical need combined with a theory of commercial advantage;[2] perhaps not unnaturally, it raised greater opposition than almost any other part of the treaty. The United States were granted the huge tract of land west of the Ohio known as the Old North-West, an area about a third the size of Europe which had earlier been deemed a part of Canada. They gained a frontier through the Great Lakes (with Lake Michigan behind it), an important chain of fortified posts, a large preserve of the valuable fur trade, and control of Indian tribes which had aided the British during the war. Such terms were bound to be highly unpopular with Canadian traders and officials, and it would have needed firm

1. The phrase is that of John Graves Simcoe, soon to be Lieutenant-Governor of Upper Canada, in a letter to Dundas of 2 June 1791 (quoted in Graham, op. cit., 232).
2. Pp. 82, 93–5 above.

control from London to see that the agreement was properly observed. But control, never easy among the distant lakes and forests, was not the strong point of the Home Secretary concerned; and Government in any case set its face against carrying the settlement into effect.

The reason given was the refusal, or inability, of the United States to pay their debts to British merchants and loyalists – the colonists who had supported us during the war –, and secure the treatment agreed for those who remained within the Union. Congress was in fact in no real position to enforce its wishes on the various states, and the terms were undoubtedly honoured as much in the breach as the observance. The result played into the hands of all those, Canadian and British, who were reluctant to cede the border, abandoning their Indian allies and losing so great a part of the fur trade. The posts were accordingly held for no less than thirteen years, until 1796; and the dispute contributed its share to the strain of Anglo-American relations.

Pitt fully supported the decision to stand fast. A matter of this kind of course fell squarely within the province of a Secretary of State, and there is no trace in the relevant papers – in Pitt's or Sydney's or the official series – of the Prime Minister intervening when the policy was hardening in the middle eighties. But that in itself is a sign that he was content to let it proceed. Sydney was not the Secretary to handle an important matter of state unaided, Pitt would act quickly enough if he felt concerned, and he showed no sign of uneasiness or of wanting a more conciliatory line. At a time when he was trying to curb military expense, he sanctioned the continuation of handsome 'presents' to the Indian tribes[1] (had he not, as a boy, seen the Mohican chiefs on their way to pay their respects to Chatham?), and he gave no hint of compromising with the Americans – very much the reverse. He dismissed their arguments on the frontier throughout the eighties, and when a more positive policy was required he began by supporting a settlement that would have reversed the peace treaty.[2]

It might have been very difficult for Pitt to have acted otherwise at the start – though if there had been the will, ingenuity might have suggested a way. There were naturally strong feelings of honour for the loyalists, whose allegiance had cost them dear. But Pitt was not in any

1. Indian 'presents' (i.e. subsidies and arms) cost the home Government over £20,000 a year on average between 1784 and 1788. It is true that the sum was increased by corruption on the spot; and that large economies were always hard to enforce on a command except by a change of strategic policy. But while Pitt scrutinised the accounts (see P.R.O. 30/8/346), this last was precisely what he seems never to have contemplated.

2. 'The Demand' he wrote at the end of 1785, 'seems itself fairly founded upon the Treaty. But there are Articles to be performed upon their Part which we must equally insist upon – Particularly this seems to be an Opportunity for urging Satisfaction respecting the Debts' (to Carmarthen, 16 December 1785; B. M. Egerton Ms 3498). For his reaction as late as 1790, see *American State Papers . . . [Foreign Relations]* I, ed. Walter Lowrie and Matthew St Clair Clarke (1832), 123–5.

case the sort of Minister to let a financial agreement go by default. It was just the kind of thing that roused him, particularly when the finances were in distress, and he had had enough to do with the loyalists' claims to appreciate their size. He was therefore ready to adopt a policy which ran counter to Shelburne's intentions. Once adopted, he encouraged its extension in a form not untypical of his general approach.

The object of the policy was still broadly that of Shelburne himself. But the situation was viewed more cautiously, and the means were more aggressive than he might have approved. It was generally agreed that America offered great outlets for British manufactures, in that search for 'new Markets' which was needed 'to afford sufficient scope and further Encouragement to the Industry of His Majesty's Subjects'.[1] The former colonies must still take goods from the source on which they had always mainly relied, and there were unknown possibilities in the hinterland beyond. But neither prospect could be properly exploited by relying on mutual goodwill. Our relations with the United States were disturbed by our methods of preserving the system of navigation, the Union itself was weak, and opportunities of commercial penetration must be seized as well as wooed. This applied to the eastern states. It applied still more to the west. For the keys to that vast, largely untapped region lay in the Mississippi and the Great Lakes, the latter now claimed in part by the Americans and the former belonging very largely to Spain. The Mississippi indeed had been for some time, and remained, a factor in British policy: we had tried in the recent peace treaty to secure free access to its lower and central reaches, and while the use of the river was now a matter for the United States and Spain alone, this did not lessen our interest in so great a highway between the Caribbean and the new lands. Both powers must be carefully watched; both were poised to spread their influence westward at our expense. It was the more necessary for us to protect the northern lines of communication, to secure the passage of the Great Lakes and a continued presence in the Old North-West.

A plan to this effect was developed by stages in 1790–1. The Nootka Sound crisis brought to a head British rivalry with Spain throughout the continent, and stimulated the prospect, already faintly stirring, of a trade agreement with the United States. The frontier dispute took on a new dimension in this sharper air. In April 1790 the Committee of Trade produced a comprehensive report on the prospects in North America, against which the problem could be reassessed. In its final form, this conceded the frontier posts to the Americans; but only in return for the establishment of an independent neutral zone south of the Great Lakes, comprising most of the disputed territory, from which both American and British troops would be excluded but in and

1. Stephen Cottrell [one of the secretaries of the Committee of Trade] to Grenville, 17 April 1790 (copy in P.R.O. 30/8/343).

through which both nations might carry on a free reciprocal trade. The British would use their good offices to conciliate the Indian tribes with the United States; British agents would therefore be free to remain in the neutral zone.

This plan may have owed something to an earlier scheme for a buffer zone when Canada was still French; it was now designed, as an American historian of the subject has observed, 'to undo the American territorial triumph of 1783'.[1] By confining the United States to an area south of the Ohio, it would have protected the passage to the west, and Canada itself, from American attack. It would have perpetuated the British influence among the friendly Indian tribes. And it would have kept the valuable fur trade of the region very largely in Canadian hands, and secured the northern base for commercial penetration. It would in fact have provided a firm foundation for a trading empire and sphere of influence, looking to the Pacific coast on the one hand and the Mississippi basin on the other. Pitt's Ministry was thus seeking a commercial goal similar to Shelburne's by a contrary territorial policy.[2] The plan failed; despite their wishes for a treaty, the Americans would not cede what they had won. They were wise in their generation, for a British success might, at least for a time, have 'cut the very heart out of the future American Middle West'.[3]

The design was brought to the point by an international crisis in all aspects of which Pitt was personally involved. But its evolution, and later its conduct, were held firmly in other hands, for in June 1789 Sydney left the Home Office and Grenville took his place. The difference was at once apparent, nowhere more so than in colonial affairs. Grenville soon gathered up the strands of the Canadian question, and proposed a clear and precise answer; and he handled its negotiation with the United States when, moving on, he became Foreign Secretary in 1791. He was indeed well fitted to do so. He knew Pitt's mind, as Pitt knew his. And this was an early example of the two men acting in concert in a policy to which they both fully subscribed.

The spirit of the new partnership was soon displayed in another way. The Government now moved openly in the direction of a largely free trade for the Canadian hinterland. In so doing, it was not departing entirely from earlier policy, for a largely free traffic already existed with the neighbouring American state of Vermont. But this had been sanctioned for political purposes – Vermont was at odds with the rest of New England, and seeking a closer connexion with Canada[4] –, and the

1. Samuel Flagg Bemis, *Jay's Treaty* (1923), 109.
2. Cf. Shelburne's arguments for the United States *enlarging* its territory in the west, pp. 93–5 above.
3. Bemis, op. cit., 109.
4. See pp. 372–4 below.

authorities in London had managed to avoid a formal endorsement. The Committee of Trade had in fact declined to pronounce one way or the other, and given the Governor-General the power to decide. Grenville's advent turned this acquiescence into a positive policy. In 1790 the Committee was led to 'permit and even encourage' existing practice,[1] and the proposals for an American treaty sought a large measure of open traffic. This may again have been partly because the Vermonters were trying to force the pace; but it was also in accord with Grenville's and Pitt's economic views. The cousins had studied Adam Smith together, and thought much alike on matters of trade.[2] Both of them were anxious to ease restrictions and act decisively where they could, and when they were brought together a new atmosphere could be sensed.

At the same time, neither Grenville nor Pitt was prepared to promote a free trade in every respect. It was in fact 'permitted and encouraged' where advantage seemed clear, and restricted or excluded where it did not. A clear test in this instance was provided by rum, the 'spirituous liquor' essential to the fur trade, demanded by 'the savages' in return for their precious pelts.[3] The Americans distilled it cheaply, largely from molasses from the French West Indies. But the Canadians were obliged to take their spirit or molasses (for they too had their distilleries) from British sources, which were more expensive than foreign supplies would have been. Both the West Indian planters and the Canadian distillers, with contrary interests, had long protested at this state of affairs; but while the latter obtained some concessions, they were not enough. More petitions were received in the later eighties, the Canadians again having some slight success, and in 1790 Grenville took up the matter. His leaven was soon at work. He questioned the parties direct, he stirred up the Committee of Trade, he brought the weight of his office to bear on a complex commercial subject. But in the end the restrictions stood. However anxious Grenville may have been to re-examine the facts, neither he nor Pitt felt prepared to gainsay arguments the force of which they respected. The old considerations prevailed; the recent concessions could not be extended without posing a threat to the carrying trade. The existing provisions were therefore repeated in 1791,[4] and continued in force throughout the long war in which maritime strength remained all-important.

British America in fact was still held firmly in the frame of the navigation system, now interpreted as liberally as possible, but not

1. Report to Grenville of 17 April 1790 (copy in P.R.O. 30/8/343).

2. 'We in truth formed our opinions of the subject together, and I was not more convinced than you were of the soundness of Adam Smith's principles of political economy . . .' (Grenville to Pitt, 24 October 1800; Stanhope, IV, 248). He added '. . . till Lord Liverpool [Jenkinson] lured you from our arms into all the mazes of the old system'. But that referred to a later time.

3. Privy Council minute of 2 December 1790 (P.R.O., C.O. 45/12).

4. 31 Geo. III, c. 31, art, XLVI.

materially weakened. Unfettered expansion inland was paralleled by continued protection in the older activities, the balance between them being determined by the home country's immediate needs. The Canadian fisheries were guardedly encouraged, with reservations for the effect on Newfoundland.[1] Forestry and agriculture were sponsored, for the sake of the West Indies and the provision – now more desirable – of British naval stores.[2] The Government did not expect too much of either – wisely so, as it turned out.[3] It agreed that Canada's greatest asset was the fact that her territory 'extends all along the back of America',[4] forming the desired natural 'vestibule of trade'. But while the passage must be opened, and all likely opportunities grasped, this must not be at the expense of the interests that made and carried the goods.

The advent of Grenville as Secretary of State, which gave fresh scope to her territorial policy, also hastened the leisurely progress of Canada's constitutional reform. In 1783, the lands now comprising the eastern part of the country were divided into two distinct entities:[5] the old colony of Nova Scotia, which also comprised New Brunswick and the island of Cape Breton (the small island of St John's, separated from Nova Scotia in 1769, also retained some dependent ties); and the province of Quebec. The governments differed in form, and still more in substance. Nova Scotia (except for Cape Breton Island, which was almost uninhabited) boasted legislative assemblies, responsible with the royal Governor of the colony for their own affairs. It was in fact administered, on paper, on the general pattern of the Old Empire; like the richer communities of the Thirteen Colonies and the British Caribbean. Quebec on the other hand was controlled by a Governor and a nominated Council, and its constitutional charter was a British Act of Parliament, the Quebec Act of 1774. The burghers of the St Lawrence towns were thus subject to a less advanced form of government than the fishermen and small farmers of the windswept Atlantic coast.

This was the case in theory; the reality was rather different. In the Maritimes, poor and sparsely populated, the assemblies laid few claims to power. The Quebec Council on the other hand, though unrepresen-

1. Pp. 342–6 above.

2. P. 355 above. The growth of hemp and flax and timber were encouraged, the first two financially by legislation (26 Geo. III, c. 53), all three materially by expert advice and help from home.

3. See p. 334 above for the doubts on the prospects for the supply of the West Indies.

4. 'Considerations on the Propriety of Great Britain abandoning the Indian posts . . .'; undated ms by an unknown author in Pitt's papers (P.R.O. 30/8/344).

5. That is to say, excluding the island of Newfoundland, which had always been separate and was not a colony, and the territories of the Hudson's Bay Company to the north.

tative, had a majority of unofficial members both French and English, some executive functions in a quorum, and certain legislative powers. The Act of 1774 was in fact a compromise in a very difficult situation, many of whose features survived to perplex Grenville and Pitt. How could a large French-speaking population best be reconciled to the British Crown? How best adjust French and English laws, Roman Catholics and Protestants?

The one recent parallel was not consoling. The conquest of the French island of Grenada in the Seven Years' War had raised similar problems for an imperial system in which representative institutions, however interpreted, were the norm. The granting of an assembly, but of Protestant membership, led to continued unrest, which was solved only by waiving the religious clause. But the subsequent recapture of the island by the French in the American War, and its return to England at the peace, left a divided embittered population in no mood to recombine. Complaints and petitions flowed in to the Privy Council in London, and in 1789 the French were declared to be legally debarred from the assembly. The French planters thereupon began to sell up and leave, and a volatile economy was further disturbed. It was not a happy precedent for revising the Canadian constitution.

Yet some revision was needed. The Quebec Act had not proved a success. It was subject to pressure even in its heyday, and now its basic condition had changed. Its main principle – an unusual one – had been to preserve the French system as far as possible, in a society in which English traditions by and large did not apply. The seigneurs and the clergy were to be recognised as the props of the state; the old civil code was retained, old clerical rights were guaranteed. The experiment worked well in many ways, but it was subject to two great weaknesses. The very strength of the French institutions meant that the British would take care to preserve their own political powers, exercised through the Governor and shaped in the last resort by Parliament. And the activities of a small but thrusting, generally unattractive, English-speaking minority led to a conflict of customs and rights, and some penetration of the old French structure itself. A major difficulty arose in the matter of commercial law. The Act had been moulded by the forceful pressure of the local Governor, Sir Guy Carleton: it had never pleased the merchant interests at home. As the American War widened, and the loyalty of the French Canadians was questioned, the Governor assumed greater control, and the balance was uneasily sustained.

But the Quebec Act was really brought in question at the end of the war. It had been based on the fact that the vast majority of the population was French-speaking. When large numbers of American loyalists migrated from the United States to Canada, the whole nature of the problem changed. By the middle eighties some 20,000 had settled in Quebec province, mostly in the western part, and another 35,000 in the colony of Nova Scotia. The English-speaking community of Canada was now nearly two-thirds the size of the French. Perhaps more important, its quality was raised – New Brunswick, it was said, was as 'polite' as Boston –, and the British Government owed it consideration.

Pitt had been much concerned from the start in the loyalists' case – one of the most urgent and controversial problems bequeathed by the war. As a member of Shelburne's Cabinet he had known something of the fight on their behalf in the peace talks, and helped defend the result against angry Parliamentary attacks. As Chancellor of the Exchequer at that time, he had examined the early claims; and he was now responsible for their settlement, and for extracting compensation from the United States. It was a long and a sad story, of the kind we ourselves know all too well. There was much real distress, some exaggeration on the part of the victims, much dissatisfaction with the Government's efforts. As usual, indeed, these were dilatory and often ungenerous: despite a promise of help from Pitt in 1785, the Treasury moved in its own ways at its own pace. But at least this was rather faster than it often showed – many seamen in the fleet would have settled gladly for such treatment –, and given the numbers involved and the lack of co-operation from America the result in the aggregate was not unworthy of the cause. Over £3 million was paid out of British funds by annual grants between 1784 and 1789, including a special grant in 1788 after long and weary investigations across the Atlantic.[1] The Minister made very clear the lines on which he had acted: he did not wish to pretend, he told the Commons, that his scheme was 'more liberal than it really was'.[2] He had not intended to try to repay the loyalists for their losses: he had rather fixed, and was now applying, a standard of compensation. And while many of the recipients no doubt laughed bitterly at his words, perhaps he was not unjustified in saying that the compensation, as a total, was 'liberal and . . . handsome . . ., all the circumstances of their case, and the case of this country, considered'.[3]

Pitt was referring in this statement to financial grants. But many of the loyalists who went to Canada received grants of land. The advent of such large numbers created a completely new situation, particularly perhaps in the Maritime Provinces, and above all in New Brunswick. The prospect of a balance to the French Canadians was welcomed in London, and Nova Scotia and its neighbours were 'henceforth regarded in England as Loyalist colonies'.[4] In 1784, New Brunswick was separated from Nova Scotia, and the dependent islands – the loyalists in

1. Exact figures are hard to compute. Probably the best estimate is a total of £3,033,091, by H. E. Egerton in the introduction (p. xl) to his edition of papers of *The Royal Commission on the Losses and Services of the American Loyalists 1783 to 1785* . . . (1915).

2. 6 June 1788 (*P.R.,* XXIV (1788), 59). The remark was provoked by a critically approving speech from Fox.

3. Ibid.

4. Helen Taft Manning, *British Colonial Government after the American Revolution 1782–1820* (1933), 55.

St John's having already set up a semi-autonomous government – were given Lieutenant-Governors, Cape Breton with a nominated Council.[1] Two years later, the inland colonies were placed on the same formal footing, all the eastern territories and Quebec coming under the Governor of the last province.

This was a step along the road which ended in the Canada Act. But there was no hint of the eventual shape of that measure at the time. The appointment of a Governor-General (the title was at first contested) seemed in fact to point in a direction contrary to that finally adopted. For the choice fell on Carleton (soon to be Lord Dorchester), the Governor of Quebec in the early seventies, and Carleton was virtually the author of the Quebec Act. He did not seem very likely therefore to move for its supersession, and he was moreover sent out to hold an increasingly difficult position while he and the Ministry decided what to do. For both sides in Quebec province were now calling for change: the loyalists with the old English-speaking minority on the one hand, their French-speaking opponents on the other. Sydney was alarmed. But he had nothing useful to propose. Ministers therefore turned to Carleton – though without marked enthusiasm – as a guarantor of order and a source of advice.

Pitt himself was still undecided, and he was not prepared to force the pace. He had found little time to spare for Canada, and he was fed with diverse reports. In the spring of 1785 he was in touch with the London Committee of Canadian Merchants, a body representing the traders of Montreal and Quebec. He seems to have expressed some sympathy with the idea of a stronger Legislative Council, or even an Assembly, and a reconstruction of the judicial system[2] – proposals also made by the loyalists with a different balance in view. But Ministers had little proper information to go on, and their instinctive reaction was to mark time. The Canadians were accordingly kept 'at a bay',[3] and Government defeated a proposal in the Commons to check the Governor-General's powers by extending those of an enlarged nominated Council.

This state of suspended animation continued for another two years. For Government was not going to move if possible until it had concrete

1. See p. 360 above.
2. The evidence is somewhat suspect; but this appears to have been the impression (see Harlow, op. cit., II, 728–30). Our information on the subject unfortunately comes mainly from the letters of an intriguing member of the committee, Pierre Roubeaud, to his correspondents in Canada and to Evan Nepean, one of the Under-Secretaries at the Home Office, in P.R.O., C.O. 42/20. The leader of the deputation to Pitt was Francis Maseres, once Attorney General of Quebec and now a Baron of the Exchequer – the Baron Maseres of Lamb's 'The Old Benchers of the Inner Temple', who 'walks (or did till very lately) in the costume of the reign of George the Second'.
3. Roubeaud to Nepean, 15 April 1785 (C.O. 42/20). Pitt's caution, and the limits to his interest, are further suggested by the fact that he failed to see the leading candidate for the Chief Justiceship of Canada, William Smith, who was then visiting London to press his claims and those of Carleton as Governor-General.

advice from Dorchester, and Dorchester was baffled and had no concrete advice to give. He preferred to govern as before, through a Council which he would dominate, possibly granting greater legal concessions to the British settlers but postponing constitutional change. In this hiatus, Ministers could only suggest a partition of Quebec province, leaving the French-speaking part as it was and giving the loyalists in the west an elected assembly. Such a temporising settlement was not very hopeful as it stood. But the authorities in London could see no farther, and Dorchester was prepared reluctantly to agree. Nothing however was done, the thorny problem was shelved once more, and the 'grievances and abuses' accordingly continued 'in an extraordinary degree'.[1]

Matters came to a head in the summer of 1788. One of the chief Canadian spokesmen for reform, Adam Lymburner, was then in London pleading the cause. His arguments stirred up Opposition – they also had some effect on Government[2] –, and an attack was launched in the Commons. The Ministry found itself hard pressed, Pitt sympathised with some of the grievances, and he was forced to state that time would be granted early in the winter session for further debate. Meanwhile the Government would again seek Dorchester's detailed advice – obviously now with a view to presenting specific proposals.[3] This was done in the summer recess; but the replies remained unsatisfactory, and in the autumn the Regency crisis arose. There was no time for Canada at such a moment, or indeed for any constitutional problem whose settlement must necessarily take account of the King's views. It was therefore not until the following summer, in 1789, that Ministers could settle down to what had now become an inescapable task.

Pitt by then was spared the need to do the work himself, for in June 1789 Grenville succeeded Sydney. The new Home Secretary was determined to tackle the difficulties – he thought 'the business of Quebec the most important and extensive of any of the subjects which [he] found in the office'[4] –, and by the autumn he had prepared a scheme. It was a comprehensive and logical attempt to meet a problem that was new on such a scale, and the result affected imperial thought over the next fifty years.

Grenville started from two propositions, one more urgent than the other. The first related to revenue. Quebec province had proved expensive to the home Government since the peace; despite post-war economies, it was costing over £150,000 a year in the later eighties after the indirect local taxes had been raised. An obvious remedy was

1. 'Observations, Political and Commercial relating to Canada'; anon., 1788 (P.R.O., C.O. 47/112).

2. Lymburner was in touch with Pitt (P.R.O. 30/8/346), as well as with the Home Office.

3. See Pitt's remarks in *P.R.*, XXIII (1788), 694.

4. Grenville to George III, 12 October 1789 (*L.C.G. III*, I, no. 555).

therefore to allow the local authorities to levy direct taxes, a power withheld from the existing Council by the Quebec Act of 1774. But this could scarcely be done except by granting representative institutions; and since the French-speaking communities were still the richest and most powerful, they should be given the privilege of a legislative assembly.

But Grenville also subscribed to a commonly held, more far-reaching creed. 'The Constitution of Great Britain is sufficient to pervade the whole world'.[1] The loyalists wished to 'partake of the forms of the British Government',[2] and were beginning to do so in some areas: could not these be extended, with suitable reservations, to cover Canada as a whole? Given the state of local opinion, it was scarcely feasible to combine the French and English-speaking populations of Quebec in one assembly – Pitt had said the year before that this 'would be to change a solid blessing into a substantial curse'.[3] The province must therefore be partitioned, as the Ministry had earlier thought, into an Upper (English-speaking) and Lower (French-speaking) Canada. But both parts should then share a broadly similar pattern of government. Each should be granted a legislative assembly, elected septennially and empowered to vote the annual supplies, which would be combined with a Legislative Council, whose members would either be hereditary or appointed for life, to form the legislature of the state. The executive in each case would still reside in an Executive Council (the successor of the existing Council), which would be nominated 'at pleasure' and assist the Lieutenant-Governor, under the Governor-General.

This was a deliberate attempt to reproduce the balance of the British constitution, the Legislative Assembly corresponding to the Commons, the Legislative Council to the Lords, the Executive Council – less closely – to the Ministry, and the Governor-General to the King. The intention could be gauged by Grenville's final draft of the plan. The Assembly was to be 'a Legislature established on the principles of the British constitution . . . competent to impose taxes for the internal purposes of the province'. The Legislative Council was to represent 'the aristocratical part of our constitution' – that 'check, both on the mis-conduct of Governors, and on the democratical spirit which prevailed in . . . Assemblies', that 'intermediate power' which had been so sadly lacking in the former American colonies. The Executive Council, though 'constitutionally distinct', might well be 'composed of members of either branch of the Legislature'; and 'the power of the Crown . . . would, of course, be represented by the Lieutenant Governors or Governor General'. The whole purpose was to 'preserve', as had not been done with due care elsewhere, 'a due admixture of the monarchical

1. P. 99 above.
2. Memorandum in Grenville to Dorchester [no. 2], 20 October 1789 (Harlow and Madden, *British Colonial Developments*, 199).
3. Speech of 16 May 1788 in the Commons (*P.R.*, XXIII, 690).

and aristocratical parts of the British constitution' with 'the establishment of a popular representation'.[1]

But this of course was the rub. How were Crown and aristocracy to exert their weight in a land 'at so great a distance from the Mother Country', where an hereditary peerage did not exist and 'the effect from the immediate presence of the Sovereign . . . was . . . necessarily lost'?[2] The answer again was presented in familiar British terms: the Governor's legislative powers could perhaps be strengthened, along the lines of the royal prerogative. But any such increase in his authority might fail in its effect without some increase in his influence. The 'want of patronage or rewards for services' in the Thirteen Colonies had contributed to the tendency 'to diminish the weight and consequence of Government itself';[3] some remedy must now be found for Canada in the absence of an hereditary revenue such as existed at home. Grenville accordingly adopted a proposal of Dorchester's to reserve substantial tracts of land to the Crown, whose lease would yield an income out of which the Governor could 'reward services' to his Government.

Such a distribution of land, moreover, would serve a further purpose. It would encourage the establishment of the landed families which were needed to fill the Legislative Council, and which – whether hereditary legislators or not – would thereby become attached to the Crown. For Grenville was well aware that a political structure similar to the English must be buttressed as far as possible by a comparable social system. A landed aristocracy was one obvious ingredient. Others were a code of law, an Established Church, and a system of education. Uniformity here of course was impossible, and indeed immediately undesirable: French Catholic institutions must be preserved, and there was a strong body of feeling (which the King himself shared) that the community's traditions should be respected. The laws and religion of Lower Canada should therefore be preserved, though the first should be amended and the second complemented to satisfy the needs of the English-speaking minority.[4] But English laws and the Anglican Church should be introduced into Upper Canada, the latter by means of Clergy Reserves on the Crown lands on which parsonages and schools would be built. Grenville indeed did his best to foster the efforts, already active, to found and disseminate a transatlantic Anglican culture. It was a process which could be traced to pre-revolutionary days. There had been talk of providing Bishops in the American and Canadian colonies in the 1760s: in the early and middle eighties the latter idea was revived. The former Under-Secretary of the American Department,

1. Memorandum in Grenville to Dorchester, 20 October 1789 (Harlow and Madden, op. cit., 197–210).
2. Loc. cit., 206.
3. Loc. cit., 208. The Governors in colonial America had often lamented their lack of patronage.
4. Legal reform in the event proved beyond the powers of the British authorities, and was left to local determination.

William Knox, produced one plan, and the loyalists another; the Committee of Trade reviewed the proposals in 1786; in 1787 a Bishop was appointed to Nova Scotia, and in 1788 a clerical teaching academy – the King's Collegiate School, the oldest public school in the overseas Empire – was founded at Windsor in the centre of that colony. Grenville now sought to enlarge it, and associate it directly with the system of education at home, by means of a board of trustees in London drawing on Exchequer funds to send Nova Scotian scholars to Oxford and Cambridge for training as ordinands. He failed, possibly because the Universities would not play. But the scheme underlined the importance he attached to sowing a seed in this virgin soil, whose growth would reflect its English parentage and produce a plant which could withstand the blasts of French Catholicism on the one hand and American radical dissent on the other.

Grenville discussed his ideas with Pitt as soon as possible; the two men talked together early in the summer recess of 1789. The Minister subscribed to the plan, leaving its handling to his cousin, as indeed he continued to do until it was about to become a bill.[1] He gave the first draft a detailed scrutiny,[2] but thereafter he seems to have stayed in the wings, and the Act was primarily Grenville's creation, as important to him as the plan for Ireland had been to Pitt. There is no reason to doubt that it was entirely in tune with the latter's thought. He kept in touch with progress – Grenville's prospect for the Anglican academy was written out at Holwood[3] –, and he announced and defended the bill persuasively when it reached the Commons. Meanwhile there were tactics to be considered, for there were three possible obstacles to overcome: the Cabinet, the King, and the Governor-General.

The Cabinet had not shown much interest in Canada – Sydney, anxious for its formal backing, had earlier lamented its indifference[4] –, and it would almost certainly follow a decisive lead. But that in turn might not be secured unless the King could first be squared. George III was not much concerned in this decade with perhaps the most significant range of imperial questions: those developments of trading policy which set the scene for so much else. His farmer's eye led him to encourage some of the experiments in cultivation, and he saw the reports from the Committee of Trade which were submitted to the Privy Council, and the Foreign Office papers on negotiations with other powers. But the royal authority was seldom involved, and he had little to say. A new constitution, however, was another matter. It concerned his prerogative,

1. See their correspondence in January 1791, in *H.M.C., Dropmore,* II, 13.

2. Three pages of his notes on Grenville's explanation, as drafted on 20 October 1789, are in Fortescue Mss, file 'Quebec'.

3. Grenville to the Bishop of Chester, 11 April 1790 (Royal Archives, Windsor; see *L.C.G. III,* I, no. 585). Harlow attributes this letter to Pitt (op. cit., II, 740–1). But it would appear to be in Grenville's hand and to be initialled by him, and there is a fair copy among his own papers (Fortescue Mss, 'Miscellaneous, 1790–92').

4. See Harlow, loc. cit., 731.

and his views must be taken into account. Ten years before, they might have given rise to serious trouble; but the fire had now been dimmed, and at this moment the embers were low. So much indeed could be surmised from the Lord Chancellor's response. For in a matter of this kind the Lord Chancellor must be consulted, and his opinion would be taken at least in part as an expression of the King's. Grenville got in touch with Thurlow at the end of August. The reply was not very encouraging – scarcely surprisingly perhaps, for quite apart from the subject Thurlow was now on bad terms with Pitt. He answered sarcastically, rather contemptuously – an exercise in which he was always proficient. But after talking to the Home Secretary, he gave a shrugging consent.[1] '. . . The application', he had written at first, '. . . would perhaps be the best way of trying [the] real worth [of the plan], and certainly of trying its expediency';[2] and he was content to let it go at that. He must have known or thought that the King would take much the same line; and so it proved. 'I own', George III remarked, 'I am sorry any change is necessary'. He would have preferred the position to be held 'in its present state for some years'.[3] But since Ministers thought otherwise, he would not try to influence them. The past decade, above all his recent illness, had taken their toll.

The way was therefore clear by mid-October to tackle Dorchester in Canada. The long despatch was sent towards the end of the month, and Ministers awaited the answer before completing their draft. But they had reckoned without the Atlantic and the Canadian winter. The document did not reach Quebec until 20 January 1790; Dorchester sent his reply on 8 February; and that did not arrive in London until 18 April.[4] It then seemed too late in a crowded session for a bill to be moved, there was a general election in the summer, and thereafter other business claimed the Government's time. The Canadian constitution was accordingly laid aside once more, and it was January 1791 before a draft was prepared for presentation to Parliament the next month.

In its final, revised version this included some of Dorchester's answers. The Governor-General had been given no real chance to question the gist of the scheme. He had been asked to comment on certain points and to fill in certain facts and figures – the lines of provincial boundaries, the size of the Chambers, electoral qualifications, laws relating to land. He made only two major proposals, one of which was heeded and one was not. He wanted greater powers for the Governor-General over the various provincial governments – a demand which the Ministry did not

1. *H.M.C., Dropmore*, I, 503–5. On receiving his answer, Grenville circulated the plan to other members of the Cabinet (see papers in Fortescue Mss, 'Cabinet Ministers' and 'Duke of Richmond').
2. To Grenville, [1–10?] September 1789 (*H.M.C., Dropmore*, I, 505).
3. To the same, 13 October 1789 (loc. cit., 532).
4. P.R.O., C.O. 42/67.

Charles Jenkinson, Lord Hawkesbury. *After Romney*

William Wilberforce. *Mezzotint after John Rising*

Lord Sydney. *Engraved after Sayers, July 1784*

accept –, and he objected (as Thurlow indeed had done, less firmly) to an hereditary Legislative Council. He had his way on the second point. Grenville and Pitt decided to substitute a Chamber of life members, reserving the Crown's right to create hereditary titles later with hereditary seats. Otherwise the plan was not materially amended, and at the beginning of March leave was given to bring in a bill.

The debate was conducted by Pitt, for Grenville himself had meanwhile been given a peerage. The fact has tended to give the impression that the Minister was more responsible for the measure than he really was. But he handled it vigorously, and the bill passed largely unchanged. Fox, predictably and not unreasonably, attacked the idea of the Legislative Council, as likely to fail in its object and give too much power to the Crown. A Canadian so-called aristocracy could not hope to carry the weight of the British: better *elect* to the upper Chamber, on the basis of property, to make it 'as much independent of the Governor as the nature of a colony would admit'.[1] He was defeated on this; but he secured some other amendments – the electoral qualifications in land were lowered, elections were fixed triennially instead septennially,[2] the size of the Legislative Assembly was increased, the granting of hereditary honours left for further review. The bill soon passed the Lords, and on 10 June it became law.[3]

The Canada Act was very much the child of its time. Its immediate object was important – to reward and reassure large numbers of loyalists who had settled in a society very different from their own. But the ways in which this was to be done were of far-reaching significance, and they embodied much reflection on the lessons of the past. For while the situation in Canada might have demanded attention in any case, this was made almost certain, and the answer was largely moulded, by the experience of the American revolt. That great event casts its shadow over the official correspondence, and pervades Grenville's final explanation of his plan. Its influence may have been reinforced at this point by another, less openly avowed but more immediate – the shadow of present, not past events, taking place a great deal nearer home. All the provisions of the Act – the Governor's patronage, the Established Church, the aristocratic Legislative Council – were designed to avoid the mistakes of earlier generations. They were also a proclamation of faith, the more deeply felt as men looked across the Channel, in 'a constitution, deservedly the glory and happiness of those who lived under it', which 'should be extended to all our dependencies as . . .

1. Speech of 8 April 1791 (*P.R.*, XXIX (1791), 74). Thurlow, on the other hand, had cast doubt on the idea as it stood precisely because it might create such an 'independent interest' (*H.M.C., Dropmore*, I, 504–5).
2. See p. 365, and cf. pp. 59, 63 above.
3. 31 Geo. III, c. 31.

circumstances . . . would admit'.[1] It was in the debate on the Canada Act in which Pitt was reported to have spoken these words that Burke broke with Fox over the French Revolution.

The fresh tribute to an old creed marked a departure of policy. It announced in effect a new principle of colonial 'assimilation'. Overseas possessions could no longer be left too much to their own devices; but neither, in reaction, should they have to depend too directly on London. A middle way must be sought between the paternalism of the Quebec Act and the *laissez-aller* of earlier decades; and the answer did not lie, as had once been suggested, in a single imperial Parliament in which the colonies' spokesmen would be absorbed. Local communities as far as possible should continue to pay their own way; local representative assemblies should remain the distinguishing feature of British rule. But they must now be restrained by a stronger executive within a balance deriving from the parent system, so that the ties with the home country were not loosened or destroyed. We must be more careful than we had been to bind our territories to ourselves. But let us do so in our own way, by the spread of our tried institutions, so that our possessions would be 'annexed to, but not merged in, the Crown of Great Britain'.[2]

In Canada it seemed, paradoxically, that this might best be achieved by partition. Immediate division was the brightest hope of achieving unity in the end. Only thus could the interests of different communities be properly protected, under the shield of a common, balancing, and eventually unifying constitution. The Canadians should certainly be 'led universally to prefer' that constitution 'and the English laws'. But the French community must not be coerced; it must rather be allowed to learn by 'experience . . . that the English laws were best'.[3]

Things did not turn out like that. The experiment did not prove a success. It worked reasonably well in Upper Canada for a time, but not in the Lower province. Confidence there, never robust, was badly shaken by more frontier troubles and another war with France; the Governor's patronage favoured the British, and the Legislative Council became an official clique. The French community remained distinct and defensive, the more so as its economic dominance became less marked; but no strong Anglicanised social structure emerged as a counteracting influence or shield. No hereditary honours were granted, the Clergy Reserves did not meet their main purpose, the squires and the parsons failed to take root. The Act survived the Napoleonic Wars, but by then it was already undermined. It met its protracted end in Durham's Report of 1839, that more conspicuous landmark of imperial

---

1. Pitt in the Commons, 11 May 1791 (*P.R.*, XXIX, 393–4).

2. The phrase is Henry Grattan's (*The Speeches of Henry Grattan . . .*, ed. by his Son . . ., II (1822), 329): cf. p. 196 above. For the Irish parallel, and perhaps influence, see W. L. Morton, 'The Local Executive in the British Empire 1763–1828', in *E.H.R.*, LXXVIII, no. 308.

3. Pitt in the Commons, 8 April 1791 (*P.R.*, XXIX, 76–7).

development. But it had enshrined genuine hopes, and it reflected the ideas of its day. It was in fact a thoroughly whiggish conception, as much so as the later Report at a later time: a monument to the belief of a governing class in its cherished institutions, which it had now been brought to the point of deciding to export. The answer was rather slow in coming, and it proved inadequate, but it was not ungenerous or irresponsible: it embodied the form of government and the values which its authors understood. And if the balance of government shifted in the end as constitutional ideas began to change, the values did not disappear. The Canada Act of 1791 was replaced by the very different Act of 1840. But something of its spirit survived, in another setting, in Macaulay's Indian Education Minute of 1835.

II

The British policies for the Caribbean and Canada, and throughout the western Atlantic, rested on old foundations and largely reaffirmed old ends. But the stimulus came from the American upheaval, and the former colonies suffered from the results. Anglo-American relations were immediately shaped – the evolution of the United States was affected – by the British regulations for the West Indian trade, the Americans' treatment of creditors and loyalists, and the related problem of the Canadian frontier. They were correspondingly troubled. But they were never entirely bleak, for there were always strong forces at least in the States anxious to grasp any chance of improvement.

Little came their way for several years. Within the compelling limits of the Navigation Acts, the British Government was inclined to congratulate itself on its commercial 'liberality' – the word often used. By an Act of 1783 for the immediate conduct of Anglo-American trade, United States' vessels could carry their goods, except whale oil and fins but now including naval stores, into British ports on the old preferential terms.[1] American foodstuffs, in British ships, were allowed into Newfoundland, and a largely free trade was established between Canada and the neighbouring state of Vermont.[2] These regulations brought some solid advantages to the United States. But it was hardly surprising that they should not have been very well received. The Americans knew that the concessions on their exports to Britain ensured cheap raw materials for an importer whose favourable balance of trade with themselves was never in doubt.[3] Their cargoes to Newfoundland were

1. 23 Geo. III, c. 39. The provisions survived the later Orders in Council for the Atlantic colonial trade, and were reincorporated in the Act of 1788 (see pp. 334–5, 337 above.)
2. Pp. 343, 358–9 above.
3. Schumpeter, *English Overseas Trade Statistics*, tables, V, VI. And see also Bemis, *Jay's Treaty*, 33–6. The United States were our largest customer apart from Ireland in the first few years of peace, and by the later eighties had outstripped Ireland itself.

confined to food, the regulations for Vermont were a two-edged weapon, and wherever the British position seemed to be threatened the Americans found themselves excluded. Their own wishes and reactions, moreover, were consistently ignored. They would have liked a reciprocal system on the lines suggested by Shelburne: as John Adams told Pitt, 'we should agree upon a liberal plan, and allow equal freedom to each other's ships and seamen'. Britain might well 'take off every duty' and America freely 'take of British productions as much as she could pay for'; and Adams proposed two draft treaties in successive years on the basis of 'equality and reciprocity'.[1] But the arguments fell on deaf ears, and counter-measures proved ineffective. In the absence of an over-riding authority, the separate American states took their separate steps. Some forbade the export of goods in British ships, some imposed retaliatory tariffs; others did virtually nothing, or nothing at all. Such divided action was not very harmful; it was not always applied strictly, and even then it could be evaded by routeing goods through a neighbouring state. As Washington admitted as late as 1788, 'One Assembly makes a system, another Assembly unmakes it'.[2]

This revelation of weakness, indeed, was part and parcel of the American scene, even after the Constitution was agreed in 1787 and Washington became President in 1789. It was a fact of which the British took note, and were prepared to take advantage. 'It will not be an easy matter', Sheffield had forecast at the end of the war, 'to bring the American States to act as a nation'.[3] Most observers came to share his view. All the interested European powers were watching closely, to see what might happen and how they should act. British policies were stiffened after a time by the idea that we must not only build on our remaining assets, but that a still undecided future might allow or require us to regain some ground.

There was one quarter in which this had always seemed possible. The farmers and lumbermen of Vermont had little use for the United States. Like the rest of their fellow Americans, they had resented British taxation. But they looked north and west towards the St Lawrence, they felt little sympathy for the eastern seaboard, and they wished to carve a state for themselves out of New Hampshire and New York. They had indeed talked of joining Canada on their own terms towards the end of the war – a prospect greeted with mixed feelings in London[4] –, and their future remained uncertain for some years after the peace. Vermont cherished the Canadian agricultural market, and the

1. Adams to Jay, 25 August 1785 (*The Works of John Adams*, VIII, 307–8). The drafts were presented to the Foreign Secretary on 29 July 1785 and 4 April 1786.
2. To the Marquis de Lafayette, 28 April 1788 (*The Writings of George Washington*, ed. John C. Fitzpatrick, 29 (1939), 477).
3. *Observations on the Commerce of the American States*, 109.
4. Where Governments were well aware that the admittance of a large and independently minded population was bound to raise fresh colonial problems; and, after a time, were embarrassed by the possible effect on the peace treaty.

growing British market for timber. It thought of itself as independent, and held aloof from the Union in and after 1787. Its spokesmen indeed were then moving in a contrary direction: towards a trading agreement with Quebec Province which was soon to be completed, and beyond that to the prospect of talks for a formal treaty with Britain itself.

The spearhead of this separatist movement was the Allen family – General Ethan Allen and his brothers Ira and Levi. Early in 1789 Levi Allen came to England on business, and stayed for the next two years. He sought a commercial treaty which would serve as the basis of continued independence, answering 'all the purposes of an alliance of neutrality' which the United States could not prevent.[1] He confirmed Vermont's resolve to stay clear of the Union, to resist its encroachments, and if need be incline to England's side. His cause was urged by Dorchester, who had been in close touch with the family, and he received 'encouragement' after a time from Grenville himself. Ministers indeed liked the thought of 'attaching the people of Vermont, sincerely to the British interest'; of gaining by this neutrality 'so considerable an accession of strength'.[2] They were even ready, in the right conditions, to 'form alliances with our neighbours, as soon as all things are well matured'.[3] But things had not matured yet, and meanwhile the Government hastened slowly.

For the Vermont affair reached its peak at an interesting time. While Levi Allen was in London, two great developments took place. First, Congress, now empowered by the states to do so, took an opening step towards erecting its own protective navigation system. In July and August 1789 it passed a set of laws regulating shipping dues, and a tariff, in favour first of American vessels and then of those built in the United States but belonging to foreign subjects. The measures were not as strong or far-reaching as had at first been intended; but they were clearly aimed chiefly at the British, they might inconvenience our Atlantic traffic, and one Act in particular, effectively restricting coastal cargoes to American ships, threatened one of the pillars of our triangular trade. The reprisals, though comparatively mild, seem to have come as a surprise. We had weighed and discounted the danger earlier, and had since seen no reason to change our views. Now we were caught in an awkward situation, to an extent indeed that was proved over the next decade. In 1790, American ships carried less than half the tonnage of cargo between the two countries: two years later they took over 60 per cent, and by 1800 95 per cent. This remarkable increase may perhaps have owed something to the early effects of the European war. It was certainly founded on a performance that was not surpassed elsewhere.

1. The wording is his brother Ethan's to Dorchester in the previous year (enclosed in Dorchester to Grenville, 16 July 1788; P.R.O., C.O. 42/60). But it perfectly expresses Levi's hopes.
2. Grenville to Dorchester, no. 23 'Secret', 6 May 1790 (P.R.O., C.O. 43/10, f. 69).
3. Same to same, 21 July 1790 (C.O. 42/68).

But that performance in turn could be planned on a basis of preferential dues, and the result could be taken as a tribute to the British example which reaped this reward.

The new laws of course caused a stir in London. The Government was perturbed. But its immediate reaction was to hold its ground. Ministers appreciated that the legislation could have serious effects – consuls' reports were unanimous on that –, but they still reckoned that they held strong cards. Our goods remained vital to the Americans, and Congress had shown itself aware of the fact: it had watered down the original proposals, and Anglophile interests had made themselves felt. And we might do a good deal more to embarrass the United States, if we meant to try. Vermont could obviously be encouraged. So might the Indians of the Old North-West. So too might the frontiersmen of Kentucky, who were also chafing at their restrictions and threatening to break away. They were not certain yet where to turn for support – possibly to Spain. We might therefore forestall any such move by offering them a trade agreement at once, which would act as a counterpoise to other powers, curb American expansion up the Mississippi, and enlarge our own sphere of interest through and beyond the Old North-West. Such a prospect had been on the cards, rather vaguely, for some time. It might now be used as a threat to Congress should the need arise. Although he remained very cautious while the options were open, Grenville was talking in October 1789 of 'the establishment of a Government [in Kentucky] distinct from that of the Atlantic States'.[1]

Vermont thus took its place within a wider range of possibilities. They lay dormant for much of the winter, while the Government gathered information and watched. But the plans sprang to life again early in the following year. For at the beginning of 1790 the second great event occurred: the news at last reached London of the Spaniards' insult at Nootka Sound. It was hard to foretell the Americans' reaction in the event of war, and it seemed possible at first that they might favour Spain. The Government's attitude therefore hardened. It prepared to dig in and disrupt. No concessions on the Canadian frontier: a treaty with Vermont: encouragement and possibly action in Kentucky: direct embargoes on American trade – this was the thinking in London in the early part of the year.[2]

But as the months went by the picture began to change. For by the end of the summer it seemed unlikely that the Americans would support Spain, and there were signs that the Anglophile party was recovering ground. We had our own means of judging, for in the autumn of 1789

1. To Dorchester, no. 15 'Secret', 20 October 1789 (C.O. 43/10, f. 59).
2. Thus Levi Allen was given his 'encouragement' in that spring (see p. 373, n2 above). He himself stated later that he had had to wait for 'more than twelve months' after arriving in London for anything to happen (to Dundas, 9 August 1791; quoted in S. F. Bemis, 'Relations between the Vermont Separatists and Great Britain, 1789–1791', in *The American Historical Review*, XXI, no. 3, 555).

we established a connexion with a leading American Minister. Our agent was Major George Beckwith, a member of Dorchester's staff who had sent confidential information from New York over the past few years. His contact was the great Alexander Hamilton, the Secretary of the Treasury. Hamilton's fervent belief in the need for a closer relationship with Britain led him to push his cause as far as he dared – and he dared a great deal. His conviction was strong, his temper masterful, and he was acting in the open conditions of those early days. It is debatable if he went so far as 'consistently' to 'mislead' the President and his colleagues in an attempt to 'commit the government of the United States to a policy at variance with that officially agreed upon'.[1] But he certainly forced his influence to the limit in a sustained attempt to swing that policy, and kept a firm grasp of his unofficial means of communication with London. In October 1789 he raised the possibility – 'which has not hitherto been the case '– of a commercial, or even a political, treaty.[2] He also gave a *bonne bouche* in the shape of advance information that an American agent might soon go to England to discuss the prospect. He repeated his sentiments in March and April 1790, as the Nootka crisis mounted; and again in July, by which time he was suggesting a formal negotiation in New York. More important at that juncture, he assured Beckwith with all his authority that the United States were 'perfectly unconnected with Spain, have even some points unadjusted with that Court, and are prepared to go into the consideration of the subject'.[3]

The British Government placed weight on these last remarks, perhaps not least because Hamilton had earlier led Beckwith to suppose that he spoke with the President's approbation. But there was further evidence to the same effect, and by mid-September, when Grenville received the report of the conversation of July, Ministers were satisfied that the Americans would keep out. Beckwith himself, from other contacts, judged 'the general disposition . . . by no means favorable' to Spain,[4] and other agents and consuls broadly agreed. There were high hopes of a rising in Kentucky if required – a trusted agent, Peter Allaire, was reporting that independence could be seized and an alliance arranged –, and the news from Spain itself suggested that the United States would remain uncommitted. Hamilton's statement, coming from such a source, fitted very well with the rest of the picture.

1. The argument is that of Julian P. Boyd, in *Number 7: Alexander Hamilton's Secret Attempt to Control American Policy* . . . (1964). It makes exciting reading. The evidence, which sometimes corrects Bemis's account in *Jay's Treaty*, demands very careful interpretation, in its own substance and in the light of European diplomatic practice and the situation in New York.
   2. Beckwith's report, enclosed in Dorchester to Grenville, no. 9, 25 October 1789 (C.O. 42/66). The text is published in *Report on Canadian Archives, by Douglas Brymner* . . . *1890* (1891), 125–6.
   3. See Brymner, op. cit., 134–6, 145–6, and Boyd, 33 n67, and ch. IV.
   4. Quoted in Boyd, op. cit., 59.

Ministers therefore counted in the end on the fact that the Americans would be neutral if we declared war on Spain. Whether we could count on their neutrality or even friendship if we carried that war to their neighbouring territory – into Florida and the Mississippi Valley – was of course another matter. Soundings were taken, the air was full of rumours; Hamilton was optimistic. But the test did not come, for the crisis passed at the end of October 1790.

All offensive plans therefore stayed on ice throughout the summer; Allen was held in play but told nothing concrete, and Dorchester kept quiet. Anglo-American relations remained correct. But they can scarcely be said to have improved. Indeed, in one respect they suffered something of a setback. In October 1789, as Hamilton had hinted, the President decided to send a representative to London.[1] The man chosen – on Hamilton's suggestion – was the celebrated Gouverneur Morris, one of the authors of the Constitution, who was then on a long visit to Paris where he stayed to observe the revolution. He received his instructions towards the end of January 1790, and reached England in mid-March. But the mission was not a success. This may have been partly his own fault. He had not hurried on his journey, and he was indiscreet when he arrived; he saw too much for his own good – or rather Washington's – of the French Ambassador and Fox. Pitt and his colleagues came to mistrust him. But even if they had not, their reaction would probably have been much the same. The grounds for dispute had not changed, and the Government saw no need for hasty concessions. The Foreign Secretary and the Prime Minister were anxious to appear amiable while the Americans' attitude remained in doubt: at the end of March, Carmarthen (now Duke of Leeds) received Morris 'with much warmth and gladness in his appearance', and two months later Pitt professed himself anxious for 'a good understanding'.[2] But he was very cautious on the subject of a treaty, and the immediate point at issue seemed to be whether or not to send a British envoy to the United States. Morris failed over the next few months to get a clear answer to this limited question, while the larger issues remained entirely in doubt. There were rumours in September that an appointment would be made. But nothing happened; Morris was now in disfavour; and when he left London late that month he had come to the conclusion, like Adams before him, that the British were 'equivocal' and unlikely to yield very much.

If Morris had proved more sympathetic, he might have had the satisfaction of seeing an envoy named. As it was, no more was done before the end of the year. The question may well have been put on one side in the final excitement of the Nootka crisis in October, and assurances from Hamilton thereafter may have reinforced the feeling

1. John Adams had returned home, thankfully, in 1788.
2. Morris to Washington, 7 April 1790 (*American State Papers, Foreign Relations*, I, 123); *The Diary and Letters of Gouverneur Morris* ... ed. Anne Cary Morris, I (1889), 328.

that there was no hurry. But there was probably a further reason for the delay. For if a Minister was sent, he must have instructions; and Government had not yet been supplied with the advice on which commercial instructions could be based. This was itself a pointer to the low priority which the subject enjoyed. For in December 1789, after the first shock of the Americans' new shipping laws had been digested, Grenville, as Home Secretary, had asked the Committee of Trade to report on the effects; and the answer, thorough as ever, was received late in January 1791. The period of gestation scarcely suggests that the problem was considered pressing in a busy year. Nor indeed was the conclusion, when it appeared, very disturbing. Contrary to the first impression, the Committee now thought that if the Americans went no farther we could accept the results. Armed with this comforting estimate, the Government at last decided that no harm would be done if an envoy was sent.

The decision was passed to the Americans early in April 1791, reaching them in June. Ironically enough, its execution was then hastened by an adverse development. For if Government first brought itself to begin discussions on the basis of a comforting report, it was soon impelled to do so by less agreeable news. In May the information reached London that, contrary to Hamilton's latest assurances, fresh and much harsher protectionist measures were being presented to Congress. These were in fact really serious, far more so than those of 1789: they would have girded the United States with the equivalent of the British navigation laws. The preparations for appointing the new envoy were speeded up at once. In the course of May, Grenville, now Foreign Secretary, ordered the acting chargé d'affaires at Madrid, George Hammond, to return home. He set out in mid-June, and his instructions were considered during the summer. They were ready early in September, and later that month he sailed for New York, bearing with him the Government's assurance of its 'readiness to enter into a negotiation' for the promotion of trade 'upon principles of reciprocal benefit'.[1]

What was Pitt's part in all this? What were his thoughts, and his feelings? One might have expected him to be touched in a rather sensitive spot – and so perhaps he was. Chatham after all had been the Americans' most distinguished champion, Pitt had been brought up against that background, and Shelburne had tried to carry the same spirit into the peace. It was not difficult of course to find a reasoned answer. Chatham had championed the Americans when, and because, they had been British subjects; he had attacked taxation without representation, but never Parliament's right to decide the shape of

1. Hammond to Thomas Jefferson [U.S. Secretary of State], 30 November 1791 (*American State Papers, Foreign Relations*, I, 189).

navigation and trade; and Shelburne's policy here had been decisively rejected. Other interests could now be said to claim prior place in the repair of an injured economy; and the growing opportunities in the Atlantic and the hinterland of Canada, enlarged in each case by the prospects in the Pacific, were strong incentives to thrust ahead and secure the areas of British interest. There were respectable arguments for a tougher approach; and Pitt's sympathy for the Americans was weakened by the fate of the creditors and the loyalists, to whom the country and he himself felt a very real obligation. This complex of policy and sentiment was far too strong for him to wish to oppose a consensus of opinion which was virtually complete, in the Ministry and beyond. For the Government's American policy commanded wide-spread assent: it was not decided by pressure from any particular quarter, above all the 'King's men' as some Americans thought. Carmarthen and Grenville, even the veteran Chathamite Camden, were concerned as well as Jenkinson, and none of the three had been associated with the 'party of the Crown' or the views of George III. The Administration as a whole reflected the overwhelming agreement in Parliament on the need to preserve the fundamentals of navigation. And since Pitt's prime concern, as John Adams noted in 1785, was to bury 'the discontents of the nation, arising from their late disappoint-ments',[1] he was certainly not going to endanger that task, or fetter renewed British expansion, by reverting to an unpopular 'experiment'[2] which did not immediately support such plans.

This attitude was fortified by pride, and a growing confidence. The United States had to deal, as Thomas Jefferson observed, 'with those who respect their own dignity so much'.[3] The immediate reaction in these disputes was to return tit for tat with interest, the more so as the Americans' troubles grew and ours appeared to recede. Pitt's own lofty dignity seemed to embody these distressing sentiments. At the same time he felt lingering sympathies, and he was not intellectually rigid. His mind was naturally open, and he was influenced by what he was told. If he was unlikely to move very fast, the fact that he found no need for haste made him a good listener when he heard the Americans' case. This was not very often. Pitt spent little time on the subject throughout the eighties. Perhaps for that reason he was the more open, or the less precise, on ways and means. No clear pattern in fact emerged – Adams wrote bitterly that Pitt 'oscillated like a pendulum'.[4] He may perhaps have felt some embarrassment, however irrational, at the thought of the famous past; if so, he could easily avoid it, for he was not pressed to think very hard. Fox cannot generally be taken as a good guide to his

1. To Jay, 31 December 1785 (*Works of John Adams*, VIII, 351–2).
2. P. 97 above.
3. To Morris, 12 August 1790 (*The Papers of Thomas Jefferson*, ed. Julian P. Boyd, 17 (1965), 127).
4. To Jay, 31 December 1785 (*Works*, VIII, 351).

rival's thoughts. But when he was asked in April 1790 what the Government's policy might be towards the United States, he was going on sound evidence when he replied that 'he did not believe Mr. Pitt would trouble his Head about the Matter'. He supposed the Prime Minister to be 'rather friendly than otherwise'; but he 'would probably leave it to Lord Hawkesbury and Mr. Grenville', who were not so well disposed.[1]

In point of fact, Pitt did trouble his head over the next few months, for every aspect of the Nootka Sound crisis engaged his close attention. He read the despatches and the agents' reports – Allaire's from Kentucky were shown to him regularly –, he took the whole business and its implications into his own hands. His attitude to the Americans in 1790 was determined entirely by its course, and the opening of formal relations likewise responded to tactical plans and needs. He was still in fact, as Fox had forecast, 'governed by Events'.[2] Events would therefore have to change, or show strong signs of changing, before he and his colleagues followed suit.

In the spring and summer of 1791, such a process seemed possible. The threat of increased retaliation undoubtedly shook the British Government, and Hammond's instructions were framed guardedly to take that prospect into account. He was empowered to enter into negotiations for a commercial treaty on the reciprocal basis of most favoured nations.[3] But even so he was given little freedom of action, his representations were to be based on the Committee of Trade's sanguine report,[4] and if Congress really seemed bent on taking fresh steps he was to let it be known that we might do likewise. He was in fact to concentrate mainly on a settlement of the Canadian frontier – along lines that would still have embarrassed the United States[5] –, and use the bait of a trade agreement, cautiously and within limits, so as to keep the American threat in check.

In the event, he did not have to do so much. The news of his appointment helped to spike the protectionist guns in Congress; the varied opposition was fortified, and the navigation bills were lost. Hammond was thus after all in a position to proceed from strength, and had little need to hasten or be unduly accommodating. His dealings with the State Department throughout 1792 (against the background of continued confidential conversations with Hamilton) were confined largely to a sterile exchange of complaints about the past. The plan for a

1. Morris to Washington, 2 May 1790; quoted in Boyd, *Number 7*, 71.
2. Ibid.
3. By which was meant a foreign nation enjoying terms at least as favourable, in the particulars specified, as those enjoyed by any other foreign nation: not necessarily the nation favoured above all others whatsoever.
4. P. 377 above.
5. Pp. 357–8 above.

neutral zone in the Old North-West made some progress – it was at least prepared and presented in detail. There was no more talk in London of promoting disaffection in Kentucky or Vermont – Allen left in 1791. But the commercial agreement showed no sign of advance. The British were not in fact prepared, unless they were forced, to take the indispensable step of amending the regulations for the West Indian trade. So matters stood at the beginning of 1793, on the eve of the war that would soon force a reluctant change of heart.

The background to the revolt of the American colonies in the 1770s has been summed up in a penetrating phrase. 'The economic frontiers of America were out of scale with its political frontiers. That was the rock on which the first British Empire came to grief.'[1] The dichotomy was still as real in the 1780s, when the former colonies were a foreign power and the Empire was settling on new foundations. It was perhaps not surprising that an early answer should not have been found to a long-term problem. But the failure proved serious for both the short and the long term. Perhaps, indeed, it did as much damage as the war itself – it certainly went far towards completing the damage already done. For it raised new barriers in place of old, which could not be overcome in the next few years; and it did much to confirm, at a critical point, the mutual suspicions of the two great parts of the English-speaking world, the effects of which lingered – and still linger in patches – into our own day.

III

The southern borders of the United States were the northern borders of Spanish territory; and beyond them the huge mass of the American continent, with a few small exceptions, was claimed by the Spaniards and the Portuguese. Portugal was sovereign in the vast area of Brazil. The Spanish possessions stretched from the 49th parallel beyond the Mississippi (apart from its extreme northern reaches) and the northern frontier of Florida, through Central and the rest of South America, almost unbroken, into Patagonia in the south. Only small British settlements – at first juridically uncertain – on the coasts of Yucatan and Honduras, and Dutch and French Guiana, remained outside this Iberian empire, and Spain also held a chain of Caribbean islands – Cuba and Pines, Hispaniola, Porto Rico, and Trinidad – interspersed among those of the British, the French, the Danes, the Swedes, and the Dutch. Spain and France remained our largest neighbours and chief rivals in the West Indies, Portugal and Spain – above all Spain – our concern on the mainland outside the United States. There was an ample historical legacy of Anglo-Spanish disputes in the New World.

1. W. K. Hancock, *Survey of British Commonwealth Affairs*, II (1940), 39.

Fresh occasions arose in the decade between the American and French Revolutionary Wars.

The quarrels of the past had turned chiefly on trade, in one form or another, and by the 1780s the terms of trade were not as favourable to the British as they once had been. Both its legal regulation and its content seemed to be changing for the worse. Our position in Central and South America was governed by a series of treaties, hinging on that of 1654 with Portugal and those of 1667 and 1670 with Spain. In differing degrees and with varying certainty, these had given us unique advantages; by the 1760s, indeed, our share of the markets was much greater than those of Portugal and Spain themselves. We paid lower duties than other foreign powers, the duties could not be raised except by agreement, we could export coin and bullion unlicensed, our representatives were allowed to settle in Brazil. Based mainly on Lisbon and Cadiz, which in theory enjoyed a monopoly of the traffic, British merchants had come to dominate the trades. But this was too good to last in the nationalistic age of the Iberian Enlightenment and, in the case of Spain, of the Family Compact with France. From the fifties and sixties to the eighties our advantages were whittled down, by stricter enforcement of the terms by Portugal, more fundamentally by Spain. For the old Anglo-Spanish treaties could be made to yield various interpretations, and the rights of either party had never been exactly framed. Later agreements failed to solve the difficulties, and throughout the third quarter of the eighteenth century the British houses in Cadiz and Lisbon found themselves increasingly harassed. Many of them indeed by then favoured the abolition of the treaties, and a general relaxation or opening of the trades.

But such steps, when they came, were not much to our liking. They did not open the markets to all comers, in a competition in which we reckoned we might well prevail, but rather weakened the force of our concessions under the existing theoretical monopoly. A Franco-Spanish treaty of 1768, and a Franco-Portuguese treaty of 1783, placed the French on the same legal footing in the Peninsula as ourselves; a series of decrees, culminating in that of 1778, opened the major ports of Spain and her American colonies to each other; and Spanish Caribbean ports were partly opened to the Americans in the American War. We were thus operating as before within a system now tilted less to our advantage; and this was the more serious because the balance of trade was in any case shifting in a new direction. The Spanish and Portuguese colonial markets had long been regarded in London as virtually one: they were handled largely by the same merchant houses, and the bullion they yielded was taken as a whole. Its value hitherto, though declining, had still been substantial, helping to pay for adverse balances elsewhere. But the decline had been hastened by the recent war, and now a new factor appeared. For as the textile mills of England and Scotland began to get into their stride, they swallowed on quite a new scale raw cotton from Brazil. Where £6 worth had been imported in 1767, £9,000 worth came in 1782, some £60,000 in 1786, and between £150,000 and £200,000 a year by the end of the decade.[1] In 1790 and 1791, gold had even to be shipped from London to Lisbon; and while this was exceptional, the Portuguese share in the influx of bullion had virtually disappeared.

The British Government was not idle in the face of this situation. It promoted various measures, some new, others well tried. There was a general reluctance to rely too heavily on foreign-grown cotton: the Committee of Trade now took steps to increase the supplies from the British West Indies. Cotton had in fact been grown there on a small scale since the early seventeenth century, and the plantations were expanding in response to the recent demands. In 1787, they sent some ¼ million lb to Britain; but this was still far from enough, and the quality was rather poor. At a meeting in February 1787, which Pitt attended, the Committee set a large-scale inquiry on foot, and Hawkesbury pursued this with vigour over the next two years. Cotton seeds were brought from India, cultivation was encouraged – largely on properties granted to loyalists from North America –, and in the early nineties the results began to show. The imports of cotton from the British West Indies then rose to an annual average of over 11½ million lb, three-quarters of which was a British-grown crop.[2]

The rest was the produce of the foreign Caribbean islands, brought in as a result of the revived free port system.[3] For this was the second, and greater, weapon on which the Government drew. Like the efforts for cotton themselves, it was partly defensive – an attempt to sustain an economy whose main staple, sugar, was disturbed.[4] But it was also a weapon of offense – a return to earlier measures designed to legalise trade from local bases with Central and South America. As such, it had a marked success. Official figures are in their not uncommon state of uncertainty; as Irving at the Custom House remarked, 'In a Trade of this kind the best Information is to be collected from Individuals'.[5] But the individuals concerned were satisfied that the traffic was growing fast. By 1791 its total value may have risen to some £4½ to £5 million a year;[6] most of the exports went to Spanish possessions; and as the free port Acts began to take effect, the Committee of Trade concluded

1. *Accounts and Papers printed by Order of the House of Commons*, XIX (1787), no. 430; P.R.O., B.T. 6/63.

2. Harlow, op. cit., II, 290. See also Frances Armytage, *The Free Port System in the British West Indies . . . 1766–1822* (1953,) appendix III, tables I, J, K.

3. See pp. 338–9 above.

4. Cotton indeed was not the only crop in mind for this purpose. Captain Bligh's famous voyage in the *Bounty* was undertaken, at the Committee of Trade's request in 1787, to collect bread-fruit plants from Tahiti for shipment to the West Indies.

5. 'A few General Observations on the Trade between Great Britain and Portugal and Spain' (n.d., but possibly 1789); B.M. Add. Ms 34429, f. 196v.

6. Armytage, op. cit., table O.

that the results had 'become an object of great National importance'.[1]

To the British, all this trade was now legal. To the Spaniards it was nothing of the kind. By their interpretation of the treaties, British goods for Spanish America must pass through the ports of Old Spain, and the island traffic was a form of smuggling, as it had been for over a century. They refused to recognise it in law. They took such counter-measures as they could. And the free ports appeared to them to be part of a system of illegitimate attack, thoroughly familiar and now resuscitated, on their exclusive claims to trade and dominion in the southern territories of the New World.

One prong of this attack was placed on the eastern shores of Yucatan and Honduras, the only piece of mainland territory on which Englishmen were actually established. Theirs had been a hard and often melancholy story, in a melancholy land, where the successors to the old privateers and pirates cut their timber around the Gulf, in scattered settlements reaching south to the malarial Mosquito Coast. Spanish attacks had gradually reduced the number of these haunts to three: the Mosquito Coast, an area round Belize, and a few of the offshore cays or islands. All were threatened or suffered in the later years of the American War. But occupation of the Belize area was recognised by the peace treaty, and Englishmen also remained on the Mosquito Coast.

The commercial value of the settlements had lain originally in the cutting of logwood (also known as dye wood or campeachy wood), which yielded the elements essential to the fixing of dyes. But as time went by, this was surpassed by the cutting of mahogany, which in 1783 accounted for ten times the tonnage of logwood felled. It was largely the shipments of Honduras timber that completed the displacement of walnut in the Georgian taste. But the Spaniards had never countenanced the activity, and did not do so at the peace. One of the objects of British policy was therefore to secure its legal recognition. The other was to see all the surviving settlements confirmed and if possible extended, so as to ensure a continuing British presence on the mainland.

Such an ambition was unlikely to be achieved in full. If the Spaniards granted one object in any degree, it would probably be at the partial price of the other. The local settlers were particularly anxious to enlarge their territory round Belize, where they had received grudging but as they deemed inadequate concessions at the peace; and the Government placed much weight on this point, as well as on the rights of the settlers on the Mosquito Coast, from the time that it raised the question in the autumn of 1784. Its case rested, as always, on the proposition that the coasts had not been inhabited earlier by Spaniards, so that under the seventeenth-century treaties (which were vaguely phrased) we had a legitimate right of settlement. Spain, as always, asserted a superior

1. Minute of 15 May 1790, quoted op. cit., 71.

jurisdiction. The exchanges were lengthy, and became a prominent feature of business for over a year. For they formed part of a general Anglo-Spanish discussion of problems outstanding from the war, and the serious period of the talks coincided with that of a negotiation for a fresh commercial treaty in Europe. The two questions indeed reacted incessantly on each other, and it was a measure of the British deter-mination on the transatlantic case that this was allowed to hold up – as it proved fatally – agreement on the European trade.[1] From the spring of 1785 to the summer of 1786 the argument was in fact a principal obstacle to better relations – the achievement of which was a prime policy of the Foreign Office at the time. The 'bare mention of the Mosquito Shore or the Bay of Honduras', according to the British Minister in Madrid, put the Spanish Foreign Minister 'in a passion' in March 1786.[2] By then indeed the situation in Europe was coming to affect the outcome of the colonial dispute, and the two Governments signed a Convention in July of that year. The settlers of Belize were granted a modest but useful extension of their holding, they were allowed to cut mahogany as well as logwood, to cultivate the land, and reoccupy and refit ships in some of the offlying islands. The British in return agreed to evacuate the Mosquito Coast, and submit to restrictions and inspection of their settlements by the Spanish authorities. A further period of bickering followed, as interpretations were worked out. Pockets of British settlers remained for some years on the Mosquito Coast, and Honduras cast its shadow intermittently over Anglo-Spanish relations down to the outbreak of war with France. But the compromise was not entirely unfavourable, and it proved significant. If the total area of the settlements was reduced, the main one at Belize was con-firmed and indeed enlarged, and the beginnings of direct Government control (at first reluctant) over the affairs of what later became British Honduras can be traced to the agreement of 1786.

This consummation lay in the future. There was a much more immediate consequence. Pitt had taken his share in the negotiation, as part of the wider talks with Spain. The Convention was brought to the point during the time in which he was interesting himself in their conduct. Its commercial advantages were plain, its potentialities of interest. But another aspect of the matter was soon revealed. In October 1790, when the Nootka Sound crisis reached its final climax, Pitt was in close touch with a certain Major-General Sir Archibald Campbell. 'I have perused the papers', Campbell wrote to him, 'sent me by Mr. Grenville regarding the Bay of Honduras, as well as the Plan . . . for an attack upon Guatimala'.[3] The settlement in fact had been listed as a

---

1. See ch. XVI, sections II, IV below.
2. Robert Liston to William Fraser [Under-Secretary at the Foreign Office], 12 March 1786 (P.R.O., F.O. 72/8).
3. 26 October 1790 (P.R.O. 30/8/120).

possible base in the event of war. The design was a comprehensive one, and such an enclave was just what the Spaniards had feared.

There was a long history of British plans for disrupting the Spanish American Empire. In their current form they went back to Walpole and the War of Jenkins' Ear, but many of the ingredients were a good deal older than that. There had always been a strong tradition – Ralegh was its first great exemplar – that the Spaniards' hold could be broken by a mixture of direct conquest and incitement of the subject peoples to revolt. The many attacks on ports and islands, stretching from the days of Elizabeth to those of George III, were often combined with plans for local risings among the coastal Indians. But more grandiose possibilities lay never far behind. The lost empire of the Incas still held men's imaginations, and dreams of independent Indian states, or even of a revived single Indian realm, found their way surprisingly often into prosaic official reports. 'El hombro dorado', the Gilded Man, figured among the exotic potentates whom eighteenth-century Englishmen found themselves taking into account. There was also the possibility, as the century progressed, that the Spanish colonists themselves might be induced to break with Spain. Plans of one sort or another were considered in almost every crisis and war from the 1740s: by Walpole, by the elder Pitt, by Bute, by North, and by Shelburne. Their attraction had not diminished in the middle eighties, for in 1781 there was both an Inca and, perhaps more significantly, a Creole revolt.

In the early years of the peace, indeed, a number of Spanish American conspirators made their way to London – a new phenomenon which henceforth continued down to the era of Liberation. Pitt saw some at least of their proposals, and while he did not encourage them he interviewed one delegation, from Mexico, in the summer of 1786. He was thus acquainted with the background when trouble threatened at the end of the decade, and when the crisis broke in 1790 he was ready to exploit the prospects. A likely instrument lay to hand. In 1785 there had appeared in England the young Francisco de Miranda, destined a quarter of a century later to found the first of the Latin American republics. Able, well informed, trained as a soldier, and burning to free the southern empire from Spain, his visit roused some interest, though the Government seems to have held aloof. He returned in 1789, after an extended tour of Europe, and was still in London when the news of Nootka Sound arrived. Within three weeks he had seen Pitt, and 'various interviews' followed in the next few months.[1] Miranda's ideas were far-reaching, and in some respects not unfamiliar. He looked to

1. Miranda to Pitt, 8 September 1791 (*The American Historical Review*, VII, no. 4, 712). The introduction was effected by Governor Thomas Pownall, the veteran politician and expert on American affairs, who was a younger brother of John Pownall of the Customs Board.

the creation of a federated empire, embracing all the Spanish American mainland and some of the islands, with a central legislature of two chambers, a system of federal justice, and an 'Emperor of Inca' as head of state. This would be preceded by an interim Government, to be set up following a British attack, which would make a treaty of diplomatic and commercial alliance with this country. Encouraged by reports of disaffection in South and Central America, and by the potentialities of a base in Kentucky,[1] Pitt and Grenville set plans on foot for the necessary expedition if required. They were entrusted to Sir Archibald Campbell, recently returned from India, under consultation with two officers – Colonel William Dalrymple and the naval Lieutenant Home Riggs Popham (later the inventor of the semaphore system) – who, like the General himself, had some knowledge of America and the Caribbean. The main attack, from the Atlantic, would fall on Mexico, protected by a flank assault on Guatemala, and accompanied by an expedition against Louisiana which might spark off a rising in the Mississippi Valley. Meanwhile an expedition from India would capture Manila in the Philippines, as the base for an operation against the Pacific coast of Mexico together perhaps with landings in Chile and Peru.

The diplomatic victory of the autumn put this extensive strategy into cold storage. It was called on later in the course of the Napoleonic Wars. The design showed several significant features. It harked back to earlier military and naval plans for both West and East, it was linked with the policies for North America, and it reflected very clearly British ambitions farther south. The old ideas of direct conquest, earlier entertained but never unchallenged, had finally given way to those of influence, yielding favoured access to states whose independence would have been founded on British arms. Spain's monopoly and rule would be broken; but we would not encumber ourselves with the results. It was one more facet of the thinking which had gained fresh strength from the American War. It was also an indication of the policy of fostering revolt in hostile countries which Pitt's Government was to repeat during the next decade.

IV

In seeking to restore the Atlantic system to a favourable state – to bury 'the discontents of the nation' in the region of the upheaval itself – Pitt was not much in the giving mood. He supported Jenkinson's measures for shipping, he conceded little to the Americans, he was happy to thrust where he could at Spain. He accepted the official forecasts, and he agreed with the prevalent view that we could not afford to gamble with our remaining sources of strength. The means varied with the conditions, as they had done indeed before the recent war: some of the

1. Pp. 374–5 above.

old restrictions were eased where an advantage could be foreseen. But altered circumstances were met by a wary and stubborn regrouping of forces; assets (as they seemed) were jealously guarded; and the process was no more free than usual of 'the skill of that insidious and crafty animal, vulgarly called a statesman or politician, whose councils are directed by the momentary fluctuations of affairs'.[1]

Yet there was one great exception to this careful respect for existing resources. The prosperity of the Atlantic traffic had long been bound up with the slave trade. The West Indian plantations relied on slave labour, and their products were exported by the vessels which carried slaves and British goods after taking British manufactures to Africa. This commerce was an integral part of the old Colonial System, and it remained important when the American colonies changed their role. West Indian sugar needed support; British shipping must retain its strength; and the greatest British ports – London, Liverpool and Bristol – had substantial capital tied up in slaves. The figures were impressive, though as usual imprecise. Taking a long average, the number of Africans transported was perhaps over 40,000 a year, of whom probably more than half were packed into British ships. Most of them went to the British West Indies, but many were landed in foreign colonies, and not a few were destined for the United States. Indeed, a new competitor had now entered the trade, for while Congress had forbidden the import of slaves along the northern American seaboard, American shipowners still carried negroes to the southern states.

Here then was a major traditional element of the British Atlantic traffic – an export, invisible to most Englishmen, on which large structures had been built. Pitt's efforts to abolish it were the more striking when viewed against his treatment of the rest. They bulked the larger perhaps because they were carried out so very much in public. For while most aspects of Atlantic policy – if one may use this term to include the Americas – fell within the normal run of Government business, and some were discussed behind closed doors, the slave trade of course became one of the issues of the day. Pitt's support of the abolitionists was in keeping with the impression he had earlier made – with Parliamentary reform, with public morality, with the virtue of a new generation.

Nor was this wrong. The campaign for abolition *was* a supreme instance of public morality, a bright shaft of light in human affairs; and Pitt volunteered and played his part readily and well. 'This was a question', Pretyman remarked, 'which called forth all the sensibilities of his heart';[2] and his later loss of enthusiasm when the war with France began, and his final defection from the cause, do not alter the fact or lessen the importance of what he did. At the same time, one must not underestimate his potential sources of strength. The campaign was an

1. Adam Smith, *Wealth of Nations*, bk. IV, ch. II, 432–3.
2. Tomline, III, 543.

exception to general policy, but the contrast was not complete. Indeed Pitt's role in Parliament would have been impossible from the start if he could not have counted on a fair measure of political goodwill. The atmosphere by the later eighties was very different from that of ten years before; and humanitarian feelings, as often, were borne on the wings of other interests. The movement could not have enlisted as wide a degree of support as it did if charity had not been beneficently linked with an appeal to commercial prospects and facts.

Apart from slaves, trade with Africa had never been important, and the continent had not entered deeply into British thought. There were plans for capturing Capetown from the Dutch in the American War,[1] as a rendezvous for India. But these were strategically defensive, in the face of a hostile alliance, and the positive value of the Cape was not rated particularly high.[2] The oceanic east coast was an Arab preserve, broken only by the Portuguese in Mozambique and now scarcely troubled by French influence, the Red Sea littoral belonged to Turkey, the north coast and the 'overland' route through Egypt were Mediterranean questions, and British resources were confined to three areas of settlement in the west. We held Fort St James at the mouth of the Gambia, and stretches of the Guinea coast, at the end of the war, and then gained access to the French settlement at Portendic, on the Gum Coast north of Dakar, as a slight return for surrendering our holding in Senegal. These regions shipped us gum and ivory and gold and dyewoods, with some hides and palm oil and indigo and wax. But the value was small – perhaps one ninth of that of our outward manufactured goods.

Nevertheless, the 1780s saw a fresh stirring of interest. The French, perhaps encouraged by the peace treaty, were active along the west coast. Between 1784 and 1789 they formed scattered settlements and made treaties with local potentates, acquired Gambia Island off Sierra Leone, and consolidated and extended their base in Senegal. They also largely displaced us in the slave trade from Portuguese Angola. Such enterprise was worrying, and it attracted the Government's notice; it may have further stimulated the new British ventures that were set on foot. But there was in any case a revival of scientific and mercantile speculation, the more so as the old Royal African Company had now disappeared and the trade was rather more open. There was some exploration in the later eighties – by Lucas from Tripoli and Daniel Houghton in Gambia –, and in 1788 an Association for Promoting the Discovery of the Interior Parts of Africa was founded in London. Its

1. P. 50 above.
2. Lower in fact than in earlier decades, before the discovery of the coppered bottom made an intermediate refit unnecessary, and allowed ships to take fuller advantage of the uninterrupted passage, with more favourable winds, down towards the South American coast and then east through the Roaring Forties, until they entered the Indian Ocean in the period of the south-west monsoon.

purpose was mainly scientific – Sir Joseph Banks was its guiding light –, but the advancement of knowledge was linked with commercial development, and the most prominent members were men of affairs. Bishop Watson, Sir John Sinclair, William Pulteney, Henry Beaufoy these were familiar Parliamentary names in the various movements for 'improvement'. The Association looked to a diversification of trade with tropical Africa, and an encouragement of tropical products, as a basis for a different but no less profitable kind of connexion. By such means, 'as peaceful as the purposes are just, the conveniences of civil life, the benefit of the mechanic and manufacturing arts, the attainments of science, the energies of the cultivated mind and the elevation of the human character may in some degree be imparted to nations hitherto consigned to hopeless barbarism'.[1] It was a statement which the abolitionists themselves might have taken as a charter, and the commercial prospects it offered formed one of the planks of their platform.[2]

At the same time the abolitionists could point to some current economic facts. The slave trade was no longer as advantageous as it once had been. King Sugar, though still very strong – and very demanding when threatened –, was not growing stronger, and the labour force available in the West Indies as a whole was now large enough to do the work. There was no longer any need to consider the needs of the American South, which was equally involved in a slave economy; indeed the revolt of the mainland colonies had removed a powerful interest from an arena in which it might have continued to play an important obstructive role. A complementary supply of sugar seemed possibly to be emerging in India, where John Company was starting cultivation in the later eighties. And this was only one of a growing number of expanding activities in the East and elsewhere – the fisheries was another – which were thought to sustain the national pool of seamen and the prosperity of the old slaving ports. Some of the busiest centres of the anti-slavery movement were in the new manufacturing towns, and it was not unsuccessful in Liverpool itself. The transatlantic commerce remained highly significant; but its proportions were changing. Traditional practices might be reviewed, new cargoes substituted for old.

All this was true. But there was of course deep-seated resistance. The new inquiries and developments were on a small scale, and meanwhile old arguments held sway. The slave trade was still very large, and it was woven into the economy of an area in which we were trying our

1. First Report of the African Association, 1790; quoted in Robin Hallett, *The Penetration of Africa . . .*, I (1965), 216.

2. The Danes, with their holdings on the Gold Coast and their plantations in the West Indies, were in fact putting such theories into partial practice in the eighties and early nineties. But the example does not seem to have attracted much notice in this country.

hardest to regain lost ground. Nor was the resistance confined to economic change. The institution of slavery was not widely looked on as necessarily evil; some of the reformers were concerned only to improve the conditions of the trade, and few of the abolitionists themselves demanded emancipation at this stage. The noble savage was a recent concept, practical men were not generally impressed, many claims could be made for the paternalistic slave owner; and what would happen if the slaves were freed? The shipments in any case took place largely out of sight, consciences were hard to rouse into action, and the excesses were for long denied.

Human kind cannot bear very much reality.

The trade had even attracted its brand of sentimental support. It was part of the fabric of life, it had built up an ethos of its own. 'I was bred in the good old school', exclaimed Nelson, defending the 'just rights' of the planters.[1] Much patient digging out of inconvenient facts, much skilled and earnest advocacy, might be needed to overcome the inertia born of such respectable tradition.

The process began to get under way in the middle eighties. Its rate of development was remarkably swift. This was at least in part a tribute to the earlier scattered efforts, dating back to Granville Sharp's protests in the later sixties and early seventies. In the seventies, indeed, the question was aired in several widely different quarters. The respected historian William Robertson in his *History of America* drew on hostile accounts of the slave system; Adam Smith dismissed its economic value in the *Wealth of Nations*; John Wesley published his *Thoughts upon Slavery*, and the Quakers bore witness. Perhaps more effective than any of these influences in rousing public attention was a tragedy on board the slave ship *Zong* in 1781, when over a hundred negroes were thrown into the Atlantic during an epidemic. Two years later the Quakers set up a committee for 'the relief and liberation' of the slaves in the West Indies and 'the discouragement of the Slave Trade' from Africa, which soon attracted a number of other active adherents. In May 1787 a fresh committee was formed, to gather 'such information as may tend to the abolition of the Slave Trade', under Sharp's chairmanship and with Thomas Clarkson, a young recruit from Cambridge, as one of its members. With its establishment the movement really took off, for Clarkson, persistent and indefatigable, had resolved to devote his life to the cause, and the gathering of accurate information was indispensable to future progress. He had been delving into papers over the past two years, and he now set out on the first of his tours of inquiry.

1. To Simon Taylor in Jamaica, 10 June 1805 (Sir Harris Nicholas, *The Dispatches and Letters of Vice-Admiral Lord Viscount Nelson (1777–July 1805)*, VI (1846), 450–1).

The ground was therefore being prepared. But the fruits might not have been shown so quickly had it not been for another, separate development. William Wilberforce had been known in society in the early eighties as a gay, amusing young man, a familiar figure at the theatre and Ranelagh, in the drawing-rooms and the clubs. He was high spirited and witty, an excellent mimic, he sang and gossiped, he was much in demand. He and Pitt had seen little of each other at Cambridge – Wilberforce had moved in faster company –, but they soon became devoted friends in London. Goostrees', Wilberforce's villa at Wimbledon, jaunts to Brighton, their holiday in France – the two young men were almost inseparable at times in those early years. Entering the Commons at the same election, they were intimate allies, and Wilberforce was one of the small and to outside eyes unnecessarily scrupulous band of Pitt's personal followers in the Parliament returned in 1784. But his interest in politics then began to ebb, and his life underwent a complete change. For in the course of 1784–5 Wilberforce suffered a religious conversion. The experience left Pitt somewhat at a loss. He respected but could not share it, and he was distressed and puzzled to find that Wilberforce thought of leaving politics altogether. He managed to dissuade him. But Wilberforce was unhappy, disliking the Parliamentary life and seeing no reason to carry on.

He did not remain quiescent for long. The slave trade had already begun to engage his interest: the final instrument of his conversion, the pastor John Newton, was himself a reformed slaver. Early in 1787 he began to make inquiries, in the spring he talked to Clarkson, and by the autumn he had found his call. 'God Almighty', he wrote at the end of October, 'has set before me two great objects, the suppression of the slave trade and the reformation of manners'.[1] He was now certain of his mission, and he embarked on the first part of it without delay.

The decision – doubtless almost inevitable – was prompted by Grenville and Pitt. Wilberforce 'began to talk over the matter' with them in the course of the year, and they urged him to go ahead. 'Pitt recommended me', Wilberforce wrote later, 'to undertake its conduct, as a subject well suited to my character and talents. At length, I well remember, after a conversation in the open air at the root of an old tree at Holwood just above the steep descent into the vale of Keston, I resolved to give notice on a fit occasion in the House of Commons of my intention to bring the subject forward.'[2] It was a solemn moment, and it made an impression on them both. The tree, which survived into this century, became venerated as 'Wilberforce's Oak'.

1. Journal, 28 October 1787 (*Life of Wilberforce*, I, 149).
2. Loc. cit., 150–1. The date of this momentous conversation is not recorded, and is hard to decide. If Grenville was there (as Wilberforce perhaps suggests) it may have been in the mid-summer, for he was in Holland and France for much of the time from late July until mid-October. But one cannot be sure that he was present, and from the entry in Wilberforce's journal of 28 October it sounds as if the resolution had been recently taken.

It was said later, after things went wrong, that Pitt had thrust the load on Wilberforce in order to avoid shouldering it himself. This was a silly argument, for which there is no evidence. The abolition of the slave trade was at best a marginal subject for a Government motion, and Pitt's Ministry at that time would certainly not have accepted it. He went to very great lengths to give the project his blessing once the motion had been made by a private Member, and in fact stretched his Ministerial influence as far as it would go. He devoted a great deal of time to the matter, and raised it with other Governments. He did as much to stimulate the Parliamentary campaign, and official inquiry and approval, as anyone in his position could possibly have done. He might of course have moved for abolition in his own name, as he had done for Parliamentary reform. But the point was that he wanted his friend to espouse the cause. Pitt indeed raised this alternative when Wilberforce fell ill early in the following year, and seemed likely to miss the chance – which might not recur for some time – of a Parliamentary occasion in the spring. He then offered to take up the business himself: he even thought it might be better if he did; 'but on this . . . your wish shall decide me'.[1] In the event he moved a resolution in Wilberforce's absence in May, for the circumstances of the slave trade to be considered early in the following session.

This was more modest progress than the abolitionists, and Wilberforce himself, had expected. But his illness was not the only reason by then for deferring a decisive debate. Pitt was anxious to prepare the ground, and involve Government in the inquiry as far as he could. He had plunged into the subject with his usual optimism in the winter of 1787 – 'the more I reflect upon it', he wrote in December, 'the more anxious and impatient I am that the business should be brought as speedily as possible to a point'.[2] Nor did he seriously question the outcome – the 'scheme', he admitted, '. . . may appear to some people chimerical, but . . . I really believe may, with proper management, be made practicable'.[3] It became clearer in the course of the winter what 'management' would involve. The abolitionists were preparing their case, with official connivance – George Rose took the 'unprecedented' step of extracting information from the Customs for Wilberforce to pass on to Clarkson.[4] But it would be unwise to rely on that alone if their opponents were to be refuted, and Pitt wished to arm himself with a full

1. Pitt to Wilberforce, 8 April 1788 (*Private Papers of William Wilberforce*, 18).
2. To William Eden, 7 December 1787 (Holland Rose, 459–60).
3. To the same, 2 November 1787 (*A.C.*, I, 266–7).
4. Rose to Wilberforce, 27 September 1787 (*Life of Wilberforce*, I, 154, n10). Pitt himself interviewed Clarkson, probably in January or February, to see how the committee's evidence was going – and by the thrust of his questions left that inexperienced enthusiast with the impression that he had hitherto been lukewarm on the subject (see Thomas Clarkson, M.A., *The History of the Rise, Progress and Accomplishment of the Abolition of the African Slave-Trade by the British Parliament*, I (1808), 472–4).

report from the Committee of Trade. It was fairly high-handed of him to implicate the Privy Council like this – and the abolitionists were rather ungrateful later to attack the decision as causing delay. But the Committee was not the only branch of Government that the Minister wished to use. It was equally necessary in his view to enlist the sympathy of the other slave powers, above all that of France, which was the next largest trader to ourselves. He had indeed started inquiries in November 1787 through the special envoy William Eden, who had gone to Paris to negotiate his famous commercial agreement, and was now trying to complete one for the Far East. They had been based, as he stressed, on his 'personal sentiments'; but he foresaw the need for 'official communication', and this began through the Foreign Office in March 1788.[1] The process was not very swift, and pending the Committee of Trade's report he was anxious to gain a more favourable response which would strengthen the case in Parliament.

Meanwhile the initial exploratory motion had to be passed. The preparations on either side had been mounting throughout the spring. The Abolition Committee stirred up public support, and petitions and subscriptions poured in – Wilberforce was sure in the early stages that *'there is no doubt of our success'.*[2] But he admitted that it was too soon to bring a motion as early as he had hoped, and as the weeks passed the opposition began to make itself felt. The slaving interests went to work, and there were strong doubts within the Government. By the time that Pitt opened the debate, on 9 May, the forces were building up. He judged it wise to be brief and non-committal: he 'studiously avoided' giving his views at this stage.[3] He wished only to commit the subject to consideration as soon as possible. His caution indeed excited some adverse comment; Fox felt free to draw attention to it, and the result could be held to prove that it had been unnecessary. For the atmosphere in the Commons had changed a great deal over the past few years: since the days when Burke, in 1780, had decided that a slave bill would be a 'chimerical object', and North in 1783 had thought it useless to present a petition from the Quakers. Pitt's motion met with virtually no opposition; there were some powerful speeches in favour; hostile interests were silent; and it passed without dissent.

Could Pitt in fact have been bolder at this point? Should he not have supported a more far-reaching motion, and in that case might it not have passed? There is some immediate evidence which may help one to decide. The rising concern over the question had recently led old

1. Pitt to Eden, 7 January 1788 (*A.C.*, I, 304); Carmarthen to Duke of Dorset, no. 5, endorsed 1 March 1788 (P.R.O., F.O. 27/27).

2. To Eden, 18 January 1788 (*A.C.*, I, 307).

3. *P.R.*, XXIII, 598. It also appears that Steele, one of the joint Secretaries of the Treasury, had sent round a circular letter stating that abolition would not be raised in the current session (see Thurlow and Richmond in the House of Lords, 25 June 1788 (*P.R.*, XXIV, 375–6).). He must have done so on Pitt's instructions.

Sir William Dolben, one of the most senior independent M.P.s, to investigate conditions aboard some slave transports which were lying in the Thames. He was horrified by what he saw, and brought a bill at the end of May to limit, for the trial period of a year, the number of negroes allowed to a vessel in proportion to its tonnage. Thus challenged on a specific instance, the supporters of the system defended themselves. But they were completely outgunned on the evidence, and could muster only five votes on the final reading.[1] So far, so good. The bill then went, in mid-June, to the Lords. It was supported by some leading members, including one Minister, the Duke of Richmond; but there was alarming opposition – 'few instances', wrote Wraxall later, had ever been of a 'more formidable' kind.[2] This was not because the House was crowded with a numerically hostile peerage: attendance was typical of the end of a session in the summer months. It was the nature of the speakers that mattered. The wartime heroes Heathfield and Rodney spoke strongly. The Duke of Chandos, the Lord Steward, might be taken as a voice from the Court. Of the Ministers present other than Richmond – Camden was a notable absentee – Howe and Carmarthen said nothing, Sydney argued for postponement, Hawkesbury (not a member of Cabinet, but officially concerned) was very cautious, and Lord Chancellor Thurlow let fly against the bill. After two days' debate, indeed, there seemed a real danger of its failing. Pitt now stepped in. He returned post-haste from Cambridge, where he was staying, he rallied his forces, and he told Grenville that he meant to 'state . . . distinctly to the Cabinet' before the Lords met again the next day, that if the measure was defeated 'the opposers of it and myself cannot continue members of the same Government'.[3] This 'discharge of high explosive'[4] had its effect in the end. But the end was not yet. The peers approved a contentious clause in the bill by 14 votes to 12 on 30 June, and Pitt followed this up by spending 'all day' in the House on 1 July.[5] But on the 2nd there was a large crop of successful hostile amendments, Thurlow continued in full spate, and the measure was returned to the Commons on the 3rd very much altered in detail.[6] Dolben at once introduced a successor, containing most of the amendments, which the House under Pitt's urging passed through all its stages in a single day. It went up to the Lords. But even then there was more trouble. The Commons in their haste had committed a technical infringement in framing the new bill, and it had to be returned and rushed through

1. Against 56. It was a thin House.
2. *Historical and Posthumous Memoirs*, IV, 142–3.
3. 29 June 1788 (*H.M.C., Dropmore*, I, 342). The mustering of support seems to have begun at White's, where Pitt went immediately on reaching town.
4. The phrase is R. Coupland's, in *Wilberforce, A Narrative* (1923), 110.
5. Edmund Burke to Richard Burke, 2 July (*The Correspondence of Edmund Burke*, V (1965), ed. Holden Furber, 406).
6. The extent of the alterations may be seen *Journals of the House of Lords*, XXXVIII, 252–5.

again on 8 July. When it finally reached the Lords in proper shape, Sydney and Hawkesbury repeated their cautions – the latter confining himself to detail –, Thurlow and others moved fresh amendments, and although these were all defeated the measure passed only a few hours before the session closed on the 11th.[1] Wraxall later stated that Pitt would not 'allow' the King to prorogue Parliament meanwhile.[2] Whether this was so or not, he had shown himself determined to stand firm, and Dolben's bill, though much altered in detail, became law.

One may draw some conclusions from this. Pitt had not expected such opposition from the upper House; but the reaction on this restricted issue showed how controversial the whole subject could be, and may be held to have justified his anxiety – no doubt the stronger from past experience – to make very sure of his ground before supporting any major change. The Commons, by contrast, had underlined their approval. But approval of what? Their action with the revised bill was no doubt clinched by a resolve to show the Lords their temper, even at the cost of accepting some unwelcome amendments. And the bill itself dealt with a specific abuse, which in the last resort it was difficult for its opponents to deny. Once the facts had been allowed, there was no real defence. Poor drafting in Dolben's first measure gave the hostile peers a good deal of scope; but it was still significant that they shifted the argument as fast as they could from the conduct of the trade to its inherent value.[3] The Commons in short had shown themselves willing, without Pitt's prompting, to consider the question as a whole, and resolved, in thin Houses, to do away with a proven scandal. But this did not necessarily mean that when they came to the larger problems they would agree on what should be done, or easily consent to limit or stop the trade itself. As Pitt had found with Parliamentary reform, it was one thing to say you would have a debate, quite another to embark on controversial legislation. And meanwhile notice had been served, with surprising force considering the circumstances, of the resistance to be expected from very powerful quarters.

If he had introduced a different motion in May 1788, Pitt would have had to decide exactly what it should be. In principle he was in favour of outright abolition. His talks with Wilberforce had led him to reject a

1. The later debates in the Lords, from 2 to 11 July, are reported in Stockdale, *Fifth Session of the Sixteenth Parliament*, III (1788), 349–83; but not in *P.R.*, XXIV, or *P.H.* XXVII (1816). Sydney's and Hawkesbury's resentment at 'the damned business' (Sydney's expression) and 'the manner in which [it] has been taken up' (Hawkesbury's) appears in the latter's correspondence (B.M. Add. Mss 38223, 38310).

2. *Memoirs*, IV, 149. His account of the whole affair is not entirely accurate.

3. For the rest, the opponents of the bill were concerned very largely simply to deny the evidence, or to state that other people – soldiers in tents, for instance – were sometimes worse off.

mere limitation of the trade, and other if weaker influences may also have been at work. There were indeed too many streams of liberal thought now flowing in the same direction for someone of Pitt's age and ideas to ignore them – it may have been significant, for instance, that William Paley, that respected and popular Cambridge figure, had recently pronounced against the institution in a book which the Minister greatly admired.[1] Pitt in short started with a moral view, on which his friendship with Wilberforce pledged him to act. But he had still to look at the facts and the prospects before committing Government to a detailed policy. He worked hard on the subject from the summer of 1788: his papers are full of reports and figures, the investigating committees' and his own. The results did nothing to shake his initial belief that 'a temporary interruption of the trade would be as full of difficulty and inconvenience as to abandon it entirely', and that if 'the principle of humanity and justice . . . is in any degree compromised, the cause is in a manner given up'.[2] When he had finished his labours, and brought his ideas to a point, he was satisfied that there was 'no part of our case that is not made out upon the strongest ground'.[3]

But by that time it was the spring of 1789, and the debate itself opened in May. This again was later than the abolitionists, or Pitt himself, had forecast. The year before, he had proposed that the matter should be raised 'early in the next session', and he thought that the session would begin in November and be over by February.[4] But things worked out otherwise. The Committee of Trade did not report until late in April, and the session in any case took an unexpected turn. The King fell ill before it began, the Regency crisis raged thereafter, and Government business and the Parliamentary timetable were completely upset. Although Wilberforce still had hopes at one time of April, he had to wait in the event until the following month.

Despite the clash over Dolben's bill, Pitt was still hopeful of the outcome. The Committee of Trade's report was a powerful document, he found the evidence 'irresistible',[5] and, confident as always of the power of reason, he thought it must have a profound effect. The Commons had shown themselves receptive so far, and would now, he believed, support the case; and although he expected resistance, he reckoned he could handle the Lords. He himself moreover was in a very strong position at that moment, his reputation enhanced by the end of the crisis and his future once more assured. The omens seemed good, and he was taking no chances: he and Grenville helped draft Wilberforce's resolutions. He was

---

1. *The Principles of Moral and Political Philosophy* (1785). Long afterwards, Lord Aberdeen recalled hearing Pitt speak of Paley as 'the best writer in the English language' (to Lord Stanhope, 1 April 1856; 'Pitt Papers, Part ii', Stanhope Mss).
2. To Eden, 7 January 1788 (*A.C.*, I, 304).
3. To Wilberforce, 20 April 1789 (*Private Papers of Wilberforce*, 35).
4. *P.R.*, XXIII, 598; *Private Papers of Wilberforce*, 21.
5. To Wilberforce, 10 April (*Life of Wilberforce*, I, 215).

'very earnest' for success.[1] But his reading of the situation proved wrong.

Wilberforce opened the debate on 12 May. He moved twelve factual resolutions, designed to show that 'no . . . inconvenience would result from discontinuing the farther importation of African slaves' into the British West Indies. The case rested on four propositions: that the conduct of the trade was both cruel and wasteful; that there were now enough negroes in the British West Indies to satisfy the needs (present and future) of the islands as a whole; that Africa's contribution to the Atlantic commerce might well be met by other of the continent's products; and – an argument which could perhaps be attacked as inconsistent – that tropical voyages were 'injurious' to the pool of British seamen. He laid some stress on the prospects if the transport of slaves was given up; for while it no longer accounted for so large a portion of the business of the old slaving ports, and other voyages were absorbing an ever growing number of ships and men, he readily conceded that the African traffic was a necessary part of our trade. But he saw no reason to despair: '. . . an extensive commerce might probably be substituted . . . and might reasonably be expected to increase . . . on that continent'.[2] It was a long and a masterly speech – 'perhaps not excelled', said Burke when he rose, 'by any thing to be met with in Demosthenes'.[3] Burke in turn was followed, almost in succession, by Pitt and Fox and Grenville. All the big guns were on one side, and there was little open opposition. But there was one great query which the abolitionists could not answer, and which clearly disturbed them throughout the debate. What was going to happen elsewhere if we gave up the trade? Would we be acting on our own, or would others follow suit? Wilberforce dwelt more than once on this point, and when he mentioned the possibility of France taking our share of the traffic 'a cry of assent' was 'heard from several parts of the House'.[4] Pitt in turn thought it necessary to devote much of his own speech to this problem; and his remarks were hardly such as to still the doubts. It was all very well to say that he believed other powers 'would be inclined to share the honour' and 'might be disposed to set about [the matter] in earnest'. He was in fact far from certain, for his approaches had met with little success, in France or in Holland or – less actively pursued – in Portugal. He had placed particular hopes on France, where the liberal Necker, now in office, was pledged to abolition; but nothing had happened yet, and what could be said if his efforts failed? 'The language' then 'must be that Great Britain had resources to enable her to protect her islands [in the West Indies], and prevent that traffic being clandestinely carried on with them, which she had thought it fit, for her own honour and

---

1. Loc. cit., 217.
2. Wilberforce's fourth resolution (*P.R.*, XXVI (1789), 151. And see also loc. cit., 148).
3. Loc. cit., 155.
4. Loc. cit., 142.

character, to abandon'.[1] This was no doubt magnificent, but many must have felt that it was scarcely war.

As the debates went on, throughout the second half of May and into June, there was indeed a disturbing tendency for less exalted speakers to hedge. Few were prepared to say that matters should be left as they were, but few seemed prepared to commit themselves to stopping the trade at once. Fear of unilateral action may have been the chief reason, or perhaps it provided a reasonable excuse. At any rate the feelings were strong enough to force a further postponement to the next session, when the Commons would hear evidence for themselves, given at the bar of the House.

The campaigners were naturally disappointed. But they were not too depressed. Their opponents had been on the defensive, many undecided Members were clearly worried, and there seemed every reason to try to clinch the issue next year. Pitt felt the same, and he was not disturbed by the fact that he lost a member of the Cabinet during the debates. For at the beginning of June the Home Secretary, Sydney, resigned. He had shown his feelings the year before,[2] and if the trade was to be abolished he would be responsible for putting the law into effect. Pitt lost no sleep, and he eased Sydney's going – he secured him a life sinecure and a step in the peerage, and gave his eldest son a seat on the Admiralty Board. Indeed he welcomed the event, for Sydney had always been something of a passenger, and his departure would kill several birds with one stone. Pitt had long wanted Grenville in the Cabinet, a suitable office was now available, and if the new Secretary of State was made a peer (as he was the next year) he could help counter Thurlow's activities in the Lords. The decision was taken on grounds wider than that of the slave trade alone. But it was noticeable that the new Cabinet Minister was at Pitt's right hand in that campaign.

Little progress in point of fact was made in 1790. The evidence which the Commons had wanted was heard at length, and with some procrastination, in a session occupied largely with other things. It was April 1791 before Wilberforce could try again.[3] The question had now been fully ventilated; but there had been some adverse developments since the earlier debates. The prospect of an alternative supply of sugar from India had receded,[4] at least on a large scale, for the West Indian

1. Loc. cit., 159. It has been argued (Eric Williams, *Capitalism and Slavery* (1944), 146) that Pitt really wanted to bring about abolition in order to ruin the French sugar trade, now larger than the British. Even unilateral action, it is claimed, would have had this effect, 'for the French were so dependent on British slave traders'. But would they have remained so if they had continued to stimulate their already growing activities (p. 388 above)? This prospect seems in fact to have been the abolitionists' greatest stumblimg block, and fear. It is in any case very doubtful if the French sugar trade was so prosperous by the end of the eighties; and from 1790 it certainly was not.
2. Pp. 394–5 above.
3. Having given notice in February.
4. See p. 389 above.

interest had defeated a proposal to lower the duties to competitive rates. Pitt's attempt to get the other major powers to abolish the trade had conspicuously failed: the Danes were moving at their own pace, but the Dutch and the Portuguese showed little interest, and the French finally refused to act. In 1789 it had begun to look as if they would do so – Necker, Brissot, Mirabeau, Lafayette, Condorcet, Sièyes were all committed to the cause. But the National Assembly, like the House of Commons, was far from convinced, and, like the Commons, defeated its leaders' efforts. Nor was that all. In the spring of 1790 there was a rising by the mulattos in Saint Domingue, the largest of the French West Indian sugar islands, and the unrest, fanned by the upheaval in France, spread in the course of the year. This was precisely the sort of thing that many British planters had feared if changes were made, and it seriously affected opinion at home. The Commons, moreover, could no longer avoid coming to a decision: Wilberforce's motion this time was 'to prevent the farther importation of slaves into the British colonies in the West Indies'.[1] Once more the big guns fired in support. But they could not carry the day. We do not know the details of voting, for no division list has apparently survived.[2] But the feelings of ordinary Members were shown as the debates wore on. 'The leaders, it was true', said the independent William Drake at the end, 'were for the abolition; but the minor orators, the dwarfs, the pigmies, he trusted, would this day carry the question against them'.[3] They did so. On 19 April the motion was defeated by 163 to 88.

The abolitionists, undaunted, resolved to try again. They redoubled their efforts in the country, with some ostensible success. This was the period of William Cowper's popular verses 'The Negro's Complaint', and Wedgwood's equally popular cameo of the suffering slave. Meetings were held, petitions mounted; when Wilberforce rose on 2 April 1792, some 500 had been received in support. But all this agitation had remarkably little effect. The retentionists were not to be drawn: only five petitions came in from the other side – Liverpool itself did not send one –, and the opponents of the motion had not openly exerted themselves in the House. But they knew what they were doing. There was no longer any real likelihood of the slave trade being abolished at once.

For if Wilberforce had failed the year before, how could he succeed now? The interval had been disastrous, though many of the campaigners would not see it. First and worst, there had been a bloody

1. 18 April (*P.R.*, XXIX, 220).

2. *The Senator; or Clarendon's Parliamentary Chronicle* . . ., which began publication in this year, gives the names of some of the leading votes on either side (II, 636); but the list is very brief. Some of Pitt's personal circle voted for the motion – Bankes, Dudley Ryder, Tom Steele (and Edward Eliot is also known to have been in favour); but some official names are conspicuous by their absence in either list, and Dundas and Steele's Treasury colleague Rose, for example (though the former was away), were now against immediate abolition.

3. 19 April (*P.R.*, XXIX, 309).

massacre in Saint Domingue, where the mulattos' rising had drawn in the negroes with terrible results. This was shocking news. 'People here are all panic-struck', wrote Wilberforce, 'with the transactions in St. Domingo, and the apprehension or pretended apprehension of the like in Jamaica and other of our islands. I am pressed on all hands', he added, '. . . except by the [Abolition] committee . . . to defer my motion till next year'.[1] The 'Black Terror' had a great effect. But the news from France was also sombre. The flight to Varennes had taken place, the Jacobins were in the saddle; and Jacobin sympathies were evident in England itself. The very successes of the abolitionists' campaign were indeed beginning to tell against them, for some at least of their supporters – and some of their methods – seemed to stem from radical sources. It was perhaps particularly damaging to the cause that the committee had set up Corresponding Societies to co-ordinate its efforts; and some of its members – very naturally, but unwisely for their immediate prospects – were showing interest in other well-meaning but increasingly suspect movements. Dundas was particularly angry with Clarkson for this, and Pitt told Wilberforce that some of their old sympathisers might desert so as 'not to encourage Paine's disciples'.[2] 'The gale of the world' was beginning to blow, and the negroes were among the sufferers.

Pitt himself indeed had been seriously disturbed by these converging developments, and he was under strong pressure to take a more cautious line. Opinion within the Government, as at Court and outside, had been hardening against immediate abolition, and there was now a strong feeling that it would be wiser to call for a gradual process, moving by stages to completion by a given date some years hence.[3] The leading exponent of this idea was Dundas, now Home Secretary, and he undoubtedly influenced Pitt. In the early spring of 1792, the Minister tried to persuade Wilberforce to substitute a less ambitious motion, which would almost certainly stand a much better chance of success. But Wilberforce, though shaken, stood firm. He repeated his call for an immediate stop to the trade in the April debate, and when it came to the point Pitt felt bound to support him. Indeed, he excelled himself – 'one of the richest specimens of his own uncommon powers', 'Memory' Woodfall's *Register* called the speech, and Fox, Grey and Windham agreed in thinking it 'one of the most extraordinary displays of eloquence they had ever heard. For the last twenty minutes he really seemed to be inspired'.[4] It was in fact, in its own vein, perhaps the finest of all his orations, and it passed into Parliamentary legend – a tale told

1. To Thomas Babington (*Life of Wilberforce*, I, 340). No date is given, but the context is early in 1792. There had in fact been a small rising in a British island already – in Dominica. But it had been quite easily suppressed.
2. Loc. cit., 343–4.
3. It is interesting that the Danes did precisely this in March 1792, fixing the final date at 1803. See also pp. 389 n2, 399 above.
4. *The Diary, or, Woodfall's Register*, 3 April 1792; *Life of Wilberforce*, I, 345–6.

by old Members in the next century, as they recalled the heroic past. Towards the end, alluding to the prospect of a new dawn in Africa, Pitt quoted the Virgilian lines:

> Nos primus equis Oriens afflavit anhelis;
> Illic sera rubens accendit lumina vesper.

I have heard it related [Lord Stanhope wrote about seventy years later] by some who at that time were Members of Parliament, that the first beams of the rising sun shot through the windows of the House in the midst of this final passage, and seemed, as Pitt looked upwards, to suggest to him without premeditation the eloquent simile and the noble Latin lines with which he concluded.[1]

It was clearly a great performance, by a great master of style. But it was more than that. In the last twenty inspired minutes Pitt opened up a new vista. 'But now, Sir, I come to Africa', he had said, and 'with these words a new chapter in history was opened'.[2] He surveyed the dark continent, scarcely known, on its own merits and for its own sake – and dealt in passing with the perennial contention that its inhabitants were perennially doomed to inferiority. 'I hope . . . we shall hear no more of the moral impossibility of civilising the Africans'; what was needed rather was 'an atonement for our long and cruel injustice' towards them. Such a survey, on such grounds, was a novel experience for the Commons as a body,[3] and it must have been intensely stirring to hear.

At the same time, however startling, the passage followed on what had gone before. For the bulk of Pitt's speech had repeated the reasoning of earlier occasions. The whole oration in fact was a striking example of the object at which he liked whenever possible to aim – the reconciliation of an ideal (in this case the answer to a moral demand) with arguments already set forth designed to satisfy the objections of

1. Stanhope, I, 145–6. This is such a well known story that it seems a shame to question it. But I must confess that I know of no conclusive evidence in its favour.

The speech was reported sparsely in the contemporary collections *P.R.* and *The Senator*; as in the surviving newspapers of the day. But a much fuller text appeared in *P.H.*, XXIX, in 1816, and this must have been copied from vol. II of W. S. Hathaway's collection of Pitt's speeches in 1806 (see Note on Sources to ch. III below). This in turn is identical with the text given in a pamphlet *The Debate on a Motion for the Abolition of the Slave-Trade, in the House of Commons, on Monday the Second of April, 1792, Reported in Detail*, published in 1793 (to be found, with another pamphlet of 1792 giving *The Speech of the Right Honourable William Pitt* . . . only, in B.M. Printed Books T. 1136), which, judging by the titles of other pamphlets given on the back, may have been produced by the Abolition Committee. Whether Pitt or Wilberforce passed that text, it seems impossible to say.

2. Sir Robert Birley, 'The Discovery of Africa' . . . (The Anti-Slavery Society, 1968), 7. The rest of this paragraph follows the sense of this address.

3. Though the point of view was not new to all its Members; see p. 389 above.

practical men. This was the faculty which, at his best, distinguished him from unpractised idealists and the average successful political leader alike. It was his peculiar strength, almost his hallmark. But the synthesis was not easy, and in this instance it was already under decisive attack. The splendid periods proved in effect to be Pitt's elegy for the cause. Feeling was now too strong – it may well have been strengthened by the knowledge that he himself had been wavering –, and the motion was thrown out by 230 votes to 85. At the same time, an amendment, proposed by Dundas, to insert the word 'gradually' into the motion for abolition, passed by 193 to 125. The way therefore was now clear for this alternative to be pursued. On 23 April Dundas moved a series of resolutions, abolishing the trade by degrees until it was ended by the year 1800. It was interesting that, in this changed context, his caution was proved excessive; for the date was advanced in the course of the debates to 1796, and the motion carried on this basis by 151 to 132.[1] The outcome was a tribute to the fact that a majority could be found for abolition, as distinct from regulation – though increasing regulation was specified for the intervening years. It also reflected the fact that Members were determined not to be rushed, in a disturbed and apparently increasingly dangerous world.[2]

But the matter had now to go to the Lords – the first chance they had had to take a hand since 1788. They did so decisively. Pitt addressed a special meeting of selected peers and Members, to report the Commons' resolutions;[3] and in the debate that followed Grenville did his best. But the peers, gratefully following the Commons' example of three years before, refused to proceed without hearing evidence for themselves in the next session. Shortly after that opened, the war with France began, and the hearings petered out. Wilberforce went on trying, with a variety of motions in the following years; but the Commons had lost interest, he spoke to thin Houses, and his hopes, though not his resolve, gradually sank.

At the end of 1792, the campaign had therefore failed. But it had produced two results – one potentially significant – to offset a total lack of

1. After an attempt to substitute 1795 had failed, by 161 to 121.

2. It was possible, of course, by this time to be thoroughly sceptical of the whole affair. 'Those who urge the immediate abolition', wrote William Eden, 'know that it is impossible; those who propose the gradual abolition mean to baffle every species of abolition; and those who vote for the continuance of the trade, know well that it ought not to be continued' (to Lord Henry Spencer, [9 April 1792]; *A.C.*, II, 400). He appears to have made an exception of Pitt, who had 'raised his own imagination to the belief' in immediate measures. But since Eden never thought that any plan for abolition stood a real chance of success (e.g. to Pitt, 12 November 1788; P.R.O. 30/8/110), this did not in his view say much for the Minister's judgment.

3. *P.R.*, XXXII, 504; XXXIII (1792), 391.

achievement. The agitation had led some of the West Indian Assemblies to scrutinise their image. An Act had been passed in Jamaica in 1781 to improve the treatment of slaves: it was remodelled in 1787 in response to criticism from England, there were further improvements in 1788 and 1792, and several of the smaller islands then followed suit. At the same time, the reformers were able to gain a foothold in Africa itself, with the Government's connivance if not with its active support. The Ministry indeed viewed the efforts with some approval at the start, for they seemed to offer a way out of an awkward dilemma. Among the loyalists from the American War were a number of negroes, whose resettlement was proving difficult. Some had gone to the West Indies, others to Nova Scotia, others to England, and this last group of immigrants was proving something of a problem. A movement, under the veteran philanthropist Granville Sharp, was formed in the middle eighties to establish them and their fellows in West Africa, and the first batch sailed for Sierra Leone in a warship in 1787, accompanied by a number of 'Whites chiefly women of the lowest sort' whom respectable men were glad to ship off to face the challenge, as they liked to put it, of 'tolerable habits'.[1] The settlement soon ran into trouble, and it clearly needed stricter control and some economic shelter. Sharp and his colleagues petitioned for a constitution and, at first, for a monopoly of trade. Rather naturally, they did not obtain the latter – strict monopoly along the coast had disappeared –, nor were they granted jurisdiction over the existing forts, which had long been administered by the Committee of African Merchants, the successors to the old Royal African Company. But when they settled for a simple authority to own land and trade freely, Government did not stand in their way. Obstruction indeed would have been inconsistent, for the object was to open up 'a general trade' in the region – exactly the sort of thing that Pitt was stressing in his arguments for an alternative to the slave trade.[2] A bill was presented to the Commons in April 1791; it passed at the end of May, and the Lords approved it in the first week of June.[3] It set up a joint stock company, the Sierra Leone Company, entirely dependent on its own capital, and receiving by charter some rather ill defined and not exclusive territorial rights – a body whose constitution drew many features from its predecessors trading to distant lands, but which made no financial grant to Government and in turn was given no monopoly or financial support. The new Company in fact was kept as independent as it well could be under Act of Parliament. The Ministry acknowledged no responsibility, as Pitt indeed had already foreshadowed in 1790, when he refused to allow temporary relief or naval protection after the

1. Report of the Directors of the Sierra Leone Company, 1791; quoted in Eveline C. Martin, *The British West African Settlements 1750–1821* . . . (1927), 104–5.
2. Cf. the peroration in his great speech of 3 April 1792.
3. 31 Geo. III, c. 55.

settlement had been attacked by its neighbours.[1] The arrangement was an attempt to steer clear of fresh commitments while taking advantage of fresh opportunities; to avoid the expense and worry of new colonies, when colonies were out of favour. But a future colony had none the less been created, whatever might be thought at the time, and the expansion of trade, fostered in this instance by philanthropic efforts, had combined once more with the effects of the recent Atlantic upheaval to saddle Government in due course with further financial and territorial concerns.

1. The evidence is in Prince Hoare, *Memoirs of Granville Sharp, Esq* . . . , II (1828), 141–9.

Trade and Empire in the East: Far Eastern Opportunities

I

Throughout the seventeenth and most of the eighteenth centuries, the territories governed by the British Crown were confined, outside the British Isles, to the western hemisphere. Even in 1783, not one inch of land was administered by the Government east of Lowestoft. All the forts and regions beyond that longitude occupied by British subjects were owned and governed, under charter, by trading associations. There was thus a strong formal contrast in Government business between East and West. There had also been a difference in the scale of trade, the greater share falling to the West.

But from the 1760s at least the outlines of this contrast were becoming blurred. If Government did not administer the Eastern possessions it found itself helping to secure them, and inextricably involved in the East India Company's affairs. Pitt's Act of 1784 was one of several possible answers to a now unavoidable problem, and the Crown's participation in Eastern business followed the growth of Eastern trade. For while the figures had remained noticeably smaller than those for the Atlantic in the past two decades, there had been a disproportionate rise in imports, and so in the volume of traffic. In the years 1761–5 the average official value of English exports and re-exports to the 'East Indies' was £976,000 a year; in 1781–5, £930,000. The comparable figures which can be extracted for the Atlantic – taking the British West Indies, North (but not Central or South) America, Newfoundland, and Africa – were £3,583,000 and £4,053,000. Imports for the same years stood officially at an average of £1,102,000 and £2,030,000 from the East, and £3,710,000 and £3,537,000 for the Atlantic as defined above. The second lot of figures in each case was affected by the American War and its aftermath, and the sharp revival of the Atlantic trade continued over the next five years. But the Eastern trade was also on the increase, though the apparent rise in imports now reflected, here more than elsewhere, a transfer of smugglers' cargoes to the Customs ledgers after Pitt's Commutation Act. In 1786–90 official exports to the East amounted to £1,914,000, compared with £5,103,000 in the Atlantic;

imports were valued at £3,310,000 and £4,671,000 respectively.[1] It thus remained true that the Atlantic commerce was much larger, and our balance there on aggregate more favourable, than that with the East. It was equally true that trade with the East was growing over the period.

All this enlargement of activity produced a new dimension in official thought. It affected naval planning and foreign policy, it demanded financial consideration and, in due course, action. It had introduced novel political forces, and a focus for political warfare, at home. It was a great new factor in national affairs. In the face of rising troubles across the Atlantic, it could also be seen as an alternative to a system whose advantage seemed more doubtful than before. There was certainly a 'swing of interest' in some quarters from the 1760s onwards, a school of thought which wanted to expand in the East and cut our losses in the West. No such policy, however, emerged from Government, before or after the American War: on the contrary, Pitt's Ministry made very great efforts in the Atlantic sphere. Nor indeed were the alternatives as sharp as was sometimes suggested: the Pacific became a factor in Pitt's American policy. The picture was larger than they represented, and it could not be so easily cut up. Government did not withdraw in the one case, *and* it was determined to press forward in the other. The postwar theme remained expansion – from a defensive posture at first in the West, by selective advance in the East. At the same time, the American experience did strengthen a theory which had been growing and was widely held – the desire to trade as far as possible without great colonial commitments. Avoid expense, limit territorial involvement, defend your interests, open up fresh commerce: this was the broad, and conscious, approach to diverse and sometimes inconsistent opportunities. The inconsistencies of course were marked, and the choice was often restricted. In the first place, there was a great difference between Government's obligations in India, which were now leading it to take over from John Company as much of the business of order and defence as it could, and those farther east, where the options still seemed more open. But even in south-east Asia and the Pacific, trade and the flag must impinge on each other, as Ministers were beginning to find and, often reluctantly, to accept. This could not be avoided, and older lessons had to be relearned. Nevertheless, there seemed to be a real contrast between the need for forces and bases on the one hand, and established dominion on the other. Expansion in the East would have gone on in any case, whether the American War had been fought or not. But the war revived and deepened old sentiments, and gave or appeared to give them fresh point.

1. Schumpeter, *English Overseas Trade Statistics*, tables V, VI; figures for England and Wales only. They must of course be regarded as highly approximate – values were often artificial, and smuggling made a different impact on different areas at different times –, and they refer to direct trade only. But they show broadly how men saw the picture at the time.

There was one place in the Pacific where events in America had a more direct effect. Among the losses which they imposed on the British Government was that of a convenient penal settlement. While transportation remained the favourite punishment for felony – while the central authorities refused to spend much money on prisons, and had no police –, America served as the dumping ground for the victims of the criminal law. It offered every advantage to the home country: it was far away, it needed labour, the convicts could be separated and controlled. The Americans, however, were not uniformly enthusiastic; there had long been protests at the practice, and by 1776 these had become part of the general revolt. In 1775, some prisoners from England had been refused permission to land. North's Ministry had therefore to consider an alternative even before the war began, and once hostilities broke out it was faced by a growing problem. Various possibilities were canvassed, the most likely for a time being West Africa; but none seemed satisfactory – West Africa itself was eventually condemned by its climate and terrain – and meanwhile the prisoners were housed as far as possible in hulks in the Thames and at the southern naval ports. Their conditions grew shameful with the growing numbers which the prisons could not accommodate, both hulks and prisons were crammed to capacity, and the authorities became alarmed. Complaints flowed in throughout the early eighties, troops had sometimes to be sent to keep order, men were escaping in growing numbers, there was a very real fear that they would get out of hand. The Commons had set up committees in the late seventies to examine the situation, and in 1784 an Act was passed to renew transportation.[1] In April 1785 another Parliamentary committee was formed to see how this might work, in other words to make recommendations as to where the convicts might go.

Plenty of recommendations had already been received. The Home Office did not lack advice. But the choice remained open until almost the last moment. The committee could not decide, and the Ministry continued to concentrate on West Africa until its disadvantages were finally proved, after a naval voyage of inspection, in 1786. In June of that year, the Cabinet was reported still to be thinking of Africa, Canada and the West Indies.[2] But it must also by then have been considering the possibility of Australia, which had been brought to the fore over the past few years. The idea indeed had been mooted in Britain almost twenty years earlier, before Cook sailed on his first voyage and while the continent (if it was a continent) was known

1. 24 Geo. III, c. 56.
2. The purported proposals made to the meeting were published in *The Edinburgh Magazine and Literary Review* for that month (III, 473). Pitt had stated in February that the subject was under Ministerial review (*P.R.*, XIX (1787), 54).

mainly from Dampier and the Dutch discoveries.[1] It was now revived more specifically in the light of his achievement, and as an answer to the current concern. In 1784, a certain James Matra, who had been with Cook, suggested to the Home Secretary that a penal settlement might be established in New South Wales. The proposal was echoed in 1785 by Admiral Sir George Young, an old East India hand, and by Sir Joseph Banks, the eminent botanist who had also sailed in the *Endeavour*, and who gave evidence to the Parliamentary committee (as he had done to its predecessor in 1779) in favour of Botany Bay. In August 1786 the Government accepted this last suggestion. On the 18th of that month, Sydney informed the Treasury that the King approved it, and preparations for a settlement went ahead from the autumn. In May 1787 the first convoy of prisoners and soldiers sailed from Portsmouth, and in January 1788 it reached Botany Bay.

The Ministry sent the ships in response to what was thought to be an urgent need. The transportation of felons must be renewed without more delay. There is no reason otherwise to suppose that a settlement would have been started at that time, let alone that Government would have been directly responsible for it. The form of government it received underlined its purely penal nature, and disclaimed any other immediate intention. The Governor was given 'a Summary Jurisd\". for Botany Bay', an expedient, wrote the old lawyer Camden to Pitt, which 'I believe in the present State of that Embryo (for I can't call it either Settlement or Colony) is necessary', although it was 'a Novelty in our Constitution'.[2] Sydney himself had stressed to Matra, in 1784, that transportation was the problem uppermost in his mind. But the choice fell where it did at least partly because New South Wales was thought to hold natural advantages, which its sponsors were advancing as reasons for other kinds of use. Botany Bay was said to be well watered and timbered, it could support a sizeable population if livestock was imported, the climate was moderate, the natives did not seem formidable. There was in fact an apparently largely empty land, of which a good deal might be made – an attractive base for settlement in a new area of the world. Joseph Banks, though he had his dreams, had judged it wise to be cautious before the Parliamentary committees: he argued only that a growing population would take more European goods and 'furnish matter of advantageous return'.[3] But Young and Matra – perhaps Young based on Matra – were more explicit to the Home Office, and they had their eyes on the East as a whole. New South Wales lay south of the Aleutians with their fur trade, of great value to

1. By J. Callender, in the first volume of his *Terra Australia Cognita*, published in Edinburgh in 1766. But the suggestion was older than that. It may first have been raised by the Frenchman de Brosses in a Paris publication of 1756.

2. 29 January 1787 (P.R.O. 30/8/119).

3. Evidence of 1 April 1779 (Harlow and Madden, *British Colonial Developments*, 426–8). Many of the eulogies in point of fact are distinctly suspect; first impressions had been much less favourable.

our traffic with China. If linked by regular communication with Britain, it could take woollen goods – also popular in China – for onward sale. We might enter the markets of Japan and Korea, hitherto scarcely tapped. And we would have a focal point for trade in the Spice Islands, to which we were allowed free access by treaty. We might thus hope to alter the commercial balance and reduce the flow of bullion to the East. But a settlement in Australia could be of strategic importance as well. It might, suggested Young, take a colony of loyalists from America. It should be able to grow the excellent variety of flax which Cook had found in New Zealand, and to import New Zealand timber, both of value to our naval stores. And it could provide a base against the Dutch, if necessary, in Java and the Moluccas, and against the Spaniards in the Philippines and Central and South America. In fact, 'the place which New South Wales holds on our globe might give it', if properly exploited, 'a very commanding influence in the policy of Europe'.[1]

Such ideas were not new, though they could now be much more precise; there was a tradition of some four decades' speculation behind them. Cook's first voyage gave it fresh life in the seventies and eighties, and the various projects, judging by the number of pamphlets, found a ready market. The public was interested. But the authorities remained wary; neither the East India Company nor the Government was prepared to risk very much. The passage to Australia could take over half a year, the foundation of a settlement could be expensive, the nature of the continent was still virtually unknown. The Company held aloof, and the Parliamentary committee of 1785 was distinctly sceptical of the commercial prospects. Some politicians, indeed, were utterly opposed even to the final limited plan. The Ministry's decision, wrote one of Pitt's normal supporters, was 'beneath the disquisition of reason; and below the efforts of ridicule'. 'Is there no part of the planet, except New Holland, to which we can have recourse?' The convicts' labour would be wasted; why not send them to cut timber for the navy in Newfoundland, or to develop the trade for which Government was calling in West Africa? We were far more likely by this measure to found a new centre of buccaneers than to reap any benefit 'either immediate, or remote'.[2]

The Ministry did not agree; but it was scarcely enthusiastic. Australia seems to have been chosen in the end because a decision was deemed unavoidable, because Africa would not do, and the remaining trans-

---

1. Matra's first Proposal, 23 August 1783 (G. B. Barton, *History of New South Wales from the Records*, I, pt. 2 (1889), 423–8). See also Young's Proposal, [January] 1785 (op. cit., 429–32). Young advocated some complementary settlement from the Friendly Islands and China.

2. *A Short Review of the Political State of Great-Britain at the Commencement of the Year One Thousand Seven Hundred and Eighty-Seven* (1787), 77–83. It was by Nathaniel Wraxall. 'New Holland' was the old name for the partially discovered continent.

atlantic possibilities would raise local discontents.[1] But having reached a decision, Government made the best of it, and Sydney's letter to the Treasury drew attention to the prospects for cultivating hemp, obtaining naval timber from New Zealand, and growing 'most of the Asiatic productions' bought at present from other European powers.[2] Pitt himself, as far as one can see, gave the subject little thought, and was content simply to fall in with the plan. As one of his biographers has remarked regretfully, 'in this matter [he] lacked the Imperial imagination'.[3] He saw Young's paper at least,[4] and he must have taken part in the discussions and in the review of the necessary bill. But there is nothing to show that he was deeply involved. His concern with the Pacific, centring on China, focused on other points of access: on the direct route from the Indian Ocean, and on north-west America linked by the South Sea islands with India and Europe. The whalers, quartering the high latitudes, found New South Wales a convenient port of call;[5] otherwise it was left on the fringe, commercially and strategically. The trade to the north passed through other channels, wartime expeditions used other bases;[6] no hemp or timber or 'Asiatic productions' reached England for many years. Time would prove the value of the settlement, as it disproved the hopes for Nootka Sound. A generation later its character had changed, and a thriving colony was taking root. But the process was bound to take time to emerge from such an origin, and London's interest remained peripheral while the distant 'Embryo' developed.

II

> When Fancy, kindling with delight,
> Anticipates the lapse of age,
> And as she throws her eagle's sight
> O'er Time's yet undiscover'd page,
> ... Sees Commerce, springs of guiltless wealth explore,
> Where frowns the western world on Asia's neighbouring shore.

1. Sydney – who in turn, it has been suggested (Eris O'Brien, *The Foundation of Australia (1786–1800)* (2nd edn, 1950), 127) may have been influenced by his able Under-Secretary Evan Nepean – was accused of having 'too hastily' turned down 'a much better plan' (Sir William Pulteney to Pitt, 14 September 1786; P.R.O. 30/8/169); and Grenville stressed the unpopularity of similar projects in 'all the colonies' (to Lord FitzGibbon, 2 December 1789; *H.M.C., Dropmore*, I, 548).

2. 18 August 1786 (Barton, op. cit., 432–5). He did not specify which productions he had in mind. Nor did he allude to the prospects for the settlement as an entrepôt for trade or as a base.

3. Holland Rose, 442.

4. P.R.O. 30/8/342.

5. See p. 348 above.

6. For one momentary but unrealised thought of a strategic use, see p. 559 below.

So sang the poet laureate,[1] with characteristic insipidity, in his New Year's Ode for 1791, after perhaps the most successful year for such exploration that the country had yet known. The financing of this Asian trade, however, was causing serious concern, as it had been doing over the past six or seven years.· For even allowing for the transfer of smuggled imports to the official accounts, our adverse balance with the East had been rising at a time when our flow of bullion from America was shrinking.[2] Pitt's Commutation Act indeed, by its very success, was underlining the difficulties. There seemed to be a real, and perhaps an urgent, need to find a greater vent for our goods.

This was a complex problem, involving questions of organisation and diplomacy. At their very centre lay the state of the China trade. For China now supplied the bulk in value of our Oriental imports, mainly through the vastly growing quantities of tea bought in the middle and later eighties. There are the usual statistical complications; but all figures agree that our declared purchases of tea rose over five times between 1783 and 1791 – from about 4 million lb to over 20 million –, and if some 4 to 6 million lb is added for contraband at the earlier date, the probable increase is still over 100 per cent.[3] It all came from China, and it accounted for something like two-thirds of the official cost of our annual purchases from the East.

This was highly beneficial in many ways. Some of the precious leaf was re-exported from England to Europe, though the great rise in domestic consumption limited the immediate rate of increase. But that was only part of the story. The Commutation Act effectively – surprisingly effectively – knocked out our competitors in the tea trade, and since tea was so important the results were widely felt. The figures are startling. In 1783, continental and American buyers were taking roughly twice as much in value, in all goods, from China as ourselves. By 1786 we were taking more than twice as much as they were, and in 1790 almost nine times as much.[4] We had in fact acquired an unrivalled dominance in a market which was crucial to the growth of trade with Asia as a whole.

But this achievement brought its problems. How were we to pay for the larger purchases without swelling our adverse balance? Partly,

1. Henry James Pye, in *The Annual Register* for 1791.

2. See pp. 381–2 above.

3. Cf. Schumpeter, op. cit., table XVII with Earl H. Pritchard, *The Crucial Years of Early Anglo-Chinese Relations 1750-1800* (1936), figure 6 and Appendix V. There was a sudden sharp drop in 1792, before the purchases resumed a less rapid upward course. They had occasionally exceeded 10 million lb earlier, in the later sixties and early seventies; but, with marked variations, had on average been much less. For estimates of contraband, see p. 241 above.

4. Pritchard, op. cit., figure 7, reckoned in Chinese taels. This success was perhaps the more notable in that fresh European competitors were testing prospects in the East. On the other hand, the United States were only beginning to develop their fast expanding marine.

perhaps, by attracting bullion from Spain through an enlarged reciprocal trade in the East – a policy favoured by Pitt and Dundas.[1] But the main answer of course must lie in increasing our transport and sale of goods, to China direct if possible, at any rate to India and south-east Asia. This did not seem out of the question, for likely means already existed. But if they were to be fully exploited, several conditions should be fulfilled.

One of the most important turned on the structure of the trade. All British commerce with the East, from the Red Sea to the eastern Pacific, was governed by the charter of the East India Company. Under its monopoly a variety of methods had grown up. The Company itself engrossed most of the Eastern traffic. But it also sanctioned a Private Trade (as it was known) carried on under licence by its sea officers, and, again by licence, a Country Trade in and from India conducted by resident Englishmen and Indians. The three kinds of activity were of course connected, but each showed certain distinct features. Company business, centred firmly on London, took far more goods from the East than it sent there – in the China trade itself, some 200 per cent more in the middle seventies, rising to well over 300 per cent in 1785–6. This would therefore, if left to itself, have resulted in a very nasty drain of bullion; but the gap was filled in part by the Company's facilities for drawing on the Private and Country trades. For here the proportions were quite different. Both Private and Country traders sold more goods to the Chinese than they bought, the first by amounts varying in the middle and later eighties between 30 and 60 per cent, the second by some 100 to 160 per cent.[2] Their combined share of the total traffic with China, moreover, was significant: in 1785–6, about a quarter in value of the purchases and about half of the sales.[3] The Company's access to the resulting balances, by virtue of its charter, was correspondingly vital to its development of business and the state of the bullion balance.

These discrepant results arose from the nature of the different trades, which had repercussions throughout the East. The Private trade had arisen to fill a gap left in the Company's activities: to take advantage of local opportunities, in the course of voyages based on England, which could be grasped only by men on the spot. It might be described, in principle at least – for it was often merged in practice with Country trading –, as supplementing by personal contact the operations of a remote control. The Country trade did more: it covered a type of business which the Company did not. It followed, in fact, the age-old pattern of commerce which the Europeans had found on

1. See pp. 460–1 below.
2. Pritchard, op. cit., 143 and Appendices XI, XII.
3. Loc. cit., Appendices VII, XI, XII. The proportions varied somewhat from year to year. It must be stressed that these figures apply to China, not to the East as a whole.

arrival, and which a distant monopoly could scarcely hope to exploit. Traffic around the Indian coasts and Ceylon, or between India and Arabia and East Africa, or between India and Malaya and through the Malacca Strait – little of this could be readily fitted into a system of long-haul passages from London. But it could easily be invaded by resident Europeans under Company licence, some supplementing their official salaries and most of them in contact with Company finance. As the century wore on, they largely ousted or absorbed the Indian and Near Eastern merchants, and in the 1780s Englishmen and Scotsmen were clearly in the lead. By then they were handling a growing complex of business, centred on the Agency Houses, as they were called, in Bombay, Madras, and above all Calcutta. Local vessels ranged from the Persian Gulf to Cochin China and, increasingly from the sixties, to Canton itself. The profits returned whence they came – the ships grew larger, so did their numbers –, they sustained fresh business – local investment, banking and insurance, for the French and Danes and Dutch as well as ourselves –, they were even remitted to England, whence credits and specie could in turn be drawn. There were close and ramifying triangular connexions between India and Canton and London: between Fairlies and Fergussons, Scotts and Macphersons; Jardines and Mathesons, Raikes's and Smiths; Goslings and Barings and Vansittarts, dealing in their private capacities at home. Without such flexible continuous exchanges, London could not have outstripped Amsterdam and Paris so decisively as 'the Emporium of the Asiatic Trade to the western world'.[1] Throughout the second half of the century, and above all in the last two decades, the Country trade was a vital element of British strength in the East.

It was not therefore very surprising that there should have been a campaign for its enlargement, at the expense of the Company's monopoly. It mounted progressively through the middle and late eighties. For Government was then once more engaged in the wearisomely familiar task of improving the Company's credit, and the charter itself was due for renewal by Parliament in 1794. The great manufacturing growth of the time, particularly in textiles, gave the protests fresh force, and much of that growth came from the fast growing volume of business with China. The machinery in London, it was said, was too clumsy, its ultimate control too distant and hampering, to cope properly with a situation in which the problems and prospects were equally great. The pressures fell on the organisation of the East India Company as a whole. But they had perhaps the greatest effect in the disputes over the China trade.

The consequences of Pitt's India Act, and the fact that the charter

1. George Smith [a merchant in Canton] to Dundas, 26 November 1786; quoted in Harlow, op. cit., II, 556.

must be re-examined, meant that Ministers were deeply involved in this argument. It had repercussions, indeed, on many aspects of their Eastern policies, commercial, strategic, and diplomatic. As early as 1783–4 Dundas was receiving suggestions for extending the trade with China, some of which he passed on to Pitt.[1] But the matter really came to the fore in 1786. In that year, two energetic merchants embarked separately on campaigns of persuasion. From Canton, and later Calcutta, the veteran merchant George Smith bombarded Dundas with reports and proposals, the latter to include a greater freeing of the trade with China as well as an embassy to the Emperor. His arguments may well have had some effect, despite his somewhat shaky status – he had got into financial trouble at Canton, and had finally had to leave. But a more powerful attack came from another quarter. In the summer of 1786, David Scott, the senior partner in the leading merchant house in Bombay, came home, after twenty-three years, determined to press for a better system. He was soon on close terms with Dundas, and through Dundas saw a good deal of Pitt.[2] The burden of his song was a recasting of the Company's monopoly. It should not be removed, for it was a necessary shield to the merchants in distant lands; but it should be eased, to allow their activities to bear greater fruit. He summed up his proposals in the spring of 1787. The Company's credit in India was very weak, and its regulations were cumbersome and rigid. It was not sending out enough manufactures – about three-quarters of the outward tonnage sailed in ballast. But the answer to these shortcomings lay largely outside the corporate activities, for the Country trade held the immediate key to greater sales. Let the Company, therefore, allow a specified list of merchants to send out goods in its ships on their own account, guaranteeing a given (and rising) amount annually over the next five years, and paying the Company freight. The Country traders, for their part, should be encouraged by permission – at present denied – to remit their fortunes home by buying Company bills of exchange; and foreigners resident in Asia should be admitted to some at least of our trading privileges. These conditions should apply to India, the base for the China trade. But there were particular steps to be taken for China itself, for which Scott foresaw a glittering future. Increased sales of goods there were essential, and there was a definite demand. They could come from England direct, and, through British agency, from Asia and the south-west Pacific. But the direct trade – which Scott thought could surpass that with India itself – needed a proper base on the Chinese coast, enjoying guaranteed security. Steps must therefore be taken by Government to negotiate conditions with the Emperor, and the settlement must continue to be under the Company's control. The

1. See the anonymous plans in P.R.O. 30/8/354, endorsed with the date 1784 and as having been forwarded by Dundas. For 1783, see Pritchard, op. cit., 232.

2. Indeed at one time, in Pitt's own words, he met him 'very often'; Pitt to Pretyman, 9 December (year unknown) (Pretyman Ms 435/42).

local trade, on the other hand, though directed to this base, would thrive best under private enterprise, centred (Scott hoped) on Bombay and enjoying wide privileges under Company protection. There should in fact be a new partnership between the Company and the private trader, which alone could grasp the enormous opportunties for growth.

These proposals, backed by Scott's influence, greatly interested the Government; and it was not long before they received a fillip from elsewhere. For early in 1788 the effects of a recession in the cotton industry began to be felt,[1] and since the East India Company was simultaneously trying to increase its imports of Indian textiles the manufacturers made it the main object of their attack. They petitioned Hawkesbury in the spring, and Hawkesbury, as always, was active. He found his colleagues disposed to listen, for the Ministry and the Company were already embroiled. Dundas and Pitt had just forced an extension of the powers of the Board of Control through Parliament, and the argument over the whalers' privileges in the southern seas was just being resumed.[2] Battle was now joined on this fresh question, which became a prominent issue in the growing debate on the Company's new charter.

That debate continued until 1793. But the result for China may be given here. The assault on the monopoly took two forms: the plans from Scott and the manufacturers (the latter more extreme) to enlarge the private trade from the south, which were discussed in growing detail between 1789 and 1793; and those, from 1791, for admitting the whalers as the spearhead of a free trade through the northern Pacific. Pitt was involved in both as part of his Eastern problems. He joined Dundas and Hawkesbury in constructing a case for the whalers, as the best means of access to Japan and Korea and China as far south as Canton. And he worked closely with them on the review of the steps to be taken for the Country trade.[3] They had to steer a middle course. On the one hand, as Scott admitted, the Company must be recognised as the responsible commercial instrument for dealing with the Chinese: conditions for foreigners were too uncertain for private merchants to manage on their own. This meant that there must still be restrictions on freedom of trade, and control – in any case desirable to aid the Company's finances – of remittances and credit. On the other hand, only local enterprise could supply the various Asiatic products which the Chinese were known to want. Raw cotton from India, in particular, was being sold direct to China on a rising scale; if the Country traders, therefore, gathering their resources at Bombay (Scott's former base), could be given free freight from that point to China in Company ships from England, they could combine with the manufacturers at home to fill the

1. See pp. 276–7 above.
2. Pp. 454–5 below, and p. 348 above.
3. Since this last raised questions much wider than that considered here, evidence for this statement is reserved for pp. 461–4 below.

vessels with profitable cargoes. The Ministers agreed, and in the end these proposals were carried. Neither the whalers nor the manufacturers were thereby given all that they might have been. The former could trade to, but not onward from, Canton, the latter were denied their own shipping, for which they had asked. The Company kept its financial supervision, and access to the Country merchants' now considerable credits. It still bought directly the great bulk of Chinese produce. The easing of the monopoly in fact fell short of the original aims; but Government had done something, in Dundas's words, to 'engraft an open trade upon . . . exclusive privilege',[1] and the commercial consequences may have partly reflected the fact. To what extent they really did so, it is hard to say. By the end of the eighties, the China trade was financing an otherwise excessive deficit in the East – without it, indeed, the Company's dividends might have ceased. But the proportion of the Country trade within that total does not seem to have risen much in the nineties, so that the Ministerial efforts on its behalf might seem merely to have helped foster its growing *volume*. This, however, in its turn sustained a growing volume of trade for the Company itself. Asian cotton, opium and spices, on an ever larger scale, combined with British textiles (and some lead and tin) to pay for purchases of tea and silks which yielded a high and fairly steady return. In the first half of the nineties, the Company's profit from China never fell below £½ million a year, and after a heavy drain in the later eighties – needed partly to make up for the stoppage in the course of the war – no bullion had to be sent from England, and very little from India, from 1792–3 to 1795–6. The virtual monopoly of the China market was held successfully at a difficult time, with results which were indispensable for India itself.[2]

If trading conditions had been easier along the China coast, Ministers might well have pressed the Company harder. But as things stood, its authority there had to be stated and maintained, and Government, as in India, was its necessary ally.

Foreigners in China had always been suspect and circumscribed. As the pressures grew in the later eighteenth century, the Empire was determined to resist them. Its methods were traditional, and partly irrelevant; but still quite strong enough to be inconveniently effective. Since Roman times, the Chinese had been used to selling more goods to the West than they took, and to receiving the balance in bullion. As European ships began to arrive in greater numbers in the sixteenth and seventeenth centuries, they were gradually confined to direct trading in one spot – Canton. The Portuguese were granted a settlement at

1. In the House of Commons, 23 April 1793 (*P.R.*, XXXV (1793), 250).
2. For the figures on which this paragraph draws, see Pritchard, op. cit., ch. IV and appendices.

Macao, on the estuary: the Dutch and British and other competitors were later allowed to join in the trade, without territorial rights, at the cost of being excluded from other ports. Canton in fact became the only market for European seaborne trade in China, and one of the only two direct points of exchange for European trade of any kind.[1] Traffic with Russia had to pass through the border town of Kiakhta, on the silk route south of Lake Baikal; and there was no land trade with the Europeans in India, or indeed any real desire for it on either side. When Warren Hastings planned to open routes to China through Tibet and Bhutan, he was told to stop by his Directors, who feared the expense and the possible commitments. So far as the British were concerned, therefore, they could sell their goods only through Canton, or by trading with Chinese junks abroad, or indirectly through the Russians.

This seemed scarcely good enough in a consciously expansionist age. It seemed less so in view of conditions at Canton. Foreigners were strictly restrained, and residents confined to specified quarters; charges, duties and 'presents' were complex and, like most of the regulations, arbitrarily applied; and the trade, after an unsettled interval when the rule was lifted, had to pass in theory through a licensed guild of Chinese merchants, the Co-Hong, themselves very much at the mercy of the local officials. The sum of these impositions, some petty, some severe, was considerable and could at times be serious. It gave rise to constant bickering, and occasionally worse. A series of incidents marked the relations between the Chinese authorities and British crews, the worst of which – the case of the *Lady Hughes* – occurred in 1784. But these fracas only stressed the uncertainties under which foreigners always laboured, and which the English merchants felt the more keenly as they engrossed the bulk of the trade. One of the greatest difficulties was the management of credit, now essential to the growing scale of business; for there was an endemic lack of Chinese capital, and the merchants must borrow in order to buy. This was not easy under Chinese law. The Co-Hong fell into difficulties and was dissolved in 1771; its members, and some of their 'private' competitors whom the British often illegally favoured, were badly in debt; and in the next few years the situation got out of hand. The Chinese purchases were financed by loans from Country traders and the Agency Houses in India, drawing on the Company's bills of exchange, and as a run of bankruptcies developed the creditors got nasty. In 1779 they induced the Admiral in India to send a warship to Canton for redress. This early instance of gunboat diplomacy – which both the Company and North's Ministry deplored – had some effect; the debts were partly paid, and the Co-Hong was refounded with rather greater powers. But the arrangements for credit remained uncertain, they continued to be made at private risk, and in the middle eighties the creditors were demanding final repayment and

1. Amoy, to the north, was nominally open to Spanish shipping, but was now never used.

a system at once safer and less restricted. It was a thoroughly awkward problem, for while the loans carried no legal sanction they involved important interests in the Company and were involved in its finance. The question of the private debts in fact, large in scope and confused in nature, was a reflection and a result of the state of the China trade as a whole.

There were thus very real obstacles in the way of exploiting this vital market. The Company's Directors, however, were prepared in the last resort to accept them. They certainly wished for better terms for their 'factory' at Canton.[1] But they did not wish to seek concessions which might affect their monopoly. They were indeed in a rather odd position, at once entrenched and exposed; for they were fighting on two fronts – to improve conditions, and their status against European competition, on the one hand, and on the other to preserve their rights against British competition in any form. The Government was also committed to this approach to some extent; but, at least initially, not nearly so far. It could not abandon the Company in its existing shape, and it did not mean to do so. But, saddled as it was with the final responsibility for financial support, and eager to increase sales in the East, it was quite prepared to seek terms more in line with current conditions and prospects. It wanted to encourage the Country trade, and even some hitherto unlicensed traders. It was also concerned to protect British seamen, so apt to find themselves in trouble, and negotiate a settlement which might help prevent the incidents.

The initiative for a move thus came from Whitehall rather than East India House. As one would expect, the prime mover seems to have been Dundas. In March 1787 he was ready to tackle the Directors with a proposal to send an embassy to Pekin. This was a bold step, which no British Government had tried before – though the Russians and the Portuguese had done so, long ago, with some success. He must have spoken to Pitt beforehand – he could not have put forward such a plan without the Minister's consent – and Pitt continued to be consulted over the next few months. It was soon decided that the embassy must be fully accredited by the King; that its leader, in fact, must rank as an Ambassador. Nothing else seemed likely to answer. Foreigners were sometimes received at Pekin, but the outcome was doubtful, and the traders themselves were now frankly apprehensive: when the Europeans at Canton were suddenly offered an audience in 1789, the first reaction of the English factory was to doubt if it dare accept. There was always the risk of humiliation, and even of no return. If new arrangements were to be sought, therefore, only an envoy with royal credentials was likely to effect anything at the Court of the Son of Heaven.

These were certainly the views of the man selected to head the mission. As Dundas's choice, he was naturally a Scot and a well-

1. 'Factory' was the name usually given to a commercial establishment in a foreign country authorised by the foreign Government concerned.

affected M.P. But he had other claims. Lieutenant-Colonel James Cathcart, Member for Clackmannan, had been Quartermaster-General in Bengal, and he had recently conducted talks with the French on Indian affairs in Mauritius. He thus had the necessary experience, he was well known to the Directors, and at the same time he was not now directly connected with the Company. On the contrary, he could be presented as a man of noble birth – he was the younger son of the ninth Lord Cathcart – and a Member of Parliament who was not engaged in trade. The Company, though not enthusiastic about the mission, approved the appointment, and finally agreed to pay the expenses. But it had doubts about the proposed instructions, which Cathcart himself had helped draw up, and which the Directors were asked to determine at the end of July. The Government concentrated mainly on one point: the establishment of a new 'depot', away from Canton. Conditions in the city were very difficult, and seemed unlikely to be much improved. The risk of incidents could be greatly reduced, and business relations placed on a new footing, if our trade could be concentrated in a 'small tract of Ground or detached Island',[1] clear of other Europeans and in which we would control our own nationals as the Portuguese did in Macao. If such an establishment were granted, it should be taken in the King's name. It should also be open to ships of all nations, on payment of fixed dues to the Chinese. Cathcart himself suggested Amoy, some 250 miles north of Canton; but if the Chinese refused, we must be content to ask for better treatment at Canton, and consider whether we should not establish a new depot 'without the [Chinese] Empire, in a Situation accessible to the Junks of the whole Coast'.[2]

The Company was unhappy about the scope of this plan, for the establishment would challenge its monopoly by falling under the Government, and by freely admitting foreign ships. The objections were taken to Pitt, who side-stepped. He was prepared to admit 'some little alteration in the wording . . . to preserve . . . a discretional latitude of Exclusion' as regards foreign ships[3] – a partial reassurance for the Directors which yet held the options open. The Government, as Dundas explained, did not wish to 'obtain a settlement from the Emperor . . . on any more limited terms than he is willing to give'.[4] It would be silly to devise a formula which might limit our freedom of action. But this did not necessarily mean that we would at once try to establish a free port, subject only to Chinese duties which would fall on all concerned. The Company appeared content with this explanation;

1. Dundas to Pitt, 'Memorandum for the Members of the India Board', n.d. but probably July 1787 (P.R.O. 30/8/355).
2. Cathcart's 'Preliminary Proposals', 20 June 1787 (see Harlow, op. cit., II, 558, n151). The text, misdated, is published in Hosea Ballou Morse, *The Chronicles of the East India Company trading to China 1635–1834*, II (1926), 156–9.
3. Cathcart to Dundas, 31 August 1787; quoted in Harlow, loc. cit., 561. He added, 'So this Point appears to be settled'.
4. To Cathcart, 26 August 1787; quoted in Pritchard, op. cit., 243.

but it must have brought further pressure to bear, for all reference to foreign shipping was excluded in the end.[1] The Ministry, however, insisted that any new depot must be received in the King's name, not the Company's; and this was a bull point for the near future, when the new charter would come up for review. The compromise was not untypical of the time; the two interests could both accept it; and the main body of Cathcart's instructions could be agreed without further dispute.

While Ministers concentrated on the new depot, they were anxious to forestall accusations that they were thereby seeking any territorial rights. Their demand was 'purely commercial', they desired 'neither fortification nor defence', and if the example of India was quoted against them, they wished to say that the British dominion there had 'arisen almost without our seeking it'.[2] Such an argument of course was necessary to try to quieten Chinese doubts. But it was not insincere, as far as it went. India was a very mixed blessing to Government, and an increase of trade in China was now sought mainly in order to set the Indian finances straight. The cry was thoroughly familiar, for the East as well as for the West, as a new Empire arose from the partial collapse of the old.

Two tricky problems remained. The first related to the trade in opium, now increasingly an element in our Eastern sales. It was proving a profitable export from India and Malaya; but its purchase was forbidden in China, and Cathcart might be asked what we proposed to do. He must be on his guard, and try to avoid discussion. But if the question was pressed, he should agree to end the trade rather than risk our demands. So this ill omened subject first found its way into a state paper. It would have been better if it *had* been discussed, and the traffic stopped.

The other awkward question, of course, was that of the private debts. When it was known that Cathcart was going, the creditors pressed him hard. Led by George Smith, of Canton and Madras,[3] with the powerful aid of Nicholas Vansittart, they tried to ensure that their claims were included in the representations at Pekin. But the Directors and the Government refused to 'load the intended Mission' with this delicate problem, and Pitt, while prepared to 'aid' the merchants, declined to give them official support.[4] Cathcart was told that he could do privately whatever he found possible, but his instructions contained no mention of the debts.

1. See Morse, loc. cit., 160–7 for the final instructions; Harlow, loc. cit., 561, and Pritchard, op. cit., 243, for the Company's earlier reaction. Why the reference was finally dropped, in these circumstances, I do not know.
2. Cathcart's instructions, 30 November 1797 (Morse, loc. cit., 164).
3. There were, confusingly, two George Smiths, both creditors, both in correspondence with Dundas, and both now living in Surrey. One (see p. 414 above) came from Canton and Calcutta, but this one hailed from Canton and Madras.
4. Dundas to George Smith, 3 August 1787; Cathcart to Dundas, 31 August 1787 (Harlow, loc. cit., 563).

The embassy sailed in December 1787.[1] But it never reached China. Cathcart was ill when he left, and he died off the coast of Malaya in the following June. A successor had therefore to be found, and the King's illness in the winter halted the search. It was the spring of 1789 before the question could be raised again. No obvious candidate was in sight, and Ministers thought of sending a mission from India chosen by the Governor-General of Bengal. They still wished to make it a royal embassy; but legal objections could be raised, and the Company now repeated its doubts of the whole idea. But it was in a weaker position than before: the Board of Control's authority had meanwhile been strengthened, and the Directors' delaying action, though still considerable, was overcome in the end.[2] Dundas was determined to go ahead – the Emperor's invitation to the foreigners in Canton was an added incentive –, the search for a suitable man went forward, and towards the end of 1791 the embassy was offered to Lord Macartney.

This raised the nature of the mission to a new level, for Macartney was not content with less. As a former envoy to Russia and Governor of Madras – and a Governor-General of Bengal had he wished[3] –, he was an altogether greater figure than anyone thought of before. His views were large, as was his ambition, and they now permeated the plans. Imaginative and incisive, he was determined to create an opportunity to place our relations with China on a more lofty footing. The embassy must be much more splendid than hitherto conceived. It should be a statement of British strength and British civilisation. Savants and soldiers, a train of artillery, scientific instruments, the finest manufactures, should be assembled in a demonstration which would surprise, inform and impress. This great show-piece, moreover, should move through the East at a much more leisurely pace, investigating staging points and markets en route. And when the mission was completed, it might travel onward to the north; Macartney was given credentials, should he require them, to the Emperor of Japan and all 'States and Princes'.[4] The expedition, on a smaller scale, was not unlike Napoleon's to Egypt a few years later; and its purpose, without force of arms and in different conditions, was partly the same. The ancient East should be given a taste of the prowess of the West, and induced to place the demonstrating power in a uniquely privileged position.

Macartney's instructions were based on Cathcart's. But they were elaborated and extended, and, as a result of prolonged discussion, set in a rather different context. The Ambassador was anxious not to blunt his object by presenting a long list of grievances, which might endanger

---

1. In a frigate commanded by Sir Richard Strachan, later to be so disastrously associated with Pitt's brother Chatham.
2. It was fought largely under the leadership of Francis Baring, who became Deputy Chairman in 1791.
3. See p. 194 above.
4. Macartney's instructions, 8 September 1792 (Morse, loc. cit., 242).

his more positive proposals and claims. The Company agreed, and suggested that a special committee (to sail with the mission) should be set up, to superintend the affairs of the Canton factory and formulate demands. Macartney concurred after some hesitation, and was thereby freed from some of the detail and able to concentrate more easily on the issues beyond Canton. Both the Company and the Government were anxious to establish better facilities to the north, where the main areas of tea growing lay and there were good prospects for expanding trade. The wording of Cathcart's instructions held; but Macartney intended to ask for several new depots, of which the largest should be at Ning-po and Chusan or Tientsin. He would also see if an entrepôt could not be gained in Pekin itself, as the Russians had once enjoyed. These requests, however, did not now mean that Canton should be abandoned. On the contrary, conditions there should be improved and the British given an offlying settlement like the Portuguese at Macao. A consul should be appointed, who would handle relations with the local officials; envoys perhaps might be exchanged between London and Pekin; and the agreements should be cemented if possible by a treaty of friendship and alliance. The Crown, for the first time, would play a part in our Chinese affairs.

The arrangements for the mission were completed in 1792. They involved a great deal of negotiation between Macartney, the Company, manufacturers, and Dundas and Pitt. The Directors had been taken aback by the embassy's expense, and they were not unnaturally reluctant at first to underwrite it. They had also to be induced to favour proposals which might seem to threaten their monopoly, for the idea of the northern depots was put forward at a time when there were wider plans for the northern trade. The Ministry's views largely prevailed, within the limits of the Company's charter: the new depots were approved 'in the King's name', and a consul would share the Company's responsibilities at Canton. But the charter itself seemed now rather less likely to be drastically amended, and the Directors were relieved of the fear that China would slip from their grasp. They had restrained the manufacturing interests which sought to press their claims on Macartney, and had ensured that the Company's views were taken fully into account. The very arguments of the past few years had indeed shown the need for co-operation, and Pitt and Dundas, and Hawkesbury, acknowledged the fact. In one respect, indeed, Macartney's instructions were stricter than Cathcart's. He was specifically ordered not to press for repayment of the private debts. 'Your Lordship', wrote Dundas, 'I know, is perfectly informed . . . of the remonstrances which the Chairman and the Directors of the East India Company have made against Your Lordship making any interference on the subject'. He should therefore see 'how far. . . any interposition can be used for the recovery of those Debts', but without risking the Company's interests.[1]

1. Loc. cit., 243.

The embassy left England in September 1792. The saga of its fortunes – or misfortunes – cannot be followed here. But when it returned two years later, it had no concrete gains to report. No concessions had been granted, Macartney had been elusively if civilly received, the objects of his instructions remained apparently as distant as before. His only achievement had been to extract some promises of reform at Canton – which did not materialise in the event. The mission had failed.[1] But the Ambassador had not been entirely disheartened. He had taken a good look at the Celestial Empire and seen that it was weak, and he was satisfied that, however reluctantly, it could not withdraw from trade with the West. Since we were far the largest trader, our continued existence was therefore assured, however hampered it might be and however liable to disturbance. If the grievances became too acute, there was probably little to stop us righting them by force. But this would be deplorable; 'our present interests, our reason, and our humanity equally forbid' it.[2] We must try 'quietly' to achieve our aims, and time might well be on our side. For, judging by the past decade, China was now increasingly involved in a traffic she could not prevent.

III

The fact that China had become so important to British prosperity in Asia pointed the problems of security and trade to the south and southeast. To Europeans, the commerce of Asia and the Pacific was indivisible, and as its scale increased so did the connexions between the parts. Geographically and historically, the East Indies lay at the centre of the arc; 'East Indies' in fact was still the name given by the Customs in London to the East as a whole. But it was precisely in this area and its approaches that the British were most vulnerable – the more so, indeed, as their position strengthened on either side. It had long been important, and it was now essential, to ensure safe passage between India and Canton. It was also desirable, as the Country trade grew, to raise its stake in the regions between. Merchants and Government alike were well acquainted with these objects. But in the conditions of the 1780s it was difficult to attain them both.

The problem hinged, as it had done for over a century, on the position of the Dutch. At the end of the American War, they were still extended through the Eastern seas. Their base of Trincomalee in Ceylon commanded the approach to the Bay of Bengal; they lay astride the Strait of Malacca, in Sumatra and at Rhio off the tip of Malaya; they were

1. Which did not prevent Macartney from being given another step in the Irish peerage. He had been made a Viscount in July 1792, before he sailed, and in March 1794 he became an Earl.

2. *An Embassy to China, Being the Journal Kept by Lord Macartney during his Embassy to the Emperor Ch'ien-Lung 1793–1794*, ed. J. L. Cranmer-Byng (1962), 213.

in Java and Borneo, the Celebes and the Moluccas – the ancient Spice Islands on whose trade Englishmen had long cast covetous eyes. On paper, they were still the barrier, and the idea died hard. The national Companies were old foes, whole generations had been nurtured on the fact, and Leadenhall Street was filled with men thirsty to seize the opportunities which they had glimpsed, and then been denied, in the recent years of war. For between 1780 and 1784 the weakness of the Dutch empire had been revealed, and British warships threatened the eastern islands freely until Suffren's French squadron appeared. As so often happens, the effects of a gradual decline had been suddenly exposed, and John Company sensed a chance which, withheld from it at the peace treaty, should now be grasped as and when conditions allowed.

But Ministers were not so sure. The weakness that excited many of the merchants worried them and made them pause. The fact that the Dutch possessions had been saved by the French meant that a new and more dangerous threat might be replacing the old. French pressure was growing fast in the Netherlands and the empire overseas. What would be the effect on the chain of Dutch bases and depots, stretching from the Cape of Good Hope to the south-west Pacific?

It was in fact the familiar story of a vacuum of power. The British reaction to it was finally dictated by events at the seat of power, in Europe. A bitter struggle, of long gestation, had been growing in Holland between opposing parties: between the old aristocratic republicans, now joined by the democratic 'Patriots', who looked to the French, and the House of Orange, headed by the Stadtholder, which was supported by the British. In 1787 the issue came to the boil. The Patriots staged a revolution, the French seemed ready to intervene, and Pitt finally determined if necessary to go to war.[1] It was his first great diplomatic crisis, and it ended triumphantly. The French climbed down, and the next year the British formed an alliance with the Netherlands and Prussia. Here then was a golden opportunity to redefine relations with the Dutch in the East. But it should now be done, so as to contain the French, by way of support rather than attack.

The possession most precious to the Dutch in the East was their monopoly of the spice trade; their greatest liability, the financial state of their East India Company. Support in either case might yield a good return. The Dutch Company was now largely dependent on the British, in one form or another, for facilities and loans in India; perhaps the links might be extended, and the two bodies brought into a closer formal relationship. It might also be wise to underwrite the Dutch position in the south-west Pacific. At the peace treaty of 1784 – signed after the Treaty of Versailles with the other powers – we had managed to extract a confirmation of free 'navigation' (free sailing) in the Eastern seas. If the Dutch could now be reassured that this did not

1. See ch. XVII, section II below.

threaten their commercial rights, we might guarantee the safety of the passage to China and of the traffic with the mainland to the south, and gain some concessions in return. These should be mainly strategic, for the Dutch held the keys to the eastern Indian Ocean, whose security must be an immediate concern. Shelburne indeed had tried unsuccessfully to win the base of Trincomalee at the peace. We might now try again, at least – if outright possession proved impossible – for guaranteed facilities and the exclusion of the French. We might also see if we could not extract something in the Malacca Strait, by cession or perhaps by lease or at worst by terms of use.

Some of these ideas had been aired before the crisis broke. As early as 1785, the British Minister at The Hague, the active and able Sir James Harris, had suggested that the two East India Companies might be brought closer together, and British support offered, perhaps through a loan, so as to strengthen his diplomatic hand. The Foreign Secretary happily agreed, as he did with most of Harris's proposals. But the matter was delicate – in fact it bristled with difficulties, political, legal and financial –, and when the tortuous arrangements were brought to Pitt's notice he quashed them at once. They deserved 'no sort of encouragement': no proper security was offered, Dutch credit was 'very doubtful', and if anything was to be done it must be properly thought out. The Dutch had offered to pledge some of their cargoes from Canton against a loan, which he thought was merely giving them 'part of our China trade'.[1] In short, he had no opinion of the scheme on its merits, and while he did not disagree with its object he was not prepared to rush matters in the interests of a struggle to which indeed he was not yet fully alert.

Harris's efforts, though perforce muted, continued over the next two years, with fluctuating fortunes as the French influence rose and fell.[2] In the autumn of 1787, Ministers took up the subject again. The Dutch position in the East was now a matter of urgent concern. At the height of the crisis, in the late summer, immediate action of course bulked large, and there was talk of taking Trincomalee and the Cape of Good Hope in the Stadtholder's name.[3] But the whole scene was also reviewed with an eye to the future, and the process continued when the crisis died down. Pitt was advised by Dundas and by Grenville, the latter of whom was the better informed, for he was sent at the end of July to Holland and again in September to France to reinforce the men on the spot. Grenville had listened to the Dutch Company's proposals

1. Pitt to Grenville, 4 October 1785 (*H.M.C., Dropmore*, I, 257). Grenville was involved, officially, as a member of the Board of Control, to which the question was referred. Dundas was in the north at the time.

2. It was during this trying period that he complained of Pitt's failure to reply to a letter from the Dutch Company's Directors (see p. 324 above).

3. Pitt to Lord Cornwallis [Governor-General of Bengal], 2 August 1787 (*Correspondence of Charles, First Marquis Cornwallis*, ed. Charles Ross, I (2nd edn, 1859), 337).

for a British loan and a closer connexion,[1] and at the end of August he asked Dundas for his views. The reply was explicit.[2] There was no point in tying ourselves up with the Dutch in this way. On the contrary, there were very good reasons for us to steer clear. We should be involved in a financial commitment which we should almost certainly regret, we were in a strong enough position in India to disregard these particular rivals, and – an argument which was much in Dundas's mind at this time – we did not want to do anything that might hinder us from reconsidering the British Company's charter during the next few years. By all means let us open the trade of India to foreign Companies, on our own terms. It was now in our interest to do so, for we were well placed to benefit from it. But that was a very different matter from forging a link with a monopoly which was struggling with growing difficulty to survive.

On the other hand, Dundas saw no objection to guaranteeing the Dutch retention of the spice trade. It was something by which they set great store, and 'an amicable footing with Holland in India would be cheaply purchased' thereby. In return, we should ask for facilities at the Cape of Good Hope and Trincomalee and 'the arsenals of Batavia' in time of war. Such an exchange should form the basis of a national treaty, which was far preferable to an agreement between the Companies.

Dundas followed this preliminary statement with a draft for the basis of a treaty.[3] This was an important paper, for it contained the views which he continued to hold over the next five years. He began by defining the 'objects' of the two countries in the East.

> That of Great Britain is to maintain and preserve the Empire, which she has acquired, in comparison of which, even Trade is a subordinate, or collateral Consideration.

The Dutch object was 'in the first Instance to secure to herself the Monopoly of the Spice Islands, and secondly to extend her general Trade by every means in her Power'. They could scarcely fight, if challenged, without French help; but with the French they could threaten India. We must therefore seek to prevent such a combination, and we could best do so by allaying the Dutch fears for their trade as it

1. Or at any rate to the Secretary's. The Directors were no more united than the rest of the country.

2. 2 September 1787 (*H.M.C., Dropmore*, III, 419–22).

3. 'Considerations on the Subject of a Treaty, between Great Britain, and Holland, relative to their Interests in India, as drawn up by Mr. Dundas, in 1787' (National Library of Scotland Ms 1068, ff. 20–37v). According to a note in Dundas's hand on this copy, it was written in October. There are several other copies in other collections, including Pitt's (P.R.O. 30/8/360). The Melville Castle Muniments in the Scottish Record Office, G.D. 51/3/23/1–8, contain copies, with Dundas's notes, of associated papers by himself and others at about this time.

stood. Dundas recognised the value of the traffic, particularly to the growing British sales of opium to China. But he was less convinced than were the English Directors of the need to attack the system direct. It would be better to admit the Dutch to a freer trade in India – perhaps asking for a share of their opium trade to China in return –, and to state that, while not conceding the right of free navigation in the Eastern seas, we would not exercise it without their agreement, and would confirm their monopoly of the spice trade. We might also, as a *bonne bouche*, restore to them the port of Negapatam (the modern Nagapattinam) south of Madras, which we had taken in the war and managed to retain, but which was really 'of no *importance* to us *political*, or *commercial*'. They for their part should sign a defensive alliance with us in the East, open their Eastern ports for 'either navigation or naval Refreshment' as we might demand, and refuse permission to all foreign troops other than British (again on demand) to garrison the Cape of Good Hope or Trincomalee or any other 'Indian possession'.

Dundas's ideas were referred to the India Board – in practice, one may suspect, to a small inner group. The result appeared in December, in the form of a 'Project for a Treaty' signed by himself, Grenville and Lord Mulgrave.[1] Although his argument was adopted, there was a certain change of emphasis from that of Dundas's original paper. It was agreed that the Dutch should be granted the monopoly of the spice trade, and greater facilities for trade in India (including that with Canton) on what amounted to the basis of a most favoured nation.[2] They should be given Negapatam, with the proviso that it must never be ceded to another power and must be kept properly defended. And the British would 'give up . . . the Navigation of the Eastern Islands by British Ships'. This renunciation, it was made clear, would not affect 'the trade to be carried on by the Inhabitants of those islands in all articles, except spices, to our own settlements', or such navigation as was necesasry to preserve contact with China. It would not be allowed to 'cramp any trade we may choose to carry on upon the coasts of Siam or Cochin China', and it did not of course affect our rights in the south-west Pacific beyond the Spice Islands themselves. But it was regarded as a real concession, not least because the Company cordially disliked it, as Dundas later had cause to emphasise to Pitt.[3] The price, therefore, should be equally real. The British demanded possession – outright possession – of Trincomalee, and of the Dutch island port at Rhio (the modern Riau) off the tip of Malaya.

1. 21 December 1787; P.R.O., F.O. 37/20. But, from a despatch of Harris's of 18 December (Secret, no. 170; loc. cit.,), the contents seem to have been already communicated to the Dutch. It has been suggested (Nicholas Tarling, *Anglo-Dutch Rivalry in the Malay World 1780–1824* (1962), 27) that Mulgrave did much of the drafting of the revised paper. Certainly, the copy that Pitt received came from him (endorsement in P.R.O. 30/8/360).

2. See p. 379, n3 above.

3. 13 August 1788 (P.R.O. 30/8/157).

Rhio, although not mentioned in his original paper, was in point of fact a cherished object of Dundas, and he set great store by it throughout the subsequent negotiation. It would ensure safe passage between the Indian Ocean and the Pacific, and it was an entrepôt for trade in the Malayan archipelago, a 'market', as the Project put it, 'which we must have . . . for the exchange or sale of the produce of Bengal'. Trincomalee, on the other hand, was a cherished object of Grenville's: as he had told Dundas a few months before, 'one's mind at once runs to Trincomalé'.[1] To judge by his later attitude, indeed, as well as by his first proposals, Dundas would have been content with some facilities there, and was alive to the difficulties of an outright claim.[2] But he was not prepared to contest the point at the outset, and he acquiesced without demur in his colleague's demand.

The Project may therefore be said to have embodied both Dundas's and Grenville's ambitions. It was the sum of what each wanted rather than a compromise between the two. It now officially left their keeping, and to some extent their immediate control; for the negotiation of a treaty was a matter for the Foreign Office, and its consideration, however formal, for the Cabinet and the King. The whole question is complicated; but certain things are clear. A full-blown treaty was an important affair, demanding the Sovereign's ratification. It was conducted in full form by a Secretary of State, through accredited agents. And it was one of the few pieces of business to be necessarily presented, at some stage and however closely or briefly, to 'His Majesty's Servants' for advice to the King. In this instance the Cabinet was involved quite fully, for the discussions were at once linked with those for the wider Anglo-Dutch alliance, on which Ministers had to be consulted and on which some of them at least held definite views. Neither Grenville nor Dundas was yet in the Cabinet, and they had to recognise the fact. '. . . It is unnecessary', wrote Dundas to Pitt at one point, on the question of Trincomalee, 'for me to say more on this Subject, for it is a Matter more Proper for the general Consideration of His Majesty's Ministers, who will consider it as it bears upon their General System of Politicks and connexion with Holland. It is not merely an India Question'.[3] This was not mere form, and in a sense it was the less so because the Foreign Secretary was not well equipped to take command. The fact that Dundas and Grenville were the experts on a subject for which Carmarthen was now responsible placed a heavier burden on Pitt than would be the case when they became Secretaries of State.

1. 26 August 1787 (*H.M.C., Dropmore*, I, 280).
2. He was even later prepared, if necessary, to substitute Cochin (in India) for Trincomalee – though neither he nor Grenville seems to have thought seriously that the suggestion would be accepted (Dundas's paper of 1 August 1789 on 'Indian affairs', with Grenville's marginal comments, in Fortescue Mss, 'East Indies, 1784–1791').
3. 13 August 1788 (P.R.O. 30/8/157).

The Project was badly received in Holland. The Dutch did not take kindly to the notion of surrendering Trincomalee. The discussions then lapsed, for both sides were anxious to conclude their European alliance, and they agreed to postpone an issue in the East that might cause delay.[1] The talks were resumed in the summer of 1788. But again they got off to a bad start, for Harris, eager to make progress in a helpful atmosphere and aware that the Dutch felt deeply about Trincomalee, seems to have departed from his instructions by proposing an arrangement of mutual defence for the base. This was disavowed in London – the Duke of Richmond protested that Harris had ignored 'what he knew to be the sentiments of the Cabinet'[2] –, and the postponement of the conversations thereafter until George III's illness ended in the spring of 1789 deepened Dutch suspicions and allowed the earlier goodwill to cool. Despite some friendly noises no progress was made in that year; Harris himself – who was very tired – went on leave, and did not return to Holland; and the outlook was bleak. But early in 1790 a fresh start was proposed. The initiative came once more from the British, who perhaps had most to gain; they clearly meant business, for the new envoy was William Eden, now Lord Auckland, and Auckland had become the recognised man to send when a commercial treaty was in sight.[3] He had negotiated the famous Anglo-French agreement of 1786, and since then had been in Spain with a similar object in view. He was a restless, persistent negotiator, he carried considerable prestige, and he showed all his known qualities over the next two and a half years.

In Auckland's hands, indeed, there was little danger of the subject being forgotten. And Pitt for his part mobilised the Government's efforts. He had to be careful how he did so, for there were strong contrasting views; and it was perhaps not surprising that some of those who held them thought that the process was being mismanaged. Auckland himself chafed (not for the first time) at the lack of prompt decision, and he was not comforted by the Foreign Secretary's soothing remark that 'although in *the Multitude of Counsellors there may be safety,* so much good company will now & then occasion delay'.[4] Hawkesbury at the Committee of Trade, on the other hand, felt that *he* was being kept on

1. Pitt's undated draft of the relevant despatch is at the end of P.R.O., F.O. 97/247.
2. To Pitt, 6 November 1788 (P.R.O. 30/8/171). He also protested at what he thought had been a secret understanding between Harris and Carmarthen, behind the Cabinet's back. Exactly what in fact had gone on it is not easy to say. Harris informed Carmarthen as early as the spring that he had written to Pitt about his proposal, and was 'anxious for his [Pitt's] ideas' (4 March 1788; B. M. Egerton Ms 3500). But I do not know what he got by way of reply: as he was called home in May, it may well have been by word of mouth. Everyone later was anxious to dissociate themselves from his action in the summer; whether they had done so at the start is not clear.
3. He did not succeed Harris directly; he changed posts with Alleyne Fitzherbert, who had been at The Hague for a year and now replaced Auckland in Madrid.
4. Leeds to Auckland, 16 November 1790 (B.M. Add. Ms 34434, ff. 78–v).

the fringe, as indeed he was in view of his known opposition.[1] Pitt relied largely on the support of Grenville, whose hand from the spring of 1790 is, literally, often to be seen – he corresponded with Auckland, he drafted or helped draft some of the most important despatches, he was unquestionably, if at first still unofficially, at Pitt's right hand in the affair. There were obvious reasons for this: Grenville knew the whole Dutch business well, he was on much better terms with Auckland than was Carmarthen, and Dundas, the other man most involved, was usually in the north for a long spell in the later summer, when foreign negotiations were apt to move.[2] But perhaps most important, Grenville, as Home Secretary, was now a Cabinet Minister, and as such could be brought more easily to the fore.[3] The Dutch negotiation at its recommencement is in fact an example of his growing influence in foreign affairs, an earnest of the time, soon to come, when he would be Foreign Secretary himself.

The renewed discussion suffered from two difficulties at the start. Harris's rejected offer on Trincomalee had soured the atmosphere, but at the same time had shown the Dutch that the British might be divided on this important point. But of greater significance – for Ministers were perhaps prepared to yield if pressed on Trincomalee –, the question of the East Indies was now included in an attempt to settle Anglo-Dutch relations on seaborne trade as a whole. As Eastern questions in fact had first been linked with the discussions on an alliance, so they were now incorporated in proposals for a new agreement on neutral rights in war. Both sides felt deeply on this problem, which had occasioned the break in 1780;[4] but it was a very hard one to settle, and, once joined, the two issues proved impossible to disconnect. The British proposals, drafted by Pitt and Grenville, were submitted by Auckland on arrival at The Hague,[5] and an amended Project was eventually produced in April 1790. It could not be considered straight away, for 'the Duke [Leeds, as Carmarthen had now become], Mr. Pitt, Mr. Grenville, & in short the whole Cabinet' were 'in the Country for the Holidays'.[6] But these were brief, and on their return a long period of discussion began.

So far as the East was concerned, the new Project provided at least the basis for a reasonable settlement. The British would guarantee the

1. See, e.g., Burges [at the Foreign Office] to Auckland, 8 January 1791 (B.M. Add. Ms 34435, f. 91v). Hawkesbury's position and feelings are suggested in his letter to Samuel Garbett of 11 June 1791, in B.M. Add. Ms 38310, f. 65, and by his undated note to the long paper which he wrote on the subject in the same year, in B.M. Add. Ms 38395, f. 172.

2. See p. 425, n1 above.

3. On the same basis, too, he had succeeded Sydney as a chairman of the Board of Control for India in 1789.

4. Pp. 49–50 above.

5. Grenville's undated paper, which seems to refer to this, is in P.R.O. 30/8/336; the 'Heads of Dispatch', in Pitt's hand and dated 1 February 1790, are in F.O 97/247.

6. Burges to Auckland, 6 April 1790 (B.M. Add. Ms 34430, f. 328).

spice monopoly, and limit their rights of navigation as already suggested; they would enlarge facilities for Dutch trade in India, and cede Negapatam. In return, they would be given access on specified terms to Trincomalee, though not possession; and the Dutch offered a port in western Sumatra, in place of Rhio which they were reluctant to yield, to protect the British position in the approaches to the Malacca Strait. This compromise had to be seen in the light of concessions which Auckland had gained on the question of neutral wartime trade. Taken as a whole, he thought it a good one, which might be accepted.

He was too hopeful. Pitt and Grenville were willing, reluctantly, to accept the offer on Trincomalee. That original stumbling block had now been virtually removed. But it soon became very clear that its partner had not, for Dundas was more determined than ever to demand possession of Rhio. He pressed his colleagues hard over the next few weeks. Rhio was 'the best, or to speak more properly, the only unexceptionable place' 'where our ships may meet the traders . . . of the Eastern Isles, and barter their commodities' on the passage between India and China. Its 'want . . . would be hourly felt in the exercise of our commerce', once we had given up 'unlimited communication' in the seas beyond.[1] These views of the Ministry's Indian expert, forcefully expressed, carried much weight. At the same time, an unforeseen and unfortunate development affected the question of neutral rights. For the crisis of Nootka Sound, mounting throughout the summer, underlined the dangers of Dutch supplies to Spain in a war in which Holland – despite signs to the contrary – might not herself be involved. It was a world-wide problem, involving Europe and the West Indies as well as the East; but the south-west Pacific, with the Spaniards in the Philippines, was a critical area. The British Government was not in a yielding mood, and some of its toughness rubbed off on the Dutch; the former stipulations on trade in the East Indies, it was now argued, were too extensive. Auckland had to return to the task in June with stiffer instructions, framed in the knowledge that his country might soon be at war.

He did his best; a revised agreement was drafted by the end of the month, reserving some of the controversial points – including Rhio – for later discussion and giving British warships free rights in Trincomalee. But the atmosphere in London was strained; the fleet had just been mobilised; and as the Ministry prepared for action a new voice was heard.

Hawkesbury had hitherto been kept out of the discussions as far as possible. But sooner or later he must be brought in, and the crisis perhaps hastened the moment. He was consulted on Auckland's emergency instructions in June,[2] and at the beginning of August was asked

1. To Grenville, 30 May 1788 (*H.M.C., Dropmore*, I, 588); 1 July 1788 (loc. cit., 591).
2. Pitt to Hawkesbury, 6 June 1790 (B.M. Add. Ms 38192, f. 72).

to give his views on the reply. He did so at once, in no uncertain terms. As the guardian of the navigation system, he looked at the proposals for neutral trading rights with a suspicious eye; and now that he knew the details, he did not like what he saw. The Dutch had taken much of our carrying trade before they had entered the late war; they must not be handed such an opportunity again. Disregarding the diplomatic and strategic implications – as he had every right to do –, he objected unequivocally to the tenor of Auckland's draft.

The effect was immediate, and serious. Hawkesbury was not a Cabinet Minister – a few months later he was seeking to become one – but he was a powerful figure in his own field, and he was stating a view that would be popular in Parliament and beyond. The Foreign Secretary expressed the dilemma, in an angry letter to Auckland's private secretary.

> The Dutch ought I think to be treated with friendly attention at least by us, and not merely as an Indifferent Power. This Sentiment, however justly prevalent among the *Cabinet* Ministers, does not seem to convince some persons of influence, beyond the Threshold, and of course may not have due weight when such are admitted to give Evidence (altho' not to decide) within the small circle above alluded to.[1]

This was the voice of a Minister who knew that his own influence was slight, and had watched Hawkesbury gaining ground at his expense for several years. But he was not alone in this instance: Pitt and Grenville also felt bound to compromise in the face of such a warning, and a stiff reply was accordingly sent to The Hague. Hawkesbury did not get all that he wanted; but he got enough to make it difficult for Auckland to reach the early agreement for which he had hoped.

Auckland indeed was so discouraged that for once he slackened pace. He could not think of a way out, and Pitt and Grenville were obliged to take the next step.[2] Their new paper differed in emphasis from some of its predecessors: Negapatam, for instance, no longer figured, and territorial questions in general were largely put aside. The issue now turned clearly on two points. The British were determined to restrict – though not necessarily to stop – Dutch carrying rights in war: the Dutch to extract a guarantee of firm, comprehensive limits to British trade and navigation in the Eastern seas. Once more a painful advance was gained, and a formula seemed possibly to be in sight; but then another international development intervened to give a fresh twist to the talks. For in the spring of 1791 the possibility of war between England and Russia suddenly arose – a war in which Holland might

1. Leeds to Lord Henry Spencer, 3 August 1790 (B.M. Add. Ms 28066, f. 173v).
2. Pitt's letter to Grenville of 11 January 1791, in *H.M.C., Dropmore*, II, 12–13, shows that the initiative and the responsibility on this occasion lay with them.

benefit in Europe from the exercise of neutral rights. Pitt, whose absorption in this crisis had already slowed down the Dutch negotiation, was not prepared to make any concession at such a time. There was no more progress until the summer, when the crisis had ended and Parliament rose. Auckland then made a further effort to bring the talks to a point. At the beginning of August 1791 he submitted yet another revised draft, and this was shown to the interested parties in London in the course of the next two months.

The result was decisive. Hawkesbury had now been admitted to the Cabinet,[1] so that his authority was confirmed. In the autumn, probably in October, he circulated his views. His 'Letter', as he termed it, was a long and powerful document, concentrating on questions of navigation and designed to destroy the prospect of a treaty. Judging by the result, it achieved its object, and Hawkesbury himself was always convinced that it was he who finally put a stop to the affair.

> The foregoing Letter [he noted later on his copy] was circulated among the Members of the Cabinet, and read by them. The late Lord Camden paid to the Writer of it many Compliments upon it, and said, after the Perusal of the Arguments contained in it, He would sooner lose his Right Hand than sign his Name to the Treaty to which it referred. Mr. Pitt never said a Word to the Author of this Letter, though written at his Desire, and though he was then in the Habit of frequently seeing him; But an End was immediately and silently put to the Negociation with Holland.[2]

This was indeed so. Virtually nothing more was heard of the matter. The discussions of the past four years had been brought finally to a halt.

Perhaps they had stood no real chance of success – though on occasions it looked as if they might. Certainly, we are told, the Dutch in the Far East never set much store by them.[3] The ground had changed a good deal from first to last. As Auckland reminded the Foreign Office towards the end, the main points at issue in 1788 had been Trincomalee, Negapatam, the degree of support for the Dutch East India Company

1. There is some difficulty in telling exactly when. Pitt proposed his inclusion in January, and the King agreed (*L.C.G. III*, I, no. 651). But it seems that he had not been admitted in April (W. Fawkener [a clerk of the Privy Council] to Hawkesbury, 25 April 1791, reporting a conversation with Pitt; B.M. Add. Ms 38226, ff. 142–v). His name, however, appears at Cabinet meetings from late in July, it would seem as a regular member (Fortescue Mss, 'Minutes').

2. B.M. Add. Ms 38395, f. 172. Both the Letter and the note are undated. But Grenville sent the document to Auckland on 29 October 1791 (*H.M.C., Dropmore*, II, 218), and the note cannot have been written before April 1794, when Camden died. The Letter occupies 49 large folio pages in Hawkesbury's copy.

It is also fair to say, however, that fresh difficulties were already arising at The Hague. Auckland was despondent in August (see B.M. Add. Ms 34439, ff. 15–20, 125–v, 183–4v).

3. Holden Furber, *John Company at Work . . .* (1948), 106.

in India, and the spice monopoly; in 1791 they were the spice monopoly, the carrying trade, and questions of neutral trade and rights in war. The discussions, shifting in emphasis, had attracted their share of bad luck: Nootka Sound and the crisis with Russia were uncovenanted setbacks. But perhaps the real cause of failure lay in the attempts to settle too many differences at once, and to make agreement on one set of problems conditional on another. The result was the reverse of what had been intended – subjects had to be dropped or postponed successively in order to reach a decision on others, but the ground was never effectively narrowed, for fresh considerations were introduced. The length and complexity of the talks showed the need to be precise, and not too ambitious, in tackling an inherently complex situation in the setting of the time.

One of the more favourable moments in the Dutch negotiation occurred in the spring of 1790, before the Nootka Sound crisis reached a peak. It was wrecked partly by Dundas's insistence on the need for Rhio.[1] In pressing his arguments, he was influenced by developments on the mainland which had been mounting in recent years. The story of the British in Malaysia over the past two decades was one of a fluctuating but, in terms of possessions, fruitless battle with the Dutch. As earlier in the islands to the east, the main settlement succumbed. Established at Acheen in western Sumatra in the early seventeenth century, and recently regarded as a possible strategic base, the entrepôt was finally closed by the ruler in 1785. Merchants' efforts on the mainland had failed to gain a formal influence in any way comparable with the extensive arrangements of the Dutch; and the Dutch drove us from the use of Rhio in 1784 – almost their only success at the end of a disappointing war – after a series of attacks on the local Sultan. By the middle eighties, therefore, we were decidedly weak in an area of increasing importance to our position in the East.

For the loss of facilities came, paradoxically, at a time when the volume and share of the British trade in Malaya were rising fast. The Dutch were maintaining their rights in a region in which their paramountcy was shrinking, and their Company's embarrassments gave its rivals their chance. The French were not conveniently placed; but British interests were well adapted to take advantage of a growing traffic and the wealth it brought. The Country trade received a fillip in the American War, when the Dutch marine was driven very largely from the seas. It drew on Indian finance, now increasingly widely employed; but much of the shipping was owned independently, not directly by Indian houses, and the combination proved practicable and profitable. The merchandise – spices and opium – formed an integral

1. '. . . There exists no serious difficulty . . . except as to the cession of the Port of Rhio' (Auckland to Leeds, no. 27 (Commercial), Secret, 5 May 1790; F.O. 37/28).

part of the China trade. Opium in particular was being smuggled on a quite significant scale to Canton, and where it was not it was sold for Malayan dollars which helped relieve the shortage of bullion. Figures once more cannot be exact, for the region was not entered separately in the ledgers; but all the evidence suggests that the merchants were doing very well. They were looking farther afield, and the suppression of the depot at Acheen led them to seek fresh bases which could serve as links between India and the China coast.

Trade was thus the main incentive in this search for a mainland base. But it could also be argued that there was a strategic need for a deep-water harbour to the east of the Bay of Bengal. It would strengthen the defences of the Indian Ocean during that part of the year when the prevailing wind blew from the east and Trincomalee could be out-flanked. The west coast of Malaya might suit this purpose, and the possibility was mentioned. But it never gained very warm support. For the ideal base seemed, at least to Ministers, to lie farther south, covering the Malacca Strait as well as the Bay itself. What was desired, in fact, was what Singapore later supplied: a focal point for trade and defence at the tip of the Malayan peninsula. It was this dual object which drew Dundas so strongly to Rhio, and induced the British Government to make such efforts on its behalf.

But in the event, even while the fate of Rhio still seemed open, the East India Company found itself presented with a harbour up the west coast. Though grateful enough, the Directors had no hand in the transaction. Their traditional policy, indeed, had been to discourage local attempts to involve them in territorial possessions which might cause expense. The war with the Dutch and the loss of Acheen altered the situation: as the Directors put it in 1786, they now wished to give 'every assistance . . . privately' to counteract 'the Policy of the Dutch in enslaving the independent Powers' of the local rulers.[1] Even so, they remained wary of committing themselves too far, and their caution was shared by Government. The accession came from the efforts of a man on the spot, Francis Light, a merchant of Acheen who had long been active in the independent states. In 1785, he had gone far towards persuading the Sultan of Kedah to cede the island of Penang, in return for a guarantee of support against attack. The authorities in London baulked at such a commitment; but, armed with their approval of his object, Light took the plunge on his own. In the summer of 1786 he

1. Instructions to the Governor-General and Council of Bengal, 2 May 1786. And cf. Board of Control to the Governor-General and Council, 28 July 1787 (signed by Pitt, Dundas and Grenville): 'We certainly wish to avoid every unnecessary expense, at the same time we must confess that we always felt the importance of every Measure which tended to facilitate our Commerce in the Eastern Seas and thereby promote a more certain intercourse of Commerce with China. As it seems the object of other Nations, particularly the Dutch, to impede our success in that pursuit, it may of course be our business by every means to counteract their attempts' (both quoted in Harlow, op. cit., II, 353-4).

made an arrangement with the Sultan, and took possession of Penang, which was soon renamed Prince of Wales Island.

Ministers' reactions to the new possession were mixed. Dundas in particular was not sure if he approved. He was glad to have a footing on, or just off, the mainland; but its usefulness was limited, for shipping from farther east must still run the gauntlet of the Malacca Strait. As the talks with the Dutch developed, moreover, he feared it might prejudice his chances of Rhio; and 'A Settlement at Rhio would make that of Penang unnecessary'.[1] While Light and his party were consolidating in the island, Ministers in fact were looking elsewhere.

Rhio was not their only object, though it was the key. They also had their eye on islands in the Indian Ocean. The Nicobars or the Andamans might serve at least one of the purposes of Penang, in providing a naval base – uncluttered by the need for agreements with a local ruler – which would help guard India from the east. In April 1785, the Board of Control had ordered a secret investigation of the Nicobars. At the end of 1788, after unfavourable reports of that group, the Governor-General of Bengal set on foot a survey of the Andamans. Six months later, he felt justified in claiming them, for use as an anchorage and a local penal colony; and if they proved suitable, he even thought of abandoning Penang, 'which we hold at considerable expense'.[2]

The Andamans were duly annexed at the end of 1789, and held, until the experiment proved a failure, for the next seven years. But Penang survived, though it was not used by the navy, and Rhio of course was never acquired. The Bengal Government ratified Light's agreement by a treaty in 1791, though still without a guarantee of protection. Thus the pattern of British possessions east of India began to take shape, by a typical mixture – compounded of elements partly complementary, partly opposed – of private and Company and Governmental effort. The design remained the same, though specific objects varied over the next quarter of a century, until it was crowned by Stamford Raffles's foundation of Singapore.

1. 'Observations on the Dutch Spice Trade'. This paper, of which there are copies in several collections, is undated, but may well have been written in 1789 or 1790. Dundas's continued insistence on Rhio made him discount the alternative – which otherwise one might have expected him to consider – of a port in western Sumatra (see p. 431 above).

2. Cornwallis to the Secret Committee of the Court of Directors, 1 August 1789 (see Harlow, loc. cit., 363).

Trade and Empire in the East: India

I

All these Far Eastern opportunities and problems centred, of course, on India. It was the British position in India which gave the related questions their shape. And in facing the commitments, ever growing and gradually changing, Government was now directly the partner of the East India Company.

The structure had been built on trade. But trade had brought territory and war in its wake. To Ministers in the eighties, the problems were largely strategic. The 'object' of Britain in the East, according to Dundas, was now 'to maintain and preserve the Empire, which she has acquired, in comparison of which, even Trade is a subordinate, or collateral consideration'.[1] His statement was made in a particular context, and then 'collateral' was the better term; but, allowing for that, his colleagues might well agree. Some of the implications were doubtless regrettable; our dominion in India might sometimes seem to have 'arisen almost without our seeking it'.[2] But it was none the less a fact, on which policy must be based. Bombay, Madras and Bengal must be guarded, hostile neighbours subdued, and communications kept open with Europe and their eastern markets. When it came to the point, moreover, Government was not unduly defensive. It often complained of the tasks, but it met them readily enough. South-east Asia was a cockpit of Europe, the British were forging ahead of their rivals, and there was no intention of surrendering the lead. Ministers might grumble at men on the spot, and sigh over the Company's affairs. They tried where they could to spare costs and commitments in pursuing likely gains. But they had their own versions of expansion – some bolder than the Company's –, and produced their own initiatives in peace as well as war.

The decade after 1783 was not in any case entirely peaceful. Dundas wrote in the uneasy aftermath of the Dutch crisis of 1787, and at a time when he was expecting trouble in India itself. There were in fact three European crises – over Holland, with Spain, and with Russia – in the

1. P. 426 above.
2. P. 420 above.

space of four years. They all had their effects on the East, the first two directly, and they linked the strategic thought of the American with that of the French Wars.

The alternative routes to India from Europe lay round the Cape of Good Hope and through the Near East – that is to say, past Dutch and French bases, and through the Ottoman Empire. The shorter passages were largely closed for all but the carrying of despatches: news of war with France reached Calcutta via Egypt and the Red Sea in 1778 and 1793, and in 1790 a messenger left London for Surat by way of Venice, Aleppo and Basrah, with despatches carrying the final result of the Nootka Sound crisis.[1] Natural hazards and Turkish intransigence were formidable obstacles, and the latter grew with the decline of the British Levant Company, which had been marked for several decades, and the advance of French influence in the eastern Mediterranean. Intermittent attempts to preserve a foothold in Egypt and open the Red Sea route – the latter pursued, characteristically, by Warren Hastings against the monopolistic wishes of the Levant Company – had ended temporarily in 1780, when the few English merchants were expelled. No vessels from India now sailed farther than Jeddah, and the British presence, never strong, disappeared from the intermediate zone.

The Government was reluctant to accept this state of affairs, particularly since the French appeared to be improving their position; and the India Board soon began to inspect the possibilities. There was one obvious source to consult – an experienced Levant merchant, George Baldwin, who had lived on and off in Cairo until the recent expulsion, and in fact transmitted the news of war to India in 1779. He was now in England, and he was sent for early in 1785 – as he put it, 'I received a summons from Mr. Dundas to attend the India Board, and I attended'.[2] The questions turned on 'the expediency of Opening the Passage to India by Suez'; Baldwin's answers seemed fairly satisfactory, and they

1. A series of letters on his journey from Lieutenant Calcraft to Dundas, between November 1790 and March 1791, is in National Library of Scotland Ms 1071. In 1778 and 1793, the British despatches were received in India well before the French.
The overland route seems to have been used fairly regularly for this purpose, and by individual travellers. There are mentions of it between the wars in the foreign correspondence from Constantinople and Vienna, and Dr P. J. Marshall informs me that British agents for the Indian rulers went overland. But of course it had its hazards. 'I am a Knight and no Knight', wrote the Governor-General from Bengal early in 1787, 'for my stars, garters, and ribbons are all lost in Arabia, and some wild Arab is now making a figure with *Honi soit qui mal y pense* round his knee' (Earl Cornwallis to Viscount Brome, 17 February 1787; *Correspondence of Cornwallis*, I, 248).
2. *Political Recollections relative to Egypt* . . . (1801), 24. There is an account, presumably of this interview, among Pitt's papers in P.R.O. 30/8/360, endorsed 'Heads of Conversation between Mr Dundas and Mr Baldwin in February 1784'. But Baldwin is explicit that the date was 1785, and from his correspondence in other sources he would seem to be right. I have found nothing surviving from the earlier year.

fitted quite well into a wider survey by the Board itself. Conducted apparently by Lord Mulgrave, this discussed the relative merits of the Suez-Red Sea route and the overland journey by Aleppo, Baghdad and Basrah, compared with the times of the passage round the Cape of Good Hope. Since each was found to have advantages over the others, inward or outward, at different seasons, Mulgrave concluded that it would be expedient to maintain them all. A British agent should be stationed in Egypt, and native agents if possible in the Near East;[1] the man in Egypt should also try to open the trade between Alexandria and Suez – a prospect which Dundas hoped might eventually contribute to the weakening of the Levant and East India Companies' monopolies;[2] and Baldwin would be the obvious candidate for the post. Dundas and Pitt agreed, and instructions were drafted accordingly. The Levant Company's qualms were overcome, and at the end of 1786 Baldwin took up his duties as consul-general under the Crown, an English vice-consul being appointed in Alexandria the next year.[3]

The commercial results were not impressive. The trade with Egypt was slight, and its scale proved too small to support a line of regular communications. Baldwin sent hopeful reports, which were taken seriously in London; but the familiar difficulties cropped up, and his credit declined. It was perhaps not surprising that Government should have resolved to close down the consulate, in February 1793. But it was ironical that the decision should have been taken then, for Baldwin had just repeated his exploit of fourteen years before, and sent on the news to India of the outbreak of war with France. To that extent, if only so far, he had justified his appointment. The next year, moreover, he went some way towards realising his hopes, for in May 1794 he signed an agreement with the Beys of Egypt allowing free British navigation of the Red Sea, and the right to land goods at Suez at reasonable rates of duty. This was on a footing with the concessions to the French; but, perhaps because of the earlier disappointments and the continued recalcitrance of the Levant Company, the authorities at home ignored the news. They may have been the more disposed to do so because Baldwin appeared to be still at his post: he had never in fact – so he claimed later – received his instructions, which did not

1. Copy of paper, n.d. but probably summer or autumn 1785, 'Prepared by Lord Mulgrave . . . For the use of Mr Dundas'; P.R.O. 30/8/360. (For Mulgrave's activity, see also Baldwin to Dundas, 4 May 1785, in P.R.O. 30/8/361.) There is also an anonymous memorandum on the subject, supposedly of 1783, in the papers of Joseph Smith, Pitt's secretary from 1787 (*H.M.C., Twelfth Report, Appendix, Pt. IX,* 343–4).

2. Dundas to Pitt, 10 or 16 November [1785?] (P.R.O. 30/8/157).

3. Pitt's part may be seen in this same letter, from Dundas, replying to his queries on Baldwin's instructions, which had to be issued by Carmarthen. The Levant Company objected to the appointment, over which it fought a rearguard action, because the consul would be responsible to Government and because, as earlier, it disliked the prospect of the Egyptian trade being opened to the East India Company.

arrive apparently for three years. Even then he hung on, after protesting to the Foreign Office and Pitt, and he departed eventually only a few weeks before Napoleon arrived in 1798.[1] With that momentous event a new chapter opened in the Near East, and the British interest and presence entered on a new phase.

The peacetime failure of the consulate in Egypt was largely due to the greater influence of the French, and the French of course posed the main threat to British communications with India. The Government was sensitive to the dangers of the ocean route: in the Dutch crisis of 1787, Dundas was alarmed that a hostile force might take St Helena as a staging post,[2] he and Pitt had earlier cast an eye on the French island of Mauritius, and the negotiation with the Dutch included a request for facilities at the Cape of Good Hope on demand.[3] There was equal concern to limit French ambitions and rights in India itself. The position had been left ambiguous by the recent peace treaty. The British undertook to 'restore' to their rivals the settlements they had held at the start of the war, and to 'take . . . measures . . . for securing' to French subjects 'a safe, free and independent trade'. But implicit in these obligations – or so it could be held – was the assumption that British rights were superior, an attitude that became explicit over the next few years. As the Foreign Secretary put it in 1786, the interests of France 'should be considered by us as purely and simply commercial, while those of England, from her territorial rights, include the greatest objects of political concern, as well'.[4] This was the context in which Pitt's Ministry wished to discuss any agreement, and its great object was to gain recognition of its claim.

But before the Government could steer the business into such a channel, the commercial questions had been raised on their own. The French had been anxious to discuss them as soon as the peace treaty was signed, and had indeed begun to do so, as a Ministerial question, while the Coalition of North and Fox was in office. When Pitt came in the pressure was renewed, and a spate of letters reached him and the Company from Paris. They were virtually ignored; but in 1785 a negotiator came to London on behalf of the French East India Company, which, after a lapse, had been revived.[5] He proposed that French

1. Copies of Baldwin to Grenville, and Baldwin to Pitt, 29 March 1796 (P.R.O. 30/8/111); Alfred Cecil Wood, *A History of the Levant Company* (1935), 174.

2. To Pitt, 20 August 1787 (P.R.O. 30/8/157). He added, 'I can never feel pleasant under the prospect of a hostile Naval Force riding unrivalled in the Indian Seas'. St Helena had been a property of the East India Company since the middle of the seventeenth century.

3. See pp. 426–7 above.

4. Carmarthen to Daniel Hailes [Secretary of the British Embassy in Paris] for Eden, 20 September 1786 (B.M. Add. Ms 34466, f. 30).

5. An account of these events is given in copy of M. Bourdieu to Dundas, 21 July 1785, in Pitt's papers, P.R.O. 30/8/360. Bourdieu asserted that the French Ministry

merchants should be able to buy British goods on better terms in Bengal, in return for payment by bills of exchange from an annual British credit on which John Company would gain an appropriate return.[1] But opinion in Leadenhall Street was divided, there were strong doubts about the new French Directors, and these were strengthened when a limited agreement between the Companies, painfully worked out, was rejected by the French Government in 1786.

Pitt had warned the British Directors that the talks 'must be looked on merely in a commercial light' – a warning to the Company not to assume political responsibilities.[2] The Ministry had also to assert its authority over the Bengal Government, which in 1786 set on foot talks, and in fact signed a 'treaty' with the French Governor in Mauritius, covering the whole range of mutual problems in India. Its envoy was Colonel Cathcart, on his way home to England;[3] and while he escaped censure, his superiors did not. The Board of Control, in the persons of Pitt, Dundas and Mulgrave, warned the Governor-General and his Council that their powers were less than they had assumed.

It was against this background that the Government decided itself to embark on talks with the French. It chose its moment deliberately and well. In September 1786 the Anglo-French commercial treaty was signed. It was highly favourable to this country, Pitt's interest in commercial agreements had been roused in the past year, and he was now prepared to seek a general improvement of relations with France. In the same month, the inner group of the Board of Control began to frame the draft for a Convention on India. Dundas 'drew the first sketch, but Mr. Pitt and Lord Mulgrave lived with me on the subject for a week at Wimbledon', and they were all of one mind.[4] In the event, the negotiation had to wait, for Eden was still engaged in the final details of the European settlement. But talks began in February 1787, and agreement was reached in the surprisingly short space of under seven months.

The British were careful throughout to base commercial terms on territorial rights; and it was this aspect of the Convention, which they regarded as accepted, that in the end pleased them most. Eden was told that he must resist any argument put forward by the French from supposed 'ancient rights'. 'We' were 'treating as the Sovereigns of the

had sent five letters between late July and late September 1784, three to Pitt and the Company or to Pitt alone, none of which the British Minister had answered.

1. Papers from the negotiator, M. Perier, loc. cit.

2. Minutes of the Secret Court of Directors, 17 August 1785 (copy in B.M. Add. Ms 34466, f. 78). There is a 'Memo' by Pitt on the talks in Clements Mss, University of Michigan.

3. See p. 419 above.

4. Dundas to Eden, 28 September 1786 (B.M. Add. Ms 34466, ff. 353–5). Pitt was determined to await the conclusion of the commercial treaty before approaching the French on this fresh business (to Carmarthen, 18 September 1786; B. M. Egerton Ms 3498).

country, they as possessing a commercial interest protected by us'.[1] No one expected to win this great point without considerable qualification, and Ministers were correspondingly delighted when the French appeared to concede. Six existing French factories were confirmed in their rights 'under the protection of the French flag'. But their laws and trading rights were stated once more, as in the peace treaty, to be 'secured' by the British Crown, and all other French commercial houses – and any new ones – were placed under British jurisdiction.[2] The Government was fully satisfied with these terms. Pitt was enthusiastic,[3] and while Dundas could not believe that our old rivals would 'always continue *bone fide* to acquiesce', he too looked on the concession as a signal achievement.[4] He was equally pleased with the commercial terms. French rights were centred once more on their Company, so that individual activities could be checked, and, within the new arrangements, Franco-Dutch co-operation on the mainland:[5] at the same time, the prospect of a more open trade between the Companies might be more easily pursued. This last was a policy which would benefit us, but which the English Directors were inclined to suspect: now they would have to make the best of the situation. The Company indeed found itself very largely overridden. Ministers kept the talks in their own hands, and went their own way. Pitt was in close control – he went through the drafts 'article by article' in April, he followed Dundas's efforts, and on 'an auspicious morning . . . at Wimbledon' in July, he, Dundas and Eden composed the final British paper.[6] When all was successfully over, the Government's authority was confimed. 'If disputes shall at any time hereafter occur, in which any of the permanent rights of Great Britain are implicated, the final arrangement of them must be left to the Government at home.'[7]

The Convention on India was signed at a moment, near the height of the Dutch crisis, when Anglo-French relations were deteriorating once more. It was indeed the last real instance of the hopes for improvement, never very robust, which had been aired over the past eighteen months. The British did not expect the agreement to remove the old causes of tension entirely, and they continued to look for the familiar signs in the familiar places. Our dominion in India, so it was stated on

1. Dundas to Eden, 26 June 1787 (B.M. Add. Ms 34467, ff. 47–8).

2. Articles 4, 5, 6 (*P.R.*, XXIII, 22–3).

3. To Eden, 8 September 1787 (*A.C.*, I, 191). See also his letter to Dundas of 8 September 1787, in which he mentions Grenville's concurrence (Clements Mss).

4. To Pitt, 19 September 1787 (quoted in Philips, *The East India Company 1784–1834*, 49).

5. Dundas later laid great stress on this point – see his notes for a Parliamentary speech, probably in 1801, in Melville Castle Documents, G.D. 51/3/25/1–2, Scottish Record Office.

6. Dundas to Pitt, 7 April 1787 (Clements Mss); Eden to Pitt, 2 September 1787 (P.R.O. 30/8/110). The Convention was signed on 31 August.

7. Secret Committee to the Governor-General and Council of Bengal, 3 November 1787 (*Correspondence of Cornwallis*, I, 338–9).

the morrow of the Convention, had arisen from 'the necessity of defending Ourselves against the Oppression of the revolted [Indian] Nabobs who entered into cabals to Our prejudice with other nations of Europe'.[1] As an historical explanation, this left something to be desired; but the connexion between native wars and European rivalries was stressed fairly enough. Trouble, in a time of European peace, would now come not so much from the French directly as from their Indian allies, particularly Tipu Sultan, Hyder Ali's successor, pursuing his ambitions from Mysore. The British were inclined to discount this danger in the later eighties, for the rapid growth of trouble at home seemed likely to deter the French from adventures abroad. Tipu was carefully watched, particularly when he visited France in 1788; but there was less misgiving in Calcutta and London than there had been earlier. As late as March 1790, Dundas was 'confident . . . that no apprehension need be entertained from any of the native Princes', and that 'France had no present views to be suddenly our rival in India'.[2] But in fact, unknown to him when he spoke, the preliminaries to the Third Mysore War had begun; Tipu had received messages of support from France, not meant perhaps to be taken very seriously, on which he was happy to act. The war continued with varying fortunes until February 1792, when Tipu was forced to make peace and surrender half his territory. It was another step along the road of sometimes unwilling but steady conquest, and it again served notice, not long before the struggle with France was renewed, that the British power in India was inexorably creating its own demands.

II

The most pervasive of these, as the product of the rest, was that of responsibility. It had now to be tackled in the light of Pitt's India Act. But one great question survived from a time when its shadow had been long indeed. The fate of Warren Hastings had to be debated in 1786.

Every schoolboy, asked what he knows about the early days of British India, would happily put the famous impeachment very near the top of his list. It had star quality at the time, and it has had it ever since. How indeed could this be otherwise, with the splendour of Burke's and Sheridan's speeches, the evocations of principle and faith which later generations took to heart, the excitement of the East, the scope of the charges, the Parliamentary drama, the setting of the trial? It was a *cause célèbre*, a great occasion, and it was moved and mounted as such. Its fame has endured as a classic document of an evolving imperial

1. Cathcart's instructions for the China mission, 30 November 1787 (Morse, op. cit., II, 164. See pp. 419–20 above).
2. Speech in the Commons of 31 March 1790 (*P.R.*, XXVII (1790), 361–2). He did refer to Tipu (not by name) as the one possible danger, but only to dismiss the immediate likelihood of attack.

attitude, and, so enshrined, its importance and value are a very real part of the national stock. Burke's audiences at the start were confident that they were watching history being made. Of course this is an agreeable sensation, which hereditary Societies are always glad to indulge; but in this instance they were right.

All the same, we must beware of attributing to contemporaries more than they really saw. Much of the symbolic significance of the trial was a later accretion. At the time, its interest was at least partly that of a gladiatorial show, and very few, if any, of those playing prominent roles shared the vision of Burke himself. To the Opposition at large it was a useful stick with which to beat Ministers, given the chance. To members of the Company, it was the latest stage in the continuing clash and balance of interests. To Pitt and Dundas and the Board of Control, it was both a complication and a massive distraction: an embarrassment coming at a moment when their relations with the Company were confused, and an unwelcome legacy from a period which was already receding into the past. For in point of fact the whole issue was now in many ways irrelevant. The personal charges furthered, but they also reflected, a shift in standards already under way, an acceptance of the fact that the British rule was moving out of its first, violent stage. And the political charges, while they underlined the difficulties which any Governor-General might expect to face, referred almost entirely to a situation that no longer existed, when Government was not involved directly in Indian affairs. They all threatened to prolong or revive old quarrels many of which were dying or dead, and the grounds of the disputes were often technical and narrow. Ministers concerned with newer problems – with changing economic and strategic patterns, and the establishment of their authority in a mixed system of government – would gladly have buried a past that was recent but in some ways curiously remote. The great business of Hastings, by the very glare of the light it threw on the Indian scene, was the first indication that, however untidily, the Act of 1784 marked a transition.

Pitt himself was unlikely to feel strongly about the issues at the start. He knew little about Indian or Company affairs before Fox's bill brought him into office, and then he disliked much of what he saw. He was not an expert in a field in which experience was needed, and his attitude to Hastings, in so far as he had one, was probably not unlike that of his mentor Dundas. He had declined to support the efforts for the grant of a peerage which the Governor-General's friends began to make in 1784, and he seems not to have answered the long letter on future policy which Hastings wrote him from India in December of that year.[1] The two men met at Downing Street in June 1785; but Pitt did not go beyond civilities, and his actions and remarks, as reported, were not particularly reassuring. The Ministry remained polite:

1. For the letter see p. 194, n. 1 above. There is a copy of it, taken for Pretyman's *Life* of Pitt, in Pretyman Ms 435/17.

it asked Hastings's opinion on various Indian questions, and it did not dissociate itself from his favourable reception at Court and elsewhere. But Pitt had now agreed to offer the vacant Governor-Generalship to Macartney, Hastings's enemy, and he remained evasive when pressed on the matter of honours and rewards.[1]

Hastings's position, moreover, was not very strong – a good deal weaker, in fact, than he was prepared to accept. He was supported by the King, and perhaps by some of the Cabinet – certainly the Lord Chancellor. But his citadel within the Company was crumbling, and this affected his support in Parliament. The 'Old Interest' at East India House, which had been so important in 1783, was a loose alliance that began to dissolve when the Coalition Ministry disappeared. Company elections showed that it was divided in 1785, and it received a final blow when Laurence Sulivan[2] died early the next year. Meanwhile, Hastings's unreconciled enemies, organised by Philip Francis and led by Burke, were hard at work preparing another appeal to the Commons. It would be difficult for Dundas to oppose them if the attempt was pressed, for he too was publicly on record as a critic, though not an outright enemy, of the Governor-General. And while Government was most unlikely to do anything that would encourage the accusations – while indeed it would obviously prefer to let the business drop –, it now had no urgent political reason to enter the lists on behalf of a man who was no longer vital to its relations with the Company or to its Parliamentary prospects.

In such circumstances, Pitt might allow the issues to be treated as a matter of conscience. He and Dundas were relieved, politically speaking, of the need to defend every aspect of Hastings's career. Dundas indeed could scarcely do so, if it came to the point. Pitt for his part was not committed, and was not obliged to act as if he was. He gave a hint of what his attitude might be when the debates began in February 1786. He refused to lay papers before the Commons on one of the questions for which they were sought – the negotiations for peace with the Marathas in 1784, which could be said to bear on current policy. But he consented in other cases, and while he praised Hastings's talents and much of his conduct, he promised not to 'screen' any crimes that were proved, and asserted that he was neither 'a determined friend or foe' of the accused.[3] No doubt he acted reluctantly – Burke thought that Ministers had 'embarrassed themselves'[4] –, and Dundas made it

1. Perhaps the more so because the pressure came largely from Thurlow. For the offer to Macartney, see p. 194 above. Pitt told Hastings's agent, Major Scott, that 'no disrespect or slight' was intended by it (see P. J. Marshall, *The Impeachment of Warren Hastings* (1965), 32). But the words could hardly be taken as outweighing the action.

2. See p. 189 above.

3. 17 February 1786 (*P.R.*, XIX, 137); 20 February (Stockdale, *Parliamentary Debates*, I (1786), 189).

4. To Sir Gilbert Elliot, [*c*. 20 February 1786] (*Correspondence*, V, 259).

clear that he himself was not going to make things easy for Opposition. But any hope of shielding Hastings from examination was reduced by his own defence at the beginning of May, when he opted to answer each charge on its merits rather than plead his general services in hazardous conditions. The decision was deplored by the solicitor to the Board of Control, and Pitt was reported to have said in the ensuing debate that Hastings had thrown away his best chance of being exonerated on the charge – one of the most prominent – relating to his treatment of the Begums of Oudh.[1] Later Pitt went farther.

> If at the commencement of the inquiry it had been urged in favour of Mr. Hastings, that if his conduct in some parts of his administration had been faulty, yet those faults were highly compensated and fully counterbalanced by the general tenor of his conduct . . ., in that case the House would have had to have weighed his crimes against his virtues.

But he 'had thought it advisable to disclaim and relinquish all [such] benefit', and accordingly 'it would be highly unjust . . . to have thrown such a shield between him and public inquiry'.[2] This was said in retrospect. But there is nothing to contradict the impression that it was a fair statement of the Minister's reaction at the time.

But while this may have been so, the impression was muted in the spring of 1786. If Pitt was holding the options open, Members in general were sure that he would come down on Hastings's side. There were good reasons for the assumption. Whatever Ministers might feel about some features of Hastings's conduct, they seemed naturally bound to protect him if pressed. The attacks were being mounted by an Opposition which had been turned out of office with the help of his supporters, and although changes might have taken place since, old ties of loyalty and advantage could still be invoked. Hastings enjoyed the favour of the Court, he had not been disavowed by Government, and a decision on his conduct, under Parliamentary attack, might well appear to be a Ministerial question. The affair had had major political repercussions at intervals ever since the late seventies. However far Pitt may have hedged, politicians now expected Government to ward off the assault.

This impression was strengthened when the attack began to get under way. It could be argued that Pitt had little option in letting the charges be brought; but when the first, on the Rohilla War of 1774, was debated at the beginning of June, he spoke and voted in Hastings's favour. It therefore came as a thunderclap when he spoke on the second – the Benares – charge on the 13th. It was generally supposed that he would repeat his performance of a fortnight before. But to

1. *The India Courier Extraordinary. Proceedings of Parliament relating to Warren Hastings, Esq.*, III, of 1786; quoted by Marshall, op. cit., 42–3.
2. 2 March 1787 (*P.R.*, XXI, 367–8).

the amazement of the House, and many of his friends, he spoke and voted with Opposition. He excused Hastings's policy; but he condemned the manner in which it had been carried out – 'repugnant to principles, which ought not to give way to any motives of interest or policy whatsoever'. The result in his view was a 'very high crime and misdemeanor', and if an impeachment was to be preferred 'this act of oppression . . . ought to be made one of the articles'.[1] His verdict proved decisive. Government supporters were in confusion, and the charge was carried by 119 votes to 79.

Why did Pitt act as he did? The question has been argued ever since. His behaviour was the more unexpected because he had given no sign of what was in his mind. He had not told the Cabinet; he may not have told any of its members; and two of his closest associates on the Board of Control, Grenville and Mulgrave, voted against him. The political world was in a ferment, and all kinds of reasons were sought. Pitt was jealous of Hastings's favour with the King; he was afraid of Hastings's weight in the Company; he had not thought that the charge would be carried, and so felt safe in appearing impartial;[2] he had been nobbled by Dundas, who took the same line in the debate. Some of these theories were almost certainly untrue. It would have been unlike Pitt to have worried excessively about Hastings's standing at Court, or perhaps in this instance even about the feelings of the Court itself,[3] and Hastings's influence in the Company was a shadow of what it had been. It was indeed precisely this freedom from pressure that allowed Pitt to take the case on its merits, and the simplest explanation, in these circumstances, was probably quite true.

1. *P.R.*, XX, 373–4.

2. This ingenious explanation was forwarded to Eden in Paris by Anthony Storer, who had close links with Opposition (16 June 1786; B.M. Add. Ms 34421, ff. 337–8).

3. Bland Burges, who supported Hastings – with the result, as he thought, that he lost Pitt's favour for a time – and held that Dundas was to blame, wrote later that Dundas had gained several notable successes: he had checked the King, destroyed Hastings's influence, and diverted Opposition to a task which left it little time for 'thwarting Ministers' in other matters. Above all he had forged a new link with Pitt, 'strengthened by the necessity of protecting themselves against the effects of the King's displeasure, under which, it was to be feared, neither of them singly would stand'. (Bland Burges Mss, Bodleian: 'Original Ms. of Hutton Bland-Burges Papers previous to Excisions'. The passage was in fact excluded from the published *Letters and Correspondence*, where a long account appears on pp. 88–92.)

It is hard to accept all these contentions. Dundas himself complained in March 1787 that Hastings's affair was 'the only circumstance unpleasing to our Friends and of course to ourselves' (to Cornwallis, 23 March 1787; *Correspondence of Cornwallis*, I, 293), which does not suggest that he and Pitt welcomed Opposition's activities. And the effect, both immediate and continued, of Pitt's 'conversion' was such that one may discount that of the King's known views. The Minister no doubt had to take them into account; but the King for his part had surely to be careful not to intrude too far in an Indian question, after his highly disputable intervention two and a half years before.

I well remember, I could swear to it now, [Wilberforce said many years later] Pitt listening most attentively to some facts which were coming out either in the first or second case. He beckoned me over, and went with me behind the chair, and said, 'Does not this look very ill to you?' 'Very bad indeed'. He then returned to his place and made his speech, giving up Hastings's case.[1]

The decision may not really have been as sudden as that. Although Pitt had been rushed, he had read the papers, and had even written to Hastings to clarify one point,[2] and the story – which soon spread – that Dundas converted him on the morning of the debate may be taken with a grain of salt. It seems more likely that the hearing in the House confirmed what he was already inclined to believe. He may have been wrong – some good authorities have held that he was. But he appears genuinely to have thought he was right.

The charge against Pitt, if a charge is to be made, may turn rather on the argument that he had allowed a thoroughly misleading impression to arise. He had not made it clear enough that he regarded each verdict as a matter for individual judgment; that they were not occasions on which Ministerial confidence was going to be involved. It can well be held that he was really trying to have it both ways: that, having done much to lead Members to think he disliked an attack on which Government might be supposed to have a policy, he then exercised the right of an independent juror to pronounce in isolation on the merits of one case.[3] It was no doubt true, as a back-bencher observed, that this was not an issue which 'affects the stability of ministry'.[4] But it could reasonably be taken as very near the line. And since this was so, it could also be argued that Pitt had at once brought impeachment closer; that his verdict in fact swayed the choice which he claimed to have opened by this means. He may have been acting – he almost certainly was – on the strict line of virtue; but it was a dangerously ambiguous thing to have done.

Exactly how ambiguous was suggested some twenty months later, when a comparable problem came to its peak. Flushed by their success over Hastings, Opposition decided in 1787 to try for the impeachment of his Chief Justice, Sir Elijah Impey. There was very little doubt that the charges were at least as damaging as those against Hastings, and probably easier to substantiate. But Pitt, lukewarm at the start, finally decided to block the attack. He managed to postpone it throughout

1. *Life of Wilberforce*, V, 341.
2. Pitt to Sydney, – June (Clements Mss); Pitt to Eden, 10 June 1786 (*A.C.*, I, 127). For his letter to Hastings, see George Bruce Malleson, *Life of Warren Hastings* (1894), 455.
3. 'He paid as much impartial attention to it as if he were a jury-man' (Wilberforce's account; *Life of Wilberforce*, V, 341).
4. Daniel Pulteney to Rutland, 8 February 1787 (*H.M.C., Fourteenth Report, Appendix, Pt. I,* 370).

1787, and when a debate could no longer be avoided the Ministry made it clear that it would muster support. '. . . It is the intention of Pitt and all his friends', wrote Gilbert Elliot, who was leading for Opposition, 'to support him [Impey] and there is every reason to fear that I shall be defeated'.[1] He was wrong about 'all' the 'friends' – many, including Dundas, stayed away. But this was equally a sign that they knew the Minister's views, and Elliot was duly beaten, on a low vote, as he had forecast.[2] There were various reasons for Pitt to wish to stop a second impeachment: Opposition had gained enough publicity and success already, quite enough of Parliament's and Government's time had been consumed, and he was currrently engaged in another fight with the Company which it might be unwise to inflame.[3] Perhaps he had also resolved not to find himself in the same position again.

After the Benares vote the atmosphere was different. Hastings's advisers were still optimistic; but when the new session began they were proved wrong. Ministers were now rather less well disposed, and back-benchers, particularly the country gentlemen, more prepared to decide for themselves. Hastings's sympathisers, moreover, continued to contribute to his downfall. Manœuvres in East India House, spreading to the Commons, greatly annoyed a Board of Control already embroiled with the Company on a wide range of subjects. The 'refractory conduct of the Indians' was believed to have been a factor influencing Pitt and Dundas early in 1787: certainly one knowledgeable member of Opposition found 'a sort of concurrence of administration with us, and a degree of *disfavour* to the *Indians* that surprised everybody'.[4] Pitt's friends, too, may have played their part – Wilberforce and Bankes were said to be 'besieging' him.[5] At all events, he was in a mood once more to judge as he found. When Sheridan moved the next charge, on the Begums of Oudh, in his famous speech of 7 February – the speech that was ranked as the greatest Parliamentary performance in living memory, and perhaps of all time –, Pitt spoke and voted in its favour. According to one account, he was not very happy at having done so. Carmarthen's friend Burges, who saw something of him during the debates, recalled a dinner party 'some time after' they began, at which the 'unlucky subject' was raised.

An accidental allusion being made to his unexpected change of sentiments respecting the Begum charge, Pitt suddenly rose from his chair and, striding to the fireplace, remarked in a dignified tone to Lord Carmarthen, 'We have had enough of this subject, my Lord. I

1. To his wife, 5 February 1788; quoted by Marshall, op. cit., 61.
2. 73 to 55. Impey himself conducted his case a great deal more adroitly than Hastings had done.
3. See pp. 454–5 below.
4. Pulteney to Rutland, 9 February 1787 (*H.M.C., Fourteenth Report, Appendix, Pt. I*, 370); Elliot to his wife, 3 February 1787 (see Marshall, op. cit., 52).
5. *H.M.C., Fourteenth Report, Appendix, Pt. I*, 369–70.

will thank you to call another.' 'With all my heart', said Lord Carmarthen, 'I am as sick of the subject as you can be. So come, Pitt, sit down and put the bottle round, for, strange to tell, it stands by you.'[1]

No doubt. But when the fourth charge – the Farrukhabad charge – came up early in March, he again voted against Hastings on some of the articles. He still maintained in February that none of these decisions (for the third charge had passed) meant that impeachment was inevitable; but a month later he changed his mind. He and Dundas now gave active assistance to the necessary Parliamentary steps; Burke's correspondence from this point is full of references to meetings with Dundas and, more occasionally, to Pitt's co-operation. This did not always take exactly the form that Burke would have wished, for indeed the Ministers acted not only in order to give Government backing to what they conceived to be the will of the House, but also to restrain Opposition from excess and to try to tidy up the wording of the charges. Pitt now hoped to ensure that the process was followed properly, and the language framed precisely: he was anxious to remove confusion and vindictiveness from what was to be a judicial case. He failed very largely, though he succeeded in excluding the virulent Philip Francis, Hastings's worst enemy, from the list of Managers for the trial. The charges, as finally presented, remained excessively long and badly constructed. The impeachment opened in Westminster Hall in February 1788.

So began the trial that was to drag on intermittently for over seven years, ending finally in Hastings's acquittal. 'The grey old walls were hung with scarlet. The long galleries were crowded by an audience such as has rarely excited the fears or gratified the emulation of an orator'.[2] The Queen and the Court, the foreign Ambassadors, the social world, the leaders of the arts: Gibbon and Reynolds, Parr and Mrs Siddons, Georgiana Devonshire and Mrs Fitzherbert, looked down on the scene of the peers in their robes, the judges and the heralds, the royal princes, the Commons, the Managers in full dress – even Fox was wearing a wig and sword – and Hastings himself, in a plain poppy-coloured suit. But Pitt was not there. He would not attend the prosecution. Apart from Lord North, who was now almost blind, he was the only great political absentee.

He could not entirely sever all connexion with the proceedings. In 1790, when there was a general election, he had to act in a dispute as to whether or not an impeachment could survive the dissolution of the Parliament that had called it. The precedents were uncertain: the Law Officers thought it could not; but Pitt sided with the prosecution,

1. *Letters and Correspondence of Sir James Bland Burges*, 90. It is possible, of course, that Burges was muddling the Begum with the Benares vote, when the 'change of sentiments' had been particularly 'unexpected'.
2. Macaulay, in the Essay on Warren Hastings.

and after what was said to be a 'most snug and amicable' meeting with Dundas, Burke and Fox,[1] saw his view prevail in the House. Interest in the trial, however, had virtually died by then. Indeed it lapsed remarkably quickly when the opening speeches were over and the detail began. It was as if the decision to embark on impeachment had acted as a sort of blood-letting, and that once it had been taken exhaustion supervened. Hastings's ordeal continued, largely unnoticed, at increasingly long intervals, and the lack of attention spread to Indian affairs as a whole. They were no longer a great political issue; the temperature had dropped, and by the early nineties the difference was marked. At the start of the Third Mysore War in 1791, Philip Francis could deplore the Commons' attitude to Indian business as 'objects ' . . remote . . . from your own immediate interests', not 'thought worthy of your care'.[2] For the time being, the old incendiary subject had been taken from the centre of the Parliamentary stage, and the authorities could pursue their mutual problems largely in the wings.

III

In the years following the India Act of 1784, its implications had to be worked out. Many questions were bound to be raised as a new pattern of authority emerged; and they were not likely to be answered quickly, given the nature of the task, the interests involved, and the prevailing conception of government. In some ways, perhaps, the Ministry was aided by its very difficulties. The demands of strategy and administration were compelling, and had to be faced. But nothing could be done without the Company's consent, and the balance between the partners was far from clear at the start.

The first problem in point of time was that of military responsibility. In the course of 1784 two awkward questions arose. The commander of the Company's troops in Madras, Major-General James Stuart, who was quarrelling with the Governor, Macartney, sought to strengthen his position with the Company by challenging the status of the Board of Control in the army's affairs. Ministers acted promptly. They reminded all parties that 'the Law' had now 'committed the Supreme Authority in all matters as well political, and Military as Civil' to the Government,[3] and with the Directors' concurrence Stuart was removed. This was a fairly simple decision, for Macartney, whose stock stood high, had already dismissed the General from his command. But a more far-reaching problem soon caused greater difficulty. In the autumn, the appointment of a new Commander-in-Chief in Bengal

1. Gilbert Elliot to his wife, 21 December 1790 (*Life and Letters of Sir Gilbert Elliot, First Earl of Minto, from 1751 to 1806*, ed. . . . . the Countess of Minto, I (1874), 373).
2. *P.R.*, XXVIII, 426.
3. Dundas drafted the letter (n.d.; John Rylands Library English Ms 929).

had to be made. The Directors wanted Major-General Robert Sloper, 'of whom', wrote Dundas, 'to say nothing is, I believe, to say the best that can be said'.[1] Pitt entirely agreed with this view, and he begged Sydney, as formal head of the Board of Control, to beware of involving Government in 'a scrape that nothing can make it prudent to incur'.[2] The Ministers were clearly not sure of their ground, and this perhaps was not surprising, for Sloper was apparently favoured by the King as well as by the Directors. In the end, indeed, they had to give way; but they were troubled by their defeat, and the next month Dundas outlined in confidence to Sydney and Pitt a possible plan for future military control.

> I cannot conceive anything more preposterous [he wrote] than that the East India Company should be holding in their hands a large European Army, exclusive of the Crown.

The remedy was to increase the size, at present modest, of the King's forces in India, and to reduce progressively that of the Company's white and native troops. Some of its officers might be given commissions on the enlarged royal establishment; the rest should continue in charge of the native forces, or be placed on half pay. Since 'the East India Company are permitted to hold the Revenue of India', the Company would meet all the expense; but even so there was no 'good reason, why the British Empire in India is to be protected by any other Troops, than those employed for the protection of the rest of the Empire'.[3]

These were bold ideas, which might not be easy to put into effect. A reorganisation of the royal troops must be agreed with the King, who already, as Dundas complained, 'difficults me much about India, . . . particularly the Indian Army'.[4] Ministers would not welcome for its own sake a fresh field for the royal prerogative. But the real difficulty of course lay with the Company itself. The Directors had been encouraged by their victory over Sloper, they were determined to hold their ground if they could, and they were in a strong position to contest any direct incursion on their rights. Pitt of all men could scarcely do much, so soon after Fox's bill and his own Act. The battle was accordingly confined for the next few years to the vexed question of appointments. There were several disputes, and in 1787 there was another major clash. It was caused by the choice of a commander of the forces for Bombay, whose officer was now to be combined with that of Governor. The Government favoured Major-General William Medows: the

1. To Grenville, 27 October 1784; quoted in Holden Furber, *Henry Dundas . . .* (1931), 37–8.
2. n.d.; Clements Mss, University of Michigan.
3. Dundas to Sydney, 2 November 1784. There are two copies of the letter, which Dundas announced he was going to discuss with Pitt, in the latter's papers, P.R.O. 30/8/157 and 361.
4. To Sydney, 10 August 1785 (copy in Rylands Eng. Ms 692).

Directors disagreed. This time Ministers stood firm, and they eventually had their way; but only after a row that infuriated Pitt and Dundas. 'The Court of Directors deserve to be hanged', wrote Pitt, and Dundas replied, 'As to the Directors who voted against him, I hope we shall consider them as objects of vengeance'.[1]

The opposition to Medows rose largely from the Company's dislike of appointing soldiers to high civil posts. It was a policy which, in an unsettled decade, the Government was determined to pursue. In 1785 it chose Major-General Sir Archibald Campbell as Governor of Madras, and the same consideration affected the appointment of the new Governor-General himself. A successor to Hastings had to be found; Macartney had turned down the offer; and in the winter of 1785 Ministers were forced to try again. They had one strong preference, who indeed had already been sounded several times. They now agreed that he should be asked once more. Lord Cornwallis, the defeated but respected commander in America, had the qualities and the standing to fit him for another difficult post. Pitt had been anxious to enlist him from the start: he had asked him to go to Ireland as Lord Lieutenant at the end of 1783, and had since suggested twice – as Dundas had done earlier, when Shelburne was in office – that he should become Governor-General of Bengal. He now repeated the offer. Cornwallis remained reluctant; but he accepted in February 1786. The Directors were not entirely happy, though some of them approved. But the appointment was too popular for them to object publicly, and Government could congratulate itself on an effective and eminent representative who was not beholden to Company interest.

Cornwallis had refused the post before partly because of the limits to its authority.[2] Like Hastings, he thought that the Act of 1784 did not go far enough. The Governor-General should not be debarred, as he was by that measure, from holding the post of Commander-in-Chief; he should be able to override or ignore his Council if necessary; and he should be given greater discretionary powers in an emergency. Eager to secure his services, Ministers agreed to meet his points, and in April 1786 they secured the passing of an Amending Act, to come into force at the end of the year.[3] Thus fortified, Cornwallis sailed in May for Calcutta, where his example soon did much to strengthen the case for filling high civil offices with military men. Four years later, Dundas ascribed to the influence of his 'good and popular government' the fact that 'the Court of Directors, and all their servants' had failed to stifle a system they still disliked.[4]

1. See p. 193, n. 2 above.
2. He also did not relish taking on something which he believed – rightly – was being offered in order to save the Ministry from having to decide between other, controversial, candidates.
3. 26 Geo. III, c. 16.
4. To Colonel Robert Abercromby, 22 April 1790 (copy in Rylands Eng. Ms 692).

All this, however satisfactory, left untouched the larger question of military control. But it had not been forgotten. In 1785, Dundas reduced the number of the Company's troops to a level below that favoured by the Directors; he was in touch with Campbell and Cornwallis, who supported his views; and in 1787 an opportunity arose to carry out his plans. The Government indeed then acted with an alacrity that sparked off a major debate on its relations with the Company as a whole; and the affair ended with another amending measure, a Declaratory Act, which did much to settle the pattern for the future within the framework of the act of 1784.

The occasion was provided by the Dutch crisis, and the possibility of war with France. In the summer of 1787, Dundas and Pitt reverted to the ideas of November 1784.[1] India should be reinforced in any case in a threatening situation, and in October the Ministry decided to dispatch four regiments – a useful lever in any proposal for a transfer of control. The King's approval was easily obtained, and the Directors were then asked to agree – a necessary move if they were to be held liable for the costs. They did so, at a day's notice, in a thin meeting, by one vote; but they soon regretted the step, and withdrew their consent. They refused to meet the costs, on legal advice, and when the Board of Control insisted the General Court of the Company formally condemned its action. In February 1788 Pitt accordingly introduced a bill 'for removing all doubts respecting the power of the Commissioners for the affairs of India' to order payment of any expenses incurred in maintaining 'the security of the British territories and possessions' in the East.[2]

The bill seemed to the Company to have dangerous implications. It would tend to give the Government 'unlimited and unrestrained power' within what had been intended to be a balanced system.[3] Such fears were strengthened by Dundas's and Pitt's behaviour in the course of the debates. Dundas made some unhappy claims at the start about the Government's right to 'apply the whole of the revenues of India' to defence, 'without leaving the Company a sixpence for their investments'.[4] And while the effect of his remarks was offset a few days later in an embarrassing defence of the Company by its counsel Erskine, who was drunk, Pitt soon made matters much worse. On 5 March, he delivered one of the worst speeches of his career. According to one account, he was suffering from a hang-over: he was certainly not his normal self.[5] After an injudicious hint of his ideas on the Company's troops – a 'consolidation' with the King's forces 'was undoubted-

1. P. 452 above. See Philips, *East India Company*, 55.
2. 25 February; *P.R.*, XXIII, 246.
3. Francis Baring, 25 February; op. cit., 246–7.
4. Op. cit., 250.
5. He was described as being 'low-spirited, and overcome by the heat of the House, in consequence of having got drunk the night before . . ., with Mr. Dundas and *the Duchess of Gordon*. They must have had a hard bout of it, for even Dundas . . . was affected by it'. (Lord Bulkeley to Marquess of Buckingham, 10 March 1788;

ly to be wished for, and sooner or later it must be attempted' –, he went on to drop a really heavy brick. 'What had been his avowed objects in framing the Act of 1784? The principal one was, to take from the Company the entire management of the territorial possessions, and the political government of the country.'[1] It was small wonder that Fox pounced on this revelation by the Company's saviour, or that some of the Ministry's independent supporters joined him and the 'India interest' to attack the speech. As the debate wore on, indeed, it began to look as if the bill might be lost. Pitt now acted quickly. In the debate on the third reading, he moved a list of amendments designed to guard against an extension of Ministerial patronage, and his speech, conciliatory and skilful, did much to repair the earlier damage. The House was willing to accept his assurances, a number of Members returned to the fold, and the bill passed the Commons by 127 to 73.[2]

The affair had several consequences. It came at a time when the Board of Control was involved in several disputes with the Company, and the business of Hastings was at its height. The mixed system of Indian government was showing real signs of strain, and both parties now paused to reflect. Dundas, who had been growing steadily more impatient and more addicted to frontal attack, appreciated that he must watch his step and move more carefully in future. The Directors, for their part, may have gained some consolation from the Government's ineptitude; but the Act had passed in the end, and they had to bow to the fact. Everyone concerned was rather chastened, and while the causes of friction remained there was a general feeling that another public clash should be avoided. The incident was the climax of a process that had recently been gathering pace, and it introduced a significant shift of emphasis in the handling of Indian affairs.

One result was the abandonment of the Government's more far-reaching scheme. Nothing more was done about the Company's control of its troops. Cornwallis again pressed for some such step after the war with France began; but his proposals, backed by Dundas, were ignored by the Directors. The Company was finally persuaded to bring its system of recruitment and pay into line with that of the King's forces; but even this did not take effect fully until 1799. It was a modest

Buckingham, I, 360–1). Bulkeley was a gossip, and he may or may not have been right. But Pitt was undoubtedly in a poor way. Grenville wrote that at the end of the debate he was 'taken so ill as not to be able to speak at all' (to Buckingham, 6 March; Stanhope, I, 361), and while in fact he did so it was only to say that he was 'much oppressed by personal indisposition' (*P.R.*, XXIII, 323). One newspaper made him add that 'he was scarcely able to put two sentences together' (*The London Chronicle*, March 6–8, 1788).

1. *P.R.*, XXIII, 301. Newspaper reports vary, as usual; but the fuller accounts give much the same impression. According to some (*London Chronicle* for 6 March – separate from the issue for 6th–8th in the note above – and *The Times* of the same day), Pitt went so far as to say that he would prefer to see British India defended by the King's forces alone.

2. On 14 March. It subsequently became law as 28 Geo. III, c. 8.

and belated achievement compared with the earlier hopes, and it stemmed from the process of compromise which distinguished the later peacetime years.

The first indications of change were to be seen in Dundas himself. Since 1784 he had been trying to ensure that the weights were fixed in Government's favour, and at times indeed seemed to deny that there should be a balance with the Company at all. He had to manoeuvre, of course, for the necessary influence, and obviously he could not always hope to win. But when he did so – which was often – his methods were sometimes unhappy, losing him supporters and protégés on whom he had relied. Frontal attack was in fact in the long run a fruitless line of approach; for it was impossible, in the end, to ignore the existence of a balance. Government now had considerable powers, which the Directors had to accept. It held the whip hand in policy, and could make the fact very clear. But the Company's powers were also substantial; its patronage was jealousy guarded, and the daily conduct of business was still effectively in its hands. The very extent to which Dundas plunged into detail meant that he must rely on the machinery of East India House. The Company's sizeable and experienced departments had no counterpart at the Board of Control, housed in a poky office in Whitehall where even Dundas had no room to himself. They and their masters still ran a system designed as one of checks and balances, and they had formidable obstructive powers, even when they knew they might have to yield. The years from 1784 to 1788 were a time of testing; they were often unhappy, and the passage of the Declaratory Act brought matters to a head. If Dundas was to consolidate his hard-won position, he would have to recognise that in Indian affairs, as elsewhere, a Minister must accept a limitation of powers.

One may talk in this way at this time of Dundas, rather than the Board of Control, because no one doubted that he was effectively in charge. Of his five colleagues, Sydney was a cypher; Walsingham, though active at first, carried little real weight, and virtually withdrew when he became a Postmaster General in 1787; and Grenville, again after an active start, did the same from 1786.[1] His influence thereafter was visible in foreign negotiations; but though he became a chairman of the Board in 1789 and remained so for the next four years, this was ex officio as a Secretary of State, and he confined himself mostly to advice, when asked, on the larger questions of policy. The other two members were Pitt and Mulgrave, and Mulgrave did a good deal. He attended the meetings, and he seems to have helped draft despatches

1. He told Thomas Coutts on 22 September 1786 that he had 'in fact quitted the India Board', continuing 'a nominal member of it only', since the establishment of 'the new board of Trade, and indeed for a considerable time before' (Fortescue Mss, 'Private Correspondence Sent & Received 1785 to 1787').

and make himself generally useful.[1] But he was a subordinate colleague, not an equal; and Pitt was not an equal, but a superior. Dundas's position was unique, he had made it entirely his own, and even when he seemed to be in difficulties it remained his for the keeping.

The strength of this position was not lessened, but rather increased, by the fact that Pitt himself was being drawn more into Eastern affairs. In his first two years of office he seems to have held aloof as far as he could; but, as the problems grew, so necessarily did his concern. The development may be seen even in the table of his attendances at the Board. He went to one of the twenty meetings in 1784, and to eight out of 57 in 1785; to eight again, out of 39, in 1786; but to 36 out of 43 in 1787, 19 out of 32 in 1788, 18 out of 25 in 1789, 12 out of 32 in 1790, and 18 out of 25 in 1791. In 1792 he attended 7 out of 21.[2] The figures suggest a story which the papers confirm. In the later eighties and early nineties Pitt was much involved in Eastern business.

But this very fact told in Dundas's favour. For the Prime Minister could not hope to move in this field without a great deal of expert advice. Dundas supplied it, as Hawkesbury did in another sphere. But his influence was more persistent than Hawkesbury's, because there was more to discuss, because he knew the detail of a large patronage, and not least because Pitt liked him and the two men thought much alike. The similarity of their views was not always fully grasped: it was the habit to point the contrast between the coarse, pragmatic Scot and the shy, high principled young Minister. But the contrast was one of character, and that in fact yielded its own mutual sympathy; in their ideas, Pitt and Dundas were closer than was often thought. Dundas held genuinely liberal views on trade, in the limited meaning that the term then had; and he was genuinely anxious to impose firm government, and restrain Company faction. He was happy to do the work and the necessary in-fighting, which Pitt could never have tackled. In return he claimed Pitt's support, which was freely given. The partnership was a real one, in which each respected the other's role. Dundas guided Pitt in forming policies which the Minister broadly approved, which fitted well with his wider objects, and some of which at least he now supervised himself.

The association was greatly strengthened by the fact that the two men got on so well. The volume of business brought them together, and Dundas's stock rose in the long and often convivial sessions. The result was soon resented, by Dundas's enemies and by Pitt's friends, and Dundas was usually blamed when Pitt found himself in any Indian unpleasantness. The critics of course were often right; Pitt's approach to Indian affairs was largely moulded by Dundas. But the extent of the Scotsman's 'ascendancy' – the word sometimes used – could be exaggerated. For these were still early days in a friendship which reach-

1. E.g. pp. 427, 439, 441 above.
2. Harlow, op. cit., II, 244, and p. 195, n2 above.

ed its full intimacy in the next decade; Pitt had his own contacts with the Company – Francis Baring in particular gave independent advice –, and he did not yet regard Dundas as a political figure of the first rank. He hesitated to give him Cabinet office even in 1791; he still looked on him rather as a first-rate man of business, loyal and experienced, who would be content with his own large sphere so long as he was given effective control.[1] Dundas knew well enough the bounds within which he worked. His influence was none the less real for the knowledge, from which indeed it drew strength.

Pitt's impact on a varied business took various forms. Now that Government was responsible for the 'management of the territorial possessions' in India,[2] he found himself drawn into Cornwallis's far-ranging administrative plans. The story of the Governor-General's efforts is a saga in itself, in which the Minister appears on occasions when his interest was engaged or his support required. He followed, and when necessary spoke in Parliament, on Cornwallis's campaign against corruption, his struggle to control appointments, his reform of the judicial system, and his 'Permanent Settlement' of Bengal. Characteristically, it was this last problem that roused Pitt's closest attention, for the issues turned on finance. The system of land ownership was chaotic, and the collection of revenue in disarray; Cornwallis wished to simplify both by turning the hereditary collectors, the zamindars, into landlords responsible for fixed annual payments from their districts. The proposal had large implications. Should collection be entrusted to Indians rather than British? How far should a British authority interfere with the system of land tenure? Should the settlement, if approved, be temporary or permanent – would the benefits of certainty of possession outweigh the loss of income from a fixed contribution if the value of the property increased? The detail was intricate, voluminous and puzzling, and Pitt 'shut himself up' with Dundas for ten days to study it.[3] He certainly plunged into the matter, though he did not need to alter the verdict. For Dundas had already spoken publicly in favour of Cornwallis's proposals, and the Ministry's approval was duly given, after Pitt's scrutiny, in August 1792.

The Company's finances altogether often claimed his attention – not surprisingly, in view of their state and his own taste for the subject. As time went by, however, they were left increasingly to Dundas. In 1784 and 1785, Pitt handled the subject in Parliament himself.[4] But

1. See the terms of Pitt's letter to the King of 29 April 1791 (*L.C.G. III*, I, no. 672), when he was trying to persuade Cornwallis to take the Home Office, placing Dundas there as a stopgap while the Governor-General was on his way home.

2. P. 455 above.

3. Dundas to Cornwallis, 17 September 1792 (*Correspondence of Cornwallis*, II (1859), 215). Charles Grant, Cornwallis's commercial adviser, stayed with them 'a great part of the time'.

4. See *P.R.*, XV, under 24 June, 2 July; *P.R.*, XVII, under 15, 24 and 28 February; *P.R.*, XVIII, under 5 May.

in 1786 it was Dundas who introduced the first of the Indian 'budgets'
– albeit incomplete in their scope – which he made a regular feature
in the next seven years, and he began to take the lead in the Indian
financial debates.[1] Pitt was closely consulted, as his papers show, and
he entered into detail. But he was content to leave the initiative to his
colleague, who came to claim it as his right.

The process was probably started by Dundas's attack on the Company's debt. At the beginning of 1784, this was thought to amount to
some £8 million in India, with a further £6 million due to be met at
home in the next six years. There was a widespread desire to tackle
the problem, and Dundas and Pitt turned to it as soon as they could.
As in the larger case of the National Debt, funding – at 5 per cent –
seemed to be the answer for the £8 million. But this could be carried
out only in England, and the creditors in India must be induced to
transfer their claims. At the same time, trading capital must be increased to sustain the opportunities for profit. Various plans were put forward, but Dundas's was finally adopted. He proposed to raise the
Company's trading capital in any one year – the investment, as it was
known – from about £1 million to £1½ million, on which he estimated
that an extra £800,000 a year could be earned. The increased income
would help service bills of exchange, drawn on the Company, which
would be issued to its creditors in India in return for their claims being
transferred to England. It would also go to meet the charges of servicing
the payment of the claims outstanding over the next few years. This
was one object; the other was to discourage profits being applied
elsewhere, and if this was to be done the rules governing remissions
home must be eased. As things stood, the Company's servants were
closely restricted in what they could send, and the earnings from the
Country trade in particular were used more easily to finance foreign
or clandestine trade. Dundas therefore urged new regulations for
drawing individual profits into the Company's net; otherwise they
might continue largely to support its competitors.[2]

The plan was highly complex, and the discussions with the Company
need not be followed. The matter, as Grenville wrote later, was one 'of
much labour, . . . the details of which have lost all their interest'.[3]
Pitt scrutinised the proposals, and took his part in the decision – his
first attendance for business at the Board of Control was in fact on this
issue. He and Dundas had their way in September 1785, and the
arrangements were put slowly into effect. They were not very successful

1. See *P.R.*, XX, XXII, XXIII, XXVI, XXVII, XXIX, XXXIII, and particularly his remarks in XXXIV (1792), 590. The term 'budget', though not used in the
debates, is sometimes given in the lists of contents to the volumes.

2. India Office Records, Home Misc. 369A, gives the fullest account of the plans
and the discussions. See also Scottish Record Office, Melville Castle Muniments,
G.D. 51/3/195/1–2.

3. Uncorrected draft in his 'Commentaries of my own Political Life . . .'; Fortescue
Mss.

over the next few years: indeed the Company's resources remained so strained that new stock had to be raised in 1786 and 1789. The creditors in India were slow to accept the bills of exchange, private profits remained and were invested largley in the East, and not enough bullion was made available, particularly at first, to support a growing trade to its full extent. Despite Pitt's and Dundas's efforts, there proved to be no painless way round this last difficulty, and larger supplies had to be shipped out towards the end of the decade. It seems doubtful indeed if the problem would have been mastered by the beginning of the war with France even if Tipu Sultan had not meanwhile caused fresh expense. But Dundas's ideas had appealed to Pitt, his advocacy proved persuasive, and it helped secure his rapid elevation to the virtual control of Indian finance.

The Prime Minister's contribution, as perhaps was natural, was sometimes more distinctive in a wider setting – in those policies bearing or centring on India which were 'not merely an India Question'.[1] Negotiations with European powers – with the Dutch or the French or the Turks –, the mission to China, the expansion of trade in the northern and central Pacific: all demanded, in differing degrees, a direction higher than Dundas could give. They all involved interests or departments beyond the Company and the Board of Control, even though the Company might lie at the heart of the matter. This was also the case, to a lesser extent, with another scheme in which the Minister played his part: a plan to allow a freer market in India for the sale of Spanish goods in return for a free sale of Indian products to Spain and the Spanish Empire. Such an exchange would have several advantages, if the terms were right. It would bring Spanish bullion direct to the region in which it was so badly needed; it would encourage British trade in the Philippines and, one might hope, throughout the East Indies; and it would provide a further means of entry to the Spanish American markets, a complement, however restricted, to the trade from the Caribbean. The idea had the added merit that it originated from the Spanish Philippine Company, which approached the East India Company late in 1785.[2] A leisurely struggle followed in London between the Government and a body of the Directors, Pitt and Dundas urging the proposals against substantial opposition. Everyone of course wanted the bullion, but the Company was inclined to suspect the price. It feared the effects of too open a market on its own position. The dissentients were finally overruled, and in December 1788 Pitt, Grenville and Dundas signed an agreement for a three-year trial. But their opponents had their revenge. Such restrictions were imposed in

1. See p. 428 above.
2. Though the East India Company had tentatively approached the Government on the possibility of 'a direct communication' with Manila, in order to attract bullion, some months before (Carmarthen to Pitt, 17 January 1785; B. M. Egerton Ms 3498).

practice that the arrangement lapsed, and was never renewed. It was an interesting trial of strength in a case which favoured the Company more than did the talks with France or Holland, where commercial considerations were combined with others and matters handled by Governments direct. No national treaty was involved here; the discussion was between Companies, on Company business; and while the British Ministers carried enough weight to have their way in principle, they proved helpless in the face of practical obstruction.[1]

The outcome indeed was not untypical of these formative years. For neither Government not its opponents in the Company could claim complete success. Politics in Leadenhall Street, as at Westminster, needed constant and detailed attention; and there were occasions when the different interests would rally as a virtually united force. There was a recognisable Company point of view on a wide range of questions, which Ministers could sometimes defeat or ignore, but to which they sometimes had to yield. Pitt and Dundas exploited their resources, and they often forced the pace; the Company's rearguard actions often slowed or stopped the advance. Each side could count its victories, against a background of compromise, and if a pattern may be traced in retrospect it could not be readily seen at the time. Hastings was impeached: Impey was not. Government fixed the terms of the talks with France and Holland: it could not build on those with Spain. It encouraged the trade with China, not as fully as it would have wished: its plans for the northern Pacific had to be curtailed. It forced through senior appointments in India: its friends in the Directorate sometimes rebelled. Much civil reform was welcomed: military reorganisation was blocked. Extensive Ministerial powers were wielded largely through the Company's machinery: Company patrons tended increasingly to listen to Dundas. The experience of a decade was finally summed up when the Company's charter had to be renewed. For this was in many ways a climax of the developments since 1784. What should be the pattern for the future, political and commercial? And how far could intentions be carried out, if it came to a trial of strength? A decision did not have to be taken until, at the latest, early in 1794; but much of the ground was being prepared from the later eighties.

The crux of the matter really lay in the provisions for trade; for these would determine the Company's standing, and so the shape of responsi-

1. The result of course affected the plan for reducing the Company's debt. It has been suggested (Philips, op. cit., 47) that the Ministry's failure to send out enough bullion for some years was deliberate, in order to force the Directors into a greater reliance on Parliamentary help. Perhaps; though one is tempted to say that this is not how successful politicians work. But bullion was short in any case (see pp. 411, 460 above), and the policy may have been affected by the hopes of extracting silver from Spain – the increased shipments followed the collapse of that prospect as well as the Ministry's unhappy experience over the Declaratory Act.

bility. The first shots were fired in 1786, when the China trade came under review and David Scott urged his radical proposals for the structure of the Company's business.[1] His remarks on China formed part of a general criticism of the existing monopoly, which should be eased so as to incorporate the expanding and diversified Country trade. Pitt and Dundas put his ideas to the Directors; but while the ensuing talks were under way the Company was attacked, with unexpected force, from outside. Hawkesbury's onslaught in 1788, precipitated by the cotton manufacturers' complaints against Indian competition,[2] developed into a campaign which continued until late in 1791. The great champion of protection was appearing in a superficially different light, as the protagonist of a freer carriage of goods, a freer access to markets, and a reduction of duties. In June 1790 he called on Pitt to arrange for a conference with the Directors, at which a start should be made on settling a policy for the new charter; meanwhile he wanted them to accept visits to India from manufacturers' agents, who would inspect the conditions and report on what they saw. Pitt agreed that the talks should begin 'without delay'.[3] But Dundas, who was no more pleased than the Company at the prospect of such an invasion, was anxious to keep the preparation of the charter under proper control. He agreed with much of Hawkesbury's argument, at least for opening the export trade, which indeed was being amplified again by David Scott. But the tone, he thought, was wild, the manufacturers were 'under a delusion' from lack of knowledge, and it was important not to let these complicated questions get out of hand.[4] It was June 1791 before the talks began, with Pitt, Dundas and Hawkesbury representing the Ministry. A committee of Directors was appointed in August to report on the export trade to India; it did so in September, and Hawkesbury commented at once. He found the gap between the Company and the manufacturers still as wide as before, and he remained unconvinced by the committee's arguments for a monopoly.[5] But he was faced by a blank wall: whatever their own differences, Dundas and the Company were determined to exclude the outsider. Hawkesbury's 'Observations' were read to the Board of Control. But nothing more was heard of them, and the matter passed firmly into other hands.

The pressures so released, however, could not be ignored. Throughout 1792 the manufacturers bombarded Dundas with petitions. At the

1. See p. 414 above.

2. P. 415 above.

3. Quoted in Harlow, op. cit., II, 513. Pitt had shown concern about the manufacturers' grievances since the start. In Dundas's papers there is a document on the subject, dated 17 April 1788 and endorsed 'Questions put by the Right Honorable William Pitt. Answered.' (John Rylands English Ms 684).

4. 'Memorandum of Instructions: Mr. Russell', endorsed 1 October 1791 (quoted in Harlow, loc. cit., 513–14). Francis Russell was solicitor to the Board of Control.

5. For the attribution of this unsigned paper to Hawkesbury, see loc. cit., 518–19, particularly 519, n71.

same time the Ministry was engaged in fighting the case of the whalers in the northern Pacific, Macartney's instructions were being drafted, and Scott and his associates were reviving their demands. The date of the charter's renewal was steadily approaching. Dundas and Pitt must make up their minds at least on its general shape.

We have a clear idea of Dundas's views in the autumn of 1791, for he then drafted detailed instructions, as a basis for discussion, to the solicitor of the Board of Control.[1] They reflected his experiences over the past three or four years. In the middle eighties he had been convinced that the Company's operations should be severely restricted. Its monopoly, if retained, must be greatly eased for both imports and exports, and its political powers might well be removed. He still thought that political direction should be strictly a matter for Government, and he still wanted the Crown to manage the finances, and gain control of the troops. But he was now prepared to leave the Company to run the civil government, subject to minor reforms, and to keep most of its commercial powers. His arguments centred on the need for a reliable agent to remit money to England; it was very difficult for this purpose to separate trade from revenue, and virtually impossible to separate the collection of revenue from the civil administration. The same reasoning underlay his growing inclination to continue the Company's control of sales from the East. He was not yet sure what should be done about the outward trade, except that the Company should retain its existing rights in China.

The Board of Control agreed that Dundas should begin discussions on this basis, and these continued throughout 1792. The Company's chief negotiator was Francis Baring; Cornwallis was kept in touch; and Pitt joined in the discussions as the business came to a point.[2] The Ministry's ideas continued to change, or shrink, as the talks went on. Cornwallis counselled caution, Baring fought hard, and the result was to be seen in the final version. Any prospect of a change in military organisation disappeared, and the minor reforms in civil government were dropped. The Company retained its rights over the outward trade – exclusively over the shipment of naval and military stores and

1. India Office Records, Home Miscellaneous Series, 413 (6), ff. 241–99; endorsed 1 October 1791 (see p. 462, n4 above).

2. E.g. Dundas to Pitt, 18 October 1792, stressing the desirability of taking Baring fully into their confidence as to 'what we mean to do. . . . If you do give him one of the papers, let him know it is done in concert with me, and that . . . we shall from time to time expect a return of unreserved communication from him' (P.R.O. 30/8/157). The use of the plural is suggestive. Six months later he wrote to Baring about the reasons which 'led me, in conjunction with Mr. Pitt, to hold a free and unreserved intercourse, both with the Court of Directors, and with other classes of men who supposed their interests at variance with the exclusive privileges of that Company' (15 April 1793; *Papers Respecting the Negotiations for a Renewal of the East-India Company's Exclusive Trade. Printed by the Court of Directors for the Information of the Proprietors* (n.d.), VII, 3–4). The same publication bears ample witness to this claim (op. cit., II, 16; III, 10, 14, 19–21, 21–4; V, 8).

copper, and over all other goods except those exported by private merchants at stipulated rates in Company shipping limited to a total of 3,000 tons a year. The same tonnage, at the same rates, was granted to private merchants' inward shipments, which must then be warehoused and sold by the Company. A restricted independent trade was allowed in China and much of the Pacific, subject to the Company's control over onward shipments home.[1] Private merchants in India might be licensed by the Company to trade with Britain or, on a separate licence, with specific foreign concerns. The Company would pay the Exchequer £½ million a year out of its revenues. The charter was granted for a period of twenty years.

This was a modest result after all the earlier talk. Some changes had been made which would prove significant as time went by. The Company's new financial obligation strengthened Government's hand. The allowance of shipping space to British manufacturers, and to Agency Houses and Country traders, was a step towards the recognition of a more open trade. So were the regulations for the Pacific trade, however far they fell short of the first design. But it was not very hard for the Directors to accept such concessions, though they did their best to reverse some of them at the last minute. Dundas introduced the bill for the charter in April 1793. Like all Indian business now, it attracted little attention. It passed the Commons, Pitt remarked, with 'a quietness unexampled in the annals of Parliament'; the Lords were equally quiescent, and the measure became law in June.[2]

The charter made one change in the direction of Indian affairs at home. It created a new, salaried office of President of the Board of Control.[3] The post very properly went to Dundas. Its creation may have had something to do with the surrender of fees by the Secretaries of State, which affected him as Home Secretary in 1792;[4] but it was an appropriate recognition in any event of the status he had won for himself. It did not give him the powers that he would earlier have wished: he did not become, as he had once hoped, Secretary of State for India. But he was now a Secretary of State in any case, so that personal ambition was not so pressing, and he could reflect that, despite its limitations, the office might be put to good use. For Dundas's elevation to the head of the Board came, appropriately, at a time when his influence with the Company was perhaps at its peak. The years 1788 to 1794 have been called those of his 'ascendancy' in its affairs,[5] and relations between the Board and the Directors were certainly easier than before. After the shock of the Declaratory Act, he had in

1. See pp. 350, 416 above.
2. *P.R.*, XXXV, 575. The act was 33 Geo. III, c. 52.
3. It also provided for two additional, salaried members of the Board who need not be Privy Councillors, for a quorum of three, and for the President to have a casting vote when required.
4. See p. 311 above.
5. Philips, op. cit., title of ch. III.

fact moved more adroitly. He was more careful in his recommendations for appointments, and he now made few mistakes. The growth of his influence was aided, moreover, by developments in the Company itself. The old India interest had broken up, and no one connexion had taken its place. There was a fairly fluid situation, from which Dundas could profit, and by 1793 he had his finger in every Company pie. The Ministry's shift of sentiment over the charter must indeed be seen against this background: recognition of the Company's case was the result of a greater intervention in its affairs. Dundas and Pitt could argue commercial policies, for which they were not responsible by statute, because the Directorate had tacitly accepted the fact of Governmental concern. It would be a great exaggeration to say that they were content to leave the Company's powers broadly as they were because they reckoned that it was now adequately under control. They ceded more than they would have wished, and, as events were soon to prove, the Directors could still revolt if they were able to combine. Government was not fully in the saddle; if it thought it was, it was mistaken. But closer co-operation had suggested that the partnership must be maintained. Dundas was not merely putting a good face on the matter when, defending the terms of the charter later, he wrote

> That a direct interference by Government in the affairs of India is necessary . . ., I am more and more convinced; but . . . the ostensible form of Government with all its consequent extent and detail of patronage . . . must remain as it now is.

So, too, must 'a monopoly of trade in the hands of the East India Company', for in the 'peculiar circumstances' of the East trade and administration could not be disentangled.[1] Government had gained a good deal since the Act of 1784: the Company was on the defensive at home, and it was being reformed in India, where Cornwallis was laying enduring foundations. But experience had shown clearly that a balance of powers must be preserved. It was perhaps ironic that Dundas's success within the Company should have been followed by the defeat of his earlier views. It would also have seemed surprising in the later eighties to be told that Pitt's statement on the new charter in 1793 would be virtually an echo of his speeches against Fox's India bill of ten years before. This was in fact largely fortuitous, for Pitt was answering an attack by Fox couched in the old terms and concerned with the old issues. He therefore passed quickly over the 'commercial arrangements' – they had been 'condemned . . . as a mere job and political delusion', but had not 'the exclusive privilege of the Company', while retained, been 'rendered subservient to the resources of the Empire?' And as for the Company's powers and patronage – well, looking back to 1783, 'the public opinion had been made up at the

1. Dundas to Sir Hugh Inglis, 2 April 1800 (copy in Rylands English Ms 929).

time, and had continued unaltered'. Legislation since that date had enabled Government to 'superintend, direct, and control': let the Directors continue, within such limits, to carry out their duties, holding their patronage, 'extending their commerce, and . . . contributing . . . to the resources of the nation'.[1] It was an adequate tactical response to a rather feeble attack. But neither the tone nor much of the content might have been expected a few years before.

1. 24 May; *P.R.*, XXXV, 579–82.

CHAPTER XVI

Diplomacy and Trade in Europe

I

In June 1784, when the great fight with Fox was over and the new Parliament had met after the election, the Foreign Secretary decided that the Ministry could now spare some time for foreign affairs.

> Were it possible [he wrote to Pitt] for England to be permitted to remain perfectly quiet and undisturbed, so as to be able by a prudent line of conduct in her domestic Government to recruit her strength almost exhausted by the late . . . war no one could hesitate a moment to adopt that system of tranquillity.[1]

But such a prospect seemed unlikely, and they must therefore consider the state of Europe. He began with the two great 'natural', but now alienated, allies.

> Could the two Imperial Courts [of Austria and Russia] be induced to take a Friendly part in the interests of England, & that of Vienna return to the old system to which she owes her present importance the prospect would indeed be brillant [*sic*] but the Coldness of Russia towards us since the accommodation of her differences with the Porte; and the very strong hold which France still retains upon the Austrian Councils render any hope of that Nature little likely to be accomplished without much delay which must inevitably prevent our profiting of any connection with other Powers which though less formidable in point of . . . strength cannot be uninteresting to this Country, in particular Denmark, & Prussia.

Both these last, he was fairly sure, were ready for 'the most friendly intercourse with England', and the Prussian envoy in London had even suggested reviving the pre-war idea of a quadruple alliance between England, Russia, Prussia and Denmark. There certainly seemed little hope elsewhere: even our traditional friends, but recent enemies, the Dutch 'must (for the present at least) be considered as

1. Carmarthen to Pitt, 9 June 1784; draft, in Carmarthen's hand, in B. M. Egerton Ms 3498.

totally out of the question'; and since 'Something should be done and as expeditiously as possible',

> Austria, Russia, & Denmark [;] Russia, Prussia & Denmark, or the two latter even alone should be attended to, and though we should be so unfortunate as to gain none of the other, do not let us throw away the last.

Carmarthen followed up this plea a fortnight later, urging that 'not an hour should be lost' in approaching the Danes, who by his information were 'now open & willing to receive any proposals from hence'.[1]

Pitt, asked for 'a line', duly replied at once. His reaction was not calculated to raise the Foreign Secretary's hopes. He subscribed politely to his 'object'. But

> The great difficulty is how to lay the foundations of such Connections, keeping clear at the same time of being too soon involved in the Quarrels of any Continental Power.[2]

Anything that could be done 'consistent with this Caution' should certainly be done 'speedily'; the more so since the Danes, whose hints must have sprung at least in part from a serious quarrel with Sweden, seemed rather less likely now than they had been to be involved in 'an actual War', so that we could perhaps afford to 'impress them with an Idea of our Friendly Disposition' – an assurance which moreover should have a good effect on Russia.

> But then the difficulty seems how to employ any thing more than very vague and unmeaning Professions, without pledging ourselves, to more than would be prudent, in case Sweden should persist in its Hostile Intentions. . . . Perhaps . . . the holding out a disposition on our Part to interfere *as far as our own Situation will permit, if the Course of Events should require our Exertions,* may be sufficient . . .

All this, however, was a 'hasty speculation, . . . neither enough digested nor distinct.' It needed 'the deliberation of Cabinet, before a Step of any Sort is taken'. Pitt was therefore at Carmarthen's disposal if a meeting was to be held.

This early exchange threw light on many aspects of the situation: on Carmarthen's thinking – and his prose style –, on the difficulties in the

1. Same to same, 23 June 1784 (copy, in Carmarthen's hand, loc. cit.).
2. Pitt to Carmarthen, 24 June 1784 (loc. cit.). And cf. his conversation with the Foreign Secretary in May, when he had agreed that 'the great object' in Europe must be to separate Austria from France; but with 'the strongest conviction', in Carmarthen's words, of 'the necessity of avoiding, if possible, the entering into any engagements likely to embroil us in a new war' (*Political Memoranda of Francis Fifth Duke of Leeds,* 101).

way of a useful foreign policy, and on Pitt's reluctance to have a European policy at all. As Carmarthen's opening remarks recognised, the Minister meant to steer as clear as possible of continental entanglements while he built up the finances and morale at home. His feelings could be gauged from a sermon that he caused Pretyman to preach, before the House of Commons in St Margaret's on the occasion of the thanksgiving for peace.[1] It was devoted largely to a reminder of the dangers of the National Debt, coupled with an attack on those who despaired of overcoming them. The country's state was critical, 'especially with respect to its revenue'; but the tasks must be tackled, and we must pray for 'a long continuance of public tranquillity, . . . happily restored to us; which alone can extricate us from our present difficulties, and raise this oppressed Country to its ancient prosperity and glory'. It was a manifesto of Pitt's attitude to affairs abroad, which was to be seen in many aspects of his immediate policies; it lay, for instance, behind his efforts for Ireland – 'Let this business of Ireland terminate well, let peace continue for five years, and we shall again look any Power in Europe in the face'.[2] That was written in 1785, and five years of peace without risk was asking a lot. Pitt was propelled into a more active foreign policy well before that period. Timetables of that kind – policy by stages – can seldom indeed be fully achieved. But this was the starting point for a career consumed in the end by alliances and war.

There was of course every reason for a cautious diplomacy in 1784. It is difficult to imagine any Minister indulging in anything else. But caution need not be synonymous with inaction, and Pitt's passivity – his hope of being left 'perfectly quiet and undisturbed' – took a good deal on trust, as such a policy always does. One must not exaggerate here. Eighteenth-century diplomacy was in many ways a very short-range affair: alliances and groupings could change very quickly, unheralded action could prove effective, and British Governments were traditionally reluctant to be involved too deeply in normal times. The old consciousness of the island, 'built by Nature for herself against infection', aroused a feeling which Pitt, with virtually no personal knowledge of Europe and immersed in his other 'permanent concerns',[3] tended at the start instinctively to share. Nor was there any issue at that moment impelling him to intervene. But that was not to say that the sky was clear. The general situation indeed was distinctly unpropitious,

1. On 29 July 1784 – a few weeks after the exchange with Carmarthen. Pitt's part in the choice of preacher may be guessed from the fact that the House instructed him and Wilberforce to convey its formal thanks to Pretyman; and Pretyman, who was by then acting as Pitt's private secretary, must have framed his remarks on the Minister's advice.

There is a copy of the published sermon in the Scottish Record Office, Melville Castle Muniments, G.D. 51/14/39.

2. P. 215 above.

3. P. 239 above.

and the apparent absence of a British policy disturbed those concerned with foreign affairs. The balance of power, broadly accepted as the regulator of peace, had been ostensibly destroyed in the past decade. Frederick the Great of Prussia was going too far when he told a British envoy in 1785 that 'France, Spain, Austria, and Russia were in alliance'[1] – he was seeking a response. But France had alliances with Spain and Austria, and Austria an agreement with Russia, and the four powers could be said at least to be disinclined to take opposite sides. This in fact was all that such combinations were generally meant to achieve: the interests of the members were always complex and partly divergent. There were certainly signs of strain in the summer of 1784. The Spaniards, so much the junior partners and never the easiest of allies, rather resented the French. The French were not on good terms with Austria, particularly over developments in the Low Countries, where the Emperor, as ruler of the Austrian Netherlands, was trying to extract serious concessions from the Dutch. The French, again, had traditional close ties with Sweden, Russia's rival once more in the Baltic; and neither they nor the Austrians had buried their fears of Russia in eastern Europe. But apart from the quarrel in the Low Countries, which had not yet reached a decisive point, there was no real sign of a break in their watchful accord; and the fact might hold various implications for England. It gave Russia a freer hand against the Turkish Empire, in which we were beginning to show some interest. It did nothing to discourage her influence in Poland, though that was still of remote concern. And it supported Austria's ambitions, and perhaps even French pressures, in Germany, where George III, as Elector of Hanover, was likely to feel himself involved. Even France's opposition to the Emperor in the Netherlands, a not unwelcome fact in itself, was designed to strengthen her position in Holland, to which we could scarcely remain indifferent. For most of the century, the Low Countries and Germany had been two of our three main interests in Europe, the Baltic being the third; and the Low Countries of course had concerned us vitally for longer than that. While there may therefore have been no issue on which Pitt was obliged to commit himself, there were good reasons for him to consider seriously 'how to lay the foundations of . . . Connections' abroad.[2]

Carmarthen continued to propound his ideas, partly in Cabinet as Pitt had suggested. He wanted to cultivate Spain and Austria, and restore good relations with Russia; and meanwhile, as he had urged, to explore the prospects with Prussia and Denmark.[3] This of course was a counsel of perfection, but events over the next few months coloured

1. Cornwallis [Special Envoy to Prussia] to Carmarthen, 20 September 1785 (*Correspondence of Cornwallis*, I, 201).
2. P. 468 above.
3. See *Political Memoranda of Leeds*, 106–13. The wooing of Spain is not mentioned there, but it appears in Carmarthen's correspondence from the end of 1784.

his hopes, particularly in the North. The key here was Denmark, which had recently become very friendly to England, since a struggle for power had ended in favour of the young heir to the throne, himself manipulated by the powerful Count Bernstorff with whom the British envoy, Hugh Elliot, had thrown in his lot. Denmark, as Carmarthen had reported, was now making overtures with the object of containing Sweden, herself on close terms with France. But the Danes would not offend the Russians, who in turn did not wish to offend the French as long as the Swedes did not move and France did not interfere with Russia's plans in eastern Europe. This was the position in the summer of 1784. But in September a rumour arose that the French and the Swedes had signed an agreement, whereby the former were given naval and commercial facilities at Gothenburg, commanding the entrance to the Baltic. The news, soon confirmed, seemed to offer an opportunity for bringing Russia into play. Carmarthen urged that England, Russia and Denmark should join in demanding an explanation from Sweden and France, and that an effort should then be made from this springboard to form a triple defensive alliance. Pitt was disposed cautiously to agree. He remained somewhat sceptical – he wanted some hard facts about Gothenburg, and he was doubtful how far Russia's co-operation might really extend. 'The Empress's politics' were unlikely to change. But this 'separate object' might not be unwelcome, and 'perhaps, if it is not imprudent for us to embark on It, It may without her intending it, lead to some more comprehensive and permanent Junction'.[1] He drafted his thoughts in October, which were sent off with the official despatch.[2] But the approach failed. The Russians, who at first had seemed alarmed at the Franco-Swedish agreement, soon began to have second thoughts, and by the time that the overture reached them they had made up their mind. They refused even to join in a demand for an explanation, which might only, as they said, precipitate an awkwardness with France. It was clear that Catherine the Great was not going to be so easily wooed.

But if one of 'the two Imperial Courts' had failed him, Carmarthen had hopes of the other. Austria indeed was, and remained for some time, his favourite object, for her alliance with France was known to be strained. In the autumn of 1784 there seemed a real chance that it might reach breaking point, for the Emperor seemed bent on imposing his main demand in the Netherlands on the Dutch. He had been putting them under severe pressure over the past three years, engineering frontier incidents, forcing them to vacate some of the old barrier fortresses, and making various territorial claims. But all these were pinpricks, designed to support his real ambition, which was to secure

1. To Carmarthen, 10 September 1784 (B. M. Egerton Ms 3498).
2. Endorsement in P.R.O., F.O. 65/12. And Carmarthen noted on his copy of the despatch, of 15 October, that it was based on Pitt's paper of the 13th (B.M. Add. Ms 28060, f. 165). The final official text is in F.O. 97/340.

free navigation of the estuary of the Scheldt, where the Dutch enjoyed control under the Treaty of Munster of 1648. This of course gave them the key to Antwerp, whose trade indeed they were slowly strangling, and the Emperor had now resolved to bring matters to a head. He made a final demand in August. It was categorically refused, and early in October the Dutch took an Austrian ship in charge on her way down the Scheldt. The Austrian Minister was at once recalled from The Hague, and it seemed possible, even likely, that war would be declared.

In that event, the French might well be involved. They had offered their good services earlier to the Dutch, they could scarcely disengage now, and in November they felt impelled to tell the Austrians that they would support Holland if necessary with force. Here then was a second opportunity by which England might hope to profit, even if Ministers could not hope to influence developments themselves. There was no real question of their mediation: they could hardly have offered their services earlier, for peace with Holland had been concluded only in May 1784. Nor would it have been easy to decide whom to favour, for support of the Dutch would have alienated Austria, and support of Austria put paid to any hope of countering French influence with the Dutch. Pitt and Carmarthen therefore agreed that they should wait and see.[1] But Carmarthen held out high hopes that events might play into our hands, for if ' the contending parties' had 'spirit to act up to their professions on either side, we probably shall be called upon by both'.[2] Pitt was not so sure. He responded to the crisis and its implications – not least in Asia, where our object was to separate the Dutch from the French.[3] He insisted on the rapid despatch of an envoy, not sent since the peace, to The Hague. But he doubted at the start if war would come, and he was inclined to think that France would reap the credit of a mediation, favouring Austria, which the Dutch in the end would accept gratefully for fear of something worse.[4] This was not in fact how things worked out, but he was right in forecasting that there would be no war. The trouble dragged on, and in the early summer of 1785

1. Copy of Carmarthen to Pitt, 8 November 1784; Pitt to Carmarthen, 9 November 1784 (B. M. Egerton Ms 3498).

2. To Sir Robert Keith [Minister in Vienna], no. 31, 23 November 1784 (F.O. 7/9).

3. He had indeed been anxious about this as early as April (to Carmarthen, 10 April 1784; B. M. Egerton Ms 3498).

4. Sir James Harris, duly installed at The Hague, recalled this 'prophecy' of Pitt's – 'I shuddered when I heard it' – in a letter of 11 January 1785 to Carmarthen (B.M. Add. Ms 28060, f. 229v). It must have been made before the end of November, when he set off, and a letter of Pitt's of 15 November (B. M. Egerton Ms 3498) suggests that Harris and Carmarthen, with William Fraser of the Foreign Office, may have dined with him on the 16th. Perhaps the prophecy was made then.

Forecasts, however, could naturally be shaken by the swing of events. On the 10th, and again on the 22nd, Pitt was by no means sure what the outcome would be (to Temple; Grenville Mss, Box 117, Henry E. Huntington Library, California).

the Ministry, stimulated by reports (which proved to be misleading) that Prussia might intervene, brought itself momentarily to suggest a joint mediation. But it was a half-hearted move, and it had no bearing on events. As a result of French mediation, Austria finally received a little territory, a sum of money in lieu of more, and possession of the Scheldt for some miles below Antwerp. But she was denied free navigation in the estuary, and the Dutch rights survived, to become in due course a question of burning importance to Europe.

The Austrian Emperor had found the climate unsuitable to his venture. Russia gave him tepid support, Prussia as always was un-friendly, though not committed, and he was unwilling in the last resort to face a hostile France. But his slow retreat was eased, and indeed he hoped might be turned to advantage, by another plan which he trusted that France would accept. It was an old idea, now revived – no less than the exchange of the Austrian Netherlands for Bavaria. The Elector was to surrender his territory to Austria, receiving the Belgic Provinces in lieu as a sovereign prince: he would gain a commer-cially more valuable possession, and Austria would consolidate her power in Germany and Italy. French approval was necessary to counter the hostility of the heir to the Electorate, and to offset the probable reaction of the other German princes.

The Bavarian Exchange was a matter of some importance, and embarrassment, to England. It was not very welcome in itself, for it would place in the Low Countries a prince ill fitted to counter French influence, particularly if he had been brought in under the shelter of France. But there was a more awkward complication for a Ministry trying to cultivate Austria; for if the German princes opposed the scheme, Hanover might be involved.

The King of England's Hanoverian policy was a matter on which his British Ministers could not claim to give advice, unless they were asked for it or a question was raised needing Parliamentary sanction or official action. If he chose to take a certain line as Elector, there was normally little to be done. George I and George II had been closely involved in German politics; and George III, though much less so, was not the man to abandon his constitutional rights. The consequence was shown in 1785. When news of the proposed Exchange had been digested – and despite a strong Austrian denial that it was proposed – the German princes began to consult, under the eagle eye of Frederick the Great. By July, Saxony and Hanover had agreed to join Prussia, and a League of Princes, the *Fürstenbund*, was formally set up. Other German states later joined this defensive alliance, which included a secret article providing for armed resistance to the Exchange. The Austrians of course were angry, the more so as they had in fact now virtually dropped the plan because the French ended by opposing it; and the Russians, anxious in any case to support Austria because of their eastern policy, were also perturbed at a Prussian success, at a

473

time when relations between the two countries over Poland were in a state of uneasy equipoise.

The British Government could not expect to escape the results. It was all very well for Carmarthen to say – as indeed was true – that we were not involved, and still sought a *rapprochement* with Austria and Russia. There was every excuse for not believing him, or pretending not to believe. It may have been rather hard that 'having . . . been totally in the Dark with respect to the Progress of the . . . Negotiation' of the *Fürstenbund,* his explanation that 'Hanover & England are not entirely synonimous' should have been received as 'rather *Athanasian* than clear or satisfactory'.[1] But, as another member of the Cabinet observed later, 'it will not do to say that England . . . may take a different part. How can it?'[2] There had indeed been no consultation; Carmarthen and Pitt had not pressed the King, and the Cabinet was not asked for, and did not give, advice.[3] 'I fear our Master', remarked Carmarthen, 'is got into a d-d Scrape'.[4] But it was one from which the Ministry could not hope to disengage itself.

The shadow of the *Fürstenbund* had already been cast by then. The negotiations were carefully watched, and the Austrians and the Russians soon reacted. When the British Minister in Vienna was told in March to ask privately for information on the Exchange, he received a snub the effects of which lasted for the rest of the year. Nor did the British fare better when, acting on a strong hint from the Russian Minister in London, they decided in June to ask the Empress to intercede with the Austrians, and open talks for a triple alliance. They were met with polite generalities, and a tacit refusal of anything more. By the late summer, there was therefore little hope of weaning the Imperial Powers from their French connexion.

In his approach to Russia, Carmarthen had hinted that, failing a reasonable response, we might have to turn towards Prussia. It was an obvious gambit, but it was not entirely untrue. We had said the same

1. To Thurlow, 5 August 1785, reporting a conversation with 'the Imperial Ministers' in London (B. M. Egerton Ms 3498).

2. Richmond to Carmarthen, 30 December 1785 (P.R.O. 30/8/151).

3. This seems to emerge fairly clearly from Richmond's letter, written after the damage was done, in which he announced that he would state his views 'if ever it becomes a Question of Cabinet'; from Carmarthen's letters to Pitt of 25 or 26 December 1785 and 4 January 1786 (also in P.R.O. 30/8/151); and from the absence of any reference to the talks, while they were going on, in the King's correspondence with his British Ministers. When the Russian Minister in London complained of the treaty, after it was signed, Pitt forwarded the papers to George III, remarking that although 'the immediate subject is not one on which it is within the province of your Majesty's servants to offer any opinion', they would be grateful for 'any more particular information' he might wish to give them. The King replied that he had acted solely in his Electoral capacity, and confined himself to sending Pitt copies of the answers already given to the Austrians and Russians from Hanover (*L.C.G. III,* I, no. 235).

4. To Thurlow, 5 August 1785 (B. M. Egerton Ms 3498).

a little earlier when rebuffed by the Austrians – 'if that House continues to be shut against us I shall perhaps be tempted to take my pipe & Sour Crout over the way'.[1] There was no great enthusiasm for the idea, either in London or at Potsdam: Prussia was regarded as a minor power, Frederick the Great was not trusted, and he for his part doubted the British Government's will to intervene in Europe. Nevertheless, he had held out guarded prospects of a closer connexion since early in the year, the British had sounded him briefly on Holland,[2] and as the German League was formed and his relations with Russia took one of their periodic turns for the worse, he decided, still cautiously, to see how the land might lie. The British, equally cautiously, decided to listen: neither Pitt nor Carmarthen wished to do more, and George III, despite the *Fürstenbund*, was suspicious.[3] The opportunity was provided by a visit of the Duke of York to Prussia to attend the summer manœuvres, attended by a small military suite which included Cornwallis. The General was authorised, as a Special Envoy, to hear what the King might have to say, and the interview took place in September 1785.

The result did not amount to much. Frederick made it clear that he did not think the time yet ripe for a fresh alliance, and indeed went out of his way to stress England's weak position. There was little prospect of the two nations challenging the Bourbon and Imperial Powers until that connexion had been further weakened and other states detached from its orbit. Meanwhile he was happy to regard himself as England's old ally,[4] and he looked forward to the day when 'Mr. Pitt['s] . . . abilities and integrity would restore his country to the importance which she had formerly held in the scale of Europe'.[5] So matters rested in the autumn of 1785.

Frederick the Great thus echoed the views which Pitt had held at the start. He also passed judgment on the Ministry's efforts over the past year. The conduct of those efforts had been unfortunate: Carmarthen was inexperienced and incompetent – the manner in which he requested information from Austria on the Bavarian Exchange invited a snub, as George III pointed out, and his subsequent approach to Russia

1. Copy of Carmarthen to Keith, Private, 12 April 1785 (B. M. Egerton Ms 3501).
2. Pp. 472-3 above.
3. I think this is suggested in Pitt to Carmarthen, 31 August 1785 (Egerton Ms 3498). It is explicitly stated in Carmarthen to Cornwallis, 2 September 1785 (P.R.O., F.O. 64/8). For the King's feelings, see Carmarthen to Thurlow, 5 August 1785 (Egerton Ms 3498).
4. He was referring to the treaty of alliance of 1756.
5. Enclosure in Cornwallis to Carmarthen, 20 September 1785 (*Correspondence of Cornwallis*, I, 203–4).

was made in a thoroughly maladroit way.[1] On the whole, he played a weak hand badly. But of course the hand was very weak, and it would have needed a combination of wisdom and luck to have made much of it. If we had thought out more rigorously the implications of the trouble in the Low Countries, and – even without trying to mediate – made our views known in good time, we might perhaps have led the continental powers to think that we were again interested in Europe. If Pitt had exerted himself over the *Fürstenbund*, its effects might have been reduced, or spared. But it would have taken a Minister of real weight and experience to have tackled George III on such a subject, and Pitt was hardly likely to venture at a time when he was hoping to win the King's support for his bill on Parliamentary reform.[2] He was content to let matters take their course in a delicate case; and the same applied to the Netherlands' dispute, in which indeed we might have done more harm than good. The facts in Europe were against us: so at first was the position at home. No foreign Court believed for some time that Pitt's Ministry would last, and even then few were certain that the young man would prove effective. And how in any case could the Government expect to achieve a substantial advance? There was a good deal in the view, held in Vienna, that 'important Events must give an accelerating Impulse . . . before any essential Alteration of System can be reasonably expected'.[3] England was paying the penalty of failure in war and financial weakness, aggravated by her 'inattention' and 'haughtiness' in earlier years. It would need 'unremitting Exertions in the Cabinet' to offset the results.[4]

But Pitt was not prepared at this point to provide those exertions – and, on the evidence, success lay beyond Carmarthen's scope. He saw the obstacles very clearly, and, as matters were handled, events could be said to have proved him right. He was intent on other concerns which rightly were more important to him: on the finances and India in 1784, on Parliamentary reform and Ireland – above all Ireland – the next year, as well as on the range of commercial and Parliamentary business which was bound to take up much of his time. It would not have been easy, and he was not going, to spend great efforts in addition on what might well prove to be a modest return – and diplomacy

1. By refusing to make the request to Austria official, he had placed the British Minister in a very difficult position (see *L.C.G. III*, I, no. 198). And his decision – influenced by advice from the unreliable Russian Minister in London – to approach the Empress secretly, through the wrong adviser, was at once known to other Russians, and again severely embarrassed the British envoy.
2. See pp. 225–6 above. The critical period here was in March and April, exactly when the talks on the *Fürstenbund* began.
3. Keith to Carmarthen, no. 47, 5 May 1785 (F.O. 74/8).
4. Same to same, no. 52, 18 May 1785 (loc. cit.). The Emperor himself two years before thought that England had descended 'for ever' to 'the rank of a second rate Power like Sweden and Denmark' (Albert Sorel, *L'Europe et la Révolution française*, I (1885), 346).

responds so readily to personal qualities that an effort might have reaped a modest reward. As things turned out, no harm was done. 'Important events' in the next few years gave Pitt the opportunity to regain 'importance in the scale of Europe'. They fell in a particular way; had they not taken the course they did, the earlier 'inattention' might have had more marked effects.

II

Pitt's first persistent contacts with European powers (and persistence was all-important) were of a different kind. In September 1784, arrangements were put in hand to negotiate a commercial treaty with France. In November 1784, the ground was prepared for talks on a commercial treaty with Spain. In November 1785 a negotiation was authorised for a new commercial treaty with Russia; and before the end of 1786 formal talks with the same object were under way with Portugal and The Two Sicilies, and there was hope – then abortive, but finally realised – of a negotiation with Prussia. To these discussions were later added others with Poland and with Holland. In all, there were negotiations with eight European states for commercial treaties between 1785 and 1792.[1]

In one sense, this was a European phenomenon. Most of the continental states were pursuing such talks in this peacetime decade. Russia led the way, with six treaties and attempts at two more at least; as the British Minister in St Petersburg remarked in 1785, there seemed to be 'a Phrenzy for concluding Treaties of Commerce with this Country, which prevails throughout Europe'.[2] But France signed five commercial treaties or conventions on European trade, as well as one continental alliance including that subject; Spain signed two, and two alliances containing reference to trade in Europe; the Austrian Emperor, two commercial treaties (one in his Italian capacity); Portugal, Denmark, Sweden and The Two Sicilies (and the Duchy of Courland, and the towns of Geneva, Danzig and Hamburg) one apiece; and Portugal, Austria, Denmark and Sweden, as well as Holland, Prussia, Poland and Turkey, included continental trading arrangements in treaties of alliance or peace. There were also limited reciprocal agreements on specific commodities and specific ports.[3] Such results may be compared with

1. And others – with the Austrian Netherlands, with Sweden, and with Turkey – were considered more or less seriously in the same period. There were also talks which led to a treaty with Morocco in April 1791. For this subject see John Ehrman, *The British Government and Commercial Negotiations with Europe 1783–1793* (Cambridge, 1962), where full references may be found.

2. Op. cit., 97, n2. This figure does not include Russian peace treaties – with Turkey and with Sweden – in which trading arrangements were mentioned; or unilateral Russian declarations concerning foreign shipping or trade.

3. For all these, see Geo. Fred. de Martens, *Receuil de Traités . . . des Puissances et états de l'Europe . . . depuis 1761 . . .*, III-VI (1791–1800), and the *Supplément* by

those attained by this country. Of the eight British negotiations, only one – that with France – ended in a peacetime treaty; one other – that with Russia – produced a treaty in 1793 recapitulating the terms of an earlier, expired agreement.

Comparisons of this kind must be qualified, of course. Some of the Europeans' arrangements could have been made more simply – by orders, for instance, on either side –, and the full treaty form may sometimes have been adopted, as indeed the British Minister to Russia hinted, so that the negotiators could enjoy the valuable formal presents exchanged. The advantages moreover were sometimes more modest, and the detail less specific, than British Governments would have accepted, for trading agreements were always very carefully scrutinised in London. This was partly because commercial treaties in Europe were often promoted for diplomatic reasons, as counters in the international game or gambits leading to an alliance. In London, on the other hand, they were apt to be approached more strictly on their merits: mercantile interests made themselves felt, and Parliamentary approval had to be secured. In the 1780s, indeed, the Foreign Secretary complained that the process could be carried too far; we must not lose sight of 'the Necessity of strictly attending to our Political, at the same time that our Commercial Interests are the more immediate (though certainly not the more important) Objects of Discussion'. The results could operate in either direction. We might lose a diplomatic opportunity through commercial caution, or, as Carmarthen now feared, the 'present Rage for Commercial Treaties' might lead us, by awkward connexions, to 'sacrifice our Political Weight upon the Continent'.[1] He was writing partly in exasperation at the talks being taken out of his hands. But he had, or might seem to have, a case, for the trade negotiations were leading Pitt for the first time to think seriously about Europe; and indeed a few years later, almost in reverse of the continental practice, he constructed largely on their behalf an important diplomatic design.

At first sight, it might have seemed in the Government's interest to have opened the European talks itself. As Adam Smith remarked at the end of the war, increased trade with the continent might compensate for the loss of the American colonies.[2] Over the years 1781–5,'fo reign Europe' – the term used in the Customs ledgers, which excluded

Frédéric Murhard, I-II (1839). My figures are confined to agreements between European states concerning continental trade: they exclude unilateral declarations – sometimes important – of foreign privileges and rights, agreements with North African authorities and with the United States, and others between European powers relating solely to trade outside Europe.

1. To Alleyne Fitzherbert [Minister in Russia], 12 November 1786 (Ehrman, op. cit., 185).
2. See p. 159 above.

Ireland, the Channel islands, and Greenland or 'the Fisheries' – took just under 50% of the exports and re-exports from England and Wales, and supplied some 55% of the imports.[1] If regarded as a unit, it was the largest single entity in the British commercial system; and since the figures represented an adverse gap of some £2½ million, and the future of the American trade was doubtful, there was a real incentive to seek better arrangements. But in the event the first negotiations were pressed by foreign Governments, impelled by a desire to take advantage of England's misfortunes and force new terms of trade. This indeed was only to be expected, for throughout most of the century England had benefited from agreements yielding exceptional privileges in some of the larger markets. The victims had been trying for some time, not unsuccessfully, to whittle away the effects; now the occasion seemed ripe to negotiate afresh. The Spaniards and the French carried clauses in the peace treaties of 1783 setting up commissions with Britain to reach new commercial arrangements.[2] These were to be concluded by 1 January 1786, and it seemed unlikely that the obligation could be ignored.

The atmosphere indeed had already been shown while the war was still in progress; and, significantly, not by an enemy but by a neutral and traditionally friendly power. Since 1781 the Portuguese had refused to import Irish woollens and linens, and had been threatening to ban all Irish manufactures, rendered distinct by North's Acts,[3] so long as they claimed the same terms of entry as those enjoyed by Great Britain. This was worrying, for it might suggest to others the idea of restricting the newly freed Irish trade and treating it differently from that of England and Scotland. It was indeed an added argument, which may have appealed to Pitt, for bringing Ireland as soon as possible into the British commercial system. But it might also perhaps presage an attack on British trade itself, an attempt 'to oblige us to enter into a new Treaty of Commerce' at an unfavourable moment.[4] Unluckily for the Portuguese, such a threat was unlikely to have much effect. The volume of Anglo-Portuguese trade had long been shrinking, and with it the flow of bullion to this country, and apart from port wine there was little the loss of which would cause great distress. The trade in cotton from Brazil, soon to be so vital to the textile industry, was still quite small,[5] and opinion in London was therefore not unduly

1. Schumpeter, *English Overseas Trade Statistics 1697–1808*, tables V, VI. The figures exclude Scotland at home, and, up to 1783, the Canaries and Madeira (as well as the foreign West Indies and Florida, also belonging to European powers) abroad.

2. So did the Dutch, in the treaty of May 1784; but there the clause applied to Africa only.

3. P. 196 above.

4. The phrase is that of Robert Walpole, the British Minister in Lisbon, in December 1781 (see Ehrman, op. cit., 9).

5. See pp. 381-2 above.

disturbed. The dispute dragged on, attracting reprisals in Dublin. But Pitt showed no sign at first of attending directly to it.

Like so much else, in fact, the problem would have been changed by his Irish Propositions. When they failed, it came up again for review. In December 1785, the Portuguese proposed a stiff 'Plan definitif' for the Irish commerce; but this soon proved to have badly overshot the mark. For the British now decided to take the initiative themselves, over the whole range of the direct (i.e. non-colonial) Anglo-Portuguese trade. In January 1786 the Committee of Trade began a detailed investigation, on lines which were fast becoming common form. Figures were collected, merchants examined, legal opinions canvassed; the result appeared in September, when the Portuguese were given their long delayed reply. It was a restatement of earlier arrangements, brought up to date. Duties under the old treaties should be confirmed, the rest should be settled at rates no less favourable than those agreed with other favoured nations, the privileges of resident British merchants must be guaranteed, the controversial Irish woollens and linens admitted as before. The Government in fact was clearly feeling strong enough to move to the offensive. It had survived the aftermath of the war, the finances were improving, Ireland no longer took up its time, and there was now the opportunity – in fact the need – to consider questions of European trade. 1786 was the year in which Pitt turned seriously to examine the subject. The reply to the Portuguese suggested that he might prove fairly tough.

The British paper ended by remarking that it would be regrettable if 'in the general Arrangements of Commerce which He [the King] is now forming with the several Powers of Europe, it should happen that His old and faithful Ally should be the only one that was averse to open Her trade with His Dominions upon a fair and liberal System'.[1] Of the other 'arrangements', the first to be debated in point of time was that with Spain. On a first estimate, the prospects might not have seemed very propitious, for relations between the two countries had long been poor, not least in matters of trade. Since the end of the sixties, the Spaniards had been attacking British commercial privileges, in Spain itself as well as in their territories overseas. Most of our resident merchants had indeed left the country; our earlier favourable balance of trade was shrinking; and so, in consequence, was the earlier flow of bullion. Nevertheless, there were strong countervailing factors to be considered. The flow of goods was still considerable – in 1784, Spain was still Britain's fifth largest customer in Europe, and Britain the largest European customer of Spain. Old trading habits were not easily lost, there was still a fund of latent goodwill, and this indeed was coming to the surface within Spain itself, as a reaction against the

1. Ehrman, op. cit., 16.

implications of the French alliance. Friendship with Spain, too, was one of the objects of Carmarthen's policy, and he had no hesitation here about trying to help over trade. He was indeed, and long remained, the most earnest advocate of a commercial treaty; and since this, like all formal foreign business, had to be conducted under the Foreign Office, there was at least the promise that the ground would be well explored.

The peace terms made it likely that the Spaniards would make the first move. They did so in 1784, and in November the British appointed their Commissioner under the treaty. He was the elderly diplomat Ralph Woodford, who had once served briefly in Madrid, and was soon to be used in some of the other, minor, negotiations. He held his first meeting three months later with the Spanish Minister in London; but the British Government was soon absorbed in the Irish Propositions and other business, and it was September 1785 before the discussions really got under way. They began on lines laid down by Pitt, and Pitt was distinctly cautious – a good deal more so, it would seem, than the Foreign Office at this stage. He made friendly noises; but he waited for details from the other side, and he was not prepared to make concessions in advance. The old trade treaties must remain in force until new arrangements were settled, 'whenever that may be'. The Spaniards would doubtless try to sell more manufactures (as distinct from produce) and this 'might perhaps be indulged at present without danger:- But it seems far from prudent to give any Encouragement to the Idea at least in the first Instance; And as to the Argument of Reciprocity, the different Circumstances of the two Countries, I think, furnish an Answer to that favourite Word'. Any reply that we might make must stress our complaints of their past behaviour, and call for redress, 'which I take to be the most of what We have to do'.[1]

The Spaniards were accordingly asked for specific proposals. But they too preferred to see the other side's cards, and suggested that the British might make some suggestions. These were duly sent, in December. But they were restricted, as Pitt had wished, to a list of grievances; and nothing much more happened for another seven months.

This perhaps was not surprising, for by the end of 1785 the festering 'Mosquito Shore' question in Honduras was coming to the boil.[2] It dominated Anglo-Spanish relations over the next six months, and no other negotiation could meanwhile expect to get very far.[3] But as soon as the issue was favourably settled, the British took up the earlier talks. Possibly they were encouraged by the outcome of the recent trial of strength; perhaps the concentration on Spanish affairs had roused

1. To Carmarthen, 12 September 1785 (loc. cit., 21).
2. See pp. 383–4 above.
3. The Spanish Philippine Company's approach on the Eastern trade, late in 1785 (p. 460 above), contained preliminary proposals only, and was not made officially on Governmental initiative.

fresh interest: certainly the course of the trade talks with France, which were under way by then, gave an added incentive for an understanding with Madrid. On the very day on which the Honduras Convention was signed, Carmarthen forecast that a 'Projet' for 'a commercial arrangement' with Spain would be ready in less than a fortnight.[1] This was optimistic; but the work was put in hand. The Committee of Trade was told to give the subject equal priority with the Project for Portugal, and despite the great pressure of similar business – for negotiations with France and Russia were also in train – Hawkesbury and Pitt studied a draft in August. The final version was soon ready, and Woodford handed it over on 7 September.

So, almost two years after the first conversation, detailed terms were ready for debate. The British paper was important, for it remained the basis of all subsequent talks.[2] It offered what it termed a reasonable reciprocity in both shipping and trade; the accompanying instructions to the British Minister in Madrid explained how the balance was reached. The proposals for shipping – 'most favoured nation' treatment[3] on either side in European and West Indian ports – would undoubtedly favour us, especially in European waters since the Spaniards' coastal marine was smaller than ours. On the other hand, the Spaniards would have the advantage in an exchange of non-colonial produce on the same terms, particularly in view of our recent measures against smuggling. Duties on colonial produce, and conditions of colonial trade, were to be regulated on a broadly similar 'most favoured nation' basis – an arrangement again likely to benefit us, though within the limits of Spain's restrictions on her colonies.[4] On the tricky subject of manufactures, which had lain at the centre of the talks with France, we would admit certain Spanish goods on duties no higher than those negotiated with that power, and others at 'moderate' rates, of which some idea was given. In return, British manufactures should pay specified duties (given in detail) on landing, which should then not be subject – as they often were in practice – to provincial additions. Resident merchants should once more be treated on the footing of earlier treaties; and arrangements were suggested in the event of war as well as for peace. These of course were fairly stiff terms. Given the conditions in the two countries – given British industrial growth – it was not difficult to guess where the balance of advantage might fall. British shipping would certainly benefit – a point taken by Hawkesbury,

1. To Robert Liston [in Madrid], 14 July 1786 (Ehrman, loc. cit., 23). 'Projet' or 'Project' was the name usually given to a paper containing formal proposals on trade to a foreign Government.
2. For the details see Ehrman, 24–7.
3. See p. 379, n 3 above.
4. I.e., in so far as Spain continued to channel Spanish American and Caribbean exports through her European ports (see p. 381 above), she would reap the advantage of the article governing European produce. For the position in the West Indies at this time, see pp. 337–9 above.

and equally well appreciated, as it proved, in Spain. But the proposals were more generous than those being offered to Portugal; and the Government was now genuinely anxious to receive an early reply.

III

Its attitude was influenced partly by the progress of the talks with France. For these had now reached the point of agreement, a treaty must then be submitted to the Commons, and it would be very helpful, politically and administratively, if Ministers could present it as part of a wider agreement.

Pitt had been no more anxious at the outset to take the initiative with France than with Portugal or Spain. The obligation to negotiate arose from the terms of the peace. This had not been opposed by the chief British negotiator at the time: on the contrary, he welcomed the chance to approach an old problem in a new spirit. In his view, a 'Liberal Peace' was essential to laying 'a foundation for a friendly discussion of reciprocal Commercial Interests'; and when the French and Spanish treaties were signed, he rejoiced to find in them 'the great principle of free trade'.[1] It is not difficult to see in these remarks the crusading spirit of Shelburne, eager in such a cause to force the diplomatic pace. Pitt, however, was not. His sardonic reference to 'the Argument of Reciprocity' may well have gained point from the memory of Shelburne,[2] and he preferred to avoid a discussion with France until he had tackled the problems nearer home. His personal connexions did not lie only with those disciples of Adam Smith who wished to apply the master's principles in every instance: if he had been Shelburne's protégé he was also the confidant of Mahon, who in 1782 had succeeded Pitt's other friend Rutland as President of the old Anti-Gallican Association, 'established for the encouragement of the Commerce and Manufactures of this Kingdom'.[3] That encouragement might now perhaps benefit from the establishment of new arrangements. Anglo-French trade (at least licit trade) had been on a modest scale throughout the century, and there might well be real advantages in a freer exchange. But France was the hereditary enemy, she was our most serious industrial rival, and it was essential in any negotiation to see that the prospects were carefully weighed.

Viewed in this light, the time was not ripe for talks in 1784 or 1785. The Ministry's behaviour was governed by the assumption. As soon as Pitt was firmly in the saddle, in March 1784, he found himself pressed to appoint a Commissioner by the terms of the recent treaty. It was

1. Quoted in Harlow, op. cit., I, 332, 448; and see p. 94 above.

2. P. 481 above. It is also suggestive that Eden, who was anxious to please, remarked to Pitt when talks were under way: 'You may smile at observing there is no such word [in the first French paper] as "reciprocity" or "reciprocal" ' (17 April 1786; Ehrman, op. cit., 49, n 1).

3. Loc. cit., 28, n 4.

difficult to refuse, and one was duly named. But the choice was not very promising – it fell on a certain George Crawfurd, who was not to be taken very seriously and whose identity indeed remains obscure – ; he was sent to Paris only in September, without any formal instructions; and soon afterwards, it seems, was told to keep out of the way.[1] This in fact proved impossible, for the French were determined to make proposals, and when these evoked no response various import restrictions were put into force. But the British remained quiescent, and in the autumn and early winter it would have been reasonable to forecast that the business would soon come to an end.

The prospects indeed looked fairly bleak. 1785 was not a good year for Anglo-French relations. British foreign policy, in so far as it existed, was devoted to weakening French influence, and if it was half-hearted in practice the intention was clear enough. In the autumn, moreover, there were growing signs of trouble in Holland, where the interests of the two countries were fundamentally opposed, and France was furthermore known to be discussing new trade arrangements with Holland and with Russia, doubtless at our expense. On the other hand, Pitt now felt more free to attend to the subject of European trade, and he had to think of the consequences if he made no move. The negotiating period with the French was due to end on 31 December;[2] it was quite possible that they would then increase the restrictions on British imports. Their example might even be copied by Spain, which had so far refrained. It was therefore only prudent to reanimate the talks. Some such thoughts as these must have carried the day, for there was a sudden flurry of activity in London, and on 9 December – three weeks before the terminal date – Crawfurd was told to ask the French for an extension of five months.[3]

At the same time, the unfortunate man found himself relieved of his commission. If he had known what was going on at home he would not have been so surprised. For an altogether greater figure had recently come on the scene, with excellent qualifications for the post – and serious disqualifications for others. Ever since he had played a leading role in defeating the Irish Propositions,[4] William Eden had been bending his considerable energies to seeking a Government appointment. He soon appreciated (as North indeed told him)[5] that their victory was not going to topple the Ministry, and he thereupon decided that if he could not beat them he had better join them. He approached Pitt in September, and negotiated through the next two months. He

1. See ibid, 30. He was probably a member of the Scottish family which had long done business in Holland; there are some letters from James and from George Crawfurd to the Foreign Office in 1791, on Dutch remittances and banking activities, in P.R.O., F.O. 97/247.
2. P. 96 above.
3. Not six, as stated in Ehrman, op. cit., 32.
4. See pp. 207–9 above.
5. Pp. 235–6 above.

could plead some perfectly reasonable arguments, as far as they applied. In the absence of a firm party structure, there was nothing extraordinary in a politician joining an Administration which he had been attacking – the attacks indeed were often a signal that their author was bargaining for a place. Nor did opposition in one instance imply the need to oppose in others. Measures were to be judged on their merits, not necessarily by their origin; and this certainly applied in those cases – large in number – which centred on normal non-party business. Eden was a distinguished 'man of business'; he had much administrative experience; and such men often looked to the system of government, and the King as its head, rather than to any specific political group. 'You are not', he had been told recently, 'an Opposition man by nature';[1] and this was perfectly true. Eden knew his worth, and, quite naturally and properly, he was seeking opportunity to exercise his talents.

But there was another side to the case. For Eden was not simply a man of business. He had been acting at least since early in 1783 as a prominent, ambitious politician, and acting moreover with a connexion that went farther than any other in its definition of party. It seemed singularly inappropriate for one who had been working so closely with Fox to plead traditional arguments of non-party behaviour. His overtures to Government, too, were made entirely on his own account; he did not pretend that he would bring over any of his friends, and the Foxites thought of themselves, and tried to act, as a group. Perhaps Eden could claim that he was not really a Foxite – he had come into the Coalition originally from North's side.[2] But that was water under the bridge after the events of the past two years. He was in fact 'ratting', by the standards of the day; and it was not surprising that his behaviour was sniffed at where it was not condemned.

Most of Pitt's colleagues, in fact, were distinctly cool to the new recruit. Pitt himself, however, was prepared to accept him. Eden was an able man, and the Ministry was not overflowing with talent; he had shown his value in opposition; and if he could be absorbed without too much fuss it would be foolish to turn him down. Pitt thought at first of the Speakership (which seems rash) or some post – perhaps a new one – to superintend financial and commercial reform.[3] But there were legal and political difficulties, the reaction was generally hostile, and meanwhile the prospect of talks with France was coming to the fore. Eden was very well fitted for the task, much better than any one else in sight.[4] His appointment was settled in December, in the rank

1. John Foster to Eden, 17 September [1785] (quoted Ehrman, op. cit., 35).
2. Pp. 207–8 above.
3. For the latter, see p. 283, n. 3 above.
4. George Rose later asserted that 'the sole Motive in that Case was getting the very fittest Man in the Kingdom to settle the Commercial Treaty with France, We having no one Friend of Government we could send' (to Pretyman, 27 November 1801; quoted Ehrman, loc. cit., 38–9). All in all, I think one may accept his statement of the final position.

and salary of a Minister, accredited for the purpose of the commercial negotiation.

He set to work at once, under the aegis of the Committee of Trade. While Jenkinson sifted the evidence on Portugal, Eden was 'passing *every* morning . . . in examination' on France.[1] By the end of March 1786 he was ready to cross the Channel, taking with him a clear indication of the different merchants' and manufacturers' views.

It could not have been easy in many cases to foresee the result of enlarging a trade which had run on a small scale, or been virtually closed, for most of the century. Not all those concerned, moreover, volunteered or were asked to attend the investigation. Pitt was very anxious, after his experience with Ireland, to avoid being faced by a single organised voice, and he instructed Eden to 'give as little employment or encouragement as possible to the Chamber of Commerce [properly, the General Chamber of Manufacturers] collectively'.[2] The separate interests were therefore treated as separately as possible, and the weight of representation varied somewhat as a result. But as the weeks went by, a picture began to emerge. Each industry and trade of course had its own demands and reservations; but most of the major sections were in favour of going ahead. The tanners and leather men, the hatters and the paper hangers, the Spitalfield silk weavers and the producers of bar iron, were by and large opposed; the West Country clothiers and the wine merchants were divided or doubtful. But the rest, in differing degrees, saw a balance of advantage in a freer exchange, and the hardware and cotton men of the midlands and north – the organised opponents of the Irish Propositions – seemed at this stage to have the fewest doubts. Not many of them were prepared to lift all restrictions: other continental ties had to be considered, no one European trade could be divorced from others, and even those who felt that 'undampted, unchecked and untaxed' they would be 'equal, if not superior, to any other manufacturer in the world',[3] were concerned not to give away the advantages that made them so. The great ironmasters and the Yorkshire woolmen, for instance, who in general were firmly in favour, insisted that the export of machinery and skilled men should be discouraged. They and their fellow supporters in fact were moved by the argument that had led them to fight the idea of a freer trade with Ireland: they expected to sell their goods more cheaply than their rivals, as the result of lower costs. So long as care was taken to mould the terms to that condition, and not prejudice sales elsewhere, they were content – some of them eager – to test a larger market.

1. To Morton Eden, 27 January 1786 (*A.C.*, I, 94).

2. Quoted by Witt Bowden, 'The English Manufacturers and the Commercial Treaty of 1786 with France' (*The American Historical Review*, XXV, no. 1, 28). See pp. 208–9 above.

3. See p. 206 above.

The Government was bound to consider these views, which indeed were not far removed from its own. Pitt himself was thinking along much the same lines. It was well worth exploring a new industrial outlet, since the opportunity was there; it would be satisfactory, as always, to ease the rigidities of the old system. We should embark on the effort in good faith. We must also see that it was carefully handled, that recognisable advantages were held and all possible objections taken into account. For Pitt was not going to give much away without a very clear return. He was still smarting from his defeat over Ireland; he was determined not to make another false move; and in any case Ireland and France were two quite separate matters. The whole point of the earlier scheme had been that it was a domestic and imperial question: the incorporation of the Irish trade on a new basis would directly aid British strength. Here we were faced by a foreign power which was also a direct competitor – far more obviously so than Portugal or Spain. 'Reciprocity' again had a different setting; again, it could not be taken as a blanket term; and there were not the same considerations as those applying to a British possession.

> I have always considered [Pitt told Eden, when the detail came to be reviewed] the general idea of abolishing on each side every hostile and invidious distinction . . . as perfectly right in itself, and a good foundation of proper settlement. But I have a great doubt whether the situation in which France has put herself does not make this principle fallacious in the application of it in the present case.[1]

This was not simply the result of pressures from forces that he had found, or was finding, too strong. It was inherent in his thinking on the matter of power and wealth.

This blend of policy and temperament underlay Pitt's reactions throughout the talks.[2] Within its limits – on its basis – he combined with Eden to see the business through. Their situations were different – Eden's fortunes hung on success in France, Pitt was determined not to risk failure in England – and there was the natural shift of vision, intensified by Eden's anxiety and drive, between the Minister in London and the man on the spot. This indeed was soon apparent, for Pitt's caution was soon roused by proposals from France, which were despatched within three weeks of Eden arriving in Paris. They contained the draft of an agreement in principle – the principle of 'reciprocity and mutual convenience' – which should be signed at once,

1. 10 May 1786 (*A.C.*, I, 481–2).
2. I should perhaps say here that, following wider study, I have brought the considerations of policy rather more to the fore than in my earlier book on the commercial negotiations, where I placed the emphasis more strongly on Pitt's reaction from his Irish defeat. It is a question of balance; both elements, I am sure, were present.

leaving the detail to be negotiated thereafter. All mutual prohibitions (that is to say, where a third party was not involved) should be abolished immediately, though the arrangements need not all be put into effect for a year; pending that limit, there should be a provisional reduction of duties, and the treaty should remain in force for a decade.

This was directly contrary to the British approach. The reasons for the proposals lay in the political conditions in France. For whatever their original expectations, the French proponents of a treaty were now on delicate ground. There were still good reasons to press for an agreement, at a time when the British economy was still perhaps vulnerable – though it was recovering fast. Increased trade and lower duties might embarrass the British talks with Portugal and Spain; and the bait of economic advantage might even be used to induce Pitt to stand aside in Holland – a danger which the British Embassy in Paris at least took seriously. On the other hand, the French economy itself was now posing growing problems. The finances, strained as always by war, had failed to recuperate, and the important wine trade was in a period of crisis. One could argue from this that a treaty with England was all the more desirable: that the wine trade must increase its exports, and that low duties on a wide range of goods would aid an ailing revenue by defeating the smuggler. One could also argue that it would now be dangerous to open the door to British imports which might easily flood an already vulnerable market. There was a sharp conflict of opinion, within the Ministry and outside. The Ministers in favour were not all-powerful, and they felt that they should move fast; but they were scarcely ready for talks on detail, for the necessary inquiry – unlike its British counterpart – had not been properly set on foot. They were therefore anxious to sign a treaty of principle, from which they might bargain in greater strength, secure from an immediate threat by their domestic opponents. The British Ministers, however, felt exactly the opposite. They were prepared for discussion on detail, they had consulted their relevant interests, and, unlike the French, they would have to defend the treaty in Parliament. They were therefore determined to seek a precise and full agreement, which could not be later argued or whittled down.

The French Projet thus stood little chance, and the British made their own proposals at the end of May. In return for agreeing to the principles of a mutual exchange on the basis of most favoured nations (a concession from their earlier attitude), they demanded the settlement of 'specific duties' in the treaty itself. They had their way in mid-June, when the French agreed to this procedure.[1] The prospects therefore looked much more hopeful, and Eden awaited detailed instructions. But, to his mounting indignation, nothing more happened for over a

1. And in so doing, yielded another important point. By accepting that the immediate settlement of the duties should be limited to 'mutual' cases, they conceded to the British the right to retain a preference on the Portuguese wines.

month. This in fact was rather surprising, for there was something of a lull at just this time. Ministers had recently been very busy. But the sinking fund and, more recently, the Navigation Act were now out of the way; so was the first shock of the debates on Hastings (Pitt had just emerged from studying the Benares charge); so was the climax of the Mosquito Shore dispute; and the drafting of the other commercial Projects – for Spain and Portugal and Russia – had not yet begun. The Parliamentary session was nearing its end. But this in itself always involved a certain amount of tidying up, there was still some other business to be seen to – the tail end (as it seemed) of the Mosquito Shore affair, and the reorganisation of the Committee of Trade; and given the limits of administrative capacity, the order of priorities was significant. Ministers let the paper for Eden take its turn because they reckoned it could afford to wait. They were no more disposed than before to rush matters of detail, and when the instructions were sent they were fairly tough. The Government was prepared to reduce the rates on French wines by over a third – which still left them higher than that on port wine. It proposed lower duties on many French products, including manufactures. But it prohibited the import of silks and re-served its position on glass and pottery, and it drove a fairly hard bargain on some of the main British manufactures. Eden, already perturbed by the news that Jenkinson had studied the draft, was naturally upset. 'The whole paper', he told Pitt, '... varies so much from the principles of all the preceding parts of the negotiation, that my heart sunk desperately from the first perusal'.[1] Nevertheless he admitted that, on this basis, he might make 'a very good and plausible' case,[2] and he set to work at once with his usual skill. The negotiations went on without pause, in close consultation with Pitt. At one point in the middle of August, Eden wrote three despatches and three long letters to London in one day. Difficulties arose until almost the end; some were still being argued on the eve of agreement. But on 26 September the treaty was signed at Versailles.

The result may be said to have been a triumph for the British cause. The French succeeded in settling the duties on their oil and vinegar at rates lower than had first been proposed, and, above all, the duties on their wines at the rates 'now levied' in England on those from Portugal. They also carried an article allowing free carriage of goods by either party if it was neutral in a war in which the other was engaged. But some of these gains were less real than they might have seemed. There was still nothing to stop the British from further reducing the duties on Portuguese wines – which in fact they soon did; and they agreed to the apparent abandonment of their traditional principle on neutral trade because they did not believe that either party would ever stand aside in a war involving the other. In return for such

1. 25 July 1786; *A.C.*, I, 147.
2. Ibid.

concessions, moreover, they carried most of their points. They managed to exclude French silks, though not glass or pottery, and secured special arrangements for Ireland – a point dear to Pitt; the reciprocal duties on manufactures opened greater opportunities to Britain than to France; the free entry and terms of residence for merchants again favoured British enterprise; and the terms for shipping in European waters pleased the Committee of Trade.[1] Ministers were in no doubt where the balance of advantage would lie. The 'issue to this business', Pitt told Eden, was 'far beyond our most sanguine wishes', and the Foreign Secretary, who had been suspicious throughout, confessed his surprise that France had been 'induc'd . . . to acquiesce so far in our wishes . . ., as she actually has done.'[2] It was an achievement which, they could feel, should be proof against attack from either extreme. They could point on the one hand to an enlargement of trade, a 'Liberal Commercial Policy', in an area hitherto virtually closed.[3] Had not Adam Smith reckoned that before the American War the lowest effective duty on the bulk of French imports was 75%? Now a much greater range could enter at reasonable rates, and 'smugglers' need no longer be 'the principal importers'.[4] Free traders might applaud. But so might their opponents, for the treaty answered the gloomy prediction that 'in the case of a free trade between France and England, . . . the balance would be in favour of France'.[5] It was pretty clear that in this instance the weights fell the other way. A carefully defined result had in fact been secured. Shelburne himself (now Lord Lansdowne) could defend the treaty as recognising the fact that 'the idea of estimating the balance of each trade was given up'. 'Commerce, like other sciences, had simplified itself'. His old opponent Sheffield could write with equal approval, 'on the first blush', that 'the reciprocity is all on one side, for I have not discovered . . . a single advantage the French have gained'.[6]

Why indeed had the French signed the treaty, and signed it so soon – for by any standard the negotiation was remarkably quick? It was a question which was asked in France increasingly over the next few

1. For details, see Ehrman, op. cit., 60–2. The treaty was to be in force for twelve years.
2. Pitt to Eden, 16 October 1786 (*A.C.*, I, 165); Carmarthen to Daniel Hailes, 29 September 1786 (P.R.O., F.O. 27/18). Carmarthen wrote in similar vein to some other envoys abroad.
3. Pitt's phrase (see p. 275 above), in his notes for the Budget speech of 1792, looking back to the 'Causes of rapid Encrease since the Peace'. It followed the note, 'Extension of Markets (French Treaty. State of France).'
4. *The Wealth of Nations*, I, 438.
5. Ibid.
6. Lansdowne in the Lords, 1 March 1787 (*P.R.*, XXII, 75); Sheffield to Eden, 4 October 1786 (*A.C.*, I, 163). Sheffield later changed his mind.

years. The answers have already been suggested : the state of the wine trade, the need for revenue, the commitment of certain Ministers; and one may add Eden's skill and persistence, in a cause vital to his fortunes. If it had not been for this combination, Pitt might well have given up. As it was, he seized his chance, moving confidently and with care. He avoided his earlier mistakes over Ireland; the whole operation was strictly controlled. Jenkinson later paid tribute to the administrative process.

> The Stipulations of this Treaty [he told his son] were formed under the immediate directions of the Committee of Privy Council for Trade: Their Sentiments on every Point were however submitted to the King's Ministers, who made such Alterations as appeared to them to be proper; and every Article of the Treaty was drawn with the Assistance either of the King's Advocate General, or the Attorney and Solicitor General; so that no Business was ever concluded with greater prudence, or on higher Authority.[1]

There spoke the expert. He could have added that the same prudence was exercised in a wider context: that the merchants and manufacturers, consulted in advance, were successfully held in play at the finish, and that Pitt took the business, on completion, commandingly through the Commons.

Pitt indeed was master of the field. He had been personally in charge at the London end, and he remained unruffled by the national and Parliamentary debate. He was fortunate, of course, in having Eden this time on his side; there was no one else in Opposition so well versed in the subject. But even Eden might have been hard pressed to make out much of a case, for the most important interests in England, Scotland and Ireland had been carefully taken into account.[2] There is no evidence in official papers, or Eden's correspondence, that leading merchants or manufacturers were consulted while the talks were going on; as in other instances, they were confined to giving their views at the start.[3] But the whole tenor of Government's policy had been in harmony with those views, to an extent in fact that eventually raised its own complications. For while the treaty pleased the larger interests of the midlands and the north, it did not remove the fears of the original objectors. Since these were mainly smaller men they were rather slow to organise, and the first articulate reaction was one of high approval. Pitt

---

1. Earl of Liverpool to Lord Hawkesbury, 31 May 1802 (quoted Ehrman, op. cit., 43).

2. For the care taken over the Scottish and Irish manufacturers, see Hawkesbury to Eden, 3 September 1786 ; loc. cit., 183, n 2.

3. The one possible exception might be Josiah Wedgwood, to whom Eden occasionally wrote from France. But only occasionally, and then to ask for facts rather than for comment or advice.

and Eden were flooded with congratulations, manufacturers passed laudatory resolutions, Consols rose, Opposition newspapers found little to say. This was too good to last. By the end of the year the hostile pamphlets were appearing, and the General Chamber of Manufacturers was split, the larger northern and midland industrialists facing an attack by some of their smaller competitors and a variety of interests centred largely on London. In February 1787 the larger men were indeed defeated on a vote. Many of them resigned, and the General Chamber, whose potentialities had once seemed so significant, virtually ceased to exist for the next seven to eight years.

This was unlikely to worry Pitt, who was no friend to the Chamber. He was the less perturbed by the end of February, because the Parliamentary debate was fizzling out. Opposition indeed had great difficulty in finding a popular cause – a defence of the tanners, the hatters and the clockmakers was not going to shake the Government. Fox and his colleagues fell back on the implications for the trade with Portugal, and to a lesser extent with Spain, and, increasingly, on the general danger of a closer connexion with France.[1] But apart from the Whig Bishop Watson of Llandaff in the Lords, no comprehensive attack was developed, and Watson succeeded only in provoking a crushing reply from Lansdowne. The debates continued into March, but the result could be clearly foreseen. Meanwhile Eden was engaged on the business of settling points of interpretation. It was still not an easy task, for both sides were trying to cover their positions: the French Ministers, increasingly assailed by their manufacturers, to save what they could, the British pushing their advantage as far as they dared. In point of fact they dared a good deal – more than Eden himself expected or wished. They not only had their way on most of the disputed issues, and forced better terms for the Irish linen trade, but – a new point at this late stage, perhaps provoked by the Parliamentary debates – they also secured an agreement allowing them to reduce the duties on Spanish wines (unlike those on the French) to the rates settled 'at any time' on the Portuguese.[2] These last two demands came from Pitt.[3] They drove home a bargain which was put into force when the ports were finally opened in May 1787.

1. This is a broad statement. Of course they made the most of any possible economic argument, and supported, though with little effect, petitions from the objectors. They also derived some sustenance from the belated fears for agriculture which some of the country gentlemen rather hesitatingly expressed. But they were forced back more and more on the possible diplomatic implications.

2. Cf. p. 489 above.

3. 'On the Spanish Point . . . I have obtained everything that Mr Pitt can possibly wish; but with as much pain and trouble as Mrs Eden or Mrs Rose ever had in Child birth' (Eden to [George Rose], 26 March 1787; quoted in Ehrman, op. cit., 69, n3). He considered that on the Irish point 'We are glaringly and grossly unfair in our Pretension'. He had earlier settled the disputed duties by a supplementary Convention. Pitt seems to have been assisted on the Spanish wines by Grenville (undated draft of despatch in the latter's hand, in P.R.O. 30/8/196).

In the course of the Parliamentary debates, Pitt made a statement which has been much quoted and admired. Replying to Burke, who had been accusing him of looking at great national questions in a counting-house spirit – of neglecting possible national dangers for purely economic considerations – he observed that 'To suppose that any nation could be unalterably the enemy of another, was weak and childish. It had neither its foundation in the experience of nations nor in the history of man.'[1] The sentiment was hedged at once with the necessary provisos: our 'watchfulness' and 'defensive preparations' would not be weakened. But since Pitt was speaking of France, it was an unusual remark. Fox said that it would have amazed Chatham; it must certainly have worried the Foreign Secretary. Of course, Pitt was deliberately raising his sights in answer to a gibe which may well have roused him. But the statement cut clean across the normal grain of foreign policy. It was not only Fox who proclaimed that France was a natural enemy; Carmarthen was equally convinced, and was saying so loud and clear. She was 'our natural and inveterate rival', to whom we must never lose 'one single political advantage, where the Views of the two Countries must necessarily clash'.[2] He judged every event from this premise, it was one that was widely accepted, and the commercial treaty did not change his mind. On the contrary, it 'revived, if not confirmed' his suspicions, for the terms were so much in our favour that the French must surely have some ulterior motive.[3] It lay no doubt in Holland, and this was not the time for conciliation, whatever the advantages in the purely economic field. He felt – he must have known – that he lacked the Minister's confidence, and at the end of the year, goaded by a piece of incivility, he was talking of resignation.[4]

Carmarthen was frightened that Pitt, having so far shown little interest in foreign affairs, was now going to approach them on the basis of a purely commercial policy. He continued to have anxious moments over the next few months. The conclusion of the French

1. 12 February 1787; *P.R.*, XXI, 175. Although these words have often been quoted, however, they were not widely published at the time. Newspaper reports seem to be sparse. But none of those I have seen gives this passage, and neither does Stockdale in his contemporary collection of the debates (I, *Fourth Session of the Sixteenth Parliament*). W. S. Hathaway, however, took *P.R.*'s text for his 'authorised' edition of Pitt's speeches (see Note on Sources to ch. III below); so did Tomline; *P.H.* followed their authority; and biographers since have done the same.

2. Carmarthen to Alleyne Fitzherbert, Separate and Confidential, 23 June 1785 (P.R.O., F.O. 97/340); to Harris, 1 December 1786 (B.M. Add. Ms 28061, f. 393).

3. Carmarthen to Harris, as above; to Hailes, 29 September 1786 (F.O. 27/18).

4. Letters between Carmarthen and Harris, December 1786; B.M. Add. Ms 28061, ff. 392–3, 398–9, 413–15. The incivility had itself been provoked by the commercial talks. Pitt had insisted on Carmarthen presenting the Portuguese Minister at Court – as protocol demanded – at a time when Pitt was anxious to show goodwill to Portugal (pp. 495–6 below), although Carmarthen was not well.

treaty led Pitt at once to take up the negotiation on India; and while this could scarcely be greeted as a sign of weakness, and the result in August 1787 was highly favourable, there was a possibly more ambiguous overture in the spring. For Pitt then suggested to the French a mutual reduction in naval manpower,[1] at a time of critical importance for British policy in Holland. The proposal could easily be defended: it might help to lower a rising temperature; it affected the running costs, not the strength, of the fleet; and, following the Government's failure a year before to gain a Parliamentary grant for the fortifications at Plymouth and Portsmouth,[2] its acceptance might suggest that French expenditure on Cherbourg, now under way, was an unnecessary financial drain. But the offer – which was not accepted – could also be seen as another sign that Pitt had not yet grasped the dangers in Europe, that he still placed economy and commercial advantage above the stern demands of the balance of power. Such fears in point of fact were soon to prove unfounded, though they might well not have seemed so then. Pitt was already making up his mind about Holland, and Carmarthen exaggerated his attachment to commercial agreements. Of course he was ready to reach them if the terms were right. But he had proved distinctly cautious, and if the issues were considered on their own merits their very isolation from other diplomatic questions meant that their effect might be slight. The commercial talks were leading Pitt, for the first time, seriously to take account of Europe, to do business with European Courts and hear European points of view. But his policies in general were still unformed; they were not always affected by his hopes for continental trade; and where these were influential they were indeed not always pacific. Among the congratulatory addresses on the French treaty of 1786 were some verses by the poet William Mason, a former Fellow of Pembroke and the author of an earlier ode to Pitt.

> Thy father's fame with thine fair Truth shall blend.
> His vigour saved from foreign foes the land,
> Thy prudence makes each foreign foe a friend.[3]

Within the next five years Pitt was three times on the brink of war; and on the last of these occasions, in central and eastern Europe, considerations of power were closely linked with his European commercial plans.

1. See p. 313 above.
2. See pp. 517–19 below.
3. To Wilberforce, 2 April 1787 (*Correspondence of Wilberforce*, I, 31).

I V

As Ministers had foreseen, one of the main lines of attack on a treaty with France was the possible effect of our trade with other countries, above all Portugal. 'Memory' Woodfall warned Eden that this was going to 'prove a bone of contention all through the debates';[1] and so it did. 'The State of the Trade with Portugal' was raised by Opposition as a necessary preliminary to considering the treaty, and the two subjects were thereafter frequently taken together. Government had hoped to avoid this danger by reaching an agreement with Portugal beforehand. It was also anxious to settle likely queries arising from the agreement with France, before Pitt turned, as he now wished, to tackle the consolidation of the Customs duties.[2] At the beginning of October 1786, soon after the British Project reached Lisbon,[3] the Portuguese therefore learned to their surprise that a special envoy was leaving London with powers to negotiate a treaty.

The parallel with the French case was underlined by the nature of the envoy's appointment. Like Eden, he was sent as a Minister 'for the sole purpose' of a commercial negotiation, working jointly with the British Minister on the spot. But with an eye to the Parliamentary session, he was given a much tighter timetable – only till the end of November –,[4] and the envoy himself was not of similar standing. He was in fact a senior clerk of the Privy Council, William Fawkener, one of the two secretaries of the new Committee of Trade: an able and knowledgeable man of a certain influence, whom Pitt was later to employ on a greater matter,[5] but clearly not carrying Eden's guns. He sailed at once, reaching Lisbon late in October.

It would have been a remarkable feat to have reproduced the success in France. After five years of battling unsuccessfully over the Irish trade, the Portuguese had been confronted by distinctly stiff proposals on a larger subject, followed by a special envoy coming to ask for a treaty within a few weeks. There was really little ground for hope, as Fawkener soon discovered. His hosts, never noted for speed, were in no mood to help. Their main concern, naturally enough, was rather to see if

1. 3 February 1787 (*A.C.*, I, 170).
2. P. 271 above.
3. See p. 480 above.
4. The overriding importance of the Parliamentary session was stressed by Camarthen when the appointment was made (Ehrman, op. cit., 70, n 1), and also by the British Ambassador to France, the Duke of Dorset, in a letter to Eden from London, where he was on leave at the time (*A.C.*, I, 392).

5. By 1791, at any rate, he was in a position to plead with Pitt Hawkesbury's claims to join the Cabinet (Fawkener to Hawkesbury, 25 April 1791; B. M. Add. Ms 38226, ff. 142–v); and he then rose to fame as Pitt's envoy to St Petersburg in the ill fated Ochakov affair.

they could not exploit the sudden British anxiety by gaining time, as Fawkener himself put it, 'to knock at other doors'.[1] They managed to avoid meeting him almost entirely for over four weeks, by which time they knew he was due to leave – though here their hopes were disappointed, for the Parliamentary timetable was delayed and he was able to stay another month. In December they had to talk. But they then confined themselves to stating detailed objections to the British Project, and returned to the Irish trade, which they seem to have decided once more might be used as a test case. For they now offered to accept the Irish linens if Irish retaliations on Portuguese goods were removed and the Irish duties on their wines cut to a third below the new rates on the French. The response on the wines, they may well have reckoned, would be a useful earnest of England's intentions; and after much correspondence with Dublin, at an already anxious time,[2] agreement was reached in the spring. The original dispute was thus settled at last. But there was nothing else to show for Fawkener's mission, which ended when he sailed home in January 1787.

With its failure, the British reverted to something like their earlier position. Anxious as they had been for a settlement, it was to be on their own terms; and when these were ignored, and the Portuguese indeed were suspected of conniving with Opposition during the debates on France, Ministers reacted strongly. Pitt sent for the Portuguese envoy in London, and, flanked by Carmarthen and Hawkesbury, 'insisted with Menaces on a complete Redress of all the Grievances of the English Merchants'.[3] The 'menaces' may have referred to the old preference on Portuguese wines, which the Government was thinking of restoring as the French treaty allowed. It decided in the end to do so, and port remained the Englishman's drink. But the concession was a useful weapon, which was brought into play in the following autumn, when another effort was made to learn the Portuguese views. For despite their irritation, the British, having taken up the business, were not prepared to let it lapse without another try, and in September 1787 they suggested some minor conciliatory modifications to their Project. At the same time, however, they threatened to cancel the preference on wines; and, whether in response to the stick or the carrot, the Portuguese made a conciliatory move. There was a series of meetings in Lisbon in the winter. But they petered out early in the new year, the British envoy could not renew them, and by the end of 1788 the negotiation seemed to be dying.

This in fact was the case. There were no more serious talks before the

1. To Carmarthen, 1 November 1786; quoted Ehrman, op. cit., 71.
2. See p. 492 above.
3. See Ehrman, op. cit., 90. The only account of the interview (or there may have been two interviews) is at third hand, from the British Minister in Lisbon retailing the Portuguese version. But since no one in London seems to have commented on it, it was presumably not far wrong.

war. The British made another, not very pressing, effort in 1789, when the Portuguese Minister in London left to become Foreign Minister. But he proved as elusive as his predecessor, and despite intermittent prodding managed to delay any response for another year. When it came, moreover, it was depressingly vague, and a further series of meetings towards the end of 1790 failed to produce anything new. The talks went on in Lisbon into 1791; but once again, and this time finally, they faded gently away. When the French war began early in 1793, no real advance had been made on the Project of over six years before.

The Portuguese negotiation failed because neither side was under enough pressure. The Portuguese were anxious to retreat from an exposed position which Pitt and his colleagues could not consolidate, for there was no compelling reason why either party should agree to terms. The Spanish talks were a different matter, for both sides were really interested at times. Unfortunately the occasions seldom coincided, and then they did not last long.

In September 1786, when they despatched their Project, the British genuinely wanted a settlement with Spain. The Foreign Office hoped that a commercial treaty might be used to foster diplomatic relations, and Pitt was also anxious, as in the case of Portugal, to blunt a Parliamentary attack on the French treaty and pave the way for a comprehensive Consolidation Act. The Spaniards for their part seemed interested, not least because the French were pressing them for a trade agreement and they wanted to strengthen their hand. This of course could cut both ways, and friendly verbal assurances were followed by a much less forthcoming official reply. But at least it was made quickly, it contained positive comments, and (despite some hostile observations on their proposals for shipping) the British persuaded themselves that there might be a clash of interest on only two major points – cotton and fish. Towards the end of October, Pitt drafted a despatch for the guidance of the British Minister in Madrid, Robert Liston.[1] While resting firmly on the basis of the Project, it was a conciliatory document, for he was inclined to think that the 'Leading Principles' of the Spanish reply might 'well be attended to, without departing from the Essential Objects of the Treaty.'[2] The Spanish Foreign Minister, Floridablanca, told Liston in return that he intended 'to make every Concession in his Power',[3] and indeed he soon made a gesture on the difficult questions of cotton and fish. Pitt was pleased. The Commissioners began to make headway in London, and in January 1787 the business really seemed to be in train.

1. There is more than one copy of the ensuing despatch of 24 October. The draft, in Pitt's hand and dated the 23rd, is in P.R.O., F.O. 72/9.
2. Ibid.
3. Liston to Carmarthen, no. 72, 2 November 1786 (Ehrman, op. cit., 77).

But there was now another delay; and one that this time proved fatal. From January to March 1787 each side again waited for the other, and when the talks revived the opportunity had been lost. The fault, which was shared by both, arose purely from negligence, and a failure on the British part to appreciate the need to maintain the pace. For the course of events at this juncture underlined the significance of timing, particularly in the conditions set by eighteenth-century European Courts. Their routines, their movements and their pleasures could be vitally important in an age when energetic action was required to overcome the natural forces of inertia. And this was nowhere more true than in Spain, 'always . . . remarkable in keeping most matters in suspense . . . the school of patience', as one sufferer observed, 'for all those who have any business to transact with the Ministry'.[1] The greatest hope of decision lay in the fact that Floridablanca was now interested; for Floridablanca was very powerful, and could probably carry the day if he wished. But he was also notoriously mercurial, a prey to 'the irritability of his nerves',[2] and it was the more important to strike while the iron was hot. It was also a very good moment to do so, for the period of mid-January to early April was one of the few times of year when business might be brought to a point in Spain. The Court's stately movements from palace to palace, its rigid social and liturgical timetable, posed an administrative problem of almost insuperable weight. When the two Governments returned to the business the occasion had slipped away, and, as it proved, the best chance of meeting the very real difficulties had vanished.

This was the more unfortunate because the British were now prepared to go quite a long way. After waiting for 'an Answer in form', they sent a fresh detailed paper in March.[3] This offered a preliminary agreement pending a final settlement; some revision of privileges for resident merchants, and some modifications of duties. It made some concessions in the matter of silks, and hinted at others if necessary on cottons; and it proposed more attractive terms for Spanish colonial produce in return for assurances on the sales of salt fish. By way of compensation, the Government wished to see British shipping rights properly safeguarded, to ensure that Spanish provincial taxes (as distinct from customs duties) were effectively limited, and to include some disputable commodities – especially glassware – in the preliminary agreement. As a final bait, it reminded the Spaniards that it was negotiating a preference for their wines with France, and that if it should withdraw the preference on Portuguese wines – as was then being threatened – Spain would be in a uniquely favourable position.[4]

1. Sir Alexander Munro [consul-general in Madrid] to Carmarthen, no. 27, 30 June 1787 (quoted loc. cit., 79).

2. Liston to Carmarthen, no. 17, 2 April 1787 (loc. cit., 80). In a covering letter he called him 'nervish, hypocondriack, and naturally hot'.

3. On the 13th. Carmarthen to Liston, no. 4 (loc. cit., 81).

4. See pp. 492, 496 above.

These were the most conciliatory proposals made by Pitt in any of the peacetime commercial negotiations. To the Ministry's surprise, they had no effect. No one expected immediate agreement; but they did anticipate progress, and they were puzzled when Floridablanca answered coolly, and disappointed when he then fell ill. The official reply came in June; it confined itself to points of detail, and stressed Spain's determination to secure complete reciprocity in matters of shipping. As Liston gloomily remarked, we seemed to be back to the position of a year before. He wondered what had gone wrong; and we may do the same. It was true that there were serious obstacles to agreement, and the recent British curb on foreign trade in the West Indies cannot have helped.[1] It was also true that the French had now begun to press harder for a commercial treaty with Spain – which they secured the next year –, and the rising tension over Holland may have begun to play its part, for the Spaniards could scarcely afford to favour England too openly in a clash with France. Such pressures must have counted, after the delay early in the year. But in view of Floridablanca's real interest at that time (and no one in London thought he was bluffing), and given his temperament, one cannot resist the conclusion that their force was heightened by the delay itself. Of course the talks might well have failed, even if they had been energetically pursued. But a sustained impetus between January and April was their best – perhaps in retrospect their only – chance. It is tempting indeed to ask if Fawkener was not sent to the wrong capital. He had virtually no hope of success in Lisbon; might he perhaps have done better in Spain?

The story was not over yet: in fact it continued for another six years. Little more happened in 1787, though the British answered the Spaniards in the autumn, and the atmosphere lightened briefly when they triumphed in the Dutch crisis. But it soon deteriorated once more, with the prospect of a Franco-Spanish agreement, and when Liston's term of office ended in the spring of 1788 his successor found the business 'in a more hopeless State than if it had never been commenced'.[2]

That successor, however, was Eden, who was not the man to let a trade negotiation die. He set to work to revive it, at first without success. He got no encouragement from Floridablanca, and not much from London, where Pitt was occupied by other matters and the summer recess was at hand. This in turn was followed by George III's illness and the Regency crisis – a period during which all foreign business came to a virtual halt. One might indeed have thought that the talks would have sunk without trace by 1789. But, after showing every sign of doing so, they suddenly revived in the spring of that year. The

1. P. 337 above.
2. William Eden to Carmarthen, no. 5, 19 May 1788 (Ehrman, op. cit., 90).

reasons may have been partly economic – the Spanish Atlantic provinces were feeling the pinch. They were also diplomatic – the Spaniards were worried by events in France. They may even have stemmed
partly from the progress of another trade negotiation, between
Britain and The Two Sicilies (or Kingdom of Naples), which the
latter had been urging for at least a year and was now seriously under
way. If successful, this would encourage Italian exports of fruit and oil
to England, in competition with those of Spain; and indeed one of the
reasons for its encouragement in London had been to 'rouse the Spanish
Minister from his lethargy'.[1] Perhaps it was now helping to do so; at
any rate Floridablanca announced in March 1789 that he was about
to make further proposals, and these followed in April. They were
distinctly hopeful as far as they went, for the Spaniards suggested that
British East India muslins (mixed silk and cotton) might be admitted
in return for better terms for Spanish West Indian produce. This
seemed almost too good to be true, for such an arrangement would
offend both the French and the Spanish Philippine Company; nevertheless, while the British were considering the point, the Spaniards
passed the necessary regulations. Floridablanca furthermore suggested
in the autumn a more 'friendly correspondence' between the two
countries, in which case trade arrangements would doubtless follow suit.[2]

All this sounded promising, though Eden himself had left Spain in
the summer, to take up his post in Holland and another commercial
negotiation.[3] But the promise soon withered, for Floridablanca's power
was in fact declining, and early in 1790 the Nootka Sound crisis arose.
By the summer the two countries were on the brink of war. But as soon
as the worst was over the persistent exchanges began again, and this
time it was the British who took the initiative. In an uncertain European
scene, in which the Spaniards were increasingly doubtful of France,
Ministers did not wish to deepen what had been a dangerous rift. As
on the occasion of the Mosquito Shore dispute, Pitt was sensible in
success. Shortly before the Convention on Nootka Sound was signed
he drafted fresh instructions to the new Ambassador, Fitzherbert,
accompanied by Projects for an alliance and a trade treaty.[4] Little
happened for some time; but in July 1791 Floridablanca (whose power
had temporarily revived) suddenly responded to the offer of an alliance.
He was obviously worried by events in France, he even wanted Portugal
to be included, and the British saw the chance of a tripartite trade

1. Ralph Woodford to Carmarthen, 16 May 1788. The negotiation failed in 1790,
after being brought apparently almost to the point. Since Pitt was not personally
involved, its course will not be followed here. But it was quite an interesting affair,
whose fate reinforces the lessons of the other negotiations. An account appears in
Ehrman, op. cit., 155–67.
2. See loc. cit., 154.
3. P. 429 above.
4. For the evidence that this initiative came from Pitt, rather than the Foreign
Office, See Ehrman, op. cit., 155.

treaty as part of a general agreement. The Cabinet referred the commercial prospects to Hawkesbury. But it soon got a dusty answer. Hawkesbury's concern lay mainly with shipping, on which the terms had always favoured ourselves. He was not disposed to weaken them now, or indeed to take any marked initiative. So far as he could see, the old difficulties remained, and if agreement was to be reached it would be only because Spain was willing to pay for an alliance. This was a typically stern reply, and the Foreign Office was prepared to try harder. But it too, while welcoming an alliance, was not going to risk commercial advantage. Carmarthen had now been replaced by Grenville, and Grenville, though much more liberal than Hawkesbury, had been introduced to the Spanish talks as Vice-President of the Committee of Trade. His views were close to Pitt's, and his proposals resembled Pitt's of the year before. A consolidation, or an aggregate, of duties on our exports at 15 per cent; a further offer on Spanish colonial produce in return for reasonable terms on salted fish; the old proposals for cotton; no further concession on shipping – this was the sum of the last serious paper, sent in September 1791. It drew a Counter-Project five months later, in February 1792; and although this was the first formal paper that the Spaniards had yet produced on the subject (the rest comprised reports from British envoys, and Floridablanca's personal replies), the delay and the contents suggested another change of climate. In point of fact they reflected Floridablanca's final decline from power – either the views of his opponents or his own attempt to outbid them. The terms were decidedly stiff; there was no mention of the domestic provincial duties, and such offers as were made on imports were linked with substantial demands.[1] The British Ambassador called them an 'Ultimatum', and they marked the real end of the business, for Floridablanca was dismissed in March and his successor was far less friendly. The Committee of Trade rejected the paper, and while the old arguments were aired for another year, all hope of a peacetime agreement had finally disappeared. The British Commissioner, Ralph Woodford, was relieved of his appointment in February 1793, and when an alliance was duly concluded after the war with France began, the articles on commerce and navigation were confined to wartime convoy and trade.

So ended the negotiation by which the British had perhaps set the greatest store. At times at least, they appeared more conciliatory than they ever appeared with France. The Spaniards, too, had sometimes shown willing. But it proved impossible to clinch the matter: one side or the other shied away, or failed to move fast enough. Given the very real difficulties – Spanish fears of British industry, and the determination in London to foster British shipping – the vacillations proved fatal. The talks indeed, by their very promise, illustrate the obstacles to achievement, the ease with which it could be denied, the great efforts

1. For brief details see loc. cit., 170–1; for the provincial duties, p. 482 above.

needed for success. They point, better perhaps than any other instance, the exceptional nature of the Anglo-French treaty of 1786.

V

In December 1786 the daily newspaper *The Public Advertiser* announced, 'There never was in the country, or perhaps in the world, a Minister who was engaged in so vast, so intricate, so complete, and consequently so difficult an undertaking, as that which at present occupies the attention of Mr. Pitt. It is no less than a general arrangement of the commerce of the greatest commercial power that ever existed, with almost all the great commercial powers in the world; – with France, with Spain, with Portugal, with Russia, with Holland, and with America'.[1] This was misleading in tone – suspiciously so indeed, for a curious change had just come over the journal, from support for Opposition to enthusiastic support for Government.[2] The initiative in the first three cases had not stemmed from Pitt, though he had built on it since; the negotiation with the Dutch about the East, if it could be so called, was still confined to talks between Harris and the Company; the response to the United States was unfriendly and largely reluctant: the design in fact was not so 'complete' or purposeful as it might appear.[3] Nevertheless, there *was* a spate of negotiations in 1786; and not the least important was that with Russia, which claimed attention towards the end of the year.

As in the cases of France and Spain, the Anglo-Russian talks were set on foot by a treaty. The trade was regulated by an agreement of 1766 which had a life of twenty years, and as the time approached both sides began to think about the future. The British were anxious to start discussions, for diplomatic as well as commercial reasons. They wished to take the opportunity – the best perhaps since the war – of seeing if Russia was friendly enough to offer any real hope of weaning her from the French connexion. They were also eager to renew, and where necessary reinforce, terms of business dating originally from 1734 – when the Russians had signed the first purely commercial treaty they ever made – which still gave the British distinct advantages in a trade of whose value they were convinced. This appreciation might seem rather surprising, for there had always been an adverse official balance with Russia, and in 1784 the gap was over £950,000. It was indeed larger than ever before, and its extent reflected a growth in mutual traffic which might only increase the drain on bullion that had always been a feature of the Baltic trade. Why then sustain it? The

1. 13 December 1786.
2. It is so noticeable from November that one may suspect Ministerial pressure or inducement; though I have found no evidence for a direct subsidy.
3. See pp. 425, 372 above for Holland and the United States.

answers were partly traditional, but partly new. Russian naval stores and timber were still accepted as necessary for the fleet, and their transport, under the Navigation Acts, as a source of strength to British shipping. Such considerations of power had always outweighed those of wealth. But as the conception of wealth itself began to change, other arguments were heard. Shipping freight was seen more clearly as an invisible earning, to use a later term; and many of the Russian goods were now regarded as directly of value to British industry – a contribution rather than an obstacle to a true balance of trade. They were imports that appealed to the liberal economists, whose definitions were influencing enlightened officials. 'It is now understood', ran a report from the Customs on the Russian trade at about this time, 'at least by Wise Men, . . . that it is of more advantage to an industrious Nation to import the Materials of Manufacture, than pieces of gold and Silver; because such Articles as Hemp, Iron, Flax, &c. pass from the Importers into a thousand hands, who each gain a profit. . . . And, if the industrious classes of a country gain by any traffic, the Nation can scarcely be said to lose'.[1] This Smithian attack on bullionism seemed the more attractive because of the prospects for British exports. For their recent increase, responding as it did to the spread of 'civilisation . . . opulence and refinement, in Russia', was unlikely to slacken, and the immediate continuation of a direct adverse balance could be accepted for the sake of future gain. In this process, legal regulation had its part to play. For while natural conditions were doubtless chiefly responsible for the boom, the treaty arrangements 'must have had their effects'.[2]

The Russians approached the talks from a different point of view. They were anxious to revise the terms which the British wished to retain. They had already reduced the force of the old arrangements, despite British objections, by granting rights to other countries; they would now seek direct concessions, particularly on shipping. In the Armed Neutrality of 1780, during the American War, they had challenged British doctrine on neutral trade and contraband. They might well try to carry some of its provisions into a new treaty, and also (as they had done in vain before the earlier agreement) to force a relaxation of the Navigation Acts. All this was recognised in London. It therefore seemed the more important to take the first step, and make detailed proposals before the Russians snatched the initiative.

The Government's notice was drawn to the problem by the British envoy Fitzherbert, in March 1785. Carmarthen referred the matter to the Russia Company – though not the Committee of Trade – and forwarded its comments in the autumn. Fitzherbert by then had heard that the French were making progress on a commercial treaty of their

1. P.R.O., B.T. 6/141, f. 33 (quoted Ehrman, op. cit., 95). Undated, but almost certainly written in 1785 or 1786; author unknown, but almost certainly the Inspector-General, Thomas Irving.
2. Loc. cit., ff. 27–8.

own, and the Ministry, as so often, responded to this threat. It at once sent Fitzherbert powers to treat; the Russians agreed to set up a Commission; and the talks began early in 1786.

'There was,' wrote Byron much later,

> just then a kind of a discussion,
> A sort of treaty or negotiation,
> Between the British Cabinet and Russian,
> Maintain'd with all the due prevarication
> With which great states such things are apt to push on:
> Something about the Baltic's navigation,
> Hides, train-oil, tallow, and the rights of Thetis,
> Which Britons deem their *uti possidetis*.[1]

It was to develop in due course into something more – the incentive for an ambitious alternative design involving the neighbouring states of Poland and Prussia, and a plan for trade through central Europe as a weapon of Pitt's policy in the rising Eastern Question. But the start – and end – of the matter was much as Byron described it, and the 'prevarication' lasted some seven years. The first round was unpromising. Fitzherbert handed in a document of his own in February 1786, incorporating the existing arrangements and some of the Russia Company's comments on their infraction. If he hoped thereby to set the terms for discussion he was disappointed, for the Russians presented within a fortnight a Projet which entirely ignored his paper and, in tone perhaps more than content, came as something of a shock. The expected demands were all there, particularly on navigation and neutral trade; but they were stated uncompromisingly, in places rudely, and the atmosphere was bleak. Fitzherbert was inclined to shrug his shoulders: the Russians were trying to play us off against the French, and he thought in any case that we should have to make some concessions. But his view was not shared in London. There was a strong British tradition of friendship with Russia, shaken but not destroyed by her behaviour in the recent war, and the Foreign Office was keenly anxious to revive it. But there was also widespread opposition to paying a high commercial price, and the general opinion in mercantile circles was that we held the whip hand. The talks on the earlier agreement in the sixties had lasted a long while, and the Russians had given way in the end. They would probably do so again, French or no French, for they still relied greatly on British goods, and also on loans and credit from the resident British merchants. Such an assessment appealed to Pitt.

---

1. *Don Juan,* Canto the Tenth, stanza XLV. The exact dating of Juan's 'secret mission' to London on this business must be granted some poetic licence. But it falls within the Second Russo-Turkish War of 1787–92, so that the 'discussion' indeed applies to the negotiation with which we are concerned. Byron knew what he was about.

For Pitt would never have called himself, as his father had done, 'quite a Russ'. He was always sensitive to pressures in the Baltic, whether from Russia or anyone else, and he was beginning to be uneasy about her activities in south-east Europe. The Ottoman Empire, which she was threatening, was a factor in the Mediterranean trade and our links with India,[1] and Catherine's ambitions were of growing, if still rather distant, concern. The Empress had been unhelpful elsewhere in Europe, notably over the *Fürstenbund*.[2] And she had been personally unsympathetic – she approved of Fox, disliked George III, and thought little of his new Ministry. Pitt, involved in any case in other urgent business, was therefore content to let the Russians wait for a firm and detailed statement of the British case.

When this came, in mid-November, it was firm indeed. The Committee of Trade had been at work since late August, and Pitt himself increasingly from October. The usual processes were followed, the Russia Company taking the place in this instance of the General Chamber of Manufacturers. In a question so largely concerned with shipping, Hawkesbury's views were of course important, and they were prominently displayed. The result was sent to Fitzherbert in six despatches, some of considerable length. The tone was unambiguous. The Russian Projet might be taken as a basis for discussion; but the Government could not accept propositions 'many of which are inimical in the last Degree to the Political as well as Commercial Interests of this Country'.[3] We could not countenance any of the articles on navigation or wartime trade, we objected to some of the proposals on duties, and demanded in our turn an extension of privileges long enjoyed. The Russians, however, did not climb down. They were inclined to doubt the British determination, for, contrary to views in London, they reckoned that if trade was interrupted they might suffer least.[4] Their varied negotiations with other countries[5] had been designed at least partly to free them from dependence on England; they were having some success; and they now speeded up the talks with France. Fitzherbert received his six despatches in mid-December 1786. On 11 January 1787, a Franco-Russian commercial treaty was signed.

This only stiffened the British Government's resolve. They took no notice of some minor concessions which the Russians offered rather guardedly, and, with the willing support of the British merchants in St

1. See pp. 438–40 above.
2. Pp. 471, 473–4 above.
3. Carmarthen to Fitzherbert, no 15, 17 November 1786 (quoted Ehrman, op. cit., 107).
4. They were encouraged in this forecast of the British attitude by their envoy in London, Simon Vorontsov. It is hard to see why he reported as he did. Carmarthen was still using conciliatory language; but Vorontsov had long discounted his importance, and Pitt had made it clear, in a long interview on 11 November, that there was no hope of agreement as things stood (see loc. cit., 109, n1).
5. See p. 477 above.

Petersburg, decided to stand firm. Fitzherbert asked for home leave, 'having now no business of importance to transact',[1] and he left accordingly in August 1787. The negotiation lapsed with his departure. It might indeed appear to have died, for there was no further serious mention of the subject until early in 1790.

When it revived, it was in a rather different setting. For in the course of 1789 the prospect had begun to emerge of a rival commercial plan. It was not Government policy yet; but Government was interested, and towards the end of 1790 Pitt made the idea his own. The raw materials of Russia could be paralleled elsewhere – in the great alluvial plains of Poland, and the forests of Poland and Prussia. Naval stores and timber, hides, linen and grain were all to be had in abundance; and the two countries in turn might offer a promise of a wider distribution of British goods. The seaports of Prussia, and the rivers of Poland, opened on central and eastern Europe. They must in any case be considered together, for to an exporter the neighbours were indissolubly linked. The 'Eastern' trade, as it was known, had always been taken as an entity in London – the figures indeed were still shown as such throughout the eighties in the Customs ledgers – and recent developments underlined the fact. The First Partition of Poland, isolating Danzig, meant that all imports up the Vistula must pass through Prussian territory, and the other major Polish seaport, Elbing, had likewise passed into Prussian hands. This raised grave complications, for Prussia levied a high duty on goods in transit, as well as separate high duties and embargoes on imports for herself. If the British trade, therefore, was to be increased with an eye to lessening dependence on Russia, the Government must seek a reconciliation between the two countries, and fresh commercial terms with Berlin.

By 1789, it was in a stronger position to do so if it wished. One result of the Dutch crisis of 1787 was the Triple Alliance of Britain, Holland and Prussia in 1788; and this in turn had a direct effect on the Poles. For in the winter of 1788-9 the Polish 'Patriots' rose against Russia, and when the revolt proved successful they looked to the West. They wished to redefine their relations with Prussia; and now that the Prussians were connected with Britain, they hoped to involve her in their fortunes, as a mediator or even an ally. Early in 1789 the Poles approached London, to secure the Government's good offices and test the ground for a request to join the Triple Alliance.

The core of any Prusso-Polish settlement was the fate of Danzig. The transit duty on the Vistula traffic made the port largely useless to Poland, and the Patriots were prepared to cede it, with some neighbouring land, in return for a lower rate. But they also expected Prussia in that event to secure them the province of Galicia, belonging

1. To Carmarthen, no. 15, 15 April 1787 (quoted loc. cit., 111).

to Austria, which was known to figure in an ambitious scheme for territorial readjustment that Prussia, confident in her new alliance, now felt free to pursue. The Prussians, however, although the authors of the plan, would not commit themselves in a constantly changing situation; and the uncertainty affected the relations between the two sides. The British were in an awkward position; for while they wished to bring the two countries together, they were themselves trying to secure a stable settlement in central and south-east Europe. Russia was now once more at war with Turkey, and Austria had joined her. But if Prussia, sympathising with the Turks, was given a free hand, hostilities might spread. Europe was in a state of growing disturbance; the tension should be reduced, and peace restored on the basis of the earlier territorial *status quo*. Galicia therefore should be left alone. But the Poles seemed unlikely then to cede Danzig; and Prussia insisted on Danzig as part of any agreement.

The British therefore were cautious. They were not going to underwrite Prussia's ambitions, or become a party to territorial change. But neither did they wish to surrender the chance of a prospective commercial advantage if this could be gained without undue risk. They had recently assessed the possibilities, and were prepared to act if they could. The stimulus had come originally, as sometimes happened, from a man on the spot – from the British consul in Memel, James Durno, a timber merchant with useful Polish and Prussian connexions. As early as 1786 he had urged the Government to open a negotiation with Prussia, an idea which was taken up after Frederick the Great died in the summer. The omens indeed had seemed not unfavourable, for the new King Frederick William II professed liberal views, his chief Minister, Hertzberg, was friendly, and the Russian Projet had annoyed the British. Nothing happened, however, for the Prussians feared a flood of 'superior' imports against which they could set no proper 'equivalent' or 'competition.'[1] But the successful Polish rising opened up fresh vistas, and early in 1789 Durno visited London to report and give his views. He stayed in England for over six months, and saw everyone concerned – Carmarthen, Hawkesbury, Grenville, Dundas (his closest supporter), and Pitt. Opinions varied – Pitt himself remained anxious to distinguish between commercial and diplomatic involvement –, but there was general interest in the prospects which Durno conjured up.[2] These were indeed exciting – and in some respects prophetic. The consul saw three major objects for a commercial initiative: to secure an alternative source of supply for the naval goods from Russia; to capture two virtually new markets, one of which

1. Viscount Dalrymple [British Minister in Berlin] to Carmarthen, 9 March 1787 (quoted in Ehrman, op. cit., 116–17).
2. See loc. cit., 119–20. Dundas's support of Durno is shown by the consul's letters to him in National Library of Scotland Ms 1075, ff. 151–6. It looks indeed as if Dundas gained him his first interview with Pitt.

moreover would give fresh entry into Russia herself; and to prevent too great a transfer of Russian and central European trade to the south, where Russia was now established in force with the prospect of access to the Mediterranean. We should therefore negotiate a Prusso-Polish agreement, for trade in general and Danzig in particular, and – an early mention of an ominous design – seek to restore to the Turks by mediation the captured Bessarabian province and the port of Ochakov on the Black Sea. Ministers listened carefully, and Durno was sent back in the autumn of 1789 to provide more facts on which 'some Commercial Arrangements' might be based.[1]

The immediate result was depressing. Durno turned out to be a nuisance; he was indiscreet and self-important, and he annoyed the British envoys in Warsaw and Berlin. He did more harm than good. But the inquiries were frustrated in any case by the deadlock over Danzig and the Galician exchange. This continued through 1790, and the British hovered on the sidelines; but the inherent difficulties, and other priorities, kept them from doing any more. Towards the end of the year, however, the picture changed dramatically. The Government was involved from the spring to the autumn in the crisis of Nootka Sound – not the best time to consider raising complications elsewhere. But it was more free to look around after October, and above all to make up its mind about Russia; for in the intervening months the situation had grown much worse. The hopes of conciliation with Turkey, and a general settlement, were fast disappearing. Catherine had earlier seemed interested in keeping the options open, perhaps even in making peace in the south-east, partly at least because she was also engaged in a war with Sweden in the north. But her attitude hardened in the summer; she rejected an offer of mediation with the Turks, she was suspected of encouraging Spain in the Nootka Sound crisis, and she continued to resent 'the unparalleled Crime', as the British envoy put it, 'of [our] being the Ally of the King of Prussia'.[2] When she made a favourable peace with Sweden in August, the prospects began to look bleak. In the winter of 1790, Pitt turned his attention to Prussia and Poland.

He did so the more firmly because the commercial talks with Russia had died again. At the beginning of February 1790, when Catherine was offering terms to Turkey, a fresh Russian Projet reached the Foreign Office, as part of 'a Prelude to a still nearer, and more intimate connection'.[3] It was noticeably discreet on the vexed subject of neutral trade – the offending articles indeed were dropped – though the paper

1. Ehrman, op. cit., 120.
2. Sir Charles Whitworth to Carmarthen, no. 32, 1 June 1790 (quoted loc. cit., 128, where the reference should read P.R.O., F.O. 65/18).
3. Same to same, no. 10, 19 February 1790 (quoted loc. cit., 126–7). The paper, which seems to have been handed in by the Russian Minister at the beginning of the month, may in fact have been sent him earlier, and kept in cold storage till the moment was ripe (loc. cit., 127, n2).

was otherwise much the same as before. But it fared no better than its predecessor: the Committee of Trade remained sceptical, and the Foreign Office was no longer prepared to argue the case. They were fortified in their views by the course of the trade in the past three years. For the expiry of the old treaty had caused little distress – the flow of goods, in both directions, had actually increased, and in so far as any one suffered it had been the Russians. The British 'factory' in St Petersburg experienced restrictions; but these rebounded on their hosts, for the loss of British credits fell awkwardly in a period of war-time expense, and the growth of contraband traffic meant a loss of revenue. The rouble, weakening in the troubled conditions of 1788, had not fully recovered by 1790. In these circumstances, the British Government had no hesitation in rejecting the proposals.

When Pitt applied himself to the Polish question he was not therefore worried about the Russian trade, the importance of which in any case he was hoping to reduce. He took the opportunity of a visit by a Polish emissary to suggest a plan. If the Poles would cede Danzig to Prussia in return for a greatly lowered transit duty on the Vistula traffic, the terms would be guaranteed by Britain and Holland as co-signatories of a quadripartite commercial treaty. He held out the prospects of an increased trade, and of a settlement of British merchants in Poland who would bring much needed financial resources and industrial and agricultural expertise. The agent, Michel Ogínski, was impressed by the Minister's manner and his knowledge. He reported enthusiastically to Warsaw, and the interview was soon followed up. In January 1791, the British Government formally offered to bring Poland into the Triple Alliance, and the Prussians and the Dutch were asked to state their views.

With this initiative, the affair moved into a new stage. It became an element in Pitt's decision to force Russia to surrender Ochakov. The fate of that ill-starred venture is another story, the first chapter of the Eastern Question which was to remain a feature of British policy throughout the nineteenth century. But the commercial implications lay near its centre, and it was typical of Pitt that they should. The wheel indeed had come full circle.: 'Political' and 'Commercial Interests' were now joined in a balance that would have seemed unlikely a few years before.[1]

VI

The same conditions governed the second stage of the negotiation with Holland. The debate on neutral rights joined that on the Far East in the summer of 1790, when it was at once affected by the Nootka Sound crisis.[2] It continued in the setting of the Ochakov crisis, as part of a

1. See p. 505 above.
2. Pp. 430–2 above.

wider problem. We may therefore pause here to point some features of the earlier talks.

The first thing that may strike one is the extent to which their conduct depended on Pitt. This may be seen both positively and negatively. In 1786, when Projects for Portugal, Spain, France and Russia were all under way, he composed some and amended others of the chief despatches and the papers themselves.[1] He superintended every move in Eden's negotiation; and the same was to be true of the talks with Prussia and Poland in 1791. But the need for his interest can be seen equally in reverse. Without his active engagement no negotiation could hope to prosper – witness the cases of France in 1784–5, Portugal and Spain until 1786, and Prussia and Poland in 1789–90. Once he entered into the subject he was usually very much in charge, working, as was his habit, with a small group of colleagues and experts. George Rose, at the Treasury, does not seem to have been much concerned. Thomas Irving at the Custom House supplied facts and figures, and perhaps – it is hard to be sure – some advice.[2] William Fawkener was a reliable official at the Committee of Trade. William Fraser, the capable Under-Secretary at the Foreign Office, had a general knowledge of the talks, and Ralph Woodford acted in some of the London conversations.[3] On a higher plane, Eden of course was essential in France, and later important in Holland, and to a lesser extent in Spain. But he carried little weight for several years - he made his way under tolerance –, and policy was formed within a group of five: Pitt Carmarthen, Jenkinson (Hawkesbury), Grenville and, less specifically, Dundas. Of these, Carmarthen was the least effective; he knew nothing about trade, he was a lightweight in his own field, and one of his subordinates lamented the loss of 'that Dignity and conse-quence which his lasiness [*sic*] and Ld. Hawkesbury's Management has contrived to take from him.'[4] Dundas was not officially concerned before 1791 except as a member of the Committee of Trade, and his influence, occasionally apparent, was confined in strictly European questions to conversation. Grenville was more directly involved, as Vice-President of the Committee and Pitt's closest confidant on matters of trade. He had personal knowledge of France and Holland, he was if anything more liberal than his cousin, he spoke on the French treaty in Parliament, and his hand may sometimes literally be seen in the drafting of papers and despatches.[5] He helped to keep the balance with Hawkesbury. For Hawkesbury was important. As working head of the

1. For the evidence, see Ehrman, op. cit., 192.

2. On the lack of evidence, see loc. cit., 12, n1.

3. See p. 481 above for Woodford. He was employed in the talks with The Two Sicilies and with Sweden (pp. 500, 477, n1 above) as well as in the more important negotiation with Spain.

4. Bland Burges to Anne Burges, 13 October 1789 (quoted Ehrman, op. cit., 187).

5. Loc. cit., 190, to which may be added notes and comments in Grenville's hand in an untitled file in the Fortescue Mss.

Committee of Trade, and President from 1786, he was in an inherently strong position which he exploited to the full. He was in charge of the preliminary work on the four Projects of that year, and partly responsible for stiffening Eden in the French negotiation, he threw his weight in 1791 into the scales against Spain, and on two critical occasions determined the course of the Dutch talks.[1] His interventions were taken seriously – indeed they were often feared – and they reinforced a contribution which had helped shape the original proposals.

The effect was substantial enough for it not to be exaggerated. Hawkesbury, important as he was, by no means always had his way. If he tightened the demands on France, he was restrained from pushing them too far; the same applied to Spain, while a treaty still seemed attractive;[2] he hardly entered into the talks with Prussia and Poland, once they really got under way; and in some other cases in which he took a tough line he was not alone. In the case of Russia, indeed, he was if anything more conciliatory than Pitt, and in that of Portugal – and at times in that of Spain – not very much less so. His influence moreover was greatest in one particular field, that of navigation: he carried a good deal less weight in questions of customs duties and merchants' rights. It was significant that the one negotiation which he finally determined – the Dutch – turned so largely on shipping and neutral trade; and the fact reflected the views and the role of Pitt himself.

For the European talks strengthen the impression, gained elsewhere, that Pitt always balanced very carefully the terms for navigation against those for an exchange of goods. One may put it like this, for while of course a trading policy comprises both elements, if a contrast had to be drawn navigation was not allowed to suffer. Protection was not always interpreted rigidly; it had indeed acquired a new dimension, for the place of freight in an assessment of value had been developed by the liberal economists. But where concessions on shipping were made, as with France and, more indirectly, with Spain, it was with a clear equivalent or advantage in mind, and there was no giving way in doubtful cases or on major issues. Russia, Spain and Holland, like the United States and Spain again in the Atlantic trade, met with a blank refusal of their major demands. Pitt knew very well that 'Englishmen were much attached to their navigation',[3] and he never lost sight of the fact in any of the peacetime talks.

There was more scope for a liberal attitude once the goods had been landed. Here again one must be clear as to what Pitt would and would not do. Lower duties and a freer traffic were to Britain's interest wherever possible; they reduced smuggling, and they fostered a growing industrial advantage. Pitt was not disposed to protect manufactures,

1. Pp. 489, 501, 431–3 above.
2. And, even more obviously, to The Two Sicilies (see Ehrman, op. cit., 163–5).
3. P. 341 above.

or agriculture, more than he had to; he subscribed to a liberal interpretation of 'advantageous imports';[1] he eased and simplified where he
could. He intended to link his commercial treaties with a consolidation
of the customs; the protection of shipping against foreign competition
was combined with attacks on monopoly at home. Pitt tried to encourage the forces of growth.[2] But if freer trade was a potent weapon, it was
not the only one to be used, and it remained a means rather than an end.
The objects were to tap the natural aids to the revenue, and open up
channels for exports; and the methods could vary a good deal with the
case. 'He makes me understand my own ideas', Adam Smith is reported
to have said after meeting him in 1787, 'better than before'.[3] The work
of '*the* great ecletic'[4] has always been fruitful in its glosses; but Pitt
could well have pointed to the limits he set to a range of options which
he also invoked. Freedom of trade in his hands sometimes meant not
much more than freedom to trade. 'Reciprocity' – Shelburne's watchword – was viewed with caution;[5] it was a servant of expansion, and in
seeking the necessary outlets the emphasis might fall elsewhere. Pitt was
often quite content to repeat old exclusive demands. He fought hard to
secure distinctive privileges, particularly for resident merchants abroad.
He sought a clear gain in a balance of exchanges which he seldom
proposed initially himself. He never abandoned the concept of the
balance of trade. His object was to bring it up to date, to apply a more
liberal definition; and he established one working model in reversing
the policy of a century with France. He was moving into more open
conditions where he judged they suited the national interest. He did
so warily, selectively, and no faster than he thought it would stand.

The obstacles to agreement were real. The European Enlightenment
found it hard to digest the early fruits of British industrialism – it
perforce sought protection against the greatest dissolvement of a system
it wished to relax. No continental state was going to admit British
manufactures without strict safeguards, unless the need seemed very
pressing or it could expect an attractive *quid pro quo*. As the Prussians
remarked, the goods from England were 'so superior' in kind and
volume that there could be 'no reciprocity', for Prussia could offer 'no
equivalent'.[6] Other countries had more to exchange; but the Spaniards,

1. There is an undated incomplete draft on the subject in his papers, in P.R.O.
30/58/1.
2. It was even claimed later – on a remark attributed to Grenville – that he
would have abolished all customs duties if war had not broken out in 1793. For
some discussion of this unlikely possibility see Ehrman, op. cit., 194, n5.
3. Pellew, *Life and Correspondence of Sidmouth*, I, 151. The story, told later, is Addington's, at first hand. Although no date is given, the occasion must have been in 1787.
4. Jacob Viner, 'Adam Smith and Laissez Faire', in *Adam Smith 1776–1926*
(1928), 117.
5. E.g. p. 481 above.
6. Dalrymple to Carmarthen, 9 March 1787; quoted Ehrman, op. cit., 116–17.

the Portuguese and to some extent the Russians shared the same apprehensions, and even France was driven into a treaty which she feared in the end. One may wonder, indeed, how well other agreements would have worked had they been reached. As it was, the British trade with Europe recovered quickly from the war. Exports rose from some £5¾ million in 1783 to over £10¼ million in 1792, and the balance for this country turned from a deficit of some £2½ million into a surplus of almost £2 million within the same decade.[1] If all the treaties had been signed, and the effects had been as the British hoped, how long would the weaker industrial nations have accepted a flood of imports? The French were soon blaming their growing distress on the 'disastrous' treaty of 1786; and while they were in fact almost certainly wrong – for the causes lay deeper – the accusations were significant, and might well have been repeated elsewhere. It was genuinely hard to reach detailed agreement when the prospects so often seemed unequal; and Pitt was not interested in arrangements that did not promise specific results.

These inherent difficulties gave greater play to those affecting any transaction at the time. The course of the negotiations points very clearly the diplomatic and administrative factors involved. One gains a vivid impression of the strength of the forces making for delay. The talks with France were completed in nine months, once they began in earnest – and those that followed on India in seven months.[2] But this was altogether exceptional: the Portuguese negotiation continued on and off for about eleven years, the Spanish and the Russian for almost eight, the Dutch for almost four, even the Polish and the Prussian (and the Sicilian) for two. Of course any matter of this kind is apt to be protracted – one can show instances from other ages; and there were some conditions favouring swift agreement, given the will or the need – when so much turned on personalities within small groups, decisions could be reached surprisingly quickly. But this was no sure foundation, and if a chance was not firmly grasped it would be lost all the more effectively in the normally ample deliberations. Timing was very important, as the fate of the talks with Spain suggests. The pace of communications, the pace of life, were natural impediments to speed, and every country could show peculiar features of its own. The inflexible timetable of the Court, and the inadequacy of the departmental system, in Spain; an equal rigidity and lassitude in Portugal; the uncertainties of Court politics in France; the fragmentation of power in Holland, chaotic rivalries in Poland; absolutism in Prussia and Russia,

1. Cf. Schumpeter, op. cit., tables V and VI with Ehrman, loc. cit., Appendix, tables 1, 2 and 3. This was not in fact a very startling achievement – though allowance must be made for the growth of sales to other parts of the world. In the early and middle seventies British exports to Europe had run at an annual average of £8½ million, yielding a favourable balance of some £3¾ million. But it was precisely the return of this state of affairs that continental Governments hoped to prevent.

2. P. 441 above.

where the ruler's will, or lack of it, was decisive – these various, sometimes contrasting, factors had always to be taken into account, and they
underlined the lesson, so familiar from the classic manuals for princes,
that there is nothing inevitable in the conduct of state affairs.

The English system had its equivalents. Some were purely administrative. The Foreign Office staff, small by the standards of the greater
western European powers, could easily find itself hard pressed. Twice
indeed, in 1787 and again in 1789, the Clerks took the unusual step of
asking for a rise in salary, because of the 'extraordinary exertions', often
into 'the midnight hours', occasioned by 'the Commencement of the
late Commercial Negotiations in particular'.[1] The department was
quickly overloaded, and its communications system was inadequate,
for there were not always enough Government messengers to carry the
despatches by the quickest route. Some distant capitals, indeed,
scarcely saw a British messenger at all: Liston in Madrid remarked
that the arrival of one in 1785 made 'a great impression', and according
to Sir William Hamilton in 1793 none had been seen in Naples for over
twenty-eight years.[2] Correspondence was often sent by the slower and
less reliable medium of the post, by Hanoverian couriers, or the returning
messengers of foreign powers. Such arrangements derived from a state
of affairs in which British envoys were often left largely to themselves:
in 1792 William Eden told his younger brother, who had just become
Minister in Berlin, that when Parliament was sitting and there was no
foreign question of immediate anxiety, 'it sometimes happen[s] with
respect to Missions even of the first rank not to receive a Syllable in
six Months'. 'When there is real Business to be done', he admitted after
watching Grenville at work, 'it is always attended to'.[3] But in foreign
affairs, quite as much as domestic, the paucity of resources in London
combined with the natural tempo to restrict the number of issues
tackled at a given time.

Eden stressed the effect of the Parliamentary session. It was certainly
noticeable in the course of the commercial talks. Occasionally it
could stimulate the efforts, as with Spain and Portugal in the autumn
of 1786;[4] far more often it was likely to interrupt them. Carmarthen in
1785, and Rose a year later, pleaded, 'the Business of Parliament' as a
cause of delay with France; Fitzherbert did the same to the Russians
in 1786, Carmarthen to the Dutch in 1790, and Woodford to Spain

1. Quoted Ehrman, op. cit., 186–7.
2. Loc. cit., 197–8.
3. Loc. cit., 201. He also recounted the experience of Sir Robert Keith,
returning home after a long spell in Vienna, who was 'under the utmost Astonishment at having been twice to the Secretary of State's Office without finding a single
Soul there, & at learning from the Door Keeper that the Principal was gone into
the Country for five or six days'. Perhaps Keith would have done better to have
gone at night, for in 1789 a regulation had been introduced that one junior Clerk
must be in residence then.
4. See pp. 495, 497 above.

in 1792.[1] The best season for all but the most pressing foreign business
was in the autumn and early winter, when Ministers and officials
returned from their holidays during the recess. It was thus peculiarly
unfortunate in 1788, when several negotiations were in progress, that
George III's 'malady' should have begun in October. The King was
not in fact involved very much in the various negotiations – there is
almost no mention of his views in the papers concerned. But he had
normally to be kept informed, no treaty could be made without his
consent, and in his absence 'the Springs of Government' virtually
ceased to play.[2] Envoys were warned not to expect 'particular or precise
Instructions' until his recovery, or alternatively a Regency, could
'restore that Part of the Constitution to its usual Energy & Effect'.[3]
An interruption of this kind, exceptional – indeed unique – as it was,
was the most dramatic of many obstructions in a process always open
to mischance. Given all the circumstances, it is perhaps not surprising
that agreement should so often have proved elusive. For they placed a
premium on will and effort, and few of those concerned, including
Pitt, wanted or needed results badly enough at any one time.

1. See Ehrman, op. cit., 200-1.
2. Woodford to Carmarthen, no. 7 [?], 11 March 1789 (quoted loc. cit., 162).
He was referring to the talks with The Two Sicilies.
3. See loc. cit., 199.

CHAPTER XVII

The Crises of Foreign Affairs: the Low Countries to Nootka Sound

I

When the Austrian Emperor Joseph II remarked at the close of the American War that England had fallen to the rank of a second rate power,[1] he voiced a view which he and his fellow European rulers continued to hold for the next three years. The abstention of Pitt's Ministry from continental issues seemed to confirm their judgment, and it was supported by the Minister's apparent personal lack of concern. Even after it was generally accepted that he was probably there to stay, he was widely regarded as no more than 'un financier impolitique'.[2] This was a judgment of 1786. By the end of 1787 it was being revised.

Of course there was considerable truth in the initial assumption. Pitt knew and cared little about European affairs at the start. He wanted to avoid continental entanglements, his interests lay elsewhere, and it took a good deal, when the time came, to make him risk his first confrontation. He carried his hopes of non-intervention as far as he possibly could. But he was not unduly pacific by nature, or prepared to yield where he thought he could stand – his early reaction to American protests on the vexed question of the northern frontier foreshadowed the later examples of his instinct to hold, and advance on, tenable ground. His object in the middle eighties was to gain a breathing space, to nurse a domestic revival; and he followed a course in which personal inclination and policy combined. When the first period of crisis arose, he could point – many did – to the results. He still had no acknowledged European partner; but Parliament was quiet, the finances looked healthy, and he enjoyed the fruits, one British envoy told him, of having 'concluded a permanent Alliance with that most formidable of all Powers, the Power of Surplus'.[3]

Prosperity is the ultimate basis of a successful foreign policy. But the

1. P. 476, n4 above.
2. See p. 280 above.
3. Hugh Elliot [in Denmark] to Pitt, Private, – August 1788 (P.R.O. 30/8/132).

immediate guarantee may have to be armed strength, and the two may conflict. In achieving a surplus Pitt was anxious to keep down the costs, and there was all the traditional reluctance to spend too much on the armed forces in peacetime. He kept a close eye on the Estimates; but if they fell less than had been hoped, the reason lay at least partly with himself. The average annual current expenditure on the forces from 1785 to 1789 inclusive (in 1784 the war establishments were still being run down) returned to the same proportion of the national total as in the last comparable period, 1771–5. The figures themselves, however, were higher by a fifth in an age of broadly stable prices, and they contained one year's expenditure on the navy, in 1786, which was considerably larger than any peacetime predecessor.[1] This represented the first outlay on Pitt's shipbuilding and repair programme, the leading feature of his defence effort in these years. But some other increased costs were accepted, particularly in the ordnance under Richmond, balanced to some extent by attempts at financial and administrative reform.[2] These were far from being invariably successful, particularly in the navy. Nevertheless, if he did not always get value, Pitt did not unduly skimp the money itself. The results did not have to be tested severely; but they met the challenges offered. The preparations for war in 1787 proved adequate, and those of 1790 were something of a triumph. In a period devoted first and foremost to economy, Pitt could claim to have achieved his limited end.

The expenditure, moreover, was less than he was prepared to accept. For in 1786 he was defeated on a substantial defence project. One of the chief factors affecting the British conduct of the second half of the American War had been the need to protect the country, and particularly the naval bases, against invasion. The Channel Fleet could not be weakened unduly, operations and supply were correspondingly hampered, and the naval effort, inevitably stretched, could not fully meet its tasks. The great scare of 1779, when the French rode the Channel, focused attention on Plymouth and Portsmouth, and one of Opposition's main cries thereafter was for stronger defences to the ports. When the Rockinghams came to office in 1782, their Master General of the Ordnance, Richmond, drew up a plan for the purpose which, he estimated under Shelburne, would cost £400,000. The first £50,000 was appropriated, but in 1783 further grants were delayed by the Commons pending expert investigation. When Richmond returned under Pitt the matter was taken up again, and in April 1785 a naval and

1. It amounted to £3,127,000. The only naval figure, not containing provision for funding debt, to approach this in peacetime during the century had been one of £2,738,000, in 1772. The overall comparative figures were: 1771–5 inclusive, an annual average of £3,988,000, comprising 72% of the current national expenditure; 1785–9, £4,788,000, or 71% of an increased current total. These figures, again, do not include the funding or servicing of debt (Mitchell & Deane, *Abstract of British Historical Statistics*, ch. XIV, table 2).

2. See pp. 312–17 above.

military board was appointed under Richmond's chairmanship. It reported in June, but, despite pressure for quick action from the King, Pitt and Richmond decided to wait until early in the following year. The estimated cost had now risen steeply to £760,000, and at the end of February 1786 Pitt moved the necessary bill.

He did so against a background of discussion. While the dockyard defences were undoubtedly weak and had caused much anxiety, the danger in 1779 had been overrated and the panic disproportionate. In Plymouth at least much of the trouble had arisen from a clash of personalities. The extent and style of the new fortifications were open to argument, and Richmond expected some opposition on strictly military grounds. But in fact it took other forms, inspired in part by his own behaviour. For Richmond, tactless and high-handed, believing fervently in his case, and well aware that political animosity could readily be disguised in military terms, had made sure that the report, as presented, supported his views. He did his best to pack the investigating board, he handled its sessions on his own terms, and he censored some unwelcome evidence on the suspect ground of security. Such proceedings invited attack. It came with an added bite because Richmond himself was already unpopular.

The Ministry was divided from the start. Within the Cabinet, Thurlow and Howe at least thoroughly disliked the bill, and Howe even canvassed opposition among Members from the Admiralty seats. Dundas, too, had his objections. But Pitt supported Richmond, and as the spokesman in the Commons he presented a strong case.[1] The proposals were expensive; but if their need could be proved, this was an occasion when the cost should be faced. Was the alternative, moreover, really less expensive in the long run? If the ports were left as they were they would be an added invitation to hostile designs, and any hope of economy would vanish in another war. And if war should break out, the forces needed to man the improved fortifications would be smaller than those required to supplement the existing defences. There was no need to enlarge the standing army now that the American colonies had gone; the militia could fill the gap, and 'was it less desirable for us to be defended by the walls of Portsmouth and Plymouth, garrisoned by our own militia, than to purchase the protection [as in the last war] of Hessian hirelings?' In the absence of other measures, we should need a larger defensive fleet – again an expensive commitment, and one that was strategically unsound. For even then the navy's freedom of operation would be hampered, and the American War had shown what the results of that could be.

Pitt's arguments were weighted to meet the feelings that had arisen. For the attack on the bill developed on a wide front. The expense – so greatly increased from the earlier estimate – frightened the country

1. Speeches in the Commons' debate of 27–8 February; *P.R.*, XIX, 176–85, 226–7.

gentlemen, the more so as it would be devoted to the army rather than the navy. Old constitutional fears were revived, of standing garrisons under the Crown; and the fact that the King was known to be in favour had its own adverse effect. Richmond's handling of the issue played into his opponent's hands, and Sheridan in particular appealed to the sense of the House. As the long debate wore on, it began to look as if Pitt would not save the day. The division was taken at seven in the morning, and the result was a tie. A great shout arose; the Speaker stood up to give his casting vote, and, 'much exhausted by fatigue', declared against the bill.[1]

It was the third time within a year that the Ministry had been defeated on a major issue.[2] Pitt was greeted with some cries of 'resign'; but the feeling was not widely held. The Cabinet was known to be divided, Richmond was held to be the culprit, and, as George III remarked, the event reflected no 'want of confidence in Mr. Pitt from the . . . House of Commons, but their attachment to old prejudices and some disinclination to the projector of the fortifications'.[3] Nonetheless, and despite the closeness of the vote, it was rash of the Minister to try again, with a slightly amended bill in May. It roused an instant reaction, and was withdrawn unheard. That was the end of the matter, and Richmond had to be content with saving some money from the Ordnance Estimates for minor improvements over the next few years.

The affair had some interesting features. It again suggested, as Eden observed, that this was 'a very loose Parliament',[4] in which Ministers might always have to watch their step. It revealed the looseness of the Cabinet structure – the two members most directly concerned were openly at loggerheads, and carried the battle into Parliament itself. The Admiralty and the Ordnance, indeed, continued to wage an open feud: naval officers in the House voted against hearing the revised fortifications bill in May, the Surveyor-General of the Ordnance thereafter spoke and voted against an Admiralty regulation, and two years later the Ordnance Members opposed Howe's proposals for naval promotions, in a debate in which the Ministry, albeit reluctantly, gave him support.[5] It was an example of the domestic conditions which Pitt had to influence and respect. It also showed that he did not ignore the factor of strength in foreign affairs.

1. Loc. cit., 227. There had been 169 votes on each side.
2. The other occasions being the Westminster Scrutiny and the Irish Propositions. Pitt's motion for Parliamentary reform was his own affair, and his defeats on tax proposals were not matters of confidence.
3. To Pitt, 28 February 1786 (Stanhope, I, Appendix, xviii-xix).
4. To John Beresford (quoted loc. cit., 288). Cf. pp. 210–11, 230–1 above.
5. See p. 315 above.

II

On 19 September 1787, the Cabinet gathered in a well attended meeting to take a decision which, as a Government, it had not had to face before. It resolved that the King should be asked to approve 'immediate orders' to 'arm' the fleet and 'augment' the army. Steps were taken to reach an agreement, already in train, for a supply of Hessian troops, and to fit out 23 ships of the line to join the 17 in service. The preparations went ahead quite briskly; but they had not been completed before their object was achieved.

The orders arose from the decision to inform the French Government that England could not 'remain an indifferent spectator of the armed interference of France' in Holland.[1] The situation there, fast deteriorating, had become critical by the summer, and from early in July civil war seemed certain. The question thereafter was the extent of foreign involvement, and whether or not the British Government would move from financial to armed support.

French and British policies vis-à-vis Holland had been broadly aligned in the past four decades with a domestic conflict for which they furnished added point. Ever since a coup d'état in the late forties had restored an hereditary Stadtholder, there had been a sharp division in the country, partly irrelevant but deeply felt. The real conflict of interest in Holland lay between a high merchant oligarchy and a middle class increasingly resentful of its own exclusion from government. But their mutual opposition was masked and distorted by the presence of the Stadtholderate, and the inadequacy of the Stadtholders themselves. The leadership of the Orange family had always rested largely on evidence of success, and this was difficult to provide in an age of declining Dutch power and, latterly, wealth. Old constitutional cries, easily raised in a state embracing powerful local rights, gained ground among the dynasty's natural supporters. The Orange allegiance was still strong, in the country nobility and gentry, the army, the peasants and the lower classes in the towns. But the gulf was narrowing between the landed and urban aristocracies; and in the early eighties a new, alarming element appeared. For the American example swept the dissatisfied Dutch bourgeoisie with a wave of revolutionary feeling. The 'Patriots', centred on Amsterdam, emerged as a highly articulate force, joining the merchant patricians in an

1. Cabinet Minute, in *Political Memoranda of Francis Fifth Duke of Leeds*, 118. The absentees were Gower (now Marquess of Stafford) and Thurlow, and the former, in answer to Pitt, had sent assurances of support for 'an active part' (17 September 1787; Grenville Papers, Huntingon Library, California). I shall use the term Holland, here as elsewhere, as a convenient abbreviation for the Dutch Netherlands or United Provinces; in point of fact, of course, Holland was one of those provinces.

uneasy but active republican alliance. It would have taken a skilled and confident ruler to have contained such a threat. But the Stadtholder was William V – 'my booby of a nephew', Frederick the Great called him –, the victim of a long minority, well intentioned, despondent and weak.

The domestic disputes had long been combined with differing foreign sympathies. The Stadtholder favoured the British, the republicans the French. Here again the Orange cause was at an immediate disadvantage, for the old British connexion, forged by William III, was now severely strained. It had suffered a shock in the War of the Austrian Succession, when financial hardship forced the Dutch to withdraw, and Britain moved closer to Prussia, herself nibbling at Dutch interests. It was severely tried in the Seven Years' War, when Dutch neutrality led to constant trouble over non-belligerent rights. And it had been virtually disrupted by the American War, when the British, goaded by the Armed Neutrality, declared war on Holland. William V, whose mother was English – she was a daughter of George II –, had made no secret of his sympathies; he was in a very difficult position by 1784. The French were able to exploit it: the Patriots had looked to them from the start, and the events of the next two years gained them wider support. By the end of 1785, the defeat of the Austrian Emperor's claims had established France as the natural protector of Holland.[1]

The British influence therefore was extremely weak. The Orange party was under pressure, we had played no direct part in the matter of the Scheldt, and our role in that of the Bavarian Exchange was embarrassed and indecisive. The rising troubles now posed a threat which it would be hard to ignore or to meet. Fortunately, there was a man at hand fully equal to the occasion.

Sir James Harris arrived in The Hague in December 1784, the first British envoy since war had broken out just over four years before.[2] Already a well known diplomat – he had been chargé d'affaires in Madrid in the Falkland Islands crisis, Minister at Berlin, and Ambassador in Russia throughout the American War – he had now, at the age of thirty-eight, risen to the height of his powers. Bold, realistic, not overburdened by scruples – 'cet audacieux et rusé Harris', Mirabeau called him[3] – he combined an easy convivial charm with a formidable professional grasp. In politics he followed Fox, a close friend since Oxford days, and as Member for Christchurch since 1780 had voted against Pitt in the recent struggle.[4] But diplomacy was his life, he

1. See pp. 471–3 above.
2. P. 472 above.
3. In 1786; quoted *G.E.C.*, VIII, 361, n(b).
4. At least according to the list appended to Stockdale's *Debates*, I, of 'those who voted against Mr. Pitt's Administration'. His name does not appear in the surviving division lists for the second reading of Fox's India bill.

carried the confidence of all parties, he was a friend of Carmarthen, knew Holland well, and could actually speak Dutch. He was an excellent choice on his merits; and even his politics had their point, for a man whom Opposition could scarcely attack might be useful in so exposed a quarter. He brought to a task which soon involved risks an appropriate response: 'I know no guide to Politicks but *events* or rather circumstances, no principles but the interests of my Court'.[1]

For some time he was a caged lion.[2] While he was convinced of the potential dangers his circumstances, and instructions, gave him little scope at first. The atmosphere in Holland was discouraging, and he had been expressly ordered to move cautiously – 'You will, on no account, whatever may be the friendly turn of your conversations with . . . well-disposed persons, make use of Our Name, without Our express command'.[3] The best, perhaps the only, immediate hope lay in a closer understanding with Prussia, herself naturally disturbed by the prospect of Austrian gains. Harris entered into a private correspondence with the British chargé d'affaires in Berlin, an energetic, confident young man called Joseph Ewart – a name that was later to become uncomfortably well known. In the early months of 1785 it began to look as if Frederick the Great might be interested, and Harris, returning to England ostensibly on leave, took the chance to press his case. He had great influence with Carmarthen, whom he always played with easy skill, and the Foreign Secretary in any case was in search of a more active policy. The Cabinet went so far in May as to propose joint action;[4] but Frederick soon put paid to any such idea. He seemed indeed quite as likely to work against Austria through France as through Britain, and Harris settled down in the autumn to a period of concealed preparation.

His prospects did not seem to improve with one important development in the winter; though in one sense this marked the first turning point in his fortunes. In November 1785 the Dutch signed a treaty of defensive alliance with France. The Ministry's first reaction was to say that nothing could be done, either by trying to persuade the Dutch to stop ratification or by supplying Harris with funds, for which he had been asking, to build up an anti-French party. But it soon changed its mind, with the King's reluctant consent; Harris was instructed to protest, and if (as was likely) this had no effect, was told unofficially that he could count on a sum of £6,000. The Government was not prepared to go too far; but a Franco-Dutch alliance was really disturbing, and Pitt told Carmarthen that his man should '*redouble every possible*

1. To Carmarthen, 11 March 1785; quoted in Cobban, *Ambassadors and Secret Agents*, 30. 'Politicks' in the context of course meant diplomacy.
2. He was later called 'lion blanc' by a French journal, from his bold eyes and white hair (*G.E.C.*, VIII, 361, n(b)).
3. Instructions of 26 November 1784, quoted Cobban, op. cit., 33.
4. See pp. 472–3 above.

effort.[1] Harris needed no prompting, and when the treaty was duly ratified he set to work with renewed vigour to cultivate his friends.

The grant from secret service funds was the first of several. They remained modest in 1786 – some £9,000 in all seems to have been spent by the end of that year.[2] The results were good as far as they went, and the knowledge that he now enjoyed some backing aided the efforts which Harris was determined to make in any case. His party began to grow, and it gained some valuable accessions as fear of the Patriots increased. But he still faced long odds. Though the French certainly had their troubles, they were in a stronger position than he was, they were spending much more money,[3] and his own support, inside and outside Holland, was not all that he could have wished. The spreading sympathy for the Stadtholderate was still unco-ordinated, leadership was lacking, and the Stadtholder himself was a liability. One could not, Harris reported, even work through his wife, the spirited Princess Frederika Sophia Wilhelmina, a niece of Frederick the Great. For while she had many of the qualities that William V conspicuously lacked, he was so jealous of the fact that her help would do more harm than good, and in any case she was looking more to Prussia than to ourselves. Nor did Harris receive much comfort from home. His proposals for commercial loans, and an association between the two East India Companies, were first rebuffed and then largely ignored;[4] and when he tried to extract a guarantee from London for funds to enable some provincial supporters to buy property giving them the right to vote in a forthcoming election, sanction for this manœuvre – perhaps hardly surprisingly – was delayed until it was too late. In the autumn of 1786 he was thus still confined to a '*prudent* line of conduct', from which he could not 'deviate, until I am commanded to do so'.[5]

The British Government's reluctance to intervene too openly was quite understandable. Harris was sure that 'till France is ready, *nothing will provoke* her to quarrel with us, and that when she is ready, *nothing will prevent* it'. The remedy was for England 'to threaten (and threaten seriously)', in which case 'France would shrink from the challenge'.[6] This was prophetic; but was it the right answer at the time? We could scarcely stand by in a revolution that made Holland entirely dependent on France. Prevention, moreover, is better than cure, and if Harris had read French intentions correctly the best treatment might well be a

---

1. 6 December 1785 (B. M. Egerton Ms 3498).

2. See Cobban, op. cit., 111–12.

3. Loc. cit., 117–20, where some of the wilder exaggerations on both sides are reduced.

4. P. 425 above.

5. To Carmarthen, 24 October 1786 (*Diaries and Correspondence of . . . First Earl of Malmesbury*, II, 246; henceforward referred to as *Malmesbury*).

6. Loc. cit., 245.

timely convincing threat. The Ministry, however, was not prepared to say that either adjective applied. 'The time may come', Carmarthen had already observed, 'when the King's mediation may be . . . the object of desire to the Republic'. But 'at present it is *impossible* for us to throw ourselves headlong into any engagement which might ultimately involve . . . England and Prussia . . . with France, and possibly Austria, and no other power whatever engaged to support them [i.e. England and Prussia]'.[1] The Government in fact, whatever Carmarthen's own reservations, echoed Frederick the Great's view of a year before; the balance of power was still too adverse for it to be risked further.[2] And although Frederick had now just died, and his successor was supposed to be more friendly, Ministers were not inclined to place as much hope in his still untested policies as was Harris himself at the start. Our relations with France, moreover, were in an interesting state. Despite Carmarthen's misgivings, Pitt was prepared to work for a wider settlement, based on his achievement in the recent commercial treaty. The options were open, and he was certainly not disposed to forgo an advantage: on the contrary, success in one instance might facilitate pressure elsewhere. Let us therefore wait and see. The troubles in Holland had not reached a crisis, and there was no point in making commitments the effect of which could not really be foreseen. 'The great object', in Pitt's view, was rather '*to keep together a party which may act with advantage . . . , on some future day, if it should arrive*'.[3]

But while he was reluctant to look for trouble, and determined to avoid a commitment, Pitt was now prepared to do a good deal to achieve his limited aim. It was probably at this point that he first became seriously interested: certainly he began to look into the problem for himself. On 5 December 1786 he called on Carmarthen to discuss the prospects – something which it sounds as if he had not done in detail before. 'He feels', the Foreign Secretary wrote in relief, '(as I knew he would do, when *properly stated*) the great and serious importance of the subject. . . .The moment that I found his apprehensions [of how to act] were only respecting the *means*, rather than the *measure*, of eventually combating the French influence, . . . I own I felt the greatest pleasure and satisfaction'.[4] The sky seemed to have lightened after the recent doubts and snubs,[5] and the great thing now was to see that the improvement was maintained. 'Now', Carmarthen urged Harris, 'that we have *raised* his attention . . ., we must, by all means, endeavour to *keep it up*'.[6]

Pitt was thus ready to step up a policy which he had so far been slow

1. To Harris, 26 September 1786 (P.R.O., F.O. 37/12).
2. See p. 475 above.
3. To Harris, 5 December 1786 (*Malmesbury*, II, 254–5).
4. To Harris, 5 December 1786 (loc. cit., 253–4).
5. See p. 493 above.
6. 12 December 1786 (*Malmesbury*, II, 258. See p. 280 above).

to indulge. It seems unlikely that his decision stemmed from a change of mind among his colleagues. The balance within the Cabinet remained much as it had been. Carmarthen wanted bolder measures, and he was supported by Richmond; Sydney was vaguely sympathetic; but others were uninterested or opposed. The King, moreover, was hostile, and harped back to the American War to show that the country was no longer fit to exert itself in Europe.[1] Nor was Carmarthen in a position seriously to influence Pitt by himself – his lack of weight indeed was so marked that he was thinking of resigning at just this time. But, recognising the fact, and excusing his action by illness,[2] he very sensibly took a step which produced the desired effect. In November he wrote to Harris, suggesting that he should write direct to Pitt. This was an unusual proposal, even though Pitt had been concerned to an unusual extent in Harris's appointment. The constitutional proprieties were strictly observed: there was no system of parallel communications as in France, and the heads of missions reported to the Foreign Secretary and the King. The First Lord of the Treasury normally corresponded with them only on subjects affecting his department, and Harris's best justification for a direct approach lay in the fact that this was a question involving finance. Following Carmarthen's lead, however, he did not confine himself to that; and the result was all that they could have hoped. Pitt was obviously impressed; he was brought into closer touch with the man on the spot, and roused to a more vivid impression of the dangers.[3] There was also a longer-term effect, which Carmarthen perhaps did not foresee. For the Minister had been introduced to a process, which was to become more marked in the next few years, of making direct contact, when he thought it desirable, with British diplomats abroad.

It was a consequence of Pitt's new interest, as well as of his policy, that he should now have kept a watchful eye on what went on. 'We wish', he told Harris, '. . . to have all the considerations . . . fully before us',[4] and this indeed proved immediately necessary to combat George III's alarm at the increased amount – £12,000 – which the envoy wished to spend. 'Where is this sum to be obtained', asked the King, 'if the hazard it may occasion of involving us in war is risqued?'[5]

1. To judge by Carmarthen's comment on George III's answer (itself not found) to a letter of 7 January 1787 (Cobban, op. cit., 123).

2. See p. 493, n4 above.

3. Harris wrote on 28 November 1786 (*Malmesbury*, II, 251–3). That he did so as a result of Carmarthen's suggestion, conveyed to him on the 21st (B. M. Egerton Ms 3500), appears certain from his letter to the Foreign Secretary of the 28th (B.M. Add. Ms 28061, f. 384v). The effect was noted by Carmarthen, who wrote that Pitt's visit on 5 December was to show him the text of Harris's letter (*Malmesbury*, II, 253).

4. 26 December 1786 (*Malmesbury*, II, 263).

5. To Pitt, 8 January 1787 (Holland Rose, *Pitt and Napoleon*, 215). He was particularly anxious that it should not be taken out of the Civil List, already under strain from his growing family expenses.

Pitt seems to have found a way, and the money was sent in the end.[1] He also followed the manœuvres of the next few months, to see that the risk was held in check. There was indeed a growing contrast from now on in the degree of control exercised by the French and the British Ministries – attributable partly to the positions and characters of the respective envoys, themselves in charge of or confronted by a miscellany of secret agents, but more to the respective circumstances and structures of government and the personalities involved. It soon became clear that there was no dominating Minister or group at Versailles, and that the Court was a scene of growing faction; Pitt, on the other hand, was able to assume effective command. His aims and his methods were soon to be tested, for Harris's efforts began to bear fruit, and in the early summer he came to London to ask for a further rise in supplies.

He arrived in May 1787. He could report substantial progress. While there had been some recent disappointments, his party was gaining strength, the republican patriciate was disenchanted with the Patriots, and the French were experiencing the difficulties of running a revolutionary party. Two developments in particular made him anxious to seek further instructions. The Princess of Orange, after holding aloof, now wished to test the prospects of British support, and had decided to ask for a loan. And the province of Gelderland, which in the autumn had defied an order from the States General to redispose its troops, on the ground that this was unconstitutional – for the States General had deprived the Stadtholder of his rights as Captain General of the Forces –, was prepared to go on doing so if it could raise the money with which to pay the men. Harris therefore wanted a sum which would detach Gelderland from its neighbours, and guidance as to what he should say to his supporters and to the Princess.

He met the Cabinet, and talked to Pitt, between 23 and 26 May. The first meeting is of interest, for Harris made notes or kept a copy of the proceedings – one of the very few records we have of a Ministerial conversation of the time.[2] Pitt was concerned to steer a middle course. He did not admit the assumption – postulated by Thurlow – that the fate of Holland might not be important, or that even if France had her way she might still not gain 'permanent' and 'solid' control of the country. But he was equally wary of the argument – which Thurlow and Richmond then advanced – that, assuming we should act, we

---

1. Together possibly with a further £4,000 a year direct to the Stadtholder; but this is obscure (see Cobban, op. cit., 125).

2. *Malmesbury*, II, 303–6. The record is in fact of the kind which the modern Cabinet adopted on the remodelling of its business in 1917, and later dropped. It gives the course of the discussion, and individual contributions, as well as the agreed decision.

The absentees were Camden and Howe; and Camden again missed the second meeting, on the 26th.

must recognise that 'half-measures' would not be enough, that war might follow 'at once' and that we should prepare accordingly. He tacitly scouted their proposal – which Richmond at least meant seriously[1] – that we should subsidise a German army, to be raised forthwith; and brought the discussion firmly onto a less inflammatory line. We could not doubt 'the *immense* consequence of Holland being preserved as an Independent State'; 'the question . . . was, which risk was the greatest, that of attempting to stop France in the progress of her preparatory designs now, or to wait to resist the execution of them when she was ready to attack us?' The first alternative, on the information so far, seemed to him unlikely to lead to war; but it might possibly do so, and we must therefore 'weigh maturely whether anything could repay the disturbing that state of growing affluence and prosperity' at home which might enable us 'to resist any force France could collect some years hence'. It was a wistful cry, which the Foreign Office had learned to fear, and Harris countered quickly. France was in no state to risk a war, but if she gained Holland without opposition she would become correspondingly stronger. Now, therefore, was the time to make a stand. We would not benefit by delay. On the contrary, immediate measures were likely to prevent a later clash.

Harris may have been unsure at the end of the meeting how far he had carried his audience. His own recipe for success contained two ingredients: 'pecuniary relief for the present, and assurances of support for the future'. He staked his reputation on the judgment that these would do the trick; but the Minister had said nothing definite about either measure, and sounded reluctant to embark on the second. By the next day, however, he had made up his mind about the first.

With Mr. Pitt [wrote Harris]. He questioned me on the *detail* of Holland; went nearly over the same ground as in the Cabinet, but with more precision; felt strongly the importance of the object; asked what Provinces I could depend on; desired me to give him my ideas on what should be done respecting France [i.e., what sort of representation to make]; sent for a map of Holland; made me show him the situation of the Provinces, &c. I proposed a squadron of frigates at Flushing: he did not object to it: talked on the money: how to be applied, and through whom.[2]

The result appeared at the second Cabinet, held on the 26th. Ministers recommended to the King that a sum not exceeding £70,000 should

---

1. There are contrasting views on Thurlow's real intentions throughout, in Cobban (op. cit., 132–3) and Robert Gore-Browne, *Chancellor Thurlow* (1953), 241–2. It seems to me that the first is probably right, and the second certainly wrong.
2. *Malmesbury*, II, 306.

be earmarked for a loan to Gelderland, and that consideration of other measures should await events.[1]

Pitt had thus decided to take the immediate calculated risk. He was still not prepared to commit himself farther. Had he tried to do so, he would presumably have had part of the Cabinet, and the King, against him; but there is no reason to suppose that he wished to try. If Harris was right and the French were likely to shrink from a strong challenge inside Holland, there would be a good chance of an agreement, which he was very unwilling to lose. It was at this time, after all, that he was offering them a reduction in naval manpower, and showing his strength in the terms proposed for a settlement in India.[2] The prospect of 'effectual exertions', as he told the King, 'being made with only *pecuniary assistance*',[3] was worth the trial; and while the argument was doubtless weighted to soothe a reluctant monarch – for George III remained unhappy – it was probably also a genuine reflection of Pitt's hopes and fears. Another war, so soon after the last, would threaten the work of the past few years, 'that state of growing affluence and prosperity' which was beginning to yield results. And his habitual optimism, playing on a still pronounced lack of experience in foreign affairs, may have urged that all would be well and nothing more would be required. This was his first real diplomatic test, and policy and temperament beckoned the same way. And if the policy looked like failing, and fresh moves had to be made in the end, he was determined to keep them firmly under Government's control. The increased financial support was a mark of confidence in Harris: in his recent achievements, and in the belief that he could hold his supporters. The decision to go no farther at the moment, and reserve judgment to London, was a sign of Pitt's anxiety to keep the options open and his resolve to remain in charge.

Over the next four weeks, things went Harris's way. The disturbances in Holland had been mounting while he was in England, and by the end of May, after riots in Amsterdam, both sides were looking to their troops. The time had come to stand and be counted, and French and British agents were hard at work in the camps. Harris was equally vigorous in the higher counsels of the provinces assembled at The Hague. The debates swung to and fro. The democratic party, led by the powerful province of Holland, called for the suspension of all officers who remained loyal to William V. But it was fast losing the support of the urban oligarchs, and by mid-June he could report that it had

---

1. The best text of the Minute is in *L.C.G. III*, I, enclosure to no. 367. The version in *Malmesbury*, II, 307 gives a figure of £20,000, which is presumably a misreading of the ms.
2. Pp. 313, 441 above.
3. 26 May 1787 (*L.C.G. III*, I, no. 368).

been narrowly defeated, and also that a majority of the troops had ranged themselves on the Stadtholder's side. French policy meanwhile was confused – 'chaotic', one of the French Ministers called it –[1] divided sharply between hawks and doves, and scarcely in control of events on the spot. When the province of Holland, on 23 June, resolved to take the plunge and call on France to mediate, it was therefore by no means certain what the response would be.

And then, at the end of the month, the issue was brought to a head. The Princess of Orange, watching carefully, had decided that the time was ripe. After talking unavailingly to her husband, who had moved the Court from the capital, she planned to re-enter The Hague in secret and announce proposals for a moderate settlement which would force the Patriots' hand. If they agreed, well and good; if they did not, they would be put in the wrong. Either way, the Stadtholder's party would have gained the initiative. Harris, who knew of the design, was uneasy, though strongly drawn by the Princess's courage. But the Orangists in The Hague approved, and she set out with a small party on 28 June. She was stopped on her way by a band of republican troops, placed temporarily under arrest, and obliged to retire to Nijmegen, in the friendly province of Gelderland.

The Princess's arrest added a new dimension to the scene. It shocked the Courts of Europe, soon to witness so much worse. If the House of Orange did nothing, it was facing defeat: if it responded, there would be civil war. But there was now a greater danger that others would be involved, for on 6 July the province of Holland, acting on its earlier resolution, asked France to mediate, and after a pause the invitation was accepted on the 18th, under the terms (as it was claimed) of the defensive alliance.[2] On the 29th the Princess appealed for protection to Prussia and to Britain. The powers were being ranged, however reluctantly, in rival camps; and a new, hitherto uninvolved, element had been introduced.

For Prussia now became the key to the situation. Could the King allow this insult to his sister to go unavenged? It was difficult to tell, for since he had succeeded his uncle in August 1786 Frederick William II had proved unpredictable, and he was not particularly fond of the Princess. His responses were due partly to his nature – he was easily swayed and easily bored –, but more to the familiar policy of *attendre* of which Frederick the Great had been a master, and which the general situation seemed to favour, or at least allow. Prussia's ambitions lay in central Europe, and her actions in the west would be governed largely by that fact. In 1787 her eyes were fixed on the east, where the old enemy Austria, though still undecided, might be drawn into supporting Russia in any fresh conflict with the Turks; for if such an

1. Cobban, op. cit., 144.
2 P. 522 above.

occasion arose and could be exploited, there might be pickings to be had in the Empire or in Poland. Friendship with France, or friendship with Britain, therefore turned on their roles in this matter; and Britain had so far been scarcely concerned, while France was known to have ambitions in the eastern Mediterranean. There were rival policies in Berlin, embodied by the Ministers von Finckenstein and von Hertzberg, the former preferring a French, the latter a British connexion. Their division was reflected in Holland, where one Prussian envoy worked in The Hague with the Patriots, and a second, sent at Hertzberg's prompting, attended the Princess. The latter could not do very much, for, as the British were forced to recognise, Frederick William, despite their early hopes, was tending to favour the French. But the King was now faced with a new development, on which he must make up his mind; and his decision might determine the outcome of the affair. If he did nothing, or – perhaps more likely – joined with France in a mediation, the British must stand aside or champion a weakened cause on their own. If he took up arms on the Princess's behalf, the French would have to fight, or accept a mediation which Britain could enter, or limit their involvement as best they could.

Throughout July it was hard to tell what the Prussians would do. Frederick William's immediate reaction was to send a stern note to the States General, demanding an apology and satisfaction to the Princess. In the middle of the month he assembled a force of 20,000 men. But he showed no immediate sign of moving, he was listening to French offers of a joint mediation, and his envoy in The Hague, exceeding instructions, assured the Patriots that all would be well. All this did nothing to still the rising storm. The Patriots redoubled their efforts, there were violent demonstrations, and by the beginning of August revolution seemed very close.

While the Prussians hesitated, the French and British Governments held back. The French Ministry was still sharply divided, and some of its agents were becoming nervous. The Patriots could not be disavowed, but they were now largely out of hand; the French finances were in disorder; and Austria – the most likely ally – was preoccupied elsewhere. Beset by uncertainties and quarrels at home, and a growing loss of control in Holland, the Foreign Minister de Montmorin was walking a tightrope. He allowed rumours to spread that a camp was being established at Givet, on the border with the Austrian Netherlands, and there were stories of preparations in the naval yards. At the same time, he was careful not to strain relations with Britain: he talked quite amicably to the Ambassador and Eden, and the talks on India went on.[1] The British, for their part, were anxious to lower the temperature. Harris had been warned on his return to Holland in June to give no pledges to his friends,[1] and throughout that and the next month the despatches

1. P. 442 above.

to Paris stressed the hopes of agreement. Steps were taken to discover the extent of the French preparations, particularly at Givet,[2] Harris was sent a military and a naval adviser, and six British warships put to sea. There were cautious exchanges with Prussia about the possibility of intervention. But at the same time Pitt tried to clear the air with France. On 27 July he proposed to the French Ambassador that both sides should suspend any further armaments; and his tone, the Ambassador noted, was remarkably friendly for a Minister not given to polite phrases. The offer was made the more easily, no doubt, because the Government now suspected that the rumours from Givet were exaggerated; but it was genuine enough, at a time when the Prussian response was still in doubt. If he had known what Montmorin was doing, Pitt moreover might have taken heart; for at the beginning of August the French Minister was trying to persuade the Patriots to apologise to the Princess of Orange, and accept a mediation in which Britain might be included.

But in point of fact the time for conciliation was running out. The Patriots were not going to listen, and the Prussians were gradually coming to the point. Opinion in Berlin was still divided, and the King was reluctant to commit himself too far: apart from anything else, the Austrian attitude was still unknown. But he was alarmed by the storm in Holland, which the French seemed unable or unwilling to quell, and early in August he repeated his demands and began to incline towards Britain. His embarrassed representative in The Hague was obliged to approach Harris; Ewart was simultaneously told from London to make an approach in Berlin; and by the 14th the British Government felt able to invite itself to a tripartite mediation. Harris could not yet 'quite solve the Prussian riddle'; but Pitt was more optimistic. As early as 2 August he suspected that Frederick William was no longer so much under 'the direction of France'.[3] Emboldened by this view, the Ministry resolved to hasten the process. On the 24th it offered France an exchange of assurances that neither Government would augment its naval preparations without informing the other. But this was conditional on a French force not being assembled at Givet; the proposal was included in a despatch protesting against

1. Several of the despatches at this time were composed partly by Pitt, and he personally added a note of warning to one of them, on the 29th (drafts in P.R.O., F.O. 97/246).

2. Where the mysterious W. A. Miles, later to become well known as a British spy in the French Revolution, made an early appearance. His activities aroused suspicion, and were, as always, complicated and unsavoury. But although Pitt seems to have held out hopes, some eighteen months before, of regular employment (correspondence in P.R.O. 30/8/159, 195), the agent may have been acting in this instance as a free lance, in the hope of an appointment or a reward.

3. Harris to Carmarthen, Private, 14 August 1787 (B.M. Add. Ms 28062, f. 328v); Pitt to Cornwallis, Private, 2 August 1787 (*Correspondence of Cornwallis*, I, 337. See p. 425 above).

French conduct, particularly in the apparent failure to influence a Dutch reply to Prussia; and on the same day Ewart was told to inform the Prussians that we supported their demands, supplies of ammunition were gathered secretly for Holland, Harris was promised more money, and the Adjutant General was sent to Hesse to negotiate for troops.

In contrast to the divisions at Versailles, and even in Berlin, opinion in London in fact was now hardening fast. By 6 August the King seemed happier to approve more positive action, and Thurlow, Pitt reported, was 'more quieted than I have ever known'.[1] Ministers were now disposed directly to try to influence events, and, by encouraging Prussia, to bring France to terms. Pitt was moving with the greater confidence because he had recently had his own emissary in Holland, one who knew his latest thoughts and whom he was prepared to trust. For at the end of July, obviously at the Minister's request, the Cabinet had sent Grenville to The Hague – the first direct diplomatic experience of a future Foreign Secretary.[2] As a reassurance to the Dutch, a check on Harris's reports, and a guide and reinforcement for him, he had an important role to play at a critical time; and he played it well. He soon confirmed Harris's views, and was calling for further indirect help; and it was clearly a sign of the feeling in London that he was able to tell the Orange leaders – as Harris had never told them – that Britain would go to war rather than abandon their cause.[3] He was back by the 23rd; and it was doubtless no coincidence that the measures on the 24th followed his 'endeavours . . . to state to the King's servants the real situation of the republic.'[4]

These were critical weeks. For by the end of August it seems clear that the British and the French were moving in divergent directions. The 'French ministers', it has been said, 'were talking of camps and war, but acting as though peace were guaranteed, Pitt and Carmarthen were talking of peace but preparing for the possibility of war'.[5] It was indeed ironical that British fears of France were growing at the very time when the French were making serious, if unco-ordinated, efforts to avoid a clash. They agreed to the British offer of assurances about naval measures – a joint declaration was signed on 30 August –, they were doing their best, while Grenville was in Holland, to bring the Patriots to heel, and on the 20th they recalled their Ambassador from The Hague as a sign of displeasure. But much of this was unknown to London – the recall of the Ambassador, for instance, was not immediately put into effect – and there was much activity of another kind: continuing talk of the camp at Givet, supplies of arms to the republicans,

1. To Grenville, 7 August 1787 (*H.M.C., Dropmore*, III, 415). The King's letter to Pitt of the 6th is in *L.C.G. III*, I, no. 382.
2. His instructions were given him on the 27th, and he arrived in The Hague on the 30th (*H.M.C., Dropmore*, III, 408).
3. See Cobban, op. cit., 169.
4. Grenville to Harris, 23 August 1787 (*H.M.C., Dropmore*, III, 416).
5. Cobban, op. cit., 173.

comings and goings of agents, an apparent lack of response to the Prussians' demands. The French in fact were in difficulties. They certainly did not want a war, which would come at the end of a summer of rising distress and discontent. The Assembly of Notables had come and gone, and the *parlement* of Paris, summoned reluctantly, was refusing at this very time to pass the Ministry's demands. On the other hand they were not prepared to lose face unnecessarily, and one could not yet tell how things would turn out. Montmorin himself was not convinced that England would risk a confrontation. He was influenced naturally by his Ambassador in London, who made some bad mistakes – he thought that the King was urging Pitt to be firmer, and he was misled by the Minister's friendly tone when making a fresh protest about French actions at the end of the month. Montmorin was also affected by the tone of the British representatives in Paris, particularly Eden, who disliked, and was known to dislike, some of his instructions; and he could learn nothing from the British preparations, for the Admiralty kept its secrets and no news leaked out. The French, like the British, were thus waiting to see how the cards fell. But, unlike the British, they could not further raise their stake.

The game still depended on Prussia; and at last the Prussians played their hand. At the beginning of September they were still anxious about a possible Austrian threat; but on the 7th war finally broke out between Russia and Turkey, and it seemed clear that the Emperor would now refuse to spare any troops for France. If there was to be a campaign, moreover, it should be launched before the autumn rains – an argument held very strongly by the Prussians' commander, the elderly Duke of Brunswick. These considerations, combined with firmer messages of British support at the beginning of the month, induced Frederick William to issue an ultimatum to the province of Holland on the 9th, giving four days for acceptance. A last conciliatory effort by the French – on the 10th they announced their intention of disbanding the camp at Givet – had no effect, for the Patriots were in no mood to climb down. On the 13th, trapped by earlier commitments, Montmorin told Eden that France would support Holland 'in whatever manner might be most efficacious'.[1] On the 14th, when no answer had been received, the Prussians crossed the Dutch frontier.

The British had now to make their position clear to the French. This did not prove easy. At the beginning of September, Eden was still talking as pacifically as he could, and was indeed trying to persuade his superiors to get rid of Harris. He had to be told off by Pitt;[2] but his continued reluctance to sound too bellicose may well have contributed significantly to the persistent hopes in France that Britain would abstain. He was brought closer to the sticking point when the

1. Eden to Carmarthen, 13 September 1787 (*A.C.*, I, 193).
2. On 8 September (*H.M.C., Twelfth Report, Appendix, Pt. IX*, 357; the passage is omitted from the letter as published in *A.C.*, I, 191–3).

Prussian ultimatum expired; for he was then told that naval preparations could no longer be suspended, and that if the Stadtholder's rights were not restored Britain would give him armed support. We still hoped to avoid a conflict, for 'the advantage of a continued peace is more to this country than anything we might gain by . . . going to war'. But 'the actual mischief of suffering France to carry its point in Holland would more than counterbalance it', and if the French did not disengage and were resolved to maintain their 'predominant influence', they would have to '*fight for it*'.[1]

These were Pitt's words; and Pitt was now in day to day charge. Since June he had been drafting some of the most important despatches to Harris;[2] he now made himself responsible for all major instructions both to Holland and to Eden in France,[3] for taking the Cabinet's opinion, and for handling the King. In the past month, with his colleagues scattered, he had worked mainly with Carmarthen and Grenville, and he had earlier covered his flank by taking Thurlow and, through him, Stafford (as Gower had become) into his confidence.[4] He now called a Cabinet meeting, which all but Thurlow and Stafford attended,[5] and the Lord Chancellor then returned and kept his friend informed. Pitt indeed still had some hopes of peace, as he prepared for war. On the 19th the Cabinet authorised a naval armament and the raising of Hessian troops; but within the next two days it also agreed, at his instance, to make a last appeal to France.[6] Since Eden could not be relied on – there was now 'great coldness' towards him[7] – Grenville was sent to Paris, and left on the 21st or 22nd. He was to try for an immediate settlement of 'all the material points',[8] in the light of the latest British measures and the developments in Holland itself.

For a while these decisions were being taken, things had been moving fast in Holland; so fast indeed that while Grenville was on his way his

1. Pitt to Eden, 14 September 1787 (*A.C.*, I, 195). The news of imminent naval preparations came from Carmarthen on the 13th (loc. cit., 527).

2. See p. 531, n 1 above; and cf. the drafts in Pitt's hand thereafter in P.R.O., F.O. 97/246 with the Foreign Office texts in F.O. 37/15–18.

3. F.O. 97/246; *A.C.*, I, 191 *et seq*. He also drafted several despatches to Ewart in Berlin (F.O. 97/323.)

4. Grenville was certainly in London a good deal late in August and early in September (*H.M.C., Dropmore*, III, 416–23), and there is an undated draft of a despatch in his hand, probably to Harris, which seems to belong to this period (P.R.O. 30/8/333). Thurlow, who left London in mid-August to stay with Stafford, had been sending the latter 'voluminous papers' on the crisis (Thurlow to Pitt, 15 August 1787, P.R.O. 30/8/183; Stafford to Pitt, 29 August 1787, P.R.O. 30/8/180). Pitt himself, who had cancelled a leisurely visit to the north in June, snatched two days for a visit to Cheveley, near Cambridge, on 10 September (William Fraser to Carmarthen, 10 September 1787; B.M. Add. Ms 28062, f. 336v).

5. P. 520, n. 1 above.

6. Pitt's lead in this is made clear in Thurlow to Stafford, n.d. but between 19 and 21 September; P.R.O. 30/29/1, packet 15.

7. Thurlow to Stafford, another undated letter loc. cit.

8. Grenville to Harris, 21 September 1787 (*H.M.C., Dropmore*, III, 425).

mission began to look out of date. The Prussian advance in the previous week had met with little opposition: Utrecht surrendered without a shot, the province of Gelderland was already friendly, and by the evening of the 17th the road seemed open to The Hague. The Patriots there were in a panic, the Orange supporters rose, and on the 18th the Stadtholder was invited to return to his capital. The news reached Pitt on the 21st, and he passed it at once to Grenville.

> One might almost be tempted [he wrote] to tell Monsieur de Montmorin . . . *que c'est une affaire terminée*. On the whole, however, it is best still to be moderate, and I do not see why you should not take the credit of having instructions which were prepared before the news of this event, and are not altered in consequence of it.[1]

His envoy in fact would be on the spot, to reap the benefit of whatever arose; for 'whether it ends in peace or war, things now cannot go ill'.[2]

It was not quite over yet. The French were determined to save what they could. Grenville, arriving on the 25th, heard that Montmorin remained undecided. He was in fact still rather in the dark about the extent of the British preparations – the French Ambassador could give him little news until the 25th – and he was naturally very reluctant to court a public defeat. But he was equally reluctant to risk a war, and as the Patriots' strength dissolved he was doing his best to make them come to terms. Failing completely, he was then reduced to making warlike noises to Grenville and Eden, while carefully abstaining from any action on the spot. On 1 October Grenville was still uncertain what the French Ministers would do; when he returned to England on the 7th he thought it possible, though unlikely, that they would be forced into war by public clamour; and as late as the 11th the Cabinet ordered reinforcements for the fleet at Spithead. But in fact events had moved too far by then for the French to rescue any advantage, and they were obliged before the end of the month to recognise the fact.

The business indeed had really been decided by 7 October. Brunswick had granted an armistice while his Government inspected proposals made by the republicans on 26 September, and on the 28th Montmorin had told them to salvage what they could for themselves. On 2 October the Prussians and the British signed a secret Convention, confirming mutual support and agreeing the terms of a settlement. On the 6th, before the armistice expired, these were read to a Dutch deputation which waited on the Princess of Orange to apologise for her arrest. They were accepted on the 10th, when the last centre of opposition surrendered in Amsterdam. Ten days later the Convention was published, and on 27 October the French disclaimed any intention of

1. 21 September 1787 (loc. cit., 426). The French phrase was taken from an earlier statement of Montmorin's, to the opposite effect.
2. Pitt to Grenville, 22 September (loc. cit., 427).

having wished to intervene, and agreed to a mutual disarmament with the British.[1]

So ended the first diplomatic crisis for this country since the end of the American War. The result was a triumph. The Stadtholder was restored, the French party defeated, and France's own offer of support exposed. The Ministry had emerged united from a period of tension which might have led to war, and without provoking dissension in, or indeed disturbing, the country. British influence in Holland might now be restored, after an unhappy decade; at any rate France's 'preponderant influence' had been dealt a heavy blow. The effect was noted throughout Europe. 'La France vient de tomber', said the Austrian Emperor. 'L'Angleterre . . . a joué un rôle brillant et ferme', wrote the Russian Minister in London. British envoys sent their congratulations from almost every Court. 'I see . . . with great pleasure', wrote Cornwallis from India, reflecting on despatches sent at the end of the year, 'that the political state of Europe is much changed in our favour since . . . 1785'.[2]

The triumph was widely ascribed to Pitt. Parallels were drawn with Chatham, and his 'strength and spirit' were generally praised – though not everyone had been so enthusiastic when the result was in doubt.[3] Eden himself, who had disapproved, acknowledged that it had been 'a glorious story', and that while he had 'shuddered at his courage', it had been a comfort 'to negotiate under the cover of such formidable exertions as Mr. Pitt was making; and we owe everything to those exertions'.[4] Allowing for the limits of his knowledge and a wish to propitiate, this was a reasonable tribute. The British policy in Holland had borne Pitt's stamp since the end of 1786: a policy not identical with Carmarthen's or Richmond's, or with Thurlow's and the King's, or yet again with Harris's or Eden's. He could not rely much on his Foreign Secretary, once matters passed beyond generalities; for while Carmarthen often knew what he wanted, he lacked the skill to achieve the probability of bringing it about. On the contrary, it was generally assumed by the end of the affair that, as Montmorin observed, 'Lord Carmarthen . . . n'est que le prête-nom de M. Pitt'.[5] There was no one

1. The texts of the final Declaration and Counter-Declaration are given in *A.C.*, I, 256–7, and the English text is also in *H.C.J.*, 43 (1803), 12.

2. For Joseph II, see *Receuil des Instructions données aux Ambassadeurs et Ministres de France . . ., XXV – 2, Angleterre, Tome Troisième . . .*, ed. Paul Vaucher (1965), 538; for Vorontsov, Tomline, II, 316 n. Cornwallis was writing to Pitt on 5 March 1788 (P.R.O. 30/8/125).

3. E.g. the Archbishop of Canterbury to Eden, 21 September 1787 (*A.C.*, I, 441).

4. To George Rose, 1 November 1787 (loc. cit., 263–4).

5. Instructions for the Chevalier de la Luzerne [Ambassador to England], 7 January 1788 (*Receuil des Instructions . . . XXV – 2, Angleterre, Tome Troisième . . .*, 552).

in fact on whom to rely except Harris and, later, Grenville;[1] and while Harris was the moving spirit he had to be supervised, and Grenville was an aide rather than a colleague. This was, or became, a Cabinet matter, and Pitt had dominated the Cabinet, and, as time went by, gained his way with George III. His relations with the King, indeed, were one of the most interesting features of the whole affair. Hitherto they had always agreed on the overriding need for peace, and Pitt may have been strengthened in his passivity by his knowledge of George III's support. He had certainly not ventured to contradict him in the awkward episode of the *Fürstenbund*.[2] But in 1787 he politely but firmly held his course. It was indeed a tribute to both that each respected the other's position: Pitt did not try to bypass the King, and the King did not bring undue pressure on Pitt. In fact he came increasingly to trust him as the business developed – he welcomed the Minister's supervision of Harris, and his reluctance to forestall events. When the crisis was at its height, he refrained from giving advice. It was not the least of the signs that Pitt had made his mark on foreign affairs.

He had had a great deal of luck. Harris was a superb envoy, patient, persuasive, bold, the very man for the job. He was the real author of a policy whose instructions he then never exceeded; there could hardly have been victory without him, and the Ambassadorship and peerage which followed – rather belatedly – were fully earned.[3] His friendship with Fox, and the fact that the crisis took place in the long Parliamentary recess, contributed largely to a general acquiescence in measures which Opposition might in any case have found it hard to attack. The French moreover were in an awkward position, politically and financially embarrassed, and increasingly baffled by a movement which they found they could not control. Suffering from divisions at home and a variety of undisciplined agents in Holland, they made the worst of a cause which was always open to risk. But Pitt's greatest stroke of fortune, the event which determined the result, was the Prussians' eventual commitment and the speed of their success. One cannot tell what he might have done otherwise – his decisions are not always easy to predict. As it was, when things came to the point he knew that they could 'not go ill'.[4] He exploited a favourable situation. But he had played his part in bringing it about, by his restrained support of Harris earlier in the year and his well controlled movements from August. Prussia was influenced, though perhaps not decisively, by the British attitude; the French were faced with a policy which progressively

1. E.g. Pitt to Grenville, 23 September 1787 (*H.M.C., Dropmore,* III, 429): 'Even in these two days I feel no small difference in not being able to have your opinion on things as they arise'.
2. P. 474 above.
3. He was raised to the rank of Ambassador, from Minister, in March 1788, and created Lord Malmesbury in June.
4. P. 535 above.

matched events. The victory did not owe 'everything' by any means to Pitt's exertions.[1] But he enabled his country to enjoy most of the prestige.

III

The declaration extracted by the British from the French at the end of the Dutch affair was a humiliating document, not calculated to improve relations. Throughout the crisis itself Pitt had tried to be moderate, and as late as 23 September he urged on Grenville the importance of entering negotiations 'readily' if they were offered.[2] He foresaw well enough the dangers of France's 'sullen acquiescence' in a forced settlement: it 'might too naturally tend to some future struggle'.[3] But when Grenville returned empty-handed, Pitt did not hesitate to make the losers pay, and while he was anxious to live at peace, and ready to sound French views on the growing Eastern Question, he was not in the mood to follow up the hint which Montmorin now dropped for a closer connexion.[4] He inclined more towards other engagements designed to check any further trouble; and his recent success may have made him more confident of his grasp of foreign affairs.

In this new atmosphere, the two immediate candidates for an alliance were Holland and Prussia. An agreement with Holland was desirable on several counts: to consolidate the ground regained from France, to settle Far Eastern questions, and – a point that was not disregarded – to balance Prussian influence in the country. The fact was recognised at once; but the talks proceeded slowly – so slowly indeed that the French could not understand the delay. But it arose from the British decision to aim for one comprehensive treaty, covering Far Eastern as well as European affairs,[5] and it was not until April 1788, when the two sides had agreed to take the problems separately, that an Anglo-Dutch treaty was signed. Britain then guaranteed the territory and constitution of Holland as they stood, and the two countries formed a mutual defensive alliance and expressed their intention of taking each other's goods on a most favoured nation basis – with the important exception that British duties on Dutch linens were not to be reduced.[6]

1. P. 536 above.
2. *H.M.C., Dropmore*, III, 428. And cf. p. 535 above. He was beginning to wonder however, how far events might affect '*the application* of the principles laid down' (to Grenville, 22 September 1787; *H.M.C., Dropmore*, III, 427).
3. Carmarthen to Grenville, 23 September 1787 (*British Diplomatic Instructions 1689–1789, volume VII, France, Part IV,* ... ed. L. G. Wickham Legg (1934), 294). The despatch was drafted by Pitt (P.R.O., F.O. 97/246).
4. I think this is suggested in a letter of Carmarthen's to Thurlow on 27 October (B.M. Add. Ms 28062, ff. 408–11). It emerges more strongly in one from Pitt to Eden on 2 November 1787 (*A.C.,* I, 266).
5. See pp. 425–9 above.
6. The English text is published in, *inter alia, H.C.J.,* 43, 500–1.

The treaty was timed to coincide with the signature of a similar Prusso-Dutch alliance. The British and Prussian Governments had agreed to make parallel arrangements with Holland rather than form a triple alliance immediately, so as not to provoke a counter-alliance which might otherwise not emerge. But they had recorded their desire for a closer connexion after the autumn crisis, and the matter was considered in the following months. The Prussians made the running in October and November, and again in the spring of 1788; they found Pitt and his colleagues well disposed, but cautious. It was of course difficult to frame a treaty while there were still questions outstanding with the Dutch – and the Prussians, too, were experiencing delays in that quarter. But the reasons were wider than that. They lay largely in the prospects, as seen from London, for central and northern Europe, where old rivalries were surfacing under the impact of a new Russo-Turkish war.

The Eastern Question in fact was now entering the orbit of British policy. Within the next three years it was to move towards the centre. This might not have happened so fast had it not been for Prussia; for the Prussians, seeing a chance to realise territorial ambitions, were closely involved in a general unsettlement into which Britain, as a result, was the more readily drawn. It was a confusing process, for the two countries' interests were by no means identical. Prussia hoped to gain at the expense of Austria, her old enemy, and all her calculations centred on the fact. At the end of 1787, stimulated by the prospect of the Austrians' joining with the Russians in the war against Turkey, the Anglophil Hertzberg resurrected an old dream of territorial exchange. The Emperor, compensated by gains in the Balkans, and threatened by Prussian support of the Turks, was to return the province of Galicia to the Poles, from whom it had been taken in the First Partition of 1772; the Poles in their turn, as a mark of gratitude, were to cede to Prussia the city of Danzig and the neighbouring province of Thorn, which would round off Prussia's territories and strengthen her eastern border. This 'complex, cynical and impracticable scheme'[1] involved an ambivalent attitude to Russia. For while it was anti-Russian in its manœuvres with the semi-subjugated Poles, the Empress might perhaps be induced to accept it if she was gratified elsewhere. Hertzberg therefore favoured Russia's acquisition of Bessarabia (on the east bank of the Dniester) and the port of Ochakov (near the mouth of the Bug), enlarging that access to the Black Sea which was Catherine's prime concern. He was in fact preparing to bring pressure on the Turks, whom he would first lay claim to support, and for whom he proposed to secure future guarantees of their territories south of the Danube; and he was also prepared if necessary to adjust Prussia's northern policy of sympathy for Sweden, hitherto a useful pinprick against Russia and a

1. M. S. Anderson, *The Eastern Question 1774–1923: A Study in International Relations* (1966), 14.

counter in the game with France. He reckoned that the plan, for all its complication, had an inherent and ingenious simplicity; for while no power could complain at gaining something, none would welcome the other's gains. The proposals for a settlement in the Balkans would give Prussia a special relationship with Turkey, while fostering dissension between the two Imperial Powers (already uneasy about each other's designs) and between them and France, with her eastern Mediterranean interests. A hostile triple alliance was thus unlikely; Prussia would emerge as an arbitrator in south-east Europe; and her influence in Poland would be greatly increased at Russia's expense.

But none of this would be easily accomplished if Prussia had to play a lone hand. She might well need the reassurance of a powerful connexion. Hence the desire for a triple alliance with Holland and, above all, Britain. The scheme as it stood, however, was not to the British taste. Pitt was anxious to remove any lingering incentive for Prussia to link up with France – a by no means impossible event, as the past year had shown – and he did not disapprove of the idea of a peaceful joint *démarche* on behalf of Turkey, or of a closer relationship between Prussia and the Poles. An Anglo-Prussian alliance might indeed prove useful, in helping to bring the Eastern war to a close, and in fostering new commercial openings and opportunities in north-east Europe.[1] But in so far as such ideas were worked out, they were aimed at Russia rather than Austria; and they were certainly not designed to risk a war for the Turks, or upset the territorial *status quo*. There was thus a fundamental difference between the two Governments' objects, partially disguised, or at least offset, by their overlapping aims. The fact became clearer as time went by, and the immediate advantages of a connexion had to be weighed more closely against the wider implications.

Throughout the winter and spring of 1787-8 the British therefore hung back. Their replies to the Prussians in December and in April were virtually the same.[2] We were anxious to combine our arrangements for Holland, and work for common ends elsewhere. But 'a formal Alliance . . . would be unpolitic' while the Imperial Powers and France were not formally connected, and while Prussia appeared to be contemplating moves of her own in the Eastern war.[3] The Government therefore drafted in April a public mutual guarantee for Holland, to follow as soon as possible the separate British and Prussian treaties with the Dutch, and suggested that the two powers should sound other well disposed nations in search of a system of defensive alliance which would be wide enough not to cause undue alarm.

1. For which, at this time, see pp. 506-7 above.
2. Cf. the despatches to Ewart of 2 December 1787 (no. 24) and 2 April 1788 (nos. 4 and 5), in P.R.O., F.O. 64/12, 64/13.
3. Carmarthen to Ewart, no. 5, Secret and Confidential, 2 April 1788 (F.O. 64/13), explaining the Cabinet's thoughts as background to instructions of the same date in no. 4.

To British eyes the most likely adherents to such a system lay in the Baltic, and its greatest merit might lie in a settlement for 'the North of Europe'.[1] If Sweden and Denmark, or either, could be included, it might be possible to talk to Russia about the whole range of problems in which the various countries were concerned. Prussian wishes in Poland, Polish trade with Prussia, Anglo-Russian trade, Russia's relations with Sweden – the whole complex might be discussed if such a confederation could be formed. The British became the more attached to the idea from a sudden impetus at the end of 1787. For late in December, out of the blue, the Swedes themselves made a secret approach for a quintuple alliance with Britain, Prussia, Holland and Denmark.[2] The proposal in point of fact was less hopeful than it looked at first – it was indeed a warlike move in search of support, for Gustavus III of Sweden was meditating an attack on the Russians to regain some former territory, in the expectation that they would now be fully occupied with the Turks. No precise answer was therefore given. But the attraction remained. In April, the British were still talking more of sounding Sweden and Denmark than of an alliance with Prussia alone.

But the picture changed in the next few months. The strongest reason for Britain to join with Prussia was to prevent her from joining with France, and in the second half of May that fear was raised again. The British proposal for a guarantee of Holland had been returned by the Prussians in April, with suggestions for additional secret articles covering mutual defensive support elsewhere.[3] These met, once more, with a cautious response: Pitt did not reject them outright, but he was not disposed to rush into an agreement, and still hankered after a wider confederation.[4] The Prussians were annoyed. They did not seem to be getting anywhere, and towards the end of the month Ewart warned that they might turn to the French. Frederick William II was about to visit Holland. He might take the opportunity to change sides. It was necessary to act soon if the Francophil party in Berlin was to be checked.

Whether this advice was sound or not, the Government was impressed.

1. Carmarthen to Ewart, no. 24, 2 December 1787 (F.O. 64/12).

2. There had been signs in the past two months that they were thinking of inclining to Britain; but this explicit proposal took us by surprise. It was accompanied by an equally sudden overture for an Anglo-Swedish commercial treaty, which was pursued intermittently over the next six or seven months (see p. 477, n1 above).

3. And also, unofficially, for 'a secret Cooperation' with Britain and Holland to acquire 'an Influence' at Liège, 'from its being the Key to all the Netherlands' (Ewart to Carmarthen, no. 24, 12 April 1788; F.O. 64/13). They may have been encouraged in this by the knowledge that a British agent had been in the city in the previous summer. It was the egregious W. A. Miles (see p. 531, n2 above), whose activities usually roused suspicion. But, while desperately soliciting Pitt for money and recognition (P.R.O. 30/8/159), he had in fact been engaged primarily on a piece of private business – the attempted restoration of the abducted son of an Irish Catholic peer – in which the Foreign Office had been asked to help.

4. Carmarthen to Ewart, no. 8, 14 May 1788 (F.O. 64/13), drafted by Pitt (F.O. 97/323).

On the last day of May, the Cabinet took the plunge. At a meeting with all members present, it resolved that a treaty of defensive alliance with Prussia must be 'forthwith concluded' if she would not wait for the negotiation of a more extensive system. Harris was present in London at the time, having been summoned home earlier in the month. He was ordered to return at once to Holland, while Frederick William was there, with powers to sign at his discretion both the mutual guarantee of the Dutch and the secret articles in the sense proposed.[1] He did so, in his best style. The King's *valet de chambre* was bribed to keep out inconvenient advisers while Harris had an audience, and a Provisional Treaty was signed at Loo on 13 June. It was a competent achievement in awkward circumstances. Prussia had been preserved from France, and by extracting a Provisional, not (as the Prussians had hoped) a Definitive treaty, the British were in a somewhat stronger position to debate the precise consequences of the secret articles.

They proceeded to do so at once; for the arrangements had to be ratified within six months, and there had already been signs that the two countries wanted different interpretations. The British were anxious not to be drawn too deeply into Prussian continental adventures; the Prussians, not to be involved in British 'maritime wars'.[2] The problem was argued in detail over the next six weeks, and agreement appeared the more likely as British hopes of a wider system finally collapsed. For in July Gustavus III of Sweden decided to risk his attack on Russia – a dangerous provocation which the two allies condemned. They both tried to bring pressure to bear, their efforts brought them closer together, and a Prussian alliance seemed the more acceptable in London as the prospect of a quintuple alliance disappeared. The Definitive Treaty was signed on 13 August. Each partner had yielded some ground. The Prussians were committed to a diversion in Europe in the case of a British war overseas; the British to land as well as financial and maritime support of Prussia, to the tune eventually of 60,000 men.[3]

The Triple Alliance (as it has always been known – it was really a triangular alliance, for there was no one treaty which Britain, Holland and Prussia signed) was widely approved by Parliament, as a proper sequel to the Dutch crisis. Fox and Burke supported a result achieved, once again, by Harris, and when the earlier naval preparations were found to have been relatively inexpensive, approval turned to enthus-

1. Cabinet Minute of 31 May; *L.C.G. III*, I, no. 450. Harris's discretionary powers are emphasised in his letter to Ewart of 13 June 1788, in *Malmesbury*, II, 421.
2. See Ewart to Carmarthen, no. 27, 19 April 1788 (F.O. 64/13).
3. The treaty is published in, *inter alia*, *H.C.J.*, 44 (1803), 216–17. The text may be compared with that of the provisional treaty of 13 June in Martens, *Receuil de Traités*, IV, 382–5, 390–3. An undated draft of the British proposals in Pitt's hand is in P.R.O. 30/8/197.

iasm. There was a general welcome for a step which in fact – whether or not this was generally understood – referred to central Europe as much as to Holland, and must lead the Ministry to watch events there if only to see that its new ally was restrained.

It was already involved in those of the Baltic, where the sudden war started by Sweden was threatening to spread in an area traditionally of British concern. The supply of naval stores was an object which no Administration could afford to ignore, and there was also the prospect now of a growing export trade. Pitt was held in London in July and August by the 'news from abroad', cancelling visits to Burton Pynsent and to the Lake District and the north.[1] By the beginning of September the situation was forcing him to intervene. For Gustavus III, after some early successes at a time of Russian weakness, had run into serious trouble and appeared in danger of defeat. His fleet was held in harbour, there had been a mutiny in the army, he himself was forced to leave the field for Stockholm; and at the end of August his old rivals the Danes seemed about to declare war. Neither England nor Prussia could allow this to pass undisturbed. They had already been in touch with the Danes, in the name of the Triple Alliance; each of them now decided to take steps on its own. Pitt sent a warning despatch to Copenhagen;[2] the Prussians moved more strongly. Annoyed by a recent Russian approach to Poland for an alliance, of which they had been belatedly informed, they were in no mood to conciliate the Empress, and their concern for Sweden was strengthened by the news that France was about to mediate on her behalf. In mid-September they told the Danes that, if they attacked Gustavus, Prussia would invade Danish Holstein; and added for good measure, with Ewart's unauthorised approval, that the British would send a fleet. This did not in fact stop the Danes; but it set the scene for a piece of spirited diplomacy. The British Minister in Copenhagen, Hugh Elliot, was in close correspondence with Ewart in Berlin. When he heard of the Prussians' decision he saw a chance to act on his own. He greeted it with obvious relish, and carried it through in high style. Crossing the Sound at once, he ran Gustavus to earth in Gothenburg, awaiting a Danish attack. The King was near the end of his tether. But Elliot told him of the allies' latest moves and, with a grandiloquent flourish – 'Sire, give me your Crown; I will return it to you with added lustre', – asked for full powers to negotiate on his behalf. Gustavus eventually consented; Elliot set off for the Danish headquarters; the Swedes, emboldened by the turn of events, presented a bold front at Gothenburg; and on 9 October the Danes accepted an armistice of eight days. During that

1. Pitt to Hester Countess of Chatham, 29 August 1788 (Stanhope, I, 381). The 'news from abroad' included disturbances in France, and the progress of the Russo-Turkish war; but, above all, the events in the Baltic.
2. Carmarthen to Elliot, no. 14, 9 September 1788; the draft is in Pitt's hand, and the despatch followed it unaltered (P.R.O., F.O. 22/10).

time the Prussians' warning reached them; the truce was prolonged, and they finally agreed to withdraw from the war.

Elliot and Ewart were naturally elated. They were annoyed to find themselves rebuked by London. This was scarcely surprising, for unlike Harris, whose example may have helped inspire them, they had acted without instructions and committed their superiors to the hilt.[1] Nor was the rebuke probably just for the record, for while the new alliance had scored an ostensible victory the British at least were propelled towards a position they wished to avoid. It was all very well for Elliot to claim that there had never been 'a more striking testimony of deference paid by a foreign prince to a King of England'.[2] The tone of his and Ewart's behaviour had forced their Government to take sides in a sensitive area at a delicate time. The result, it was true, was what had been hoped. Sweden was saved from humiliation. But Britain's relations with Denmark were weakened by this 'deference', and the Russians, already disgruntled,[3] were encouraged in the suspicions which had been growing over the past four years. Pitt was not looking for that kind of triumph. He was not looking for trials of strength in central Europe at all. He was rather, in this instance, trying to escape being drawn into any camp; and indeed, on first learning of Ewart's and Elliot's activities, he wondered if he could not invite France and Spain to join in a mediation – in a case in which Prussia had moved largely with the object of forestalling France.[4]

For Pitt was still, above all, very wary of being identified with Prussia. His efforts in 1789 were directed to making that clear. It proved increasingly hard to do so as the situation became more disturbed. In the north the Government tried to steer a middle course. Gustavus was warned that he could not always count on British support, beyond sympathy and some money; and while the Danes, now neutral, were warned of our displeasure when they conveyed a Russian squadron through Swedish waters, the Ministry's 'earnest desire' was to 'conciliate' them, and still indeed attract them to the Triple Alliance.[5] Relations

1. Harris's example may have operated particularly on Ewart, who had become a protégé of the older man's over the past two years. He may indeed have been emboldened by a private letter from his mentor, who had just been staying with Pitt and Carmarthen, informing him that 'Our Idea is that the King of Sweden must not be crush'd, or the balance of the Baltick overset' (29 August 1788; Ewart Mss, Kirtlebridge, Dumfriesshire). Nevertheless, Harris had added that they also wished that Prussia had not sounded so bellicose, which might have given him a warning.

Elliot, despite his elation, may have felt rather nervous about what he had done. 'Write everything about me to London;' he urged Ewart on 16 October, 'I have never written myself, having acted hitherto without Instructions' (Ewart Mss).

2. To Carmarthen, 15 November 1788; quoted in Holland Rose, 500.

3. See pp. 505–6 above and 546 below.

4. To George III, 19 October 1788; *L.C.G. III*, I, no. 485.

5. Carmarthen to Elliot, 5 December 1788, 24 June 1789 (when Carmarthen had become Leeds). The protest about the convoy was sent on 21 August 1789. See Holland Rose, 498–9, 501–2.

with Russia were formal and cool, though both sides showed occasional interest in a thaw: the Regency crisis in the winter raised Catherine's hopes that Pitt would disappear, and the commercial negotiation remained mostly at a low ebb. The northern situation developed with only spasmodic comment from London. Meanwhile events farther south left the Government embarrassed and often perplexed.

The first of these followed in the course of the winter. Between November 1788 and May 1789 the Poles freed themselves from Russian control. The Great Diet (as it became known), meeting in October, demolished the edifice of government guaranteed by Russia, and, aided by the demands of the Turkish war, procured the withdrawal of Russian troops. These were startling achievements, which surprised the Poles themselves. They would not have been possible without the support of Prussia, which offered the Poles a connexion or alliance in place of one recently proposed, unsuccessfully, by Catherine II.[1] It was not immediately clear what form it might take, or indeed if it would come about at all. There was still the possibility that Prussia and Russia would patch up their differences and reach a fresh agreement, in which of course the Prussians would improve their position without recourse to the Poles. But the Russians vacillated; the Poles forced the pace, with overtures to Berlin; and by the late summer the Prussians could not resist the lure. The time seemed both demanding and ripe. The Imperial Powers were doing well in the Eastern war, and might soom be more free to act strongly elsewhere. Meanwhile, however, they were fully engaged, Austria was harassed by troubles in the Empire and the Netherlands, and France, the third possible partner, seemed to be sinking into revolution. It was the sort of occasion for which Hertzberg was waiting. He revived his old scheme in extreme form, and in August 1789 proposed that it should be presented to the Imperial Powers, backed by a military demonstration and an ultimatum on behalf of the Turks.

Any such event was bound to rouse the British, for under the terms of the alliance we might be involved. Pitt had had little time to follow European affairs closely during the Regency crisis of the winter, and in the spring and early summer the situation was still obscure. But the Ministry was thoroughly alarmed by the prospect of a war in such a cause, the more so because British and Prussian interests overlapped even while they diverged. The Government was interested in the Austrian Netherlands, now accepted as a region of British concern.[2] It was also becoming concerned in the commercial possibilities of Poland under the new regime, as an alternative source of supply and market to Russia.[3] Both issues involved consultation with Prussia: it was the more important to see that they were not used by the Prussians for

1. See p. 506 above.
2. See pp. 547-8 below.
3. Pp. 506-8 above.

their own ends. Our relations with Russia, and to a lesser extent with Austria, were already strained by the war: Catherine had accused Pitt of inciting the Turks at the start (a claim to which the activities of the British envoy in Constantinople lent colour), and his very efforts to be strictly neutral caused intermittent trouble, particularly when they led him in March 1788 to stop Russian agents from hiring transports in England. The prospect of awkward decisions now made it the more necessary not to risk our freedom of manœuvre by being associated too closely with the Prussian schemes. The Cabinet gave clear notice in June of its dislike of policies aimed apparently at 'aggrandisement rather than security'.[1] It repeated its warnings in September, when it learned of Hertzberg's latest plan. The Prussian Minister wished, so Ewart reported, to urge 'the expediency of combining the Affairs of the East with those of the North'.[2] He was told that this was acceptable only if it referred to the desirability of a peaceful negotiation.[3]

The British representations had their effect. They supported military objections within Prussia itself to an immediate, largely unprepared campaign, and Frederick William was veering in any case towards an even more distasteful scheme. Rather than confine himself to a territorial exchange not wholly unfavourable to his 'natural enemy' Austria,[4] he was thinking of preparing for a war in the spring with much greater gains in view. To this end he would ally himself with the Turks in the winter, discourage Sweden from making peace, and press steadily forward for a closer connexion with the Poles. Hertzberg's proposals were therefore rejected, and the British breathed again. But in point of fact the prospects were no brighter than before.

The Prussians' new design was pursued over the next few months, against the usual background of feints and diversionary conversations. Gustavus III was encouraged to persevere,[5] the growing troubles in the Austrian dominions were encouraged, and meanwhile talks proceeded with the Turks and with the Poles. The former resulted in January 1790 in a treaty, negotiated by the Prussian Minister in Constantinople, promising intervention in the spring of 1791 if the Imperial Powers had not returned their conquests by then. This in fact went well beyond the envoy's instructions, and it caused a great stir:

1. Leeds to Ewart, 24 June 1789 (Holland Rose, 509). The despatch noted that Prussia thought the continuation of the Swedo-Russian war *'in some degree advantageous'* as a *'diversion in case the Allies should take part in a Turkish War'*. This was 'an object by no means in our view.'

2. To Leeds, no. 48, 10 August 1789 (P.R.O., F.O. 64/16).

3. Leeds to Ewart, no. 16, 14 September 1789 (loc. cit.).

4. His own phrase – 'He could not bring himself to do so little harm to his natural enemy'; quoted in Robert Howard Lord, *The Second Partition of Poland: A Diplomatic History* (1915), 118.

5. Partly by assurances, renewed despite earlier discouragement from London (see pp. 543–4 above), that England would send a fleet to the Baltic in his support.

the Prussian Government indeed was soon forced to state that the terms would not be ratified. But the event did not help to lower the temperature, and neither did its sequel at the end of March, when after three months of hard bargaining Prussia signed an alliance with the Poles. The scene was now set to her liking, ready for any move she might care to make.

All this was serious enough. It made the British thoroughly uneasy. Even the Prusso-Polish alliance, favoured in principle, seemed dangerous in such a context. But there was a further development, of more direct concern, which added to the growing difficulties of these winter months.

Since early in 1789 there had been signs of revolt in the Austrian possessions. Joseph II's far-reaching reforms, coupled with the need to raise supplies for the Turkish war, were provoking widespread regional – often conservative – reactions. Galicia, Hungary, Bohemia, Lombardy, were in a state of unrest in varying degrees; so were the Austrian Netherlands, where the distant suzerainty of Vienna was tolerated only on the assumption that it remained remote. But in June 1789 – at the very moment when the Estates in France were asserting their rights – the Emperor removed the privileges of the Estates in Brabant. As in Holland a few years before, an unnatural coalition arose, of democrats looking to Paris and conservatives resenting monarchical assumptions. In July it declared for a Belgic Republic under the protection of the Triple Alliance, and in the autumn and early winter sent emissaries to London to press its case. It also approached the Dutch and the Prussians: the former were mildly in favour; the latter, as might have been expected, were prepared to force the pace. Here was a splendid chance to weaken Austria, and with the aid of their allies. It would commit Britain, enlarge Prussia's influence, and raise her prestige at a critical time. A successful guarantee of Belgium would be noted in Galicia and Hungary; it would also show the whole of Europe that the Triple Alliance carried weight. These feelings grew stronger as the revolution gathered strength. By the end of November, the Prussians were pressing for recognition of the Belgic Republic.

The British, once more, disagreed. Pitt had been opposed from the start. He set down his views in August, and they did not change. Our great object in the Austrian Netherlands was to prevent them from being added to the power of France; this was – in his prescient words – 'worth the risk, or even the certainty' of war.[1] It followed therefore that they should be held within the sphere of Dutch and British interest; it did not necessarily follow that they should become an autonomous power. The earlier position in fact suited us well – semi-independent

1. Memoir of 27 August 1789 (B.M. Add. Ms 28068; quoted by J. H. Clapham in *The Cambridge History of British Foreign Policy 1783–1919*, I (1922), 188).

provinces under Austrian rule – and our best policy was to try to restore it by supporting the restoration of Belgian rights. If the Emperor decided on force, the Triple Alliance must oppose him. But Ministers on the whole thought this unlikely, and then precipitate action would be unwise. What, in the first place, should we be recognising? A confused and client state, a target ripe precisely for French adventure or intrigue. And what should we do if, once committed, we found that Austrian policy changed? The Emperor was known to be ill; he was in fact rumoured to be dying, and his successor was suspected of holding very different views. The Prussians talked at the end of the year of the need to be 'Masters of the Events'. But if we moved as they wished 'the Consequence . . . would . . . be, that instead of rendering Ourselves Masters of the Events, . . . we may find Ourselves entangled in such a Manner as to prevent Our improving the different Occurrences which may arise to the best Advantage.'[1]

By the end of December, both allies were roused. Each was angry with the other, and Hertzberg made matters worse by seeking to involve the problem in his perennial Galician exchange. The British, who held 'the Question of the Netherlands to be perfectly distinct from any other',[2] now decided that Prussia must be firmly restrained. Enlisting Dutch help, they managed in January to produce a tripartite agreement. There should be no intervention by the allies without Austrian consent, or unless circumstances made it necessary for them to maintain the Netherlands' privileges. They reserved the right to recognise Belgian independence if this was required. But there was to be no unilateral action by any of the partners, and they would all stand by the agreed result.[3] This seemed to check the wild men in Berlin. But the affair was not over yet. The Prussians continued to press for recognition, and Ewart caused a furious reaction in London in February 1790 by seeming to favour a bargain with Austria in return for the Galician exchange.[4] In March, as the central European crisis seemed about to come to a head, allied relations were still embittered by the Netherlands' problem.

British policy over Belgium naturally pleased the Austrians; and at the beginning of 1790 the Imperial Powers decided to cast a fly. After

1. Ewart to Leeds, no. 85, 31 December 1789 (F.O. 64/16); Leeds to Ewart, no. 4, 26 February 1790 (F.O. 64/17, where the draft carries some marginal corrections by Pitt. There is also a copy in his own papers, P.R.O. 30/8/338). These views had by then been put into practice. In October, and again in November, Pitt had refused to deal with Belgian emissaries.

2. Leeds to Ewart, 15 December 1789 (copy in B.M. Add. Ms 28064, ff. 408–9v). And see also same to same, no. 22, 14 December 1789 (F.O. 64/16).

3. There is a copy of the Convention, signed at The Hague on 11 January 1790, in F.O. 64/17.

4. The correspondence is in B.M. Add. Ms 28065.

a successful campaign in the summer they were sounding Turkey on the prospects for peace, and as the Anglo-Prussian disputes became more open they saw a chance to exploit them. In mid-January a sudden offer of defensive alliance reached London from Vienna, coupled with a request for British mediation in the Eastern war. Soon afterwards an equally sudden offer of alliance came from St Petersburg, accompanied by renewed proposals for a commercial treaty.[1] Neither was taken very seriously so far as an alliance was concerned; but the Austrian opening for a mediation was a different matter. The Government informed the Prussians,[2] and replied cordially to Vienna. But a few weeks later it received a more pressing invitation to act.

The Emperor Joseph II had been ill since early in 1789; by the winter it was doubtful if he would recover, and now, on 20 February, he died. He was succeeded by his brother Leopold, Grand Duke of Tuscany, who was known to dislike the war. On the 24th the British Minister in Florence was summoned from his normal duties of entertaining English travellers to hear and report some important news. The new Emperor – or King of Hungary as he remained pending the Imperial election – asked for British 'Mediation & Assistance' for a general peace. He did so, moreover, in distinctly promising terms. He called the Russian alliance 'unfortunate', asserted that he disliked his brother's recent policies, and announced his intention of approaching Prussia forthwith.[3] Here was a real chance for the Ministry to intervene. At the end of March, against an ominous background of Prussian military preparations, the British envoys in Vienna, St Petersburg and Constantinople were told to propose an immediate armistice in the Eastern war, to be followed by a negotiation for a general settlement.

The British concentrated their hopes on Austria, which had made the approach. Since Russia might procrastinate, and the reply in any case would take longer to reach London, they suggested an immediate armistice between the Austrians and the Turks. They also proposed – as they had long thought – that the basis of a settlement should be the territorial *status quo* as it had been on the eve of the war. There were several reasons for this. It would of course help the Turks, who in return might join an extended alliance; it might, by precedent, help the Swedes if peace came to the north; it would effectually curb the Prussians' manoeuvres; and – a chain of reasoning still rather tentative, but

1. For the former see Leeds to Keith, Secret and Confidential, 12 January 1790 (F.O. 7/19); for the latter, Leeds to Alleyne Fitzherbert, Private, 2 February 1790 (copy in B.M. Add. Ms 28065, ff. 95–6), and pp. 508-9 above. The Government suspected that the Austrian offer, which bore an earlier date, had in fact been antedated so that it appeared to have been composed before a recent run of further reverses in the Netherlands.

2. Taking care to point out that they had not kept us officially informed of their own discussions with Austria and Russia in recent months (Leeds to Ewart, no. 3, Secret and Confidential, 9 February 1790; F.O. 64/17).

3. Lord Hervey to Leeds, no. 6, 28 February 1790 (F.O. 79/6).

gradually hardening – it might induce the Poles to make an easier settlement with the Triple Alliance, which would satisfy Pitt's hopes. For the Poles, now drawing closer to Prussia,[1] still hankered for Galicia in exchange for losing Danzig; and this awkward ambition was an obstacle to a comprehensive commercial scheme. If the *status quo* was accepted, they might then agree to more modest compensation, which Britain could guarantee as the basis for an enlarged Anglo-Prusso-Polish trade. Since one of the objects of such an arrangement was to curb Russian commercial expansion to the south,[2] it was also associated directly with the maintenance of the former Turkish borders. This was all still in the background, and the Prussians were still holding the options open; their alliance with the Poles in March made no mention of the Galician exchange. But it was an element in the British thinking, which reinforced the more pressing reasons for a general recognition of the territorial *status quo*.

The proposals were not easily accepted. The Austrians, perhaps hardly surprisingly, objected at first to an armistice without Russian consent. Their immediate reaction indeed was so cool that the Prussians were able to discount it, and throughout April and most of May it looked as if they would still attack. Pitt had to repeat his familiar warnings to Berlin, and define his conditions of support.[3] But by the end of that month the prospects began to look brighter. The Prussian preparations were not going well – transport and supplies were proving inadequate –, the Austrians were massing troops on the Silesian frontier, and they for their part were feeling disappointed with the Russians. For in April the Poles, excited by the Prussian alliance, showed signs of invading Galicia, and when the Austrians asked the Russians for a promise of support they received an evasive reply. Catherine was more interested in a fresh campaign against the Turks: she would only mount a diversion against Poland, leaving the defence of Galicia to the Austrians themselves. This news strengthened the new Emperor in his determination to talk to Prussia, and the Prussians themselves were now more in the mood to agree. On 27 June their envoys met at the village of Reichenbach, and a direct negotiation began.

Agreement was reached a month later, on 27 July. As a result of some hard bargaining,[4] a Convention was signed recognising the

1. See pp. 545, 547 above.

2. P. 508 above.

3. He was at particular pains to stress that if Prussia was involved in a war which she had not herself started, and was attacked by France or Denmark, British support would be forthcoming at once; but that this must not be taken as in itself a general guarantee against attack from any quarter. Since the most likely quarters in point of fact were Austria and Russia, the promise was in effect a discouragement, as well as reflecting the continuing British concern at any threat from France. (Leeds to Ewart, no. 7, 26 March 1790, no. 12, 21 May 1790. The final version of the latter is in F.O. 64/17; drafts of both are in Pitt's papers, P.R.O. 30/8/338).

4. Pitt was particularly upset at one point when the Prussians threatened, after their earlier denial, to ratify the treaty with Turkey which their envoy had signed

status quo. Austria consented to an immediate armistice on her own account with Turkey, and to attend a Congress for final peace terms under the mediation of the Triple Alliance. If she then gained minor territorial advantages, the Prussians reserved the right to claim equivalent concessions. Austria agreed to take no further part in a continuing Russo-Turkish war; the Triple Alliance would use its good offices to bring such a war to an end; and also to reconcile the Netherlands to Austrian rule. At the beginning of August 1790 the immediate danger of war in central Europe had thus been averted, and in the various Courts of Europe the effects were being assessed.

At first sight, the result appeared to be a humiliation for Austria; and it was so regarded in Vienna itself. Any minor gains she might win from the Turks might be balanced by losses to Prussia, and she was placed in uneasy isolation, and in debt to the Triple Alliance. Nevertheless, she had in fact saved a good deal from a weak position. She could still bargain with Turkey, and her possessions remained intact. Galicia had not changed hands, the Belgians had failed to achieve independence, and there was now a chance to settle unrest elsewhere. These achievements and opportunities were a measure of Prussia's failure; for if Prussia dictated the terms, they were not those she would have liked. She had not gone to war when brought to the point; she had secured nothing concrete; and she had emerged from the Convention having failed to satisfy the Poles. Her schemes perhaps had gained her prestige: she was a guarantor for the Turks and the Belgians. But she had gained nothing else, and the future was full of doubt. She had forced the pace; her threats and manœuvres had set the scene for the negotiation. But the outcome was ostensibly as much to the advantage of the Triple Alliance as to herself.

For it was the alliance that emerged as the mediating instrument; and the terms which it guaranteed were those that Britain had proposed. At first sight, she had come out best. The *status quo* had been preserved, and the Turks, the Belgians, the Austrians themselves, were placed in the setting she had wished. It might really seem, as one British diplomat put it even before this event, that she was 'now incontestably in possession of the balance of Europe' – a 'happy change' from the position of a few years before.[1] France, in her troubles, was almost out of the running; the Imperial alliance had at last been weakened; British influence was high in the Low Countries, though the Dutch remained stubborn in matters of trade; the Prussians' plans of the past few years had been effectively restrained. Even the fact that the Poles were now angry with Prussia was a not inconvenient bonus

on his own responsibility at the beginning of the year (see pp. 546–7 above). The draft of the long and furious despatch to Ewart (no. 19, 23 July 1790), in his own hand throughout, is in B.M. Add. Ms 28066, ff. 120–126v.

1. Alleyne Fitzherbert [at The Hague] to Leeds, 1 January 1790 (B.M. Add. Ms 28065, f. 1).

for any future initiative that Britain might wish to take. Such deductions could be easily drawn, and they were legitimate. But their value could be overestimated in a situation in which no one had really won much. For the real legacy of Reichenbach was 'dissatisfaction, disillusionment, growing estrangement',[1] and in such a state of affairs the British contribution raised its own dangers. Prussia and Poland were still dissatisfied; and if Austria had stopped fighting, Russia had not. Indeed a run of successes against Sweden, leading in August to peace in the Baltic, left her more free than before to carry on against the Turks. There was much unfinished business in eastern Europe; Britain was now more directly involved; and she had taken her stand on the preservation of the *status quo*. As Pitt entered more deeply into the ramifications, spreading outwards from the problem of Poland, he found himself challenging Russia on a principle he refused to drop. Given the conditions of 1790, which the Convention failed to remove, it was not a long step from Reichenbach to the Ochakov crisis in the following spring.

All these events may seem rather petty when one considers what was happening elsewhere: the meeting of the States General, the fall of the Bastille, the march on Versailles, the Jacobin Club. The Triple Alliance and the Convention of Reichenbach pale against the fires of the French Revolution; the diplomats' preoccupations were soon to be so largely swept away. In September 1788, in what proved to be the dying months of the *ançien régime* in France, Lord Malmesbury – Sir James Harris – gave Pitt a general survey of continental problems. The most urgent need was for a Congress to settle the Baltic war; and this might then consider 'all other subjects, which as far as human foresight can reach may lead on some future day to disturb the tranquillity of Europe: . . . the Election of a King of the Romans – the fixing of the nature of the Bavarian succession – the determining of the doubtful points in the constitutions of Sweden & Poland', which, with 'various other less important Objects', might all be settled in 'a kind of *new Treaty of Munster*'.[2] The emphasis was to shift in the next twelve months more largely to eastern and central Europe. But there it remained until the summer of 1791.

This did not mean that events in France were not followed attentively elsewhere: in England, at first with widespread sympathy, later with growing concern. Nor of course were the diplomatic implications

1. Lord, *The Second Partition of Poland,* 152. He is referring specifically to Prusso-Polish relations; but the description may be generally applied.

2. 29 September 1788, from The Hague (P.R.O. 30/8/155). The reference, strictly speaking, was to one of the treaties in 1648 which comprised the Peace of Westphalia that brought the Thirty Years' War to a close. Malmesbury was doubtless thinking of the Peace as a whole.

ignored: in Holland, in Germany, throughout the Austrian possessions, the leaven could be seen at work. The British Government was less likely than others to worry much about domestic unrest; but it now had as much reason as any to consider the prospects for the balance of power. Despite the recent commercial agreement France was still the prime suspect in London. The Triple Alliance had owed its existence to the fact, and the position did not alter in the various crises that now arose. In the Baltic, in Belgium, in central Europe, the possibility of French action evoked the same British response. It was in order to lessen the risk of French domination that Pitt discouraged Belgian independence, and he was more ready to promise aid to Prussia if she was attacked by France than by the Imperial Powers.[1] But while the British did not lose sight of France, it was now as a factor in situations in which she was not at the centre, and indeed was often on the fringe. At first it seemed possible that her internal troubles would make her risk diversions abroad; but by the end of 1789 such intermittent fears were dying away. It seemed far more likely by then that the old enemy could be discounted; that she had ceased for the time being to carry weight in European affairs. This rising feeling was universal. While the Revolution provoked increasing alarm, it removed France from serious consideration in the period of the eastern crisis.

This was an irony of history. But historical irony is seldom complete. The distraction of interest, as it now seems, had its relevant effect.

> It was in the north and east of Europe [wrote the great Sorel] that the crisis occurred which, from 1789 to 1795, stirred up the great powers of Europe against each other, revealed the antagonism of their pretensions, called forth their rivalries, demonstrated the vice of their public interests, turned their attention from the affairs of France until the close of 1791, for long delayed their coalition, paralysed it when formed, and eventually broke it up.[2]

There is no total break in human affairs. The balance of power was a continuing theme, the Eastern Question was about to become one. And while, on the eve of the climacteric, both were viewed in traditional ways; while the statesmen of Europe, including Pitt, measured strange currents for familiar purposes, they did not abandon their standards and instruments when the flood waters broke, and recent attitudes survived to help shape a reluctant readjustment.

IV

In May 1790, when the British Government was anxiously defining its

1. See p. 550, n3 above.
2. Translated from *L'Europe et la Révolution française*, I, 502.

obligations to Prussia in the event of her being involved in a war with the Imperial Powers, it sent a reminder to Berlin of Prussia's obligations in the event of Britain going to war with Spain.[1] For the Ministry's desire for peace in central Europe was heightened in this uneasy period by a fast developing crisis of its own. Throughout May and June and much of July, during the preamble and course of Reichenbach, it was mustering its forces in the confrontation over Nootka Sound.

The first news that the Spaniards had seized a British ship on the remote north-west coast of America had reached London from Madrid on 21 January, some eight months after the event.[2] It was soon followed by a rumour that more than one vessel had been involved, and that a Spanish squadron had been reconnoitring the neighbourhood to prevent or warn off foreign settlements.[3] The whole story was not yet known – there had in fact been a series of incidents, culminating in a proclamation of Spanish possession in June and further arrests in July – and what was known was very confused. But this did not stop either Government from protesting to the other at once. On 10 February the Spanish Ambassador, acting on instructions, declared that a British ship had tried to 'take possession of Nootka Sound in the name of the British King', and demanded that 'such undertakings' should be punished, and prevented in future. Three days earlier, Leeds had peremptorily demanded the immediate release of the ship, pending which there could be no discussion of territorial rights.[4]

Both these protests were strongly worded. Pitt indeed was disturbed by Leeds's phrasing. The first orders sent in answer to the reports from the chargé d'affaires in Madrid had been to obtain more information – both of what had happened and of the Spanish defences in America –, to be guarded in what he said, but to assert in the necessary terms the right of British subjects to trade and settle in lands not already in European occupation.[5] Now the Foreign Secretary had categorically linked an immediate condition with a discussion of principle at the very start of the dispute. He had also, as it happened, failed to circulate the papers to the Cabinet, which had met on the subject before he

1. Leeds to Ewart, no. 11, 7 May 1790 (F.O. 64/17).

2. Date of receipt endorsed on Anthony Merry [chargé d'affaires in Madrid after Eden's departure] to Leeds, no. 1, 4 January 1790 (F.O. 72/16).

3. E.g. same to same, enclosure to no. 2, 7 January, no. 6, 15 January (loc. cit.). See p. 349 above. The Spaniards were in fact thought to have been aiming at the Russians as much as any one else, particularly because they had earlier recognised Russian settlements in the extreme north, in Alaska, and were anxious to prevent a southern extension.

4. The translated text of the Ambassador's letter, from the French in which it was written, is in William Ray Manning, 'The Nootka Sound Controversy', in *Annual Report of the American Historical Association for the Year 1904* (1905), 367–8. The draft of Leeds's letter to the Marquis del Campo [the Ambassador] of 7 February 1790 is in F.O. 72/16. The former was sent, independently of the latter, on receipt of instructions which would have been despatched more than three days before.

5. Leeds to Merry, no. 3, 2 February 1790 (F.O. 72/16).

wrote his letter.[1] The opening move had been clumsily handled. The Prime Minister therefore decided to take charge himself, and Leeds became at the outset, as he had done in the course of the earlier Dutch crisis, little more than the, sometimes reluctant, 'prête-nom de M. Pitt'.[2]

He was naturally not best pleased. 'The unanimous sense of the Cabinet', he thought, had been 'that this business was to be taken up with a high hand'; and that he had done.[3] The snub increased his resentment at his obvious lack of influence, and the effect was to be seen as the crisis came to a head. But there was really no difference of substance between the two men at this point. Pitt was quite as ready as Leeds to seek proper satisfaction and defend the principle of open trade, and Leeds on reflection was ready to agree that we needed more facts before we spelled out our demands. On 26 February a reply was sent to the Spanish Ambassador.[4] It called for the surrender of the seized property and compensation for the insult, and stated that the violent nature of the action precluded any larger discussion meanwhile. The language was more restrained than that of Leeds's earlier letter; the timing and details of redress were avoided; so was any contingent declaration of rights. The ball was returned to the Spaniards' court. Some freedom of manœuvre was recovered. But, taken in conjunction with the instructions to Madrid, the British Government was giving nothing away.

Not much more happened for some time, and the affair began to show signs of following a familiar course, in which neither side was really anxious to force the pace. The Spaniards were known to have presented their case to the French, and suspected of talking to the Austrians and the Russians. They were certainly reinforcing their American garrisons, and fitting out some ships of the line. There was a precautionary move in England too. A hitherto rather vague plan was taken out of the locker, for a small naval expedition to north-west America which would 'lay the foundation of an establishment for . . . the prosecution of the fur trade'.[5] Such a design of course was what the Spaniards had been fearing, and trying to guard against; both parties knew what was at stake, and were disposed to test their claims. Nevertheless, neither wanted at this stage to provoke a war. The British expedition was approved, but it would take more than a year to reach its goal, and meanwhile the immediate dispute might be settled and talks started on the problems of trading and territorial rights. In March, while it was considering the naval instructions, the Ministry seems to

1. Pitt to Leeds, 23 February 1790 (copy in P.R.O. 30/8/151).
2. P. 536 above.
3. Leeds to Pitt, 23 February 1790 (P.R.O. 30/8/151).
4. Copy of Leeds to del Campo, 26 February 1790 (F.O. 72/16).
5. Draft instructions, Grenville to Vice-Admiral Arthur Phillip, March 1790 (quoted in Harlow, op. cit., II, 440). See p. 349 above.

have hinted as much to the Spaniards; and they in turn were probably genuine in hoping – though the hope was expressed, as so often, ungraciously – that the incident would not be allowed to become 'a ground for quarreling'.[1] The two Governments, after all, had several good reasons not to let this happen. Despite lingering differences over the Mosquito shore,[2] their relations were now quite amicable and might indeed well improve. The Spaniards were worried by events in France, and on rather bad terms with Russia – they were anxious to be neutral in the war with Turkey, and had refused to allow Russian naval ships to use Spanish ports. They had recently shown signs of wishing to revive the commercial negotiation with England, and the earlier mutual suspicions seemed on the whole to be dying down.[3] The British for their part remained genuinely anxious to reach an understanding, and when they were invited to mediate in central Europe they even thought momentarily of asking Spain to help.[4] Throughout February and March 1790 each side therefore waited on the other, not relaxing their pretensions but hoping that a formula might be found.

But in the middle of April the business took a new turn. Early in that month the principal owner of the seized ships, John Meares, returned home. Meares was a retired naval lieutenant, who since 1786 had been involved in one of the various enterprises to north-west America which were a feature of the time.[5] After a preliminary visit to Nootka for the East India Company in 1788, he had erected some buildings in 1789, established relations with the inhabitants, and explored and traded up and down the coast. The British ships which figured in the incidents had been under his general orders, and as far as the British were concerned his was the first full account of the affair. It gave disturbing information, and made some important claims. The Government now learned definitely for the first time that more than one ship had been seized, that the crews had been badly treated and imprisoned in Mexico, and that the Spaniards had formally proclaimed their possession of the whole area. It was also informed that Meares had himself already claimed some territories in the King's name, established a permanent settlement, and made treaties with the local chiefs. His report was handed to the Home Secretary probably in the middle of April, and published to an excited public early the next month.[6]

1. Leeds to del Campo, draft of a letter dated March 1790 (F.O. 95/7), which however I cannot be certain was sent; Merry to Leeds, no. 24, 29 March 1790 (F.O. 72/16). Other despatches from Madrid at this time stressed the Foreign Minister Floridablanca's stiffness and suspicions; but the former was a Spanish characteristic, and the latter were familiar by now (see p. 498 above).

2. P. 384 above.

3. Pp. 499–500 above.

4. Cf. p. 544 above.

5. P. 349 above.

6. On 5 May. It was then entitled *Authentic Copy of the Memorial of Lieutenant John Meares to the Right Honourable William Wyndham Grenville, dated 30th April 1790*. But it

Some of these statements proved greatly exaggerated, and others were misleadingly presented. The report was meant to force the Government to extract compensation, and the account of his voyages which Meares himself published later in the year threw a rather different light on several aspects of the dispute.[1] He was not in fact a reliable witness; he was soon quarrelling with his associates; like other not dissimilar figures on comparable occasions, he was an unpromising victim to support. But his story shocked the Ministry, and on 20 April it was also roused by the Spanish Ambassador's answer to the earlier reply to his initial protest. An order had now been given to free the British crews. But this was to be taken as an act of courtesy only, there was no mention of redress, and Spanish rights were reaffirmed. To underline the point, moreover, the Ambassador complained of other intrusions by British vessels as far afield as Cuba and Peru.[2] Such a message might earlier not have seemed impossibly discouraging: the release of the crews, after all, was a hopeful step. But coming when it did, it added fuel to the flames of Meares's report. On 30 April the Cabinet resolved, at a full meeting, that a Memorial should be presented to Spain 'demanding immediate and adequate satisfaction for the outrages committed', and that 'to support the demand, and to be prepared for such events as may arise' the King should give orders to fit out a squadron of ships of the line. On 3 May a Privy Council was held to authorise a press for the navy; on the 5th, the day that Meares's report was published, Parliament was informed; and on the 6th Pitt asked the Commons for the necessary supplies.[3]

He had clearly decided, in these altered conditions, to concentrate on the basic problem. After announcing quite briefly what had happened, he turned to the implications. The seizures had taken place in an area in which British subjects had 'an incontrovertible right of trading, and . . . to which no country could claim an exclusive right of commerce and navigation'. Nevertheless Spain had levied a claim (so he was reported as saying)

the most absurd and exorbitant that could well be imagined; a claim which they had never heard of before, which was indefinite in its extent, and which originated in no treaty, or formal establishment

was probably ready well before that, and may have reached Ministers as early as 13 April (see John M. Norris, 'The Policy of the British Cabinet in the Nootka Crisis', *E.H.R.*, LXX, no. CCLXXVII, 569).

1. *Voyages Made in the Years 1788 and 1789 from China to the North-West Coast of America* . . . (1790). For the possible date of publication, see Harlow, op. cit., II, 447, n58.

2. Del Campo to Leeds, 20 April 1790 (F.O. 72/16).

3. *H.M.C., Dropmore*, I, 579–80; *L.C.G., III*, I, no. 589; *P.R.*, XXVII, 562–6. In agreeing to hold a Council, the King suggested that it should consist of 'the Cabinet Ministers', so as to ensure no leakage of news and thus collect more men from the press 'in the first attempt' (to Grenville, 2 May 1790; *H.M.C., Dropmore*, I, 580).

of a colony, nor rested on any one of those grounds on which claims of sovereignty, navigation and commerce, usually rested. If that claim were given way to, it must deprive this country of the means of extending its navigation and fishery in the Southern Ocean, and would go towards excluding His Majesty's subjects from an infant trade, the future extension of which could not but prove essentially beneficial to the commercial interests of Great Britain.[1]

Here was the crux of the matter. We had never admitted the Spanish pretension, advanced under the famous Papal Bull of 1493, to all non-European territories not then occupied by another European power. On the contrary, we adhered to the natural sanctions of discovery and trade, and of possession based on settlement.

> Your right so to do which you claim from the Pope
> We Britons dont value the end of a rope!
> It's a farce you may make your weak Subjects believe,
> But our right's equal to yours from Adam and Eve.[2]

This was the principle; and it was now invoked to support a new interest. For the significance of Nootka lay in its role in the fast developing whaling industry, and all that this might imply for the growth of trade and influence in the Far East. The Southern Whale Fishery was 'perhaps an object of full as much importance . . . as Nootka Sound itself'; they were facets of a single policy, and they were linked at once in the Ministry's plans. It was not just a question of claiming some territory which Englishmen had occupied – though the Spaniards' actions in any case would have provoked a response of some kind. The occupation, while not directed by Government, had occurred against a background of Governmental concern; the Admiralty's tentative plans to follow up Cook, the projected protest to Spain about the treatment of British whalers in Patagonia, the Ministry's discussions with the chartered Companies in support of the whalers' demands[3] – all this lay behind the force with which the incident was now taken up, and accounted for Pitt's language in the Commons. Of course Meares's revelations might have precipitated a crisis in any case. 'The din of war ran through the country like wild-fire',[4] and the Ministry had to reckon with the probability that Opposition, and perhaps the House in general, would have made the running if it had not. But, faced with those revelations

1. *P.R.*, XXVII, 564–5.
2. Print of 12 May 1790, 'The English Ambassador and his Suite before the King at Madrid, 1790'; *Catalogue of Political and Personal Satires Preserved in the Department of Prints and Drawings in the British Museum*, ed. Mary Dorothy George, VI (1938), no. 7646.
3. Pp. 346–50 above.
4. *Letters and Papers of Admiral of the Fleet Sir Thos. Byam Martin*, I (1903), 139. (In his recollections, the Admiral antedated Meares's account to March).

and the Spaniards' recent reply, Pitt seems to have needed no such prompting to react strongly, impelled by that determination to extend a 'beneficial infant trade' which he had held persistently over the past few years.[1]

The Spaniards themselves gave ample weight to this impulse. Their suspicions indeed were extensive and precise. The incursion into Nootka, Floridablanca told the British Ambassador in June, was meant to strike at the trade of Mexico; the Southern Whale Fishery was aimed at that of Chile and Peru; the settlement at Botany Bay presaged an attack on the Philippines: there was every indication that such activities were part of a far-reaching design.[2] Spain was used to infiltration of her trade in the Atlantic – in and from the Caribbean and in Honduras. Now there seemed to be a sudden renewal of activity in the Pacific, far more serious than the earlier probes. Such fears would doubtless have been intensified had the Spaniards known that the proposed naval expedition to north-west America was planned to be routed via Botany Bay, where it would victual and pick up a frigate from India.[3] Although it was largely by chance that they had picked on the British at Nootka – they were equally sensitive to threats from others, particularly the Americans and the Russians –, having done so, they were ready to make the occasion the point at which a stand must be made. Neither side in fact was going to give way lightly, having been brought into collision, for both were convinced that there were large issues at stake.

The mobilisation of the fleet had now to be followed up, and an answer given to the new Spanish note. Pitt remained anxious to take the business in two stages: to extract immediate compensation for the injury, and then to negotiate a comprehensive agreement. He had made it clear in Parliament what the argument in this second stage would be, and he now spelt it out in detail to the Ambassador in Madrid. A withdrawal of Spanish claims to exclusive rights in hitherto unoccupied American territories; the return of the depot at Nootka Sound to the British, and free settlement by Europeans along the north-west coast; the recognition of the Southern Whale Fishery, and a definition

1. The potential pressures from Opposition and public opinion are stressed by John M. Norris, loc. cit., 572–5. He emphasises the point that a general election was to be held soon. But Pitt was not in fact worried by this, there is no evidence that he was influenced by it, and while I do not doubt that he was glad to take the sting out of any possible attack by Opposition, there were other sufficient reasons for him to have acted as he did.

2. Fitzherbert [who arrived as Ambassador on 9 June] to Leeds, Private, 16 June 1790 (B.M. Add. Ms 28066, ff. 27–8); Secret and Confidential, no. 4, of the same date (P.R.O., F.O. 72/17).

3. See Harlow, op. cit., II, 439–40. When the expedition sailed finally in 1791 (see p. 354 above), it was however sent via the Sandwich Islands, not Australia.

of its activities; no settlement by either power in the unoccupied parts of South America, except to prevent occupation by a third power; mutual freedom to trade in each other's settlements – these should be the guiding lines for a new relationship.[1] Pitt in fact wanted to clear up all the difficulties which had led to piecemeal policies in the past – to the large-scale smuggling, the consequent decrees and countervailing legislation – and were currently affecting the course of the talks on a new commercial treaty in Europe. He wanted to seize this opportunity to move into a new system; and he was quite prepared to pile on the pressure in such a cause. It was a typical example of his approach when he had a major object in view: a reluctance to be confined to a negative issue, an anxiety to use a quarrel constructively, a dislike of clumsy provocation, and a readiness to be tough where conditions allowed.

The proposal was bound to raise problems for Spain, which had just refused to admit obligation, and would now find it difficult to concede one point without appearing to yield the rest. It also raised problems for Pitt, some of whose colleagues thought it far too weak. Leeds had been simmering for some time; on 2 June he exploded, and if his reasoning was confused his attitude was clear. Spanish reparation for the immediate insult should not be eased by the offer of talks, which indeed (according to his thinking) would not give Floridablanca 'time to breathe'. It would be better, instead of 'cramming' proposals 'down [his] throat' by stages, to make our main demands in one piece. No doubt this would mean war; but war was probably unavoidable, and everyone presumably preferred it to 'Disgrace'.[2] The line of argument was not very impressive – no wonder Pitt preferred to handle foreign crises himself –, and this bellicosity might seem curious in a Foreign Secretary who had always advocated friendship with Spain. But Leeds was disgruntled by his recent treatment, he was always looking for a strong policy, and he was influenced at this moment by his view of the European scene. Early in June, this looked quite bright; the Triple Alliance could be called in support, while Spain had so far failed to rally her most likely allies. The French, though excited, were not committed, and the Imperial Powers were busy elsewhere.[3] But this might not last, the future was uncertain, and the United States in particular, on strained terms with Britain, might, given time, take the Spanish side. 'Before we know where we are', wrote Leeds's Under-Secretary Burges, 'we shall have the Americans, and possibly the Russians, on our backs'. Better go to war at once, with 'some vigorous and decisive stroke'.[4] This view found support in the Cabinet – certainly

1. Leeds to Fitzherbert, no. 2, 16 May 1790 (F.O. 72/17). The accompanying no. 1, of the same date, was corrected extensively by Grenville, and slightly by Pitt.
2. Leeds to Pitt, 2 June 1790 (P.R.O. 30/8/151).
3. See pp. 563-4 below.
4. To Leeds, 27 June 1790 (B.M. Add. Ms 28066, ff. 55-6). He thought moreover that 'in two months' time' the French would have joined in.

The Marquess of Carmarthen. *Attributed to G. Knapton*

William Eden, Lord Auckland *by Lawrence*

Downing Street, the 'Square' and Number 10 on the right
by J. C. Buckler

Holwood House. *Engraved by Smith*

with Thurlow and Camden – and it was reflected in Parliament and in a spate of pamphlets and prints.[1] A month later Pitt yielded some ground. Despite some hints from Madrid of a compromise, including neutral arbitration of territorial rights,[2] he drafted early in July a more uncompromising demand. There must be a full and immediate satisfaction which would 'amount to an Admission, that the Court of Spain was not in Possession of an actual known and acknowledged Sovereignty and Dominion at Nootka'. This was indispensable, and 'No subsequent Discussion can therefore take place on this Point'. At the same time, he tried to soften the blow by adding that 'Any other Grounds of Claim, founded on anything short of such an actual known and established Possession . . ., will still be open to Discussion, and will in no Degree be precluded from [i.e. by] the Satisfaction'. On this basis, he enclosed forms of words for the two powers to sign a Declaration and Counter-Declaration respectively.[3]

Leeds, not surprisingly, was scarcely happy with the new proposals.[4] But they gave him part of what he wanted, he agreed reluctantly, and so did the Spaniards towards the end of the month. On the 24th, Floridablanca signed a Declaration virtually following the British wording, and Fitzherbert signed the Counter-Declaration for his Government. Spain thereby promised to restore the captured ships and indemnify the owners for injury and insult, without prejudicing 'the ulterior discussion of any [Spanish] right . . . to form an exclusive establishment at the port of Nootka'. The British for their part signed a Counter-Declaration accepting this redress, but similarly without prejudicing their right to reclaim an establishment at Nootka, or form one in future.[5]

Both sides could claim an advantage. The Spaniards had been very unwilling to sign, and were forced to do so by Fitzherbert employing mounting threats. But they had escaped a final surrender in the matter of sovereignty, and had made no overt concession on the conduct and rights of trade. The 'ulterior discussion' thus remained to be held, now without an intervening issue. The armaments were assembled, and it was still possible that they would be used.

The British had gained their immediate point – the release of the ships, and compensation – thanks to the range and vigour of their preparat-

---

1. Thurlow's attitude is implied in Leeds's letter of 2 June (p. 560 n2 above); Camden's is stated in Camden to Pitt, 29 June 1790 (P.R.O. 30/8/119). For a list of pamphlets over the year, see Norris, loc. cit., 574 ns 4, 5, 575 n1.

2. Floridablanca to Merry, 4 June 1790 (translation in P.R.O., F.O. 185/6).

3. Leeds to Fitzherbert, no. 7, 5 July 1790 (F.O. 72/18). The draft of the despatch in Pitt's hand is also there.

4. To Pitt, 5 July 1790 (B.M. Add. Ms 28066, ff. 67–8).

5. The English texts are published in, *inter alia*, P.R., XXVIII (1791), 35–6, and P.H., XXVIII (1816), 914–16.

ions for war. At the beginning of May they had set large-scale movements on foot. The naval mobilisation went ahead on a Parliamentary credit of £1 million: 40 ships of the line were being fitted out, and by the end of June 25 sail were at sea. The work was marked by 'uncommon celerity and unparalleled dispatch',[1] and meanwhile the strategic dispositions were strengthened. Two men of war sailed for the Caribbean and another three for India; four regiments of foot were sent to the West Indies, and one to Gibraltar;[2] the Governors in the western Atlantic, from Newfoundland to Barbados, were told to look to their defences; and various plans were drawn up for colonial attack. The reinforcements for India carried orders to prepare an expedition against the Philippines, and a more extensive strategy was considered for the New World. On 6 May, the day on which Pitt spoke in the Commons, he and Grenville had a long talk with the Latin American Miranda, and more were held in the next few weeks.[3] They discussed the prospect of supporting a rising in South America, and Pitt showed Miranda's papers to the Cabinet.[4] He also consulted a former adjutant-general in Jamaica, Colonel William Dalrymple, about operations in the Gulf of Mexico, against Louisiana or Mexico itself.[5] These might be linked with movements from Kentucky, and from Honduras against Guatemala.[6] Old plans were refurbished, in new conditions, for an attack on the Spanish possessions overseas.

The greatest of these new conditions was the existence of the United States, whose attitude might well be crucial in a fresh American war. Not the least of the immediate effects of Nootka, indeed, was its effect on Anglo-American relations, poised uneasily at this point after the last few unhappy years. The Ministry manœuvred in more than one direction. A scheme was produced for settling – to the British advantage – the dispute over the American-Canadian frontier; an American envoy was received in London to discuss a commercial treaty, and held in play throughout the critical months; above all, the Governor of Quebec, Lord Dorchester, who was about to leave on a visit to England, was ordered to stay and continue the secret correspondence which he had earlier started with Alexander Hamilton, to learn the American Government's intentions and try to bring the two countries closer together.[7] At the same time, plans were considered for risings in the dissident frontier States if necessary. The Allen brothers from Vermont,

1. George Vancouver, *A Voyage of Discovery to the North Pacific Ocean, and Round the World . . . Performed in the Years 1790, 1791, 1792, 1793, 1794, and 1795*, ed. John Vancouver, I (1798), 48.

2. Four regiments had been sent to India at the time of the Dutch crisis (p. 454 above.)

3. Pp. 385–6 above.

4. *American Historical Review*, VII, no. 4, 712.

5. Dalrymple to Pitt, 10, 12 and 16 May 1790 (P.R.O. 30/8/128).

6. Pp. 374–5, 384–6 above.

7. Pp. 357–8, 374–6 above.

who had been kicking their heels in London for over a year, were suddenly encouraged in their proposals for a separatist movement, and fresh soundings were taken in Kentucky about an insurrection, an attack on the Spaniards across the Mississippi, the creation of an independent State, and an alliance with Britain.[1] All these activities, mostly subterranean, were continued throughout the summer until the crisis ended and they were allowed to subside.

It was also necessary to move in Europe. Efforts were made to play on French apprehensions in their domestic troubles – Fitzherbert saw Montmorin on his way to Spain, and the new Ambassador, Lord Gower, kept up the pressure after his arrival in June. There was probably little to be done about Russia. But the Austrians were now more friendly, and responded pacifically to the first British representations. Under the new Emperor, they would probably stay neutral. So probably would Portugal and Turkey and the smaller powers, though the first might bend its neutrality in Spain's favour, as might Naples and Turin. Two of the Barbary States on the other hand – Tunis and Morocco – might act the other way or even break with Spain, and their neighbours along the coast were unlikely to give her facilities. But of course the main hope for England lay in the Triple Alliance, and as soon as the crisis broke calls were made to the Prussians and the Dutch. Both responded well. Although the Prussians had cause to feel sore with the British for their lack of support over central Europe, and had always disliked the thought of being drawn into overseas quarrels, they announced on 20 May that they would meet their obligation if required. Their aid in such a case would take the form of land operations in Europe.[2] But the Dutch would be more closely affected, since they might hope to gain in the event of a purely maritime war. On 4 May they were asked, as a start, if they would fit out a naval force at British expense, and place it at our disposal even if hostilities had not begun. They agreed, to the tune of ten ships of the line, and decided later to meet the cost themselves; and early in July the squadron joined the British fleet. It thus seemed probable to the Spaniards by then not only that Britain meant business, but also that she would be able to count on her allies.

It was not so clear, on the other hand, if Spain could rely on immediate support. While the Spanish naval preparations went ahead, Floridablanca had been doing his best to enlist sympathy. He circularised the Courts of Europe with a statement of his case, and proposed a neutral arbitration of rights. He also approached the most likely candidates for an effective alliance. British envoys sent news of his attempts from Vienna and St Peterburg, Copenhagen and Stockholm. But there was little response from those invited, in an already troubled year. These however were marginal efforts, whatever return they might

1. Pp. 372–4 above.
2. See p. 542 above.

yield. The Spaniards' real hope lay in France, under the shelter of the Family Compact. At first the prospects looked not unpromising: the French Ministry was divided, but there was a powerful party in favour of a demonstration which might divert attention from internal troubles and avenge the humiliation of 1787. On 14 May Louis XVI gave orders to fit out fourteen ships of the line. But his action soon gave rise to trouble. The National Assembly was already casting eyes on the royal prerogative of making war, and the Girondins seized the opportunity to bring the issue to debate. On 22 May the delegates decided that the King could not declare war without their concurrence, and a new element was thus introduced. British observers were relieved. But still the Assembly had not vetoed the armament, and the Spaniards could hope to build on the fact. On 16 June they made a formal demand for French assistance. Ten days elapsed before they had an answer, and then it told them little; under the new arrangements, the King must submit the request to the Assembly. Nothing more was heard in the next six weeks, in the critical period of July. It was perhaps not surprising, therefore, that the Spaniards should have signed the Declaration on the 24th.

In trying to dispose of the incident at Nootka Pitt had been about as restrained as he could, given the excitement which the affair, and above all Meares's account, had provoked. He had adopted a line which he hoped would allow him to tackle the larger issues on his own ground, and now that this point had been reached he was not going to let them fade away. On 14 August, when the Spaniards proposed (as indeed they had done earlier) that the fleets should disarm, they were told that this was impossible until the unresolved questions had been settled.[1] Three days later Fitzherbert in Madrid was sent 'a tremendous Dispatch, not much more voluminous than Postlethwayt's Dictionary'.[2] It contained the sense of the proposals to which the Government thereafter adhered. The principle was explained in the preamble: British traffic with Spanish possessions would be regulated, and illicit trade prevented, in return for an assurance of agreed rights of trade and fishing in the Pacific. The British ships and settlement at

1. *A Narrative of the Negotiations Occasioned by the Dispute between England and Spain in the Year 1790* (1790), 199. This was written by Bland Burges at the Foreign Office, for the King and the Cabinet (Burges to Hawkesbury, 11 December 1790; B.M. Add. Ms 38226, f. 9). It was later printed with a *Continuation*, as was a selection of *Official Papers relative to the Dispute* . . . (1790). The Government also commissioned or supported a number of pamphlets, by named and unnamed authors. The news of the signing of the Declaration and Counter-Declaration had been received in London on 5 August.

2. Copy of Leeds to Fitzherbert, Private, 16 August 1790 (B.M. Add. Ms 28066, f. 27v). The allusion was to Postlethwayt's two volume *Universal Dictionary of Trade and Commerce*.

Nootka must be restored, and Spanish claims of sovereignty over the coast were to be dropped. Spain, after all, had earlier recognised Russian settlement in the extreme north, so that her pretensions had already been exposed;[1] she should now work out with Britain the geographical limits of her suzerainty, leaving other areas open to free trade and occupation. If this was agreed, the British would ensure that their merchants did not settle or trade freely with recognised Spanish territories along the coast, or indeed approach them within a given distance – five leagues was suggested, though Fitzherbert was told privately that he might go to ten. The boundaries proposed were the latitudes of 31 degrees North and about 45 degrees South, which would give the Spaniards the southern peninsula of California to south of San Diego and the coast down to within about ten degrees of Cape Horn; and again Fitzherbert was told that he might go farther if necessary, in the north perhaps to 40 degrees, beyond San Francisco. Outside these limits of latitude and territorial waters British and Spanish subjects should have equal freedom of navigation and fishery, and equal rights of settlement on hitherto unoccupied soil. But the earlier proposal that both should abstain from competition in the extreme south of America was repeated, though the British privately did not regard that as a material point.[2]

The whole of this argument was built on the assumption that there had been a declared British occupation at Nootka Sound: indeed rights arising from discovery alone were specifically stated, or acknowledged, to be not enough.[3] It was not, as it happened, a very sure foundation, and the Spaniards continued to contest it; for the Government had accepted Meares's story without investigation, and some of it was later found to be misleading. It was very doubtful, in fact, if he had formed a proper settlement and claimed territory as he said, although one of the ships arriving slightly later under his general orders had undoubtedly made the beginnings of an establishment. The exact position was ambiguous; neither power was 'wholly right nor wholly wrong' in its account;[4] but the British Government bargained on the evidence being strong enough to support its larger case.

Fitzherbert presented the new paper on 8 September, and Floridablanca replied in the course of the next week. He suggested a temporary agreement while the boundaries were examined on the spot. The British proposals were accepted in principle, and the Southern Whale Fishery was recognised; but the wording was imprecise, nothing definite was said about Nootka, and British fishing crews were not to make landings on the coast.[5] Fitzherbert was not unhopeful of this reply: he

1. See p. 554, n3 above.
2. Leeds to Fitzherbert, no. 11, 17 August 1790 (P.R.O., F.O. 72/18).
3. Article 1 of the Project.
4. W. R. Mannings' conclusion, loc. cit., 444.
5. Fitzherbert to Leeds, no. 26, 16 September 1790 (F.O. 72/19).

thought it foreshadowed a concession of 'substantially all the Objects for which we have been contending', and he suspected that European opinion would in general support his view.[1] But opinion in London did not. The counter-proposals, Leeds wrote on 2 October, 'have not been relished here'.[2] They did not remove 'all causes of Misunderstanding', and we were not prepared to admit 'any further delay'. We were accordingly sending two drafts of a treaty, differing only in providing for an immediate definition of boundaries or not, which was to be taken as an ultimatum and should be accepted within ten days.[3]

The Government took this harder line in the light once more of the diplomatic situation. Its own mobilisation was now complete: from a total of 93 ships of the line, of which 40 had been brought to the ready, 37 were at sea.[4] The plans for an attack on Spanish America had been further advanced: a potential commander had now been chosen, and measures were being studied for invasions from west and east. The British strength was thought to be adequate, if Spain alone was considered. But much turned on the position in Europe if others were to be involved. The Triple Alliance was standing the strain – even though the crisis was increasing the toughness with which the Dutch were being treated in the Far Eastern negotiation.[5] The Prussians had repeated their assurances, and the Dutch squadron had been replenished. The Spaniards, by contrast, were still uncertain of their friends. The Americans now seemed unlikely to help them, and the British were aware of the fact. The Imperial Powers were not going to move, and neither was Sweden or Denmark. But the great question of course remained that of France. Spanish hopes revived towards the end of August, for on the 26th the National Assembly approved a proposal to raise the naval armament, which was settled finally at 45 ships of the line. It did so in response to an appeal from Mirabeau, now moving to the centre of affairs, and Mirabeau had already set on foot talks with Spain to re-establish the Family Compact as a revised National Compact. The decision naturally caused concern in London, even though it was regarded as possibly only for show – 'meant [rather] to appear on *Paper* than the *Sea*'.[6] The British Ambassador was told to demand an explanation, and when (thanks to a muddle) no reply was received, was instructed to warn the French that the ships must make no move to join the Spanish fleet. Pitt also took other, secret, steps. In July he had sent the agent W. A. Miles[7] to Paris to work against the conclusion of the National Compact, and in October he

1. To Leeds, Private, 16 September 1790 (B.M. Add. Ms 28066, ff. 265-v).
2. Copy of Leeds to Fitzherbert, Private, 2 October 1790 (loc. cit., f. 285).
3. Same to same, no. 19, 2 October 1790 (F.O. 72/19).
4. *Letters and Papers of Byam Martin*, III, 302; I, 149.
5. See p. 431 above.
6. Copy of Leeds to Fitzherbert, Private, 1 September 1790 (B.M. Add. Ms 28066, f. 241).
7. See pp. 531 n2, 541 n3 above.

encouraged Hugh Elliot, home on leave from Denmark, to try his hand as well.[1] Miles was a friend of Lafayette, and ostensibly in sympathy with the Revolution – he even succeeded in becoming a member of the Jacobin Club. Elliot was an old friend of Mirabeau. Their transactions are obscure. 'There are few matters in diplomatic history more wrapped in mystery', it was said some sixty years ago,[2] and time has shed no fresh light on the affair. It is possible that Mirabeau was bribed:[3] at any rate the emissaries were active, and their efforts were aided by disaffection in the dockyards and the hesitation of Floridablanca himself. For the Spanish Minister was becoming dubious of a further French embrace; he feared the spread of 'democratical' ideas, and was sceptical if the ships could put to sea. Many Frenchmen – including Montmorin, still Foreign Minister – were openly pacific, and if Mirabeau was really prepared to gamble on a war, the spreading paralysis and disorder were serious impediments. The British therefore decided to press on and ignore the risk from France; and by the middle of October, if Miles was to be believed, it had effectively disappeared.[4]

The risk of war itself, however, had not. For the Spanish Government was far from being unanimous for peace. The British ultimatum reached Fitzherbert on 12 October. He at once had several meetings with Floridablanca, and by the 16th had gained the impression that the Foreign Minister would accept something approaching its terms. This indeed was so. But there were other Ministers to be considered, and on the 19th they met in a 'Junta' on their own. They remained in session until the 25th, and then, to Floridablanca's annoyance, declared for war. Britain was claiming more than she had ever done, even at her moments of greatest success: more than in 1715 or 1763. If her pretensions were admitted, they would only lead to future incidents: better to accept the challenge at once, and rely on the preparations which were now complete. This was a categorical answer. But meanwhile Floridablanca was making further efforts, and by the time that the Junta ended its meetings he had gained just enough to risk the rest. One of the Spaniards' main objections – the point on which the Junta indeed expressed itself most strongly – was to a precise demarcation of boundaries; and the alternative proposal, for access to the whole unoccupied coast pending such a decision, was equally disagreeable.

1. Miles to Marquess of Buckingham, 15 July 1790 (*The Correspondence of William Augustus Miles on the French Revolution 1789–1817*, ed. the Rev Charles Popham Miles, I (1890), 150); Pitt to George III, n.d. but in October (Holland Rose, 579–80).

2. Oscar Browning in *The Cambridge Modern History*, VIII (1907), 291.

3. See Holland Rose, 578–81.

4. 'The great object of my mission is in general much liked. The business is realised'; Miles to George Rose, 11 October 1790 (*Correspondence of Miles*, I, 170–1). He may have been talking of his own pet object, a Franco-British alliance. But if this was chimerical, he was at least confident by implication that a new Franco-Spanish alliance would not be pursued.

Floridablanca now succeeded in rejecting the earlier latitudinal limits: indeed, while accepting a *de facto* line in the north, he avoided a specific geographical limit at all. Free settlement was to be allowed 'to the north of the parts of the . . . coast already occupied by Spain' in April 1789, which preserved most of California; and a definite boundary in the south was likewise dropped in favour of the first British proposal, for mutual abstention in that area unless a third power showed signs of intervening.[1] These stipulations mitigated the effects of British landings along the coast, and Floridablanca also managed to extend his territorial waters to ten leagues.[2] He had to rest content with these and a few minor verbal concessions; but he reckoned that they might give him enough room to gain agreement in private before worse should befall. A final British paper, drawn up by the Ambassador, was presented on 23 October. Floridablanca obtained his King's approval the next day, and, without telling the Junta, signed a Convention with Fitzherbert on the 28th.[3]

The Spaniards had saved something, as Floridablanca argued. Nor indeed was the settlement complete, for the detail of compensation and restoration at Nootka had still to be worked out, and by exploiting the need for an inquiry on the spot, and to find out exactly what Meares had done, they managed to spin out the talks for more than another three years. It was not until January 1794, in a changed atmosphere, that the British were given all that they wanted.[4] But none of this could disguise the immediate fact that Spain had suffered a severe defeat. She had twice signed Conventions reluctantly, under threat of war. She agreed in October to give redress without the reservation allowed in July,[5] and ceded land and buildings hitherto claimed as her own. If she had avoided the demand for specific boundaries, she had yielded the north-west coast to free occupation between northern California and Alaska. And if she kept British merchants from trading directly with her American markets, and British fishermen from landing on the coasts in the extreme south, she recognised their rights to navigate and fish 'in the Pacific Ocean or in the South Seas'.[6] It was indeed the principles thus admitted, rather than the actual territorial gain, that Pitt and his colleagues valued most. The acquisition of Nootka was to lead in due course to the establishment of British Columbia, on foundations far more advantageous than had recently been gained

1. Cf. pp. 560, 565 above. The quotation is from article V of the subsequent Convention, which followed Floridablanca's suggestion here.
2. Cf. p. 565 above.
3. For the English text, see *P.R.*, XXVIII. 36–8, *P.H.*, XXVIII, 916–18.
4. See Manning, loc. cit., 469–70.
5. P. 561 above. The relevant wording in the July Convention was not repeated in October.
6. Article III of the Convention of 28 October.

for the Mosquito Shore.[1] It was to farther the consolidation of British North America. But this was not foreseen at all precisely, or even much wanted, at the time. The Convention, so Fitzherbert was reminded later while the details of restitution were still in dispute, 'was certainly never intended to set up any claims . . . to the exclusive possession of the port of Nootka'. What *had* been intended was the acceptance of 'the right . . . to settle or trade on these coasts', and this had been 'sufficiently established by the actual restitution of any tract however small'.[2] Although Pitt was momentarily inclined to dispute the rejection of precise territorial limits,[3] he was thinking less of possible occupation than of enlarged opportunities for trade. And when the point was raised by Opposition in the debate on the Convention, it was answered effectively by Dundas. 'We were not contending for a few miles, but a larger world', one which was 'founded upon the skill of our manufacturers, and the adventures of our merchants'. 'We ought then to proceed upon another principle . . . We do not insist on any right to invade the colonial rights of other nations, in order to extend our commerce; but the spirit of commercial adventure in this country is unbounded'.[4] Colonies in fact were not much in favour; open trade and fisheries offered an alternative; Spain had always resisted such encroachments; and she had now (as a Spaniard recognised) 'conceded what has always been resisted and refused'.[5]

All this was very important. But the Nootka crisis is of wider interest in a study of Pitt. For it clarified, by sharpening, many of his policies and attitudes. There is no sign here of the reluctance or caution with which he approached some of the strictly European problems; his interest was deeply engaged, and he pressed for a definite result. If he did not get all that he wanted, he got a good deal, and his moderating tactics at the start were designed to serve his main attack. The affair was part of the variegated campaign which he was waging for overseas

1. Cf. p. 384 above.
2. Instructions to Lord St Helens [Fitzherbert], 9 August 1793; quoted in Lennox Mills, 'The Real Significance of the Nootka Sound Incident', in *The Canadian Historical Review*, VI, no. 2, 122. And cf. the instructions to Vancouver of February 1791 (p. 354 above), envisaging 'an intercourse' between the British possessions on either side of the continent, 'for the purpose of commerce' by way of a North-West Passage.
3. See Leeds to Pitt, 21 November 1790 (B.M. Add. Ms 28066, f. 347). Leeds sensibly urged him to leave well alone, even if the formula was 'not completely adequate'.
4. Speech of 14 December 1790 (*P.H.*, XXVIII, 98–9). According to the report in *The Senator* (see p. 399, n2 above), though not to *P.R.*, Pitt made an equally suggestive remark later in the same debate. 'But what opens a new source of wealth to the industry of this nation, is the advantage of the Fisheries in the Pacific Ocean or South Seas, without any disturbance or molestation. In these few words may be comprehended the whole essence of the treaty . . .' (*The Senator; or, Clarendon's Parliamentary Chronicle. . .*, I (n.d., but 1791), 126).
5. Iriarte [secretary of the Spanish Junta of Ministers] to Floridablanca, 28 October 1790; quoted by Manning, loc. cit., 457.

expansion, and if it has often seemed to historians – as it has – an exception to a pacific European policy, it served the objects at which he was aiming in a wider world. It had something of the flavour of Chatham: old echoes indeed might almost be heard. 'Sir, as to the . . . searching your ships – . . . On the part of Spain, an usurpation . . . claimed and exercised over the American seas; on the part of England, an undoubted right, by treaties, and from God and nature'. 'Spain knows the consequence of a war in America'. 'When Trade is at stake it is your last Retrenchment, you must defend it or perish'.[1] These were not the sort of phrases which Pitt would use; they were hardly his style. But the sentiments were familiar, and the occasion brought them forth.

The crisis is also of interest as marking something of a stage in Pitt's conduct of overseas affairs. It brought together, under pressure, many separate strands. The fact that Nootka stood, on the lines then projected, at a meeting place of West and East, meant that many different interests were involved and reflected in the result. The affair tested Britain's standing in Europe after the developments of the past few years: it revealed the current state of the balance of power. It threw light on the British attitude towards the United States, and to a developing system of trade. Its reverberations were felt in the policies for Canada, for central and south America, and the Far East. It tested Pitt's efforts on behalf of the navy.[2] And it marks a certain point in his own career. For Nootka came after three years of foreign policy in which Pitt had increasingly taken personal control. Since the end of 1786 the main decisions had been his, in a period which saw a change from isolation to intervention. Carmarthen was carrying progressively less weight, he counted for very little throughout this crisis, and even the first move towards a reconciliation thereafter came from Pitt rather than himself.[3] A replacement indeed was becoming discernible, for Ministries, like nature, abhor a vacuum, and in 1790 William Grenville may be seen intruding on the position he was soon to fill. His influence, visible since 1787, had grown fast since he became Home Secretary in 1789, and the largely imperial nature of the Nootka dispute allowed him officially to be involved. He was consulted on the plans for attacking Spanish America; he was in touch, through the Governor of Quebec, with the United States; he corresponded with the King – like the old Secretaries of State – on some of the military and naval movements.[4] He was also, from his point of vantage, concerned in the diplomacy itself: he saw some at least of Pitt's despatches,

1. Speeches of 8 March 1738 and 8 March 1739. And cf. his speech on the Falkland Islands' crisis of 22 November 1770.

2. See p. 517 above.

3. See p. 500 above.

4. Pp. 384, 374–5 above; *L.C.G. III*, I, nos. 609, 617, 621 (a more doubtful instance), 627, 630, 633. But the Foreign Secretary, too, may have given an order to the fleet on at least one occasion (see *Letters and Papers of Byam Martin*, I, 150–1).

and he had a much closer connexion than did the Foreign Office with Miles.[1] But he was not Foreign Secretary yet, and meanwhile Pitt was in detailed charge, working to some extent with the envoys abroad – though in this respect Eden remained unique in degree – and against the background of an imperial policy worked out with the trio of Jenkinson, Grenville and Dundas. He encountered little opposition in the Cabinet, partly because the objects were generally agreed, and partly because there was no personal focus for discontent. Thurlow, the most likely rebel, held largely aloof in this case; Richmond had lost influence, and in any case was friendly; and the rest were generally prepared to leave matters to himself. He was careful to inform and consult his colleagues at the point of their acknowledged responsibility. But foreign affairs were now firmly in his hands, and it was he who reaped the credit.

By the end of 1790, Pitt was indeed in a powerful position. He was strong at home, and had gained confidence in his judgment overseas. Nootka in some ways was his peak in diplomacy; certainly in his personal direction of it. For in 1791 he was to suffer his first major diplomatic reverse, and then Grenville was transferred from the Home to the Foreign Office. The ground indeed was not as firm as he may have thought at this prosperous time. He was being drawn along a slippery path in central Europe, and self-confidence had its dangers. But when the Nootka crisis ended he could look back on a line of achievements ever since the crisis in Holland had raised his interest in foreign affairs. There was plenty of trouble ahead; but if Pitt's career had finished then, diplomatic historians might have acclaimed it as one of virtually unbroken success.

---

1. See Miles to Buckingham [Grenville's brother], 15 July, 13 December 1790 (*Correspondence of Miles*, I, 150, 178–82), and Miles's correspondence with Grenville in 1791 ('Private Correspondence Received 1791', Fortescue Mss). He had been told 'to have no communication whatever . . . with the King's Minister at Paris'. This would not necessarily mean that the Foreign Secretary was ignorant of what was going on. But he may well have been, for Leeds had apparently dropped Miles in April (B.M. Add. Ms 28095, ff. 299–300).

Part Five

CHAPTER XVIII

Public and Private Life

I

The atmosphere of Downing Street today is still curiously un-obtrusive and retired. At times there are excitements – a demonstration in Whitehall, or people drawn into the street itself by an occasion; and in summer it has its share of tourists and passers-by. But often it is almost deserted, and then one senses the con-tinuing flavour, masculine, experienced, matter of fact, of an earlier style.

The strength of this impression is rather surprising, for the street has changed a great deal since it was first completed in the course of the eighteenth century. One side vanished in the bulk of the Victorian Government buildings, part of the other had earlier gone in Soane's (later Barry's) new offices, and while there is still that quiet air of a cul-de-sac which gives the closes of Westminster and St James's their character, the cul-de-sac too disappeared, almost a century ago. In the 1780s, as indeed much later, there were houses across the end, recessed in a little square where the flight of steps now runs down to the park. Like all the rest except number 10, they had no official connexions then, although in the nineties Government offices started to creep in. In 1793 the Foreign Office moved, from the nearby Cockpit where it had recently settled,[1] to the 'small, dark, inconvenient premises' which served until after Palmerston's day; and five years later the Colonial Office was put into number 14, in the square. Their heads were Grenville and Dundas, so that the street was beginning to witness that Ministerial intimacy which it has known ever since. But when Pitt first went to live there he had private neighbours, in the establishments backing on the park and the Horse Guards, and the pokier dwellings off Whitehall. It was from his father's windows at number 14 that William Eden in 1785 watched the shop tax riot outside the Minister's house.[2]

Number 10 itself was already bigger than it looked from the street. It had in fact just suffered one of the largest extensions of its long career. Then as now the works were expensive, and raised a Parliamentary fuss; one of Pitt's early tasks, as Chancellor of the Exchequer, was to defend the cost incurred by North and the Rockinghams. This had risen

1. See p. 173 above.
2. P. 254 above.

to double the original estimate of some £5,500; but the foundations had proved faulty, and the accommodation was greatly improved. If the Commons had foreseen a bachelor occupant for most of the next quarter of a century they might have been even more annoyed, and Pitt's own first impression, rather ungratefully, was of a 'vast awkward House'.[1] But there were good stables, the garden was agreeable, his study and dining room overlooked it where the Cabinet Room and private secretaries' rooms are now, and there were 'comfortable lodging-rooms' above.[2] He had a first taste of these amenities in 1782–3, and it was one of his homes for nineteen out of the next twenty-two years.

One does not know very much, in this earlier phase, about his domestic surroundings. He presumably put his books – still largely confined to the classics, mathematics and history of his Cambridge days[3] – in the library separated by his secretary's room from the larger study. Did the latter already have the nineteen mahogany chairs, the Turkey sofa covered with green leather, the five Pembroke tables, the large library table, and the brown holland spring blinds that were later there?[4] One also knows little, at this stage, about his working Ministerial day; the best source would be Pretyman, who became his private secretary,[5] and Pretyman seldom tells. It was certainly un-methodical: Pitt was apt to answer letters as he felt inclined, and he seldom kept copies – he never, for instance, employed the early copying machine then coming into use.[6] He worked quickly on his papers, and

1. See p. 84 above.

2. 'The best Summer Town House possible' (Pitt to his mother in July 1782; see ibid). The stables and coach-house were across the open ground (then a stable yard) that leads from the street to Treasury Passage (see *London County Council Survey of London*, XIV (1931), fig. on p. 92 and Plate 61). For Pitt's speech in 1782, and the alterations of 1781, see loc. cit., 121 and Plate 111.

3. There are some additions on public affairs, however, suggestive of these years: *The Annual Register* for 1784 to 1791 (after which, curiously, it seems to have stopped), a volume of *Observations on Reversionary Payments for Providing Annuities*, some *Tables of Interest*, and a run of the *Parliamentary Debates* (Pretyman Ms 562:21). In April 1785 he bought (or paid for) '3 Volumes of Monsure Neckars Finances', and in 1786 and 1787 paid for purchases from various booksellers (Arnott, Thompson, Debrett, Cadell, and Flack). In February 1791 he had '44 Volumes of the Journals' bound – simply, one imagines, as the cost was 6/8d (P.R.O. 30/8/205).

4. Pretyman Ms 562:22.

5. Pitt had also considered the family's former private tutor Wilson, 'But I must do something for Pretyman' (to Wilson, 6 February 1784; Duke University, North Carolina. I am indebted to Professor W. B. Hamilton for this information). William Bellingham, 'from the *Army*' (p. 84 above), who had been appointed his private secretary at the Exchequer in 1782 at his brother Chatham's request, became an MP at the election in 1784. He was later made a Commissioner of Victualling, and a baronet in 1796, and was Chatham's train-bearer at Pitt's funeral. Mrs Pretyman Tomline, in some notes in 1801, mistakenly calls him Sir James ('Mr. Pitt II', Stanhope Mss).

6. Whose products may be seen, for example, in the faded copies of Orde's letters on the Irish Propositions, in the Bolton Mss.

held the arguments easily in his head. Speeches appeared to give him little trouble: Mrs Pretyman Tomline tells a story to illustrate the point. On the day on which Pitt introduced his bill for reducing the National Debt – the climax of his financial policies – he asked his sister Harriot and the Pretymans to dine, though the ladies had thought he would prefer to be alone.[1] 'Never, never can I forget this Dinner!' Pretyman's 'countenance was that of *extreme* & *affectionate* anxiety'. Pitt however was 'as gay and unconcerned as ever'. He teased Mrs Pretyman, 'talked on indifferent subjects', and said that he had been over the final details of the scheme that morning but had not yet planned what he was going to say. Pretyman was 'exceedingly startled'. But Pitt went for a walk in the park, and when he returned it was apparently 'all settled'. There was not much more time for preparation, for some of his friends called in on their way to the House. He remained 'lively and considerate', and then went down himself, to deliver a memorable speech on a complicated technical subject.[2]

Pretyman's anxiety was understandable. But in fact Pitt's confidence was explicable here, given his temperament and his debating powers. The sinking fund scheme was one to which he had given a very great deal of thought; he had been considering it for over six months, and working on it for two,[3] and his mastery of the detail was such that it needed only a rapid final survey. Speeches came naturally to him: he had lisped in numbers and the numbers came, and he often spoke easily on complicated policies with far less solid preparation. He had the power from the very start to digest a subject with dazzling speed; and speed did not preclude thoroughness, more often than not. It was perhaps his most conspicuous gift, and it brought its own penalties and rewards in this period, when his Cabinet colleagues were of little help and the Secretaries of State in particular almost no help at all. The circumstances increased his natural propensity to range increasingly far and wide; for if the field of government was limited so were the means of handling business, and the burden fell, with his willing consent at this stage, largely on Pitt himself.

The fact made for constant pressures, and at times for crowded days. Such terms of course are relative. The 1780s saw a steady growth of business, particularly perhaps on overseas affairs, and Pitt of his own volition added to the process in certain respects. His financial measures involved a great deal of work, and he covered many aspects of government more fully than the average First Lord of the Treasury. On the other hand he excluded certain areas which had been of interest to

1. Dinner, it must be remembered, was generally taken in London society at this period at four or five o'clock.

2. Tomline Mss, Box 29, 1, 35:3; Pembroke College, Cambridge. Pretyman himself later recalled Dundas's astonishment at Pitt's lack of ostensible preparation for a speech he was about to make in 1784 (Rosebery, *Bishop Tomline's Estimate of Pitt*, 29, n3; henceforth cited as *Tomline's Estimate*).

3. See pp. 261-7 above.

them: compared with Newcastle, for instance, or indeed most Ministers, he skimped the detail of patronage and Parliamentary management, and he did not exchange ideas with kindred spirits on the scale, or in the style, of Shelburne. His surviving correspondence and papers for these years, large as they are, are not exceptionally so by current standards, although the files do not contain – but do those in other cases? – all that he saw. Like most public men of the age, he had little secretarial help. Pretyman remained private secretary from 1784 to 1787, when he was made Dean of St Paul's and (simultaneously) Bishop of Lincoln,[1] and he was succeeded by a young Cambridge man from the Treasury, Joseph Smith, who apparently had acted as his assistant.[2] But they could do only so much: men of affairs were accustomed then to conducting their own correspondence, and while the secretaries relieved their master of some minor interviews, and Pretyman, as a mathematician, was sometimes of use on finance,[3] they did not materially ease the load of papers and meetings which were the staple of Pitt's life.

Even so, the burden was not overwhelming in the years before the war. If it prevented Pitt from going far afield, it did not deprive him of all his leisure. He generally tried, however, to keep evenings free for papers, engagements and Parliament permitting. In Downing Street, he liked to 'lounge' for a spell after dinner, and then settle down to work, going to bed if possible at about eleven. The same applied in this early period if he was staying at Putney, or at Wimbledon with either Wilberforce or Dundas.[4] Even with the latter, Mrs Pretyman Tomline tells us of the years of which she knew, 'notwithstanding Reports, the Evenings were *usually* spent in *business*'.[5]

In these same years, Pitt spent his free time as much as possible with '*his old set* of friends'.[6] He managed to do so a good deal. Though he still went about more than he was to do later, in the first stage of the French

---

1. Succeeding Bishop Thomas Thurlow, a younger brother of the Lord Chancellor, who had held both positions simultaneously. Pitt had tried much earlier to secure Pretyman's appointment as Dean of Worcester (to Shelburne, 13 January 1783; Clements Mss, University of Michigan), and had made him a Canon of Westminster in 1784.

2. Smith, who was some two years older than Pitt, was a nephew of the Master of Gonville and Caius College, Cambridge, and had been taken into the Treasury as a temporary Clerk by Orde. He did well out of the appointment. Over the years Pitt made him Secretary to the Lord Warden, and a Serjeant of the Admiralty, of the Cinque Ports, Receiver-General of Stamps, and Paymaster of the Out-Pensioners at Chelsea and of the Irish Pensioners resident in England. He also had 'a lucrative appointment' in Jamaica. He married as his second wife Margaret Cocks, a co-heiress of the Somers family, who brought him a reputed £100,000. (Notes and deeds of appointment in the papers of Mr W. H. Saumarez-Smith.)

3. See pp. 264–6 above.
4. See p. 105 above.
5. Notes written in 1801 ('Mr. Pitt II', Stanhope Mss).
6. Ibid.

wars, he seems quite soon to have retired very largely from his earlier ventures on the general round. Of course his position brought him into contact with the various circles of that small world; but he remained at arm's length, and kept his private life apart. He was seldom seen in society. George Selwyn, the veteran diner out, was invited to meet him once, at – to his disgust – Sir Sampson Gideon's, the son of the great Jewish financier.[1] But such mentions are rare in the diaries and letters of the day, unless the writer was a colleague or an intimate friend.[2] Nor did Pitt see anything, by way of alternative, of the writers or artists who were socially respectable: his indifference to them indeed has often been condemned. Macaulay later accused him of positive hostility, citing the refusal to increase Dr Johnson's pension when the great man was ill and in need of funds. This in fact was probably not Pitt's doing – it is unlikely that he saw the petition, which was made to the King in confidence through Thurlow –, but the point is rather that he may not have been consulted because he would not have been personally concerned.[3] 'I do not know Pitt', the Doctor said himself, ('Fox', he added, condemning his politics, 'is my friend'),[4] and the young man never sought, or was asked to share, the company of The Club. Gainsborough disliked him when he painted his portrait in 1787 – he was struck by Pitt's 'hauteur and disrespectful manner', and though Pitt was said to like his nephew, Gainsborough Dupont, he was not in touch with that world.[5] He did not go to the Academy banquets, as 'Lord North, in his administration had done';[6] he showed no inclination for private patronage, or for the relations which patronage brought. Considering the age in which he lived, and his own background – for the Grenvilles and Chatham were instinctive patrons – his lack of personal contact was remarkable, and remarked.

Much the same applied to his relations with interests more important to him. He does not seem to have seen much of the City men whose advice he sought or heard. There were of course social lines to be drawn, and Pitt ranked socially as a young man of fashion; but they were often subtle, and always being bent, and this was not the main reason for his reserve. The banker Robert Smith, later Lord Carrington, was an intimate. But then he was in politics, much of an age with Pitt, and

1. '. . . to meet Mr. *Pitt*, and to eat a *turtle: quelle chére!*' (*George A. Selwyn, his Letters and his Life*, 253). He did not go. Gideon had in fact just changed his name, on marriage, to Eardley.

2. Or had been at the Bar with him in his early days (see p. 24 above).

3. For a discussion of the affair, see Dr L. F. Powell's notes to *Boswell's Life of Johnson*, ed. George Birkbeck Hill, IV (1934), 348–50, 542–3.

4. Loc. cit., 292.

5. *The Farington Diary*, I, 260, for Gainsborough – a later story, but detailed and likely enough; William T. Whitley, *Thomas Gainsborough* (1915), 339, for Gainsborough Dupont.

6. *Farington Diary*, I, 146. The reason, according to his friend Charles Long, was 'private'. But Reynolds had earlier noted that he paid 'not much attention to the arts' (to the Duke of Rutland in 1787; *H.M.C., Fourteenth Report, Appendix, Pt. I*, 229).

a member of Goostree's club. No one else of his kind at this time crossed the guarded boundary of friendship; Francis Baring was probably too old, and in any case still had connexions with Shelburne, and Pitt's amicable dealings with Coutts never ripened into anything more. The Mansion House and Livery Companies might furnish entertainment, and support for Government, but that was all. There was no equivalent in this phase of Pitt's life of a Ralph Allen or even Beckford in Chatham's. His personal relations with the merchants and bankers were as restricted as with almost everyone else.

For the picture was not very different in the field of politics itself. Pitt did not meet his opponents socially – the 'Foxite houses'[1] indeed were distinct, and Burke for instance was not asked to dine until he had broken with Opposition.[2] But neither did he see much of his supporters apart from his small group of friends, and some of those saw less of him now than they had done at the start. Goostree's closed down because Pitt hardly ever went there,[3] and while he retained his connexion with White's few visits are recorded, and then they had a definite object in view. He called in to organise support for Dolben's slave trade bill, and during the Regency crisis, and attended the club's victory ball at the Pantheon when the crisis was over;[4] but although he welcomed the emergence of a political stronghold in opposition to Brooks's, he seems to have acted as a *deus ex machina*, unlike Fox across the street.[5] Seen little in general company, and entertaining his own circle at home, he relied on others to keep him in touch with the larger political world.

At the other end of the scale there were the King and the Cabinet, demanding regular attention of course, but not receiving much more. As a Minister of the Crown, Pitt was naturally present at Drawing Rooms and Levees when the monarch was in London, to pay his duty and to have an audience in the Closet.[6] The Court was a centre of

1. Or 'kennels' as Pitt's mother's old friend Catherine Stapleton referred to them, clearly using a familiar term. She was surprised to find herself in one in 1791 (to Hester Countess of Chatham, 30 April 1791; P.R.O. 30/8/59).

2. *The Correspondence of Edmund Burke*, VI, ed. Alfred Cobban and Robert A. Smith (1967), 363, 376–7, 388, 410. The hosts were Dundas and then Grenville, Pitt being present.

3. P. 107 above.

4. For the first see p. 394, n3 above; for the second – when he was said to be 'in high spirits' – Lord Bulkeley to Buckingham, 25 November 1788 (Buckingham, II, 14); for the third, in March 1789, *Gleanings from an Old Portfolio, Containing some Correspondence between Lady Louisa Stuart and her Sister Caroline, Countess of Portarlington, and some other Friends and Relations*, ed. Mrs Geoffrey Clark, II (1896), 122.

5. By the middle nineties elections to membership were being largely controlled in Pitt's interest by his young men; so much so, indeed, that he intervened to stop excessive blackballing.

6. And he was sometimes summoned on his own, if need be 'in morning dress' (e.g. *L.C.G. III*, I, no. 574) and not the full dress required when he appeared in company at Court, or in Parliament.

business, and of conversation; attendance was no mere formality, and it often confined him or brought him to town. He also went down to Windsor, and to Weymouth when the King began to go there. But neither he nor George III was inclined for a closer relationship; both guarded their private lives, and the King was in any case likely to be cautious with Chatham's son and a nephew and cousin of the Grenvilles. Pitt was equally wary; he had no wish to enter the royal circle, and it was three years, for instance, before Fanny Burney, in the seclusion of the Queen's household, saw him at all.[1]

The Cabinet also seems to have had its own social habits, obviously less formal and probably far less well established. But Cabinet dinners had certainly been known at least since the 1760s, though their regularity and frequency may well have varied with different Administrations.[2] Chatham himself had scarcely seen his colleagues in his last disastrous Ministry. But that was quite exceptional, and Pitt appears to have taken his share in a normal routine from the time that Ministers held a 'very merry' dinner at the end of the struggle with Fox.[3] By 1792 he was circulating printed cards for some of his dinner invitations, which by their form may have referred to Ministerial gatherings.[4] Different members acted as hosts in their houses, though how often one does not know – perhaps quite regularly when Parliament was sitting, and occasionally when it was not. It may also have been at about this period that the famous fish dinners at Greenwich began; tradition ascribes them to Pitt's initiative, although this may not have been so.[5] He sometimes dined in private with a Cabinet colleague – with Sydney and Carmarthen, it seems, in particular. But none,

1. *Diary and Letters of Madame D'Arblay (1778–1840)*, ed. Charlotte Barrett, III (1905), 309.

2. I am indebted to Professor Christie for some evidence on this point.

3. See p. 142 above. For one reference by Pitt to 'a Cabinet dinner', undated, see Ashbourne, 335; for another to a dinner with 'only the Cabinet present', Pitt to Carmarthen, 31 August [1784] (B. M. Egerton Ms 3505). Wilberforce mentions dining with him late in 1785 at a 'sort of Cabinet dinner' (*Life of Wilberforce*, I, 98) – perhaps the kind of occasion that Burges described for a slightly later date (p. 449 above).

4. There is one in the Kenyon Mss at Gredington, Flintshire, noted in A. Aspinall, *The Cabinet Council 1783–1835* (1952), 177, n1.

5. The usual story (repeated in the article on George Rose in *D.N.B.*) is that Pitt was invited once a year, on Rose's suggestion, by the MP Robert Preston to dine with the two of them at Preston's 'fishing cottage' on Dagenham Reach. This may have been in the eighties, for Preston is described as Member for Dover, and he changed his seat after 1790. But the distance from London proved inconvenient, the dinner was moved to a tavern in Greenwich, and Pitt then asked if he might bring Camden (presumably his friend John Pratt, the son of the old Lord Chancellor, who may or may not have succeeded his father by that time) and later Charles Long. The company grew, each member paying his share, and at some point it turned into a Cabinet dinner. But the date of this last change is again uncertain, and may even not have been in Pitt's lifetime – it was possibly as late as 1812. I am indebted to Mr David Leggatt, borough librarian of Greenwich, for investigating the matter.

except his brother Chatham in due course, was of his private circle. The '*old set* of friends' was distinct, the inheritance of Cambridge and Goostree's, and it was in their company that he felt free to unbend.

In 1784 and 1785 this private life centred on Downing Street, particularly perhaps when Pitt's sister Harriot came to act as hostess in the latter year. He had the villa which he rented at Putney from August 1784, where he went for a night or more when he could, and there was Wilberforce at Wimbledon if he wanted a convenient change. But more often he was held in town, and when Harriot was there her presence made the 'vast awkward House' a home. She must have been a delightful person, and her vivacity and wit are said to have been like her brother's. The two were very close. Pitt 'was attached' to her, wrote Mrs Pretyman Tomline, 'with a degree of affection a character so like his own could alone deserve'. 'I used to tell her', she continued, ''twas a pity She was his *Sister*, for no other woman in the World was suited to be his wife'.[1] She gave him the companionship and understanding he needed, and the links were not weakened when she married his friend Edward Eliot in September 1785, for the couple lived at number 10. This was the focal point of a circle which remained much the same as it had been since Pitt came to London, and of a life which followed the same course so far as his position now allowed.

But in 1786 the scene began to change. Pitt had bought a house at Holwood, near Hayes, in the previous autumn, and when it was ready he went there as much as he could. In the autumn of 1786, too, Wilberforce gave up his villa at Wimbledon, a move which set the seal on his religious conversion and closed a chapter for the two friends. But an even more serious event occurred at the same time, for in September 1786 Harriot died after having a child. Pitt was momentarily overwhelmed, and the blow had longer consequences. For Harriot's loss left a gap that was never properly filled, and some of the results began to be shown in the next few years.

Of course neither Harriot not Pitt could have expected to live their lives unaltered. Pitt was likely to see more of some of his working associates as the work increased, and if Harriot had survived, and had a family, she might have moved, or things might have changed. But any such process would have been more gradual, and this sudden death left him without his most familiar and perhaps closest kindred spirit. It may not have meant the loss of an influence; it certainly meant the loss of a presence, and the effects were bound to be felt. Eliot continued to live with him for a time, but old habits were further weakened when Pretyman left London in 1787.[2]

There was an earlier association of fish dinners with Greenwich, from the banquets of the Tudor Privy Council at the Palace (The Rev A. G. L'Estrange, *The Palace and the Hospital; or, Chronicles of Greenwich*, II (1886), 355–6.)

1. Notes of 1801; 'Mr Pitt II', Stanhope Mss. And see also her remarks in Tomline Mss, Box 35:3, Pembroke College, Cambridge.

2. See p. 578 above. He took up residence as Bishop of Lincoln.

And so in the later eighties a rather different pattern began to emerge; not completely or dramatically, but unmistakably in some respects. Two new figures in particular became more important. Pitt was now without a hostess, and he was ill fitted to find one. But he soon found that he had got one, whom he was glad enough to accept. She was very different from Harriot – indeed she could hardly have been more different, for this was Jane Duchess of Gordon, one of the stormier characters of her time. Some ten years older than Pitt, she had brought down from Scotland the husband from whom she was later to be parted, and settled in Pall Mall, leasing Buckingham's (Temple's) house. Handsome, ambitious, high spirited, bold, and long a leader of Edinburgh society, she set out to conquer London as a political hostess. Her position buttressed a formidable nature. The Duke of Gordon was once described – by a Scot – as the greatest subject in Britain, a powerful, still semi-feudal, chieftain with one of the largest rent rolls in the country. She herself was wild and headstrong – as a girl she shocked the good citizens of Edinburgh by riding a pig bareback down the High Street, and she always bounced and rode pell-mell towards her goal.[1] A 'perfect Divle', and a 'horrid violent woman', one of her Scottish enemies called her;[2] but she had a way with her, and at least to her friends a lively ready charm. It must have been rather overpowering, and she was certainly coarse –

> The Duchess triumphs in a manly mien;
> Loud is her accent, and her phrase obscene[3] –

but she was clever, unconventional and witty, and could keep an evening going. She had known Pitt for some years; but she moved in on him in 1787, and he soon found her an amusing supper companion and an energetic ally. Politically committed, she was (as was shrewdly observed) 'of Infinite service among the Young Men', holding nightly gatherings of them in Pall Mall and acting as a 'whipper-in'.[4] Indeed, she did something to keep in being a recognisable group of contemporaries and supporters, and she seems to have brought Pitt himself into such company rather more than he had recently been. She perhaps reached her height in 1789, when she took the lead in organising the victory ball for White's after the Regency crisis, and presided at 'a

1. 'Her Grace of Gordon bounced away according to custom'; Lady Louisa Stuart to Lady Carlow, May 1785 (*Gleanings from an Old Portfolio*, 23).
2. *Lord Fife and his Factor: Being the Correspondence of James Second Lord Fife 1729–1809*, ed. Alistair and Henrietta Tayler (1925), 186.
3. From *The Female Jockey Club*, of 1794; quoted in *G.E.C.*, VI (1926), 6, n (a). And see also Wraxall (who knew her well), *Historical and Posthumous Memoirs*, IV, 458.
4. Catherine Stapleton to Hester Countess of Chatham, 29 April 1789 (P.R.O. 30/8/59); introduction to *An Autobiographical Chapter in the Life of Jane, Duchess of Gordon* (privately printed, 1864).

very jolly supper party' with Pitt.[1] She was then thought to be working hard to marry him to her eldest daughter; but that failed, and by 1791 their relations seem to have been less close.[2] They probably continued to see something of each other over the next ten years, but '*the* Duchess' was no longer the regular hostess for what she called 'Bachelor Hall'.[3]

The other name that now began to be heard was altogether more important. Dundas did not burst suddenly on Pitt's life; but if his progress was slower, it endured. He had of course been present since 1784, but not prominently at first. It was the steady growth of Far Eastern business, and above all Hastings's impeachment, that brought him forward. The fact that Wilberforce gave up his villa at just about this time was also a help; for when Holwood seemed rather too far from London, Dundas could still offer some country air at Wimbledon. Grenville was also nearby;[4] but he was stiffer company, and the older man provided better entertainment. Dundas knew how to appeal to Pitt; and while he had his eye on the main chance, the two men were, or became, genuinely fond of each other. Their friendship was still in the making: it was the war years that really sealed it; but by the turn of the decade it was an acknowledged fact.

Pitt's old circle disapproved, and understandably. They feared, and came to deplore, the effect on 'a mind as yet altogether unsullied by habitually associating with men of worldly ways . . ., in short, with . . . trading politicians'. No one, 'however originally pure', could escape from such a habit, 'especially in the hours of friendly intercourse and of social recreation, without contracting insensibly more or less defilement'.[5] This was Wilberforce's verdict, and others felt the same. 'When most of *his first set* of friends were gradually withdrawn from . . . almost daily intercourse . . . new habits were acquired and *various circumstances* unhappily tended to *foster* rather than *correct* them'.[6] The withdrawal in point of fact was still far from complete, and Dundas in

---

1. *Gleanings from an Old Portfolio*, 118, 122.

2. The daughter, Charlotte, was married instead (it was said, with Pitt's assistance) to Colonel Charles Lennox, later 4th Duke of Richmond. The Duchess was a great matchmaker: of her five daughters, three became English Duchesses and one a Marchioness.
For this episode, see Catherine Stapleton to Hester Countess of Chatham, 29 April 1789 (P.R.O. 30/8/59), and Lady Louisa Stuart to Lady Portarlington, 5 June 1789 (*Gleanings from an Old Portfolio*, 141); also Wraxall, loc. cit., 462. For a possible decline in relations by 1791, Catherine Stapleton to Hester Countess of Chatham, 30 April 1791 (P.R.O. 30/8/59).

3. Wraxall implies (loc. cit., 457) that she remained in touch with Pitt until 1801. But there are fewer references to her after 1790, and Pretyman mentions Pitt's seeing less of her after a time, though he gives no date (*Tomline's Estimate*, 33, n2).

4. See p. 105 above. He bought a villa at Wimbledon, in fact, at about the same time as Dundas.

5. *Private Papers of William Wilberforce*, 72.

6. Mrs Pretyman Tomline in 1801 ('Mr. Pitt II', Stanhope Mss). Her incessant underlinings were almost on a par with Queen Victoria's.

any case was not an ogre. He understood Pitt better than they thought, and may have come to meet a need better than they knew. But he was of course a very different kind of companion, and he was fatal in one way. For it was he more than any one else who encouraged Pitt to drink.

Exactly how much and how regularly Pitt was drinking by the early nineties, it is impossible to say. There is indeed a good deal of doubt as to when he first showed the effect. Pretyman said that he never saw him the worse for drink until 1798;[1] but if this was so, it was more a sign of Pitt's desire to avoid causing embarrassment than anything else. Macaulay told Lord Stanhope in the 1840s – and his source would doubtless have been Holland House, and so originally Fox – that the first time Pitt was affected in the Commons was in February 1793, when, accompanied by Dundas, he brought down the King's Message for war with France. This elicited a verse in *The Morning Chronicle* which caused much amusement:

> I cannot see the Speaker, Hal, can you?
> What! Cannot see the Speaker, I see two.[2]

But there may have been a precedent, perhaps less obvious, in March 1788, in the first debate on the Declaratory Bill for India.[3] Such occasions were rare – there is no hint that Pitt's other upsets in the House were ascribed to drink –[4] and there are few other public indiscretions to go on. *The Rolliad* seized on a story, of which there must have been gossip, that Pitt, Dundas and Thurlow, returning from dinner with Jenkinson at Addiscombe, galloped drunkenly through an open tollbar gate and were fired on for their pains.[5] But one cannot really tell how far dull and deep potations had yet replaced the brisk intermperance of youth.[6] Pitt had always liked a convivial evening – his friend Rutland had been a hard drinker – and by the later eighties he clearly had his share. It may have been of this time, when he knew him best, that Bland Burges later wrote of 'his extreme easiness, his boist'rous familiarity and drinking with his intimates'.[7] Figures of

1. Ibid.
2. Holland Rose, 279. It has been attributed to Porson, who became brother-in-law to the part-proprietor, James Perry (see *Notes and Queries, 2nd Series*, VI (1858), 118).
3. P. 454 above.
4. See pp. 29, 106 above.
5. See Holland Rose, 289. Pitt's drinking is specifically the theme here –
    His reason drowned in Jenkinson's champagne.
But a rather similar story was told, in a ballad of 1784 entitled 'Billy Pitt and the Farmer', in which Dundas also figured but there is no mention of drink or a tollgate, and the two are simply said to have lost their way (Stanhope, I, 285; and see also Wraxall, op. cit., III, 219–20 and n).
6. E.g. p. 108 above, in 1783.
7. Notes for a character sketch, in 'Concise Diary of Events by Sir James Burges, 1752–1806' (Bland Burges Mss; Bodleian Library).

consumption, however, are hard to come by; none seem to have survived for this period from Downing Street, and those for his country house at Holwood, which start in 1789, are not particularly startling. Port of course was easily the main item – a port lighter than we know it and in smaller bottles, but still, compared with other wines, what Boswell called 'a very heavy and a very inflammatory dose'.[1] Sometimes five or six bottles were drunk by the 'parlour', with three or four of madeira and two or three of claret; but the size of the company is unknown, and the average is two or three of port, one of madeira, and one of a red table wine. Quite often one bottle of port was drunk and one of madeira with no other wine in the 'parlour', and the overall quantity for an evening, which was generally more than double this, was accounted for the rest by the 'steward's room'.[2] By current standards, and Pitt's reputation, this is nothing much, and it may have been that he drank more in London, and when he was with those who set out to drink. Dundas certainly sat down to do so, and the tragedy was that Pitt thus became accustomed to sessions on a scale which was exceptional even by the practice of the day. For Dundas brought to London the habits of the Scottish Bench and Bar, the hardest drinking fraternity in the British Isles. He had been trained – on claret rather than on port – in the dining rooms and inns of Edinburgh, in the company of those hard-bitten judges who would preside in court the next morning apparently untouched by their all-night sittings. It was a perilous example, and Pitt must have had quite a strong head to compete: Burges indeed noted 'His possession of faculties when drunk or when just awaken'd from sleep'.[3] It helped kill him in the end; but in the eighties and early nineties his constitution appeared to be showing little sign of strain.

How did Pitt reconcile, so easily, such very different kinds of company? For a man of his description it may indeed seem strange. From Harriot to the Duchess, from Wilberforce to Dundas – these were large transitions, remarkable, it might appear, in someone known to be chary of his friendship. He was always confined to a small private group; but no one

1. *Boswell's London Journal 1762–1763*, ed. Frederick A. Pottle (1950), 303.

2. 'Hollwood Cellar Book'; P.R.O. 30/8/203. Between 14 July 1784 and 14 July 1785, Pitt bought the following wines (to the nearest dozen): 200 dozen of port, 71 dozen of madeira, 48 dozen of claret, 15 dozen of burgundy, 5 dozen of white champagne, 10 dozen of red champagne, 12 dozen of hock, 37 dozen of lisbon, 4 dozen of red hermitage, 23 dozen of sherry, 4 dozen of mountain, 1 dozen of red cape, 1 dozen of white cape, 1 dozen of malmsey, 8 dozen of brandy, and 2 bottles of tokay; also 4 dozen of rum, 3 bottles of hollands [gin], and 2 bottles of perry (P.R.O. 30/8/219.) The cellar at Holwood in September 1789, when the first surviving book opens, shows rather the same variety and proportions, with a few bottles of barsac added.

3. 'Concise Diary of Events', Bland Burges Mss.

could say that the birds were of one feather, or furthermore that he himself, whatever the company, was greatly changed. There was no doubt apt to be a difference in his conversation with, say, Pretyman on the one hand and Dundas on the other; but in all essentials he remained, throughout his life, much the same. Such accounts as we have are consistent, from the beginning almost to the end. 'Kindness and good-humour', 'playful facetiousness'; 'playfulness, urbanity, and good-humour' – this is from one quarter.[1] 'His laugh – love of fun – playful tricks': this is from another, less well disposed.[2] Men who had never met him, or come across him only in public, were amazed when they caught a rare glimpse of him in private, and his friends, of whatever description, mourned him bitterly when he died. There was no 'diminution of regard' by those who 'were gradually withdrawn', and the memory he left to those who knew him was of someone 'singularly amiable; his spirits . . . naturally buoyant and even playful; his affections warm'.[3] He was the same with all his intimates; and yet, distrustful of larger acquaintance, he seemed unconcerned who his intimates might be.

But perhaps the answer is suggested by the question: by this very catholicity of affection in one who found it difficult to seek out and choose his friends. Amiable and warm, he was happy from the start to take what circumstances offered: shy and haughty, he was unable to take the initiative himself. The family combination of simplicity and pride, the power to charm or repel, must have been given a peculiar impress by his upbringing and was set hard by his early fame. His background and Cambridge gave him a first set of friends, with almost no effort on his part. Political fortune gave him Dundas, and it may have been Dundas who opened a chink of the door (which was all that was needed) to the Duchess of Gordon. The contrast between his circle and Fox's has often been drawn, and the inferiority of Pitt's attributed to his fear of competition and his desire to lead. He may well not have been averse to flattery, perhaps particularly as he grew older – Burges stresses the fact, and Wilberforce seems to concede it.[4] But he was not vain, and his companions were drawn precisely not by choice so much as by chance. He was unlikely to admit a political figure with a standing or following of his own – Dundas at the outset was definitely of the second rank. But otherwise he was happy with anyone whom he had got used to, whom he found congenial, and with whom he could relax.

For the key to Pitt's private life was his wish to separate it from the public business which, paradoxically, was his ruling passion. He always kept the two as much apart as he could. He was bored on his visit to

---

1. *Private Papers of Wilberforce,* 68, 63; *Tomline's Estimate,* 33.
2. Burges, loc. cit., Bland Burges Mss.
3. Mrs Pretyman Tomline, in 'Mr Pitt II', Stanhope Mss; Brougham, *Historical Sketches of Statesmen,* 208.
4. Loc. cit., Bland Burges Mss; *Private Papers of Wilberforce,* 68.

France when they questioned him about Parliamentary reform.[1] He preferred to talk on 'indifferent subjects' to Mrs Pretyman when she expected him to be thinking about the sinking fund bill.[2] When Burke met him in 1791, and was asked to stay the night, 'neither at dinner supper or breakfast did a single word pass which had the smallest reference to foreign or domestick politics'.[3] Perhaps this was not as odd as Burke thought it, in the somewhat delicate circumstances; but it was of a piece with Pitt's normal habits. In the right company he could be brilliant – one would like to know more about that particular conversation. But he liked very simple pleasures: horseplay and nonsense and repartee. When he met the Duchess of Gordon after an interval in which they had stopped seeing much of each other, 'Well, Mr. Pitt', she asked, 'do you talk as much nonsense now as you used to do when you lived with me?'[4] And the young men of the next generation, Canning and his contemporaries, recalled and rather deplored his 'quizzing' and bad jokes. Austere and chilly in public, he could be like a boisterous schoolboy in private; and he can hardly have been fastidious to have enjoyed the company of the Duchess and Dundas. He often accepted the tastes that he found, and he was very much a man of his time. But he retained a singular innocence, not unlike that of the children whom he loved. We hear more about them later in his life; but there is a glimpse of his little niece, Harriot's daughter, being carried to a window at Burton Pynsent to see her favourite uncle driving home from cricket at 'almost *full speed*'.[5] There was indeed something young and untouched in his nature, which he never lost, and on which different observers again commented in different ways. He was 'originally pure', 'unsullied' – the attributes of childhood sprang to the minds of those who loved him. Others, less affectionate, noted his 'Inexperience of men and the world'.[6] He was not the only one of his family to show a remoteness and lack of understanding of his fellows;[7] and, in this form, it was both a source of weakness and a source of strength. It further detached him from large areas of life; but it also helped preserve in an unlikely setting a remarkable peace of mind. While those who worked with him knew well enough the mercurial treatment of his policies, his tendency to be 'either in a garret or a cellar',[8] they were also struck, without exception, by his buoyant and

1. See p. 111 above.
2. P. 577 above.
3. To Richard Burke, 1 August 1791 (*Correspondence of Edmund Burke*, VI, 376–7).
4. He replied, 'I do not know, madam, whether I talk so much nonsense, I certainly do not *hear* so much'. This is one of Pretyman's few personal stories (*Tomline's Estimate*, 33, n 2.)
5. Hester Countess of Chatham to Edward Eliot, 9 October 1788 (Pretyman Ms 435/40). She does not say whether he had been watching or playing.
6. The last quotation is from Burges, loc. cit.
7. See p. 4 above.
8. See p. 110 above.

even temper; by the way he slept soundly whatever his troubles, and the ease with which he threw them off. The picture which Wilberforce drew at the start was not altered for many years.

> I fancy [he wrote to Pitt, referring to his ability to 'throw off all your Load . . . & rest yourself',] it must have been this which when I am with you prevents my considering you as an Object of Compassion, the prime Minister of England, for . . . when I am at a Distance, out of Hearing of your foyning & Play & such other proofs of a light Heart, I cannot help representing you & myself as oppres't with Cares & troubles.[1]

He remained in truth, as he had been called in his early teens, in many ways a 'wonderful youth'.[2]

One is thus faced, in describing Pitt, with something like a reversal of normal practice. For it was in his public, not his private, life that much of his character emerged. It was there that he showed the pride, the fighting qualities, the power to dominate, the changes of mood, the shrewdness and the vacillations, that were entirely laid aside when he was off duty.

μή μοι τὰ κόμψ', ἀλλ' ὧυ πόλει δεῖ
No subtle arts for me, but what the state requires.[3]

But the state required many, and it is in Pitt's policies and his politics that one may trace the springs of action which were otherwise hidden from sight.

II

The pressure of business, or rather its incidence, prevented Pitt from often going far from London. It stopped him from ever crossing the Channel again after 1783. In 1784 and 1785 he went down to Brighton when he could, but thereafter he stayed for the most part even closer at hand except for his visits to his mother at Burton Pynsent, usually once in the late summer and sometimes briefly at about Christmas. He could not manage two or three days at the 'famous place of Mr. Drummond in the New Forest' in the best months of the summer recess of 1784,[4] and when he planned a tour to the north a few years later it

1. 2 August 1785; P.R.O. 30/8/189.
2. P. 10 above.
3. Jowett's translation; from Aristotle in the *Politics*, 111, 4.8, quoting from the lost play the *Aeolus* of Euripides.
4. To Hester Countess of Chatham, 7 October 1784 (Stanhope, I, 233). This would have been Robert Drummond, of Drummond's bank, and the place was Cadland, on Southampton Water.

had twice to be called off.[1] He had a round of 'excursions' in the late autumn of 1789, finishing up at Stowe;[2] but his only real chance of going far afield lay in the journeys to Somerset, which he sometimes broke in the earlier years with Bankes in Dorset, and later with Rose at his new property near Lyndhurst. Even these, however, were not always possible, at least for any length of time. Harriot's death, and the need to stay with Eliot, delayed him in 1786 until November; he could not go down later that winter, or in the winter of 1788–9, and in 1790 could spare only a few days in the autumn, although he snatched the inside of a week at the end of the year. His plans were frequently being changed, often by despatches from abroad – there was the Portuguese commercial treaty, or the Dutch business, the Northern War, the Nootka crisis, or the news from France.[3] There were also Levees and Drawing Rooms, and the habitual uncertainty of the Parliamentary session – when it was going to end, or, sometimes, to begin. These were not excuses; Pitt set much store by his visits to the west. They were part and parcel of a constantly interrupted life.

His other – his only other – regular visits were to Cambridge. Even though they were not frequent, he liked to go there from time to time. His duties as Burgess for the University gave him little trouble, and he did not give them much attention, but he was fond of his College and enjoyed the occasional Feast. He did what he could for Pembroke – in 1784 he gave a particularly handsome piece of plate, and he used his good offices at the Treasury to forward a notable benefaction in the same year. He also became High Steward of the University in 1790. But it was pleasure quite as much as business that took him that way. Cambridge moreover was near Cheveley, Rutland's estate, and even though Rutland was in Ireland Pitt could go there and have a little shooting.[4] He was among familiar faces on these visits, and in familiar haunts.

But the difficulties of leaving London meant that he, like other Ministers, should really have somewhere of his own within easy distance. In August 1784 he rented a house near Putney; but that lasted only a year. For in the summer of 1785 the opportunity arose to buy a property after his own heart, Holwood House near Keston, only a mile or two from Hayes where he had been born and brought up.[5] It had been sold in 1784 to a Mr John Randall, a London shipbuilder, who fortunately soon changed his mind, and by August 1785 Pitt was in search of the

1. See p. 543 above for 1788, and Stanhope, I, 345–6 for 1787.
2. To Hester Countess of Chatham, 21 November 1789 (P.R.O. 30/8/12).
3. Loc. cit. *passim*. These foreign questions affected his plans in the winter of 1786-7 and the summers of 1787, 1788, 1790, and 1791 respectively.
4. To Hester Countess of Chatham, n.d. but endorsed 13 September 1787 (P.R.O. 30/8/12). See p. 17 above.
5. 'Holwood' is the usual spelling. Pitt wrote indifferently 'Holwood' or 'Hollwood'; usually 'Holwood (or Hollwood) House', and occasionally 'Holwood (or Hollwood) Hill'.

necessary money. He would have to borrow, for the purchase was well beyond his means – as he told Wilberforce, it was an extravagance. He had to find £5,000 for the house and estate, some £568 for contents, and another £509 for farm stock and gear. But he soon learned that there was also the chance of including a small neighbouring farm for £750 – it was Downe farm, near the house of that name which Charles Darwin was to make famous – and in that case the total cost would be over £6,800 for an estate of some 200 acres. He decided to try for both properties, raising as much as he could on their security. By the end of August he had the promise of £3,000, and it was raised to £4,000 by the end of the year. On that basis he went ahead, buying Holwood in November 1785 and Downe farm in January 1786.[1]

The house itself was quite small, a sixteenth or early seventeenth century brick lodge. Pitt seems to have left it much as it was, though he doubtless redecorated and made a few alterations; there is a tradition that he took a cottage in the nearby village of Westerham from which to supervise the work, but this may conceivably have been later, in 1797, when he enlarged the house.[2] He could put up a small party of friends, for there were five bedrooms apart from his own and the servants'; downstairs there were a drawing room, dining room and study, the last hung with Gillray's prints over the years.[3] It must all have looked rather refreshing; the drawing room had green cotton curtains and green and white striped covers to the sofa and chairs, the dining room green curtains and a green and pink Wilton carpet, the study green curtains again, while Pitt's bedroom had white curtains and white coverings to the four-poster bed. The furniture in the larger rooms was mahogany almost throughout. There were five more bedrooms in the back quarters and the garret, and the offices included a still-

1. For the purchases, see Holwood Estate, bundle 1216 docs. 1 & 2, 3, bundle 1215 docs. 1 & 2, 3 (photostat in the Kent County Record Office, Maidstone, of summaries of documents in the Earl of Derby's Mss at Knowsley, Lancashire); for the finance, loc. cit., bundle 1215 doc. 4, and notes from Augustine Greenland to Pitt, 26 August, 25 and 29 November, 1 and 3 December 1785 (miscellaneous notes on Pitt, Stanhope Mss.)

The £4,000 was in the form of a mortgage with William Hornby, who had returned to England in 1784 from being Governor of Bombay. Two years earlier Dundas had demanded his recall with that of Warren Hastings. But the two Governors were not closely connected, the demand failed, and when Hornby finally came home the fact seems to have aroused no particular political interest. The transaction with Pitt was probably quite normal; retired East Indians not infrequently invested money in loans, to politicians as well as others.

2. The cottage, still known as 'Pitt's Cottage', is now a restaurant and tearoom. If he stayed there in 1785 it must have been over quite a short period, for at the end of November Harriot and Edward Eliot went to stay with him at Holwood (or 'Holly Wood', as Harriot called it) for several days. She also remarked that her brother was lucky in having 'a small House that will not allow of many Visitors', which does not sound as if he had done very much (to Hester Countess of Chatham, 21 November [1785]; *The Letters of Lady Harriot Eliot*, 120–1).

3. Frederick Sidney Gammon, *The Story of Keston in Kent* (1934), 26–7.

room, dairy and laundry. There were also a coachman's room, and a grooms' room with two beds, over the stables.[1]

The property, unlike the house, was soon enlarged by degrees, for in the usual way of landowners Pitt was anxious to round it off. Several further purchases followed: in August 1788, July and October 1790, and October 1793.[2] One of them involved a major alteration, for in July 1790 he was allowed to enclose part of Keston Common in return for an annual payment of £10 to the parish and the re-routeing of the main road to Westerham, which hitherto had run through the park close to the house. He had probably in fact wished to do this for privacy, and he turned the old road into a drive. But it was only one of the works which he undertook. For Pitt shared with his father the prevalent taste for 'improvement', for planting and clearing and well contrived views; and it now became his favourite recreation. 'Tomorrow', he told his mother in November 1786, 'I hope to get to Holwood, where I am impatient to look at my works. I must carry there, however, only my passion for planting, and leave that of cutting entirely to Burton'.[3] But there was in fact plenty of cutting as well: the removal of shrubs, turning of walks, and a clearance of the woods to make a view to the north. Not all the 'improvements' were equally fortunate. The crest of Holwood hill is the site of one of the most important Iron Age forts in Kent, an extensive earthworks covering about 100 acres and traditionally known as Caesar's Camp. Pitt was wholly indifferent to its fate. He levelled a section of the fortifications, planted firs in others, and, as his friend Long later told him, 'ruined the camp'. Protests had no effect. 'He laughed', another friend, Bathurst, recalled, 'when I remonstrated ... All the Roman remains among us, and whatever related to Gothic or ancient times, he held in no great respect'.[4] He seems to have been entirely untouched by antiquarian interest or by the dawning of the Romantic taste.

In the early days at least, he took part in the cutting and planting himself. Lord Mornington (later Lord Wellesley) watched him 'working ... with his labourers for whole days together, undergoing considerable bodily fatigue, and with so much eagerness and assiduity, that you would suppose the culture of his villa to be the principal occupation of his life'. A 'great many people' were involved at first, and the work was said to have gone on sometimes after dark under lanterns. And when the larger plans had been carried out, Pitt still liked to make small improvements; he and his friends would go out with spuds and

1. Inventory of 4 July 1794 (P.R.O. 30/8/219).
2. Holwood Estate, bundles 1214 docs. 5 & 6; 1207 docs 4 & 5; 1211 docs. 21 & 22, 23; 1214 docs. 1 & 2. Lord Cranworth, who owned the property in the middle of the nineteenth century, told Stanhope that there was a further acquisition of land in August 1794 (5 September 1860; 'Pitt Papers, Part ii', Stanhope Mss).
3. 13 November [1786] (see Stanhope, I, 321).
4. See the admirable account by Gammon, op. cit., 24–5.

billhooks, grubbing up shrubs and pruning thickets.[1] He also supervised his farming, which seems to have centred on sheep.[2] In short, he enjoyed '*the pleasures of the Country*' and '*improvements on his Grounds*'.[3]

These were happy days. Pitt was a good host, and he liked to take down a friend or two to stay. When they were not busy in the woods or garden, or with their papers, they walked or rode or talked or read. Pitt himself devoured the classics, as he had always done; the house was 'strewed' with Greek and Latin authors, and if the weather compelled him to travel by carriage he would take one with him to pass the time.[4] They were his great love; he was not so well read in other directions, and does not seem to have kept up much with the new books. Although Mrs Pretyman Tomline claimed that he 'read almost everything worth reading', the general impression does not bear this out.[5] There were considerable gaps, ascribed usually to the fact that he had been plunged into office so soon, and he certainly showed no sign of encouraging the authors of his own time. He had a high opinion of Paley, and is said to have shared the fashionable taste for Burns – the more so in this last case, perhaps, because the poet had been a protégé of the Duchess of Gordon.[6] But even allowing for the decline of the office, and the absence of obvious rivals, it was disgraceful – and was so regarded – to appoint the recently retired MP Henry James Pye Poet Laureate in 1791.[7] Pitt in fact seems to have had an academic rather than a living interest in literature, and an uneven knowledge of the broader range, though his remarkable memory enabled him to remem-

1. Wellesley in *The Quarterly Review* in 1836, reprinted in *Diaries and Correspondence of George Rose*, II, 293; *Tomline's Estimate*, 35 and n1; Gammon, loc. cit., 25–6.

2. The stock included 211 sheep and 4 lambs in July 1794, as well as 5 cows, a few cart horses, 6 pigs, and a number of ducks and hens. In the following April, at lambing time, there were 660 sheep all told. (P.R.O. 30/8/219.)

3. Mrs Pretyman Tomline's notes of 1801 ('Mr. Pitt II', Stanhope Mss). She excepted hunting and shooting from these pleasures. In point of fact Pitt seems to have liked shooting, and he is known to have hunted occasionally. But he tended to give up field sports as time went by (*Tomline's Estimate*, 34), and had other things to do at Holwood.

4. *Diaries and Correspondence of George Rose*, II, 292; *Tomline's Estimate*, 35.

5. Notes of 1801 (Stanhope Mss). But cf. Wraxall, op. cit., III, 223–4; Burges, 'Concise Diary' (Bodleian Library); and the impression recorded later by Brougham in his *Historical Sketches of Statesmen*, 196.

6. But the post in the Excise which Burns was given in 1788 came primarily from the activities of his patrons in Scotland, not those of Pitt at the Treasury. For Paley see p. 396, n1 above.

7. 'Eminently respectable', as Sir Walter Scott remarked, 'in everything but his poetry'. He had been publishing his uninspired verse since the sixties, and after leaving the Commons, where he had supported Government, at the election of 1790, was looking for a place. Although he took the offered Laureateship, he was in fact far from satisfied – not unnaturally, in view of its small value – and continued to ask for other posts (letters in Pitt's papers, P.R.O. 30/8/169). Unfortunately he was conscientious, and insisted on producing the annual Odes required of him at the New Year and for the King's birthday.

ber and quote what he read.[1] By all accounts his taste was less eclectic than Fox's, and when he took a book into the garden, to sit under the tree long known as 'Pitt's Oak', it was often no doubt a volume of Homer or of Horace.

The country life of Holwood, and his journeys there, helped to keep Pitt in reasonable health. He rode to and fro whenever he could – the Dutch Ambassador indeed once complained of 'Mr. Pitt . . . riding on Horseback & being so much in the Country'[2] – and there were other opportunities when he called on Jenkinson or Eden nearby. He led an active life at this time, and while still thin and rather light in weight,[3] showed no real sign of his later disorders at least until 1789. There are mentions of the occasional bad cold, and early on, more disturbingly, of spasms of sickness.[4] But the latter seem to have been infrequent, particularly in the middle eighties, and the only trouble of note in those years was a swelling in one of his cheeks, which led to an operation. He had had a slight attack of it when he was up at Cambridge, and it recurred more seriously early in 1786. The doctors found 'an encysted tumour', and the celebrated John Hunter removed it at Downing Street. Pitt showed a sangfroid equal to the standards of a pre-anaesthetic age. He would not let Hunter tie his hands as was normally done, assured him that he would not move, and asked how long the surgeon would take. On being told six minutes he fixed his eyes on the Horse Guards' clock, and remained motionless until it was over, when he remarked cheerfully 'You have exceeded your time half a minute'.[5] The pain returned briefly in August 1788;[6] but that is the last we hear

1. E.g. p. 15 above; and in 1801 he astonished a party at Mrs Pretyman Tomline's by his quotations and remarks on English poetry (copy of letter to Bishop Pretyman Tomline, 22 December 1801; 'Mr. Pitt II', Stanhope Mss). He is said (Rosebery, *Pitt,* 273) to have thought *Gil Blas* (presumably in Smollett's translation) the best of all novels.

2. Carmarthen to Harris, Private, 1 July 1788 (B.M. Add. Ms 28063, f. 205v). Pitt also rode to and from Cambridge on at least one occasion (Pitt to Hester Countess of Chatham, 13 September 1787; Stanhope, I, 346). And he seems to have exercised in the park in London (Pitt to Grenville, 10 or 12 February 1789; *H.M.C., Dropmore,* I, 411).

3. Judging by the record of Berry Brothers' scales: 11 stone 6¼ lb in 'boots &c.' in March 1785; 12 stone, again in boots, in 1786. Cf. pp. 105–6 above.

4. E.g. pp. 29, 106 above. He also had an exhausting cold, which made him lose his voice, in December 1788, during the Regency crisis. But that was scarcely surprising.

5. The story was written down later by W. E. Tomline, Pretyman's son, from his father's account. Hunter is said to have remarked that he had never seen 'so much fortitude & courage in all his practice'. (Edward Stanhope's copy from a commonplace book in the Pretyman Tomline papers; Stanhope Mss.) Harriot mentions the Cambridge attack (*Letters of Lady Harriot Eliot,* 137).

6. Harris to Pitt, 28 August 1788 (P.R.O. 30/8/155); Pitt to Hester Countess of Chatham, 29 August, 1 September 1788 (P.R.O. 30/8/12); George III to Pitt, 19 September 1788 (*L.C.G. III,* I, no. 482, n2).

of it, and in general Pitt seems in this period to have been free of serious illness.

In 1789, however, the first symptoms appeared of the disease which was to plague him increasingly in the next decade. In mid-July he was troubled with 'a Lameness, which is just enough to confine Me, and to justify some Pretensions to the Name of Gout'.[1] As he said, he was 'very well entitled to it'; it had been Chatham's disease, and he himself had been thought to be affected by it as a child. The attack soon passed, and while he had another in October 1791 that too was slight and there seemed no particular need to worry.[2] It was not until 1793 that his health began noticeably to change. In the early nineties, to all appearance, he had weathered his years in office pretty well.

III

The money spent on Holwood further embarrassed Pitt's shaky and confused finances. The position remains as obscure as it did when his friends first tried to clear it up. It is not even certain exactly how much he received by way of income from his official posts. From December 1783 he was First Lord of the Treasury, and Chancellor and Under Treasurer of the Exchequer. From August 1792 he was also Lord Warden of the Cinque Ports, an appointment which the King conferred on him upon the death of the former Warden, Lord North. Various computations have been made of the net monetary value of these offices – that is to say, when all monetary incidents are added and tax and duties subtracted. While the broad picture is clear, no one acquainted with eighteenth-century finance will be surprised if some of the details are imprecise. As First Lord of the Treasury, Pitt was paid a gross salary of £5,622: £1,600 as one of the Treasury Commissioners and £4,022 in addition as First Commissioner. He also received, until 1797, a small sum by way of New Year's Gifts[3] – some £46 in 1784, an average of £33 by a later calculation. Certain duties and taxes had then to be deducted from the two parts of this salary, amounting in theory, it would seem, to about £1,077. But these were always adjusted to leave a net total of at least £5,000, and in his case of some £5,033.[4] With the addition of New Year's Gifts, he may thus

1. Pitt to Hester Countess of Chatham, 14 July 1789 (see Stanhope, II, 38). Pretyman later noted that his first attack of gout was in that year (Tomline Mss, Box 29, 1, 35.2; Pembroke College, Cambridge).

2. Same to same, 4 October 1791 (P.R.O. 30/8/12). Since these two attacks were mentioned in the newspapers (which was why Pitt mentioned them to his mother), they were perhaps the only ones in that period.

3. They were abolished in the department by a Minute of 10 October 1797; *Reports from Committees*, XIII (1803), 724.

4. There are complications in these sums, all of which I give to the nearest £. I have followed Appendix (B) to the Fifteenth Report of the House of Commons' Select Committee on Finance of 1797 (*Reports from Committees*, XII, 290–1). There is

have enjoyed a net income of just under £5,100. As Chancellor and Under Treasurer of the Exchequer, his gross salary was £1,800. He also received New Year's Gifts said to have been some £79, and fees which it is difficult to specify – £200 a year according to a statement of 1782, £800 a year according to a retrospective statement of 1831.[1] After deducting duties and tax, perhaps the most reliable account of his net income from this office gives it as £1,898.[2] Taking these calculations, his annual net income from the Treasury and the Exchequer was accordingly £6,931. From late in 1792 he also received a gross salary of £4,382 as Lord Warden of the Cinque Ports (£4,100 on the Civil List, £282 on the Army Vote), from which he paid some £1,329 in duties and taxes and salaries to subordinates, leaving a net total of £3,053.[3] From 1784 to 1792, therefore, his official incomings on this reckoning would have been in the region of £6,900 a year, and thereafter just short of £10,000.

These were large amounts. When Wraxall wished to illustrate Pitt's haughtiness, he remarked that there were men with £5,000 a year who would have been grateful for a nod or a glance; and Shelburne told Boswell that 'a man of high rank' who looked after his affairs might 'have all that he ought to have' for the same annual sum.[4] This, then, was wealth; but Pitt's salaries exceeded it, and he paid no rent or 'coals and candles' at Downing Street. He was a bachelor, with a quite modest estate after 1785. Yet he was seldom, if ever, out of debt.

It is impossible to say at all exactly why this was so. Part of the reason in this period may have lain in his efforts to help his mother. She had been left in poor straits at Chatham's death; her reversionary pension from the Crown was often in arrears; and when Pitt first came to London she had supplied half his income.[5] He now did what he could, using his influence to get the pension paid, and on at least two occasions

a slightly different, and less extensive, account in Appendix 47 to the Second Report of the Commissioners for Enquiring into Fees in the Public Offices, of 1786, published in *House of Commons Accounts and Papers*, VII (1806). Rosebery, in Appendix C to his *Pitt*, produced his own summary of salaries and deductions, with the aid of a Treasury official who also consulted some later statements. But his deductions do not tally exactly with those of the Commissioners in 1786, or with the total given in 1797.

1. For the fees, see Appendix 31 to the Sixth Report of the Commissioners for Examining the Public Accounts, of 1782, published in *H.C.J.*, 38; and Rosebery, op. cit., 296, citing 'House of Commons Paper, No. 322 of 1831', which I have failed to trace.

2. Select Committee on Finance, 1797; *Reports from Committees*, XII, 290–1. Cf. Rosebery, op. cit., 296.

3. Ibid. There were also small miscellaneous payments attached to the office, which varied from year to year. Nevertheless, according to one authority, some of Pitt's friends spoke of his 'actual income' from it as £2,500 (The Marquess Curzon of Kedleston K.G., *The Personal History of Walmer Castle and Its Lords Warden* (1927), 39, n2).

4. P. 231 above; Boswell's *Life of Johnson*, III, 265, under 10 April 1778.

5. See pp. 19–20 above.

giving more direct support. In 1783 he gave her, or repaid, the sum of £500, and in 1793 he advanced £300, apologising that it was not more because he had had to apply his new salary as Lord Warden to his own debts.[1] This was nothing much; but in 1786, when he could ill afford it, he seems (though the evidence is incomplete) to have made a very real sacrifice, allotting her the sum of £5,800 which he had just raised by loan from their banker Coutts. This was in fact all the capital that he might hope himself ever to receive, the residue, as yet unpaid, of his share of his father's inheritance.[2] The loan was raised on Burton Pynsent, and Pitt thereafter paid the interest.[3] If the money went (as seems likely) to his mother, it added substantially to the difficulties in which he was already plunged.

Another contributory factor, at least at first, may have been the irregularity of payments from the Exchequer. Pitt's bank account and the Exchequer books agree that this was so from 1784 to 1786. In 1784 he received his salaries as First Lord and Chancellor for the two first quarters of the year in September and for the third quarter in December, and only one quarter's salary, it seems, as an ordinary Commissioner of the Treasury.[4] He waited until late July and early August 1785 for the next payments, which covered his various salaries up to the end of the first quarter of that year; and another twelve months – until late July 1786 – for a further instalment, which again brought him up to the end of the first quarter of the year. It was late January 1787 before he received anything more, and then it was only the salaries for the second quarter of 1786. Thereafter matters seem to have settled down, and payments were more regular, though still behindhand, over the next six years.[5]

None of these disbursements was related to the minor items of income, fees and gifts, and it is indeed very difficult to tell what happened to all the £6,900-odd which Pitt was supposed to receive until late in 1792. That calculation was presumably not excessively inaccurate, for most of the figures of which it is made up appeared in a Parliamentary report which Pitt himself must have seen.[6] But according to the

1. Messrs Coutt's Ledgers, under Countess of Chatham, 15 June 1783; Pitt to Hester Countess of Chatham, 11 November 1793 (Ashbourne, 160).

2. See p. 19 above.

3. The deed of assignment and bond to Coutts's Bank, of 2 August 1786, are in Pretyman Ms 50/3/182. There is no proof from Messrs Coutts's Ledgers, or from Thomas Coutts's personal memorandum book in the Bank's archives, that the £5,800 went to Lady Chatham. But there is some later evidence; for when Pitt's affairs were under review many years later, the transaction puzzled George Rose, and Pretyman then told him that, to the best of his knowledge, the money went to her, and that she should have repaid Pitt the annual interest which Coutts's ledgers show that he met. See J. Holland Rose, *William Pitt and the Great War* (1911), 475–6.

4. There seems to be no trace of the other three quarters' salary under this head at any time.

5. Messrs Coutts's Ledgers; P.R.O., E. 403/1174–80.

6. That of the Commons' Select Committee on Finance in 1797. See pp. 595–6 above.

Exchequer books for the middle eighties he was being paid £1,805 a quarter, or £7,220 a year, and once the payments settled down his bank account shows a credit from official sources of some £6,240 a year. Since the Treasury payments, in the Exchequer books, are clearly gross salary before duties are deducted (£1,600 a year as a Commissioner, £4,022 as First Lord), one may subtract some £600 from this first figure, leaving about £6,620. But since the Treasury salaries were thus paid in full, this leaves a salary of only £1,600 as Chancellor of the Exchequer, whereas according to the calculations it should have been at least £1,800.[1] £1,600 was moreover what Pitt was actually paid, in equal quarterly instalments, from the Exchequer books; so that either all the later calculations were wrong (which would be odd) or he was not receiving, or taking, his full income as Chancellor in these years. And even then he was paying into his bank account £6,240 instead of £6,620, a further deficit of almost £400 a year. The discrepancies have defeated me. I can find no evidence that Pitt allotted a regular sum at source to anyone else – to his mother, say, or a creditor; but anything between 6 and 10 per cent of his official income – probably nearer the former figure, allowing for the great delay in receiving fees and gifts,[2] and for clerks' and agents' fees – appears to have been diverted between the Exchequer and Coutts. Perhaps it went to Pretyman, and later Joseph Smith, towards immediate needs.

In a sense, however, these calculations are academic. For none of the delays or irregularities of income, or family undertakings, was allowed seriously to affect Pitt's expenditure. He was in fact entirely unworried whether the money was there or not. As early as 1785 his banker friend Robert Smith found unpaid bills for almost £8,000, though Pitt had told him that his arrears of salary for that year would be enough to clear off any debts. He spent as he felt inclined, and he seldom looked at his accounts – Pretyman sometimes asked him to do so, but he 'rarely' did, and would then promise economies which he never carried out.[3] The result was that he was robbed, by his servants and his tradesmen; and such accounts as survive suggest that this sometimes happened on a large scale. It is impossible to tell what his full outgoings were in any year: only occasional lists are preserved. But we have an idea of some of his running expenses. The housekeeping accounts for Downing Street and Holwood cover food and oddments in the first case, with the addition of garden and farm expenses in the second. At Downing Street they are said to have amounted to £2,848 in 1785 (and there was a further £865 spent on wine between July 1784 and July 1785), £2,105 in 1786, £1,348 in 1787, £1,479 in 1788, £1,890 in 1789,

1. See p. 596 above.
2. Some of which seem in fact to have reached his bank account after 1789.
3. *Tomline's Estimate*, 36.

£1,665 in 1790, £1,609 in 1791, and £1,276 in 1792. On (presumably) the same basis, Holwood cost less, for Pitt was there less often: £1,119 in 1785–6, £446 in 1787, £775 in 1788, £536 in 1789, £1,175 in 1790, £871 in 1791, and £1,258 in 1792.[1] A few of the items are rather suspicious, such as a butcher's bill for some £96 for January–February 1785, a sum which was equivalent to perhaps 34 cwt of meat; and there are said to have been curiously high deliveries of meat sometimes on Saturdays, when Pitt was often at Holwood.[2] It is possible in fact that this particular abuse was checked, for the butcher's bills dropped after a period; but in spite of fresh instructions to the servants,[3] the waste and fraud clearly continued.

We do not know how many of these servants there were at all times, or how much they cost. There are odd references to some of them, but no regular or complete accounts. In 1785 Pitt paid duty on four servants, and in 1786 on eleven; but it is not clear if the numbers continued to rise. Wages in any case were low, and all these expenses, though on the large side for a single man, were not enough to cause Pitt distress. They may not of course have been recorded in full, and we have no idea what he spent in some other ways – on wine and clothes, in taxes on Holwood, on furniture and decorations, above all on repairs and improvements. But there was one field of activity where the costs were astonishingly high, at least for a time – high enough in fact for them to account by themselves for his running into debt. For between July 1783 and July 1786 – the only period recorded – Pitt spent £37,930 on his stables' account: £16,813 in 1783–4, £12,470 in 1784–5, and £8,647 in 1785–6.[4]

1. P.R.O. 30/8/204, 205 respectively, and P.R.O. 30/8/219 for the wines in 1784–5; figures to the nearest £. The variations in the running expenses of Holwood were caused mostly by the garden and farm. In 1790, 1791 and 1792, there were particularly large bills to a nurseryman, John Russell.

Social historians might like to have the names of Pitt's regular London tradesmen for these years. They were: Lock (butcher), Payne (baker), Pratt (fishmonger), Gay (cheesemonger), Gunter (confectioner: this was T. Gunter of 31 New Bond Street – an ancestor of the celebrated Victorian confectioner?), Fisher (greengrocer), Godson and Company (poulterer), Cousins (grocer in 1785) and Whittingham (thereafter), Hedges (tallow chandler), Willson (milkman), Pattison (turner), Blakiston (tea dealer, 1785–7) followed by Arnaud (in 1788) and Kilvington (thereafter), Mackay (oilman). There is also the odd mention of George Heming (silversmith), Pearson (china), Swan (earthenware), Gray (cutler), Egg (gunsmith), Hart ('Lace Mender'), James Moore and also William Croft (cabinet makers), Robert Perryman (coachmaker), Samuel Crowther (wigmaker), William Hobard and also Francis Bristowe (shoemakers), Robert Foulder and also John Walter (stationers – probably the printer John Walter who founded *The Times*), Garratt or Garrett ('Newsman'), Arnott, Thompson, Debrett, Cadell, Flack (booksellers). I have found no tailor or wine merchant named in this period.

2. P.R.O. 30/8/204; Holland Rose, 287–8.

3. Undated paper in P.R.O. 30/8/219. Perhaps they were issued by Joseph Smith, on taking over from Pretyman in 1787.

4. P.R.O. 30/8/219.

Horses and coaches, and all that went with them, were always apt to be a large item. Much care and expense were lavished on a good turn-out, and travelling costs could be heavy. Even so this is an amazing sum, and its detail is equally surprising. For of the five heads of expenditure listed – purchase of horses, their purveyance and keep, hackney-work and posting (meaning posthorses or chaises), tradesmen's bills and carriages etc., and disbursements to servants – the first two amounted to no less than £21,835.[1] The quarterly figures varied wildly: rising to over £2,000 on one occasion, to between £3,000 and £4,000 on three others, and to over £4,000 for the last quarter of 1785; falling sometimes to under £1,000, to under £500 on one occasion, and for the last quarter recorded, so we are told, to nothing. Despite the substantial sums under tradesmen's bills and carriages, there do not seem always to have been many of the latter: in 1785 Pitt paid a year's duty on two carriages.[2] Why then was he spending such enormous sums on horses? He did not keep a racing stable – his purchases were purely for riding and carriage (and perhaps farm) work. Nor did the numbers actually in hand apparently warrant more than a coach-man and two grooms at Holwood;[3] and the stables at Downing Street, though good, were not huge. The amounts spent regularly on 'hackney-work and posting', moreover, suggest that he, like most people, often used horses other than his own. What can have happened to the beasts which were bought and kept at an average cost of over £7,000 a year?[4]

One can only conclude that in this instance he was being grossly cheated: perhaps indeed that is why the account was retrospectively drawn up. The unpaid stables' bills must have formed a good part of those that Robert Smith found in 1785, as their successor doubtless did of the later debts. They contributed to a situation which was becoming potentially serious. For what with running costs on a scale (to take the clearest examples we have) of at least £16–17,000 in 1785 and £11–12,000 in 1786, the purchase and improvement of Holwood, aid to his mother, and irregular receipt of salary, Pitt was coming to rely increasingly on loans – an exercise, of course, which in turn involved him in fresh expense.

For while Pitt had a sizeable official income, he still had no private resources. In 1785 he was paid just under £4,400 of the £10,244 which was his nominal fortune; and shortly afterwards he seems to have

1. They cannot be separated after April 1784; before that date the ratio of expense was 1 to 3 and 1 to 4.
2. P.R.O. 30/8/205, under 12 September 1785.
3. To judge by the furnishing of rooms over the stables (P.R.O. 30/8/219).
4. For comparison, this sum was equal to the entire expense of one of the leading Newmarket racing establishments – an outlay which was recognised as lying beyond the reach of all but the richest men.

received a further very small sum.[1] In 1787 he was left £3,000 in his friend Rutland's will. That was the extent of his capital, with another £5,800 in theory to come. It was therefore a question of finding security on which to borrow.

The borrowing had been going on since 1780. By the end of 1783, as far as one can tell, Pitt seems to have raised something in the region of £4,800: two loans, in company with his elder brother, of £1,500 each from Solomon Henry, the first on the security of chambers in Lincoln's Inn; and two from Coutts, one of £1,000 on the security of a legacy (unpaid) from his father, and another of £800, security unknown.[2] The first loan from Henry had just been repaid,[3] so that some £3,300 was still owing. Over the next few years, the process was stepped up. There seems to have been a fresh loan of £4,000 from Coutts's Bank in March 1784 (though the details are obscure) which was entered to his credit early the next year;[4] in January 1786, Pitt received his £4,000 from William Hornby, taking out a mortgage on Holwood for that sum;[5] he then paid off the second loan from Solomon Henry, presumably out of that money (and contemplated, but did not ask him for, a further loan);[6] and in August 1786 raised a sum of some £11,611 from the bank, part of it on the security of his remaining unpaid fortune of £5,805, and the rest for a bond of £6,000.[7] The £5,800 may have gone to his mother; and, again perhaps using the remainder, he paid off Coutts's old loan of £1,000 and the balance of the loan of £4,000.[8] In 1787 he was therefore paying interest on a total of some £15,805,[9] in return for which he had mortgaged a large part of Holwood and pledged the rest of his nominal inheritance, and then still owed the bank £6,000. Thereafter the pace died down, though the commitments did not. It was not until July 1791 that Pitt entered, with his brother, into a fresh bond with the bank for £6,000, apparently replacing the

1. See p. 19 above for the £4,400, and Pretyman Ms 50/3/182 for the small sum, of about £42.

2. For the first loan from Henry, and the £1,000 from Coutts, see p. 20 above; for the second loan from Henry, and the £800, Messrs Coutts's Ledgers. This last possibly included the £100 borrowed from Coutts in 1780 to help pay for the rooms at Lincoln's Inn (p. 20 above).

3. Pretyman Ms 50/3/180. It may have been then that the second was raised (Pretyman Ms 435/36).

4. In March 1784 Pitt signed a bond to Coutts for £2,000, apparently in return for a sum of £4,000 (Pretyman Ms 435/36). In January 1785 (Messrs Coutts's Ledgers) he received £4,000 via Augustine Greenland, who was looking after his financial affairs at the time (miscellaneous notes on Pitt, Stanhope Mss).

5. Holwood Estate, bundle 1215 doc. 4. See p. 591, n1 above.

6. Messrs Coutts's Ledgers; Greenland to Pitt, 20 January 1786, Stanhope Mss.

7. Pretyman Ms 50/3/182; Messrs Coutts's Ledgers.

8. Messrs Coutts's Ledgers.

9. Loc. cit. The early loan of £800 may have been regarded as repaid by Pitt's bond of March 1784, when he raised a further sum. At any rate, the payments of interest in 1787, and for some time thereafter, relate to Hornby's mortgage and the two bonds to Coutts of 1786.

loan of that sum to himself of five years before; and, again with his brother (though his own share is unknown), borrowed £7,000 from Thomas Coutts in person.[1] But he was also receiving regular advances from Coutts in these years on his official income, and in June 1793 was eventually forced to assign to him his salary as First Lord of the Treasury.[2]

This tale of borrowing, and repayments made on the occasion of fresh borrowing, is rather sad. One is watching Pitt trying to keep his head above water, and preserve enough good faith to raise further loans. He was managing in part to honour the bonds he signed, sometimes belatedly and at renewed expense; but only, after a time, at the cost of part of his salary. Less well secured creditors, however, were less fortunate, and had to take their chance. There seem to have been two major efforts to meet their claims, in 1786 on the strength of one of Coutts's loans, and again in 1793.[3] But even then they were probably not paid in full, and the victims seem to have been pretty patient: I know of only one action being brought against Pitt in this period for recovery of debt.[4] One can form no idea of what he owed to tradesmen by the early nineties, and it is highly unlikely that he had much idea himself.[5] It is a strange picture: the guardian of the national finances so regardless of his own, the scrupulous and dedicated Chancellor so ignorantly profligate in private. It is also a commentary on a moral code which enshrined Pitt as a model of virtue; as a shining example, indeed, to be contrasted with Fox. This of course was entirely true in one vital respect: he resolutely refused to enrich himself from public funds. The only sinecure post that he ever filled, the Lord Wardenship of the Cinque Ports, was at the King's express gift, and with the command that it was not to be refused;[6] and moreover he did his best, when occasion arose, to honour his obligations, by carrying

1. For the new and old £6,000 see Messrs Coutts's Ledgers, 19 August 1791; for the £7,000, the 'Memos of Thos. Coutts 1795 to 1809' (Coutts's Archives no. 466), relating to his personal affairs. Since all details concerning this second loan are given there under Chatham's name, and Chatham is said to have repaid it in July 1804, it may have affected him more than Pitt.

2. Messrs Coutts's Private Ledgers, 16 July 1791; deed of assignment of 3 June 1793, Coutts's Archives no. 157; Thomas Coutts to Pitt, 17 November 1792 (P.R.O. 30/8/126). This last shows that Pitt was having to consider assigning his salary both as First Lord of the Treasury and as Chancellor of the Exchequer to Coutts in the previous winter, action being taken with the Exchequer 'when . . . Prudence suggests'. Coutts himself in point of fact was not anxious to hasten such action, in view of the possibility of 'observations that are as well avoided'. The reason to be given was Pitt's *arrears* of salary; but in fact these had not been serious for the past five years, with the exception of 1790.

3. For the latter occasion see p. 597 above; for the former, Messrs Coutts's Ledgers, under August 1786, when he paid over £7,600.

4. Augustine Greenland to Pitt, 12 December 1785 (notes on Pitt, Stanhope Mss). The amount is not stated. Pitt paid, with costs.

5. He seems at this period to have been paying his servants without much delay.

6. Stanhope, II, 160.

out its ancient and largely lapsed duties of defence. His hands were publicly clean, and they remained so despite his notorious lack of money.[1] Nor were his embarrassments the result of vice as that was generally understood. He did not gamble, or by all accounts make doubtful speculations or spend his money on women. He was financially pure, except that he failed to pay all that he owed. And this was not considered unduly reprehensible – tradesmen could wait and meanwhile salvage what they could, as tailors continued to do until much more recent times. They were not indeed the only people to be in that position: it applied to many of their patrons as well, including those in Government service or enjoying grants from the Crown. Pitt himself sometimes waited for his salary, as his mother had to wait for her pension. Private debt of this kind, unrelieved by public assistance, was widely regarded as a quite venial sin.[2]

It also appeared, to Pitt's friends, as an aspect, unfortunate in this instance, which yet was typical of a character they loved and admired. He should of course have paid more attention, and cut his coat according to his cloth; but then he was 'generous and liberal',[3] and without thought for his personal concerns. His debts, deplorable as they were, arose from that same simple and elevated spirit, that same disdain of private interest, which were so attractive in other respects. So his intimates argued; and in their way they were right. Pitt's attitude to his financial affairs did reflect these qualities, as also his perennial hopefulness, his inactivity when bored, and his untroubled belief in himself. It was symptomatic of his temperament. It also owed much to his childhood impressions: to Chatham's lordly disregard of money, and his conception of his role. Despite some contrasts in its application – Chatham lived grandly, Pitt quite modestly; Chatham accepted loans from his friends, Pitt preferred to put the matter aside – they shared a common approach to this tiresome subject, a seigneurial dismissal carried, typically, to extremes. They stamped their different hallmarks on the same metal, each in unmistakable style. For Pitt's serene rejection of his financial problems was indeed a function of his nature: of his exclusive concentration on public issues, his impersonal devotion to his public standards, and the accompanying, almost monklike, detachment and suspension of choice in his private life.

1. And according to George Rose, writing later, he also declined any private help which could be construed as coming from an interested quarter. Rose cited an offer of £100,000 from 'the London merchants' in 1788 (misdated 1787) (to Pretyman Tomline, 21 July 1801; Holland Rose, *William Pitt and the Great War*, 475. See also Stanhope, II, 16–17).

2. The qualification should be stressed. It differentiated Pitt's case, for instance, from that of a debtor such as the Prince of Wales, whose embarrassments had to be met by the public.

3. *Tomline's Estimate*, 36.

CHAPTER XIX

Westminster Revisited

I

In 1787 a pamphlet appeared, entitled *A Short Review of the Political State of Great-Britain*. By an anonymous author who was in fact the Ministerial back-bencher Sir Nathaniel Wraxall, it went through at least eight editions in the course of the year. Wraxall was not an original or a penetrating writer; but he could catch the tone of the day – it is this which excuses and sometimes gives value to the prejudices and inaccuracies of his celebrated memoirs. Progressing through the leading figures, he gave a character sketch of Pitt, much on the lines of his later more ample picture. But he did not bother with the rest of the Government, for

> When I have thus finish'd the portrait of the Minister, I may be said in it to have comprehended almost the whole administration.

Pitt in fact stood, 'like Ajax, single and alone'. He had capable advisers in Jenkinson and Dundas, but, apart from Thurlow's oratorical powers, there was 'a vast vacuity' in the Cabinet itself, and all was 'sustained, as it appears to be, by the ... talents of one individual'.[1] Not everyone would have gone as far as this, or agreed with all the implications. Some would have criticised the emphasis on the Cabinet compared with other influences. But Wraxall, as so often, seems to have been voicing a widespread impression, and one that probably increased over the next few years. How accurate, and significant, was it? What *was* now the nature of Pitt's power, and support? In what ways had they developed since he came into office, and with what effects on the political scene?

The emphasis in Wraxall's assessment was on the Minister's performance in the Commons, and of course this bulked large in the impression he made. So far as the country in general was concerned, indeed, he was fortunate in his time; in the fact that his debating powers could be conveyed, however feebly, to a growing public. There is always apt to be a danger in talking of a widespread impression or of the country in general, and the danger may well be greater when the audience is hard to define. The political public in the 1780s is both recognisable and elusive: recognisable in the acceptance of an effective

1. Sixth edn, with additions; 28–30.

body which was 'the well-informed and weighty parts of the community', whether enfranchised or not;[1] elusive in the drawing of its boundaries and the extent of its concern. It would probably be unwise to exaggerate the latter when there were no pressing issues at stake: the final stages of the American War had been an exceptional time. But for that very reason they had hastened a real if partial change of atmosphere, focusing a number of converging developments, in thought and education, in communications and wealth. Not all the results were new, either in kind or in their objects: on the contrary, conscious reform hankered largely after a return to the past. In various, sometimes contrasting ways, its supporters were as traditional as their opponents – many of them would have said a good deal more so – and the stirring of interest was often reminiscent of an earlier age. But whatever its tone or its causes or objects, there was one real innovation in the conditions for political concern. For in a manner unknown in the middle of the century, or at any earlier period, the public of the seventies and, still more, the eighties could follow the work of Parliament.

This was evident in a number of ways. The House of Commons itself, for the first time, began after 1780 to print some of its papers for sale or circulation beyond the House. The regular customers seem to have been the public offices and departments, but on certain occasions at least there was a rather wider distribution. Some of the reports from its committees, moreover, were reproduced independently by the booksellers, and even its standing orders were published commercially in or by the nineties.[2] There was a growing need for such information, which was beginning to be met. But more important was the demand for the debates, shown by the spread of the newspapers which made it possible. Their numbers rose significantly in the course of Pitt's first decade. By the end of 1792, seven London daily journals, including *The Times* and *The Observer*, had been added to the nine dailies (five mainly advertising journals) and ten others produced there in 1783.[3] Their great attraction was their political news and comment centring on the accounts of the Parliamentary proceedings; it was this that distinguished them from earlier journals, and from the provincial press. It had long been the habit – as Montesquieu noted – to circulate the newspapers from hand to hand, and provide them in the coffee houses and inns. In the middle seventies, a few years after the legal decision which opened the way to regular Parliamentary reporting, they began to be hired out, and by 1789 it was reckoned that a single copy might pass to twenty or thirty readers in London alone.[4] With

1. P. 145 above.

2. Sheila Lambert, 'Printing for the House of Commons in the Eighteenth Century' (*The Library, Fifth Series,* XXIII, no. 1), 44–6.

3. See p. 143 above.

4. This was George Rose's estimate, in the debate on the Ministry's motion to increase the newspaper stamp duty (3 July 1789; Stockdale, *Debates,* II, 421–2).

all its inadequacies and distortions, in all its venality and ignorance, the press[1] was serving a rising interest in Parliamentary affairs and Parliamentary form which was to add a new dimension to politics in the course of the next half century.

The process was soon noted, ostensibly applauded, disliked and fed by the politicians themselves. Since it could not be denied, it had best be controlled; and where it could not be controlled it had better be influenced. The lines were sometimes indistinct: hence perhaps the often genuine conviction that newspapers, subsidised, bribed or intimidated, were yet a palladium of English liberty. Like the electorate, in fact, they might be bought or bullied because they had rights – much less firmly based – to sell or to yield. They were certainly open to pressure, for, apart from *The London Gazette* which published the official notices, none was financially secure, and all those connected with their production followed a risky calling. The Foxite journals (as they may conveniently be labelled) were vigorous in the early eighties. Pitt's Government redressed the balance by the end of the decade. One cannot be sure exactly how much the Ministry spent, for even when there are recorded accounts they may be incomplete; but regular subsidies almost certainly rose steeply between 1784 and 1790. In an account attributed to the earlier year, £500 out of £1,238 devoted to publications was named as going to five London newspapers.[2] Similar intermittent accounts in the years 1788 to 1793 show regular subventions to nine such newspapers amounting to £2,800–2,850 a year, and there were certainly three others being paid on occasions during that period.[3] Other sums went to writers (about a dozen can be identified, including the inevitable Miles) for contributions to the press, and for the familiar business of composing pamphlets and verses; and by the time that printing, Government advertisements, and smaller items have been added, the totals for 1790–1 and 1792–3 come respectively to almost £4,600 and £4,900.[4]

Several members of the Government were concerned to varying

1. *O.E.D.* cites an early use of the word in this sense in 1797.

2. *L.C.G.*, III, I, no. 158; and see Aspinall, *Politics and the Press*, 68. Another £200 went to a sixth newspaper; but not in that case as a subsidy, but to reimburse the purchase of a share in the property by one of the managers, John Benjafield. Benjafield also received £110 for 'expenses of various sorts'.

The account, which also includes election expenses, is incomplete: £150 is not accounted for at all, and another £350 went to two men who cannot now be identified. But supposing that both these last sums were devoted to publications – which is pure conjecture – one would arrive at a total for such purposes of £1,738.

3. For details, see Aspinall, 66–83, and *The History of The Times*, I (1935), 60–1. Not all the payments to the nine regulars began or ended at the same times.

These figures do not refer to, or take account of, subsidies to Scottish newspapers from 1792, and Ireland was a separate matter. The English provincial newspapers appear to have been ignored (Aspinall, op. cit., 350–1); if Pitt ever had recourse to them (see op. cit., 353), this would seem to have been a wartime development.

4. Op. cit., 69, 163–7.

extents in these transactions. Grenville later recalled how the adverse reporting of debates had early been 'the subject of complaint amongst us';[1] and his name, together with those of Jenkinson, Carmarthen, Dundas for Scotland, and Eden towards the end of the period, appears fleetingly at different times in this shadowy world. Burges was active in his years at the Foreign Office, giving exclusive news and writing anonymous articles,[2] and Rose and Steele, and later Charles Long, were the Treasury paymasters. Pitt himself is more in the background, but of course he was in touch. He naturally knew what had been done, for he was in charge of the funds – our information for the years 1788 to 1793 indeed comes largely from the copies of accounts in his papers[3] – and he must presumably have known what was going to be done, for the Treasury Secretaries would scarcely have spent such funds without his consent. His presence can occasionally be glimpsed – approving a publication, or receiving an appeal when a writer or proprietor found himself in trouble[4] –, and it can be felt more strongly, if indirectly, in the difficult periods of the Regency crisis and 1792. Usually, however, he would seem to have sanctioned a business which he found rather distasteful (he would seldom agree, for instance, to vet or prepare the reports of his speeches for the press), and to have avoided, as one disgruntled proprietor put it, 'any commitment of yourself'.[5]

The results doubtless did something to help his image in the country. The Ministry probably acquired more space in the newspapers than did Opposition in the middle and later eighties, and it had advantages in feeding its favourites with news and in farthering their distribution. The effect, however, should not be exaggerated. The very venality of the press cut both ways: if journals could be won they could also be lost, and even among the faithful, as Pitt complained later, there was really 'little means . . . to keep printers in order'.[6] Not all those receiving payments from Government were equally indebted or equally consistent. And the contempt which all politicians still felt for the products was probably shared in varying degrees by less well informed readers. No one at the centre took the newspapers seriously, except in some cases as propaganda; it is impossible to say, in the pre-war period,

1. To Tomline, 26 March 1818 ('Pitt Papers: Autograph Letters from Colleagues &c II'; Stanhope Mss). See p. 144 above.
2. Aspinall, op. cit., 184, 203.
3. P R.O. 30/8/229.
4. E.g. for the first pp. 39, n2 and 564, n1 above; for the second Miles's correspondence (P.R.O. 30/8/159), and two letters from Edward Topham of the newspaper *The World* (P.R.O. 30/8/183). Pitt followed the correspondence when John Walter of *The Times* landed in Newgate in 1790, although this was addressed to other members of the Government (see *History of The Times*, I, 56–60).
5. Edward Topham to Pitt, 25 November 1794 (quoted in Aspinall, op. cit., 73).
6. To Chatham, 30 December [1800]; Stanhope, III, 255. He was referring to an unfavourable article in what had long been a Ministerial newspaper.

how seriously they were taken elsewhere. Their growth was a symptom of the times: of a growing desire for information, and of the politicians' determination to keep it under control. But government and politics remained senatorial; the reaction to the pressure was reluctant and limited, and the pressure itself spasmodic and still quite easily met.

The tone of the effective political public, in fact, remained much what it had been for a generation. Pitt was judged on broadly familiar standards by a broadly familiar if widening audience. Having said that, it is not at all easy to go beyond generalities, for shades of opinion do not emerge clearly from a run of prosperous years. There were a few fierce, largely sectional, attacks on his fiscal and commercial policies: against the Irish Propositions and to a smaller extent the Eden treaty, against some of the taxes, and certain West Indian measures. But even when they were widespread – as not all were – they were mostly short-lived, and did little to disturb the general satisfaction as the economy improved. There was sometimes disappointment of a rather different kind in another quarter: among liberal economists, surveying measures which together made up a regrettably mixed bag. The new Navigation Act, the East India Company's new Charter, some of the other safeguards of the navigation system, even some of the terms for Government loans and for the redemption of Government debt – these were regretted, as Grenville put it later, by some 'enlightened individuals, in the silence of the closet' and more occasionally in public. Even so, he may well have been right in saying that such men 'did justice to [Pitt's] intentions, applauded His triumphs over some . . . inveterate prejudices . . ., and Lamented, but perhaps without greatly condemning, His compliance with others too powerful to be then resisted'.[1] They felt that he was on their side, even in a case in which perhaps he was not, and were prepared to forgive his errors or defeats for the sake of what was achieved. Others among his early supporters may have felt more disillusioned as time went by. The Kentish Committee for Parliamentary Reform, for instance, censured its member in 1786 for his complacency over the continued influence of the Crown;[2] and the charge reflected a wider impression that the general pattern had not been changed. Parliamentary reform itself had been defeated; there had been no further direct attack on places; and the handling of the Commons, and often of policy, showed no great break with the recent past. Many reformers – some of Pitt's own friends – regretted these facts. Elsewhere they were shrugged off, or mildly or keenly welcomed. To some they marked a surrender to stronger forces, to others a proper rejection of faction. But whether deplored, applauded or simply noted, they add a complication to the appraisal of opinion about Pitt himself.

---

1. 'Commentaries of my own Political Life . . .'; Fortescue Mss. He was talking of the peacetime years.

2. *Morning Post*, 15 May 1786. See p. 69 above. Pitt had recently been reported as saying in Parliament that its extent need not cause immediate anxiety.

For it is very difficult sometimes to isolate the Minister from the views expressed about the Ministry; some of the praise in the eighties, for example, rubbed off on George III. One must remember after all that Pitt was still comparatively a newcomer at this time: that while he had certainly captured the public's imagination, he was still in the early stages of what we know became a long career. The contemporary perspective was not ours, and when his name is used as a synonym for Government one cannot always be sure exactly how much that meant.

Within these rather nebulous limits, certain things can be said. There was general astonishment and admiration that so young a man had done what he did, and had consolidated a position gained so unexpectedly. There remained a lively interest in Chatham's son, and much ready goodwill. It was generally held that he remained incorrupt. There was a general pleasure in his speeches, among a public that followed the debates; even Foxites like Dr Parr admitted that 'the dog talks grammar'.[1] It was agreed that in this vital sense he towered above his colleagues. There was widespread, though not universal or continuous, admiration for his finance. There was much satisfaction in the later eighties that the country's prestige was rising, without a war. There was a feeling, often doubtless superficial and held with whatever qualifications, that he had aided, and in some ways fostered, a revival of fortunes from a low ebb. When Gibbon visited England in 1787 after a lapse of four years, he 'rejoyced in the apparent encrease of wealth and prosperity which might be fairly divided between the spirit of the nation and the wisdom of the minister'.[2] Many would have agreed with this verdict, and with the way in which it was put. For in congratulating Pitt many sensible men were also congratulating themselves.

II

Such varied attitudes can be followed, as they were stated, more clearly in Parliament. For whatever the effects of opinion outside – and in the light of the election of 1784 Pitt may have felt that he could draw on a real if intangible support[3] – they were normally experienced at best at one remove, and it was in Parliament, and above all in the Commons, that he could test and hope to guide the reactions to his policies and himself.

The honeymoon was over in 1785. But the succeeding years were

1. Henry Richard Vassall Third Lord Holland, *Further Memoirs of the Whig Party 1807–1821 With Some Miscellaneous Reminiscences,* ed. Lord Stavordale (1905), 330.
2. 29 July 1787; *Memoirs of My Life,* ed. Georges A. Bonnard (1966), 181. On proper reflection, the historian had added the word 'fairly' in the margin.
3. See p. 153 above.

calmer and a more predictable relationship emerged. From 1786 to the summer of 1790, when there was a fresh general election, Pitt was defeated on one major Governmental measure which he introduced to the Commons, the dockyard fortifications bill; and in that case it was widely recognised that the responsibility was Richmond's rather than his own. He had to withdraw one tax – the shop tax – which he had passed earlier, and to alter the terms of one loan – a tontine –, though in the second case this was not mainly as the result of Parliamentary opposition. He was obliged to accept a bill for the east coast turbot fishery which was pressed upon him, and gradually to limit his support of Palmer in the Post Office. And, having failed to persuade the Ministry to view it as a Ministerial subject, he was forced to acquiesce in the postponement of Wilberforce's slave trade bill.[1] These were his only Parliamentary reverses in a period of five busy years. They may be compared with the results in 1784–5;[2] so too may the occasions – Hastings's impeachment at once springs to mind – on which his advocacy may have been decisive.

Avoidance of defeat in a division, or debate, was not of course the whole story; sometimes indeed it could mark a partial defeat in itself. It might well have sprung from earlier compromise, or an earlier acceptance of unwelcome pressures; it could mean that the Minister had dropped or watered down something he would have liked to do. Given the state of the House – the limits to party coercion, the variety of sentiments, the tone of that particular Parliament – this argument should not be carried too far; for if Pitt had changed course drastically in mid-stream he would have forfeited much of his earlier support. But, given those same factors, many of the measures could be widely taken on their merits, and if the exact nature of support was apt to vary, so too was that of the approach.

Pitt's Parliamentary success in the later eighties resulted in fact from a combination of causes: from his policies, his handling of party, and his personality. Each acted on the others, and the sum was the test of a Minister, as it always is in the setting of his time. It was in the balance which he struck in those years, and the ensuing degree of confidence, that his personal contribution – his personal achievement – must be judged.

1. Pp. 518–19, 253–4, 258, 352, 294–8, 392–6 above.
2. Which, it may be recalled, had included the Ministry's defeat on the Westminster scrutiny and its need to modify the Irish Propositions; the dropping of Pitt's proposed taxes on coals and on hop planters' licences, and of his tax on linens and calicoes; his unwilling acceptance of a simplification of the salt tax; his partial remodelling of the terms for funding the navy bills; and his personal defeat on Parliamentary reform. The Government also lost a proposal, introduced by the Solicitor General in 1785, to reform the London police.
All these instances, in both periods, are drawn from public bills or bills on public measures. I have not pursued the fate of strictly private bills (numerically much greater), some of which may have had party connotations.

Much of it turned, of course, on his oratory. He was by now at, or very near, the summit of his powers. He soon purged himself of the few flaws that were noted at the brilliant start; of some verbosity and diffuseness, and an occasional straining after effect.[1] The descriptions of his style soon settled down into a repetitive pattern: they hardly vary between the later eighties and the recollections after his death. 'Clear enunciation, uninterrupted fluency, correctness of language, perspicuity of arrangement, cogency of reasoning' – these keynotes are sounded again and again.[2] The 'magical effect', as Brougham was to recall it, was set off by the 'sonorous voice' and the dignity, ungraceful but impressive, which proclaimed 'a ruler of the people'.[3] The appeal above all was to the reason; imagination and 'conviction' were built on that base.[4] Windham later called it a 'state-paper style';[5] but it was the epitome of what a state paper should be, and it could be raised and sometimes transformed by a closely argued passion. When one thinks of the effect on Members that a successful speech can have in the Commons today, one may imagine the impact of such a series at a time when the House was indisputably the centre of attraction.

These great set occasions, moreover, did not exist in a vacuum. While the speeches were conscious works of art, they were not divorced from Pitt's day to day performance. Pretyman indeed thought that his greatest strength lay in his replies, when he could be conciliatory, impartial, lofty, contemptuous or cutting in turn. 'He sometimes indulged in pointed ridicule, severe invective, and bitter sarcasm'; and when he did so, it was apt to produce 'most visible effect'.[6] He destroyed the career in the Commons of the rising Whig lawyer, and future Lord Chancellor, Thomas Erskine by a gesture at the outset, and thereafter managed him by 'the ascendancy of terror'.[7] He was very formidable; trained from childhood, he quickly grasped every aspect of the game, and he knew and could usually master the moods of the House. 'Mastery' indeed is a word that also recurs in the descriptions of him, applied to an assembly which held its share of tough, idiosyncratic men. If he lacked Chatham's petrifying quality, he too could quell as well as impress.

Father and son indeed were equally cast in a classic mould – a fact

1. E.g. the opinion of John Nicholls, an experienced Member, in *The Farington Diary*, I, 138.

2. Pretyman, in his unpublished chapter (*Tomline's Estimate*, 28). Cf. Wraxall in his pamphlet of 1787, 25–6, and Brougham's *Historical Sketches* of 1839, 202–3.

3. Brougham, ibid.

4. Cf. again Wraxall and Brougham.

5. Brougham, 203.

6. *Tomline's Estimate*, 28. There are complaints about his sarcasm from Opposition, and sometimes from independent Members, from the start.

7. The Duke of Wellington's phrase (Stanhope, IV, 347). Sheridan had earlier said much the same. The incident took place in the debates on Fox's India bill, when Pitt, sitting with paper and pen in hand to take notes of Erskine's eagerly awaited maiden speech, ostentatiously lost interest and finally threw away the pen.

of which they and their hearers were equally well aware. Both men drew support for their instinctive behaviour from high antique models, and at moments, facing an audience many of whom had 'read the great books', however scantily, they established an almost Periclean relationship of claim and acceptance. Each stood there as

> one who, as I believe, is second to no man either in knowledge of the proper policy, or in the ability to expound it, and who is moreover not only a patriot but an honest one.

And his speeches were not the least part, for

> A man possessing that knowledge without that faculty of exposition might as well have no idea at all on the matter.[1]

Here in spirit was the younger Pitt addressing the country gentlemen, and suggesting, without undue modesty, a difference between himself and Fox.

The country gentlemen, the independents and the more solidly independent of the party back-benchers, were indeed his favourite audience, the kind of men he wanted to convince. Like so many in the House he came originally from the smaller gentry himself, and like Chatham he sought and claimed a wide ranging, deep rooted support. The uncommitted Members represented the ideal, and most nearly approached it in practice. He valued their approval, and he got it more often than not. Sometimes of course they were dubious, and at times they turned against him, when they sensed the pressures and impatience of power. But usually he held their sympathy, and he came to command their trust as the evidence mounted that he was both competent and sound.

For competence, of course, was immensely important. One does not need always to agree with a Minister to admit that he is being successful, and in the 1780s, after the war, men were in the mood for some success. Pitt was supplying a run of consistently good immediate results, and his reputation naturally thrived on the fact. It may also have benefited from the recognition that few of his measures were now notably controversial, and the two aspects of the case reacted on each other. The Parliamentary temperature declined under the impact of successful policies many of which were introduced in a way calculated to encourage Parliamentary peace. As the earlier disturbances died away, and the national economy and prestige visibly improved, the country gentlemen settled comfortably into the feeling that Pitt was safe.

1. Thucydides, *The History of the Peloponnesian War*, bk. II, 60; R. W. Livingstone's translation. The continuation might also be quoted, if one had the 1790s rather than the '80s in mind.

At the same time, the feeling persisted that he was exciting; and this rare combination indeed held much of the secret of his appeal. It was one that infuriated his opponents, and it can worry historians for rather different reasons, for the combination is of a kind particularly open to doubt or attack. Many Foxites – and some others – were quite genuine in their belief that Pitt was a hypocrite, who moreover often took credit for what was scarcely his due. It was not only that he was reaping the reward of a naturally favourable change of circumstances; they also held that he was regularly abandoning his principles for the sake of quick, often easy success. The first point is very largely true, though it should not be an accusation: if there are tides in the affairs of men, they must be taken at the flood. And as they look closely at Pitt's policies historians can see that they often resembled his predecessors', that many were more traditional than might have been expected, and that when something new was done the sense of continuity is still strong. Neither in reform nor in conservation is there a distinctive break, and Pitt himself seems quite often uncertain in advance what he is going to do. Did he in fact have any coherent style of government – and if it is true that his character may best be seen in public affairs, it would be here that one can say that the style was the man? Or was he producing, as has been asked, no more than 'a series of responses to circumstances'[1] – pragmatism raised to an exceptionally articulate level?

Most men at the time appear to have thought that there *was* something more. Not that many were anxious themselves to move too fast in the larger fields of policy. Much of Pitt's work was of marginal interest to the average Member, unless it had direct political repercussions. The Foxites' accusations, indeed, concentrated mainly on the strictly political area, and their suspicions that Pitt was surrendering, for instance, to the King's persistent influence often confused familiar controversies with the more impersonal problems of government. Fox for his part had not proved conspicuously radical as a Minister – the treatment of West Indian trade in 1783 is one example –,[2] and few would have denied or seriously quarrelled with the obstacles to major change. When men came into office

> they must have done with mere words, and must come to things; they must set down to work by line and rule; must search Laws, hunt precedents, examine minutes of proceedings, consult and discuss, and pursue a detail; often submitting themselves to the advice of subordinate persons . . .

1. Richard Pares, 'The Younger Pitt', in *The Historian's Business and Other Essays*, 129.
2. See p. 334 above. And he was sometimes content, for that matter, to be distinctly conservative when it suited his book in opposition – witness his speeches on the Eden treaty. He also of course, like many good Whigs, upheld a conservative view of liberty, as he showed in his speeches on the inquiry into sinecures (when he defended places for life), and on the fortification of the dockyards.

'All Parties' in fact 'must conform to the established order of things' in great degree. This was the language of a lawyer and official;[1] but much of what he said was unexceptionable, and the most obvious quality required of a Minister was that his policies should work.

But it was precisely here that Pitt satisfied the feeling that he was doing more than the average pragmatist. If he was responding to circumstances, the circumstances needed a response which they did not seem to have been getting very clearly in recent years. There had been plenty of talk about what should be done, and the Rockinghams and Shelburne had done something; but they were working in adverse circumstances, some of their effort was misdirected, and there remained very large gaps. Pitt tackled many of the outstanding problems which had not been tackled effectively before, and at many of the points which seemed to be important. In a period of buoyant economic activity he solved a crisis in financial confidence, by restoring budgetary surpluses, improving the system of accounts and borrowing, and containing debt. He drastically reduced smuggling, and did much to tidy up the collection of the revenue. He put forward a comprehensive plan for Ireland. He reversed the system of trade with France, our largest European competitor. He repaired the fleet, and restored the British voice on the continent after a period of silence. This was exciting stuff within the passage of a few years, and in a generation not accustomed to sustained movement. When expounded as Pitt expounded it, there was a new air of purpose and promise. Of course he had his full share of luck – of the luck which he often earned – and the facts on examination are often rather different from the appearance. Like all achievements, it was partly illusory. But as in most serious achievements, the illusion stemmed from what was real. Pitt appeared to have mastered the small, decisive difference between failure and success; and to have done so by exploiting events in a way that transcended piecemeal reaction.

This was a style of government, demanding a sure touch. It was embellished by qualities which fitted the time particularly well. 'Our Constitution is so happily tempered, and its machinery so well constructed, that it requires less *skill* than it does *good intentions*, to keep it in order.' 'In the administration of Government, party-principles are nothing, but personal qualification is everything. Where there is more understanding, more attention to business, and more honesty, there, and there only, will the Administration be distinguished from others'.[2] Pitt seemed to have these qualifications, and good intentions as well as

1. John Reeves, a former Chief Justice of Newfoundland, in his anonymous pamphlet *Thoughts on the English Government* . . . (1795), 68, 69. Reeves had also worked with Hawkesbury and shared his views, and it was typical of him to add, in his passage on 'subordinate persons', 'who, though never heard of, do more perhaps to keep the machine a-going than their Principals'. Nor did he qualify the statement that 'all Parties must conform to the established order of things'.

2. William Knox, pp. 47–8 above; Reeves, *Thoughts on the English Government*, 69.

skill. He appeared to the central body of Members to be not only well equipped, but also to be seeking the country's interest as that was generally understood.

All this was doubtless true, and it was important. It gave Pitt the distinctive place he held on the political stage. But such confidence was a tender plant; it had to be carefully nourished, and in any case it could not secure him in office by itself.

The swings of strictly independent sentiment were illustrated in 1788. In the early months of that year Pitt ran into a rather bad patch in the Commons. In February and early March he found himself temporarily in trouble over the Declaratory Act for India, and in April facing the storm over naval promotions which led to the later replacement of Howe at the Admiralty.[1] In both cases he gave the initial impression of trying to override back-bench opinion; and while he recovered swiftly in March, the April battle left its mark, and would seem to have aggravated a growing feeling that the Ministry, and indeed both front benches, were losing touch with the House. A letter was circulated in May calling for the formation of a party independent of both Pitt and Fox, which was signed by six peers and 24 MPs.[2] Perhaps by the nature of the case few of the names were particularly prominent, though they included some respected knights of the shire and some men hitherto friendly to the Minister – Sir Edward Astley, John Pollexfen Bastard, John Walker Heneage, John Stanley. Nor indeed could the episode be called important; it came in the later stages of the session, had little visible effect, and was soon overtaken by events. There was always an inherent paradox in the idea of an independent party, and the limits to independent mediation had been exposed in 1784. Within a year of the circular letter Pitt was stronger than ever. But the incident underlined the ready suspicions of those to whom he always liked to appeal, and the sometimes contrasting need to rely on more disciplined troops.

The contrast was not invariable, for the ethos of independence was a reality which permeated the parties themselves. The lines were not rigidly drawn, and a Minister had ideally to strike the right balance between conducting himself as a master and as a servant of the House. Automatic majorities could not be taken for granted; if majorities were secured consistently, that was in part at least a tribute to the leader's flexible skill. But the more consistently they occurred the greater the tendency to think in terms of a party, and to associate it with the leader who secured the votes. When Pitt came into office a recognised

1. See pp. 454–5, 315 above.
2. There is a copy in the Braybrooke Mss at the Essex County Record Office, the meat of which is reproduced in Namier, 'Monarchy and the Party System', in *Personalities and Powers*, 31–2. I am indebted for the names of the MPs to Mr John Brooke.

Ministerial system existed, centring on the habitual resources of the Crown. Did his achievements in the course of the decade significantly farther the process, and in so doing modify it in any way?

Was there in fact, in the first place, any difference between the early and the late eighties? In one way at least it seems undoubtedly that there was. To some extent at any rate developments in the system of Ministerial support are likely to be echoed, where they have not been affected, by developments in Opposition. And between 1780 and 1790 the Opposition leaders made a deliberate and quite successful attempt to catch up on Government's organisation for elections. They were determined in the late eighties not to be caught again by a sudden dissolution, and in their preparations were able to secure a more obvious cohesion than before. In doing so they must in turn have been able to count on some identity of purpose among the various groups, to be perpetuated, one might suppose, by the discipline of the election itself. Here then, one might say, was a specific advance in the definition of party, a significant development which was not to be reversed.

The evidence of activity is impressive.[1] Serious preparation began in the winter of 1788-9, co-ordinated by the MP William Adam (a nephew of the architect brothers), who had been an expert on elections since the seventies as a follower of North, one of the negotiators of the Coalition, and a manager of Hastings's impeachment. An active, honest and experienced man of business, he was the 'shadow' Secretary of the Treasury in the Regency crisis, operating from Burlington House, the London house of the Duke of Portland, and charged with the co-ordination of constituency effort, work which he continued throughout the following year. When the general election eventually came in the summer of 1790, the extent of his labours could be seen. It has been reckoned that 83 seats had by then attracted the attention of himself and Portland and their Scottish allies; and that out of these 83 seats they proposed candidates in 46, and were approached by patrons or candidates in the other 37. The central initiative varied in the 46 constituencies; but definite bargains were struck with the patrons or candidates in six cases, candidates were chosen and to some extent supervised (and independent alternatives discouraged) in perhaps another 22, and in a further two or three their expenses were formally underwritten. The same varying interest and activity applied to the other 37 seats, once the central organisation had been approached, even to the extent of expenses being underwritten in six or seven cases.[2]

Although comparable detail is lacking for the election of 1784 – partly because there was then no one central agent as there was in 1788-90 – one does seem to be faced here by a difference in kind. In the

1. See *Whig Organization in the General Election of 1790* . . ., ed. Donald E. Ginter (1967).
2. Ginter's introduction, op. cit., xxxviii-xli. In a few cases (according to his findings, in 5 of the 46, and 5 of the 37) the evidence is scanty or unclear.

first place, a party fund was built up in the middle and later eighties, more centralised and elaborate than had been known before. Devoted at first primarily to the continued subsidising of newspapers, it also embraced the publishing of pamphlets, the upkeep of an office at a Pall Mall bookseller's – Thomas Becket's, where the celebrated *Rolliad* was probably composed –, the payment of a small staff, and later the expenses of a small group of election agents. At elections themselves this fund had to be supplemented: in 1788, when there was a by-election for one seat in the ruinously expensive constituency of Westminster, a sum was raised retrospectively to help meet the costs, and this served as a precedent for the raising of more money on which to fight the forthcoming general election.[1] The result in 1790 was disappointing; Westminster perhaps had taken its toll. But such efforts, managed centrally and based on the conception of a continuing fund, showed a new impetus in the organisation of Opposition.

The fact that the fund had had its origin largely in newspaper subsidies – including, unlike the Government, a few provincial newspapers[2] – moreover suggests an important aspect of this party appeal. The greater facilities for public information, the potentialities of public associations, the insensible spread, perhaps the greater persistence – though not necessarily the heightening – of political concern: these significant if uncertain phenomena marked a step in the growth of the political nation which had some effect on the politicians themselves. There was a more regular basis on which to identify the familiar connexions, when an issue arose on which they held identifiable views. If groups wished to fight together, if patrons and Members found a common banner, it was rather easier to project a party image than it had been ten or fifteen years before.

Opposition in fact could look outwards from Parliament towards the country at large with a more confident feeling that an organised message would evoke an organised response. There was a difference of atmosphere in this respect between 1780 and 1790, although the earlier election took place at a time of national crisis and the later did not.[3] But if this was true, much would turn on the presence or absence of a recognised question with which party rivalry could be readily identified. The most obvious of such issues in the 1780s, as for some time past, was the powers of the Crown and its relations with Parliament. Many

1. Donald E. Ginter, 'The Financing of the Whig Party Organization, 1783–1793' (*The American Historical Review*, LXXI, no. 2), 424–8. For Government's financial activities in the by-election, see Laprade, 'William Pitt and Westminster Elections' (*American Historical Review*, XVIII, no. 2), 270–1. The high costs of what was virtually a repetition of the contest of 1784 led both parties to agree in 1790 to a formula for the future which in effect gave the constituency to the Foxites.

2. See p. 606, n3 above.

3. Cf. Ginter's account of *Whig Organization in . . . 1790* with Ian R. Christie's of the earlier general election in *The End of North's Ministry 1780–1782*. Professor Christie has confirmed to me that he sees a real change here.

of the other questions of government – the questions, indeed, which had taken up the bulk of Parliamentary debates since 1784 – fell outside this spectrum, and often outside party definition. But it so happened that the general elections of 1784 and 1790 took place after major clashes on this exciting topic. Such a fact could not but facilitate, and indeed in the later instance it led to, increased activity by a central Opposition organisation. It was not a matter of chance that this began, in 1788–9, at a time when the Regency crisis seemed quite likely to end in a change of Ministry, although the efforts thus initiated did not flag when the prospect disappeared. The debates of that winter obliged Members to stand up and be counted in full Houses in a way that was reminiscent of 1783–4; and the connexions thus strengthened or formed would not disappear entirely when the immediate issue had again died down.

The two occasions – Fox's India bill, and the Regency crisis – thus had an importance which certainly should not be underestimated. They excited intense public interest, and made their impact on the attitudes to party inside the House. The extent of that impact may be measured, if roughly, by its limits, both at the time and when set within the surrounding quieter periods. For even in 1788–9 Opposition's electioneering activities were far from complete, if Adam's records give anything like a comprehensive picture. It was a considerable achievement to have covered 83 seats in varying degrees; but in May 1788, a few months before the Regency crisis arose, it had been reckoned by one of the leaders that Opposition could count on 125 Members, 108 Foxites and 17 attached to North.[1] A different calculation in the same month put the figure at 155, compared with 108 independents and 280 Government supporters.[2] The central managers – unless Adam's papers are incomplete, either in themselves or because he did not personally cover all the ground – thus imposed a known control of some kind, by their own reckoning, on two-thirds at most of their more reliable supporters; and the proportion may have been less. Unless there was quite a large number of constituencies with which they did not bother because the seats were completely safe – and from those covered by Adam's list, this seems unlikely – they were operating still within fairly well defined bounds.

The picture produced by the estimates of 1788 – the broad threefold

1. *H. of I*., I, 534, citing North's calculation of 1 May in the North Mss at Waldershare, Kent.

2. Braybrooke Mss (see p. 615, n2 above). This accounts for 543 Members out of the total of 558. Fourteen of the other fifteen were classed as 'Absentees and Neutrals'.

These contemporary accounts may be compared with the careful analysis given in F. O'Gorman, *The Whig Party and the French Revolution* (1967), Appendix 1, which gives Opposition 132 members – much more evenly divided between the Foxites and North – immediately after the election of 1784, and 144 on the eve of the election in 1790.

division, the variation between the figures – did not indeed differ fundamentally from that of a few years before. In the lists for Opposition, the old private connexions had been absorbed into the followers of Fox and North. But private loyalties were still present even when they lay beneath the surface, they had still always to be taken into account, the number of independents had not greatly shrunk, and from the tone of many of the debates the voting pattern was not always predictable. It cannot be properly followed, for division lists are known for only three occasions between the spring of 1784 and the winter of 1788, and one of those – relating to Pitt's motion for Parliamentary reform in April 1785 – was far from typical of the normal alignment.[1] But the normal alignment itself seems to have been flexible in that 'very loose' Parliament, it applied only to certain questions, and not all the candidates mustered by Opposition in the country could be automatically relied on in the House. Can one be sure that the advance in their central organisation was itself an inevitable process? The clarification born of 1783 and 1788 was carried farther after 1792, when Fox and his faithful supporters broke away from their associates. Party, in the Foxite sense, then hardened, even while its leader's fortunes withered in the war. But if there had been no war, and Pitt had continued in the nineties as in the eighties, and moreover with the issue of the Crown then removed; or even if Fox had reacted differently (as he might have done) to the French Revolution, and the Parliamentary situation had shaped itself accordingly: would the lines then necessarily have come to be drawn as they were, so that earlier developments could later be seen as irreversible?

This of course must be a matter of guesswork, and the question may be wrongly put. Given the spread of public interest, however slow and partial, and the effects of the French Revolution, new questions must sooner or later have made their influence felt. But within the framework of the older questions, the pace of development could not be foreseen. The Ministerial benches themselves had a familiar look in 1788. In their circular letter of May 1788,[2] the independents analysed the major elements of the Government's majority. The 'Party of the Crown' was put at 185, a figure which included 'all those who would probably support His Majesty's Government under any Minister, not peculiarly unpopular'. 'The Party attached to Mr. Pitt' was given as 52, and 'Of this Party were there a new Parliament, and Mr. P. no longer Minister, not above twenty would be returned'.[3] 'Detached Parties' in support

1. The other two occasions were the motion to adjourn in committee on the Irish Propositions, on 13 May 1785; and the second reading of the bill to fortify the dockyards at Portsmouth and Plymouth, on 27 February 1786. See *H. of P.,* I, 534.

2. P. 615 above. Pitt had a copy – see his secretary Joseph Smith's papers, in *H.M.C., Twelfth Report, Appendix, Pt. IX,* 373.

3. One may compare this with Grenville's statement, much later, that in the Parliament of 1784–90 Pitt's 'personal friends were numerous, and warmly attached' ('Commentaries of my own Political Life', Fortescue Mss).

were said to provide another 43: ten for Dundas, nine for Lansdowne (Shelburne; a rather shaky ally, it might be thought), nine again for Lonsdale (Lowther; also very shaky, as was shortly to be seen), and fifteen 'East Indians'. This accounted for just over half the seats in the House, and the sum was added up in the traditional way.

The structure of politics within the Commons had thus not altered greatly since 1783. Pitt and Fox had to play with the usual pieces. But pieces, it must also be remembered, are the means by which players develop their styles. The conjunction and clash of the two men gave the game its character from the middle eighties, in the ebb and flow of 'the combat between Achilles Pitt and Hector Fox'.[1] It was very unusual – one might say unknown – to find two politicians of that calibre at the same time and so prominently opposed. It was unusual to find two opponents each raised clearly above his colleagues in the House, and each prepared to take responsibility. It gave a new flavour to the proceedings, and perhaps a more vivid sense, even to independents, of a persistent clear-cut division into two major groupings. Heightened, indeed made possible, by the great clashes of 1783 and 1788, it fostered a more intense and continuous feeling of gladiatorial support.

Their different roles, in Ministry and Opposition, set the two leaders rather different tasks. Fox had to keep together in adverse circumtances a party made up of private interests, grown used now to working together, but with its full share of private animosities and in part at least liable to break off. Aided, perhaps largely, by the very size of the defeat which had placed it where it was, by the sense of identity forced on the survivors of 1784, his patchy but remarkable qualities as a party leader – often careless or indecisive, a most uncertain tactician, but living 'with as well as by his connections, attentive to the Discipline, even to the smallest Minutiae of the Corps he commands'[2] – did much to counter the situation which his shortcomings had helped bring about. The repeated reverses in the lobbies, and his own blunders, could not diminish his personality, or its effect on a highly personal scene. Opposition's strength might vary with the issue, and the prospects might generally seem dim; the evidence of a trend towards party cohesion would very often have seemed absurd. But a sizeable if not always readily mobilised force remained constant nevertheless, and the auxiliaries could expect more often than not to find Fox giving fire to the attack. This was his invaluable contribution to a party of which he was not formally or indeed actually the head; for the prospective First Lord of the Treasury was Portland, who had held the post before,[3]

1. Gibbon to Sheffield, 1 October 1785 (*Letters of Edward Gibbon*, III, 34).

2. Leeds's description, possibly in 1792 (B.M. Add. Ms 27916, f. 63). The judgment perhaps reflected the natural fears of a former opponent; for criticisms from within the party itself, see 'The Diary of Georgiana, Duchess of Devonshire', in Walter Sydney Sichel, *Sheridan . . .*, II (1909), 400, and *The Life and Letters of Sir Gilbert Elliot*, I, 257.

3. P. 104 above.

and Portland, a harder worker, was in charge of the organisation in the country. Pitt in this sense was in a stronger position, for he had no great magnate with whom to share his power – he was himself the First Lord of the Treasury: Fox and Portland, as it were, in one. But on the other hand he relied normally for his majorities on 'the Party of the Crown,' that substantial body which 'would probably support His Majesty's Government under any Minister, not peculiarly unpopular'.[1] He had attracted a certain following of his own, as a successful Minister was apt to do, and even a hard core of twenty (if the figure is correct) was a bargaining force. Nor of course was the party of the Crown a uniformly reliable body; the means of influence were on the decline, partly as a result of his own exertions, and there were shades of difference between its members, as in other groups. It could fail to follow the Minister wholeheartedly in a matter on which he and the King (but not all the Cabinet) were agreed, as was shown by the bill for the fortifications of the dockyards. It could even be sufficiently confused, when caught unawares, to allow him to survive the Court's displeasure, as in the motion for Hastings's impeachment. But these were exceptional cases; Pitt could not persistently challenge its feelings, and the fate of his bill for Parliamentary reform showed what could happen when the King withheld his favour. A balance, a compromise, had to be struck, as had traditionally been the case: the Minister depending on the Crown for support, the Crown depending on him to manage its followers, to bring in reinforcements from elsewhere, and to lead them all to victory in debate. There were weights in either scale: the King's prerogative and influence on the one side, Pitt's qualities and achievements, and the fact that he stood against Fox, on the other. He could invoke his appeal and, increasingly, his record to fortify his own position, and hope thereby to gain a larger following for himself. But his record and appeal included, and his position could turn on, the way in which he handled his relations with the Crown.

III

These same relations governed the management of the House of Lords. Pitt's Ministry had little trouble there in its first four years. At first sight this was perhaps surprising, for there were some able speakers in Opposition – Stormont, Carlisle, Norfolk (from 1786), Bishop Watson, above all Loughborough – and the Ministerial spokesmen, particularly at first, were distinctly weak. Although every member of the Cabinet apart from Pitt was a peer until 1789, with one notable exception they were an unimpressive team. Howe scarcely spoke – and his successor Chatham was also fairly silent –, Sydney and Carmarthen were lightweights, Gower (Stafford) and Camden elderly and casual, and

1. P. 619 above.

Richmond, though active, was unpopular. The Ministry depended heavily on Thurlow, as prominent here as was Pitt in the Commons; and this, combined with the royal favour, accounted for his indispensability. In 1786 he was joined by Hawkesbury, who brought material strength, and Chief Justice Kenyon was a useful addition in time for the Regency crisis. But no other prominent member or servant of Government was available until Mulgrave and, more important, Grenville appeared in 1790.[1]

This lack of debating strength, however, did not prevent the Ministry from winning the divisions. Its supporters were more regular in attendance than their opponents, they could be more easily mobilised, and they habitually outnumbered Opposition in a reasonably full House. On seven major occasions between March 1785 and March 1788, including divisions on the Irish Propositions, the Anglo-French commercial treaty, and the arrangements for Hastings's impeachment, Government's smallest majority was 16, with 99 peers present, and its largest 55, from an attendance of 136.[2] None of these occasions moreover turned directly on the powers of the Houses or the powers of the Crown; and when such questions were involved in the forms which they took in 1783 and 1788-9, the outcome, allowing for some initial confusion in the earlier instance, was not seriously in doubt.

For the temper and make-up of the Lords remained significantly different from that of the Commons. Although the great Whig families remained at the centre of a sizeable body of Opposition peers, the majority of the House had not forgiven Fox for his language in the early months of 1784, and felt it as much as ever a natural duty to 'co-operate with the Crown'. Some also recognised the need to do so, for in a number of cases it was a literal truth that 'they derived their consequence' from the Crown 'alone'.[3] 'The thanes, high priests and household cavalry' were a common object of Opposition abuse, and in large

1. William Eden, who was raised to the Irish peerage in 1789, did not become a British peer with a seat in the House until 1793 (and for that matter Mornington, a junior Lord of the Treasury from 1786, was also an Irish peer whose British peerage, that of Wellesley, came only in 1797). Harris was likewise not available as Lord Malmesbury until December 1788, and he then reverted in the Regency crisis to his old Foxite connexion. Rutland was in Ireland from 1784 until his death in 1787, and his successor (and predecessor) Buckingham (the former Temple) had been keeping very quiet since the end of 1783. Cornwallis, though regularly wooed before he became Governor-General in India, had consented only to be Constable of the Tower, and could not be regarded as an active Ministerialist.

2. D. Large, 'The Decline of the "Party of the Crown" and the Rise of Parties in the House of Lords, 1783-1837' (*E.H.R.*, LXXVIII, no. 309), 672; and see also 670-1 for the method of calculation, and 673-4. The first occasion was on a motion of 18 May 1787 (which the Ministry defeated) to disbar Scottish peers who held British peerages from voting in the elections of Scottish representative peers, the second on a motion of 21 February 1788 (also defeated by Government) to agree with the mode of proceedings for Hastings's impeachment proposed by the Managers for the Commons. On the first occasion 13, and on the second 15 peers abstained.

3. See p. 44 above.

measure they looked to the King himself. The Scottish representative peers, 16 in all, were mostly dependent on the Ministry for election, some of course bringing their own local bargaining power to bear. But it would require a politician of quite exceptional influence to bind more than a few of them to himself, and while Dundas could have done this in the 1790s, and actually did so in 1806 and 1807, he could not rely on such a personal following for Pitt in the middle eighties. The Scottish peers were Ministerial fodder mainly because they were attached to the Crown. So too were most of the Bishops and the Household officers. Some of the latter, it was true, had recently been treated as political appointments, to be changed on changes of Ministry – the Lord Steward, the Master of the Buckhounds, the Captain of the Gentlemen Pensioners were cases in point. But the offices remained in the King's hands for the most part, and some of the political appointments themselves – still debatable – were arranged whenever possible in accordance with his preference. So too, more often than not, was the choice of Bishops. The Minister of the day could sometimes place a friend or supporter who looked primarily to himself or his party, as Pitt did with Pretyman until he aimed too high, at Canterbury itself.[1] But George III was always on the watch for such efforts, which impinged on the prerogative, he disliked the thought of 'my bishops [being] party men and politicians',[2] and he was still generally successful in defence. Although the episcopal bench was not quite as tame as it was usually said to be, it provided a dependable vote for the secular policies of the head of the church. These various categories were numerically significant: 16 Scottish representative peers, at least 20 Household officers, and 26 Bishops made a rough total of 62, and of these Government could count on some 53 and the King personally on a probable minimum of 43 out of that number.[3] Nor were most of the 53 peers passive or occasional supporters: on the contrary, many of them seem to have attended regularly and been prominent in the lobbies. They accounted for over half the Ministerial peers who were present on more than twenty occasions in 1785 and 1786, and for almost two-thirds of that total in 1787–8; and in the seven representative divisions already cited, for an even higher average proportion. On five of those occasions they could have outvoted Opposition without further assistance, and on the other two they supplied the bulk of the

1. See p. 14 above.
2. Quoted in Large, loc. cit., 684. Even when the King gave Edward Wilson a canonry at Windsor in 1784, specifically on the ground that he 'had educated Mr. Pitt' (*L.C.G. III*, I, no. 194), he did so of his own volition as a mark of favour, and did not let Pitt overlook the fact.
3. I.e. in the King's case on say 10 of the 12 Ministerial Scottish peers, say 16 of the 20 Household officers (including those of the Queen's and the Prince of Wales's Households, the last containing only one member of the House of Lords), and say 17 of the 26 Bishops (one perhaps being strictly Ministerial and 8 rather doubtfully in Opposition, 5 of the latter owing obligations originally to North).

majority.[1] Without such a steady and active cohort, very largely devoted to the Crown, the Minister could thus not have relied so confidently on the House of Lords.

If he wished to balance this influence, Pitt must call on the other placemen and the new creations, as well as on a proportion of the less active, uncommitted peers. He must in fact join, and if necessary oppose, the influence arising from his own tenure of office with, and if necessary against, the powers of the King and the Court. His situation was broadly the same in essence as in the Commons; but by the nature of the case it was perhaps less favourable in the Lords. Placemen varied greatly, as in the lower House, spanning much of the political spectrum: from some of the Minister's colleagues and personal appointments to incumbents for life with their own opinions. Many holders of posts, from the great territorial magnates seeking their Lord Lieutenancies to the lesser peers in lesser positions, again looked largely to the Crown; some were survivors of earlier Ministries, who kept their earlier loyalties; and any Minister's influence here would grow the longer he stayed in office. The best test of Pitt's success in these circumstances was therefore the nature of the new creations, particularly because in this respect he came to be accused of swamping the House. Much indeed has been heard of 'Pitt's peers', at the time and later; the complaints seem to have started seriously in the nineties, and they became something of a chorus after his death. Almost everyone agreed that the character of the Lords had by then altered with the numbers, and most observers were prepared to say that the change had been for the worse. Many of Pitt's friends, such as Wilberforce and Pratt, joined with his enemies in deploring the outcome, and their views were widely echoed over the following century. The complaints were both political and social: at first against the elevation of borough proprietors, and then – a deeper note – against the quality of the new men. Disraeli, as so often, put his characteristic stamp on an accepted tradition: 'He made peers of second-rate squires, and fat graziers. He caught them in the alleys of Lombard Street, and clutched them from the counting-houses of Cornhill'. Or as an acute, sympathetic, detached and patrician historian put it, 'He did, indeed, ennoble with unsparing hands'.[2]

The process began at once; in fact, it was more noticeable towards the beginning than at the end. In all, there were 119 creations and promotions in the peerage of Great Britain or of the United Kingdom during Pitt's periods as a Minister,[3] and of these 5 dated from his second Ministry of 1804–6. Of the 119, 89 were creations – 87 in the first long Ministry – and there were no fewer than 45 creations and promotions between December 1783 and the general election in the

1. See the tables in Large, loc. cit., 672, 674.
2. *Sybil*, bk. I, ch. III; Rosebery, *Pitt,* 275.
3. I.e. excluding the peerage of Ireland in its separate existence before 1801.

summer of 1790.[1] When one considers that there were 212 temporal peers at the end of 1783, one can see the size and pace of the activity that was so much condemned.

For it was the magnitude and regularity of the process that caused the grumbles and, in the end, alarm. It was true that the pace had been rising since 1776, when there was a sudden enlargement of both the British and the Irish peerage, and that there had been 36 creations and promotions in the former from that year to the end of 1783. Even so, the largest number of changes in any one of those years had been 16, of which 2 had affected women, and there had been a virtual gap until 1780, with only one intervening creation. In 1784 there were 22 changes, there was then no gap in the process except in 1785,[2] and it was this rather than the nature of the men affected that began to seem disturbing. Socially, indeed, the 45 creations and promotions made very little difference. There had been second-rate squires and fat graziers before, and in this period not a single man was snatched from Lombard Street or Cornhill. The 9 Scottish and Irish peers were not barbarians, and neither were the 18 commoners:[3] Carteret, Eliot, Egerton, Cocks, Parker, Dutton, Lowther, Griffin, Harbord, Percy, Pitt – Thomas Pitt – were respectable names. The men of talent – Elliott, the hero of Gibraltar, the colonial Governor Carleton, the diplomats Yorke and Harris, the lawyer Kenyon – were of a familiar kind; and Jenkinson, it was often forgotten, came of an established county family. Only Noel Hill, created Lord Berwick of Attingham, whose grandfather had been a draper in Shrewsbury, might be said to have had a connexion, if indirect, with trade. It could be argued, however, that some of the creations might have been to the Irish, not the British, peerage, and it was in fact the political aspect that gave rise to the greatest complaint at this stage. Opposition could point to the elevation of borough owners by the advocate of Parliamentary reform: to the fact that 6 out of the 14 patents in January and May 1784 went to men of this description.[4] They also objected to the preponderance of political supporters in the elevations within the peerage, 'an engine of alarming corruption'[5] which could be as potent as the creations themselves. Much of the alarm was of course factitious; they had

1. Of those 45, 29 were creations (2 conferments of Royal Dukedoms on sons of the King, 18 creations on behalf of commoners, 9 conferments of a British peerage on Scottish or Irish peers), and 16 were promotions within the British peerage. I have omitted one peer, Lord Ducie, claiming (not having created for him, as in another case) a seat by special limitation; and the terminal date has been taken as that of the Parliament, 10 June 1790. See A. S. Turberville, *The House of Lords in the Age of Reform 1784–1837* (1958), 45 and Appendix III.

2. There were many more changes in the Irish peerage, however, between 1776 and 1783 than between 1784 and June 1790: 60 compared with 44.

3. See n1 above.

4. See p. 151 above.

5. Egerton Brydges in 1798; quoted in Turberville, op. cit., 45.

done the same thing in their day, particularly in rewarding patrons after an election. But it was true that the changes were now becoming more continuous, and were not confined to the more obvious occasions.

What lay behind them? Several explanations have been given. It has been said that Pitt set out to swamp the Whig oligarchy, and render the Lords subservient to the Crown; that he used the peerage as a substitute for the waning influence of Government in other directions, brought about by Economical Reform and his own administrative measures; that he was building up his own party, distinct from if allied with the King's; that individual demands simply forced his hand, and he gave in to pressure. There may well be some truth in each of the first three answers, various as they are. The decline in the number of places of profit perhaps tended to make Government look more towards the peerage, as it looked also to the Garter – though not, in comparable degree, to the other forms of favour in the baronetage and the orders of knighthood.[1] The Crown and the Ministry would obviously like to strengthen their position in the upper House as much as they decently could, an achievement that would moreover have repercussions, through patronage, on the House of Commons. And Pitt himself would not be averse to strengthening his own position, in so far as he could do so – which was still not very far – independently of the King and the private magnates. But while such reasons are valid as far as they go, it seems doubtful if they can really account for the result. It seems probable, indeed, that the growth and disturbance of the Lords was largely forced on both Pitt and the King. Neither, particularly George III, always looked with great pleasure on the process. Like all sovereigns in the era of the classical constitution he deplored the dilution of the peerage, and, despite its provocations, felt protective towards the order. He kept a sharp eye on demands and supplications, not infrequently imposing his veto – he refused, for instance, to allow Temple and Shelburne to become dukes. He was active as the fountain of honour in denials as well as in grants, and by 1790 was growing restive at the increase in numbers. And Pitt for his part was not always happy about his recommendations: 'a variety of circumstances', he wrote in 1786, was responsible for 'a larger addition to the British Peerage than

1. The Order of the Garter was enlarged in 1786, and there were 10 new Knights from 1784 to 1790 compared with 5 from 1780 to 1783 and 6 in the seventies. On the other hand there were 2 new Knights of the Thistle from 1784 to 1790 compared with 6 in the seventies and none from 1780 to 1783, and 8 new Knights of the Bath as against 25 in the seventies and 7 from 1780 to 1783. The new Irish Order of St Patrick, founded in February 1783, began with 15 Knights, to whom only one was added from 1784 to 1790. Seventy Knights Bachelor were dubbed in the 1770s, 35 from 1780 to 1783, and 74 from 1784 to 1790. The figures for the British and Irish baronetage were 58 and 17 respectively in the seventies, 38 and 13 from 1780 to 1783, and 18 and 18 from 1784 to 1790.

I like, or than I think quite creditable'.[1] Sometimes, however, he found those circumstances 'unavoidable', whether they were political or social, and it was this fact more than anything else that suggests a key to his response. For Pitt did not really care very much about the composition of the House of Lords. He subscribed to the orthodox view of its role as a balancing element in the constitution: he wanted to introduce a counterpart to Canada in 1791.[2] He had no pronounced radical thoughts about it, although he would have liked to contain its patronage by his scheme of reform for the Commons, and expected its influence to sink in the course of time.[3] He respected the institution, and likewise the weight of the peerage in the country. But he did not venerate the great magnates, or the peerage, as a caste. He could be sarcastic about the 'old nobility'[4] – not in general so very old – and like his father, and many country gentlemen, did not mind reducing its pretensions. His creations, particularly in the early stages, hardly suggest a set purpose. Their political advantage had limits in the long run, for while some might increase his immediate power in the Lords, an elevation from the Commons, as George Rose noted, could open the way to replacement by an opponent, and, as John Pratt later observed, the upper House itself gradually swelled to an 'ungovernable . . . size'.[5] The social dilution, too, was insignificant at first, as was the introduction of men of talent. It was not so much, in fact, that Pitt was embarking on a policy to swamp or change the Lords as that he did not mind enough about them to avoid or control the beginnings of the process. Bored by patronage in all its forms, and unable here to rely so heavily on his agents at the Treasury, he surrendered to many of the demands which he found it hard to refuse – though within bounds set in the last resort by the King – and the advent of new conditions in the nineties furnished new reasons for continuing the practice. Rose remarked that many of Pitt's creations and promotions were due to his 'most uncommon share of good nature'.[6] It was a quality which in this instance might equally well have been called indifference.

---

1. To Rutland, 19 July 1786 (*Correspondence between Pitt and Rutland*, 150–1). He was admittedly giving this reason to avoid meeting a demand from the Lord Lieutenant for the elevation of two Irish peers. For George III in November 1790, see Stanhope, II, Appendix, xiii.

2. Pp. 365–71 above.

3. See p. 136 above.

4. See *The Farington Diary*, III, 14.

5. Lady Spencer to Lord Spencer, 28 January 1811, quoting the second Lord Camden (*English Historical Documents*, XI, 205). George III had remarked much earlier that too great an increase would be 'found inconvenient' (to Pitt, 21 November 1790; Stanhope, II, Appendix, xiii). For Rose's view, see *Diaries and Correspondence of George Rose*, II, 260.

6. Ibid.

IV

The House of Lords was one of the stages on which Pitt encountered his colleagues and the King. The fact that so many of the Cabinet were in the upper Chamber – all of them except himself in the first five and a half years – meant that their mutual relations might be tested or revealed in its proceedings; and it was indeed in order to control his fellow Ministers as well as the peers in general that he acted so vigorously in 1788 when the Lords were threatening Dolben's slave trade bill.[1] It was to counter Thurlow's growing lack of co-operation that he secured a peerage for Grenville in 1790, with the express object of leading the Ministry in the House. And peerage questions formed one of the subjects on which he had continually to deal with George III, testing their relations often more directly than did the conduct of divisions and debates.

The Cabinet as a body had its recognised responsibilities, though it would be hard to say precisely what they might or might not be. In Pitt's first seven years in office certain features may be seen. The most obvious subjects of formal consultation lay in the field of foreign affairs. They did not, however, cover it fully; the various talks on European trade attracted only intermittent attention, and then usually at the point when a treaty seemed closely in the offing or had to be formally proposed, and the King's German policy as Elector of Hanover was reserved largely to himself, subject only to the implications for British alliances or expenditure. Alliances and questions of peace or war in fact provided the most likely occasions for the Cabinet's scrutiny, and overseas problems seem most often to have reached it at that, sometimes late, stage. There are examples in the conversations with the Dutch over the Far East, and in the commercial negotiations with France, Prussia, Poland, and Russia; conversely, Pitt talked of consulting the Cabinet (though he may not actually have done so) before deciding on a policy for northern Europe in 1784, and he was happy for it to be kept informed from the start of the growing threat to the Scheldt in 1784–5.[2] The major diplomatic problems – the Mosquito Shore, Holland in 1787, the Prussian alliance and the Northern war in 1788, Nootka Sound in 1790 – involved discussions and sometimes Minutes, though in markedly varying degrees. They could also involve naval or military preparations which occasioned further Minutes. Out of 66 references to Cabinet decisions or meetings (other than dinners) which I have found for the periods January 1784 to October

1. See pp. 393–5 above.
2. See pp. 468, 470, for the north, and Pitt's correspondence with Carmarthen from August 1784 to August 1785, in B. M. Egerton Ms 3505, for the developments centring on the Low Countries.

1788 and March 1789 to June 1790 – in other words, when the system was functioning regularly during the life of that Parliament with both King and Cabinet in operation – 40 concern foreign affairs and preparations rising from them; and 12 of the 18 Minutes similarly found relate to those subjects.

It is harder to say how far domestic affairs came under review. Pitt once wanted to make a list of 'all the Points both Foreign and domestic that require the immediate Consideration of the Cabinet',[1] but the list has not survived, and such a general allusion is rare. Much of the difficulty arises from the nature of the evidence. For the Cabinet as a body met to give advice to the King on 'the King's service': as has been well said, this was its primary concern, not 'the improvement of social conditions or political machinery'.[2] The topics thus considered might be highly varied; but they tended also to be specific, and so did the occasions and method of giving advice. The most reliable record of a meeting was a Minute, sent to the King after the discussion,[3] and a Minute was by no means always required. It usually contained a recommendation for action, rather than a report of the Cabinet's views; it was not in fact a regular communication, and there was no guarantee in any case that it would be preserved. For instance, in the 18 Minutes found for this period of some six and a half years three relate to Ireland, and one each to India, the colonies, and home affairs; but there are a good many references to these same subjects other than those in the Minutes – in the 66 mentions of decisions and meetings ten relate to Ireland, three to colonies, three to India, and nine to home affairs.[4] One would therefore be unwise to rely too much on this particular type of report for a true impression of the Cabinet's business.[5]

1. To Carmarthen, 29 July 1785 (loc. cit.).

2. Pares, *King George III and the Politicians*, 163.

3. Sometimes of course there is a useful letter from the Minister principally concerned; but more often not.

4. With the 40 references to foreign affairs (above) this makes a total of 65. There was one meeting in October 1784 about which we know nothing in detail, but which from the attendance and description was probably devoted to domestic business (see *English Historical Documents*, XI, 95).

These 65 references do not include any to 'Grand Cabinets', which now met mostly to hear a prior reading of the King's Speech at either end of the session (see p. 181, n1 above). Nor do they include mentions of past decisions on a subject already covered in the calculation itself. It is also possible that the Cabinet did not meet on every occasion for which there is a reference: in a few cases one finds the King or a Minister suggesting consulation, but no evidence that it then took place.

5. Professor Aspinall, the leading authority, found 74 Cabinet Minutes for the whole of Pitt's first Ministry, from December 1783 to March 1801 (*The Cabinet Council 1783–1835*, 195). That is an average of only four a year over a period half of which was spent in war, when Cabinet meetings were apt to be more frequent than they were in peacetime. Professor Christie informs me, moreover, that the sending of Cabinet Minutes to the King was exceptional before 1779. The change thereafter in fact reflects an elaboration of the administrative system, as well as the greater personal involvement of George III, both brought about by war.

Nor of course can one claim that all the references together give the full story. I have doubtless missed or misconstrued some of the evidence, and there must have been meetings – perhaps many meetings – of which we shall never know. Still, something of a picture emerges, and the pattern is fairly clear. The references to the colonies and to India concern the royal functions – constitutional changes, and the movement of ships or troops. In the cases of Ireland and the United Kingdom they are of various but similar kinds: in four out of the 19 instances they relate to the King's Speeches to Parliament (usually simply to note the contents), in six others to business that might be called semi-Conciliar (legal instruments or procedural forms for certain political appointments, and the examination into an attempt on the King's life in 1786),[1] in one case to the prosecution of a pamphlet, required because a colonial Governor (a royal appointment) was attacked, and in one other case to the Prince of Wales's debts. This leaves seven instances in which a particular Ministerial policy or piece of Parliamentary business came under review; and five of those concerned Ireland – the Irish Propositions and Parliamentary business.

The remaining two occasions fell during the political crisis of 1783–4.[2] It may seem curious that there are so few references to the Cabinet at such a time, and perhaps the surviving evidence is again incomplete. Ministers certainly met, perhaps frequently, to discuss tactics and take decisions; but how many Ministers, and how formally, is another matter. The recorded meetings appear very often to have been of either more or less than a Cabinet, and in some such cases it is hard to tell which of its members were there. But this state of affairs is not really so surprising when one remembers the circumstances. The Cabinet was a scratch assembly, collected with difficulty and of no great political weight. It was far from being a coherent body, and in any case had little to do with the Commons, where the main battle was being fought. Dundas, Grenville, Rose, Mahon, Robinson – these were the kind of men who really mattered in the crisis, and with whom Pitt was consulting from day to day. The Cabinet of course must have been kept informed, and brought into play on certain necessary occasions. But there was only limited help to be got from the miscellaneous group of peers who had been persuaded to act, in some cases reluctantly, together.

The other great crisis, of 1788–9, was a different matter, for by then the Cabinet had settled down and a formal responsibility was thrust

1. The Lord Chancellor in fact called this last an examination by the Council. It was perhaps more like a process of the now virtually defunct Grand Cabinet.

2. On one, the Cabinet met at the King's behest to advise if the time had come for him to dissolve Parliament. The other is rather interesting. Just after the dissolution, Richmond referred to a past 'decision' of the Cabinet to 'circulate' Ministerial and uncommitted peers in the course of the debates as having been a matter of Cabinet 'responsibility' (to Sydney, 27 and 29 March, 7 April 1784; Sydney Mss, Brotherton Library, Leeds).

upon it by the nature of the occasion. The very fact that the circumstances were exceptional, indeed, underlined its function; for the removal of one element in the constitution illuminated, even while it distorted, others. Ministers had now to be viewed collectively, in a way that was normally not so explicit but that could be seen as both a recognition and potentially an advancement of the Cabinet's role. Their collective identity was certainly recognised at moments by the Prince of Wales; he summoned them as a body to Windsor at the outset, and later, when Pitt sent him on their behalf the outline plan for a Regency, snubbed him by replying in a letter handed to the Lord Chancellor 'to be communicated to the K's Ministers'.[1] 'The King's Ministers' – the Cabinet[2] – in point of fact met often during the crisis, and seem to have approved each major stage in Pitt's handling of the case. They were sometimes assisted by the legal advisers, above all the new Lord Chief Justice Kenyon on whom Pitt was largely relying, and with whom, as well as his usual confidants, he was acting throughout. For despite the necessary shift of emphasis, Pitt remained personally in charge here as elsewhere, shaping policy in concert with a picked body of friends and experts. There was indeed some danger in too intimate a disclosure of tactics to all his colleagues, for it was soon suspected that there was a traitor in the camp – and no less a one than the Lord Chancellor –, and if this was so it could obviously hamper 'Cabinet measure[s] or instructions'.[3] Allowing for the exceptional circumstances which were fostering an exceptional collective responsibility, Pitt in fact still managed to hold his cards close to his chest; even Grenville, who was much in his confidence, confessed at the height of the upset that he had 'no means of knowing or guessing at General Pitt's intentions'.[4] Once again, though much more than usual, the Minister consulted the Cabinet where the system demanded. But when the crisis was over it was soon clear that the system had not changed.

The Cabinet's role in 'the King's service' could be interpreted in short in a variety of ways, and the choice would be determined largely by the relations between the King's servants. At one end of the scale there might be a Ministry like North's in the later stages of the American War, whose members functioned strictly within the limits of their primary obligations to their royal master; at the other end, one like

1. Not actually 'directed *to the Cabinet*', as Grenville told Buckingham on 4 January 1789 (Buckingham, II, 87. See also 80–1). See *The Correspondence of George, Prince of Wales 1770–1812*, I, ed. A. Aspinall (1963), nos. 371, 375, and n1 on p. 439. For the Prince's summons in November 1788 and the ensuing Cabinet Minute, see loc. cit., nos. 320–1, 329, and the editorial notes.

2. Both descriptions are used, and in cases where it is pretty clear that they mean the same thing.

3. Grenville to Buckingham, December 1788 (Buckingham, II, 60). He may well have been echoing Pitt, with whom (though not yet himself a Cabinet Minister) he was in close touch.

4. Same to same, 25 December 1788 (loc. cit., 77).

Rockingham's in 1780–2, where there may have been little discipline but the obligations were felt to lie much more strongly between Ministers themselves. Depending on the circumstances, therefore, Cabinet conversations could doubtless take different forms. Fox once made the point: there were Cabinet meetings, he said, 'for affording to the members an opportunity of consulting with each other and stating their ideas reciprocally on points connected with their several departments, but with no intention of communicating the result to his Majesty', and others when 'the Cabinet Council meets to advise His Majesty in person'.[1] Fox thought more than most men in party terms, and he was naturally gregarious. Pitt's position and personality were different, and one senses a rather different approach. There were almost certainly times when Cabinets were called on foreign policy without a report to the King directly in view: for instance, Ministers agreed to meet twice a week for a spell early in 1786 in the dispute over the Mosquito Shore,[2] and if they did so the fact is not reflected in further communications with the sovereign. Judging indeed by the proportion of surviving Minutes to surviving mentions of decisions and meetings, the latter may in general have outnumbered the former by at least three to one; and it is always possible that Ministers, summoned on one matter, may have gone on to talk about others. They also doubtless talked business on occasions at the King's Levees and Drawing Rooms, and, even if perhaps less formally, at the Cabinet dinners, which during the American War at any rate had been business occasions.[3] But there is no sign of any such practice being regular or deliberate, and indeed the tone and scale of the correspondence suggests the reverse.

For as one follows public affairs through the middle and later eighties one gains the impression that Pitt managed his colleagues as much by exclusion as by direct control. The conventions of government made this perfectly possible. The fact that the Cabinet existed in reference to the King, and that its responsibilities could justifiably be limited to that purpose, meant that large areas of policy need not be discussed. It was a situation that suited Pitt well for a time, and he pursued a legitimate traditional course. Many of the policies by which he set the greatest store were not necessarily Cabinet business, and since his closest advisers were not yet members of that body he ignored it as much as he could. Of course the matter was not entirely in his hands: any member could call a meeting without prior notice, and sometimes (though it would seem not very often) Pitt found himself summoned unawares. The conventions, too, could cut the other way. There were

---

1. Speech in the Commons in 1806; quoted by Pares, *King George III and the Politicians,* 168–9. Pares dismisses the contention that Fox was here distinguishing between two different bodies.
2. Carmarthen to George III, 30 January 1786 (*L.C.G. III,* I, no. 275).
3. I am indebted to Professor Christie for this last piece of information.

occasions when Pitt would have been glad of a more powerful collective voice to bring a colleague to heel – as in the case of Lord Howe. There were others when he would have liked his colleagues to accept a policy as a matter of Ministerial responsibility, and they refused to do so; he failed with Parliamentary reform and the slave trade, as anyone less optimistic might have expected. Hints of resignation were then of doubtful avail;[1] these were not traditionally measures of Government, and he was forced to accept the fact. But the balance of advantage was in his favour, leaving him free to exploit a situation which allowed him, if he was capable, to secure his primacy by other means.

Pitt in fact controlled the Cabinet by his success in other directions: by his handling of the Commons, and his consequent importance to the King. The effect could be seen as time went by. At the start, when he had not yet settled firmly into the saddle, he was rather uncertain, and sometimes seemed quite anxious to consult his colleagues about the unfamiliar problems of foreign affairs. There were rumours, indeed, that all was not well: Rutland seems to have heard them in Ireland in the summer of 1784, they were current a year later, and Pitt was then at pains to deny that there was 'a spirit of disunion in the Cabinet'.[2] The main trouble at that moment was the Irish Propositions; but the year was altogether rather unhappy. By the end of 1786, however, things had changed very much for the better. 'There never was so firm an administration', wrote one MP then, 'We don't here [*sic*] of their quarrelling among themselves or of the King quarrelling with them';[3] and this state of affairs lasted over the next two years. That period in fact saw Pitt at the height of his prestige in his original Cabinet; he carried his colleagues on the questions referred to them, and even in the vexed matter of Dolben's slave trade bill, which they would not make a matter of Ministerial confidence, he finally bullied them out of Ministerial opposition.

The impress of those years indeed was such that it was extended in retrospect. To the Foreign Secretary, 'whatever was remiss in your mode of administering Govt. till the fatal period of 1791 [when he himself left office], is scarce worthy of recollection much less of being recorded'; and Bland Burges, a quite percipient and, for a time, well informed if partial observer, thought that 'From 1783 to 1789 he had no person in the Cabinet to influence or oppose him, and things went on prosperously'.[4] This last comment was broadly true, if one

1. See p. 394 above.
2. Rutland to Pitt, 15 August 1784 (*Correspondence between Pitt and Rutland*, 41); Lansdowne to Francis Baring, 25 July 1785 – 'I will tell you in confidence, that I hear of nothing but distractions among the Cabinet' (Northbrook Mss); Pitt to Rutland, 8 August 1785 (*Correspondence*, 111).
3. George Dempster to Sir Adam Fergusson, 10 November 1786 (*Letters of George Dempster to Sir Adam Fergusson*, 159).
4. B.M. Add. Ms 27916, f. 46; 'Concise Diary of Events by Sir James Burges' (Bodleian Library).

moderates the eulogy for the early phase. Thurlow, always potentially awkward, was comparatively quiescent until the Regency crisis, and thereafter chastened until 1791–2. Richmond was losing his early influence by 1786. Howe confined himself to the navy, though he in turn resisted interference until he was replaced. Gower and Camden – who was now something of an invalid – remained quietly in the wings, lending their experience and advice when required. And the two Secretaries of State were not of a calibre to influence events, although Carmarthen sometimes fretted at his insignificance. When Wraxall wrote his pamphlet in 1787 it was thus quite reasonable to say, as far as the Cabinet was concerned, that Pitt 'comprehended almost the whole administration'.[1]

This was one way of running affairs, and it worked satisfactorily while things went well. Given weak colleagues, Pitt could exploit the system of dispersed departmental powers. But it was a strain in more anxious times, and he began to feel the need for more effective support, particularly as the European scene became more confused. It would doubtless have been possible to continue on the old lines, at least until war broke out; but after 1788 events began to play into his hands, and he was able to make some changes. There had been very few of these since 1783. An early attempt to move Carmarthen from the Foreign Office in order to make room for Camden and his friend Grafton failed, and Camden could be added only when Rutland (who had briefly been Lord Privy Seal) went to Ireland and Gower took his place.[2] Howe was eased out in the summer of 1788, making way for Chatham.[3] But otherwise membership remained the same throughout these years. In June 1789, however, Sydney resigned on the slave trade question, and Pitt seized the opportunity to bring in Grenville;[4] and two years later the Foreign Secretary resigned, opening the Foreign Office to Grenville and the Home Office (though Pitt hesitated on this at first) to Dundas.[5] At about the same time the membership was enlarged to include Hawkesbury from the Committee of Trade;[6] and in June 1792 Thurlow was at last forced to go and was not immediately replaced. In those three years the composition of the Cabinet therefore changed materially, and in every case to Pitt's liking and with new appointments of his choice.

The shift of emphasis had some repercussions on his own position. It brought him much needed co-operation in the two main offices, and three effective Ministers into the Cabinet itself. Real and formal weight were thus combined and represented on the same body, and the Min-

1. P. 604 above.
2. See pp. 131, 198 above. For the attempt on Carmarthen, see *L.C.G., III*, I, no. 150, n2.
3. P. 315 above.
4. P. 398 above.
5. See p. 458 above.
6. See p. 433 above.

istry's voice was strengthened in the Commons with the elevation of Dundas. Pitt could now bridge the gaps between departmental powers by greater personal understanding and contact; he could tackle the system in a rather different way. At the same time, by placing those powers in the hands of more considerable men, he altered the balance at least potentially and to some extent, as it proved, in practice. Burges, observing from the Foreign Office, may have gone too far in thinking that Pitt's 'free agency was [now] more and more restrained';[1] his policies had long been shaped in concert with the same advisers, representing varied pressures and modes of thought. But their added stature was bound to tell: they could bring their views to bear more directly, and in the two chief cases from departments with very real independent rights. The later history of Grenville was to underline the point. But it was as yet of limited importance, for the immediate result of the changes was to reinforce Pitt's standing. If the old Secretaries of State went of their own accord, the new ones were of his choosing, indebted to him for their advancement and, almost ostentatiously, to nothing else. Dundas might be a powerful political agent in Scotland, Grenville was a member of a political clan; but neither was a natural member of Cabinet, and the combination, traditionally speaking, was weak. They brought no 'acres to their abilities',[2] they could not be looked on as King's men, and while Hawkesbury had always been regarded as such he too owed his inclusion in fact to Pitt. The removal of Thurlow a year later drove the lesson home; for the Lord Chancellor was traditionally the guardian of the prerogative, he himself had stood close to George III, he had never believed that the King would let him be forced out, and the King, though unhesitating, was upset.[3] In an age when appointments were tests of strength, and Cabinets variously, often finely, proportioned, these major changes were a tribute to the position which Pitt had achieved in the peacetime decade.

They were the more so perhaps because there was no question of 'storming the Closet': no concerted move by a group or a party to force its nominations on the King. Pitt was acting on his own, his reinforcements were chosen for their efficiency rather than their influence, and the operations took place against a background of support for, and partial dependence on, the Crown. In so far as he had managed to have his way it was as the result of his own kind of service, not of overt and successful hostility, to George III.

1. 'Concise Diary of Events', Bodleian Library.

2. Lord Chesterfield's comment in 1792. 'He hoped the present Ministers might be entitled to places in Heaven, as he was sure their Kingdom was not of this world, adding "We cannot go on well unless we have some acres added to our abilities" ' (*Political Memoranda of Leeds*, 199).

3. A 'decision', he wrote, '. . . revolting to my feelings' (to Thurlow, 17 May 1792; quoted by Aspinall, *The Cabinet Council*, 233, n1).

Every Ministry in turn had to work out its relations with the King, and the whole question had been thrown into confusion towards the end of the American War. Pitt's hope, here as elsewhere, was essentially to calm things down, and considering the circumstances he achieved a marked success. It was much easier said than done, for after the crisis of 1783–4 he could easily be represented as the King's creature, which suited neither his object nor himself. By upbringing and character he was far from being a King's man, and if the charge was too widely believed he could lose much of his appeal. He was well aware of the danger; but he owed his office to a defence of the Crown, and he was equally well aware of the dangers of continuing faction. If the country was to recover quickly political passions should be allowed to cool, and the constitution, with its healing powers, to resume a subtler beneficent course. He was a servant of the constitution; he accepted its limits and its possibilities. It was from this starting point that he approached his dealings with the King.

Everyone of course claimed to be serving the constitution: Fox and the Rockinghams had done so no less than George III. There was much room for interpretation, and Pitt was in no position, and did not really want, to force the pace. But by the same token there was room for manœuvre, and – a point of sometimes hidden substance – there were important sectors of government where direct confrontation need seldom arise. The conventions which fastened on certain areas of business tended to ignore some others; and it was in these last that Pitt, like any First Minister, was doing much of his work. It was work of growing potential constitutional significance, an as yet imperfectly measured force behind a rising tide. For the loss of influence by the Crown to the Cabinet, and the emergence of the Prime Minister himself, were to be determined eventually as much by the growing irrelevance as by the solution of earlier issues. The nature of the increase in the scale of government was only one of the factors involved; but it was a factor, and in the course of his career Pitt advanced and profited from the process.

The areas of business concerned in this decade were those of finance and commercial policy. In neither was the Minister strictly obliged to be in frequent contact with the King. Economical Reform had been aimed primarily at the political powers of the Crown, and some of Pitt's administrative measures impinged on the same target. There were the questions of the Crown lands, of revenue places, of the Civil List itself. But the ways in which he tackled the whole subject took much of the steam out of the argument; by depersonalising the issues as far as possible, he further advanced the slowly growing distinction between the Crown and the King. It was necessarily a gradual movement, and it had not gone very far as yet; but the steady, quiet shift of emphasis was to prove of major importance. For the removal of the problem from the centre of controversy was more effective than open attack, and much could be done, given knowledge and patience, within Pitt's own undisputed sphere. His powers as First Lord of the Treasury and Chancellor of the Exchequer gave him scope for action without troubling the monarch, or tangling too much with the party of the Crown. He used them directly and indirectly, in reforms to the machinery on the one hand, and on the other by the impact of his strictly financial policies. This was his departmental right; the consequences were far-reaching; and a skilful Minister could do a great deal without being disturbed by his colleagues or his master.

So far as the King was concerned, much the same could be said about commercial policy. George III seems to have been drawn in here only at the point where his rights were involved. He certainly followed what was going on when a formal negotiation was under way, for it then entered into the Foreign Office despatches which he normally read. His illness in the winter of 1788-9 delayed the discussions with several European powers. But this was because the 'Intermission in the executive Part of the Government' prevented 'particular or precise Instructions' to envoys[1] rather than because he had personally contributed anything to the talks. It was in fact a good illustration of the position in this sphere: the royal prerogative demanding regular information on, and assent to, policies the detailed pursuit of which the King was in practice content to accept. The forms here, moreover, applied to business involving 'the King's Ministers abroad' and those 'about his person'.[2] There was other important work of essentially the same nature, much of which fell into different channels. Trading policies in the Far East, and for that matter in Africa, were not handled primarily by a Cabinet Minister until the early nineties, let alone by a Secretary of State except, again, when they became the subject of negotiation with a foreign power. They therefore normally followed a process in which the prerogative was not automatically concerned, and there is little sign of the King's intervention, or even of his receiving detailed information, in a field of business which proved to be one of the most significant of Government's activities.[3] If the affairs of India had recently led to a major constitutional crisis, the expansion of an Eastern commercial empire was now largely bypassing the older forms.

The fact needs to be stressed, in an age of dispersed powers, when rights and procedures – always objects of attention – were watched with particular care. But this being so, what about those questions in which the King *was* more directly involved? His formal powers were extensive and varied, and the application of some of them was a matter for arrangement. How in practice was the combination handled in a situation which included Pitt?

There are few instances of a direct clash over policy in these years,

1. P. 515 above; Ehrman, op. cit., 199.
2. P. 170 above.
3. For some implications arising from this, see pp. 403-4, 420, 435-6 above.

or of Pitt's going against the King's known inclination. He did so in the case of Hastings's impeachment, and George III was powerless to intervene. But when Impey's impeachment came up for debate, it was noticeable that Pitt did not pursue it, and indeed threw his weight into the opposite scale.[1] He raised or supported two essentially private questions – Parliamentary reform and suppression of the slave trade – which the King disliked, and failed to get his colleagues or the party of the Crown to give them Ministerial backing. All these were marginal cases in the sense that the Minister and the King were free respectively to press and reserve their positions. They lay outside the recognised responsibilities of 'His Majesty's confidential servants' in submitting advice and securing Parliamentary support. So too did the case of the German *Fürstenbund*, on which George III acted without consulting his Ministers, and in a way which they deplored.[2] Where there were clear obligations on either side, however, it is difficult to cite examples of open disagreement. Pitt went faster than the King would have liked over Holland at the end of 1786 and early in 1787, and he and Grenville later pushed through their Canada Act despite the King's rather weary reservations.[3] But there was no prolonged or fierce dispute; reciprocal pressures were held in check; and in general the course of collaboration ran smooth on strictly Ministerial policies.

Different, indeed contrasting, explanations have been advanced for this fact. It has been argued on the one hand that such results show that Pitt was having his own way; they have also been held to suggest, on the contrary, that he was moving within limits set by George III. He was regularly securing agreement for his policies; but was this because the King was not in a position to disagree, or because the policies were perforce tailored in advance to the King's requirements? The latter contention stresses the extent of the royal powers, latent and actual. The sovereign had considerable latitude in his relations with his First Minister, and with his Cabinet: he could initiate business, consult Ministers separately, and even temper their counsel, though cautiously, with advice from others.[4] He had his own sources of information from those appointed in his name – he kept closely in touch with the army and the navy, and talked to his senior diplomats and Governors when they visited London –, and could bring the findings to bear, and urge his preferences, whenever he wished. All this was strictly legitimate, if the situation allowed. And this particular Ministry was beholden to him: it had been formed in answer to his appeal, and contained some members who looked as much to the throne as to their Parliamentary leader. The party of the Crown was indispensable to Ministers, in face of a substantial Opposition. It was therefore not surprising that their

1. Pp. 448–9 above.
2. See pp. 473–4 above.
3. Pp. 524–6, 367–8 above.
4. See pp. 181–2 above.

policies should have proved broadly congenial to the King. A pacific foreign policy in a period of weakness, yielding to a stronger attitude at a time of growing power; a due regard in imperial and commercial affairs for the elements of strength in an inherited system – managed in detail largely by an expert who had been known as a King's man; a settlement of India which naturally avoided the more obnoxious of Fox's proposals, and secured the growing participation of the Crown; the dropping of the more aggressive of the plans for Economical Reform: such developments were certainly not unwelcome to him, and it would really be immaterial if they all fell directly under his eye or not. They were brought about by an able young Minister who had gained the confidence of the Commons, and whose personal enthusiasms could be tolerated for the sake of greater gains. On such an argument, the rather uneasy period of 1784–5 could be seen as 'The Best Years of William Pitt', and its successor to 1789 as 'The Best Years of George III'.[1]

It is useful to have a corrective to an uncritical acceptance of the nineteenth-century view. But the reasoning goes a long way with the Foxites', and the Foxites, it has already been suggested, largely missed the point. It was, and remains, very easy to see problems of government in this political light: to ignore them until they raised political debate, and then look for this particular explanation. But matters were not as simple as that, either in government or in politics themselves. The pressures on Ministers were far more diffuse; they came from diverse facts and quarters, and the King's wishes often reflected a situation already taken into account. It is not indeed easy, on a closer view, to ascribe specific policies to him at this time, notably in foreign affairs where his role was most directly marked. He may have found his Government's ideas broadly congenial; but within those broad limits he accepted developments and changes without much ado. If he was happy with Pitt's early caution over Europe, he appeared content with the later interventions once he was used to the idea, and if the first of them had led to war over Holland it is hard to see what he could have done. He seems to have expressed no opinion on the various changes of attitude to the United States: on Shelburne's policy of friendship – and Shelburne was *his* Minister quite as much as Pitt – or on Pitt's later coolness or later still on the Ministry's sudden thaw. He showed no preference, again, on the choices open in the Far East, where they involved matters submitted to him. He made no comments, as far as can be seen, about the contents of the King's Speeches. This is not to say that he had no views, or was always entirely happy: errors in the conduct of business, in particular, could earn a shrewd rebuke. It was rather that his views, like Pitt's, were shaped partly by the situation as it was presented, and partly by the interplay of political forces which neither of them could

1. Chapter headings in Donald Grove Barnes, *George III and William Pitt, 1783–1806.*

fully control. For if the problems of government were largely impersonal, compounded of inherited policies and accepted facts, the attitudes to them, as found in Parliament, were not wholly amenable to guidance from any one quarter. The King would respond to feeling in the party of the Crown, itself far from monolithic, as the party of the Crown would rally to him in extreme cases; and beyond its ranks lay the House at large, in which his Ministers had to work. In the middle and later eighties, when Pitt had stilled the clamour of the past few years, there was much to be said from the King's point of view for staying quietly in the wings.

He was probably in any case now disposed to do so. For while the partnership between Crown and Ministry could vary greatly with the partners, it was unusual – and was so regarded – for the King to try to weight the scales of policy too much. The exceptional suspicions of the early eighties had sprung largely from an exceptional situation in the American War, when North's virtual breakdown had brought George III into the forefront of business. He had been almost his own Prime Minister at times; but this was generally felt to be undesirable, and he himself had sometimes been unhappy about his role. The result was that he had been named and attacked for Ministerial decisions, and the personal hostility thus aroused was not easily assuaged. But Pitt was in a position much more like that of North before the American War, when the Minister had been looked on as a good House of Commons man. Like North at that time, he enjoyed the confidence of the average uncommitted Member as well as the King; like North at that time, he sought where possible, and guided, a substantial consensus of opinion. His early setbacks, with one exception, had not indeed been at the hand of George III. The King had helped block Parliamentary reform by ostentatiously favouring a free vote; but it was not thanks to him that the Minister had lost on the Westminster scrutiny or the Irish Propositions. On the contrary, Pitt had then suffered from a different process: from a widespread loss of support for the King's Government which was not confined to any one sector.[1] He was careful thereafter to avoid this mistake, and he succeeded very largely in doing so. But the achievement can scarcely be explained simply by an implicit surrender to the King.

The royal influence in fact was seldom felt at its strongest in the sphere of policy. North's case, and in a different sense the treatment of Fox's India bill, really were exceptions to something like a rule. They showed that the prerogative could be made to cover some unusual situations; but no one, including the King, was particularly anxious for them to arise. For George III's duty, like that of his Ministers, was to make the constitution work, and he was quite prepared – indeed he thought himself anxious – to respect his conventional limits provided

1. And it was this again which briefly put him in danger over the India Declaratory Act in 1788, a matter on which George III held views very much like his own.

always that others, on his interpretation, did the same. Those limits could be wide: the King could make his suggestions, and urge his views, and cause delay. In the last resort he could use his veto in certain cases, and make his views publicly known. But he would have to be careful, and sure of his case, if he encountered real Ministerial objections; and normally if he disliked what was being done he could act more correctly from a neighbouring sphere. For the monarch's most consistent source of strength lay in his powers in the field of appointments: it was here that he could hope to lay his impress on a Ministry, and make his influence felt. The pressure could be positive or negative; it could be used to secure an agreeable man or group of men in office, or to block the opposite, or if that failed – as with the Coalition – to obstruct their recommendations. The influence that might not fall directly on the choice of measures might well fall on the choice and treatment of men; and, more rarely, there was the possibility of dismissal if the King was free to indulge it. The effects spread beyond the Ministry, the Court and Parliament themselves. There were appointments to be made to deaneries and bishoprics, to the fleet and to the regiments, in embassies and colonies, schools and academies, the counties, the universities, the law. There were pensions to be granted, reversions to be promised, honours and privileges to be bestowed. Such matters, which had become the staple of public life in an age when public business was small, did not lose their importance when larger issues revived and the work of government began again to grow.

It was in this field, accordingly, that expert observers were apt to form their impressions of a Minister's strength, or of the degree of favour that he was enjoying. The two were not necessarily the same, for the King might want to bolster a weak Ministry by showing his support; this indeed was so with Pitt at the start, but then a more normal pattern supervened. It included both co-operation and challenge, in an area in which neither party would give way too much; but, in these years, more of the first than of the second. This was not because of any particular friendship between George III and Pitt. The King was spared the treatment he received from other members of that awkward clan: Chatham's ornate and terrifying humility, the Grenvilles' ungracious and persistent demands. But even when Pitt was being helpful, as he often was, the relationship was correct rather than cordial, and if the atmosphere was easier than it had been for some time this was due to the political rather than the personal situation. The King was obviously not going to be as difficult as he had been with the Rockinghams and the Coalition. If he sometimes objected to Pitt's nominations for peerages, for example, he did not refuse to make peers as in 1783; and he assented sometimes to appointments that must have disturbed him – to Harris's and Eden's among the diplomats (even though they were removed thereby from immediate Opposition), and to some of the naval promotions in 1788 which caused such an unseemly Parliamentary row. And Pitt for his part was not going to be as aggressive as some of his predecessors. He did not attack the exercise of the prerogative on principle, like the Coalition and the Rockinghams, and he did not nag persistently as George Grenville had done. He usually accepted George III's wishes in areas where they should be respected, just as George III usually accepted his recommendations in the areas of direct Ministerial importance. On the whole, then, the arrangements ran quite smoothly in such potentially sensitive discussions. Nevertheless they did not always do so, and when they did not Pitt could sometimes be stubborn. He was not always successful; the result depended largely on the ground he chose, and George III was not the man to be easily coerced. The most open (at any rate the noisiest) quarrel that the two men ever had was over Pitt's abortive recommendation of Pretyman for the Archbishopric of Canterbury – an appointment which the King rightly looked on as his own. But the Minister quite often had his way, and sometimes without much consideration for his master. Almost the first piece of business which he submitted after George III's recovery from his illness in the spring of 1789 was a promotion in the army for a nephew of his cousin Buckingham, then once again Lord Lieutenant of Ireland; and, faced with an outburst of fury from that nobleman and a threat of resignation, he pressed it despite the King's expressions of 'personal uneasiness' and the plea that his 'mind was not strong enough as yet to stand little ruffles'.[1]

The same forbearance – perhaps in this case one might say caution – was exhibited by George III in his treatment of the Ministry as a whole. If in the sphere of appointments he showed that he regarded it as an acceptable Government, he did not act within its ranks as he had come to act with North. At various times in his reign he had been accused of excessive private dealings with separate Ministers, and also of encouraging divisions within a Cabinet. The first charge was certainly true of North's Administration, and the second may well have applied to some of the Cabinets which the King disliked or feared – George Grenville's, for instance, and Rockingham's. It was also true that in North's later years George III turned increasingly to two office holders outside the Cabinet itself – Robinson and Jenkinson –, and it was then indeed that the accusation of 'secret influence' was revived with greatest force. But that practice probably arose at least in part from a not unreasonable desire to get something done, and to bring pressure and encouragement to bear on North in a form which he would accept; and in the different circumstances of Pitt's first decade, and after his own recent chastening experiences, the King showed little sign of repeating such manœuvres. Written evidence of course would not give the whole story here, and he may well have tried sometimes

1. See *L.C.G. III*, I, nos. 502, 504, and Stanhope, II, Appendix, viii. The quarrel over Pretyman took place in 1805.

to influence Ministers by expressing his views in private conversations with them. But there was no complaint of favouritism or interference from Pitt himself; even Thurlow failed to profit from the royal friendship; and with the exception of Sydney at the time of the Parliamentary reform bill in 1785 no record appears to have survived of a royal correspondence with another Minister on a question over which the King and Pitt disagreed.[1] Both men in fact were keeping within their limits as far as they could, and off debatable ground, and achieving a very reasonable partnership thereby. Pitt proceeded within his own large sphere as far as possible without disturbing George III, and otherwise so handled matters that there was little occasion for the monarch's interference; George III, relieved to be spared further attacks and grateful for a spell of stability, gave his Minister as much latitude as he thought the prerogative would allow. The constitutional framework was not altered, and this balance could always be upset. Later events were to show that the King's powers could be effectively used. But in the early years of the Ministry's life a working relationship was established which, perhaps in its very lack of intimacy, met the needs of the day. George III relied on Pitt to defeat his enemies in Parliament, to rally moderate opinion, and pursue that group of policies which was bringing popularity and success.[2] Pitt relied on George III for support in Parliament and, preferably by inference, within the Ministry, and on a continuation of the royal favour which secured and conceded him freedom to act. Each depended in his own degree on the other, and profited thereby, and as long as he remained in effective operation each reckoned that he could hold his own. So matters stood in the prosperous middle years of the decade. And then in November 1788 the future was suddenly thrown into doubt.

1. See p. 224, ns3, 4 above.
2. As Wraxall noted in his pamphlet of 1787, 'It has fallen to the lot of few Princes . . . to enjoy so considerable a portion of the personal attachment, respect, and adherence of their subjects, after the unprecedented disgraces and calamities of his reign, as George the Third appears to possess at the present moment' (*A Short Review of the Political State of Great-Britain*, 3). Ministerial success played its part in this 'extraordinary and improbable' (op. cit., 11) result.

CHAPTER XX

The Regency Crisis

I

On 22 October 1788 Pitt received a note from Sir George Baker, the King's physician, who had just paid a call at Windsor, as he had been doing regularly for some days. His Majesty, Baker wrote, was in a state 'nearly bordering on delirium', and that evening he went round to Downing Street to give a full report.[1] It must have come as a shock, though all had not been well for a week or more. The King's health indeed had been bad throughout the summer, and a stay at Cheltenham had brought only intermittent relief; he was rather weak and in pain again early in October. Still, Baker did not diagnose anything of this kind, and in the past two days Pitt had received two letters from the monarch which, although one was rather excited, could scarcely have aroused real suspicion.[2] He may even have seen George III on the 21st, for he had then been summoned to Windsor to discuss foreign affairs; and it may have been on this occasion that he was kept standing in a long conversation of over three and a half hours.[3] He certainly had a chance to judge the new alarming development for himself on the 24th, after a Levee at St James's which the King courageously decided to hold. This was done, George III wrote the next day, 'to stop further lies and any fall of the Stocks'; but he was aware that the Minister 'really seemed distressed at seeing my bodily stiffness'.[4] The general impression was that the King was 'in a bad state of health', but nothing 'material',[5] and for some days thereafter, when he was back at Windsor, there were momentary spells of improvement. On 3 November he wrote to Pitt that, while he still found it hard to concentrate, he was eating and sleeping better and feeling rather less tired.[6] But this was the last letter for four months,

1. Baker's diary, quoted in Charles Chenevix Trench, *The Royal Malady* (1964), 16.
2. Stanhope, II, Appendix, iii-iv; *L.C.G. III*, I, third letter of no. 485. Although the first of these letters has been held to have borne 'clear indications of [a] disturbed state' (John W. Derry, *The Regency Crisis and the Whigs 1788–9* (1963), 6), I cannot see, despite its acknowledgements of illness, that it was of a kind seriously to suggest derangement; and the second letter was written in a more relaxed frame of mind.
3. *L.C.G. III*, I, no. 485. *The Diaries and Correspondence of George Rose*, I, 186 mention the long conversation, but give no date.
4. George III to Pitt, 25 October 1788 (Stanhope, II, Appendix, iv).
5. *Life and Letters of Sir Gilbert Elliot*, I, 225.
6. Stanhope, II, Appendix, v-vi.

for on the evening of the 5th the King had a bad attack, and by the end of the following week he showed every sign of being insane.

The attack indeed was so severe that it was thought for some days that the King might die; but when the immediate danger receded it remained obvious that he could not carry out his duties. Pitt and his friends saw at once what that could mean. 'If this lasts beyond a certain time', the Minister wrote to Pretyman on the 10th, 'it will produce the most difficult and delicate crisis imaginable in making provision for the Government to go on.' It was indeed 'the effect . . . on the understanding' that was 'to be dreaded'.[1] If George III died, there was an end of it. The immediate future was fairly predictable. But if he was incapacitated there must be a Regency; and its powers, hard to define in any case, would be peculiarly so in this instance because they must surely be exercised largely or solely by the heir to the throne.

The Prince of Wales had come of age in 1783. Since then he had been a constant source of worry, and his relations with Pitt were badly strained. The Minister had so far escaped lightly from the King's growing troubles with some of his younger sons – he had to take notice of Prince William's debts, but Lord Howe bore the burden of his naval escapades; George III himself dealt with Prince Edward's embarrassments in Hanover, where he was supposed to be learning his trade as a soldier; and although the Duke of York's finances eventually demanded some attention from Government, the King coped as best he could with his favourite son's growing hostility. But this relief was more than balanced by the incessant confusion of the Prince of Wales's affairs, which soon outgrew the normal resources of the Civil List. Subsisting nominally on an allowance of £50,000 a year from that source and £12,000 from the Duchy of Cornwall – and granted £30,000 by Parliament in 1783 to pay off what he owed when he came of age – he was in debt to the tune of £150,000 by the end of 1784 and £250,000 early in 1786, and appeared most unlikely to confine himself to that. Pitt was kept informed of the King's unsuccessful efforts to learn the details in 1785, and in 1786, as the muddle grew, he became increasingly involved. He countered a plea from Opposition for a larger allowance in April, on the ground that he could not interfere without the King's instructions; in May he drafted a message from George III, again demanding details from the Prince before anything could be done; in June he asked the King's permission to consult the Cabinet – which may or may not have been given; and in July, when the Prince dismissed his Household and announced the sale of his racing stud, the Minister composed a further message from the King and collected 'the whole correspondence' for future reference.

1. Holland Rose, 411, from the Pretyman Mss. Tomline, II, 363 n gives a slightly different version, with no precise date. Sir George Baker, however, was less hopeful (diary, quoted Trench, op. cit., 22). For Grenville's thoughts in those same days, see Buckingham, II, 432–44.

He also seems, as might have been expected, to have been approached by at least one unprepossessing intermediary on the Prince's behalf, with a scheme with which – as might have been expected – he would have nothing to do.[1] In 1787 matters came to a head. The Prince could no longer survive on his own, and his friends in Parliament pressed once more, and now more vigorously, for his relief. Pitt and Thurlow had already been in touch with the King in an effort to find a settlement, and early in May, Dundas having acted as a go-between, the Minister went to see the Prince at Carlton House. After two conversations, the second attended by Dundas and Sheridan, an arrangement was reached. The Prince at last agreed to furnish details of his affairs, Pitt in return consulted his colleagues, and after a spate of explanations and forecasts he asked the Commons for a grant of £161,000 to pay off past debts and £60,000 to complete the works, still unfinished, at Carlton House. The King also agreed to allow his son an additional £10,000 a year from the Civil List, a settlement which produced a temporary reconciliation between them.[2] The outcome may also have temporarily eased the Prince's animosity towards Pitt;[3] but, given the circumstances and his own character, not very much and not for very long.

The King's worries and obduracy had been increased by his son's politics and his matrimonial affairs, both of which were suspected of contributing to the financial drain. In the usual manner of Hanoverian heirs the Prince had thrown in his lot with Opposition, and, to his father's great distress, made a boon companion of Fox. Fox indeed gained some unmerited suspicion for plunging the young man into wicked habits: his personal and political influence, while hardly reassuring, were in fact more limited than George III supposed. The Prince had got into plenty of scrapes on his own account, he did not pay much attention when Fox (perhaps rarely) counselled caution, and he listened readily to others when 'dear Charles' was not there. He believed what he wanted to believe, and behaved as he wished to behave; and some of Opposition's trouble in the winter of 1788 arose from his disregard of Fox's advice. He had already embarrassed them profoundly by lying about his marriage to Mrs Fitzherbert, which had been performed in strict secrecy in December 1785. For she was then given £50,000 a year, the Prince could not afford it, and yet the ceremony had to be denied when his friends asked for a larger allowance from Parliament. Pitt had behaved correctly in the Commons when the rumour of the wedding was raised, in 1786 and again in 1787. While

---

1. *L.C.G. III*, I, nos. 181, 190 (and 192), 292, 305, 309, 313. Pitt's draft of the letter of July 1786 is in P.R.O. 30/8/105.

2. *L.C.G. III*, I, nos. 343, 352, 354, 358, 360, 362, 364–6; *Correspondence of George, Prince of Wales*, I, nos. 219, 221, 223–8, 240, 242; P.R.O. 30/8/105. There are calculations and proposals among Pitt's papers in P.R.O. 30/8/228.

3. See *H.M.C., Dropmore*, I, 362.

he suspected the truth from the start,[1] he refused to discuss it or to include it in the financial calculations. Nevertheless he could not prevent the matter from being debated, whereupon Fox, quite sincerely, denied the allegation; and although the episode was scarcely the Minister's fault, the Prince, having behaved badly, was furious, and the affair deepened his bitterness against the Government and particularly against Pitt.

If there was to be a Regency, therefore, the prospect for Ministers was bleak. They were genuinely perturbed by the thought of the Prince exercising the royal functions, and their own position was unenviable whether they were turned out (as they expected) or not. For either they would lose their offices, and moreover have to face some awkward decisions on their future conduct, or they would have to act with an avowed opponent and perhaps in concert with his advisers. It was extraordinarily difficult to see ahead, when every course of action carried obvious dangers; and the dilemma was not lessened as November wore on by the doctors' puzzlement over the illness itself.

II

For after the first onset of apparent madness, which continued unbroken for about a fortnight, George III showed symptoms of a partial and fluctuating improvement. On some days he was quite sane, he would then revert to his former state, and no one could pronounce with any confidence on the cause. The diagnosis was of crucial importance, since the nature of the Regency might well depend on how soon and how far the King was likely to recover. What then, it was asked with growing clamour, *was* really wrong? And were the medical forecasts entirely professional, or were the doctors – as was widely supposed – beginning to play politics themselves?

No doubt some of them were – medical politics at least. But we can look on their dilemma with fresh sympathy in the light of fresh evidence. A layman cannot properly judge; but medical opinion is now disposed to the view that George III was suffering from a disease which has been diagnosed only within the last sixty years. Acute intermittent porphyria, a rare hereditary disorder of the metabolism, endemic in the Stuarts and so transmitted to the Hanoverians through the Electress Sophia, has been authoritatively put forward, and appears to have gained general acceptance, as an explanation that will meet all the salient facts of the case.[2] If the argument holds, it is not surprising that the physicians at

1. See Holland Rose, 397–8.
2. *Porphyria – A Royal Malady, Articles published in or commissioned by the British Medical Journal* (1968). The historical research was the work of the physicians Drs Ida Macalpine and Richard Hunter, whose first article in January 1966 opened the discussion.

the time disagreed, that most of them were evasive, and that the politicians could choose between them according to taste. For this strictly physical disorder – whose nature can be detected by physical means – can produce mental symptoms indistinguishable from those of hysteria, psychoneurosis, paranoia or schizophrenia; from insanity, in fact, in the commonly accepted sense of the word. Its onset and disappearance can be sudden, serious attacks may be widely spaced, and the mental effects may vary greatly in the course of an attack with the progress of the physical cause. Small wonder, perhaps, that the best qualified observers could recall no parallel case, or find an 'exact precedent in the records of insanity'.[1]

Meanwhile, however, insanity of some kind was perforce accepted. There must be a Regency, however temporary, and the question arose how it should be framed. The case bristled with difficulties, political and legal, as the rare instances of past Regencies had always done. Three issues in particular could be seen immediately. Should insanity be treated as equivalent to a royal minority? Should it be taken alternatively as equivalent to an absence of the sovereign? And how was a Regency to be brought into being – in other words, on whose authority did it rest? This last problem was of pressing importance, for a new Parliamentary session was due to start, and how was it to be opened if the King could not act?[2]

The answer in each case must be influenced by precedents, and Pitt set to work to inspect them.[3] There were several on which to draw for either of the first two possibilities. If the King's incapacity was to be treated as absence, several parallels arose over the past hundred years. In the late seventeenth and early eighteenth centuries Lords Justices (usually leading Ministers) had generally been appointed, when William III was abroad,[4] when provision had been made for the interval that would arise between Queen Anne's death and the arrival of her successor, and sometimes when the first two Georges visited Hanover. But a member of the royal family could also be named: the Prince of Wales in 1716, Queen Caroline in 1732. This combination of examples was not particularly helpful if a specific answer was required, for the extent of the authority given to the caretakers varied in different cases. In 1716, for instance, the Prince of Wales was given sharply restricted powers; in 1732, on the other hand, they were much more widely defined. All that could really be said, if absence was to be taken as the criterion, was that 'no set procedure, no order of precedence or line of succession, was acknowledged'.[5]

1. Quotation from the doctors towards the end of the King's life, loc. cit., 8.
2. For the following paragraphs see the analysis by Derry in *The Regency Crisis and the Whigs*, 10–20.
3. The papers at his disposal are in P.R.O. 30/8/228.
4. Queen Mary had been given powers to act for the future in 1689; but of course she was sovereign with William in her own right.
5. Derry, op. cit., 18.

The stronger analogy, however, seemed to lie in a minority. There were two eighteenth-century precedents here, those of 1751 and 1765. On the first occasion the Princess of Wales (George II's widowed daughter-in-law) had been named guardian of her children by Act of Parliament, and Regent, accompanied by a Council of Regency, if any of those children should succeed to the throne while under age. She was given the exercise of the prerogative with certain exceptions which followed those laid down in 1707 for the prospective Lords Justices: consent to a bill altering the succession, or repealing the Act of Uniformity, or the Scottish Act securing the Presbyterian form of church government. These same restrictions were laid down in 1765 for a prospective Council of Regency, when George III suffered a short-lived illness – perhaps of the disease which attacked him in 1788 – and provision was made against his early death. There had been no need to proceed farther on that occasion, but Ministers had persuaded the King to restrict the choice to members of his family, although he himself had wanted an unfettered discretion.

There were also precedents, however, to be considered from more distant ages. The pundits turned their attention to the events of 1326, 1377, 1422, and 1454–5. Of these the two last, affecting Henry VI, seemed particularly applicable; for the Regency in 1454–5 was caused by the King's madness, and its provisions were greatly influenced by what had happened in 1422, when he came to the throne as a child. The Duke of Gloucester, the King's uncle, had then been empowered by Parliament to act as Regent,[1] assisted by a Council whose assent for his actions he was likewise obliged to secure. Such restrictions, however, did not suit him, and he soon claimed an unfettered jurisdiction as of right. The House of Lords refused to concede this, Gloucester was rejected, and Parliament replaced him by the Duke of Bedford, giving the latter a group of titles – Protector and Defender of the Realm and Church, and Principal Counsellor to the King – which did not include the word Regent. Gloucester was named as substitute for Bedford if the latter was abroad, but the Protector was again given a Council of Regency whose powers were prescribed. Six years later Gloucester tried once more, this time directly through the House of Lords; but he was once more rebuffed, and the minority ended much as it had begun.

The role of Parliament was equally important in 1454–5, on the two occasions when Henry VI was insane. In 1454 the two Houses chose the Duke of York as Protector, and the King was just capable of signifying his assent by handing the Great Seal to a leading Privy Councillor, the Earl of Salisbury. In 1455 the Houses appointed a Council with the Duke at its head, but this time with a clause stipulating that he could be relieved by the King in Parliament or when the baby Prince of Wales came of age. While the Council as a body, moreover,

1. The royal assent being signified by the nine months old King being given the Great Seal to hand to the Master of the Rolls.

was given the widest authority, sovereignty was stated to reside inherently in the person of the King.

The precedents of those years were studied anxiously in November 1788. A Regency must clearly be sanctioned by Parliament; but the new session had not begun, and how was the royal assent to be secured to a bill if the monarch could not act? Since sovereignty resided in his person, how could he be bypassed? The answer was taken to lie in the authority conferred in those same years on the Great Seal. Although the sovereign was thereby excluded in person from a constitutional process, this had been done before in an emergency, and had not been subsequently challenged.[1] The procedure was therefore repeated now; the session was postponed for a fortnight with the Prince of Wales's agreement, and after meeting and adjourning on 20 November at the end of the summer prorogation, the two houses reassembled on 5 December.

III

Such was the legal background to Pitt's political problems. The Ministry's first reactions were naturally hesitant and confused. It was assumed that the Prince of Wales must be Regent, with or without a Council; but beyond that point the possibilities were obscure. One immediate question at the very start was what should be done if he suggested a Coalition, bringing in some of his own adherents to join some of his father's Ministers. Grenville, for one, was much perplexed by this between 7 and 20 November, and nothing could be learned from the Prince's conversations with Pitt, in which he showed 'civility, but nothing more'.[2] By the 13th Pitt's friends, and it would seem Pitt himself, were inclined to hope that he would be 'removed at once' if the Regent on his appointment pressed for some such arrangement. But there was one great obstacle to what they 'all' agreed would be 'desirable', for Pitt would then be abandoning the King, who might recover to find Fox in office.[3] The problem in fact was part and parcel of the wider problem of the Regency itself: the form that it should take, and the limits that should be imposed.

To a great extent these decisions would be influenced by the doctors' forecasts. Pitt went down several times to Windsor in mid-November, and was distressed by what he saw. But he was far from satisfied with the medical reports as the month went by, particularly as he himself

1. The legal argument turned on the relationship between his natural and political capacities, the deficiency in the former being held not to invalidate the latter, which was exercised through an instrument originating from himself.

2. Grenville to Buckingham, 9 November 1788 (Buckingham, I, 440, 441). See also same to same, 20 November 1788 (op. cit., II, 4); and in general op. cit., I, 432–55 and II, 2–4.

3. Same to same, 13 November 1788 (op. cit., I, 451–2).

noted marked signs of improvement on the 22nd when he again visited the King. The Prince of Wales had earlier sought a second opinion, calling in Dr Richard Warren, a leading practitioner favoured by many of the great Whig families. There is no reason to suppose that this was done with a political motive, for the Prince was genuinely upset by his father's condition at the start, and Warren was a natural enough choice. But he proved to be very pessimistic, a third doctor, Reynolds, was indecisive, and the King disliked a further consultant, Sir Lucas Pepys, whom the Prince also sent. The surgeon Rennel Hawkins, who was also in attendance at times, seems to have taken a less gloomy view; but all in effect were baffled, and Pitt resolved to call in fresh advice. He chose Dr Addington, his family's old doctor, who had kept a lunatic asylum some twenty years before; and Addington reported that the King might well recover, and recommended his removal to Kew for a change of surroundings. The royal family and the Cabinet agreed, Pitt was asked to inform His Majesty in writing, and the move took place on the 29th. On 3 December the five physicians were summoned before the Privy Council, to answer the questions that must guide Parliament, now about to meet. All agreed that the King could not attend to business; all, except Warren at first, were prepared to say that his recovery was probable, and Warren was eventually obliged to support them; but none cared to predict when recovery might come. A further question established the fact that Addington alone had more than a smattering of experience – ancient though it was – in the treatment of lunacy.

The atmosphere of this examination was political, for the political situation was now developing fast. The Prince had won much popularity, and rather surprised respect, for his unfeigned emotion at the beginning; but, as was soon observed, his distress was 'not of that deep and rooted sort for which "no physic of the mind" can be found',[1] and it proved unable to weather the political temptations and the nervous gloom of Windsor, where he had taken up quarters. His relations with the Queen soon deteriorated – there was a furious quarrel over the safekeeping of the King's private possessions – and as always he listened readily to the worst advice. Fox might not have been a very wise counsellor; but he was in Italy when the crisis broke, and in his absence Sheridan and Grey and the lesser fry of Carlton House took charge. Stories began to reach London of the Prince's behaviour – of heartless rudenesses and indiscretions; the minor politicians began to cabal, and speculate on the possible spoils; and by the time that George III was moved to Kew his heir had returned to his old form. The Prince's reappearance in town was marked by a spate of gay evenings and wild talk with his cronies at Brooks's, and a readiness, as it seemed, 'to go to all the lengths to which that party are pushing him'.[2] The party as a

1. Sir William Young to Buckingham, 30 November 1788 (op. cit., II, 25).
2. Grenville to Buckingham, 7 December 1788 (loc. cit., 37).

whole was not, in point of fact, as elated as the Ministry thought; Portland and Fox himself, who reached home on 24 November, were becoming worried by Sheridan's and Grey's influence. But the Prince was now in full cry, the sweets of office beckoned, and by the time that Parliament met talk of a Coalition had died away.

Over the same period the Ministry's attitude was hardening. Despite some differences of emphasis within the Cabinet over the desirability of a Coalition – which Camden and Richmond were at first inclined to consider – members presented a united front throughout, with one great exception. Thurlow's dislike of Pitt had been growing steadily, and he was now a thoroughly awkward colleague. He had played his part in the Dutch crisis in 1787 – he wrote several useful memoranda for Pitt on the legal aspects – but the affair of Dolben's slave trade bill put him in an ugly humour, and he now took a line of his own. His position as Lord Chancellor – the 'Keeper of the King's Conscience' – gave him a responsibility and a point of view which he was fully astute enough to interpret to his advantage. Summoned by the Prince on his own at the start, on 6 November, he played an ambiguous waiting game, watching the likely course of events. He could justify his conduct by pleading the need for the Lord Chancellor to remain in office whatever form the Administration might take; indeed the more distasteful it was going to be to his master, the more necessary for him to be there.[1] But it seemed highly doubtful if he would have come to this conclusion had he not been on bad terms with Pitt, and his behaviour was worrying at a time when it was so important for the Cabinet to be solid. Even if he did not relay Cabinet conversations, as was suspected, he had many interviews with the Prince and some with Opposition, and his advice to his colleagues on 26 November to join a mixed Government was not well received. For Ministers were now increasingly resolved in these uncertain conditions that they should act as the King would approve on his recovery, and although contact with Opposition had been maintained through Richmond – probably with Pitt's knowledge, for Richmond was loyal –, and Pitt himself had a friendly talk on the 27th with Lord Stormont, the Coalition's Lord President of the Council in 1783, it seemed pretty clear by the end of the month that no immediate accommodation was going to take place.

When Parliament met on 5 December, therefore, some sort of fight seemed likely. Pitt had gained one point from the doctors' examination, and he was about to be given another of the same kind. The admission that the King would probably recover, and that Addington, who held that view most openly, was the best qualified to do so, were cogent arguments for restrictions on a Regency. They were strongly reinforced within the next forty-eight hours by the appearance of a new figure on the scene. For on the 5th the Queen called in Dr Francis Willis, a

1. See his reported conversation with William Knox, in *H.M.C., Various Collections,* VI, 279.

clergyman and physician who kept a private madhouse in Lincoln-shire, where he had built up a reputation for his unusual treatment of mental disorders. He was indeed the first doctor to attend the King who was actually practising in that field, which gave his opinion a certain weight, and his first effect on the patient was distinctly favourable. The King, enjoying a better spell at that moment, said that Willis had settled his mind; he seemed to respond to the doctor's personality; and the doctor – who was not of a doubting nature – was confident of a cure. He told Pitt so on the 6th at Kew, and again sent good news on the 8th, and by that time the other physicians had agreed to place him mainly in charge. On the very eve of the debates the situation thus seemed to be changing, and Pitt faced Opposition with an apparently strengthened hand.

Even so, he must have been in great difficulties if Opposition had not mishandled its case. For the Ministry had still not decided exactly what line to pursue. Although the precedents suggested that the appointment of a Regent was open to choice, and was not a matter of right – and indeed there was some thought among Ministers early in December of naming the Queen –, it had been generally accepted at the outset that the Prince must hold office, and restrictions had not been considered in any detail.[1] Pitt was anxious as always to carry with him the bulk of opinion in the Commons, and when they met he proceeded firmly but cautiously. His first action, on 8 December, was to move for a committee of the House to examine the doctors – a proposal raised by Fox, which the Minister turned to his own use by choosing the members. Pitt indeed took the opportunity to show that he intended to remain in control while he lasted; when he read out the names he paused before the last, and in reply to cries of 'Burke' quietly proposed Lord Gower.[2] On the 10th he took the next step by moving for the appointment of a committee to examine precedents; and it was at this point that he had his first and perhaps greatest stroke of luck. For when Fox rose to speak he challenged the authority of the House to examine the case at all.

In his firm opinion, his Royal Highness the Prince of Wales had as clear, as express a right to assume the reins of Government, and exercise the power of Sovereignty, during the continuance of the illness and incapacity with which it had pleased God to afflict His Majesty, as in the case of His Majesty's having undergone a natural and perfect demise . . .

1. For the possibility of the Queen, see Buckingham, II, 40–1.
2. *Life and Letters of Sir James Bland Burges,* 118. Gower was the eldest son of Lord Stafford, the Lord Privy Seal.

The function of the two Houses was to pronounce 'when the Prince ought to take possession of, and exercise, his right.'[1] Pitt, listening closely, is said to have slapped his thigh, and, turning to his neighbour, whispered 'I'll *un-Whig* the gentleman for the rest of his life!'[2]

Why did Fox make what seemed at once to be an elementary mistake? The Prince's cause was best served, as Thurlow indeed had told him, by letting 'everything . . . flow to him of itself'. 'He could only interrupt its course by impatience to receive it'.[3] Now Opposition was being propelled along precisely this second course, and an unexceptionable search for precedents had been incontinently challenged. It has always been held that Fox was led away by eagerness to seize what could be a fleeting chance; to secure himself in office before anything intervened. The party, resigned to a long stay in the wilderness, had suddenly glimpsed the promised land, and they, and he, could not bear the thought and dangers of delay. He may also have felt under pressure to equal or outbid the Prince's advisers who had taken charge while he was abroad; and in any case he was far from well at this critical juncture. He had travelled across Europe at breakneck speed, and was suffering from dysentery: he could not attend the Privy Council's examination of the doctors on 3 December, and by the 5th he was so ill that he thought he was dying. Never conspicuous for his judgment, and operating in a highly excitable atmosphere, the debate of the 10th found him at his worst.[4]

The speech gave Pitt an opportunity which he was quick to press home. It committed his opponents to a division on ground they could ill defend. A question of principle had been raised, and one which could cause some delay – precisely what Fox had been so concerned to avoid. In the long debate which followed the Minister made the most of his advantage, and a second speech by Fox could not undo the damage. Burke made matters worse by an angry attack; the feeling of the House was with Pitt; the motion was carried, and the Ministry obtained a majority on the committee. Almost incredibly, Opposition repeated its mistake two days later, when Pitt proceeded to his next step with a motion for the Commons to form themselves into a committee on the state of the nation. After another embarrassed effort by Fox, Sheridan tried his hand. But in the course of a speech intended to be conciliatory he undid any good he might have done. Arguing that excessive discussion of principle could 'create dissensions and animosities',

1. *P.R.*, XXV (1789), 24.

2. The story appears in Thomas Moore's *Memoirs of the Life of the Right Honourable Richard Brinsley Sheridan* (1825), II, 38. It is said to have been 'authentic'.

3. Thurlow's account to William Knox, *H.M.C., Various Collections*, VI, 279. And cf. J. Nicholls, *Recollections and Reflections, Personal and Political, as connected with Public Affairs during the Reign of George III* (1820), 71–2.

4. He himself seems to have appreciated his blunder at once, if the Duchess of Devonshire is to be believed (diary for 10 December, in Sichel, *Sheridan*, II, 414). For Pitt's condition in the same month see p. 594, n4 above.

he went on to 'remind' Pitt 'of the danger of provoking that claim to be asserted which he observed had not yet been preferred'.[1] Once again the Minister seized on the remark to 'unwhig the gentleman', and when the debate was adjourned to the 16th it was clear that his remarks had told.

More predictably perhaps, Government had also done well in the Lords. Helped by Fox's blunder of the day before, it secured agreement on the 11th for a committee to examine precedents, and a further debate on the 15th went decidedly its way. The occasion was notable for Thurlow's speech, in which he suddenly interrupted his constitutional argument with a sobbing declaration of gratitude for the King's 'many favours . . . which, when he forget, may God forget him!' The Chamber was crowded with Members from the Commons, who were stupefied by the performance. 'Forget you', Wilkes is supposed to have muttered, 'He'll see you damned first'; Burke, so the story goes, exclaimed 'The best thing that can happen to you'; and Pitt, repeating 'Oh what a rascal', walked out of the House.[2] The speech was a sign of the effect of the Commons' debates; so too was one by the Duke of York, disclaiming his brother's intention of claiming the Regency as of right. As the opening period of the new Parliament ended, the Ministry could therefore feel relieved.

But the future was still full of hazard, and Opposition still full of hope. Its leaders were far from united, their intrigues and backbiting continued, the first sanguine expectations had lessened; but the situation had not really changed. The King was still incapable, the Regency must come, and Pitt could not avoid for very much longer the task of proposing what form it should take. Despite fleeting moments of depression Fox remained sublimely confident, and on the eve of the next debate the betting at Brooks's on the division was even. Thurlow may have been veering away – not that that worried Fox, who had always opposed his inclusion –, but there were signs that others were beginning to veer towards the Prince. Carlton House was active, and had hopes (some justified) of some wavering peers and MPs and boroughmongers; and, as in 1784, a central uncommitted group was beginning to emerge. Known as the 'Armed Neutrality', under the leadership of Lord Rawdon and the Duke of Northumberland, this was rumoured by mid-December to include about 20 peers and 30 MPs. When the Commons' debate was resumed on 16 December, Opposition was therefore confident of better results.

The formation of the Armed Neutrality was hastened by the belief that Pitt was about to propose his long awaited restrictions on the Regency. Opposition and the Prince himself were under the same impression. The Prince complained through Thurlow on the 15th (as he had done ten days earlier) that he had been given no information

1. *P.R.*, XXV, 45.
2. Stanhope, II, 10. See *P.R.*, XXVI, 29–30 for Thurlow's speech.

in advance, and the Lord Chancellor argued in the Lords against 'the discussion of unnecessary questions'. But Thurlow was not in the Minister's confidence, and Pitt did not in fact intend, as he now informed the Prince, 'to lay before the House' in the forthcoming debate 'the particulars of . . . a plan'.[1] His tactics were still to delay, and to pursue the question of right; and the resolutions which he moved on the 16th centred on that point. He asked the Commons to vote for two resolutions: that the King's 'personal exercise of the Royal authority' was 'interrupted'; and that it was 'the right and duty' of the Lords and Commons 'to provide the means of supplying the defect'. These objects allowed him to concentrate on the arguments suggested by precedents; and despite good speeches by Fox and North, and the emergence of a body of 'neutrals and wavering people', at the end of a long day he won the division by 268 to 204.[2]

It was the worst blow yet for Opposition. On the eve of the debate they had been hoping for just short of 250 votes, and they had certainly not expected to be 'shockingly beat'.[3] Their first reaction was to trust that the restrictions which Pitt would now advance would prove acceptable, and the Ministry for its part was delighted and surprised at the result.[4] Sheridan tried to rally the forces, and persuade the Armed Neutrality to bring forward amendments; but the dissensions flourished more strongly than ever, and over the next fortnight Government clinched its success. Amendments and postponements were moved in the Commons on the 18th and 19th and 22nd; but when the vote was taken they were defeated, by 251 to 178. The resolutions then passed through the Lords on 26 and 29 December, the vital second resolution by 99 votes to 66.[5] A further sign of the way things were going was furnished on the 25th, when Thurlow met Fox to tell him that he was ending his talks with Opposition. By the end of the year Pitt had thus won the first stage of the Parliamentary battle. He must now move to the delicate business of framing his detailed proposals.

While the debates were under way, public opinion was shaping, in much the same way that it had done in 1784. There are indeed strong similarities between the two occasions, particularly as far as Pitt

---

1. For the exchange of letters (and the date of the Prince's) see *Correspondence of George Prince of Wales*, I, nos. 361–2; for Thurlow's remark in the Lords, *P.R.*, XXVI, 34.

2. *P.R.*, XXV, 48–90. For the neutrals and waverers see Buckingham, II, 63.

3. Sir Gilbert Elliot to Lady Elliot, 18 December (*Life and Letters*, I, 248). For the earlier calculation of numbers see *Correspondence of George Prince of Wales*, I, no. 364, n1.

4. *Correspondence of George Prince of Wales*, I, no. 364, n5; Grenville to Buckingham, 17 December 1788 (Buckingham, II, 63).

5. *P.R.*, XXV, 95–153; XXVI, 40–88. Camden (a former Lord Chancellor), not Thurlow, had been placed in charge of the business in the Lords.

Lord Thurlow *by Reynolds*

The Choir of St Paul's, 23 April 1789. *Engraved by R. Pollard*

himself was concerned. In December 1788 he won his Parliamentary divisions, as he could not do five years before; but his strategy was essentially the same, to hang on and delay in the hope that the King's power and, as far as possible, feeling in the country would come to his aid. No effort was spared by either side to enlist popular support. The Ministry made full use of its newspapers, and advised and spent freely in the cause. Opposition of course did the same, and with some success. There were signs of wobbling in some Government journals – *The Morning Chronicle* and *The World* are interesting examples –, and at the end of the year Carlton House pulled off a notable coup. Acting through the Prince's *maître d'hôtel*, the Dutchman Louis Weltje, it managed to buy *The Morning Post*, hitherto a Ministerialist organ. It now had at least three major London dailies firmly committed; it produced its full share of pamphlets and leaflets; and in the course of December, after a slow start, its caricaturists published a spate of prints.

But despite these vigorous efforts, the tide swung relentlessly towards Pitt. One of the main uses of the newspapers was to report the meetings in the country, held, as in 1784, to send addresses to Parliament. The battle of the addresses began late in December, the corporation of Cambridge taking the lead, and Government's victory there was a foretaste of what was soon to come. The City of London was also stirring: a meeting of merchants and bankers voted a favourable address early in January 1789, and a subscription of £100,000, promised a week or two before with the object of meeting Pitt's debts, was an impressive earnest of personal support even though the Minister refused to accept it.[1] Preparations were also on foot in the constituencies, in case there should be a general election. Opposition's efforts have already been noted: they began seriously in December, when William Adam took charge.[2] Ministerialists were equally alert: Grenville was thinking about Buckinghamshire as early as November, and the next month the Pittites in York were busy distributing coals to the poor.[3] Such signs of impending developments multiplied in January, as the Parliamentary fight moved towards a climax.

But Government's efforts would have lost much of their force if Pitt could not still have counted on important medical support. Only so long as this was available could the Ministry be sustained. Willis, aided by his son, was now firmly in charge, and, secure in the Queen's confidence, he commanded enough weight to balance the indecision or pessimism of his colleagues. Despite frequent setbacks he remained optimistic, he hailed every hint of recovery, and on 18 December Pitt received a particularly sanguine report. The Ministry's hand was thus greatly strengthened in the first phase of the Parliamentary struggle, as the politicians waited to see how the King progressed.

1. See p. 603, n1 above.
2. P. 616 above.
3. Buckingham, I, 434; Derry, op. cit., 117.

On 30 December, the day after the Lords passed his resolutions, Pitt sent his plan for the Regency to the Prince of Wales. It is hard to tell for how long it had been discussed in detail – possibly, in specific form, for not more than a week, but the final provisions were vetted by Chief Justice Kenyon and the Cabinet was fully involved[1]. The Prince was to exercise the royal authority, subject to four restrictions. The care of the King's person and the direction of his Household should be vested in the Queen; the Prince should not be empowered to grant any part of the King's real or personal estate; he should not have the power to grant any office in reversion, or any pension or office whatever, except those that by law must be filled for life or on good behaviour, other than on the term of His Majesty's pleasure; and he should not be able to bestow any peerage except on the King's issue, when any of them had attained the age of 21.[2] These were tough conditions indeed, and it was not surprising that the Prince should have protested strongly to the Cabinet, in an able and dignified letter drafted, it would seem, mainly by Burke.[3] The limitations placed on the granting of offices and pensions, and the refusal to allow the creation of peers, removed some of the most effective and intimate attributes of the prerogative, and must hamper severely any Ministry that the Regent might appoint.[4] Pitt was framing his proposals openly 'on the supposition that his Majesty's illness is only temporary and may be of no long duration'. If unfortunately recovery was delayed 'to a more distant period', Parliament could then always 'reconsider' them.[5] The whole policy in fact was an uncompromising assertion of Parliamentary right, and the provisions were pointed unambiguously against the Prince.

Pitt presented the resolutions to the Commons on 16 January 1789. Some delay – the Prince having replied on the 2nd – was caused initially by a sudden piece of business. For on that same day, the 2nd, the Speaker died, and a successor had to be chosen forthwith. The result

1. The evidence of dates is slender. Pitt wrote on the evening of Christmas day asking Kenyon to call on the 26th, as he wanted very much to see him on the 'legal question' (Kenyon Mss). Kenyon's diary for December (Kenyon Mss) shows him dining or breakfasting three times with Thurlow from the 23rd to the 30th (as he did quite regularly throughout the crisis), which may have been significant, and Grenville suggests that Ministers had agreed on 'the outlines of their plan' by the 28th (to Buckingham; Buckingham, II, 80). But it is difficult to say exactly when the provisions, in the form that they were sent, began to be drawn up.

2. Pitt to the Prince of Wales, 30 December 1788 (*Correspondence of George Prince of Wales*, I, no. 371). His draft of the letter is in P.R.O. 30/8/105.

3. Prince of Wales to Pitt, 2 January 1789 (*Correspondence*, I, no. 375; and see also no. 373). For the letter's address, see p. 631 above.

4. Professor Aspinall states (*Correspondence of George Prince of Wales*, I, 353) that a fifth and even more serious restriction, that the Regent should be debarred from dissolving Parliament, had also been thought of, but dropped.

5. To the Prince of Wales (loc. cit., no. 371).

once again was a triumph for Government. Opposition, uncertain of its aims, was slow to move, and by the time that it did so clearly, on the 4th, the Ministerial candidate had been known and canvassed for two days. He was William Grenville, who bowed rather reluctantly to the Cabinet's, and particularly no doubt to Pitt's, pressure; and he was duly elected on the 5th by 215 votes to 144.[1] It was a Ministerial success in two respects: Pitt had placed a close confidant in the chair for the critical debates, and he had hurried through a process which might have been opposed on constitutional grounds in the absence of the normal royal approbation. The way was now open, on the 6th, for discussion of the restrictions. But Opposition then postponed this further by a change of tactics. The situation indeed was becoming more and more curious. The old party roles were already reversed, Fox appearing as the champion of the prerogative and Pitt of the liberties of the two Houses:[2] now the Prince's supporters, recently so determined to force the pace, appeared to be playing for time. They called, though cautiously and rather confusedly, for a fresh examination into the King's health before the Regency plan was considered – a move perhaps designed to give them time to solve their continuing disputes and rally their dispirited forces, and also to make Pitt appear evasive if he would not comply. He was not in fact anxious to do so; he probably wished to build on his recent successes, and it was always possible that the assembled doctors would give Opposition an excuse to throw doubt on Willis's views. But he thought it best to give way, in order no doubt to placate the neutrals, and the examination, by the same Commons' committee,[3] began on the 7th.

It lasted five days, and the proceedings filled some 400 folio pages. Though Willis had some bad moments, he emerged essentially unscathed. When Pitt presented the report to the Commons it passed the House without a division, despite an attempt by Burke to move for its recommitment. Three days later the Minister introduced the restrictions of which he had informed the Prince over a fortnight before. They followed exactly the digest in his letter.[4] The ensuing debate opened with an amendment proposed by Powys, the veteran independent, giving the Prince the power to exercise the royal authority in full. It was defeated by 227 votes to 154, and Pitt's motion to consider the resolutions then passed unopposed. Further amendments by Opposition were rejected on the 19th – in two cases by 229 to 165, and 220 to 164 –,[5] the resolutions were then passed, and went up to

1. *P.R.*, XXV, 158.
2. In mid-December the MP Sir William Young saw handbills stuck up on Devonshire House 'in which a few words of *Fox for the Prince's prerogative*, and of Pitt, in reply for privilege of Parliament and liberties of the nation, were not badly selected' (to Buckingham, 13 December 1788; Buckingham, II, 58.)
3. Pp. 653–4 above.
4. See *P.R.*, XXV, 188–96.
5. Loc. cit., 245, 286–7.

the Lords. Over the 22nd and the 23rd they were passed by the upper House, the majorities ranging between 94 to 68 and 92 to 64.[1] A method however had still to be found of giving an equivalent of the royal assent to a bill, and debates took place on that problem in the Commons from 2 to 5 February. Despite a last-ditch effort by Burke, Government then carried a motion to put the Great Seal into commission and affix it to measures passed by both Houses. With this 'necessary fiction', again suggested by precedents,[2] Pitt was able to introduce the bill on the 5th. It passed the Commons on the 12th, and on the 16th the Lords began their debates.

Opposition had thus failed again, on ground that might reasonably have been expected to be more favourable to them. Pitt's policy of restrictions, one might have thought, would have brought them added strength from the neutrals and waverers, whether all these had joined the Armed Neutrality or not. Some of the respected independents who had been uneasy in the spring were indeed being heard again now, and by the beginning of February the leaders of the Neutrality felt strong enough to bargain for some posts when the Regent took over.[3] But in the event the numbers, in rather lower divisions, showed no proportionate increase from those in December, and the Ministry carried its tough provisions with remarkable success. The reason lay partly in the tactics and behaviour of the Opposition leaders. By his blunders at the start Fox had made much the same mistake (though by an opposite approach) as in 1784: he had scared much respectable opinion, and achieved the fatal combination of alienating many country gentlemen as well as the Crown. His claims for the Prince indeed appeared particularly odd coming when they did, at the end of a year in which the Whig clubs had been actively preparing for the centenary of the Glorious Revolution. The more moderate speeches from Opposition in January, the formal acceptance of the restrictions by Carlton House, the hard terms of some of the restriction themselves, could not wholly undo this damage; and the position was not made any better by the continued manœuvring and bickering among the Prince's advisers. Their incessant and feverish Cabinet making, and the accompanying quarrels, were widely known, and Fox's own behaviour put the seal

1. *P.R.*, XXVI, 128, 150.

2. See p. 650 above, and, for a legal explanation, Holdsworth, *A History of English Law*, X, 443–4.

3. It would be interesting to know more about the composition and discipline of this body, to see how far it incorporated the peers and MPs who had figured in the abortive movement of May (p. 615 above). In mid-December it was said to comprise 'about thirty in the Commons & twenty in the Lords', and among the former were said to be Sir John Sinclair and John Pollexfen Bastard. (Sir John Eden to William Eden, 15 December 1788; quoted in Derry, op. cit., 93–4). The three division lists that survive for the crisis (*P.R.*, XXV, 90–5, 289–96, 465–71; Stockdale's *Debates*, XVI, 89–98) show several of the signatories of May voting against Government at different times.

on this impression. Unable to throw off his illness, which dogged him throughout January, he retreated to Bath at the end of the month. In his absence, which lasted several weeks, the lack of control became ever more obvious, and in the debates of February only Burke, taking an increasingly independent line, made much of a stand. The genuine uneasiness with which some of the neutrals viewed the Ministry's policy was thus allowed very largely to run to waste.

The feeling in both Houses was perhaps further affected, and Opposition's troubles were certainly heightened, by the growing signs of its unpopularity in the country. In the first shock of George III's illness the public seems suddenly to have woken up to the fact that, by and large, it had become fond of the King. His popularity had been rising for some time, notably so since 1786 when there had been an attempt on his life by a lunatic. It was increased by the rising dislike of the Prince of Wales, with his debts, his rumoured marriage, and his rudeness to his parents. The rackety ménage of Carlton House was by no means to everyones taste, and in 1787 he was already said to have 'contriv'd . . . to shake the affections, and to diminish, if not forfeit the respect' of the people.[1] His behaviour now – the jokes and gibes at Brooks's, the quarrel with the Queen, the eager expectation of power – shook and disgusted a public well supplied with rumour and news. His friends as usual made their contribution to the feeling of uneasiness: Sheridan for instance managed to be evicted from his lodgings in the middle of the crisis, and took up quarters at Mrs Fitzherbert's. It was all grist to the mills of the caricaturists and the Government pamphleteers, and it must have played its part in swelling the tide of petitions and addresses that were now gathering pace. Opposition had its successes – a large meeting at the St Alban's Tavern in London went decidedly in its favour – but the Ministerialist efforts brought much greater rewards. By 16 January 45 addresses of support had been received, and the flow continued over the rest of the month. Fox's ill-health and Opposition's disunity wrecked the plans for a great meeting in his stronghold of Westminster, and, just as in 1784, he could never claim proof of popular support. Adam's preparations for an election, and the party's hopes for a belated swing of fortune, could not disguise the fact that by February they had lost every stage of the campaign so far.

IV

But when all this has been said, in the first half of February Pitt was running out of time. His success in January had been due mainly, in the last resort, to the continued uncertainty about the King. As long as there seemed to be a real chance of George III's recovery before the

1. *A Short Review of the Political State of Great-Britain*, 16–17.

Regency began, the 'rats' would tend to stick to the ship. Some, it is true, were showing signs of leaving, and a few had already done so, most notably Lord Lonsdale, the great boroughmonger to whom Pitt had once owed his seat and whom he had made a peer. His members had voted with Opposition since December, and others were beginning to waver as they or their patrons recalculated the odds. But the Ministry's ranks in general remained steady, and Opposition's mistakes kept 'them so as the deadline came closer with the last debates on the Regency bill. For Pitt, triumphant as he had proved himself, had now done all he could: indeed his very triumph ensured that he could do no more. He had exploited his opponents' follies, he had kept the Prince out of power for three months, and, whatever might happen in the future, had effectively clipped the Regent's wings. But the Regency could now be delayed no longer, for the Lords went into committee on 16 February and the final outcome was not in any doubt. The Great Seal would be affixed to the bill, as the Minister had proposed, and it was pretty certain that the Government would then be changed and he himself dismissed.[1] Pitt had put a good face on the prospects;[2] but he had always assumed that he would go once the Prince took over, and he was indeed supposed to have made his arrangements to return to his practice at the Bar.[3] By the middle of February his moral victory was virtually complete. But it had not removed – indeed it had virtually ensured – his probable removal from office.

And then, at the last moment, the King recovered, as dramatically as he had fallen ill. He had shown signs of improvement early in the month; but this had happened before, and no one, except perhaps Willis, was prepared to bank on the fact. By the 13th or 14th, however, the other doctors were cautiously optimistic, and on the 17th they announced that the patient was convalescent. On the same day the King sent for the Lord Chancellor, although the latter was warned to avoid talking business, and on the 19th, after a Cabinet meeting, the House of Lords was informed that further discussion of the Regency bill was postponed until the 23rd. It was never resumed. Thurlow saw the King again on the 20th, and gave him a general account of Parliamentary events. It was calmly received, and the Chancellor had another audience on the 22nd. On the 23rd the Prince of Wales and his brother the Duke of York saw their father; and that same evening George III wrote to Pitt, in terms which showed clearly enough that he grasped what had been going on.

---

1. There was a rumour in mid-February that Portland, 'like an honest man', was opposed to a change of Ministry when the Prince became Regent (Lord Herbert to the Reverend W. Coxe, 21 February 1789; *Pembroke Papers* (*1780–1794*), 406–7). But this seems rather unlikely, and in any case the Prince himself was firmly believed to favour dismissal.

2. See p. 580, n4 above.

3. Holland Rose, 413.

It is with infinite satisfaction I renew my correspondence with Mr. Pitt by acquainting him of my having seen the Prince of Wales and my second son. Care was taken that the conversation should be general and cordial: they seemed perfectly satisfied. I chose the meeting should be in the Queen's apartment, that all parties might have that caution which at the present hour could but be judicious.

I desire Mr. Pitt will confer with the Lord Chancellor, that any steps which may be necessary for raising the annual supplies, or any measures that the interests of the nation may require, should not be unnecessarily delayed; for I feel the warmest gratitude for the support and anxiety shown by the nation at large during my tedious illness, which I should ill requite if I did not wish to prevent any further delay in those public measures which it may be necessary to bring forward this year, though I must decline entering into a pressure of business, and indeed for the rest of my life shall expect others to fulfil the duties of their employments, and only keep that superintending eye which can be effected without labour or fatigue.

I am anxious to see Mr. Pitt any hour that may suit him to-morrow morning, as his constant attachment to my interest and that of the public, which are inseparable, must ever place him in the most advantageous light.[1]

The interview took place the next day. 'The King spoke of his disorder as of a thing past';[2] and so indeed it was, for no further disturbance occurred. On 27 February the medical bulletins ceased, and despite Opposition's hopes of a relapse the crisis in fact was over.

The political situation returned to normal at once. 'The vessel has righted again', wrote one of William Eden's correspondents on the day that Pitt saw the King,[3] and the waverers and renegades were quick to make their peace. A similar process took place in Dublin, where the Irish Parliament had been causing great difficulties, stimulated by the prospect of asserting its independence. Government had in fact been defeated there early in February, and while the British Commons were passing Pitt's final measures the Irish had been busy composing a loyal address to the Prince. Now all such hopes of a separate line – of making a reality of the constitution of 1782[4] – had been dashed, and the Lord Lieutenant and Pitt himself prepared to take revenge. The experience of 1789 indeed did much to strengthen Pitt's dislike of the Parliament in Dublin, already aroused by his experience in 1785, and it was to affect his treatment of Ireland in the next decade. Meanwhile the rats ran

1. Stanhope, II, Appendix, vi-vii.
2. Grenville to Buckingham, 24 February 1789, relaying Pitt's account of the conversation (Buckingham, II, 125).
3. Anthony Storer to Eden, 24 February 1789; quoted in Derry, op. cit., 190.
4. See p. 196 above.

for cover, the Irish Opposition retreated, and on both sides of the water the Ministry resumed its sway.

After a pause for breath, the celebrations began. On 10 March the session of Parliament was formally opened with the reading of the King's Speech, and that night London was illuminated in 'a blaze or masses of light'.[1] The crowds were so great that Gilbert Elliot, on his way from Brooks's, could make his way down St James's Street only 'by creeping under horses and coaches', and William Windham and his party could not get into 'the best streets' at all.[2] The festivities and illuminations continued at intervals throughout the country for the next six weeks, and in the capital itself there was a series of set pieces. On 26 March the Queen held a Drawing Room at St James's to celebrate the King's recovery, for which Pitt and others gave dinners in advance. The rooms were crowded, and the ladies wore 'caps' and ribbons with loyal inscriptions, the Whig ladies making a point of attending in force. On 2 April there was a concert and supper at Windsor, the tone of which aroused Opposition's wrath. The supper table in St George's Hall was decorated with devices, including the Lord Chancellor's arms and, before Pitt's place, a frame supporting his arms 'and the number 268, the first Majority in the House of Commons, written in sugar-plums or sweetmeats'. 'All this', wrote one Opposition Member, 'is quite new at Court, and most excessively indecent, as the King is always expected to be of *no party*'.[3] Thurlow himself may perhaps have been relieved, and Pitt quietly amused, by the conjunction of their devices after all that had passed.

Meanwhile at the end of March White's had held a victory ball at the Pantheon, which by all accounts was a very splendid affair. The building was illuminated and hung with devices, some 2,000 people were present, and dancing – mostly country reels and dances – went on into the early hours. The Ministerialist ladies wore white and gold dresses, with loyal inscriptions as at the Drawing Room, but on this occasion the leading Opposition ladies stayed away. Pitt, in high spirits, supped in a party which included the Duchess of Gordon, Dundas, and Dr Willis – a very different appearance from the evening nine years before when he stood in his domino unrecognised and alone.[4] Some three weeks later Brooks's staged a rival ball at the Opera House, attended

1. *Life and Letters of Sir Gilbert Elliot*, I, 281.
2. Ibid; *The Diary of the Right Hon. William Windham 1784 to 1810*, ed. Mrs Henry Baring (1866), 166–7.
3. *Life and Letters of Elliot*, 300. And cf. *Gleanings from an Old Portfolio*, 123. The decorations were widely ascribed to the Queen, who had earlier infuriated the two elder Princes by suggesting that they might wish to stay away.
4. See p. 22 above. *Gleanings from an Old Portfolio*, 122; *The Public Advertiser*, 2 April 1789; *The Diary; or, Woodfall's Register*, 3 April 1789.

by some 1,200 people, to which the Ministerialist ladies were careful to go.

The Opposition's ball was held on the eve of the climax of the celebrations. On 23 April, St George's day, the King and Queen went to St Paul's for a thanksgiving service. They passed through crowded streets to the firing of guns and the ringing of church bells, and up the great nave, lined with grenadiers and beefeaters, and beneath the dome to their seats in the choir. The King's demeanour was closely watched – he was in Windsor uniform, looking thin and worn, but appeared calm and cheerful and 'perfect in his Manner'.[1] His elder sons' behaviour, on the other hand, was widely condemned. They had put as good a face as possible on the events of the past few weeks, and the Prince of Wales escorted his father to the Queen's house for the procession to the City. But once inside the Cathedral he could not contain himself. 'The Prince of Wales', by one account, 'caught the Duke of York by the shoulder and, pointing to his Royal father and mother, burst into a fit of laughter. The Duke followed his example and laughed so violently that he was obliged to cover his face with his hands'.[2] It was indeed a 'Most offensive' exhibition, a final 'savage instance of heartlessness' which did them 'no good with the public'.[3] When the service was over the King and Queen drove back through the cheering crowds, and London was again illuminated that night, more splendidly than before.

Amid the excitement one figure went his way as quietly as he could. The House of Commons was seated as a body in the choir stalls and galleries, flanking the peers, and Pitt took his place with other Privy Councillors to one side of the floor. He drove to the Cathedral in the Members' procession in a carriage 'with three other gentlemen' and his back to the horses, unnoticed until they reached Fleet Street, 'when a shout of applause burst forth'.[4] On the return journey, however, the people were waiting; they surrounded the carriage and drew it back to Downing Street. It was a repetition of 1784, and a contrast to his experience in 1785;[5] and no doubt he was not much impressed by the fickleness of the mob. But the day was in truth his triumph as much as the King's, and the commentaries recognised the fact. He had again captured the imagination of the country, and even more firmly than five years before. He had never been 'in such high Estimation as he now is'; he had 'reached the summit of human glory'; the Whigs

1. Mrs Stapleton to Hester Countess of Chatham, 24 April 1789 (P.R.O. 30/8/59).

2. Bland Burges's account, unpublished in his *Letters and Correspondence,* in transcript of 'Original Ms. of Hutton Bland-Burges Papers previous to Excisions', 108 (Bodleian Library).

3. Ibid; Mrs Stapleton to Hester Countess of Chatham, 24 April 1789 (P.R.O. 30/8/59).

4. *The Public Advertiser,* 27 April 1789. Thurlow is said to have been cheered, and Fox hissed, along the route.

5. Pp. 140–1, 254 n4 above.

themselves had found that 'Pitt is the only object the nation can perceive'.[1] He had shown an indisputable control of Parliament: Opposition was discredited and depressed, and in his defence of the Crown the Minister had greatly consolidated his own position. The King was his debtor, domestic peace had been preserved and its future was identified with himself; and his victory had its effects abroad as well as at home. Despite recent events it was hailed in France, where Fox was feared as a dangerous enemy, and Hertzberg in Prussia wept with relief on learning that Pitt could continue in office. As he left the Cathedral on that April morning for the thronged and noisy streets, he was the master of the English political scene and a major figure on the European stage. 'This was the moment at which his fame and fortune may be said to have reached the zenith'.[2] Five weeks later he was thirty years old.

1. Lady Stafford to Granville Leveson Gower, 12 February 1789 (*Lord Granville Leveson Gower . . . Private Correspondence*, I, 13–14); Hannah More to her sister, 6 January 1789 (*Memoirs of the Life and Correspondence of Mrs Hannah More*, I (1834), 303); *Life and Letters of Elliot*, I, 248.
2. Macaulay, Essay on William Pitt.

Note on Pitt's Papers

T he papers and correspondence of a leading statesman are liable to be found in a variety of places. Pitt's are no exception. Apart from a group of early letters to Edward Eliot in the Pretyman Mss, a few files among the Chatham Papers at the Public Record Office (some containing originals and others copies), and odd copies and drafts of outgoing correspondence scattered in the departmental archives, his out-letters are to be found in the recipients' papers or in the collections of copies made from them. This note is concerned with the surviving collections of the documents which were in his own possession, and these follow a pattern imposed very largely soon after his death. The bulk of Pitt's papers went to his elder brother and senior executor Chatham, who died childless in 1835. They were then divided between Chatham's two executors, William Henry (later Lieutenant-General Sir William) Pringle, who was the husband of Harriot Hester Eliot, the daughter of Pitt's sister Lady Harriot Eliot, and William Stanhope Taylor, the eldest son of Pitt's other sister Lady Mahon's third daughter, Lucy Rachael Stanhope. Pringle's portion, which was much the larger, was deposited by his son John Eliot Pringle in the Public Record Office in 1888, and forms the Chatham Papers, or Class P.R.O. 30/8 as they are now known, which also include (from Pringle's collection) the papers of the first Earl and Countess and the second Earl of Chatham. The younger Pitt's papers comprise volumes P.R.O. 30/8/101–363 of this archive, and volume 373, acquired more recently from a different source. Taylor's portion descended to Sir Timothy Hoare, Bart. Its contents are listed in report 6139 of the National Register of Archives.

A further substantial collection of Pitt's papers, however, went to his former private secretary, and second executor, Bishop Pretyman Tomline. Some of them appear to have been sold or escaped, and can be traced elsewhere; but the main body remained with his family, and is now deposited almost in its entirety in the Ipswich and East Suffolk Record Office. This is the collection referred to in this book as the Pretyman Mss.

Some other papers were acquired later (partly, it would seem, from the Pretyman Mss) by the fifth Earl Stanhope. They remain at Chevening, in Kent.

There are also a few documents which belonged to Pitt among George Rose's papers at the British Museum (Add. Ms 42772), among those of Pretyman's successor as private secretary, Joseph Smith (listed by the National Register of Archives as being in the possession of Mr W. H. Saumarez Smith, and largely calendared in *H.M.C., Twelfth Report, Appendix, Pt. IX*), and in the library of Duke University, North Carolina. Finally, some were removed from 10 Downing Street immediately after Pitt's death by his last secretary, William Dacres Adams. They have now been deposited by a descendant in the Public Record Office (Class P.R.O. 30/58).

Copies were made of some of these papers at different times. The largest collection, assembled from the second Earl of Chatham's archive for Bishop Pretyman Tomline when he was writing his life of Pitt, is in the Cambridge University Library (Add. Mss 6958–9). Copies of George III's correspondence with Pitt are in the English Mss at the John Rylands Library, Manchester, and others are in the William L. Clements Library at the University of Michigan.

A useful guide to the subject has been published by the Historical Manuscripts Commission, *The Prime Ministers' Papers 1801-1902* (1968), compiled by John Brooke. It applies to Pitt's earlier as well as to his later career.

Notes on Sources

For the Pitt family, see Sir Tresham Lever, *The House of Pitt* (1947). There is no comparable history of the Grenvilles, and their collective character may best be studied in *The Grenville Papers* . . ., ed. William James Smith (4 vols., 1852–3); Buckingham (4 vols.) (see Abbreviations, p. xv above); and *H.M.C., Dropmore* (7 vols.) (see Abbreviations).

The history of Hayes Place, referred to in many works of local interest, is given rather more fully in Edward Hasted, *The History and Topographical Survey of Kent* . . . (2nd edn, 1797), and C. Greenwood, *An Epitome of County History* . . ., I (1838). There is a chapter on the Pitts' tenure of the property in Canon [H.P.] Thompson, *A History of Hayes in the County of Kent* (1935). A more detailed picture of Chatham's acquisitions, and of the house itself, may be gained from the following sources in the Kent County Archives at Maidstone: Till Mss U.468, Q.5/1; Norman Mss U.310; Miscellanea, U.47/26, T.1–6. See also John Andrews and A. Drury's 'Topographical-Map of Kent' of 1769 (B.M. Maps, K.1 TAB. 21), and, for a view of the house in the later period of the Pitts' tenure, B.M. Maps 25, c.26, p. 31. There is a contemporary description and view of Burton Pynsent in the Reverend John Collinson, *The History and Antiquities of the County of Somerset*, I (1791), and a later account by Christopher Hussey in *Country Life*, LXXVI, no. 1968.

The main source for Pitt's early years is the correspondence of Chatham, Lady Chatham, William Pitt, Dr Anthony Addington, and the Reverend Edward Wilson, in the Chatham Papers at the Public Record Office: P.R.O. 30/8/1–5, 7–13, 15–16, 67. P.R.O. 30/8/196 and 198 contain scattered notes of his reading at Cambridge. Other early letters and financial memoranda are in the Stanhope Mss at Chevening, in 'Pitt Papers, Part i', 'Mr. Pitt, II', 'Letters from Hester Lady Chatham to Revd. Dr. Wilson, 1765–99', and folders of 'Notes by William Pitt'. Some of Pitt's letters to Wilson, from Cambridge days onwards, are at Duke University, North Carolina. Early verses are in Sir Timothy Hoare's Mss, c/o the National Register of Archives. Some of Mrs Pretyman Tomline's reminiscences are in 'Mr. Pitt, II' at Chevening; others, with some of her husband's, among a section of the latter's papers at Pembroke College, Cambridge (Mss 29, I, 35:3). In the Pretyman Mss themselves, deposited at the Ipswich and East Suffolk Record Office, are letters, notes, and account books relating to Pitt at Cambridge (nos. 435/41, 503:1, 562:26), early financial documents (including the transaction with Solomon Henry) (nos. 435/14, 50/3/177–181), letters from Pitt to Edward Eliot (T.435/39), reminiscences of Pitt on the Western Circuit (no. 562:1820), and the catalogue of his books at his death (no. 562:21).

There is a Ms catalogue at Orwell Park House, Nacton, Suffolk (made by Messrs Hatchards in 1911) of the part of Pitt's library which is now there. Tomline, Stanhope, Ashbourne, and Holland Rose (see Abbreviations) drew in varying degrees on these collections.

Pembroke College, Cambridge, contains other material on Pitt's years at Cambridge. The Sizing Books (exceptionally detailed for the period) may be checked against his correspondence to show, week by week, when he was there and when he was not; the Admission Book gives information on entries to the College during his time; and there is a small collection of correspondence, including Chatham's letter to Turner of October 1773, and a letter from Pitt himself of April 1773 announcing his entry on the books of the College. Much of this material has been used in an article, 'William Pitt and Pembroke', in the *Annual Gazette* of the Pembroke College Society, no. 8, June 1934. The library of Sidney Sussex College, Cambridge, contains John Hey's Ms of his lectures on Morality, in which the preface refers to Pitt's attending some of them from November 1778, on the introduction of J. C. Villiers. For Pitt's attendance at George Atwood's lectures, see *The Gentleman's Magazine*, LXVII, Part II (1807), 690. The *locus classicus* for life in the University in the eighteenth century is D. A. Winstanley, *Unreformed Cambridge* (1935). See also J. P. C. Roach's account in the Victoria County History of *Cambridge and the Isle of Ely*, III (1959), Sir Charles Mallet's ch. XXII in vol. II of *Johnson's England*, ed. A. S. Turberville (1933), and M. L. Clarke, *Classical Education in Britain 1500–1900* (1959). Some valuable light is thrown on the Cambridge ethos by Norman Sykes, *Church and State in England in the XVIII Century* (1934), Caroline Robbins, *The Eighteenth Century Commonwealth Man* (1950), and J. G. A. Pocock, *The Ancient Constitution and the Feudal Law* (1957).

Brian Tunstall, *William Pitt Earl of Chatham* (1938) discusses Chatham's financial expedients in the 1770s. Messrs Coutts's Ledgers for 1779 to 1781 give details of the dealings between Thomas Coutts and his bank on the one hand and Lady Chatham and her children on the other. The Parliamentary debates which Pitt attended from 1778 to 1780 may be established by collating his correspondence with vols. XIX-XXI of *P.H.* (1814) (see Abbreviations). Pembroke College, Cambridge, and Duke University, North Carolina, possess specimens of his letters requesting support for election as one of the Burgesses for Cambridge University in 1780; Daniel Cook's unpublished thesis, 'The Representative History of the County, Town and University of Cambridge, 1689–1832' (1935) sketches the background. On the general election itself, see Ian R. Christie, *The End of North's Ministry 1780–1782* (1958).

CHAPTER II

The two most reliable accounts of the Parliamentary buildings in the old Palace of Westminster are Maurice Hastings's *Parliament House* (1950) – which should, however, be used with some caution in its remarks on the procedure of the Commons – and an unpublished monograph by Orlo Cyprian Williams, 'The Topography of the Old House of Commons' (1953). There are three copies of the latter, of which I have consulted the one in the library of the Ministry of Works at Lambeth. The clerical organisation of the

House is described in the same author's *The Clerical Organization of the House of Commons 1661–1850* (1954). *H. of P.*, I (see Abbreviations) is an authoritative general survey, as II and III are the source of biographical detail, from 1760 to 1784. For membership, procedure and customs see also Edward and Annie G. Porritt, *The Unreformed House of Commons* (2 vols., 1909), Josef Redlich, *The Procedure of the House of Commons* (3 vols., 1908), and, for the conventions of the later eighteenth century in particular, John Hatsell's *Precedents of Proceedings in the House of Commons* (4 vols., 1781; new edn, 1818). Eight articles by A. Aspinall, 'The Old House of Commons and its Members (c. 1783–1832)' (*Parliamentary Affairs*, XIV and XV), give a vivid impression of life in the Chamber. For the constituencies, see, in addition to *H. of P.* and Porritt, T. H. B. Oldfield, *The Representative History of Great Britain and Ireland . . .* (6 vols., 1816). A. S. Turberville, *The House of Lords in the XVIII Century* (1927), is the standard authority on the subject to 1784.

Recent research into Parliamentary history in the second half of the century has been profoundly affected by the two books of Sir Lewis Namier, *The Structure of Politics at the Accession of George III* (for which the second edition of 1957 should be used), and *England in the Age of the American Revolution* (1930). Of his many reviews and addresses, 'Monarchy and the Party System' and 'Country Gentlemen in Politics, 1750 to 1784' may be noted particularly: both are published in *Personalities and Powers* (1955). Some of the inferences drawn from these and other works are challenged by Herbert Butterfield in *George III and the Historians* (1957), and by W. R. Fryer in 'The Study of British Politics between the Revolution and the Reform Act' in *University of Nottingham Renaissance and Modern Studies*, I (1957). Richard Pares, *King George III and the Politicians* (1953) is a stimulating study of political behaviour throughout the reign. Betty Kemp, *King and Commons 1660–1832* (1957) links recent research into the anatomy of politics with an older constitutional tradition. Archibald S. Foord examines the problems from the point of view of *His Majesty's Opposition 1714–1830* (1964); Corinne Comstock Weston discusses *English Constitutional Theory and the House of Lords 1556–1832* (1965). Sir William Holdsworth's account of 'The Historical Background' in ch. I, vol. X of *A History of English Law* (1938) is a classic. Christie (see ch. I) is indispensable for the Parliament elected in 1780.

CHAPTER III

There is no single reliable source for Pitt's speeches. The standard collection is *The Speeches of the Right Honourable William Pitt, in the House of Commons*, ed. W. S. Hathaway (4 vols., 1806), which however ŏmits almost all the budget speeches. This drew principally on 'the journals of Debrett and Woodfall [see below], and . . . other public reports of admitted authenticity'; in a few cases on reports revised by Pitt himself; and in others on those of Members who had been present. The 'public reports of admitted authenticity' are themselves of various kinds. The best single text for the 1780s is probably that of *The Parliamentary Register* published by Debrett for the years 1781 onwards [*P.R.*], which normally gives a fuller account, and one brought out much nearer the time, than that of *The Parliamentary History of England* [*P.H.*] edited by William Cobbett and published (first by him and then by T. C. Hansard) between 1806 and 1820. Debrett and Cobbett, however, should always be compared, for they do not always draw on the same material. (For debates from 1784 onwards, see also Note on Sources to ch. VIII below.)

This material is to be found mainly in newspaper reports, supplemented – particularly in the case of *P.R.* – by drafts and corrections on the part of Members, by their reminiscences, and possibly by notes taken during, or in the early eighties more often immediately after, a debate, which the editors were unable to use fully in the space available. The most reliable reports in the early eighties are probably those in 'Memory' Woodfall's *The Morning Chronicle, & London Advertiser* (supporting the Rockingham, later Foxite, party), and in *The Morning Herald, & Daily Advertiser* (supporting the Government of the day). Both were daily journals. *The London Evening Post*, appearing twice a week, generally follows *The Morning Herald*, but occasionally has its own material, which sometimes appears in *P.R.* The files of these three papers are reasonably complete in the Burney Collection in the British Museum: those of others, such as *The Morning Post,* much less so. The monthly *Gentleman's Magazine* and *London Magazine*, which had earlier furnished the best Parliamentary reports, had now been overtaken in this respect by the daily and bi-weekly papers.

There is a list of published collections of debates in H. Hale Bellot, 'General Collections of Reports of Parliamentary Debates for the Period since 1660' (*Bulletin of the Institute of Historical Research*, X, 171–7). It is supplemented by A. Aspinall, 'The Reporting and Publishing of the House of Commons' Debates 1771–1834' (*Essays Presented to Sir Lewis Namier*, ed. Richard Pares and A. J. P. Taylor (1956), 227–57), which also gives an excellent account of the conditions under which Parliamentary reporters worked. The effect of newspapers' political bias is discussed more fully in ch. XIX below.

Brian Tunstall's *William Pitt Earl of Chatham* (see Note to ch. I), ch. XVIII, gives a brief, lucid account of Chatham's final views on peace with America. Sources for Shelburne are contained in the Note to ch. IV below. Evidence of his support for Pitt in the Cambridge by-election of 1780 is to be found in a letter from Pitt to Shelburne of March 1780, in the Shelburne Papers at the William L. Clements Library, University of Michigan, and in one from the Duke of Grafton to Shelburne, 7 or 9 November 1780, in Lord Lansdowne's papers at Bowood (microfilm in the archives of the History of Parliament Trust). For Rutland's support on the same occasion, see *H.M.C., Rutland,* IV, 239–40, and *H.M.C., Fourteenth Report, Appendix, Pt. I,* 18–19, 30–1. For Pitt's visits to Shelburne and Camden between 1778 and 1781, and Shelburne's part in the affair of James Charles Pitt, see correspondence in P.R.O. 30/8/12.

The two best works on the intricate history of the reform movement in the late 1770s and the '80s, and the various groups' relations with the Parliamentary parties, are those by George Stead Veitch, *The Genesis of Parliamentary Reform* (2nd edn, 1965), and I. R. Christie, *Wilkes, Wyvill and Reform* (1962). Caroline Robbins (see Note to ch. I), and Eugene Charlton Black, *The Association; British ExtraParliamentary Political Organization 1769–1793* (1963), are very useful for background and organisation. H. Butterfield, *George III, Lord North and the People 1779–80* (1949) discusses the events of the movement's most exciting period. The Reverend Christopher Wyvill's *Political Papers . . . chiefly respecting a Reformation of the Parliament of Great Britain . . .* (6 vols., 1794–1804) are the main published source for the Yorkshire Association and its links with Pitt: volume II contains Wyvill's own publications, including his open letters to Pitt. Their correspondence in the Chatham Papers (P.R.O. 30/8/192) contains nothing of substance that has not been published; nor is there anything of interest in that collection from other prominent reformers. P.R.O. 30/8/234 has two undated drafts in Pitt's hand on matters affecting electoral reform, and a paper of 1 May 1783 on the proposal for an extra hundred members. In view of the newswriters' absence from the gallery, Romilly's account of Pitt's speech of 7 May 1782, in *Memoirs of the Life of Sir Samuel Romilly . . .* ed. by his Sons, I (1840), 221–3, is of interest. *The Life and Correspondence of Major Cartwright*, ed. by his niece, F. D. Cartwright (2 vols., 1826) has a few references to Pitt from the point of view of the founder of the Society for Promoting Constitutional Information. For Mahon, see Ghita Stanhope and G. P. Gooch, *The Life of Charles Third Earl Stanhope* (1914); for Richmond, Alison Gilbert Olson, *The Radical Duke* (1961). The views of the Rockinghams may be gathered from George Thomas, Earl of Albemarle, *Memoirs of the Marquis of Rockingham and his Contemporaries* (2 vols., 1852), and N. C. Phillips, 'Edmund Burke and the County Movement, 1779–1780' (*E.H.R.*, LXXVI, no. 299). For Fox, see Note to ch. IV below.

CHAPTER IV

There is a good survey of the political events of this confused period in Steven Watson, *The Reign of George III 1760–1815* (1960), ch. X. The most searching examination of Shelburne's peace negotiations is in Vincent T. Harlow, *The Founding of the Second British Empire 1763–1793*, I (1952), chs. VI–IX; Richard B. Morris, *The Peacemakers, The Great Powers and American Independence* (1966) covers the whole European field. For Rockingham, see also the Note on Sources to ch. III. Shelburne provoked much contemporary discussion: for an interesting view from a senior official, see the account by William Knox of the American Department in *H.M.C., Various Collections*, VI, 281–6. Shelburne's own attitude appears in Lord Edmond Fitzmaurice, *Life of William, Earl of Shelburne, afterwards First Marquess of Lansdowne* (3 vols., 1875–6), particularly vol. III, and in John Norris, *Shelburne and Reform* (1963). Peter Brown, *The Chathamites, A Study in the Relationship between Personalities and Ideas in the Second Half of the Eighteenth Century* (1967) discusses Shelburne's role in the transmission of policies and attitudes. For Fox, see *Memorials and Correspondence of Charles James Fox*, ed. Lord John Russell, (2 vols., 1853), particularly vol. II: of the various biographies – none entirely satisfactory – those by Christopher Hobhouse (1934) and Edward Lascelles (1936) are the most useful. *The Autobiography and Political Correspondence of Augustus Henry Third Duke of Grafton*, ed. Sir William Reynell Anson (1898), Cyril Matheson, *The Life of Henry Dundas* (1933), Buckingham, I (see Abbreviations), and *H.M.C., Dropmore*, I (see Abbreviations), throw various lights on the decline of Shelburne's Ministry. *A.C.*, I (see Abbreviations), and Reginald Lucas, *Lord North, Second Earl of Guilford . . . 1732–1792*, II (1913), assess events from the point of view of North's party. The King's position is very clearly stated in *The Correspondence of King George III from 1760 to 1783*, ed. the Hon. Sir John Fortescue, VI (1928), the contents of which need to be checked with the originals in the Royal Archives at Windsor. Some additional information can be obtained from Charles Jenkinson's correspondence in B.M. Add. Mss 38309 and 38567, from John Robinson's correspondence in B.M. Add. Ms 37835 and *H.M.C., Tenth Report, Appendix, Pt. VI*, and from Shelburne's papers in the William L. Clements Library, University of Michigan, and in the possession of Lord Landsowne at Bowood. The main collections of Dundas's papers, in the National Library of Scotland, the Scottish Record Office and the John Rylands Library, Manchester, contain nothing of importance for this period that is not published. Pitt's position is fully covered in Stanhope, Holland Rose, and the publications mentioned above. There are some notes by him on the peace treaties in P.R.O. 30/8/196. Edmund C. Burnett has published from the Pretyman Mss some 'Observations of London Merchants on American Trade, 1783' (*The American Historical Review*, XVIII, no. 4), which Pitt may have used in preparing his bill on the subject.

For the Rockinghams' and Shelburne's administrative reforms, see, in addition, the articles by Keir and by Foord in Note on Sources to ch. VII below; Betty Kemp, 'Crewe's Act, 1782' (*E.H.R.*, LXVIII, no. 267); I. R. Christie, 'Economical Reform and the Influence of the Crown' (*The Cambridge Historical Journal*, XII, no. 2); and Binney (Note on Sources to ch. VII). The Treasury Board Minutes in P.R.O., T. 29/52, 29/53 are useful for Shelburne's Administration, and Pitt's part in the administrative programme is illuminated by papers in P.R.O. 30/8/231 and 285. *P.R.*, IX–XI (1783–4) and *H.C.J.* 39 should be consulted for the fate of Pitt's two bills from April to July 1783.

CHAPTER V

For the repairs and alterations to 10 Downing Street, see *Survey of London*, XIV (1931), 121–2; for the sale of Pitt's chambers in Lincoln's Inn, Augustus Greenland's bill for 1783 in miscellaneous notes on Pitt in Stanhope Mss. The date of Pitt's joining White's is given in *The History of White's . . .* pubd. by the Hon. Algernon Bourke, II (n.d. but 1892), Pt. II, 70. The story of James Goostree and his club is best told in *Survey of London*, XXIX (1960), 334–5, XXX (1960), 469. Robert Isaac Wilberforce and Samuel Wilberforce, *The Life of William Wilberforce*, I (1838), ch. II, and his *Private Papers*, ed. A. M. Wilberforce (1897), are the prime sources for Pitt's social life at this time, to which may be added the other sources quoted in the chapter's textual notes. Mrs Pretyman Tomline records Pitt's weight at the age of fourteen in her notes of 1806 ('Mr. Pitt II', Stanhope Mss); H. Warner Allen, *Number Three Saint James's Street* (1950), 111, his weight in March 1783. His height may be inferred from the suit of his clothes in the London Museum.

For the holiday to France, see Wilberforce, I, and *Mémoires, Correspondance et Manuscrits du Général Lafayette, publiés par sa Famille*, II (1837), 160–1, where Pitt's visit is wrongly attributed to 1786; for Madame Necker's matrimonial plan, Le Vicomte d'Haussonville, *Le Salon de Madame Necker . . .* (1882), II, 52–7. Pitt's ideas of going abroad in 1781 and 1782 are mentioned in his letters to William Meeke of 29 August 1781 and (probably) June 1782, both in 'Pitt Papers, Part I' in Stanhope Mss. *P.R.*, IX-XI, and *P.H.*, XXIII (1814) cover the period April–July 1783. For Fox's suspicions of Pitt in June and his view of the Coalition's prospects in July, see *Memorials of Fox*, ch. II, 113, 118–9; for the King's approach in July, and Pitt's view of the situation in September, Earl Stanhope, *Miscellanies, Second Series* (1872), 23–31, 33–5, *H.M.C., Dropmore*, I, 214–18, and Buckingham I, 303–5. Adam's and Portland's political estimates are cited in *L.C.G. III*, I, xxiii (see Abbreviations).

CHAPTER VI

On the East India Company's affairs I have relied largely on an unpublished paper, 'Pitt and India', by Miss Jean Dawson. Lucy S. Sutherland, *The East India Company in Eighteenth-Century Politics* (1952), and C. H. Philips, 'The East India Company and the English Government, 1783–4', in *Trans. R.H.S., 4th Series*, XX, are authoritative. For Pitt's papers on India, see Note on Sources to ch. VIII below.

The literature on the crisis of 1783–4 is extensive. To the memoirs and biographies cited in Notes to earlier chapters may be added Robert Gore-Browne, *Chancellor Thurlow* (1953); Robinson's papers in B.M. Add. Ms 38567, in B.M. Fascimiles 340 (2) and (5) – some of which are published in *H.M.C., Tenth Report, Appendix, Pt. VI*, and in *Parliamentary Papers of John Robinson 1774–1784*, ed. William Thomas Laprade (1922) – and in the National Library of Scotland, Ms 63B (Dundas's copy); I. R. Christie, 'The Political Allegiance of John Robinson' (*Bulletin of the Institute of Historical Research*, XXIX); Jenkinson's papers in B.M. Add. Mss 38309, 38567; George III's in *L.C.G. III*, I (and the introduction by Professor Aspinall), and in J. Holland Rose, *Pitt and Napoleon, Essays and Letters* (1912), Part II (A); *The Political Memoranda of Francis Fifth Duke of Leeds . . .*, ed. Oscar Browning (1884); *Correspondence between the Right Honble. William Pitt and Charles Duke of Rutland . . . 1781–1787* (1890), and *H.M.C., Fourteenth Report, Appendix, Pt. I;* Keith Grahame Feiling, *The Second Tory Party 1714–1832* (1938), Appendix I. There is nothing in Pitt's own papers, except a few letters in P.R.O. 30/8/12. Opposition's view of the St Alban's negotiations may be followed in *Memorials and Correspondence of Fox*, IV, and B.M. Add. Ms 47561. For Temple's resignation, see E. Anthony Smith's article in *The Historical Journal*, 6, no. 1, as well as the introduction to *L.C.G. III*, I; and William Wyndham Grenville's retrospective draft of his proposed memoirs, 'Commentaries of my own Political Life . . .', in the Fortescue Mss at Boconnoc in Cornwall. I have also benefited from an unpublished paper by Dr Murray S. Downs, 'The British Constitution in 1783: George III Dismisses the Coalition'. Donald Grove Barnes, *George III and William Pitt, 1783–1806* (1939) discusses – to my mind, not entirely convincingly – the roles of the King and the Minister throughout. For caricatures, see M. D. George, *Catalogue of Prints and Drawings in the British Museum: Division I. Political and Personal Satires*, V and VI (1938).

The debates are covered in *P.R.*, XII-XIV (1784), and *P.H.*, XXIII-XXIV (1815). There was a spate of compilations for the period, published mostly by Stockdale, which may be found in the British Museum Catalogue. Dundas held some interesting 'Notes', mdae by someone else, of the debates between 18 November and 17 December 1783 (Scottish Record Office, G.D. 51/3/11/3). For division lists, see *H. of P.*, I, Appendix III.

There is a lively modern literature on the general election. Laprade (see above) first challenged the assumption that the result was a purely popular victory, in articles in *The American Historical Review*, XVIII, and *E.H.R.*, XXXI. His findings are discussed by C. E. Fryer in *History, New Series*, IX, by Mrs Eric George in *Trans. R.H.S., 4th Series*, XXI, and by N. C. Phillips in *Yorkshire & English National Politics 1783–1784* (1961). The most recent view is that of John Brooke in *H. of P.*, I. Some payments for the election are recorded in P.R.O. 30/8/229. For Pitt's fortunes at Bath, see Sir Jerom Murch, *The Elder and Younger Pitt, their Connection with Bath* . . . (privately printed, 1873).

P.R.O. 30/8/315 and B.M. Add. Ms 35382 throw some light on the election for Cambridge University. Details of the poll are to be found in John Beverley's compilation noted on p. 150 above, a synopsis of which appears in Charles Henry Cooper, *Annals of Cambridge*, IV (1852), 412, n2. Daniel Cook's unpublished thesis (see Note on Sources to ch. I above) is also useful.

CHAPTER VII

National statistics are to be found in B. R. Mitchell and Phyllis Deane, *Abstract of British Historical Statistics* (1962), Phyllis Deane and W. A. Cole, *British Economic Growth 1688–1959: Trends and Developments* (2nd edn, 1968), and Elizabeth Boody Schumpeter, *English Overseas Trade Statistics 1697–1800* (1960). For some stimulating comments on the first two works, see J. F. Wright, 'British Economic Growth, 1688–1959', in *Ec.H.R., 2nd Series*, XVIII, no. 2, and articles in the University of Sydney's *Business Archives and History*, IV, no. 1, and VI, no. 2. On the National Debt, see also the book of that name by E. L. Hargreaves (1930). Attitudes and arguments at the end of the American War are still the subject of active debate; for an interesting summing up see Peter Marshall, 'The First and Second British Empires: A Question of Demarcation', in *History*, XLIX, no. 165. Harlow, I, ch. V (see Note on Sources to ch. IV above) is a major contribution.

The literature on the Industrial Revolution is of course enormous. Perhaps the best guides are T. S. Ashton's *The Industrial Revolution 1760–1830* (1948), M. W. Flinn's *Origins of the Industrial Revolution* (1966), and David S. Landes's ch. V in *The Cambridge Economic History of Europe*, VI, Part I (1965). There has recently been much discussion of some of the arguments in a series of articles in *Ec.H.R.* and other journals, of which R. M. Hartwell has edited a selection in *The Causes of the Industrial Revolution* (1967). Two stimulating commentaries by economists are A. J. Youngson's *Possibilities of Economic Progress* (1959), and W. W. Rostow's *The Stages of Economic Growth: A Non-Communist Manifesto* (1960).

There is no detailed comprehensive survey of the system of government in the later eighteenth century, and much of the work on its various aspects lies in articles in journals. For convenience a select list is given here, although some of the subjects are treated more fully in other chapters. Lists of offices and office-holders are to be found in the annual editions of *The Royal Kalendar*. Some general issues are discussed by Holdsworth in ch. III ('The Executive') of *A History of English Law*, X, by D. L. Keir in 'Economical-Reform, 1779–

1787' (*The Law Quarterly Review*, L, no. CXCIX), by Archibald S. Foord in 'The Waning of the "Influence of the Crown"' (*E.H.R.*, LXII, no. 245), by S. E. Finer, 'Patronage and the Public Service' (*Public Administration*, XXX), by G. Kitson Clark, ' "Statesmen in Disguise" . . .' (*The Historical Journal*, 2, no. I), by Franklin B. Wickwire, 'King's Friends, Civil Servants, or Politicians' (*The American Historical Review*, LXXI, no. 1), and, from the vantage of a slightly later period, by J. R. Torrance, 'Sir George Harrison and the growth of bureaucracy in the early nineteenth century' (*E.H.R.*, LXXXIII, no. 326). Dora Mae Clark sheds some light on 'The Work of the Secretary to the Treasury in the Eighteenth Century' in *The American Historical Review*, XLII, no. 1, as does I. R. Christie in 'The Political Allegiance of John Robinson, 1770–1784' (ch. VI above). The financial system itself was examined in detail by Statutory Commissions and Parliamentary Committees on several occasions between 1780 and 1797: their reports are listed in the Note on Sources to chs. X and XI below. An authoritative modern survey is J. E. D. Binney's *British Public Finance and Administration 1774–92* (1958). Sir John Craig gives a good description of *The Mint* (1953). The work and composition of some of the revenue departments is reviewed by W. R. Ward in *The English Land Tax in the Eighteenth Century* (1953), 'The Office for Taxes, 1665–1798' (*Bulletin of the Institute of Historical Research*, XXXV), 'The Administration of the Window and Assessed Taxes, 1696–1798' (*E.H.R.*, LXVII, no. CCLXV), and 'Some Eighteenth-Century Civil Servants: the English Revenue Commissioners, 1754–98' (*E.H.R.*, LXX, no. 274); by Edward Hughes, *Studies in Administration and Finance 1554–1825* (1934), for the salt duties; by Elizabeth E. Hoon, *The Organization of the English Customs System 1696–1786* (1938), and R. B. Leftwich, 'The Later History and Administration of the Customs Revenue in England (1671–1814)' (*Trans. R.H.S.*, Fourth Series, XIII); and by Kenneth Ellis, *The Post Office in the Eighteenth Century* . . . (1958), the best of several books on that subject. C. M. Clode, *The Military Forces of the Crown* . . . (2 vols., 1896) may be supplemented by Olive Gee, 'The British War Office in the Later Years of the American War of Independence' (*The Journal of Modern History*, XXVI, no. 2). The best account of the Board of Ordnance appears in Arthur Forbes, *A History of the Army Ordnance Services*, I (1929). For the militia, see J. R. Western, *The English Militia in the Eighteenth Century* . . . (1965). Naval administration is patchily served for this period; but the relevant articles in Sir Oswyn Murray's series on 'The Admiralty' (*The Mariner's Mirror*, XXIII, no. 1, XXIV, no. 3) are useful, as are Franklin B. Wickwire, 'Admiralty Secretaries and the British Civil Service' (*The Huntington Library Quarterly*, XXVIII, no. 3), Admiral Sir Vesey Hamilton, *Naval Administration* (1896), Bernard Pool, *The Navy Board Contracts 1660–1832* . . . (1966), and *The Private Papers of John, Earl of Sandwich* . . ., ed. G. R. Barnes and J. H. Owen (4 vols., 1932–8). Piers Mackesy, *The War for America 1775–1783* (1964) is a magisterial review of its subject. Mark A. Thomson's *The Secretaries of State 1681–1782* (1932) is the standard account of those important Ministers. For the colonial side of their work, with that of other authorities, see also Margaret Marion Spector, *The American Department of the British Government 1768–1782* (1940), Arthur H. Basye, 'The Secretary of State for the Colonies, 1768–1782' (*The American Historical Journal*, XXVIII, no. 1), Helen Taft Manning, *British Colonial Government after the American*

Revolution 1782–1820 (1933), Arthur Herbert Basye, *The Lords Commissioners of Trade and Plantations . . . 1748–1782* (1925), Mary P. Clarke, 'The Board of Trade at Work' (*The American Historical Review*, XVII, no. 1), Dora Mae Clark, *The Rise of the British Treasury* (1960), and Franklin B. Wickwire, *British Subministers and Colonial America 1763–1783* (1966). For the Secretaries' duties and organisation in foreign affairs, before and after the foundation of the Foreign Office, see also Sir John Tilley and Stephen Gaselee, *The Foreign Office* (1933), E. Jones Parry, 'Under-Secretaries of State for Foreign Affairs, 1782–1855' (*E.H.R.*, XLIX, no. CXCIV), and D. B. Horn, *The British Diplomatic Service 1689–1789* (1961). For the Home Office, see Sir Robert Troup's book of that name (1925). On the vexed questions raised by the evolution of the Cabinet, the best summaries are by Trevor Williams in *The Making of English History* (1952), revising his earlier account in *History*, XXII, and by D. B. Horn and Mary Ransome in *English Historical Documents*, X, and A. Aspinall and E. Anthony Smith, op. cit., XI (1957, 1959 respectively). All three contain detailed bibliographies. The history of Whitehall itself, palace and street, is well told in George S. Dugdale's *Whitehall through the Centuries* (1950).

For Pitt's Cabinet colleagues in 1783-4, see, in addition to the memoirs and biographies cited earlier, *D.N.B.* and *G.E.C.* There is a mass of literature on George III: four appraisals based on more recent research are by Barnes, ch. II (see the Note on Sources to ch. VI above), by Sir Lewis Namier in 'King George III: A Study of Personality' (*Personalities and Powers*, 1955), by J. H. Plumb in 'George III' (*Men and Places*, 1963), and by W. R. Fryer, 'King George III: His Political Character and Conduct, 1760–1784; A New Whig Interpretation' (*Renaissance and Modern Studies*, VI; University of Nottingham, 1962).

CHAPTER VIII

There are two detailed connected accounts of political events in 1784–5, based on diaries or memory: *The Historical and Posthumous Memoirs of Sir Nathaniel William Wraxall 1772–1784* [in fact to 1789], ed. Henry B. Wheatley, (6 vols., 1884), III and IV; and the unpublished last journal of Horace Walpole, in Mr Wilmarth Lewis's collection at Farmington, Connecticut. Neither, however, can be accepted uncritically. *P.R.*, XIII (1784) – XVIII (1785), *P.H.*, XXIV, XXV (1815), and John Stockdale's new publication of the *Debates and Proceedings of the House of Commons, First Session of the Sixteenth Parliament*, I (1785) – *Second Session*, VI (1786), cover the Parliamentary debates.

On India, I have again drawn largely on Miss Jean Dawson's unpublished account of 'Pitt and India', which itself draws on Pitt's papers in P.R.O. 30/8/102, 157, 196–7, 353, 355–6, 358, 361–2; on those of Pitt and Dundas in the William L. Clements Library, University of Michigan; and on India Office Library, Home Misc. Ms 290 and Board of Control Minutes, vol. I. C. H. Philips, *The East India Company 1784–1834* (1940, 2nd edn. 1961) is the standard account, and Harlow, *The Founding of the Second British Empire*, II (1964), ch. III, is valuable. See also C. H. Philips, 'The New East India Board and the Court of Directors in 1784' (*E.H.R.*, LV, no. CCXIX); Holden Furber, 'Henry Dundas and the East India Directors in 1784'

(*The Journal of Modern History*, V, no. 4); Sophia Weitzman, *Warren Hastings and Philip Francis* (1929); and C. C. Davies, 'Warren Hastings and the Younger Pitt' (*E.H.R.*, LXX, no. CCLXXVII). The Ley Mss, from which I have taken a quotation, are on deposit at the Institute of Historical Research in the University of London.

Pitt's policy for Ireland has also been the subject of an unpublished account by Miss Jean Dawson. His papers at the Public Record Office (P.R.O. 30/8/188–9, 196, 320–5, 328–30) are rather disappointing, although P.R.O. 30/8/329 contains some of Orde's correspondence and P.R.O. 30/8/330 some of Rutland's; nor is there anything substantial in the other collections of his papers. The main sources lie in P.R.O., H.O. 100/1–17, in the published correspondence of Pitt and Rutland – *Correspondence between the Right Honble. William Pitt and Charles Duke of Rutland 1781–1787* (see ch. VI above), and *H.M.C., Fourteenth Report, Appendix, Pt. I –*, and in Orde's papers (particularly Letter Books I and II) among Lord Bolton's Mss at Bolton Hall in Yorkshire. Some of these last are published in Ashbourne, chs. III and IV. The Cabinet's heads of proposals in January 1785, and correspondence with the King, are in *L.C.G. III*, I, and J. Holland Rose, *Pitt and Napoleon, Essays and Letters* (ch. VI above), Part II, A; the text of the first Resolutions, in Vincent Harlow and Frederick Madden, *British Colonial Developments 1774–1834, Select Documents* (1953), 252–55. A little further information for the summer of 1785 can be found in *The Correspondence of the Right Hon. John Beresford*, ed. the Right Hon. William Beresford, I (1854), and *H.M.C., Dropmore*, III is also useful. Lecky's treatment of the subject in his great *History of Ireland in the Eighteenth Century* (1892 edn.), II, should be compared with that of Harlow, I (see Note on Sources to ch. IV above), which deals more fully with Sheffield, Eden and the English manufacturers. On the last, see also Witt Bowden, 'The Influence of the Manufacturers on Some of the Early Policies of William Pitt' (*The American Historical Review*, XXIX, no. 4), and J. M. Norris, 'Samuel Garbett and the Early Development of Industrial Lobbying in Great Britain' (*Ec.H.R., 2nd Series*, X, no. 3). Some of the pamphlet literature may be followed in B.M. Printed Books 08218 bb 35; there is a more ample collection in the Baker Library at the Graduate School of Business Administration, Harvard University. Oscar Browning, 'Adam Smith and Free Trade for Ireland' (*E.H.R.*, I, no. II), Alice Effie Murray, *A History of the Commercial and Financial Relations between England and Ireland from the Period of the Commonwealth* (1903), George O'Brien, *An Economic History of Ireland* (1918) – which should be read with L. M. Cullen, 'Problems in the Interpretation and Revision of Eighteenth-Century Irish Economic History' (*Trans. R.H.S., 5th Series*, 17) –, R. B. McDowell, *Irish Public Opinion 1750–1800* (1944), and Edith M. Johnston, *Great Britain and Ireland 1760–1800: A Study in Political Administration* (1963), give useful background information. Eden's papers in B.M. Add. Mss 34420, 45728, and Thomas H. D. Mahoney, *Edmund Burke and Ireland* (1960), ch. V, help fill in the picture for Opposition.

CHAPTER IX

The debates are covered – incompletely, as so often – as in the Note on Sources to ch. VIII above. For a vivid picture of the Westminster election of 1784, see Joseph Grego, *A History of Parliamentary Elections* . . . (2nd edn, 1892), which draws largely on the contemporary compilations *History of the Westminster Election* (1784) and *The Wit of the Day, or the Humours of Westminster* . . . (1784). John Simeon, *A Treatise on the Law of Elections* . . . (1789) is useful on the subject of writs. The Hon. George T. Kenyon, *The Life of Lloyd, First Lord Kenyon* (1873), and John Lord Campbell, *The Lives of the Chief Justices of England* . . ., III (1857), present contrasting views of Kenyon's legal opinion on the scrutiny. Some of his papers on the subject are among Lord Kenyon's Mss at Gredington in Flintshire. Pitt's motives in the affair have been inconclusively argued from that day to this, but never enthusiastically defended. William T. Laprade discusses them, most unfavourably, within a wider context in 'William Pitt and Westminster Elections' (*The American Historical Review*, XVIII, no. 2).

For Parliamentary reform see the Note on Sources to ch. III above. The account of Mortlock's affair is based on the biography in *H. of P.*, III, and on the sources quoted there and the material assembled for that purpose.

CHAPTER X

The most convenient retrospective summary of the tangled figures of national income and expenditure is in B. R. Mitchell and Phyllis Deane, *Abstract of British Historical Statistics* (see Note on Sources to ch. VII above), ch. XIV. Detailed figures were compiled for *House of Commons Accounts & Papers 1868–9*, XXXV, with a valuable explanatory 13th Appendix by F. W. Chisholm. On the shortcomings of the revenue figures see also R. C. Jarvis, 'Official Trade and Revenue Statistics' (*Ec.H.R., 2nd Series*, XVII, no.1). Contemporary findings appear in *H.C.J.* 41, 66, in *Reports from Committees of the House of Commons 1715–1801, Reprinted by Order of the House*, XI (1803), and, in scattered form, in the rarer *Papers Printed by Order of the House of Commons from the Year 1731 to 1800 in the Custody of the Clerk of the Journals* (1807), of which there are catalogues in the P.R.O. (Round Room) and the B.M. (State Paper Room).

Binney (see Note on Sources to ch. VII above) is an indispensable guide to the period, with interesting comments on the various finance Ministers. The Treasury Board Minutes, P.R.O. T.29/55–65, are a primary source.

A succinct introduction to smuggling is given in Neville Williams, *Contraband Cargoes* (1959). There is material in Hoon (see ch. VII above), in Henry Atton and Henry Hurst Holland, *The King's Customs . . . to 1800* (1908), and in A. L. Cross, *Eighteenth Century Documents relating to the Royal Forests, the Sheriffs and Smuggling* (1928). Two valuable articles are those by G. D. Ramsay, 'The Smugglers' Trade: A Neglected Aspect of English Commercial Development' (*Trans. R.H.S., 5th Series*, II) and by W. A. Cole, 'Trends in Eighteenth-Century Smuggling' (*Ec.H.R., 2nd Series*, X, no. 3). The report of the Parliamentary Committee on Frauds on the Revenue, 1783–4, is in *Reports from Committees of the House of Commons 1715–1801*, XI. P.R.O. 30/8/283 contains some of Pitt's papers on the subject; P.R.O. 30/8/295, 296–9, some on spirits, wine and tobacco; P.R.O. 30/8/318–19, some on the Scottish distilleries. Hoh-Cheung and Lorna A. Mui, in 'William Pitt and the Enforcement of the Commutation Act, 1784–1788' (*E.H.R.*, LXXVI, no. 300), give an excellent account of that story, documents for which are in P.R.O.

30/8/293-4 and 111, and in Francis Baring's letters to Henry Dundas, 1785-1795, in the Northbrook Mss and the Melville papers at the National Library of Scotland, Ms 1069.

On taxation, see William Kennedy, *English Taxation 1640-1799* . . . (1913), Stephen Dowell, *A History of Taxation and Taxes in England* . . . (4 vols., 1884), Richard D. Richards, 'The Lottery in the History of English Government Finance' (*Economic History* (*A Supplement to The Economic Journal*), III), E. R. A. Seligman, *Progressive Taxation* (1908), and F. Shehab's book of the same title (1953). Contemporary suggestions submitted to Pitt are in P.R.O. 30/8/264-272, 274; other papers on taxes, in P.R.O. 30/8/302-4; papers on lotteries and tontines, in P.R.O. 30/8/277; on the malt tax, in P.R.O. 30/8/292; on the coal tax, in P.R.O. 30/8/301.

The classical introduction to the subject of the public debt is E. L. Hargreaves, *The National Debt* (see ch. VII above). J. J. Grellier's *The History of the National Debt, from the Revolution of 1688 to the Beginning of the Year 1800* . . . (1810), and *The Terms of All the Loans Which have been Raised for the Public Service during the Last Fifty Years* . . . (1799), are useful. Mitchell and Deane (see above), ch. XIV, give figures based on a series of later investigations in *House of Commons Accounts & Papers 1868-9*, XXXV, *1890-1*, XLVIII, *1898*, LII. Contemporary inquiries and recommendations are contained in the Report of the Parilamentary Finance Committee of 1782 (*Reports from Committees 1715-1801*, XI), and in the Eleventh Report of the Commissioners for Examining the Public Accounts (*H.C.J.* 39). From the various pamphlets on the debt, those of Richard Price mentioned in the textual notes – and collected in William Morgan's edition of *The Works of Dr Richard Price, with Memoirs of his Life* (1810) –, Lord Stanhope's *Observations on Mr Pitt's Plan* . . . (1786), Lord Grenville's *Essay on the Supposed Advantages of a Sinking Fund* (1828), and *Tracts on the National Debt*, ed. J. R. McCulloch for Lord Overstone (1857), may be mentioned. P.R.O. 30/8/169, 196, 275, 282 contain some correspondence and papers of Pitt's, Pretyman's and Price's; Pembroke College, Cambridge, Tomline Ms 35:3, Mrs Pretyman Tomline's interesting reminiscence of the events of 1786. These are also discussed in Carl B. Crone, 'Richard Price and Pitt's Sinking Fund of 1786' (*Ec.H.R., 2nd Series*, IV, no. 2), which attributes to Pitt a greater dependence on Price than I have done.

The Thirteenth Report of the Commissioners for Examining the Public Accounts (*H.C.J.* 40) is indispensable for the Consolidation Act. *House of Commons Accounts & Papers 1829*, VI, and *1831*, XIV, review past methods of accounting. Binney (see above) is particularly helpful here. P.R.O. 30/8/305 contains some of Pitt's papers.

Other financial papers of Pitt's, of greater interest for administration or trade, are listed in the Notes on Sources to chs. XI-XV below. Of the many commentaries on his policies, George Rose's *A Brief Examination into the Increase of the Revenue . . . since the Conclusion of the Peace in 1783* (1792), and *A Brief Examination into the Increases of the Revenue during the Administration of Mr. Pitt . . .* (2nd edn, 1806); Tomline, I and II; and Sir John Sinclair's *History of the Public Revenue of the British Empire &c., with a Review of the Financial Administration of William Pitt,* (2 vols., 1785), (republished, with a 3rd vol. of 1790, in 1803-4), may be noted particularly. For economic conditions in the 1780s, see T. S. Ashton, *Economic Fluctuations in England 1700-1800* (1959).

CHAPTER XI

Publications on the revenue departments are given in the Note on Sources to ch. VII above. Binney is again very useful throughout. For the tax offices, see W. R. Ward; for the Customs, Hoon; for the Post Office, Ellis (all ch. VII above), and Howard Robinson, *The British Post Office, A History* (1948). There is much contemporary information in the reports of investigating bodies: in the First, Second, Thirteenth, Fourteenth, and Fifteenth Reports of the Commissioners for Examining the Public Accounts (*H.C.J.* 38, 40, 41, 42), in the Tenth Report of the Commissioners for Enquiry into Fees in the Public Offices (*House of Commons Accounts & Papers* 1806, VII), in the seventeen Reports of the Commissioners for Enquiry into Crown Lands (*H.C.J.* 42–8), and in the Fourth to Thirteenth Reports of the House of Commons' Select Committee on Finance in 1797 (*Reports from Committees*, XII (1803)). More information on Palmer's case is in the *Report of the Committee who were Appointed to Consider the Agreement made with Mr. Palmer, for the Reform and Improvement of the Posts* (1797). There is material in Pitt's papers in P.R.O. 30/8/230 (Crown Lands), 232–3 (Post Office), 282 (Land Tax), 284–5 (Customs), 290, 296, 298–9 (Excise). Letters to and from individuals mentioned in the text are scattered through P.R.O. 30/8/102 –187. P.R.O. T.43/7 and 44/10–12, and Customs 18/410 onwards, give quarterly establishments of the Customs and the Excise.

On the Mint, see Craig (ch. VII above). A copy of the inquiry of 1782 is in P.R.O. 30/8/231, which also includes some papers on the Treasury. Binney is the best guide to that department and the Exchequer; see also the Second Report of the Commissioners for Enquiry into Fees, and the Fifteenth and Twenty-Second Reports of the Finance Committee of 1797 (as above), and J. C. Sainty, 'The Tenure of Offices in the Exchequer' (*E.H.R.*, LXXX, no. 316). P.R.O. 30/8/282 and 306 contain Pitt's papers on the Commissioners for Auditing the Public Accounts (whose Minutes are to be found in P.R.O., A.O. 6/1–8); P.R.O. 30/8/239, 247, some on the army, ordnance and naval accounts. See also the Third to Fifth, Seventh to Tenth, and Twelfth Reports of the Commissioners for Examining the Public Accounts (as above). The papers of William Molleson, one of the Commissioners for Auditing, are in National Library of Scotland Mss 5496–5508.

There are some papers of Pitt's on the Royal Household and the Civil List in P.R.O. 30/8/229. See also Norris, *Shelburne and Reform* (ch. IV above), ch. X, The Rt Hon. George Rose M.P., *Considerations on the Debt of the Civil List* (1802), and the articles by Keir and by Foord (ch. VII above). Minutes and correspondence of the first decade of the Stationery Office are in P.R.O. Stat. 3/1. For the Committee of Trade, see Anna Lane Lingelbach, 'The Inception of the British Board of Trade' (*The American Historical Review*, XXX, no. 4).

For the Secretaries of State and their offices, see the books by Thomson, by Troup, by Tilley and Gaselee, and by Horn (ch. VII above): also the First Report of the Commissioners for Enquiry into Fees, and the Sixteenth Report of the Finance Committee of 1797 (as above). P.R.O., H.O. series 31, 35, 36, 42, and F.O. series 83, 90, and 95/9, give an idea of those departments' relations with other domestic authorities. F.O. 95/591 relates to the internal arrangements of the office.

There is useful material on the Ordnance in Forbes (ch. VII above), Olson (ch. III above), and Richard Glover, *Peninsular Preparation, The Reform of the British Army 1795–1809* (1963). There are also a few papers in P.R.O. 30/8/241–2. The bulk of Middleton's correspondence on naval reform in the eighties is published in *Letters and Papers of Charles, Lord Barham . . . 1758–1813*, ed. Sir John Knox Laughton, II (1910); the Third to Ninth Reports of the Commissioners for Enquiry into Fees (as above) contain very largely the fruits of his labours. A few of his unpublished letters to Pitt are in P.R.O. 30/8/246; others to Chatham in P.R.O. 30/8/365. There are other naval papers of Pitt's in P.R.O. 30/8/250. I have also had the benefit of reading some unpublished work by Miss P. K. Crimmin on naval administration during this period.

CHAPTER XII

Harlow, *The Founding of the Second British Empire 1763–1793*, I (see ch. IV above) and II (ch. VIII above), though alas not completed by his own hand, are outstanding among recent studies of British empire and trade in a period which he has shown to be interesting and significant. Selected documents are published by Harlow and Frederick Madden in *British Colonial Developments 1774–1834* (see ch. VIII above). Gerald S. Graham, *Sea Power and British North America 1783–1820* (1941) is also required reading for the subjects of this chapter. There is an interesting article on 'Adam Smith's Project of an Empire' by E. A. Benians, in *The Cambridge Historical Journal*, I, no. 2. The same author's ch. I, and Harlow's ch. II, of volume II of *The Cambridge History of the British Empire* (1940) offer useful general surveys, as does K. E. Knorr, *British Colonial Theories 1570–1850* (1944). Ralph Davis, *The Rise of the English Shipping Industry in the Seventeenth and Eighteenth Centuries* (1962) is of value, with an excellent note on statistics in Appendix A.

There is no full-length study of Charles Jenkinson. Wraxall (see ch. VIII above) gives a suggestive character sketch in his first volume, pp. 415–20, and Jenkinson attracted his share of adverse or derisory allusions in the current rhymes and Opposition journals. His own voluminous papers in the B.M., particularly Add. Mss 38191–2, 38218–28, 38309–10, 38395, 38471, 38566–7, 38570 for correspondence, and many volumes of copies of official documents (some with his own comments), give an impressive picture of his activities. His role is discussed in A. F. McC. Madden's 'The Imperial Machinery of the Younger Pitt', in *Essays in British History Presented to Sir Keith Feiling*, ed. H. R. Trevor-Roper (1964).

The Home Office's colonial papers (P.R.O., C.O. series) are concerned mainly with questions of government, which are surveyed by Helen Taft Manning in *British Colonial Government after the American Revolution* (ch. VII above). They contain less on trade. But this is covered admirably by the Committee of Trade's papers, to which the Minutes in B.T. 5/1–8 form a useful guide for the period. Commercial statistics must, as always, be handled with care. Elizabeth Boody Schumpeter's *English Overseas Trade Statistics 1697–1808* (ch. VII above) is the safest guide, and T. S. Ashton's introduction underlines the limits of their scope and reliability. David Macpherson's *Annals of Commerce, Manufactures, Fisheries, and Navigation . . .* (1805), IV, cannot be neglected.

Lowell Joseph Ragatz, *The Fall of the Planter Class in the British Caribbean 1763-1833* . . . (1928) treats fully of its subject, and Richard Pares's *Merchants and Planters* (*Supplement No. 4 to Ec.H.R.*, 1960) provides a typically stimulating background. See also Lilian M. Penson, 'The London West India Interest in the Eighteenth Century' (*E.H.R.*, XXXVI, no. CXLIII), and Herbert C. Bell, 'British Commercial Policy in the West Indies, 1783–1793' (*E.H.R.*, XXXI, no. CXXIII – the latter, however, more reliable for the years 1783 to 1787 than for their successors). Frances Armytage treats of *The Free Port System in the British West Indies, A Study in Commercial Policy, 1766-1822* (1953). The islands' value to the British economy is a disputable topic: see particularly D. A. Farnie, 'The Commercial Empire of the Atlantic, 1607–1783' (*Ec.H.R., 2nd Series.*, XV, no. 2), and, for one important aspect, R. B. Sheridan, 'The Wealth of Jamaica in the Eighteenth Century' (*Ec.H.R., 2nd ser.*, XVIII, no. 2). Official papers on West Indian trade are to be found in P.R.O., C.O. 325–6, and B.T. 6/75–7, 84–7; Pitt's papers, in P.R.O. 30/8/348–52. There is a useful file, 'West Indies', in Grenville's papers in the Fortescue Mss at Boconnoc in Cornwall.

P.R.O., B.T. 6/96 contains material on the Navigation Act of 1786. There are papers on the Newfoundland fishery in C.O. 194/37 and 41, in B.T. 6/89–90, and P.R.O. 30/8/195 (Pitt's précis of the Committee of Trade's report of 1785) and 346. See also the Reports of the Select Committee of the House of Commons on the State of the Trade to Newfoundland, 1793, in *Reports from Committees*, X (1803). Harold Adams Innis, *The Cod Fisheries: the History of an International Economy* (1940) is an important pioneering work. For government, see C.O. 194/35–41, 195/15, and John Reeves, (legal adviser to the Committee of Trade), *History of the Government of the Island of Newfoundland* . . . (1793).

For the whale fisheries, see B.T. 6/93–5. There are letters to Pitt from the Enderbys in P.R.O. 30/8/133, and from Charles Greville in P.R.O. 30/8/140, and some Admiralty papers in P.R.O. 30/8/259. Gerald S. Graham has an article on 'The Migrations of the Nantucket Whale Fishery: An Episode in British Colonial Policy', in *The New England Quarterly*, VIII, no. 2. Harlow, II, ch. V, section III, is particularly valuable, and Glyndwr Williams, *The British Search for the North-West Passage in the Eighteenth Century* (1962) gives an excellent account of the background to the Nootka Sound crisis. Sources for the crisis itself may be found in the Notes to ch. XVII below.

For the British fisheries, see the Reports of the House of Commons' committees in *Reports from Committees*, X. Edward Hughes (see ch. VII above) gives an interesting study of the problems. *Letters of George Dempster to Sir Adam Fergusson 1756–1813, With some Account of his Life*, ed. James Fergusson (1934), is useful for the Scottish fisheries, on which there is also some material in Dundas's papers in National Library of Scotland Mss 354 (a), 640, 6602.

CHAPTER XIII

The main materials for Canada lie in the Home Office colonial papers: for Quebec Province, and Upper and Lower Canada, in P.R.O., C.O. 42/11–12, 16–21, 47–51, 58–73, 82–3, 89–93, 316–17, and (collections of the Secretary of State's correspondence with Governors) 43/3–4, 8–10, 16, 37. C.O. 47/112 is also of interest. For Nova Scotia and the other north-eastern territories, C.O. 189/1–3, 189/10, 217/11–12, 217/25–7, 227/6 are the most convenient collections. The Treasury papers P.R.O., T. classes 50 and 79, and the Foreign Office papers P.R.O., F.O. 4/1, cover the loyalists' claims, of which there are also early accounts in John Eardley Wilmot, *Historical View of the Commission for Enquiring into the Losses . . . of the American Loyalists . . .* (1815), *The Royal Commission on the Losses and Services of the American Loyalists, 1783 to 1785 . . .*, ed. Hugh Edward Egerton (1915), and *Report of the Bureau of Archives for the Province of Ontario* (1905).

Pitt's files on Canada (P.R.O. 30/8/346–7) are disappointing. P.R.O. 30/8/156 has one letter to him from Francis Maseres. The small collections of Sydney's papers in the Huntington Library at San Marino in California and in the Brotherton Library at the University of Leeds yield no information; nor do the few letters from him at the University of Michigan, or in the main archives of Pitt's papers here. But Grenville's correspondence published in *H.M.C., Dropmore*, I–II contains something, and there is more among his unpublished papers in the Fortescue Mss at Boconnoc ('Quebec', 'Cabinet Ministers', 'Duke of Richmond', 'Miscellaneous 1790–92', 'West Indies', and – for Adam Lymburner – 'Private Correspondence Received and Sent 1788'). There is nothing of importance on this subject from him in the Grenville papers at the Huntington Library. Of the many secondary accounts see particularly Harlow, II; A. L. Burt, *The Old Province of Quebec* (1933); *The Cambridge History of the British Empire*, VI (1930); Gerald M. Craig, *Upper Canada: The Formative Years, 1784–1841* (1963); *The Diary and Selected Papers of Chief Justice William Smith 1784–1793*, ed. L. F. S. Upton, I (1963), II (1965); Brig.-General E. A. Cruikshank, 'The Genesis of the Canada Act', in *Ontario Historical Society, Papers and Records*, XXVIII (1932); and W. L. Morton, 'The Local Executive in the British Empire, 1763–1828' in *E.H.R.*, LXXVIII, no. 308. Documents are published in the *Report[s] on Canadian Archives* from 1885, and in *Documents Relating to the Constitutional History of Canada 1759–1791*, ed. Adam Shortt and Arthur George Doughty (1907).

A useful account of Anglo-Canadian-American relations appears in A. L. Burt, *The United States, Great Britain and British North America from the Revolution to the Establishment of Peace after the War of 1812* (1940). Samuel Flagg Bemis, *Jay's Treaty, A Study in Commerce and Diplomacy* (1923), is central to the same theme in this decade. Julian P. Boyd, *Number 7: Alexander Hamilton's Secret Attempts to Control American Foreign Policy . . .* (1964), which goes carefully over some of the ground from its own point of view, is a separate publication of one part of the same author's edition of *The Papers of Thomas Jefferson*, 17 (1965). Volumes 7–16 (1953–64) cover the rest of this period. Other collections of American documents are in *American State Papers, Documents, Legislative and Executive, of the Congress of the United States [Foreign Relations]*, I, ed. Walter Lowrie and Matthew St Clair Clark (1832); *Diplomatic Correspondence of the United States, Canadian Relations 1784–1860*, ed. William R. Manning, I, (1940); *The Writings of George Washington*, ed. John C. Fitzpatrick, 27–32 (1938–9); *The Papers of Alexander Hamilton*, ed. Harold C. Syrett, III–VII (1962–3); *The Works of John Adams . . .* by His Grandson Charles Francis Adams, VIII (1853); Jared Sparks, *The Life of Gouverneur Morris . . .*, I–II

(1832), and *The Diary and Letters of Gouverneur Morris* . . ., ed. Anne Cary Morris, I (1889). For Grenville's correspondence with Dorchester, see the P.R.O., C.O. papers above; P.R.O., F.O. 4/2–16, 115/1 contain the official Foreign Office papers. Pitt's papers in P.R.O. 30/8/343–4 are of little help; there are some notes in his hand, endorsed 1783, on the repayment of British merchants' wartime claims and on the loyalists, in P.R.O. 30/8/195. Carmarthen's (Duke of Leeds's) correspondence and papers while Foreign Secretary (but only to the end of 1790) are in B.M. Add. Mss 28060–6 and Egerton Mss 3498–9, 3500–5; they are not very important for this subject, and I would ascribe less initiative to him here than does Joanne Loewe Neel in 'The Marquess of Carmarthen and the United States, 1783–1791' (*History Today*, XIII, no. 2). Of Grenville's papers in the Fortescue Mss, the file 'Quebec' has some material on Vermont, 'Private Correspondence Received 1791' some on the decision to send an envoy to the United States in 1791. A varied selection of documents is published by Frederick J. Turner in 'English Policy towards America in 1790–1791' (*The American Historical Review*, VII, no. 4; VIII, no. 1).

For the background to Anglo-Latin American trade, see Richard Pares, *War and Trade in the West Indies* (1936), ch. II, A.K. Manchester, *British Pre-eminence in Brazil, Its Rise and Decline* (1933), and Allan Christelow, 'Great Britain and the Trades from Cadiz and Lisbon to Spanish America and Brazil, 1759–1783' (*The Hispanic American Historical Review*, XXVII, no. 1); for the British West Indian free ports, Armytage (ch. XII above). Useful papers on Honduras are published in *Archives of British Honduras, Volume I* . . . ed. Major Sir Alder Burton (1931); the negotiation with Spain may be followed in P.R.O., F.O. 72/3–8. P.R.O. 30/8/345 contains Pitt's files on Central and South America, and P.R.O. 30/8/120, 128, some letters from General Campbell and Colonel Dalrymple. There are some letters from Pitt to Carmarthen on Honduras in B.M. Egerton Ms 3498. The best account of his dealings with Miranda is in William Spence Robertson's 'Francisco de Miranda and the Revolutionizing of Spanish America', in the *Annual Report of the American Historical Association for 1907*, I, (1908).

The background to European activity in Africa is well sketched in J. D. Hargreaves's Part 2 of ch. VIII in *The New Cambridge Modern History*, VIII (1965), and in Robin Hallett, *The Penetration of Africa* . . ., I (1965), which treats fully of the subject and is particularly good on West Africa. Robin Hallett has also edited the *Records of the African Association 1788–1831* (1964); other useful collections of documents are in Harlow and Madden (see ch. VIII above), and C. W. Newbury, *British Policy towards West Africa, Select Documents 1786–1874* (1965). Judith Blow Williams, 'The Development of British Trade with West Africa, 1750 to 1850' (*Political Science Quarterly*, L, no. 2) is useful. For the anti-slavery movement, see R. Coupland, *The British Anti-Slavery Movement* (1933), Frank J. Klingberg, *The Anti-Slavery Movement in England* (1926), and G. R. Mellor, *British Imperial Trusteeship 1783–1850* (1951). Eric Williams, *Capitalism and Slavery* (1944) provides a stimulating Marxist critique, which in turn is criticised by Alan M. Rees in 'Pitt and the Achievement of Abolition' (*The Journal of Negro History*, XXXIX, no. 3), and by Roger T. Anstey, 'Capitalism and Slavery: A Critique' (*Ec.H.R., 2nd Series*, XXI, no. 2). Sir Robert Birley, 'The Discovery of Africa, Some Lessons for Today' (The Anti-Slavery Society, 1968) contains a fine analysis of the culminating passage of Pitt's speech in the Commons in 1792. For Wilberforce, see *Private Papers of William Wilberforce*, and the *Life*, I (ch. V above), *The Correspondence of William Wilberforce*, ed. by his Sons, Robert Isaac Wilberforce . . . and Samuel Wilberforce, I (1840), and R. Coupland, *Wilberforce, A Narrative* (1923). There is one unpublished letter from him to Pitt on the pre-war slave trade campaign in P.R.O. 30/8/189. Thomas Clarkson's *The History of the Rise, Progress, and Accomplishment of the Abolition of the African Slave-Trade by the British Parliament* (2 vols., 1808) is a prime source from an important and controversial figure. Some interesting documents are published in Elizabeth Doonan, *Documents Illustrative of the History of the Slave Trade to America*, II (1931). The debates on the trade, and on Sierra Leone, from 1788 to 1792 are covered in *P.H.*, XXVII-XXIX (1816); *P.R.*, XXIII, XXIV (1788), XXVI-XXIX (1789-91), XXXII, XXXIII (1792); Stockdale, *Fifth Session of the Sixteenth Parliament*, II, III (1788) – the latter valuable for the House of Lords –, *Sixth Session*, I-III (1789), and *Seventh Session* (1790), when the series ceased for thirteen years; and *The Senator; or Clarendon's Parliamentary Chronicle* . . ., I, II (n.d.) for 1791, which adds marginally to *P.R.* The Committee of Trade's Report of April 1789 is published in *Accounts & Papers* . . ., XXVI, *1789*: evidence presented to the Commons from 1789 to 1791, in *Accounts and Papers* . . ., XXIV, XXV, *1789*; XXIX, XXX, *1790*; XXXIV, *1790–1*. Pitt's papers on the slave trade are to be found largely among his 'Notes' in the Stanhope Mss at Chevening, and in his files for the West Indies at the P.R.O. (see ch. XII above), particularly P.R.O. 30/8/348, 351; those on Sierra Leone are in P.R.O. 30/8/363. His inquiries of foreign powers may be followed in *A.C.*, I (see Abbreviations), and the P.R.O., F.O. series 22, 27, 37, 63. An adverse view of his role is given in Barnes, *George III and William Pitt* (see Note on Sources to ch. VI above), 176–80, 205–12. For the early days of the Sierra Leone Company, see Eveline C. Martin, *The British West African Settlements 1750–1821, A Study in Local Administration* (1927).

CHAPTERS XIV & XV

Harlow, I and II (see chs. IV, VIII above) are again indispensable for the regions covered by these chapters. Harlow & Madden (ch. VIII above) contains significant documents. Peter Marshall (see ch. VII above), Gerald S. Graham, *The Politics of Naval Supremacy* (1965), ch. II, and Ronald Hyam, 'British Imperial Expansion in the Late Eighteenth Century' (*The Historical Journal*, 10, no. 1), comment on the thesis, which is Harlow's, of 'the swing to the East'.

The incursion of European powers into the Pacific may be followed in J. C. Beaglehole, *The Exploration of the Pacific* (2nd edn, 1947), and in the same author's masterly general introduction to the first volume of his edition of *The Journals of Captain James Cook* . . . (1955). The settlement of New South Wales is discussed in Eris O'Brien's *The Foundation of Australia (1786–1800)* (2nd edn, 1950), in C. M. H. Clark's *A History of Australia*, I (1962), in Geoffrey Blainey's *The Tyranny of Distance* (1966), and – a commentary on this last – in G. C. Bolton, 'The Hollow Conqueror: Flax and the Foundation of Australia' (*Australian Economic History Review*, VIII, no. 1). The debate continues. The concluding pages of Michael Roe's 'Australia's Place in "The Swing to the East", 1788–1810', in *Historical Studies Australia and New Zealand*, 8, no. 30, pose the questions in the context of the whaling trade. For some of the documents, see G. B. Barton, *History of New South Wales from the Records*, I, pt. 2 (1889), and Clark, *Select Documents in Australian History 1788–1850* (1950). Pitt's papers on the subject in P.R.O. 30/8/342 reveal very little.

The China trade has been the subject of one of the great historical works of our time, the 3 volumes (1964) of Louis Dermigny's *La Chine et L'Occident, Le Commerce à Canton au XVIIIe siècle, 1719–1833*. This is an achievement of almost Gibbonian weight and quality, balanced on a seemingly restricted topic like the medieval theologians' angels on a pin. But most of the material relevant to my ch. XIV was already available in Earl H. Pritchard's *The Crucial Years of Early Anglo-Chinese Relations 1750–1800* (1936). See also Hosea Ballou Morse, *The Chronicles of the East India Company trading to China 1653–1834*, II (1926), and his 'The Provision of Funds for the East India Company's Trade at Canton during the 18th Century' in *Journal of the Royal Asiatic Society of Great Britain and Ireland for 1922*, Part II – April. M. Greenberg, *British Trade and the Opening of China 1800–42* (1951) contains observations applying to the earlier period. Holden Furber, *John Company at Work, A Study of European Expansion in India in the later Eighteenth Century* (1948) surveys the Country trade, and C. H. Philips contributes a useful introduction to his edition of *The Correspondence of David Scott . . . Relating to Indian Affairs 1787–1805* (2 vols., 1953–4). Earl H. Pritchard has published 'The Instructions of the East India Company to Lord Macartney on his Embassy to China and his Reports to the Company, 1792–4', in *Journal of the Royal Asiatic Society . . . for 1938*, Parts II, III, IV – April, July, October. J. L. Cranmer-Byng has edited *An Embassy to China, Being the Journal Kept by Lord Macartney during his Embassy to the Emperor Ch'ien-Lung 1793–1794* (1962). The unpublished material is to be found in the mass of documents on Indian affairs, noted briefly below. But P.R.O. 30/8/354 contains a collection of Pitt's papers on China, and P.R.O. 30/8/121 and 154 include his correspondence from Cathcart and Macartney respectively – the latter very sparse. Macartney's reports to the Home Secretary are in P.R.O., C.O. 77/29. National Library of Scotland Mss 1060, 1069 contain many of Dundas's papers on the Chinese debts, and a large number of letters from George Smith of Canton and Calcutta.

Affairs in the East Indies are again covered largely in the collections on India. But the negotiations with the Dutch may be followed in P.R.O., F.O 37/13–38 (particularly 23–35), 97/247; P.R.O. 30/8/110 and 336, as well as Pitt's papers on the East (below); B.M. Add. Mss 28062–6, 34429–40, 34466–8, 38310, 38395, and Egerton Ms 3500; National Library of Scotland Ms 1068; Scottish Record Office, G.D. 51/3/23/1–8; Fortescue Mss, 'East Indies, 1784–1791'; *H.M.C., Dropmore*, I–II. Harlow, II, ch. VI, goes carefully into the subject, and see also Alfred Cobban, *Ambassadors and Secret Agents, The Diplomacy of the First Earl of Malmesbury at The Hague* (1954), and H. R. C. Wright, 'The Moluccan Spice Monopoly, 1770–1824' (*Journal of the Malayan Branch Royal Asiatic Society*, XXXI, Part 4). On Sumatra and Malaya, see John Bastin, *The British in West Sumatra (1685–1825)* (1965); Nicholas Tarling, *Anglo-Dutch Rivalry in the Malay World 1780–1824* (1962);

and K. G. Tregonning, 'Factors in the Foundation of Penang' (*Journal of the Greater Indian Society*, XVII, nos. 1 & 2).

There is a vast documentation on India, to which I can only point. In my treatment of the subject I have relied much, as in ch. VIII above, on an unpublished paper by Miss Jean Dawson; also on C. H. Philips, *The East India Company 1784–1834* (ch. VIII above); Holden Furber's two books, *John Company at Work*, and *Henry Dundas, first Viscount Melville, 1742–1811* (1931); H. R. C. Wright, *East-Indian Economic Problems in the Age of Cornwallis and Raffles* (1961); B. B. Misra, *The Central Administration of the East India Company 1773–1834* (1939); *The Cambridge History of India*, V (1929), particularly ch. XXVI; and Harlow, II, particulary ch. III. James Mill's great *History of British India* (3 vols., 1817) can never be neglected. Halford Lancaster Hoskins, *British Routes to India* (1928) is useful for that topic; for the Egyptian consulate, see also George Baldwin, *Political Recollections relative to Egypt* . . . (1801), and Alfred Cecil Wood, *A History of the Levant Company* (1935). The impeachment of Warren Hastings is examined with authority in the book of that title by P. J. Marshall (1965); see also the *Life* by Keith Feiling (1954), Sophia Weitzman, *Warren Hastings and Philip Francis* (ch. VIII above), and vol. V of *The Correspondence of Edmund Burke*, ed. Holden Furber (1965). The *Correspondence of Charles, First Marquis Cornwallis*, ed. Charles Ross (2 vols., 1859), contains letters to and from Pitt and Dundas covering a range of subjects.

The Parliamentary debates and reports are of course full of Indian affairs; for the reports, see the bibliographies in Philips, *The East India Company* and Furber, *John Company at Work*. These also contain lists of the Company's publications, some of the most important of which (including the *Papers Respecting the Negociation for a Renewal of the East-India Company's Exclusive Trade* in 1793) are bound up in B.M. Printed Books 581 h 22 – a collection made by William Eden. Pitt's surviving papers on India have been gathered in P.R.O. 30/8/353–63; other letters, from Francis Baring and from Dundas, are in P.R.O. 30/8/111 and 157. For Baring's papers, see ch. X above; Dundas's – voluminous indeed – are scattered between the various collections (at least thirteen of them, of which seven are overseas) into which his great archive has been split over the years. Some of these have been described in institutional lists of acquisitions and in journals: the most reliable pointer to all known sources is in the typescript introduction to vol. I of the inventory to the Melville Castle Muniments, in the Scottish Record Office at H.M. General Register House in Edinburgh. The John Rylands Library at Manchester, the National Library of Scotland, and the Scottish Record Office contain the largest proportion of this material in the British Isles; it is best to consult the custodians for effective use. The records of the Board of Control, and the bulk of the East India Company's papers, are in the India Office Records: there are several catalogues to consult, of which Joan C. Lancaster's *A Guide to Lists and Catalogues of the India Office Records* (1966) gives an authoritative survey. Current acquisitions are noted in the *Annual Reports* of the India Office Library (now Records).

CHAPTER XVI

The European diplomatic scene after the War of American Independence is described in the first volume of Albert Sorel's classic *L'Europe et la Révolution française* (1885); the fruits of later research are summed up in volume VIII of *The New Cambridge Modern History* (1965), particularly ch. IX by M. S. Anderson, and in David Bayne Horn's *Great Britain and Europe in the Eighteenth Century* (1967). The older *Cambridge History of British Foreign Policy*, I (1922), has a chapter by J. H. Clapham on 'Pitt's First Decade 1783–1792'; Felix Salomon briefly discusses the main features in 'The Foreign Policy of William Pitt in the First Decade of his Ministry in its European Significance' (*Trans. R.H.S., New Series*, X (1896)), and treats the subject at greater length in the first volume of his uncompleted *William Pitt der Jüngere* (1906). The Ms sources used for section I of this chapter are given, in context, in the Note on Sources to ch. XVII below. For the material on the trade negotiations see John Ehrman, *The British Government and Commercial Negotiations with Europe 1783–1793* (Cambridge, 1962).

CHAPTER XVII

For the Duke of Richmond's fortifications plan, see Olson (ch. III above), where sources are given. The debates are in *P.R.*, XIX-XXI (1786–7).

The publications mentioned in the Note on Sources to ch. XVI above hold good for this chapter; and there is of course useful material in Tomline, Stanhope, and Holland Rose. Ephraim Douglas Adams, *The Influence of Grenville on Pitt's Foreign Policy 1787–1798* (1904) has a few useful remarks on this period. The best recent guide to the literature on European history is in J. S. Bromley and A. Goodwin's *A Select List of Works on Europe and Europe Overseas 1715–1815* (1956) – and a fresh edition of this valuable aid would be very welcome. The authoritative account of the Dutch crisis of 1787 is A. C. Cobban's *Ambassadors and Secret Agents* (see chs XIV & XV above). There are also two articles by J. Holland Rose: 'Great Britain and the Dutch Question in 1787–1788', in *The American Historical Review*, XIV, no. 2; and 'The Missions of William Grenville to The Hague and Versailles in 1787', in *E.H.R.*, XXIV, no. XCIV. Oscar Browning's article, 'The Triple Alliance of 1788', in *Trans. R.H.S., New Series*, II (1885), is really concerned with the crisis. Much primary material on the British side is published in *A.C.*, I, *H.M.C., Dropmore*, I and III, *Diaries and Correspondence of James Harris, First Earl of Malmesbury . . .*, ed. by his Grandson, the Third Earl, II (1844), *Despatches from Paris 1784–1790*, ed. Oscar Browning (2 vols., 1909–10), and *British Diplomatic Instructions 1689–1789, France, Part IV*, VII, ed. L. G. Wickham Legg (1934). *The Political Memoranda of Francis Fifth Duke of Leeds* (see ch. VI above), *L.C.G. III*, I, and *H.M.C., Twelfth Report, Appendix, Pt. IX*, have some relevant information. *Receuil des Instructions données aux Ambassadeurs et Ministres de France . . ., XXV-2, Tome Troisième . . .*, ed. Paul Vaucher (1965) is also useful. The Foreign Office papers are in P.R.O., F.O. 27/16–26 (France), 37/5–20, 97/246 (Holland and Netherlands), 64/7–12, 95/1, 97/323 (Prussia and Germany); Pitt's papers on the subject, and correspondence from envoys and colleagues, in P.R.O. 30/8/110, 155, 180, 183, 197–8, 332, 333, 336. Eden's (Auckland's) papers in B.M. Add. Mss 34420–7, and Carmarthen's in B.M. Add. Mss 28059–62 and Egerton Mss 3498, 3500, have valuable unpublished material; P.R.O. 30/29/1, packet 15, contains Thurlow's interesting reports to the absent Stafford, and the

Grenville Papers in the Huntington Library, California, Stafford's letter of support to Pitt in September 1787.

The affairs of northern, central and eastern Europe, and the Belgic provinces, in this period have received much detailed study. There is a good introduction to *The Eastern Question 1774–1923* by M. S. Anderson (1966). Friedrich Karl Wittichen, *Preussen und England in der Europäischen Politik 1785–88* (1902), Sir Richard Lodge, *Great Britain & Prussia in the Eighteenth Century* (1923), and Robert Howard Lord, *The Second Partition of Poland . . .* (1915) are very useful. So is Dietrich Gerhard, *England und der Aufstieg Russlands* (1933), and I understand that, for those who can read Russian, there is a good guide to relevant works in the successive lists of *Ministerstvo Cultury SSSR, Vsyesoyouznaya Knijnaya Palata, Yejegodnik Knigi SSSR*. The main Foreign Office papers are in P.R.O., F.O. 7/13–21, 97/58 (Austria), 22/9–12 (Denmark), 37/21–30 (Holland and Netherlands), 64/13–18, 97/323 (Prussia and Germany), 65/15–19, 97/341 (Russia), 73/6–11 (Sweden), 78/8–11, 12B (Turkey), 79/6 (Tuscany). P.R.O. 30/8/338 is the most useful of Pitt's files, which are otherwise disappointing. Carmarthen's (Leeds's) papers are in B.M. Add. Mss 28064–6, 28068, Egerton Ms 3500. *Diaries and Correspondence of Malmesbury*, II, is valuable for the making of the Triple Alliance. Emma Eleanor Elizabeth Elliot-Murray Kynynmound, Countess of Minto, *A Memoir of the Right Honourable Hugh Elliot* (1868) gives an account of that envoy's career; his private letters to Ewart (together with those of other British envoys) are in the Ewart Mss, the property of Mr Hector Monro, of Kirtlebridge, Dumfriesshire, a collection which gives a good picture of the continuing crisis as seen by the men in most of the capitals directly concerned.

There are several studies of the Nootka Sound crisis. William Ray Manning, in 'The Nootka Sound Controversy' (*Annual Report of the American Historical Association for the Year 1904* (1905)), examines the background to the affair, as well as its course, making use of Spanish documents. John M. Norris investigates 'The Policy of the British Cabinet in the Nootka Crisis' in *E.H.R.*, LXX, no. CCLXXVII, and elucidates contemporary publications, for the period January to July 1790; so does Harlow, with sometimes different conclusions and carrying the story to its end in October, in *The Founding of the Second British Empire*, II, ch. VII. Another interpretation of 'The Real Significance of the Nootka Sound Incident' is given by Lennox Mills in *The Canadian Historical Review*, VI, no.2. Harlow and Madden, *British Colonial Developments* (see ch. VIII above) publish some interesting documents in section I, B. The missions of W. A. Miles and Hugh Elliot have often been discussed, and Holland Rose's account (see Abbreviations) is probably still the best; some of Miles's letters are published in *The Correspondence of William Augustus Miles on the French Revolution 1789–1817*, ed. the Rev. Charles Popham Miles, I (1890), and there is earlier correspondence with Pitt in P.R.O. 30/8/159. Volume II of *Despatches from Paris 1784–1790* (see above), and *The Despatches of Earl Gower, English Ambassador at Paris from June 1790 to August 1792 . . .*, ed. Oscar Browning (1885), are also useful for the French scene, and *H.M.C. Twelfth Report, Appendix, Pt. IX* contains, on pp. 366–7, a letter from Fitzherbert to Pitt on his way through Paris to Spain. The King's correspondence on the crisis is in *L.C.G. III*, I, and *H.M.C., Twelfth Report, Appendix, Pt. IX*, 368. Some of Grenville's communications with

Auckland in Holland, and other papers on events, will be found (in whole or in part) in *H.M.C., Dropmore*, I; others again are in the files 'Lord Auckland', 'Miscellaneous, 1790–92', and 'Private Correspondence Received 1791' (containing letters from Miles, demanding payment for his recent services), in the Fortescue Mss at Boconnoc. B.M. Add. Mss 34430–33, and 'Letters to Sir James Burges about Foreign Affairs, Undated, & – 1790' in the Bland Burges Mss, Bodleian Library, contain some of Auckland's correspondence for the period (*A.C.*, II (see Abbreviations) is disappointing); B.M. Add. Ms 28066 contains Leeds's; there are a few relevant letters to Pitt from Cabinet colleagues in P.R.O. 30/8/119, 151, 171; and other papers in P.R.O. 30/8/198 and 341. But the main files are official. The F.O. papers in the P.R.O. may be consulted by country for the reactions throughout Europe and in America (and see also Notes to chs. XII-XIV above); F.O. 72/16–20, 95/7, 185/6 for Spain itself; and P.R.O., B.T. 5/6 and P.C. 2/135 for Meares's evidence on his activities to the Committee of Trade and later to the Cabinet sitting as a Privy Council.

CHAPTER XVIII

Information for this chapter is naturally to be found in a wide range of sources: in the various Ms collections containing Pitt's correspondence, and the published letters, diaries and memoirs of the day. More directly, Stanhope and Holland Rose, and occasionally Ashbourne (see Abbreviations), have valuable material, which is reinforced by those letters from Pitt to his mother that remain unpublished from P.R.O. 30/8/12. *The Letters of Lady Harriot Eliot 1766–1786*, ed. Cuthbert Headlam (1914), *The Life of William Wilberforce* and his *Private Papers* (see Note on Sources to ch. V above) are also helpful. *Bishop Tomline's Estimate of Pitt together with Chapter XXVII from the Unpublished Fourth Volume of the Life*, ed. The Earl of Rosebery, K.G. (1903), is full of interest. So are his wife's recollections, in 'Mr. Pitt II' in the Stanhope Mss and Box 29, 1, 35:3 in the Tomline Mss at Pembroke College, Cambridge; and James Bland Burges's notes for a character sketch, in his 'Concise Diary of Events . . ., 1752–1806' in the Bodleian Library. The unpublished papers of Joseph Smith, listed by the National Register of Archives as being in the possession of Mr W. H. Saumarez Smith, add little to those printed in *H.M.C., Twelfth Report, Appendix, Pt. IX*. There are a few items in the fifth Lord Stanhope's notes on Pitt at Chevening.

The *London County Council Survey of London*, XIV (1931), gives a careful account of Downing Street and Number 10. I have searched in vain for evidence of connexions between Pitt and the City: Baron Heath, *Some Account of the Worshipful Company of Grocers of the City of London* (3rd edn, 1869), and Sir Walter Sherburne Prideaux, *Memorials of the Goldsmiths' Company*, II (1896), are the sources for his two favourite Livery Companies. *The Farington Diary by Joseph Farington R.A.* ed. James Greig, I (1922), and William T. Whitley, *Thomas Gainsborough* (1915), mention his relations with the arts. There is a discussion of his part, if any, in the matter of Dr Johnson's pension in *Boswell's Life of Johnson*, ed. George Birkbeck Hill, Revised and Enlarged Edition by L.F. Powell, IV (1934). Laureate Pye's letters to Pitt are in P.R.O. 30/8/169.

Lord Fife and his Factor: Being the Correspondence of James Second Lord Fife

1729–1809, ed. Alistair and Henrietta Tayler (1925), has some hostile references to the Duchess of Gordon. Lt.-Colonel Alex. Fergusson, in *The Honourable Henry Erskine . . . with Notices of Certain of his Kinsfolk and of his time* (1882), gives a more friendly account. *An Autobiographical Chapter in the Life of Jane, Duchess of Gordon* (privately printed, 1864) is of little use for this period; so is P.R.O. 30/8/139, containing her letters to Pitt. There is more of interest in *Gleanings from an Old Portfolio . . .*, ed. Mrs Godfrey Clark, II (1896), and Mrs Catherine Stapleton's letters to Hester Countess of Chatham in P.R.O. 30/8/59 are also useful. On the questions of Ministerial dinners, and Pitt's health, see the textual notes to the chapter. For his Cambridge business see P.R.O. 30/8/315, and *The Victoria History of the Counties of England: A History of the County of Cambridge . . .*, III (ch. I above), under Pembroke College.

The Holwood cellar books are in P.R.O. 30/8/203, and an inventory of contents of the house and farm in P.R.O. 30/8/219. The purchase of the estate may be followed in the Earl of Derby's papers, 'Holwood Estate Deeds and Conveyances', at Knowsley, the contents of which are summarised in a photostat in the Kent County Record Office at Maidstone. There is also some very useful information on the subject, including the loan from William Hornby, in letters from Augustine Greenland to Pitt among the notes on Pitt in the Stanhope Mss. Frederick Sidney Gammon, *The Story of Keston in Kent* (1934) is good. He draws largely on *The Life of William Wilberforce* and the *Diaries and Correspondence of the Right Hon. George Rose . . .*, ed. the Rev. Leveson Vernon Harcourt (2 vols., 1860), and on a succession of articles in *Archaeologia Cantiana: Being Transactions of the Kent Archaeological Society*, of which those by C. Roach Smith in XIII (1880) and Philip Norman in XXIV (1900) may be mentioned particularly. Hasted's *History of Kent*, I (ch. I above), 111, may also be consulted.

P.R.O. 30/8/204–7, 219, throw fitful light on the problems of Pitt's private finances. So do Pretyman Mss 50/3/182, 435/36 and 503:6 (and see also ch. I above), and the letters from Augustine Greenland in the notes on Pitt among the Stanhope Mss. Ernest Hartley Coleridge, *The Life of Thomas Coutts, Banker* (2 vols., 1920) is of marginal interest, and so, with one exception in November 1792 (see p. 602 above), are Coutts's letters to Pitt in P.R.O. 30/8/126. But there is much of value in the archives at the head office of the bank: the Ledgers and Private Ledgers (the former with contemporary indices of names), the personal 'Memos. of Thos. Coutts 1795 to 1809' (which are also retrospective; Coutts's Archives, no. 466), and the deed of assignment to Coutts of Pitt's salary as First Lord of the Treasury in 1793 (Coutts's Archives, no. 157). The dates of payment of that salary and his salary and fees as Chancellor of the Exchequer, from 1784 to 1792, may be followed in the Pells' Issue Rolls of the Exchequer, P.R.O. E.403/1174–1190, from which I have concentrated on Rolls 1174–1180.

CHAPTER XIX

The main study of the relations between politicians and the newspapers in this period is A. Aspinall's *Politics and the Press c. 1780–1850* (1949). *The History of The Times*, I (1935) is also useful, and Pitt's papers in P.R.O. 30/8/229 throw some light on payments. Sheila Lambert, 'Printing for the

House of Commons in the Eighteenth Century' (*The Library, Fifth Series,*
XXIII, no. 1), and Black, *The Association* (see ch. III above), are of interest
for related developments.

The progress of party is discussed in several of the publications cited earlier,
particularly in Foord, *His Majesty's Opposition,* Feiling, *The Second Tory Party
1714–1832,* and the concluding pages of John Brooke's Introductory Survey
to *H. of P.,* I (see respectively chs. II and VI above, and Abbreviations).
*Whig Organization in the General Election of 1790, Selections from the Blair Adam
Papers,* ed. Donald E. Ginter (1967), and the same authority's 'The Financing
of the Whig Party Organization, 1783–1793' in *The American Historical Review,*
LXXI, no. 2, are of great value, as also is the opening chapter of F. O'Gorman's *The Whig Party and the French Revolution* (1967). Valerie Cromwell,
'The Losing of the Initiative by the House of Commons, 1780–1914' (*Trans.
R.H.S., Fifth Series,* 18) surveys some aspects of the period from a later
vantage point. W. A. Laprade's article in *The American Historical Review,*
XVIII, no. 2, cited in ch. IX above, deals briefly with the Westminster
by-election of 1788, for which there is some material from Pitt's point of view
in P.R.O. 30/8/236, 237. Lists of M.P.s and peers and their voting habits are
widely scattered in various collections; some are to be found among Pitt's
papers in P.R.O. 30/8/234.

The standard work on the House of Lords at this time is A. S. Turberville,
The House of Lords in the Age of Reform 1784–1837 . . ., (1958), the continuation
of the same author's *The House of Lords in the XVIII Century* (see ch. II
above). D. Large, 'The Decline of the "Party of the Crown" and the Rise of
Parties in the House of Lords, 1783–1837' (*E.H.R.,* LXXVIII, no. 309) is
most helpful. Wm. A. Shaw, *The Knights of England . . .* (2 vols., 1906) gives
the dates of enrolments in the orders; Robert Beatson, *A Political Index to
the Histories of Great Britain and Ireland* (3 vols., 3rd edn, 1806), of those to the
British and Irish baronetcies.

A. Aspinall, *The Cabinet Council 1783–1835* (1952) is the *locus classicus* for
composition, habits and procedure. It may be supplemented by his edition
of *L.C.G. III,* I (see Abbreviations), and by the Introduction to Part I of
English Historical Documents 1783–1832 – volume XI in that series –
by Aspinall and E. Anthony Smith. But this remains a subject, well trodden
though it is, which may yet yield to further study. It is of course involved in
the vexed question of the King's role, on which much has been written.
Barnes, *George III and William Pitt, 1783–1806* (see ch. VI above), which is
wholly devoted to the problem, is based mainly on the papers now published
in *L.C.G. III,* I, and on Pitt's correspondence with and concerning the royal
family in P.R.O. 30/8/101, 103–6. Richard Pares's *King George III and the
Politicians* (ch. II above) is indispensable.

CHAPTER XX

The King's illness in 1788-9 has been diagnosed by Ida Macalpine and
Richard Hunter in 'The "Insanity" of King George III: A Classic Case of
Porphyria' (*British Medical Journal,* 8 January 1966). The article, together
with another by themselves, one by John Brooke, and one by Professor Abe
Goldberg, is reprinted in *Porphyria – A Royal Malady,* published by the
British Medical Association (1968). Their argument runs counter to that in

M. Guttmacher, *America's Last King. An Interpretation of the Madness of George III* (1941), which is repeated in Charles Chenevix Trench, *The Royal Malady* (1964). This latter work, however, contains much of interest on the course of the illness, although its examination of the political crisis is not to be compared with John W. Derry's in *The Regency Crisis and the Whigs 1788–9* (1963), which supersedes earlier accounts. Dr Derry is also very helpful on the legal problems, as is Sir William Holdsworth, *A History of English Law*, X (ch. II above). Lecky's classic *History of England in the Eighteenth Century*, ch. XVI, gives a powerfully hostile view of Pitt's behaviour; Robert Gore-Browne's *Chancellor Thurlow* (see ch. VI above), and the Hon. George T. Kenyon's *The Life of Lloyd, First Lord Kenyon* (see ch. IX above), are favourable to Thurlow. Much valuable material is to be found in William Grenville's letters published in Buckingham, I, II (see Abbreviations), and P.R.O. 30/29/384, containing Stafford's papers, throws light on the Cabinet's support of Pitt. There is nothing in *H.M.C., Kenyon Mss (14th Report, Appendix, Pt. IV)*, but the Chief Justice's Ms diary and correspondence, in the possession of Lord Kenyon, are more useful. *The Correspondence of George Prince of Wales 1770–1812*, I (1963), ed. A. Aspinall, is very important. The views of many politicians may be followed in the published editions of their letters and diaries, and the Ms collections cited in earlier chapters.

Catalogue of Political and Personal Satires . . . in the British Museum, VI (see ch. VI above) covers the caricatures of the day; Aspinall, *Politicians and the Press c. 1780–1835* (ch. XIX above), the dealings with the newspapers. The Parliamentary debates are contained in *P.R.*, XXV, XXVI (1789), Stockdale's *Debates*, XVI (1789), and *P.H.*, XXVII (1816). Pitt's papers on the crisis are to be found mainly in P.R.O. 30/8/196–7, 228, those dealing with the Prince of Wales's affairs in P.R.O. 30/8/105, and with his younger brothers' in P.R.O. 30/8/106. Published diaries and correspondence, and the London newspapers preserved in the Burney Collection at the British Museum, give impressions of social attitudes and descriptions of events. In volume K. XXIII, 36 f and g in the Maps Department at the British Museum there are views and a plan of the arrangements in St Paul's on 23 April 1789.

Index

Names of persons are given as far as possible in the style by which their owners were generally known in the period of this volume.